Lecture Notes in Computer Science 9741

More information about this series at http://www.springer.com/series/7409

Pei-Luen Patrick Rau (Ed.)

Cross-Cultural Design

8th International Conference, CCD 2016
Held as Part of HCI International 2016
Toronto, ON, Canada, July 17–22, 2016
Proceedings

Springer

Editor
Pei-Luen Patrick Rau
Tsinghua University
Beijing
China

ISSN 0302-9743 ISSN 1611-3349 (electronic)
Lecture Notes in Computer Science
ISBN 978-3-319-40092-1 ISBN 978-3-319-40093-8 (eBook)
DOI 10.1007/978-3-319-40093-8

Library of Congress Control Number: 2016940346

LNCS Sublibrary: SL3 – Information Systems and Applications, incl. Internet/Web, and HCI

Printed on acid-free paper

This Springer imprint is published by Springer Nature
The registered company is Springer International Publishing AG Switzerland

Foreword

The 18th International Conference on Human-Computer Interaction, HCI International 2016, was held in Toronto, Canada, during July 17–22, 2016. The event incorporated the 15 conferences/thematic areas listed on the following page.

A total of 4,354 individuals from academia, research institutes, industry, and governmental agencies from 74 countries submitted contributions, and 1,287 papers and 186 posters have been included in the proceedings. These papers address the latest research and development efforts and highlight the human aspects of the design and use of computing systems. The papers thoroughly cover the entire field of human-computer interaction, addressing major advances in knowledge and effective use of computers in a variety of application areas. The volumes constituting the full 27-volume set of the conference proceedings are listed on pages IX and X.

I would like to thank the program board chairs and the members of the program boards of all thematic areas and affiliated conferences for their contribution to the highest scientific quality and the overall success of the HCI International 2016 conference.

This conference would not have been possible without the continuous and unwavering support and advice of the founder, Conference General Chair Emeritus and Conference Scientific Advisor Prof. Gavriel Salvendy. For his outstanding efforts, I would like to express my appreciation to the communications chair and editor of *HCI International News*, Dr. Abbas Moallem.

April 2016 Constantine Stephanidis

HCI International 2016 Thematic Areas and Affiliated Conferences

Thematic areas:

- Human-Computer Interaction (HCI 2016)
- Human Interface and the Management of Information (HIMI 2016)

Affiliated conferences:

- 13th International Conference on Engineering Psychology and Cognitive Ergonomics (EPCE 2016)
- 10th International Conference on Universal Access in Human-Computer Interaction (UAHCI 2016)
- 8th International Conference on Virtual, Augmented and Mixed Reality (VAMR 2016)
- 8th International Conference on Cross-Cultural Design (CCD 2016)
- 8th International Conference on Social Computing and Social Media (SCSM 2016)
- 10th International Conference on Augmented Cognition (AC 2016)
- 7th International Conference on Digital Human Modeling and Applications in Health, Safety, Ergonomics and Risk Management (DHM 2016)
- 5th International Conference on Design, User Experience and Usability (DUXU 2016)
- 4th International Conference on Distributed, Ambient and Pervasive Interactions (DAPI 2016)
- 4th International Conference on Human Aspects of Information Security, Privacy and Trust (HAS 2016)
- Third International Conference on HCI in Business, Government, and Organizations (HCIBGO 2016)
- Third International Conference on Learning and Collaboration Technologies (LCT 2016)
- Second International Conference on Human Aspects of IT for the Aged Population (ITAP 2016)

Conference Proceedings Volumes Full List

1. LNCS 9731, Human-Computer Interaction: Theory, Design, Development and Practice (Part I), edited by Masaaki Kurosu
2. LNCS 9732, Human-Computer Interaction: Interaction Platforms and Techniques (Part II), edited by Masaaki Kurosu
3. LNCS 9733, Human-Computer Interaction: Novel User Experiences (Part III), edited by Masaaki Kurosu
4. LNCS 9734, Human Interface and the Management of Information: Information, Design and Interaction (Part I), edited by Sakae Yamamoto
5. LNCS 9735, Human Interface and the Management of Information: Applications and Services (Part II), edited by Sakae Yamamoto
6. LNAI 9736, Engineering Psychology and Cognitive Ergonomics, edited by Don Harris
7. LNCS 9737, Universal Access in Human-Computer Interaction: Methods, Techniques, and Best Practices (Part I), edited by Margherita Antona and Constantine Stephanidis
8. LNCS 9738, Universal Access in Human-Computer Interaction: Interaction Techniques and Environments (Part II), edited by Margherita Antona and Constantine Stephanidis
9. LNCS 9739, Universal Access in Human-Computer Interaction: Users and Context Diversity (Part III), edited by Margherita Antona and Constantine Stephanidis
10. LNCS 9740, Virtual, Augmented and Mixed Reality, edited by Stephanie Lackey and Randall Shumaker
11. LNCS 9741, Cross-Cultural Design, edited by Pei-Luen Patrick Rau
12. LNCS 9742, Social Computing and Social Media, edited by Gabriele Meiselwitz
13. LNAI 9743, Foundations of Augmented Cognition: Neuroergonomics and Operational Neuroscience (Part I), edited by Dylan D. Schmorrow and Cali M. Fidopiastis
14. LNAI 9744, Foundations of Augmented Cognition: Neuroergonomics and Operational Neuroscience (Part II), edited by Dylan D. Schmorrow and Cali M. Fidopiastis
15. LNCS 9745, Digital Human Modeling and Applications in Health, Safety, Ergonomics and Risk Management, edited by Vincent G. Duffy
16. LNCS 9746, Design, User Experience, and Usability: Design Thinking and Methods (Part I), edited by Aaron Marcus
17. LNCS 9747, Design, User Experience, and Usability: Novel User Experiences (Part II), edited by Aaron Marcus
18. LNCS 9748, Design, User Experience, and Usability: Technological Contexts (Part III), edited by Aaron Marcus
19. LNCS 9749, Distributed, Ambient and Pervasive Interactions, edited by Norbert Streitz and Panos Markopoulos
20. LNCS 9750, Human Aspects of Information Security, Privacy and Trust, edited by Theo Tryfonas

21. LNCS 9751, HCI in Business, Government, and Organizations: eCommerce and Innovation (Part I), edited by Fiona Fui-Hoon Nah and Chuan-Hoo Tan
22. LNCS 9752, HCI in Business, Government, and Organizations: Information Systems (Part II), edited by Fiona Fui-Hoon Nah and Chuan-Hoo Tan
23. LNCS 9753, Learning and Collaboration Technologies, edited by Panayiotis Zaphiris and Andri Ioannou
24. LNCS 9754, Human Aspects of IT for the Aged Population: Design for Aging (Part I), edited by Jia Zhou and Gavriel Salvendy
25. LNCS 9755, Human Aspects of IT for the Aged Population: Healthy and Active Aging (Part II), edited by Jia Zhou and Gavriel Salvendy
26. CCIS 617, HCI International 2016 Posters Proceedings (Part I), edited by Constantine Stephanidis
27. CCIS 618, HCI International 2016 Posters Proceedings (Part II), edited by Constantine Stephanidis

Cross-Cultural Design

Program Board Chair: **Pei-Luen Patrick Rau, P.R. China**

- Zhe Chen, P.R. China
- Pilsung Choe, Qatar
- Paul L. Fu, USA
- Zhiyong Fu, China
- Sung H. Han, Korea
- Toshikazu Kato, Japan
- Pin-Chao Liao, P.R. China
- Dyi-Yih Michael Lin, Taiwan
- Rungtai Lin, Taiwan
- Jun Liu, P.R. China
- Yongqi Lou, P.R. China
- Liang Ma, P.R. China
- Alexander Mädche, Germany
- Katsuhiko Ogawa, Japan
- Teh Pei Lee, Malaysia
- Yuan-Chi Tseng, Taiwan
- Lin Wang, Korea
- Hsiu-Ping Yueh, Taiwan

The full list with the program board chairs and the members of the program boards of all thematic areas and affiliated conferences is available online at:

http://www.hci.international/2016/

HCI International 2017

The 19th International Conference on Human-Computer Interaction, HCI International 2017, will be held jointly with the affiliated conferences in Vancouver, Canada, at the Vancouver Convention Centre, July 9–14, 2017. It will cover a broad spectrum of themes related to human-computer interaction, including theoretical issues, methods, tools, processes, and case studies in HCI design, as well as novel interaction techniques, interfaces, and applications. The proceedings will be published by Springer. More information will be available on the conference website: http://2017.hci.international/.

General Chair
Prof. Constantine Stephanidis
University of Crete and ICS-FORTH
Heraklion, Crete, Greece
E-mail: general_chair@hcii2017.org

http://2017.hci.international/

Contents

Culture and Mobile Interaction

Culture in Smart Environments

Culture and User Experience

Use of Cultural Intelligence to Measure Influence of Online Social Networks on Cultural Adjustment

Shalinda Adikari(✉)

School of Computing,
National University of Singapore, Singapore
shalinda@comp.nus.edu.sg

Abstract. When people are crossing the borders for studies, business and migration purposes, they have to face the culture shock during the mingling of new cultures. However, as online social networks can be reached anytime, from anywhere in most cases where access to traditional networks is impossible, this makes online social networks, particularly important to the sojourner who will have to constantly resort to social support sources to cope with the difficulties and psychological stress of cross-cultural adjustment. Nevertheless, the use of online social networks in the context of cultural adjustment is an under explored area. This study draws upon social network theory, social capital theory and cultural adjustment perspectives, to develop a new model which can contribute to the sparse literature on the impact of online social networks on cross-cultural adjustment and serves a foundation for future research in this vital area of influence of online social networks.

Keywords: Online social networks · Cultural adjustment · Social network ties · Cultural intelligence · Supportive messages

1 Introduction

There is extensive research currently conducted to understand and explain the notion of cross-cultural adaptation, mostly from psychological and sociological aspects. These research works and theories attempt to explain how an individual moving from one culture to another culture (mostly crossing the borders of the country) align his life to the new culture, rules, customs and perceptions. The number of people crossing the borders yearly for studies, business and migration purposes are increasing gradually [18]. Therefore, an analysis on factors that contributes to the sojourners' [18], people who are temporarily residing in countries other than their home country, cultural adjustment is important.

Previous research work has explained cultural adjustment as a staged model of recovery from the cultural shock [4], a learning process [3], a hybrid of both recovery and learning [17], and equilibrium model as a dynamic and cyclic process for tension reduction [4]. Cross-cultural adjustment is also viewed from a social support perspective, in which most of the interaction, learning and recovery related to cultural adjustment is explained via an interaction framework [2]. These literatures have highlighted

P.-L.P. Rau (Ed.): CCD 2016, LNCS 9741, pp. 3–15, 2016.
DOI: 10.1007/978-3-319-40093-8_1

that an immigrant or a sojourner will face resistance and shock during a cultural switch. Individuals use various methods, and tools to accept the new environment and feel habitual in the new culture. Acculturation [11], a process the society and people undergo when two cultures mingle, has been studied in depth in order to determine the most suitable process for a sojourner to be comfortable in the new environment. Online social networks can be considered as a good support structure for acculturation because they provide an opportunity to interact with the new environment and maintain the sojourners' old contact as well. Social networking sites have become an everyday tool in our lives. Social network sites have received a tremendous amount of attention recently by individuals and it is argued in this paper that social networks can influence cultural adjustment. This research will study the social support perspective in multicultural adjustment using the Social Network Theory [7, 22, 31] and attempt to show how a sojourner for acculturation can use online social networks, the indispensable tool used for networking in the present day.

As mentioned earlier, the number of people crossing borders is increasing. They will undergo the cultural shocks discussed in the previous section, which has been studied in psychology in depth. This study contributes to the above literature by understanding how online social networking can be used for acculturation. It combines the psychological theory on the social support perspective of cultural adjustment with existing social networking theories, using today's popular social networking media. Apart from the theoretical contribution, the implications of the study recommends different types social ties for sojourners to find various social supports to overcome depression, obtain affirmation, improve skills and get tangible assistance, in the process of adapting to the new culture. Based on the above theoretical and practical implications of this study, it can be considered that this research makes a significant contribution to the existing cross cultural adjustment literature.

The rest of this report is organized in the following manner. Section 2 discusses the theoretical background and the Sect. 3 discusses the theoretical framework, including the hypotheses. Section 4 explains the data collection, analysis and results. The Sect. 5 discusses the importance and implications of this study.

2 Theoretical Background

Cultural adjustment has been used interchangeably with cultural adjustment in the literature. It has also been variously defined. [17] defined cultural adjustment as a process in which a person familiarizing with and is able to function effectively in a new culture. Adelman [2] considers cultural adjustment as coping with uncertainty in and attaining perceived mastery or control over the new cultural environment. According to Searle and Ward [34], cultural adjustment includes a socio-cultural sense of adjustment and psychological feelings of wellbeing. Ang, Van Dyne et al. [5] concur with Searle and Ward [34] as they consider cultural adjustment as a person's attainment of interactional adjustment and general wellbeing. Earlier research has looked at the phenomenon of cultural adjustment from an individual perspective. One of such key research is Black and Stephens [16] which has contributed greatly to the literature on understanding the acculturation of expatriates. This work was based on the threefold classification: general adjustment, interaction adjustment and work adjustment by Black [13] and it became the foundation for later research: [6, 14, 27, 33, 35–37]. However, [17] has proposed an enhanced model which helps to measure adjustment in different dimensions while distinguishing between cognitions and emotions [10, 15, 24–26]. This model explores the outcomes of adjustment in a cross-sectional sample of expatriates via the definitions of constructs like novelty, discretion, self-efficacy, and social networks.

In contributing to prior research, Ang, Van Dyne et al. [5] have developed the constructs of cultural intelligence (CQ) [23] based on contemporary theories [20] in the offline settings. They have enhanced the theoretical precision of cultural intelligence [23] by developing a model which posits differential relationships between the four dimensions of CQ (metacognitive, cognitive, motivational and behavioral) and three intercultural effectiveness outcomes (cultural judgment and decision making, cultural adjustment and task performance in culturally diverse settings). Testing the model through several substantive studies, they have established a consistent pattern of relationships between the four CQ dimensions and the three intercultural effectiveness outcomes where metacognitive CQ and cognitive CQ predict cultural judgment and decision making; motivational CQ and behavioral CQ predict cultural adjustment; and metacognitive CQ and behavioral CQ predict task performance. Therefore, according to Ang et al. [5], a sojourner to be culturally adapted, he or she needs to be achieved cultural adjustment, cultural judgment, decision making and task performance essences. However, the cultural intelligence has only been tested in offline setting and not applied to the online setting at all.

From a social network perspective, a social network involves a set of actors and the relations that connect them [38]. The social network of actors (i.e., individual people, organizations or families) consists of strong ties and weak ties. A tie is the relationship between individuals in the network. Strong ties such as family or close friends [2, 29], are more intimate and involve various forms of resource exchange. Weak ties such as friends of friends, past colleagues, or other acquaintances [21], on the other hand, involve fewer intimate exchanges and less frequent maintenance. They are considered as valuable conduits to diverse perspectives and new information [21]. According to Birnie and Horvath [12], social network theory is able to apply to describe human relationships developed through either face-to-face communication or electronic means. It is particularly relevant to the examination of how the Internet helps maintain old ties and establish new ties [38]. SNSs, aside facilitating the maintenance of pre-existing social ties and the creation of new connections [38], are considered to be an important platform for individuals to manage a wider network of weak ties [21]. Social network theory is therefore applicable to examine online social networks developed through SNSs.

Social capital has been used to describe the latent aggregated resources and benefits entrenched in the relationships with other people [19, 21], such as tangible assistance, emotional support, assurances and skill acquisition [2]. Two kinds of social capital have been discussed by Putnam [32]. Bonding social capital comes from strong ties (i.e., close friends and family) in the form of emotional support [29] and tangible resources [21]. Bridging social capital, conversely, "consists of loose relationships (i.e., weak ties) which serve as bridges connecting a person to a different network, allowing the person access to new perspectives and diffuse information" [29].

3 Theoretical Framework

The research question addressed in this study is how cultural intelligence can be used to measure online social networks of a sojourner influence on cross cultural adjustment. The study has adopted the social support perspective of cultural adjustment from the psychology literature and combines it with the social network theories in the information systems literature to deliver a comprehensive model to analyze the influence of the online social networks on acculturation.

Based on the social support perspective of cultural adaptation discussed by M.B. Adelman [2] cultural adjustment is an indication of (1) coping with uncertainty and (2) perceived mastery or control. The support of the society is classified into two notions such as (1) supportive messages and (2) supportive sources. As earlier mentioned, the cultural intelligence [23] by Ang, Van Dyne et al. [5], can be defined as a measurement of sojourner's capability to function and manage effectively in a culturally diverse setting through meta-cognitive CQ, cognitive CQ, behavioral CQ, and motivational CQ. This measurement has been further enhanced to demonstrate a consistent pattern of relationship where motivational CQ and behavioral CQ predict cultural adjustment. Combining the above two models, we argue that cultural adjustment that is motivational CQ and behavioral CQ of the cultural intelligence is equivalence to coping with uncertainty and perceived mastery or control of Adelman's model. Therefore, the equivalence to coping with uncertainty and perceived mastery or control can be achieved through the relevant supportive messages. Furthermore, the supportive messages received related to the cultural adjustment from the social network could allow a sojourner to be adapted to the multi-cultural environment by adjusting to the new culture and then have a sound cultural judgment and decision-making process. As a fact that, the remaining two intercultural effectiveness outcomes that are specified in the cultural intelligence (cultural judgment and decision making and task performance) can only be achieved after a sojourner becomes adjusted to the new culture. We also argue that different social support groups in the online social network will provide support in the cultural adjustment process at different levels. This suggests that different types of supportive messages will be provided by different groups, which is mainly categorized as weak ties and strong ties based on the tie strength.

Based on the aforementioned arguments and the theoretical background, we provide the following model, which ultimately uses cultural intelligence to answer the several sub-questions in the current research which are, (a) Does cultural intelligence ample to measure cultural adjustment via social network settings? (b) Does a social network allow an individual to have more cultural adjustment in the multi-cultural environment? (c) Does the supportive messages received via social networks relate to an individual's multi-cultural adjustment. (d) How does strong and weak ties related to different kind of supportive messages.

3.1 Proposed Model

Based on the social support perspective on coping with uncertainty of cultural adjustment theory [2], we have identified four message types that can be considered as the support received by the network/surrounding for a sojourner. We have considered these four messages as the independent variables of our model [4]. These four message types support an individual to

1. Have perspective shifts on cause-effect contingencies: We have defined this variable as Overcome Depression(OD)
2. Enhance control through skill acquisition: We have defined this variable as Skill Improvement(SI)
3. Enhance control through tangible assistance: We have defined this variable Tangible Assistance(TA)
4. Enhance control through acceptance and assurance: We have defined this variable as Acceptance and Assurance(A&A)

The model describes that these messages are received by different types of supportive sources in the sojourners' network/surrounding. We consider these supportive sources as the ties [22] in the network of the sojourner and identify it as a moderator that supports an individual at different levels in cultural adjustment using the aforementioned messages. The dependent variables we measure are, motivational CQ and behavioral CQ, which we define as the cultural adjustment and it is measured by the cultural intelligence of an individual [5]. Figure 1 depicts the complete proposed model.

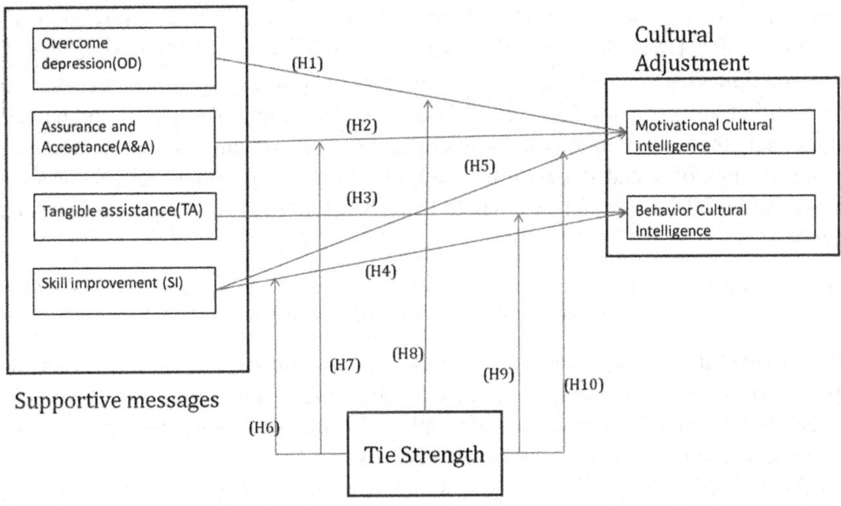

Fig. 1. Proposed theoretical model

3.2 Hypotheses

As per the model above, there are seven constructs, and following are the hypothesis we have derived in order to find answers to the initial research questions.

Overcoming Depression. Essentially, these messages aid the individual in modifying negative causal attributions that contribute to feelings of being overwhelmed or depressed. For example, spouses can be overwhelmed by the enormous task of family relocation, resulting in feelings of personal helplessness in organizing for the move. Pre-departure assistance can function to help prospective sojourners in developing realistic expectations and beliefs about personal capabilities that mediate stress [4]. Using online social networks sojourners can reduce their stress well by playing games, simple conversation of similar experience and do other activities. Therefore the following hypothesis can be derived.

(H1) The extend of supportive messages received from the online social network to overcome depression is positively related with the motivational cultural intelligence

Assurance and Acceptance. Emotional support in the form of validation of self-worth, affirmation of personal relationships, and a sense of belonging is a critical function of these messages. Cross-cultural, adjustment, particularly given the disruption of old ties, is dependent on the acceptance and reassurances of others in the new setting. Membership groups, of people undergoing similar changes, often serve to alleviate the stress of culture-shock and provide an ersatz community [4]. Therefore, the following hypothesis can be derived.

(H2) The extend of supportive messages received from the online social network for assurance and acceptance is positively related with the motivational cultural intelligence

Tangible Assistance. This straightforward assistance of personal resources (e.g., time, money, labor) cannot be underestimated in the initial and long-term adjustment to a new environment. However, what makes such concrete assistance "supportive" are the interpersonal messages which accompany this help. The old adage, "It's not what you say (give), but how you say (give) it" applies to offering tangible help to another. For example, neighbors who offer to assist in childcare while moving into a new home can promote feelings of social integration based on communal exchange or a contractual arrangement based on monetary exchange [4]. Therefore the following hypothesis can be derived.

(H3) The extend of supportive messages received from the online social network for tangible assistance is positively related with the behavioral cultural intelligence

Skill Improvement. These supportive messages function to increase the skills of a recipient to achieve desirable out-comes. Orientation programs for developing cross-cultural communication skills and problem solving are representative of this type of instructional support. Among informal networks, such as sojourning students' ties with host nationals, these message types function instrumentally to facilitate the academic and professional aspirations of the sojourner [4]. Therefore, the following hypothesis can be derived.

(H4) The extend of supportive messages received from the online social network for skill improvement is positively related with the motivational cultural intelligence.

(H5) The extend of supportive messages received from the online social network for skill improvement is positively related with the behavioral cultural intelligence.

Strong Ties. The strong ties in the social network will be the community who the sojourner interacts frequently, and who knows themselves in detail. These groups in the social network will help the sojourner to overcome the shock in the new environment by helping to overcome depression. Furthermore, since they are more close to the sojourner they will understand the sojourners' feelings on the new environment and will provide reassurance and affirmation. Therefore, we derive the following two hypotheses.

(H6) If the tie strength is stronger, then the relationship between the overcome depression and motivational cultural intelligence will be stronger.

(H7) If the tie strength is stronger, then the relationship between the affirmation/assurance and motivational cultural intelligence will be stronger.

(H8) If the tie strength is stronger, then the relationship between tangible assistance and behavioral cultural intelligence will be stronger.

Weak Ties. The weak ties in the social network will be the community who the sojourner does not interact frequently or the people from the new community. There are groups in the social network will main assist the sojourner in acquiring new skills and to get tangible assistance.

(H9) If the tie strength is weaker, then the relationship between the skill improvement and motivational cultural intelligence will be stronger.

(H10) If the tie strength is weaker, then the relationship between skill improvement and behavioral cultural intelligence will be stronger.

4 Data Collection and Analysis

As stated above, the main emphasis of this research is to find out the use of cultural intelligence to measure the influence of online social network: the Facebook, on these students to become culturally adjusted when they first arrived in Singapore. Therefore to conduct the survey on the above mentioned research question, we have used the given questionnaire in the appendix that formulated according to the proposed hypotheses. The questionnaire was created as the measurement instrument in-order to measure the influence of online social networks on cultural adjustment. After an extensive literature review, 29 items were selected to measure the 7 constructs. Since it was required to measure which type social network ties provide each of the supportive messages, there was a need to repeat the tie strength measurement questions for each supportive message type. The validity of the questionnaire was checked using two techniques; they are Face validity and Pretest. As the initial step, to evaluate the Face validity, the developed questionnaire was given to several experts in the field of Information System (including senior PhD students) to review. The main purpose of this step was to ensure the consistency of items and the constructs. After that, the questionnaire was refined based on their comments. As the second step, the questionnaire was distributed within 10 university town residents to complete as a pre-test. This group consisted of graduate students and exchange students in the National University of Singapore. The purpose of this test was to check the understandability of the questions. Based on their feedback, the questionnaire was finalized as shown in the appendix. As the next step of our study, the questionnaire was designed electronically and distributed among the residents of University Town. 148 residents responded to the survey, but only 130 cases were selected for analysis. To check whether the selected sample is good enough to carry out the analysis, we have conducted the KMO and Bartlett's Test. According to the analysis results the KMO value is 0.799 and it is well above the recommended value of 0.5 [30]. To further understand the underlying relationships of the proposed factors and items, we have conducted Exploratory factor analysis (EFA) and Confirmatory factor analysis (CFA) [36]. Once AA1, OD4, MOT5, BEH5, BEH4, BEH3, MC5, and MC4 items were removed remaining items are satisfied the both convergent and discriminant validity.

The hypotheses were tested using LISREL. According to the Table 1, we can see that only the hypotheses H3 and H8, is supported. That is the relationship between Tangible assistance and Behavioral CQ. This implies that, the constructs Overcome depression, Acceptance and Skill improvement, which were the antecedent for Motivational CQ, did not surprisingly show any statistically significant relationships. Also, the effect of Skill improvement does not contribute to the Behavioral CQ. Aligned with the H8, we can say that the tie strength is stronger sojourners receive more supportive messages related to the tangible assistance and that leads to better achieve the behavioral CQ.

Table 1. The hypotheses that significant with the direct effect and the moderator effect

Hypothesis	t-value	Coefficient	Outcome
H3	3.36	0.23	Supported
H8	3.526	0.251	Supported

5 Discussion

The study finds that certain types of supportive messages from the online social network assist in improving different aspects in cultural adaptation. As sojourners who have come to a foreign country for studies, they have understood the possible supportive sources in the online social networks and used it to become more culturally aware and adjusted to the new environment. By being engaged in online social networks during the transition period from one culture to another culture across borders the sojourner can expect to receive different types of supportive messages which can help him be better prepared for the new environment. However, they should understand that these supportive messages are capable of assisting in cultural adjustment only if the sojourner is willing to act upon the information and emotional support received.

Intention to use online social networks for acculturation will increase over the time due to high usage of social media amongst the society. As identified via the survey most of the sojourners have received messages for tangible assistance via their social network during the cultural adaptation. The survey only captures the extension of messages received via the online social network for tangible assistance. It does not indicate that the sojourner received the particular tangible assistance. However, as the there is a positive correlation between the behavioral CQ and the tangible assistance messages received via the online social network, it can be inferred that sojourners use the online social network during the transition period to overcome certain cultural difficulties.

The rest of the results as shown above indicates that there is no significant relationship between the supportive messages received for depression, affirmation, skill improvement with the motivational or behavioral CQ. This result contradicts the existing literature and our initial model predictions. Therefore, it is required to explore the reasons for this contradiction.

The focal reason for the low significance of the model could be due to the relationships build in the theoretical framework with the supportive messages and the cultural adaptation. Even though previous studies have clearly indicated and justified that cultural adjustment can be measured by the cultural intelligence measurements, since many of the hypotheses are not supported in this framework, we suggest to explore other measurements of cultural adjustment. Different measurements to measure the uncertainty level and the perceived mastery the new environment could improve these results [5]. Furthermore, there are other social network theories, which captures the social capital of the sojourner [9] which could be considered as level of cultural adjustment. We argue that these results could be made more significant if a better measurement of cultural adjustment can be devised based on certainty level and perceived mastery in the new environment.

Therefore, for the future studies, it needs to be explored if a different measurement for cultural adjustment can be obtained if the significance of the model can be improved. These two future actions are mandatory for this study in order to validate the framework with high significance levels. Also, from the theoretical perspective, the framework is capable of capturing only the supportive messages received from the online social networks. There could be a negative effect based on the messages received via the online social network. Therefore, it is required to explore the negative messages that can be given from an online social network to a sojourner, which could tamper the effect from the positive supportive messages received from the social network.

The objective of this study is to develop a comparative, theoretical model to determine the use of cultural intelligence to measure the influence of the online social network for acculturation in a sojourner's life. The theoretical model was mainly built upon the theory of social supportive perspective of cultural adjustment and social network theories. Our results show that online social networks provide supportive messages for tangible assistance, which leads to the behavioral CQ of a sojourner. In conclusion, we attempt to explain the insignificance of relationships by highlighting that the cultural intelligence score might not be the most suitable cultural adjustment measurement in this context since the supportive messages received via the online social network could have less influence on the cultural intelligence on the sojourner. Therefore, we propose a revision to the measurement of cultural adjustment that should be captured by the uncertainty level and perceive mastery of the sojourner in the online settings.

Appendix

Construct	Item	Description
Motivational cultural intelligence [5]	MOT1	I enjoy interacting with people from different cultures
	MOT2	I am confident that I can socialize with locals in a culture that is unfamiliar to me
	MOT3	I am sure I can deal with the stresses of adjusting to a culture that is new to me
	MOT4	I enjoy living in cultures that are unfamiliar to me
	MOT5	I am confident that I can get accustomed to the shopping conditions in a different culture
Behavioral cultural intelligence [5]	BEH1	I change my verbal behavior (e.g., accent, tone) when a cross-cultural interaction requires it
	BEH2	I use pause and silence differently to suit different cross-cultural situations
	BEH3	I vary the rate of my speaking when a cross-cultural situation requires it
	BEH4	I change my nonverbal behavior when a cross-cultural situation requires it
	BEH5	I alter my facial expressions when a cross-cultural interaction requires it
Tie strength derived from [28]	TS1	On average how close was your relationship with the people who sent messages indicated in Section X, prior to receiving the messages
	TS2	On average how often did you communicate with the people who sent messages in Section X, prior to receiving the messages
	TS3	On average to what extent did you typically interact with the people who sent messages in Section X, prior to receiving the messages
OD derived from [9]	OD1	Did some activity together to help me get my mind off of things and made me feel less bored
	OD2	Conducted discussions to make me feel less disappointed about myself when I had difficulties in the new environment
	OD3	Talked with me about some interest of mine and made me feel interested in the new environment
	OD4	Joked and kidded and tried to cheer me up
A&A derived from [1]	AA1	Expressed esteem and respect for a competency or personal quality of yours, and what you are doing
	AA2	Listened to you talk about your private feelings, and listened when you wanted to confide about things that were important to you
	AA3	Let you know that he/she will always be around if you need assistance and cared about you as a person

(*Continued*)

(*Continued*)

Construct	Item	Description
	AA4	Agreed that what you wanted to do was right and appreciated it
SI derived from [1, 39]	SI1	Directed you to useful information on how to do something in the new environment
	SI2	Suggested some action you should take to improve your skills
	SI3	Gave you feedback on how you were doing without saying it was good or bad
	SI4	If I wanted to learn a new word in the Singapore culture my social network helped me to find that information
TA derived from [8]	TA1	Agreed to loan you something that you needed
	TA2	Pitched in to help you do something that needed to get done
	TA3	Agreed to come with you to someone who could take action on a particular situation
	TA4	Agreed to provide you with a place to stay or lend some money

References

1. Abbey, A., Abramis, D.J., Caplan, R.D.: Effects of different sources of social support and social conflict on emotional well-being. Basic Appl. Soc. Psychol. **6**(2), 111–129 (1985)
2. Adelman, M.B.: Cross-cultural adjustment: a theoretical perspective on social support. Int. J. Intercultural Relat. **12**(3), 183–204 (1988)
3. Adler, P.S.: Culture shock and the cross-cultural learning experience. In: Luce, L.F., Smith, E.C. (eds.) Toward Internationalism: Readings in Cross-Cultural Communication (1987)
4. Anderson, L.E.: A new look at an old construct: cross-cultural adaptation. Int. J. Intercultural Relat. **18**(3), 293–328 (1994)
5. Ang, S., Van Dyne, L., Koh, C., Ng, K.Y., Templer, K.J., Tay, C., Chandrasekar, N.A.: Cultural intelligence: its measurement and effects on cultural judgment and decision making, cultural adaptation and task performance. Manage. Organ. Rev. **3**(3), 335–371 (2007)
6. Aycan, Z.: Expatriate adjustment as a multifaceted phenomenon: individual and organizational level predictors. Int. J. Hum. Resour. Manage. **8**(4), 434–456 (1997)
7. Barnes, J.A.: Class and committees in a Norwegian island parish. Plenum, New York (1954)
8. Barrera, M., Ainlay, S.L.: The structure of social support: a conceptual and empirical analysis. J. Community Psychol. **11**(2), 133–143 (1983)
9. Beck, A.T., Ward, C.H., Mendelson, M., Mock, J., Erbauugh, J.: An inventory for measuring depression. Arch. Gen. Psychiatry **4**, 561–571 (1961)
10. Berger, C.R., Gudykunst, W.B.: Uncertainty and communication. Progress Commun. Sci. **10**, 21–66 (1991)
11. Berry, J.W.: Immigration, acculturation, and adaptation. Appl. Psychol. **46**(1), 5–34 (1997)

12. Birnie, S.A., Horvath, P.: Psychological predictors of internet social communication. J. Comput.-Mediated Commun. **7**(4) (2002)
13. Black, J.S.: Work role transitions: a study of American expatriate managers in Japan. J. Int. Bus. Stud. **19**(2), 277–294 (1988)
14. Black, J.S.: O Kaerinasai: factors related to japanese repatriation adjustment. Hum. Relat. **47** (12), 1489–1508 (1994)
15. Black, J.S., Gregersen, H.B.: Antecedents to cross-cultural adjustment for expatriates in Pacific Rim assignments. Hum. Relat. **44**(5), 497–515 (1991)
16. Black, J.S., Stephens, G.K.: The influence of the spouse on American expatriate adjustment and intent to stay in Pacific Rim overseas assignments. J. Manag. **15**(4), 529–544 (1989)
17. Brewster, C., Suutari, V., Haslberger, A.: Facets and dimensions of cross-cultural adaptation: refining the tools. Pers. Rev. **34**(1), 85–109 (2005)
18. Church, A.T.: Sojourner adjustment. Psychol. Bull. **91**(3), 540 (1982)
19. Coleman, J.: Social capital in the creation of human capital. Am. J. Sociol. **94**, S95–S12 (1988)
20. Earley, P.C., Ang, S.: Cultural intelligence: Individual interactions across cultures. Stanford University Press, Palo Alto (2003)
21. Ellison, N.B., Lampe, C., Steinfield, C.: Feature social network sites and society: current trends and future possibilities. Interactions **16**(1), 6–9 (2009)
22. Granovetter, M.S.: The strength of weak ties. Am. J. Sociol. **78**, 1360–1380 (1973)
23. Gross, R., Acquisti, A.: Information revelation and privacy in online social networks. In: Proceedings of the 2005 ACM Workshop on Privacy in the Electronic Society. ACM (2005)
24. Grove, C.L., Torbiörn, I.: A new conceptualization of intercultural adjustment and the goals of training. Int. J. Intercultural Relat. **9**(2), 205–233 (1985)
25. Gudykunst, W.B.: Uncertainty and anxiety. In: Theories in Intercultural Communication, pp. 123–156 (1988)
26. Gudykunst, W.B., Nishida, T.: Attributional confidence in low-and high-context cultures. Hum. Commun. Res. **12**(4), 525–549 (1986)
27. Kraimer, M.L., Wayne, S.J., Jaworski, R.A.A.: Sources of support and expatriate performance: the mediating role of expatriate adjustment. Pers. Psychol. **54**(1), 71–99 (2001)
28. Levin, D.Z., Cross, R.: The strength of weak ties you can trust: the mediating role of trust in effective knowledge transfer. Manage. Sci. **50**(11), 1477–1490 (2004)
29. Lin, J.-H., Peng, W., Kim, M., Kim, S.Y., LaRose, R.: Social networking and adjustments among international students. New Media Soc. **14**(3), 421–440 (2012)
30. Massey Jr., F.J.: The Kolmogorov-Smirnov test for goodness of fit. J. Am. Stat. Assoc. **46** (253), 68–78 (1951)
31. Milgram, S.: The small world problem. Psychol. Today **2**(1), 60–67 (1967)
32. Putnam, R.D.: Bowling alone: The collapse and revival of American community. Simon and Schuster, New York (2000)
33. Robie, C., Ryan, A.M.: Structural equivalence of a measure of cross-cultural adjustment. Educ. Psychol. Measur. **56**(3), 514–521 (1996)
34. Searle, W., Ward, C.: The prediction of psychological and sociocultural adjustment during cross-cultural transitions. Int. J. Intercultural Relat. **14**(4), 449–464 (1990)
35. Selmer, J.: Practice makes perfect? International experience and expatriate adjustment. MIR: Manag. Int. Rev. **42**(1), 71–87 (2002)
36. Straub, D., Boudreau, M.C., Gefen, D.: Validation guidelines for IS positivist research. Commun. Assoc. Inf. Syst. **13**(1), 63 (2004)

37. Takeuchi, R., Yun, S., Russell, J.E.: Antecedents and consequences of the perceived adjustment of Japanese expatriates in the USA. Int. J. Hum. Resour. Manage. **13**(8), 1224–1244 (2002)
38. Taylor, S., Napier, N.: Working in Japan: lessons from women expatriates. Sloan Manage. Rev. **37**, 76–84 (1996)
39. Ye, J.: Traditional and online support networks in the cross-cultural adaptation of chinese international students in the United States. J. Computer-Mediated Commun. **11**(3), 863–876 (2006)

HCI Within Cross-Cultural Discourses of Globally Situated Rhetorical and Etymological Interactions

Daniel G. Cabrero[1(✉)], Arminda Guerra Lopes[2], and Barbara Rita Barricelli[3]

[1] School of Computing and Engineering, University of West London, London, UK
daniel@personas.technology

[2] Madeira Interactive Technologies Institute, Madeira, Portugal
aguerralopes@gmail.com

[3] Department of Computer Science, Università Degli Studi Di Milano, Milan, Italy
barricelli@di.unimi.it

Abstract. About forty years of thriving Human-Computer Interaction (HCI) have expanded into an affluent and apparent diverse and enriching field-for-all. Subsequently this has given way to other fields such as Human-Work Interaction Design (HWID), where a main focus stands on human-centred practices at work regarding productivity and the final fulfilment of humanly aims and goals. This is in stark contrast with other ways of accepting the world, thus of work. HCI for Development (HCI4D) often shows interdependences proposed in the Global North often fail in settings like in the East or also in the Global South. This is while technology permeates at rapid and unstoppable paces everywhere. If HCI4D thus-far shows scant positive results, traditional HWID is seemingly stagnated into modes of production having little to do with promoting actual satisfaction, nor environmental sustainability, to mention a few further options. As younger, novice participants enter academic and practitioner HCI grounds, concepts, definitions and terminology resemble confusion at times, while in occasions these appear to depict archaic modes of distribution, self-empowerment and development as inevitable in today's technologically connected world. Questioning thus existing globalised status-quos related to concepts, definitions and deployments sparks into proposing fairer, more sustainable and micro-cultural approaches to life via and by HCI. To achieve the above, the disentanglement of established meanings through the dissemination of objects, concepts and HCI definitions and terminologies is proposed by applying a theoretical and a pragmatic analysis. This is done with the aim of shedding clarity via reflection and comprehension into mindfulness of ethical and integral possibilities.

This paper presents, proposes and discusses an approach to concepts and words in everyday life such as work, interaction and development, as seen from a myriad of cultural perspectives, cases and understandings. The ultimate objective is to keep discerning past, present and future meanings in HCI, and the connotations of such commonly used terms and expressions.

Keywords: HCI · Rhetoric · Etymology · HWID · HCI4D · Cultural Usability · UX · Participatory Design · Personas · Micro-Cultures

P.-L.P. Rau (Ed.): CCD 2016, LNCS 9741, pp. 16–25, 2016.
DOI: 10.1007/978-3-319-40093-8_2

1 Introduction

About forty years now have got HCI thriving and expanding into an apparent diverse and enriching field-for-all. It is well known computers back then got initially disposed to facilitate efficient and effective ways, though more recently they aim to evolve into striving for a satisfactory usage. Subsequently this also gave way to several subfields such as HWID, where the main focus stands on the integration of work analysis and interaction design methods for pervasive and smart workplaces, and where the intended aim is in promoting human-centred practices in work places in regards to productivity to fulfil humanly aims and objectives. With the breakthrough of cross-cultural HCI, smart work places and philosophies from the Global North have recently trespassed frontiers. This is so, for example, with HCI4D as a form of crossing and cutting into cultural milieus whereby technology permeates at a rapid, ubiquitous, and unstoppable pace. Such speed of this evolution, though, is all problematic to firmly catching-up with by academic and practitioner spheres alike. This is while, often, agendas and interests from some 'other' parties prevail. As a result of a lack in epistemological adaptation HCI4D so-far shows scant positive results (Blake et al. 2014), whereas traditional HWID can be somewhat seen as stagnated into modes of production having little to do with promoting actual satisfaction, nor gratification beyond the financial means, nor environmental sustainability to mention but few aims. It is then that HCI, from its Global North lieu of inception, seemingly keeps promising endless technological supplies and innovations based on a swaying capitalistic system of depleting resources. This is a system where many, at best, undergo competition issues even if not desiring to contend at all. As younger novice participants permeate HCI academic and practitioner grounds, contexts, concepts, definitions, and terminology often resemble confusion at times, while in occasions they appear to depict archaic modes of distribution, self-empowerment and development as inevitable in today's connected world. Some of such apprentices, thus, question the existing globalised status-quo of concepts, definitions and deployments, while they propose a fairer, more sustainable and micro-cultural approach to life through HCI (Löfstrom 2010). A way to strive towards achieving the above objectives is by means of disentangling established terms and meanings through the dissemination of the significance of objects, concepts and HCI definitions, and terminologies, by applying a pragmatic analysis that scaffolds from the theory. Another way is by looking at synonyms and antonyms so as to shed clarity via exemplification, reflection, open-mindedness and an ultimate mutual comprehension. Thus, a study of the evolving of words and meanings is hereby proposed into mindfulness, ethicality and integrity among other possibilities for, and toward a better HCI-for-all.

This paper hence introduces first, proposes later, and eventually, if constructively, criticises and discusses a rhetorical and etymological approach to concepts and terms of everyday life such as work, interaction and development as seen from a myriad of cultural perspectives and understandings. This is then contextualised and intertwined into HWID and HCI4D, together with concepts of HCI such as Usability and UX, as well as with some of the methods, tools and techniques utilised in the field of HCI such personas. The objective is to keep discerning past, present and future meanings, and the connotations of such commonly used terms and expressions. This is done by means of exemplification of different signifiers and signifies of the terms aforementioned, and the questions these provoke when seen from a kaleidoscopic viewpoint within, but also beyond the understanding in the Global North. The ultimate aim is to establish HCI advancements and to propose HCI in-the-making via reflecting the use of terms and communicational tools and their meanings across cultures.

2 A 'Bit' of HCI History: The Proposal of a 4th 'Gratifying' Wave

The need to continuously reflect upon the history of HCI has to do with rapid changes on the field's focus, together with its very recent emergence. Understanding reasons for different outcomes, we can then assess today's visions more realistically, and tomorrow's views, perhaps, more lucidly and sympathetically with us and others.

After the initial HCI wave of technical rationality, Grudin (2005) began to focus on the cultural barriers that still today separate HCI and IS: HCI discovered the limitations of laboratory studies and surveys to understand discretionary use of methods and the focus of IS in research as based on the economic, organizational, and marketing theory and practice of today.

The third wave of HCI claimed to expand from the working and computer-based context into a broader environment of the mobile and the home, the everyday lives and also into culture (Bødker 2006). This then meant to break the boundaries between work and leisure, arts and the home. In other words, between rationality and emotion.

Grudin (2012) goes on arguing HCI as a field amalgamating disciplines: human factors, information systems, computer science, and library and information science. He concludes that HCI, wherever studied, it will be in its early days of research. Reasons to such a statement are changes on influences: new waves of hardware enable diverse ways to support same activities; email changed the way we communicate; social networking came along; the desktop computer has lost the spotlight to portable devices; government and industry invest on parallel computing; different patterns of technology use emerge in different cultures and in different industries; accessibility and sustainability are development areas; digital technologies changed people's behaviors.

In their part, Sanders and Stappers (2014) argue the way design is done, and who is responsible it, have evolved based on a move from the designing of things to interactions to systems, and from designing for laypeople to designing with and by people.

As such, recent issues about the disciplinary of HCI have been debated because of the prevalence and resistance of 'the old modes'. Scaffolding from CHI publications over the past 20 years, Kostakos (2015) shows HCI seemed to follow technical fashions rather than long-term research themes, and argues HCI does not seem to have a solid intellectual or methodological core. Reeves (2015) then recommends thinking of HCI not as a discipline, but rather as an inter-discipline. This Rogers and Blackwell (2012) agree upon, while they go deeply on the discussion stating there is a hole at the center of HCI research. To explain this hole they focus on two case studies: one as a systematic analysis of 180 collaborative projects on research in interdisciplinary design toward understanding the insights into human behavior; a second case study comes as a survey of interdisciplinary innovation. These studies allowed to reflecting on the use of theories and methods on other disciplines to do HCI work. Pan et al. (2012) are equally concerned about HCI becoming a fashion-driven discipline. They propose to examine and explore what might happen if HCI becomes a fashion-driven discipline.

Finally Rogers and Blackwell (2012) problematize whether HCI is a discipline or not. It might not be, as Kim (1990) already advised, due to the need of interdisciplinary cooperation, as HCI is not discipline but an interdisciplinary field, thus a generality.

A contemplation of a fourth wave in HCI may well hence come-by and emerge from, for example, problematizing methods, tools and techniques that do not make it into the proceedings of big conferences such as CHI (Cockton 2013); also by propositioning to solidly moving from User-Centered Design (UCD) philosophies of professional designer and top management self-empowerment into a more Participatory Design (PD) involvement of laypeople (Sanders 2002) in the construction of sustainable and gratifying futures. It must not though be forgotten that wide participation is not it all, and that innovation at times comes making a worthy breakthrough (Cockton 2013).

What seems clear to many more by the day is that there must be a liaison and a humanly attuning in the adoption of human values towards a gratifying UX (Harper et al. 2008), as well as a carefully drafted agenda toward an HCI research and practice based on human needs and social responsibility (Muller et al. 1997).

As technology strives to connect with the human body and soul, we must now think about the world as a small portion of the Universe, thus act with responsibility in developing life and the human race with a set of values, ethics, and integrity that are coherent with Gaia and all things in the world being interconnected (Laurel 2011).

3 Communication in HCI: Is It Issued or We Make It Ourselves?

Since as humans we are societal beings, communication is paramount ground for society formation, information, comprehension, and at times for transgression too. Communication though is greatest yet challenge in HCI in that, at its core, HCI strives to find out how to overcome a fundamental design challenge: how to draw on user-data to effectively communicate relevant needs, requirements and aspirations to the design of technologies (Grudin 2003). Cultural Usability emphasizes this challenge outside the Global North, while it argues western prevailing methods as ill-suited beyond their realm (Winschiers-Theophilus 2009). Thus if living in an interconnected world, methodologies, methods, tools and techniques need of a further analysis and potential adaptation, perhaps also a greater redesign when deployed "out there".

Drawing on the HWID'15 pre-conference meeting held at the British Computer Society (BCS) in London UK, a discussion took place about what the word work means. Themes and proposals emerged as: aging users, independent lives and work modes, happiness by purpose, long-term usage together with interest/change of technology, boredom because of automatizing, current and new technologies, redundancy, smart university/analytics and visualization, UX in factory, create work, phases in life, co-creation, experience based products and value assessment, and the word work per-se.

While such conceptualizations are open to interpretation, we tackle them in the section below by analyzing the origin and evolution of terms such as work, interaction and development, and in the ensuing section we then propose some empirical understandings across projects and cultural milieus as well.

4 An Approach to Signifiers and Signified Across Cultures

This section introduces and analyses terms as follows: work, development and interaction. This is in order to offer some understandings across cultures and settings, and to find out what sustainability, social change and empowerment are or can be.

4.1 Work

In his seminal work "Keywords: A Vocabulary of Culture and Society" Williams (1983) analyzed the historical evolution of many major terms for culture and society. Not surprisingly most of these expressions are still very common, while their meaning continuously evolves through cultures and along societal changes and agendas.

The sense of the word *Work*, in particular, is described by Williams as changed from "*activity and effort or achievement*" to "*steady or timed work*" (Williams 1983, p. 103) underlining its peculiarity of imposed condition. This leads to the consideration of Work as an activity performed for a wage or a salary, therefore strictly related to being hired.

The word *Career*, in contrast, is described as focusing on the relationship the concept has with a person's progress in life, without only being the Work activity (ibid, 1983). Given his political inclinations, Williams' opinions about pursuing a career are very strong, especially when efforts to reaching promotion are compared with a *rat race*.

A further publication very critical on today's economic scenario and that criticizes how work is considered in a capitalistic society is "The Corrosion of the Character" (Sennett 2000). Here people are specifically described as individuals now used to concepts like flexibility, teamwork, delayering, and ever-changing working conditions being presented as new opportunities for self-fulfillment. For Sennett, however, these are to be seen as new forms of oppression leading to damages in workers' well-being.

The cause on the above might be found, among others, in the depletion of world natural resources, as much as in the long working hours for many which, paradoxically, contrast with the large amount of poverty and unemployment in many sites worldwide. In Knopf (2014), the need of adopting new technologies for implementing renewable energies, and sectorial strategies in the electricity and transport sector is considered mandatory to keep the 2-degree limit in our future.

Some of the HCI research community is hence being attentive about environmental sustainability. An example of research work comes from Dourish (2010), who focuses on discussing the use of ICTs to promote and support environmental sustainability and ecological awareness in the technology user. This shakes and pushes the idea of a new way of being HCI designers and developers, and to improve consciousness about the impact and consequences of the use of technology and IT in general in the World.

4.2 Development

Development as a term originates in the Global North, though it was initially contextualized as a word of technological possibilities (Williams 1983) rather than for diminishing and disempowering (Escobar 1995). Synonyms such as unfold and unroll (Williams 1983, p. 103), though, entice to think of the possibility of recounting from the myriad of perspectives and viewpoints that the world provides nowadays.

Then, antonyms of such a term are *undeveloped* or *underdeveloped*, which, *through these verbal tangles, an often generous idea of 'aid to the developing countries' is confused with wholly ungenerous practices of cancellation of the identities of others, by their definition as underdeveloped or less developed, and of imposed processes of development for a world market controlled by others* (ibid, p. 104).

Development as expressed in an old/new meaning scaffolds precisely from the contrary to what Williams (1983) presents above. Development thus has to do with the development of all people's educational intellect to allow, encourage and empower this type of growth, rather than the one of suppression as understood by mechanisms of suppression and agendas of colonial interest.

Development, then, as a term applied to HCI4D, must be analytically reassessed. This is because it otherwise (1) symbolizes a constructed set of meanings, whereby dependency is the norm from historical agendas that encourage systematic workings and variations serving imperialistic plans and schemas; and (2) a sense of underdeveloped societies in relation to the developed economies (ibid, 1983, p. 103).

Development as evolutionary acquires sense if/when localities are taken into account as per specific sets characteristics shaping livelihoods in particular geographical milieus, and in a way that, when *Nations proceed in a course of Development, their later manifestations being potentially present in the earlier elements* (ibid, p. 103).

4.3 Interaction

Etymologically, interaction refers to a mutual or reciprocal action, e.g. communication among people, or actions of people that affects others. The study, thus, of rhetoric advanced from being focused exclusively on discourse, in Ancient Greece, to the inclusion of interactive audiovisual elements in the 20th century.

Nowadays, a ubiquitous digital world releases a new field of research, which might be called "rhetoric of interaction". Rhetorical possibilities can be analyzed in interactive design by some of the aspects in traditional rhetoric studies: ethos, logos and pathos, while a rhetorical approach to design can provide methods and principles to understand people's culture and context.

Care must though be taken, as looking to synonyms and antonyms of interaction one finds communication, contact, collaboration, as much as apathy, triviality or lethargy.

In our analysis and proposal interaction is then expressed as an old/new meaning based on the origins of human-to-human interaction with participatory values of integrity and ethicality based on respect and fraternity.

Sennett (2000) argues the personal consequences of work in the New Economy have led to disorientation of the individual because of the use of concepts like *flexibility*, *decentralization and control*, *flextime*, *change* and *long-term commitment*, as well as *work ethics and teamwork*. People, Sennet argues, have to cope with new concepts of *flexibility*, *flextime*, *teamwork*, *de- layering* and *ever-changing working conditions* that superficially present new opportunities of self- fulfillment to workers, but that in reality they create new forms of subjugation, confusing individuals and deteriorating their emotional and psychological well-being. Ultimately, the solution proposed by Sennett is to do with the necessity of people to rely on communities to build-up their own identities.

Scaffolding from the above, several aspects of HCI research such as UX, aesthetics and design thinking are then more problematic to research in a traditionally scientific way. Pan (2012) argues that fashion in relation to interaction design has a place in HCI, as it becomes an influence on the decisions and judgments made by HCI practitioners and researchers. Other authors subscribe this approach in that fashion affects interaction designers' design thinking in relation to functionality, appearance, UX and visual experience.

5 Exemplifying HWID Together with HCI4D

Portraying diverse ways of doing this section exemplifies work on HWID together with HCI4D to convey the above terms via pragmatic examples from literature.

5.1 Work

Irani and Silberman (2013) designed and developed Turkopticon as a system that allows workers to publicize and evaluate their relationship with their employers. This work is considered as activism as it stems from a strong critique to the invisibility of workers in the human computation domain, as represented by the popular Amazon Mechanical Turk system. Workers have been provided for two years with an anonymized integrated system allowing them to rate their experience with the employers.

Unfortunately such a worker-oriented perspective is not as common. Exceptions are mostly related to activist groups or non-profit organizations. For example, WWF published "Common Cause: The Case for Working with our Cultural Values" (Crompton 2010) to promote an ethical approach defining causes "bigger-than-self".

In these regards, there is still a rather amount of work to be done in unmasking powers and forces of oppression that neither allow for full values, nor for a sustainable and integral way of working in an ethical, integral and constructive manner.

5.2 Development

Promising and uplifting examples of ways forward in development are found in places that, due to the utter scarcity of resources, enable leeway and flexibility in creating and molding from quasi-blank canvases. An instance of this comes from informal settlements like Havana in Katutura, in the outskirts of Windhoek, Namibia. In such an underdeveloped and uncared for locality, there are major defies such as a paucity of basic living facilities typical of slums. These correspond to inadequate housing, and a lack of electrical reach, access to potable water, and hygiene resources like proper showers to serve sanitation. Besides, wastelands surrounding inhabitants' shanties, abusive drunkenness, and a great lack of education are the daily encounters for the inhabitants in such local (Cabrero et al. 2015).

To improve the above, and to allow scope to generate bottom-up possibilities straight from the ground, a project that combines partakers such as a university and some of its students, designers, researchers, facilitators, ONGs, political bodies such as embassies to foreign countries, and the local councilors is developing educational efforts specifically to do with the development of the community's intellect to allow, encourage and empower a sustainable, culturally-aware type of growth by means of skill provision and training, as well as of a community center (Winschiers-Theophilus et al. 2015a; b).

In such environments, besides, HCI forms an important part in that, by means of User-Created Personas (Cabrero et al. 2015), regular youth in Havana gain advantage in creating representations of themselves via person-like representatives that convey their needs, requirements and ambitions towards the design of logistics and, in particular, of technologies that aim to ameliorating their situations and progression in life.

6 World Machines: Providing Definitions to Sharing Economies

Nowadays, given the complexity of many design problems, the "*participation of more knowledge than any single person possesses*" (Fischer 2005, p. 1) is fundamental for creating a successful project, idea, or artifact. Such a collaborative approach stems from several years of research progresses led to the definition of Reflective Practitioners and Reflective Communities (ibid 2005). The idea beyond these concepts is to support not only collaborative design and development in HCI, but to help all partakers in overcoming the communication distance between different minds, expertise, and points of view. Reflective Communities are based on what is called Shared Understanding that needs to be created ad hoc for specific communities that collaborate and share a common objective.

In the recent years, the need of addressing UCD processes is becoming more common than not. With such paradigm shift from UCD to PD, a natural need comes to form the new generation of "Universal Access Designers" (Keates 2011). For doing this, upcoming and existing generations need be informed on Usability, Accessibility and User Experience as pinpointing the significance in considering the widest possible range of users in a specific workplace or situation.

At the basis of this approach, there is a socio-technical design methodology that considers both the technical aspects and the human factors as a very interrelated matter. The concept of World Machines introduces an archetype and a way to design a group of tools able to combining computational powers with a so-called social agenda for cross-cultural collaboration (Light et al. 2015), which specifically focuses its attention in the connection between Sharing, Environment and Ecological Thinking.

7 Conclusion

This paper has presented rhetorical and etymological approach to concepts and words of everyday life such as work, interaction and development seen from a myriad of cultural perspectives and understandings. In order to continue developing technological means that can satisfy the very final user, a coherent understanding of the peoples' agendas must be bore in mind at all times.

To empower laypeople with HWID and HCI4D methodologies, methods, tools and techniques can enable new ways of making concepts of HCI such as Usability and UX to evolve in diverse and varied ways that make the world to progress under a myriad of viewpoints and perspectives.

This will in turn allow for a richer understanding of the past, the present and the future to come in HCI, while reflecting upon the use of terms and communicational tools, and their respective meanings across cultures.

References

Abdelnour Nocera, J., Barricelli, B.R., Lopes, A., Campos, P., Clemmensen, T. (eds.): HWID 2015. IFIP AICT, vol. 468. Springer, Heidelberg (2015). doi:10.1007/978-3-319-27048-7

Blake, E., Glaser, M., Freudenthal, A.: Teaching design for development in computer science. Interactions **21**(2), 54–59 (2014)

Bødker, S.: When second wave HCI meets third wave challenges. In: Proceedings NordiCHI 2006, pp. 14–18. ACM, New York (2006). http://doi.org/10.1145/1182475.1182476

Cabrero, D.G., Winschiers-Theophilus, H., Mendonca, H.: User-created personas – a micro-cultural lens into informal settlement's youth life. In: Abdelnour Nocera, J., Barricelli, B.R., et al. (eds.) HWID 2015. IFIP AICT, vol. 468, pp. 57–70. Springer, Heidelberg (2015). doi: 10.1007/978-3-319-27048-7_4

Cockton, G.: A load of Cobbler's children: beyond the model designing processor. In: Proceedings of the CHI 2013, pp. 2139–2148. ACM Press (2013)

Crompton, T.: Common Cause: The Case for Working with our Cultural Values London, WWF-UK, Climate Outreach and Information Network, Campaign to Protect Rural England, Friends of the Earth, Oxfam 100 (2010)

Dourish, P.: HCI and environmental sustainability: the politics of design and the design of politics. In: Proceedings of the DIS 2010, pp. 1–10. ACM Press (2010). http://dx.doi.org/10.1145/1858171.1858173

Escobar, A.: Encountering development: The making and unmaking of the Third World. Princeton University Press, Princeton (1995)

Fischer, G.: From reflective practitioners to reflective communities. In: Proceedings of HCII 2005 (2005)

Grudin, J.: The west wing: fiction can serve politics. Scandinavian J. Inf. Syst. **15**(1), 73–77 (2003)

Grudin, J.: Three faces of human-computer interaction. In: IEEE Trans., 2–18 (2005)

Grudin, J.: A moving target — the evolution of human-computer interaction. In: Jackson, J. (ed.) Human-Computer Interaction Handbook, 3rd edn., p. 40. Taylor & Francis (2012)

Harper, R., Rodden, T., Rogers, Y., Sellen, A. (eds.) Being Human: Human-Computer Interaction in the Year 2020 (A3). Microsoft Research Ltd. (2008)

Irani, L., Silberman, M.S.: Turkopticon: interrupting worker invisibility in Amazon mechanical turk In: Proceedings of CHI 2013, 28 April – 2 May 2013 (2013)

Keates, S.: Teaching the next generation of universal access designers: a case study. In: Stephanidis, C. (ed.) Universal Access in HCI, Part I, HCII 2011. LNCS, vol. 6765, pp. 70–79. Springer, Heidelberg (2011)

Kim, S.: Interdisciplinary cooperation. In: Laurel, B. (ed.) The Art of Human-Computer Interface. Addison-Wesley, Reading (1990)

Knopf, B.: RealClimate: Mitigation of Climate Change – Part 3 of the new IPCC report, 17 April 2014. http://www.realclimate.org/index.php/archives/2014/04/mitigation-of-climate-change-part-3-of-the-new-ipcc-report/#more-17217. Accessed 21 April 2014

Kostakos, V.: The big hole in HCI research. Interactions **22**(2), 48–51 (2015)

Laurel, B.: Gaian IxD. Interactions **18**(5), 38–46 (2011). http://dx.doi.org.ezproxy.uwl.ac.uk/10.1145/2008176.2008187

Light, A., Bardzell, J., Bardzell, S., Cox, G., Fritsch, J., Hansen, L.K.: Making 'World Machines': discourse, design and global technologies for greater-than-self issues. In: Proceedinigs of the Aarhus Series on Human Centered Computing 2015, vol. 1, Aarhus, Denmark (2015). http://doi.org/10.7146/aahcc.v1i1.21326

Löfstrom, A.: What is culture? toward common understandings of culture in HCI. In: Forbrig, P., Paternó, F., Mark Pejtersen, A. (eds.) HCIS 2010. IFIP AICT, vol. 332, pp. 133–141. Springer, Heidelberg (2010). http://doi.org/10.1007/978-3-642-15231-3_14

Muller, M.J., Wharton, C., McIver Jr., W.J., Laux, L.: Toward an HCI research and practice agenda based on human needs and social responsibility. In: Proceedings of the ACM SIGCHI Conference on Human factors in computing systems, pp. 155–161 (1997)

Pan, Y., Roedl, D., Blevis, E., Thomas, J.: Re-conceptualizing fashion in sustainable HCI. In: Proceedings Of the DIS 2012, pp. 813–815. ACM (2012)

Reeves, S.: Human-computer interaction as science. In: Proceedings of 5th Decennial Aarhus Conference (Critical Alternatives). ACM Press (2015)

Rogers, Y.: HCI theory: classical, modern and contemporary. Synth. Lect. Hum.-Centered Inform. **5**(2), 1–129 (2012)

Sanders, E.B.-N.: From user-centered to participatory design approaches. In: Frascara, J. (ed.) Design and the Social Sciences: Making Connections, pp. 1–8. Taylor & Francis (2002)

Sanders, L., Stappers, P.J.: Designing to co-designing to collective dreaming: three slices in time. ACM Interactions **21**(6), 24–33 (2014)

Sennett, R.: The Corrosion of Character: The Personal Consequences of Work in the New Capitalism. W.W.Nort. Co., New York (2000)

Williams, R.: Keywords: A vocabulary of culture and society, 2nd edn. Fontana Paperbacks, London (1983)

Winschiers-Theophilus, H.: The art of cross-cultural design for usability. In: Stephanidis, C. (ed.) Universal Access in HCI, Part I, HCII 2009. LNCS, vol. 5614, pp. 665–671. Springer, Heidelberg (2009)

Winschiers-Theophilus, H., Cabrero, D.G., Angula, S., Chivuno-Kuria, S., Mendonca, H., Ngolo, R.: A challenge-based approach to promote entrepreneurship among youth in an informal settlement of windhoek. In: Proceedings of the SATN 2015, Technology Vaal University Science Park, Sebokeng (2015)

Winschiers-Theophilus, H., Keskinen, P., Cabrero, D.G., Angula, S., Ongwere, T., Chivuno-Kuria, S., Mendonca, H., Ngolo, R.: ICTD within the discourse of a locally situated interacion: the potential of youth engagement. In: Steyn, J., Van Belle, J.P. (eds.) Proceedings of the 9th IDIA conference, pp. 52–71, Nungwi (2015)

How to Develop a User-Friendly Chinese Hand Input System for the Touch Device? A Case Study

Zhe Chen[1], Pei-Luen Patrick Rau[2], and Lin Ma[1(✉)]

[1] School of Economics and Management, Beihang University, Beijing, China
malin2014@buaa.edu.cn

[2] Department of Industrial Engineering, Tsinghua University, Beijing, China

Abstract. The purpose of this study is to find how to develop a user-friendly Chinese hand input system for the touch devices. A case is studied to discover the factors which influencing the users' experience in the Chinese hand input. In the case, three personas are developed to test the usability of Chinese hand input systems of three different touch devices (i.e. smartphone, tablet personal computer and all-in-one computer). The typical personas and process for Chinese hand input are established according to the result of the case study. This study also indicates the usability consideration for a Chinese hand input system. The results of this study can be applied to product design of Chinese hand input system and future research on Chinese hand input.

Keywords: Case study · Chinese hand input · Touch device

1 Introduction

Chinese input system is widely used in the touch-sensitive devices such as smartphones or tablet personal computers. People input Chinese characters by their fingers including the thumb, index finger and middle finger. Comparing to Chinese Pinyin (i.e. Chinese Phonetic Alphabets) input, hand input is friendlier to users who are not familiar with Chinese Pinyin. In fact, Chinese Pinyin is studied from 1955, authorized by Chinese National People's Congress in 1958 and became an international standard in 1982 (ISO 7098:1991 1991). This standard is revised in 2015 (ISO 7098:2015 2015). Thus, although Chinese Pinyin is the most frequently-used approach in Chinese input on the touch devices currently, it is difficult to input with Chinese Pinyin for many users who are not familiar with or even have never learned Chinese Pinyin. In this situation hand input provides a good alternative to those users who have difficulties in inputting Chinese characters with its Pinyin. Previous studies indicated that Chinese calligraphy (i.e. the beautiful handwriting of Chinese characters on paper) brought positive emotions (Kwok et al. 2011; Yang et al. 2010). Considering aesthetic aspects of hand input on mobile touch devices may improve the user experience (Chen et al. 2014).

Previous studies have made much effort on Chinese hand input but most of the researchers focus on the algorithms and their purpose is to recognize the handwritten Chinese characters. Chinese user in the hand input system doesn't attract enough attention. It is shown that input positions, fingers' dimensions, fatigue of fingers' movements

P.-L.P. Rau (Ed.): CCD 2016, LNCS 9741, pp. 26–33, 2016.
DOI: 10.1007/978-3-319-40093-8_3

and other factors related to the user of Chinese hand input system will have influence on the performance of the Chinese handwriting (Chen et al. 2013; Tu et al. 2012; 2015). Input positions, including one-hand held input, two hand-held input and on hand-held input depends on the dimension and weight of the touch devices. For the small size of mobile touch device such as smartphone, both of one-hand held and two-hand held positions are possible to the hand input users. For the large size of mobile touch devices such as tablet personal computers, two-hand held is the most appropriate position to input. And for the large size of touch devices such the KIOSK or touch screen on the automatic teller machine or library information center, no hand-held position is used when the touch device is fixed and supported. Fingers' dimensions, including the width of the fingers, the length of the fingers, the area of the fingers and etc., will also affect the Chinese handwriting (Chen et al. 2014). The width of the fingers and area of the fingers reflect the size of the input box as it difficult to input when the input box is smaller than the area of the input finger. The length of the finger affects the location of the input box especially when one-hand held position is adopted. As Chinese characters are composed of multiple strokes and radicals, a lot of fingers' movements are required to complete one character and consequently fatigue of fingers should be studied. The acceptable level of fatigue of fingers should be studied to improve the user's experience of handwriting. The thumb is used to input while one-hand held position is adopted and index finger or middle finger is used to input while two-hand held position is adopted. Current research studied the interface for thumb touch on the smart devices but thumb input on Chinese handwriting still need more attention (Park and Han 2010, p. 8; Parhi et al. 2006).

On the other hand, individual differences require more attention when developing a user-friendly touch device for Chinese handwriting. Users with different education backgrounds may have different cognitive process when handwriting a Chinese character into a touch device. Users with different ages may have different movement abilities to hand input Chinese characters. For example, the fingers' movements of the elderly people are quite slower than other people (Zhou et al. 2012) and meanwhile it should not be neglected that slow and clear handwritten scripts lead to higher accuracy.

Interface design is the key issue in the interaction of Chines hand input. The size of the input box, the location of the input box, display of handwritten script, display of alternative recognized characters and so on will have a possible effect on the user experience of Chinese handwriting. It is examined that an optimized interface can improve the input time and accuracy of Chinese handwriting (Chen et al. 2013; 2014; Ren and Zhou 2009; Tu et al. 2013). A good interface design lead to higher performance and users' satisfaction.

2 Method

The purpose of this study is to discover how to design a user-friendly hand input system for Chinese character on the touch devices. The method of persona is developed to find the usability design considerations of Chinese hand input systems on three devices.

Persona is created through the result of open interviews of 5 Chinese users. The descriptions of the interview participants are shown in Table 1.

Table 1. Description of the interview participants

Participants	Age	Education level	Job	Touch devices experience
1	22	College	Student	8 years
2	30	Ph.D	Professor	10 years
3	18	Middle school	Student	8 years
4	50	Middle school	Housewife	6 years
5	54	Middle school	Operator	3 years

The interview questions focus on the following items.

- Background (age, education level, job, years of using touch devices).
- Description of the situations of using hand input for Chinese on the touch devices, including mobile phones, tablet personal computers, all-in-one computers.
- Difficulties of using Chinese hand input systems.
- Suggestions for Chinese hand input systems.

Persona 1: JIANG Yu is a housewife. She is 54 years old. She had a middle school educational experience. She comes from Hujiang Providence in the south of China and she has some accent, so she is not good at Pinyin of Chinese characters. She enjoys in playing iPhone and iPad. She send the text message directly and send the message via online chatting platforms including Tencent QQ. She likes cooking very much so she usually searches recipes on iPad to help her cooking. In her spare time, she also likes watching TV shows on All-in-one computer. The romantic story is her favorite type. So she searches the keywords of opera type or star name in online TV websites.

Persona 2: ZHANG Ming is an operator in a steel factory who is responsible to making molds. He is the husband of Yu, 57 years old. He also had a middle school educational experience. But he took a computer skills training for three years in his 30 s and he is proficient in using CAD, Photoshops, and other graphics software. He uses touch mobile phone to send short e-mails to his colleagues. He spends most of his time in the all-in-one computer for his work and entertainment. He makes short comments when he read news on websites.

Persona 3: ZHANG Hua is now a senior college student who major in software engineering. Hua is the son of Yu and Ming. He almost has his smartphone with him no matter where he is. His social life is through his mobile phone. He comments on the photos and status of his friends. He uses mobile search engineering to look up interesting things. He also likes pop songs and he always has a long song list on his music applications and he likes to make personal tags to these songs. Labels he used is “Shower song” (i.e. 洗澡歌), “to my girlfriend” (i.e. 女友爱听), “study times”(i.e. 学习时间), “keep silent for moment”(i.e. 冷静一下), “think alone” (i.e. 独自思考). He often uses his mobile phone with his right hand.

Three touch devices are used in this study, which are a 4.7-in. mobile phone, a 9.7-in. tablet personal computer and a 21.5-in. all-in-one computer with touch screen (Fig. 1).

Fig. 1. Three touch devices in this study

A focus group including four experts and three real users is established to discuss the usability problems in hand input systems of three touch devices. Two experts are professors in the college school who study human-computer interaction. One expert is a professor who studies human behavior modeling. One expert is a software engineer. Table 2 shows the decryptions of participants in the focus group.

Table 2. Participants in the focus group

Participants	Age	Education level	Job	Touch devices experience
1	30	Ph.D	Professor	8 years
2	34	Ph.D	Professor	10 years
3	32	Ph.D	Professor	8 years
4	40	M.D	Engineer	11 years
5	50	Middle school	Worker	3 years
6	54	Middle school	Housewife	6 years
7	25	College	Student	9 years

3 Results and discussion

Based on the persona and their stories the focus group creates three typical scenarios for Chinese hand input on the touch devices.

- Sending text message via mobile phone or mobile chatting applications.
- Searching keywords in online applications, including search engine, musical application, video websites via the touch devices.
- Short comments on the news, friends' status, and photos.

Figure 2 shows the hand input process for Chinese character in three scenarios. This process is iterative, when user find all of the recognized characters are not their target character they would choose to rewrite the character. And user touches the functional button on Chinese hand input system to switch to another input system such as symbol input system, number input system, and alphabetic input system. These actions assist the user to combine hand input with another input method.

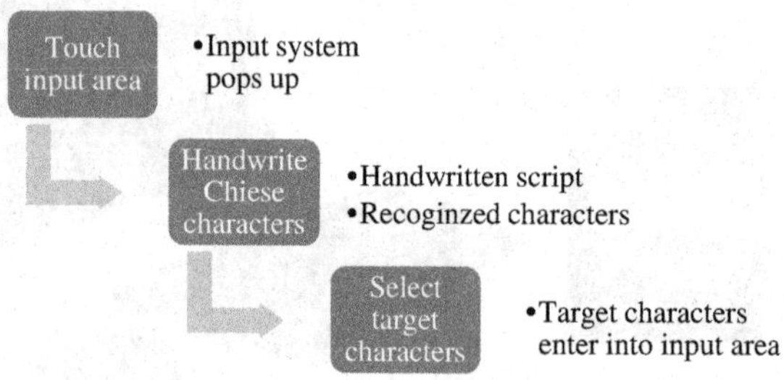

Fig. 2. Hand input process for Chinese character

The typical interface of Chinese hand input system on the touch devices includes the input area, recognized character area and functional area. The recognition algorithm and dataset are also essential to Chinese hand input. In the physical level, the texture of the touch screen and reactions time of touch action is also important to the Chinese hand input users. Table 3 shows the list of usability considerations of Chinese hand input system based on the results of focus group. The results are useful to improve the usability of current Chinese hand input system and make the system user-friendlier.

Table 3. The list of usability considerations of Chinese hand input system

Type	Considerations
Interface	• Input box: shape, size, location, background color/photo, script weight, script color, feedback • Recognized area: size and location of shown character, number of shown characters, words, sentence, character mixed with alphabetical letters, numbers, symbols, Chinese sentence • Functional area: delete, confirm, input system swift, send, ignore
System	• Recognition algorithm: reaction time, minimum strokes • Dataset: character, words, sentence • Physical realization: touch technology, screen texture, response time

Input Area. The design of input area is the most important interface design. Beside the general interface design considerations such as color, color, shape, value, direction, there are some design considerations for the Chinese handwriting. First, the size of input box is the critical factor for the effective handwriting area. The size of input box should be suitable to users' finger size no matter which finger user use to handwrite Chinese characters. And meanwhile the input box should be large enough so that users can see clearly of the handwritten scripts in the process of handwriting. The size of input box also has a connection to the size of handwritten scripts. Although handwritten script is individually different, the input box size limits the handwriting area and consequently influences the input performance such as input time. The national and international standards have demonstrated the finger size for Chinese (CNIS 1988; 1996). But updated and detailed dimensions of finger size for Chinese are still working in progress currently. Previous studies have indicated the optimal size of input box on hand-held devices should be 30 mm × 30 mm (Chen and et al. 2013; 2014). However, it is not clear that the optimal input size for Chinese handwriting on small display size such as smart watch or large display size such as Kiosk.

The location of input box is the key issue that probably has a significant influence on the handwriting performance and users' subjective ratings. The location of input box reflects to the distance between the relaxing position to the handwriting position. The distance will reflect to the input time in handwriting. And it should be taken into consideration that the necessary information can display on the screen while handwriting. For example, user may check the name and phone number of the contact person when handwriting the text message to them. Inappropriate location design for input box may lead to blocking the sight for display. Thus design consideration on location of input box is important to balance display and input. And the dominant hand may be another factor related to the location of input box. Location design for the right-handed users may not suitable for the left-handed users.

It is probably better if the background of input box has similarity to the paper in paper and pen-based handwriting task. Chinese users learn and train their handwriting skills in the paper using pen. The familiarity of the system will increase if the design of the background of input box is close to the paper, for example, imitating the texture and color of paper for the background of input box. It is shown that "米" style or "Nine block box" is the assistive way that young Chinese learn handwriting Chinese characters (Chen and et al. 2014), as shown in Figure 4. Thus it is better to consider to add this photo to the background of the input box so that the handwriting on touch devices are consistent with users' mental model and expectations.

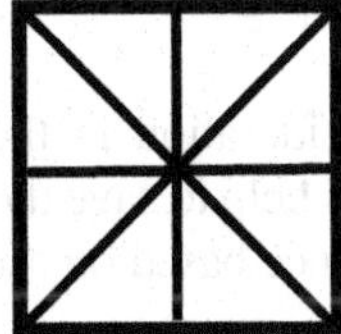
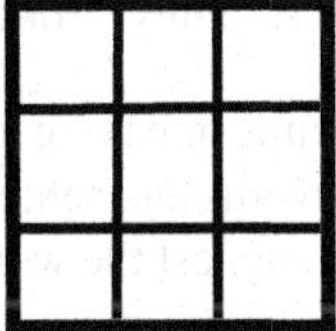

Fig. 4. Background design in paper-pen based Chinese handwriting

Script weight is another issue should be specially considered in the input area. If the script weight is too low it will not match the users' mental model as user expect the script weight should be consistent with the tip of handwriting finger. This expectation results from users' experiment in paper and pen based handwriting experience as the script weight is connected to the thickness of the tip of pen. The script weight should not be too high because it is hard to distinguish each stroke especially when in some cases Chinese characters with dozens of strokes are used in handwriting task.

Recognized Area. Like the input box, the size and location of shown characters, the script weight should be taken into considerations when designing a user-friendly Chinese handwriting system. These design factors have direct connections to the handwriting performance. Since the main task in the recognized area is to select the target character, there are some special design considerations for the recognized area, such as the style of shown characters, number of shown characters, words and sentence, characters mixed with alphabetical letters, numbers, symbols, Chinese sentences. Taking the number of shown characters for example, how many of recognized characters should be shown in the recognized area is one of the key factors. In an idea situation, the recognition system and recognition algorithm will correctly understand users' intention and there is no need to shown any recognized character to let user select the target character. However, due to the handwriting style and connecting strokes and other reasons, it seems impossible to skip the selecting step with the current recognition system. The more shown characters there are, users have more choice to select but will spend more time on visual search and finger movements. Thus the number of shown characters depends on many other factors such as handwriting scenarios, display size.

Functional Area. There is a functional area in the Chinese handwriting interface which leave the space for the button of delete, confirm, input system swift, send, ignore and etc. The key to design functional area is to find users' specific handwriting requirement and design for it. For example, when user are exploring the Internet and searching the keywords with the Chinese handwriting system. The keep a button named "search" is appropriate.

Recognition Algorithm. Recognition algorithm is critical to the input accuracy and input time and directly influence users' subjective rating on the whole Chinese handwriting system. Using an adequate and fast algorithm may reduce the reaction time and even minimize the strokes user need to handwrite. It is essential that one of the most important reasons influencing users' satisfaction on Chinese handwriting is that some Chinese characters have so many strokes to handwrite.

Dataset. Chinese semantic meaning needs consideration in the design. Chinese is composed of character, words and sentence. It will help to save the input time when the handwriting system can suggest the word or sentence based on uses' writing history or usage history.

Physical Realization. It is also important to consider the physical features of the touch devices such as touch technology, screen texture, system response time.

References

International Organizational for Standardization: ISO 7098:1991: Information and Documentation – Chinese Romanization. International Organization for Standardization, Genève (1991)

International Organizational for Standardization: ISO 7098:2015: Information and Documentation – Chinese Romanization. International Organization for Standardization, Genève (2015)

China National Institute of Standardization: Human Dimension of Chinese Adults, Vol. GB/T 10000-1988. Statistics and Product Press of China, China (1988)

China National Institute of Standardization: Hand Sizing System e Adult, National Standard of People's Republic of China, Vol. GB/T 16252e1996. Beijing China (1996)

Kwok, T.C.Y., Bai, X., Kao, H.S.R., Li, J.C.Y., Ho, F.K.Y.: Cognitive effects of calligraphy therapy for older people: a randomized controlled trial in Hong Kong. Clin. Interv. Aging **6**, 269–273 (2011)

Yang, X.L., Li, H.H., Hong, M.H., Kao, H.S.: The effects of Chinese calligraphy handwriting and relaxation training in Chinese Nasopharyngeal Carcinoma patients: a randomized controlled trial. Int. J. Nurs. Stud. **47**(5), 550–559 (2010)

Chen, Z., Rau, P.L.P., Chen, C.: How to design finger input of Chinese characters: A literature review. Int. J. Ind. Ergon. **44**(3), 428–435 (2014)

Chen, Z., Rau, P.L.P., Chen, C.: The effects of human finger and Chinese character on Chinese handwriting performance on mobile touch devices. Hum. Factors J. Hum. Factors Ergon. Soc. (2013). 0018720813503007

Park, Y.S., Han, S.H.: Touch key design for one-handed thumb interaction with a mobile phone: Effects of touch key size and touch key location. Int. J. Ind. Ergon. **40**(1), 68–76 (2010)

Parhi, P., Karlson, A.K., Bederson, B.B.: Target size study for one-handed thumb use on small touchscreen devices. In: Proceedings of the 8th Conference on Human-Computer Interaction with Mobile Devices and Services, pp. 203–210. ACM (2006)

Ren, X., Zhou, X.: The optimal size of handwriting character input boxes on PDAs. Int. J. Hum. Comput. Interact. **25**(8), 762–784 (2009)

Tu, H., Ren, X., Zhai, S.L.: A comparative evaluation of finger and pen stroke gestures. In: Proceedings of the SIGCHI Conference on Human Factors in Computing Systems, pp. 1287–1296. ACM (2012)

Zhou, J., Rau, P.L.P., Salvendy, G.: Use and design of handheld computers for older adults: A review and appraisal. Int. J. Hum. Comput. Interact. **28**(12), 799–826 (2012)

Tu, H., Ren, X.: Optimal entry size of handwritten Chinese characters in touch-based mobile phones. Int. J. Hum. Comput. Interact. **29**(1), 1–12 (2013)

Tu, H., Ren, X., Zhai, S.: Differences and similarities between finger and pen stroke gestures on stationary and mobile devices. ACM Trans. Comput. Hum. Interact. (TOCHI) **22**(5), 22 (2015)

Group Participation Influence on Members' Gifting Behaviors in a Social Game

Na Chen and Pei-Luen Patrick Rau(✉)

Department of Industrial Engineering, Tsinghua University, Beijing 10084, China
chenn06@mails.tsinghua.edu.cn, rpl@tsinghua.edu.cn

Abstract. This study investigated whether group members' participation influence individuals' gifting behaviors. The experiment was conducted on the platform of WeChat Red Packet, which is a currently prevalent money gifting social game. Forty-eight participants were recruited. Two studies were conducted. Study 1 focused on the ratio of group partners who participated in the gift exchange (participation ratio) and Study 2 focused on the total frequency of gifts sent by partners (partners' frequency). The results of Study 1 showed that in a friend group, higher friends' participation ratio in gifting social games motives individuals to send gifts more times; whereas in a stranger group, group members' participation ratio does not influence the individual's gifting behaviors. Study 2 suggested that in both friend and stranger groups, higher partners' frequency motives participants to send more gifts but shows no influence on the amount of monetary value of the gifts sent by participants.

Keywords: Money gifting · Social games · Group participation

1 Introduction and Background

The "red packet war" during the 2015 Chinese Lunar New Year holiday between two of China's Internet giants, Tencent and Alibaba, has attracted the attention of billions of Chinese people. Red packet is a kind of prevalent money gifting social games and these games are usually designed as an in-app function. The name of red packet literally means a red packet filled with money, given as a gift to friends and families. The competition reached its peak on New Year's Eve. More than one billion digital red envelopes (authorized to connect with users' bank cards) were sent through Tencent's Wechat Lucky Money users on that night, compared with 240 million by Alipay Wallet (Chen 2015).

The kind of money gifting social games is traceable to Chinese traditions. Gifting red packet is one of the most ancient Chinese traditions and is frequently employed in various interpersonal interaction situations, such as festivals and celebrations. As a unique cultural phenomenon, the tradition is always referred to as a cultural case in research in the fields of cultural study (Millington et al. 2005; Wang 2015), business (e.g. Luo 2008), and doctor-patient relationship (e.g. Huffman and Hochster 2007; Hurst 2009).

P.-L.P. Rau (Ed.): CCD 2016, LNCS 9741, pp. 34–42, 2016.
DOI: 10.1007/978-3-319-40093-8_4

The red packet is usually gifted in a group chat context and group members share the amount in the packet. Group-level factors will influence money gifting behaviors (Dholakia et al. 2004). Previous research indicated that membership (Yoo et al. 2002), group norms and social identity (Dholakia et al. 2004; Zhou 2011), reciprocity and pro-social behaving duty (Wasko and Faraj 2000) influence member participation in group activities, but little research ever took consideration of other group members' participation in the investigation of individual's gifting behaviors. Research indicated that people participate out of reciprocity and they increased the participation if others contribute more participation (Wasko and Faraj 2000). In addition, previous study indicated that interpersonal relationships influence both behaviors on social media (Aral and Walker 2014; Burke and Kraut 2014) and money offering behaviors (Chen and Rau 2016). This study focused on the effects of interpersonal relationships on money gifting behaviors in social games.

Therefore, this study aimed to investigate in different group contexts in which individuals have different interpersonal relationships with the group members, how group participation influenced individuals' behaviors in money gifting social games. Two studies were conducted and focused on different aspects of group participation. Study 1 focused on the ratio of group members who participated in the lucky money gifting game and Study 2 focused on the total frequency of lucky money sent by group members. For a clear description, the focus of Study 1 is shorten to the term of group participation ratio and the focus of Study 2 is shorten to the term of partners' frequency. Two typical interpersonal relationships were selected as the subjects, including close friends and strangers. The two studies followed the same experiment design and procedures.

2 Experiment Design

This study chose WeChat™ as the experiment platform. WeChat is one key mobile instant messaging application developed by Tencent™ and it is the winner in the red packet war. WeChat launched its money gifting social game, WeChat Lucky Money, on 17 January 2014 (Liu et al. 2015). Lucky Money can be gifted in WeChat group chat as a group message. Group members click the message and received a sub-packet of the Lucky Money. WeChat divided the amount of Lucky Money into several sub-packet randomly. The number of the sub-packet is identified by the sender. Group members share the Lucky Money and reciprocate it.

To manipulate a group chat context for participants, the role of four "fake participants" were design who cooperated with the real participation. Two fake participants were male and the other two were female. Fake participants behaved following standard behaving processes. The real participant in this experiment was informed that he/she should complete experimental tasks with other four group members but they five were separated in five room so that they could communicate via a WeChat group chat rather than face-to-face contact.

This study developed two typical scenarios for the close friend and stranger scenarios respectively. Participants experienced both scenarios in the experiment. In the close friend scenario, participants were asked to discuss gathering during the festival holiday which would come soon. In the stranger scenario, participations were asked to discuss a piece of teamwork about each others' hometown food.

3 Study 1

Study 1 investigated whether lucky money gifting behavior was influenced by tie strength and group participation ratio in lucky money gifting.

3.1 Variables

The independent variable of group participation ratio was a between-subject one and had two levels: complete and partial. The complete level meant that in this condition, all the four fake participants gifted a five-RMB lucky money packet once in both scenarios. The partial level meant that in a partial condition, two fake participants gifted five-RMB (equal to around 0.77 US dollars) lucky money packets twice in both scenarios. Both the total value (20 RMB equal to around 3 US dollars) and count of lucky money packets gifted by the four fake participants in two conditions were the same, in order to avoid the influence of the amount and frequency of lucky money gifted by group members on participants' behaviors.

The amount and frequency of lucky money offered by participants in each scenario were recoded as two dependent variables. The two variables were shortened to the terms of participant gifting amount and participant gifting frequency.

Tie strength with the fake participants were recorded as a control variable before each scenarios using the scale developed by Gilber and Karahalios (2009). Participant's background information, previous WeChat and Lucky Money experience were also recorded.

3.2 Participants

Forty-eight participants were recruited and were divided into two group participation ratio conditions, 16 participants in the complete condition and 32 participants in the partial condition. Two samples were gender balanced. There was no significant difference in the ages between to samples (complete: Mean = 20.81, SD = 0.90; partial: Mean = 20.41, SD = 1.24; $p > .05$).

3.3 Results

3.3.1 Manipulation Effectiveness Check

The results of the independent sample t-test indicated that there were no significant differences in previous WeChat and Lucky Money experience between the two conditions (all $p > .05$). The results of the analysis of variance (ANOVA) test indicated that in both conditions, there were no significant difference in the tie strength among the four fake participants according to scenarios (all $p > .1$) and in both sceneries, there was no significant difference between the tie strength in the two conditions (all $p > .05$). These results suggested the effectiveness of experimental manipulation and thus further comparisons between the two conditions were conducted. The results of the paired sample t-test indicated that in both conditions, the tie strength with close friends was higher than the tie strength with strangers (complete: $t = -9.584$, $p < .001$; partial: $t = -19.180$, $p < .001$); this suggested that participants indeed perceived the differences the interpersonal relationships between the two scenarios.

3.3.2 Gifting Behaviors

The data of participant offering amount and frequency did not follow the residual normality and homogeneity of variance, and thus non-parametric Mann-Whitney was used for the analyses of participant gifting behaviors. In the close friend scenario, participant gifting frequency in the complete condition was lower than the frequency in the partial condition ($p < .05$) whereas in the stranger scenario, there was no significant difference in participant gifting frequency between two conditions ($p > .1$). In both scenarios, there were no significant differences in participant gifting amount between two conditions (both $p > .1$). The detailed analyses results are listed in Tables 1 and 2. Table 3 shows the frequency analyses of the lucky money participants offered.

Table 1. Non-parametric Mann-Whitney testing results of participant gifting amount (RMB) in Study 1

Scenario	Condition	Mean	SD	Z	p
Stranger	Complete	4.23	3.05	−0.297	.766
	Partial	5.37	4.30		
Close friend	Complete	6.27	4.11	−1.505	.132
	Partial	8.10	4.30		

Table 2. Non-parametric Mann-Whitney testing results of participant gifting frequency in Study 1

Scenario	Condition	Count per person	Z	p
Stranger	Complete	0.94	−0.308	.758
	Partial	0.94		
Close friend	Complete	1.13	−2.310	.021
	Partial	1.41		

Table 3. Frequency analyses of the lucky money participants offered in Study 1

Scenario	Condition	Frequency	No. of persons	%
Stranger	Complete	0	3	18.8
		1	11	68.8
		2	2	12.5
	Partial	0	7	21.9
		1	22	68.8
		2	1	3.1
		3	2	6.3
Close friend	Complete	1	16	100.0
	Partial	0	1	3.1
		1	20	62.5
		2	8	25.0
		3	3	9.4

4 Study 2

Study 2 investigated whether individuals' lucky money gifting behavior was influenced by the total frequency of lucky money gifted by the fake participants.

4.1 Variables

The total sum of lucky money was related to the total frequency. It is reasonable to assume that sum amount of lucky money sent by the fake participants would influence participants' gifting behaviors. Considering that, we asked two fake participants to send a large amount of lucky money and the other two to send a small amount more times. Hence, the effects of total sum sent by the fake participants would be decreased. The independent variable of partners' frequency was also a between-subject one and had two levels: high and low. The high level meant that in this condition, two fake participants gifted a twenty-RMB lucky money packet once and the other two fake participants gifted one-RMB lucky money packets three times in both scenarios. The low level meant that two fake participants gifted a twenty-RMB luck money packet once and the other two fake participants gifted a one-RMB lucky money packet once in both scenarios. In high level the total sum of lucky money gifted by partners was 46 RMB (equal to around 7.1 dollars), whereas in the low level this figure was 42 RMB (equal to around 6.5 dollars). The small variation in the total sum of lucky money sent by partners could be ignored in a WeChat group chat context. Participants' evaluation of the value of the lucky money was assessed with one post-scenario question: "How appropriate was the total amount of money sent by other partners during the discussion using lucky money?" Responses were given on a seven-point Likert scale ranging from 7 = 'far too many' to 1 = 'far too little'. Perceptions of the amount sent in conditions 4 and 5 were similar ($p > .1$). The dependent variables were the same as those in Study 1.

4.2 Participants

Sixty-four participants were recruited and were divided into two partners' frequency conditions, 32 participants in the high condition and 32 participants in the low condition. Each condition was gender balanced. There was no significant difference in the ages between to samples (high: Mean = 20.13, SD = 1.34; low: Mean = 20.56, SD = 1.37; $p > .1$).

4.3 Results

4.3.1 Manipulation Effectiveness Check

There were no significant differences in previous WeChat and Lucky Money experience between the two conditions (all $p > .1$). In both conditions, there were no significant difference in the tie strength among the four fake participants according to scenarios (all $p > .05$) and and in both sceneries, there was no significant difference between the tie strength in the two conditions (all $p > .05$). These results indicated that we could conduct further analysis. In both conditions, the tie strength with close friends was higher than the tie strength with strangers (high: $t = -18.236$, $p < .001$; low: $t = -15.705$, $p < .001$); this suggested that participants had a correct understand of the interpersonal relationships between the two scenarios.

4.3.2 Gifting Behaviors

We used non-parametric Mann-Whitney for the analyses of participant gifting behaviors. In both scenario, participant gifting frequency in the high condition was higher than the frequency in the low condition (both $p < .05$). In both scenarios, there were no significant differences in participant gifting amount between two conditions (both $p > .1$). The detailed analyses results are listed in Tables 4 and 5. Table 6 shows the frequency analyses of the lucky money participants offered.

Table 4. Non-parametric Mann-Whitney testing results of participant gifting amount (RMB) in Study 2

Scenario	Condition	Mean	SD	Z	p
Stranger	High	10.81	9.24	−0.697	.486
	Low	10.73	6.05		
Close friend	High	13.97	6.12	−0.182	.855
	Low	14.01	6.84		

Table 5. Non-parametric Mann-Whitney testing results of participant gifting frequency in Study 2

Scenario	Condition	Count per person	Z	p
Stranger	High	1.44	-2.664	.008
	Low	1.03		
Close friend	High	1.84	-2.966	.003
	Low	1.31		

Table 6. Frequency analyses of the lucky money participants offered in Study 2

Scenario	Condition	Frequency	No. of persons	%
Stranger	High	0	3	9.4
		1	14	43.8
		2	13	40.6
		3	2	6.3
	Low	0	2	6.3
		1	27	84.4
		2	3	9.4
Close friend	High	1	12	37.5
		2	13	40.6
		3	7	21.9
	Low	1	23	71.9
		2	8	25.0
		3	1	3.1

5 Conclusions

Based on a money gifting social game, this study investigated the effects of group participation on members' gifting behaviors. For a general consideration of the effects, the experiment involved two group contexts in which individuals have different interpersonal relationships with the group members. The two group contexts included a close friend group context and a stranger group context. We conducted two studies to investigate two aspects of gift exchange behaviors, including group participation ratio and partners' frequency of gifting. The results of Study 1 indicated people will participate more in maintaining the relationships with a friend group in which more members participate in the inter-group relationship maintaining but they will not invest more resources. In a stranger group, other group members' participation does not influence people's money gifting behaviors. Study 2 suggests that when the amount of money involved in the gift exchange interaction is fairly small, interpersonal relationship is the main influence on individuals' gifting behavior; in contrast if the amount involved exceed a certain threshold, reciprocal norms are a better predictor of individuals' gifting behaviors than tie strength. Friendships usually involve multiple forms of interaction in addition to gifting and it is this multiplicity of interaction which gives friendships their robustness. This means that even if a friend sends a low-value gift, individuals will reciprocate a large-value gift or a favor of equivalent value. Because relationships with strangers are more sensitive to reciprocal norms, individuals tend to respond rapidly to an increase in the value of gifts; gifting to friends is more robust against changes in other partners' behavior, as noted above. When the amount of money involved in the interaction reaches a certain threshold, however, tie strength has a less explicit (we did not mean less important) influence on gifting behavior than reciprocal norms. The effects of tie strength on gifting behavior warrant further investigation. The two studies were both conducted on a group-level factor and intragroup-level factors warrant further investigation.

Acknowledgement. This study was funded by a National Natural Science Foundation China grant 71188001.

References

Aral, S., Walker, D.: Tie strength, embeddedness, and social influence: A large-scale networked experiment. Manage. Sci. **60**(6), 1352–1370 (2014)

Burke, M., Kraut, R.E.: Growing closer on facebook: changes in tie strength through social network site use. In: Proceedings of the SIGCHI Conference on Human Factors in Computing Systems, pp. 4187–4196. ACM (2014)

Chen, N., Rau, P.P.L.: How Guanxi sources influence closeness? The moderating effects of reciprocal norms on feeling closeness. Soc. Behav. Pers. Int. J. **44**(7) (2016)

Dholakia, U.M., Bagozzi, R.P., Pearo, L.K.: A social influence model of consumer participation in network-and small-group-based virtual communities. Int. J. Res. Mark. **21**(3), 241–263 (2004)

Gilbert, E., Karahalios, K.: Predicting tie strength with social media. In: Proceedings of the SIGCHI Conference on Human Factors in Computing Systems, pp. 211–220. ACM (2009)

Huffman, S.B., Hochster, M.: How well does result relevance predict session satisfaction? In: Proceedings of the 30th Annual International ACM SIGIR Conference on Research and Development in Information Retrieval, pp. 567–574. ACM (2007)

Hurst, W.: The Chinese worker after socialism. China Q. **198**, 459–493 (2009)

Liu, W., He, X., Zhang, P.: Application of red envelopes–new weapon of wechat payment. In: 2015 International Conference on Education, Management, Information and Medicine. Atlantis Press (2015)

Luo, Y.: The changing Chinese culture and business behavior: The perspective of intertwinement between guanxi and corruption. Int. Bus. Rev. **17**(2), 188–193 (2008)

Millington, A., Eberhardt, M., Wilkinson, B.: Gift giving, guanxi and illicit payments in buyer–supplier relations in China: Analysing the experience of UK companies. J. Bus. Ethics **57**(3), 255–268 (2005)

Chen, L.: Red Envelope War: How Alibaba and Tencent Fight Over Chinese New Year, Forbes, 19 February 2015. http://www.forbes.com/sites/liyanchen/2015/02/19/red-envelope-war-how-alibaba-and-tencent-fight-over-chinese-new-year/#42daf0de7826. Accessed 18 February 2016

Wasko, M.M., Faraj, S.: "It is what one does": why people participate and help others in electronic communities of practice. J. Strateg. Inf. Syst. **9**(2), 155–173 (2000)

Wang, S.Y.K.: Policing in Taiwan: From authoritarianism to Democracy. J. Contemp. Asia **45**(3), 553–556 (2015)

Yoo, W.S., Suh, K.S., Lee, M.B.: Exploring the factors enhancing member participation in virtual communities. J. Global Inf. Manage. (JGIM) **10**(3), 55–71 (2002)

Zhou, T.: Understanding online community user participation: a social influence perspective. Internet Res. **21**(1), 67–81 (2011)

The Influences of Culture on User Experience

Tales Rebequi Costa Borges de Souza(✉) and João Luiz Bernardes Jr.

School of Arts Sciences and Humanities – EACH, University of São Paulo, São Paulo, Brazil
{tales.rebequi,jbernardes}@usp.br

Abstract. In the last years, some studies about how cultural differences influences user experience (UX) have started being published. Most of these studies concluded that cultural differences really affect UX. These studies were conducted in different countries, using different methods and led by researches with different cultures. Observing these points, the main objective of this review is to map the work in this area and to suggest a research guideline for similar work. First, a systematic literature review was conducted in the main academic search engines, using many related keywords. The search engines returned 1227 studies and all abstracts were read and evaluated according to the acceptance criteria. Twenty three remaining studies were analyzed in detail. Results showed that the Hofstede's definition of culture and cultural differences is the most commonly used definition in this area, most studies used questionnaires to evaluate if the culture really influences UX and regarding the results, the majority, 87 %, confirm that it does. Based on this analysis, we identify and propose a guideline to replicate this kind of work in other scenarios. This guideline may represent a significant contribution to the area, perhaps enabling an increase in the number and standardization of certain cross-cultural studies, in the development of new techniques and in the relevance of this subject during UX projects.

Keywords: Culture · User experience · Usability

1 Introduction

In the last years, some studies about how cultural differences influences user experience (UX) have started being published. Most of these studies concluded that cultural differences really affect UX, whether in product development [1], systems such as internet banking [2] or games [3]. These studies were conducted in different countries, using different methods and led by researches with different cultures. Observing these points, the main objective of this review is to map the work in this area, listing the methods and results around the world, and to suggest a research guideline for similar work.

A systematic literature review is a method to identify, evaluate and interpret all relevant research available for a specific research question, subject area or phenomenon of interest. The main reasons and advantages for conducting a systematic review are: to summarize the information about a particular topic, find gaps in subject areas or provide a background to a study [4]. Therefore, a systematic literature review was conducted to answer these following questions:

P.-L.P. Rau (Ed.): CCD 2016, LNCS 9741, pp. 43–52, 2016.
DOI: 10.1007/978-3-319-40093-8_5

- How do the user experience studies define "cultural difference"?
- Which methods exist to assess whether cultural differences influence UX?
- What are the results of this type of study?

Based on the results, we identified and propose a guideline to replicate this kind of work in other scenarios. This guideline may represent a significant contribution to the area, perhaps enabling an increase in the number and standardization of certain cross-cultural studies, in the development of new techniques and in the relevance of this subject during UX projects.

2 Methodology

The review was conducted in five academic databases IEEE Digital Library, ACM Digital Library, Capes Periodicals, Capes Thesis and USP Thesis.

Twelve keywords in English and two keywords in Portuguese were used on the search engines (Table 1).

Table 1. Keywords used on the systematic literature review

Keyword	Language
Cultural Usability	English
Cultural "User Experience"	English
Cultural UX	English
Cultural "Interface Design"	English
Culture Usability	English
Culture "User Experience"	English
Culture UX	English
Culture "Interface Design"	English
Cross-Cultural Usability	English
Cross-Cultural "User Experience"	English
Cross-Cultural UX	English
Cross-Cultural "Interface Design"	English
Cultural Usabilidade	Portuguese
Cultural Experiência do Usuário	Portuguese

Search strings were built with the keywords that were submitted to the search engines of the mentioned bases. Based on reading the abstracts, the criteria for inclusion and exclusion listed below were applied.

Inclusion criteria:

- Works that address cultural differences related to usability or synonyms were included.

Exclusion criteria:

- Papers that present ratings without presenting the method used were excluded.

The full text of the papers included through these criteria was read and the criteria for final selection were reapplied. Then the following information was extracted from the selected works:

- Definition of "cultural difference";
- Method to evaluate cultural difference;
- Method to evaluate user experience;
- Result of the study;
- Countries that the study covers;
- Audience;
- Number of participants;
- Statistical methods used.

Finally, there was a quantitative and qualitative analysis of the information extracted.

3 Results

The search results for each of the sources of research were recorded and are shown in Table 2.

Table 2. Results by search source

Academic Bases	Results	Accepted	Rejected
ACM DL	711	29	682
IEEEXplore	276	2	274
Capes Periodicals	236	14	222
Capes Thesis	2	0	2
USP Thesis	2	0	2
Total Results	**1227**	**45**	**1182**

After reading the abstracts, the 45 accepted papers were classified into two categories: type and media as shown in Table 3. The type category refers to the phase of the product lifecycle in the cultural influence is analyzed: development, testing, final user experience or in research of new methods. The media category refers to which type of interface was explored in the study.

We then decided to focus on the papers with the UX type. Among the 28 papers included in this type, 5 were excluded because they were studying user experience with objects instead of software, focusing on reliability instead of a broader definition of UX or were a precursor study of a final study already present in this review. Then the 23 remaining papers were analyzed fully [5–27].

In order to answer the first research question, "How do the user experience studies define cultural difference?", we sought to examine how each study categorized the culture of the participants and how it defined this concept. As shown in Fig. 1, the work of the anthropologist Hofstede [28] predominates as the basis of the definition of culture, followed by the study Nisbett [29] with only three entries.

Table 3. Accepted papers categorized by type and media

Media/Type	Development	UX	Tests	Research	Total
Electronics	–	1	–	–	**1**
Games	–	2	–	–	**2**
Mobile	–	6	–	–	**6**
TV	1	–	–	–	**1**
Cars	–	1	–	–	**1**
Web	6	18	8	2	**34**

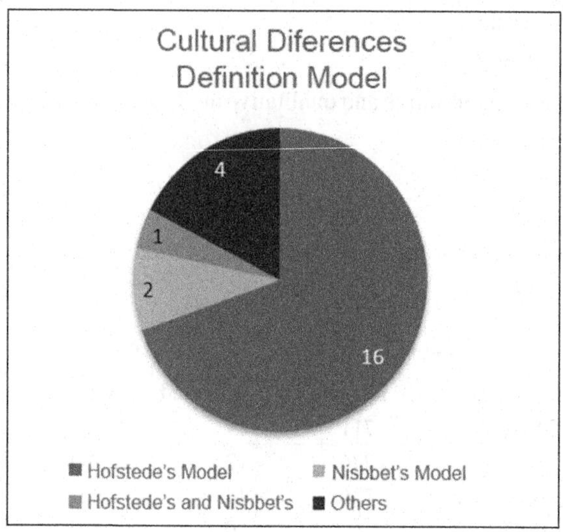

Fig. 1. Cultural difference definition models

The Hofstede perspective is methodologically advantageous to work that wishes to map the behavior of cultural groups, especially highlighting the focus on measuring cultural traits. Hofstede follow a particular line of thought in anthropology, according to which there are generalizable cultural traits [30].

Although Hofstede's analysis is based on cultural dimensions, the dimensions are calculated by territories and, therefore, continue to use political divisions as part of its foundation. Some studies [5, 7, 21] considered the birthplace and the time and place of residence to set the culture of the individual, while other studies [13, 16, 23, 27] used only the birthplace. It is understood that it is appropriate to analyze where the individual lives, if the current reality has influenced the culture derived from the birthplace.

Then we analyzed the second research question "Which methods exist to assess whether cultural differences influence UX?". As shown in Fig. 2, the most widely used method to evaluate the influence of cultural differences in user experience is the use of questionnaires, followed by performance measurement in predefined tasks.

Questionnaires play a key role in usability evaluation [31]. In the papers evaluated in this review, questionnaires were very popular and used to identify the importance of

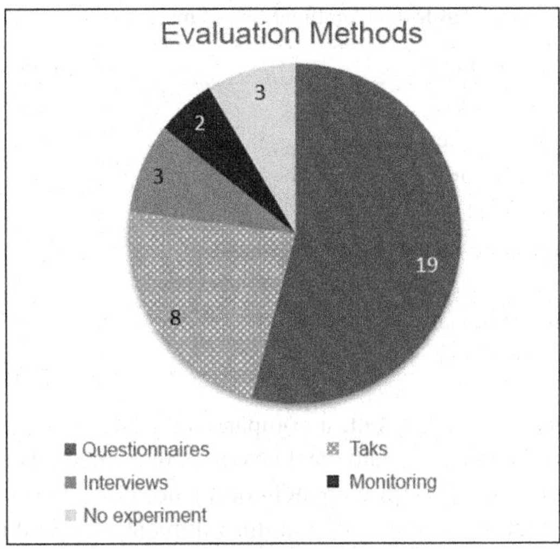

Fig. 2. Evaluation methods

usability attributes, such as effectiveness, efficiency and satisfaction, in finished products [5, 6, 11, 24, 25] and to investigate the user experience [10, 14, 16–21, 26, 27]. Questionnaires were also used in a less conventional way, in tests in which the user completed sentences according to their understanding [22], in initial mapping of user culture [7, 8] and to recognize icons [23].

The second most used method, measuring performance in tasks, constitutes successful evaluation in tasks in relation to time and/or amount of hits. This method, used in some studies [7, 10, 13, 17, 18, 21, 26, 27], was conducted by asking users to execute activities or perform tasks in different interfaces to correlate the performance of any given interface with the culture of a certain group.

The method of conducting interviews, used in some papers [8, 16, 26], is similar to applying the questionnaire in relation to the purpose of raising the awareness of the user, but adopting a personal interaction as a strategy to capture more information.

The last method listed, monitoring, analyzes the user experience through the capture of user signals. In this set of papers there are two examples, the traditional eye-tracking [16] that monitors eye movements and gaze direction in order to assess several factors, including user satisfaction, and the less conventional FunToolKit [19], which analyzes children's facial expressions and smiles to measure satisfaction.

The higher number of evaluation methods in relation to the number of papers occurred because some combined more than one method. Table 4 shows the combinations of methods were used.

Three of the papers included did not perform user experiments themselves [9, 12, 15], but based their conclusions only on literature reviews and annotations.

The third research question, "What is the result of the study?", focuses on how many studies have indicated that cultural differences impact on user experience and how many got the opposite result. The vast majority of studies, 87 %, conclude that there is influence.

Table 4. Combinations of methods

Combinantion	Quantity
Questionnaires	9
Tasks and questionnaire	6
Questionnaires and interviews	1
Tasks and logs	1
Tasks, questionnaires and interviews	1
Eye-tracking, questionnaire and interview	1
Fun Toolkit and questionnaire	1
No experiment	3

For a better analysis of this result, a comparative analysis of the papers follows, highlighting some of the strengths and weaknesses in their methods and definitions, in order to indicate which results inspire greater confidence.

Among the 20 articles that claim that culture influences UX, three performed no experiment [9, 12, 15] and three did not discuss which statistical methods were used [21, 26, 27]. All other studies conducted user experiments and showed the statistical methods used, including the three that could not find evidence of culture influencing UX.

Of the papers that performed experiments and showed their statistics, 16 adopted young people such as students, trainees, gamers etc. as their target group. There is only one exception [19], which used children as target audience. It is considered appropriate to choose as target users of the same general age group, or to control for it, since age is one of the factors that influences culture.

One study selected numerically equal groups of men and women [17]. This control is important since gender may interfere with both culture and UX. The amount of target audience for the studies varied within the range of 40 [7, 8, 19] to 5000 [22] participants. Studies using online questionnaires had larger samples.

Among the papers that claim to have found significant influence of culture in UX, two stood out for demonstrating through the experiment that there was effective performance improvement in the activities when using the culturally appropriate interface [7, 13]. This type of analysis has high added value because it not only shows that the performance differs between cultures but also using a culturally appropriate interface can improve both performance and UX.

These studies measured user experience and performance on tasks exposing the same interfaces to groups with different cultures and analyzed these measurements with statistical methods and methodologies typical of reliable research.

On the other hand, the two papers that claim to have found no influence [10, 18] may present small methodological divergences. One of them [19] said the experiment was inconclusive, but used a relatively small sample of young children as subjects in two different countries and with considerably different sample sizes in each country, which complicates data analysis. It also used the Fun Toolkit to measure satisfaction, along with self-reported questionnaires (which may also be more problematic for children to answer). Other two articles [10, 18] used a different research procedure: instead of subjecting users of different cultures to the same interface, as most of the articles made, they chose to show two significantly different user interfaces to users of a single culture, and were then unable to detect any difference.

4 The Guideline

Based on the results and in the best practices adopted on the studies we analyzed, a guideline was created to help researchers in future studies that aim to investigate whether cultural differences between two or more specific groups are deep enough to affect user experience.

The first step is to choose the population to the study. It is recommended to choose a population with very similar characteristics, in which only one factor influences cultural differences, to minimize the interference of other factors (or one must be aware of these other factors and control for them during data analysis). When analyzing differences in regional culture, for instance, which is a very common type of study, one should attempt to choose people within the same ranges of age, income and education. Profession (or general professional area) may also play a large role in culture, particularly in aspects related to that profession, so it should also be as uniform as possible or controlled for. Gender may or may not have an influence but since analyzing for a single gender is usually undesirable, we recommend controlling for it, and choosing the same number of men and women in each cultural group may also alleviate this problem. Finally, for regional differences, it is interesting to confirm that the study participants live in the same region they were born and never lived for long periods in other regions to avoid the adoption of other cultural traits.

The second step is to evaluate if the groups of the study really shows cultural differences. In the attempt to pick a population as uniform as possible aside from one factor such as regional culture, one might end up picking from a group, such as "computer science students aged between 20 and 25" which has its own more uniform subculture that supplants the influence of other factors, such as where they live. To verify whether the different cultural groups in the population do show cultural difference, we recommend the use of Hofstede's Values Survey Module [28], because it is methodologically advantageous, giving clear, numerical results through the application of a questionnaire, and easily replicable.

The third step is to choose the system or interface that will serve as a basis for the UX evaluation. It is important to equalize or control for previous knowledge and experience with the system, to avoid that users with more familiarity obtain results significantly different compared to those that have no practice. Therefore, we recommend creating a new system or interface if feasible, used only for the experiment, ensuring that all users will have no familiarity with it, unless one wishes to test experienced users, in which case training before the experiment may alleviate these differences in experience.

The fourth step is to choose the methods to evaluate the user experience and satisfaction about the system. We recommend the use of questionnaires and task performance measurements, frequently used in studies analyzed in this review, as ways to get quantitative results to compare. Standard questionnaires such as QUIS [32] or others could be used, and are preferable since they have already been vetted by the research community. If possible, we also recommend the application of some form of interview to get further results and explanations, including qualitative results.

The fifth step is to define the tasks to be measured. It is recommended to choose different system features and, in some of these, place some "traps" (i.e. instances where uses may easily commit errors or purposefully ill-designed elements of interaction) to analyze user reaction to these elements.

The sixth step is to define questions for the interview. Common options are asking about what users liked best and liked least, what they would change in the interface and letting them make general comments.

The seventh, and last, step is to apply the experiment and to compute the results. If the VSM results and the UX tests results shows statistically significant difference between the different cultural groups but statistically converge between the users of a same group, this strongly suggests that the cultural differences between these groups is deep enough to impact the UX. It is then possible to analyze which aspects of the experience differ mostly between groups and to begin to understand and design for these differences.

5 Conclusion

Our goal was to map the work in this area, discussing the methods and results around the world, and to suggest a research guideline for similar work.

Our results indicate that Hofstede has the most accepted definition of culture and his method to calculate cultural differences using cultural dimensions is methodologically advantageous, easily replicable and largely utilized in this kind of study.

Questionnaires and task performance measurements are the most used methods to evaluate the UX in this kind of study.

Most of the studies analyzed on this review, 87 %, concluded that the cultural differences really affects the UX.

To help researchers that want to replicate this kind of study in other groups of user we elaborated a guideline with seven steps:

1. Choose the population
2. Evaluate cultural differences
3. Choose a new system/interface
4. Choose the methods to evaluate UX
5. Define the tasks
6. Define the interview questions
7. Apply the experiment and compute the results

We believe that culture is an important part of UX and, the more studies are performed, the more techniques that account for culture in the UX process will evolve. With this work, we contribute with futures studies by making experimental design less complex with a guideline based on success studies.

References

1. Lachner, F., von Saucken, C., 'Floyd' Mueller, F., Lindemann, U.: Cross-cultural user experience design helping product designers to consider cultural differences. In: Rau, P. (ed.) CCD 2015. LNCS, vol. 9180, pp. 58–70. Springer, Heidelberg (2015)
2. de Souza, T.R.C.B., Morandini, M., Bernardes Jr., J.L.: Brazilian cultural differences and their effects on the web interfaces user experience. In: Rau, P. (ed.) CCD 2015. LNCS, vol. 9180, pp. 209–220. Springer, Heidelberg (2015)
3. Wang, H., Xia, B., Chen, Z.: Cultural difference on team performance between chinese and americans in multiplayer online battle arena games. In: Rau, P. (ed.) CCD 2015. LNCS, vol. 9181, pp. 374–383. Springer, Heidelberg (2015)
4. Kitchenham, B.: Procedures for performing systematic reviews. Keele Univ. **33**, 1–26 (2004)
5. Young, K.L., Bayly, M., Lenné, M.G.: Cross-regional in-vehicle information system design: the preferences and comprehension of Australian, US and Chinese drivers. IET Intel. Transport Syst. **6**(1), 36–43 (2012)
6. Wallace, S., et al.: Culture and the importance of usability attributes. Inf. Technol. People **26**(1), 77–93 (2013)
7. Reinecke, K., Bernstein, A.: Improving performance, perceived usability, and aesthetics with culturally adaptive user interfaces. ACM Trans. Comput. Hum. Interac. (TOCHI) **18**(2), 8 (2011)
8. Shin, D.-H., Choo, H.: Exploring cross-cultural value structures with smartphones. J. Global Inf. Manag. (JGIM) **20**(2), 67–93 (2012)
9. Clemmensen, T., et al.: Cultural cognition in usability evaluation. Interact. comput. **21**(3), 212–220 (2009)
10. Chang, C.-L., Yelin, S.: Cross-cultural interface design and the classroom-learning environment in Taiwan. Turk. Online J. Educ. Technol. TOJET **11**(3), 82–93 (2012)
11. Zaharias, P.: Cross-cultural differences in perceptions of e-learning usability: An empirical investigation. Int. J. Technol. Hum. Interact. **4**(3), 1 (2008)
12. Zahed, F., van Pelt, W.V., Song, J.: A conceptual framework for international web design. IEEE Trans. Prof. Commun. **44**(2), 83–103 (2001)
13. Rau, P.-L.P., Choong, Y.-Y., Salvendy, G.: A cross cultural study on knowledge representation and structure in human computer interfaces. Int. J. Ind. Ergon. **34**(2), 117–129 (2004)
14. Zaharias, P., Papargyris, A.: The gamer experience: Investigating relationships between culture and usability in massively multiplayer online games. Comput. Entertainment (CIE) **7**(2), 26 (2009)
15. Hillier, M.: The role of cultural context in multilingual website usability. Electron. Commer. Res. Appl. **2**(1), 2–14 (2003)
16. Cyr, D., Head, M., Larios, H.: Colour appeal in website design within and across cultures: A multi-method evaluation. Int. J. Hum Comput Stud. **68**(1), 1–21 (2010)
17. Noiwan, J., Norcio, A.F.: Cultural differences on attention and perceived usability: investigating color combinations of animated graphics. Int. J. Hum. Comput. Stud. **64**(2), 103–122 (2006)
18. Ford, G., Gelderblom, H.: The effects of culture on performance achieved through the use of human computer interaction. In: Proceedings of the 2003 Annual Research Conference of the South African Institute of Computer Scientists and Information Technologists on Enablement Through Technology. South African Institute for Computer Scientists and Information Technologists (2003)

19. Sim, G., Horton, M., Danino, N.: Evaluating game preference using the fun toolkit across cultures. In: Proceedings of the 26th Annual BCS Interaction Specialist Group Conference on People and Computers. British Computer Society (2012)
20. Yan, Q., Gu, G.: A remote study on east-west cultural differences in mobile user experience. In: Aykin, N. (ed.) HCII 2007. LNCS, vol. 4560, pp. 537–545. Springer, Heidelberg (2007)
21. Marcus, A., Alexander, C.: User validation of cultural dimensions of a website design. In: Aykin, N. (ed.) HCII 2007. LNCS, vol. 4560, pp. 160–167. Springer, Heidelberg (2007)
22. Walsh, T., Nurkka, P., Walsh, R.: Cultural differences in smartphone user experience evaluation. In: Proceedings of the 9th International Conference on Mobile and Ubiquitous Multimedia. ACM (2010)
23. Lin, C.J., Sung, D., Yang, C.-C., Jou, Y.-T., Yang, C.-W., Cheng, Lai-Yu.: Designing globally accepted human interfaces for instant messaging. In: Aykin, N. (ed.) HCII 2007. LNCS, vol. 4560, pp. 150–159. Springer, Heidelberg (2007)
24. Frandsen-Thorlacius, O., et al.: Non-universal usability?: a survey of how usability is understood by Chinese and Danish users. In: Proceedings of the SIGCHI Conference on Human Factors in Computing Systems. ACM (2009)
25. de Angeli, A., Kyriakoullis, L.: Globalisation vs. localisation in e-commerce: cultural-aware interaction design. In: Proceedings of the Working Conference on Advanced Visual Interfaces. ACM (2006)
26. van Dam, N., Evers, V., Arts, F.A.: Cultural user experience issues in e-government: designing for a multi-cultural society. In: van den Besselaar, P., Koizumi, S. (eds.) Digital Cities 2003. LNCS, vol. 3081, pp. 310–324. Springer, Heidelberg (2005)
27. Ahtinen, A., et al.: Design of mobile wellness applications: identifying cross-cultural factors. In: Proceedings of the 20th Australasian Conference on Computer-Human Interaction: Designing for Habitus and Habitat. ACM (2008)
28. Hofstede, G.H., Hofstede, G.: Culture's Consequences: Comparing Values, Behaviors, Institutions and Organizations Across Nations. Sage (2001)
29. Nisbett, R.: The Geography of Thought: How Asians and Westerners Think Differently… and. Simon and Schuster, New York (2010)
30. de Salgado, C., Cardoso, L., Leitão, C.F., de Souza, C.: A Journey Through Cultures: Metaphors for Guiding the Design of Cross-Cultural Interactive Systems. Springer Science & Business Media, London (2012)
31. Alva, M.E.O., Martínez P., A.B., Cueva L., J.M., Hernán Sagástegui Ch., T., Benjamín López, P.: Comparison of methods and existing tools for the measurement of usability in the web. In: Lovelle, J.M.C., Rodríguez, B.M.G., Gayo, J.E.L., Ruiz, M.D.P.P., Aguilar, L.J. (eds.) ICWE 2003. LNCS, vol. 2722, pp. 386–389. Springer, Heidelberg (2003)
32. Questionnaire For User Interaction Satisfaction. Questionnaire For User Interaction Satisfaction. Web, 20 February 2015. http://www.lap.umd.edu/QUIS/index.html

The Brazilian HCI Community Perspectives in Cultural Aspects in HCI

Isabela Gasparini[1], Luciana C. de C. Salgado[2(✉)], and Roberto Pereira[3]

[1] Department of Computer Science, Santa Catarina State University (UDESC), Florianópolis, Brazil
isabela.gasparini@udesc.br

[2] Department of Computer Science, Fluminense Federal University (UFF), Niterói, Brazil
luciana@ic.uff.br

[3] Department of Informatics, Federal University of Paraná (UFPR), Curitiba, Brazil
rpereira@inf.ufpr.br

Abstract. We consider culture as a concept and a concern that permeates the 5 HCI Grand Challenges identified in 2012 by the Brazilian HCI community, and that should be understood and considered from a broad and systemic perspective. In this sense, we conducted a workshop about cultural issues to investigate and promote the topic in the HCI Brazilian community. In this paper, we present and discuss some results from the workshop, highlighting as primary empirical evidence the participants' survey responses. The results allow us to develop a panorama of how the Brazilian HCI community is interested in the subject of culture understands and makes sense of the subject in their practices.

Keywords: Culture · HCI Brazilian community · Workshop

1 Introduction

We live in a globalized and constantly changing world where technology, culture, society and nature are on a constant move. Thus, understanding the complex cultural context in which people live is becoming increasingly critical and necessary in order to clarify a problem and design a solution for it. However, one of the greatest challenges to Human-Computer Interaction (HCI) practitioners is to turn interfaces universally accessible and usable, on one hand, and to respect and promote culture-determined aspects of the user's experience, on the other hand. Big companies all over the world share this challenge and concern. Google, for instance, claims that "they are working toward a web that includes everyone", but recognizes that "they are still not where they want to be when it comes to diversity" [12].

Over the years, cultural issues in technology design have been receiving attention from the HCI community [7, 10]. In Brazil, specifically, different research groups with different approaches have been working on artifacts, methods, tools, theoretical background and models to incorporate cultural issues in the interaction design process [11, 14–16, 20]. Salgado [17], for instance, has proposed a Semiotic Engineering conceptual tool, namely, Cultural Viewpoint Metaphors (CVM) for guiding the design

P.-L.P. Rau (Ed.): CCD 2016, LNCS 9741, pp. 53–62, 2016.
DOI: 10.1007/978-3-319-40093-8_6

of cross-cultural interactive systems. Gasparini et al. [10] presented a survey of cultural-aware issues in HCI to establish background and some basic concepts for helping designers incorporating cultural issues in HCI. Pereira and Baranauskas [14], in turn, propose artifacts and methods for a value-oriented and culturally informed approach to design, recognizing the cultural nature of values and favoring the identification of relevant cultural aspects to the design context, process and stakeholders.

On the one hand, all the previously cited works have been focused on the importance of including and understanding cultural issues in HCI. On the other hand, each research group has adopted different theoretical foundations and different methodological frames to conduct its research. This is due to at least two reasons: (i) Brazil is a multicultural country with continental dimensions; (ii) the Brazilian HCI community has been founded in different approaches. In such a plural scenario, the key question is why just a few researchers, in Brazil, explicitly recognize the cross-cultural nature of their research.

In 2013, in a dataset composed by 236 full papers published in fifteen years of the Brazilian Symposium on Human Factors in Computer Science (namely "IHC"), Gasparini and co-authors [11] found only 6 papers focused on cultural issues. In the following year (2014), the same symposium ("IHC") had just one full paper explicitly focused on this theme. The "IHC" is the major HCI conference in Brazil and it is supported by the HCI Special Interest Group of the Brazilian Computer Society. In the same year and conference, we organized the first Workshop on Cultural Aspects in HCI (WCIHC) aimed at: (i) identifying challenges and interests about this theme by the Brazilian community, (ii) sharing different concepts, theories, methodologies and knowledge, and (iii) raising the participants' awareness to the importance and relevance of the topic. The workshop was attended by 23 participants from 20 different Brazilian organizations (18 universities and 2 Information Technology companies). From the participants, 8 are PhDs, 3 PhD candidates, 1 master, 7 graduates, and 3 undergraduate students. The research question that motivated the workshop was: What are the Brazilian community perspectives in Cultural aspects in HCI?

The workshop included different activities, such as paper presentation session; practical and participatory activity about design in a cultural critical context, focus groups, and a final discussion. In order to find out the researchers' profile and background we invited all the registered attendees to answer a pre-workshop survey. It aimed at collecting evidence regarding: research activities, areas of concentration, research interests in Culture and HCI, what the participants understand by culture and cultural issues in HCI; previous experiences with cultural issues; and which cultural questions they believe to be relevant.

In this paper, we present and discuss some results from the workshop, highlighting as primary empirical evidence the survey responses. The results allow us to develop a panorama of how the Brazilian HCI community is interested in the subject of culture, understands and makes sense of the subject in their practices. Furthermore, we outline what the Brazilian HCI community thinks of when culture plays a leading role in interaction design.

This paper is organized as follows: Sect. 2 presents the foundation and concepts about culture and HCI. Section 3 details the workshop structure and dynamics.

Section 4 presents and discusses the initial results from the workshop. Section 5 presents our final remarks and directions for future research and activities.

2 Foundations and Concepts about Culture and HCI

Every technology triggers positive and/or negative impact on the environment in which it is inserted and on the people that are living in it – even in a indirectly way. Winograd [22] has stated that the task of designing interactive systems goes beyond building an interface to cover all the "interspace" in which people live.

In fact, HCI field needs to deal with universal issues and aspects that are also matter of other (computing or not) areas and, at the same time, consider specific aspects of the environment (e.g. cultural, social, economic, political, and geographic) in which the application occurs. Several authors as Bannon [1], Baranauskas [4], Bødker [5], Sellen and co-authors [19] claimed that the relationship between people with technology has changed intensely in last years. Currently, interactive systems can be anywhere and used anytime. These changes are profound enough to require a review of HCI field, its theories, methods and practices, and require consideration and explicit involvement of cultural issues related to context in which technology is designed, disseminated, evaluated and used.

Interactive systems need to support an increasing amount of materials and make them accessible to different populations Worldwide. A key challenge for the interaction designer is to design, build and evaluate systems that understand the cultural diversity of its stakeholders and answer a wide variety of needs and expectations.

Recently, the HCI Brazilian research community has developed an initiative to identify Grand Research Challenges for HCI in Brazil for the next decade [3]. Five Grand Challenges were presented: 1. The Future, Smart Cities and Sustainability; 2. Accessibility and Digital Inclusion; 3. Ubiquity, Multiple Devices and Tangibility; 4. Human Values and 5. HCI Education and the Market. This initiative shows the need to understand, consider and deal with cultural issues when doing scientific research in HCI. More than that, Salgado and colleagues affirm that culture topic is crosses the 5 suggested Great Challenges [18], requiring an understanding of Culture and an approach from a broad and systemic perspective.

Most research on culture and HCI performed in the last 15–20 years has investigated the impact of cultural differences on the users' experience and aimed to define the cultural issues in the HCI design process (de Souza et al. [8]; del Gado [9]; Vatrapu & Suthers [21]). Other studies have proposed alternatives to the evaluation processes and design to accommodate cultural factors in the conceptualization and construction of multicultural systems interfaces (Barber & Badre [2]; Bourgues-Waldegg & Scrivener [6]; Gasparini et al. [10]; Pereira & Baranauskas [13]). In addition, new research showed interest in helping HCI professionals in developing multicultural systems that expose and communicate cultural diversity (Salgado and co-authors [17]).

However, while the importance of dealing with cultural issues is obvious and is often present in debates around the course of the HCI area, the treatments given to this issue have been so far mostly fragmentary, guided by practical and specific problems (e.g., the need to develop Web applications for an international and culturally diverse audience). There is an urgent need to discuss and generate new knowledge that will help HCI professionals to find the necessary balance between cultural accessibility – allowing users from one culture to use software produced by other cultures, and preservation of cultural diversity – producing technology that respect, express and strengthen the identity and cultural values (Salgado et al. [17]). Indeed, there is still a lack of theoretically and methodologically informed work (artifacts, methods, tools, examples, experiments) to support the understanding of cultural issues and its explicit consideration in the technology design. The very notion of the meaning of culture, its role in the HCI, and the existing theories and methods used must be put into perspective, shared, reviewed and discussed.

Our initiative in this direction was to establish a place to discuss cultural issues in the practices and research with HCI Brazilian community. For that to happen, we proposed a workshop held jointly with the Brazilian Symposium on Human Factors in Computer Science ("IHC").

3 WCIHC: The Workshop on Cultural Aspects in HCI

In recent years, unwanted impacts of computer systems on economic, ethical, political and social life have become more evident. Such kind of problems generally stem from a software development vision that does not privilege the social world in which solutions are used and people live, i.e., that ignore the complex cultural context of life. Therefore, we argue that research and developments in twenty-first century HCI must respond to the cultural challenges brought about by globalized societies. There is an urgent need to generate a body of knowledge that will help HCI designers to recognize the importance of cultural issues in the design and evaluation of interactive technologies, reaching a proper balance between cultural accessibility and the preservation of cultural diversity. Indeed, the very understanding of culture, its role in the design of technology, the existing theories and methods to deal with cultural issues are topics that need to be discussed, disseminated and revisited. Therefore, the first workshop WCIHC (acronyms of I Workshop on Cultural issues in Human Computer Interaction) aimed at sharing knowledge, experiences and practical results on the research undertaken by the HCI community on this issue and discussing the cultural dimensions in Human-Computer Interaction.

Because the WCIHC happened jointly with the "IHC" event, it had the potential to promote a current discussion forum for the HCI community in Brazil, favoring not only research in the Great Challenges context, but contributing to the development of researches in line with the challenges of a society mediated by Information and Communication Technologies.

The objectives of the WCIHC workshop were twofold: (a) Promote discussions, share knowledge, experiences and concrete results of the research carried out on the cultural dimensions in Human-Computer Interaction; and (b) Disseminate existing research on the topic in the Brazilian community, stimulating the development of new initiatives.

People interested in participating with a paper submission were invited to submit a paper, justifying their interest in the topic and describing experiences related to cultural issues in HCI, including topics such as: Theories, methods, techniques for the design/ evaluation of interactive systems; Design and/or evaluation of multicultural systems; Internationalization-Localization; Culture-Sensitive Design Process; Culture-sensitive Interaction; Cultural accessibility; Cultural awareness; Cultural Diversity and its effects on HCI research; Cultural Perspectives on HCI; Usability, HCI and Culture; Adapting the design and evaluation of interactive systems based on cultural issues; Cultural issues in HCI education; Multi and intercultural Collaboration; Intercultural encounters in HCI.

Each submission was evaluated by two reviewers, and the criteria for selection were: quality of data, arguments about the relevance of the topic, practical implication of the results for HCI, and potential for promoting constructive discussions during the workshop. Five papers were accepted for presentation and discussion at the Workshop, related to: (1) Survey of cultural aspects in HCI Research; (2) Culture in iDTV Projects; (3) Investigating the cultural aspects in the group formation of collaborative learning; (4) Digital Inclusion in a Kaingang Community; and (5) The investigation on elderly, games and motivation.

Among the five papers, the papers 1 and 2 provided general discussions on the subject, and the papers 3, 4 and 5 showed more specific discussions, addressing specific and local topics. The first work presented a comprehensive literature review and contributes to present an overview of some of the major works on the subject in the HCI. This was especially important to place the participants in relation to the existing work and to promote a common basis for discussion. The second work also presented a literature review and contributed to propose a set of questions to support the identification of requirements related to cultural issues involved in a practical context. These issues were important to promote critical thinking about cultural aspects and to show their direct relationship with design requirements. The third work showed the importance and relevance of considering cultural issues when forming groups to promote collaborative learning. This work contributed to relate culture with education, including questions about its practical applications, and suggested an agenda on the issue. The fourth work reported a direct experience of working with an indigenous tribe in southern Brazil, contributing to the workshop by showing a reality of great cultural difference and to the discussion of the methods and theories to be used to support the work in this kind of context. Finally, the fifth work highlighted the importance of understanding culture when designing solutions to specific groups, but not restricted to them, promoting discussions on the need to understand a specific user group, but located in a more complex and comprehensive context.

Besides the call for papers, we invited all the participants of our workshop (both presenters and the general audience) to answer a survey, before the workshop take place, to discover how culture is understood by Brazilian HCI practitioners. The workshop had 22 participants (researchers, masters and PhD students, industry professionals engaged in HCI and interested in cultural issues) and all of them answered the survey before the workshop.

The workshop was held on 27 October 2014, being organized as follows: Opening, with a brief summary of the objectives and the presentation of the agenda; Oral Presentations and discussions of selected papers; Panel with the organizers; Practical activity in groups; Discussion with the audience; and workshop closure. In the practical activity, the participants were exposed to a problem situation and were invited to reflect on the cultural issues involved in it. The activity intended to bring the discussions developed at the workshop into a practical context, promoting the critical reasoning and inviting the participants to think about real problems and the way they would deal with it.

The pre-WCIHC survey. The survey was available online for all the people who had subscribed to the WCIHC. Initially, the survey explained its goals, and presented an informed consent term. Only after this step people could answer the questions. The survey was composed by personal and demographic questions (e.g., background, field, institutions of work and jobs, professional activities, topics of interest, research interest), workshop expectations (e.g., what topics related to culture they would like to see in the WCIHC, their expectations about the workshop) and their previous knowledge about culture in HCI (e.g., information about their knowledge on the topic, what references and authors they knew, what culture means for them, which cultural aspects did they consider relevant in HCI study, as well as their previous experiences when dealing with cultural issues in HCI). In the next section we present and discuss some results from survey.

4 Preliminary Results

All the 22 participants answered the survey before attending to the workshop. The first set of questions was about the participant's profile. Most of them have some background in computer science/informatics field (academic education, e.g. undergrad or Master/PhD; or teaches/researches in the field), and one participant has academic education and works in Arts. When asked about their institution (in the past 3 years), as all participants are located in Brazil, only Brazilian' institution (universities and research centers) were described. The participants work in different regions of the country (at least 1 participant from each one of the 5 regions in Brazil). This is quite an interesting aspect, because Brazil has continental proportions, each region has different traditions and costumes, and these cultural differences could be investigated and applied in HCI field.

In relation to their research topics of interest, although all the participants research in HCI in some extend, different topics emerged. The main topics are presented in Fig. 1, which highlights "Accessibility", "Computers and Education", and "Semiotic Engineering".

About the reasons that led them to enroll in the workshop, most of them (21) stated that they have interest in Culture and HCI, and one participant want to know the topic. Eight participants already research in the topic and six participants claimed they still do not research on the topic but they want to start.

When asked which themes related to culture and HCI they would like to see addressed in the WCIHC, there were different suggestions: Ongoing research on the subject in Brazil; systems evaluation focusing on culture; perception of cultural

Fig. 1. Participants' main topics of research

differences (cultural awareness); cultural diversity and its effects on research in HCI; cultural perspectives on HCI; cultural identities, values, ethical issues, cultural accessibility and preservation of cultural diversity in HCI; research in the area of Online Social Networks, where there are users from different cultures and nationalities; privacy and cultural issues; relation of Culture, Web and Mobile; Approach to virtual learning environments; Semiotics Engineering Evaluation Methods (e.g., MIS and MAC); Methods, models and challenges to identify and realize cultural issues in system design; ethical issues, implicit coding of cultural meanings in software artifacts; cultural reframing software (can software produced and used in a primary culture change the meaning [and use] in another culture?); Interdisciplinary Contributions to address cultural aspects; Culture of Deaf people and its impact on the design of Universal User Interfaces; New approaches and methodologies; Main cultural aspects that influence technological artifacts; Analysis of cultural aspects in Collaborative Learning; Digital Aesthetics; and the main influences of culture in teaching and learning context.

About the participants' expectations related to the workshop, it is interesting to note different aspects, related to their research and to HCI community, such as: meet people interested in the topic; know the current research; know theories and techniques of culture in HCI; learn more about the topic; observe possible intersections of interest and potential collaborators; gain experience in research and evaluation of multicultural systems methodologies, as well as exchange experiences with others facing the same research problems; contribution to improvement of their research; a comprehensive insight into the cultural aspects in HCI, etc.

When asked to report their previous knowledge about cultural issues in HCI, a few people stated having no knowledge about culture. Most of the participants have only little contact with the theme, most from a lecture or reading some papers related to the topic, and few people from a discipline in the field. In relation to the main authors that are frequently referenced in the literature related to cultural and HCI issues, we presented a list of well-known authors in the field and asked the participants to check the ones they already knew. Figure 2 presents the cited authors.

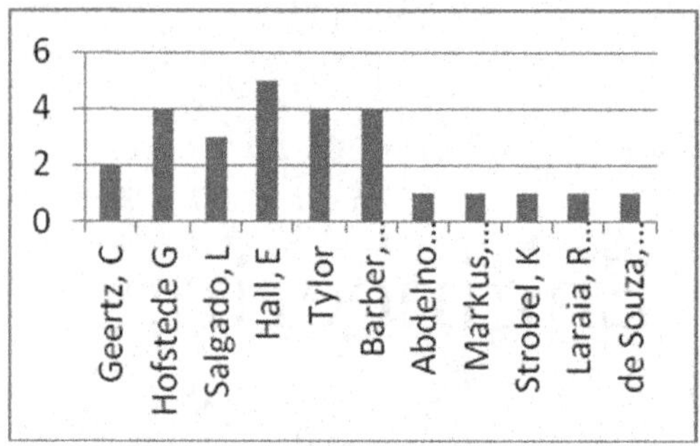

Fig. 2. Cited authors

When we asked participants what is culture to them, the answers were diverse, but all related to each other. Here we show 3 participant's responses (translated by the authors), with distinct ways of writing, probably related to their knowledge of the topic:

Participant 1: *"Aspects of a society."*; Participant 2: *"It is a set of conventions established over time in a community, influenced by factors such as tradition, laws, territories, values etc.*"; Participant 3: *"A higher order signification system which determines how the expression and content from multiple lower order signification systems used by one or more social groups are associated with each other. It is my interpretation of the term signifying order' proposed by Danesi and Perron in the book that deals with culture in a semiotic perspective."*

Finally, about the question "What cultural issues do you consider relevant for HCI studies?", the answers were varied: Cultural plurality questions; Microcultures; organizational culture; Language and behavioral differences; How countries deal with the lack or excess of privacy; All the issues related to beliefs, values and customs of a group or society, at the technical, formal and informal levels; All issues related to culture and its implications in the interaction of people with the new technologies; Beliefs, habits, values, customs; Accessible interfaces to language groups; Localization of interfaces; diversity of aesthetic and logical paradigms; The formation of culture, cultural diversity and how different values can impact HCI; Styles of thought and communication, etc. These answers indicate that Cultural issues are still a new topic to discuss in the Brazilian community, which has different interested, purposes and ways of understanding the role of culture in HCI.

5 Final Remarks and Directions for Future Research

Nowadays we need to discuss the course of HCI area and to rethink the theories, methods and practices adopted to support the design of computing solutions in a culturally informed manner. It is a two-way road, once revisiting theories, practices and methods to become "culturally aware" will be useful, and even possible, only if the HCI community changes its mindset, i.e., its culture of research and practice.

In fact, we need to understand and recognize that cultural aspects directly influence how an interactive system is created, perceived, understood and used. The lack of understanding and knowledge about the need for considering cultural differences in HCI has led to the design of products that do not meet the demands of their users, do not make sense, and that often cause unwanted impacts on the environment in which they are available and on the diverse stakeholders.

The WCIHC was an initiative to promoting such discussion in the HCI Brazilian community, highlight the importance of cultural issues in HCI research, and promoting the exchange of experiences and practices between the participants. The initial results from this workshop suggested that our community is diverse, and that although many participants do not consider (or do it at a minimum level) cultural issues in HCI research and practices, they are aware of their importance, and prone to advance in this direction. For that, background material, examples of practices and further discussions to understand concepts, share experiences, practices, challenges, and practical problems are welcome and necessary. We hope this is initiative to be the first step to more people to get involved on the topic.

Acknowledgement. The authors would like to thank all participants who participated in WCIHC and con-tributed to the research reported in this paper. Additionally, the authors thank CNPq, FAPERJ and FAPESP (#2013/02821-1) for the financial support.

References

1. Bannon, L.: Reimagining HCI: toward a more human-centered perspective. Interactions **18**(4), 50–57 (2011)
2. Barber, W., Badre, A.: Culturability: the merging of culture and usability. In: Proceedings of the 4th Conference on Human Factors & the Web, Basking Ridge, NJ, 5 June 1998
3. Baranauskas, M.C.C., de Souza, C.S., Pereira, R.I.: GranDIHC-BR – Grand Research Challenges for Human-Computer Interaction in Brazil. Human-Computer Interaction Special Committee (CEIHC) of the Brazilian Computer Society (SBC) (2015). ISBN: 9788576692966
4. Baranauskas, M.C.C.: Social awareness in HCI. Interactions **21**(4), 66–69 (2014)
5. Bødker, S.: When second wave HCI meets third wave challenges. In: 4th Nordic Conference on Human-Computer Interaction: Changing Roles, Norway, pp. 1–8 (2006)
6. Bourgues-Waldegg, P., Scrivener, S.A.R.: Meaning, the central issue in cross-cultural HCI design. Interact. Comput. **9**(3), 287–309 (1998)
7. Clemmensen, T., Roese, K.: An overview of a decade of journal publications about Culture and Human - Computer Interaction (HCI) - Department of Informatics Howitzvej DK. Working Paper nr. 03-2009 (2009). http://openarchive.cbs.dk/bitstream/handle/10398/7948/WP_2009_003.pdf
8. de Souza, C.S., Laffon, R., Leitão, C.F.: Communicability in multicultural contexts: a study with the international children's digital library. In: Forbrig, P., Paternò, F., Pejtersen, A.M. (eds.) HCIS 2008. IFIP, vol. 272, pp. 129–142. Springer, Boston (2008)
9. Del Gado, E., Nielsen, J.: International User Interfaces. John Wiley and Sons, New York (1996)

10. Gasparini, I., Pimenta, M.S., de Oliveira, J.P.M.: Vive la différence!: a survey of cultural-aware issues in HCI. In: X Brazilian Symposium on Human Factors in Computer Systems (IHC 2011), pp. 13–22 (2011)
11. Gasparini, I., Kimura, M.H., Moraes Jr., S.L., Pimenta, M.S., de Oliveira, J.P.M.: Is the Brazilian HCI community researching cultural issues? An analysis of 15 years of the Brazilian HCI conference. In: The Fourth International Workshop on Culturally-Aware Tutoring Systems (CATS 2013). Proceedings of the Workshops at the 16th International Conference on Artificial Intelligence in Education AIED 2013), Memphis, pp. 11–19 (2013)
12. https://www.google.com/diversity/. Accessed in October 2015
13. Pereira, R., Baranauskas, M.C.C.: Value pie: a culturally informed conceptual scheme for understanding values in design. In: Human-Computer Interaction. Theories, Methods, and Tools, pp. 122–133 (2014)
14. Pereira, R., Baranauskas, M.C.C.: A value-oriented and culturally informed approach to the design of interactive systems. Int. J. Hum Comput Stud. **80**, 66–82 (2015)
15. Salgado, L.C.C., et al.: Conceptual metaphors for designing multi-cultural applications. In: LA-WEB 2009 - Latin American Web Congress, pp. 105–111 (2009)
16. Salgado, L.C.C., Souza, C.S., Leitão, C.F.: On the epistemic nature of cultural viewpoint metaphors. In: X Brazilian Symposium on Human Factors in Computer Systems (IHC 2011), pp. 23–32 (2011)
17. Salgado, L.C.C., de Souza, C.S., Leitão, C.F.: A Journey through Cultures: Metaphors for Guiding the Design of Cross-Cultural Interactive Systems. Springer, London (2012)
18. Salgado, L., Pereira, R., Gasparini, I.: Cultural issues in HCI: challenges and opportunities. In: Kurosu, M. (ed.) Human-Computer Interaction, HCII 2015, Part I. LNCS, vol. 9169, pp. 60–70. Springer, Heidelberg (2015)
19. Sellen, A., Rogers, Y., Harper, R., Rodden, T.: Reflecting human values in the digital age. Commun. ACM **52**, 58–66 (2009)
20. Silva, M.A.R., Anacleto, J.C.: An end user development environment for culturally contextualized storytelling. Int. Rep. Socio-Inform. (IRSI) **6**, 4–8 (2009)
21. Vatrapu, R., Suthers, D.: Intra- and Inter-cultural usability in computer supported collaboration. J. Usability Stud. **5**(4), 172–197 (2010)
22. Winograd, T.: The design of interaction. In: Beyond Calculation: The Next Fifty Years of Computing, pp. 149–161. Springer, New York (1997)

Cross-Cultural Study of Tactile Interactions in Technologically Mediated Communication

Lalita Haritaipan and Céline Mougenot[✉]

Tokyo Institute of Technology, Tokyo, Japan
haritaipan.l.aa@m.titech.ac.jp mougenot.c.aa@m.titech.ac.jp

Abstract. In order to design tactile devices for technologically mediated communication, we investigated what tactile and gestural interactions would be spontaneously used for sharing emotions in mediated communication. In an experiment with 40 participants, we identified relations between hand gestures performed with a concept device and emotions that a "sender" intends to convey to a "receiver". Among others, our results show that squeezing and shaking are the most popular chosen hand gesture interaction. Gesture intensity and speed follow the arousal (intensity) and temperature follows the valence (pleasure). Emotions that subjects are most are willing to share with such a tactile are gratitude, love, happy, sad, astonished, excited, angry and worried.

Keywords: Tactile interactions · Emotion · Communication · Culture · Design

1 Emotions and Tactile Communication

A number of communication devices have been designed to explore tactile interactions in communication [Picard 1997], as ComTouch [Chang et al. 2002], Hand Data Glove [Piyush et al. 2012], a vibro-tactile device [Rantala et al. 2013], a mid-air haptic device [Obrist et al. 2015]. A comprehensive review of 143 communication devices for mediating intimate relationships, which includes touch-based devices, has been reported by [Hassenzahl et al. 2012]. Indeed, it has been shown that touch is an effective way to communicate emotions [Hertenstein et al. 2006, 2009]. From a biological point of view, there is some evidence that touch triggers the release of oxytocin hormone, which decreases stress [Uvnas-Moberg and Petersson 2005]. In this context, our goal is to find a systematic way to design touch-based long-distance communication devices. More specifically we aim at identifying correlations between tactile interactions and emotions that are felt by the users of such a device.

In all aforementioned studies, the participants were people from one single cultural background. In a study by Nummenmaa et al. [2013], the focus was on the differences between cultures. The authors proposed maps of bodily sensations associated with different emotions and they did not observe any differences between European and East Asian subjects. They concluded that emotions were represented in the somatosensory system as culturally universal categorical somatotopic maps. With a similar approach applied to technologically mediated communication, our study aims at identifying

P.-L.P. Rau (Ed.): CCD 2016, LNCS 9741, pp. 63–69, 2016.
DOI: 10.1007/978-3-319-40093-8_7

differences between two groups of people, Japanese and French, in the way the would use such a tactile device for mediated communication.

In this study, we specifically focus the gestures of a sender who is willing to share emotions with another person, through a handheld technological device, as described in Fig. 1. Thus we conducted an experiment to identify the characteristics of such hand gestures and analyzed the results with a special focus on the differences between the Japanese participants and the French participants.

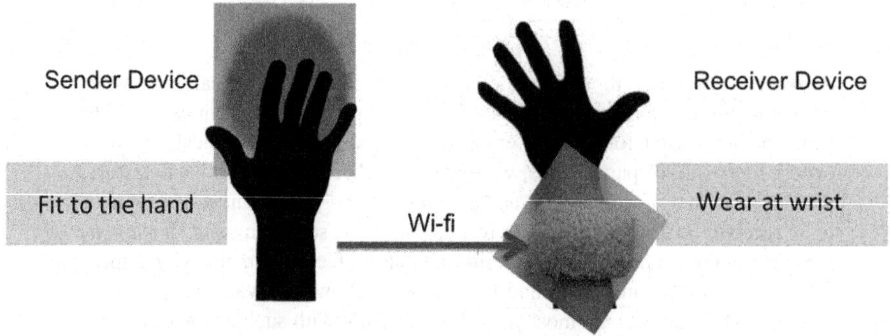

Fig. 1. Design concept of our tactile communication device

Fig. 2. Experimental setting

2 Experiment

Participants. 40 people participated in the experiment, half were French nationals, the other half Japanese nationals, aged 21 to 37 years (M = 24.9). In both groups, around half of the subjects were female subjects.

Procedure. In an individual one-hour session, the participants received a list of 35 emotions extracted from [Paltoglou et al. 2013], an extended version of the Circumplex Model of Emotion [Russell 1980]. Three interpersonal emotions, gratitude, love and sympathy, were added to the list, as in [Obrist et al. 2015]. For each emotion, the subjects were individually asked to perform one hand gesture that they thought was the best way to communicate the given emotion and to describe the properties of the gesture they performed: type of gesture, intensity (5-point Likert scale), speed (5-point Likert scale), temperature that they would like the receiver to feel (cold /neutral /hot). The participants were also asked to select the emotions they would like to be able to communicate with a tactile long-distance emotional communication device.

Data Analysis. Data were analyzed with SPSS software, two-way between-groups ANOVA and Fisher's test, and in some cases independent samples t-test.

3 Results

Types of Gesture. The most chosen gestures are mapped on the Circumplex Model of Emotions, with percentage of subjects who chose the gesture (Fig. 3). The most popular gestural interactions are squeezing, for intense emotions, and shaking, for pleasant emotions. Fisher's Exact Probability Test is used for comparing the differences between nationalities. French and Japanese subjects have differences in choosing gesture types for 6 out of 35 emotions: bored, determined, disgusted, frustrated, pleased and sleepy.

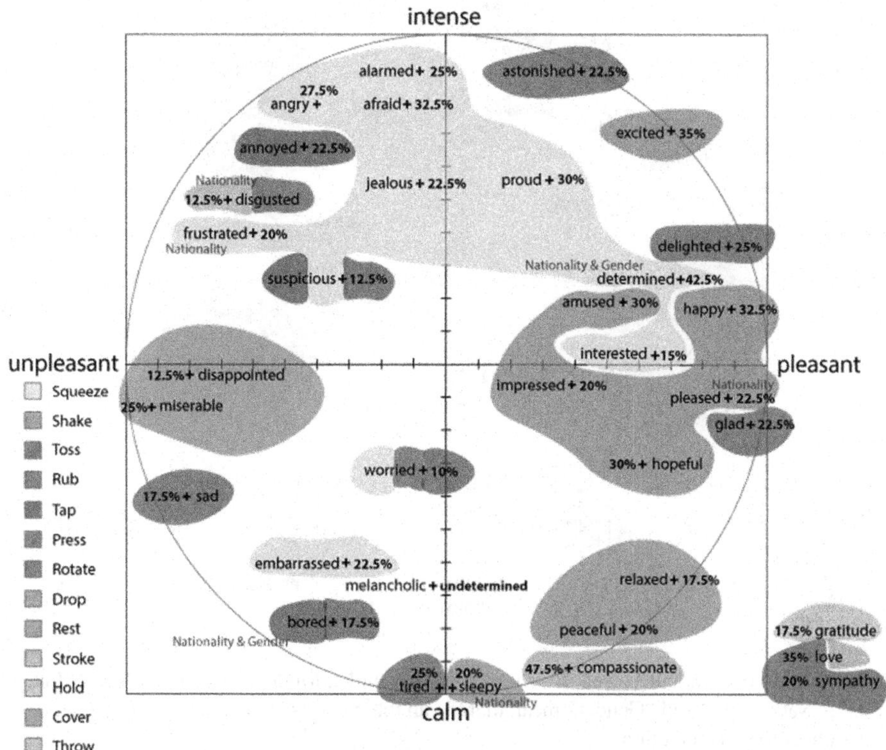

Fig. 3. Most frequent types of gesture shown on the Circumplex Model of Emotions Note: "Nationality" and "Gender" mean that this gesture was significantly used differently across nationalities or genders.

Gesture Intensity. Gesture intensity tends to follow the arousal (intensity), gesture intensity increasing with the emotion intensity. There is a nationality effect in 7 out of 35 emotions: astonished, bored, compassionate, frustrated, hopeful, sympathy, and worried. Between Japanese and French subjects, there was a significant difference in gesture intensity for only astonished emotion t(38) = 2.77, p = .01.

Gesture Speed. Gesture speed tends to follow the arousal (intensity), speed increasing with the intensity. Between Japanese and French subjects, there was a significant difference for 'determined': t(38) = −2.58, p = .01, and 'excited': t(38) = −2.18, p = .04.

Temperature. Temperature tends to follow the valence (pleasure), with high temperature chosen for pleasant emotions and low temperature for unpleasant emotions. Between Japanese and French subjects, there was a significant difference in gesture speed for embarrassed t(38) = 4.04, p = .00, two-tailed), and sympathy t(38) = −4.64, p = .00, two-tailed).

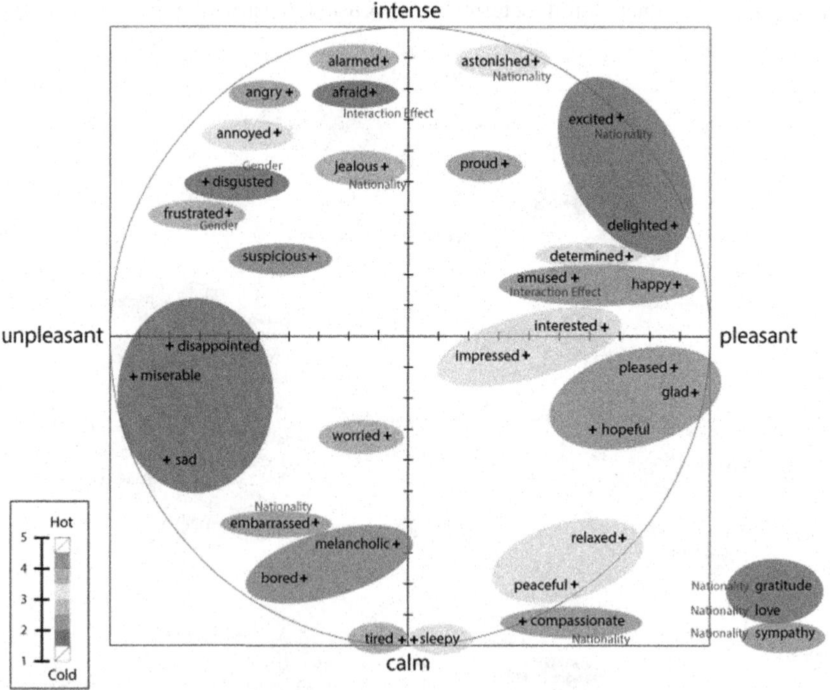

Fig. 4. Gesture temperature levels shown on the Circumplex Model of Emotions Note: "Interaction", "Nationality" and "Gender" mean there is an interaction effect, a nationality effect, or a gender effect for each emotion.

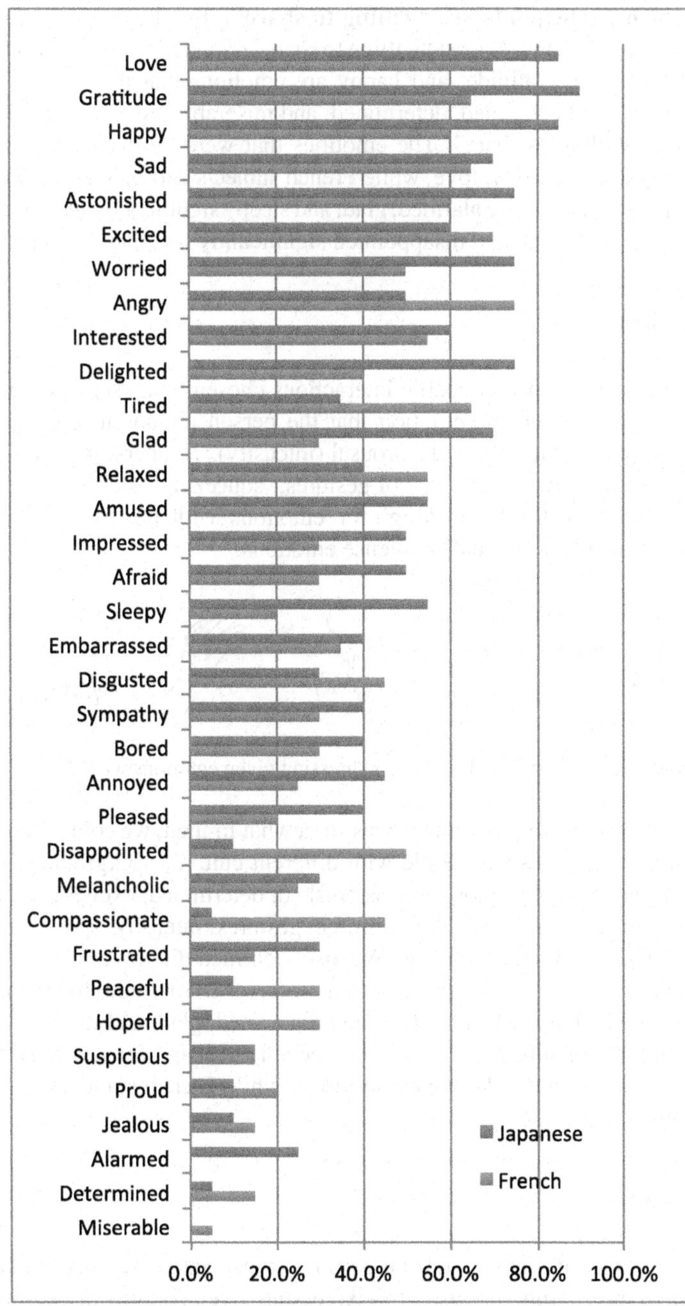

Fig. 5. Percentage of respondents who are 'Willing to Share' the emotion with a tactile device

Emotions which participants are "willing to share". Emotions in Fig. 5 are listed from most "willing to share" to least "willing to share" (counted from the total frequency of all subjects). Love, gratitude, and happy are emotions that participants are most "willing to share", while alarmed, determined, and miserable are emotions that participants are least "willing to share". The emotions that were most chosen by Japanese subjects were gratitude, happy, love, while French subjects chose: angry, excited, love. Japanese subjects want to share alarmed, glad, and sleepy significantly more than French subjects, but compassionate and disappointed significantly less than French subjects.

4 Discussion

We identified relations between tactile interactions chosen by a user of a touch-based communication device and the emotion that the person intends to convey. Gesture intensity and speed tend to follow the arousal (intensity). Temperature tends to follow the valence (pleasure). As for the type of gestures, 'squeezing' is chosen for emotions with positive intensity level; 'shaking' for emotions with positive pleasant level; 'tossing' for extreme pleasant and/or intense emotions.

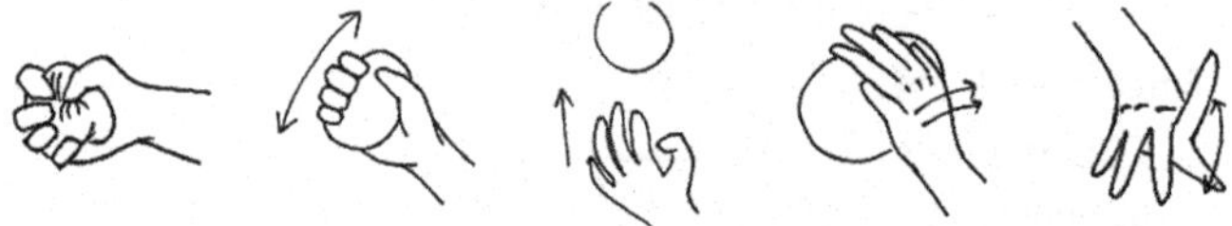

Fig. 6. Most popular gestures chosen for expressing given emotions with a tactile device

Although the sample of participants was somewhat limited, we could identify some significant differences between people with different cultural backgrounds, i.e. Japan and France in this study. Emotions like astonished, determined, excited, embarrassed, sympathy were express in significantly different gestures (intensity, speed and temperature) by Japanese and French subjects. We also identified differences in the emotions that participants were willing to share with a 'receiver'. Gratitude, love, happy, sad, astonished, excited, angry, worried, delighted, interested, glad, and tired are emotions that more than 50 % of subjects would like to be able to share. Interestingly, Japanese subjects mostly chose gratitude, happy and love, while French subjects chose angry, excited and love.

5 Conclusion

Our study allows identifying which hand gestures (types, intensity, speed, and temperature) would be most intuitively used for expressing given patterns of emotions when using a device for mediated long-distance communication. We found some significant differences between the Japanese subjects and the French subjects, especially in the selection of emotions that people are willing to share with a tactile communication device. The findings can inform the design of future tactile communication devices.

Acknowledgements. This study was supported by a Grant-in-Aid to Tenure-track Researchers from the Japan Science and Technology Agency (JST).

References

Chang, A., O'Modhrain, S., Jacob, R., Gunther, E., Ishii, H.: ComTouch: design of a vibrotactile communication device. In: Proceedings of DIS 2002, the 4th ACM Conference on Designing Interactive Systems: Processes, Practices, Methods, and Techniques, pp. 312–320 (2002)

Hassenzahl, M., Heidecker, S., Eckoldt, K., Diefenbach, S., Hillmann, U.: All you need is love: current strategies of mediating intimate relationships through technology. ACM Trans.Comput.-Hum. Interact. **19**(4), Article 30 (2012)

Hertenstein, M.J., Holmes, R., McCullough, M.: The communication of emotion via touch. Emotion **9**(4), 566–573 (2009)

Hertenstein, M.J., Keltner, D., App, B., Bulleit, B., Jaskolka, A.: Touch communicates distinct emotions. Emotion **6**(3), 528–533 (2006)

Nummenmaa, L., Glerean, E., Hari, R., Hietanen, J.K.: Bodily maps of emotions. Proc. Nat. Acad. Sci. **111**, 646–651 (2013)

Obrist, M., Subramanian, S., Gatti, E., Long, B., Carter, T.: Emotions mediated through mid-air haptics. In: Proceedings of CHI 2015. ACM (2015). http://dx.doi.org/10.1145/2702123.2702361

Paltoglou, G., Thelwall, M.: Seeing stars of valence and arousal in blog posts. IEEE Trans. Affect. Comput. **4**(1), 116–123 (2013)

Picard, R.W., Healey, J.: Affective wearables. Pers. Technol. **1**(4), 231–240 (1997)

Piyush, K., Verma, J., Prasad, S.: Hand data glove: a wearable real-time device for human-computer interaction. Int. J. Adv. Sci. Technol. **43**, 39 (2012)

Rantala, J., Salminen, K., Raisamo, R., Sarakka, V.: Touch Gestures in communicating emotional intention via vibrotactile stimulation. Int. J. Hum. Comput. Stud. **71**, 679–690 (2013)

Russell, J.: A circumplex model of affect. J. Pers. Soc. Psychol. **39**, 1161–1178 (1980)

Uvnas-Moberg, K., Petersson, M.: Oxytocin, a mediator of anti-stress, well-being, social interaction, growth and healing. Z Psychosom Med Psychother **51**(1), 57–80 (2005)

The Different Attachment to Virtual Possession Between Young and Elder Adults

Chia-Sui Hsu and Yuan-Chi Tseng(✉)

Cognition, Experience and Behavior Design Lab, Department of Industrial Design, National Cheng Kung University, No. 1 University Road, Tainan, Taiwan
Anita.chiasui.hsu@gmail.com, yctseng@mail.ncku.edu.tw

Abstract. This research explores emotional relationship between individual among different ages and their virtual possessions. We conducted 24 in-depth interviews with younger adults (under 20-year-old) and elder adults (above 40-year-old) in Taiwan. Data were collected and analyzed following grounded theory coding method. By understanding usage behaviors and feelings about participants' important virtual possessions, we induced several differences of virtual possession attachment among different ages. We concluded four types of virtual possession, the causes of attachment development and usage behaviors among different ages. Finally, several similarities and dissimilarities between elder and young adults were discussed. Some guidelines of designing for improving virtual possession attachment for people in these two generations are proposed.

Keywords: Attachment · Virtual possession · Different generation

1 Introduction

We are surrounded by an enormous amount of objects in everyday life. As technology developing, the relationship between objects and us has become more and more complicated [1]. The interaction between an individual and his/her objects has not only involved functionality but also the perception and the entire context. In this regards, Bowlby [2] addressed the Attachment Theory, describing an emotional-laden target-specific bond between two persons. This concept has been echoed with studies in various fields, opening a novel perspective toward how we interact and develop relationship with our objects [3–6].

To date, we have increasingly acquired virtual objects in our daily life. New types of virtual objects have not only change our behavior and perception but also change the whole experience. New experience such as reading electronic books and playing video games that we may not even imagine in the past are possibly gained nowadays. Researchers in various domains have gradually focus attention on the relationship between human and their virtual possessions [7, 8]. However, rarely has researchers investigated how individual develop emotional relationship with their virtual possessions.

The attachment development to virtual possessions is based on how individual perceive their virtual possessions. Hence, there are many influencing factors of it.

P.-L.P. Rau (Ed.): CCD 2016, LNCS 9741, pp. 70–78, 2016.
DOI: 10.1007/978-3-319-40093-8_8

Although Klein and Baker [9] had claimed that material possession attachment is a dynamic concept and might be influenced by age and gender, it might be different on virtual possession attachment. Odom (2011) investigated how teenagers preserve their virtual possessions and addressed several issues that are different from the material possessions [8]. Also, Cushing found age has an effect on some differences to her findings of personal digital information preservation [10]. Therefore, for getting better understanding of attachment to virtual possessions, it is necessary for us to learn how people in different age develop the emotional relationship to virtual possession.

2 Background and Related Works

In the following section we reviewed the background to the questions addressed in this article, including self-extension and attachment to virtual possession, virtual possession usage among different age, and related HCI researches.

2.1 Self-Extension and Attachment to Virtual Possession

Belk (1988) claimed that people are able to develop certain self-extension to their material possessions and feel attachment to them [11]. He proposed that self-extension is a perception that people transfer their personal identity to their possessions and consider the possessions could stand for their representation in the world. Therefore, we always feel a sense of losing ourselves when we accidentally loss our treasured possessions. For this reason, possessions seem to have stronger relationship than ordinary products with individuals [11, 12]. Hence, in this study we focused on the emotional relationship to possessions instead of products. On that account, self-extension would be a vital factor when we explored the relationship.

As we acquiring more and more virtual possessions nowadays, the issue of how we consider virtual objects has become important. Cushing (2012) addressed four characteristics of digital possessions and claimed that digital objects could be able to be considered as a possession [10]. However, as we know the characteristics of virtual possessions are very different from physical ones, the virtual attachments with individual may be also different. Belk (2013) updated his theory of self-extension, presenting the differences of extended self in digital world. He reviewed the relevance studies and claimed that people indeed extend their selves to virtual possession [13]. However, there are some slightly differences between them. As a conclusion, the notion of "attachment to virtual possession" here is yet a complicated concept and has various characteristics. Belk's self-extension is one of the characteristics of the attachment to virtual possession and will continually need to be improved.

2.2 The Usage of Virtual Possessions Among Different Ages

Based on the literature, age may be a factor influencing self-extension and attachment to virtual possessions [10, 13], Thus, we refer the theory Digital Native and Digital Immigrant for our theoretical sampling.

The concept of digital natives and immigrants was proposed by Prensky [14], an American education consultant, investigated two types of generations to explain the gap between American teachers and their modern students. The Digital Native was defined as people who were born after the existence of digital technologies. They are familiar with technology and have different brain activities when they are using digital device. On the contrary, Digital Immigrants are those people who born before the existence of digital technologies and adopted it to some extent later in life. In Prensky's article, there are many differences between these two generations. For example, instead of digital books, Digital Immigrants still prefer material books although they also use Internet. Digital Natives are used to interact with people and search information on Internet. The different attitudes of these two generations may influence how they consider and preserve their virtual possessions. Therefore, in this study, both Digital Natives and Digital Immigrants were included in sampling so as to investigate the difference between people in different ages. Nevertheless, the exact age boundary between these two generations was not clearly defined in Prensky's research. But, children born after 1980 was later applied as Digital Native because computer bulletin board systems and Usenet has already been in use at the time.

However, in this study, because the different technology development of Eastern and Western culture, we considered 1985, five yeas later than America, as our boundary of Digital natives and Digital immigrants. Moreover, in order to distinguish the differences, we tried to increase the gap between these two generations by adding and cutting ten years of them. Consequently, the two generations of participants in this study were participants who are elder than 40 years old and participants who are younger than 20 years old.

3 Method

Our goal is to explore the emotional relationship between individuals and their virtual possessions among different ages by Grounded Theory. Figure 1 shows the process of this research [15].

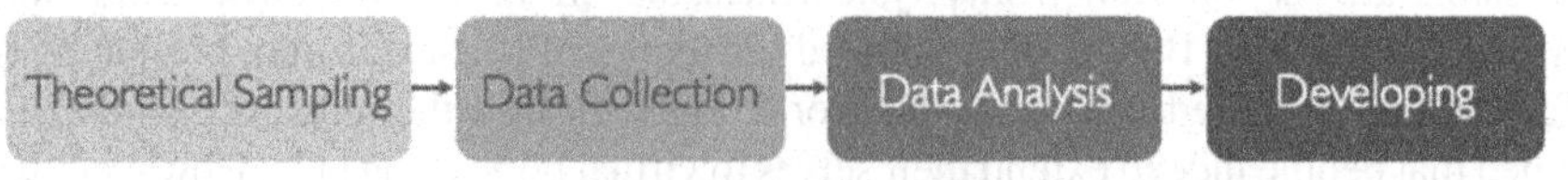

Fig. 1. Research process of this study

3.1 Data Collection

The study conducted 24 in-depth interviews with younger adults (13–20 years old; coded as capital Y) and elder adults (40–51 years old; coded as capital E). Participants were all Taiwanese and the gender was selected equally. All participants were recruited from Internet. People were asked to fill a prescreen questionnaire to make sure their qualification in this study. Eventually, 24 participants were selected. Emails were sent to schedule in person interview with the researcher. Every participant was offered 300NTD and a MUJI notebook. All interviews were audio recorded and transcribed. Field notes and photos were taken when necessary during the interview. Participants could choose their preferred interview places as long as they are quiet enough for audio recording. Therefore, most of interviews were conducted in public café or restaurant. Five of them were conducted in participants' home and work place. The interviews were conducted in semi-structure and approximately 1.5 to 2 h. Participants were encouraged to bring and share their virtual possessions while answering the questions.

3.2 Data Analysis

All vocal data from the interview were transferred into transcripts in order to be analyzed by coders. There were three stages in data analyzing: open coding, axial coding and selective coding. First, the interview data were labeled by a code team with open coding process. The code team consisted of three graduate students from different backgrounds and the first author. All data were reviewed and discussed by coders repeatedly so as to be more objective.

4 Findings

4.1 Four Types of Possession

Based on the characteristics of possessions, we classified virtual possessions into four types: valuable memory, personal creation, collectible and utility item. A virtual possession might be classified into more than one type. For example, digital photos could simultaneously be a valuable memory and a personal creation. For instance, Participant E09 and Y12 regarded their digital photos both as record and creation. Therefore, we will focus on the type of possessions in the following discussion, instead of each single possession that was mentioned in the interview.

Type 1: Valuable Memory

Almost all participants indicated that their "most important virtual possession" contains valuable memories. Among our participants, such virtual possessions included digital photos, messages and records in videogames.

Figure 2 shows mostly digital photos are attached to elder participants and chat logs and screenshots are attached to young participants in this study. Although the possessions are distinct, the main reason of attachment is similar: the valuable memories contained in the possessions are mostly about their treasured significant others, feelings and events.

Type 2: Personal Creation

Personal creations and works such as Facebook posts, personal writings and photographs were categorized into this type. Most possessions in this type were from elder participants. All elder participants presented certain ability and passion of creating something to manifest their personality. Figure 3 shows only elder participants attach to their Facebook posts and writings and both elder and young participants attach to their photographs. To clarify, photograph here is regarded as personal creation instead of valuable memories in the previous section.

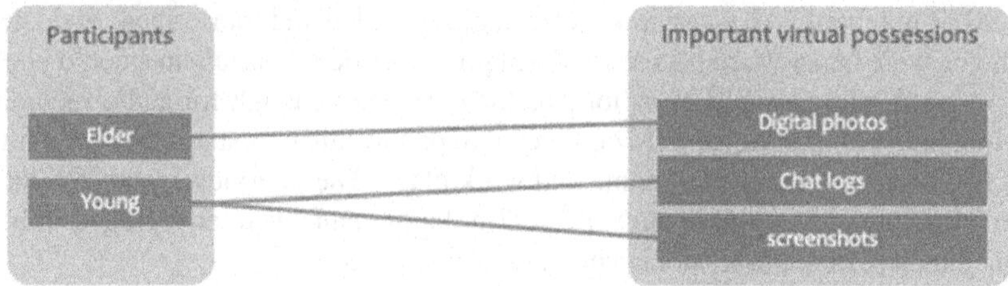

Fig. 2. Relationships between participants and their valuable memories

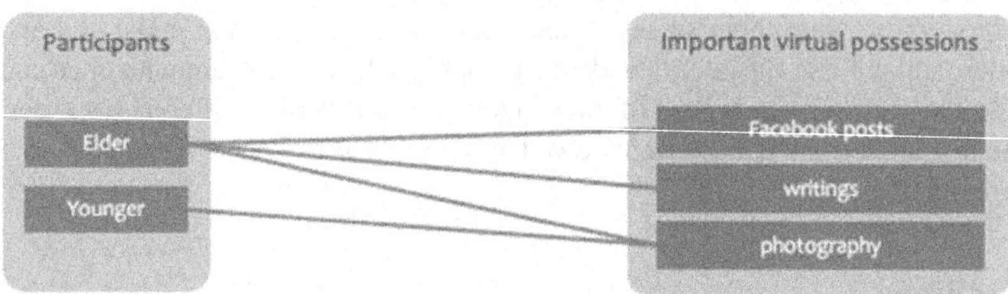

Fig. 3. Relationship between participants and their personal creations

Type 3: Collectible

Collectible is defined as a set of perceived valuable items that are collected by an individual including music collections and pictures of a specific idol. Figure 4 shows all possessions in this type were from young participants. Young participants collected virtual objects that they are interested in and keep them in a good order. They expressed that those collectibles can not only inspire and encourage them to become who they want to be but also help them feel a sense of belonging.

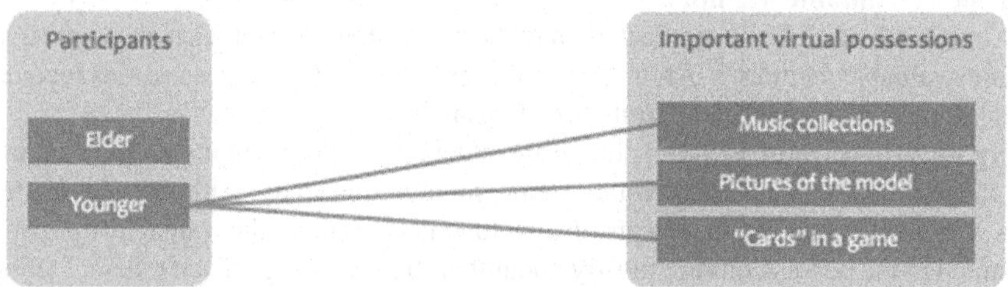

Fig. 4. Relationship between participants and their collectibles

Type 4: Utility Item

Items collected for some functional purposes were categorized into this type, such as screenshots and bookmarks of useful information. Also, some social interaction records by screenshots and embarrassing photos of friends, which used as social tools for teenagers, were also classified into this type.

Figure 5 illustrate both elder and young participants attach to their screenshots. Only one elder participant shared attachment to her bookmarks and the other one young participant expressed her attachment to a specific video application on her iPod. People preserve this type of possessions because they want to prepare for their future needs.

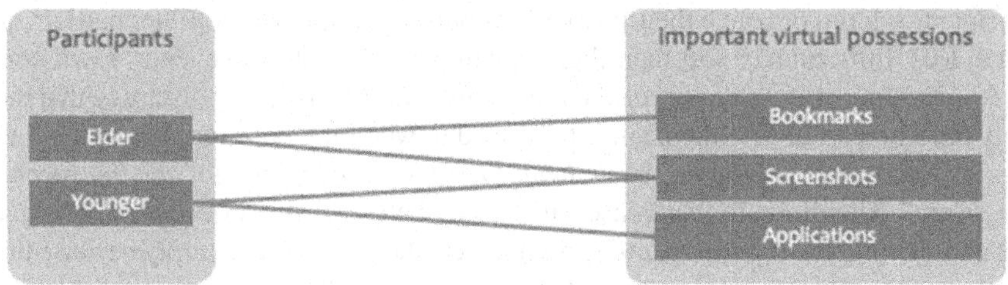

Fig. 5. Relationship between participants and their utility items

4.2 Usage Behavior

We observed four major usage behaviors in our data. We introduce each of them and presented some similarities and dissimilarities between two age groups in the following section.

Creating a Controllable Place to Preserve the Possessions. We observed all of the participants have tried to create a controllable and safe place for preserving their possession. However, there are still some differences between different ages.

(1) *Elder participants: backup and duplicate in multiple places*
This phenomenon was found mostly in elder participants who have preserved their digital photos for at least 8 years. They all preserve the photos in good order and duplicate them in multiple places such as Cloud and portable hard-drive. *"These are gradually… I always feel they are important to me, so I keep looking for better places to preserve them. To avoid losing them" (E10).* On the contrary, surprisingly, young participants in this study seldom backup their possessions. It seems that they are very unfamiliar with the digital technology. Several young participants expressed that they even do not know how to import information from their mobile to desktop. Some of them revealed they would love to do the backup if they had had the ability. *"I don't preserve them (chat logs) on purpose. But I don't delete them on purpose, either. Because it (Facebook) doesn't provide the function… If I had choice, I would love to do that" (Y02).*
(2) *Young participant: mobile phone is the safest place*
Several young participants expounded that persevering all the virtual possessions on their mobile phone and carrying it with them everywhere can make them feel safe and convenient. On the contrary, several elder participants preserve their possessions on Cloud. However, none of them take Could as the safe place for the preservation. Participant E08 and E10 preserve their photo on Cloud in good order. They both expressed that accessibility is the main purpose to preserve photos on Cloud. *"I can look for the photo by application easily if I need to share to others"*

(E10). For these participants, everywhere in digital world is temporary for them. They believe the digital world is always changeful and insecure.

The Frequency of Reviewing and Organizing. In this study, our elder participants usually organize their possessions very well but seldom review. On the contrary, young participants seldom organize their possessions but review them a lot. Elder participants such as E02, E08 and E10 sort their digital photos files by date and event. *"I will name files as some interesting titles related to the events" (E08)*. Also, they disclosed that they barely have time to review them since they need to work and raise families at the same time. As E07 said, *"I seldom review them. I am busy for fighting for my life recently (Laughing)"*. Therefore, in these cases, reviewing behavior always occurs with organizing and sharing. Elder participants seldom review the possessions simply because they do not eager to review. *"I can review them when I am home. It's not urgent. I believe they (the digital photos) will stay there stably and will not disappear" (E02)*. However, there are still a few elder participants review their possessions very often. For example, participant E01 and E06 who publish their works on social media seem to review more frequently than the others. On the contrary, young participants review their possession very often. Since they have more spare time than elder participants, reviewing the important possessions becomes a relaxation and recreation in their daily life. They review the possessions when they have spare time or when they think of specific people and events. They usually review photos on mobile phone which they can access anytime, and anywhere.

Present Their Selves by Sharing. This study shows that elder participants enjoy share their selves in a digital environment and younger participants tend to share different selves in different digital environment. Elder participants share the possessions as spreading their thoughts to others. E06 considers his Facebook page as a platform spreading the positive thinking. *"I would like to share my positive power to everyone. I hope people would like to follow this (Facebook posts with his wife)...and it might help people to improve their relationship"*. Moreover, E07 shared her creations related to social issues and hopes they will have some slight influences to society. Both of them mentioned that they know they have followers on Facebook. It seems that this situation make them feeling influential. Also, they care about the comments and responses of their posts. As E01 said, *"It is boring if you posted something and there is no response. You make people satisfied and you feel satisfied too. This is the meaning of sharing."* Even some participants would plan their activities for sharing. *"Sometimes it is like ...we go out in order to create new post"* (E06). For young participants, they tend to separate the content on different platform in order to share to different audiences. Sometime they even do not use their real name on Internet. *"Because I can share to everyone on YouTube. Sharing to strangers... I create a fictitious name so people would not know that is me" (Y14)*.

5 Conclusion and Design Guidelines

This study explores attachment between individuals and their virtual possession among young and elder adults in Taiwan. We found people in different generations use and attach to their virtual possessions differently. The different backgrounds of generations, such as technology knowledge and personal values of the different generations, result in the different virtual possession attachment found in this study. Also, the type of virtual possessions could also result in the difference. Therefore, in order to customize digital service and virtual possession for different generations, the background of participants and the type of virtual possessions need to be concerned in the future design process. Here, we proposed several design guidelines for designing attachment to virtual possessions among different age.

For all users, consider the attribute (type) of virtual possession that user attaches to and create a controllable space for him/her to preserve it when designing virtual possession with attachment. For young users, consider the function of reviewing and selected sharing. Contrarily, for elder users, consider the function of organizing and public sharing. However, personal value and technology knowledge should be considered while designing attachment to virtual possessions for both generations.

Overall, this work contributes to our understanding of attachment development to virtual possessions among different ages. As noted, virtual possession attachment is a complicated concept and its influencing factors are interrelated. Therefore, in future work, more factors should be discussed together in order to understand the whole picture of attachment development to virtual possessions.

Acknowledgements. This research was supported by a grant, MOST 104-2628-E-006 -013 -MY3, from Ministry of Science and Technology, Taiwan.

References

1. Bilton, N.: I Live in the Future & Here's How It Works: Why Your World, Work, and Brain are Being Creatively Disrupted. Crown Business, New York (2010)
2. Bowlby, J.: Attachment and Loss, vol. 3. Basic books, New York (1980)
3. Norman, D.A.: Emotional Design: Why We Love (or Hate) Everyday Things. Basic books, New York (2004)
4. Mugge, R.: Product attachment, TU Delft, Delft University of Technology (2007)
5. Chapman, J.: Design for (Emotional) Durability. Des. Issue **25**, 29–35 (2009)
6. Page, T.: Product attachment and replacement: implications for sustainable design. Int. J. Sustain. Des. **2**(3), 265–282 (2014)
7. Blevis, E., Stolterman, E.: Ensoulment and sustainable interaction design. In: Proceedings of IASDR, Hongkong (2007)
8. Odom, W., Zimmerman, J., Forlizzi, J.: Teenagers and their virtual possessions: design opportunities and issues. ACM (2011)
9. Kleine, S., Baker, S.M.: An integrative review of material possession attachment. Acad. Mark. Sci. Rev. **1**, 1–29 (2004)

10. Cushing, A.L.: Possessions and self extension in digital environments: Implications for maintaining personal information. The University of North Carolina At Chapel Hill (2012)
11. Belk, R.: Possessions and Self. Wiley Online Library, New York (1988)
12. Borgmann, A.: Technology and the Character of Contemporary Life: A Philosophical Inquiry. University of Chicago Press, Chicago (1984)
13. Belk, R.: Extended self in a digital world. J. Consum. Res. **40**(3), 477–500 (2013)
14. Prensky, M.: Digital natives, digital immigrants. On Horiz. **9**(5), 1–6 (2001)
15. Strauss, A.L., Corbin, J.M.: Basics of Qualitative Research, vol. 15. Sage Newbury Park, CA (1990)

Social Things: Design Research on Social Computing

Jun Hu(✉)

Department of Industrial Design, Eindhoven University of Technology, Eindhoven, The Netherlands
j.hu@tue.nl

Abstract. In the era of social networking and computing, things and people are more and more interconnected, giving rise to not only new opportunities but also new challenges in designing new products that are networked, and services that are adaptive to their human users and context aware in their physical and social environments. A research vision on social things is needed, that addresses both the technological and social aspects in design, and that requires a social approach to the Internet of Things.

Keywords: Social things · Internet of things · Social computing · Design research

1 Introduction

In the concept of Internet of Things, things start to communicate with other things, forming an "Internet of Social Things", allowing things to have their own social networks, enabled by communication technologies that are both fixed and ad hoc, and both wired and wireless. These "Internet of Social things" are further in connection with their environments and users through sensors and actuators, communicating with the social networks of humans, interacting in social networks with humans and other objects, forming a "Social Internet of Things". These two levels of social networks of things and humans give rise to not only new opportunities but also new challenges in designing new products (that are networked) and services (that are adaptive to their human users and context aware in their physical and social environments). Therefore, the design research to meet these new opportunities and challenges needs a social approach to the Internet of Things, which brings our attention to a research area, namely "social things", that address both the technological and social aspects of the Internet of Things.

2 Social Things

2.1 Social Things for Data Driven and Service Centric Design

The merge of the social networks of people and the Internet of things leads to a shift from product or system oriented design to service centric design. Systems, products and the related services are more connected than ever. Products have become the terminals of the services and systems have become the platforms to deliver the services. Social computing started in late 1990's and early 2000's serving as platforms not only for

P.-L.P. Rau (Ed.): CCD 2016, LNCS 9741, pp. 79–88, 2016.
DOI: 10.1007/978-3-319-40093-8_9

sharing online content and conversation, but also for processing the content of social interaction and feeding back into systems [1]. The difference is that the social interaction and feedback are tied to things, sensors, and information intertwined in the social channels. These channels create touch points between services and customers, and the feedback from the customers to the services has become quicker, driven by a more flattened and bottom-up social structure. Along with this development, products with embedded connectivity and identification technologies have become part of the Internet of Things, and with embedded sensing technology these products have been integrated into people's lives in a more adaptive and social manner, learning human activities and behavior from the big data in the networks of both humans and things. Figure 1 shows an in-flight entertainment system that collects not only the music preference of the passenger, social recommendations of the music, but also the heart rate to detect the stress level and to reduce it through adaptive music [2].

Fig. 1. Heart rate controlled music recommendation for low stress air travel [2]

With the facilitation of social things, service design can be carried out in an interactive and sustainable process. In this process data and input can be collected social interaction among the users; and the stakeholders and from the behavior of the users and the products, analyzed and quickly or directly fed back to the process. The quicker this feedback loop is, the more the design cost can be reduced. This research area needs to investigate how to tightly combine and coordinate these computational, physical and social elements to facilitate the service and the design process of it. Traditional new product design and development methods become insufficient when dealing with the shift towards service centric design, the power from the flattened and bottom-up social structure, and the complexity of the social systems of humans and things. Adaptivity of the intelligent systems and services has to be reinvestigated in the context of social things and social innovation in a larger scale eco-system in which the social networks of people and the Internet of things are intertwined.

2.2 Social Things for Social Innovation

The growth and development of distributed and pervasive computing, social networks and mobile technologies have dramatically increased the complexity of the systems, products and the related services, but also the complexity of the design itself. Social things that merge the social networks of humans and the Internet of things, on the other hand, brings up new solutions against the complexity, towards social innovation, by harvesting the collective intelligence from the social networks of humans, including the designers, the users and the organizations, and the collective intelligence from the Internet of Things, in order to realize greater value from the interaction between people and things, which in turn, inventing innovative and hopefully also sustainable ways of living. In this context, design has become a social activity – design is a result of social innovation; design drives social innovation and leads social transformation.

In this context, the design research on social things aims at developing methods, tools and techniques to support design as social innovation and design for social innovation. In the case of design as social innovation, the research should investigate how social things can be used to support the collaborative design activities by the designers as well as other stakeholders including the end users and to enable collective creativity and intelligence in dealing with the complexity of the systems of today. In this case open source hardware and software are good examples of today (Fig. 2), but more can be expected to happen to other end user products and systems. In the case of design for social innovation, the research shall investigate how to use social things for design to trigger and support social innovation that leads to societal transformations, by introducing design perspectives and design intervention in a social context. The penetrating of social things to the society creates possibilities in creating collective awareness platforms for possible solutions that need collective efforts and shared knowledge, enabling new forms of social innovation.

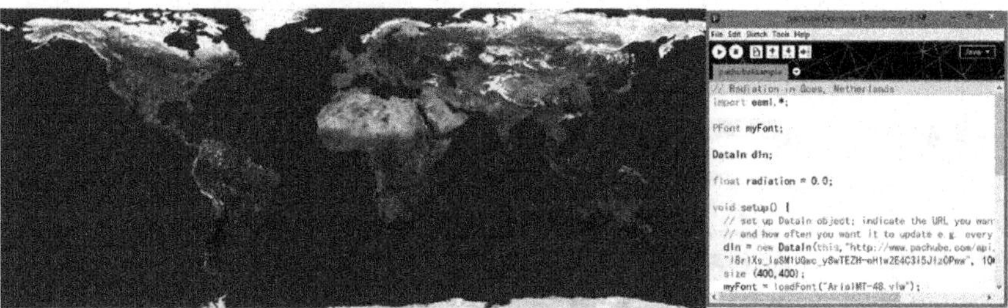

Fig. 2. Open data from internet of things, accessible using open source software tools

2.3 Social Things as "Simulation" Platforms for Design

The integration of the networks of humans and things gives the opportunity to bring design much closer to the end users, to other stakeholders and to its social and situational context, and vice versa. It sheds a promising amount of lights on improving the validation process of design, as computational simulation has done to electrical and mechanical engineering when computer was introduced to these disciplines.

Social things have their physical forms, but also can be easily captured and represented in digital means. It enables them to be used for validating design in earlier phases of the process. It is interesting to investigate how social things could be utilized as "simulation" platforms for earlier concepts – in this case physical prototypes might still be necessary but the situational context (people, other things and the environment) can be brought in or closer in order to quest the concept earlier (Fig. 3 shows a project in which the early concepts of a physical clock was evaluated with potential users in a virtual world [3]).

Fig. 3. Digital model of a physical clock is evaluated in a virtual world [3]

2.4 Social Things as a Competency and as a Tool in Design Education

New types of designers have to be equipped with systematic understanding and perspectives, be competent in utilizing the social things to harvest the creativity, the input and the feedback through social interaction. The developments also bring up new opportunities in utilizing social things in facilitating the learning to make learning a more effective and more enjoyable social experience. Figure 4 shows a set of open source software, hardware and learning environment used in the design education at the department of industrial design, Eindhoven University of Technology.

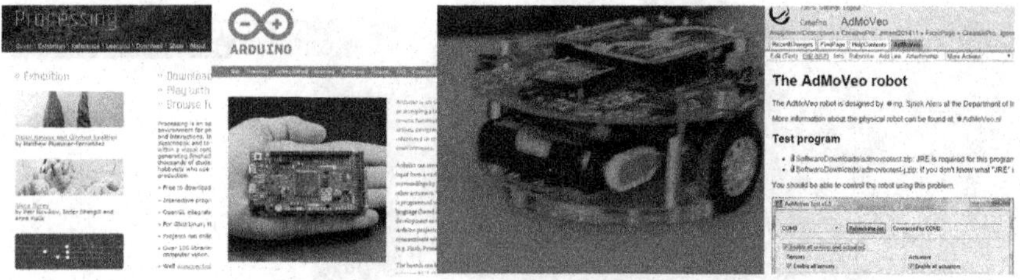

Fig. 4. Open source software, hardware and learning environment in a design education [4]

The perspective and the ability of utilizing social things as an enabler in design should be implemented in the design education. This research area should investigate how this can be carried out in a self-driven learning process, and how to utilize the social things and social computing technologies to facilitate this process.

2.5 Research Methods

Social things as a research topic is at the intersection of computational systems and social behavior. This research should employ engineering and empirical research methodologies, or a research-through-design approach, depending on the subject under investigation.

Social things can be used to empower end-users, for example in the medical field, where patients get faster and more accurate information about their personal health status, exchange experiences, and keep track of the performance of medical institutions. The research question is how to design such social systems, and how to measure their performance, which includes the perceived quality. The measurement instruments themselves can be designed as social tools (on-line questionnaires, data logging with the social things, network-oriented data visualization, distributed data mining, and crowd wisdom).

Not only the end-users will change their way of working, also the design community itself will change when adopting the power of social things and social computing. The effect is already visible in the communities around Arduino, Processing, and DIY 3D printers. Whereas most of the present-day tools are still traditional editors, compilers and CAD tools, the next generation of tools will be designed as social tools. This asks for a research-through-design approach: creating new tools, co-creating and sharing them inside the design community, and evaluate their performance and perceived quality with appropriately designed new tools. State-of-the-art engineering and design methods should be deployed to bootstrap the design of these new tools.

3 Research Areas and Activities

With the above mentioned research vision, we have been involved in a number of research projects in related areas. "Social things" as a research area is broad, as seen from the examples to be introduced next. It is not our intention to give a complete overview here, rather it is to demonstrate our effort in its two-fold focus on both technological and social aspects.

3.1 Social Things to Connect the Digital and the Physical

Social things can be utilized to connect the digital and the physical, employing and developing computational technologies such as distributed multimedia and interaction for entertainment in ambient intelligent environments [5–7], semantic web for interoperability of smart objects in intelligent environments [8–10], augmented and mixed reality for installations in social and cultural computing [11–14], virtual reality for serious games as learning or diagnostic tools [12, 15, 16] (Fig. 5 shows an augmented home that integrates a digital game with the physical environment), tangible interfaces

Fig. 5. Augmented home: integrating a virtual world game in a physical environment [12]

to digital systems [9, 17, 18]. All these research activates have been engaging sensing and actuating technologies, or embedded technologies that integrate both for an integrated system that merges and blurs the digital and the physical.

3.2 Social Things for Health and Care

Sensors, actuators, smart objects and integrated systems have been utilized in several projects in delivery simulators for medical training [19, 20], comfort and bonding in perinatology research [21], reducing stress in long haul flights [2, 22], emotional care for elderly with dementia [23, 24], social connectedness through unconscious and peripheral data [25, 26] (Fig. 6), and relaxation with bio-feedback [27–29]. In recent years, both the ageing society and the general needs of improving the quality of life and well-being have lead policy makers in many countries to turn to individuals at home and the social networks of the individuals, and to deliver the service over the networks, as an important source of long-term health care, where social things and social computing would play important roles.

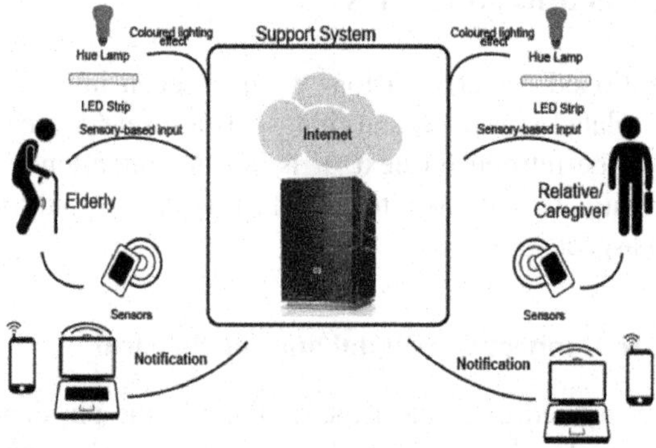

Fig. 6. Social connectedness through unconscious and peripheral data [25, 26]

3.3 Social Things in Public Spaces

Social things are often situated in public spaces, enabling social interaction among multiple users and systems, and the analysis of the social behavior based on the collected data [30–33]. Several research carriers in our projects are interactive and participatory public installations, either functional or artistic [11, 34–36]. These interactive installations require gathering input, data and information using computer vision, mobile devices, connected or embedded sensors from either the physical space or social networks. For output, many of these installations using projection mapping to augment the physical objects or spaces with a digital layer, being a good example for designing systems that integrate the physical with the digital. These installations often aim at an environment or connected spaces, being a very good research carrier for the Internet of Things as situated and large scale objects, and for studying the group user behavior and experience [37]. Figure 7 shows the installation designed for the city of Taicang, China.

The installation is roughly 10 by 10 meters on its base and 8 meters high. On top of the base are constructions that give the impressions of a large sail, and the moon rising from the waves. Images, animations and videos can be projected onto the inner surface of sail in the evenings, allowing the public to contribute their photos from social media to induce the feeling of social connectedness [11, 35].

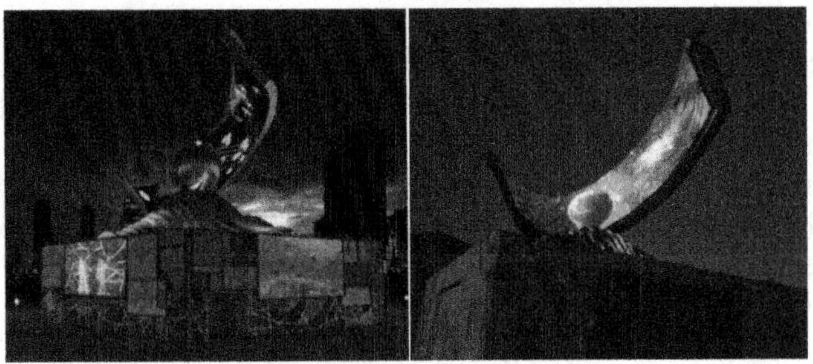

Fig. 7. Moon rising from sea [11, 35]

3.4 Social Things for Sustainability

Several projects have been carried out in the TU/e DESIS lab, part of the DESIS (Design for Social Innovation and Sustainability) association, a "network of design labs, basked in design schools and design oriented universities, actively involved in promoting and supporting sustainable change". Next to the research activities in designing for social interaction in public spaces as already mentioned, activities are mostly educational with student projects. Recently together with two Ph.D. students we started our research activities in a social recipe recommendation system for food sustainability, with the help of the Internet of Things (Fig. 8, mobile devices and intelligent trash bins) [38, 39].

Fig. 8. Intelligent trash bins for a social recipe recommendation system [38, 39]

4 Concluding Remarks

The research area "social things" focuses more on social computing as tools and platforms for design. The design context of social interaction, social innovation and service centric design requires close cooperation with other expertise. It is expected to closely collaborate on social interaction with colleagues from the user centered design and research, on tangible and physical interaction as well as social innovation with colleagues in interaction design and social design, and on the service centric design process with the colleagues with a business perspective. The Internet of Things elements of this research will not only generate data for data driven design, but also blend the analyzed results into the physical forms in the created designs.

The research focus is more on designing social computing tools and platforms than it is on developing the enabling technology itself, which requires collaboration with computer science and electrical engineering.

It is also expected to contribute to key societal issues such as energy, health and mobility. Possibilities in contributing to other areas shall be considered, for example the environment and energy domain offers many opportunities for exploring crowdsourcing; techniques and social intelligence in systems design; social networking can provide ad-hoc yet real time information from the drivers and vehicles for a more efficient traffic, or for a better experience on move.

References

1. Wang, F.-Y., Carley, K.M., Zeng, D., Mao, W.: Social computing: from social informatics to social intelligence. IEEE Intell. Syst. **22**(2), 79–83 (2007)
2. Liu, H., Hu, J., Rauterberg, M.: Follow your heart: heart rate controlled music recommendation for low stress air travel. Interact. Stud. Soc. Behav. Commun. Biol. Artif. Syst. **16**(2), 303–339 (2015)
3. Xue, Y.: Magnetic clock: contextual information exchange, B22 Project report, Department of Industrial Design, Eindhoven University of Technology (2009)
4. Alers, S., Hu, J.: AdMoVeo: a robotic platform for teaching creative programming to designers. In: Chang, M., Kuo, R., Kinshuk, Chen, G.-D., Hirose, M. (eds.) Learning by Playing. LNCS, vol. 5670, pp. 410–421. Springer, Heidelberg (2009)
5. Hu, J., Feijs, L.: Synchronizable objects in distributed multimedia applications. In: Pan, Z., Cheok, A.D., Müller, W., Zhang, X., Wong, K. (eds.) Transactions on Edutainment IV. LNCS, vol. 6250, pp. 117–129. Springer, Heidelberg (2010)
6. Hu, J., Feijs, L.: IPML: structuring distributed multimedia presentations in ambient intelligent environments. Int. J. Cogn. Inf. Nat. Intell. (IJCiNi) **3**(2), 37–60 (2009)
7. Hu, J.: Design of a distributed architecture for enriching media experience in home theaters. Ph.D. thesis, Department of Industrial Design, Eindhoven University of Technology, Eindhoven (2006)
8. Hu, J., van der Vlist, B., Niezen, G., Willemsen, W., Willems, D., Feijs, L.: Designing the internet of things for learning environmentally responsible behaviour. Interact. Learn. Environ. **21**(2), 211–226 (2013)

9. van der Vlist, B., Niezen, G., Rapp, S., Hu, J., Feijs, L.: Configuring and controlling ubiquitous computing infrastructure with semantic connections: a tangible and an AR approach. Pers. Ubiquitous Comput. **17**(4), 783–799 (2013)
10. Niezen, G., van der Vlist, B., Hu, J., Feijs, L.: Using semantic transformers to enable interoperability between media devices in a ubiquitous computing environment. In: Rautiainen, M., et al. (eds.) GPC 2011. LNCS, vol. 7096, pp. 44–53. Springer, Heidelberg (2012)
11. Hu, J., Funk, M., Zhang, Yu., Wang, F.: Designing interactive public art installations: new material therefore new challenges. In: Pisan, Y., Sgouros, N.M., Marsh, T. (eds.) ICEC 2014. LNCS, vol. 8770, pp. 199–206. Springer, Heidelberg (2014)
12. Offermans, S., Hu, J.: Augmenting a virtual world game in a physical environment. J. Man Mach. Technol. **2**(1), 54–62 (2013)
13. Hu, J., Bartneck, C., Salem, B., Rauterberg, M.: ALICE's adventures in cultural computing. Int. J. Arts. Technol. **1**(1), 102–118 (2008)
14. Hu, J., Bartneck, C.: Culture matters - a study on presence in an interactive movie. CyberPsychol. Behav. **11**(5), 529–535 (2008)
15. Langereis, G., Hu, J., Gongsook, P., Rauterberg, M.: Perceptual and computational time models in game design for time orientation in learning disabilities. In: Göbel, S., Müller, W., Urban, B., Wiemeyer, J. (eds.) GameDays 2012 and Edutainment 2012. LNCS, vol. 7516, pp. 183–188. Springer, Heidelberg (2012)
16. Gongsook, P., Hu, J., Bellotti, F., Rauterberg, M.: A virtual reality based time simulator game for children with ADHD. In: 2nd International Conference on Applied and Theoretical Information Systems Research (ATISR), Taipei, Taiwan (2012)
17. Kwak, M., Niezen, G., van der Vlist, B., Hu, J., Feijs, L.: Tangible interfaces to digital connections, centralized versus decentralized. In: Pan, Z., Cheok, A.D., Müller, W., Yang, X. (eds.) Transactions on Edutainment V. LNCS, vol. 6530, pp. 132–146. Springer, Heidelberg (2011)
18. van de Mortel, D., Hu, J.: ApartGame: a multiuser tabletop game platform for intensive public use. In: Tangible Play Workshop, Intelligent User Interfaces Conference, Honolulu, Hawaii, USA, pp. 49–52 (2007)
19. Hu, J., Peters, P., Delbressine, F., Feijs, L.: Distributed architecture for delivery simulators. In: International Conference on e-Health Networking, Digital Ecosystems and Technologies (EDT 2010), Shenzhen, pp. 109–112 (2010)
20. Hu, J., Feijs, L.: A distributed multi-agent architecture in simulation based medical training. In: Chang, M., Kuo, R., Kinshuk, Chen, G.-D., Hirose, M. (eds.) Learning by Playing. LNCS, vol. 5670, pp. 105–115. Springer, Heidelberg (2009)
21. Chen, W., Hu, J., Bouwstra, S., Oetomo, S.B., Feijs, L.: Sensor integration for perinatology research. Int. J. Sens. Netw. **9**(1), 38–49 (2011)
22. Liu, H., Hu, J., Rauterberg, M.: iHeartrate: a heart rate controlled in-flight music recommendation system. In: Measuring Behavior, Eindhoven, The Netherlands, pp. 265–268 (2010)
23. Gu, J., Zhang, Y., Hu, J.: Design for elderly with dementia: light, sound and movement. In: 8th International Conference on Design and Semantics of Form and Movement (DeSForM 2013), Wuxi, China, pp. 152–158 (2013)
24. Gu, J., Zhang, Y., Hu, J.: Lighting and sound installation for elderly with dementia. In: 4th International Conference on Culture and Computing-ICCC 2013, Kyoto, Japan, pp. 169–170 (2013)

25. Davis, K., Jun, H., Feijs, L., Owusu, E.: Social hue: a subtle awareness system for connecting the elderly and their caregivers. In: 2015 IEEE International Conference on Pervasive Computing and Communication Workshops (PerCom Workshops), pp. 178–183 (2015)
26. Davis, K., Owusu, E., Regazzoni, C., Marcenaro, L., Feijs, L., Hu, J.: Perception of human activities: a means to support connectedness between the elderly and their caregivers, pp. 194–199 (2015)
27. Yu, B., Hu, J., Feijs, L.: Design and evaluation of an ambient lighting interface of HRV biofeedback system in home setting. In: Hervás, R., Lee, S., Nugent, C., Bravo, J. (eds.) UCAmI 2014. LNCS, vol. 8867, pp. 88–91. Springer, Heidelberg (2014)
28. Holenderski, K., Hu, J.: Enriching reading experience with dramatic soundtracks. Adv. Multimedia Technol. **2**(1), 24–31 (2013)
29. Yu, B., Feijs, L., Funk, M., Hu, J.: Breathe with touch: a tactile interface for breathing assistance system. In: Abascal, J., Barbosa, S., Fetter, M., Gross, T., Palanque, P., Winckler, M. (eds.) INTERACT 2015. LNCS, vol. 9298, pp. 45–52. Springer, Heidelberg (2015)
30. Brenny, S., Hu, J.: Social connectedness and inclusion by digital augmentation in public spaces. In: 8th International Conference on Design and Semantics of Form and Movement (DeSForM 2013), Wuxi, China, pp. 108–118 (2013)
31. Funk, M., Hu, J., Rauterberg, M.: Socialize or perish: relating social behavior at a scientific conference to publication citations. In: ASE International Conference on Social Informatics (SocialInformatics 2012), Washington, DC, USA, pp. 113–120 (2012)
32. Wang, C., Hu, J., Terken, J.: "Liking" other drivers' behavior while driving. In: AutomotiveUI, Seattle, WA, USA, pp. 1–6 (2014)
33. Wang, C., Terken, J., Yu, B., Hu, J.: Reducing driving violations by receiving feedback from other drivers. In: Adjunct Proceedings of the 7th International Conference on Automotive User Interfaces and Interactive Vehicular Applications, Nottingham, United Kingdom, pp. 62–67 (2015)
34. Hu, J., Le, D., Funk, M., Wang, F., Rauterberg, M.: Attractiveness of an interactive public art installation. In: Streitz, N., Stephanidis, C. (eds.) DAPI 2013. LNCS, vol. 8028, pp. 430–438. Springer, Heidelberg (2013)
35. Hu, J., Wang, F., Funk, M., Frens, J., Zhang, Y., van Boheemen, T., Zhang, C., Yuan, Q., Qu, H., Rauterberg, M.: Participatory public media arts for social creativity. In: 4th International Conference on Culture and Computing-ICCC 2013, Kyoto, Japan, pp. 179–180 (2013)
36. Wang, F., Hu, J., Funk, M.: Practice and experience evaluation of interactive digital public art design. Zhuangshi **2015**(269), 96–97 (2015)
37. Lin, X., Hu, J., Rauterberg, M.: Review on interaction design for social context in public spaces. In: Rau, P. (ed.) CCD 2015. LNCS, vol. 9180, pp. 328–338. Springer, Heidelberg (2015)
38. Lim, V., Yalvac, F., Funk, M., Hu, J., Rauterberg, M.: Can we reduce waste and waist together through EUPHORIA? In: Third IEEE International Workshop on Social Implications of Pervasive Computing (2014)
39. Yalvaç, F., Lim, V., Hu, J., Funk, M., Rauterberg, M.: Social recipe recommendation to reduce food waste. In: CHI 2014 Extended Abstracts on Human Factors in Computing Systems, pp. 2431–2436 (2014)

Cross-Cultural Design Learning Tool: Cross-Cultural Design (CCD) Approach: A Study of South Korean Student Projects in Collaboration with Goldsmiths, University of London, UK

Dong Yeong Lee(✉) and Mike Waller

Goldsmiths, University of London, London, UK
{d.lee,m.waller}@gold.ac.uk

Abstract. This paper explores how design can develop an innovatory practice that builds the skills needed to design with cultural sensitivity. It is relevant to designers, researchers, and developers interested in extending the capabilities of innovating in relationship to culture. This paper presents a series of learning projects and outcomes that demonstrate the development of a cultural design tool. The project took place between Goldsmiths University of London in the United Kingdom and (KDM) Korean Design Membership in South Korea.

Keywords: Innovation methods · Cross-Cultural design · Teaching cultural understanding · CCD · Innovation tool · Cultural design · Global design · Service design

1 Introduction

Design engages with many aspects of life, from the design of the sound and experience of an alarm clock that wakes us up in the morning, to the underlying cultural knowledge that informs the design of mobile phone interfaces in different socio-cultural contexts. Sherry Turkle (2011) discusses that it is important to understand the complex cultural connections we have with things. We need to build a critical understanding of the cultural context to be able to design successfully, particularly for a wider global context, not only to conserve but also to develop cultural identities. Therefore, although a design can often have universality, it must be sensitive to cultural nuances. The underlying focus of the proposed experimental Cross-Cultural Design (CCD) tool is to learn, develop and apply skills in engaging designers culturally and their understanding of 'cultural difference'. It is not only design that is concerned with understanding culture, but other subject areas like contemporary critical, social, and cultural theory can also support the activity of Cross-Cultural Design (Diehl and Christianns 2006). In today's multicultural societies, understanding this cultural difference is a skill required by designers to engage meaningfully with users, particularly with the increased use of consumer technologies. As a result of globalisation, considerable efforts are being made to explore and understand cross-cultural relationships. This paper takes the specific example of cross-cultural design innovation projects held at Goldsmiths, University of London, in the United

P.-L.P. Rau (Ed.): CCD 2016, LNCS 9741, pp. 89–97, 2016.
DOI: 10.1007/978-3-319-40093-8_10

Kingdom and at the KDM design center in Seoul, South Korea. The aim of the paper is to present the proposed learning tool and discuss the development of cultural knowledge capital by the participants. There were 150 participants in total from the Korea Design Membership- a Korean Government organisation, the Regional Design Center in Gwangju, Daegu, Pusan cities, South Korea.

A series of case studies comparing a range of projects, briefs, outcomes, and evaluations will be presented in the paper. These case studies explore the implementation and ongoing development of Cross-Cultural Design (CCD). The projects explore learning that requires students to identify and explore different cultural backgrounds of a range of users. Here, the cultural difference could be between countries, genders and the like. How to define this 'cultural difference' is the very first task assigned to students in order to understand the context of the individual design activity and reinterpret it in its actual context (Curedale 2012). By analysing, comparing, displacing and repositioning their original meaning, students can attain a cohesive understanding of their function, role, cultural values, beliefs, aspirations and ideals; whilst learning about the rationale behind current designs and finally reinterpreting them in contemporary contexts.

From the initial workshops and project briefs a model was developed to help the students explore cross cultural concerns within their work. This learning tool helped students understand the nuances of cultures, and understand and interpret different cultures with the aim of developing new directions to explore, creating cultural innovations, and evolving design concepts. The model was divided into categories of approach to cultural formations;

1. Combination and Harmonisation - Design process based on sharing ideas and facilitating communication between two or more cultures.
2. Hybrid and Fusion - Design process based on sharing ideas. Similar to combination and harmonisation, Hybrid and Fusion will lead to a synergy of ideas and innovative results.
3. Transform/Translate/Transplant - Design process based on the idea of adopting one culture into another, and analysing the effects.
4. Inclusion and Exclusion - Design process based on defining boundaries examined from two different angles: protecting your own culture, and disregarding another culture.

We are witnessing the rapid development of many technology based products and services, and simultaneously global audiences are becoming more sophisticated and complex, as different cultural expectations and social needs need to be considered. Design is rapidly developing with many innovative products and services that combine manufactured hardware and software which require cultural knowledge to be well received by their user communities. Theorist Theodore Levitt (1983), in his Harvard Business Review article, *The Globalization of the Markets*, paid particular attention to the phenomenon of 'standardised products and brands'. Several observations were made including; (Levitt, 1983 IN Douglas and Wind 1987, p. 419);

1. Customers in the global markets' needs and interests are becoming increasingly homogenous worldwide;

2. People around the world are willing to sacrifice preferences in product features, functions, design, and the like for lower prices at high quality; and
3. Substantial economies of scale in production and marketing can be achieved through supplying global markets.

The proposed model of cultural engagement should help address this shifting requirement of innovation. There is an interest to support the hyper-local, regional and national to promote their own cultures, whilst respecting and understanding the cultures of others. At a national level governments are aware that their own creative industries can have a major impact on their economies. Consumers and prosumers are becoming more sophisticated and want to access and be part of the formation of a wider and more culturally rich range of products and services.

2 The Importance of Cross-Cultural Design

The benefits to the users of cross culture design are that products and services can engage with exposing users to cultural fashion, other cultural practices that they may want to learn more about. These practices may be about how we would like to live our lives, be different from others, and adopt other cultural practices that add something to our own lives. Often when designs of products and services are exported to other cultures their understanding can be misinterpreted as cultural values can be very different. In each culture there are different thoughts on what is fashionable, interesting and what quality might mean. What one culture may find amusing, another might find offensive. This is why understanding other cultures is so important for designers to engage with. There are also good arguments to suggest that local designers should be involved in innovation teams, that bring some of their own cultural understanding to a particular project.

3 Current Status of Design Education and Why Learning About 'Culture' Is Important

Common teaching methods within undergraduate higher education design include briefs within set themes, creating a basis for students to make sense and solve problems practically, individually, or in groups. Implementing novel and playful methods into design processes allows students to step out of their comfort zone and follow often-unexpected routes to a new way of developing a design outcome. Current trends in design education across industry encourage use of interdisciplinary design and collaborative practice. A cross-cultural approach to collaborative projects enables use of group work through a multicultural way of thinking, and opens doors to exciting new ways of combining design ethics and processes developed within individual design discipline backgrounds.

As Kolko (2010) declared, broader design and a diversity of methods should be an integral tool for educating future designers that should be sought out by educators. By introducing innovative methods of teaching students about design issues and giving a wider view on the affordance of design, the trained designers of the future will be able to tackle design problems and briefs with an open view of the designer's roles and responsibilities.

At Goldsmiths there are a series of tools used to identify the relationship between the designer and user, and the contexts of site, event, society and culture were used in all of the cross-cultural design briefs. What is central to this relationship diagram is the dialogical relationship being developed between designer and user, identified as an empathetic understanding built on an engaged connection with the user. In the centre of the diagram below is a mediating lens through which the designer sees the context of user and the object of innovation. This lens encourages the designer to acknowledge that they have particular cultural biases or influences that they see the the project through. They can also invest in exploring particular ways to look or understand the culture of the user, citizen or participant (Fig. 1).

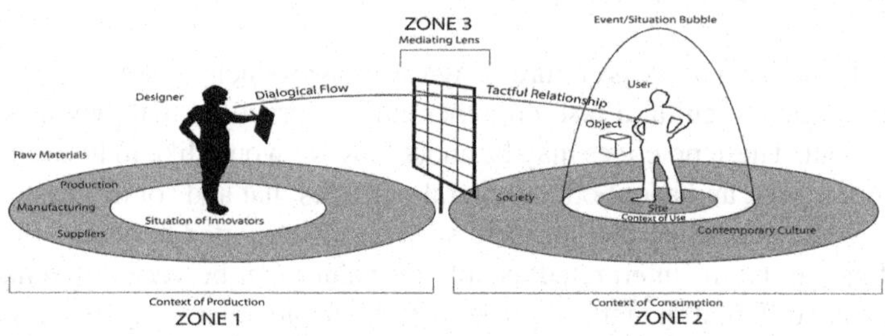

Fig. 1. Terry rosenberg context of design diagram (drawing mike waller)

We adopted Runco's playful approach to the design briefs for these cross-cultural projects. (2013, p. 111) Runco reminds us that the notion of creativity is not new; it is practised, accepted, and shared across cultures. However, using creativity as a starting point, or a means to instigate cross-cultural exchange, relationships and collaboration can encourage more solid learning, understanding, and appreciation of new (i.e. different to one's own) culture. "Given that there are often large differences in the prevailing ideas and practices between different cultures, a product/idea judged as being very creative in one culture might be perceived very differently in another culture" (Wolbers 2013, p. 86).

Rajeshwari Ghose is a Hong Kong-based critic featured in Buchanan and Margolin's '*The Idea of Design* (1995b)'. She discusses the pace and attitude towards design and development in Asia compared with that of the Western world, saying that, "China had no modern design education until the late 1970s. Design education has been formed mainly in western countries" (Buchanan and Margolin 1995a, p. 192).

It is apparent that there is a need for a platform that enables creative collaboration between cultures, so that an appreciation of a wider set of properties can be established between cultures. As Buchanan and Margolin (1995a,b) highlight, it will result in the introduction of new possibilities of collaboration because of an in-depth understanding of what others do.

4 Setting up CCD Learning Programme

We have been running Cross-Cultural Design programmes and teaching students from a variety of Korean design universities within the Design Department at Goldsmiths, University of London for the past five years. The Cross-Cultural Design programmes have been developed around different themes related to different cultural concerns, from tourism to cultural practices. From this experience, we found that students were able to engage and understand cultural difference through the design project brief, and they were able to develop new types of Cross-Cultural Design enquiries. Through the delivery of these cross-cultural design projects it is clear that cross-cultural design activities within the design curriculum help students understand and respect cultural difference, and support the success for the future development of a culturally enriched design field.

The programmes used the developed CCD learning tool, which were evolved and iterated at the Pi Studio (Prospecting and Innovation Design Research Studio) at Goldsmiths, University of London for the students from Kyung Hee University, Korea. As with all of the project design briefs, the teaching teams have tried to focus on a clear and meaningful topic, identified as requiring exploration through designing (Table 1).

Table 1. Brief of 4 CCD short courses since 2011

	Programme title	Brief
1	Colonial of cultures	The aim of this project brief was to introduce a new approach to socio-cultural 'difference' through design and designing
2	Bon voyage	This project is about a journey or a variety of journeys, which were geographic and creative. During this particular project, the impact, implications, and counter-arguments of globalisation were researched, with the aim of developing these issues whilst still enjoying the celebration of cultural differences through the design concepts
3	Tourism of the ordinary	As designers we are interested in understanding, exploring and reinventing the world. This project engages with a number of lost cultural practices in Korea, drawing on them to invent new cultural practices as well as reinventing existing ones
4	Future shopping	This brief introduces students to a live project exploring the positive disruption that design can make in proposing new and future forms of retail cultures. Designers think about 'positive disruptions', as well as how to work with ideas that address change and transformation caused by emerging technology

5 Development of Cross-Cultural Design Learning Tool

The cross-cultural design tool is introduced within each of the projects to assist the students in deconstructing their understanding of culture. The four approaches to cultural enquiry include; (1) Combination and Harmonisation, (2) Hybrid and Fusion, (3) Transform/Translate/Transplant, (4) Inclusion and Exclusion.

Combination and harmonisation involves sharing and communicating ideas between cultures with a view to be able to create cultural forms that span one or more cultural practices from different cultures and encourage communication and interest from the other cultures, including practices, behaviours, materials and artefacts. Hybrid and fusion is intended as a way to inspire more radical collisions of culture. The lace bowls, designed by Ching-Ting Hsu, and craft art by Tsun-Jen Lee are examples of what happens when an oriental embroidery pattern is combined with western aesthetic lace. Through transform/translate/transplant, students endeavour to carry a cultural practice from one context into another, and explore the possible impact. Inclusion and exclusion focuses on building cultural bridges to invite the other into, or creating cultural fences that guard one's own culture and traditions, therefore exclude other cultures. In some cases it is possible to create a new culture that includes some members but excludes others, like a subculture.

6 Testing the Cross-Cultural Design Learning Tool

The CCD learning tool has been tested firstly to verify the viability of the Cross-Cultural Design concepts, and secondly to test the Cross-Cultural Design programme, analyse the design outcomes, and develop Cross-Cultural Design tools. There were 38 CCD design outcomes by 150 participants in total from KDM (Korea Design Membership-a Korean Government organisation), with support of MA Design students from Goldsmiths, University of London. The outcomes of the CCD learning tool in the four categories can be seen in the case studies below.

6.1 Exploring the Category 1. Combination and Harmonisation

Global-wall public display for a street market in London and Seoul.

This project explored how a new form of public market media display could allow market traders to communicate with people in different markets globally. The aim was to open up new forms of trade or harmony between market stall holders in Seoul and in

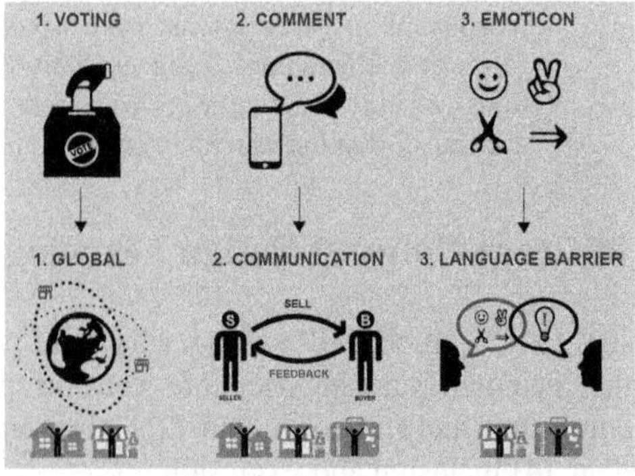

Fig. 2. Globalwall system (Source: student project outcome)

London. Building a specific located communication technology or platform could create the conditions to stimulate inter-cultural trade (Fig. 2).

6.2 Exploring the Category 2. Hybrid and Fusion

This Tea Explorer example is an electronic plugin tool that creates the smells of a particular type of tea. It also includes a media application that explains the culture of brewing, and delivers a service to access the supply of different teas from different countries. This is about combining cultures to make a cross-cultural tool to sample multiple cultures of tea (Fig. 3).

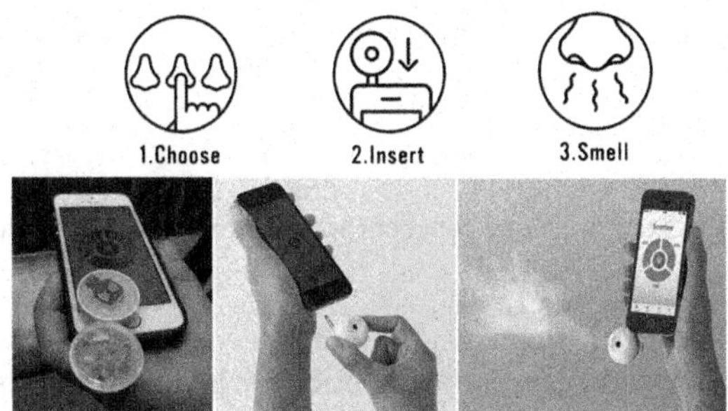

Fig. 3. Tea scent taster system (Source: student project outcome)

6.3 Exploring the Category 3. Transform/Translate/Transplant

Picnic bag for a city, London version.

The concept of the Picnicking bag of London is that the traditional Korean 'BOJAKI-wrapping cloth' can be merged with the British picnic culture by creating a picnic mat which also transforms into a map of the city (Fig. 4).

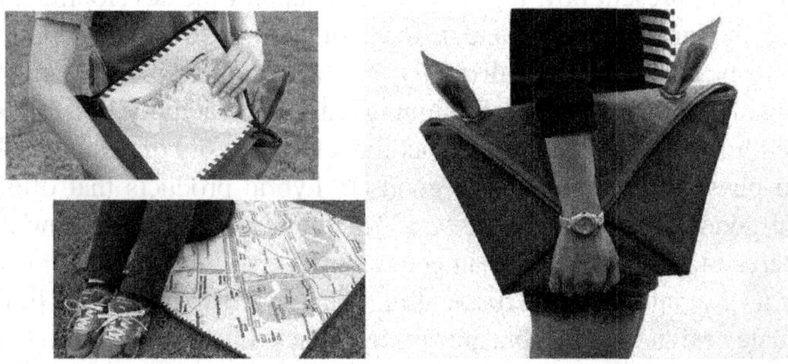

Fig. 4. Picnicking bag of London (Source: student project outcome)

6.4 Exploring the Category 3. Inclusion and Exclusion

Digital Mirror of Shame

Different meanings shame in Europe and South Korean - Shame of Korean: beauty, Shame of European: obesity (Fig. 5)

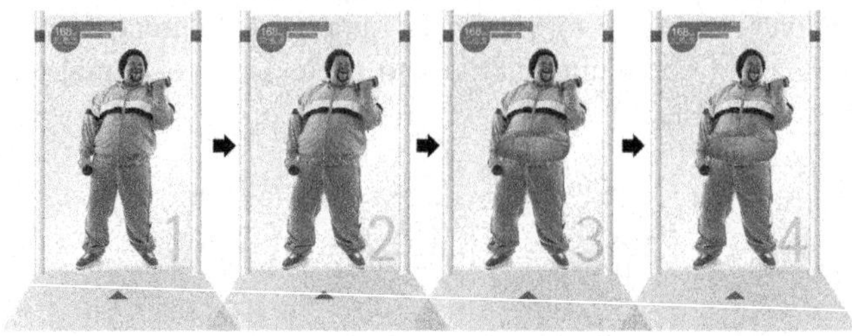

Fig. 5. The door of shame concept (Source: student project outcome)

This example from a student response to a brief that juxtaposing two different cultural sensibilities towards the concept of shame in the UK and in Korea. Interestingly while this would never become a product as it could offend its users, it exposes the nuances of Korean and British cultural attitudes to shame. This more in depth exploration of culture permits the students to explore the possible collisions of these attitudes within their design projects. There are clearly limitations to this approach, as it can often rely on preconceived notions and cultural stereotypes, which requires tutor encouragement to understanding culture through better contextual research.

7 Conclusion

This paper aimed to present how design tools can support the development of creative synergies and the understanding and respect of cultural diversities. Cross-cultural design, whilst respecting cultural diversity, can also protect and enhance particular cultures, national, regional and local. Designing is a cultural activity, and this tool locates the study of culture within the design curriculum. The territory of design is also rapidly shifting from physically manufactured goods to hybrid products that often combine manufactured goods, service and software. The audiences for these new designs are culturally interesting as they often span geographies, and create new forms of cultures through their user communities. Cross-cultural design tools are not just limited to use in undergraduate design learning, but are also relevant to innovation within multicultural communities, governments, organisations and businesses.

References

Buchanan, R., Margolin, V.: Discovering Design. The University of Chicago Press, Chicago (1995a)

Buchanan, R., Margolin, V.: The Idea of Design. Massachusetts Institute of Technology Press, Cambridge (1995b)

Curedale, R.: Design Methods 2: 200 More Ways to Apply Design Thinking. Design Community College, Inc, Topanga (2012)

Diehl, J., Christianns, H.: Globalisation and cross-cultural product design. In: International Design Conference - Design 2006, Dubrovnik, Croatia (2006)

Douglas, S., Wind, Y.: The myth of globalization. Columbia J. World Bus. **Winter**, 19–29 (1987)

Ghose, R.: Design Development, Culture, and cultural legacies in Asia, Issues. Presented in International Conference, Design and Development in South and Southeast Asia (1988)

Hennessey, B.: Nurturing Creative Mindsets Across Cultures: A Toolbox for Teachers. Billund: The LEGO Foundation (2013). http://www.legofoundation.com/en-us/research-and-learning/foundation-research/cultures-of-creativity/. Accessed 10 Oct 2014

Kolko, J.: Thoughts on Interaction Design. Morgan Kaufmann, Burlington (2010)

Runco, M.A.: Fostering Creativity Across Cultures. Billund: The LEGO Foundation (2013). http://www.legofoundation.com/en-us/research-and-learning/foundation-research/cultures-of-creativity/. Accessed 10 Oct 2014

Turkle, S.: Evocative Objects: Things We Think With. MIT Press, Cambridge (2011)

Wolbers, T.: Three Pathways By Which Culture Can Influence Creativity. Billund: The LEGO Foundation (2013). http://www.legofoundation.com/en-us/research-and-learning/foundation-research/cultures-of-creativity/. Accessed 10 Oct 2014

The Usability of Hand Pose and Gestures for Spaceflight Training System

Wanhong Lin[1,2(✉)], Jiangang Chao[1,2], Jin Yang[2], and Ying Xiong[2]

[1] National Key Laboratory of Human Factors Engineering, China Astronaut Research and Training Center, Beijing 100094, People's Republic of China
acclwh@hotmail.com, 85365060@qq.com
[2] China Astronaut Research and Training Center, Beijing 100094, People's Republic of China

Abstract. Virtual hand pose and gestures for manipulation is one of the hardest interactive problem in Spaceflight Training System. This paper researched the usability of hand pose and gestures, proposed a couple of non-contact action determining rules and an action states transition method based on finite state machine (FSM) to control the manipulation process of virtual hand. Meanwhile, a gesture recognition method based on hand pose data was proposed. The experiment result shows that the proposed method has a high success rate and efficiency for manipulation. It can be used for the way of manipulation in Spaceflight Training System.

Keywords: Usability · Hand pose and gestures · Spaceflight training system

1 Introduction

With the rapid development of computer technology in the field of spaceflight training, Augmented and Virtual Reality Environments arise and become part of training system. The role of human computer interaction with these system, or HCI, is becoming more important. In particular, an approach that involves adapting the way humans communicate with each other for HCI is considered to be the most promising. Potential spaceflight training systems which use these new technologies require input devices that can be easily carried along with the user and instantly available when needed (or made available by the environment). Such technologies pose several challenges on the GUI (Graphical User Interface) paradigm designed for desktop interaction, particularly on current input devices such as keyboards and mouse [1–4].

Especially, spaceflight training systems inherently requires controls with a high degree of freedom. For instance, manipulation of a 3D object with using user's hand directly rather than with a mouse can offer an ideal alternative and more comfortable and easier way than using mouse and keyboard for such systems [3–5]. In this way, users can control the position and orientation of a 3D object directly by simply moving their hands.

P.-L.P. Rau (Ed.): CCD 2016, LNCS 9741, pp. 98–107, 2016.
DOI: 10.1007/978-3-319-40093-8_11

Although wearable devices might be an option, a computer vision based gesture recognition system seems to be a more natural alternative since it can be considered as part of the environment and operates remotely, it does not require the user to wear or have any physical contact with a device. A gesture based interface has the potential of eliminating the need of pointing devices, thus saving the time and effort in using such devices for the interaction process. As a result, the interaction with AR/VR system based on gestures motivated us to develop a method for tracking a user's hand in 3D and recognizing hand gestures in real-time without using any invasive devices attached to the hand [5]. In this work, referring to the previous method [2] we proposed a new technique for estimating the 3D gesture based on the 3D pose of a user's hand by using depth camera in real-time. In addition, the proposed technique is able to recognize predetermined hand gestures in a fast and robust manner by using Machine Learning which has been properly trained beforehand. Meanwhile, because performing gestures for long periods of time can be physically stressing, the understanding of how gestures can be more effectively and more comfortably used to communicate with training systems becomes more important.

2 Hand Pose and Gestures Lexicon

In terms of hand pose, the user uses a virtual hand based on the data of hand pose to manipulate the virtual object as human do in the reality world. Hand gestures are different. The virtual system captures hand movements and then hand movements will be recognized as corresponding gestures that can generate command to control virtual objects or 3D menu.

In the previous study, we found that the system needs to carry out the physical collision detection between virtual hand and virtual objects when using hand pose to manipulate the virtual object. It is well known that physical collision detection is a very complicated process. In this paper, we will merge these two modes to make an interface with the virtual reality system.

In term of object manipulation, there are several kinds of actions that need to be carried out by the astronaut in the training system:

- Push the button on the menu: The astronaut usually need information which is triggered by buttons on the 3D menu to control the training process.
- Select: Select the object.
- Grab: Grab the object.
- Rotate: Rotate the object.
- Move: Move the object.
- Release: Release the manipulated object.

So the commands generated by hand pose and gestures includes Push, Select, Grab, Rotate, Move and Release. According to our study, we defined the hand pose and gestures as following Table 1.

Table 1. Hand pose and gestures Lexicon

Command	Hand pose and gestures
Push	Palm push forward after selected
Select	Use index finger to point
Grab	Thumb and index or middle fingertips come together
Rotate	Point forward using index and middle fingers, and then cycle the hand.
Move	After grab, movement of object is determined by absolute location of center of hand
Release	Thumb and index-middle fingertips separate

3 Action States Transition Based on FSM

When the astronaut is training, those actions are continuous. So those actions need to be distinguished based on the state of the different movement. According to the special virtual weightless environment of astronaut virtual training, this paper proposed a couple of non-contact action determining rules and an action state transition method based on finite state machine (FSM). Finite state machine (FSM) [6, 7] is a good tool for states control of the virtual hand action. The interactive model of FSM for virtual hand action is shown in Fig. 1, where S represents the state, c represents the states transition conditions.

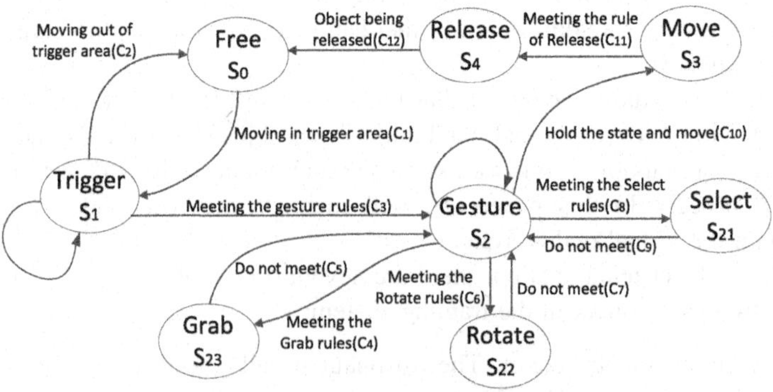

Fig. 1. The finite state machine of action

As our previous research results [8], we proposed some action determining rules which are a kind of rules that used to determine whether a virtual hand manipulates the object in virtual training world.

Because all of the objects in the training system are weightless, a slight touch from virtual hand would lead to the movement of objects, which will result in failure to manipulate. Traditional determining rules based on collision detection are not suitable for weightless virtual environment. We developed two non-contact determining rules based on hand pose and gestures.

Rule One: the distance between the object and the virtual hand must be less than a certain critical value.

Rule Two: the character value of the hand gesture is must be less than a certain critical value, which is called the object action trigger area.

It is determined that action is successful only if the virtual hand and the object meet the condition of Rule One and Rule Two at the same time. After successful action, the object is attached to the virtual hand and moves with it together. The object will be released when the virtual hand does not satisfy Rule Two.

According to the principle of FSM, the constituent elements of FSM are defined as: states (*S*), input events (*X*), output (*Y*), states transition function (*f*) and output function (*g*).

States (*S*): action states of virtual hand. There are five states, Free State, Trigger State, Gesture State, Move State and Release State. Each state corresponds to a kind of action state between the virtual hand and the object.

Input events (*X*): correspond to the five states shown in Fig. 1. There are six conditions which are the virtual hand moving into the object action trigger area, the virtual hand moving out of the object action trigger area, the virtual hand meeting the rules of gesture, the virtual hand meeting the rules of move, the virtual hand meeting the condition of release and the object being released.

Output (*Y*): the rendering results displayed to the operator.

States transition function (*f*): defined as the determination function which determines the states transition from the current state to the next one. Equation (1) shows its relationship with the states and time, where $X(t) \in X, S(t) \in S$.

$$S(t+1) = f(X(t), S(t)) \tag{1}$$

Output function (*g*): defined as a mapping relationship between the current state and the output. Equation (2) shows its relationship with the states, where $Y(t) \in Y$.

$$Y(t) = g(X(t), S(t)) \tag{2}$$

Free State (S_0): the virtual hand does not touch any object. In this condition, virtual hand can move freely and the finger joints can bend freely.

Trigger State (S_1): the virtual hand moves into the object action trigger area, but does not meet the action determining rules. At this time, the virtual hand does not touch the object, the object does not be manipulated.

Gesture State (S_2): the virtual hand can manipulate the object stably by following the gesture determining rules. The object is adsorbed to virtual hand in the gesture state.

Move State (S_3): the virtual hand can manipulate the object stably by following the two determining rules. The object is adsorbed to virtual hand moving with the virtual hand together as a child node.

Release State (S_4): the virtual hand converts to the release state when it does not satisfy Rule Two of the action determining rules after manipulating the object. In this state, the virtual hand releases the object and then converts to the free state.

4 The Gesture Recognition Method

There are many devices provide the data of hand pose such as Intel RealSense, Leap Motion, Kinect etc. Due to the high accuracy of Leap Motion [9], we choose the pose data provided by the Leap Motion for gesture recognition.

4.1 Gesture Recognition Algorithm

As already reported the Leap Motion device provides only a limited set of relevant points and not a complete description of the hand shape [10]. But the device provides directly some of the most relevant points for gesture recognition and allows to avoid complex computations needed for their extraction from depth and color data. The Leap Motion sensor mainly provides the following data, as depicted in Fig. 2:

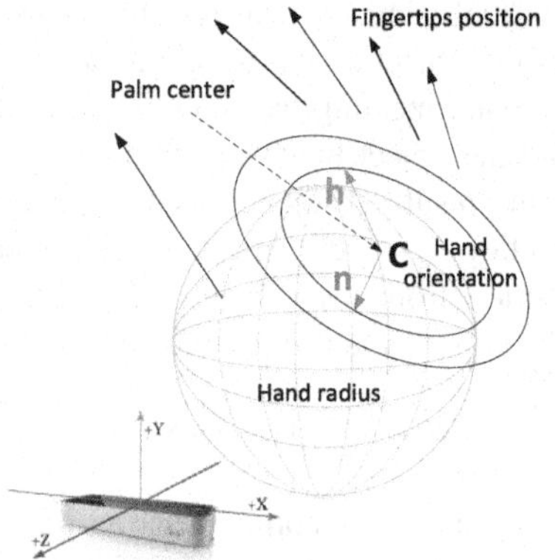

Fig. 2. The pose data from Leap Motion

- Number of detected fingers N ∈ [0, 5].
- Position of the fingertips Fi, i = 1… N.
- Palm center C.
- Hand orientation, h points from the palm center to the direction of the fingers, n is the normal to the plane that corresponds to the palm region pointing downward from the palm center.
- Hand radius r.

Note that the accuracy is not the same for all the reported data vectors. The 3D positions of the fingertips are quite accurate: according to a recent research [9] the error is about 200 um. While the localization of the detected fingers is accurate, their detection is not too reliable. There are some situations in which the sensor is not able to recognize all the fingers such as fingers folded over the hand, hidden from the sensor viewpoint, fingers touching each other and the hand not perpendicular to the camera, etc. These issues are quite critical and must be taken into account in developing a reliable gesture recognition approach since in different executions of the same gesture the number of captured fingers could vary. For this reason simple schemes based on the number of detected fingers have poor performance. As previously proposed approach [10] we deal with this issue by sorting the features on the basis of the fingertip angle with respect to the hand direction h. In this paper, we also consider the ratio of circumference and area.

In order to account for the fingers misalignment, we consider the projection of the hand region into the palm plane described by n and passing through C, as depicted in Fig. 3. In this work we analyze 5 different types of features computed from the Leap Motion data that will be described in the rest of this section:

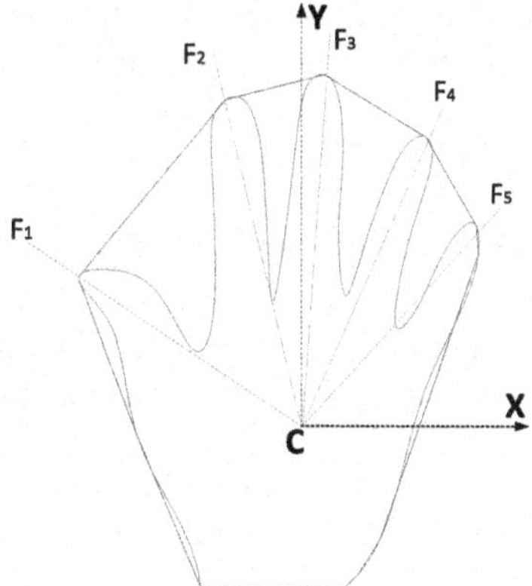

Fig. 3. The features of hand

- Fingertip angles: angles corresponding to the orientation of each fingertip projected onto the palm plane with respect to the hand orientation h.
- Fingertip distances: 3D distance of the fingertips from the hand center.
- Fingertip elevations: distances of the fingertip from the palm region plane.
- Fingertip 3D positions: x, y and z coordinates of the fingertips.
- Circumference and area ratio: Circumference is the sum of the connections between the five fingers and the palm of the hand. Area is the middle part of the five fingers and the center of the palm.

All the features values (except for the angles) are normalized in the interval [0, 1] by dividing the values for the distance between the hand center and the middle fingertip length $S = \|F_{middle} - C\|$ in order to make the approach robust to people with hands of different size. The scale factor S can be computed during the calibration of the system.

After the completion of the feature extraction, we need a classifier to classify the features. Due to the small number of samples, the SVM (Support Vector Machines) classifier [11] was selected for feature classification. In SVM, the sample space is mapped to a high dimensional space through a nonlinear mapping method, which makes the original nonlinear problem transform into the linearly separable problem in the feature space. Then the optimal hyper plane is found in the high dimension space.

In this way, the features are classified. Because the radial basis kernel function can realize the nonlinear mapping and need fewer parameters, the radial basis kernel function model is selected in this paper.

4.2 Noise Suppression

Although the tracking accuracy of Leap Motion is less than submillimeter in theory, Leap Motion still can produce identification unstable phenomenon. Device resolution, thermal magnetic noise, hand shake [12], visual and numerical block singular value solvers are likely to introduce noise signal. In this paper, the literature [13] proposed an adaptive cut-off frequency of the low pass filtering method, the cutoff frequency of the low pass filter will be changed by detecting the real-time speed of palm. Equation (3) gives adaptive filter parameters and calculation expression.

$$\hat{X}_i = a_i X_i + (1 - a_i)\hat{X}_{i-1} \tag{3}$$

X_i is a high-dimensional vector which is composed of the coordinates and vector values returned from Leap Motion.

$\hat{X}_i$ is a vector after adaptive filtering, a_i, as Eq. (4), can be calculated by the sensor data update interval T_i and time constant τ_i, as Eq. (5), is a smoothing factor between [0,1]:

$$a_i = \frac{1}{1 + \tau_i / T_i} \tag{4}$$

$$\tau_i = \frac{1}{2\pi f_{ci}} \tag{5}$$

The cut-off frequency f_{ci} is determined by the Eq. (6). $\hat{V}_i$ represents the linear velocity and angular velocity of the palm movement is the derivative of $\hat{X}_i$. In this paper it takes the empirical value $f_{c\min}$ = 1 Hz, β = 0.5.

$$f_{ci} = f_{c\min} + \beta \left| \hat{V}_i \right|. \tag{6}$$

5 Experiment and Result

For verification of the method, an action rules sub-experiment and an equipment assembly training sub-experiment were designed. Then subjective evaluation and objective evaluation were carried out [14].

This experiment has a total of 40 subjects, including 30 researchers who develop the space flight simulator and 10 graduate students who major in graphics and virtual reality. They understand the basic principles and application of virtual reality, computer graphics and the interaction with virtual reality system. But they didn't have the experience of the orbit assembly training.

5.1 Action Rules Experiment

In order to test our action rules and simulation FSM model, we designed a grab experiment. We analyzed 358 times grabbing operation from 40 subjects. We took the average number of grabbing operation every successful grab and the average grabbing time as the evaluation. The result is shown in Table 2.

Table 2. Evaluation of virtual hand grab

Evaluation	Average	Standard deviation
Numbers of grabbing operation every successful grab	1.50	0.984
Grabbing time (seconds)	4.41	3.364

From the evaluation above we can conclude that the virtual hand grabbing operation, which following our action determining rules and FSM model, has a high success rate and efficiency. This method can be used as astronaut operation training method in a virtual weightless environment.

5.2 Equipment Assembly Training Experiment

The experiment system is shown in Fig. 4. The subjects complete the gas generator for exercise assembly training according to the predefined process.

Fig. 4. The experiment system main view

To verify the effectiveness of the astronaut virtual assembly training, the assembly training method which guided by the learning manual were compared. The manual of assembly learning is a standard handbook. The specific assembly steps are introduced in detail by words and pictures. The manual of learning as the traditional way of training and virtual assembly training were compared to verify the efficiency and effect of the method of training.

Subjects were divided into control group and experimental group. Each group has 20 subjects. Control group does experiment by learning assembly manual training, and then have a real assemble. Learning training manual required time and the real assembly time were recorded. After the completion of the real assembly, the control group of experimenters transfer to virtual assembly training experience, experience after the completion of the fill in for virtual training methods of subjective evaluation questionnaire. While in the experimental group, in reverse order, assembly training through the virtual assembly training system, then the assembly objects, recorded both in manual training experience and fill in the questionnaire.

Through the calculation and analysis of the recorded data, we can find that, the average time required for the control group to training is 287.83 s, the experimental group is 183.81 s, the average time required for the control group and experimental group to manipulate are 87.13 s and 77.52 s, which indicates that the training efficiency and training effect of the experimental group are significantly better than that of the control group. Other results of subjective evaluation questionnaires are as shown in Table 3.

Table 3. Manipulation subjective evaluation questionnaires results

Evaluation	Means (0–5)	Standard deviation
Degree of alternative manual	3.875	0.68641
Interactivity	3.350	0.73554
Realistic	3.325	0.99711
Gesture recognition effect	4.025	0.76753
Operability	3.400	1.12774
Weightlessness effect	3.625	0.89693
Immersion	4.175	0.74722
Overall evaluation of virtual training	3.950	0.55238

It can be seen from subjective evaluation results and questionnaire that the proposed method is effective and can be used into the virtual training system.

6 Summary

Our experiments show that the advantage is obvious with using hand pose and gestures for HCI. As a new way to interact with VR system, it provides a more natural way to manipulate the virtual objects in the VR environment, reduces the user's learning time, improves operational efficiency and can very harmoniously embedded in training system. But there are also some disadvantages, such as the time to finish a menu operation is slower than using a mouse and as is the case usually occurs as likely to cause fatigue. Further research will be conducted to reduce the discomfort fatigue.

Acknowledgments. This work was supported by China Astronaut Research and Training Center within the following research programs: Advanced Space Medico-Engineering Research Project of China (2013SY54A1303, 9140c770204150c77318, 2013SY54B1301, FTKY201302).

References

1. Sen, F., Diaz, L., Horttana, T.: A novel gesture-based interface for a VR simulation: Re-discovering Vrouw Maria. In: 2012 18th International Conference on Virtual Systems and Multimedia (VSMM), pp. 323–330 (2012)
2. Sato, Y., Saito, M., Koike, H.: Real-time input of 3D pose and gestures of a user's hand and its applications for HCI. In: Virtual Reality, 2001. Proceedings, pp. 79–86. IEEE (2003)
3. Lee, C.-S., Oh, K.-M., Park, C.-J.: Virtual environment interaction based on gesture recognition and hand cursor. Electron. Resour. (2008)
4. Nasser, N.H., Alhaj, M.: Hand gesture interaction with a 3D virtual environment. Res. Bull. Jordan ACM **II(III)**, 186–193 (2011)
5. Ming, A., Yuqing, L., Bohe, Z., Fuchao, H.: Study on real-time interactive simulation of rotating top in weightlessness. Manned Spaceflight (2014)
6. Chen, Y., Lin, F.: Safety control of discrete event systems using finite state machines with parameters. In: Proceedings of the American Control Conference. Arlington: American Auotmatic Control Council, pp. 975–980 (2001)
7. Feng, Z., Yan, B., Xu, T., et al.: 3D direct human-computer interface paradigm based on free hand tracking. Chin. J. Comput. **37**(6), 1309–1323 (2014)
8. Hu, H., Chao, J.G., Liu, J.G.: Grab simulation based on FSM for astronaut virtual training. In: 3rd International Conference on Mechatronics, Robotics and Automation (ICMRA 2015), pp. 1060–1064 (2015)
9. Weichert, F., Bachmann, D., Rudak, B., Fisseler, D.: Analysis of the accuracy and robustness of the leap motion controller. Sensors **13**(5), 6380–6393 (2013)
10. Marin, G., Dominio, F., Zanuttigh, P.: Hand gesture recognition with jointly calibrated Leap Motion and depth sensor. Multimedia Tools Appl., 1–25 (2015)
11. Chang, C.-C., Lin, C.-J.: LIBSVM: a library for support vector machines. ACM Trans. Intell. Syst. Technol. **2**, 27:1–27:27 (2011)
12. Vaillancourt, D.E., Newell, K.M.: Amplitude changes in the 8-12, 20-25, and 40 Hz oscillations in finger tremor. Clin. Neurophysiol. **111**(10), 1792–1801 (2000)
13. Casiez, G., Roussel, N., Vogel, D.: 1€ filter: a simple speed-based low-pass filter for noisy input in interactive systems. In: Proceedings of the 2012 ACM Annual Conference on Human Factors in Computing Systems, pp. 2527–2530 (2012)
14. Ledda, P., Chalmers, A., Troscianko, T.: Evaluation of tone mapping operators using a high dynamic range display. ACM Trans. Graph. **24**(3), 640–648 (2005)

Characterizing Intercultural Encounters in Human-Computer Interaction

Luciana C. de C. Salgado[1(✉)], Clarisse Sieckenius de Souza[2], Catia M.D. Ferreira[3], and Carla Faria Leitão[2]

[1] Department of Computer Science, Fluminense Federal University (UFF), Niterói, Brazil
luciana@ic.uff.br

[2] Department of Informatics, Pontifical Catholic University of Rio de Janeiro (PUC-Rio), Rio de Janeiro, Brazil
{clarisse,cfaria}@inf.puc-rio.br

[3] Diretoria de Informática, Instituto Brasileiro de Geografia e Estatística (IBGE), Rio de Janeiro, Brazil
catia.ferreira@ibge.gov.br

Abstract. This article presents a two-step study, which is part of a project that aims at investigating how cross-cultural systems, intentionally or not, express and promote *indirect intercultural encounters* in Human-Computer Interaction. Previous research have proposed five Cultural Viewpoint Metaphors, a Semiotic Engineering conceptual tool to support HCI designers to understand and organize communicative strategies in the interactive discourse to promote such encounters. At this stage of our research we investigated the design of cross-cultural systems using CVM and one of the best known among numerous classes of signs proposed by Peirce – icons, indices and symbols, aiming at supporting the semiotic engineering (specifically, the choice of signs, i.e. the interface elements) of these kind of applications. Our findings point at the power of an alignment of the semiotic characteristics of Cultural Viewpoint Metaphors with theoretical semiotic elements from Peirce's typology of signs in the interaction design cycle of cross-cultural systems.

Keywords: Culture · HCI · Cultural viewpoint metaphors · Semiotic engineering · Intercultural encounters

1 Introduction

The ever-increasing World Wide Web (Web) and its wide variety of cross-cultural applications (i.e. systems that intentionally expose foreign material to their users [16]) and users from different cultures have established a growing interest and need in research about Culture and Human-Computer Interaction (HCI). Over the years HCI research has been conducted aiming at investigating methodological [1, 6, 14, 17] and practical challenges [2, 10, 12, 21] about international and cultural aspects of HCI, such as the effect of culture in interaction [4, 11], intercultural collaboration [21], solutions to HCI design and culture-sensitive interaction [15].

P.-L.P. Rau (Ed.): CCD 2016, LNCS 9741, pp. 108–119, 2016.
DOI: 10.1007/978-3-319-40093-8_12

This work is part of a broader research about how cross-cultural systems may, intentionally or not, express and promote indirect intercultural encounters with signs and traces of foreign values, practices, heritage, and so on, in HCI. Intercultural encounters in HCI may direct or indirect [15]. Direct intercultural encounters may happen when users make contact by interacting with users from others cultures with CMC technology. Indirect intercultural encounters, in turn, take place when users are exposed and/or may explore cultural diversity (belief, law, customs, language, symbols and so on) by interacting with cross-cultural systems.

The two-step study presented in this paper investigated such indirect intercultural encounters with concepts of Cultural Viewpoint Metaphors (CVM) and Peirce's typology of signs (icons, indexes and symbols). CVM is a Semiotic Engineering [4, 5] conceptual tool to support designers in stimulating users to engage in different levels of intercultural contact (if it is desirable), which may increase their perception about cultural diversity in the particular domain where the system is placed. So, the intercultural contact potentially causes a level of perception of cultural diversity. The adoption of each metaphor invite designers to follow a specific combination of communication features and cultural variables to achieve effects on interactive discourse.

Previous studies with CVM focused on the communication of culture investigating HCI practitioners' [15], users' [8] perspectives and methodological issues [9]. Among others, the results show two main contributions: (i) CVM have strong epistemic power for guiding the choices of communicative strategies in the design of cross-cultural application; (ii) CVM may be used as a vocabulary to reach users' cultural perspectives at evaluation time. In this paper, we are focusing on the semiotic engineering of cross-cultural applications regarding to how designers may protocol cultural components in the interface to promote intercultural encounters in HCI.

In order to address the research question presented above, we conduct a two-step study to understand the different ways of promoting intercultural contact with cultural diversity by using CVM (and their respective effects) in the light of Peirce's typology of signs. We aim at discussing and contrasting different ways to promote intercultural encounters in HCI as well as investigating users' perceptions about them.

The paper is structured in four sections. After the introduction, we present our theoretical foundations, with a brief explanation of CVM and Peirce's typology of signs. Next, the two-step study to answer our research question. Finally, our conclusion and possibilities for future work.

2 Theoretical Foundations

This paper presents a theoretical characterization of possible indirect intercultural encounters that may take place in HCI.

2.1 Cultural Viewpoint Metaphors

CVM is a Semiotic Engineering conceptual tool to support the decisions on dimensions of intercultural encounters in HCI design cycle of cross-cultural systems. Semiotic

Engineering, a semiotic theory of HCI, which is rooted in Peirce's [18, 19] and Eco's view [8] of Semiotics, a comprehensive study of culturally-determined codes and signs production, at all levels of human experience. According to Eco culture is the basis of two fundamental process: signification and communication.

Following these foundations, Semiotic Engineering theory supports the study of a distinctive unit of investigation: HCI as a particular kind of computer-mediated communication. Besides the cultural aspects of users and systems (itself), the theory involves the designer in the communication and signification process in HCI. In Semiotic Engineering terms, interaction designers need to choose and use (codify in the interface) signs to say how, why and what for the users may use the interactive system to reach their purposes. The combination of signs (interface elements, communicative strategies and styles and so on) will compose the interactive language.

Designers need, therefore, to be mindful of how (un)powerfully the interactive language may be due the choices they made (at design time) to communicate specific messages to be differently understood and perceived by individuals from multiple cultures. The five conceptual metaphors lead HCI practitioners to think about interaction as a journey in which the users are the travelers. CVM are plotted in a continuum of cultural approximation that goes from the user culture to a visited foreign culture (see Fig. 1). Each metaphor represents a different intensity of intercultural contact (between users and cultural signs from foreign cultures).

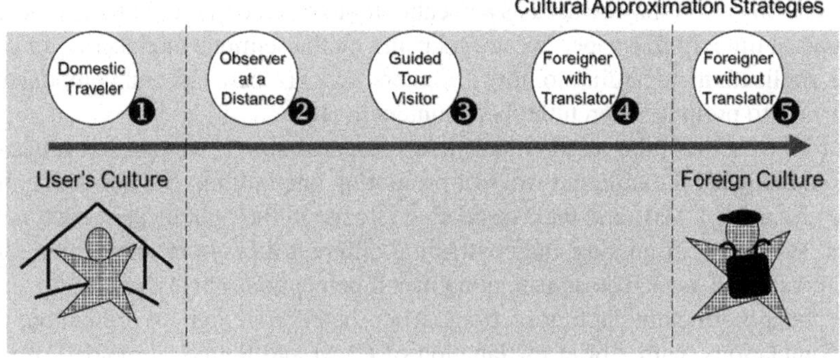

Fig. 1. Cultural Viewpoint Metaphors [15]

The domestic traveler metaphor keeps the user isolated in their own culture, the foreign culture is invisible to the user and communication is performed in users' own native language, with no references to foreign practices and cultural values [16]. On the opposite site, with the foreign without translator metaphor the user may have contact with foreign culture as it is, with no mediation. There is an absence of cultural mediation in these two extremes.

In the three intermediary metaphors, different levels of cultural mediation influence the intercultural encounters. With the observer at a distance metaphor, cultural markers of another culture are communicated as "bits of information": small facts about the foreign culture are presented for users interested in learning more about the subject (the native users' culture and language dominate).

The guided tour visitor metaphor provides a contrast between the two cultures (the user and the foreign culture), so the foreign culture is illustrated and explained in the user's language through cultural markers that illustrate the foreign culture: there is a strong cultural mediation and approximation.

The foreigner with translator metaphor allows the foreign culture to be experienced directly, but with language translation of the verbal content, i.e., the cultural markers can be experienced directly, but in the user's language. Thus, the three metaphors situated between the two extremes (observer at a distance, guided tour visitor and foreigner with translator) indicate how does the intercultural encounters may take place according to the different levels of cultural mediation.

The adoption of each metaphor entails a different organization of the interactive discourse, including the design of communication features and the combinations of values assigned to two cultural variables: language (native or foreign) and cultural practices (with several domain-dependent values).

2.2 Peirce's Typology of Signs

Signs have been defined by Peirce [18] as "Something which stands to somebody for something in some respect or capacity. It addresses somebody, that is, creates in the mind of that person an equivalent sign, or perhaps a more developed sign. That sign which it creates I call the interpretant of the first sign. The sign stands for something, its object. It stands for that object, not in all respects, but in reference to a sort of idea, which I have sometimes called the ground of the representamen".

Peirce defines a triadic model for a sign where: the representamen is the form which the sign takes (not necessarily material); the interpretant is not an interpreter but rather the sense that a human mind makes of the sign; and the object, to which the sign refers and thus provides *grounding* for it. In the following definition, Peirce clarifies the determination relationship among the elements of the semiotic triangle: "Sign is anything which is so determined by something else, called its Object, and so determines an effect upon a person, which effect I call its Interpretant, that the latter is thereby mediately determined by the former" [18].

For instance, ⚠ is a sign that represents 'warning' by virtue of a conventional contemporary Western culture interpretation (interpretant). It signifies some risk to a person. A sign exists whenever some interpreter takes a representation to mean something. Moreover, according to Peirce, the meaning of a representation (its interpretant), is also another sign. Then, each sign has another sign that corresponds to its meaning. The interaction between the representamen, the object and the interpretant is referred to by Peirce as 'semiosis'. Eco uses the term 'unlimited semiosis' to characterize this process as potentially infinite [8].

Peirce defined a fundamental typology of signs that can be manipulated to help communicators achieve their intent – symbols, indexes and icons. It is intrinsically related to Peirce's phenomenological categories of semiotic interest (firstness, secondness and thirdness), which are meant to provide the basis for explaining any phenomena of interest, i.e., of all possible experiences to acquire knowledge [20].

The following interpretation of Peirce's view by Santaella gives us the notion of what these phenomenological categories are: "Firstness is allied to the ideas of chance, indeterminacy, freshness, originality, spontaneity, quality, immediacy, monad… Secondness is associated to the ideas of brute-force, action-reaction, conflict, here and now, effort and endurance, dyad… Thirdness is linked to the ideas of generality, continuity, growth, advocacy, mediation, triad" [20].

3 Two-Step Study

Firstly (in Step One), we contrast the concepts and effects proposed by each metaphor with each Peirce's phenomenological categories and typology of signs. We aimed at understanding the relationship between them and the effects in the promotion of intercultural encounters. We, thus, arrived at three levels of effects in intercultural contact: cultural diversity unawareness, cultural awareness, and cultural diversity experience. Secondly (in Step Two), we studied what users perceived at interaction time at an intercultural encounter situation. We, thus, triangulated the results from Step Two with the three levels of intercultural contact (achieved in Step One).

3.1 Understanding the Effects of Intercultural Encounters (Step One)

To begin, the domestic traveler metaphor stays out of question, since it does not intend to promote intercultural contact. The intended design effect is, thus, that of cultural unawareness, i.e., the condition of being uninformed or unaware about other culture (unconsciousness resulting from lack of knowledge or attention).

The definition of observer at a distance metaphor says that "the cultural markers of another culture are communicated as 'information' (not as an experience the use can 'feel')". It is achieved by a narrative about the foreign culture to provide factual information about what is different from one's own culture. So, design intent is to give the seed for cultural semiosis, but not the experience of cultural diversity itself. In Peirce's semiotic terms, the idea of this metaphor is to present an index for the presence of other culture, so the user will be contact with other culture in a secondness way. We are not saying that the whole interface is created with indexical signs, but that the general idea is that a design with this metaphor usually evokes the secondness of the referents of cultural diversity.

The Guided tour metaphor, in turn, usually evokes the thirdness, since designer's deputy mediates intercultural contact by giving meaning to foreign referents. The definition says that the cultural markers from another culture are 'illustrated' to the user (aspects of cultural issues are exemplified and explained in the user's language). It is achieved by an interpreted view and commentary on the foreign culture which mediates the user's approximation and contact with cultural diversity. The idea of this metaphor is to guide the user's interpretation by thirdness signs, thus reaching the maximum mediation.

In both cases (in the observer at a distance and guided tour visitor metaphors) the intended effect is that of cultural awareness. But the effects on cultural diversity perception are potentially different, since the strict associations evoked by secondness representation in observer at a distance metaphor are not mediated by the designer's deputy.

The idea of the foreign with and without translator metaphors is to represent cultural diversity by evoking the firstness of their referents, since according to their definitions the cultural markers of another culture can be directly 'experienced' by the user. With firstness signs there is no mediation, but we also see secondness elements with the foreign with translator metaphor, since the interface in the users' language acts as a reference to their native culture when making relations to the foreign cultures. In both cases, the design intent provokes a cultural experience, since it represents the nearest point of contact with a foreign culture where the designer may try to offer to the user.

As a whole, in Peirces' semiotic terms, design represents cultural diversity by signs to users. If we consider that the correspondence between CVM and the Peirce's categories is plausible, with CVM designers may work thinking about different levels of knowledge in terms of firstness, secondness, and thirdness. So, designers may consider that users' semioses may walk through the continuum of cultural approximation by reflecting how intercultural encounters may stem from rationality to sensorial experiences with different levels of cultural diversity perceptions (see Table 1).

Table 1. Potential effect on cultural diversity perception

Metaphor	Cultural Diversity is represented by	Description	Effect
Domestic traveler	Not applicable	Not applicable	Cultural diversity unawareness
Observer at a distance	Secondness signs	the strict associations evoked by secondness representation **are not mediated** by the designer's deputy	Cultural diversity awareness
Guided Tour Visitor	Thirdness signs	designer's deputy mediates intercultural contact by **giving meaning** to foreign referents	Cultural diversity awareness
Foreigner with translator	Firstness and Secondness signs	The language is the unique cultural mediator	Cultural Diversity Experience
Foreigner without translator	Firstness signs	There is no mediaton	Cultural Diversity Experience

The next section presents how users perceived the promotion of cultural diversity in intercultural encounters at interaction time.

3.2 Exploring User's Perception (Step Two)

We ran two empirical studies, the Study One (S1) with Englishtown[1] (ET website), an online English school, and the Study Two (S2) with Wikipedia[2], a collaborative on-line free encyclopedia. Our research question was: How users perceive the promotion of cultural diversity (with intercultural encounters) in HCI?

ET website has not been designed with CVM, but it is clearly a cross-cultural application that exposes and exploits opportunities to intercultural encounters. The ET mission, as clearly stated in the website "is to use technology to create a fundamentally better way of learning English". Wikipedia website is also a cross-cultural application: a multilingual, web-based, free-content encyclopedia project with more than 31,000,000 articles in 285 languages.

Each study (S1 and S2) was divided in two steps. In Step One, a Brazilian HCI evaluator inspected the selected website using CVM to identify portions where different levels of cultural approximation were explored and interactive resources used to promote indirect intercultural encounters. Seven scenarios of inspection were then created for user sessions in the next step of the study.

In Step Two, five potential users were recruited to evaluate (in individual sessions) the selected portions of the website (in each study). The participants belong to different areas of expertise: Statistics, Informatics, Education or Law. All of them were Brazilian, with college or university graduation. They all had at least a basic knowledge of English and are interested in learning more about this language (in S1) and had an interest in Encyclopedia information (in S2).

Step Two had, therefore, 3 (three) phases: recruitment, empirical study and empirical data analysis. In the empirical study (of each study), five different participants (P1, P2, P3, P4 and P5) were briefly introduced to the specific website and to the concept of intercultural contact (with examples and illustrations). Then, participants listened to an explanation of the evaluation activity they should perform. There were seven scenarios for inspection, each involving one or more tasks. At the end, participants described and classify detected intercultural encounters enabled by the interaction, with their own words. After completing the evaluation activity, during the post-test interview, participants reported verbally on what they had just done and experienced. This stage aimed at collecting evidence of their perceptions about how the interaction scenarios promoted intercultural encounters (or not).

Empirical data analysis was carried out in two stages using discourse analysis techniques [13], a systematic exploration aiming to find out major meaning categories in discourse with intra-participant and inter-participant analysis. Firstly, we looked for evidence of each participant's usage and signification of intercultural encounters during the evaluation activity and post-test interviews. In this stage, we investigated how participants perceived intercultural encounters according to Peirce typology of signs and what perceptions they expressed with regard to such encounters.

---

[1] http://www.englishtown.com.br.

[2] http://www.wikipedia.com.

We conduct a research to see, thus, which category of sign (firstness, secondeness, thirdness) the representations (interfaces signs to promote intercultural encounter) have evoked to users. For that to happen we drawn on the process of signification in an interaction context scenario.

Synthesis of Results From Study One (with Englishtown). Results from the empirical data in Study One pointed at a main category of meanings: specific interactive resources promoted particular contacts with foreign culture. For lack of space, we selected only some pieces of evidence to illustrate the kind of qualitative data we used.

Evidence from participants show how they could be closer from the other culture. P1, for instance, observed that they can see how natives from other culture (American) really speak from videos. P4, also commented about the opportunity to have contact with native's accent.

> *P4: "The video is better because you see the situation, I mean, it gives tips about how you can behave. One's gets nervous like me (laughs), shy and became confused there. It shows the one's tension, which is something that one can not reveal in an interview. [...] In this video, it is simulating an interview situation. [...] Then you get the accent."*

By using pictures, in a learning situation, the ET website shows interesting places to take an English course abroad. Excerpts from P1, P2 e P3, for instance, showed us that this type of interface element attracted attention and sparked the curiosity of them.

> *P1: "It [the website] wants to sharpen your curiosity in cultural life of the city and not in the English itself. It calls your attention to their culture to create curiosity."*

> *P2: "So, this is a dynamic way. He puts a text, a very short content about what is better and the advantages of studying in that city. So, it is a very dynamic to give you that information and to motivate you. And it repeats [the cities]. So, if you move quickly, you can come back and see again. I found it interesting..."*

Participants also highlighted the potential of some interface elements. P2, for instance, said that the quiz give the opportunity to going deeper into other culture. P3 identified in lessons (using video) many possibilities to be in touch with foreign issues (subtitled texts, accent, and figures). P5, in turn, said that the articles are good for students that do not speak English well.

> P2: *"[About the quiz 'Your English is good enough to get around in London'] It put very specific things there, slangs. So you can go deeper into their culture."*

Additional evidences, showed that the interface kept participants not so close to others cultures, but mediated the contact.

> *P1: "So funny! [...] It [the website] is explaining the meaning of each situation. '-' The meaning of this expression. Is going to be different if you translate literally. You have to use the expression from that place."*

> *P3: "It explains exactly what is the meaning (which is an expression when you get surprised by something), he explains what it is (without translating)."*

In conclusion, Study One showed that firstness signs helped users to get closer to the other culture and thirdness signs mediated the approximation. The quizzes and videos, for instance, promoted an intercultural experience. Participants verbalized that they could be closer with other culture by having contact with translations, accent and other specificities. The articles and tips, in turn, improved their cultural awareness, because they perceived the opportunities to learn more by having contact with foreign material with cultural mediation.

Synthesis of Results From Study Two (with Wikipedia). Results from Study Two also showed us how participants perceived traces of others cultures, semiotically. For the lack of space, we selected excerpts from participant's discourse which compose the following category of meaning: different signs evoked different reactions and perceptions.

The P1 and P3 perceived the other culture when they saw a table with countries, which the official language is Portuguese. The website also shows a map that reinforces this contrast.

> P1: *"The table gives you the opportunity to make a comparison between Brazil, which is my country, and the other countries that speak the same language. [...] This contrast is always very interesting. [...] Even here, for example, on the map you can see the contrast regarding the size. You see the size of Brazil and the size of the other countries [who speak Portuguese as the official language]*".

In other situation, P1, P2, P4 and P5 realized that some links were indexes to learn more about the other culture.

> *P1: "You became interested in Poland cooking? Great! You have also other different cuisines in the same continent [Europe]. If you want to check them, you have a link here that allows you take a look at there. So he's always encouraging you to take a look, experience the culture of another country or another region*".

> *P5: "He [the site] expands the possibilities of knowledge from this small cultural issue (that is the food). So, if you want to know how is the food in Northern Ireland, Romania, the links enables you..[to the cuisine of these countries]*".

The sounds also called attention of participants to some details from other culture. P1 and P2 said that the sound allow them to go deep into other culture. P3, P4 and P5 realized that it is a good strategy to put them closer to foreign cultures.

> P3: *"I think that when you listen the sound you are you coming closer to this cultural aspect. One thing is to describe something, but there is no way to describe the sound of the berimbau"*.

Some participants S2.P4 and P5 revealed their sensation when in touch with an article from a very different culture.

> P4: "*He put me in a specific language, which I do not know which one is. Yeah, I 'm a little lost, but I would guess that here [in the top left], for example, was the amount of articles that it has [in that language*]".

> P5: "*I suppose, strongly, that it is Poland [this Wikipedia page] and then it makes me feel illiterate, that is the feeling I have. I look and this is not telling me anything. I imagine they have relevant information of Polish culture here, historic landmarks, people who were important to that country or events that were important.*"

The Study Two showed us that different signs (tables, links, images, sounds, links, and language) promoted different intercultural contacts to users. Moreover, the participants discourse showed how they promoted different levels of intercultural contact.

3.3 Triangulation

The triangulation stage aims at validating our qualitative analysis [3, 7], by looking for consistencies and inconsistencies among our findings From Step Two (Empirical Studies) and Step One (Exploration of CVM and Pierce's Typology of Signs). After comparing and contrasting both results, we found evidence that interactive discourse promoted different levels of intercultural encounters due to the type of sign used by designer.

Discourse excerpts from participants showed us that iconic representations (which evokes the firstness of their referents) such as sounds, images and so on promoted an intercultural experience to participants. When P5 told us that he was lost when interacting with Polish material, is an example of *Foreigner without translator metaphor*.

Indexes representations (which evokes the secondness of their referents) such as links lead participants to anticipate possibilities to learn more about a foreign culture. Finally, symbolic representations (which evokes the thirdness of their referents) strongly mediated the contact with foreign elements by giving explanations, comparisons to the users.

In conclusion, our findings point at congruencies among the user's perceptions at interaction time and our categorization of cultural diversity perception (see Table 1).

4 Conclusions

Given the multifaceted nature (beliefs, values, ethnicity, regional and so on) of HCI, this paper presents a characterization of possible *indirect intercultural encounters* that may take place in HCI by using two related approaches: Peirce's type of signs and CVM, a conceptual tool of Semiotic Engineering [4, 15].

This research worked on the effects the elaboration and protocol of cultural components (signs, in Semiotic terms) in the interactive discourse may promote on users' perception. This research demonstrated the causal relation between the semiotic engineering with icons, indexes and symbols and the potential consequences of them to the users' levels of perception and knowledge about cultural diversity.

Others HCI researches have used Peirce's Semiotic approach. Mihai Nadin, for instance, applied that paradigm to interface design in the late 1980s with a fundamental conclusion for interface design as such: 'since the technology upon and for which we build interface changes very rapidly, pan-logical semiotic principles, in their breadth and depth, provide a foundation for improved interface design [22]. Joost and Hemmert, in Design, also investigated Tangible User Interfaces in light iconic, indexical and symbolic representations [23].

In conclusion, this work shows that semiotic engineering of cross-cultural systems, i.e., the elaboration of an interactive discourse that communicates opportunities for intercultural encounters, may be viewed as a matter of promoting cultural unawareness,

awareness or experience. The current Semiotic Engineering ontology considers (so far) three classes of signs in the designer's deputy's interaction discourse: static, dynamic, metalinguistic [18]. With this view we are opening a theoretical implication of thinking in classes of cultural signs in terms of the promotion of cultural unawareness, awareness or experience. This allow us to characterize HCI more precisely and deeply, illuminating subtle issues in cross-cultural HCI design research.

In the near future, we will be working on the improvement of CVM scaffolds in order to improve this epistemic tool usability and explore the categories proposed in this work in design studies.

Acknowledgement. The authors would like to thank all participants who participated in empirical studies and contributed to the research reported in this paper. Additionally, the authors thank CNPq and FAPERJ for financial support received for this research.

References

1. Barber, W., Badre, A.: Culturability: the merging of culture and usability. In: Proceedings of the 4th Conference on Human Factors and the Web, pp. 1–14 (1998)
2. Clemmensen, T., Roese, K.: An overview of a decade of journal publications about Culture and Human - Computer Interaction (HCI)- Department of Informatics Howitzvej DK. Working Paper nr. 03-2009. (2009). http://openarchive.cbs.dk/bitstream/handle/10398/7948/WP_2009_003.pdf
3. Creswell, J.W.: Qualitative Inquiry and Research Method: Choosing Among Five Approaches. Sage, Thousand Oaks (2007)
4. de Souza, C.S.: The Semiotic Engineering of Human-Computer Interaction. The MIT Press, Cambridge (2005)
5. de Souza, C.S., Leitão, C.F.: Semiotic engineering methods for scientific research in HCI. In: Synthesis Lectures on Human-Centered Informatics, vol. 2, no. 1, pp. 1–122. Morgan & Claypool, Princeton (2009)
6. del Gado, E.M., Nielsen, J. (eds.): International User Interfaces. Wiley, New York (1996)
7. Denzin, N.K., Lincoln, Y.S.: The landscape of qualitative research. Sage, Thousand Oaks (2008)
8. Eco, U.: A Theory of Semiotics. Indiana University Press, Bloomington (1976)
9. Ferreira, C.M.D., de Castro Salgado, L.C., de Souza, C.S.: A vocabulary to access users' cultural perspectives in human-computer interaction. In: Kotzé, P., Marsden, G., Lindgaard, G., Wesson, J., Winckler, M. (eds.) INTERACT 2013, Part IV. LNCS, vol. 8120, pp. 314–322. Springer, Heidelberg (2013)
10. Gasparini, I., Pimenta, M.S., De Oliveira, J.P.M.: Vive la difference!: a survey of cultural-aware issues in HCI. In: Proceedings of the 10th Brazilian Symposium on on Human Factors in Computing Systems and the 5th Latin American Conference on Human-Computer Interaction. Brazilian Computer Society, pp. 13–22 (2011)
11. Lindgaard, G., Dudek, C., Chan, G.: Cultural congruence and rating scale biases in homepages. In: Kotzé, P., Marsden, G., Lindgaard, G., Wesson, J., Winckler, M. (eds.) INTERACT 2013, Part IV. LNCS, vol. 8120, pp. 531–538. Springer, Heidelberg (2013)
12. Marcus, A.: Global and intercultural user-interface design. In: Jacko, J., Sears, A. (eds.) The Human-Computer Interaction Handbook, pp. 441–463. Lawrence Erlbaum Associates, Mahwah (2002)

13. Nicolaci-da-Costa, A.M., Leitão, C.F., Romão-Dias, D.: Gerando conhecimento sobre homens, mulheres e crianças que usam computadores: algumas contribuições da psicologia clínica. In: IV Workshop sobre Fatores Humanos em Sistemas Computacionais, IHC 2001, pp. 120–131. Anais SBC, Florianópolis (2001)
14. Oyugi, C., Dunckley, L., Smith, A.: Evaluation methods and cultural differences: studies across three continents. In: Proceedings of the 5th Nordic Conference on Human-Computer Interaction: Building Bridges, pp. 318–325. ACM (2008)
15. Salgado, L.C.C., de Souza, C.S., Leitão, C.F.: A Journey Through Cultures: Metaphors for Guiding the Design of Cross-Cultural Interactive Systems. Springer, London (2012)
16. Salgado, L.C.C., de Souza, C.S., Leitão, C.F.: On the epistemic nature of cultural viewpoint metaphors. In: Proceedings of the 10th Brazilian Symposium on Human Factors in Computing Systems and the 5th Latin American Conference on Human-Computer Interaction, pp. 23–32. Brazilian Computer Society, Porto Alegre (2011)
17. Winschiers, H.: The challenges of participatory design in a intercultural context: designing for usability in namibia. In: PDC, pp. 73–76 (2006)
18. Peirce, C.S.: The Collected Papers of C.S. Peirce, vol. 1–6, Hartshorne, C., Weiss, P. (eds.) vol. 7–8, Burks, A.W. (ed.). Harvard, Cambridge, 1931–1958
19. Peirce, C.S.: The essential peirce: selected philosophical writings. In: Houser, N., Kloesel, C.J.W. (eds.) vols. I, II. Indiana University Press, Bloomington, 1992–1998
20. Santaella, L.: Teoria Geral dos Signos – Semiose e Autogeração. São Paulo, Ática (2000)
21. Vatrapu, R.: Explaining culture: an outline of a theory of socio-technical interactions. In: Proceedings of the 3rd ACM International Conference on Intercultural Collaboration, Copenhagen, Denmark (2010)
22. Nadin, M.: Interfaces design and evaluation*semiotic implications. In: Hartson, H.R., Hix, D. (eds.) Advances in Human-Computer Interaction, vol. 2, pp. 45–100. Ablex Publishing, Norwood (1988)
23. Joost, G., Hemmert, F.: In touch with representation: iconic, indexical and symbolic signification in tangible user interfaces. In: Design Research Society Conference 2010, 7 July 2010 (2010)

Do You Trust One's Gaze? Commonalities and Differences in Gaze-Cueing Effect Between American and Japanese

Saki Takao[1(✉)], Atsunori Ariga[1], and Yusuke Yamani[2]

[1] Department of Psychology, Rissho University, Tokyo, Japan
s08013477615@gmail.com, atsu.ariga@gmail.com

[2] Department of Psychology, Old Dominion University, Norfolk, VA, USA
yyamani@odu.edu

Abstract. Direction of others' gaze can guide one's attentional orientation, an effect called the gaze-cueing effect. The present study examined relationships between the gaze-cueing effect and general trust (i.e., a cognitive bias in benevolence of human nature) across participants in the United States and Japan. American participants voluntarily followed the non-predictive cueing gaze irrespective of their general trust, while Japanese participants voluntarily ignored the gaze in response to the levels of their general trust. These results were largely consistent with the previous suggestion that Westerners tend to focus on an object independent of its context while Asians tend to attend the context and implies that individuals' general trust levels may modulate early-stage visual processing such as detecting a visual object.

Keywords: Gaze cueing effect · General trust · Visual attention · Cultural difference

1 Introduction

A basketball player can pass the ball to another player without directly looking at the player (so-called "no-look pass"), to trick opponent players. This example shows one aspect of human visual processing in the context of interpersonal nonverbal communications. More specifically, the visual system serves to modulate attentional orientation in response to others' social cues, i.e. socially relevant stimuli, such as pointing gesture, eye-gaze direction, head orientation, or body orientation [1–7].

Previous research examined how the gaze perception influences observers' attentional orientation [2, 3]. Friesen and Kingstone [3] presented the face stimulus with gaze directed to the left or right side at the center of the display, and then a target dot on either the left or the right side of the face. They asked participants to press a button as soon as they detected the dot regardless of the direction of the cue. They found that when the target appeared at the cued direction, the reaction times (RTs) were shorter, as compared to when the target appeared at the opposite side from the gaze direction, an effect termed the gaze-cueing effect. The fact that this effect occurred even when a stimulus-onset asynchrony (SOA) between the gaze and target was short (around 100 ms) indicates that the visual system automatically and involuntarily directs attention to a side of the visual

P.-L.P. Rau (Ed.): CCD 2016, LNCS 9741, pp. 120–129, 2016.
DOI: 10.1007/978-3-319-40093-8_13

field that the gaze is directed to. In other words, the visual system automatically and involuntarily directs attention to the direction of the gaze, potentially demonstrating the reflexive nature of human sociality. Advancing this knowledge, Bayliss and Tipper [8] reported the evidence that the reliability of gaze direction (i.e., how often each face stimulus looked to the target location) can influence observers' personality judgments of each facial identity. Their experiment contained three types of faces; faces always directing their gaze to the target (predictive-valid faces), faces always averting their gaze from the target (predictive-invalid faces), and faces directing and averting their gaze to/from the target with equal proportions (non-predictive faces). After the experiment, participants evaluated predictive-valid faces as more trustworthy than predictive-invalid faces. Their results indicate that their perception of the gaze that contains behaviorally relevant information can modulate evaluation of trustworthiness.

Although the previous study has shown that gaze perception alters observers' personality judgment [8], it is unclear how the observer's personal tendency affects gaze perception or the following cognitive processing. The present study examined the relationship between the gaze-cueing effect and observers' general trust. General trust is a cognitive bias or a belief in benevolence of human nature in general, a construct known to differ across individuals in Japan and the United States [9]. Also, it is suggested that people who have higher general trust are more likely to be deceived by others [10]; in contrast, people who have lower general trust are less likely to be deceived by others. Therefore, investigating whether general trust predicts the magnitude of the gaze-cueing effect would provide us an important clue about at which stage of visual processing personal tendency, or general trust, is determined.

To achieve this goal, two independent approaches were adopted in this study. First, we manipulated gaze-target SOAs to investigate at least two types of attentional orientation [11, 12]. One is top-down, or goal-directed, selection of information, in which the visual system directs attention based on the observer's current goals or intentions. This type of attentional orientation is achieved endogenously or voluntarily, and thus requires a long gaze-target SOA (around 700 ms). The other is bottom-up, or stimulus-driven, selection, in which stimulus properties exogenously or involuntarily capture attention, irrespective of the observer's current goals or intentions. This type of attentional orientation is achieved with a short gaze-target SOA (around 100 ms). Therefore, the first goal of this study is, by manipulating the SOAs, to isolate the influence of general trust, if any, on visual processing that is involuntary or voluntary.

Second, this study further examined cultural effects on the relationship between the gaze cueing effect and general trust. Previous research indicates that Westerners tend to focus on a salient object independent of its context while Asians tend to attend the context [13]. More specifically, individuals engaging in North American cultures are more capable of ignoring contextual information and those engaging in Asian cultures are more capable of incorporating contextual information [14]. If so, American observers should process the cueing gaze analytically (or in a stimulus-driven manner), and thus the effect of general trust (or context) may not emerge whether visual processing is voluntary (with shorter SOAs) or involuntary (with longer SOAs). On the other hand, Japanese observers should process the cueing gaze holistically (or in a context-based manner), and thus the effect of general trust (or context) may emerge especially when visual processing is voluntary with longer SOAs.

2 Experiment 1: Effects of General Trust and SOAs on Attentional Orientation for Japanese Participants

2.1 Method

Subjects. Thirty Japanese adults (14 males, age range 18–23 years) were recruited from Rissho University, Japan. They reported normal or corrected-to-normal visual acuity. They were blind to the purpose of the study.

Stimuli. Stimuli mirrored those used in [3], and were drawn in black on the white background. A round face subtending 6.8° contained two eyes (two circles subtending 1.0°), one nose (one circle sub-tending 0.2°), and one mouth (one straight line of 2.2° in length). The two eyes were separated by a gap of 2.0° with each other, and were located 0.8° above the central horizontal axis. The nose was located at the center of the display and the mouth was located 1.3° below the nose. The black pupils (two filled-in circles subtending 0.5°) were used as cues, by just touching left or right in the eyes. A black dot subtending 0.6° were used as a target, which located 5.9° left or right from the fixation (a red dot).

Procedure. First, general trust was measured using the general trust questionnaire [9] that contains 6 items as below.

- Most people are basically honest.
- Most people are trustworthy.
- Most people are basically good and kind.
- Most people are trustful of others.
- I am trustful.
- Most people will respond in kind when they are trusted by others.

Participants answered these questions with 7-point Likert scale respectively (1 = strongly disagree, 7 = strongly agree). Next, participants were asked to perform a speeded detection task with gaze cueing that was task-irrelevant. After participants pressed the space key, the fixation point was presented at the center of the display for 500 ms (Fig. 1). Then, the face outline without black eyes was presented. After the duration of 900 ms, black pupils were added to the face outline and indicated the gaze direction, left or right. With an SOA of either 117 ms or 700 ms, the target dot was presented at the left or right side of the face. Participants reported the location of the dot as quickly and accurately as possible. Participants were informed in advance that gaze direction did not predict the target location (validity = 50 %). The catch trials were also intermixed, in which an open circle was presented on behalf of the face outline, and participants were required to withhold their responses. Participants performed 384 experimental trials in total (128 trials in each the valid, invalid, and catch condition).

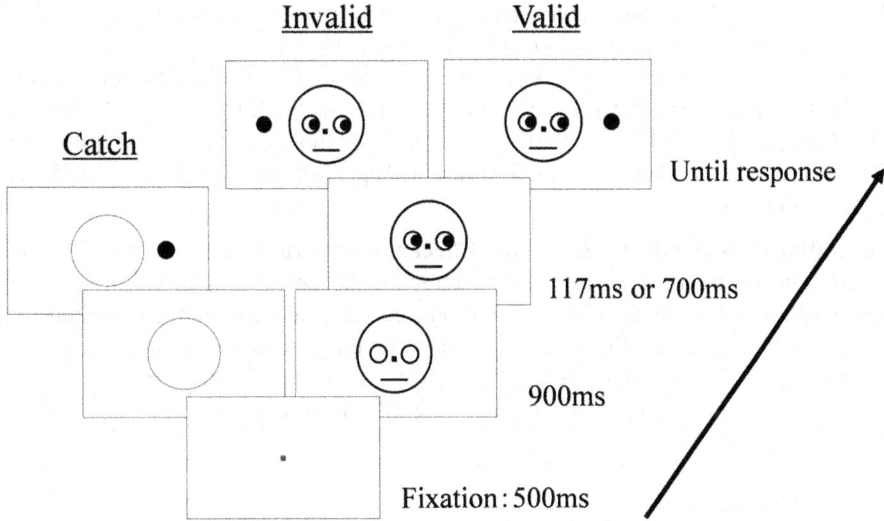

Fig. 1. Schematic illustration of each condition in Experiment 1 (Color figure online)

2.2 Results

The Gaze-Cueing Effect. For each participant and condition, the median RT was calculated. Figure 2 shows the median RTs averaged over participants. A within-subject 2 (condition: valid and invalid conditions) × 2 (SOA: 117 and 700 ms) analysis of variance

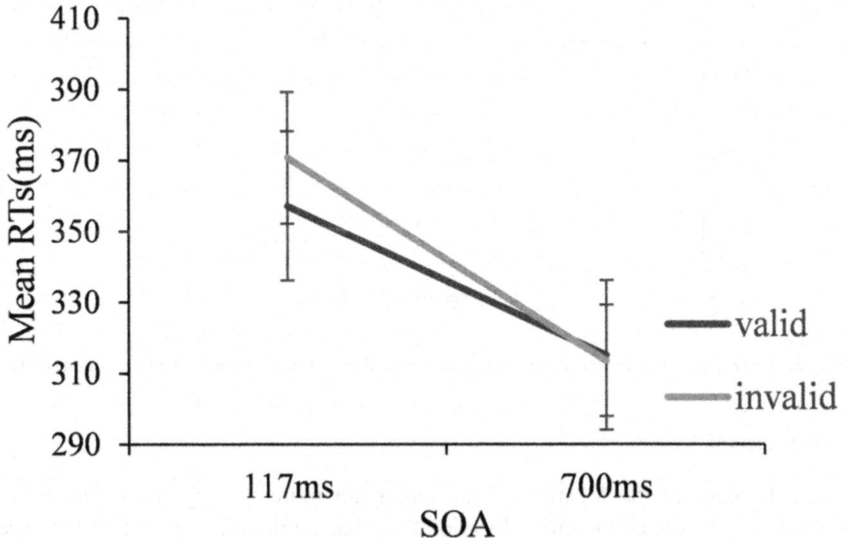

Fig. 2. Averaged median RTs as a function of SOAs and gaze validity in Experiment 1. Error bars indicate 95 % confidence intervals.

(ANOVA) with these data demonstrated the significant main effects of condition [$F(1,29) = 8.69, p < .01$] and of SOA ($F(1,29) = 160.46, p < .01$]. The interaction was significant [$F(1,29) = 23.17, p < .01$], which was elicited by the significantly shorter RTs in the valid versus invalid condition at the 117-ms SOA [357.12 ms (valid) vs. 370.72 ms (invalid); $F(1,29) = 35.02, p < .01$], and by no significant difference in the RTs between the conditions at the 700-ms SOA [315.08 ms (valid) vs. 313.55 ms (invalid), $F(1,29) < 1$].

Correlation Between the Gaze-Cueing Effect and General Trust. The magnitude of the gaze-cueing effect was calculated by subtracting the mean RT in the valid condition from the mean RT in the invalid condition. The correlations between the magnitude of the gaze-cueing effect and the general trust score (average score for the six items) were shown in Fig. 3, for each SOA respectively. There was no significant correlation for the 117-ms SOA [$r = .02$, *ns.*] but the marginally significant correlation for the 700-ms SOA [$r = .30, p < .10$].

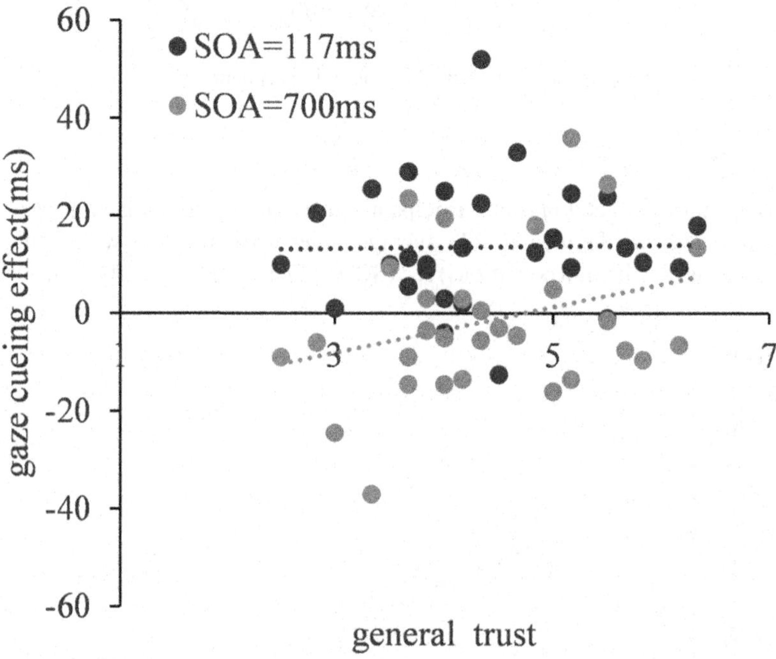

Fig. 3. Correlations between the general trust and the gaze-cueing effect in Experiment 1

2.3 Discussion

Participants reported the location of the target dot more quickly when the shortly preceding gaze predicted the target location than when it did not, replicating the gaze-cueing effect. On the other hand, the gaze cueing effect was not observed for the long SOA. This absence of the effect was likely because the participants who reported lower general trust would voluntarily and more successfully suppress perception of the gaze, which was consistent with our prediction derived from the suggestion that Asians tend to attend the context [13, 14]. That is, Japanese participants in Experiment 1 processed the cueing gaze holistically (or in a context-based manner), and thus the lower general trust helped participants with suppressing visual processing of the non-predictive gaze direction, in order not to be deceived.

Previous research indicates that Westerners process visual items more analytically than Asians. This hypothesis predicts that participants in the United States will demonstrate the gaze-cueing effect regardless of SOAs because they process the face stimulus more analytically. Furthermore, preceding studies on general trust and cultural differences indicate that general trust scores are higher among Americans than Japanese individuals [9]. Experiment 2 repeated Experiment 1 with American participants to examine these points.

3 Experiment 2: Effects of General Trust and SOAs on Attentional Orientation for American Participants

3.1 Method

Subjects. Thirty American adults (4 males, age range 18–22 years) were recruited from Old Dominion University, VA, U.S.A. They reported normal or corrected-to-normal visual acuity. They were naïve as to the purpose of the study.

Stimuli & Procedure. The stimuli and the procedure were identical to those used in Experiment 1.

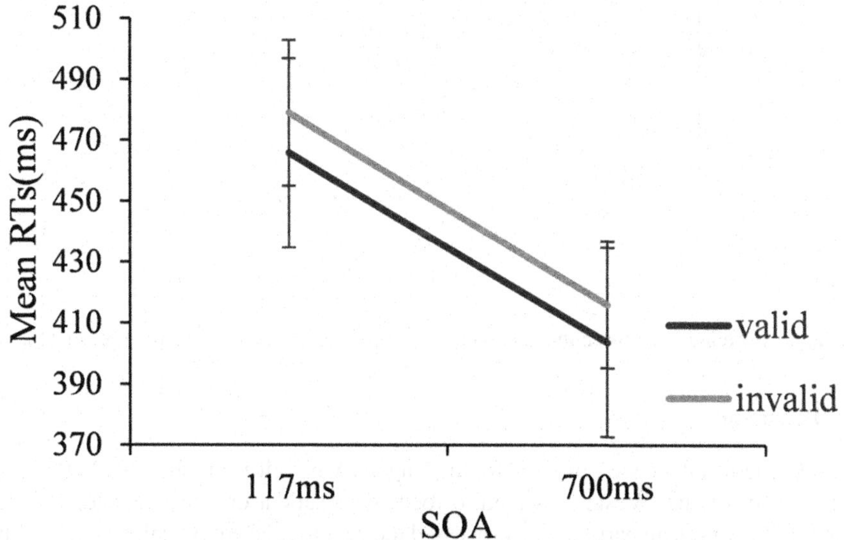

Fig. 4. Averaged median RTs as a function of SOAs and gaze validity in Experiment 2. Error bars indicate 95 % confidence intervals

3.2 Results

The Gaze-Cueing Effect. The analysis identical to that of Experiment 1 was performed. Figure 4 shows the median RTs averaged over participants. The data demonstrated the significant main effect of condition [$F(1,29) = 11.95, p < .01$], and also the significant main effect of SOA [$F(1,29) = 232.05, p < .01$]. The interaction between these factors was not significant [$F(1,29) < 1$]. That is, the magnitude of the gaze cueing effect did not differ between the 117-ms [465.85 ms (valid) vs. 478.92 ms (invalid)] and the 700-ms SOA conditions [403.72 ms (valid) vs. 416.03 ms (invalid)].

Correlation Between the Gaze-Cueing Effect and General Trust. The magnitude of the gaze-cueing effect and the general trust score were calculated as in Experiment 1. The correlations between the gaze-cueing effect and the general trust were shown in Fig. 5, for each SOA. A negative correlation was significant for the 117-ms SOA [$r = -.36, p < .05$], but no correlation for the 700-ms SOA [$r = .05$, *ns.*].

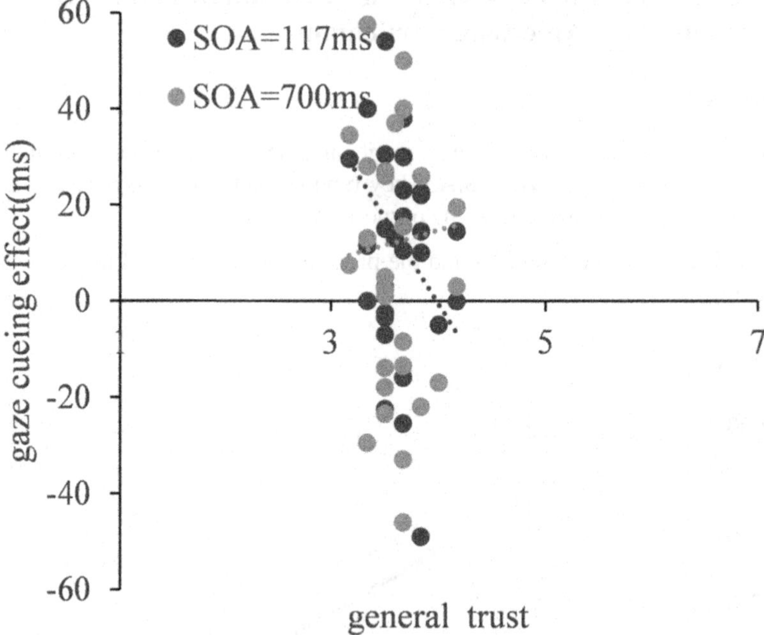

Fig. 5. Correlation between the general trust and the gaze-cueing effect in Experiment 2

3.3 Discussion

The gaze-cueing effect was observed for the long SOA as well as the short SOA. Because it was suggested that Westerners tend to focus on a salient object independent of its context [13], American participants processed the cueing gaze analytically (or in a stimulus-driven manner), thus endangering the gaze-cueing effect irrespective of SOAs. That is, American participants were unable to suppress perception of the gaze direction, even though they reported lower general trust.

Interestingly, the participants with lower general trust elicited larger cueing effects when attentional orientation was triggered involuntarily with the short SOA. This evidence presumably suggests that personal tendency, or general trust, would potentially underpin Westerners' analytic, or stimulus-driven, visual processing, and that the lower general trust might reflexively accelerate participants to make an (over)analytic strategy of visual processing. That said, further investigations are warranted as regards this issue.

4 General Discussion

The present study examined relationships between the gaze-cueing effect [2, 3] and observers' general trust [9], focusing on cultural influences between Japanese and American.

In Experiment 1, Japanese participants demonstrated the gaze-cueing effect for the short SOA irrespective of individual general trust, but no effect for the long SOA. As for the long SOA, the weak positive correlation between the effect and the general trust suggests that participants with lower general trust would voluntarily and more efficiently suppress the non-predictive gaze direction in a context-based manner. On the other hand, American participants in Experiment 2 demonstrated the gaze-cueing effect with both the short and long SOAs in a stimulus-driven manner. Furthermore, the effect was negatively correlated with the general trust when attentional orientation was triggered involuntarily with the short SOA; though no correlation was elicited for the long SOA. This evidence interestingly suggests that participants who reported lower general trust might reflexively accelerate to make an (over)analytic processing of visual information, which might underlie Westerners' analytic strategy of visual processing.

In general, the obtained results are well consistent with the suggestion that Westerners tend to focus on a salient object independent of its context while Asians tend to attend the context [13, 14]; American participants voluntarily followed another's gaze irrespective of a context (or general trust), and Japanese participants voluntarily suppressed perception of another's gaze in response to a context (or general trust). However, it is noteworthy that American participants potentially incorporated contextual background, or lower general trust, into reflexive attentional orientation. This new finding clearly shows the different strategies in visual processing between Japanese and American.

Additionally, recent studies have shown that the representations of conventional, communicative symbols, such as pointing arrows and words, can be overlearned, thus leading to the reflexive orienting of visual attention [15–18]. Because the gaze-cueing effect was correlated with the general trust differently between Japanese and American in this study, our evidence would support the concept that the gaze-cueing effect is also caused by overlearning, not by an innate tendency.

The current study has at least three caveats when interpreting the data. First, inconsistent with the previous works on general trust and cultural difference, American participants rated general trust scores lower than Japanese participants [$t(58) = 4.41, p < .001$].

At the two sites, due to the requirements of each institution, participants were recruited differently, which might have caused this unexpected difference on general trust scores. Second, the variance of the general trust scores for American participants appears smaller than the Japanese participants (0.99 vs. 0.53), which could have contributed to the significantly negative correlation between the gaze-cueing effect and general trust for the 117-ms SOA condition for American participants. Future research should ensure that the variances of the scores between the two sites are comparable. Finally, the grant mean RTs were substantially longer for American participants than Japanese participants [441.13 ms vs. 339.12 ms; $t(58) = 7.14, p < .01$] although the experimental settings such as timing of stimulus presentation and response collection were identical. Speculatively, American participants might have been more conservative in making a judgment especially when they voluntarily controlled their attention at the longer SOA. In fact, American participants did show the gaze cueing effect at the longer SOA, which could have contributed to this difference in the grand means. Nevertheless, future research could explore the source of the difference in the speed of visual judgment for individuals across different cultures.

Acknowledgements. This research was supported by Grant-in-Aid for challenging Exploratory Research (#26590075), the Japan Society for the Promotion of Science to AA. Correspondence should be addressed to S. Takao, Department of Psychology, Rissho University, 4-2-16 Osaki, Shinagawa-ku, Tokyo 141-8602, Japan (e-mail: s08013477615@gmail.com).

References

1. Ariga, A., Watanabe, K.: What is special about the index finger?: the index finger advantage in manipulating reflexive attentional shift. Jpn. Psychol. Res. **51**, 258–265 (2009)
2. Driver, J., Davis, G., Ricciardelli, P., Kidd, P., Maxwell, E., Baron-Cohen, S.: Gaze perception triggers reflexive visuospatial orienting. Visual Cogn. **6**, 509–540 (1999)
3. Friesen, C.K., Kingstone, A.: The eyes have it! Reflexive orienting is triggered by nonpredictive gaze. Psychon. Bull. Rev. **5**, 490–495 (1998)
4. Kingstone, A., Friesen, C.K., Gazzaniga, M.S.: Reflexive joint attention depends on lateralized cortical connections. Psychol. Sci. **11**, 159–166 (2000)
5. Langton, S.R.H., Bruce, V.: Reflexive visual orienting in response to the social attention of others. Visual Cogn. **6**, 541–567 (1999)
6. Langton, S.R.H., Bruce, V.: You must see the point: automatic processing of cue to the direction of social attention. J. Exp. Psychol. Hum. Percept. Perform. **26**, 747–757 (2000)
7. Langton, S.R.H., Watt, R.J., Bruce, V.: Do the eyes have it?: cues to the direction of social attention. Trends Cogn. Sci. **4**, 50–59 (2000)
8. Bayliss, A.P., Frischen, A., Fenske, M.J., Tipper, S.P.: Affective evaluations of objects are influenced by observed gaze direction and emotional expression. Cognition **104**, 644–653 (2007)
9. Yamagishi, T., Yamagishi, M.: Trust and commitment in the United States and Japan. Motiv. Emot. **18**, 129–166 (1994)
10. Garske, J.P.: Interpersonal trust and construct complexity for positively and negatively evaluated persons. Pers. Soc. Psychol. Bull. **1**, 616–619 (1975)
11. Posner, M.I., Cohen, Y.: Components of visual orienting. In: Bouma, H., Bouwhuis, D.G. (eds.) Attention and Performance X, pp. 55–66. Erlbaum, Hillside (1984)
12. Yantis, S.: Stimulus-driven attentional capture. Curr. Dir. Psychol. Sci. **2**, 156–161 (1993)

13. Nisbett, R.E., Miyamoto, Y.: The influence of culture: holistic versus analytic perception. Trends Cogn. Sci. **9**, 467–473 (2005)
14. Kitayama, S., Duffy, S., Kawamura, T., Larsen, J.T.: Perceiving an object and its context in different cultures: a cultural look at new look. Psychol. Sci. **14**, 201–206 (2003)
15. Friesen, C.K., Ristic, J., Kingstone, A.: Attentional effects of counter predictive gaze and arrow cues. J. Exp. Psychol. Hum. Percept. Perform. **30**, 319–329 (2004)
16. Hommel, B., Pratt, J., Colzato, L., Godijn, R.: Symbolic control of visual attention. Psychol. Sci. **12**, 360–365 (2001)
17. Ristic, J., Friesen, C.K., Kingstone, A.: Are eyes special?: it depends on how you look at it. Psychon. Bull. Rev. **9**, 507–513 (2002)
18. Tipples, J.: Eye gaze is not unique: automatic orienting in response to uninformative arrows. Psychon. Bull. Rev. **9**, 314–318 (2002)

Usability Comparison of Text CAPTCHAs Based on English and Chinese

Junnan Yu(✉), Xuna Ma, and Ting Han(✉)

School of Media and Design, Shanghai Jiao Tong University, Shanghai, China
{Junius,Hanting}@sjtu.edu.cn

Abstract. Text CAPTCHAs are widely deployed in nowadays for websites to defend malicious attacks. Although most text CAPTCHAs employ alphanumeric characters, there are emerging interests in designing CAPTCHAs based on regional languages. Here, we conducted experiments to compare the usability of CAPTCHAs based on English and Chinese. The results indicate that, comparing with CAPTCHAs that employ random English or Chinese characters, those based on frequently-used English or Chinese words provide the best usability in terms of efficiency, effectiveness and satisfactory for participants who are native Chinese speakers while familiar with English. CAPTCHAs based on random Chinese characters, however, is least user-friendly from a comprehensive perspective. The evaluation method and results presented here may shine a light for the design of CAPTCHAs that employ characters other than alphanumeric.

Keywords: CAPTCHAs · Usability · Human-computer interaction · Cross-culture design

1 Introduction

CAPTCHA (Completely Automated Public Turing test to tell Computers and Humans Apart), with its aim to distinguish human behavior from automatic scripts, is now widely used for online systems, particularly in registration and password verification scenes [1, 2]. For instance, Gmail employs it to filter out spammers; Facebook would benefit from preventing fake accounts and junk messages; PayPal utilizes it to enforce the financial security of its users and so on.

Principally, a well-designed CAPTCHA is expected to be easily recognized by humans while hard for bots to crack. Since its invention in 2002, CAPTCHAs in nowadays generally fall into three categories [3]: Text, Image and Voice. Given that Text form is the dominant one [4] and the focus of this paper, the word CAPTCHA mentioned afterwards represents only the text kind unless otherwise specified. Typically, a CAPTCHA includes several alphanumeric characters which are distorted and/or overlapped with each other, together with strikethrough lines and noise backgrounds [5, 6]. In this way, computer algorithms will have difficulty separating characters from one another and identifying them individually. With the increased complexity of those designs, it is more efficient to defend automatic scripts [5] but also at the cost of degraded

P.-L.P. Rau (Ed.): CCD 2016, LNCS 9741, pp. 130–138, 2016.
DOI: 10.1007/978-3-319-40093-8_14

usability. Therefore, it's essential to study the usability of text-based CAPTCHAs with a variety of design complexities.

For instance, Chellapilla et al. [7] investigated the design factors that could balance between usability and security. Elie Bursztein et al. [8] identified a set of features of alphanumeric CAPTCHAs and classified them in to three categories—visual features (character sets and counts, font sizes, etc.), anti-segmentation features (character overlaps, random dot sizes, etc.), and anti-recognition features (rotated character counts and degrees, etc.), then further investigated their effects on the usability of alphanumeric CAPTCHAs. Lee [9] compared the usability of alphanumeric CAPTCHAs for native Chinese speakers of different ages and revealed that young group had better performance than the old group. Belk et al. [10] evaluated the effects of cognitive styles on people's performance of CAPTCHAs. They pointed out that, when designing a user-friendly CAPTCHA, not only should the intrinsic factors like noise, mask line, etc. be taken into account, but also some variables on a user's side such as his/her cognitive style, culture background, etc.

However, all those studies on the design and usability of CAPTCHAs are predominantly focused on those employing alphanumeric Characters. Under the background of globalization, there is also an increasing concern about designing localized CAPTCHAs that employ the regional languages. Shirali-Shahreza [11] designed a type of text CAPTCHA that employed Persian/Arabic characters with improved security and usability. Yang [12] explored the application of Korean characters in text CAPTCHAs, their results showed that the Korean CAPTCHAs could be easily understood by native Korean speakers while difficult to be defeated by OCR (Optical Characters Recognition) programs. Banday [13] investigated the usability of CAPTCHAs based on Urdu, one of the regional languages used in India. The results indicated that, for native speakers of Urdu who had few or no familiarity with English, they solved Urdu CAPTCHAs significantly faster and more accurately than those based on English. Shortly, localized CAPTCHAs are generally believed to provide better usability because people are intuitively more comfortable with their native languages.

Meanwhile, CAPTCHA designs that employ Chinese characters are also emerging and have already been deployed by leading internet companies, such as Baidu.com and Renren.com, the counterparts of Google and Facebook in China, respectively. Paralleling with those deployments, Wang [14] proposed a Chinese CAPTCHA design that added a semi-transparent layer of Chinese characters as the background of the main layer and further experimentally proved that it was an effective means against OCR. Shen et al. [15] explored a multiscale corner structure model that was capable of hacking Chinese CAPTCHAs, which was insightful to improve the security of Chinese CAPTCHAs. Studies of Chinese CAPTCHAs are mainly about their mechanism [16–18], the usability of such localized CAPTCHAs, however, has hardly been explored, particularly, its difference with respect to those based on English characters.

Here, we investigated and compared the usability of CAPTCHAs based on English and Chinese for Chinese users. This study focuses on the following questions: Would the subjects have better performance when interacting with CAPTCHAs that use their native language? What are the subjects' perceptions about those localized designs?

2 Method

2.1 Participants

Thirty participants (13 males and 17 females), who are native speakers of Chinese with English as a familiar second language, were recruited for current studies. Their average age was 21.6 with a standard deviation of 1.3. All participant were students from Shanghai Jiao Tong University, 9 of them were undergraduate students and the remaining were graduate students. All participants had passed the College English Test Band 6, a language proficiency test held by the Ministry of Education of China. Therefore, they were all familiar with the English words appeared in current experiments. In addition, each participant was an experienced computer user who spent at least 2 h per week on word processing with keyboard and mouse. During online activities, all subjects had encountered English CAPTCHAs, and 29 of them had experienced Chinese CAPTCHAs. None of them had trouble reading on the screen or operating the input devices of computer.

2.2 Apparatus

The experiments were conducted in a lab environment. All participants were instructed to solve CAPTCHAs on a same setup, which included a 20-inch liquid crystal display with a resolution of 1440 * 900, a computer running Windows 8.1 system, a set of regular QWERTY keyboard and mouse as the input devices. The input software for Chinese characters was Microsoft Pinyin, which was daily-used input method for all participants and also the pre-installed input method of Windows 8.1. The tilt angle, height and distance of the display and chair were adjusted by participants to comfort themselves. The CAPTCHAs were generated on a remote server and loaded in the form of a webpage to the local browser, which was Google Chrome in this study. After the CAPTCHA test, each participant was also required to finish an online questionnaire and interviewed to learn their subjective opinions regarding those CAPTCHA designs.

2.3 Tasks

All participants were required to finish three consecutive tasks: Firstly, each participant was required to get familiar with the experimental apparatuses through solving five CAPTCHAs prepared for testing purpose. After that, four types of CAPTCHAs were presented for participants to solve one by one and each type of design included 12 randomly generated CAPTCHAs. Finally, participants were asked to finish an online questionnaire and interviewed to learn their subjective perceptions about the CAPTCHA designs in the experiments.

2.4 Study Design

To compare the usability of English and Chinese CAPTCHAs for Chinese users, four types of CAPTCHAs, which were based on Random English Characters (REC),

Frequent English Words (FEW), Random Chinese Characters (RCC) and Frequent Chinese Words (FCW) and illustrated in Fig. 1, respectively. REC and FEW designs utilized English characters RCC and FCW employed Chinese characters. For each language, the characters were presented as either random characters (REC, RCC) or words (FEW, FCW) that are frequently used in daily life. All other design factors were kept the same. For instance, each CAPTHCA was 230 pixel in width and 70 pixel in height. The font size was the same for all designs and the font family employed was Microsoft Yahei, which supports both English and Chinese Characters. The characters displayed on each CAPTCHA had a transparency of 25 % while were surrounded by 3 random lines and the same background noise levels. The distortion of each character was also kept the same by setting the same parameter. Furthermore, although each English CAPTCHA included 8 letters while the Chinese one included 3 or 4 characters, the average keystrokes [19] required for their inputs were the same under current experimental setting. Therefore, it maintained a similar workload to input different CAPTCHA types and was expected to provide a similar condition to evaluate the solving time of different designs.

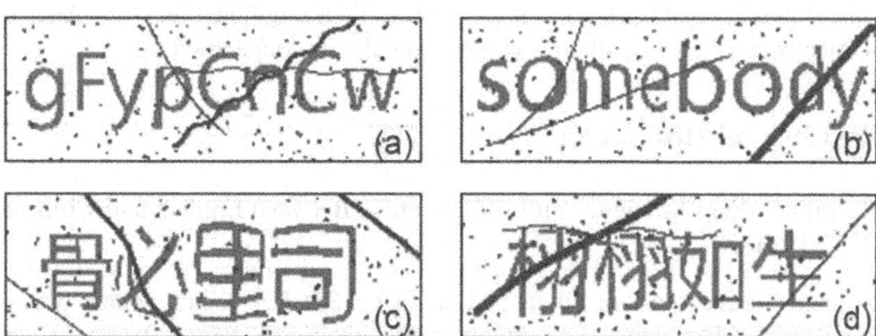

Fig. 1. Illustration of Text CAPTCHA styles explored in current study: (a) Random English Characters (REC); (b) Frequent English Word (FEW); (c) Random Chinese Characters (RCC); (d) Frequent Chinese Word (FCW). These CAPTCHAs were generated through a re-developing of the widely-used Securimage code [20].

During the experiment, only one CAPTCHA was presented on the web interface each time. Each participant was instructed to recognize, input and submit the characters shown on that CAPTCHA, which simulated the general CAPTCHA verification scene used by most websites in nowadays. After submitting his/her recognition result, a record will be generated on the remote server, indexing the solving time, the user input and whether the CAPTCHA was correctly input. Meanwhile, the webpage refreshed automatically and the participant was directed to solve the next CAPTCHA till the end of the task cycle, which included 48 CAPTCHAs in total, 12 for each kind. The collected data were further analyzed to obtain the average solving time and correction rate for each type of CAPTCHA design.

The usability of each CAPTCHA design was evaluated by three independent variables of usability [21]: effectiveness, efficiency and satisfaction. The effectiveness and efficiency were measured by the average solving time and correction rate for each type of CAPTCHA, respectively. The satisfaction was obtained through an online questionnaire and a face-to-face interview with each participant.

2.5 Procedure

The experiment was carried out in three stages—experiment preparation, testing and interview. During the preparation stage, we reset the testing apparatuses and described the purpose and tasks of the experiment to each participant, who was also informed that this test was anonymous and any data collected would be restricted for the use of current study only. After that, a participant was instructed to get familiar with the experiment apparatuses through solving five CAPTCHAs prepared for testing purpose. In the testing stage, a participant was left alone in the lab to solve four consecutive CAPTCHA sections and one online questionnaire without any disturbances. However, the experiment instructor would wait outside the lab in case the participant would need any tech support. For the final stage, participants were interviewed to learn their additional comments about the different CAPTCHA designs as well as their emotional feelings. After that, each subject was given a small gift to appreciate his/her cooperation.

3 Results and Discussion

3.1 Comparison of Efficiency and Effectiveness Between English and Chinese CAPTCHAs

The average solving time for all four kinds of CAPTCHA design, which based on Random English Characters (REC), Frequent English Words (FEW), Random Chinese Characters (RCC) or Frequent Chinese Words (FCW), were illustrated in Fig. 2.

The solving time of FEW (M = 4.68 s, SD = 1.4 s) is essentially the same as that of the FCW (M = 4.46 s, SD = 2.7 s). This same solving time can be explained by the fact that all those participants were familiar with both the English and Chinese words appeared in this study. Therefore, participants had a similar response to both kinds of CAPTCHA design. It is also indicated in Fig. 2 that, solving RCC designs (M = 9.38 s, SD = 4 s) takes the longest time, followed by REC designs (M = 7.75 s, SD = 2.3 s). The results of both RCC and REC are much longer than those of FEC and FCC results. The longer solving time for CAPTCHAs based on both random English and Chinese characters reveals that, it took more time for participants to recognize each characters individually and then type them into the test interface. The similar solving time for both FEC and FCC further shows that it took basically the same effort for participants to response to their native language and a familiar second language. In general, CAPTCHAs based on frequently-used English and Chinese words have better efficiency than those employ random characters while there are no significant difference for the solving time of frequent English and Chinese words.

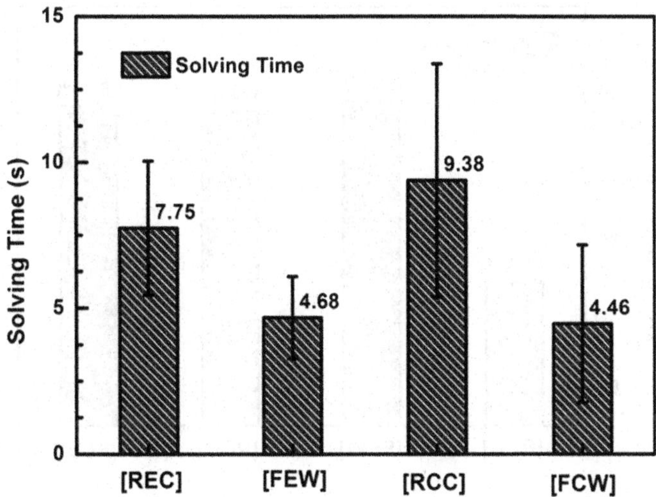

Fig. 2. Average solving time for all four kinds of CAPTCHA design: Random English Characters (REC), Frequent English Words (FEW), Random Chinese Characters (RCC), Frequent Chinese Words (FCW)

The effectiveness of those four CAPTCHA designs are represented by the percentage of CAPTCHAs that were correctly solved. As shown in Fig. 3, solving accuracy for FEW (99.22 %), RCC (97.66 %) and FCW (98.44 %) are almost the same, while REC (74.68 %) gave a significantly lower correction rate. The high correction rate for CAPTCHAs based on Chinese language and English words demonstrated that there is no intrinsic difference for participants to recognize those kinds of English and Chinese CAPTCHAs. To understand why the correction rate is much lower for CAPTCHAs based on REC, we further analyzed the user inputs for such kind of CAPTCHA. It turned out that, a majority of incorrect inputs were due to the confusion of similar English letters, such as "I" and "L". Therefore, we removed CAPTCHA inputs that contained any confusion letters and reanalyzed the correction rate of REC, which is illustrated in Fig. 4. It is clear that, without those confusion letters, the correction rate of CAPTCHAs based on REC has been improved by more than 10 %. Even without those confusion letters, however, the correction rate of REC is still at least 10 % lower than the other three designs. This is because the random lines and back ground noises, which were integrated for an improved security, sometimes would partially merge with the English characters, making them difficult for participants to identify correctly. While for English words, even though one or two letters of a word were masked, it was still possible for participants to recognize that word as a whole and correctly solve it. Therefore, the effect of random lines and background noise is more pronounced on REC design than FEW one. Furthermore, due to its complexity, even if most part of a Chinese character was blurred by the random line and background noise, participants had no difficultly recognizing it as a whole and therefore it maintained a high correction rate. Briefly, the correction rate is lowest for REC while quite good for FEW, RCC and FCW CAPTCHAs.

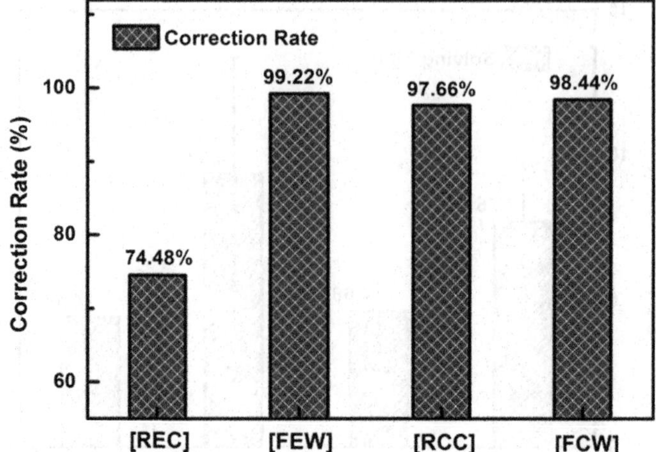

Fig. 3. Average correction rate for all four kinds of CAPTCHA design: Random English Characters (REC), Frequent English Words (FEW), Random Chinese Characters (RCC), Frequent Chinese Words (FCW)

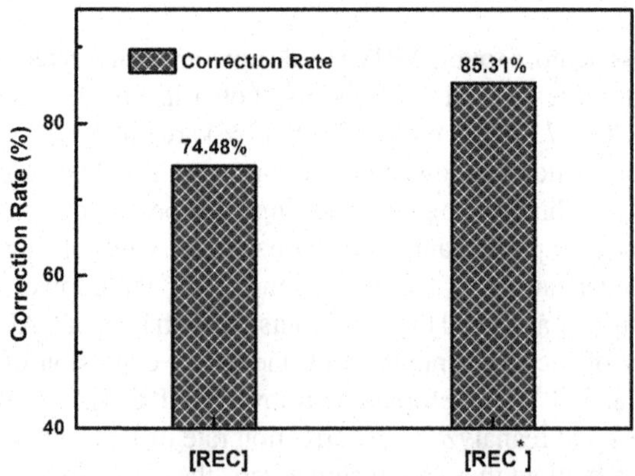

Fig. 4. Correction rate of CAPTCHAs based on Random English Characters. REC or REC* represents the correction rate with or without confusion letters appeared in a CAPTCHA, respectively.

3.2 Satisfactory Questionnaire and Interview

In addition to the efficiency and effectiveness studies, each participant was also required to finish a questionnaire and interviewed to acquire their subjective opinions toward those four types of CAPTCHA designs. The results reveal that more than 97.3 % of the participants preferred to solve CAPTCHAs based on frequently used words rather than random characters. They believed that those CAPTCHAs could be easily recognized with just a single glance. On the contrary, for CAPTCHAs based on random characters, they would have to recognize each character individually and therefore it took more efforts to solve them. When asked which of the four kinds of CAPTCHAs they prefer to solve the most, 56.07 % of the subjects were in favor of CAPTCHAs based on English words while the remaining 43.3 % were in favor of Chinese. The subjects who supported English words felt it was more natural and straightforward to type English words because they do not need to switch the input method between English and Chinese. For those who preferred CAPTCHAs based on Chinese words, they felt more comfortable with native language and the Pinyin input methods in nowadays are smart enough to make it fast to type Chinese. Although more than 78 % of the participants believed that CAPTCHAs based in random Chinese characters provided the most security, there were hardly any participant who was willing to encounter such type of CAPTCHAs.

4 Conclusion

The usability of CAPTCHAs based on English and Chinese were compared through a usability study conducted with participants who were familiar with both languages. Within the framework of similar design factors such as font size, font family, amount of distortion, random lines, background noise level and typing workload, it was found that, the effectiveness and efficiency of CAPTCHAs based on frequently-used English or Chinese words are similar while better than those based on random English or Chinese characters. CAPTCHAs based in random Chinese characters, however, turned out to provide the least overall usability. And the satisfactory questionnaire and interview showed that participants also preferred to encounter CAPTCHAs based on frequently-used words. In a word, comparing with English CAPTCHAs, Chinese also boasts the potential of serving a user-friendly CAPTCHA design. Therefore, the study presented here supports the application of Chinese CAPTCHAs to a large extent.

Acknowledgements. Junnan Yu gratefully thank Dr. Runze Li for helpful discussion. This work was supported by Shanghai Pujiang Program under Grant No. 13PJC072, Shanghai Philosophy and Social Science Program under Grant No. 2012BCK001, and Shanghai Jiao Tong University Interdisciplinary among Humanity, Social Science and Natural Science Fund under Grant No. 13JCY02.

References

1. von Ahn, L., Blum, M., Hopper, N., Langford, J.: CAPTCHA: using hard AI problems for security. In: Biham, E. (ed.) Advances in Cryptology — EUROCRYPT 2003, vol. 2656, pp. 294–311. Springer, Heidelberg (2003)
2. Von Ahn, L., Blum, M., Langford, J.: Telling humans and computers apart automatically. Commun. ACM **47**, 56–60 (2004)
3. Yan, J., Ahmad, A.S.E.: Usability of CAPTCHAs or usability issues in CAPTCHA design. In: Proceedings of the 4th Symposium on Usable Privacy and Security, pp. 44–52. ACM, Pittsburgh (2008)
4. Jeng, A.B., Tseng, C.-C., Tseng, D.-F., Wang, J.-C.: A study of CAPTCHA and its application to user authentication. In: Pan, J.-S., Chen, S.-M., Nguyen, N.T. (eds.) ICCCI 2010, Part II. LNCS, vol. 6422, pp. 433–440. Springer, Heidelberg (2010)

5. Bursztein, E., Martin, M., Mitchell, J.: Text-based CAPTCHA strengths and weaknesses. In: Proceedings of the 18th ACM Conference on Computer and Communications Security, pp. 125–138. ACM (2011)
6. Moradi, M., Keyvanpour, M.: CAPTCHA and its Alternatives: A Review. Secur. Commun. Netw. **8**(12), 2135–2156 (2014)
7. Chellapilla, K., Larson, K., Simard, P., Czerwinski, M.: Designing human friendly human interaction proofs (HIPs). In: Proceedings of the SIGCHI Conference on Human Factors in Computing Systems, pp. 711–720. ACM (2005)
8. Bursztein, E., Moscicki, A., Fabry, C., Bethard, S., Mitchell, J.C., Jurafsky, D.: Easy does it: more usable captchas. In: Proceedings of the 32nd Annual ACM Conference on Human Factors in Computing Systems, pp. 2637–2646. ACM (2014)
9. Lee, Y.-L., Hsu, C.-H.: Usability study of text-based CAPTCHAs. Displays **32**, 81–86 (2011)
10. Belk, M., Fidas, C., Germanakos, P., Samaras, G.: Do human cognitive differences in information processing affect preference and performance of CAPTCHA? Int. J. Hum Comput Stud. **84**, 1–18 (2015)
11. Shirali-Shahreza, M.H., Shirali-Shahreza, M.: Persian/Arabic baffletext CAPTCHA. J. UCS **12**, 1783–1796 (2006)
12. Yang, T.-C., Ince, I.F., Salman, Y.B.: A korean CAPTCHA study: defeating OCRs in a new CAPTCHA context by using korean syllables. Int. J. Contents **5**, 50–56 (2009)
13. Banday, M.T., Shah, N.A.: Challenges of CAPTCHA in the accessibility of Indian regional websites. In: Proceedings of the Fourth Annual ACM Bangalore Conference, pp. 1–4. ACM, Bangalore (2011)
14. Wang, T., Bøegh, J.: Multi-layer CAPTCHA based on Chinese character deformation. In: Yuan, Y., Wu, X., Lu, Y. (eds.) ISCTCS 2013. CCIS, vol. 426, pp. 205–211. Springer, Heidelberg (2014)
15. Shen, Y., Ji, R., Cao, D., Wang, M.: Hacking Chinese touclick CAPTCHA by multi-scale corner structure model with fast pattern matching. In: MM 2014 – Proceedings of the 2014 ACM Conference on Multimedia, pp. 853–856 (2014)
16. Chen, D.: Research of the Chinese CAPTCHA system based on AJAX. WSEAS Trans. Circ. Syst. **8**, 53–62 (2009)
17. Hai-kun, J., Wen-jie, D., Li-min, S.: Research on security model with Chinese CAPTCHA. Comput. Eng. Des. **6**, 023 (2006)
18. Xu, S., Lau, F., Cheung, W.K., Pan, Y.: Automatic generation of artistic Chinese calligraphy. Intell. Syst. IEEE **20**, 32–39 (2005)
19. MacKenzie, I.: KSPC (Keystrokes per Character) as a characteristic of text entry techniques. In: Paternó, F. (ed.) Mobile HCI 2002. LNCS, vol. 2411, p. 195. Springer, Heidelberg (2002)
20. Securimage. https://www.phpcaptcha.org/
21. Standard, I.: Ergonomic requirements for office work with visual display terminals (vdts)–part 11: guidance on usability. ISO standard 9241-11: 1998. International Organization for Standardization (1998)

Measuring Disengagement and Chaos in Multitasking Interaction with Smart Devices

Yubo Zhang, Pei-Luen Patrick Rau(✉), and Runting Zhong

Department of Industrial Engineering, Tsinghua University, Beijing 100084, China
rpl@mail.tsinghua.edu.cn

Abstract. In this study we developed an instrument to measure disengaged and chaotic experience of multitasking interaction with multiple smart devices. An online survey was conducted in a sample of 380 valid respondents. Via exploratory and confirmatory factor analysis in equal-size subsets of the collected sample, we constructed a model with five factors with an acceptable goodness-of-fit. The five factors were: Confusion (CF), Flow experience (FE), Complexity and disorientation (CD), Time distortion (TD), Situation awareness (SA). This instrument provides a method to gain insight on how people behave and feel in multitasking contexts and it is beneficial for designing and evaluating information infrastructure to support people's multitasking behaviors.

Keywords: Ubiquitous and mobile devices · Disengagement · Chaos · Multitasking · Instrument

1 Introduction

Multitasking interaction with multiple smart devices has become a prevalent phenomenon in the era of ubiquitous computing. The development of various smart devices makes it possible to sequentially or simultaneously interact with multiple smart devices. A survey by Hollywood Reporter showed that 79 % of the respondents always or sometimes visited Facebook while watching TV and 41 % tweeted about the show they were watching and three quarters said that they posted about TV while watching live shows [1]. American teenagers from 8 to 18 years old spent 29 % of the media use time using two or more media concurrently [2]. Besides for entertainment purposes, multitasking is prevalent in working contexts. It is shown that people's attention duration on the computer screen is only 1.25 min on average [3], meaning that people are easy to switch their attention away from their primary task and attend to interruptions.

Although multitasking interaction with multiple devices serves various needs of multitaskers [4, 5], evidence suggests that multitasking has negative impacts. Multitasking happens accompanied by attention switching between primary works and interruptions. As people resume working from irrelevant interruptions from a different device, they need to exert effort to reorient to the original context. This extra cognitive workload generated in this process hinders individuals' motivation, ability and opportunity to process the primary media content [6]. As people's limited attention resources are strained in this process, their performance is degraded [7]. In addition,

P.-L.P. Rau (Ed.): CCD 2016, LNCS 9741, pp. 139–150, 2016.
DOI: 10.1007/978-3-319-40093-8_15

multitasking causes high levels of stress [8], described as "a complex and often stressful media experience" [9].

Due to the potential harm to multitaskers, an understanding of how people's attention gets distracted and how the negative experience is produced is necessary for helping multitaskers better interact with multiple devices and manage multiple tasks. In previous studies concerning multitasking, physiological data collected by bio-sensors have been used to reflect multitaskers' stress levels [10] and experience sampling has been adopted to measure accompanied mood during the multitasking process [11, 12]. These shadowing methods are suitable to monitor the trend of stress or mood for a period of time in field studies. However, we are not aware of any psychological measurement, i.e. an instrument, to directly measure the negative experience in multitasking contexts. Therefore, this study aims at developing an instrument consisting of multiple key constructs to measure negative experience of multitasking interaction. The instrument provides a method to gain insight on how people behave and feel in multitasking contexts and it is beneficial for designing appropriate information infrastructure to support people's multitasking behaviors.

2 Literature Review

One study summarizes the negative experience of media multitasking from four dimensions: inefficiency, enslavement, disengagement and chaos [9]. Inefficiency, caused by shifting of attention from one stimulus to another, reflects on the deterioration of task performance, which can be defined and measured objectively in different contexts. Enslavement refers to addictive habits, consequences, feelings and corresponding attitudes of a multitasker from the long-term perspective. As we aimed at developing an instrument to measure the extemporaneous negative experience on the spot in a multitasking setting, we did not take the two dimensions into consideration in this study. The current study merely focused on disengagement and chaos. In the following section, we first review previous studies of disengagement and chaos.

2.1 Disengagement

In multitasking contexts, multiple stimuli from different devices compete for individuals' limited attention resources. Multitaskers become "disengaged and disconnected from attending to any particular media task" [9]. When people use computers and televisions concurrently, they attend to computers primarily compared to televisions, and they switch between such two media with a frequency they are not even aware of [13].

Disengagement is defined as "when participants made an internal decision to stop the activity, or when factors in the participants' external environment caused them to cease" [14]. Its opposite facet, engagement, is characterized by a series of attributes including challenge, positive affect, endurability, aesthetic and sensory appeal, attention, feedback, variety/novelty, interactivity, and perceived user control [14]. A similar concept with engagement, flow experience, is an "optimal experience" when an individual completely concentrates in an activity [15]. The flow experience is the combination of feeling fully challenged and skillful [16]. An operational decomposition of the flow experience in multitasking contexts includes sense of control, focused attention, curiosity, intrinsic interest and interactivity [17]. Another concept, which has delicate difference with flow experience, is cognitive absorption. It refers to total immersion into an activity, with deep enjoyment, a feeling of control, curiosity and not realizing the passing of time [18]. Engagement, flow experience and cognitive absorption all emphasize individuals' fully concentrated state, the opposite of which describes disengagement when processing content from multiple media.

2.2 Chaos

Chaos is defined as "an experience of disorder and upheaval" [9] accompanied by multitasking activities. Chaos is a complicated concept consisting of various connotations. The first one is negative emotions caused by interruptions. As found in previous studies, frequent interruptions cause increasing working speed and more stress, no matter in laboratory settings [8] or in real life [10]. Besides, frustration [8] and sense of guilty [9] are often generated in the process of multitasking.

The other connotation refers to the inability because of mental overload. Mental workload in multitasking contexts is higher than in single-task contexts because people not only need to process content on each device, but also exert extra efforts to manage and coordinate different tasks [19]. It can increase the inability to process content effectively in multitasking contexts and make the interactivity between the individual and multiple devices complicated [17]. For example, when people interact with multiple devices, they need to navigate tasks on each single device and switch between multiple devices. Hence, people may feel the sense of disorientation and process content less effectively. Besides, stimuli from multiple devices can cause interruptions to multitaskers, creating an "attentional residue" [20], which means the residual cognitive resources for a prior task when the individual has begun to work on the subsequent task. Thus, multitaskers have to expend extra cognitive effort to reorient back to the original task and the overall cognitive workload in the multitasking process is increased [21].

No matter from emotional perspective or from the cognitive perspective, all the studies consistently indicate that multitasking interaction with multiple devices creates is associated with higher levels of stress and lower levels of positive mood, which is concluded here as "chaos".

3 Method

Based on previous studies, we summarized variables regarding disengagement and chaos in multitasking contexts and adapted them into questions for composition of a questionnaire. The questionnaire was surveyed online for data collection and then for factor analysis so as to extract a multi-factor model to develop the instrument.

3.1 Questionnaire Design

All the questions were 5-point Likert scales. They were translated into Chinese before being included in the questionnaire. The translations and wordings were checked and modified by one human factors engineering PhD student and one research assistant on psychology. The ambiguity issues were cleared up as well. The questionnaire consisted of two parts. The first part was a general paragraph describing multitasking interaction with multiple smart devices followed by three concrete scenarios. It was emphasized that multitasking interaction in real life had a much broader spectrum beyond the three examples. So we reminded that the quantity and type of devices in multitasking contexts were not limited to the three examples. The second part contained 32 questions with 16 questions regarding disengagement and 16 regarding chaos. They were adapted from the existing literature with syntactical structure and context changes as the main modifications. For instance, an item measuring the flow experience is "I had a strong sense of what I wanted to do" [21]. In the questionnaire, we embodied it in the multitasking scenario as "I have a strong sense of what I want to do while engaging in such multitasking activities". The questions were adapted from studies by [9, 17, 18, 22, 23]. All the items can be found in Table 1, with "ENGX" or "CHAX" as the code. "X" stands for the sequence number of its appearance in the questionnaire, and "ENG" and "CHA" stand for disengagement and chaos respectively.

Six questions were added according to the results of an interview carried out with three college students in China respectively who have rich experience in multitasking. The interview was to make up for the literature's lack of focusing on multitasking scenarios. The interview lasted for 30 to 40 min. The participants were encouraged to describe their real multitasking experiences and their accompanying feelings during the process. The moderator encouraged them to elaborate their feelings related to multitasking contexts. The interview was transcribed and the extracted items were noted in Table 1 as well.

3.2 Data Collection

The online questionnaires were distributed via social media in China. RMB 5-worth of mobile phone credit was rewarded to each respondent. Ultimately we collected 437 responses, among which 380 copies were valid.

Among the valid copies, 205 of the respondents were males, while 175 were females. 15 respondents were not older than 20 years old, 322 respondents were between 21 and 30 years old, and 43 respondents were older than 30 years old. 20 respondents have an education level of high school or lower, 160 of them have a university/college degree, and 200 have a graduate or higher degree. 192 of the respondents were students.

All the valid responses were randomly divided into two groups with an equal size. The data in the two groups were for an exploratory factor analysis and a confirmatory factor analysis respectively. Before the factor analysis, the two groups were compared in terms of age, gender and education level. The results suggested no significant difference in age ($t = .347$, $p = .729$), gender ($\chi^2 = .011$, $p = .918$) and education level ($t = .124$, $p = .902$) between the two groups.

Table 1. Rotated component matrix of EFA about negative experience of multitasking interaction with multiple smart devices.

Abbreviation in questionnaire	Description	Factor loading					
		CF	FE	CP	TD	SA	DO
Confusion (CF)							
CHA11	I feel guilty when I engage in such multitasking activities	0.951					
CHA10	I feel like I am going around in circles when I navigate multiple devices	0.84					
CHA13	I feel disoriented when I engage in such multitasking activities	0.69					
CHA12	After navigating multiple tasks for a while I have no idea where to go next	0.671					
Flow experience (FE)							
ENG6	Engaging in such multitasking activities excites my curiosity		0.778				
ENG15	Compared to completing one task with one device, I feel that my control ability over devices and tasks is strengthened when I use multiple devices to deal with multiple tasks		0.736				
ENG11	Involving in such multitasking activities is intrinsically interesting		0.659				

(*Continued*)

Table 1. (*Continued*)

Abbreviation in questionnaire	Description	Factor loading					
		CF	FE	CP	TD	SA	DO
ENG7	When I engage in such multitasking activities, I am challenged and I feel I can meet the challenge		0.627				
ENG3	Engaging in such multitasking activities provides me with a lot of enjoyment		0.555				
Complexity (CP)							
CHA16	Navigating between devices is a problem			0.885			
CHA4	Navigating multiple tasks with multiple devices is not very intuitive			0.661			
CHA15	When I engage in such multitasking activities, the interruptions between tasks make me restless			0.609			
Time distortion (TD)							
ENG1	Time appears to go by very quickly when I engage in such multitasking activities				0.768		
ENG14	I lose track of time when I engage in such multitasking activities				0.689		

(*Continued*)

Table 1. (*Continued*)

Abbreviation in questionnaire	Description	Factor loading					
		CF	FE	CP	TD	SA	DO
Situation awareness (SA)							
ENG9	I have a strong sense of what I want to do while engaging in such multitasking activities					0.826	
ENG5	When engaging in such multitasking activities, I feel in control of what I am doing					0.597	
ENG4	I feel that engaging in such multitasking activities allows me to do more things, but limit my understanding of one specific thing					0.589	
Disorientation (DO)							
CHA1	I don't know how to get to my desired location on a certain device						0.829
CHA2	It is difficult to find the content on a certain device that I have previously viewed when I engage in such multitasking activities						0.828

Note: Items ENG14, ENG15, CHA15 were extracted from interview results.

4 Results

4.1 Exploratory Factor Analysis (EFA)

The EFA was conducted to find the structures of the factors with regard to negative experience in multitasking contexts. The results of the Kaiser–Mayer–Olkin (KMO) test and Bartlett's test of sphericity were .805 and $\chi^2 = 1278.57$ ($p < .001$), suggesting being suitable for factor analysis. In the factor extracting and screening phase, the following rules were carried out: extracting components with eigenvalues larger than 1 as principal component; deleting items with loadings smaller than .45 on all common factors; deleting factors containing only one item; making the whole model explicit and simple to explain [24–26]. All the procedures were conducted with SPSS v20.

Finally, 19 items were retained and the component matrix was obliquely rotated to acquire a meaningful explanation of the model. The 19 items composed of six factors and explained 66.63 % of the total variance. The six items and their corresponding items were listed in Table 1. They were named: Confusion (CF), Flow experience (FE), Complexity (CP), Time distortion (TD), Situation awareness (SA), Disorientation (DO).

4.2 Confirmatory Factor Analysis (CFA)

The CFA was conducted to test the model's goodness-of-fit. The CFA was conducted with SPSS Amos v22. The models were improved according to the modification indices provided by Amos and the professional meanings of each factor. Besides that, the correlation coefficients between the following factors were set zero as their correlation relations did not reach the significant level in the output of the full correlated model: (CF, FE), (SA, DO), (CP, SA), (FE, DO), (FE, CP), (DO, TD).

Goodness-of-fit index (GFI), adjusted goodness-of-fit index (AGFI), comparative fit index (CFI), Tacker-Lewis index (TLI) and root mean square error of approximation (RMSEA) were calculated. The results were summarized at the original model row in Table 2.

Table 2. Model's goodness-of-fit

Model	χ^2	*df*	GFI	AGFI	CFI	TLI	RMSEA
Original model	270.47	141	.87	.83	.90	.87	.07
Modified model	275.98	143	.86	.82	.92	.91	.06

Previous research suggests that a model with GFI greater than .90 and AGFI larger than .80 demonstrates an acceptable fit [27]. It has also been indicated that RMSEA value between .05 and .08 is acceptable. Another study has indicated that >.90, >.90 and <.06 are cutoff values for CFI, TLI and RMSEA, but the criteria for TLI and RMSEA tend to overreject true population models when the sample size is small [28]. The model satisfied the criteria of the AGFI, the CFI and the RMSEA, but not the GFI and the TLI.

4.3 Reliability and Validity

The Cronbach's alpha coefficients of the six factors were .852 (CF), .835 (FE), .589 (CP), .593 (TD), .546 (SA) and .601 (DO). For constructing a theoretically reliable instrument, .7 is the cutoff threshold for the Cronbach's alpha coefficients. The results showed that there were four factors in the model failing to meet the requirement.

The discriminant validity was tested on the original model. Any two factors in the model were combined into one factor, forming a restricted model. Then the chi-square value differences between each restricted model and the original model were compared. As shown in Table 3, the five-factor model combing CP and DO did not have a significant difference with the original six-factor model in the chi-square value. That indicated a direction of model improvement.

4.4 Model Improvement

Inspired by the results of the discriminant validity, we merged CP and DO, forming a new dimension-reduced model. The Cronbach's alpha coefficient of the new factor was .679, which showed improved internal consistency.

The goodness-of-fit is shown at the modified model row in Table 2. It can be seen that the modified model showed improved goodness-of-fit compared to the original model.

Table 3. Chi-square value changes between different models

Models	χ^2	*df*	χ^2 Difference
Six-factor partially correlated model	270.47	141	N/A
CF_FE combined	627.24	143	356.77***
CF_CP combined	303.04	144	32.57***
CF_TD combined	337.29	145	66.82***
CF_SA combined	386.47	144	116.00***
CF_DO combined	292.61	143	22.14***
FE_CP combined	409.64	144	139.17***
FE_TD combined	319.84	145	49.37***
FE_SA combined	290.65	144	20.18***
FE_DO combined	328.76	143	58.29***
CP_TD combined	327.57	145	57.10***
CP_SA combined	382.89	144	112.42***
CP_DO combined	275.98	143	5.51
SA_DO combined	335.59	143	65.12***
SA_TD combined	336.49	145	66.02***
DO_TD combined	335.22	145	64.75***

Note: (1) ***$p < .001$; (2) The Chi-square value differences were calculated between each five-factor model and the six-factor partially correlated model.

5 Discussion

5.1 Explanation of Factor Connotations

Via the EFA and the CFA, we constructed a five-factor model measuring negative experience of multitasking interaction with multiple smart devices. The five factors include: Confusion (CF), Flow experience (FE), Complexity and disorientation (CD), Time distortion (TD), Situation awareness (SA).

'Confusion' describes the vacant and upheaval feelings in the engagement of multitasking. Due to the mutual interruptions of multiple tasks and unfocused attention, multitaskers tend to lack a clear goal and corresponding strategies and tactics. Thus, they suffer a divided dedication and feel guilty and frustrated during the involvement. The second factor, 'Flow experience', describes the extent to which multitaskers show interest, happiness and curiosity in the multiple tasks they are involved in. The third factor, 'Complexity and disorientation', is the sum of aforementioned Complexity and Disorientation. It contains items reflecting the task complexity in multitasking contexts, especially the disorientation brought by navigating between multiple devices. Multitaskers not only need to cope with navigation tasks within one device, but also need to manage the coordination between multiple devices. The fourth factor, 'Time distortion', describes the phenomenon of losing track of time in multitasking contexts. Time distortion is usually accompanied by flow experience and it happens on game players very frequently [29]. The last factor, 'Situation awareness', refers to the perception, understanding and control of what happens in a multitasking context. The five factors all describe the extemporaneous experience on the spot in a multitasking setting.

5.2 Usage of Instrument

This instrument can provide multitaskers with a useful tool to self-exam their states in multitasking contexts. It can benefit the design of smart device and information technology service provision. It can serve as a series of design guidelines for the design of products or services targeting at collaborative working with multiple devices. Besides, it can be used as an evaluation tool for corresponding products or services, especially for those products aiming at providing integrated functions across multiple platforms. Last, this instrument can be used to evaluate the effect of intervention on multitaskers to manage their distracting behaviors in a multitasking context.

5.3 Limitations and Future Work

The current sample size is not large enough and has a limited representativeness because of collecting data only via social media. We cannot arbitrarily regard social media users as multitaskers in real life. Besides, the indices adopted in this study do not reach the realistic standard for constructing a mature psychometric instrument. The items in each factor should be selected based on a more systematic and comprehensive literature summarization. More thorough calculations of various psychometric indices should be performed. Sampling in a broader range of population should be adopted in the future research.

6 Conclusion

In this study we developed an instrument to measure disengaged and chaotic experience of multitasking interaction with multiple smart devices. Via exploratory and confirmatory factor analysis, we constructed a model with five factors with an acceptable goodness-of-fit. The five factors were: Confusion (CF), Flow experience (FE), Complexity and disorientation (CD), Time distortion (TD), Situation awareness (SA). This instrument provides a method to gain insight on how people behave and feel in multitasking contexts and it is beneficial for designing and evaluating information infrastructure to support people's multitasking behaviors.

Acknowledgement. This study was funded by a National Natural Science Foundation China grant No. 71188001 and State Key Lab of Automobile Safety and Energy.

References

1. Godley: THR's social media poll: How facebook and twitter impact the entertainment industry (2012). Accessed http://www.hollywoodreporter.com/gallery/facebook-twitter-social-media-study-302273#3
2. Rideout, V.J., Foehr, U.G., Roberts, D.F.: Generation M2: Media in the Lives of 8-to 18-Year-Olds. Henry J. Kaiser Family Foundation, Menlo Park (2010)
3. Mark, G., Voida, S., Cardello, A.: "A pace not dictated by electrons": an empirical study of work without email. In: Proceedings of the 2012 ACM Annual Conference on Human Factors in Computing Systems - CHI 2012, p. 555 (2012). http://doi.org/10.1145/2207676.2207754
4. Jeong, S.-H., Fishbein, M.: Predictors of multitasking with media: media factors and audience factors. Media Psychol. **10**(3), 364–384 (2007)
5. Wang, Z., Tchernev, J.M.: The "myth" of media multitasking: reciprocal dynamics of media multitasking, personal needs, and gratifications. J. Commun. **62**(3), 493–513 (2012)
6. Ophir, E., Nass, C., Wagner, A.D.: Cognitive control in media multitaskers. Proc. Natl. Acad. Sci. **106**(37), 15583–15587 (2009)
7. Kahneman, D.: Attention and effort. Am. J. Psychol. **88** (1973). http://doi.org/10.2307/1421603
8. Mark, G., Gudith, D., Klocke, U.: The cost of interrupted work: more speed and stress. In: Proceedings of the SIGCHI Conference on Human Factors in Computing Systems, pp. 107–110. ACM (2008)
9. Bardhi, F., Rohm, A.J., Sultan, F.: Tuning in and tuning out: media multitasking among young consumers. J. Consum. Behav. **9**(4), 316–332 (2010)
10. Mark, G., Wang, Y., Niiya, M.: Stress and multitasking in everyday college life: an empirical study of online activity. In: Proceedings of the 32nd Annual ACM Conference on Human Factors in Computing Systems, pp. 41–50. ACM (2014)
11. Mark, G., Iqbal, S., Czerwinski, M., Johns, P.: Capturing the mood: facebook and face-to-face encounters in the workplace. In: Proceedings of CSCW 2014. ACM, Baltimore (2014a)
12. Mark, G., Iqbal, S.T., Czerwinski, M., Johns, P.: Bored mondays and focused afternoons: the rhythm of attention and online activity in the workplace. In: Proceedings of the SIGCHI Conference on Human Factors in Computing Systems. ACM, Toronto (2014b)

13. Brasel, S.A., Gips, J.: Media multitasking behavior: concurrent television and computer usage. Cyberpsychology Behav. Soc. Networking **14**(9), 527–534 (2011)
14. O'Brien, H.L., Toms, E.G.: What is user engagement? A conceptual framework for defining user engagement with technology. J. Am. Soc. Inform. Sci. Technol. **59**(6), 938–955 (2008)
15. Csikszentmihalyi, M.: Beyond Boredom and Anxiety. Josey-Bass, San Francisco (1975)
16. Csikszentmihalyi, M.: Flow: the psychology of optimal performance. In: Optimal Experience: Psychological Studies of Flow in Consciousness (1990)
17. Park, J.H.: Flow in multitasking: the effects of motivation, artifact, and task factors. University of Texas at Austin (2014)
18. Agarwal, R., Karahanna, E.: Time flies when you're having fun: cognitive absorption and beliefs about information technology usage. MIS Q. **24**(4), 665–694 (2000). http://doi.org/10.2307/3250951
19. Xie, B., Salvendy, G.: Review and reappraisal of modelling and predicting mental workload in single-and multi-task environments. Work Stress **14**(1), 74–99 (2000)
20. Leroy, S.: Why is it so hard to do my work? The challenge of attention residue when switching between work tasks. Organ. Behav. Hum. Decis. Process. **109**(2), 168–181 (2009). http://doi.org/10.1016/j.obhdp.2009.04.002
21. Dabbish, L., Mark, G., González, V.M.: Why do I keep interrupting myself?: environment, habit and self-interruption. In: Proceedings of the SIGCHI Conference on Human Factors in Computing Systems, pp. 3127–3130. ACM (2011)
22. Jackson, S.A., Eklund, R.C., Martin, A.J.: The Flow Manual. Mind Garden Inc., California (2010)
23. Ahuja, J.S., Webster, J.: Perceived disorientation: an examination of a new measure to assess web design effectiveness. Interact. Comput. **14**(1), 15–29 (2001)
24. Hair, J.F., Anderson, R.E., Tatham, R.L., Black, W.C.: Multivariate Data Analyses with Readings. Englewood Cliffs, New Jersey (1995)
25. Smith, B., Caputi, P., Rawstorne, P.: The development of a measure of subjective computer experience. Comput. Hum. Behav. **23**(1), 127–145 (2007)
26. Stiggelbout, A.M., Molewijk, A.C., Otten, W., Timmermans, D.R.M., Van Bockel, J.H., Kievit, J.: Ideals of patient autonomy in clinical decision making: a study on the development of a scale to assess patients' and physicians' views. J. Med. Ethics **30**(3), 268–274 (2004)
27. Lattin, J.M., Carroll, J.D., Green, P.E.: Analyzing Multivariate Data. Thomson Brooks/Cole, Pacific Grove (2003)
28. Hu, L., Bentler, P.M.: Cutoff criteria for fit indexes in covariance structure analysis: conventional criteria versus new alternatives. Struct. Equ. Model. Multi. J. **6**(1), 1–55 (1999)
29. Rau, P.-L.P., Peng, S.-Y., Yang, C.-C.: Time distortion for expert and novice online game players. CyberPsychology Behav. **9**(4), 396–403 (2006)

Cross-Cultural Product and Service Design

From "Illustration" to "Interpretation"—Using Concrete Elements to Represent Abstract Concepts in Spatial Design

Li-Yu Chen[1(✉)] and Ya-Juan Gao[2]

[1] Department of Interior Design, Chung Yuan Christian University, Taoyuan, Taiwan
chenly99@gmail.com

[2] Graduate School of Creative Industry Design, National Taiwan University of Arts, New Taipei, Taiwan
78343821@qq.com

Abstract. Spatial art and spatial design both requires the exploration of the formation and elements of space before creating a physical space by combining the elements. Then, perceptual space is formed after the incorporation of the designer's subjective concepts in order to gain the approval of participants or users. Creating a spatial design mode from concrete to abstract is an issue that should be researched to establish captivating and meaningful space. This study explores the illustration of spatial abstract concepts and abstract time metaphor of spatial representation from the formation of space, the definitions of physical space and perceptual space, and the temporal factors in spatial context, proposing a spatial design mode of concept-element-interpretation-design with different spatial designs.

Keywords: Metaphor · Spatial design · Interpretation · Design model

1 Introduction

The difference between art and design is that art allows for self-expression via mediums while design addresses stated needs and solves problems. Art is subjective to the eyes of the beholder while design is objective. However, in both spatial art and spatial design, the formation and elements of space should be explored first before creating a physical space by combining the elements. Then, perceptual space is formed after the incorporation of the designer's subjective concepts.

Space is formed from the relationship between forms. Space represents the location, direction, area, and distance of forms through the hollow part of a 3D structure. Therefore, space is not a part of design; it is created from the interaction of styling elements and design principles (Jiang et al. 2007).

Elements and composition define the existence of space. For example, the porosity of roofs and walls determines the composition of space, which can be enclosed, partitioned, or combined. The enclosure of space is determined by its elements and opening. These elements have a major impact on the perception of spatial style and orientation. To some degree, the partitioning and enclosing of space are different but with closely related features. Partitioning involves roofs, walls, and the floor and combination applies

P.-L.P. Rau (Ed.): CCD 2016, LNCS 9741, pp. 153–162, 2016.
DOI: 10.1007/978-3-319-40093-8_16

enclosing and partitioning interchangeably for richer spatial changes. The formation of physical space utilizes styling elements such as ceilings, walls, and the floor to express real-life dimensions and spatial functions.

Perceptual space is presented using size of forms, layering, color contrast, and material transformations to depict the distance, position, and lighting of space and express the imaginative spatial perception. Constructing physical space with concrete elements is simple, but using concrete elements to express abstract perceptual space requires developing conceptual creation into creative design.

Time is represented through space; therefore, time also requires space to be remembered. Time transports through changes in the land and colors. Space is the remains of time in the natural world and is human activity in humanity (Jian 2005). As people move in the environment, they become aware of the temporality of space, not simply by the vastness of space, but mainly by manifesting temporal and spatial changes through the perception of changes (Liu 2010).

According to French Marxist philosopher and sociologist Henri Lefebvre, there are three levels in the production of space: perceived space (spatial practice), conceived space (representations of space), and lived space (representational spaces). Perceived space is physical place, conceived space is mental place, and lived space is social place. Art and literature present representational spaces using imagination to rewrite space controlled by the objective world. Poets write poems by using their imagination through reality, which also results in the creation of metaphors. Artists create artworks by using their imagination in reality and their works of art are a metaphor of the artists' imagination.

The properties (character) and course of time (history) of space and social factors (people in motion) are correlated. How is the character of space shaped? Time (history) is an important factor. All things on earth need time to be created (Chen 2008).

As such, by using time factors as an inspiration for design creativity to explore the transformation of the significance of space caused by temporal changes, innovation and new ideas can be evoked, forming a close connection with the local environment.

2 Spatial Design: From Abstract to Concrete

Design activities are considered as a series of complex design related problem-solving processes (Goldschmidt 1997). In terms of its organization and presentation, design problems are passive in which designers provide an active response based on the design objective. Design problems are solved by searching and finding the solution. Jones (1992) asserted that a design process can be classified into data collection, idea generation and development, detailed designs, and project implementation. Archer (1984) proposed an operable design model where he divided the design area into three stages and six procedures while emphasizing the correlation and feedback behavior between each procedure. The three stages include analysis, creation, and evaluation and the six procedures include architectural planning, data collection, analysis, integration, development, and communication.

Form is a method in which design concepts are expressed by constructing. When an exterior form expresses an interior meaning, this certain form then becomes an element that represents the interior meaning.

Space refers to the perception of atmosphere created from architectural elements. The perception of atmosphere in space plays an important role in architectural design; it is the internal representation of an exterior form. By organizing and arranging architectural elements, spatial perception can conform to the conceptual perception and imagination (Hwang 2007).

Abstraction is a conceptual process in which general rules and concepts are derived. Therefore, abstract is not just a simplification of contour, but also includes the extraction of essence and meaning (Norman 1998). Symbols refer to the delivery of an abstract meaning through a certain meaningful agent, which is the symbol. However, a direct correlation is not always evident between the meaning and symbols; sometimes it is established by convention.

Visual message can be categorized into three functions: (1) Representation: exploring the things people see and identify in the environment and from past experiences (in particular, photos); (2) abstract: reducing certain visual elements and emphasizing direct, emotional, or original messages; (3) symbol: giving meaning. Therefore, a spatial abstract design model involves extracting styling elements from spatial concept, using symbols to interpret the meaning to complete the design process, as shown in the Fig. 1.

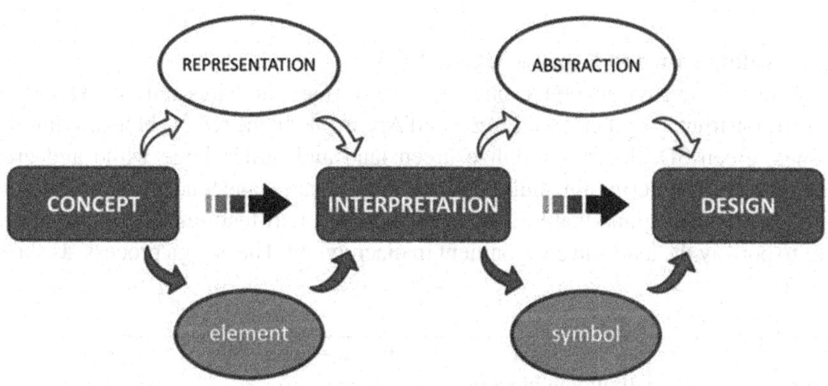

Fig. 1. Spatial design model from Representation to Abstraction

3 Interpreting Abstract Perceptions with Concrete Elements

Using concrete elements to interpret abstract perceptions include illustrations of abstract concepts and spatial metaphors of abstract concept of time. In terms of the former, illustrated abstract concepts can be expressed by scaling up or down to display the observer's location, using 2D to determine 3D space or spatial contour for conversion of meaning. Temporal dimensions are used to explore the historical meaning of space, using temporal factors in spatial context as materials for interpreting and creating new space.

3.1 Using Illustrations to Express Abstract Concepts in Space

Spatial illustrations are products of designers' thinking and spatial interpretation further enhances designers' creative thinking. Illustrations are tangible and visually comprehended by observers while interpretations are intangible and require observers to perceptually experience.

In order to express space and convey ideas, designers or artists utilize various perspectives to draw different views. Views are produced based on the principle of graphics, presenting real-life space or styles on paper via parallel protection according to the observed position and direction, thereby producing top views and elevations. Perspective drawings are produced through perspective principles. Therefore, the viewpoint and position of observers determine the way with which space is presented in views.

Views determine perspectives. Thus, spatial design is not just a concrete illustration; it requires the use of interpreted perspectives and methods to allow space to be easily understood. Ways to expressing abstract concepts with illustrations include scaling down, scaling up, 3D projecting, 2D space, and contouring.

The following sections are descriptions of land art, memorial space, installation art, exhibition, and interior design.

3.1.1 Scaling Down to Express Macro Views

Think of our living environment as puzzles of various architectures and use 3D building blocks to construct Taoyuan Land Puzzle and Art, in which the red 3D blocks symbolize buildings, green 3D blocks symbolize green land and farms, large white and green squares symbolize intertwining buildings and green spaces, and blue glass square plates symbolize Taoyuan's land feature, ponds. This work of art features the use of building blocks to portray the land and environment in macro view. The design process, as shown in the Fig. 2.

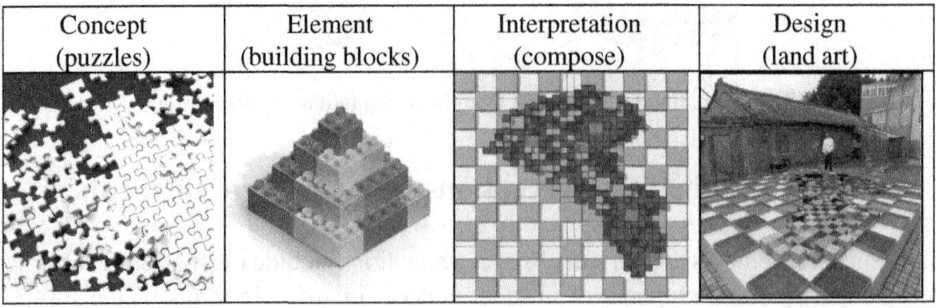

Concept (puzzles)
Element (building blocks)
Interpretation (compose)
Design (land art)

Fig. 2. Design process for scaling down to express macro views (Color figure online)

3.1.2 Scaling up to Emphasize the Concept of Memory

In order to search for the concept of "memory" in the history of Chung Yuan Christian University (CYCU), enlarged books are used as the styling element to enclose the space of Chung Yuan Christian University Chang Ching Yu Memorial Library using ceilings and walls layered with books and pages. The purpose is to seek for the memory of history. The physical environment of books is not the purpose of design; rather, the main significance of design is establishing the abstract spatial concept of restoring memories to reconstruct history. The design process was shown in the Fig. 3.

Concept (reading)	Element (book)	Interpretation (file)	Design (memory space)

Fig. 3. Design process for scaling up to emphasize the concept of memory

3.1.3 Using Projection to Establish 3D Drawings

Scaled up doorknob are used as elements to be projected on walls to present top views. A set of doorknob cut in half metaphorized the section that cannot be seen in space. The spatial installation art of graphics interpret the 3D projection and the undetected section in space. The design process was shown in the Fig. 4.

Concept (drawing)	Element (doorknob)	Interpretation (section/projection)	Design (installation art)
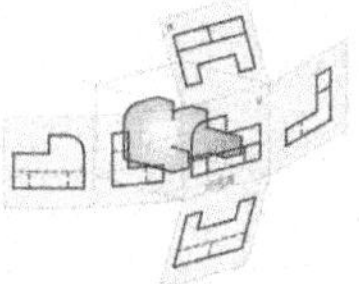	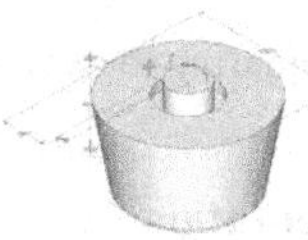	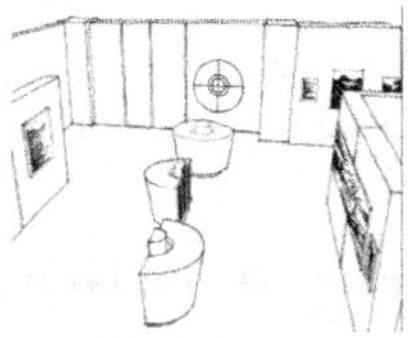	

Fig. 4. Design process for using projection to establish 3D drawings

3.1.4 Using 2D Views to Define Space

Here, walls, sliding doors, and windows are the elements. The exhibition space of Space in Painting vs. Drawing for Space is divided and enclosed with walls or with drawing symbols on the floor to present the abstract doors and windows and portray the different divisions of space. The floor plan presented on the floor creates a perceptual space of seeing drawings through space and establishing space with drawings. The design process was shown in the Fig. 5.

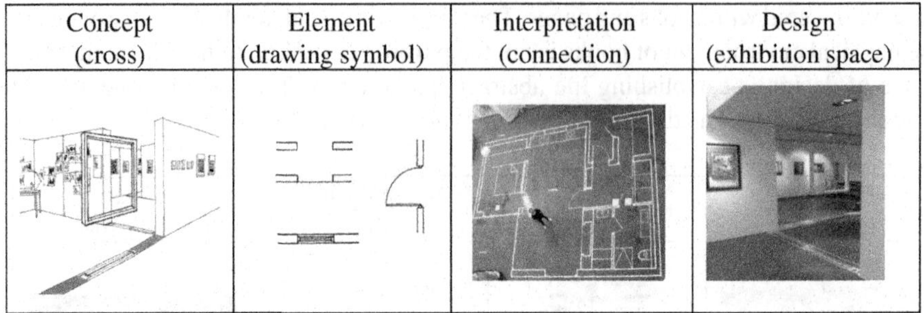

Concept
(cross)
Element
(drawing symbol)
Interpretation
(connection)
Design
(exhibition space)

Fig. 5. Design process for using 2D views to define space

3.1.5 Using Contouring to Extract Styles

Irrigation ditches are chosen as the elements and contours are used to symbolize flowing water. The Taoyuan City Library uses the ceiling and floor patterns, bamboo slips, and wavy design counter irrigating the books in the library to symbolize the features of irrigation ditches in Taoyuan. The design process was shown in the Fig. 6.

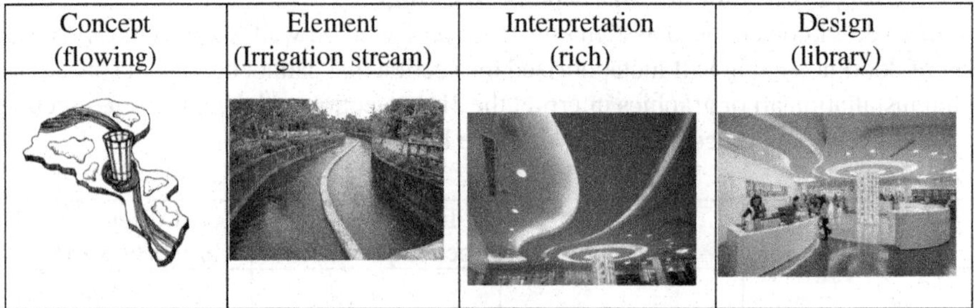

Concept
(flowing)
Element
(Irrigation stream)
Interpretation
(rich)
Design
(library)

Fig. 6. Design process for using contouring to extract styles

3.2 The Temporal Factors in Spatial Representation

"Representation, or exhibition, aims to allow people to understand its inner meaning as well as its exterior appearance by displaying. Here, the presenter, or exhibitor controls the initiator, not the audience" (Han 2000).

Representation refers to the whole manifestation, not the sum of exhibits. People are closely related to space. From a user-centered perspective, this study explores people's purpose and demands towards appreciating art or design in different spaces. Exhibitions can be viewed as text, using a unique language to convey its desired message (Chang 2011).

Exhibition design preserves and interprets different cultures by displaying historical events or current nature and art so as to connect visitors with culture and promote exchange. Curation is an important part of exhibition design. A creative way to develop exhibition design from theme planning and storylines to spatial design is to influence people with the atmosphere and narrate with space.

Spatial presentation, circulation arrangement, narrative text, and spatial shaping create resonance with the audience, further giving visitors a better understanding towards the occurrence of the event. Designers need to consider the interaction between the audience and the environment and pay attention to the connection between exhibits and space. As a result, space is able to deliver information on the exhibition by interacting.

Temporal factors control spatial context, exploring the meaning of space through the sequence of time to interpret and create new spaces.

3.2.1 The Reading Sequence of History

Commemorative space is used to honor or preserve the memory of a historical figure or event. The reading sequence of a person's life or an event represents time. The Chang Ching Yu Memorial Hall in Chung Yuan Christian University was designed with the concept of "turn a page of history and open the door to his life." The life of Chang Ching Yu is narrated in 12 chapters, which are designed as panels place on the walls for visitors to read as if reading from the pages in a book.

By means of telling a story on 3D pages and using digitally processed portraits on glass doors, visitors can get an insight into the life of Chang Ching Yu, surrounded by a sea of books on the ceiling and walls. Space shown as Fig. 7.

Fig. 7. The reading sequence of history (Chang Ching Yu Memorial Hall, CYCU)

3.2.2 Contrast of a Historical Figure and Scene

In Space in Painting vs. Drawing for Space, the difference between the years in which the artworks were completed serves as a metaphor for the changes of the divisions at the exhibition venue reflecting history. With paintings and drawings as the main characters of a story, each space contains different paintings and designs to explain the meaning of the divisions. The four divisions include the space of history, the space of modern, the space of imagination (designer), and imagination of space (artist). Space shown as Fig. 8.

Fig. 8. Contrast of a historical figure and scene (Art Exhibition)

In the space of history, a painting by Song Dynasty artist Zhang Zeduan *Along the River During the Qingming Festival* and the version by five Qing dynasty court painters and *One Hundred Stallions* by Guiseppe Castiglione in the Qing Dynasty are displayed to portray the historical changes of Chinese paintings in the interpretation of space and the viewpoints of painting in different times in history including visual angles, graphics, and lifestyles.

In the space of modern, hand-drawn maps of Taipei by British talent Tom Rook and Chen Chien-Jung's masterpiece of modern city from an architectural perspective serve as metaphors for the changes in exhibition divisions and time with the sliding doors and fixed window drawings.

In the exhibition, cities painted by artists and space created by the designer form a drawing that represent time, giving visitors the chance to personally experience the drawing and space from the works of art.

3.2.3 Changes in Life

Ponds vs. Houses explores temporal factors in spatial context. "Shinwu" is a current geographic name and also the record of past development. New houses in history transforming into ancient houses in geography represents an exchange of time. Fan-jian Clan Ancestral Shrine, located in Shinwu, and apartment buildings create a contrast of old and new, traditional and modern. Space shown as Fig. 9.

Fig. 9. Changes in Life (Land art- Ponds vs. Houses)

Ponds vs. Houses Part 2—Rediscover Shangri-La continues the concept of "weaving," adding 3D blocks with recycled calendars and shopping mall advertisements and the colors red, blue, yellow, white, and black to symbolize diversified thinking to compose a *Rediscover Shangri-La* landscape puzzle with temporal elements and living content.

Rediscover Shangri-La aims to inspire the audience to take action towards the environment. All participants choose the environment they wish to live in. "Time" is an important element of the exhibition and "participation" changes artwork. The exhibition displays photos taken every day and the original versions for the audience to compare the different changes every day and recognize their roles in the environment (Fig. 10).

Fig. 10. Changes in Life (Land art- Rediscover Shangri-La) (Color figure online)

4 Conclusion

The creative concept of space can be expressed with 2D drawings. The meaning behind space can be interpreted by changes in style. Using concrete elements to depict abstract thinking refers to the use of existing images from illustration to interpretation, which can also be said as the different levels of design creativity. Presenting space by storytelling is the process of organizing the order of space, using temporal factors in spatial context to enrich the hidden elements in works of art. The transformation from the physical space of using materials, colors, and styles to the perceptual space of using metaphoric interpretation can enhance the levels of design to substantial perception to psychological perception, enriching the outcomes of spatial design.

References

Jiang, J.L., Lin, F.M., Chen, C.S.: Design Principal and Practice. Pingtung University of Science and Technology, Pingtung (2007)

Jian, Z.Z.: The space image and metaphor in Taiwan urban poetry. J. Taiwan Poetry **6**, 7–33 (2005)

Liu, Y.Z.: Timeliness of space field: a discuss of time description in Hsien-yung Pai's record of flowery bridge. Da-Yeh J. Gen. Educ. **6**, 39 (2010)

Chen, L.M.: Space. J. Cultural Study **10**, 1–3 (2008). @Lin-Nan

Archer, L.B.: Systematic method for designer. In: Cross, N. (ed.) Development in Design Methodology, pp. 57–82. Wiley, Chicester (1984)

Goldschmidt, G.: Capturing indeterminism: representation in the design problem space. Des. Stud. **18**, 441–445 (1997)

Jones, C.J.: Design Methods, 2nd edn. Van Nostrand Reinhold, New York (1992)

Hung-Hsiang, W., Hung, J.-L.: A metaphorical method for product design in cultural and creative industry. J. Des. **16**(4), 35–55 (2011)

Hwang, Z.Y.: The role of the physical models in the digital design process, Master thesis, NCTU (2007)

Hsu, C.C., Wang Regina, W.Y.: Redefining abstraction in visual art and design. J. Des. **10**(3), 35–55 (2005)

Norman, D.: Design of Everyday Things. MIT Press, London (1998)

Han, B.D.: Theory and Practice of Display. Garden City Publish, Taipei (2000)

Chang, W.Z.: Story-telling structure analysis, part of The landscape of Library exhibition, pp. 31–56 (2011)

The Management Model Development of User Experience Design in Organization

A Case Study for Taiwan Technology Industry

Henry Been-Lirn Duh[1], Jim-Jiunde Lee[2(✉)], Pei Luen Patrick Rau[3], and Mu Qing Chen[2]

[1] School of Engineering and ICT, University of Tasmania, Private Bag 129, Hobart, Tasmania 7001, Australia
Henry.Duh@utas.edu.au
[2] Graduate Institute of Communication Studies, National Chiao Tung University, 1001 University Road, Hsinchu 300, Taiwan, ROC
jiulee@mail.nctu.edu.tw, mini50321@hotmail.com
[3] Department of Industrial Engineering, Tsinghua University, Room South 525, Shunde Building, Beijing, China
rpl@tsinghua.edu.cn

Abstract. This study aimed to develop a holistic user experience management model for companies to evaluate and advance their management status. The research started with qualitative interviewed with corporations in Taiwan, then we used affinity diagrams to organize interview materials, through matching interview findings with Total Quality Management (TQM), Total User Experience Management (TUXM) is constructed to apply in local corporations. To provide corporations with a more effective management tool, TUXM is further paired with Corporation UX Maturity Model to generate tactical UX management guidelines. Our model provides assessment of user experience management from three dimensions:

1. Include all local corporations in our model to obtain a holistic view of the corporation UX development status in Taiwan.
2. For each corporation to examine its UX resource allocation.
3. Combine international advanced UX development cases into the checklist, local corporations can realize the UX development gap when compared with international competitors in the same industry.

Keywords: UX management · User experience design · Activity theory · Corporate User-Experience maturity mode · TUXM

1 Introduction

Companies must embed the concept of user-orientation into their core management strategy, with every department from product design to business planning and marketing motivated to optimize user experience (UX). By emphasizing user interface or

P.-L.P. Rau (Ed.): CCD 2016, LNCS 9741, pp. 163–172, 2016.
DOI: 10.1007/978-3-319-40093-8_17

product appearance, companies can highlight the importance of UX to all levels of management.

In Taiwan, upper-level management and design teams are often divided over the concept of user experience design (UXD). The emergence of UX teams has also changed the original roles and responsibilities of divisions such as marketing and development. Even senior executives who genuinely want to promote UX often have difficulty fully understanding the problems faced by product designers, who in turn struggle to comprehend how design is limited by profit and efficiency requirements.

User experience management is a concept of design managements, which in turn is part of business management. In this discipline, the concept of Total Quality Management (TQM) is considered by many developed nations to be an important indicator of production quality. The term is also used to describe an ideal environment in which every facet of an organization, from staff to strategy to information transfer, is committed to ensuring quality. The objective of this study is to develop an ideal UXD management model, like TQM, that executives can benchmark against when executing strategy.

2 Literature Review

2.1 Tqm

Ishikawa (1986) credits TQM (Total Quality Management) for the development of quality management into a comprehensive system covering all areas beyond product quality. 'Total' means that quality management is intended to encompass as many processes and staff at every level possible. Quality refers to satisfying the requirements and expectations of customers. Management means maintaining the ability of the organization to strive for continuous improvement (Cohen and Brand 1993). In summary, TQM "is a management approach to long term success through customer satisfaction. In a TQM effort, all members of an organization participate in improving processes, products, services, and the cultural in which they work".

According to Westcott (2005), the key principles of TQM are as follows: Customer-focused., total employee involvement, process-centered, integrated system, strategic and systematic approach, continual Improvement, fact-based decision making, and communications.

2.2 From Design to UX Management

Design management is a business discipline that uses management theory and methodology to manage design behavior. In the process of design and production, there are many factors that can lead to design quality issues. Apart from senior executives failing to properly manage product quality, design teams may also have gaps in technology and management techniques. For example, they may not have clear design objectives, specifications, or technology standards. They may lack knowledge and experience in design management, or fail to properly evaluate and deliberate on design.

Quality inspections at each stage of the design process offer the obvious benefit of monitoring and controlling quality; however, they also facilitate discussion and exchange that can enhance design quality. Consistent quality management, from initial design to final production, is essential to ensuring that product design is effectively realized.

When reviewing international case studies on design management, researchers found that many large corporations have utilized UXD management to improve their company value. The strategy adopted by Google is 1. Integrated company design index; 2. Development of localized design; 3. Quantitative HEART framework; 4. Design objective – GSM model; 5. Diverse portfolios for designers, and 6. Quantification of team performance in order to improve management.

Tencent Holdings Ltd takes the approach of 1. Integrating development with design processes; 2. Assessing each department against integration of UX metrics; 3. Setting UX metrics for products; 4. Creating the role of UX General Manager, and 5. Making UX the responsibility of all staff.

In his book *Undercover User Experience Design*, Cennydd Bowles (2011) highlights the four development stages of UX: Undercover UX, Emergent UX, Maturing UX, and Integrated UX.

At the initial stage, companies are focused only on controlling costs, and executives are entirely unfamiliar with the concept of UX. Product functions are driven by marketing demands. During the emergent phase, companies begin to recognize UX principles and engage experts to conduct usability testing on a small budget. Relevant stakeholders also begin to take note of UX, however at this point, UX techniques and knowledge have not yet matured.

At the maturing phase, companies have recognized the importance of UX experts and have begun to establish UX teams and define their job descriptions, goals and responsibilities. Executives are willing to allocate a reasonable budget to UX management, and UX teams have access to various tools and methodologies to achieve business objectives. In the final integration phase, executives have acknowledged the value of UX and believe that it is the responsibility of all employees. Senior management work to integrate UX with corporate development strategy, product development is driven by user requirements, and the entire company progresses towards becoming a customer-centric organization.

Van Tyne (2009) developed the Corporate User-Experience Maturity Model to assist companies in more effectively managing UX. The model progresses through a sequence of stages: (1) Initial stage; (2) Professional Discipline;(3) Managed; (4) Integrated UX, and (5) Customer-Driven Corporation. Aaron (2009) further defined each development phase. Companies can evaluate the maturity of their UX teams by comparing them against the indicators of different development phases (Table 1).

Judging from previous studies, many companies in Taiwan still lack a comprehensive UX management tool. Although the corporate UX maturity model discussed earlier is a management tool for UX-integrated design processes, it does not provide specific evaluation criteria for each development phase. Also, because the model was based on international contexts, we must consider whether it requires modification to suit the industrial environment of Taiwan.

Table 1. Corporate user-experience maturity model

Maturity level	User-centric design processes	Human resources and training	Organizational restructuring	Involvement from management	Company objectives
Initial	1. Basic UX practice 2. Awareness of users 3. Few practice	Limited number of UX staff	External UX experts	Traditional production team	Optimize existing products
Professional Discipline	1. Model design 2. User awareness.	UX team	Project management	1. UX process. 2. Budget allocated	UX leads to tangible benefit
Managed	Design standards	Appointment of UX manager	Delegation of UX duty	Integrated business processes	UX management strategy
Integrated UX	1. Develop different design processes 2. Measurable, controllable, predictable UX outcomes	UX executive's responsibilities are expanded	Involvement from senior management	1. UX Architect. 2. UX management tools	1. UX is at the core of competitiveness 2. UX creates differentiation
Customer-Driven Corporation	1. Design processes are optimized 2. Quantitative UX index is optimized	UX gets into the core business decisions	UX is integrated into criteria for other divisions	1. Commercial strategy includes UX. 2. Third party collaboration	1. UX is integrated into company vision 2. Company evolves into customer-centric organization

Using TQM and the corporate UX maturity model as prototypes, this study built a Total User Experience Management (TUXM) model for industry in Taiwan, incorporating interview data from local companies that have already embedded UX.

3 Methodology

In the qualitative research phase, we filtered subjects by theme and conducted intensive, unstructured interviews that allowed subjects to freely express their personal viewpoints on specific topics. These interviews provided us with high quality data to analyze and interpret (Stokes and Bergin 2006). The advantage of this method is that interviewers can focus on exploring a single topic in-depth (Bainbridge 1989). During March to October 2015, we interviewed 18 subjects from 13 companies.

3.1 Questionnaire Design

According to the design strategy study conducted by Bell Lab in 2011 (Ebenreuter and Geerts 2011), design teams utilize management strategies to solve business problems. They pointed out that design teams generally encounter four major types of event in carrying out their everyday responsibilities:

Table 2. Corporate information (2015)

Company code	Industry type	Occupational level	Companies capital (NT)	Date (2015)
A	Hardware	Manager	8.2 billion	3/29
B	Hardware	Executive, Manager	44.1 billion	4/30
C	Hardware	Executive, Manager	22 billion	4/30
D	Hardware	Manager, Stuff	37 billion	5/04
E	Internet	Manager	The market value of 4.6 trillion	6/15
F	Hardware	Manager	5 billion	7/01
G	On-line service	Executive	700 million	7/20
H	On-line service	Manager	300 million	7/24
I	On-line service	Executive	100 million	9/25
J	Software	Stuff	100 million	8/12
K	Hardware	Stuff	1.1 billion	8/14
L	Internet	Executive	50 million	8/19
M	Hardware	Stuff	31 billion	3/28
Total	13 companies, 18 interviewers			

Decision-making, simplifying problems, exploring solutions, and convergence of differing opinions. We hypothesized that UX teams in Taiwan also encounter these types of event, which we incorporated into our questionnaire development.

Bødker (1995) applied activity theory to the field of Human-Computer Interaction (HCI). This theory provides a set of principles that can be used to analyze and interpret human activity. Activity theorists believe that we develop an object-oriented consciousness of activity from our everyday doings. The activities a person engages in indicate what objects he/she desires to understand and interpret.

An activity comprises the following six key elements: object, subject, community, division of labor, rules, and instruments. The small triangle in the theoretical model represents the links and intermediary effects between elements. This concept can be used to analyze activities in the discipline of UX management.

We drafted the interview questionnaire based on the four types of event described above and the six main elements of activity theory. This draft questionnaire was pre-tested by experts twice and revised four times before finalization.

3.2 Affinity Diagram

Also known as the KJ method, the Affinity Diagram was developed by Kawakita Jirou in 1953. After field interviews, all the participant notes are collated and audio or visual files are converted into transcripts. Keywords, phrases, or sentences relevant to the activity theme are recorded on cards or notes, and then sorted into groups.

Researchers are then able to discuss common ideas or meanings, and identify classes and group relationships. Our Affinity Diagram has three main groups: Company assets, management, and market, as shown in Fig. 1.

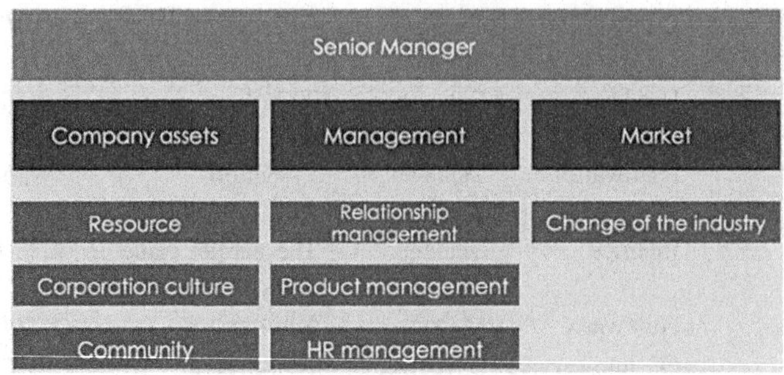

Fig. 1. Affinity Diagram collated from interview data

1. Company Assets: Clouding tangible resources, such as space and budget, as well as intangible resources such as discourse right and company emphasis on UX.
2. Management: The experience and expertise of middle management, including the inter-departmental management of relationships, products, and human resources.
3. Market: The UX manager must continually monitor market and industry trends, and evaluate what threats and opportunities caused by the external environment relates to the UX development.

4 TUXM

We matched the eight key components of TQM with the results of the affinity diagram to create the Total User Experience Management (TUXM) model, comprising the following six elements: UX objectives, Integrated-Design System, strategic communication, Continual Improvement, Fact-Based Decision making, and a T-Type design team (see Fig. 2).

5 Corporate User-Experience Maturity Model

The TUXM model represents the ideal elements of comprehensive UXD, while the Corporate UX Maturity Model provides more specific benchmarks to measure capabilities. We matched the interview results and TUXM elements to the Corporate UX Maturity Model, in order to break UX maturity down into more practical criteria.

Using the method of Aaron (2009), we categorized the companies interviewed into Fig. 3. We then re-classified the companies as shown in Table 2 based on their management methods (Table 3).

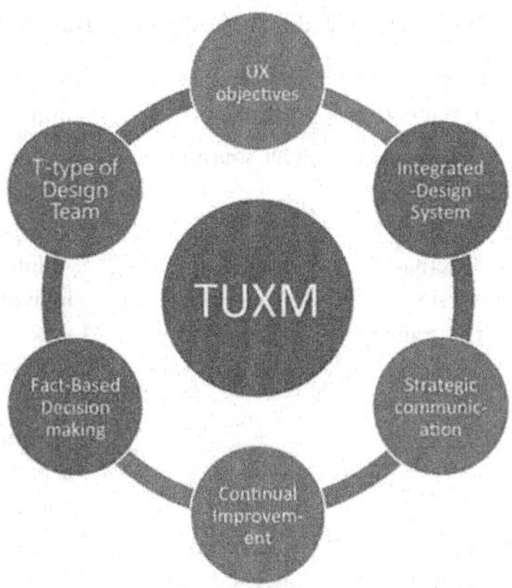

Fig. 2. Six key elements of TUXM

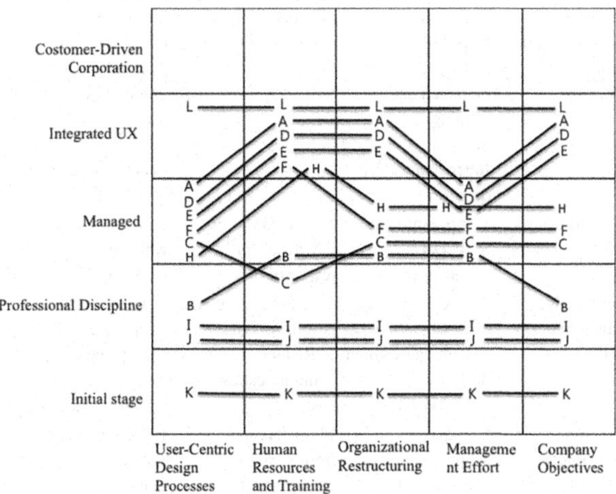

Fig. 3. Distribution of UX maturity among companies interviewed. (The letters A-L represent companies codenamed).

6 Discussion

After incorporating interview data into the revised corporate UX maturity model, we discovered that the model can be used for three purposes:

6.1 Evaluate UX Development in Taiwan

We matched the interviewees to the corporate UX maturity model (Fig. 4), illustrating the extent of UX development in each organization. According to the curve, technology

Table 3. New corporate user-experience maturity model

Maturity level	User-Centric design processes	Human resources and training	Organizational restructuring	Involvement from management	Company objectives
Initial stage	1. Basic UX 2. Limited UX experience	Limited number of UX staff	Out souring.	Traditional production team	Optimize existing products
Solutions	1. Repeatpractice UX 2. Document design 3. Integrate UX into existing processes	1. Externa-l professionals 2. UX training	Delegate responsibility for UX to product manager.	1. Integrate individual UX expertise 2. Visualize UX results 3. Other departments notice UX	Understand the value and benefits of UX
Professional Discipline	1. Model design 2. User awareness 3. Surveys	Other departments are assigned responsibility for UX	1. UX is not integrated with other departments	1. Budget allocated 2. UX satellite products developed	1. UX increase steady benefits 2. Project decision requirements
Solutions	1. User data management 2. Design criteria 3. Process monitoring	1. More resources 2. Designers' responsibilities 3. Project management training 4. Independent UX division	1. Collaboration between designers and project teams	1. UX integrated into business processes 2. Executives take initiative in managing UX 3. Designers develop UX philosophy	Top-down UX promotion
Managed	1. Unified design standards	1. Appointment of UX manager.	1. Delegation of UX tasks and responsibilities	1. UX integrated with business processes	1. UX management strategy
Phased solutions	Quantify UX management criteria	1. UX direct link to executives 2. Cultivate skilled designers 3. UX criteria	1. Cross-divisional design processes 2. Reduce communication costs	1. Executives participate in UX management 2. UX test standards 3. UX Architecture	1. Customize UX 2. Flexible application of UX design
Integrated UX	1. Different design processes 2. UX outcomes are Measurable, controllable, predictable	1. Expand scope and responsibilities of UX executive	1. Involvement from senior management	1.UX Architect. 2. UX management tools	1. UX is at the core of competitiveness 2. UX creates differentiation
Phased solution	1. Optimize design processes 2. Interact with external organizations	UX performance index	Non-UX divisions plan UX management policy	1. UX is integrated into commercial strategy 2. Non-UX departments establish UX evaluation criteria	1. High-level vision and strategy is established for UX
Sustainable development	1. Design processes are optimized 2. Quantitative UX index is optimized	1. UX team provides input into core business decisions 2. UX is prioritized	UX is integrated into criteria for other divisions	1. UX is integrated into commercial strategy 2. Third party collaboration	1. UX is integrated into company vision 2.Customer-centric organization

companies in Taiwan that have integrated UX can be roughly divided into three types. In the upper Fig. 3., companies in the same field have the same level of maturity in UX.

Type 1: Companies in this category are developing evenly across all five management constructs, and are mostly situated in the standardization and predictive control phases. They are less mature in user-centric design and investment from management.

Type 2: Companies in this category are also progressing equally across all five constructs, but are positioned mostly in the foundation and standardization phases.

However, because nearly 80 % of the companies in this table are technological firms, the sample is not representative of the general state of UX development in Taiwan. Once updated with further data on other industries, this table will better represent the general trend of UX development in Taiwan, providing the government with reference in developing UX-related policy. Study the allocation of UX resources in companies.

Companies can use the corporate UX maturity model to (1) self-assess their level of UX maturity, and (2) analyze their competitiveness against industry peers.

6.2 Examine Best Practice

We integrated UX best practice from international firms into this model. Companies in Taiwan can compare their own UX development against these standards, and identify the gap between themselves and their peers overseas.

Although we did identify several generalizable constructs from the data available, we were unable to find a comprehensive case study to compare all management constructs. Nevertheless, we hope that companies can use this model to identify their current phase of development and where they should be investing their efforts in the future.

Two reasons for integrating these international case studies into the model were:

1. The model could be used as an international instrument of design management.
2. Companies wanting to define their position with regards to UX development can compare their results against model companies and identify where improvement is needed.

7 Conclusion

The corporate UX maturity model can be used to illustrate the gap between a company and its competitors with regard to UX development. This visualization of weak areas highlights to other departments the necessity and practicality of corporate UX development, encouraging cross-divisional collaboration.

Although we have identified the key constructs of UX maturity, we do not know whether these constructs should be implemented in some type of optimal sequence, and if so, what this sequence might be. Companies can currently use this model to evaluate their development status, but the next step would be to order these constructs by priority. Due to time limitations, we were unable to explore this aspect.

We hope that the corporate UX maturity model will be used to provide guidance via three types of mechanism: testing, consulting, and training.

1. Testing: The complete model allows companies to more accurately identify their UX development status.
2. Consulting: A quantitative questionnaire could be developed to conduct a wider survey of UX design teams in Taiwan. The results could then be used to form a specific management plan to supplement the UX maturity model. This would assist companies in executing strategy and engaging suitable consultants).
3. Education and training: The results of this model can be used as the basis for developing UX Strategist training courses or corporate workshops.

References

Marcus, A., Gunther, R., Sieffert, R.: Validating a standardized usability/user-experience maturity model: a progress report. In: Kurosu, M. (ed.) HCD 2009. LNCS, vol. 5619, pp. 104–109. Springer, Heidelberg (2009)

Bainbridge, W.S.: Survey Research: A Computer-Assistant Introduction. Wadsworth, California (1989)

Bødker, S.: Applying activity theory to video analysis: how to make sense of video data in human-computer interaction. In: Context and Consciousness

Bowles, C., Box, J.: Undercover User Experience Design. New Riders Publishing, pp. 144–166, San Francisco (2011)

Cohen, S., Brand, R.: Total Quality Management in Government: A Practical Guide for the Real World. Jossey-Bass Inc., Pub., California (1993)

Ebenreuter, N., Geerts, M.: Design Strategy: towards an understanding of different methods and perspectives. In: Proceedings of the 2011 Conference on Designing Pleasurable Products and Interfaces, pp. 51:1–51:8. ACM, New York (2011)

Ishikawa, K.: Guide to Quality Control. Asian Productivity Organization, Second Revised Edition, Tokyo (1986)

Westcott, R.T.: The Certified Manager of Quality/Organizational Excellence Handbook. ASQ, Quality Press, Wisconsin (2005)

Stokes, D., Bergin, R.: Methodology or "methodolatry"? An evaluation of focus groups and depth interviews. In: International Conference on Economics and Finance Research IPEDR, vol. 4 (2011). Qualitative market research: An international Journal 9(1), 26–37 (2006)

Van Tyne, S.: Corporate user-experience maturity model. In: Kurosu, M. (ed.) HCD 2009. LNCS, vol. 5619, pp. 635–639. Springer, Heidelberg (2009)

SYSTEMATEKS: Scalable Interactive Modular Simulation (SIMS): Towards Sustainable Design

Luigi Ferrara and Nastaran Dadashi(✉)

Centre for Arts, Design and Information Technology, George Brown College, Toronto, Canada
{lferrara,Nastaran.dadashi}@georgebrown.ca

Abstract. Design, in the context of Sustainable Interaction Design (SID) is defined as "an act of choosing among or informing choices of future ways of being" (Blevis, 2007). The present paper introduces SYSTEMATEKS (SIMS) as an evolutionary design thinking concept that has been developed and practiced by the lead author on numerous successful and sustainable design projects for more than two decades. These physical products have a wide range of applications ranging from furniture, exhibitions and architectural designs that embodied ethical, sustainable and universal values and design principles. The overarching aim of the present paper is to document the process implicit in SIMS in a way that it can also be practiced by Sustainable Interaction Designers. The findings of this paper can be used as a guide to designers to ensure that the design process will lead to sustainable and "transfigurable" designs that could meet a wider range of user requirements and that also can shift application depending on the context of use. Furthermore, this process framework can be utilized as a method of evaluation to assess the sustainability of a user interface.

Keywords: Sustainable Interaction Design · Human Computer Interaction

1 Introduction

Design, in the context of Sustainable Interaction Design (SID) is defined as "an act of choosing among or informing choices of future ways of being" (Blevis 2007). Blevis (2007) has proposed five principles for SID that includes:

Linking invention and disposal;
Promoting renewal and reuse;
Promoting quality and equality;
De-coupling ownership and identity; and
Using natural models and reflections.

These principles, even though inspired from Human Computer Interaction (HCI) domain, share commonalities with the sustainable design principles of any physical object.

The ultimate goal of a sustainable design (whether a physical object, a landscape, and a piece of jewellery or a digital interactive interface) is to assure that a meaningful

P.-L.P. Rau (Ed.): CCD 2016, LNCS 9741, pp. 173–181, 2016.
DOI: 10.1007/978-3-319-40093-8_18

and continuous relationship between user and the object is maintained and in doing so, the product (physical or virtual) is reusable, transformative and adaptive.

The present paper introduces the philosophy of SYSTEMATEKS with its methodology of Scalable Interactive Modular Simulation (SIMS) as an evolutionary design thinking paradigm that has been developed and practiced by the lead author on numerous successful and sustainable design projects for more than two decades. These physical products have a wide range of applications ranging from furniture, exhibitions and architectural structures that incorporate ethical, sustainable and universal values and design principles. The overarching aim of the present paper is to document the process followed by SIMS in a way that it can also be adapted by Sustainable Interaction Designers.

This paper introduces SIMS and reviews examples of physical objects that were developed in-line with SIMS. This review has led to development of sustainable design processing framework. Parallels with physical and digital design realms have been considered and their synthesis has led to development of a framework that can be adopted by both physical/industrial designers as well as digital/HCI designers.

The findings of this paper can be used as a guide to designers to ensure that the design process will lead to a sustainable and transfigured designs that could meet the wider range of user requirements and that also can shift application depending on the context of use. Furthermore, this process framework can be utilized as a method of evaluation to assess the sustainability of a user interface.

2 Background

Sharing is the predominant way of communicating and design is the way users, designers and developers share. It's the interface between the inner and outer, turning sentiments into the embodiments in the world around us. Design as a method of making things allows us to share the world and understand the world in a harmonious and integrated way.

Communicating design objectives are driven from epochs of three economies (Esping-Andersen 1999), the economy of representation, the economy of abstraction and this new economy, which we refer to as the economy of transfiguration where the world is dematerialized and then rematerialized again through digital technologies. A significant challenge persists as often these digital transfigurations are approached and embodied through traditional design practices: a sequential method where designer envisions and materializes solutions, often without considering the sociological impact of their design and expects users (who are living in this new epoch) to welcome the design.

Current technological advancements have allowed designers to imagine a whole host of different worlds, but they are often more unsuccessful than not, because they don't recognize all of the fundamental problems in the world. There is an urgent need for a systems shift. A new more equitable model based on sharing is required, where users have equal access to resources, means of production and can develop for themselves designs that help them realize their full potential. This new model encourages new understanding of the sense of ownership.

Traditional Human factors approaches define user engagement as the predominant way of enhancing user ownership and to consequently increase the system usability (O'Brien and Toms 2008). Co-design (Sanders and Stappers 2008), human centred design (Huang and Chiu 2016), usability testing and many similar disciplines are at their peak to support better end user engagement and potentially more efficient user interaction. Ideally this will lead into high revenues, more satisfied users and change in consumer culture. However, none provide thorough universality, as it appears that these approaches offer piecemeal solutions and lacks a holistic philosophy for design. Ownership implies property and goods, exchange and markets, accumulation and profits; sharing implies commons and a format for sharing the commons, it implies access and data pools, and an economy of usage and experience versus an economy of goods. The notion of economy of experience suggests the shift from physical products (which previously could be measured through numeracy and literacy) to sensory aspects of design. True sustainability supports this aspect of experience over possession and in doing so promises a new type of ownership, equity, and universality while providing at the same time individualism.

To achieve these goals there is a need for an ecology of innovation. Social innovation (e.g. impact of mobile devices in our daily lives) and technical innovation (e.g. Internet of Things, wearable products) are to be utilized and understood in order to develop an understanding of business innovation (e.g. apple, android) and perhaps political innovation (e.g. Uber). The essential question is how do we make the right kind of changes. Instead of looking at what is possible with the available technology, we need to understand what is desired and how technology can be utilized to allow us to achieve these desires.

The evolution of design is moving away from the designer who designs for everyone on everyone's behalf. There is a need to design with people, where the design is no longer monopolized under the designer, but through the creation of systems allows the designer to empower people to create designs for themselves. This philosophy is called SYSTEMATEKS and to do that we need to create scalable, modular, simulations for interactions, called SIMS.

Within SIMS the process of design (although inspired from a top-down approach), explores the bottom-top components of knowing, sharing and believing and thus forms a balanced creation (i.e. a system of systems).

SIMS is inspired by systems thinking where design should be scalable, interactive, modular (or "modulable") and optimal. The idea is generally rooted in the fact that in order to develop sustainable design, it is possible to reverse-engineer the design acceptability process by users. This mainly points to the concept of design and sharing, where users not only contribute to design (i.e. co-design), but also design has the capability to be accessed and used by different users (i.e. customizable) and hence allow for a wider range of users to share a particular design proposition. This is also applicable where user needs change over time. The resilience of a sustainable design makes it a very attractive characteristic for digital interface designers.

More specifically there is a paradigm shift, from ownership to sharing, towards the perception, utilization and application of new interactive interfaces (physical or digital) and to support this neo industrial perspective it is important to emphasize commonalities, access requirements and usage (applicability). Ultimately the future of design lies in creating systems that allow people to personalize and co-create designs for themselves (Ferrara 2015).

3 Case Studies

The current paper explores two successful exemplars of sustainable product designs that have stood the test of time. The lead author responsible for leading these design projects reported on the evolutionary and iterative process associated with the design and development of the selected interfaces and searched for patterns and characteristics that formed these designs. These case studies are briefly introduced in this section.

3.1 The Benchmark

The project was started with a single dot, then turned it into a line, moved it into the second plane, until it became a substantiated, three dimensional object. The objects were further joined with one another, replicated again and again until an archetype element or conceptual building block was arrived at. The archetype (Fig. 1) is like a piece of code, it's something that can be interpreted and used in various ways.

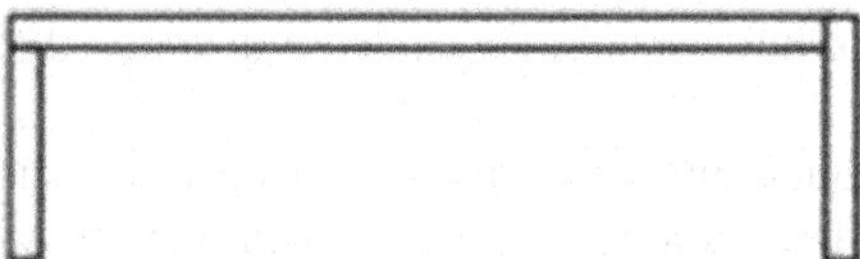

Fig. 1. Archetype: everything begins somewhere and ends here

The archetype was developed as a bench; this bench could be stacked to form a shelf. Turned laterally it becomes a wall. Rotate it and suddenly you have a chair. Array them you have a stairway. Arrange them and you have a bedframe. With other combinations, you can have a couch and table, a kitchen, even a desk.

Benchworld can be altered, re-used, re-purposed without waste. Different users create different meanings and contexts from the archetype. Put the archetype in a system, and then users can generate their own worlds. Users can re-interpret these benches in any shape and form imaginable (Fig. 2). A sustainable design that meets all of the criteria that Blevis (2007) envisioned.

The design was utilized in many ways and forms and for completely different applications than it was originally created for. The transfiguration of the design allowed for no waste and since it was interpretable in many forms, it was adaptable in different contexts and environments. It satisfied users and promoted individualism through its universality of adaptation.

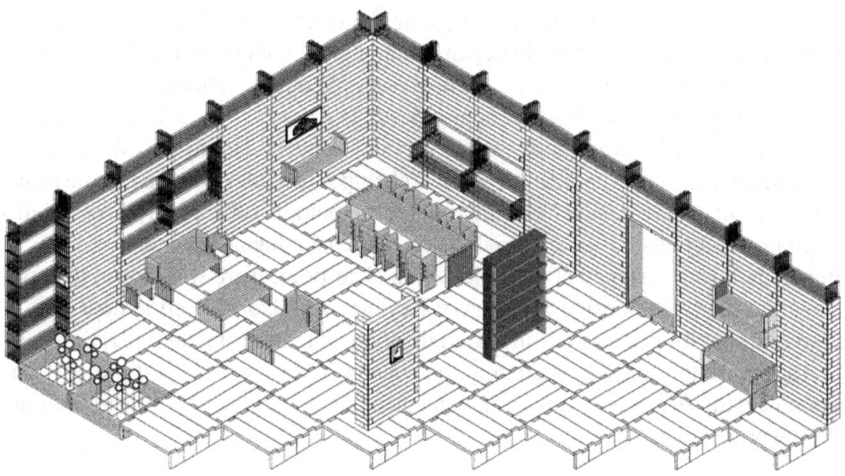

Fig. 2. Populate

The design process can be summarized in (Fig. 3) below. It is a truly iterative and holistic approach, where there is no sequence and all elements inform one another. The process can start from either of the components, but the important aspect is that all dimensions/factors (context, archetype, organization and integration) should be considered and explored.

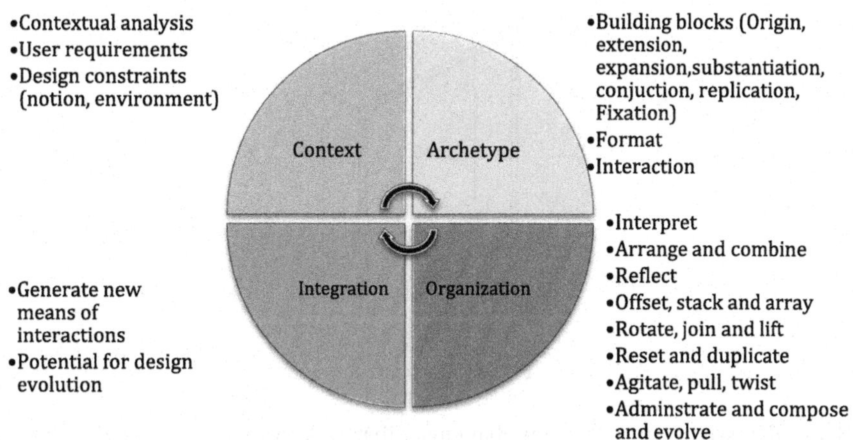

Fig. 3. SIMS process

Context refers to understanding the work domain; list the range of high level user requirements, breakdown of potential activities, system functions, system and product purposes and priorities. Archetyping lets one search for fundamental building blocks and invites the designer to think about shape, format, material, modes and forms of interaction and in doing so develops an understanding of interaction constraints.

Archetypes are derived from understanding the origin, extending the elements and gathering momentum, expanding the features until they become tangible and substantial, until they become recognizable using the processes of conjunction, replication and then finally fixation until the archetype is finally developed.

The next two dimensions apply archetype and context. The first explores various forms of structuring and organization of the archetypes to achieve a transfigured design. Examples of such activities include: interpretation, rotation, offset, arrays, reset, reflection, agitation, administration, materialization, dimensioning and population.

Benchmark was designed at the time with a clear brief: there was a need to furnish a space, and hence the design albeit very flexible was also very structured and this structured format limited successful materialization and range of materialization. Users could transfigure the shape by changing the content of design. The next project aimed to manipulate the structure in a way that enhanced the flexibility and transfiguration of the design process itself.

3.2 The Open Lattice

The open lattice (Fig. 4) was the second project that was designed based on the idea of SIMS and lessons learned were incorporated. Open Lattice is made of two elements, a small cross and a frame. The lattice was inspired by the identity or lack of one implicit in the Canadian psyche, a place that would accept all and allow others to flow through it, to be changed and transformed over time.

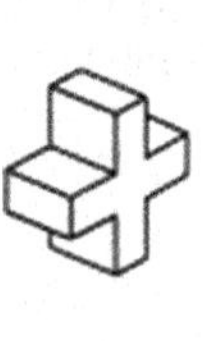
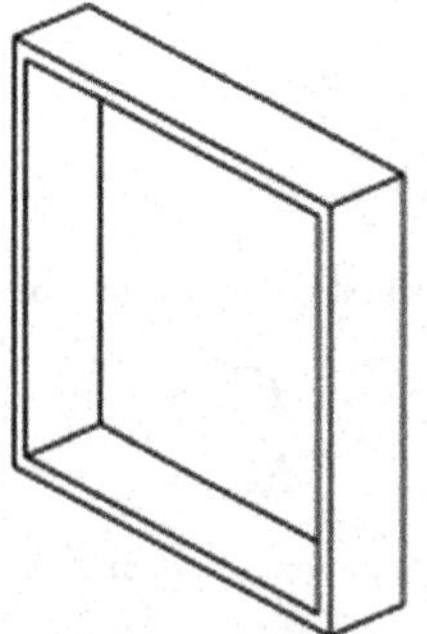
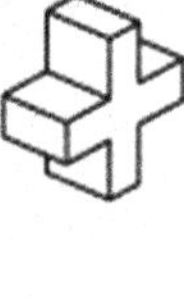

Fig. 4. Open lattice

This addressed one of the key challenges that was faced during the Benchmark project, where the content was somewhat fixed in Benchmark by the re-contextualization, in the Open Lattice (due to its empty frame) the archetype itself allowed for infinite content interpretation. The increased flexibility enabled a greater degree of possibilities and transfiguration without loosing any of the capabilities that Benchmark offered. Example of versatility of open lattice is shown in Fig. 5 below.

Fig. 5. Open lattice in architecture (The transportation EXPO 2012)

The only concern that resulted from the increase in flexibility was a loss of structural simplicity and consequently some of the practicality of the design. Benchmark, due to being very structured was also very predictable and therefore more practical. The Open Lattice due to its openness (an empty frame), is structurally more fragile and seems to be weaker and therefore the manufacturing and assembly process needs to compensate for this limitation. However, once it's used, it is more resilient even though it's not as practical to re-arrange, it is more flexible and allows content to be introduced and swapped out over time. The risk is that it be used in so many different ways and not all of them can be perfectly predicted since the manufacturing requires some expert skills.

In comparison to Benchmark, Open Lattice has a user learning curve associated with it. The question becomes whether the values offered by this form are sufficient to encourage users to invest in learning (acquiring some level of manufacturing skills) and to further own the design.

4 SIMS Characteristics and Link to Digital Design

Looking at the two examples stated above, SIMS characteristics are identified as generative, transformable, supports multiple materials and forms and supports alternative designs. These characteristics should be explored and assessed during the design of digital interfaces to ensure that the elements have the potential to be transfigured so that a sustainable design is supported. It must be noted that these characteristics are mutually exclusive and depending on the context of design various aspects of these characteristics can be limited. However, the awareness of the extent of status of these characteristics within the digital interface allows designers to be cogniscient of the sustainability and ideally universality of their end digital products.

1. Generative. It can generate complex objects, environments, communications and organizationsby capturing sentiments that can be transfigured into embodiments.
2. Transformable. The holonic elements are able to transform across multi-dimensions interacting tomake larger compositions and can be manipulated by a co-creator.
3. Multiple materials. The elements can be made of multiple materials singularly on in combination withthe material governing the scale of the element.
4. Alternative design. The elements can be stretched dimensionally and selectively altered to response tovaries locals and the personal preferences of the co-creator.
5. Multiple forms. The combination of base elements generate multiple forms, serves various functions,combine types of matter to create multiple effects for an array of purposes and in doingso can continue to evolve both sentiment and embodiment.

Looking at these characteristics as well as the process framework suggested in Fig. 3, it is evident that there are many commonalities that can be adopted from SIMS into designing digital interfaces to ensure that they are flexible, universal, resilient and consequently sustainable.

Digital interfaces are fundamentally limited to their platforms of design; designers follow the context of use (often a very specified one) and derive detailed user requirements based on available guidelines (e.g. W3C) or as a result of specific user analysis (e.g. usability testing, Human Factors evaluation). They ensure that the forms and shapes are noted and feasible within the digital environment and are in-line with the system functions, purposes and priorities.

The two aspects missing in designing digital interfaces are those that contribute to its transfiguration. What we have called (organization and integration) in Fig. 3 are dimensions that mainly contribute to this transfiguration. Having these dimensions digital designers can explore potential transformation and possible generative aspects of their designs and finally pursue a true sustainable digital interface.

5 Discussion

SIMS refer to a process for a generative design comprised of holonic recombinant elements, guided by formal, dimensional, and material systems to create evolutionary products, scenarios, and communications that allow for collaborative creation in production and consumption.

SIMS can generate complex objects, environments, communications and organizations by digitally capturing sentiments that can be transfigured into embodiments. These processes consist of developing archetypal elements or holons that have been generated by an originating concept, which can be materialized in the physical world. These holonic elements are able to transform across multiple dimensions, interacting to make larger compositions and can be manipulated by a co-creator.

The elements can be made of multiple materials, singularly or in combination with material governing the scale of the element. The elements can be stretched dimensionally and selectively altered to response to varied locales and the personal preferences of the co-creator. The combination of base elements generates multiple forms, serves varied functions, combines types of matter to create multiple effects for an array of purposes and in doing so can continue to evolve both sentiment and embodiment.

Historically, our literate means of communication started from symbols that were first pictographs and then alphabetic and most recently binary. The work of Alan Turing and his Turing Machine showed that how with less (0 and 1) we could produce the most (almost everything in the universe). This insight has inspired SYSTEMATEKS, where you arrive at the fundamental building block and allow it to develop the most diverse range of design possibilities. With Benchmark it was the dot and the line (which later formed a bench) and with Open Lattice it is the frame and the cross, like a 1 and 0, allowing you to build an infinite world from the way these interact with each other.

In order to develop true sustainability, it is important to promote resilient and flexible design, however this flexibility calls for user learning and the values of a design might not be very clear to the users in order to justify their investment in the learning required to have an impact on their lives.

6 Conclusion and Future Work

In the next phase of research and as a result of the fundamental goals of Systemateks it will be critical to merge the physical expression of SIMS with the digital tool set and interface that manages and controls it. The potential is for a digital interface that can manipulate physical reality and help turn that physical reality into an endlessly generative and responsive one to the evolutionary needs of people and at the same time to allow physical reality to inform and alter the digital tool set by collecting the intelligence of interactions in the living physical world. The result would be two generative universes in constant relation with the other, influencing and changing each other over time.

References

Blevis, E.: Sustainable Interaction Design: invention & disposal, renewal & reuse. In: Proceedings of the SIGCHI Conference on Human Factors in Computing Systems, pp. 503–512. ACM (2007)

Esping-Andersen, G.: Social foundations of postindustrial economies. OUP Oxford, Oxford (1999)

O'Brien, H.L., Toms, E.G.: What is user engagement? a conceptual framework for defining user engagement with technology. J. Am. Soc. Inf. Sci. Technol. **59**(6), 938–955 (2008)

Sanders, E.B.N., Stappers, P.J.: Co-creation and the new landscapes of design. Co-design **4**(1), 5–18 (2008)

Huang, P.H., Chiu, M.C.: Integrating user centered design, universal design and goal, operation, method and selection rules to improve the usability of DAISY player for persons with visual impairments. Appl. Ergon. **52**, 29–42 (2016)

Ferrara, L.: SYSTEMATEKS evolutionally design thinking and practice. In Proceeding of the Ninth International Conference on Design Principles and Practices (2015)

Design in Everyday Cooking: Challenges for Assisting with Menu Planning and Food Preparation

Atsushi Hashimoto[1(✉)], Jun Harashima[2], Yoko Yamakata[3], and Shinsuke Mori[1]

[1] Kyoto University, Yoshida Honmachi, Sakyo-ku, Kyoto 606-8501, Japan
ahasimoto@mm.media.kyoto-u.ac.jp
[2] Cookpad Inc, Yebisu Garden Place Tower 12F, 4-20-3 Ebisu, Shibuya-ku, Tokyo 150-6012, Japan
[3] The University of Tokyo, 7-3-1 Hongo, Bunkyo-ku, Tokyo 113-8656, Japan

Abstract. In this study, we introduce challenges for assisting with everyday cooking activities. Menu planning is the first step in daily cooking, and there are many commercial services available. We introduce the case study of "cookpad," one of the largest recipe portal sites, and illustrate their efforts to maintain an up-to-date recipe search system. As an academic challenge, situated recipe recommendation is also introduced. Food preparation is another important topic. We present our perspective based on the relationship between recipe texts and cooking activities, along with related studies.

Keywords: Recipe · Cooking activity

1 Introduction

Cooking is a fundamental activity in our daily lives. A good meal enriches our quality of life, and it promotes wellness as well as provides pleasure. It can act to ease family budgets. In some cases, a meal can have specific religious or cultural meanings. To address these multifaceted needs, various types of improvement to cooking and meal planning might be possible by designing systems with the support of information and communication technology.

Daily cooking activities include regular repetition of planning a menu, preparing food, and eating. For eating, the main target for improvement concerns health administration [1–6]. The challenge of these studies is to recognize a menu and estimate a user's nutritional intake from a photo taken by the user's mobile phone. To encourage good eating habits, Takeuchi et al. [7] designed an interactive tool on a social network service; users can share photos of their meals and receive remarks from their friends via this tool. This communication tool is designed to prompt users to make healthier menu choices, by secretly sorting positive remarks based on the healthiness of the meal.

P.-L.P. Rau (Ed.): CCD 2016, LNCS 9741, pp. 182–192, 2016.
DOI: 10.1007/978-3-319-40093-8_19

Although there are a multitude of interesting studies concerning eating, it is difficult to introduce them all. In this study, we focus on recent attempts to design modern applications for assisting with menu planning and food preparation, as these are activities of interest for us.

There are many recipe portal sites, and they are accessible from all over the world, because menu planning is a task that is directly related to people's purchasing behavior. In spite of the universal need of recipe sites, there are large cultural differences in recipes. As is clear from the fact that "Washoku" (Japanese cuisine) won world heritage status in 2013, cooking has deep cultural aspects. Religions, histories, climates, and industrial progress are all related to local foods. A typical cross-cultural problem is translation of recipes, which is one of the desired applications. Ingredients, culinary arts, cooking devices, and equipment are subject to translation as well as language. In this sense, cooking is a challenging target for cross-cultural computing.

This manuscript is organized as follows. Section 2 introduces the technical efforts of a recipe portal site "cookpad"[1] as a case study of a commercial assistive service for menu planning. Academic challenges for menu planning are overviewed in Sect. 3. Section 4 summarizes assistive systems for food preparation from the viewpoint of the relationship between recipe texts and human actions. Finally, Sect. 5 presents the conclusion.

2 Challenges in a Company

In this section, we describe challenges faced by cookpad, an Internet site comprising over 2.2 million recipes as of January 2016, making it one of the largest recipe sites in the world. Of the many challenges faced by the site, we specifically introduce those that are closely related to academic research.

Recipe Search. Like general recipe sites, cookpad provides users with a search box to help them find recipes efficiently. Because recipes in cookpad are written in Japanese, which is a language that does not delimit words by white-spaces, morphological analysis is necessary to recognize words in the recipes. The analyzer in cookpad uses a manually maintained dictionary consisting of a vast number of food-related words. In the recipe search, synonymous expressions are also recognized using a domain-specific synonym dictionary, which is also maintained manually.

Recipe Classification. To find recipes, it is not sufficient merely to provide a search box. In cookpad, recipes are automatically classified into various categories (e.g., meat dishes, seafood dishes, vegetable dishes) and users can limit their search results using this information. The classification is based on a machine learning method (using support vector machines) where tens of thousands of recipes are used as labeled data. To ensure service quality, the precision for each category is maintained at 90 % or above so that users can find relevant recipes easily.

[1] http://cookpad.com/.

Content Selection. Search results consisting only of recipes may not always satisfy the user's information need. According to users' queries, major search engines show not only web pages but also other content (e.g., YouTube videos in Google search results). Likewise, the cookpad shows not only recipes but also various other content (e.g., tips, news, and videos related to the user's queries). For each query, content is selected based on a multi-armed bandit algorithm to maximize its click-through rate.

Research Promotion. To promote food research, cookpad has made its recipes available [8] through the National Institute of Informatics (NII), a Japanese Research Institute with the goal of advancing informatics research. The 1.7 million recipes involved in this challenge are those that were uploaded to cookpad by the end of September 2014. This data collection was released in February 2015.[2] Any researcher in public institutions (e.g., university) can obtain access to the collection for research purposes and as of January 2016, 82 research groups at 56 universities had already done so.

3 Academic Challenges for a Smart Recipe Search

3.1 Cooking Recipe Recommendations Using Surrounding Information

One of the most stressful issues for homemakers is to decide the day's menu [9]. Many homemakers browse the web to decide what they are going to cook each day. Although most existing recipe search systems request that the user submits a query, such as the name of the menu that they want or names of the ingredients that they want to use [10–12], people cannot always explain the property of the recipe that they are looking for, even if they have a preference for a recipe. To deal with these issues, we considered that what people want to eat must strongly depend on their daily circumstances and that a recipe cooked in a given situation must be preferred by someone who is in a similar situation. Therefore, we have proposed a method that recommends recipes not only according to a recipe's properties but also according to the user's situation.

On the web, there are many blog-type recipes that describe not only the recipe itself but also the reason why the recipe was selected. We analyzed 2,074 blog-type recipes which were randomly collected from "RECIPE BLOG" [13]. We found that 48.2 % blog-type recipes describe at least one reason for selecting recipes and that these reasons could be classified into 18 categories. We then devised an algorithm that extracts situations corresponding to the 18 categories from a user's life log, such as his or her tweets, and recommends recipes that have similar reasons to the extracted ones. We evaluated the proposed method under three fictitious scenarios; in two of them, the user had vague requirements for recipes and they could only describe their situation as "it was so busy today." We call it as "situational scenario." The other had concrete requirements such as

[2] http://www.nii.ac.jp/dsc/idr/cookpad/cookpad.html.

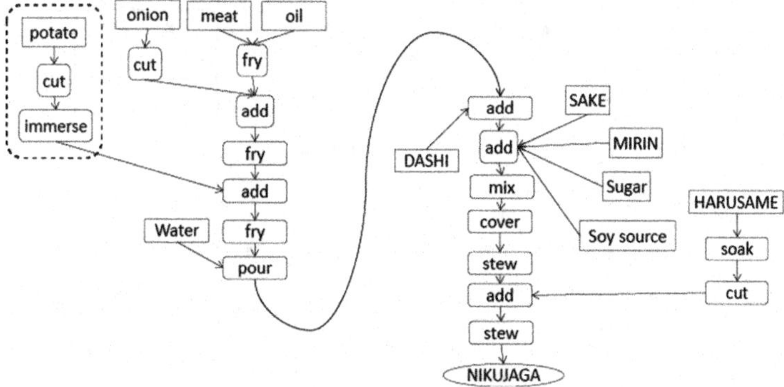

Fig. 1. A recipe tree of one "NIKUJAGA" recipe.

"I bought Pacific saury for a good price." We call this a "procedural scenario." We input the description of each scenario into the proposed system and obtained the top ten results. As a baseline method, we also made queries derived from each scenario and found ten recipes that contained the queries as a part of the recipes. Five examinees evaluated each recipe recommended by the two methods using a five-point scale. The proposed method obtained a higher score than the baseline method in the two situational scenarios, while the baseline method obtained a higher score in the procedural one. Therefore, the proposed method is useful when a user cannot make his or her requirements clear as mentioned above. For details, please refer to [14].

3.2 Recipe Comparison Using a Recipe Flow-Graph

As will be shown in the next section, we are constructing a method to translate the procedural text of a recipe into a flow-graph, which will represent the procedural workflow of a recipe, such as which cooking actions are performed to which ingredients, and which ingredients are mixed with each other. Although the flow-graph introduced in the next section can be described as a Directed Acyclic Graph (DAG), it can be simplified to an ordered labeled tree, as shown in Fig. 1, which we call a recipe tree, as we focus on the flow related to ingredients, tools and cooking actions. A recipe tree has significant advantages over a recipe flow-graph because it has multiple fast and effective graph-matching algorithms, including the editing distance calculation. Therefore, we have proposed a method to calculate similarities (distance) between two recipes by calculating the editing distance between their recipe trees.

In general for unordered labeled trees, including recipe trees, the problem of computing the editing distance between two trees is difficult (more precisely, the problem is known to be NP-hard [15]). Therefore, we developed heuristic algorithms specialized for cooking recipe trees. The proposed method not only calculates the distance between two recipes but also derives the details of their differences. Figure 2 shows the mapping result between two "NIKUJAGA"

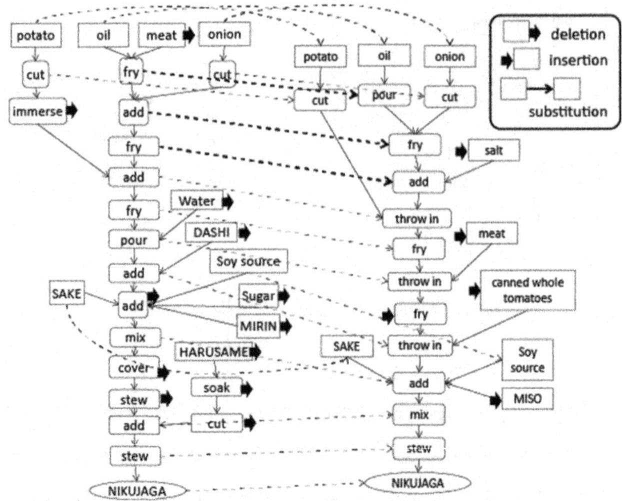

Fig. 2. Result of mapping one "Nikujaga" recipe to another.

recipes when one recipe is mapped onto the other, with minimal operation costs. According to the result, we can easily note differences such as "the timing of mixing meat differs between the two recipes" and the action "immerse the cut potato" in the left recipe is omitted in the right one. Moreover, we have proposed a method to find a common cooking flow of a specific dish by extracting the common structures of recipe trees that are translated from the top ten search results from the name of that specific dish. The details of these methods are provided in [16]. In a related study, Wang et al. [17] also proposed flow-graph representations of recipes. They defined the similarity between two recipes based on the number of common subgraphs shared by two recipes.

4 Assistive Applications for Food Preparation

Recipes are important information sources in food preparation. People prefer to eat a different menu everyday. Some external factors, such as childbirth or a sick family member, may force us to change our repertoire of dishes. Both a variety of recipes and comprehensive recipe presentation are important to enrich our food preparation experience.

Figure 3 shows our image of the applications and agendas in this topic. This perspective is inspired by machine translation via an intermediate model; this is, once we map the recipe text and observed food preparation activities onto a semantic model, we can directly compare the text and activities. In this sense, the semantic model of the working process corresponds to an intermediate language model in the machine translation problem.

A typical application is **recipe generation from observation**, which is achieved by agendas C→B in Fig. 3. There are many challenges to recognizing

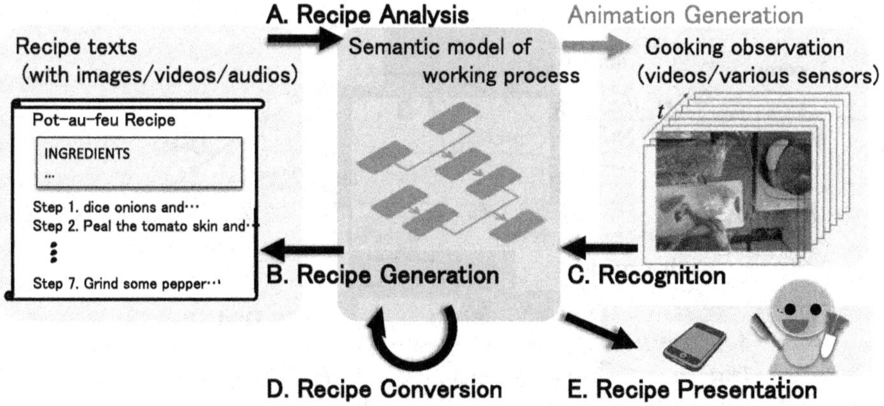

Fig. 3. Translation of Recipe/Observation into an intermediate model and its applications.

food preparation activities (agenda C) [18–27] and some to generating recipe texts (agenda B) [28].

Recipe translation is realized by A→D→B. Agenda D has not yet been studied in detail; a comparison in the structured recipe representation in Fig. 2 is the first step of D, i.e. this study is front-line research toward this goal. As mentioned in Sect. 3.2, the DAG (or tree) representation of a recipe is a natural structural organization of the cooking process, and some research teams have proposed methods to extract the structure from recipe texts (agenda A) [29–31]. Most of the challenges facing processes A and B are addressed in the Japanese language [16,30,31], and but little in other languages [29]. For recipe translation and localization, it is important to develop these techniques in multiple languages.

An example of a workflow structure provided by [30] is shown in Fig. 4 with vertex labels (Table 1) and edge labels (Table 2). This is the flow extracted from a recipe posted on cookpad. Because recipes on cookpad are user-generated, texts are informal and there are many difficulties: disparate notation, non-regularized manners of reference, and broken contexts of descriptions.

To extract the complete structure from informal recipes, it might be useful to complement the recipes with information derived from observation. One of our recent trials attempted to match recipe texts and cooking observations in the semantic model to obtain reliable and informative structural representations of the recipes. The number of matched pairs results in statistical information concerning human activities, i.e., the human tendency to cook a dish following a recipe. Such information should enhance performance in systems involving agendas A-E.

While the above applications contribute to increasing the variety of recipes, there are a series of proposals to improve recipe presentation [18,32–38]. Most of them [32–35,37,38] assume a simple recipe structure, which is a sequence

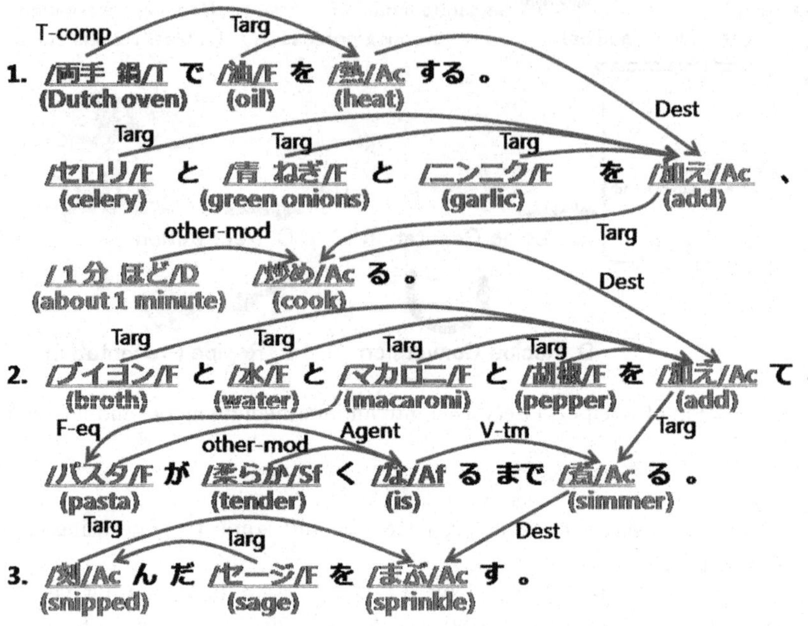

Fig. 4. An example of flowgraph.

Table 1. Named entity tags.

NE tag	Meaning
F	Food
T	Tool
D	Duration
Q	Quantity
Ac	Action by the chef
Af	Action by foods
Sf	State of foods
St	State of tools

Table 2. Edge labels.

Edge label	Meaning
Agent	Action agent
Targ	Action target
Dest	Action destination
F-comp	Food complement
T-comp	Tool complement
F-eq	Food equality
F-part-of	Food part-of
F-set	Food set
T-eq	Tool equality
T-part-of	Tool part-of
A-eq	Action equality
V-tm	Head verb of a clause for timing, etc.
Other-mod	Other relationships

of steps. A few other studies use the DAG or tree structure for a more intelligent recipe presentation [18,36].

In [18], we have forecasted the next intended step of a user via human-object interaction on a cooking surface. A human interacts with objects to proceed with cooking tasks. Simultaneously, the human puts objects aside if they are in his or her way. The challenge was to identify the intended step even while such out-of-context interactions are observed with informative interactions. The proposed method estimates the progress of the cooking process from the history of the interactions together with the intended next step. The estimated progress narrows down the options for the next step. In the experiment, the proposed method achieved more than 70 % accuracy in its forecast. Because forecasting is generally a difficult task of pattern recognition, this is a remarkable score, nonetheless the accuracy should be enhanced by more sophisticated semantic models with statistical information.

5 Conclusions

In this study, we introduced challenges for assisting with everyday cooking activities, particularly menu planning and food preparation. There are many commercial websites that provide recipes. Accurate and easy-to-use recipe search and recommendation tools are important to increase the number of customers. We introduced challenges by cookpad as a practical example. An accurate and large corpus is critical to achieve a practical recipe search engine. Companies pay a lot of efforts to maintain their corpus and keep the system up-to-date.

We also introduced academic challenges for menu planning. There is a lot of room for academic researchers to enhance recipe recommendation. Food preferences are influenced by the user's day; therefore, a highly customized recipe recommendation requires a daily context of the family members. From this perspective, both web mining and Life logging are within the scope of this application.

While there have been several assistive systems and related methods for food preparation, one of the most important challenges is to obtain a highly informative semantic model of the food preparation process. We believe that matching the recipe text and cooking observations will provide a breakthrough in this topic. Finally, more challenges in non-Japanese languages are waited for cross-cultural applications in everyday cooking.

Acknowledgement. This work was supported by JSPS KAKENHI Grant Numbers 24240030, 26280039, 26280084.

References

1. Wang, X., Kumar, D., Thome, N., Cord, M., Precioso, F.: Recipe recognition with large multimodal food dataset. In: Proceedings of IEEE International Conference on Multimedia & Expo Workshops, pp. 1–6 (2015)

2. Anthimopoulos, M., Gianola, L., Scarnato, L., Diem, P., Mougiakakou, S.: A food recognition system for diabetic patients based on an optimized bag of features approach. IEEE J. Biomed. Health Inform. **18**(4), 1261–1271 (2014)
3. Sudo, K., Murasaki, K., Shimamura, J., Taniguchi, Y.: Estimating nutritional value from food images based on semantic segmentation. In: Proceedings of the 2014 ACM International Joint Conference on Pervasive and Ubiquitous Computing: Adjunct Publication. UbiComp 2014 Adjunct, pp. 571–576 (2014)
4. Kitamura, K., Yamasaki, T., Aizawa, K.: Foodlog: capture, analysis and retrieval of personal food images via web. In: Proceedings of the ACM Multimedia 2009 Workshop on Multimedia for Cooking and Eating Activities, pp. 23–30 (2009)
5. Khanna, N., Boushey, C.J., Kerr, D., Okos, M., Ebert, D.S., Delp, E.J.: An overview of the technology assisted dietary assessment project at purdue university. In: Proceedings of 2010 IEEE International Symposium on Multimedia, pp. 290–295 (2010)
6. Kawano, Y., Yanai, K.: Food image recognition with deep convolutional features. In: Proceedings of ACM UbiComp Workshop on Workshop on Smart Technology for Cooking and Eating Activities (CEA), September 2014
7. Takeuchi, T., Fujii, T., Narumi, T., Tanikawa, T., Hirose, M.: Considering individual taste in social feedback to improve eating habits. In: Proceedings of IEEE International Conference on Multimedia & Expo Workshops, pp. 1–6 (2015)
8. Harashima, J., Ariga, M., Murata, K., Ioki, M.: A large-scale recipe and meal data collection as infrastructure for food research. In: Proceedings of the 10th International Conference on Language Resources and Evaluation (2016, to appear)
9. Mynavi Corporation: Cooking related questionary investi-gation reported by Mynavi woman on 27th (in Japanese). http://woman.mynavi.jp/article/140227-44/. Accessed 1 Feb 2016
10. Oyama, S., Kokubo, T., Ishida, T.: Domain-specific web search with keyword spices. IEEE Trans. Knowl. Data Eng. **16**(1), 17–27 (2004)
11. Tsukuda, K., Yamamoto, T., Nakamura, S., Tanaka, K.: Plus one or minus one: a method to browse from an object to another object by adding or deleting an element. In: Bringas, P.G., Hameurlain, A., Quirchmayr, G. (eds.) DEXA 2010, Part II. LNCS, vol. 6262, pp. 258–266. Springer, Heidelberg (2010)
12. Chung, Y.: Finding food entity relationships using user-generated data in recipe service. In: Proceedings of the 21st ACM International Conference on Information and Knowledge Management, pp. 2611–2614 (2012)
13. Ai-Land Co., Ltd.: Recipe blog (in Japanese). http://www.recipe-blog.jp/. Accessed 1 Feb 2016
14. Kadowaki, T., Mori, S., Yamakata, Y., Tanaka, K.: Recipe search for blog-type recipe articles based on a users situation. In: Proceedings of ACM Conference on Ubiquitous Computing, pp. 497–506 (2014)
15. Zhang, K., Jiang, T.: Some MAX SNP-hard results concerning unordered labeled trees. Inf. Process. Lett. **49**(5), 249–254 (1994)
16. Yamakata, Y., Imahori, S., Sugiyama, Y., Mori, S., Tanaka, K.: Feature extraction and summarization of recipes using flow graph. In: Jatowt, A., et al. (eds.) SocInfo 2013. LNCS, vol. 8238, pp. 241–254. Springer, Heidelberg (2013)
17. Wang, L., Li, Q., Li, N., Dong, G., Yang, Y.: Substructure similarity measurement in chinese recipes. In: Proceedings of the 17th International Conference on World Wide Web, pp. 979–988 (2008)
18. Hashimoto, A., Inoue, J., Funatomi, T., Minoh, M.: How does user's access to object make HCI smooth in recipe guidance? In: Rau, P.L.P. (ed.) CCD 2014. LNCS, vol. 8528, pp. 150–161. Springer, Heidelberg (2014)

19. Shimada, A., Kondo, K., Deguchi, D., Morin, G., Stern, H.: Kitchen scene context based gesture recognition: a contest in ICPR2012. In: Jiang, X., Bellon, O.R.P., Goldgof, D., Oishi, T. (eds.) WDIA 2012. LNCS, vol. 7854, pp. 168–185. Springer, Heidelberg (2013)
20. Iscen, A., Duygulu, P.: Knives are picked before slices are cut: recognition through activity sequence analysis. In: Proceedings of the 5th International Workshop on Multimedia for Cooking and Eating Activities, pp. 3–8 (2013)
21. Rohrbach, M., Amin, S., Andriluka, M., Schiele, B.: A database for fine grained activity detection of cooking activities. In: Proceedings of 2012 IEEE Conference on Computer Vision and Pattern Recognition, pp. 1194–1201 (2012)
22. Packer, B., Saenko, K., Koller, D.: A combined pose, object, and feature model for action understanding. In: Proceedings of 2012 IEEE Conference on Computer Vision and Pattern Recognition, pp. 1378–1385 (2012)
23. Lei, J., Ren, X., Fox, D.: Fine-grained kitchen activity recognition using RGB-D. In: Proceedings of the 2012 ACM Conference on Ubiquitous Computing, pp. 208–211 (2012)
24. Hashimoto, A., Inoue, J., Nakamura, K., Funatomi, T., Ueda, M., Yamakata, Y., Minoh, M.: Recognizing ingredients at cutting process by integrating multimodal features. In: Proceedings of the ACM Multimedia 2012 Workshop on Multimedia for Cooking and Eating Activities, pp. 13–18 (2012)
25. Ueda, M., Funatomi, T., Hashimoto, A., Watanabe, T., Minoh, M.: Developing a real-time system for measuring the consumption of seasoning. In: Proceedings of IEEE ISM 2011 Workshop on Multimedia for Cooking and Eating Activities, pp. 393–398 (2011)
26. Hashimoto, A., Mori, N., Funatomi, T., Mukunoki, M., Kakusho, K., Minoh, M.: Tracking food materials with changing their appearance in food preparing. In: Proceedings of ISM 2010 Workshop on Multimedia for Cooking and Eating Activities, pp. 248–253. IEEE (2010)
27. Miyawaki, K., Sano, M.: A virtual agent for a cooking navigation system using augmented reality. In: Prendinger, H., Lester, J.C., Ishizuka, M. (eds.) IVA 2008. LNCS (LNAI), vol. 5208, pp. 97–103. Springer, Heidelberg (2008)
28. Yamasaki, T., Yoshino, K., Maeta, H., Sasada, T., Hashimoto, A., Funatomi, T., Yamakata, Y., Mori, S.: Procedual text generation from a flow graph. IPSJ J. **57**(3) (to appear). Written in Japanese
29. Kiddon, C., Ponnuraj, G.T., Zettlemoyer, L., Choi, Y.: Mise en place: unsupervised interpretation of instructional recipes. In: Proceedings of the 2015 Conference on Empirical Methods in Natural Language Processing, pp. 982–992 (2015)
30. Maeta, H., Sasada, T., Mori, S.: A framework for procedural text understanding. In: Proceedings of the 14th International Conference on Parsing Technologies (2015)
31. Karikome, S., Fujii, A.: Improving structural analysis of cooking recipe text. IEICE Tech. Rep. Data Eng. **112**(75), 43–48 (2012)
32. Sato, A., Watanabe, K., Rekimoto, J.: Shadow cooking: situated guidance for a fluid cooking experience. In: Stephanidis, C., Antona, M. (eds.) UAHCI 2014, Part III. LNCS, vol. 8515, pp. 558–566. Springer, Heidelberg (2014)
33. Matsushima, Y., Funabiki, N., Zhang, Y., Nakanishi, T., Watanabe, K.: Extensions of cooking guidance function on android tablet for homemade cooking assistance system. In: IEEE 2nd Global Conference on Consumer Electronics, pp. 397–401 (2013)
34. Halupka, V., Almahr, A., Pan, Y., Cheok, A.D.: Chop chop: a sound augmented kitchen prototype. In: Nijholt, A., Romão, T., Reidsma, D. (eds.) ACE 2012. LNCS, vol. 7624, pp. 494–497. Springer, Heidelberg (2012)

35. Uriu, D., Namai, M., Tokuhisa, S., Kashiwagi, R., Inami, M., Okude, N.: Panavi: recipe medium with a sensors-embedded pan for domestic users to master professional culinary arts. In: Proceedings of the SIGCHI Conference on Human Factors in Computing Systems, pp. 129–138 (2012)
36. Hamada, R., Okabe, J., Ide, I., Sakai, S., Tanaka, H.: Cooking navi: assistant for daily cooking in kitchen. In: Proceedings of the 13th Annual ACM International Conference on Multimedia, pp. 371–374 (2005). Written in Japanese
37. Bradbury, J.S., Shell, J.S., Knowles, C.B.: Hands on cooking: towards an attentive kitchen. In: Proceedings of CHI 2003 Extended Abstracts on Human Factors in Computing Systems, pp. 996–997 (2003)
38. Ju, W., Hurwitz, R., Judd, T., Lee, B.: Counteractive: an interactive cookbook for the kitchen counter. In: Proceedings of CHI 2001 Extended Abstracts on Human Factors in Computing Systems, pp. 269–270. ACM, New York (2001)

QUALIA into the Fashion Show Case Analysis

Shu Hui Huang(✉), Ming Chw Wei, and Tzu Chiang Chang

Graduate School of Creative Industry Design, National Taiwan University of Arts, Banqiao District, New Taipei City 22058, Taiwan
shhuang@textiles.org.tw, ntua10070801@gmail.com, chang.tc0214@msa.hinet.net

Abstract. "A sense of qualia experience" provides an emotional quality by a well-designed strategy to amuse the Target Audience (TA). Nowadays, the fashion industry supplies its TA with high value-added experiences that include a variety of sensitivity, touching, and qualia, into their daily lives. The purpose of this research is to explore the exhibition design of fashion industry activity applied by differentiation and specialization through five aspects of QUALIA, including attractiveness, beauty, creativity, delicacy, and engineering, for future references. Based on the analysis of the data research, the audience has shown internalization of the culture and creativity through building an atmosphere, storytelling, perceptual-space creating, and visual-experiences, shaping from curatorial design of fashion show industry.

Keywords: Qualia · Fashion show · S-O-R model · Cultural creativity

1 Introduction

Creative Life Industry, which integrates experiences of livelihood industries and high quality aesthetics, plays an important role in guiding enterprises to apply the concepts of experience economy. There are various competitive elements that play significant roles within the economic development from industrial to experience-economy. These include quality, function, brand, service, and information. Additionally, the key factors that create the experience-economy are the "service space" and "qualia." According to Lin (2011), in order for the development of economy and culture to flourish, "experiences" are applied to four dimensions which include space, service, product and promotion of an enterprise.

After integrating culture with "design creativity," a form of "aesthetics economics" was produced and transformed into a "design industry." There are many components that influence the design stages of brand-name fashion. These range from cultural strengths, integration of unique creativity, and emphasis of QUALIA traits. For this reason, the success of a product in the fashion market is closely related "QUALIA." As a result, Taiwan has begun to shift into a cultural and creative industry by creating their own brands and QUALIA products. Fashion brand companies realized that product success depended not only on its market and technology aspects, but also innovation in service.

P.-L.P. Rau (Ed.): CCD 2016, LNCS 9741, pp. 193–204, 2016.
DOI: 10.1007/978-3-319-40093-8_20

The features of QUALIA enables users to become subjective of all the qualities that contribute to the product's uniqueness. To explain, level of attraction, beauty, creativity, and engineering are all features of QUALIA that trigger interaction within the mind. Previous research mainly focused on applying QUALIA in the area of product design. This study extends that perspective to exploring curatorial design of fashion activity and proposes differentiation and specialization for future references.

2 The S-O-R Paradigm Perspective

Studies on how the environment affects human behavior has its roots in Psychology. For instance, Schacter (2011) argued that in order to understand the environment, perception is necessary and defined as the organization, identification, and interpretation of sensory information. Similarly, Goldstein (2009) states that all perception involves signals in the nervous system, which in turn, results from physical or chemical stimulation of sensory organs. Perception is not the passive receipt of these signals, but is shaped by learning, memory, expectation, and attention (Gregory 1987; Bernstein 2010).

Atmospherics is a qualitative construct that encompasses four of the main senses, with the exclusion of taste. In marketing terms, Philip Kotler (1973) defines "Atmospherics" as the conscious designing of space to create certain effects in buyers. He also argued "Atmospherics" as a tangible product and is only a small part of the total consumption package. Buyers respond to the entire product, which include services, warranties, packaging, advertising, pleasantries, images and so on.

Stimulus-response theory was the first to suggest a link between environment and behavior. In Marketing research, Kotler (1973) initially referred to the importance of environmental atmospherics as a marketing tool. The Mehrabian-Russell Model is based on the Stimulus-Organism-Response(S-O-R) paradigm, which includes components of the environment (S) that induce approach-avoidance behaviors (R) within the environment. They are mediated by the individual's emotional states (O) aroused by the environment. Mehrabian and Russell (1974) states that responses to an environment are classified as either approach or avoidance behaviors. Lazarus (1998) criticized this behavioristic psychology perspective by arguing that "a person in this interchange is a passive creature, reacting to an environment that stimulates him or her, and that person's influence on the environment is ignored."

Commercial space is divided into three different atmospheres: intended atmosphere, designed space, and perceived atmosphere. Kotler presents atmospherics as an important concept that largely influences position when determining value. Kotler proposes that applying brand fashion show to connecting atmospheres will produce a causal chain:

- Effect of perceived sensory qualities
- TA's perception of the sensory qualities
- Impact of TA's modified information and affective state
- Sensory qualities of space surrounding object of purchase.

3 The Branded Service Space Perspective

Service space is a concept that was developed by Booms and Bitner (1981) to emphasize the impact of the physical environment when a service process takes place. Booms & Bitner defined a servicescape as "the environment in which the service is assembled and in which the seller and customer interact, combined with tangible commodities that facilitate performance or communication of the service." The servicescape divides into the exterior (landscape, exterior design, signage, parking, surrounding environment) and the interior (interior design and decor, equipment, signage, layout, air quality, temperature and ambiance). Bitner (1992) coined the term 'servicescapes' in reference to the physical surroundings, as fashioned by service organizations, to facilitate the provision of service offerings to customers.

A brand encompasses the name, logo, image, and perceptions that identify a product, service, or provider in the minds of customers. It takes shape in advertising, packaging, and other marketing communications, and becomes a focus in the relationship with consumers. Brand equity is defined as the value of a brand. According to cognitive psychology, brand equity lies in consumers' awareness of brand features and associations, which drive attributions and perceptions. Branded environments extend the experience of an organization's brand, or distinguishing characteristics as expressed in names, symbols and designs, to the design of interior or exterior physical settings (Bertil 2011). It uses space as a physical embodiment of the brand to create a "brand space." This is achieved through "architecture, interiors, lighting, graphics, landscape" in spaces such as retail stores, showrooms, trade-fair booths and office environments.

Servicescape comprised of ambient factors, design factors and social factors (Ezeh and Harris 2007). Similarly, fashion show environmental stimuli are comprised of both ambient and design factors. Creators of branded fashion show environments leverage the effect of the physical structure and organization of space to help deliver their TAs' identity attributes, personality and key messages. In fashion shows, the catwalk servicescape involves exterior space (exterior design, signage, surrounding environment) and interior space (interior design and decor, stage, equipment, signage, layout, air quality, temperature and atmosphere). Various benefits of a fashion branded environment include improved brand position and communication, greater audience recognition, differentiation from competitors, and higher perceived value. The concept of fashion show servicescape and audience experiences help assess the difference between a fashion brand and a fashion industry.

4 QUALIA Perspective

The former Chief Executive Officer of Sony Corporation, Nobuyuki Idei, believes that market products and "QUALIA" are closely related. Qualia design is considered to be one of the pivotal components in cultural and creative life industries. It has a significant impact on consumer perception of innovation. Until now, research investigating use the QUALIA were more focused in the area of product design. According to the study conducted by Ko et al. (2009); Lin (2011), examined a cultural product design model that internalizes the awareness of culture and creativity through atmosphere building, storytelling, perceptual-space creating, and touch-experience design. Based on the analysis above, the conclusion is that the TA internalizes all these features and information that are shaped from curatorial design of fashion industry and have an impact on their experience and interpretation. Research on QUALIA design factors of the fashion exhibition environment display that QUALIA design provides a deep understanding of the link between target audience behaviors and new ways of interpreting feature-responses. To investigate the effect of QUALIA empirically, it is necessary to analyze participants' emotions and interactions within the fashion show. This article analyzes the psychological processes that produce the various emotional expressions that occurred throughout the fashion show of emotions references the emotional expressions produced in the fashion show and analyzes the psychological processes.

4.1 Attractiveness Perspective

Visual attractiveness, produced primarily by visual stimuli, is a quality that produces a strong desire. It generates emotions of interest and attracts attention to an object, event, or process.

4.2 Beauty Perspective

Beauty is a quality that is visually pleasing. The experience of "beauty" often involves an interpretation of some entity as being in balance and harmony with nature, which may lead to feelings of attraction and emotional well-being. Because this can be a subject experience, it is often said that "beauty" is in the eye of the beholder. For instance, in a fashion show, visually stimulating experiences are created and influenced by sensational clothing showpieces, external elements, fashion model, stage style, music levels, etc. Therefore, the performance effect and emotional expression embodies psychology and consciousness.

4.3 Creativity Perspective

Creativity is a phenomenon in which something new and valuable is formed. Re-search by Dr. Mark Batey of the Psychometrics at Work Research Group at Manchester Business School has suggested that the creative profile can be explained by four primary creativity traits with narrow facets within each. "Idea Generation" (Fluency, Originality, Incubation and Illumination). "Personality" (Curiosity and Tolerance for Ambiguity). "Motivation" (Intrinsic, Extrinsic and Achievement). "Confidence" (Producing, Sharing and Implementing). Creativity in fashion shows involves performance strategy, theme, media application and originality.

4.4 Delicacy Perspective

Exhibition layout and design offer service and activity flow. The importance of delicacy perception and its influence can be seen in fashion shows. These factors consist of atmosphere creation, visual performances, fashion show space imagery, runway type, model type, clothing display techniques etc. We expect that the delicacy results can be used as a reference for relevant fashion runway design in the future.

4.5 Engineering Perspective

Kansei Engineering aims at the development of products and services by translating the customer's psychological feelings and needs into the domain of product design (i.e. parameters). Kansei Engineering parametrically links the customer's emotional responses (i.e. physical and psychological) to the properties and characteristics of a product or service. In consequence, products can be designed to bring forward the intended feeling. Kansei Engineering can be considered as a methodology within the research field of 'Affective Engineering'. Aside from the functional traits, the visual qualities engineering design may affect perception.

Fashion shows incorporate affective attributes such as brand attractiveness, style aesthetics, performance creativity, service delicacy and space engineering which are key factors consumers seek when selecting brand products. Therefore, fashion designs must consider not only audience products needs but also need offer qualia mentality and emotions.

5 Method

This study presents review of fashion-show environmental psychology articles based on the stimulus-organism-response paradigm. The paper follows the sequence of the Stimulus-Organism-Response(S-O-R) framework starting with environmental stimuli in fashion show settings. Then, audience's inner organism theories are reviewed, followed by behavioral responses. Fashion show target audience (TA) under the stimulus-response paradigm are viewed as machines which react automatically to stimuli. Therefore, the S-O-R suggests that when a person is exposed to external stimuli, 'inner organism changes' precede behavioral responses.

According to the S-O-R model, to investigate the effect of QUALIA empirically, it is necessary to analyze participants' interactions and emotions produced within the fashion show. The purpose of this research is to explore the exhibition design of fashion industry activity and apply the five aspects of QUALIA: attractiveness, beauty, creativity, delicacy, and engineering. Figure 1 describes the SOR model of QUALIA perception and processing involved in brand-fashion exhibition. The research method consists of three steps: sense environmental variables to understand participants emotional state information, then behavioral responses to design elements, and finally to apply QUALIA design into fashion show; and four stages: (1) Brand Showpieces design concept (translating fashion features into curatorial information and design elements), (2) exhibition set (project design, target, objective), (3) exhibition design (Strategy, theme, originality), and (4) designing exhibition layout (activity flow, environment visual). Therefore, QUALIA are elements of discourse between a participant and a brand. The aim of this paper is to review fashion exhibition environments, TA emotions, and cognition in fashion show experiences.

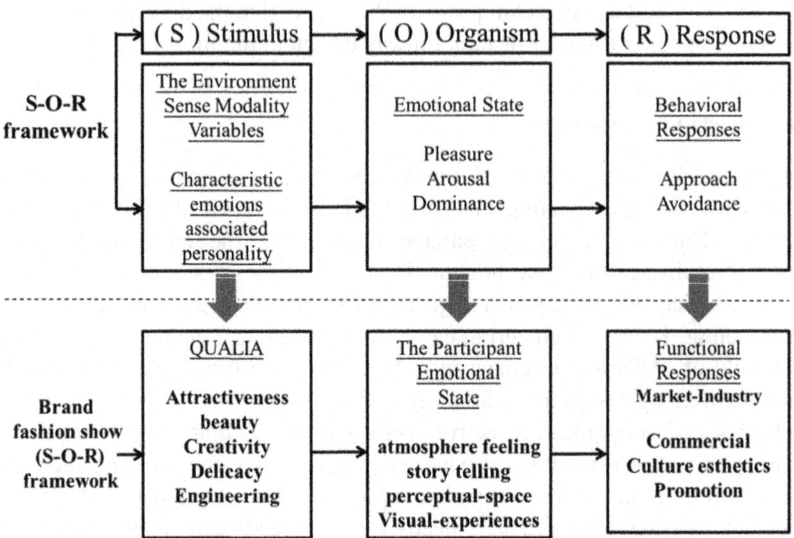

Fig. 1. Mehrabian and Russell Model (1974) A approach to environmental psychology; A conceptual framework for exploring the fashion show turning (S-O-R) into QUALIA.

The Stimulus-Organism-Response(S-O-R) paradigm dominated consumer behavior literature and has been widely employed in marketing. In recent years, the rapid development of Taiwan's creativity in the living industry began to promote service innovation; which also became a core competitive strength for the fashion industry. In order to match the requirements of innovative service, the process of QUALIA design has not only been introduced to the industry, but also created total experiences for the audiences and consumers.

6 Experimental Samples

This study is from the brand curatorial design of fashion show pragmatic experience and formality. Fashion brands trace back to the essence of new creative design concepts, showpieces, and curatorial works. Interpretations can be affected by attractiveness, relationship between brand, curatorial, operation of an art space, etc. In other words, the direction of curatorial and adjustments result from different experiences.

In this study, the experimental samples were based on the brand curatorial design of fashion shows. KERAIA not only offers combinations of ordinary clothing and party dresses, but also makes high-end fashion apparels and formal outfits. Following the international trend, they also launched brand-fashion shows to promote various seasonal products such as accessories, fashion leather products, shoes, hand-bags, and jewels. Given the research purposes, KERAIA's fashion show events over the past two years were observed.

Experimental Sample 1: Brand Fashion Show in Taipei IN Style (2014). Taipei IN Style's (TIS) core value is to promote the fashion industry in Taiwan by supporting not only the popular brands, but also the individual designers for their creativities and aspirations. KERAIA attended the new collection fashion show in TIS with the clear goal of introducing Taiwan fashion with the professionals worldwide. TIS strives to pull an all-in-one trade fair where a variety of events, ranging from press conferences, house shows, seminars, trunk shows, and business matching meetings, are all delicately presented for the numerous visitors. Table 1 is KERAIA curatorial design of fashion show with 2014 new collection- British Luxury beauty. Ms. Tsai Li-Yu, design director, chose to adhere to the new artistic aesthetics fusion. The Brand curatorial design of fashion show was a process consisting of showpieces design concept while setting the British Sweet and romantic theme as the visual environment. Plan atmosphere and show space imagery. The purpose is to promote Taiwan's designer brand. Target is especially for brand exposure for the international fashion media, business partners, and brand VIPs.

Table 1. KERAIA curatorial design of fashion show in Taipei IN Style, 2014

QUALIA into 2014 KERAIA curatorial design of fashion show British Luxury beauty			
Brand Showpieces Design concept	**Exhibition set**	**Exhibition design**	**Exhibition layout**
Color, Style, Shape **Atmosphere imagery** **Show space imagery**	**Project design** **Target** **Objective**	**Strategy** **Theme** **Originality**	**Activity flow** **Environment** **Visual**

TIS is a platform for Asian brands that also acts as a bridge connecting KERAIA with buyers. This is beneficial for both parties as they provide opportunities to meet, exchange of ideas, business discussions, and introduction of new potential friends from different parts of the world. Table 2 displays the types of QUALIA elements and Participant emotion definitions involved in the KERAIA fashion show. In relation to the performance effect, the artistic taste and emotion expression presented in the fashion show can stimulate the audience psychologically. In addition to media exposure and previously listed benefits, TIS also offers KERAIA VIPs the most up-to-date fashion and market trends, new product launchings, and special promotions through the TIS official website or Facebook. The QUALIA show also maintained the media and VIPs as significant roles.

Table 2. The types of QUALIA elements and Participant Emotion definitions in 2014 KERAIA fashion show.

Definition KERAIA Brand Fashion Show in Taipei IN Style, 2014 Venue: Song-Shan Cultural Park in Taipei, Taiwan			
Aspects of QUALIA	**Connotation**	**Design Element**	**Participant Emotional**
Attractiveness	Topic attraction Brand image design style Brand Equity		Famous Designer Fashion luxury brand Brand fans and VIPs
Beauty	Clothing Fashion Exhibit Design Senses emotion Aesthetic style		Supermodel Luxury design Visual beauty Fashion showpiece rend
Creativity	Novelty Interesting Surprise Pleasure Sense		Famous Actress Vocal Performance Art Ballet Dance
Delicacy	Business Services Internal space Event Planning		Professional trade fair Business Exchange Media Interview
Engineering	Field experience Atmosphere tone Comfortable		International trade show Professional show International runway

Experimental Sample 2: Brand Fashion Show in Mandarin Oriental, Taipei (2015). QUALIA branded environments consist of improved brand position and communication. KERAIA demonstrates this in their 20th anniversary brand festival by becoming renowned for providing "great customer service" to repay VIPs. The fashion show's high quality brand servicescape includes many features such as catwalk show venue, exterior space (exterior design, signage, surrounding environment) and interior space (interior design, decor, stage layout, air quality, temperature and atmosphere). Table 3 is KERAIA's curatorial design of fashion show in 2015, involving a new collection in a British Modern Chic style fashion. The process is comprised of showpieces design concepts, elegant vogue and low-key luxury, along with a British chic visual setting. Plan modern atmosphere and show space imagery. The purpose is to promote brand image. Brand curatorial fashion show target is especially for brand exposure to the local fashion media and fashion celebrities.

Table 3. KERAIA curatorial design of fashion show in Mandarin Oriental, Taipei, 2015

QUALIA into 2015 KERAIA curatorial design of fashion show British Modern Chic			
Brand Showpieces Design concept	**Exhibition set**	**Exhibition design**	**Exhibition layout**
Color, Style, Shape Atmosphere imagery Show space imagery	Project design Target Objective	Strategy Theme Originality	Activity flow Environment Visual

Wide ranges of creativity were presented in the fashion show, sourcing from audiences, curators, and fashion designers. Their integration of performance strategy, theme, media application and originality form provided KERALA's design for the 20th festival to become a truly unforgettable experience for participants. The types of QUALIA elements and Participant emotion definitions are summarized in Table 4. The KERAIA 2015 AW fashion catwalk show begins its performance through a symphony to exhibit light and sound sensation. Exhibition layout and design consists of British modern chic style. Activity flow and quality service prioritized to ensure delicacy perception in the fashion show. Delicacy atmosphere provides visual performances on the catwalk show. Perceived higher brand servicescape quality. KERAIA fashion show is summarized by affective attributes, attractiveness, style aesthetics, performance creativity, service

Table 4. The types of QUALIA elements and Participant Emotion definitions in 2015 KERAIA fashion show.

Definition KERAIA Brand Fashion Show in Mandarin Oriental, Taipei 2015 Venue: Mandarin Oriental in Taipei, Taiwan			
Aspects of QUALIA	**Connotation**	**Design Element**	**Participant Emotional**
Attractiveness 個人風格(感動與認同) 情感連結(追求與經典)	Topic attraction Brand image design style Brand Equity		Designer Brand 20th anniversary Fashion luxury brand Brand diehard Fans
Beauty	Clothing Fashion Exhibit Design Senses emotion Aesthetic style		Beautiful style Luxury design Fashion Famous ladies
Creativity	Novelty Interesting Surprise Pleasure Sense		Symphony perform light and sound sensation
Delicacy	Business Services Internal space Event Planning		British style decoration Visual atmosphere Social environment
Engineering	Field experience Atmosphere tone Comfortable		Five-star luxury hotel Comfortable seating Fresh temperature

delicacy, and space engineering. All of which are key factors that consumers seek when selecting brand name products. Customer relationship management, building brand image while maintaining VIPs feelings, is also very essential in becoming established among customers.

7 Conclusion

This article is to understand the process of how the "QUALIA" concept is formed in audience's minds and how they estimate this "QUALIA". Research is also trying to build a framework for the target audiences to calculate the qualia level of fashion show experience and services through S-O-R model literature review. These factors can also influence the comprehension of S-O-R model by participants and curators. Furthermore, we conclude this study of applying QUALIA in curatorial design in fashion shows.

1. For the audiences qualia perception and experiences:Creative Life Industry integrates experiences and quality aesthetics. The quality of the fashion show may be perceived as higher quality based on the environment in which the service is provided. An important role in guiding the fashion industry is to apply the concepts of the experience economy. In the fashion industry, curatorial design of the catwalk show should be expanded into a product that applies QUALIA into the designing experiences process such as Atmosphere building(topic attraction, design style, brand image, brand Equity), Sense-experiences (clothing style, exhibits design sense, sensory emotion, aesthetic appearance), Pleasant emotions (novelty, interesting, surprise, pleasure, sense of innovation), Practical functions (show service details, event space arrangement, external event planning, media exchanges PR), and Servicescape (field engineering experience, create an atmosphere of tonality, external environment planning). QUALIA in the fashion show relates to the performance effect in which the emotion expression embodies psychology and the consciousness.
2. For the Market-Industry functional responses:Based on the analysis above, the conclusion is that the TA is capable of internalizing the culture and creativity through building an atmosphere, storytelling, perceptual-space creating, or visual-experiences shaping from curatorial designs of fashion industry. In the fashion show emotion expression relates the performance effected, the emotion expression can embodies psychology and consciousness. According to this perspective, this study extends the view to explore the exhibition design of fashion industry activity by applying fashion art aesthetics, commercial functions, and the promotion of differentiation and specialization through the five aspects of QUALIA: attractiveness, beauty, creativity, delicacy, and engineering. This conclusion can serve as a reference for future interests in applying QUALIA to enhance industrial competitiveness.

This article demonstrates an established QUALIA curatorial fashion show model and can be utilized as a valuable reference when designing a cultural creative experience. With the development of industrial tendencies, fashion industry companies gradually realize that the keys to product innovation are not solely depend on market and technology aspects, but should also improve service innovation. Fashion brands are more focused on adapting with consumers by discovering ways to create new experiences and establish value. The KERAIA QUALIA fashion exhibition contributed a deep understanding regarding the link between target audience behaviors and new methods of interpreting specific features responses in the fashion show exhibition.

Acknowledgements. The authors would like to express their sincere gratitude to the KERAIA International Development Co. Ltd. and Taiwan Textile Federation for this study. We would also like to thank anonymous reviewers and the editor for their comments.

References

Aaker, D.A.: Managing Brand Equity. The Free Press, New York (1991)

Bernstein, D.A.: Essentials of Psychology. Cengage Learning, pp. 123–124 (2010)

Bertil, H.: Sensory marketing: the multi sensory brand-experience concept. Eur. Bus. Rev. **23**(3), 256–273 (2011)

Bitner, M. J.: Servicescapes: the impact of physical surroundings on customers and employees. J. Mark. 7–71 (1992)

Booms, B.H., Bitner, M.J.: Marketing strategies and organization structures for service firms. In: Donnelly, J., George, W.R. (eds.) Marketing of Services. American Marketing Association, Chicago (1981)

Bradford, J.: Fashion Journalism. Routledge, p. 129 (2014)

Cassidy, L., Fitch, K.: Beyond the catwalk: fashion public relations and social media in Australia. Asia Pac. Public Relat. J. 15(1) (2013)

Crawford, C.M., Benedetto, C.A.D.: New Product Management, 6th edn, pp. 10–11. McGraw-Hill, Irwin (2000)

Dalto, A.: Brands tempt female bloggers with 'swag'. O'Dwyer's Commun. New Media Fashion Issue **24**(9), 12–13 (2010)

Ezeh, C., Harris, L.C.: Servicescape research: a review and a research agenda (2007)

Farris, P.W., Bendle, N.T., Pfeifer, P.E., Reibstein, D.J.: Marketing metrics: the definitive guide to measuring marketing performance. Mark. Rev. **7**(1), 59–78 (2010)

Goldstein, E.: Sensation and perception. Cengage Learning, pp. 5–7 (2009)

Gregory, R.: "Perception" in Gregory, Zangwill, pp. 598–601 (1987)

JExperian.: Getting the most from social: An integrated marketing approach (2012)

Keller, K.L.: Brand synthesis: the multidimensionality of brand knowledge. J. Consum. Res. **29**(4), 595–600 (2003)

Ko, Y.-Y., Lin, P.-H., Lin, R.: A study of service innovation design in cultural and creative industry. In: Aykin, N. (ed.) IDGD 2009. LNCS, vol. 5623, pp. 376–385. Springer, Heidelberg (2009)

Kotler, P.: Atmospherics as a marketing tool. J. Retail. **49**(4), 48–64 (1973)

Lazarus, R.S.: Fifty years of research and theory by RS Lazarus: an analysis of historical and perennial issues: Lawrence Erlbaum (1998)

Mehrabian, A., Russell, J.A.: An Approach to Environmental Psychology. MIT Press, Cambridge (1974)

Neumeier, M.: The Brand Gap: How to Bridge the Distance Between Business Strategy and Design. New Riders Publishing, Berkeley (2006)

Lin, R.: From Service Innovation to Qualia Product Design (2011)

Rosenbaum, M.S.: The symbolic servicescape: your kind is welcomed here. J. Consum. Behav. **4**, 257–267 (2005)

Schacter, Daniel: Psychology. Worth Publishers (2011)
Sherman, G., Perlman, S.: Fashion public Relations. Fairchild Books, New York (2010)
Taipei: Brand Fashion Show in Mandarin Oriental. Taipei (2015)
Westfield, A.M.: The Role of Public Relations in Redefining Brands in the Fashion Industry. University of Southern California, Los Angeles (2002)
Yang, K.: Using the SOR model to understand the impact of website attributes on the online shopping experience (2012)
Yen, H.Y., Lin, C., Lin, R.: A study of applying Qualia to business model of creative industries. In: Cross-cultural design. Methods, practice, and case studies, pp. 148–156 (2013)

The Effect of the Transition Design of Artwork to the Purchasing Demand - A Case Study of Apparel Design

Chi-Ying Hung(✉) and Chung-Liang Chen

Graduate School of Creative Industry Design,
National Taiwan University of Arts, Ban Ciao City, Taiwan
yumeeiren@gmail.com

Abstract. Under the standard of mass production, how to apply different elements to the apparel in customized space is an issue concerned by the designer. The energy from the artist is inexhaustible. If it can be extended to apply to the apparel, such policy selection shall create the demand of customers. The purpose of this study is to evaluate and compare the effect of the transition design of artwork to the purchasing demand of the customers. There were thirteen apparels chosen and divided into three groups. Except for the art group, which was the test group for the artwork conversion, pop group and memorial group were selected for comparison. From the result of the study, we found that the elements coming from the artwork and converted the design on to the T-shirt having higher demand evaluation in "Artistic atmosphere", "cultural connotation", and "special design". The conclusion was that art group implied more proportion in the demand factor of "souvenir". In contrast, the basic demand factors such as "figure modification" and "product price" obtained lower evaluation levels. At last, this study offers four proposals including price-oriented mode of production, functional fabrics material value added, joint brand marketing planning and cross-border cooperation in apparel design, and wishes to popularize the art of living through apparel.

Keywords: Artwork transition design mode · Apparel design · Souvenir · Purchasing demand

1 Introduction

Transferring the poetry with cultural thickness into artistic painting to reflect poetic feeling to people is the artistic conception through "painting" illustrated by artists who construct creative mode to transmit the situational poetry (Lin and Lin 2015). Such creative concept is that the artists, after passing inner transformation, perform the external form of aesthetics on the work. They use the characters codes of the poetry as a bridge to shorten the communication distance between the painters and the viewers. In addition, it contains the depth of the cultural creativeness. If it is transferred into art products, it must have development value with commercial mode. However, the artists take full-time in personal creation and usually they have insufficient knowledge in experiencing the art products and market transactions. The common way they use

P.-L.P. Rau (Ed.): CCD 2016, LNCS 9741, pp. 205–216, 2016.
DOI: 10.1007/978-3-319-40093-8_21

usually is selling to the customers through gallery or the manager. Therefore, they do not consider concretely how to commercialize the art commodities. And the application of the cultural creativeness is limited to traditional souvenir only (Lin et al. 2016).

Hsieh and Guan (2011) had taken the artists' works as the subjects and proposed the design mode to transorm the artistic products. Thus, taking the artwork as a media to design the artistic products was becoming a trend of cross-boundary cooperation between the art and the design. By the value exchange between them, the market of artistic products was created. In addition, the reading people could collect artistic products which were more affordable than the original works after enjoying the exhibition of paintings. Thus, it could provide another incoming source for the artists to extend the creation of life.

At present, historical relics from museum or with local characteristic such as aboriginal culture or Hakka culture always become the major research and design objects for the cultural products of apparel. Also, there were observations and discussion (Lu 2011) for the type of apparel design which used the elements of character art and aesthetic feeling. It is seldom to use the mass-production of apparel, through the carrier of conversion work of art, as related study spindle. The purpose of this study, by discussing the art transition design applied in mass-production apparel, is to know if there is any influence of the transition design of artwork to the purchasing demand, to expect the artistic life having broader commodity options and make people dress & walk with good feeling of art.

2 Literature Review

2.1 Way of Artwork Transition Design

Henrik and Vanessa (2008) thought the artwork was not created for functionality, but expressed the human experiences and was ingenious creative work. If the painting was printed on T-shirt or the furniture was designed with artistic sense, then the art would be a kind of integrated product. Therefore, the combination of art and apparel would not damage the appreciation value of the artwork existed alone. Clever conversion and combination could make product and artwork have synergistic effect. On way the artistic aesthetics can be extended to the general public by using the propagation force commodity economy; the other way the product can continue to be innovated through the art. Then the demands of different consumer groups will be satisfied.

Artwork belongs to cultural assets. By utilizing the cultural features and characterization, the artwork could be regarded as the elements for product design. It could promote self-recognition and personalized consumer experience, which was the way (Yair et al. 2001) to highlight local culture under globalization market competition. Hsu and Lin (2014) used the multivariate ethnic and cultural characteristics in Taiwan as the source of creativeness and concept for development. Through the literature review and expert opinion, collecting scenario approach and product semantics, cultural product design program was proposed. Such program constructed three cultural spaces and levels; the factors to be considered in product design were separated as the design properties. These properties are: (1) External or physical level: including color, texture, lines and shape, surface ornamentation, process of details, and components composition; (2) Middle or behavior level: including easy for use, structure, operability of binding relationship, security and functionality; (3) Internal or psychological level: including the special meaning, story and feeling, or cultural characteristics of product, and so on. Such program is the cross-referencing among cultural space, cultural level and cultural products; and it can be referred when cultural products are designed.

For the purpose of applying to the articles in modern life, Yeh (2014) discussed the cultural connotation of traditional and classical poetry. With the emotional demand of modern design and the angle of experiencing the beauty of poetry, she designed and built "the mode of transition design for poetry shape". Such mode used the discussion of related conception and variations in classical poetry culture to carry out the creative conversion for industry application; and built a bridge foundation for oriental culture and arts and product design. Apparel is just like canvas. The designers can use the platform to express various elements on apparel. By means of the important theory and basis of design conversion, how to execute and practice is the aim of this study.

2.2 Purchasing Demand of Souvenirs

The artwork itself was provided with appreciation value; besides, it had implied value of souvenir when it was transformed into consumer products. Gordon (1986) thought that souvenir was "admission or the admission for getting into the memory". It has the same function as buying the apparel which printed with artwork. For most of the people liked to recall special time or event of the memory, the souvenir had the reminded effect to express the same feeling or resonate. Littrell et al. (1993) had proposed 8 phases to investigate the truth cognitive research of crafts souvenirs for the tourists. They were (1) uniqueness and originality, (2) manufacturing method, (3) aesthetic sense, (4) functionality and usability, (5) meeting the cultural and historical meaning, (6) manufacturer and material, (7) personal shopping experience, and (8) credibility. The criteria of these phases had considerable relevance with the purchasing intention assessed by the customer. The apparel with artwork transition design had the monumental value. If the same assessment index was used, the significance found by this study might be influenced in certain degree.

2.3 Purchasing Demand of Apparel Design

The difference between the apparel and the clothes with high quality was that the latter was the clothes for one person or few people customized by a tailor. It valued fitness and particularity. However, the apparel (ready-to-wear, apparel, ready-made garments) was done quickly and pre-finished sewing or "Apparel which is done before sold" (Hsiao 1988). Apparel was one of the representatives of the popular products; and popularized by industrial mass production. It would change the design pattern by following different social culture and economic environment and fashion trends. Nowadays, apparel becomes indispensable necessities in daily life.

Le (1997) thought the following factors might influence the quality of apparel, cognitive or impression of the value: epidemic, design details, performance means, main ingredient material, accessories material, structure, work, ease, logos, brand image, after-sales service and so on. On the above factors, brand and after-sales are the business areas of marketing planning. The others are important factors considered in the phase of design and manufacturing. (Chen and Chen 2011) had researched for the demand effect assessment of customers of apparel design. They listed 23 items of demands for assessment from three phases, design expression, sewing work and consumer behavior by using Analytic Hierarchy Process (AHP) to calculate the weight. The result showed that the top five evaluated demands, the most important factors for customers, were "design taste and aesthetic sense", "able to modify figure defect", "applicability of commodity", "commodity price", and "combination offer of commodity" sequentially. For the apparel designers or marketing planning staff, such result offered the reference and basis in evaluating the customer demand factors.

3 Research Methods

To evaluate the purchase demand of the customer for the apparel after conversed the design with artwork and to further understand the difference between the original and the product without design conversed by artwork, we used the three layers of cultural product design proposed by Hsu and Lin (2011) and the top five factors for apparel demand proposed by Chen (2011) plus eight demand elements in souvenirs, the research framework of costume design conversion was integrated and displayed as shown in Fig. 1. Test and comparison research was executed to observe the influence of purchase demand of the customers.

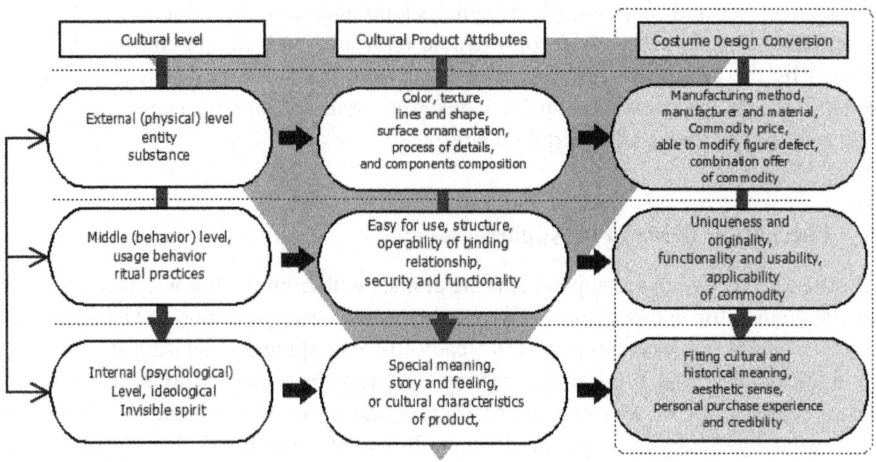

Fig. 1. The research framework of costume design conversion

3.1 Sample Selection

The range of apparel was complicated and multivariate in many fields such as gender, function, material, category, pattern, age and application. In order to focus on the research of design conversion, we planned to use single item of upper outer garment which was less obvious and highlights design style. In addition, to avoid the interference from style and level of apparel and the pattern and decorative accessories, T-shirt was selected as the sample of this research. Such type of commodity had the features of easy structure and not significant gender in wearing. Most important factor was that it could be easy to mass production and meets the objects and scopes discussed by this research.

Table 1. Commodity research samples

*Art category (A.B.C.D),Popular category(E.F.G.H.I),Souvenirs category(I.J.K.L),Others(M)

This research selected 13 garments as shown in Table 1, divided into three groups. Each group was composed of 4 garments. Except that the art group was transition design of artwork; pop group and souvenirs group were selected for comparison. The commodities of artwork transition design contained four artworks of international famous artists: (A) PIET MONDRIAN, (B) JEAN-MICHEL BASQUIAT, (C) ANDY WARHOL and (D) PAULA SCHER. And commodities manufactured for that season and designed by general costume designer were selected for the pop group. In which, plain garment without figure or pattern was put into the pop group. Besides, T-shirt which had characteristics of intersection between art group and pop group, often seen in museums or tourist site, was chosen as the comparison group. The 13th garment, maternity dress, was selected for individual comparison due to the special purpose. All of the samples for such research were in mass-production; and they were the commodities which were public in physical store or virtual online store. Because the samples were consuming commodities, so the price would be an important index for further observation. Therefore the prices for these three groups of commodities would be displayed on the samples of the research. The principle of marked price was based on the mean value of market price for each group; consistent price would be made. If promotions or other combination offered caused the price fluctuations, it was beyond the range that this research could control.

3.2 Questionnaire Design and Testee

The questionnaire contained basic information, description and test questions with the figure of commodities. It was scored by five rating scales. The testees evaluated subjectively the fitting degree of the eight purchasing demands according to thirteen images of garments; one score for Strongly Disagree; five scores for Strongly Agree. Choose three types of commodities that the testees wanted to buy most in sequence. In this research, the testees were divided into two parts: (1) there were 18 experts in design field and web questionnaire was chosen; (2) there were 57 general students from college who finished the questionnaire in the classroom in school. First the testees would be informed about the purpose of the questionnaire. The images and description of the commodities with price marked would be displayed by brief report. Later, the students should fill the questionnaire to evaluate the eight assessment attributes of the commodities. The valid questionnaires included 74, in which 23 for males and 51 for females.

4 Results and Discussion

Table 2 listed the mean value, between 2.91 and 3.52, for eight demand assessment for the whole testees. The mean value was 3.20. The standard deviation for all items was smaller than 1, which meaned the opinion of the testees under such structure was consistent.

Table 2. Results of the customers demand

Design conversion	Demand phase	Demand assessment items	Investigation		Significance
			Mean	SD	Verification value: 3
External level	Commodity price	I can accept the price.	3.03	0.78	0.880
	Able to modify figure defect	Wearing can modify the figure.	3.03	0.30	0.207
Middle level	Uniqueness and originality	I think the design is special.	3.52	0.35	0.000
	Functionality and usability	I think the design is tasteful.	3.30	0.29	0.003
	Applicability of commodity	I will wear and use it frequently.	2.91	0.42	0.438
Internal level	Meet the cultural and historical meaning	I think it has cultural connotation.	3.41	0.33	0.001
	Aesthetic sense	Wearing can increase aesthetic sense.	3.06	0.27	0.413
	Artistic connotation	I think it has artistic atmosphere.	3.32	0.31	0.003

4.1 Comparison for the Demand Items in Purchasing Apparel

Figure 2 was drawn by using different line sections for comparison according to the related information from Table 3. The difference among three groups was made through the analysis and comparison. From Fig. 2, it was obviously that except the item of "wear and use it frequently" had closer differences, the remaining items had significant differences. Table 3 listed relevant information of comparing apparel categories with three different design conversions, briefly introduced below:

1. The mean value for artistic atmosphere for art group was 3.53. It met that artwork, after converted to apply in apparel design, still kept the advantage of art vision. The second was 3.33 (memorial group) and the last was 2.99 (pop group). From here, we found that the reputation of the artist and the artwork with expensive price converted on T-shirt definitely could establish the vision of art appreciation for the customers. If cross-matching for "artistic atmosphere" and "price" with these three groups, the order of "price acceptance" for them would be pop group (3.96), memorial group (3.02) and art group (2.12) sequentially. The interesting thing was that the testee generally did not agree with T-shirt with high price. Though "artistic atmosphere" for art group obtained high rating, yet the high price of the artwork would not reflect on the price of the apparel equally. It also explained the customers understood the price of T-shirt. No big difference occurred due to the converted design with artwork or other figure. From the view point of complete competition

market, no matter website online shopping or purchasing via traditional channel, the design value of the T-shirt added by brand business would be never stopped. High quality with low price became the normality of the market. Therefore, under the multi-choice of the customer, the high acceptance of price of the pop group was the inevitable result in competition.

Table 3. Relevant information for three groups of commodities

Items	ALL		Art group①		Pop group②		Memorial group③		
	Mean	SD	Mean	SD	Mean	SD	Mean	SD	Sequence
Q1	3.41	0.33	3.44	0.14	3.07	0.34	3.70	0.15	3 > 1 > 2
Q2	3.52	0.35	3.67	0.15	3.17	0.41	3.60	0.11	1 = 3 > 2
Q3	3.30	0.29	3.32	0.17	3.11	0.36	3.33	0.18	1 = 3 > 2
Q4	3.32	0.31	3.53	0.14	2.99	0.32	3.37	0.18	1 > 3 > 2
Q5	3.03	0.30	2.80	0.26	3.06	0.22	3.06	0.17	2 = 3 > 1
Q6	3.06	0.27	3.02	0.22	3.10	0.27	2.95	0.28	2 = 1 > 3
Q7	2.91	0.42	2.90	0.35	3.11	0.35	2.75	0.60	2 > 1 = 3
Q8	3.03	0.78	2.12	0.21	3.96	0.14	3.02	0.35	2 > 3 > 1

*Q1: I think it has cultural connotation. Q2: I think the design is special. Q3: I think the design is tasteful. Q4: I think it has artistic atmosphere. Q5: Wearing can modify the figure. Q6: Wearing can increase aesthetic sense. Q7: I will wear and use it frequently. Q8: I can accept the price.

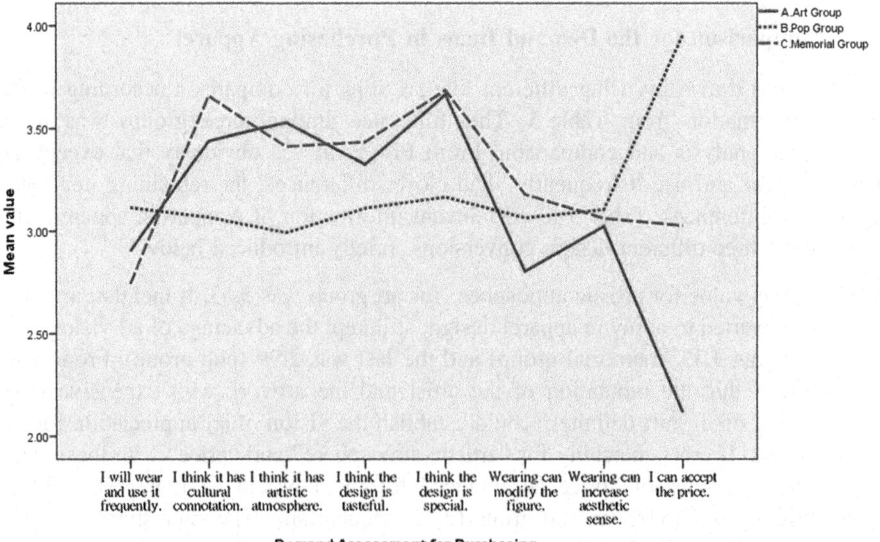

Fig. 2. Comparison of demand assessment for three groups of commodities

2. If viewing the point of "design is tasteful", the mean value for "Art group" (3.32) equaled to the "Memorial group" (3.33), which was higher than the "Pop group" (3.11). The definition of design taste might be changed due to trend or preference of customers and it was subjective assessment. From the evaluation in terms of scores, the "Art group" expressed personal style of the artist; the "Memorial group" must fit the subject of tourism or sightseeing. Topics for both groups might have consistency. If the material of the design came from artwork or landscape feature, the reputation of the material might influence the judge of the testee on the design taste. That the evaluation for both groups would be the same and be higher than the "Pop group".
3. If viewing the point of "cultural connotation", the mean value for three groups would be "Memorial group" (3.70), "Art group" (3.44) and "Pop group" (3.07) in sequence. If classified by commodity function, the products of memorial group had the concept of souvenir. The design idea was based on landscape feature which was used to express the local culture or popular culture to satisfy the request of the customer. However, art group expressed the unique style of the artist. It implied cultural and historical background. It was an age of painting, also is the model of art. The cultural thickness is undoubtedly. Therefore the evaluation for memorial group and art group would be higher.
4. If viewing the point of "increase aesthetic sense", the mean value for "Pop group" (3.10) was higher than "Art group" (3.02) and "Memorial group" (2.95). The biggest function of the apparel was to let the people have characteristics such as young, vivid, thin, handsome, beautiful, and so on. They were important factors of apparel that people chose to purchase. Therefore, the products of pop group would ingratiate the market demand. To the supplier of apparel, the proportion for "wearing to increase aesthetic feeling" must be higher than other groups. In addition, due to the limitation of material in design, the evaluation of aesthetic feeling for the memorial group was low.
5. If viewing the point of "wear and use it frequently", the mean value for three groups would be "Pop group" (3.11), "Art group" (2.90) and "Memorial group" (2.75) in sequence. Sample selected in this research was the single product of T-Shirt. The style of such product was simple structured without big change. It would be suitable for artwork or other totem printed on it. Hence, on the market, many museums and tourist places would make T-shirt as the souvenir. As a result, it had high memorial nature but not be put on frequently. So the evaluation for Art group and Memorial group was the lowest. Apparel popular in season must accept the high test in the market and focus on the demands of the customer in changing and innovating. Thus, it would focus on applicability requirements.

4.2 Comparison for the Commodities that You Most Want to Purchase

From thirteen products, selected three of products based on purchasing intention. After classified and added up, they could be distributed and shown as Table 4. Overall, F(15.3 %), D(14.0 %), I(10.8 %) and J(10.8 %) were the ones that people would like to purchase. If classified by gender, D(16.9 %), I(20.0 %) and L(10.8 %) were the ones that men wanted; F(17.9 %), D(12.8 %) and J(12.8 %) were the ones that women wanted. The only one that men and women liked was D. The product design of PAULA SCHER was conversed by painter and art educator. The sequence for these three commodities counted in accordance with purchase intention would be art group, memorial group and pop group. The most popular commodity was F(15.3 %) for the pop group of Disney product. The least popular commodity was K(1.8 %) for the memorial group of auspicious product released by Imperial Palaces of the Ming and Qing Dynasties in Beijing. Both were designed with traditional totem. It could be inferred that the design of F style tends to be cute and lovable, with famous figure on the product of T-shirt. Additionally, it was relevant that the majority of testees were female.

Table 4. Products that people most want to buy

Category and product		Overall favorability		Gender	
		Items	Percentage	Male (30 %)	Female (70 %)
Art group	A	14	6.3 %	6.2 %	6.4 %
	B	13	5.9 %	6.2 %	5.8 %
	C	16	7.2 %	7.7 %	7.1 %
	D	31	14.0 %	16.9 %	12.8 %
Pop group	E	9	4.1 %	3.1 %	4.5 %
	F	34	15.3 %	9.2 %	17.9 %
	G	9	4.1 %	3.1 %	4.5 %
	H	11	5.0 %	0	7.1 %
Memorial group	I	24	10.8 %	20.0 %	7.1 %
	J	24	10.8 %	6.2 %	12.8 %
	K	4	1.8 %	3.1 %	1.3 %
	L	17	7.7 %	10.8 %	5.8 %
Others	M	16	7.2 %	7.7 %	7.7 %
Total		222	100 %	100 %	100 %

5 Conclusions and Suggestions

In recent years, influenced by large and international apparel chain brand set such as ZARA, H&M, UNIQLO, GAP, and the competition of low-priced apparel from China, the apparel industry in Taiwan was facing the severe test. Observing from the consumer's point of view, if people could have high-quality and diversity of choice, then such challenge would be healthy competition for promoting the customer's value. The purpose of this research, by using the direction of multi-material, expected to create customer's demand and discussed the demand assessment influence of the customer due to the apparel with design conversed with artwork. The research structure basis was made according to the literature document; then built the customer assessment index to meet the apparel demand index. Thirteen items were selected and divided into three apparel commodities with different design and materials. The purpose of this research shall be analyzed and confirmed via questionnaire.

The result showed that the element coming from the artwork was converted as a design in T-shirt. The demand assessment for "I think it has artistic atmosphere", "I think it has cultural connotation", and "I think the design is special" was higher. It could be inferred that such kind of commodity implied proportion of "souvenir" with more demand factors. But, the level of demand assessment for the basic apparel of "Wearing can modify the figure" and " I can accept the price" was lower. Therefore in addition to satisfying the economies scale and price problem in manufacturing, the design plan was more important if we wanted to make artistic life popularly via apparel. Below listed some observations and proposals:

1. Price-oriented mode of production: Though machines were helpful for manufacturing apparel, yet the sewing work still could not replace human processing. So, labor-intensive still could not be broken away. To effectively reduce the cost and the selling price, in the field of apparel technology, the manufacturing of T-shirt was easy and suitable for mass-production. Due to less change in style, the transferred printing for applying the artwork design on the apparel played the key role. Combining modern technology, the printing technique expressed the art of the culture and the beauty of the apparel. As said by Lin (2014), it reflected "considering the tradition and ancient time; transferring into modern elegance".
2. Functional fabrics material value added: For the style change in T-Shirt is less, it might be better if value can be added onto the material of the cloth and embraced with artwork topic. For example, artwork with environmental awareness could match with yarn recycled from styrofoam. Artwork with natural water and mountain could join with cool feeling yarn or warm yarn. Even the apparel series with pure cotton also could be made by using organic cotton. Under the policy of value added but price not increased, the purchasing intention for people would be increased.
3. Joint brand marketing planning: The brand factor was excluded in this research for everyone knew it would influence the purchase intention in various fields of commodities. The cooperation of apparel brand and the artist was just like the combination of culture and the industry. At present, the international famous brand, e.g., Uniquo, had similar commodity plan and that was worthy to learn
4. Cross-border cooperation in apparel design: Trend of fashion and the textile technology were the important factors to be referred in apparel design plan. But the cooperation of artwork and the artist was few. If art and culture could be integrated into the apparel industry, such kind of apparel business might become one of new creative industries due to the art authorized.

If apparel, just like canvas, can make artist enjoy playing, and beautiful patterns or harmonious colors can be expressed while people wear and move, then the target of artistic life or life art can be spread through the perfect combination of apparel with high usage and exposure. This is the largest motivation of this study. The age of making quantity instead of quality in the market of apparel in Taiwan had gone for a long time. If brand business is fabulous to many SMEs, then original intention of exploring customer needs shall be the unchanged strategy.

References

Chen, W.L., Chen, T.H.: A study on the customer requirement impact factors of apparel design. J. Des. Sci. **14**(1), 1–22 (2011)

Gordon, B.: The souvenir: messenger of the extra ordinary. J. Popular Cult. **20**(3), 135–146 (1986)

Hsiao, M.L.: Apparel industry. Fashion design. Shih Chien University, Taipei (1988)

Hsieh, M.H., Guan, S.S.: Applying "Associative forced relationship of formative elements" in artistic commodities design. J. Des. **16**(4), 57–73 (2011)

Hsu, C.H.: Construction of cultural and creative products design patterns. Graduate School of Creative Industry Design, National Taiwan University of Arts, Taipei (2014)

Huang, C.Y.: The relationships among cultural tourism authenticity, experiential value, and place attachment – a case study of Lukang old street. Shih Hsin University. Taipei (2014)

Le, Y.Y.: The total quality control system for the apparel industry. China Textile Testing & Research Center, Taipei (1997)

Lin, C.L., Chen, S.J., Hsiao, W.H., Lin, R.: Cultural ergonomics in interactional and experiential design: conceptual framework and case study of the Taiwanese twin cup. Appl. Ergonomics **52**, 242–252 (2016)

Lin, C.H.: Innovational model of fashion design from the viewpoint of aesthetic economic. Taiwan Text. Res. J. **2009**(19), 27–41 (2009)

Lin, R., Lin, H.M.: Experience sharing, Taipei (2015)

Lin, R., Kreifeldt, J.G.: Do not touch: the conversation between technology and humart, Taipei (2014)

Littrell, M.A., Anderson, L.F., Brown, P.J.: What makes a craft souvenir authentic? Ann. Tourism Res. **20**(1), 197–215 (1993)

Lu, T.C.: Research into the Chinese character and its application-within contemporary fashion design. Des. J. Shih Chien Univ. **5**, 90–103 (2011)

Yair, K., Press, M., Tomes, A.: Crafting competitive advantage: crafts knowledge as a strategic resource. Des. Stud. **22**(4), 377–394 (2001)

Yeh, M.L., Lin, B.H., Hsu, C.H.: Cultural and creative design and application in poetry form and spirit transformation. J. Des. **16**(4), 91–105 (2011)

Yeh, M.L.: Creative design applications for poetry culture. Graduate School of Creative Industry Design. National Taiwan University of Arts, Taipei (2014)

Uniqlo. http://www.uniqlo.com/

Lativ. http://www.lativ.com.tw

Cafepress. http://www.cafepress.com/+womens-maternity

Universal Orlando. https://www.universalorlando.com/

Yumeeiren. http://www.ymr.com.tw

The Behavioral Analysis for Cross-Cultural Understandings Using Place Oriented Internet Radio

Ayaka Ito(✉) and Katsuhiko Ogawa

Graduate School of Media and Governance, Keio University, Fujisawa, Japan
{ayk,ogw}@sfc.keio.ac.jp

Abstract. Japan is accepting a number of foreign visitors in the trend of cultural diversity and building mutual understanding with who have different cultural background becomes essential. To support foreigner's better quality of living, we propose internet radio "CCR (Cross-Cultural Radio)", which provides place oriented contents including international listener's comments. Sequentially, "CCUS (Cross-Cultural Understanding Scale)" was invented and evaluation experiment was conducted in Tokyo to measure the effectiveness of CCR. Experiment result illustrates that CCR is effective in certain dimensions of cross-cultural understandings. This paper intends to explore the cultural exchange amongst foreign visitors to Japan by the behavioral analysis of individual experiment participants.

Keywords: Internet radio · Place orientated contents · Measurement · Evaluation · Cross-cultural understandings

1 Introduction

General knowledge of the host culture such as language or values and attitude toward the host culture and its members has been consistently posited to play an important role in influencing effective communication across cultures [1]. Although historically it has been regarded as mono-lingual/cultural country, with a drastic increase of foreign visitors [2], Japan is no exception to appreciate cultural diversity. We have to be aware that all foreigners are unique individuals, and we should not generalize them by nationality, race, and religion. Foreigners are visiting Japan for several purposes such as sightseeing, studying abroad or working. Likewise, depending on their cultural backgrounds, problems they encounter greatly vary, and there will never be a solution applicable for everyone. To propose a way to solve their problems individually, creating new media to provide foreigners opportunities to know Japanese culture at a deeper level is meaningful from a cross-cultural viewpoint.

Previous literatures have shown in terms of tourists revisiting places, the effect of motivation and satisfaction is prominent according to Yoon [3] and Bramwell [4]. Alegre [5] and Ekinci et al. [6] also pointed out the eagerness of tourists' visiting in relation to the characteristics of places. In terms of information system, Masuda [7] and Takagi [8] suggested a recommendation system for tourists, which provides customized tour information depending on user's need, including using smartphone applications. However,

P.-L.P. Rau (Ed.): CCD 2016, LNCS 9741, pp. 217–228, 2016.
DOI: 10.1007/978-3-319-40093-8_22

there is almost no research of using internet radio specifically as a tool for building cross-cultural understandings in Japan. In this paper, we propose place-oriented internet radio called "CCR (Cross-Cultural Radio)", which helps foreigners to recognize Japan from a cross-cultural perspective by providing several types of place oriented contents, including local people's interview, international listener's impression, opinion and comments. In addition, we created original criteria "CCUS (Cross-Cultural Understanding Scale)" and conducted an evaluation experiment in Tokyo to measure the actual effectiveness of contents and CCR. The crucial aim of this paper is to analyze the cultural exchange amongst individual experiment participants through the observation of their behaviors.

2 Design of Cross-Cultural Radio

2.1 Concept

CCR works in three steps (Fig. 1): contents design by the personality, listening process by various listeners such as international tourists, studying abroad students and multinational corporations employees who are not familiar with Japanese culture, and getting feedback plus revision of the contents. There are three types of contents available for international listeners, which are "Guidebook" (audio information from famous guidebook such as Lonely Planet), "Locals" (story or tips from local people's interview), and "Tourists" (opinions including self reflection or sympathy to the other tourists who listened to the previous two types of contents). In this paper we explicitly focused on first two aspects of the cycle, listening process by international tourists through evaluation experiment, followed by the contents design of Guidebook, Locals and Tourists.

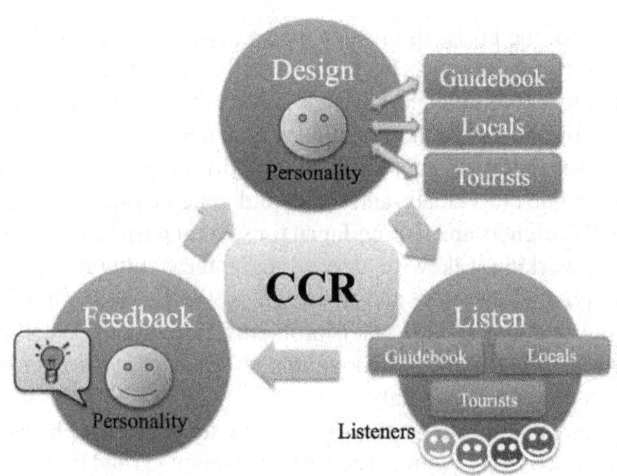

Fig. 1. Concept of Cross-Cultural Radio "CCR"

2.2 System

Previous research [9–12] show that acceptable duration of contents should be around 1 minute to 1 and half minutes. Several companies deal with production of audio guide player support the architecture of contents too.

1. Selecting Location. As CCR is designed for internationals visit Japan, the selection of place where contents are mapped is undoubtedly important. In this research, Asakusa, one of the most famous and popular tourist spots in Tokyo was chosen. The reason is that Asakusa has rich cultural heritages such as Japanese traditional temples or shrines, as well as dining venues and souvenir shops that attract many international tourists. Besides Asakusa is located in the heart of Tokyo and has great accessibility, which enables us to conduct fieldwork effortlessly.
2. Contents “Guidebook”. For contents Guidebook, several tips of accommodations, introduction of restaurants and explanation of famous architecture were picked from Lonely Planet Tokyo [13] and recorded using voice synthesize software (Fig. 2).

> “Asakusa Engei-hall”
> Have you ever seen standup comedy in your country? If you want to experience Japanese traditional comedy performance, here is the place. This is called Asakusa Engei-hall, provides humorous talking by classic rakugo speakers. The audience also enjoys stage arts unique to the theater, including the paper cutout and funny music played by carpenters tool.

Fig. 2. Example of contents “Guidebook”

3. Contents “Locals”. For contents Locals, a couple of interviews for locals were conducted in Japanese and story related to their daily lives in Asakusa was selected. Each story was translated into English and supplementary explanation about cultural activity was added if needed (Fig. 3).

> “Future of Asakusa”
> (After the local’s interview in Japanese) Before World War II, Asakusa has been one of the most energetic, cutting edge cities in Japan. But unfortunately nowadays it’s taken over by other big cities like Roppongi or Shinjuku. She feels to revitalize Asakusa as a vivid city, collaboration with local community is important, not only bringing lots of tourists from outside. Using social networking service can be one of them; so young generation helps older shop owners to introduce these up-to-date technologies into traditional Japanese shops.

Fig. 3. Example of contents “Locals”

4. Contents “Tourists”. Design of contents Tourists is slightly different from the other two contents. After the listeners listened to either contents Guidebook or Locals, they had free discussion about comparison with their own culture. Listener‘s

conversation is recorded and certain parts including their opinion or impression of the place are selected, then added to the previous two types of contents (Fig. 4). Therefore, this type of contents encloses the real voice of listeners, both spoken in English or Japanese (in this case the conversation is roughly translated into English).

> "Asakusa's current problem"
> (After the local's interview about subsidy for Asakusa dwellers in Japanese) "I was talking like, 'This place is very packed' and my friend said 'No no what's happening is actually quite opposite.' and I asked 'Really? Why?' and he said 'Because there is not enough young people to take on the jobs to kind of keep infrastructure that country going.' And I didn't even know that was an issue. As for in Britain, I really don't know. I hear occasionally people talks about how they are worried like, as they are getting older there is gonna be more people on pensions and such…"

Fig. 4. Example of contents "Tourists"

5. Mapping Contents into CCR. Once place oriented contents are prepared, they are mapped into CCR website (http://web.sfc.keio.ac.jp/~ayk/ccr/map.php, see also the QR code in Fig. 5) using JavaScript and are available for smartphones or tablets. Each contents are connected into one speech icon relevant to the place and when users click or tap the icon corresponded contents are played.

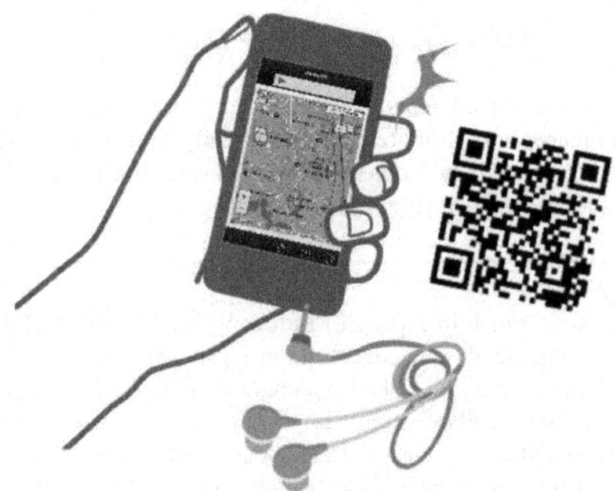

Fig. 5. CCR available for smartphone and website QR code

3 Measurement Cross-Cultural Understanding Scale "CCUS"

To validate the credibility of CCR, evaluation process with appropriate criteria is essential. Since CCR has a unique concept, inventing new and suitable measurement is more realistic rather than using conventional criteria without localization. Measurement design and cross-cultural adjustment are demonstrated by Benson [14], Cui & Awa [15] and Yellen [16]. In the reference of related literature, Ito [17] determined ten dimensions of cross-cultural understandings, which are:

1. Mobility. An individual's ability to find his/her way around in the foreign place is one of the most important dimensions of cross-cultural understandings. Knowing local geography and usage of public transportation systems are two potential items for this dimension. Capability to ask staff around in the face of uncertainty for directions, or usage of appropriate tools such as map application on smartphone is included. When mobility is improved, an individual feels more confident to explore new places and shows an enthusiasm to find cultural aspects in unfamiliar venues.
2. Food/Diet. Although food allergy is not the case, this dimension involves being open-minded to try new food, and how he/she can be adaptable for the change of diet. Accepting foreign food and culinary manners cannot be omitted when understanding certain culture, as for many people eating food is an entrance of cultural exchange. In relation to CCR contents, information such as recommendation of restaurants or grocery stores might affect this dimension, and ideally an individual would represent an appetite for certain food, connected to either his/her own or host culture.
3. Flexibility. As Hofstede defined "uncertainty avoidance" in his prominent work [18], more or less people from any cultural background may face culture shock and attempt to escape from that anxiety. Being flexible and patient for such uncertain activity or unexpected cultural norm is one dimension. Listening to local people's story which is exotic to his/her own culture or having an interaction with them will cultivate a tolerance of general matters and help them to hold positive image for foreign culture.
4. Knowledge. Whether he/she accepts it or not, acknowledgment of host culture is an essential aspect of cross-cultural understandings. In terms of socially appropriate behaviors, host country nationals have certain expectations as to how foreigners in their country should behave includes avoiding offensive actions toward locals. Webb et al.'s unobtrusive measure [19] could be useful in this regard, including the shared notion of "common sense". Compared to other dimensions, cultural knowledge is visible and recognizable information, which is easily gained by contents Guidebook.
5. Language Skills. This dimension appears consistently as a core factor of mutual understandings as former literatures are reviewed. However we should be aware that when cultural adaptation or acculturation occurs, adapted individual will learn the language, but individual who learn the language may or may not adapt. It is worth clarifying that this dimension is not about calculating an individual's language proficiency like speaking or listening, but it is rather about how open

he/she is to learn host language regardless of the level. For instance, in Japan visitors only use English manage to survive but whoever tries to learn Japanese will make life easier.

6. Interaction. The nature and frequency of interactions with host country individuals is an indication of cross-cultural understandings. This involves one's ability to initiate interaction, as well as the extent of his/her eagerness to communicate to Japanese people, regardless of language ability. This dimension is closely connected to mobility, because when individuals feel comfortable to start interaction with locals (mainly conversational greetings such as "Excuse me" or "Thank you") their mobility will surely be enhanced.
7. Awareness of Cultural Difference. A question such as "to what extent are you aware of Japanese culture/society is different from yours?" is asked in this dimension. Recognition of cultural difference between their own is a starting point to build mutual understandings in any circumstances. The bigger the difference becomes the more obvious of the awareness, and an individual with an experience of traveling to foreign countries tend to improve this dimension. However, not only difference between the home culture but also similarities can contribute to its change.
8. Nonverbal Communication. In addition to one's language, there are a variety of ways to communicate nonverbally. Understanding letters or characters, visible gestures such as eye contact, and appreciating personal space are some of them. Also having a reasonable repertoire of "communicative currency" may be useful. As an example, in a communicative setting Japanese use euphemism often. For foreign individuals sometimes it is hard to "read between the lines", but at least demonstrating an attitude to accept these context differences can boost this dimension.
9. Respect. Being interested in the host country citizens and casual friendliness towards them should be relevant as cross-cultural understandings. For instance, willingness to participate in activities distinctive to the host country will raise a fundamental respect for others and might lead to an appreciation of his/her current state. It is likely that CCR listeners will raise respect toward locals after they recognize the cultural difference. It is also greatly connected to the self-reflection process.
10. Relationship. Inclination to establish and maintain a relationship regardless of the skills is one crucial dimension. Even though this can be influenced by an individual's personal character such as being extrovert or introvert, we should be aware that every individual has his/her own pace for building it. For instance, not all introverts are weak in relationship building than extroverts; they will establish deeper and more stable relationship with others.

After the correspondent literatures are reviewed and dimensions mentioned above were rationalized, this new criteria was named "CCUS (Cross-Cultural Understanding Scale)". In the evaluation phase, measurement users score each dimensions from 1 to 10, using self-evaluation method. This evaluation is conducted twice, before and after any related experiment such as fieldwork or interview. Afterwards two score results are compared and discussed.

4 Evaluation Experiment

4.1 Method

We conducted fieldwork for three international tourists as CCR listeners (participant CH2, CH3 and UZ), using the same scheme to explore how the cycle of CCR works. CH2 and CH3 are 24 and 25-year-old females, both from China. UZ is 22-year-old male from Uzbekistan. CH2 and CH3 are close friends and took part in the fieldwork together in November 2015. Later they participated in the fieldwork again, focused on the contents Tourist this time.

First, we distributed an experiment instruction sheet to the participants. Fieldwork route is printed and they were asked to walk and listen to the contents (Guidebook and Locals in first fieldwork and Tourists in second fieldwork) mapped into the route in the numeric order (Fig. 6). Before they start to walk, they filled in the CCUS form. We took pictures of participants while they are walking (Fig. 7). Fieldwork was done either in English or Japanese, depending on participant's language ability. Conversation was recorded and after they listened to all contents numbered, they filled in the CCUS form again.

Fig. 6. Fieldwork route with an instruction. (Color figure online)

Fig. 7. Participants taking evaluation experiment in Asakusa

4.2 Result

Figure 8 is the average score of three participants' CCUS ten dimensions, the blue line is before the fieldwork, and the red line is after they listened to the contents Guidebook and Locals, and the green line is after they listened to the contents Tourists. We see some dimensions such as "language skills", "interaction" and "nonverbal communication" were improved after the fieldwork. On the contrary, we also see the decline in "mobility" and "awareness of cultural difference".

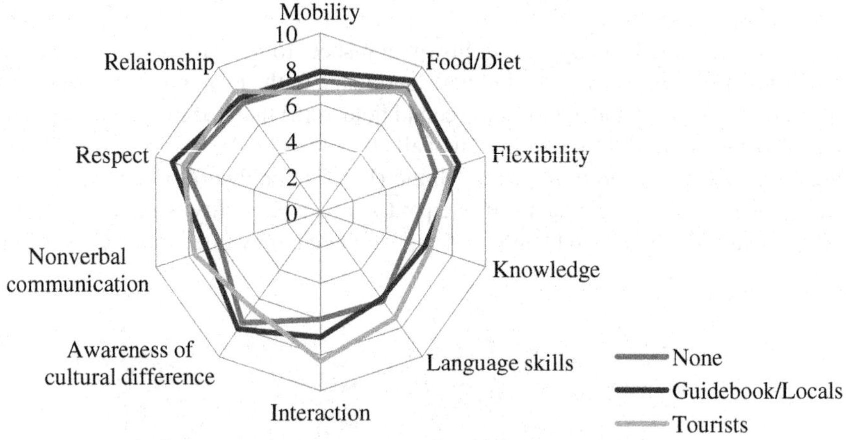

Fig. 8. Three participants' average CCUS score. (Color figure online)

"Fortune slip"
(After the explanation) "Yeah, you can try." "Okay." "This is the second best." "Second best? Oh!" "Daikichi (best luck), kichi (good luck), chukichi (average good luck) syokichi (small luck), suekichi (least luck)." "Oh this is kichi?" "Yes."

Fig. 9. Transcription of contents Tourists CH2 listened to

5 Behavioral Analysis of Participants

As shown in the result, CCR has enriched some aspects of cultural dimensions. We will have a closer look at individual participant's score focusing on the contents Tourists, referring comparative study by Ito [20], particularly dealt with the contents Guidebook and Locals.

5.1 Participant CH2 (Fig. 10)

Figure 6 indicates the most touristy district in Asakusa, a major temple called Senso-ji and its premises shown as a green area on top, and the main street aiming at there called

Nakamise-dori. As illustrated in blue line in Fig. 6, walking along Nakamise-dori and going through Senso-ji premises is the most popular route of Asakusa sightseeing. Since CH2 has never been in Asakusa until first fieldwork, she is a beginner tourist in a way. It is reasonable to assume that she was delighted with the route recommendation as her first visit and had positive impression for the fieldwork.

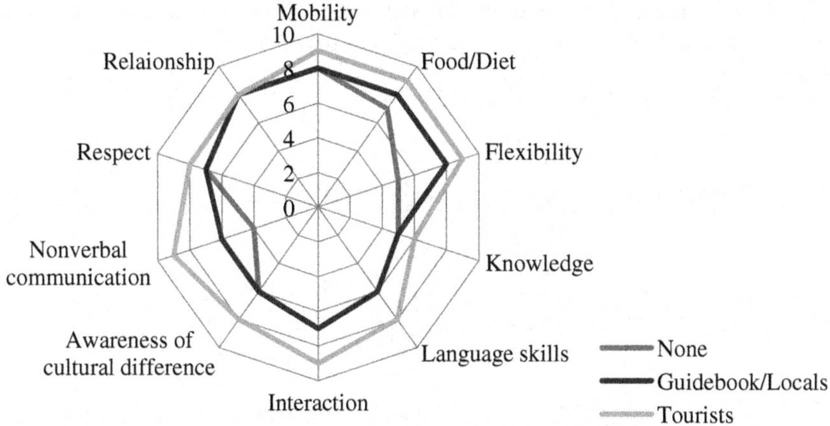

Fig. 10. Participant CH2's CCUS score. (Color figure online)

At Senso-ji she listened to the contents Tourists about the fortune slip, a previous fieldwork participant buying one influenced by the contents Guidebook (Fig. 9).

CH2 thought she might try it too, and purchased her own fortune slip after she listened to the contents. The slip's front was written in both Japanese and English, and she found its back was all in Chinese, saying "all flowers bloom when spring is approaching, if you are having something bad, it's time to be patient until the spring". She seemed quite surprised and said "it's comfortable to know the meaning of the fortune exactly right in my language". For her, getting the essence of Japanese culture in her own language must have been an event to promote "nonverbal communication" and "awareness of cultural difference" between China and Japan, as well as a trigger to interact with host culture which are illustrated as improvement in Fig. 10. Besides, from the guidebook tips she learned Senso-ji has a lot of bad (or worse) fortune slips while she actually got the second best. Hypothetically, a fun moment when she got lucky carried on until the end of the fieldwork, and affected to the overall positive evaluation after the fieldwork.

5.2 Participant CH3 (Fig. 11)

CH2 and CH3 are both studying abroad students and CH3 has arrived in Japan a year before CH2, so she knows more about Japanese society, lifestyle and culture than CH2. Although Fig. 11 shows some dimensions have declined after listening to the contents Tourists compared to Guidebook and Locals, CH3 has improved "interaction", "nonverbal communication" and "relationship" amongst ten dimensions. She did not purchase any fortune slip like CH2 but was watching her buying one, talked about the result in Chinese. Knowing Japanese culture through the conversation with CH2 counts as indirect cultural exchange and affected her relative improvement of dimensions. At the same time, interaction with CH2 in her own language actually worked as a homogeneity booster rather than recognizing a difference between Japanese culture, which explains a drop of "awareness of cultural difference". After the fieldwork, she commented "this time the explanation in English (contents Tourist) is more interesting than last time (contents Guidebook and Locals) because we could know what other foreign tourists think about Japanese culture" and told the fieldwork experience was enjoyable.

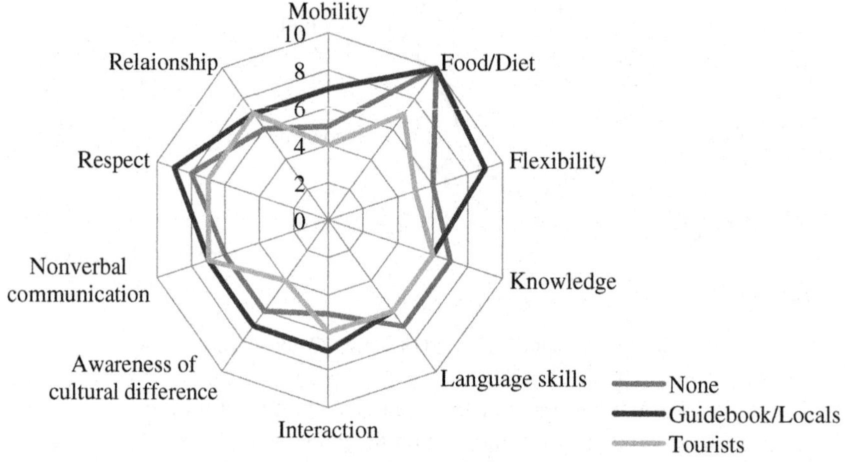

Fig. 11. Participant CH3's CCUS score. (Color figure online)

"Religion in Japan"
"(Japanese) monks usually try to be in solitude, but this (Senso-ji) is very busy." [...] "We really don't have a specific religion even though it's Buddhism, people don't practice it. We Japanese are spiritual, but not that religious." "Hmm."

Fig. 12. Transcription of contents Tourists UZ listened to

5.3 Participant UZ (Fig. 13)

In Ito's previous study focused on contents Locals, after UZ listened to the local person's interview about the future of Asakusa (Fig. 3), he mentioned his hometown Samarkand. Because of financial reason lots of residents are leaving the city and flowing into Toshkent, the capital of Uzbekistan nowadays and he feels sad about it. He wishes people in Samarkand will love their city just like as Asakusa locals. He felt something in common with Japanese people and cultivated affinity toward host culture, which has appeared as the improvement of "awareness of cultural difference". After the fieldwork he commented, "It was a great time with you, and I think it's unique chance to learn Japanese culture and chance to compare to Uzbek culture".

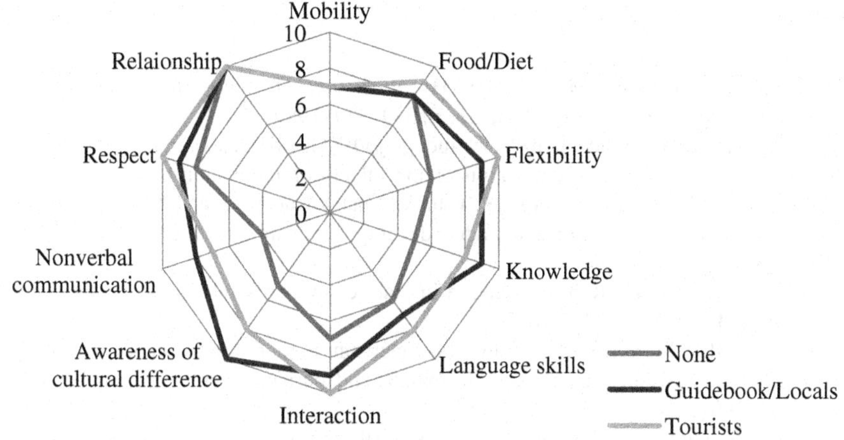

Fig. 13. Participant UZ's CCUS score. (Color figure online)

On the other hand, after he listened to the contents Tourists about religion in Japan (Fig. 12), he observed Japanese visitors throwing coins into the offertory box of Senso-ji. He told he is respectful of Japanese religious style, yet as a Muslim he wants to stick at his belief and would not to offer coins. This experience might have improved his "interaction" and "respect" by raising awareness of how people in different cultural backgrounds connect their religious beliefs into their daily lives.

6 Conclusion and Future Studies

In this paper we proposed place oriented internet radio called "CCR (Cross-Cultural Radio)" by providing three types of contents; "Guidebook", "Locals" and "Tourists". To validate the effectiveness of this unique media, we also suggested "CCUS (Cross-Cultural Understanding Scale)" as new criteria to measure the level of cross-cultural understandings. According to the result of evaluation experiment conducted in Tokyo for three participants, it is reasonable to assume CCR has contributed to the enhancement of several aspects of culture. Besides, through advanced behavioral analysis for individual participants focused on the contents Tourists, we found a certain listening experience can be triggers of participants' voluntary action or contemplation of themselves, which helps them to gain new cultural perspectives.

For the future work, we will design and develop a variety of place oriented contents especially focuses on Tourists, which includes defining process of contents promote affinity towards culture. Recruiting more participants for the evaluation experiment is crucial to make CCR more solid and reliable media. To enhance cross-cultural understandings for foreign visitors in Japan, we should test if the same scheme works not only in Asakusa but also in different cities of Japan, or it significantly varies depending on the characteristics of the place. One possibility of the evaluation experiment is employing Japanese tourists as participants for a comparative research to internationals.

References

1. Wiseman, R., Hammer, M., Nishida, H.: Predictors of intercultural communication competence. Int. J. Intercultural Relat. **13**(3), 349–370 (1989)
2. Japanese Ministry of Justice. http://www.moj.go.jp/ENGLISH/index.html
3. Yoon, Y., Uysal, M.: An examination of the effects of motivation and satisfaction on destination loyalty - a structural model. Tourism Manag. **26**(1), 45–56 (2005)
4. Bramwell, B.: User satisfaction and product development in urban tourism. Tourism Manag. **19**(1), 35–47 (1998)
5. Alegre, J., Cladera, M.: Repeat visitation in mature sun and sand holiday destinations. J. Travel Res. **44**(3), 288–297 (2006)
6. Ekinci, Y., Riley, M., Chen, J.: A review of comparisons used in service quality and customer satisfaction studies: emerging issues for hospitality and tourism research. Tourism Anal. **5**(2), 197–202 (2001)
7. Masuda, M., Izumi, T., Nakatani, Y.: A system that promotes repeat tourists by making sightseeing unfinished. Hum. Interface Soc. **14**(3), 259–270 (2012)
8. Takagi, S., Masuda, M., Nakatani, Y.: Tour navigation system using landmarks customized by personal preferences. Inform. Process. Soc. Jpn. **3**, 305–306 (2012)
9. Hatala, M., Wakkary, R.: Ontology-based user modeling in an augmented audio reality system for museums. User Model. User-Adap. Inter. **15**(3), 339–380 (2005)
10. Bodker, S.: Through the Interface: A Human Activity Approach to User Interface Design. Lawrence Erlbaum Associates Inc., Malwah (1990)
11. Dean, D.: Museum Exhibition: Theory and Practice. Routledge, London (1994)
12. Hummels, C., Helm, A.: ISH and the search for resonant tangible interaction. Pers. Ubiquit. Comput. **8**(5), 385–388 (2004)
13. Hornyak, T., Milner, R.: Lonely Planet Tokyo (Travel Guide), 9th edn. Lonely Planet, New York (2012)
14. Benson, O.: Measuring cross-cultural adjustment: the problem of criteria. Int. J. Intercultural Relat. **2**(1), 21–37 (1978)
15. Cui, G., Awa, N.: Measuring intercultural effectiveness: an integrative approach. Int. J. Intercultural Relat. **16**, 311–328 (1992)
16. Yellen, T.: The cross-cultural interaction inventory: development of overseas criterion measures and items that differentiate between successful and unsuccessful adjusters. Natl. Tech. Inf. Serv. **3**, 1–19 (1975)
17. Ito, A., Ogawa, K.: The evaluation of place oriented internet radio “CCR”, using measurement of cross-cultural understandings. In: 10th International Conference of Digital Society (2016, Submitted)
18. Hofstede, G.: Cultures and Organization: Software of the Mind. McGraw-Hill, New York (1991)
19. Webb, E., Campbell, D., Schwartz, R., Sechrest, L.: Unobtrusive Measures – Nonreactive Research in the Social Sciences. Rand McNally and Co., Illinois (1966)
20. Ito, A., Ogawa, K.: “Re:Radio”, the place oriented internet radio to enhance the cross-cultural understanding in Japan. In: Stephanidis, C. (ed.) Human Computer Interaction International 2015 Posters, vol. 1, pp. 249–255. Springer, Switzerland (2015)

The Relationship Between Robot Appearance and Interaction with Child Users: How Distance Matters

Weijane Lin[1(✉)] and Hsiu-Ping Yueh[2]

[1] Department of Library and Information Science, National Taiwan University, Taipei, Taiwan, ROC
vjlin@ntu.edu.tw

[2] Department of Bio-Industry Communication and Development, National Taiwan University, No. 1., Sec. 4., Roosevelt Rd, Daan Dist., Taipei 10617, Taiwan, ROC

Abstract. This study intends to explore child patrons' interaction with robots by assessing the interpersonal distance under a specific context of library. In addition to the general exploration on human preference and performance in HRI, it is expected to understand more profoundly the activities and intentions people possessed through the systematical investigation of interaction context and structural measurement of interpersonal distance. Previous studies in human-robot interaction have suggested several factors that are important including robots' appearance, users' features and their perceptions of robots. However, studies regarding child users are few, and the understanding of children's attitudes toward robots remains limited due to insufficient or unempirical supports. Studies regarding the human-robot interaction support that the personal space also appears inevitably that reflects human intentions to interact with the robots. In addition, another critical but less-explored factor that affect human-robot interaction is contextual effect. Contextual cues are what people sense and rely on to proceed with conversations, and cannot be overlooked in the exploration of any interaction.

This study recruited 77 elementary students from 3rd–6th grade and assigned the task to be recommended the book from the robot in the library. The personal space that the participants kept with different appearance robots and the attitude they had to the robot were recorded and analyzed. The result showed that the participants had positive attitude to the robots and felt comfort when interacting with robots. Among them, girls were more positive than the boys. Additionally, the one that interacted with human-like robot kept the personal space closer than the one that interacted with machine-like robot. The former one interacted with the robot in intimate space that indicates that the participants took the library as a private space and thought the robot as their close friend.

Keywords: Library robot · Reader service for children · Personal space

P.-L.P. Rau (Ed.): CCD 2016, LNCS 9741, pp. 229–236, 2016.
DOI: 10.1007/978-3-319-40093-8_23

1 Introduction

For many public libraries, child patrons are one of the major user groups, and they are also the most active users in the library [1]. Viewing children as the future clients, public libraries actually devote many efforts to do researches or activities for child patrons. However, difficulties may be encountered due to child patrons' physical limits or literacy skills that hindered their use of the library resources. It is often that child patrons need and require librarians or adults' help to get library services and resources, therefore an assistive agent is of help to child patrons' library use.

Human interaction involves various intentions and actions that reflected these intentions. A typical representation of the phenomena is described by Hall [2] as the "personal space," where people stay in a certain distance in an interaction to show their intentions to interact with the others and the current situation [3]. When the distance between two people is short that may mean their relationship is close, and vice versa. Studies regarding the human-robot interaction support that the personal space also appears inevitably [4] that reflects human intentions to interact with the robots. In addition, another critical but less-explored factor that affect human-robot interaction is contextual effect [5]. Contextual cues are what people sense and rely on to proceed with conversations, and cannot be overlooked in the exploration of any interaction.

Motivated by the aforementioned issues, this study intends to explore child patrons' interaction with robots by assessing the interpersonal distance under a specific context of library. In addition to the general exploration on human preference and performance in HRI, it is expected to understand more profoundly the activities and intentions people possessed through the systematical investigation of interaction context and structural measurement of interpersonal distance.

2 Research Design

This study investigates the personal space and the attitude that child patrons possessed under different kinds of contexts in order to better understand child patrons' thinking toward the library robots. To obtain valid data, a designated experiment was conducted to extract insight from users' actual behaviors instead of reported opinions and impression without actual experience. Also, to better understand how child patrons' behave in different contexts, this research used the factors that discussed in previous studies: users' age, gender, and robots' appearance as variables to see the difference. Quasi-experiment was therefore adopted as the proper research method to approach the context targeted by this research.

To understand child patrons' feelings and movements in the interaction with the robot, this study used two robots of different appearance: the human-like robot named "Julia", compared to the machine-like robot named "Book Smile". Except for the appearance, the technical specs of the two robots were identical. Both robots were equipped with lasers to detect obstacle and participant's feet for measuring distance data automatically.

During the experiment, the users' personal space would be measured and the movement of the participant would be observed through the task. First, the users' personal space would be measured and taken by the robot during the book recommending and retrieving tasks. Also, the action of the participant would be observed and recorded during the entire experiment process by the video camera to see what kinds of facial expressions, movements, or other body languages the participant had to the robot.

This study also developed the paper-based questionnaire after the experiment task to investigate the participants' attitude to robots, the participants' robot appearance preference, and the participants' demographic information. The instruments were modified versions from the robot anxiety scale (RAS) and Negative attitudes toward robots scale (NARS) from Nomura, Kanda, Suzuki, and Kato's research [6]. The reliability and validity of the instrument was tested and sufficient (Cronbach's $\alpha = 0.77$).

3 Preliminary Findings

This study recruited 77 participants from 3rd grade to 6th grade (age 9–12) from an elementary school in Taipei. And the experiments were conducted in the library of this elementary school. The ratio of gender was 34:43 (boy: girl). All participants participated in the experiments under their free wills and parents' consents, and one participant dropped out during the experiment, which made the valid sample of 76 persons. These participants were divided into two groups to interact with robots with human-like appearance and machine-like appearance respectively.

3.1 Participants' Personal Space and Attitude Toward Robots of Different Appearance

To investigate whether the robot's appearance will affect the personal space the participants' keep from the robot. The study used the data from human-like robot (Julia) group and machine-like robot (Book Smile) group to run independent groups of T-test to see the difference. The descriptive statistics shown that when the participant interacted with the human-like robot, the average personal space was 0.35 m, which was the level of intimate space according to Hall (1966) (distance < 0.45 m). On the other hand, the participant who interacted with the machine-like robot, Book Smile, performed the personal space in 0.75 m. Although the later one was relatively far than the former one, the personal space that the participant shown was still in the level of personal space (distance < 1.2 m) which represented that the participant were willing to interact with the robot from social space to the closer space—personal space.

Table 1. Personal space when Interacting with robots of different appearance

Appearance	N	Mean	S.D.	t
Human-like	36	.35	.54	-3.25^{**}
Machine-like	40	.75	.54	

**Result is significant at 0.01 level (2-tailed)

There were significant differences existed in the personal space between the human-like robot (Julia) group and the machine-like robot (Book Smile) group. The personal space the participants kept when interacting with Julia was significantly closer than the other group. In addition, participants would approach the human-like robot (Julia) to take the book, and stayed in front of the robot to read the content. However, the participant would backward immediately after taking the book from the machine-like robot (Book Smile), and read the content in certain distance away from the robot (Table 1).

To investigate whether the robot's appearance will affect the attitude the participants' had to the robot. The study used the questionnaire data from human-like robot (Julia) group and machine-like robot (Book Smile) group to run independent groups of T-test to see the difference. Different groups of the participants' comfort attitude to the robot were shown in Table 2.

Table 2. Participants' attitude when interacting with robots of different appearance

	Appearance	N	Mean	S.D.	*t*
I feel relax interacting with the robot	Julia	37	4.14	1.48	−1.35
	Book Smile	40	4.55	1.22	
I feel easy when the robot moves toward me	Julia	37	3.97	1.40	−0.25
	Book Smile	40	4.05	1.36	
I feel comforted interacting with the robot in front of other people	Julia	37	4.16	1.48	−0.36
	Book Smile	40	4.28	1.30	
I feel comforted being with robots that have emotions	Julia	37	4.59	1.61	1.17
	Book Smile	40	4.15	1.72	
If the robot had emotions, I would be able to make friends with them	Julia	36	4.44	1.68	−0.02
	Book Smile	40	4.45	1.36	

The results showed that the comfort attitude that participants had were positive. Among all the questions, the Julia group scored the "I feel comforted being with robots that have emotions" highest (M = 4.59). Also, the participants felt least comfortable when the robots approached them. This may because that the participants didn't know they were going to interact with the robot before the experiment and felt confused. However, there was no significant difference between two groups of the participants.

In the feeling of the library tasks, the results were positive which showed that the participants were willing to have robots to recommend readings. Also, the scores of the feeling of the task were higher than the robot attitude. The participants regarded robots as communicable and trustworthy, also they felt the conversations with the library robot were relevant. The overall data showed that the participants' attitude toward the two robots was not significantly different. Despite of different appearance, a possible inference was that the both robots had the features and functions that the children preferred. While Julia and Book Smile robot used cartoon-like design concepts and elements, the results might not reflect significant difference in the two groups.

3.2 Gender Difference in Personal Space and Attitude Toward Different Robots

To investigate whether the participants' gender would affect the personal space the participants' keep from the robot. The study used the data from boy and girl groups to run independent groups of T-test to see the difference. The results showed that when the boy interacted with the robot, the average personal space was 0.72 m, which was the level of personal space (distance < 1.2 m). On the other hand, the girl who interacted with the robot (girl features) performed the personal space in 0.43 m, which was in the range of intimate space (distance < 0.45 m), and was closer than the former one. It may be said that the girl was more willing to interact with the robot than the boy (Table 3).

The results of the t-test analysis showed significant difference between the boys and girls groups. The personal space the girls kept when interacting with the robot was significantly closer than the boys. This could also be translated as that girls regarded the robot as their close friends or family more than the boys. Similar results also applied when the participants interacted with the machine-like robot, Book Smile. The girls also stayed in closer distance with the robot than the boy.

Table 3. Participants' personal space when interacting with the human-like robot

Gender	N	Mean	S.D.	*t*
Boy	34	.72	.66	2.25*
Girl	42	.43	.45	

*Result is significant at 0.05 level (2-tailed)

To investigate whether the participants' gender will affect their attitudes toward the robot, the result showed that participants' attitude toward both robots was positive. And the girls had better comfort attitude to the robots than the boy. Additionally, although both gender were willing to make friend with a robot of emotions, the results showed that the girl (*M = 4.71, S.D. = 1.37*) were more willing than the boy (*M = 4.12, S.D. = 1.63*). However, there was no significant difference between two groups of the participants in the comfort attitude part. In the feelings of the library tasks, the girls were more positive than the boys to have the robots recommended readings. In addition, girls perceived the conversations with robots as significantly more relevant than boys ($t\ (76) = -3.44$, $p < .01$).

The participants liked the robot with no human-like appearance, arms, and emotion. However, in the monitor and facial features parts, there were significant differences between the boys and the girls: girls liked the robot with monitor (M = 4.60, S.D. = 1.94) and facial features (M = 3.83, S.D. = 1.82) more than the boy felt about the monitor (M = 2.71, S.D. = 2.02) and the facial features (M = 2.71, S.D. = 1.95). The results showed that the boys had less positive attitude than the girls in all attitude parts. This may be the reason that the boys stayed farer than the girls when interacting with the robot (Table 4).

Table 4. Gender difference in attitudes toward robots

	Gender	N	Mean	S.D.	*t*
I feel relax interacting with the robot	Boy	34	4.18	1.42	0.96
	Girl	43	4.49	1.30	
I feel easy when the robot moves toward me	Boy	34	3.79	1.27	0.71
	Girl	43	4.19	1.44	
I feel comforted interacting with the robot in front of other people	Boy	34	4.00	1.37	0.50
	Girl	43	4.40	1.38	
I feel comforted being with robots that have emotions	Boy	34	4.18	1.62	0.59
	Girl	43	4.51	1.71	
If the robot had emotions, I would be able to make friends with them	Boy	34	4.12	1.63	0.10
	Girl	42	4.71	1.37	

To summarize, both gender and robot appearance would affect the personal space that the participants kept from the robot. Participants would interact with human-like robot in the intimate space ($m < 0.45$) despite of the robot's gender. On the other hand, when interacting, the participants would stay in a farther space (personal space, $m < 1.2$) with machine-like robot. The results regarding gender difference supported findings of the previous studies [7, 8], and proved that participants perceived a same-gender robot more positive and psychologically close than the opposite-gender robot.

4 Conclusion

This study has discussed the personal space and the attitude in interaction between child patrons and robots under different contexts. It was established by analyzing the distance, video, and questionnaire data of the child patrons' attitude and the behaviors. The results showed that the child patrons were willing to interact with the robots for the book recommending services. Also, they are willing to read the book with and from the robot. The appearances of the robots affected the interaction between the child patrons and the robot. When the participants interacted with the human-like robot, they tended to interact in intimate space; on the other hand, the participant who interacted with the machine-like robot would prefer to interact in personal space.

The results also suggested gender differences in the child patrons' interaction with the robots. The personal space that the girls interacted with the robot was closer than the boys. And the attitude that the girls had to the robot was also more positive than the boy. That is to say that the robots' appearance and the child patrons' gender factor would affect the personal space that the child patrons and the robot interacted with.

The study was distinct from previous studies of HRI space [9, 10] by its context-specific research design. With the direct and automatic measurement of the distance, bias and ambiguity could be avoided. And the personal space was examined in the real world, where the library context, robot instruments and interaction were all genuine, the findings contributed to provide empirical evidence for the research and practices of the field.

This study started from Taiwan to establish one aspect of the child patrons' personal space in the library with the robot. The results showed that the gender and the robots' appearance do affect the personal space; also the gender would affect the attitude that the child patrons have. This may be the reference for the library to conduct the robot service and its content. However, it should be noted that the study was limited by the participants' background. In this study, the participants were all the students from Taiwan, where the students may feel less familiar than other countries that develop robots maturely. As Bartneck [11] indicated, the cultural background had a significant influence on people's attitude to robots. Hence, the opinions and the personal space of the robot may be different when the experiment is conducted in other countries. Yet, the study's results are still the good references when the library is considering introducing the robot service in the future.

References

1. Benton Foundation. Buildings, books and bytes: libraries and communities in the digital age (1996). https://www.ideals.illinois.edu/bitstream/handle/2142/8130/librarytrendsv46i1o_opt.pdf?sequence=1. Accessed 2 Sept 2015
2. Hall, E.T.: The hidden dimension: man's use of space in public and private. The Bodley Head Ltd, London (1966)
3. Reeves, B., Nass, C.: The media equation: how people treat computers, televisions, and new media like real people and places. Cambridge University Press, New York (1996)
4. Walters, M. L., Dautenhahn, K., Boekhorst, R., Koay, K.L., Kaouri, C., Woods, S., Nehaniv, C., Lee, D., Werry, I.: The influence of subjects' personality traits on personal spatial zones in a human-robot interaction experiment. In: Proceeding of IEEE International Workshop on Robot and Human Interactive Computing (ROMAN), pp. 347–352 (2005)
5. Ham, J., van Esch, M., Limpens, Y., de Pee, J., Cabibihan, J.-J., Ge, S.S.: The automaticity of social behavior towards robots: the influence of cognitive load on interpersonal distance to approachable versus less approachable robots. In: Ge, S.S., Khatib, O., Cabibihan, J.-J., Simmons, R., Williams, M.-A. (eds.) ICSR 2012. LNCS, vol. 7621, pp. 15–25. Springer, Heidelberg (2012)
6. Nomura, T., Kanda, T., Suzuki, T., Kato, K.: Prediction of human behavior in human-robot interaction using psychological scales for anxiety and negative attitudes toward robots. IEEE Trans. Robot. **24**(2), 442–451 (2008)
7. Eyssel, F., Kuchenbrandt, D., Bobinger, S., de Ruiter, L., Hegel, F.: If you sound like me, you must be more human: on the interplay of robot and user features on human-robot acceptance and anthropomorphism. In: Proceedings of the 7th ACM/IEEE Conference Human-Robot Interaction (HRI 2012), pp. 125–126 (2012)
8. Nomura, T., Suzuki, T., Kanda, T., Han, J., Shin, N., Burje, J., Kato, K.: What people assume about humanoid and animal-type robots: cross-cultural analysis between Japan, Korea, and the USA. Int. J. Humanoid Robot. **5**, 25–46 (2008)
9. Banik, S.C., Gupta, A.K.S., Habib, M.K., Mousumi, R.N.: Determination of active personal space based on emotion when interacting with a service robot. Int. J. Adv. Robot. Syst. **10**, 1–7 (2013)

10. Balasuriya, J.C., Watanabe, K., Pallegedara, A.: ANFIS based active personal space for autonomous robots in ubiquitous environments. In: Proceedings of the 2007 International Conference on Industrial and Information Systems, pp. 523–528 (2007)
11. Bartneck, C., Nomura, T., Kanda, T., Suzuki, T., Kato, K.: Cultural differences in attitudes towards robots. In: Proceedings of Symposium on Robot Companions (SSAISB 2005 Convention), pp. 1–4 (2005)

Service Design Strategies for Long-Term Effects that Individual Moments Have on the Whole: A Case Study of "Persephone"

Muqing Niu(✉) and Linong Dai(✉)

Shanghai Jiaotong University, No.800 Dongchuan Rd., Shanghai, People's Republic of China
mqniu@hotmail.com, Lndai@126.com

Abstract. The essay targets at exploring the strategies on service design for promoting the long-term effects that generated by every individual moment through probing into design strategies of every single part of the real-time user experiences of an aftermath rescue service system "Persephone".

Keywords: Group effect · Long-term effect · Group consciousness · Persephone · Service design · User experience

1 Introduction

Earthquake is one of the most powerful disasters in the world. More than 300 million people have been seriously affected in the earthquake at 20 century. There are more than 18 % areas, and 12 % populations on earth are under the risk, and the earthquake may come suddenly without any advancing warning. No matter how advanced technology we have, human lives remain fragile in the face of earthquakes, because major survival technologies may corrupt.

In China, the underdeveloped western areas often suffer from deadly earthquake made worse by poor infrastructure and planning. It takes time for the outside rescue resources to reach the stricken areas, making the existing resources become far more inessential in the golden rescue areas. Ensuring the supply of food and safe drinking water and trying to restore good sanitation are critical, which help save more lives. However, every single resource allocation is based on the efficiency of communication. Taking the 2008 Wenchuan earthquake, for instance, the damages of the base stations, the lacking of electricity, and the traffic jam caused by exceeded number of users all exacerbated the efficiency of communication. The main goals of designing Persephone rescue system is to make every user stays notices, informed and connected in case of severe aftermath situations. Persephone helps users stay noticed, informed and targeted by opening up an entrance for the first time rescue and information exchange among victims. Based on the combination of P2P meshed network and the traditional cellular services, the success and efficiency of Persephone are based on mutual

P.-L.P. Rau (Ed.): CCD 2016, LNCS 9741, pp. 237–245, 2016.
DOI: 10.1007/978-3-319-40093-8_24

help, a number of participants and the delayed data accumulation. As a result, our design purpose is to increase user participation and increase the time user stay online. Users take advantages of Persephone to get access to the information they need. The concealed meaning, which is hard detected by users in the process of interaction. When a user is trying to connect others, he or she is also the crucial bridge of information delivery. In the other words, when a user is sending out a message asking for help, meanwhile the user himself or herself is also a significant node help others exchange information in the whole system. The resource data generated by groups of users could also help government and organizations conduct the resource allocation management. Consequently, it is crucial to promote user participation and residence time on Persephone app thus to promote better group effects. In order to develop a comprehensive approach to the user experience of Persephone, authors probe into user demands and psychology through a series of user research.

2 Research Methodology

When the presence of every individual user is a significant part of the whole rescue system, and the benefit from this group value may also return to the user, the key point of getting better group benefits is to make the long-term effect and group benefit perceivable and foreseeable by the participated users in the process of service receiving. The authors accumulated the data to analyze social-related thinking models, rescue concepts and current rescue behaviors of various victims survived in Wenchuan earthquake by the methodology of persona analyze. Then we organized the data with the framework of POMES (people, object, environment, message, service), structured the user needs, and sort out the relationship between users role-related behaviors and their corresponding mental perceptions. Then the authors explored the possible development of Persephone service design guidelines to help users have better emotional control, perspective taking, and to show expression of respect. On the purpose of the conversion from the user demands to design guidelines, the research applies the model of Means-end Chain and uses it to transform different kinds of user demands to the corresponding guidelines for service design.

2.1 Data Accumulation

Survey. A survey of 28 survivors from 2008 Wenchuan Earthquake through persona analyze by the in-depth interview and a five-person focus group. They are college students, government officers, merchants, and soldiers. Each in-depth interview is about 40 min. We ask people to describe their experiences of Wenchuan Earthquake. Following, we designed several scenarios by showing them video documentaries and coming up with questions. We ask them about their choices, demands, behaviors, and psychological movements. For the focus group, the researchers displayed some typical problems and demands gathered from the in-depth interviews, and came up with some design proposals. The researchers piled up rich data with tones of video, photos and recordings.

Questionaire. Methods to conduct the survey by sending out a questionnaire to 514 people of different ages and occupations came from earthquake belt areas like Wenchuan, Beichuan, Mianzhu, Chongqing, Baoji, and Xian. We greatly enriched data by questionnaires.

2.2 POEMS and Personal Analysis

After research of data collection, we input all the data into an Excel spreadsheet in accordance with the construction of POEMS (Fig. 1). POEMS considers people, object, environment, message, service and other factors synthetically. It is suitable for analysis of large amounts of qualitative data [3].

1	Behavior	Time After Earthquake	Self Description	Actor Gender	Actor Age	Object	Environment	Behavior Motivation	Service	Confusion	Advice
22	打电话给母亲	20m	我打电话给我妈，电话都打不通。	女	22	手机，电力	房子倒了，断电，没有信号	亲情	联系亲友，通信需求	寻找手机信号位置	无
23	挖掘被掩埋受害者	4h	很多人在叫喊，我就冲过去，很多人和我一起，并不知道什么情况	男	34	人力，组织，通信	房子倒了，断电	自我实现，群里意识	提供帮助，发现被救者，救援组织	信息咨询模糊，救援组织混乱	更明确的信息，更高效的救援
24	发出求救信息	10h	外面很多脚步声，说话声，我喊不出来，拿石头敲地，一直没有人发现我，过了很久才有人说这里好像有个人	男	35	人力，通信	废墟，被掩埋，	求生	提供求救信息，明确自身地理位置	如何被发现	无
25	等待外援	2d	我们那边路都坏了，两天后一些当兵的才进来，大部队进来都是很多天后	女	45	人力，外援，	道路损坏，地理位置位于山区，震后第一时间外援无法到达	生存需求	震区内外的通信，基础设施的恢复，自救人力资源，物质资源	外援到来之前如何展开自救	合理展开自救，分配现有资源
	提供救助	1d	我们刚开始自顾不暇，和大家集中在一	男	49	人力	房子倒了，断电	生存需求，群	联系亲友，通信需	亲友信息检索	无

Fig. 1. User needs in aftermath scenarios

We categorized user demands into 11 dimensions (Fig. 2). The diameter of each axis is the influence of such user need, which is positively correlated to the certain numbers of times user mentioned directly and indirectly. Location- relating communication are the universal demanding shared by all users, no matter they are the people who need help, who offer help, who can only help themselves, organizations, government, reporters and other kinds of data collection volunteers. The second rank comes to the resource sharing, which are food, water, medical treatment and other kinds of life supporting materials. The third rank comes to the feeling statement including the senses of existence and emotion expression.

It is found that users demands are according to their roles in the situation (Fig. 3). We analyzed all the needs of types of users and narrowed down user roles and characters into three typical persona, resource demanders, resource providers and observers. As time goes by, user roles can convent from one to the other. The shape of the groups is relating to the tendency of role changing. The group of “I am safe” is the buffer pole of the community. The amount of people who are offering help increases from the buffer pole. Meanwhile, the number of people who need help decreases and add numbers to the buffer pole. There are also a group of people like reporters and college students who are the roles like the bridges and speakers of the information broadcasting. They link the disastrous areas and outside areas together, offer the information and news on both sides, and help organizations and governments make rescue strategies and

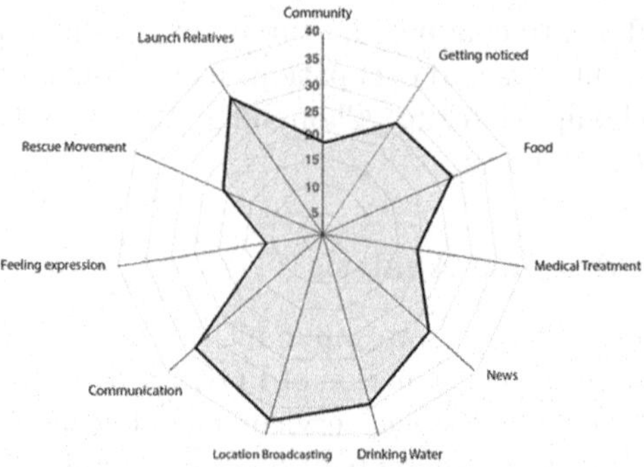

Fig. 2. User demands statistic map

allocate resources. By thinking about the needs of the fictional personas, we are better able to infer what a real person might need. Such inference assisted with our latter brainstorming, case specification and features definition.

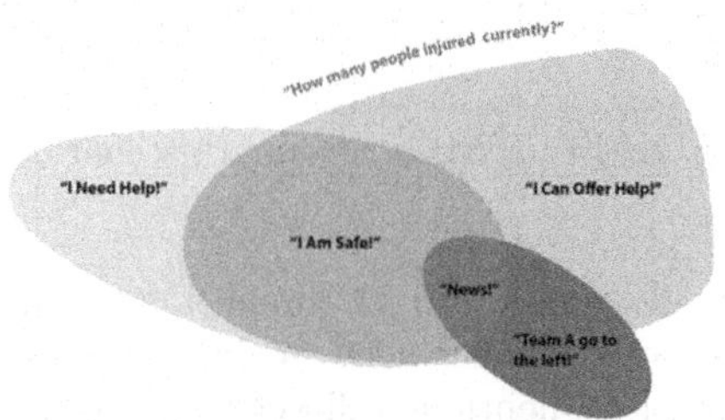

Fig. 3. Characters and roles

We classified user needs and related them into four social cognitive and psychological need categories, the norm of reciprocity, empathy, self-actualization and the sense of security (Fig. 4). Resource demanders are the users who're behaviors of getting resources are dominating in their whole movement. They can be the victims who are injured looking for medical support, who are starving searching for food or water, who are helping others finding life- supporting materials. This group of users could have the possibility to be changed into resource providers or observers once their resource demanding are relieved. The resource providers are the group of people whose main movements are providing life-supporting materials to people who need them. The resources they are providing can be physical stuff like food, water, medical equipment, as well as labour power. They can be individuals, group, organizations. Once the resource is running out, they may turn into observers. Observers mainly consist of people who are currently safe, do not need extra support but also do not have extra resources to share with others in general. They are the people survived and observe the situations. They could turn into the resource supporters due to the organizations, guidances and self-emotional will. There are also some people who can be essential in terms of macroscopic data generation, the journalists and information collectors, who belongs to the group of observers. They are the most active and up-and-coming groups in the disastrous areas, who link data and information as well as peoples mental relationship. There are some demands like "Communication", "location broadcast", and "launch relatives", which are demanding to connect people together into collaboration.

	The norm of reciprocity	Empathy	Self-actualizaion	The sense of security
Resource demanders	resource launch getting connected location launch	building confidence receiving notification getting attention	expression of emotion updating self information	real-time oriented getting informed comfort
Resource providers	notification broadcast explicit guide	real-time oriented information getting attention encouragement	resource info updating complement feedback	getting accessed given authority
Observers	public opinion news	broadcast notification	micro monitoring authority building trust	system reliability real-time oriented information tendency statistics

Fig. 4. User need of Persephone service and user experience

The norm of reciprocity is the expectation that users will respond favorably to each other by returning benefits for benefits, and responding with either indifference or hostility to harms [4]. The norm of reciprocity could be the motivation and also the surveillance to promoting users be a part of the system. Even if a user is neither seeking for help or offering help, it is sensible to stay online in terms of "Norm of Reciprocity". Embedding the idea of the core technique of the P2P meshed network in the service design is a good way to chase for the "Norm of Reciprocity". Every user is a significant node for the whole information change, especially for the users who is a single bridge between two group of users, which is indispensable. However, for the government, public opinions supervise their behaviors when they do the resource statistic and allocating and strategy making.

Self-actualization is a term that has been used in various psychology theories, the quest for spiritual enlightenment. The concept was brought most fully to prominence in Abraham Maslow's hierarchy of needs theory as the final level of psychological development that can be achieved. Showing how much influence a single users behavior has on the whole. Every small step of further approaching on help offering deserves a feedback, which is a subconscious and implicit motivation that encouraging users to explore more.

The sense of security is essential and for the people who is calling for help, which offers them courage and patience in the severe situation. The sense of security is essential. For the people who is calling for help, the sense of security offers them courage and patience in the severe situation. One of a good way to chase the sense of security is to enhance the frequency communication and decrease the chances that messages had been sent out but had no return. Each users status will be visible to all users in the same area, users can tap the note to see every users current status.

3 Service Design Strategies for Promoting User Experience in Individual Moments

3.1 Roles and Characters

There are three roles, "I need help", "I am safe" and "I am safe and I can offer help". In addition, to being themselves (Presenting their own name and contact information), users can choose the roles representing their current status according to their dominating behaviors in the aftermath situation. During the chaotic situation, as resources are limited to access and people are more sensitive to the uncertainty than usual, message exchanging should be more accurate, brief and comprehensible. We should enable users who are in severe situations using as fewer operations as possible to send out the crucial life-supporting information. When selecting "I need help", the tags of "medical", "water", "food", and "electricity" appear for them to select, and multi-selection is supported. The "medical" tag will be selected by default, users can touch the tag to remove selection (Fig. 5).

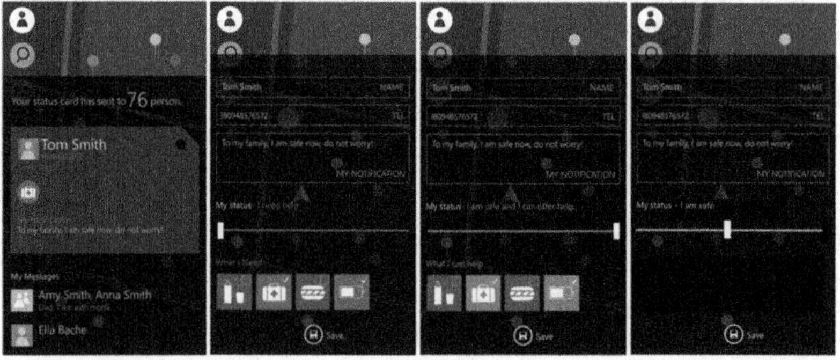

Fig. 5. User Roles and Characters; 3–1 User Centre; 3–2 "I need help"; 3–3 "I am safe and I can offer help"; 3–4 "I am safe"

This design is in perspective of building the sense of security, which means the more severe and emergency the situations are, the fewer operations the users need to do, and the most crucial information will always be launched to the public. The same tags go for the role of "I am safe and I can offer help", by means of achieving the sense of consistency, and making everything comprehensible and efficiency. Three roles can be changed due to the slider bar by very easy operations as users role could change over time. The updated information of users role will be broadcasted to the public one minute after user editing to prevent false operation, and to increase information change efficiency by minimizing information load over the whole system.

3.2 Location and Resource Launching

For people to pay attention to something, they must first perceive it [6]. Everything is based on Bing map, including who is nearby, and their roles related resource status (Fig. 6). According to the norm of reciprocity, the expectation that users will respond favorably to each other by returning benefits for benefits [4].

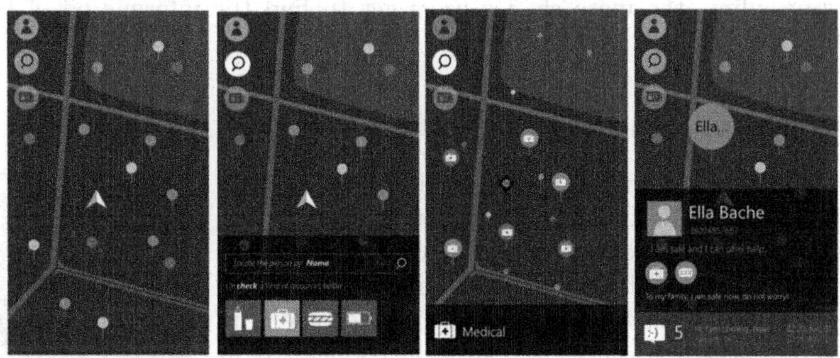

Fig. 6. Location, resource launch, and people nearby

Every movement of a single user can be accessed by the nearby users made the norm of reciprocity visible by each user. In real situations, a user can have a dominating role as "I need help" or "I am safe and I can offer help", and also be an observer on the third perspective. Being a part of the system and out of the system at the same time, users will get attentions of other and get noticed by others at the same time. People are motivated by progress, mastery and control. When they feel they are learning and mastering the situation, they are more motivated to be part of it [6]. Also perceiving something does not mean paying attention to something, the existing features of making everyone feels a sense of control in the chaotic situation could not only motivate people reacting more in the dimensions of information sharing and exchange, but also help resource supporters getting the sense of self- actualization, and encourage them to explore more.

3.3 Emotional Design Respect: People, Families and Friends

After earthquakes, people are scared, hurt and helpless. They want to contact their families, friends, people they are familiar with. They want to obtain food, water and other life-supporting resources. They want to help and help others. No matter the resource demanders, the resources supporters or the observers, the safety of their friends and relatives is one of the universal demanding. Users can send out a sentence of words to families and friends in from self-information editing centre (Fig. 3). Meanwhile, how far the information could reach could be told by users on the user centre page through the sentence "Your status card has been sent to X Person", which is based on the norm of reciprocity and empathy for each other. Users creating bridges for information exchange with people nearby, and they help each other survive. Users can sense what another person is experiencing from within the other person's frame of reference, and the capacity to place oneself in other's position [5]. Making people become bonds of information delivery for each other, motivate people to stay online. The success and efficiency of Persephone are based on mutual help, a number of participants and the delayed data accumulation. Based on the norm of reciprocity, the more users stay online, the more chance users get to find the information of their relatives and friends.

3.4 Communications and Notifications

Users can launch a targeted user on the resource map to do the information exchange, using other users as the bridge of message delivery. "The Group chat" is added to the system as one of the communication features. Doing things together bonds people together, and people who engaged in synchronizing activities are more cooperative in completing subsequent tasks (Scott Wiltermuth and Chip Heath, 2009). Group activities could be organized in group chat, and build the sense of security for each single user. Notification (Fig. 7) is the window to receive information from the outside of the disastrous areas. The notification could be editing from Perseboard, which is the data buffer running on Azure.

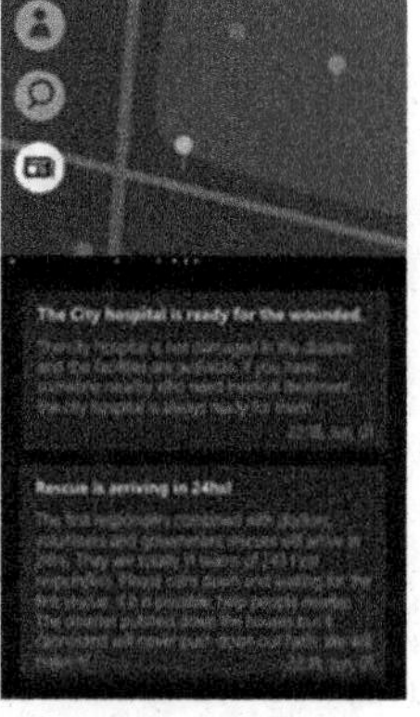

Fig. 7. Notification

4 Conclusion

This research is based on the service design of Persephone, an aftermath rescue system taking advantage of P2P meshed network. Through user research based on the methodology of persona and POEMS, and sort out the relationship between users role-related behaviors and their corresponding mental perceptions, and transform different kinds of user demands to the corresponding guidelines for service design in the perspectives of "The norm of reciprocity", "Empathy",

"Self-actualisation" and "The sense of security". By probing into design strategies of every single part of the real-time user experiences of an aftermath rescue service system "Persephone", the authors explored the possible development of Persephone service design to help users have better emotional control, perspective taking, to show expression of respect in the process of service receiving, thus promotes the long-term effects that individual moments have on the whole. However, the study has its limits in data supporting because of the few amount of data samples. Although typical, the aftermath situation Wenchuan earthquake cant represent the whole China. Enrich the source of data accumulation could help us explore more possibilities of design strategies that could promote long-term effects by enriching user experiences in individual moments.

Thanks. This study was completed by the cooperation of Imagine the world, and Shanghai Jiaotong University. All the products presented above are original designs from Imagine the World.

References

1. Lidwell, W., Holden, K., Butler, J.: Universal Principles of Design. Rockport Publishers, Beverly (2010). p. 182, ISBN 978-1-61058-065-6
2. Pruitt, J., Adlin, T.: The Persona Lifecycle: Keeping People in Mind Throughout Product Design. Morgan Kaufmann, Burlington (2006). ISBN 0-12-566251-3
3. Huang, X., Dai, L.: Chinese cultural values in user experience design of kids home products. In: Rau, P.L.P. (ed.) CCD 2015. LNCS, vol. 9180, pp. 49–57. Springer, Heidelberg (2015)
4. Gouldner, A.W.: The norm of reciprocity: a preliminary statement. Am. Sociol. Rev. **25**(2), 161–178 (1960)
5. Barrett-Lennard, G.T.: The empathy cycle: refinement of a nuclear concept. J. Counselling Psychol. **28**(2), 91 (1981)
6. Weinschenk, S.: 100 things every designer needs to know about people. Pearson Education, Upper Saddle River (2011)
7. Balakrishnan, H., et al.: Looking up data in P2P systems. Commun. ACM **46**(2), 43–48 (2003)

Exploring the Multilingual Efficiency of Urban Online Spaces: Implications for Culture-Centered Design

Antigoni Parmaxi(✉), Anna Nicolaou, Salomi Papadima-Sophocleous, and Dimitrios Boglou

Language Centre, Cyprus University of Technology, Limassol, Cyprus
{antigoni.parmaxi, anna.nicolaou, salomi.papadima, dimitrios.boglou}@cut.ac.cy

Abstract. This paper builds up a picture of how multilingualism is supported in various aspects of urban online spaces. The main assumption of this study is that language is an indispensable element of culture; thus, understanding how a multilingual city facilitates multilingualism in terms of provision of and access to information, can deepen our understanding for supporting cross-cultural Human Computer Interaction (HCI). This study explores how multilingualism is supported in urban online spaces of Limassol, a location of increased inward migration and a city that holds a prolonged multilingual character. Data include manifestations of multilingualism or monolingualism in various online contexts, such as official websites and digital media. Findings demonstrate several aspects of multilingualism, as well as implemented policies and practices for promoting a multilingual online locus. As a result of the findings, suggestions for best practices for the online spaces of multilingual cities are put forward, as well as implications for cross-cultural HCI.

Keywords: Language · Multilingualism · Interculturalism · Multilingual online locus · Language visibility · Cross-cultural HCI

1 Introduction

The multicultural and multilingual character of today's communities is reflected in day-to-day encounters with people, in business transactions, in education, in advertisements, road signs, media and online spaces. As cultural diversity has become a new challenge for Human Computer Interaction (HCI), there is a need for reviewing and evaluating the study of culture in HCI in a systematic way [1, 2]. The main assumption of this study is that language is a fundamental element of culture; thus, understanding how a multilingual city facilitates multilingualism in terms of provision of and access to information, can deepen our understanding for supporting cross-cultural HCI. This study explores how multilingualism and plurilingualism are supported in the urban online spaces of Limassol, a location of increased inward migration and a city that holds a prolonged multilingual character [3]. The study is an attempt to bring forward important aspects of cross-cultural HCI, such as language visibility and invisibility, linguistic support at the level of governance or policy, as well as social inclusion and

P.-L.P. Rau (Ed.): CCD 2016, LNCS 9741, pp. 246–256, 2016.
DOI: 10.1007/978-3-319-40093-8_25

intercultural dialogue in online spaces. The study also looks into the challenges and obstacles involved in creating and managing multilingualism in linguistically diverse online spaces. The purpose of this paper is to provide an overview of the current situation of multilingualism as this is manifested in urban online spaces in significant spheres or aspects of the city life; that is (a) the public sphere, (b) educational sphere, (c) economic life and (d) the private lives of citizens. The aforementioned four key spheres are delineated in order to provide for comprehensive exploration of how multilingualism is depicted in online spaces of city life. Ultimately, this paper builds up a picture of how multilingualism is supported in significant online aspects of multilingual citizen communities. The study is related to the research activities of a wider network of different European cities who attempted to sketch multilingualism in different cities (see also, [4, 5]).

2 Short History of Language Diversity in Limassol

Cyprus has historically had a multilingual and multicultural character since ancient times. This, however, is now more evident than ever before. The population composition of Cyprus today is largely heterogeneous as the country is inhabited by people of diverse cultural backgrounds. In the past, migration in Cyprus used to be associated with large-scale emigration of Cypriots abroad in the early twentieth century in search of jobs and better standards of living; and later between 1960 and 1975, especially following the Turkish invasion of the island in 1974, to countries such as the UK, the USA and Australia [6]. More recently, however, Cyprus has experienced a large wave of inward migration due to various world events and situations that have sent numerous groups of people in Cyprus searching for relocation opportunities.

For historical reasons, the most commonly spoken languages in Cyprus in general are Greek by Greek-Cypriots, and Turkish by Turkish-Cypriots since the Ottoman Era (1571–1878). Under Article 3 of the Constitution, Greek and Turkish are both official languages, but de facto they are used as such in the Republic of Cyprus and the occupied area respectively. As a principle, the Republic of Cyprus government recognises to members of all religious groups and communities the right to use their own language in private and in public, and to receive instruction in it. The Greek Community in Cyprus use both Standard Modern Greek (SMG) – the official language in Greece – and the Greek Cypriot dialect, which belongs to the South-Eastern Greek subgroup and is considered to have remained closer to ancient Greek because of its isolation.

Greek has no legal status in the occupied area. The Turkish currently spoken in Cyprus is the Turkish Cypriot dialect and mainland Turkish, the latter mainly imported by settlers and troops. Before 1974, Turkish was used in all services (together with Greek and English) in the Republic of Cyprus. Since the 1974 division, the use of Turkish has been discontinued, as most Turkish-Cypriots were displaced to the occupied area of the island. However, in the Republic of Cyprus it is still used in passports, identity cards, birth certificates and other official documents. It is also offered as an elective language in government schools.

Other languages and cultures also left their mark on Cyprus. English has always had a strong presence on the island because of the island's colonial history. English was the official language during the British Administration in 1878–1960. As a result, it has left a strong linguistic influence on the island. English has been used as the lingua franca, by both communities along with Greek, and by other people who now live in Cyprus. It is used in many domains such as business, tourism and education. French was used during medieval times (1192–1489), and Italian during the Venetian Rule (1489–1571). Assyrians, Persians, Arabs and others also spent some time in Cyprus during different times for various reasons and left their linguistic and cultural mark on the island. All these languages and cultures have enriched the linguistic and cultural mosaic of Cyprus through the centuries.

Limassol is the second largest city in Cyprus, with a population of 235.056 [7], the largest city on the island in geographical size, and also the largest port in the Mediterranean transit trade. Limassol today includes five municipalities. In the last decades, Limassol has developed into one of the most important maritime, tourism, commercial and service centres in the area. Limassol is also known for its long tradition in cultural issues. It gives the possibility to the visitors to attend a great number of activities and visit many museums and archaeological sites. Foreign populations residing in Limassol are of a diverse cultural and linguistic background. Greece and the UK are among the top countries sending immigrants to Cyprus in general and to Limassol in specific. Other foreign populations hail from countries such as Russia, Poland, Romania, Slovakia, Bulgaria, Latvia, Ukraine, Belarus, Syria, Egypt, Lebanon, Jordan, Sri Lanka, the Philippines, India, Bangladesh and China (Limassol: Results of the Intercultural Cities Index, 2011). Due to the geographic location of Limassol, people from all over the world call Limassol their home. Although the majority of Limassolians are Greek-speaking, other languages like English, Russian, Arabic, Chinese, Indian, or Vietnamese are also heard in the street, and a mixture of cultures is evident in everyday life.

3 Multilingualism in Online Spaces

To be able to explore important aspects of cross-cultural HCI in online spaces and find out whether people communicate interculturally effectively, we needed to examine if there is evidence in online space for understanding cultural differences and share cultural information and meanings effectively. But what does an online space, a website entail? According to Papadima-Sophocleous [8], "a web page is usually a combination of text and visuals, sometimes accompanied by sound, and in more sophisticated cases information is presented in a multimedia form (text, buttons, images, photos, animation, sound, video, and special effects)". In terms of text, one needs to consider which language or languages are used and which form of the language(s). Visuals and symbols complementing or supporting the meaning of the text need to be carefully selected as they may have a different meaning in different cultures. And if a web site is more sophisticated, one needs to consider how much this helps understanding the message by users from different linguistic and cultural backgrounds.

Communication with people from different cultures is not a new phenomenon. People have been travelling for centuries, transacting and exchanging culturally and linguistically. Fast travel, international media and the Internet have made world communication much more accessible. Communication occurs not only between people who travel, but also between people of different cultures who live together in the same spaces such as in the public sphere, economic life, the private life of citizens, and the educational sphere, locally and internationally. Knowledge of other cultures is of vital importance in order for communication between people of different cultures to be effective and in order for all parties to be able to emerge with the same understanding. To achieve that, both the web developer and the web visitors need to be interculturally competent, in other words they need to have the "…abilities to understand different modes of thinking and living … and to reconcile or mediate between different modes present in any specific interaction …" [9].

Over the years, some sort of common cyber culture was developed. Aspects such as netiquette were designed to guide internauts into how to behave online and neticons accompanied people's messages. However, as more and more people of diverse linguistic and cultural background cultures used the Internet, cultural misunderstandings started to occur. This led to the development of approaches towards a web of more effective intercultural communication. Elements such as language, culture, layout and design were taken into consideration in this light.

Although English seems to be the most dominant language on the web, more and more websites are developed in many languages [10]. Wherever English is used, either as mother tongue or as a lingua franca, and since there is no standard English, every effort needs to be taken to use a form of English comprehensible to most site visitors (writing style, short and simple sentences, use of specific words, idioms, slang, and turns of phrase, similes and metaphors, that may have different cultural connotation in another language, etc.). The aims of each site should be to reach as many of its intended visitors as possible, in the best possible way. This should determine the choice of language(s). Very often, organisations opt to provide translated versions of their sites. In such cases, caution needs to be exercised for the message to be mediated appropriately, both linguistically and culturally in order to avoid cultural misunderstandings.

According to Schneiderman [11], a website's interface intermediates between a system and users, therefore it is important that it accommodates the need of the users and makes it easy to use. Website user interface needs to take into consideration the users' cultural differences [12]. In general, organisations need to ensure sensitive presence on the Internet. This extends to the website presentation, the site layout and design, which also send messages of meanings that could be misunderstood. These include interface, navigation and screen design, images, and colours. According to Marcus and Baumgartner [13], "people from different countries/cultures use user-interfaces (UIs) in different ways, prefer different graphical layouts, and have different expectations and patterns in behaviour".

Cultural misunderstanding in online spaces may be caused by elements such as reading order; length of words and phrases may cause difficulties with graphical navigation methods and may lead to screen redesign ([16]; as cited in [8]). Images may also be the source of cultural misunderstanding. Images can have different meaning in different cultures. Images must be appropriate, clear and non-insulting to their intended audience [8]. Colour is another aspect that may cause cultural misunderstanding as different colours have different meanings among cultures as well as within a culture ([14, 15]; as cited in [8]). Site development and management are also important and need to take into consideration where the audience comes from, locally or internationally and accommodate their needs as well, and take into consideration other aspects such as downloading time, and streaming ([16]; as cited in [8]).

Successful multilingualism in online spaces is based on human and technical factors; in other words, it requires cultural competence and appropriate software solutions. Parameters such as language, culture, layout and design need to be taken into consideration in order to have effective online intercultural communication. A standard user interface is and can no longer be used in the design of a website. Cultural differences are now also being explored. Several studies explored interface designs. Husmann [17], for example, investigated the localisation of web user interface by examining the cross-cultural differences in home page design. SD Erişti [18] explored the cultural factors in web design of 15 university web sites chosen randomly from 11 countries. Cyr and Trevor-Smith [19] investigated the localisation of web design by comparing German, Japanese, and U.S. website characteristics. Cyr et al. [20] also carried out a four nation study which addressed differences in preference and perception of website design across cultures.

Intercultural online design entails the manifestation of elements of language, culture, layout and design. For the purposes of this study, we explored intercultural online design with an emphasis on the use of language/s in various websites accessed and utilized by users coming from different cultural backgrounds.

4 Methodology

As noted earlier, the aim of this study is to create a multiplicity of up-to-date narratives on the multi/plurilingual realities of the online space of Limassol in terms of provision of and access to information. Four key spheres were explored related to the public sphere, education sphere, economic life, and the private lives of citizens. Examples of online spaces varied in each sphere, but included digital artefacts which illustrated the multilingual reality of the online spaces of the city, like websites and social networking pages or communities.

(a) The public sphere included online spaces, such as websites, of the local municipality/city council, public services (health, transport, tourism) and media (television, newspapers, digital media). Types of data collected in this sphere included the websites of the municipalities of Limassol, the website of public services and local media.
(b) The educational sphere included online spaces, such as websites of public schools (from day nursery to adult education), vocational schools, non-governmental organisations (NGOs) involved in formal or informal education, independent/private schools (including bilingual schools), complementary schools (language academies), and cultural organisations/societies/associations. Types of data

collected in this sphere included websites of public and private schools, as well as complementary schools and cultural organisations.

(c) The economic sphere included online spaces, such as websites of large local/national companies and multinationals companies based in Limassol, industries and manufacturing corporations, SMEs, service providers (professional services), and financial transactions' companies. Types of data collected in this sphere included information from the website of chambers of commerce and employers' associations as well as companies and SMEs based in Limassol.

(d) The private sphere included online spaces, such as websites and communities within social media, that demonstrated local or city-wide activities (such as festivals) that were not initiated by the public sphere (although they may have received public funding) but were organised instead by local community groups, online spaces of services that are offered by local communities (including volunteer activities), local support networks and religious activities and organisations/structures. Types of data in this sphere included examples of social network groups and websites of festivals, religious activities, networks of migrant groups, clubs, sports, and other cultural activities (theatre, music, etc.).

A reporting template was employed in order to facilitate data recording and language visibility in online spaces. The template captured concise information from websites related to (a) language options in online spaces, and (b) access to information in the different languages in online spaces.

We articulated the following research hypotheses, with regard to multilingualism in online urban spaces in Limassol:

- Visibility. We hypothesise that some languages are more visible than others in online urban spaces, and that this visibility/invisibility is meaningful. We hypothesise that sometimes, when languages are visible, the visibility operates at a symbolic level. This symbolism is seen and understood by some, and largely ignored by others. Languages which are highly visible in online space may not be the languages in which the various transactions and policies of city life are enacted.
- Challenges/obstacles. We hypothesise that both challenges and obstacles will appear inhibiting or facilitating communication in online urban spaces.

5 Findings

This study explored language visibility in online urban spaces in the four spheres (public sphere, educational sphere, the economic life, and the private life of citizens) demonstrating the strong presence of Greek, English and Russian. Although the official languages in Cyprus are Greek and Turkish, English is more visible in online spaces in Limassol than any other language, whilst Greek dominates in the educational sphere and English and Russian in the economic life (see Table 1).

Table 1. Language provision in the online spaces of Limassol in the four spheres (public sphere, educational sphere, economic life, and the private life of citizens).

Sphere	Language provision in online urban spaces examined							
	Monolingual				Bilingual		Three or more languages	Total
	Greek	Turkish	English	Russian	Greek/Other[a]	English/ Other[a]	Three or more languages	
Public sphere	4	0	0	0	9 (English[b] [9])	1 (Russian [1])	5 (Greek, English[b], Russian[b] [4], Greek, English[b], Russian[b] and German[b] [1])	19
Educational sphere	52	0	7	2	4 (English [4])	1 (Chinese[b] [1])	2 (Greek, English[b], Spanish[b], French[b], German[b], Italian[b], Russian[b] [1], Greek, English, Russian [1])	68
Economic sphere	0	0	27	0	5 (English [5])	6 (French [1], Russian [4], Arabic [1])	8 (Greek, English, Russian [6]; Greek, English, Russian, Hebrew, Romanian [1]; Greek, English, Russian, Chinese [1])	46
Private lives of citizens	3	0	12	0	7 (English [7])	1 (Russian [1])	2 (Greek, English, Turkish [1]; Greek, English, French, Italian, Portuguese, German, Chinese, Spanish [1])	25
Total	59	0	46	2	25	9	17	158

[a]In brackets other(s) language(s) used; in square brackets number of online spaces using the specific language (s).
[b]Limited information is provided in these languages.

5.1 Online Spaces in the Public Sphere

In the public sphere, language provision appears to be balanced between monolingual, bilingual and multilingual online spaces (see Table 1). Greek, English, Russian and German are the languages that gain visibility in the online spaces in the public sphere, yet languages that need to be boosted include Turkish, Arabic, Bulgarian and Romanian.

The integration of foreign languages in online spaces in the public sphere (e.g. in the websites of local municipalities) is often made through an information guide provided by the national authorities in English and Russian. All websites have a Greek and an English version. However, some important documents are available only in Greek and in many cases the English version of the website is not working, is under construction or has a limited amount of information available in English compared to Greek. Application forms and documents are always available in Greek and in English in most cases, but no document is provided in Turkish -the second official language of Cyprus.. Yet, migrants do not only need shortened information, but to be able to access regulations and information in their mother tongue (or at least in a lingua franca).

On local level, Limassol is making efforts to improve its welcoming policies by implementing a welcoming policy instrument. The city has published a comprehensive package of information to aid newly arrived foreign residents. However, the attainment rate of Limassol's policy goals is still quite low according to the Intercultural Cities Index [3].

5.2 Online Spaces in Educational Sphere

While intercultural education is an official aim of the Ministry of Education in Cyprus, measures to implement it in online spaces are unfavourable with limited information available in languages other than Greek. Having a vast majority of public schools' websites being monolingual, de facto excludes migrant children and their parents from access to important information related to their education. Symbolic use of language in one public school is provided by having the school's director's salutation translated in 6 different languages (Spanish, French, German, Italian, English, Russian). Such symbolic use of these languages enacts familiarity with the visitor of the website. Private schools are more sensitive in providing information in more than one languages -as they follow an English curriculum. A good practice noticed is the provision of information in different languages in an information pack-instead of providing the whole translated version of the website. Such a practice provides a cost-efficient way to facilitate easy access of the majority of information in another language.

Languages other than Greek and English are visible in the educational online spaces such as French, Russian, Spanish, Chinese and German. Neglected languages are Arabic, Romanian, Bulgarian, Spanish, Chinese and German, in spite of the large population of these ethnicities that reside in Limassol. Regarding languages that deserve a boost in the educational online spaces include English, together with Turkish, Russian, Chinese, Arabic, Bulgarian and Romanian.

5.3 Online Spaces in Economic Life

Cyprus has always been an attractive migration pole, and labour market conditions are among the reasons that make migrants decide to settle in Cyprus. With regard to language visibility in online spaces in economic life, English, Russian and German sketch the economic linguistic profile of Limassol. The English language is used widely within various private companies and in many industries, such as banking, financial services, legal firms, tourist organisations, hotel and hospitality enterprises, and many others. Taking into account the economic profile of the city, English, German and Russian are the strongest financial partners in Limassol, thus the visibility of these language is meaningful in terms of their presence in the economy. Remarkably the multicultural character of Limassol is also formulated by people of Asian or African origin; however, their languages appear to be neglected and thus less visible within economic online spaces.

5.4 Online Spaces in the Private Sphere

Various clubs, organisations and associations geared towards the promotion of interculturality and cooperation, human rights, multilingualism and equality exist in Limassol. Some examples of such institutions are: the Filipino Overseas Contract Workers Association of Limassol, the Cyprus-Bulgaria Business Association, the Association of Bulgarians in Cyprus, the Association of Russian-speaking Residents of Cyprus, the The Middle East Council of Churches, the Association of Recognised Refugees in Cyprus, the Bi-communal Community Centre in Limassol, etc. In these online spaces, English is dominant as these associations bring together migrants from different countries and follow the lingua franca approach for promoting their activities. Less visible languages in the online spaces in the private sphere are Arabic, Bulgarian, Romanian, Turkish, Sri Lankan, Vietnamese, Chinese, Polish, Hungarian, German, French, Slovakian and Serbian. Languages that need to be boosted, are Turkish (as official and equal state language), Bulgarian, Romanian, Roma, and Arabic.

6 Discussion

Limassol is a city of increasing inward migration receiving in the last years many immigrants of diverse cultural, linguistic and economic background. This unprecedented change in the demographic character of the city has happened in a short span of time and has found the people and authorities unprepared to deal with it. Although online spaces welcome visitors from several different cultural and linguistic backgrounds, many of these spaces only represent the dominant Greek language, thus not being able to cater for the needs of culturally diverse visitors.

With regard to the languages' visibility, our primary hypothesis that some languages are more visible than others in online spaces, and that this visibility/invisibility is meaningful has been confirmed. Greek and English appear to be the most visible languages; however, this does not reflect the overall linguistic mosaic of online spaces Limassol. In general, the wide use of English – being an international dominant language - and the neglect of other languages is one of the key themes that has emerged. English is an effective way of handling overall communication and information provision in online spaces; on the other hand, it is perceived as a danger of national languages extinction. Moreover, Russian emerged as the most visible language in the economic sphere. Therefore, we could mention that certain languages have established themselves and gained visibility based on their financial strength in the city.

Our second hypothesis relates to challenges and opportunities in language provision in online urban spaces. Online urban spaces demonstrate multiple ways of linguistic diversity, either by translating all contents of the page in more than one language, by providing an information pack with the majority of the content in several languages or by demonstrating symbolic use of language.

7 Conclusion

Through the analysis of the online urban spaces of Limassol, various suggestions have emerged. In general, online urban spaces need to adopt a more pluralistic perspective. To achieve this, online urban spaces need to reassess the needs of their visitors and provide a broader linguistic support in terms of access to information. Moreover, the city needs to explore the efficiency of performance of online urban spaces towards migrant citizens.

Designers may adopt cost-effective ways to involve the cultural and linguistic context in the design of their artifacts. A cost effective way for supporting linguistic diversity is to provide an information pack with the whole component of the website, and thus facilitate their visitors' access to information. Providing the opportunity to visitors to understand that the developer catered for their needs can be an important step for fostering their engagement on the website.

Limassol's linguistic support at the level of governance or policy is overall limited. A multilingual online locus needs to make an effort to accommodate its diverse citizens. The actions and initiatives to be taken include assessment of online visitors' needs and linguistic background and a vision in accommodating -even at a symbolic level- the needs of multilingual citizens. As noted by Bourges-Waldegg & Scrivener [21], a central issue in cross-cultural HCI is representations and meaning mediate action. Designing and sharing an online locus that intends to be shared by culturally diverse users needs to entail the cultural diverse needs of its users, in terms of culture and language provision.

8 Limitations

This study sketches multilingualism in Limassol in online urban spaces by exploring a substantial number of online spaces in four key spheres. This study does not provide a holistic understanding of all cultural aspects in online spaces in the city of Limassol. The intention was to bring to the surface current aspects of handling language barriers in online spaces. The data of this study is available to anyone that may be interested to conduct a further research on the topic. The results of the current study are limited to the particular online spaces; yet they may reflect both present and future trends of multilingualism in terms of provision of and access to information in online spaces.

References

1. Kamppuri, M., Bednarik, R., Tukiainen, M.: The expanding focus of HCI: case culture. In: Proceedings of the 4th Nordic Conference on Human-Computer Interaction: Changing Roles, pp. 405–408. ACM (2006)
2. Parmaxi, A., Zaphiris, P.: Computer-mediated communication in computer-assisted language learning: implications for culture-centered design. Univ. Access Inf. Soc. **15**(1), 169–177 (2016)
3. Limassol: Results of the Intercultural Cities Index (2011). http://www.coe.int/t/dg4/cultureheritage/culture/cities/Index/Limassol_en.pdf
4. Nicolaou, A., Parmaxi, A., Papadima-Sophocleous, S., Boglou, D.: Landscaping multilingualism in the urban community of Limassol: policies, practices and visions. In: Proceedings of INTED2016 Conference, Valencia, Spain (2016)
5. Carson, L.: The LUCIDE network: languages in urban communities-integration and diversity for Europe. Eur. J. Appl. Linguist. **1**(2), 305–312 (2013)
6. Gregoriou, P., Kontolemis, Z., Matsi, Z.: Immigration in cyprus: an analysis of the determinants. Cyprus Econ. Policy Rev. **4**(1), 63–88 (2010)
7. CYSTAT (Statistical Service of the Republic of Cyprus). Population and social conditions—Census—2011. Nicosia, Cyprus (2011)
8. Papadima-Sophocleous, S.: A web of intercultural communication. Informatologia **36**(3), 166–241 (2003). Croatia
9. Byram, M., Fleming, M.: Language Learning in Intercultural Perspective. Cambridge University Press, Cambridge (1998)
10. Pimienta, D., Prado, D., Blanco, Á.: Twelve years of measuring linguistic diversity in the Internet: balance and perspectives. United Nations Educational, Scientific and Cultural Organization (2009)
11. Schneiderman, B.: Software Psychology: Human Factors in Computer and Information Systems. Winthrop Computer Systems Series. Winthrop, Cambridge (1980)
12. Nasrul, M.A., Norb, K.M., Masromc, M., Syariefd, A.: Website fit: an overview. Procedia Soc. Behav. Sci. **40**, 315–325 (2012)
13. Marcus, A., Baumgartner, V.J.: A visible language analysis of user-interface design components and culture dimensions. Vis. Lang. **38**, 1–65 (2004)
14. Boor, S., Russo, P.: How fluent is your interface? Designing for international users. In: INTERCHI 1993 (1993)
15. Kravitz, R.: Going Global On-Line: What You Need To Know (2002). http://www.ibm.com/us-en/
16. Gaine, F.: Globalisation: The Challenges to Usability (2001). http://www.frontend.com/
17. Husmann, Y.: Localization of web user interfaces. Cross-cultural differences in home page design. Wissenschaftliche Arbeit zur Erlangung des Diplomgrades im Studiengang Sprachen-, Wirtschafts-und Kulturraumstudien (Diplom-Kulturwirt) (2001)
18. Erişti, S.D.: Cultural factors in web design. J. Theor. Appl. Inf. Technol. (JATIT) **9**(2), 117–132 (2009)
19. Cyr, D., Trevor-Smith, H.: Localization of web design: a comparison of German, Japanese, and U.S. website characteristics. J. Am. Soc. Inform. Sci. Technol. **55**(13), 1–10 (2004)
20. Cyr, D., Bonanni, C., Bowes, J., Ilsever, J.: Website design and culture: an empirical investigation. In: Proceedings for the International Workshop for the Internationalisation of Products and Systems Conference, Vancouver, Canada (2004)
21. Bourges-Waldegg, P., Scrivener, S.A.: Meaning, the central issue in cross-cultural HCI design. Interact. Comput. **9**(3), 287–309 (1998)

Bridging Personal Adaptations to Urban Landscape Design

Tatsuya Shibata(✉)

School of Information Environment, Tokyo Denki University,
2-1200 Muzai-Gakuendai, Inzai, Chiba 270-1382, Japan
tshibata@mail.dendai.ac.jp

Abstract. This paper describes how affective engineering approaches contribute to urban design methods for street and urban landscapes. I focus on (1) differences attributed to individualism of the English and the Japanese in urban landscapes, (2) differences between information and the environment and the current information environment, and (3) introduction of Symbiosis Communicator for Advanced and Preserved Environment (SCAPE), the design support system that includes Kansei, knowledge, and augmented media. A case study highlights a landscape designed in a resident participation project in Chiba, Japan. I conclude that SCAPE may help with designs that promote local diversity and resident participation.

Keywords: Personal adaptation model · Urban landscape · Affective engineering · Augmented reality

1 Introduction

This paper describes how affective engineering approaches contribute to urban design functions and methods from the viewpoint of street and urban landscape design. Integration and diversity are important for street pattern structures and urban landscapes. The space syntax theory espoused by Hillier [1] shows integration of streets in London, Venice, Detroit, etc. Psarra [2] indicates that Venice is a city with locally and globally balanced combinations of street patterns based on the space syntax method. The street patterns in Venice look complicated, indicating that it would be easy to become lost. In the center of Detroit, street integration is unbalanced, causing people to leave this area and move to the suburbs.

Physical street structures differ in terms of balance for local and global integration. An orderly balance of private and public streets and urban landscape design is quite important. Japan faces many problems in street and urban landscape design that must be solved. Especially, the two types of individualism that differentiate English and Japanese cultures influence urban landscape design. The next chapter provides examples of landscape differences between England and Japan. I introduce Symbiosis Communicator for Advanced and Preserved Environment (SCAPE), an innovation of Kansei information technology [3–5], to promote resident participation for an orderly urban landscape design. I think that balance and order play important roles in urban design.

P.-L.P. Rau (Ed.): CCD 2016, LNCS 9741, pp. 257–265, 2016.
DOI: 10.1007/978-3-319-40093-8_26

2 English Individualism Versus Japanese Individualism

The prominent difference in urban landscapes in England and Japan pertains to the order of streets. English urban designs are based on regulations concerning building height and setback space width, so each street is characterized by uniformity in these areas. Regulations ensure that the skylines in England are either straight or curved (Fig. 1). Urban landscape design in England is based on maintaining order. On the other hand, there are some regulations in Japan, but building heights and widths of setback space are not constant except in some new towns. Therefore, skylines are typically not linear or curved in Japan (Fig. 1). Urban landscape design in Japan is based on disorder.

Fig. 1. Urban landscapes in England and Japan

In terms of historical landscape scenes, buildings in London are generally older than in Tokyo. Historical buildings in Tokyo are frequently destroyed and replaced with high-rise office and residential buildings. However, there are a few historical towns in Tokyo, such as Asakusa.

What are the reasons for the visual differences between Tokyo and London? I attribute the differences to the various concepts regarding public and private land use. For example, the address system in the UK is based on streets (lines), whereas the address system in Japan is based on land (areas). Land in Japan is generally owned by individuals and land developers, so it is possible that a low-rise housing area is situated next to a towering residential building in Chiba New Town, Japan, for example. Land in the UK used to be state-owned but is now privately owned, whereas most land in Japan is privately owned. Urban landscape design in the UK is based on a public order, in contrast to the private order that characterizes Japan's urban landscape, so there are stronger regulations for buildings in the UK than in Japan.

In terms of social behaviors, the Japanese work hard and tend to devote themselves to work rather than to their personal lives, whereas the English reverse these priorities. Moreover, the order when writing name and address in England is first name, surname, house number, street, town, and country; in Japan, the address begins with the country and is followed by the prefecture, house number, surname, and first name. The address format supports the observation that priority is given to the private or personal over the public in the UK, whereas the public viewpoint is more important in Japan. Japanese people strive for public order, but the English focus on their private lives. English behavior is more private, though the English urban landscape has a public order that is homogeneous. The Japanese behave publicly, but the Japanese urban landscape has no order and is heterogeneous. It would seem that Japanese people are quite selfish rather than individualistic in urban landscape designs.

There is a clear difference and contradiction between behaviors and urban landscape designs in Japan. I think that the Japanese have misunderstand the concept of individualism, which affects urban design strongly. The Japanese novelist Soseki Natsume, who visited London, indicated that the concept of individualism is perceived differently in the UK than it is in Japan [6].

3 Information and Environment Versus Information Environment

Figure 2 shows the relationship between information and the environment and the corresponding link to the body. Information from media includes language, images, movies, and music. Language is representative. For example, no apples are identical, but everyone recognizes an apple as an apple. Language treats different apples homogeneously. Invariant features play an important role in recognizing objects in our brains to name objects. The information can be homogeneous, though the environment seems to be heterogeneous. The environment is twofold: natural and built (artificial). Natural environments are neither constant nor homogeneous because climates change based on daytime and nighttime and the four seasons. Thus, there is no identical natural environment in the world. However, a built environment controls temperature and brightness for constancy. The homogeneous structure of the built environment is similar to the structure of information. Differences between information and the environment involve (1) movability, (2) independence of places, and (3) existing entity (or weight), as Fig. 2 shows. The body looks homogeneous but is heterogeneous.

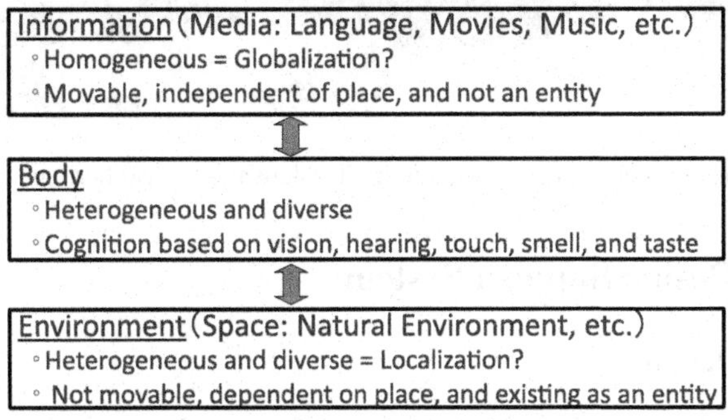

Fig. 2. Relationship between information and the environment

Homogeneously built environments in Japan include buildings, shopping centers, and convenience stores. Figure 3 refers to a tower residential block in Kunitachi, Tokyo. Residents there protect the street landscape design with straight skylines and trees, although a land developer built the tower block similarly to other buildings that had already been constructed. Built environments become homogeneous, as there are numerous 7-Eleven retail shops and AEON shopping malls in Japan. Figure 4 shows a natural landscape with a heterogeneous environment. Shirakawago, a village surrounded and segregated by mountains, has a beautiful landscape with wooden detached houses featuring steep roofs. The landscape shown in Fig. 4 is opposite that shown in Fig. 3. A built environment should be in harmony with the surrounding regional environment, and people must protect and maintain their landscape. Therefore, resident participation plays an important role, and residents in Kunitachi and Shirakawago maintain their environment by themselves. The Japanese tend not to care for the public landscape order, as I talked about the Japanese selfishness.

Fig. 3. A homogeneous and information-oriented environment in Tokyo, Japan

Fig. 4. Heterogeneous environment in Shirakawago (world heritage), Japan

4 SCAPE: Design Support System

4.1 Interface Design

Figure 5 shows the previous and current interface environment for accessing and displaying information. Figure 5a shows an environment in which, for example, people go to a fixed telephone to communicate with others or to a desktop PC to input information via the keyboard. A body has to go to the interface to input and receive information. On the other hand, Fig. 5b shows an environment in which people do not have to go to an interface; the environment or space can be an interface (i.e., ambient environment). A smartphone and Kinect (Microsoft) are user interfaces for accessing data and information. The interface is independent of place, and it is wearable. There is no boundary between the body and the interface, as Fig. 5b shows.

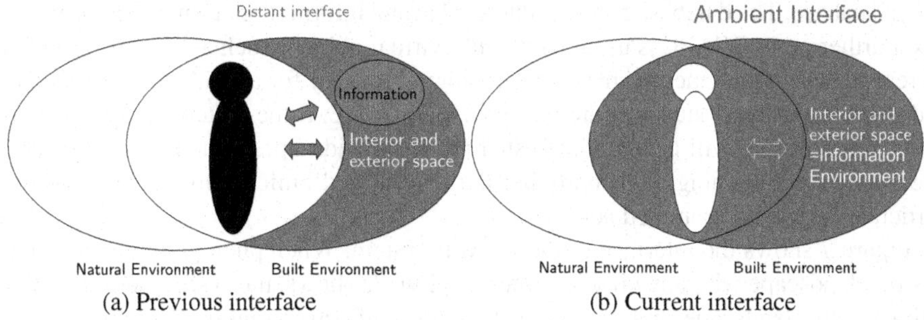

(a) Previous interface (b) Current interface

Fig. 5. Previous and current interface design

4.2 Interface Supporting Personal Design

I refer to "human media"—including Kansei media, knowledge media, and augmented media, as Fig. 6 shows. Kansei media are based on personal adaptation models developed through deep learning methods [4, 5]. For example, street landscapes taken on a user's smartphone are evaluated with a personal affective model automatically, as Fig. 7a shows. It means that the evaluations are different for individuals. Knowledge media are based on collections of multimedia databases that are structured by models. Augmented media are tools to represent 3D objects in the real world. The three media technologies are integrated as an interface to support personal design. Creations by individuals are shared and distributed to create new values and services.

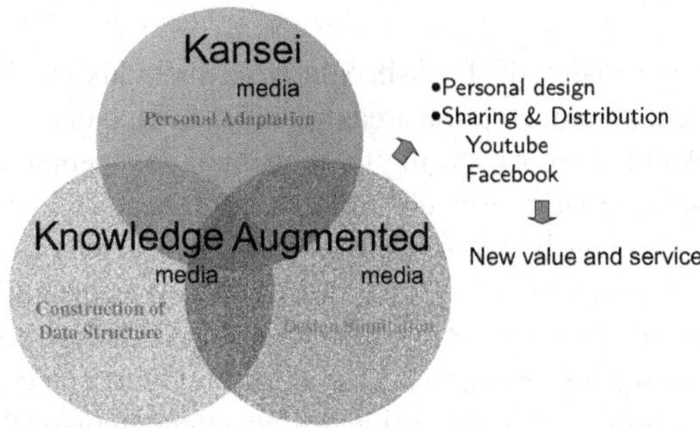

Fig. 6. Human media technology to unite three media technologies

4.3 SCAPE System

SCAPE stands for Symbiosis Communicator for Advanced and Preserved Environment; it integrates Kansei knowledge with augmented media technology. The basic idea is (1) to model residents or designers' Kansei, and (2) to construct the relationship between subjective responses to multimedia data and feature descriptors of multi-modal data such as images, 3D models, sounds, etc. The system is used to construct buildings, street furniture, and textures for pavement; professionals' and designers' models are included in the database. The database contains knowledge and information from various specialists. Furthermore, SCAPE is used (3) to build virtual objects, such as objects designed on real sites using augmented reality technology. It is easy for a resident to understand and share the images once they are retrieved via SCAPE. If the system is used by residents, more people will become interested in urban landscapes, thus fostering greater attention on maintaining and improving the natural and built environment. Resident participation can be promoted actively.

Figure 7 shows the interface of the SCAPE system. When photographing any kind of street landscape with any kind of camera, as Fig. 7a shows, the system automatically estimates the landscape and output by Kansei or affective rankings according to a personal Kansei model. Figure 7b indicates 3D light retrieval results harmonized in the target 2D street image. There are 2D and 3D models with features for colors, shapes, and Kansei or affective rankings. Figure 7c indicates virtual 3D light object alignment on the real site using augmented reality technology [7]. The advantages of SCAPE are the selection of various types of data from multimedia databases and the simulation of any kind of 3D data at the real site.

5 Resident Participation in Landscape Design Project

I think resident participation will be a key point for keeping and protecting urban landscapes because residents can create their environment actively and independently. However, residents generally have no knowledge about environmental design. Since they do, however, have the desire to protect the environment, SCAPE would be an effective tool to support them. Thus, they would not have to rely on architects and designers.

A resident group in Japan —Kobayashi Sumiyoi Machidukuri Group—designed a small pavilion in a Dosaku mound tomb area in Inzai, Chiba. Nobody has cared for this area except the resident group. According to questionnaires, people requested a small pavilion as a rest area so that they could reflect on the beautiful surrounding, which include woodlands and cherry blossoms. The project is supported by the resident group, students from Tokyo Denki University, and an architect. We carried out several workshops to design the pavilion, as Fig. 8a shows. We used SCAPE to check the 3D CAD model of the pavilion (Fig. 8b). Residents were able to imagine and explore many kinds of pavilions. Figure 9 shows the final pavilion design agreed upon by the resident group.

Local governments or developers design urban landscapes to keep them clean and follow design guidelines that meet local regulations. Typically, local governments or developers determine urban landscape designs. Moreover, residents usually have no knowledge of the designs and no tools for presenting their desired images. However, many projects involving resident participation in urban landscape design are underway in Japan. SCAPE could be a useful tool to help them design their towns and cities independently.

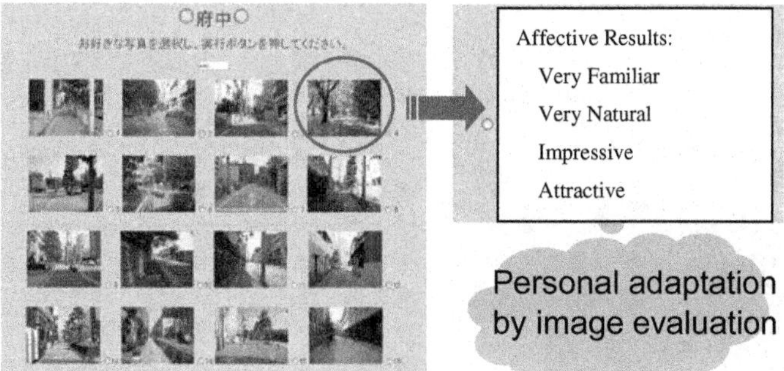

(a) Estimation of affective judgment regarding 2D street image with a personal Kansei model

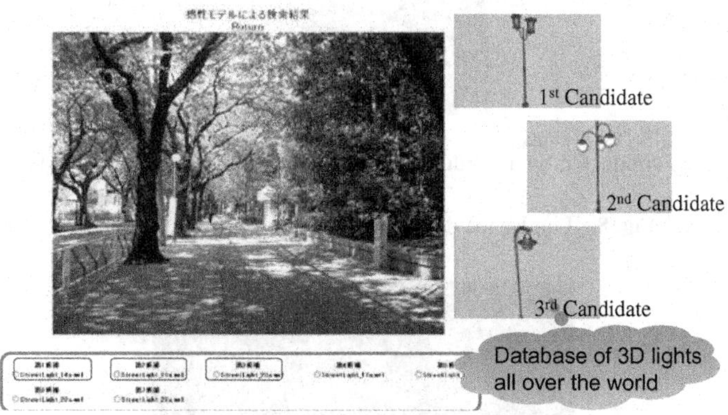

(b) 3D light retrieval results harmonized in the target 2D street image

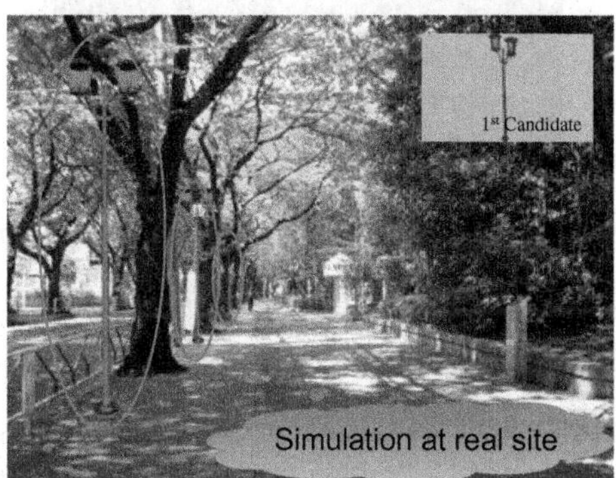

(c) Virtual 3D light object alignment on a real site

Fig. 7. SCAPE system interface

(a) Workshop conducted by a resident group (b) Design check at real site using SCAPE

Fig. 8. Landscape design project undertaken by residents

Fig. 9. Completed pavilion built in Dosaku mound tomb area

6 Conclusions

SCAPE will support town and city designs by individuals and residents in local and regional areas. Designs are shared through the Internet to unite residents and maintain a sustainable society. Therefore, we can promote diversity and heterogeneous environments and societies throughout the world. However, there is currently more disorder in urban design than before in Japan because of selfishness by landowners. We need to accept the diversity of towns and ensure order in town designs. I believe that SCAPE will promote resident participation in designing landscapes that reflect diversity.

References

1. Hillier, B., Hanson, J.: The Social Logic of Space. Cambridge University Press, Cambridge (1984)
2. Psarra, S.: Beyond analytical knowledge: the need for a combined theory of generation and explanation. A|Z ITU J. Fac. Archit. **11**(2), 47–68 (2014)
3. Shibata, T., Kato, T.: Modeling of subjective interpretation for street landscape image. In: Quirchmayr, G., Bench-Capon, T.J., Schweighofer, E. (eds.) DEXA 1998. LNCS, vol. 1460, pp. 501–510. Springer, Heidelberg (1998)
4. Shibata, T., Kato, T.: Image retrieval system for street-landscape images using adjectives. Trans. Inst. Electron. Inf. Commu. Eng. D-I **82**(1), 174–183 (1999)
5. Uchiyama, N., Shibata, T.: Analysis and model on harmonization between urban landscape and buildings—method of multi-modal kansei retrieval system. J. Archit. Plann. **73**(623), 241–248 (2008)
6. Natsume, S.: My Individualism. Kodansha, Tokyo (1978)
7. ARToolKit. https://www.hitl.washington.edu/artoolkit/

A Study of Relationship Between Personality and Product Identity

Wen-Zhong Su(✉) and Po-Hsien Lin

Graduate School of Creative Industry Design,
National Taiwan University of Arts, Ban Ciao District,
New Taipei 22058, Taiwan
orpheussu@gmail.com, t0131@mail.ntua.edu.tw

Abstract. There are many researches show that product have personified personality, in recently years, the cultural & creative products has emphasize the direction of personalized merchandise to cater demand from consumer and thereby satisfied the maverick consumer which have distinctive psychological needs. The purpose of this study is investigated the cognition of cultural & creative products are identical between the consumer who have different personality traits and learn more about the consumer preferences and purchase intentions. The research process of this paper is divided into four phases. First, according to the literature reviews define the correspondence between "Personality", "Personalized Product" and "Consumer Perception" as first phase. In second phase, this paper collected the winner's works of cultural & creative award during 2010 to 2015 as test sample to implement expert pre-questionnaire. Researcher reconstructed next phase questionnaire through comparison the "Personalized Product" awareness from expert into formal survey. During the third phase, each examinee will answer Professional DynaMetric Programs and finish "Personalized Product and Purchase Intention questionnaire". The fourth phase will be data analysis and result. This study is going to verify the relationship between "Personality of Cultural & Creative Product" and "Consumer Perception", and discuss the correlation of "Consumer Perception" and "Personality". Above factor will be affected the consumer purchase intention or not. This result would be provided to product planner, designer or marketing for reference.

Keywords: Products personality · Personality traits · Consumer perception · Purchase intentions

1 Introduction

The Cultural and Creative Industries Development Act was passed in 2010. The Council for Cultural Affairs of the Executive Yuan was elevated to become the Ministry of Culture in May 2012. Thus, Taiwan has advanced toward the development stage of cultural and creative industries. During this stage, the design of cultural and creative products was catered to consumer requirement. Thereby, products of personality were adhered to in order to satisfy consumer's unique and different psychological requirement. Consequently, a host of research found that consumers have added

P.-L.P. Rau (Ed.): CCD 2016, LNCS 9741, pp. 266–274, 2016.
DOI: 10.1007/978-3-319-40093-8_27

personal traits to products, including positive and negative ones, that is, personification of products (Sirgy 1982). The literature of emotion research for product design assessment also underscores product identity. The ergonomics designers also explore how different consumers correlate personality with product identity, and made products become unique and interesting, for instance, hinting the gender of products (McDonagh and Weightman 2003). Whether product identity matches with the designer concept eventually hinges on the cognitive foundation of consumers and further generates purchasing willingness. Kotler and Kotler (2000) thinks that "cognition" refers to the process of generating internal significance from outside information of personal selection, organization and interpretation. "Cognition" is being given environmental significance, a process of gaining impression through sensing and organizational interpretation (Robbins 2000). This shows cognition is being influenced by external situations in different environments and also influenced by the personal traits and internal factors of the consumer.

In developing a new product, the creative designer shall focus on aesthetics and emotional factors (Jordan 2000). Concomitantly, it is essential to further the relation between product identity and consumer cognition, and act as reference for creations by future designers. Cognitive research of product identity involves too many uncontrollable external environmental cognitive factors and made the interference variable to research too complicated. Henceforth, this study uses the controllable personality of consumers as the variable for product identity and consumer cognition, and hopes to comprehend the extent of influence between the two. This is planned for next stage research foundation.

2 Literature Review

2.1 Cultural and Creative Product and Product Identity Study

The rise of global cultural and creative industries is the result of highlighting the culture industry. Under this mindset, as well as under the influence of the consumption process of modern culture, more importance is attached to developing the spiritual value of products, thereby developing toward artistic creations of a fine culture (Chen 2009). Thus, product design no longer stresses on function, rather it diversifies toward attraction of consumers with feeling for the product. Moreover, each product is formed by a set of attributes such as outward appearance, brand, function and after-sales service and so on, which formed a part of the product attributes (Wenxian and Qinfu 2000). In the current consumer society, the aesthetical experience of cultural and creative products will play a considerable role.

Norman (2004) thinks that utilizing emotion for product design allows stirring up the positive emotions of people with its attraction, therefore, such products will be more useful. Rahman (2012) also mentions that the generation of aesthetics may be defined as physical stimulus, that is, experience obtained through vision or feeling. It is thus understood that study of aforementioned literary documents, the cultural and creative products attach more importance to aesthetics and emotion than other products.

H1: Different cultural and creative products have different product identity.
- H1a: Item 1 cultural and creative product has personal traits.
- H1b: Item 2 cultural and creative product has personal traits.
- H1c: Item 3 cultural and creative product has personal traits.
- H1d: Item 4 cultural and creative product has personal traits.
- H1e: Item 5 cultural and creative product has personal traits.

2.2 A Study of Relationship Between Personality and Product Identity

Regarding study of cognitive influence from consumption behavior, scholars have found that personality can have significant direct influence if the product type has a high level of linking symbolically, and the product brand personality matches with consumer personality (Aaker 1997). Study points out that in using certain brand product, consumer personality would engage in dialogue and communication with certain brand, share and co-construct its symbolic value and extend its self-conception. A study by Zang (2008) found that throughout the process of system recommendation by consumer, latter's degree of acceptance for system recommended products differs from personality. Henceforth, a host of studies show that different personality can have significant correlation with consumer cognitive judgment. This study hopes to comprehend the degree of correlation between product identity and consumer cognition.

H2: Significant correlation between cultural and creative product identity and consumer cognition.

2.3 Study of Consumer Personality and Product Purchasing Willingness

In purchasing a product the consumer chooses a product and image matching his or her personality. Sometimes, the consumer chooses not to buy a product even though he or she likes the shape of the product but dislikes its symbolic significance. (Creusen and Schoormans 2005). Henceforth, prior to purchasing the consumer would try to know the outward appearance or content of the product, and the decisive factors in cognitive psychology are as follows: (1) Past experience, (2) Personal need and wish, (3) Current personal physiological and psychological situation, (4) Personal situation, (5) Characteristics of the observed object, (Zhong 1990). (Norman and Ortony 2006) also proposed that the human information processing system may be divided into the "cognitive" system and the "emotional" system. Both differ in function: The emotion system controls judgment and swiftly makes efficient positive and negative appraisal toward the environment while the cognitive system interprets and endows meanings to external happenings. A host of studies by scholars show that consumers have comparatively positive appraisal for products similar to his or her personality.

H3: Significant correlation between consumer cognition and purchasing willingness.

H4: The extent of matching the product and consumer personality will positively affect his or her purchasing willingness.

3 Methodologies

3.1 Study Flow

This study uses the award-winning articles of 2010–2015 Creative Expo Taiwan as specimen. First, two experts carried out classification of personality for all articles, and then picked out articles of similar classification and used as specimens for expert questionnaire of the first stage. After analysis, a stage 2 questionnaire will be carried out on consumer personality and consumer cognition, and find out the correlation between product identity and consumer cognition, as well as the influence on product identity and consumer cognition from five major personalities. Eventually, survey will be carried out on consumer purchasing willingness. The study flow is shown in Fig. 1:

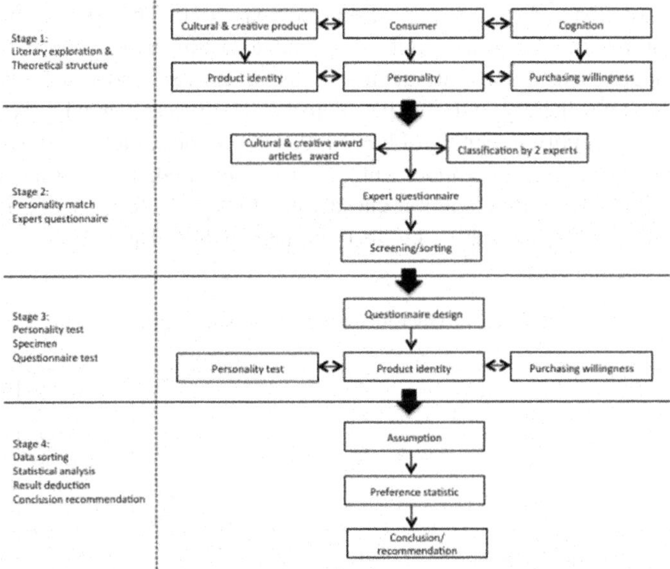

Fig. 1. Study flow

The study flow and steps are described below in four stages:

1. First stage: Find out the structure and special characteristics of cultural and creative products, consumer personality, and relevant theories of consumer cognition through collection and exploration of relevant literary data, and consequently find out whether such would affect consumer purchasing willingness.
2. Second stage: Take the award-winning articles for 2010–2015 as testing specimens, and prepare questionnaire by two experts matching the specimen personality, then carry out a preliminary expert questionnaire, and eventually compare expert's cognition for product identity, and again screen out, sort and design the questionnaire for the next stage.

3. Third stage: Questionnaire design and actual survey. Those receiving test of the study are primarily college juniors, including students of the day and evening sections, a total of 101 students participating. Age distribution is from 19–21 years old and those receiving test are primarily students of the broadcasting and design departments and business administration departments.
4. Fourth stage: Questionnaire data analysis.

3.2 Products Winning Cultural and Creative Products Award: https://creativexpo.tw/

To enhance the synergy of Taiwan cultural and creative industries, promote the outstanding creative talents, and encourage enterprises emphasizing research and development and innovation, the Council for Cultural Affairs of the Executive Yuan planned the Taiwan Excellence Award starting from the year 2010. The Award aims to build quality living for the Chinese people, accumulate innovative synergy for Taiwan industry through contest, construct quality living in Taiwan, and made it the highest honor for Taiwan's literary and creative industry. The researcher will carry out preliminary product identity screening of the shortlisted products, then carry out first stage questionnaire, and pick out a product with comparatively higher scores, and eventually usher in the final consumer cognition questionnaire stage. Refer to Table 1 for correlation of product identity, creative product and personality (Table 2).

Table 1. Product identity & personality sorting

Product identity	Product identity preliminary screening					First stage Questionnaire result	Personality
Lively		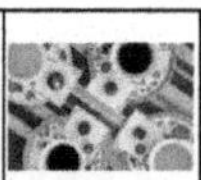	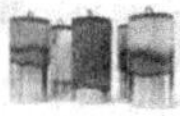				Peacock
Steady							Tiger
Peaceful							Koala
Elegant							Owl
Kind			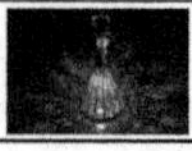				Chameleon

4 Result and Discussion

A total of 115 people took part in the PDP aptitude test during the consumer questionnaire stage. Valid questionnaires are 102 and the final statistics are: Koala (32 people), Owl (21 people), Peacock (25 people), Tiger (13 people), Chameleon (11 people), and the gender distribution is shown in the Figure below:

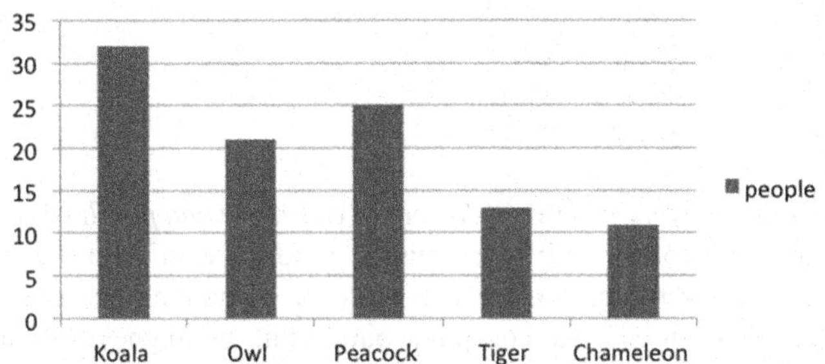

Fig. 2. Personality distribution

In the five sub-assumptions of H1, we found that t-values are greater than 2. Under 95 % of confidence level, product identity of the five creative products are significantly higher than the median value. In other words, these five creative products have personality traits (Fig. 2).

Table 2. Creative product personality test

	T-value	Degree of freedom	Significance (dual tail)	Median difference	95 % of difference within trust zone	
					Lower limit	Upper limit
com1	14.700	101	0.000	0.971	0.840	1.102
com2	13.061	101	0.000	0.912	0.773	1.050
com3	7.935	101	0.000	0.598	0.449	0.748
com4	22.740	101	0.000	0.941	0.859	1.023
com5	15.000	101	0.000	0.863	0.749	0.977

H2:Significant correlation between creative product identity and consumer cognition.

Testing result shown in Table 3 shows that comparing to other low profile creative products with stable, peaceful, elegant and kind quality, only the lively creative product can comparatively highlight personality with ease (Table 4).

Table 3. Correlation Testing between Product Identity and Consumer Cognition

Product identity < - > Cognition	Relative coefficient
com1 < - > con1	0.258[b]
com2 < - > con2	0.060
com3 < - > con3	–0.185
com4 < - > con4	0.007
com5 < - > con5	0.001

[a] p-value < 0.05;
[b] p-value < 0.01;
[c] p-value < 0.005

H3:Significant correlation between consumer cognition and purchasing willingness. From testing in Table 3, only the creative product with lively personality can stimulate consumer purchasing willingness while the remaining peaceful and elegant creative product also can enhance consumer purchasing willingness (Table 5).

Table 4. Correlation Testing of Product Identity and Purchasing Willingness

Product identity < - > purchasing willingness	Relative coefficient
com1 < - > pur1	0.305[b]
com2 < - > pur2	0.122
com3 < - > pur3	0.145[a]
com4 < - > pur4	0.131[a]
com5 < - > pur5	0.109

[a] p-value < 0.05;
[b] p-value < 0.01;
[c] p-value < 0.005

H4:Matching of product and consumer personality can positively affect his or her purchasing willingness.

Table 5. Correlation testing of product identity matching with purchasing willingness

Product identity < - > purchasing willingness	Relative coefficient
con1 < - > pur1	0.381[b]
con2 < - > pur2	0.222[a]
con3 < - > pur3	0.329[a]
con4 < - > pur4	0.402[b]
con5 < - > pur5	0.287[b]

[a] p-value < 0.05;
[b] p-value < 0.01;
[c] p-value < 0.005

Compared to testing of H2 and H3, matching of creative product and consumer personality can stimulate consumer purchasing willingness.

5 Conclusion and Recommendation

The questionnaire analysis shows that the four assumptions of this study have significant correlation and testifies to the personality of creative products and general merchandise, and different personalities stimulate purchasing willingness if different personalities match with product identity. This study draws following conclusions:

1. Experts have screened out classified creative products using personality traits, and picked out five representative products with different identities. Such products will form the next stage questionnaire. Consequently, through questionnaire analysis statistics, we can see that the five creative products boast different identities and testify to the personality of creative products with general merchandise.
2. Judged by analysis of the five products with different identities, those creative products with "lively" personality are more pronounced in personality trait, comparing to the comparatively low-profile creative products which are stable, peaceful, elegant and kind.
3. Apparently, the degree of matching between creative products and consumer personality is an important factor in consumer purchasing willingness. It is a critical and vital factor in knowing consumer personality and designing products with identity for the market.
4. This study only uses pictures of creative products and personality traits for description in a bid to testify the correlation between creative product and personality with purchasing willingness. Despite progress in preliminary study, there is a plethora of factors to consider throughout the entire purchasing process of creative products. This will be the future direction of study.

In recent years, creative products sprouted up on the market. Nevertheless, only very few products have become popular. How to satisfy consumer psychology will be an issue for most designers aspiring to comprehend. Conclusions of this study found close correlation between different consumer personalities and identities of creative products and purchasing willingness. This is worth for further study. In the future, this study will further explore how the intrinsic emotion of creative products, outward appearance and function could affect personalities of different consumers. This will benefit future product planning by designers and provide reference to consumer in buying products with matching identities.

References

Aaker, J.L.: Dimensions of brand personality. J. Mark. Res. **34**, 347–356 (1997)

Creusen, M.E.H., Schoormans, J.P.: The different roles of product appearance in consumer choice. J. Prod. Innov. Manage **22**(1), 63–81 (2005)

Jordan, P.: Designing Pleasure Products: an Introduction to the New Factors. Taylor & Francis, London (2000)

Kotler, N., Kotler, P.: Can museums be all things to all people?: Missions, goals, and marketing's role. Mus. Manage. Curatorship **18**(3), 271–287 (2000)

McDonagh, D., Weightman, D.: If kettles are from Venus and televisions are from Mars, where are cars from?. In: 5th European Academy of Design Conference, Barcelona, Spain, pp. 151–162, April 2003

Norman, Donald A.: Emotional Design: Why We Love (or Hate) Everyday Things, pp. 63–98. Basic Books, New York (2004)

Norman, D.A., Ortony, A.: Designers and users: two perspectives on emotion and design. In: Bagnara, S., Crampton-Smith, G. (Eds.) Theories and Practice in Interaction Design, pp. 91–103. Lawrence Erlbaum Associates, Mahwah (2006). Accessed 11 March 2010

Rahman, Osmud: The influence of visual and tactile inputs on denim jeans evalation. Int. J. Des. **6**(1), 2012 (2012)

Robbins, S.P.: Fundamentals of Management. Prentice Hall, Upper Saddle River (2000)

Sirgy, M.J.: Self-concept in consumer behavior: a critical review. J. Consum. Res. **9**(3), 287–300 (1982)

Wenxian, Z., Qinfu, Z.: Joint Analysis of Product Design. Management Science Series, vol. 9. Hwatai Cultural Enterprise Limited, Taipei (2000)

Chen, X.: A Study of Information Design for Cultural Product. Master's thesis of Ming Chuan University Design Management Research Institute (2009)

Zang Z.: Unpublished master's thesis. Department of Computer Science and Information Management of Providence University. Title of thesis: "Recommendation and Product Identity–Influence on Consumer Purchasing Online Recommended Products." (2008)

Zhong S.: Cognitive Psychology. Psychology Publishing House in Taipei City (1990)

Digital Display and Transmission of the Culture of Traditional Chinese Furniture

Xinxin Sun(✉) and Chao Li

School of Design Arts and Media, Nanjing University of Science and Technology, Xuanwu Area, Nanjing 210094, China
sunxinxinde@126.com, 260082785@qq.com

Abstract. This paper explores the knowledge structure of traditional furniture culture, which contains aesthetic culture, technology culture, function culture, national culture and art culture. By conducting investigation on user groups via the depth interviews and personas method, established user role model and indicate the demands of different user groups for traditional Chinese furniture. And then the digitization model of display and dissemination of the culture of traditional Chinese furniture is established, according to the theories of User Centered Design and knowledge dissemination. Therefore, the interactive digitization form, which is funny and vivid, is adopted to display and disseminate traditional Chinese furniture. The purpose is to spread the culture of traditional Chinese furniture via top-down model of culture dissemination and get the culture of traditional Chinese furniture inherited and spread in a "live" status.

Keywords: Traditional Chinese furniture · Cultural diffusion · Digital display · Interaction design

1 Introduction

Cultural development is the source of life of a country and a nation. Technology and innovation, the important engine of cultural development, is the source of cultural innovation. Cultural heritage, which condenses the quintessence of national culture and shows the spirit of the regional people, is a symbol of national culture and plays a key role in the inheritance of regional culture. As one of the important components of the material and cultural heritage in China, traditional Chinese furniture is a wonderful work among world classical furniture system, especially the furnitures in the Ming and Qing Dynasties. Traditional Chinese furniture with rich varieties, exquisite material, excellent workmanship, beautiful shape and delicate patterns is an important component of the Chinese traditional culture, which carries abundant information about ancient Chinese, such as lifestyle, ideology and value orientation etc.

However, foreign culture is having an impact on the national culture in the era of globalization. The relationship between culture and the development of science and technology is inseparable [1]. With the development of Internet, cloud computing, big data and 4G, the popularity and prosperity of mobile intelligent equipment and public resources platform construction, it should be taken into consideration that how to display

P.-L.P. Rau (Ed.): CCD 2016, LNCS 9741, pp. 275–287, 2016.
DOI: 10.1007/978-3-319-40093-8_28

the traditional culture confronted with the advanced science and technology [2]. There is a significant difference about the possession quantity of cultural knowledge in different groups of people, which brings challenges and opportunities to the protection and heritage of cultural heritage. There are also problems in the display and dissemination of traditional Chinese furniture culture: (1) the methods of gathering information about traditional Chinese furniture are single, mainly from related research institutes and museums; (2) the contents displayed are single, and the gap among the audience groups of traditional Chinese furniture culture is large while most of the display of the content currently is an explanation of physical furniture with a lack of systematic display of furniture culture relevant. (3) the form of display and dissemination of traditional Chinese furniture culture is single. Most physical furniture now is stored in museums or possessed by collectors. As a result, t is difficult for people who have an appetite for furniture around the world to learn deeply about the characteristics and cultural connotation of the furniture. Meanwhile, it is a barrier to spreading the Chinese traditional culture. (4) the display form of physical furniture is single. People usually get familiar with furniture in a static view so that there is a lack of an interaction between audience and the traditional furniture. It is more difficult to arouse people's enthusiasm for the traditional furniture culture.

Based on the Above Problems, This Paper Launches the Following Research: Study on the display form of traditional Chinese furniture culture under the background of digital medium and technology; Study on characteristics and category of audience groups of traditional Chinese furniture culture; Study on the model of acquisition, display and dissemination of Information about traditional Chinese furniture culture.

The Purpose and Significance of This Study: By sorting out the culture of traditional Chinese furniture and carrying out stratification research on the user groups, to dig the needs of different groups of the user towards traditional Chinese furniture and establish user demand model. The interactive digitization form is introduced into the display and dissemination of furniture culture. Establish the display and dissemination model of the culture of traditional Chinese furniture and put forward the application methods and paths. The digitization medium for display and dissemination provides a good platform for traditional Chinese furniture. Therefore, the interactive digitization form, which is funny and vivid, is adopted to display and disseminate classical Chinese furniture. It will arouse people's interest in Chinese traditional culture, and make people who have an appetite for traditional Chinese furniture around the world get acquainted with the culture of classical Chinese furniture conveniently and quickly. In this way, the culture of traditional Chinese furniture will be inherited and spread in a "live" status.

2 Background

2.1 The Cultural Connotation of Traditional Chinese Furniture

Development: Traditional Chinese furniture has a long history, dating back to the seventeenth Century BC. After thousands of years of development, Chinese furniture always has a unique national style. Chinese furniture has always been dominated by wooden products. And furniture modeling is affected by architectural modeling so that furniture modeling is a transformation of constructions. From the point of view of the history of the furniture development, due to the changes in people's living habits, traditional Chinese furniture experiences the process from the low-type furniture which needs kneeling on the ground from Shang and Zhou dynasty to Qin and Han dynasty, the sitting-on furniture in transition period from Wei Jin dynasty to Sui Tang dynasty, to the sitting-on furniture high-type furniture of the Northern Song Dynasty. The traditional Chinese furniture reached a historical peak in the Ming Dynasty. Whether the varieties of furniture or the making technology, furniture workshops and specialized market is in the heyday of the development of China's ancient furniture. The furniture in Ming Dynasty creates a superb furniture production technology and exquisite art form [3]. As a whole, Chinese antique furniture has experienced the process of changing from low to high with the furniture varieties becoming richer and production process level gradually increasing. It forms a relatively perfect furniture system.

Cultural Connotation: From a certain sense, the furniture is a cultural integration. It marks the level of the social productivity of a country or region in a certain historical period. It is the epitome of a certain lifestyle and the manifestation of a culture. On the basis of its rich cultural and historical tradition, traditional Chinese furniture is changing all aspects of human culture constantly and profoundly. Traditional Chinese furniture culture is influenced by ritual system (it reflects the political and social attributes of furniture), folk customs (such as festival and wedding feast customs), religion (for example, a large number of high-type furniture of Buddhist Tianzhu inflow into China), ancient literati, painting, architecture, hundred worker skills, society and other multiple factors. When ultimately reflected in traditional Chinese furniture culture, it is mainly manifested in three aspects: furniture technology culture, furniture humanistic culture and furniture art culture (Fig. 1) [4]. Taking the furniture of Ming Dynasty which is in its heyday as an example: in furniture technology culture, it appears to be using exquisite timber and paying attention to the natural texture fully reflecting the wood's natural color and texture, with scientific structures and sophisticated tenon and mortise; in furniture humanistic culture, it appears to be embodied for decorative patterns. The patterns must be intentional and the intention must be auspicious. The dimension of the furniture is suitable for the human body engineering; in furniture art culture, it appears to be decorated moderately. It is a combination of decoration and structure. And the modeling is minimalist with moderate proportion.

Features: The culture of traditional Chinese furniture is regional, professional, multiple and contemporary. Influenced by Chinese ancient philosophy, traditional Chinese furniture Itself is the product of the unity of heaven and man and the material carrier of its cultural spirit, whether in furniture design, or in furniture fabrication.

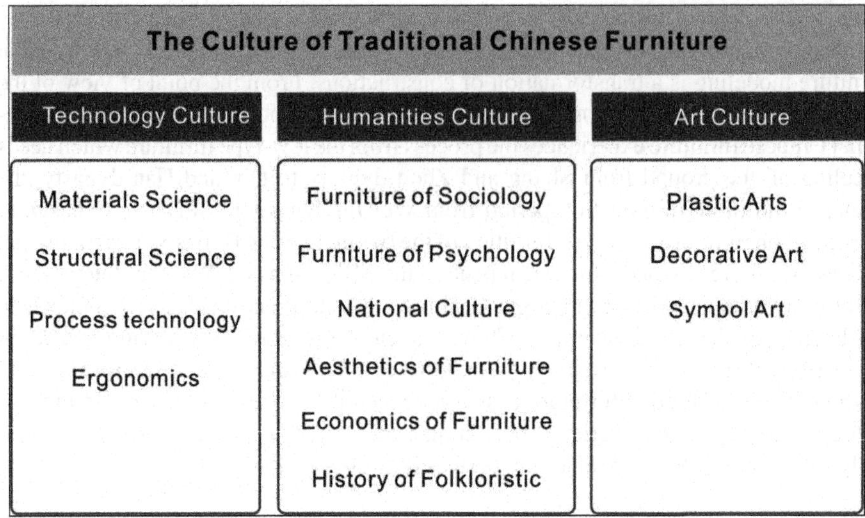

Fig. 1. Chinese traditional furniture culture connotation

2.2 The Medium and the Technology of Digital Display:

As a new research method, digitization is introduced to the research on traditional furniture. The medium of digitization, which is of transmissible, Interactive and interesting, brings a new experience for the display and dissemination of traditional Chinese furniture culture. At present, there are the following medium and technology:

PC Network Platform: The medium of digital display, which is based on PC network platform, is one of the most traditional medium forms in the digital display medium. And it is also the earliest form of application and popularization. Based on the personal computer terminal, through the Internet online browsing furniture cultural heritage resources, digital resources can be presented via images, video, music and other imaging methods. In the meanwhile, with the development of computer technology, all kinds of interactive virtual display also tend to be more popular.

Mobile Smart Devices: The popularity of smart mobile devices has been gradually changed the people's life. Beginning from smart phones, the emergence of mobile smart devices such as smart watches, smart bracelet, smart wearable device, have a great impact on human lifestyle. As a kind of new medium of the display and dissemination of the traditional furniture culture heritage, digital display medium, based on mobile smart devices, has a wider application platform and audience groups. As the medium of digital display, the application of mobile smart devices is an important channel for the display and dissemination of furniture culture.

Public Platforms: Traditional medium such as museums, art galleries, shopping centers and other public cultural platforms, also provides a good platform for the dissemination of furniture culture relying on the digital construction. Taking the museum as an example, digital means are integrated into the design of exhibits display to enhance the audience's sense of participation by means of holographic projection, touch screen, 3D images, sensing devices and other interactive devices. And it can achieve the simultaneous transmission and share of images and information through the Internet.

Virtual Reality Technology: As a kind of digital technology, it is widely used in many fields in recent years. With the aid of the computer simulation, Virtual Reality could create a virtual environment so that the user will be immersed in the virtual environment and produce the feeling of be personally on the scene. Through specific operation, the user can be able to interact with the multi-dimensional information environment, acquire knowledge, improve awareness and germinate ideas. By means of Virtual Reality technology, the research on traditional Chinese furniture is mainly used in the demonstration of the products and virtual space of classical furniture.

The diversity of digital medium and technology provides a new opportunity for cultural display. The digital display medium of traditional furniture cultural heritage, from PC to mobile smart device application and from the social network to the public cultural platform, achieves comprehensive and three-dimensional digitization information transmission and interactive experience with multiple sensory involvement including vision, hearing and touch. In the meanwhile, digitization plays an active role in promoting the protection and inheritance of cultural heritage.

3 Research Method

Based on the survey and analysis of user groups whom the display and dissemination of traditional Chinese furniture culture is intended for, this study establish three types of user groups according to the knowledge level and attention degree of traditional Chinese furniture culture. In addition, this study establishes Character Model to guide the follow-up study so as to determine the models and ways of information collection and digital display and dissemination of traditional Chinese furniture culture.

The research process is divided into three steps: Firstly, start the start research and screening the information obtained to organize and form forceful user information via Interview method. Secondly, summarize similar user information and establish three types of user groups. Finally, establish Character Role Models for the three types of user group respectively.

3.1 Preliminary User Investigation

Preliminary user investigation is divided into three steps: user selection, user interview and an arrangement of interview information.

User Selection: Nanjing is an ancient capital of China, which has a profound cultural heritage. There are many universities, large museums and communities in Nanjing. Therefore, the study is carried out in Nanjing, China. We visited University (Nanjing University of science and technology, Nanjing Forestry University), museums

(Nanjing Museum) and communities (Xiaolingwei community, Vanke community and other four residential community. Finally, 30 Chinese users is chosen as the final interviewees, including collectors, college students, primary and secondary school students, retired workers, white-collar workers and etc. These users use smart phones and have a certain cultural knowledge base.

The Way of Interview: This study learns the users' real thoughts and experience demands by asking questions. In the interview, the combination of structured interview and non-structured interview is adopted. At the same time, part of the users' studios and living environments is observed to understand the users' behaviors and lifestyle (Fig. 2).

Fig. 2. The way of interview

Interview Contents: Determine the Interview contents according to the subject. The contents are divided into general questions and deep questions depending on content level. Firstly, by means of Interview with basic questions, to learn the recognition degree of traditional Chinese furniture culture among users. Secondly, by means of Interview with deep questions, to dig opportunities for the display and dissemination of Chinese furniture culture.

Sort Out the Interview Information: Weigh and analyses the users' problems systematically. In the meanwhile, label and classify all of the data according to user viewpoint, motivation, demographics and other factors.

Find the Common Mode: Seize important labels of the users and describe these labels in categories.

3.2 The Analysis of User Roles

Through the preliminary user investigation, a lot of user information is gained, including attention degree, loyalty, and awareness degree of different user groups towards traditional Chinese furniture culture. After ordering and summing up the data of 30 users, different factors were typical combined. In the meanwhile, transform user demands into characters and establish three types of user groups from top to bottom according to the user's academic background, interest, motivation, loyalty and other important factors (Fig. 3).

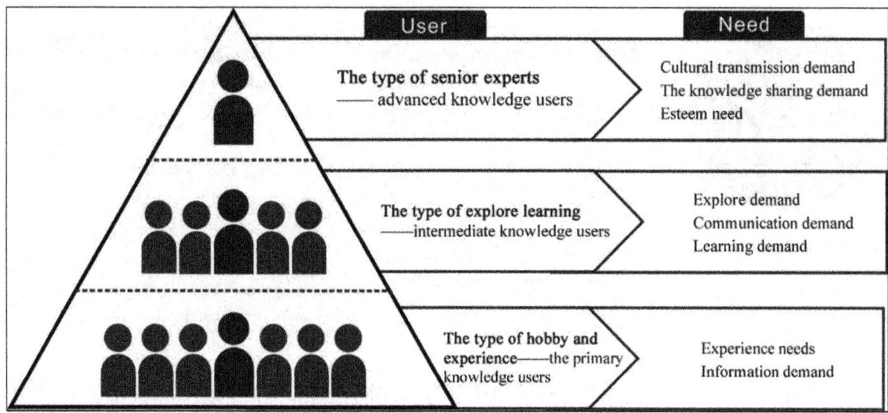

Fig. 3. User roles

"The Type of Senior Experts"—— Advanced Knowledge Users: The principal members are people with have higher educational level and social status, including collectors, scholars in the direction of the furniture, researcher on traditional Chinese furniture and etc. They are in possession of abundant professional knowledge and have great enthusiasm for traditional Chinese furniture and its culture based on a deep research on traditional Chinese furniture. And they are willing to devote time and energy to the study and dissemination of Chinese traditional furniture culture. The dominant demands of this kind of user groups consist of the demand for culture dissemination, the demand for knowledge sharing, and the demand for respect.

"The Type of Explore Learning"—— Intermediate Knowledge Users: Students with a certain knowledge of Chinese traditional culture, white collars and people from all walks who love Chinese traditional culture. They have a bachelor degree or above with good cultural quality and eager to learn the related knowledge of traditional Chinese furniture culture. In addition, they are willing to share the spread furniture culture. The dominant demands of this kind of user groups consist of the demand for exploring, the demand for knowledge exchange and the demand for learning.

"The Type of Hobby and Experience"—— The Primary Knowledge Users: This type of user groups refer to people who grasp a certain cultural knowledge but don't understand the culture of Chinese traditional furniture. For these people, they are willing to learn to accept the traditional culture. These users mainly include primary and secondary school students, college students and the following education adults, parts of the elderly and other user groups. The dominant demands of this kind of user groups consist of the demand of knowledge experience and the demand for information.

Sun Lin
"willing to through their own strength to carry forward the Chinese traditional furniture culture everbright."
The type of senior experts—— advanced knowledge users
Name: Sun Lin
Age: 50
Profession: professor
Education: doctor
Interest: handwriting
Character: Kindly
Attitude towards the traditional culture: proficient in ancient Chinese traditional furniture culture, is committed to the research and spread of furniture culture.
Knowledge acquisition way: paper books and Internet.
Lifestyle: furniture teaching and scientific research, often lectures on furniture culture,published several monographs, likes calligraphy and going to the museum in spare time.
User attitudes: willing to through their own strength to carry forward the Chinese traditional furniture culture everbright.

Zhang Ran
"Traditional Chinese furniture culture is a need to study and develop, "
The type of explore learning——intermediate knowledge users
Name: Zhang Ran
Age: 21
Profession: Student
Education: Undergraduate
Interest: Reading
Character: Open and clear
Attitude towards the traditional culture: willing to understand and learn traditional culture, like China painting, chinese classical novels.
Knowledge acquisition way: paper books, e-books, APP
Lifestyle: gives priority to study at ordinary times,has strong ability to learn, pays attention to new things,happy to share with friends. Sometimes goes to the museum or gallery, also use APP to understand cultural knowledge.
User attitudes: traditional Chinese furniture culture is a need to study and develop, he is willing to participate in the study of furniture culture, and spread knowledge.

Xue Jia
"I am willing to take daughter go to the museum or library to know and learn."
The type of hobby and experience——the primary knowledge users
Name: Xue Jia
Age: 39
Profession: Housewife
Education: Junior college student
Interest: Climbing
Character: Optimistic and hopeful
Attitude towards the traditional culture: willing to understand traditional culture knowledge, especially recognize her daughter should learn Chinese traditional culture from an early age.
Knowledge acquisition way: Internet.
Lifestyle: 8-year-old daughter, elementary school;Her husband do business. She is responsible for housework,her daughter's study and life.
User attitudes: do not know much about chinese traditional furniture culture, but is willing to take daughter go to the museum or library to know and learn.

Fig. 4. The User Model

3.3 Establish the User Model

The establishment of the User Model is to refer to transform the user in the future into lifelike people and build the future product system model for these real "people" [5]. By creating User Model, we can reduce the subjective assumptions and understand what the real users' demands are so as to learn how to serve for different types of users better. Therefore, based on the previous research, the elements are abstracted and the above three types of user groups are built into Character Model Cards respectively. In the meanwhile, the user demands above are introduced into the User Model. Model Cards consist of User profile, the attitude towards traditional culture, the way of knowledge acquisition, lifestyle and etc. (Fig. 4). Model Cards are the basis for the subsequent design model.

4 Results and Discussions

4.1 Establish Digital Display and Dissemination Model of Traditional Chinese Furniture Culture

According to the "user-centered" design concept, pay attention to the object of display and dissemination of traditional Chinese furniture culture, that is, "the user". And taking it as the center, to build the model of display and dissemination of traditional Chinese furniture culture, combined with the theory of knowledge dissemination. "The dissemination of knowledge" is such a process of social activities: in the specific social environment, a part of the social members spread the specific knowledge and information to another part of the members of the society by means of specific media of knowledge dissemination, and they look forward to receiving the desired effect of the spread [6]. After being created by members of human society through social practice and creative thinking, the knowledge and information of traditional furniture culture is obtained selectively by those members of society who have the awareness of knowledge dissemination and the duty of social knowledge dissemination. After they release and encoding code, it becomes culture knowledge products that are available for dissemination. Then in specific social backgrounds and

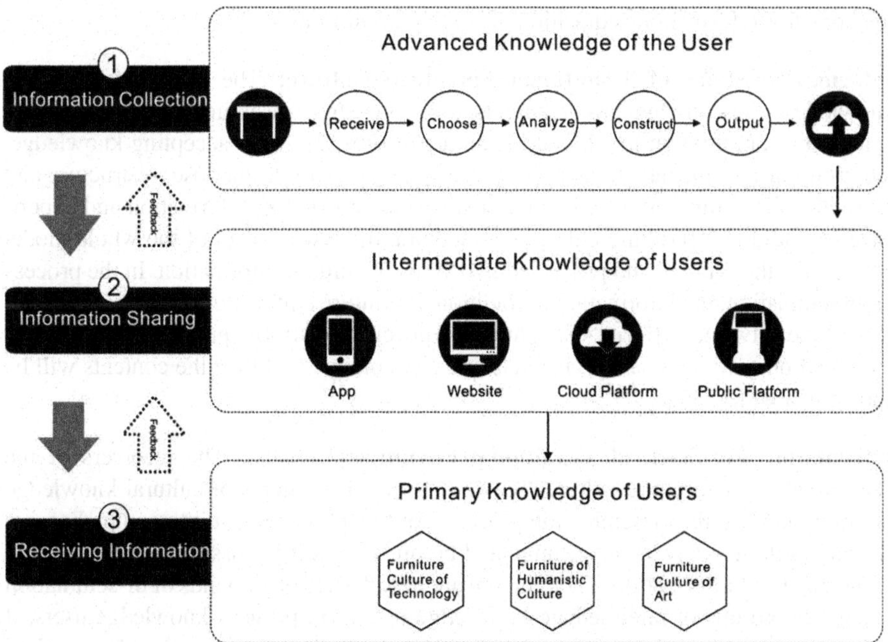

Fig. 5. Digital display and dissemination model of traditional Chinese furniture culture

environments, it will be spread to another part of society members through the specific dissemination medium of traditional furniture culture knowledge. That is the process of knowledge dissemination of traditional furniture culture. In brief, the process of digital dissemination of traditional Chinese furniture culture is: information acquisition of traditional furniture culture, information share of traditional furniture culture and information feedback of traditional furniture culture (Fig. 5). The three steps are coincident with the design demands of three user groups from experimental result. In this way, establish the display and dissemination model of traditional Chinese furniture culture.

Information Acquisition of Traditional Furniture Culture: The prerequisite condition of the cultural dissemination activities in the human society is to produce the cultural knowledge information which could be spread by people. The culture of traditional Chinese furniture is a huge system. As a result, the acquisition of furniture culture is an important work because it is the starting point of the whole model. "The type of senior experts"(advanced knowledge users) including collectors, furniture scholars and other professional persons, through their social practice and creative thinking, acquire abundant culture knowledge, experiences and skills of the furniture. These are the cultural knowledge of furniture, which can be spread by people. After choosing, analyzing, processing and constructing, this cultural knowledge of furniture will rise to theoretical cultural knowledge and which can be used as the contents for display and dissemination. In the meanwhile, advanced knowledge users such as collectors and furniture scholars are a relatively stable social group. They upload the cultural knowledge of furniture to the digital platform and establish information database of furniture culture to form abundant culture resources. Therefore, advanced knowledge users are important members for information acquisition of traditional furniture culture.

Information Share of Traditional Furniture Culture: The group of advanced knowledge users implements behaviors of knowledge dissemination to knowledge communicators through the digital medium platform [7]. After accepting knowledge, the group of intermediate level users processes it so as to decompose, restructure and reproduce the culture information. By sharing the knowledge, information and experience of traditional furniture culture via medium, the lowest level of the whole model can receive the original and processed two kinds of cultural information. In the process of dissemination, the information of traditional furniture culture could be share with the help of the network platform, social media, App, cloud platform, public terminal equipment and other dissemination channels and technology. And then the contents will be spread in a wider range.

Information Feedback of Traditional Furniture Culture: The receivers of the dissemination of furniture culture receive the specific contents of cultural knowledge information from the dissemination process. And then they take it into comprehensive account with the knowledge accumulated before so that it is possible to produce new knowledge and information. Then if there are new desires or demands of dissemination among the groups of intermediate knowledge users and primary knowledge users, it enters into a new knowledge dissemination process when put into practice. The original receivers of knowledge dissemination actually become the "culture disseminator" because of their own innovation and dissemination behaviors of original furniture culture knowledge. As for the original culture disseminator, it has been converted to "the receivers of the culture dissemination" as a result of the demands and acceptance of the knowledge spread by the original receivers of the knowledge dissemination. The knowledge contents spread by the culture disseminator in this process is such an innovation based on the knowledge and information received and the knowledge accumulated before. And it is spread not only to the original culture disseminator, but also to other members of the society. Therefore, such a new process of knowledge dissemination is also the process of cultural information feedbacks.

The three links above build the process of the digitization of traditional furniture culture. In the process, the dissemination of traditional Chinese furniture culture has shown a trend of spread by groups. And furniture culture is displayed in digitization with the help of digital medium. This process is sustainable, cyclical, constantly updated. The knowledge of traditional furniture culture is able to get decomposed and restructured and meet the knowledge demands of different user groups so that the dissemination model of traditional Chinese furniture culture is formed with information collection, information sharing, and information reception and information feedback.

4.2 Strategies for Digital Display and Dissemination of Traditional Chinese Furniture Culture Display in Digitization

The display of traditional Chinese furniture culture is supposed to combine with the social environment, regional characteristics and humanistic spirit. Only create such a cultural background will the traditional Chinese furniture show its material content and spiritual culture and be known by more people. It requires us to refine, classify and summarize the contents of traditional Chinese furniture culture. In addition, t requires us to show the cultural characteristic features of "express the meaning by the form" and "reach the meaning by the scene" combined with digital display technology to embody the furniture culture. As a kind of technical means, the digital display will penetrate in all aspects of the display and dissemination of traditional Chinese furniture culture. Different display scenarios and dissemination stages need different mediums. In addition, it could be useful to exploit the advantages of the information dissemination in Internet era and the functions of information dissemination of Mobile Internet terminal products.

Experience and Share: After experiencing the industrial age that is characterized by material consumption and occupation and emphasizes the function of the product, the information society provides services and non-material products. As a result, the design object is from substance to substance, from the product to service, from occupation to share emphasizing the attributes of User Experience. It is the results of returning to the original aims of design, cogitating on design and understanding the relationship between user and product from a higher level. The relatively profound knowledge of traditional culture concentrate in the "Loyal Fans" in the above study. These knowledge could not only builds the "experts" experience for themselves by sharing, but also create funny experience of acquiring knowledge for other knowledge receivers.

The Co-creation of Group Knowledge: In the future, the entity museum may disappear and develop sustainably in other forms. There will be a more equal and mutually beneficial relationship between the entity places of furniture culture dissemination such as museums and the user. Knowledge becomes means of production shared jointly, and the driving force of innovation comes from the joint efforts of both parties. That is, the user and the museum to create together. Therefore, the user is the most valuable productive assets cultural display and dissemination in the future [8]. In the meanwhile, it will change from individual behavior to group behavior, and also transform from personal knowledge to group knowledge through tapping, building and sharing the culture resources of traditional Chinese furniture culture together by groups of all classes of society.

5 Conclusion and Future Works

Starting from the problems in the display and dissemination of traditional Chinese furniture culture, this paper analyses the cultural connotation of traditional Chinese furniture and points out that the display of traditional Chinese furniture culture can be combined with PC network platform, mobile intelligent equipment, public platform, Virtual Reality technology under the background of the digital medium and technology. In order to understand the characteristics of the audience of traditional Chinese furniture, this paper launches the investigation and analysis on the target user group and according to the user's academic background, interest, motivation, loyalty and other important factors, divide the audience groups of traditional Chinese furniture into three types of user groups from top to bottom: "the type of senior experts"— advanced knowledge users, "the type of explore learning"— intermediate knowledge users and "the type of hobby and experience"—the primary knowledge users. According to the "user-centric" design concept, the paper establishes the display and dissemination model of traditional Chinese furniture culture combine with the theory of knowledge dissemination. The hierarchy of this model corresponds to the demands of the three user groups for information acquisition of traditional furniture culture, information share of traditional furniture culture and information feedback of traditional furniture culture. In addition, this paper points out strategies for digital display and dissemination of traditional Chinese furniture culture: display in digitization, experience and share and the co-creation of group knowledge. What this paper discusses is not only the digital display means, but also analyses the cultural audiences and establishes different character models. What's more, the display model of furniture culture dissemination is also built from top to bottom. In the process, the digital medium is kind of means, which services for the whole model of culture display and dissemination.

The traditional furniture,which inherits from ancient advanced productive forces and advanced culture, is so abundant and bright. The designers and researchers are supposed to devote wisdom and strength into the traditional furniture. The purpose of the digital display and dissemination of traditional Chinese furniture culture is, taking advantages of modern digital media technology, to make more people make full use of the aging characteristic of network resources and mobile Internet media through the mobile terminal devices. By taking advantages of fragmented time, to realize and learn the connotation and value of furniture culture, to establish a general national confidence and to enhance the context of furniture culture. The final purpose is to turn the protection of intangible cultural heritage into people's conscious behaviors of culture Inheritance.

Acknlowledgment. The authors are grateful for the financial support provided by "the Fundamental Research Funds for the Central Universities"(No. 309201140132024).

References

1. Yinyin, Z., Xiping, S., Jingyan, Q.: Service oriented sustainable experience design of museum. Packag. Eng. **22**(36), 1–4 (2008)
2. Dicks, B.: Culture on Display: The Production of Contemporary Visitability. Peking University Press, Beijing (2012)
3. Wang, S.: The Study of Ming Dynasty Furniture. SDX Joint Publishing Company, Beijing (2013)
4. Yushu, C.: The History of Furniture, pp. 175–196. China Light Industry Press (2012)
5. Creswell, J.W.: Research Design: Qualitative, Quantitative, and Mixed Methods Approaches, 4th edn. SAGE Publications, Inc., Thousand Oaks (2013)
6. Stickdorn, M., Schneider, J.: This is Service Design Thinking: Basics, Tools. Wiley, New York (2012)
7. Solomon, S., Weisbuch, G., de Arcangelis, L., Jan, N., Stauffer, D.: Social percolation models. Phys. A **277**, 239–247 (2000)
8. Yang, J., Leskovec, J.: Modeling information diffusion in implicit networks. In: ICDM, pp. 599–608 (2010)

Survey on Campus Landscape Construction and Study on Suitability Comprehensive Evaluation

Based on the Perspective of the Sustainable Development of Green Campus in China's Urbanization Process

Wei Wang(✉), Zhongwei Shen, and Huayi Zhou

School of Architecture and Design, Southwest Jiaotong University, Chengdu 610031, Sichuan, China
{wangwei31, shenzhongwei}@home.swjtu.edu.cn

Abstract. Scientific and rational designing and construction of green infrastructure is an important part of the sustainable urbanization of China. In view of this, deeper insights into the actual condition of campus landscape construction in China's urbanization process were gained by investigating 10 primary and secondary schools on the spot and interviewing 20 experts and scholars. A 12-experts panel Delphi questionnaire survey on the evaluation indexes of Campus Landscape was conducted, and the suitability comprehensive evaluation index system was established. By the division of suitability grade, the set pair analysis theory was applied to the suitability comprehensive evaluation of Campus Landscape. Finally, taking the Zundao School in Mianzhu as an example, the school ground suitability comprehensive evaluation was made.

Keywords: Primary and secondary schools · Campus environmental landscape · Urbanization · Ecological civilization · Suitability · Evaluation

1 Introduction

China is known as one of the countries experiencing fastest urbanization development, and the statistic from National Bureau of Statistics shows that the urbanization rate rose from 51.27 % in 2011 to 52.57 % in 2012 and then to 53.73 % in 2013. Experts predict that the urbanization rate will arrive at 80 % in 2030 [1]. Despite having made significant achievements, urbanization also suffers a lack of ecological civilization [2]. The problems such as the out-of-control land use, the lower quality of regional environment, and the ecological destruction in urbanization construction, etc. [3], have posed a severe challenge to the sustainable and healthy development of cities.

The urbanization of China must consist with China's national condition and the concept of sustainable development, since it is the inevitable choice in the path toward ecological civilization. As a result of this, the development of urban green infrastructures is thought of as a significant measure to address urbanization problems and relevant urban problems by Chinese governments at all levels and the workers of

P.-L.P. Rau (Ed.): CCD 2016, LNCS 9741, pp. 288–298, 2016.
DOI: 10.1007/978-3-319-40093-8_29

landscape architecture, who have achieved remarkable effects through the successive implementation of landscaping projects as well as the protection and utilization of scenic spots [4].

Campus green space is the second largest green space in cities behind park. Notwithstanding the smaller area, campus is likely to make greater ecological contributions than the park as a habitat because cities are always brimming with a large quantity of homogeneous and scattered campuses. Provided campus landscape is properly built as a friendly habitat and connected through ecological corridor to shape an ecological network where living beings can shuttle between different habitats, it is inevitable that campus will play an irreplaceable role in protecting urban ecological safety, highlighting urban characteristics, and guaranteeing urban sustainable development.

The construction of eco-friendly campus landscape not only helps to maintain campus biodiversity, but also takes into account campus beautification and greening. Besides offering the teaching materials required by the education of natural science as the ideal place of outdoor teaching, campus landscape can contribute to physical and mental health of children. The outdoor experiential education can motivate children to learn, and involve them in the significant learning in campus learning habitat regarding new knowledge and skills to broaden their vision. Campus landscape can enable children to become aware of the life value, understand and respect universal living beings in learning process, develop their outlook on ecology and fully realize the beauty of nature. In this way, children will endeavor to strive for an agreeable environment in the future.

2 Survey on Campus Landscape Construction of Primary and Secondary Schools

2.1 Investigate Primary and Secondary Schools on the Spot

In order to gain deeper insights into the actual condition of campus landscape construction in China's urbanization process, the researcher has devised a biological habitat questionnaire, made a field survey on 10 local schools (see Table 1), and used the result obtained as the reference for Delphi method questionnaire.

- As shown by the field survey, the floor space of these schools ranges from 10,000 to 40,000 m^2, with over 50 % of the ground made up of hard pavement.

Table 1. 10 Local schools

School Name	Location
Daxijie Elementary School, Ziyan Elementary School, Zundao School, Xiaode Secondary school	Mianzhu, Sichuan
Xiaoquan National Primary School, Deyang Experimental Primary School, Deyang High School	Deyang, Sichuan
Wenchuan First Primary School, Wenchuan Yanmen school, Wenchuan First Secondary school	Aba Prefecture

- 60 % of campuses are adjacent to streets, and a lower number of biological species and living beings are allowed to enter campus from outside. However, a minority of schools neighbor uncultivated land or agricultural land, but the enclosure cannot stop the living beings from jumping into campus. As a result, the uncultivated land or agricultural land naturally becomes the heartland of schools, and besides, biodiversity is also raised as the living beings shuttle between school and outside environment.
- While designing and constructing a building, few schools take into consideration biological channels. In view of this, the researcher carries out an investigation into campus road system, finding that only 30 % of schools take advantage of natural materials. The footpath paved by Xiaoquan National Primary School with abandoned stones, for instance, shows distinct characteristic, whereas most of primary schools tend to make use of asphalt or cement, which is adverse to the activity of organisms in campus.
- In terms of plants selection, the researcher finds that 40 % of schools incline to grow native plants, and others prefer growing plants based on visual landscape. Though such plants are not ecologically meaningless, schools are heavy with landscape streets, which have obviously occupied the survival space of native plants.
- In order to maintain the beauty of campus, 90 % of schools assign weeding task to special person regularly, 70 % of them resorting to pesticide.
- Though 70 % of schools are equipped with a pool, none of them has built a creek. The bottom of the pool is made of cement and tile, without pores or side slopes for organisms, thus going against the requirements of ecological pool.

2.2 Interview with the Workers of Environmental Education Affairs

An interview with the management experts and environmental education workers of the schools above is conducted, and their working experience has educated the researcher about the concept and methods of campus landscape construction. According to the analysis on the identical and different views of the interviewees, the consistent opinions and conclusions are included in Delphi method questionnaire as reference. The interviewing result is summarized as follows:

- The interviews believe that campus biodiversity can contribute to building a new less-polluted Chinese town on the way to sustainable development.
- 60 % of interviewees argue that campus should be equipped with the habitats such as tree, grassland, and pond to attract varieties of organisms, whereas the remaining interviewees insist that there is no need to classify habitats, and the campus should be let develop naturally to attract the organisms.
- In terms of management, human intervention in organisms should be lessened, and the environment should be let develop naturally within permission limit. For instance, there is a need to sweep the fallen leaves, as well as reduce the weeding frequency and the use rate of pesticide. Besides, schools are supposed to arrange

special person or group to protect and monitor school's ecological environment so as to guarantee the sustainability of the biologically diverse campus environments.

- The interviewees hold that campus landscape construction requires multiparty participation. Administrative director is of great importance, since campus management is in the charge of administrative director. Additionally, a group of like-minded teachers are required to make environmental plan and design the course with joint efforts for the sake of the education about natural ecology. Besides, to seek the sponsorship of relevant units is also of vital significance; otherwise, it will be difficult to carry out the education of natural ecology based on a utopian scheme. While establishing the habitat design course, campus could provide an environment more suitable for learning if experts offer consultation service and assistance.
- The eco-friendly campus landscape is usually beneficial to environmental teaching, since teachers and children can often see the ecological natural phenomena such as about natural evolution, survival of the fittest, and the law of the jungle. Besides, the eco-friendly campus landscape can realize the functions such as life education, ecological teaching, and design of teaching situation.

3 Methods of Suitability Comprehensive Evaluation

3.1 Building of Evaluation Index System

As an outdoor learning place, campus landscape can inspire children to make discoveries, explorations, interactions, and individual communications in environment, and enhance the relationship with environment and the sense of ownership. To evaluate campus landscape is of vital practical significance [5, 6]. Suitability evaluation, frequently used in environmental planning, is primarily applied to urban construction land, agricultural land, natural reserves or tourism land, regional planning and landscape planning, project site, and environmental influence, etc. [7–9]. Considering that campus landscape is a combination of humanistic education, social economy, and eco-environmental system, the quality of environmental landscape construction is judged by means of suitability evaluation.

According to the information obtained through the field survey on the schools above and the interview with the workers of environmental education, this study complies the candidate index list for the comprehensive evaluation on campus landscape suitability as well as the Delphi method questionnaire. Then, 12 experts are invited to participate in the questionnaire survey until the questionnaire survey result converges. Afterwards, a statistical analysis is performed to build an evaluation index system.

Comprehensive Evaluation Index System of Campus Landscape Suitability includes four grades. Grade-I Index is comprehensive evaluation on campus landscape suitability. Grade-II Indexes are Inclusivity, Natural Environment, Place and Property, Flexibility and Changes. The Grade-II Index Weight corresponding respectively are A1 (0.285), A2 (0.222), A3 (0.358), A4 (0.135). The Grade-III Index and Grade-IV Index are shown in Table 2.

Table 2. Comprehensive evaluation index system of campus landscape suitability

Grade-III Index (Weight)	Grade-IV Index (Weight) – Case Evaluation Result
Universality A11 (0.063)	universality of users q1 (0.018) - Suitable
	fairness of campus landscape use q2 (0.018) - Highly suitable
	multicultural element utilization q3 (0.015) - Suitable
	embodiment of school history and background q4 (0.012) - Unsuitable
Accessibility A12 (0.08)	no use limitation on the disabled q5 (0.015) - Suitable
	the offering of route and location map q6 (0.015) - Highly Suitable
	the design of a proper space based on the frequency and size of children activity q7 (0.018) - Highly Suitable
	the dynamic flow and the requirement of silent children group q8 (0.018) - Suitable
	the selection of multi-functional facilities q9 (0.014) - Suitable
Participation A13 (0.069)	the participation of teachers and children in design and construction q10 (0.018) - Suitable
	the openness of participatory process to interest group q11 (0.018) - Suitable
	the role and function of children participation q12 (0.015) - Suitable
	the representativeness and reasonable operation of corresponding participating organizations q13 (0.018) - Suitable
Interaction A14 (0.073)	different types of interactive space q14 (0.022) - Suitable
	corresponding interactive space for different age groups q15 (0.018) - Suitable
	interactive space suitable for group size q16 (0.018) - Suitable
	space for self-expression and observation q17 (0.015) - Suitable
Biodiversity A21 (0.088)	different plant arrangements q18 (0.022) - Suitable
	the preservation and integration of existing plants to the largest extent q19 (0.018) - Highly Suitable
	the integration of natural elements into artificial environment q20 (0.018) - Suitable
	the offering of the habitat suitable for animals q21 (0.015) - Suitable
	the construction of an entire ecosystem with regional section jointly q22 (0.015) - Highly Suitable
Soil Conservation A22 (0.04)	topsoil conservation q23 (0.012) - Suitable
	topsoil conservation and reuse q24 (0.008) - Suitable
	excavation and filling q25 (0.008) - Suitable
	reduction of soil erosion risk q26 (0.012) - Suitable
Microclimate A23 (0.045)	the offering of natural sheltering to the largest extent q27 (0.015) - Suitable
	the reduction of cement pavement q28 (0.015) - Suitable
	maximization of greening area q29 (0.015) - Suitable
Water Resource A24 (0.049)	the collection of site water q30 (0.012) - Unsuitable
	the collection of water resource for site greening q31 (0.009) - Unsuitable
	the reduction of landscape water wastage q32 (0.012) - Suitable
	purification and drainage of surface water q33 (0.008) - Unsuitable
	the integration of campus landscape with site water design q34 (0.008) - Unsuitable
Landscape Environment A31 (0.075)	the combination of shelter, color and space q35 (0.015) - Suitable
	emotional design and expression q36 (0.015) - Suitable
	the creation of location awareness and sense of ownership q37 (0.018) - Suitable
	readability, diversity and graphic expression of guiding system q38 (0.015) - Highly Suitable
	the reasonable allocation of trees, and the requirement for shelter and light q39 (0.012) - Suitable

(Continued)

Table 2. (*Continued*)

Grade-III Index (Weight)	Grade-IV Index (Weight) – Case Evaluation Result
Outdoor Learning A32 (0.057)	the use of campus site in combination with teaching activity and course q40 (0.018) - Suitable
	the support and encouragement for outdoor learning q41 (0.015) - Suitable
	the seamless transition and convenient pass between indoor and outdoor environment q42 (0.012) - Suitable
	the integration of new technologies into campus site and its application q43 (0.012) - Suitable
Activity A33 (0.1)	the satisfaction of children's requirement for outdoor exercise q44 (0.032) - Highly Suitable
	children's gender, age, and confidence level q45 (0.025) - Suitable
	formal sports exercise space and affiliated facilities q46 (0.025) - Suitable
	the safety of children's outdoor play and sports field q47 (0.018) - Suitable
Silence And Reflection A34 (0.024)	the region of self-recovery and reflection in campus q48 (0.012) - Suitable
	space for children's pressure alleviation q49 (0.012) - Suitable
Display A35(0.054)	reasonable display of school image in campus q50 (0.015) - Highly Suitable
	the openness and hospitality expression of campus q51 (0.015) - Suitable
	opportunities for the display of children's achievements and skills q52 (0.012) - Suitable
	the influence of display site and pass way on school order q53 (0.012) - Highly Suitable
Safety A36 (0.048)	good visual field for monitoring q54 (0.018) - Suitable
	avoidance of hidden space resulting from greening q55 (0.015) - Suitable
	well-defined sign and clear control over entrance and exit and traffic route q56 (0.015) - Suitable
Space Requirement A41 (0.03)	the satisfaction of the requirement for spatial function and use in campus site q57 (0.018) - Suitable
	individual space size q58 (0.012) - Suitable
Multi-Purpose A42 (0.07)	the recognition of surrounding communities and sense of ownership q59 (0.015) - Highly Suitable
	monitoring over free access and activity safety of community members q60 (0.012) - Unsuitable
	the opportunities of children's class activities, after-class activities and weekend activities q61 (0.016) - Suitable
	the benefit for the exchange and interaction between children and adults q62 (0.015) - Unsuitable
	the utilization of campus site as community resources q63 (0.012) - Unsuitable
Functional Diversity A43 (0.035)	the satisfaction of current and future diversity requirement of teachers and students q64 (0.015) - Suitable
	serving the activities such as about teaching, sports, exchange and festival q65 (0.012) - Highly Suitable
	the use of non-exclusive space q66 (0.008) - Suitable

3.2 Set Pair Analysis

Set pair analysis (SPA) is a systematic analysis method that processes identical-discrepant-contrary quantitative analysis in the indeterminate system. Set pair analysis, proposed by Zhao Keqin-a Chinese scholar-in 1989, performs an analysis on the system from identical, discrepant and contrary angles, as well as studies the mutual transformation among them. The comprehensive evaluation on campus landscape suitability faces varieties of uncertainties, which can be effectively eliminated by means of set pair analysis.

The basic thinking of set pair analysis is: in the face of a certain question, two correlated sets X and Y are given to form a set pair (X, Y), and then, an analysis is performed on the set pair to figure out N characteristics, with S characteristics shared by the two sets X and Y, P characteristics contrary between the two sets X and Y, and F = N-S-P characteristics unclear (they are neither contrary nor commonly owned). S/N is defined as the identical degree H(X,Y), denoted by a; F/N is defined as discrepant degree or uncertain degree H(X,Y), denoted by b; P/N is defined as contrary degree H(X,Y), denoted by c. The correlation degree [10] of every different characteristic weight is expressed as follows:

$$\mu = a + bi + cj = \sum_{k=1}^{S} \omega_k + \sum_{k=S+1}^{S+F} \omega_k i + \sum_{k=S+F+1}^{N} \omega_k j \qquad (j = -1, i \in [-1, 1], a + b + c = 1) \tag{1}$$

Where $\omega_k \left[k = 1, 2, \cdots, N, \sum_{k=1}^{N} \omega_k = 1 \right]$ refers to weight of characteristic. In this paper, the weight of each index in the comprehensive evaluation index system of campus site suitability in urban primary and middle schools is determined by means of AHP [11].

3.3 Grading of Suitability

The evaluation has three grades, namely, highly suitable, suitable, and unsuitable. When the weights of all the indices at the same grade are added together, the suitability evaluation result of the campus site can be obtained through Eq. (1) and denoted by correlation degree μ. As shown by Eq. (1), j = −1, and the value of i is obtained from [−1,1]; according to principle of equipartition, i = 0. Since the value range of the normalized correlation coefficient μ is [−1,1], the suitability grade corresponding to correlation coefficient can be seen in Table 3.

Table 3. Grading standard of suitability

Grade	Unsuitable	Suitable	Highly Suitable
Correlation Coefficient	$-1 \le \mu \le -0.333$	$-0.333 < \mu \le 0.333$	$0.333 < \mu \le 1$

In suitability evaluation, i has different values, which can reflect not only the suitability of campus site, but also the design, construction, and management level of this site. When $i = 1$, μ corresponds to the highest suitability of the site; when $i = -1$, μ corresponds to the lowest suitability of the site. The parties of campus site planning, construction, and management may on the one hand find out the vulnerabilities and non-sustainable factors according to the evaluation result of each index in index system, and on the other judge the grade of site suitability and work out the suitability degree of the campus site according to the value range of μ. On this basis, they can upgrade the suitability of the site through corresponding measures.

When $c \neq 0$ in $\mu = a + bi + cj$-the equation of correlation degree, a/c-the ratio of the identical degree a to contrary degree c means the set pair trend against the background of a specific question, i.e., shi (H) = a/c. The order of the set pair trend that is arranged according to a/c value is termed as set pair trend order, with the relationship between the grade and order of set pair trend shown in Table 4 [12]. The set pair trend has revealed the development trend of site suitability, which has provided a direction for the parties of campus site planning, construction, and management.

Table 4. Relationship between grade and order of set pair trend

Grading	Relationship	Set Pair Trend (Meaning)
Equipollence	$a = c, b > a$	Slight Equipollence (The identical trend is equal to contrary trend in the system)
	$a = c, b = a$	Weak Equipollence (The identical trend is equal to contrary trend in the system)
	$a = c$, $a > b > 0$	Strong Equipollence (In the system, though the identical trend is equal to contrary trend, but they are uncertain)
	$a = c, b = 0$	Quasi-Equipollence (In the system, though the identical trend is equal to contrary trend, but they are weak)
Identical Trend	$a > c, b = 0$	Quasi-Identical trend (The system has a certain identical trend)
	$a > c, c > b$	Strong Identical trend (The system is dominated by identical trend)
	$a > c$, $a > b > c$	Weak Identical trend (The system has a weak identical trend)
	$a > c, b > a$	Slight Identical trend (The system has a very weak identical trend)
Contrary Trend	$a < c, b = 0$	Quasi-Contrary trend (The system has a certain contrary identical trend)
	$a < c$, $0 < b < a$	Strong Contrary trend (The system is dominated by contrary trend)
	$a < c, b > a$, $b < c$	Weak Contrary trend (The system has a weak contrary trend)
	$a < c, b > c$	Slight Contrary trend (The system has a very week contrary trend under the influence of uncertainties)

4 Case Study

Mianzhu Zundao School is a nine-year compulsory education school, and Zundaochang Town is 8 km away from the west of Mianzhu City. The 5.12 Wenchuan Earthquake in 2008 has delivered a heavy blow to Zundao School, 99 % of the teaching building turned into dilapidated building, all teaching facilities destructed. Following the urbanization of China after disaster, the renowned real estate company China Vanke donated a large sum of money to Zundao School for the sake of rebuilding. Covering a floor space of 35,666.67 m^2 and a built-up area of 11,793.00 m^2, the campus is equipped with web-based teaching facilities suitable in the 21st century, and the buildings are constructed with the advanced earthquake-proof technique that can resist against the seismic magnitude up to 9 degree. Meanwhile, the campus, near the mountain and by the river, highlights environmental landscape and comes out as a representative new urbanized school. Characterized by beautiful environment, modernization, humanistic care, and safety, the campus develops into the paradise where children learn knowledge (see Fig. 1).

Fig. 1. Environmental Landscape of Manzhu Zundao School (Source: Author)

This study carries out a comprehensive evaluation on the suitability of this campus site by means of the abovementioned suitability evaluation system, with the evaluation result shown in Table 2.

According to the evaluation method above, the correlation degree can be figured out through Eq. (1):

$$\mu = 0.185 + 0.727i + 0.088j \quad (2)$$

When i = 0, μ = 0.097; the grade of environmental landscape suitability of Mianzhu Zundao School will be suitable, as shown in Table 3.

When i = 1 and i = −1, μ1 = 0.824 and μ2 = −0.63, respectively, with the value range of μ being [−0.63, 0.824]. This suggests that the campus site will be most suitable when μ1 = 0.824, and its grade will be highly suitable; however, the parties of campus site planning, construction and management should not feel satisfied with the present suitability degree of the campus site, but find out the vulnerabilities and identify the non-sustainable factors according to the unsuitable evaluation index and then upgrade the comprehensive level of campus site suitability with corresponding measures.

Analysis on set pair trend: in Eq. (2), a/c = 2.10, a > c, and b > a, which suggests that the system has a very weak identical trend; that is, the campus site is at suitable grade, but there is a very weak highly suitable trend. Additionally, b has a high value, which means that the index weight of suitable grade accounts for a large proportion. However, these indexes, which are seemingly suitable, will face grade decline as the campus site requirements and evaluation requirements increase; therefore, to avoid the unsuitable grade, there is a need to check these indices carefully and take corresponding measures to attain the highly suitable grade.

5 Conclusion

By investigating present construction situation, it was found that the Campus Landscape which was consistent with biodiversity and suitable for environmental education should possess the following 4 conditions: (1) building the comprehensive landscape site; (2) building the diverse biotopes environment; (3) implementing environmental education; (4) taking multi-participative construction and management measures.

Comprehensive evaluation index system of campus landscape suitability was conducted. There were 66 indicators involved in 4 categories being built: (1) inclusivity; (2) natural environment; (3) place and property; (4) flexibility and changes. In accordance with the Analytic Hierarchy Process and Set Pair Analysis, a scientific and objective platform was created for green campus decision-making operability in China's urbanization process.

Acknowledgements. This work is supported by the Sichuan Research Center of Applied Psychology (No. CSXL-152219), the Center for Early Childhood Education Research in Sichuan (No. CECER-2015-B11), and the Sichuan Landscape and Recreation Research Center (No. JGYQ201437), P. R. China.

References

1. Guanghua, W.: China's urbanization by 2030. Int. Econ. Rev. **19**, 99–111 (2011)

2. Jiyao, L., Houming, J.: Ecological civilization–Chinese new urbanization historical considerations. Soc. Sci. **29**, 50–53 (2014)
3. Hongqing, R.: The construction of new urbanization and ecological environment protection in China. Mod. Econ. Res. **32**, 5–9 (2013)
4. Baoxing, Q.: Constructing green infrastructure toward an ecological civilization era through the sound urbanization approach with Chinese characteristics. Chin. Landscape Archit. **26**, 1–9 (2010)
5. Ling, S., Hongjun, L., Borong, L.: Research and application of green campus evaluation system suitable for Chinese national situation. Build. Sci. **26**, 24–29 (2010)
6. Na, G., Tao, Z., Shaoxia, G.: Comprehensive evaluation of children's outdoor play ground in residential area based on the grey system theory—taking children's outdoor play ground of Shundeju residential district in Qingdao as an example. Build. Sci. **26**, 98–101 (2010)
7. Junyan, Y., Yi, S., Xin, S.: New city spaces zoning suitability evaluation in landscape environment: exploration of Nanjing Riverside new city. J. SEU (Nat. Sci. Ed.) **42**, 1132–1138 (2012)
8. Wang, Y., Yin, X., Li, G.: Delimitation of urban growth boundary based on land ecological suitability evaluation: a case of Shenshan special corporation zone. Urb. Dev. Stud. **19**, 76–82 (2012)
9. Mingyu, Z., Wang Lixiong, S., Xiaoming, S.J.: Adaptability analysis of lighting luminance of Chinese ancient architecture in urban core areas. Chin. Illum. Eng. **23**, 29–33 (2012)
10. Keqin, Z.: Set Pair Analysis and Its Preliminary Application. Zhejiang Science Technology Press, Hangzhou (2000)
11. Jingxion, W., Junfeng, L., Jia, L.: AHP-based ecological suitability analysis on Yunmen mountain region. Huazhong Archit. **29**, 87–90 (2011)
12. Jiahong, Z., Kaili, X., Shijun, X.: Analysis on the risk of the logistics system of dangerous articles. Saf. Environ. **7**, 150–153 (2007)

Evaluation and Research on Interior Decoration Design of Automobile Cabins Based on Intention Recognition – Taking Control Panel Design for an Example

Chaoxiang Yang, Jianxin Cheng(✉), Zhang Zhang, and Xinhui Kang

East China University of Science and Technology, Shanghai, People's Republic of China
{darcy_yang, nbukxh}@foxmail.com, cjx.master@gmail.com, zhangzhang@ecust.edu.cn, 670614462@qq.com

Abstract. The Article tries to apply Kansei Engineering theory to build up a relationship between the design elements for control panel design of automobile cabins and the perceptual evaluation of users. By integrating design features of the automobile control panel with the evaluation procedure for perceptual image design, an association model is finally established between the design elements for the control panel relating to the interior decoration of automobile cabins and the perceptual evaluation of users through screening of design patterns for the control panel, cognitive study on the perceptual image and by using the composition of design element system. During the study, perceptual evaluation data of test samples is obtained with the method of semantic differential. Combined with the design decomposition elements obtained via morphological analysis, an association model between the design elements and the perceptual evaluation is obtained with factor analysis method to determine the relationship of them and help to forecast the perceptual evaluation value. The article establishes a forecast that the association model can be used for the perceptual evaluation value of cabin interior decoration, and forms a set of systematic and scientific evaluation methodology for the interior decoration design of automobile cabins by describing and verifying the design methods for the control panel in cabins.

Keywords: Control panel design · Intention recognition · Kansei Engineering

1 Introduction

People began to transfer attention to the automotive interior gradually from the born of car when they tirelessly pursued the automotive mechanical properties and appearance in Nineteenth Century. Whether the auto control design was good or bad directly related to the evaluation of people driving experience, the comfortable, entertaining and easy operation affected the automobile industry development greatly [1]. Different interior systems been placed in the environment of man - cockpit took different levels of impact to the driver's psychological and physiological, thereby affected the drivers' operation. In the field of design, using the method of Kansei Engineering could

P.-L.P. Rau (Ed.): CCD 2016, LNCS 9741, pp. 299–304, 2016.
DOI: 10.1007/978-3-319-40093-8_30

combine the design elements and the user's feelings, and establish the model of the relationship between the two [2]. TANOU in Japan [3], HSIAO in Taiwan, China etc. [4] all used these research means.

Therefore, this paper used the theory of Kansei Engineering, took the central console of the intermediate car in the market as the research object of the design evaluation, in order to produce the product design evaluation method which was in line with the consumer's perceptual demand.

2 Introduction of Kansei Engineering

The term of "Kansei Engineering" was first proposed by Japanese scholars in the speech of "the theory of automobile culture" at the University of Michigan in 1986 [5]. It was a theory or method to explore the relationship between the "human" sensibility and design characteristics of the "object" by using engineering technology [6, 7]. In the process of product design, the core part of the emotional design was to take emotional images and feelings into the elements of product design, help designers to grasp the product characteristics, understand its relationship with consumer sensory images, so as to determine whether these evaluations were in line with the designers' intentions at image.

3 The Design Overview of Car Cockpit Interior

Central control console, door trim, instrument panel, seat, steering wheel, etc. all belonged to the automotive interior. The dashboard, door trim, seats were paid more attention by people. In contrast, the console was often easy to be ignored, and was rarely involved even in the automotive related research. But with the development of automobile industry, console was given more functions, for example: giving drivers more driving information, improving the comfort and automatic operation, increasing more control panel and display, all kinds of audio equipment, air conditioning equipment switch, glove box, cup holder and so on, which made it become a very important part of the automobile interior design. As a result, it should be paid more attention in the automotive development and design phase.

Console layout mainly included two forms, the one was independent existence between the driving seat and the deputy driving seat which was common in the mini car or truck; another was connected together with the dashboard, which was common in high-grade car, this paper took the console in this form as the research object.

4 Research Scheme Design under the Framework of Kansei Engineering

Research method of the Kansei Engineering was introduced in this paper, it took four steps to establish the evaluation model of the automobile control platform. First of all, collecting the representative samples of the vehicle console which took a clear design orientation, next building the control system and the related model of console based on on the perceptual image cognition of the central control station, so as to determine the relationship between the user's perceptual evaluation and the design elements of the central control station, and use the obtained perceptual evaluation to guide the design of the automobile control platform.

1. *Collecting samples the car console which took a clear design orientation.* The console design evaluation from the perceptual image started from the target user's demand survey research, the difference of design positioning meant that the corresponding user perceptual cognition and demand were different. Therefore, it should clear the design and positioning of the console samples firstly, clear product target user group. Secondly, it should collect 58 sample table modeling pictures of console extensively, classify these pictures preliminary, subjective screen on the basis of clarity and angle, determine a set of representative sample pictures, and use gray treatment to remove the color factor, as shown in Fig. 1.

Fig. 1. The representative samples of the console

2. *Determining the representative perceptual vocabulary.* Collecting emotional adjectives which were descriptions of console as much as possible according to the manufacturer's website, books, magazines, newspapers and consumer interviews and other ways, excluding semantic fuzziness vocabularies by screening, selecting residual perceptual describe words through questionnaire and cluster analysis, and choosing 6 groups most from a hierarchical perceptual vocabulary descriptions of the console. As shown in Table 1:

Table 1. The representative perceptual vocabulary

Code	Y1	Y2	Y3	Y4	Y5	Y6
perceptual vocabulary	quality	technological	novel	concise	eye-catching	streamline

3. *Determining user questionnaire.* Determining the representative quotations by the numbers of representative samples and combination, and establishing the semantics difference scale table of vehicle console. Controlling the reliability and validity of the scale table in order to ensure the accuracy of the survey.
4. *The evaluation and analysis of the user to the automobile console.* Through Users evaluated the representative samples of the console by the questionnaire, so as to obtain the user's perception of the console.

5. *Establishing the relationship model between the model elements and the perceptual evaluation of the vehicle console and drawing the conclusion.* Determining the main product features and design elements of the representative samples, and transforming the perceptual evaluation to the engineering scale by the gray data theory and multiple regression analysis. Summarizing the corresponding relationship between the modeling elements and the perceptual evaluation of the car console, and concluding the evaluation method of the vehicle console based on the perceptual image.

5 Method Validation

The car console design was taken as a case in this paper, it determined that the target consumers of car were college graduates about 5 years, their consumption patterns were dominated by their internal psychological factors with distinctive psychological characteristics. The representative sample in this experiment were determined through this method, and were classified and analyzed by using the method of multiple scales, design personnel classification standard and coordinate value were found through the SPSS software, the pictures of final samples were obtained through clustering analysis.

The evaluation of users to the car console were got by the network questionnaire in this time, the questionnaire contained personal information, the car console evaluation and the car console needs these three parts, as shown in Fig. 2.

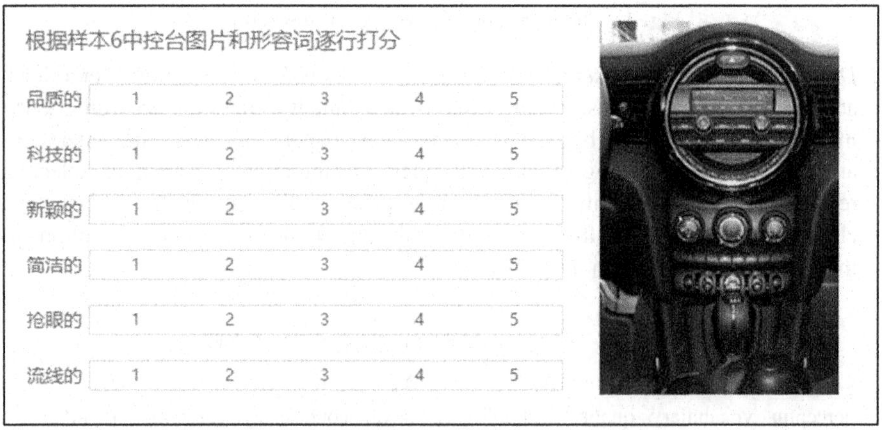

根据样本6中控台图片和形容词逐行打分

品质的	1	2	3	4	5
科技的	1	2	3	4	5
新颖的	1	2	3	4	5
简洁的	1	2	3	4	5
抢眼的	1	2	3	4	5
流线的	1	2	3	4	5

Fig. 2. The questionnaire about car console

The questionnaire data and descriptive statistical analysis were done, and the data matrix of the console sample was obtained, as shown in Table 3. 6 sets of perceptual vocabulary were setted as the variable X to make the decision of the principal component analysis, and the main component of the contribution rate and the high load factor of the common factor were obtained.

As shown in Table 2, the rotated component matrix was obtained through the initial component load matrix of varimax orthogonal rotation, it could be seen the first common factors of high load variables were Y2, Y3, Y5, which were classified as form factor according to the semantic. The second the high load factor on the high load was Y1, Y6 was the second common factor on the high load of variables, which defined as the quality factor. Y4 was the variable of high load on the third factor, which was defined as the value factor. Thus, the semantic core of the 6 groups perceptual words were summed up, and potential factors were dug out.

Table 2. Common factor data sheet

Common factor	Perceptual vocabulary	Factor load	Characteristic value	Variance contribution rate/%	Cumulative contribution rate/%
Factor 1 (form factor)	Y2	.805	4.141	69.021	69.021
	Y3	.941			
	Y5	.932			
Factor 2 (quality factor)	Y1	.766	1.172	29.530	88.550
	Y6	.947			
Factor 3 (value factor)	Y4	.999	.624	10.397	98.948

The component score coefficient matrix was obtained according to the Thomson regression method, and the spatial model of console perceptual image was set up as follows:

Form factor = −0.202Y1 + 0.259Y2 + 0.562Y3 − 0.013Y4 + 0.500Y5 − 0.300Y6.

Quality factor = 0.357Y1 − 0.097Y2 − 0.210Y3 − 0.031Y4 − 0.230Y5 + 0.956Y6.

Value factor = −0.129Y1 + 0.172Y2 + 0.032Y3 + 0.963Y4 − 0.134Y5 + 0.026Y6.

Perceptual image spatial model described the constitution of the automobile console from the perspective of semantics. The console design elements and image spatial were explored further in this paper, as shown in Table 3, the function mapping relationship between design elements and emotional semantic were established through multiple linear regression method, and emotional design concept model of console was proposed.

As shown in Table 4, the relevance amount of design elements to the emotional vocabulary could be found according to the design factor regression analysis coefficient table. Taking the quality of sense as an example, when a user needed a "sense of

Table 3. Data samples

Sample	Perceptual vocabulary value						Design elements								
							Navigation radio panel(X1)			Air outlet of air conditioner(X2)			Control button configuration(X3)		
	Quality	Technological	Novel	Concise	Eye-catching	Streamline	Square (C11)	Polygon (C12)	Arc line (C13)	Trapezoid (C21)	Circular (C22)	Quality (C23)	Technological (C31)	Novel (C32)	Concise (C33)
T1	3.2	2.93	2.33	3.07	2.13	2.93	1	0	0	0	0	1	0	0	1
T2	3.13	3.07	2.97	3	2.73	2.7	1	0	0	0	1	0	0	0	1
T3	2.8	2.73	2.4	2.53	2.37	2.5	0	0	1	1	0	0	0	0	1
T4	2.8	2.7	2.4	2.43	2.4	2.67	0	1	0	1	0	0	0	1	0
T5	3.13	3.23	2.8	3.2	2.9	2.63	0	1	0	1	0	0	0	1	0
T6	3.47	3.4	3.3	2.57	3.67	3.2	0	0	1	0	0	1	1	0	0

Table 4. Linear regression coefficient table of design elements

Perceptual vocabulary Y	The design elements of the automobile console								
	C11	C12	C13	C21	C22	C23	C31	C32	C33
Y1	0.232	−0.373	0.141	−0.763	0.08	0.746	0.73	−0.373	−0.192
Y2	0.028	−0.126	0.154	−0.487	0.106	0.433	0.689	−0.126	−0.395
Y3	−0.099	−0.199	0.298	−0.468	0.339	0.229	0.754	−0.199	−0.375
Y4	0.556	0.036	−0.592	−0.268	0.299	0.047	−0.344	0.036	0.223
Y5	−0.381	−0.071	0.452	−0.286	0.027	0.282	0.866	−0.071	−0.579
Y6	0.133	−0.374	0.241	−0.746	−0.139	0.901	0.832	−0.374	−0.268

quality", the design relationship between elements according to: The C23 = 0.746 > C31 = 0.73 > C11 = 0.232 > C13 = 0.141 > C22 = 0.08 > C33 = −0.192 > C12 C32 = −0.373 > C21 = −0.763, that the importance sort which affected the users' "sense of quality"was shown: air conditioning out tuyere half arc, a control button cylindrical, navigation radio square panel, navigation radio panel arc shaped, air out of round outlet, a control button hybrid, navigation radio panel polygon, control button forms mixed type, air conditioning out tuyere ladder.

6 Conclusion

The automobile console design was analyzed from the perspective of industrial design in this paper, the quantization value of automobile console form image was found by using of artistic psychology with perceptual image theory, the semantic core and potential factor were summarized which under the perceptual meaning by combining with factor analysis method, the form image model of automobile console was established. Subsequently, the correlation model was got through multiple regression analysis design elements and perceptual image, which provided a scientific reference for automobile console design, and helped designers design car console which could meet users' psychological needs.

References

1. Jing, Z., H, Y.: The development and prospect of the experience design in the automotive interior design. J. Mech. Eng. **3**, 77–81 (2014)
2. Nagamachi, M.: Kansei engineering: a new ergonomic consumer-oriented technology for product development. Int. J. Ind. Ergon. **15**, 3–11 (1995)
3. Tanoue, C., Ishizaka, K., Nagamachi, M.: Kansei engineering: a study on perception of vehicle interior image. Int. J. Ind. Ergon. **19**, 115–128 (1997)
4. Hsiao, S., Chen, C.: A semantic and shape grammar based approach for product design. Des. Stud. **18**, 275–296 (1997)
5. Jonathan, C., Craig, M.V.: Creating Breakthrough Products Innovation from Product Planning to Program Approval, pp. 1–31. Prentice Hall, New Jersey (2002)
6. Jianning, S., Pingyu, J., et al.: Study on the application of Kansei Engineering and its application in product design. J. Xi'an Jiao Tong Univ. **38**, 60–63 (2004)
7. Leong, B.D.: Culture-based knowledge towards new design thinking and practice-A dialogue. Des. Issues **19**, 48–58 (2003)

CJM-Based Service Design Process

Fuli Yang(✉) and Lili Qu

Ant Financials (China) Co., Ltd, Hangzhou, China
xunfei@alibaba-inc.com, lili.qu@alipay.com

Abstract. As the current service design process is not suitable for Alipay O2O service due to the particularity of users, product and service in China, our own service design process that is based on the Customer Journey Map (CJM) has been formed. This process forms five concepts (Steps, Matters, Contents, Details, and Sensory) according to the process of confirming the five user experience elements (The Strategy Plane, The Scope Plane, The Structure Plane, The Skeleton Plane, and The Surface Plane). This paper takes Chinajoy as an example to introduce the process on basis of five concepts in detail. The complete process begin with making CJM, then ascertaining Steps and listing Matters, furthermore proposing and overviewing Contents, clearing Details, finally accomplishing Sensory. Refinement in each phase is not a linear movement, but a to-and-fro and interactive process. When designing the contents on each phase, information at the former steps should be iteratively optimized so as to create better user experience.

Keywords: Service design process · Customer journey map · E-Ticket · Alipay

1 Introduction

Since 2013, a fundamental change from online payment product to online-to-offline (O2O) payment service is discernable in Alipay, which is the biggest Third-Party Payment platform in China. As a result, we start to explore with service design methodology in O2O payment service, and the tool we used most is Customer Journey Map (CJM).

However, we gradually realized that we don't know how to transform the contents of CJM into the services. While a large number of literatures focused on the definition, methods and tools of service design, and the method of how to make a CJM [1–8], **the process of how to use CJM is still lacking. And the current service design process is not suitable for Alipay O2O service due to the lack of localization to China**, for the two reasons: (1) The difference of the number of users: Services come to existence at the same moment they are being provided and used. That means the huge difference of the number of users possibly result in huge differences in terms of designing the services [8]. And the current service design process hasn't been verified by the situation of large population. (2) The difference of the products and services: Alipay is morphing into all-in-one banking tool: a savings bank, wire service and investment house. Most importantly, it's all done via mobile device. Using Alipay app, you can buy anything

P.-L.P. Rau (Ed.): CCD 2016, LNCS 9741, pp. 305–315, 2016.
DOI: 10.1007/978-3-319-40093-8_31

you want online and in brick and mortar stores, send money to friends, make cross-border transactions, and earn a healthy interest on your balance. Alipay is unique worldwide.

In order to filling up the blank, we reviewed and found that the traditional experience design process is the process to establish the contents of the five elements of user experience (Surface, Skeleton, Structure, Scope, and Strategy) [9] in essence. On this aspect, it is in line with service design. So we decided to form the service design process according to the process of confirming the five user experience elements. Finally, our own service design process, which is CJM-based, has been formed.

This paper will take Chinajoy (China International Digital Interactive Entertainment Products and Technology Exhibition, hereinafter referred to as "CJ") as an example to introduce the process in detail. CJ is held in Shanghai every summer. It lasts four days, and up to about 200 thousand people participates every year. Every participant typically needs to line up for a long time due to the huge number of people. In peak hours, the queue for checking can cost up to 2 to 3 h. We used our service design process to design the CJ electronic tickets' selling and checking process. The result has proven to be a success in 2014 and 2015. And this is also the first significant success for Alipay to provide E-tickets' checking service in large-scale offline event.

2 Five Concepts Through CJM

In The Elements of User Experience: User-Centered Design for the Web, Jesse James Garrett gives a detailed introduction about the five elements of user experience [9]. As these five elements are proposed in traditional experience design, to make them more applicable in service design, we've done some simple revisions (see Fig. 1).

Revised Definition of the Five Elements for Service Design

Elements	The Strategy Plane	The Scope Plane	The Structure Plane	The Skeleton Plane	The Surface Plane
Original definition in Traditional Design	The core strategic concerns are who the critical stakeholders are and how to balance the major stakeholders' interests and users' needs.	This plane deals primarily with functions and contents transferred from users' needs and product.	This plane defines patterns and sequences in which options will be presented to users, namely, address problems related to information architecture (classification and presentation) and flow.	This plane deals primarily with arrangements ,namely, optimization of interface layout to realize the best presentation of information and effective communication of certain elements (buttons, fields, pictures or texts).	Be it in traditional experience design or service design, this plane is dealing with the ***Sensory*** design and presentation of the logical arrangements that make up the skeleton of the Details in five senses (vision, hearing, touch, smell and taste).All goals on other planes will be archived on this plane. The final deliverable of this plane will be in the form of products or service recognizable to users in pictures, words, sound, taste or other elements.
Revised definition for Service Design	In spite of a wider range and more major stakeholders, service design has the same core concern on the strategy plane.But the CJM is more effective to extract users' needs than stakehold- ers'. Therefore, this paper is not going to discuss the Strategy Plane.	As service process always involves complex offline scenario, functions and contents are indivisible. We should to pack them and name them ***Matters*** so as to clear goals of the structure plane. In order to confirm Matters in a more comprehensive and accurate way, we have to design ***Steps*** first.	It also defines touchpoints in which channels will be presented in Service Design. To be more specific, we should know: 1. Which touchpoints will be used? 2. What are the necessary ***Contents*** in each touchpoints in order to accom- plish Matters? 3. How to put these Contents under systematic management?	There's huge difference in online and offline part, Contents should be considered separately. As for the online part, interface layout should be organized and wireframe be created; while for the offline part, the specific form, location and number of people or objects in each segment should be designed, namely, ***Details***.	
Concepts	No Concept Extracted	**Steps,Matters**	**Contents**	**Details**	**Sensory**

Fig. 1. The Definition of the Five Planes

2.1 The Strategy Plane

Generally speaking, the needs of major stakeholders are in the back and front stage of service [10], but CJM tends to show the front stage more [4]. Therefore, extract users' needs, rather than the stakeholders', from CJM is effective. The upside is the stakeholders' interests already become relatively clear before a service being carried out.

2.2 The Scope Plane: Steps and Matters

When using the CJM to complete Steps and Matters on the scope plane, the contents of "Phase", "Do", "Hear", "See", "Say", and "Thoughts" in CJM will be referred to. The steps are as follows:

- Steps Design

  (a) Review the variety and location relevant centralization of touchpoints in different phases of CJM, which will decide that we may have to use a different method to design the Steps. Here, location relevant centralization refers to the distance between touchpoints and users. If users take mobiles wherever they go, then location relevant centralization of mobiles is high. Generally speaking, the smaller the distance, the higher the location relevant centralization, and the lower the mobility costs for users, the easier design becomes.
  (b) For phases where touchpoints exist in fewer than three types and have centralized locations, Steps design can directly refer to "Do" in CJM. In the phase of E-ticket buying in CJ project, touchpoints are mostly mobiles, so the contents of "Do" in CJM can be directly referred to. In this process, unreasonable Steps from "Do" should be optimized and simplified to the largest extent on the basis of being in line with user cognition and habit.
  (c) For phases where touchpoints exist in more than three types and have disperse locations, location should be factored. In this case, other methods such as circulation design should be selected to design Steps according to the on-site environment.

- Matters Design

The Steps needs to be decomposed into possible Matters based on "what users' and stakeholders' need" from the Strategy Plane and the lanes from the CJM.

(a) In this process, users' needs should be detailed by delving into "Thoughts" and "Feelings" in CJM and taking "Issues" and "Opportunities" as supplement, while stakeholders' needs will be clarified by their representatives during the project.
(b) New ideas that may be generated during the above process need to complement the Steps.
(c) Determine the priority of Matters. Matters with the highest priority are which will cause process suspension without being accomplished; Matters with second high priority are which frequently take place in each Step. When project resources are limited, accomplishing Matters with high priority is the precondition to basic user experience.

Take E-ticket buying (the phase in which touchpoints have limited variety and centralized locations) as an example, the four Steps in this phase all come from "Do" in the CJM. From the thoughts that users have in each Step, we can know their possible needs. For example, in Step "Place Orders", from the thought "Know more about invoice information." or "Can I buy one for my friend?", we can create the Matter "Learn more about E-ticket buying rules." If E-ticket sellers want personal information of users so as to promote notifications, we can create the Matter "Fill in personal information." Therefore, we come to the following Fig. 2:

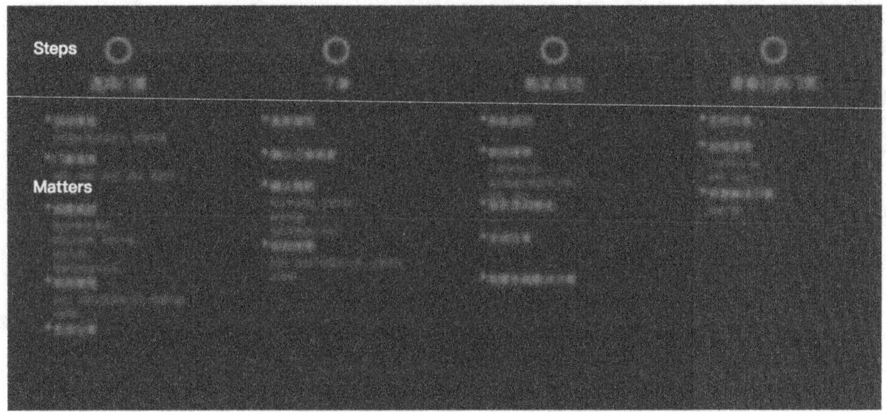

Fig. 2. The example of Steps and Matters: CJ E-ticket buying

In the phase "Yet-To Enter" of CJM, we can make use of circulation design in designing Steps and Matters. If to combine the "Do" contents with the circulation map about how users get to the convention center, we can find out key points in the route, namely, Steps. For example, the only entrance-No.1 Entrance of exhibition this time is a very important Step, not only because that all users have to enter through this entrance, but also because it is a target location of all users (see Fig. 3).

Matters in every Step will be decided by "Do" and "See". For example, at the No.1 Entrance Hall, users may look around for Alipay E-ticket Check while walking ahead, so we can create the Matter "Search Alipay E-ticket Check".

2.3 The Structure Plane: Contents

While completing Contents on the structural plane with CJM, the contents of "Touchpoints", "Environment" etc. in CJM will be used. The steps are as follows:

(d) To classify touchpoints according to the people and physical objects for management convenience.
(e) To rename the classified touchpoints and set separate lane for them. Finally, to complete the Touchpoints Lane according to the Fig. 4 below.

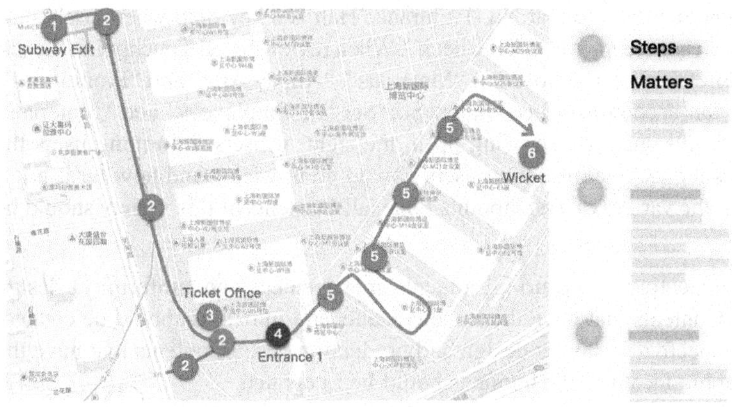

Fig. 3. The Circulation Design of CJ

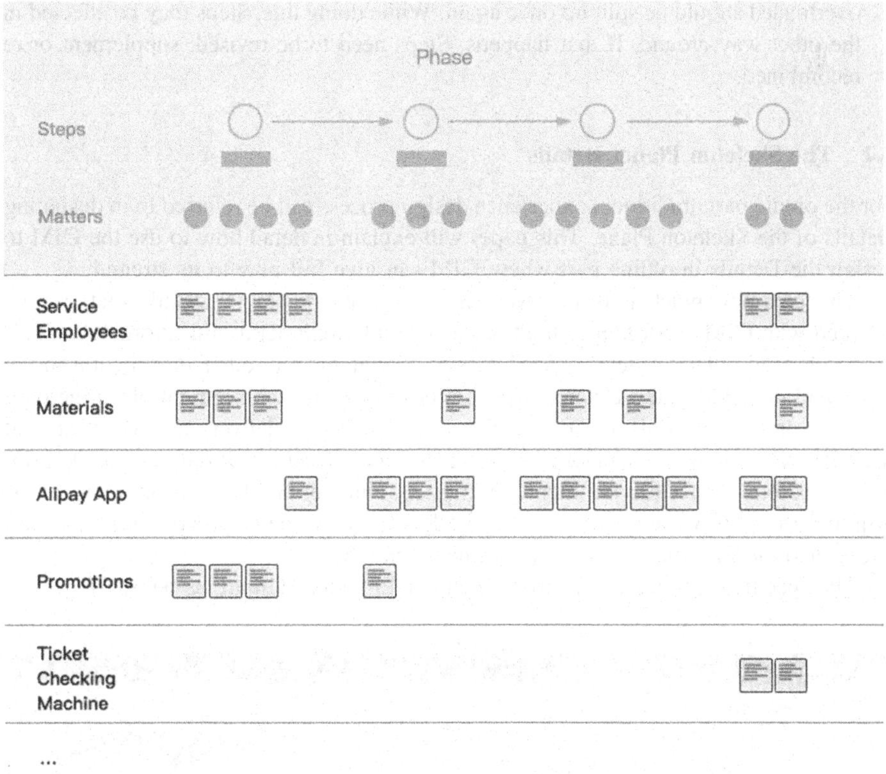

Phase

Steps

Matters

Service Employees

Materials

Alipay App

Promotions

Ticket Checking Machine

...

Fig. 4. The Touchpoints Lane

(f) To consider the relevance of "Touchpoints" and "Environment" while designing Contents from Matters in each Step. Generally speaking, to design the Contents needed in each touchpoints based on the two questions: "Are these touchpoints suitable to accomplish these Matters?" and "How to accomplish them?".

We have mentioned before that No. 1 Entrance Hall is a key Step where users may have the Matter "Search Alipay E-ticket Check". When reviewing all Touchpoints Lanes, we can find that in "Service Employees", "Materials", "Alipay APP" and "Promotions", the former two can accomplish this Matter. So "Service Employees" and "Materials" should have Contents such as "showing up in the sight of users /informing users the location of E-ticket checking/informing users how to go to wicket and how far it is".

According to the variety of Touchpoints Lane, all Contents of this variety should be reviewed:

- From the perspective of ensuring contents management and uniformity, design modules for Contents that have the same contents and functions should be created.
- From the perspective of saving design and production costs, Contents that have the same geographic location touchpoints should be integrated.
- From the perspective of ensuring the completeness of process, breaks between each Step should be modified, and the whole process be improved.
- From the perspective of information load of each touchpoints, Contents that are overloaded should be split up once again. While doing this, Steps may be affected in the other way around. If that happens, Steps need to be revised, supplement or re recombined.

2.4 The Skeleton Plane: Details

For the online part, traditional experience design process can be referred to in designing Details of the Skeleton Plane. This paper will explain in detail how to use the CJM to design the Details in offline part where CJM can give full play to its strength.

The common practice is to reversely deduce every single Details that can be clarified with CJM according to the final deliverables, extract useful information from "Environment", "Do", "Hear", "See", "Say", "Thought" and other information in the CJM, and thus design the Details of people or objects in each segment of offline part.

Take on-site materials as an example, things needed in delivery are: Wireframe of materials, Functions, Dimension, Number, Position, Specifics, Environment Description, and Note. As for Environment Description, Number and Dimension, they can be acquired from "Environment" of CJM; the Positions can be acquired from "Do" and "See"; and the Specifics, from "Environment" and "Do"…

The specific Contents of materials in No. 1 Entrance Hall are as below (Fig. 5).

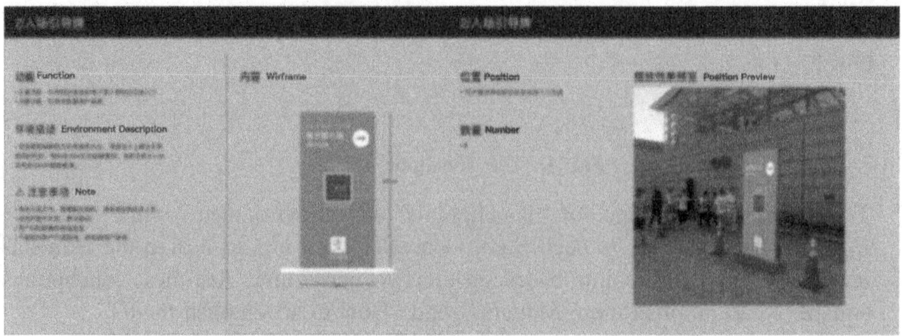

Fig. 5. The Contents of materials in No.1 Entrance Hall

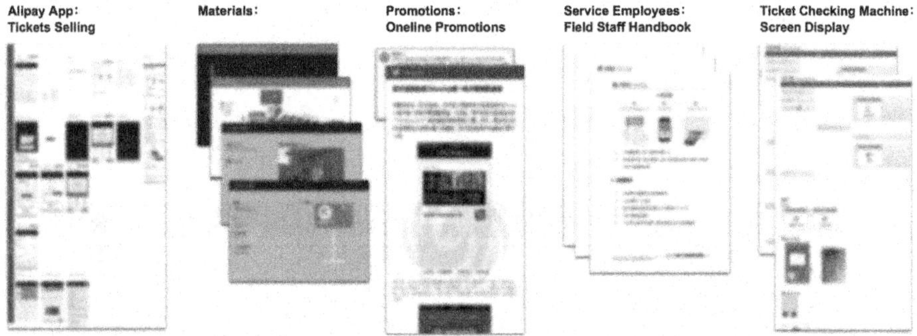

Fig. 6. The deliverables of Details for CJ

Ultimately, the deliverables (Fig. 6) we will output are corresponding to every Touchpoints Lane that were obtained from the Structure Plane.

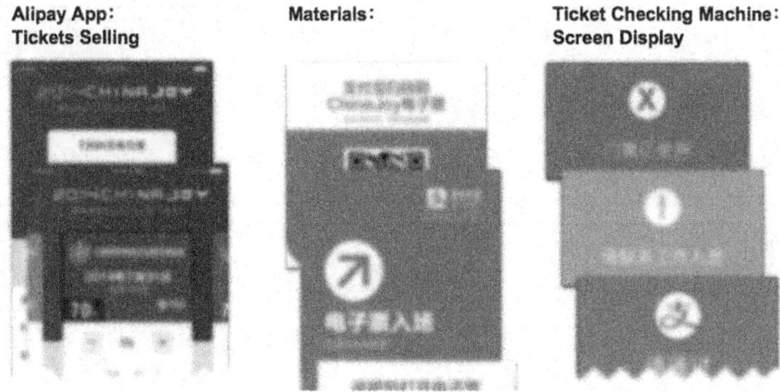

Fig. 7. The deliverables of Sensory for CJ

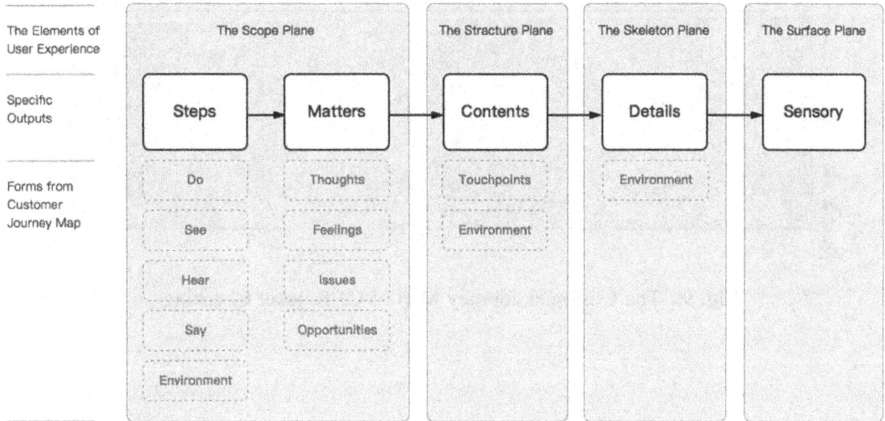

Fig. 8. The Five Concepts

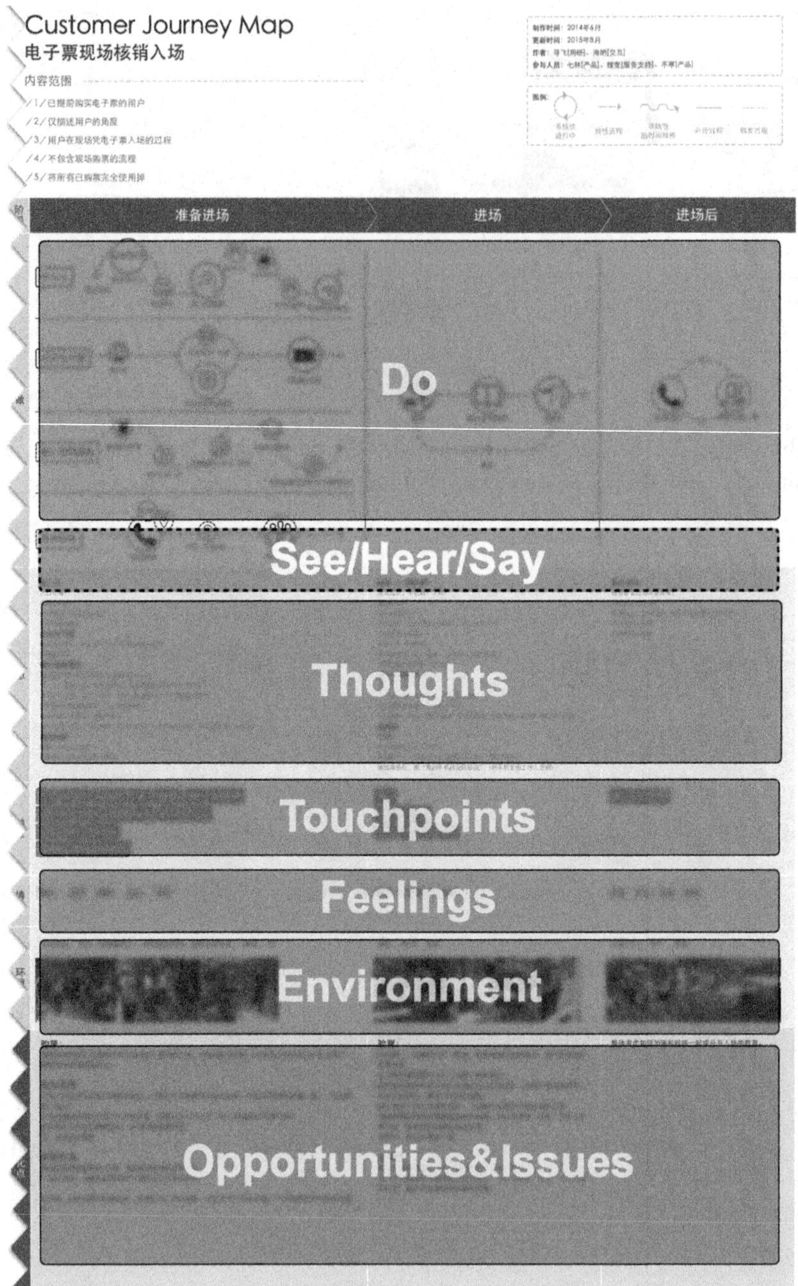

Fig. 9. The Customer Journey Map of CJ E-ticket Checking

2.5 The Surface Plane: Sensory

The success of design for the Surface Plane depends on the designers' experience and inquisitive mind. CJM has a quite limited role on this plane.

As for how to do the five sensory design, there are large number of literatures available in relevant subject, so we will not dilate upon this topic.

Some deliverables of Details may need to be visualized on this plane. Finally, we obtained 3 sets of visuals for CJ program (Fig. 7).

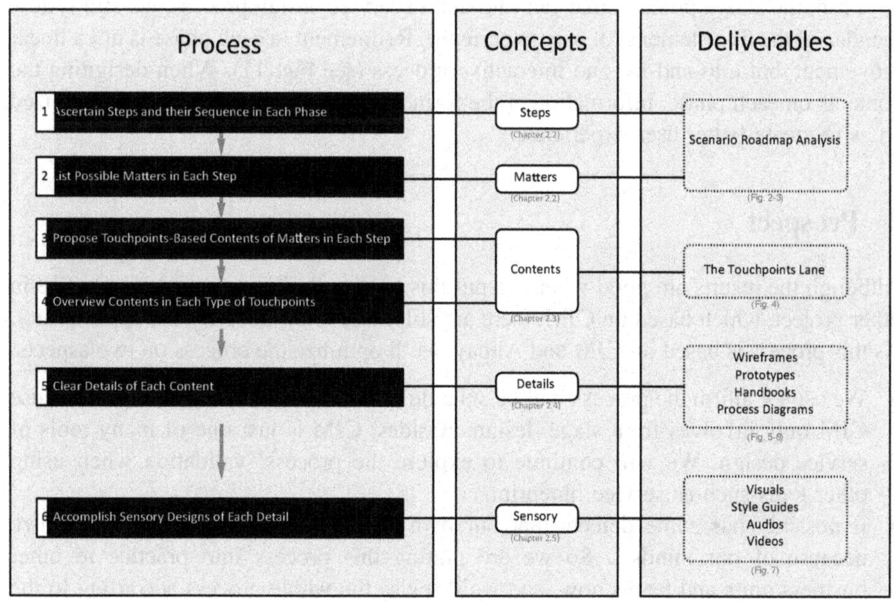

Fig. 10. The Process of Service Design

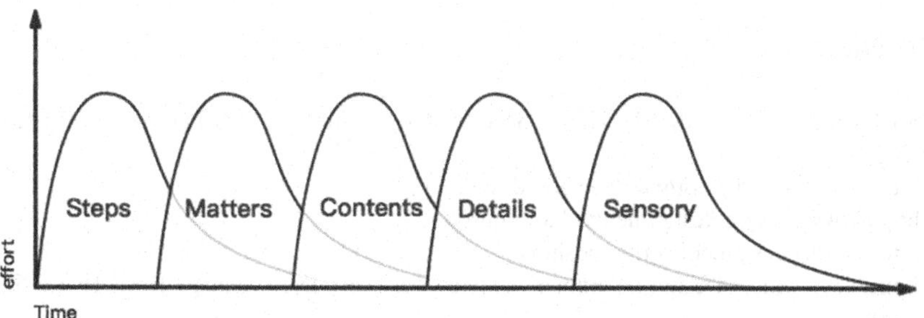

Fig. 11. The Interaction of Service Design Process

3 Conclusion

Obviously, five significance concepts-Steps, Matters, Contents, Details, and Sensory-are formed according to the process of confirming the five user experience elements from CJM (see Fig. 8).

Before design, we need to reconstruct the real scenario—make the CJM first. The Fig. 9 is a draft of CJM in the CJ E-ticket checking segment.

Next, we can start describing the process of service design on the basis of this draft. The whole process and its deliverables are as follows (see Fig. 10).

From the above process, one can find that in service design process, we still follow the idea of the five elements of user experience. Refinement in each phase is not a linear movement, but a to-and-fro and interactive process (see Fig. 11). When designing the contents on each phase, information at the former steps should be iteratively optimized so as to create better user experience.

4 Prospect

Although the results are good when we put this service design process into practice in other project, which based on CJM, there are still more to do to verify the applicability. As this process is based on CJM and Alipay, we'll optimize the process on two aspects:

- We cannot affirm the process will be suitable also for the back stage design, because CJM only involves front stage design. Besides, CJM is just one of many tools of service design. We will continue to explore the process' validation when using other tools such as service blueprint.
- It possibly has some defects that our own business and team could not realize because of our mindset. So we are putting this process into practice to other business units and teams now, and we'll revise the whole process according to the outcome.

References

1. Stickdorn, M., Schneider, J.: This is Service Design Thinking. BIS Publishers, Amsterdam (2010)
2. https://en.wikipedia.org/wiki/Service_design
3. http://www.service-design-network.org/intro/
4. http://servicedesigntools.org/repository
5. Eckersley, M.D.: Designing human-centered services. Des. Manag. Rev. **19**(1), 59–65 (2008)
6. Harri, P.P., Kukkonenb, O., Kapteinc, M.: E-selling: A new avenue of research for service design and online engagement. Electron. Commer. Res. Appl. **14**(4), 214–221 (2015)
7. Camerea, S., Bordegonia, M.: A strategy to support experience design process: the principle of accordance. Theor. Issues Ergon. Sci. **16**(4), 347–365 (2015)

8. Nousiainen, A.K.: Service Design Outcomes in Finnish Book Industry- From Transition to Transformation. Laurea University of Applied Sciences. Degree programme in Service Innovation and Design Master's thesis, October 2013
9. Garrett, J.J.: The Elements of User Experience: User-centered Design for the Web and Beyond, 2nd edn. New Riders, San Franciso (2010)
10. http://www.cooper.com/#work:parker

A Study on the Comparison and Inspiration for Operation Mode of the Maker Space Brand in China and America

Minggang Yang, Xinhui Kang(✉), Yixiang Wu, and Chaoxiang Yang

School of Art, Design and Media, East China University of Science and Technology, NO. 130, Meilong Road, Xuhui District, Shanghai 200237, China
nbukxh@163.com

Abstract. Maker space could be simply understood as the place where the guests doing things together. This concept could be traced back to the source-"hacker space" in the European, now it developed into a new form of organization and service platform. It promoted knowledge sharing, cross-border cooperation, creative achievement and even product through providing open space physics and prototype processing equipment to makers and organizing relevant meetings and workshops. According to a maker space list in Wikipedia, it shown that currently there were 2001 invasive space totally in the global. Among them, 1225 maker spaces were recorded as creative space, 355 maker space were planed to be build. These maker spaces were different in styles: some maker spaces mainly were centralized of Geek for coding technology, music recording and technical design; some maker space mainly focused on art design and hand-made; some maker space covered two forms which could create hybrid. According to the service object and function of maker space, it could be divided into the following four types: FabLabs, Hackerspaces, TechShops, Makerspaces operation mode, and it shown the characteristics of specialization, commercialization, etc. According to the difference among operation mode of maker space, investment and business service system etc., the following several modes of maker space existed currently in China: training investment, aggregate type and new type of real estate, the media driven, financing service, industry chain service and integrated business ecological system type.

This paper used the research and comparative analysis method, it made a comparison for brand operation mode of maker space in China and America, compared and analyzed development goals, talent team construction and organization operation mechanism of maker space between China and America. It focused on understanding the latest developments and implementation strategy of innovative talents training and maker space in the United States, put forward development strategy of maker space in China with American maker space brand operation and management experience, and provided reference for Chinese new geek culture mode.

Keywords: Maker space · Brand · Operation mode · Comparative study

1 Introduction

Makers initially were groups with innovative talent and hobby who focused on designing prototype products by use of digital technology, after they became maker groups who were keen for practice, shared technology and exchanged ideas for innovative. Makers

P.-L.P. Rau (Ed.): CCD 2016, LNCS 9741, pp. 316–325, 2016.
DOI: 10.1007/978-3-319-40093-8_32

were the representatives of the individual design and manufacturing groups who were most passionate and dynamic, they created a better life with their own creativity. The former chief editor of "Wired"-Anderson forecast in "Makers:The New Industrial Revolution" that people would use the wisdom of the network in the real world in the next ten years. The future not only belonged to network companies which based on the virtual principle, but also belonged to those industries deeply rooted in the real world. "Maker movement" was a booster which let the digital world truly overthrew the real world, it was new wave with landmark significance. The world would realize the creation of the whole people, and set off a new round of industrial revolution.

With the popularity of global maker culture and the rising demand of public innovation and public entrepreneurial, it took the talent aggregation, classification, and management operation mode into national policy making system, and became an important part of maker movement in different countries. As the earliest nation who implemented the maker culture-America, it had the latest research trends and practical strategies in construction, development and operation mechanism of the maker space. On the basis of this, it could provide theoretical reference and inspiration for the development of China's maker space.

2 The Development and Representative Model of the United States Maker Space Brand

2.1 The Development and Reason of the United States Maker Space Brand

2.1.1 Development History of the United States Maker Space Brand

"Maker" was derived from the comprehensive interpretation of words Maker and Hacker, it referred to software and hardware products which DIY their own creativity. 1984 Hamburg, Germany established the largest and earliest Chaos Computer Club at that time. "The godfather of maker"- Mitch Altman was inspired after participating the Chaos Communication Camp in Germany at 2007, in the San Francisco he founded the most famous maker space brand -Noisebridge after returning to the United States. Subsequently, under the promotion by Mitch Altman, maker space had a rapid development in the global. TechShop, who was called as "the first national open public workshop in the United States", was a profit-making organization founded in California in 2006. maker space- Attisan's Asylum in Auckland was found by the maker-Gui Cavalcanti in 2010, as a non-profit service organizations, members could use different public tools for 24 h only need to pay the membership fee.

2.1.2 The Reason of the United States Maker Space Brand Development

The United States was a paradise for thinker, inventor, and entrepreneur, it seemed that American were full of innovation spirit. There were many high tech industries in Silicon Valley, it originated from the early garage makers in the United States. The success of a large number of well-known enterprises, such as the United States CISCO, Intel, Amazon etc. all promoted the success of the United States "garage culture". At the same time, the United States was the first country to pay attention to entrepreneurship education, it provided different channels of entrepreneurship education, entrepreneurship competition and entrepreneurship education institutions. In recent years, more and more Americans created any products through the 3D printer, laser cutting machine, design software which was easy to use and desktop manufacturing equipment. They expected to enjoy the pleasure of creating production by own hands, shared the results through the network, and created the future of open source together.

2.2 Three Representative Models of the United States Maker Space Brand

2.2.1 Hobby Gathering Model – Taking NoiseBridge as an Example

NoiseBridge in the United States was located on the west coast of San Francisco City, it was a non-profit educational institutions for the public interest. 5200 square feet of space was located in the city center, the monthly operating expenses was more than 5000 U.S. dollars. As an open maker space, there was no need to pay fees and free to participate in training courses, and even directly went into the maker space to start work. Funding mainly come from the donation by the members, the members had a periodic donations payment of $10, $30 and $60 in a monthly, it could also be a one-time donation. Every week NoiseBridge would open training courses or seminars and other activities attract a large number of like-minded makers to participate, while promoted the culture of maker.

2.2.2 Profit Oriented Model – Taking TechShop as an Example

TechShop was the largest maker space linkage mechanism in the United States, it contained 8 branches, and planed to open a number of branches in the future. Funding sources mainly relied on membership fees and course training fees, membership fees could be paid $150 for a month or $1650 for a year. TechShop provided more than $1 million professional equipment and software, and it had comprehensive guidance of professionals to ensure the safety of members.

2.2.3 New Type of Real Estate Model – Taking WeWork as an Example

Adam Neumann and Miguel McKelvey founded a service platform to provide office space rental for small and micro enterprises, startups and free profession person in 2010 in the United States, with the operation mode of second landlord, it obtained more than 50 billion market value in a short span of four years. Wework was not real estate developers and never did other large investment, instead it leased vacant office in American economic depression as the second landlord identity, and made simple segmentation and re-decoration, then rented to the number of start-up companies, also provided leisure, entertainment and social public space for startups. Wework charged for membership fees and rents to maintain normal operation, and invited venture capital companies and executives to come to visit and exchange from time to time, provided different parties for members, it expected to seek communication platform and obtain more funds cooperation projects.

3 The Development and Representative Model of the China Maker Space Brand

3.1 The Development and Reason of the China Maker Space Brand

3.1.1 Development History of the China Maker Space Brand

Li Dawei who returned from the United States established a "New workshop" maker space in a storey house at the junction of Yongjia Road and South Shanxi road in Shanghai with software engineer Wu Sili couples on March 25, 2011. This workshop was the first maker space in Shanghai even in China. After the introduction of maker to our country, the provinces and cities created a variety of maker platforms for promoting the integration of creativity and manufacturing. To May 2015, Beijing had more than 50 maker space, Shanghai had more than 60 maker space, Tianjin and Wuhan had 30 to 40 maker space, the development of maker space was rapid at Suzhou, Hangzhou, Nanjing, Chengdu, Chongqing and other cities.

3.1.2 The Reason of the China Maker Space Brand Development

With the change of global industrial structure, China begun to focus on cultivating its own brand of excellent enterprises and personnel, and tapped the public's ability to innovate. Many makers carried dreams, they hoped to their own creativity could be industrialization. The development of electronic commerce and internet made people easy access to information and resource sharing, they were difficult to form a scale and dispersed motivated by interests, this kind of folk spontaneous creativity practice was just accorded with the Chinese government's macro development. Chinese government provided policy guidance and built platforms for exchange and innovation to mobilize the power of the public, and promoted the transformation and upgrading of industrial structure.

3.2 Three Representative Models of the China Maker Space Brand

3.2.1 Investment Driven Model – Taking Beijing Garage Coffee as an Example

April 7, 2011 in Zhongguancun, the world's first business theme cafe house was established on the street in Beijing. This maker space provided the most open platform for exchanges and cooperation with the cheapest office environment for the early entrepreneurial team, entrepreneurs could enjoy a free day of open office environment here with the cost only a cup of coffee [6]. Garage coffee did not provide angel investment or shareholding to maker team, it only provided a platform for communication and exchange for entrepreneurs and investors. At present, the main profit model of the garage coffee included advertising and self media, activity venue rental, entrepreneurship training and the normal operating income, etc.

3.2.2 The Polymerization Activity Model – Taking Shenzhen Firewood Space as an Example

January 2015, the premier of the State Council- Li Keqiang who did a inspection in the Shenzhen and came to Shenzhen firewood maker space [7], which ignited China maker space boom instantly. Firewood maker space belonged to Seeed Studio Technology Co., Ltd., CEO- Pan hao transformed old company into a maker space initially, then he felt the atmosphere was too depressed and moved to overseas Chinese city's creative industry park. The ordinary membership fee in firewood maker space was 200 yuan per month, members could enjoy the laser cutting machine, 3D printers and other ordinary work space. VIP membership fee was 1500 yuan per month, members could enjoy a small CNC, engraving machine, Taiwan drilling machine and other advanced equipment VIP work space. Firewood maker space focused on exchange and cooperation for members, held creative projects exhibition weekly, and published business activities party.

3.2.3 Training Guidance Model – Taking Tsinghua i-Center as an Example

Some colleges in our country setted up maker space with their advantages in hardware, such as maker space in Tsinghua University-i.Center was transformed from based industrial training center which was responsible for organization and coordination of the students' metalworking practice and teaching practice. 16500 square meters physical space were equipped with hundreds of digital control lathes, 3D printers, laser scanners and other infrastructure facilities for makers. In January 2013, professor Gu Xueyong in department of industrial engineering opened "cross disciplinary system integrated design challenge" course in i.Center maker space, students could experience skills and practical method required in the project development process deeply and reality, it let students understand the challenges which makers should face. In may 2014, i.Center launched "Building a dream - the United States and China youth maker competition" activity, the purpose was to enhance the cultural exchanges between China and the U.S. and deepen the friendship.

4 Comparison and Enlightenment for the Brand Model of Maker Space Between China and America

4.1 Comparison for the Brand Model of Maker Space Between China and America

4.1.1 Comparison for Brand Model Target of Maker Space

The mission of many maker spaces in the United States was to provide open space and advanced prototype processing equipment for the public, and to promote global manufacturing innovation. The goal was to shorten the distance for the tourists to communicate and cooperation, and strive to save resources, protect the environment at the same time of localization. The rising of China maker space came from government "bonus system", as early as September 2014, Premier Li Keqiang proposed to set off a new wave of "public entrepreneurship", "entrepreneurial roots" at the summer Davos forum opening ceremony, formed new situation of "everyone innovation" and "peoples business". Brand goal of China maker space was to comply with the requirements and the characteristics of the network of innovation and entrepreneurship, construct the low cost and convenience new business service platform through professional services and market mechanism, provide work space, resources sharing space and project incubator space for entrepreneurs, be able to provide technical funds, team building, business counseling and other support for grassroots entrepreneurs so as to revitalize China's manufacturing industry.

4.1.2 Comparison for the Brand Policy of Maker Space

In June 18, 2014, U.S. President Barack Obama held the first carnival in the White House, it aimed to foster and encourage the spirit of innovation, and achieve "the root rejuvenation of the U.S. Manufacturing". President Obama also announced new measures to let more Americans who was young or old use technology and tools to live their own lives easily. More than 13 federal government agencies and companies including Etsy, Kickstarter, Indiegogo and local automotive manufacturers provided business guidance, training and start-up funding for U.S. manufacturers and major retailers. Ministry of education and other five institutions, more than 150 colleges and universities, more than 130 libraries and large companies including Intel, Autodesk, Disney, Lego, 3D systems committed to create more maker space, and launch more students and educators to join them. Ministry of defense, the Department of energy, the National Aeronautics and Space Administration, the National Science Foundation and other 11 federal agencies provided 2 billion 500 million $ a year to finance small business innovation research (SBIR) and the small-medium enterprises technology transfer (STTR) project. The United States Department of agriculture would launch two new competition to encourage the agricultural technology and production of the surrounding colleges and universities. Competition helped to promote the development of agricultural technology and entrepreneurship, and promote food, agriculture, natural resources, rural development and other related issues.

In terms of maker space in our country, in March 2015, the general office of the State Council issued "The guidance for development of maker space to promote public innovation and entrepreneurship". The idea mainly focused on accelerating construct public record space, promoting maker space, entrepreneurship coffee and innovative workshops; Reducing the threshold for innovation and entrepreneurship, simplifying the business registration process, local governments gave appropriate financial subsidies; encouraging scientific-technological personnel and students to entrepreneurship, encouraging high school to open the innovation and entrepreneurship education, increasing the training of college students; improving the venture investment and financing mechanism, carrying out Internet public equity financing pilot measures etc. China's current rapid development of the maker space did not form a scale yet. The integration of enterprise and university entrepreneurial team was not deep.

4.1.3 Comparison of the Construction for the Brand Team in Maker Space

The MIT Media Lab in Massachusetts Science Institute was founded in 1985, it belonged to of architecture and design institute of Massachusetts Institute, it had profound attainments in the field of transformation for achievements of science, technology, multimedia, including touch user interface and wearable devices. The foundation of media lab team building was strong, there were nearly 40 senior researchers, 48 cooperative enterprise researchers, 75 visiting scientists and post doctoral, 80 technical and administrative personnel.There were more than 100 graduate students, these people had different disciplines background and work experience, while more than 200 students worked in the laboratory through the undergraduate research opportunity program (UROP) each year.

Beginning in 2014, "basic industrial training center" in China's Tsinghua University was upgraded to "i.Center"- specifically belonged to the Tsinghua people's "maker space". i.Center was the world's largest campus maker space which covered 16500 square meters, all the students in Tsinghua University should be trained with creative thinking in this factory. They need to do a hammer, because it was a collection which all the tools should be used in the workshop, so that students could grasp the creative ability of the product quickly. There were a total of 107 faculties and staffs in Tsinghua University basic training center, staff who directly engaged in teaching were 81 people, a professor and seven associate professors existed in 8 people. There were a large number of high-quality experimental guidance teachers in i.Center, they communicated with the world's leading maker actively, and understood the forefront of the creative practice. Including firewood space founder Pan Hao, he was hired as a maker teacher, he exchanged the growth process of maker space with students. NoiseBridge founder Altman Mitch and more than ten countries-outside maker talents were serve as guest mentors in i.Center.

4.1.4 Comparison for the Business Model of Maker Space Brand Government Agency Business

U.S. Defense Advanced Research Projects Agency (DARPA) reached a cooperation agreement with the Department of Veterans Affairs. Techshop would establish new maker space in Pittsburgh, Pennsylvania, and Washington, DARPA's new adaptive vehicle manufacturing projects worked with the techshop together, made cooperation with experimental platform for the development of advanced manufacturing technology. At the same time, the Department of Veterans Affairs and Ge Corp provided free membership for one year and $350 worth of professional guidance and training for more than 1200 veterans in the country. Our country maker space was based on priority policy, the Shanghai science and Technology Committee, the Communist Youth League in Shanghai Committee and other units started the "business Pujiang" action plan. Shanghai maker space alliance established and initiated by nearly 40 venture service organizations jointly would become a new incubator resource sharing, exchange and cooperation platform in Shanghai. Beijing issued "Entrepreneurship China" ZhongGuanCun venture leading engineering (2015-2020), the main task was to support Zhongguancun business organization and the innovation resources docking, played advantages in the field of intelligent hardware industrial, and provided entrepreneurial projects and professional personnel.

Manufacturing Enterprise Business. Fujitsu Corporation with and the United States Laboratory of Fujitsu and TechShop held "TechShop inside" activities together. A move maker space was opened to children of all ages, which was equipped with many 24 foot trailers of the prototype processing equipment, it aimed to enhance the students' interest and creativity in the field of science, technology, engineering, art and Mathematics (STEAM), advocated "learning by doing", improved students practice activities and access technology. At the beginning of most maker space establishment, it was non profit and aimed to manufacture DIY and share knowledge, created maker space development environment, provided project incubation space. Maker activity remained in the initial stage of industrialization production and creative realization, therefore it was not really fusion with the China manufacturing enterprise deeply.

Comparison and Analysis for the Business Model of Maker Space Between China and America. Cooperation between our country maker space and government agencies still stayed in policy support stage, it mainly provided incubation environment for makers, while maker space in the United States helped and solved the military project development and Veterans Service with the financial assistance from government, mutual benefit and win-win formed industrial virtuous circle. United States maker space had cooperation with Ford Motor which opened a brand maker space, established the partnerships encouraged employees to develop new car technology by changing the innovative environment. TechShop and Standford D.School had cooperation to open innovation center in order to train students hands-on ability and scientific interest. In China,maker space business development existed "entertainment" phenomenon. Therefore, it was an urgent problem need to be solved that how to strengthen the cooperation business model of maker space, manufacturing enterprises and institutions of higher learning.

4.2 Inspiration from the Comparison for the Brand Model of Maker Space Between China and America

4.2.1 Understanding Maker Space Brand Concept

"The godfather of maker"-MitchAltman said that although he visited different maker spaces around the world, Noisebridge was still his favorite. A lot of maker motions were gathered together by "creative changed to be reality" spontaneously in the United States, it took the maker space as a storm of the entertainment paradise. Compared with the original intention of maker space in China and America, it could be seen that there were still a lot of shortcomings in our country. The maker space in China after "localization" received supports from technology companies and real estate developers, established the entrepreneurial coffee shop and project incubator, it aimed to launch a better idea and get greater commercial value. Too strong idea of starting a business bounded the infinite of creativity, so many fantastic but interesting products of foreign countries were difficult to see in the Chinese market. The future Chinese maker space development needs market leading incubator,also need priority and pure maker space.

4.2.2 Developing a Good Maker Space Brand Team

Counting world-renowned maker space collar army brand, TechShop found by Mark Hatch and Artisan's Asylum found by Gui Cavalcanti could be thought in people's mind. We should enhance the training quality and service level, build a space brand management practice could not be separated from the construction and cultivation of high-quality personnel. With the opening of our country's business services market and policy system, the competition of innovation and entrepreneurship was becoming more and more intense. In this process of competition,cultivating high-quality talent team to develop brand development strategy and seeking greater space for development were problems that our country's makers need to think about.

4.2.3 Improving Brand Security System of Maker Space

NoiseBridge and techshop respectively through member donations, appropriate tuition training courses, as well as strict membership system maintained its own operations, it solved the contradiction between expensive rent and the using of high quality hardware for members, while our country's maker space dependent on government subsidies heavily. Our country should draw lessons from the successful case of the United States, studying and formulating sustainable development of the ecological circle, providing a basis for the development of other space with flexible mode of financing and sound management system.

5 Conclusion

The spirit of maker was collaboration, open source, sharing and cooperation with the entrepreneur to take the ideal into reality. Now the pace of global integration was accelerating, the United States maker activity was rising, the maker culture in China began to take root. China's political environment, investment channels, the training concept of the different formed f a unique development model of localization maker space. Finding the similarities and differences of maker space operation mode between China and America through the network investigation and literature comparison method, get the enlightenment conclusion that our country should clear maker space brand concept, improve maker space brand system construction, cultivate outstanding maker space talent team and improve maker space brand guarantee system. Cultivating a good environment for growth was conducive to the development of our country's maker movement, promoting the innovation of China's industrial and technological level, and achieving the great rejuvenation of the Chinese nation.

References

1. Anderson, C.: Makers: The New Industrial Revolution. Random House Business Books, London (2012)
2. Deyu, W., Jianxin, Y., Shuangshou, L.: Analysis for the operation mode of the domestic maker space. Mod. Educ. Technol. **25**(5), 33–39 (2015)
3. Lina, W., Junmin, F., Qianfei, T., et al.: Study on the maker operation mode in the United States. Sci. Technol. **183**(5), 7–9 (2015)
4. NoiseBridge. https://www.noisebridge.net/wiki/Noisebridge
5. TechShop. http://www.techshop.ws/index.html
6. Garage Cafe. http://www.chekucafe.com/aboutUs
7. ChaiHuo Makerspace. http://www.chaihuo.org/
8. Shuangshou, L., Jianxin, Y., Deyu, W., et al.: The practice of maker space construction in Colleges and universities. Mod. Educ. Technol. **25**(7), 5–11 (2015)
9. Guidance formulated by the general office of the State Council on the development of maker space and promotion of public innovation and entrepreneurship. http://www.gov.cn/zhengce/content/2015-03/11/content_9519.htm
10. Jianxin, Y., Hongbin, S., Shuangshou, L.: Innovative education laboratory of American colleges and the social maker space investigation. Mod. Educ. Technol. (2015)
11. TsinghuaUniversity. http://www.icenter.tsinghua.edu.cn/publish/gyxl/1061/index.html
12. TechShop and Fujitsu Partner to Empower Maker Movement. http://www.fujitsu.com/global/about/resources/news/press-releases/2014/1208-01.html

Cultural Ergonomics

The Influences of Children's Temperament and Their Parent-Child Reading Environment on Their Preferences Regarding Parent-Child Reading

Jo-Han Chang[1(✉)] and Tien-Ling Yeh[2]

[1] Graduate Institute of Innovation and Design, National Taipei University of Technology, Zhongxiao E. Rd., Taipei, Taiwan
johan@ntut.edu.tw

[2] Doctoral Program in Design, College of Design, National Taipei University of Technology, Zhongxiao E. Rd., Taipei, Taiwan
tienling0303@gmail.com

Abstract. Taipei City Government and New Taipei City Government have been actively promoting the project of "one parent-child center per district" to provide parents and children different choices for parent-child reading. Thus, this study aimed to explore the influences of children's temperament and reading environment on children's preference regarding parent-child reading, so that care takers can choose the most appropriate reading environment based on children's preference. A questionnaire survey was conducted in August, 2011 with the subjects being children aged 3 to 7. A total of 119 questionnaires were retrieved. The questionnaire contains three parts: (1) demographic information, (2) children's temperament scale; and (3) parent-child reading environments and scenarios. After field observation, reading environments were categorized into: (1) home: living room and bedroom; and (2) public space: exclusive reading area, subsidiary reading area, and park. And there were 34 scenarios summarized. These categories were used for further analyses. The analysis results are as below: (1) The children of 6 different types of temperament all preferred a bedroom at home and they loved to sit with their parent on the bed or on the floor. In the aspect of public space, the children preferred the subsidiary reading areas in bookstores or wholesale stores and parks. They loved to sit on a chair and face their parent. (2) Children's reading environment and scenario would influence their preference regarding parent-child reading. They preferred a reading area or a subsidiary reading area in a public space.

Keywords: HCI and children · Children's temperament · Parent-child reading · Reading environment

1 Introduction

The earlier a child can form his reading habit, the earlier his reading ability is developed, and the more he is able to enjoy reading (Ke 2006). This trend of developing the reading habit earlier started in 2006, when Hsin-Yi Foundation, Cultural Affairs

P.-L.P. Rau (Ed.): CCD 2016, LNCS 9741, pp. 329–337, 2016.
DOI: 10.1007/978-3-319-40093-8_33

Bureau, Taichung County Government, and Taipei Public Library cooperated on the movement "Bookstart" to encourage parent-child reading, increase children's reading experiences, and help them to develop a habit of life-time reading. In this movement, public libraries play a key role (Chen 2006). However, parent-child reading can be performed not only indoors, but also outdoors as parents can use a park or a balcony as the parent-child reading space, so that children can feel refreshed (Chen 2015). The influence of environments on children's reading is strong. If children can read in a good environment, their interest in reading and the corresponding effects can be increased. Most parents, during their school days, read only text books and nothing else. They didn't form a reading habit before. As a result, their expectations for their children and the school their children go to are all about "grades". For most parents, "reading" equals to reading "extracurricular materials". They don't care about building a reading environment for their children and helping their children to form a reading habit, so that their children can develop the ability to explore (Chen et al. 2010). Ke (1995), a scholar, suggested that reading comprehension covers identification of words, meaning extraction, sentence integration, article comprehension, meta-cognition, and reading attitude. And reading attitude covers preferences for contents and colors of books and reading contexts. Thus, based on the previously described background and motivations, this study explores children's temperament and their preferences for reading contexts, so that their parents can understand what a proper reading environment is to help their children form a reading habit. The main purpose of this study is to explore the influences of children's temperament and their parent-child reading environment on their preferences regarding parent-child reading.

2 Literature Review

2.1 Children's Temperament

A person's temperament is the characteristics of his disposition. Some scholars believed that temperament is inherent (Thomas and Chess 1977). A scholar proposed that a person's temperament is the presentation and response of his individual behaviors (Martin 1988). And another scholar indicated that a person's temperament is the performance of his individual emotions (Chang 1989). Foreign scholars Thomas and Chess started a long-term study from the medical viewpoint, to explore the development and stability of children's temperament. After continuous follow up, it was found that the difference in temperament between early childhood and childhood wasn't significant. The trend was stable. However, individual maturity and interactions with external environments might also leads to changes in children's temperament (Chess and Thomas 1989). According to the previous related studies, a person's temperament can influence him in various ways, including his social interactions with his peers (Wang 1995; Chou 2008; Rudasill 2011). Based on Martin's theory (1996), Wang (2003) modified the child temperament scale used abroad to develop a model for children aged 5 to 6 in Taiwan. In this model, there are 6 temperament dimensions, including distractibility, emotion intensity, approach or withdrawal, activity level, adaptability, and persistence. The validity and reliability of the child temperament scale modified by Wang (1995) were very good. Then, based on the combinations of the temperament dimensions, Wang (2003) proposed 6 major types of temperament, including being concentrated, being quiet, being ordinary, being energetic, being social, and being free. Table 1 shows the characteristics of these temperament types based on the above-mentioned dimensions. This study adopted the child temperament scale modified by Wang as the research tool.

Table 1. The characteristics of the temperament types based on dimensions

Dimension/type	Ordinary	Social	Concentrated	Free	Energetic	Quiet
Activity level	Medium	Medium	Low	Low	High	Low
Adaptability	Medium	High	Medium	High	Medium	Medium
Approach or withdrawal	Medium	High	Medium	High	Medium	Low
Emotion intensity	Medium	Medium	Low	Medium	High	Low
Distractibility	Medium	Low	Low	Low	High	Medium
Persistence	Low	Medium	High	High	Low	Medium

2.2 Context

Schools are the first unit children ever learn about socialization. Thus, in terms of promoting children's reading, besides home, school learning environments are also essential. Other than at home, children can also read in a library (Lin 2002; Yen 2002). The research by Von Sprecken and Krashen (1988) with the students from the reading courses found that if books are easy to access, 90 % of children would choose to read. In a reading area, placing some soft materials such as mats, carpets, and bolsters and a lot of books and making the environment warm with decorations can help increase children's willingness to enter this area (Huang 2004; Lo 2005; Yen 2008; Liao 2011). Furthermore, good lighting helps to increase motivations to read, as children can be more concentrated, and their reading effects can be improved (Shiao 1995).

- Parent-Child Reading Space
  According to the previous description, children need a rich collection of books and warm reading atmosphere for reading. It would be even better if there can be an exclusive reading space (corner) for children. Setting up a reading corner can not only motivate children to read, but also help them to form a reading habit. A reading corner should be set up within the range of children's activities, such as a study room or a place next to the bed in a bedroom at home and the children's reading area in a library or a bookstore. In cases such as having an outing, some children's books can be brought alone in order to build an environment where books which can be accessed conveniently, so that children's reading habit and attitude can be developed easily (Wan 2013).
- Furniture for Parent-Child Reading
  When reading, children can hardly sit upright in the same place for a long time. Thus, it is important that the furniture used for parent-child reading must be able to attract children, of the proper size, and with many variations. When children read on

the floor, some mats, soft cushions, and bolsters can not only offer them support but also keep them safe. When children read in a place like a living room, a study room, or a library, a sofa or a set of classroom table and chair can be considered based on the reading atmosphere. During the time for a bed time story, a cozy bed and a pillow can help to create warm and comfortable atmosphere and improve the interactions and intimacy between parents and children (Wan 2013).

3 Research Methods

The research methods adopted include the questionnaire survey method and statistical methods. After considering the interactions between children and their caretakers and their ability to understand the content of the books for parent-child reading, this study decided to issue the questionnaires to the caretakers of children at pre-school age (children at 3–7 years).

3.1 Questionnaire Survey

1. Questionnaire Design

The questionnaire contains three parts, basic information, child temperament scale, and parent-child reading contexts.

- Basic information: The items in this part include gender and age of the child and his caretaker as well as the relationship between them.
- Child temperament scale: This study focused on the children of ordinary temperament. Thus, the "Child Temperament Scale" developed by Lin, Tung, and Wang from National Taiwan Normal University based on the scale proposed by R. P. Martin from the University of Georgia, USA was used. This scale is for children of 3–7 years. There are 48 items in total. They are categorized into 6 categories: activity level, adaptability, emotion intensity, distractibility, approach or withdrawal, and persistence. Each category contains both positively and negatively worded items. The assessments are based on the Likert 7-point scaling. After the assessments, children can be classified into 6 categories: children of ordinary, social, concentrated, free, energetic, and quiet temperament (Wang 2006).
- Parent-child reading contexts: According to the literature, this study made some assumptions regarding parent-child reading contexts with parents and children in different spaces with different relative positions (Fig. 1). The assumed contexts include home spaces and public spaces. Home spaces include a living room (or a study room) and a bedroom. Public spaces include an exclusive reading area (in a library or a public childcare center), a subsidiary reading area (in a bookstore or a hypermarket), and a park (open space). Each of them is represented by a capital letter. For every space, there are cases with and without furniture (chairs or a bed). Each case is represented by a lowercase letter. The parent-child relative positions include the child sitting in the parent's arms, the child sitting next to the parent, the child sitting opposite to the parent, and the child sitting 90 degrees to the parent.

Each relative position is represented by a number. Table 2 shows an example. After excluding the contexts which are less likely to happen due to space limitations, there are a total of 34 parent-child reading contexts. The Likert 5-point scaling was used for assessments, with 5 options: strongly agree, agree, neutral, disagree, and strongly disagree. The participants were asked to answer the questions based on their previous parent-child reading experiences.

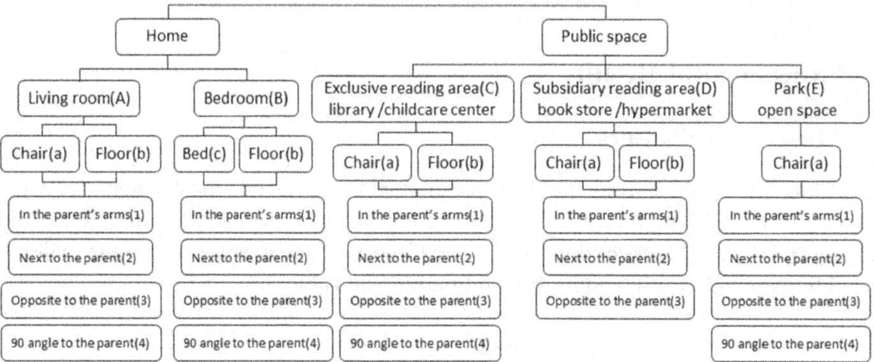

Fig. 1. The parent-child reading context assumptions

Table 2. An example of a parent-child reading context

Context	Code
The child sitting in the parent's arms on the chair in the living room	1 A a 1

2. Participants and Survey Duration

- Subjects: Caretakers with experiences with children aged 3 to 7 (pre-school age)
- Number of questionnaires issued: 119
- Duration: August, 2013
- Sampling method: Convenience sampling

3.2 Statistical Analysis

1. Descriptive statistics: Basic statistics of the data.
2. Descriptive Statistics and ANOVA:
   - Whether there is an influence of child temperament on children's preferences regarding parent-child reading
   - Whether there is an influence of reading contexts on children's preferences regarding parent-child reading.

4 Experimental Result

4.1 Descriptive Statistics

According to the data from the 119 questionnaires retrieved, most caretakers were female (74.79 %). Children were mostly accompanied by their mother in parent-child reading (68.07 %). Most children were male (56.3 %). The average age of the children was 4.9 years old. These results are summarized in Table 3.

Table 3. Basic information statistics

Variable\statistics	Option	Number of people	Percentage
Gender of caretaker	Male	29	24.37
	Female	89	74.79
Caretaker-child relationship	Father and son/daughter	28	23.53
	Mother and son/daughter	81	68.07
	Grandparent and grandchild	2	1.68
	Other	5	4.2
Gender of child	Male	67	56.3
	Female	51	42.86
Age of child	(Average)	4.9	–

4.2 Results of ANOVA

Children's temperament did influence their preferences regarding parent-child reading. The homogeneity passed the test ($P > 0.05$). And the ANOVA result showed significant differences ($P < 0.05$). Items with significant differences are summarized in Tables 4, 5 and 6.

Table 4. One-way ANOVA of the preference test results regarding children's temperament

Context code		Sum of squares	Degree of freedom	Sum of mean squares	F test	Significance
10	Room, bed, set next to parents	6.698	5	1.340	3.011	.015
14	Bedroom, floor, next to parent	6.581	5	1.316	2.455	.044
27	Subsidiary reading area, chair, opposite to parent	23.263	5	4.653	6.046	.000
33	Park, chair, next to parent	12.732	5	2.546	2.579	.049

Table 5. Descriptive statistics of the preference test results regarding children's temperament

Context code	Child temperament	Average	Standard deviation	Min	Max
10	Ordinary	3.3333	1.92605	.00	5.00
	Social	3.1111	2.36878	.00	5.00
	Concentrated	3.3636	2.20330	.00	5.00
	Free	3.8889	2.20479	.00	5.00
	Energetic	**4.5000**	.70711	4.00	5.00
	Quiet	4.4583	2.06375	.00	5.00
14	Ordinary	2.4127	2.12993	.00	5.00
	Social	1.6667	2.50000	.00	5.00
	Concentrated	1.7273	2.41209	.00	5.00
	Free	1.6667	2.50000	.00	5.00
	Energetic	**4.5000**	.70711	4.00	5.00
	Quiet	2.9167	3.34816	.00	5.00
27	Ordinary	1.0952	1.62356	.00	5.00
	Social	1.5556	2.35112	.00	5.00
	Concentrated	2.1818	2.52262	.00	5.00
	Free	.1111	.33333	.00	1.00
	Energetic	**3.0000**	.00000	3.00	3.00
	Quiet	2.4167	5.56321	.00	5.00
33	Ordinary	.9683	1.52367	.00	5.00
	Social	1.0000	2.00000	.00	5.00
	Concentrated	1.6364	2.33550	.00	5.00
	Free	.5556	1.66667	.00	5.00
	Energetic	**3.0000**	1.41421	2.00	4.00
	Quiet	2.1250	6.75865	.00	5.00

Table 6. The preference test results regarding reading contexts

Context code		Sum of squares	Degree of freedom	Sum of mean squares	F test	Significance
17–24	Exclusive reading space (library or childcare center)	43.015	7	6.145	7.830	.000
25–30	Subsidiary reading space (bookstore or hypermarket)	28.946	5	5.789	6.604	.000

5 Conclusion and Discussion

5.1 Child Temperament Preferences

According to the statistical analysis results, among the home spaces, the children of the 6 different types of temperament all preferred to read in a bedroom. They liked to sit on the floor or the bed with their parent. Among the public spaces, the children preferred the reading area in a bookstore or a hypermarket or a park. They liked to sit on a chair opposite to their parent's seat. The descriptive statistics showed that the energetic children's preference for parent-child reading environments was significant, while the preference of the children of all the other temperament was not. The research subjects of this study were pre-school children aged 3–7. The differences among the children of different types of temperament weren't significant. They hadn't yet been influenced by interactions from environments. The differences in the preference for a parent-child reading environment among the children of different types of temperament were small. These findings are consistent with what the study by Thomas and Chess had found. Future studies can focus on children aged 7 or above, as the differences in reading preferences among children of different types of temperament in this age group may be more significant due to the influences of their maturity and environmental factors.

5.2 Parent-Child Reading Space Preferences

The most common parent-child reading space was a space at home, followed by an exclusive reading area in a library or a public childcare center. Similar to the findings of the two previously mentioned scholars (Lin 2002; Yen 2002), parent-child reading has become a common practice. Children prefer subsidiary reading areas in bookstores and hypermarkets. To create a reading space, besides making it comfortable, if books in that space are easy to access, 90 % of children would read in that space (Von Sprecken and Krashen 1988). This way, it would be easier to help children form a reading habit and improve their reading attitude.

References

Chan, C.C., Li, Y.C., Tseng, P.F.: A study of developing indicators and evaluation tools for reading literacy of children in Taiwan. RDEC Bimonthly **34**(1), 48–61 (2010)

Chan, Y.C.: Public library and babies' reading campaign: bookstart as an example. Bull. Taipei Public Library **24**(1), 97–100 (2006)

Chen, Y.H.: Benesse (2015). http://www.benesse.com.tw/educate/essay.asp?vid=4280

Chou, S.Y.: The Relationship between temperament and problem behaviors in elementary school children. Master's dissertation, Graduate Institute of Family Education and Counseling, National Chiayi University, unpublished, Chiayi City (2008)

Huang, Y.W.: The Post-Occupancy Evaluation of Using and Planning of Instructional Resource Centers: A Case Study of An Elementary School in Chiayi City, Graduate Institute of Educational Technology, National Chiayi University, Chiayi City, pp. 154–155 (2004)

Ke, H.W.: "Reading Ability Development". In: Tseng, J.S (ed.) An Introduction to Language Pathology, p. 80. Psychological Publishing, Taipei City (1995)

Ke, H.W.: Teaching Reading Literacy, Common Wealth, books.com.tw (2006). http://www.books.com.tw/products/0010346607. Accessed 8 Feb 2015

Liao, Y.L.: "Give Me Five Happy Reading" – a study on improving children's reading activities in order to increase their interest in reading. Early Childhood Educ. **301**, 25–41 (2011)

Lin, M.C.: An investigation of elementary students' interests in reading in ping-tung county. In: Master's dissertation, unpublished, Pingtung (2002)

Lo, C.F.: The Use of Reading Environment among Preschool Teachers in Taichung City, Graduate Institute of Early Childhood Development and Education, Chaoyang University of Technology, Taichung City, pp. 112–115 (2005)

Martin, S.R.: The Relationship between temperament ratings and behavior problems in preschool children. Unpublished Doctoral dissertation, State University of Georgia (1996)

Martin, R.P.: Assessment of Personality and Behavior Problems: Infancy Through Adolescence. Guilford Press, New York (1988)

Rudasill, K.M.: Child temperament, teacher–child interactions, and teacher–child relationships: a longitudinal investigation from first to third grade. Early Childhood Res. Q. **26**, 147–156 (2013)

Shiao, H.C.: The current status and improvement solutions regarding classroom lighting. Educ. Mon. **333**, 13–17 (1995)

Thomas, A., Chess, S.: Temperament and Development. Brunner, New York

Thomas, A., Chess, S.: Temperament and its functional significance. Course Life **2**(7), 163–228 (1989)

Von Sprecken, D., Krashen, S.: Do students read during sustained silent reading? Calif. Readers **32**(1), 11–13 (1988)

Wang, P. T.: Early Childhood Development and Counseling Assessment Amount. Psychology, Taipei (1995)

Wang, P.T.: Infant Temperament: the Basic Characteristics and Social Composition. Psychology, Taipei (2003)

Wang, P. T.: Children Feeding on Story Books, Taiwan (2013)

Xing, Z.C.: Zhang psychology dictionary. Donghua, Taipei (1989)

Yan, L., Zhang, J.: On influence of developmentally appropriate book comer upon children's reading interest and habit. Early Childhood Educ. **10**, 25–29 (2008)

Yen, M.F.: An Investigation of Elementary 6th-grade Students" Intertests in Reading in Taipei County. Master's dissertation, in-service master's program, Department of Adult & Continuing Education, National Taiwan Normal University, unpublished, Taipei (2002)

Influence of Media Forms on Painting Appreciation Experiences

Si-Jing Chen[1], Chih-Long Lin[2(✉)], Sandy Lee[3], and Yen-Yu Kang[4]

[1] Graduate School of Creative Industry Design, National Taiwan University of Arts, New Taipei City 22058, Taiwan
Jing0503@gmail.com

[2] Department of Crafts and Design, National Taiwan University of Arts, New Taipei City 22058, Taiwan
CL.Lin@ntua.edu.tw

[3] Painter, Lee Studio, New Taipei City 24301, Taiwan
slee@mail.mcut.edu.tw

[4] Department of Industrial Design, National Kaohsiung Normal University, Kaohsiung City 82446, Taiwan
yenyu@nknu.edu.tw

Abstract. This study mainly investigates the influence of different media presentation forms on viewers' perception, preference, and viewing time. This study enrolled 15 male and 15 female subjects to participate in the experiment. The independent variables included gender (male and female) and media forms of paintings. The media forms included four factors: original paintings, planar presentation of paintings, screen presentation of paintings, and picture book of paintings. The experimental results showed that, the gender factor did not have significant influence on all the measurement variables. Media forms had significant influence on 4 indices; "viewing paintings arbitrarily," "paintings reflected a sense of value," "preference for paintings," and "viewing time" ($p < 0.05$). According to the research results of this study, the sense of value reflected by original paintings was the highest, and they were most preferred by viewers. It is advised to provide proper painting titles and good viewing environment during exhibition of paintings to help viewers develop pleasant emotions and further increase their preference for paintings.

Keywords: Painting · Media forms · Viewing time · Preference

1 Introduction

From the point of ergonomics, the human performance and preference would be affected by media form. For text reading task, Mayes et al. (2001) show that subjects take longer to read text on a screen than on paper. As for accuracy, Egan et al. (1989) report that students using digital hypertext on a screen to find out specific information in the text had higher accuracy than students using the paper text. For reading comprehension, Dillon and Gabbard (1998) conclude that comprehension when reading from a screen is better than reading from paper when performing substantial searching or manipulation and comparison of visual details among objects. However, Cushman (1986) finds that

P.-L.P. Rau (Ed.): CCD 2016, LNCS 9741, pp. 338–344, 2016.
DOI: 10.1007/978-3-319-40093-8_34

visual fatigue is significantly higher with when reading black objects on a white screen background than reading paper. In addition, Martin and Platt (2001) also found that the medical school students still prefer to read from paper rather than from a screen.

Moreover, the better image quality of display could improve visual task performance and reduce visual fatigue. Menozzi *et al.* (2001) reported that using liquid crystal display (LCD) caused fewer errors in visual search tasks than using cathode ray tube (CRT) display. Wang and Huang (2004) also found that using LCD display for after etching inspection (AEI) showed less eye fatigue and better accuracy than using CRT display. This is due to the better image quality and higher refresh rate of the TFT-LCD display. Further, Takahashi (2006) compared the display effect on visual acuity after one-hundred minutes TV program watching, and found that watching LCD display had a significantly higher decrease in visual acuity than that of watching plasma display. The behavior of TV program watching is different from TV game playing, and the users tend to have higher motivation, attention and concentration on video game playing. However, information about the evaluation of a plasma display and CRT display for video game playing on visual fatigue and mental workload is lacking. For visuospatial task, Van Orden and Broyles (2000) compared the visuospatial task performance of participants who used seven types of two-dimensional (2-D) and three-dimensional (3-D) displays. The authors reported that, overall, the task performance of participants who used the 2-D plan, or side-view, display type was more favorable than the task performance of participants who used any other display system, but the 3-D volumetric display type was more suitable for participants performing integration and prediction tasks in a limited 3-D space.

However, previous studies did not consider whether the human behavior and preference of the painting watching would be similar to that of the functional visual task. This study mainly investigates the influence of different media presentation forms on viewers' perception, preference, and viewing time while watching a painting.

2 Methods

2.1 Subjects

This study enrolled 15 male and 15 female subjects to participate in the experiment. The ages of the participants ranged from 18 to 40 years (mean = 23.23, SD = 4.41). The mean age of male participants was 22.20 (SD = 3.85) years. The mean age of female participants was 24.27 (SD = 4.71) years.

2.2 Experimental Design

The independent variables included gender (male and female) and media forms of paintings. The media forms included 4 factors: original paintings, planar presentation of paintings, screen presentation of paintings, and picture book of paintings. For original paintings, this study used 21 pieces of oil paintings of Ms. Li, a novice painter who had learned painting for 5 years, as the experimental samples; 9 of the paintings were landscape paintings, and 12 were abstract paintings, and all of the paintings were

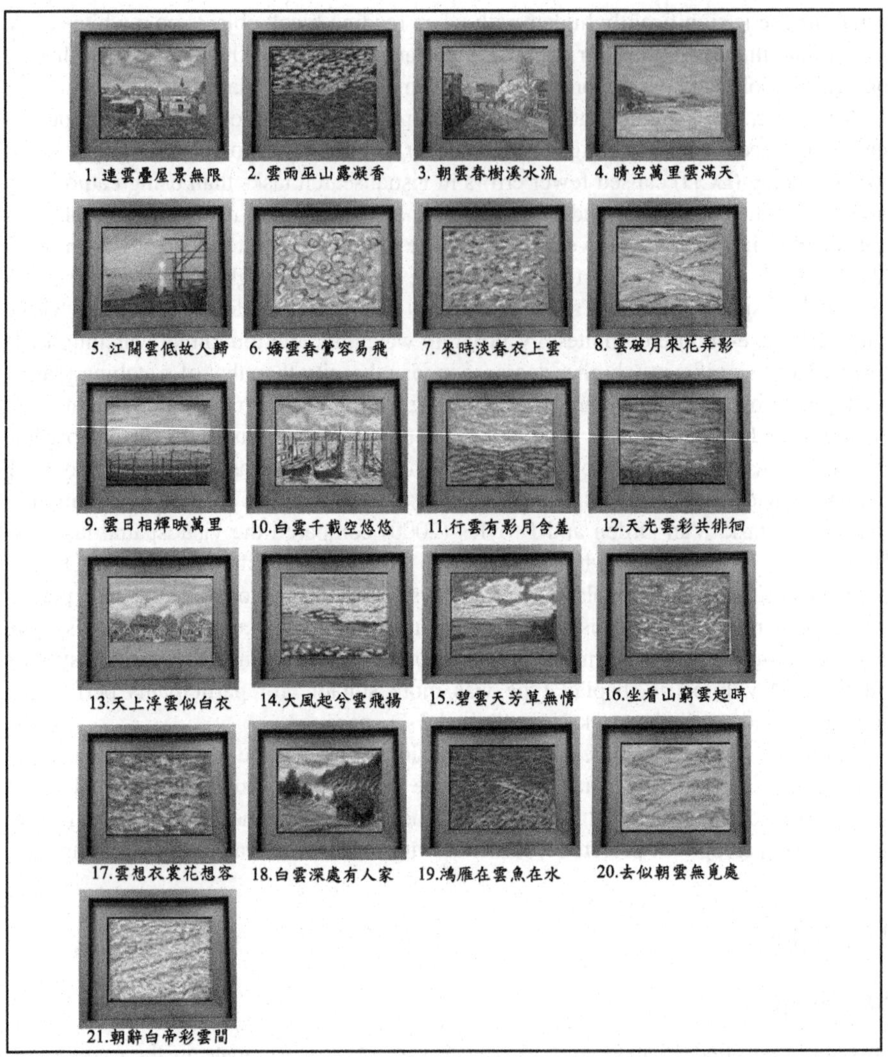
1. 連雲疊屋景無限
2. 雲雨巫山露凝香
3. 朝雲春樹溪水流
4. 晴空萬里雲滿天
5. 江闊雲低故人歸
6. 嬌雲春鶯容易飛
7. 來時淡春衣上雲
8. 雲破月來花弄影
9. 雲日相輝映萬里
10.白雲千載空悠悠
11.行雲有影月含羞
12.天光雲彩共徘徊
13.天上浮雲似白衣
14.大風起兮雲飛揚
15..碧雲天芳草無情
16.坐看山窮雲起時
17.雲想衣裳花想容
18.白雲深處有人家
19.鴻雁在雲魚在水
20.去似朝雲無覓處
21.朝辭白帝彩雲間

Fig. 1. Twenty-One original paintings and corresponding titles

displayed in frames of the same style (as shown in Fig. 1). Regarding the planar presentation of paintings, 21 original paintings pieces were scanned into electronic image files using the scanner (CRUSE-CS185ST 1100), which were output into planar images of A1 size (84.1 cm * 59.4 cm) using the HP designjet 5000. Afterwards, they were displayed in the same aluminum frames (as shown in Fig. 2). Regarding the screen presentation of paintings, the electronic image files of paintings were converted into a briefing file, and presented using a 37-inch LCD TV (Panasonic TC-37MPJ), as shown in Fig. 3. Regarding the picture book of paintings, the paintings were bound in a picture book with a spread page size of 60 cm * 30 cm. Each painting piece was presented on a

Fig. 2. One sample of planar paintings (right side: a painting displayed in aluminum frames; left side: the planar painting zooms in partly).

Fig. 3. The screen presentation of paintings (right side: a painting displayed in a 37-inch LCD TV; left side: the screen painting zooms in partly).

Fig. 4. The picture book of paintings (upper side: a painting displayed in a book; lower side: a partial enlarged view).

spread page and a partial enlarged view on another spread page. Therefore, the picture book included 21 paintings pieces, and 84 pages in total (as shown in Fig. 4).

There were two measuring variables in this study: one was the questionnaire survey on subjective perception, and the other was the record of viewing behavior. The questionnaire included basic information (gender, age, and the highest level of education) and the scale on painting viewing experience (6 items on the perception of the viewing process and 5 items on evaluation of paintings). The latter used a 5-point scale for scoring, where 1 denoted strongly disagree, 2 denoted disagree, 3 denoted neutral, 4 denoted agree, and 5 denoted strongly agree. Moreover, in order to evaluate viewing behavior, this study concurrently used a stopwatch to record the time spent viewing the 21 painting pieces by the subjects.

2.3 Experimental Procedure

The experimental sites of this study were the exhibition space and office. The original pieces of paintings and planar presentation of paintings were displayed in an exhibition space, while a screen presentation of paintings and the picture book of paintings were viewed in the office. Every subject was randomized to determine their order of experimental combination. The subjects could adjust the time spent viewing each piece of painting according to their preference. During the appreciation of original paintings or planar presentation of paintings, the subjects had to walk around in the exhibition space. When reading the picture book, the subjects had to turn the pages with their hands. When watching the screen, the subjects had to hold the wireless presenter (Logitech R400) and press "Page Up" and "Page Down" buttons to present the paintings. After viewing the 21 pieces of paintings, the subjects recorded the viewing time and completed the questionnaire. Afterwards, the subjects viewed the paintings under another experimental condition. The subjects only received two experimental combinations each time, and received the other two experimental combinations one week later.

3 Results

The analysis of variance results in Table 1 reveal that the gender factor did not have significant influence on all the measurement variables, suggesting that the opinions on issues and viewing behaviors between male and female subjects were the same. Media forms had significant influence on 4 indices; "viewing paintings arbitrarily" ($p < .05$), "paintings reflected a sense of value" ($p < .01$), "preference for paintings" ($p < .05$), and "viewing time" ($p < .001$).

The Duncan grouping results indicate that the "viewing paintings arbitrarily" for the four media forms can be classified into two groups. The first group, with the higher scores was for original painting and planar painting. The second group, with the lower scores was for screen painting and book painting. As can be seen in the table, the average "viewing paintings arbitrarily" scores for the original painting and planar painting is 4.43 and 4.40, respectively; the scores for the screen painting and book painting is 3.97 and 4.10, respectively. In other words, the original painting and planar

Table 1. The corresponding mean values of measurements under media forms and gender effects.

Measurements		Gender		Media Forms				
		Female	Male	Original painting	Planar painting	Screen painting	Book painting	Significance
Questionnaire (1 ~ 5 score)	Emotional delighted	3.87	3.57	3.90	3.77	3.70	3.50	
	Emotional relaxation	3.97	3.92	3.93	3.93	4.07	3.83	
	Emotional calmness	4.05	4.12	4.10	4.07	4.17	4.00	
	I can view paintings arbitrarily	4.22	4.23	**4.43**[a]	**4.40**[a]	**3.97**[b]	**4.10**[b]	*
	The painting is unique	3.43	3.62	3.67	3.50	3.30	3.63	
	The paintings are attractive	3.50	3.38	3.63	3.23	3.47	3.43	
	The paintings reflected a sense of value	3.22	3.50	**3.80**[a]	**3.00**[c]	**3.33**[b]	**3.30**[b]	**
	I can feel cloud meaning	3.78	4.05	3.97	3.87	3.93	3.90	
	Painting titles can help improve preference	3.53	3.55	3.73	3.43	3.53	3.47	
	I want the painting in my house	3.73	3.93	4.03	3.73	3.80	3.77	
	Preference for paintings	3.57	3.55	**3.77**[a]	**3.47**[b]	**3.57**[b]	**3.43**[b]	*
Viewing behavior	Viewing time (second)	364.97	420.13	**412.17**[b]	**364.73**[b]	**282.17**[c]	**511.13**[a]	***

*Significant at $p < .05$, **Significant at $p < .01$, ***Significant at $p < .001$. a, b, c means Duncan grouping results.

painting score is about 0.5 higher than that for the screen painting and book painting. The Duncan grouping results indicate that the "paintings reflected a sense of value" for the four media forms can be classified into three groups. The first group, with the highest score was for original painting, followed by screen painting, book painting and planar painting. The original painting score is about 0.8 higher than that for the planar painting. The Duncan grouping results indicate that the "preference for paintings" for the four media forms can be classified into two groups. The first group, with the higher scores was for original painting. The second group, with the lower scores was for screen painting, planar painting and book painting. The Duncan grouping results indicate that the "viewing time" for the four media forms can be classified into three groups. The first group, with the longest time was for book painting, followed by original painting, planar painting and screen painting. The viewing time for the screen painting is about 55 % shorter than that of the book painting.

The present results provide evidence that the media form affects some painting viewing experience and viewing behavior. The painting value was substantially decreased under the planar painting compared with that the original painting. In addition, viewing time was greatest when participants watch the book painting than when they watch the other three painting forms.

4 Conclusion

According to the research results of this study, the sense of value reflected by original paintings was the highest, and they were most preferred by viewers. It is advised to provide proper painting titles and good viewing environment during exhibition of paintings to help viewers develop pleasant emotions and further increase their preference for paintings.

Acknowledgements. The authors gratefully acknowledge the support for this research provided by the Ministry of Science and Technology, Taiwan under Grants MOST-103-2410-H-144 -003 -MY2. The authors also wish to thank those who contributed to the research.

References

Cushman, W.H.: Reading from microfiche, a VDT, and the printed page: subjective fatigue and performance. Hum. Factors **28**, 63–73 (1986)

Dillon, A., Gabbard, R.: Hypermedia as an educational technology: a review of the quantitative research literature learner comprehension, control, and style. Review of Educational Research **68**(3), 322–349 (1998)

Egan, D.E., Remde, J.R., Landauer, T.K., Lochbaum, C.C., Gomez, L.M.: Behavioral evaluation and analysis of a hypertext browser. In: Proceedings of CHI 1989, Association for Computing Machinery, pp. 205–210, New York (1989)

Martin, L.A., Platt, M.W.: Printing and screen reading in the medical school curriculum: Guttenberg vs. the cathode ray tube. Behaviour and Information Technology **20**, 143–148 (2001)

Mayes, D.K., Sims, V.K., Koonce, J.M.: Comprehension and workload differences for VDT and paper-based reading. Int. J. Ind. Ergon. **28**(6), 367–378 (2001)

Menozzi, M., Lang, F., Naepflin, U., Zeller, C., Krueger, H.: CRT versus LCD: effects of refresh rate, display technology and background luminance in visual performance. Displays **22**, 79–85 (2001)

Takahashi, M.: Ergonomic issues in picture quality improvement in flat panel TVs. In: Nikkei Microdevices' Flat Panel Display: 2006, pp. 58–63. InterLingua Educational Publishing (2006)

Van Orden, K.F., Broyles, J.W.: Visuospatial task performance as a function of two- and three-dimensional display presentation techniques. Displays **21**, 17–24 (2000)

Wang, M.J.J., Huang, C.L.: Evaluating the eye fatigue problem in wafer inspection. IEEE Trans. Semicond. Manuf. **17**, 444–447 (2004)

From "Idyllic" to "Living Space"—Turning "Art Work" into "Interior Design"

Ya-Juan Gao[1(✉)], Yun Lin[2], Li-Yu Chen[3], and David Chang Hsi Dai[4]

[1] Graduate School of Creative Industry Design, National Taiwan University of Arts, Ban Ciao City, Taipei 22058, Taiwan
78343821@qq.com

[2] TOFF Group, Fuzhou, People's Republic of China
linyun@toff.com.cn

[3] Department of Interior Design, Chung Yuan Christian University, Taoyuan, Taiwan
chenly99@gmail.com

[4] Department of Liberal Studies, California State University, Pomona, USA

Abstract. "Idyllic", which literally means a quality suggestive of the poetic and picturesque, is used as the criterion with which to evaluate a Chinese painting. For living space, the product should also fit into a context of living environment and meet user requirements. Idyllic describes the arts striving toward perfection, beauty and refinement in all aspects of life. Transforming "idyllic" into "living space" involves more than considering the interior design itself. It remains a challenge to represent use contexts and user needs in a way that designers with technical backgrounds are able to make direct use of them. When designing "arts" into "business", we need a better understanding of human-art interaction not just for taking part in the humanity context, but also for developing the interactive experience of arts. Therefore, a general framework is proposed for interior design that applies to representing human-art interactions and translating aesthetics into user requirements in an interior design case. The intended purpose of this paper is to provide a framework for examining the way designers interact across the art and interactive experiences of users in the design process.

Keywords: User experience · Interior design · Idyllic style · Aesthetics

1 Introduction

In an era emphasizing aesthetics experience, both the developed countries with mature economic and cultural development and the newly emerging countries which try to break through the industry positioning aggressively have all sensed that cultural creativity can increase the entire economic growth, enhance industry competitiveness, inherit cultural assets and create high added value in the country's image. Many international enterprises, in this trend of industry transformation, have devoted themselves to the guidance of local culture the global market (Chang et al. 2013). In the global market - local design era, connections between arts and aesthetic design have become increasingly close. For local design, culture and arts value-adding creates the core of local design value. It's the same for the global market; local design is the motivation for pushing culture and arts

P.-L.P. Rau (Ed.): CCD 2016, LNCS 9741, pp. 345–354, 2016.
DOI: 10.1007/978-3-319-40093-8_35

forward in global market development (Lin and Chen 2012). When we think about "globalization" we must think "localization" for the market (Lin 2011).

Multiple studies in the areas of cross-cultural behavioral and cognitive psychology continue to uncover significant differences in the way people behave, think, assign value, and engage others (Lin 2007, 2009, 2011). Understanding culture and cross-cultural behavioral is thus vital in the design field. "Culture" plays an important role in the design field, and "cross cultural design" will be a key design evaluation point in the future. Designing "culture" into modern products will be a design trend in the global market. Obviously, we need a better understanding of cross-cultural communication not only for the global market, but also for local design. While cross-cultural factors become important issues for product design in the global economy, the intersection of design and culture becomes a key issue making both local design and the global market worthy of further in-depth study (Lin 2007).

Despite the recognized importance of aesthetic design in cultural and creative design industries, they lack a systematic approach to it (Monk and Lelos 2007). Obviously, we need a better understanding of human-arts communications not only for the global market, but also for local design. While cross-cultural issues become important for product design in the global economy, the intersection of design and culture becomes a key issue making both local design and the global market worthy of further in-depth study (Lin and Lin 2010). Therefore, this study focuses on the analysis of art works in which the aesthetic elements are used. Then, a framework is proposed to provide designers with a valuable reference for designing a successful cultural product (Smyth and Wallace 2000). Results presented herein create an interface for examining the way designers communicate across art work as well as the interwoven experience of incorporating design and aesthetics into the design process.

2 Framework for Turning "Art Work" into "Interior Design"

Based on Lin's studies (Chen et al. 2014, 2015), turning poetry into painting involves complex issues that are interdisciplinary in nature. The issues are with nature: it appears to be suitable for "reading" in different ways, and multiple perspectives are available by analyzing them. A research framework was proposed as shown in Fig. 1 – this is used in a continuous search for a deeper understanding of the nature of turning poetry into painting, and for which some conjectures can be tested. Some of the outstanding notes state here. (1) Significance: the art work and interior design can express a kind of significance; that is, the designer's intentions can indeed be expressed through the art work and interior design. (2) Expression: Interior design may represent the poet and artist's feelings; through the art works, the artist's imaginations, thoughts, and feelings can be reproduced. Designers can express through artwork for Idyllic style to turn into the interior space presented. (3) Communication: the results of signification and expression can be sent to the viewer only when the Interior Designer and the viewer's thoughts are identical (Fiske 2013; Norman 2004).

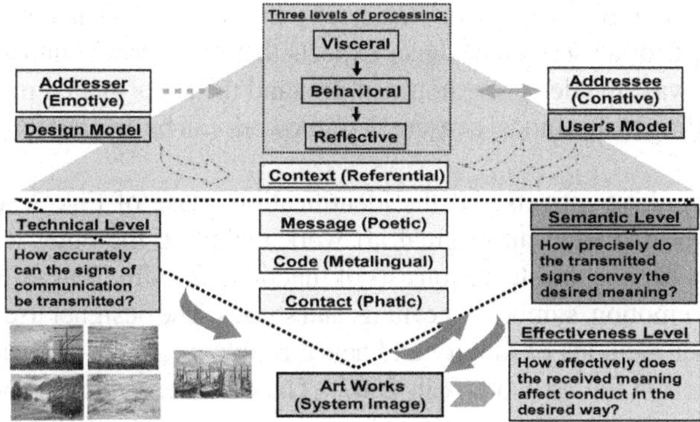

Fig. 1. Communication model for turning poetry into painting (Lin et al. 2015)

It is worthy of our curiosity - How do artists express themselves through "Poetry" and how do they create landscapes, poetry, lyrics, or drawings through "Painting." Professor Lin's study (Lin 2007, 2009, 2011; Lin and Chen 2012; Lin and Lin 2010), described a research framework combining communication theory with communication and mental models. The framework was proposed to explore the issue of turning poetry into painting as shown in Fig. 1. An artist (addresser) sends a message to an audience (addressee) through his/her artwork, through the analysis of the four constitutive factors context (referential), message (poetic), code (metalingual), contact (phatic). Norman (2004) proposed three levels of processing: visceral, behavioral and reflective.

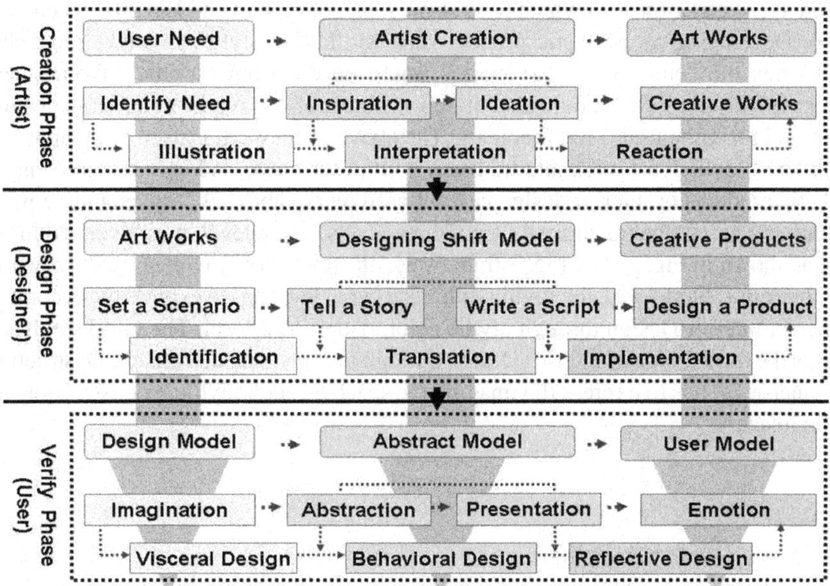

Fig. 2. Research framework for turning poetry into painting (Lin's teaching materials 2016)

This communication model is for turning poetry into painting. Thus, when a designer designs a product for a user, the designer expects that the user will understand and use it in the desired way; the designer should understand the use's mental model as Shown in Fig. 2. According to this model a research framework can be created for turning poetry into painting.

From the cognitive models and the identification phase of Fig. 2, art and design features are identified from an original art work including the outer-level of colors, texture, and pattern. The mid-level consists of function, usability, and safety. The inner-level consists of emotion, symbolic meaning, and stories. The designer uses the scientific method and other methods of inquiry and hence is able to obtain, evaluate, and utilize art information from the art work (Lin 2007). The designer achieves some depth and experience of practice in these art features and at the same time is able to relate the art elements to design problems in modern society. This produces an appreciation for the interaction between arts, technology, and society (Lin 2007). It expresses the art elements that are associated with the artistic features, the meaning of the chosen art work, the aesthetic sensibilities, and the flexibility to adapt to various designs. Good use can be made of it in design practice by converting artwork into interior design products. Thus, in the deep design space of Poetry and Painting, how designers turn the poetic mood into living space and how "Art Work" is turned in "Interior Design are worthy of study and practice and may be based on the above theoretical basis and practical methods (Chen et al. 2014, 2015).

"Poetry" comes from "Painting," "Painting" displays "Poetry," "Poetry" overflows in "Painting," and "Painting" surpasses "Poetry." "Idyllic" is commonly used to describe the beauty of natural landscape and the mood of paintings. The idiom of the "Idyllic" (詩情畫意, shi-qing-hua-yi), which literally means the quality of poetry and picturesque, is used as the criterion with which to evaluate a painting (Yeh and Lin 2014; Yeh et al. 2014). Developing an aesthetic product such as "Idyllic style", involves more than considering the "culture" or "art work." Based on the word "Idyllic", the aesthetic product or "Idyllic style" should also fit into a context of "art work" or cultural meaning in use and meet the users' requirements. The above framework is used as an approach to explore "Idyllic" art work and translate it into user needs and user requirements in aesthetic products or interior design cases. Based on the above theory, cognitive mode and cultural art can be transformed from three levels: outer-level, mid-level and inner-level as shown in Fig. 3. The Fig. 3 framework illustrates how to transform "Art work" into "Interior Design" with the Idyllic style. The outer-level has to express the decorative surface of interior Design through idyllic color, pattern and form. The mid-level has to express the furnishings of interior Design through idyllic elements and idyllic structure. The inner-level has to express the imaginative space through idyllic reconstruction and idyllic imagery.

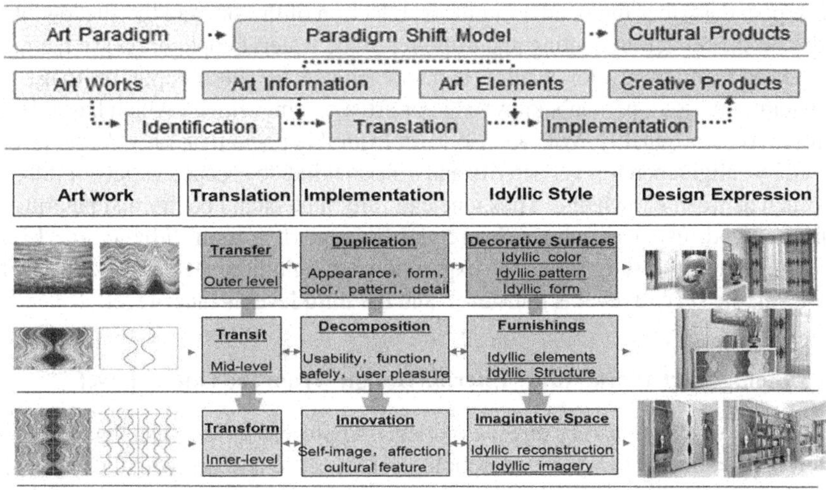

Fig. 3. Framework for turning “art work” into “interior design”

3 A Case Study of Turning “Idyllic” to “Living Space”

Based on Lin’s research (Chen et al. 2014, 2015), after the experimental analysis of the results during the exhibition, the painting entitled “Reflected Sunlight and Cloud Shadow Lingered Over and Over” as shown in the right at Fig. 4 was chosen from a painting exhibition (at the left of Fig. 4).

Fig. 4. Exhibition for turning poetry into painting

This poem comes from the Southern Song Dynasty poet Zhu Xi’s concept of “The Book”. Professor Xu Yuanchong (Xu 1997) translates and decodes for the poet:

There lies a glassy oblong pool. (半畝方塘一鑒開)
Where light and shade pursue their course. (天光雲影共徘徊)
How can it be so clear and cool? (問渠哪得清如許?)
For water fresh comes from its source. (為有源頭活水來)

The poet describes the pond as a mirror reflection of the sky and the shadow of the clouds and the reflection floating and dripping in the water. People often use the metaphor to keep learning new knowledge, and to reach new heights. People like to use Zhu Xi's poem to praise a person's knowledge or artistic achievement, which has a deeper definition to its originality. We can also learn from this poem that, only thoughts were inspired by enlightened forever activity and a broad mind, to accept a variety of different ideas such as fresh knowledge. Thus, one can fully understand poetry and paintings in the background, using the above theoretical framework – from "Idyllic" to "Living Space". The framework explains the expression through three levels: the first level is outer-level, the second level is mid-level, and the third level is inner-level.

3.1 Turning "Art Work" into "Interior Design" from the Outer- Level

The Outer-level can be a very direct experience to present its tangible element. It is a direct manifestation of visual and morphological aspects combined with the conversion mode for color, texture, pattern conversion, and analysis and poetry paintings in the scenic description. It can pick up color paintings and graphics for design conversion purposes. Based on the Outer-level theoretical study (Chen et al. 2014, 2015), the analysis of color, texture and pattern can be directly converted to designing color or patterns for interior design spaces such as indoor decorative paints, wallpaper, decorative materials, decoration, as well as carpets, curtains, lamps and other soft furnishings installed. The analysis of "Reflected Sunlight and Cloud Shadow Lingered Over and Over" painting, the sky and clouds reflected on the water surface. Create an image and pattern from this painting, used as decorative pattern in interior design. The patterns of the painting directly used for indoor curtain, shown in Fig. 5. Additionally, the paintings

Fig. 5. Overall tone, decorative painting and curtain, color of the hanging basket chairs and patterns.

can still be used as home fabric patterns and colors as well as presenting other patterns in lamp shade design. In summary, the method of extraction and pattern painting color analysis is a direct quote, and it is a direct manifestation of "poetic" in the "outer-level" (Lin 2007, 2009, 2011).

3.2 Turning "Art Work" into "Interior Design" from the Mid-Level

In fact, the mid-level is Function. It considers the usage do conversion. The main concerns are: functional properties, artificial function, the use of performance, function combined with other attributes, the poetic combination of pictorial integration of indoor space, using "sky clouds hover" poetry paintings as the basis for giving full consideration to the reasonable function, human factors design, functionality and performance to achieve multi-purpose conversion, dynamic and static optimization and so on. Therefore, in the study of space on a desk design would be reflected according to the "Art Work" to find the rule, the elements and structures applied to the design as shown in Fig. 6. Curved lines from the "Reflected sunlight and cloud shadow lingered over and over" form the design elements for a movable, sliding cabinet which can be slid around to change the use of the space. This maximizes function, easy to use to provide a reasonable performance(Chen et al. 2014, 2015).

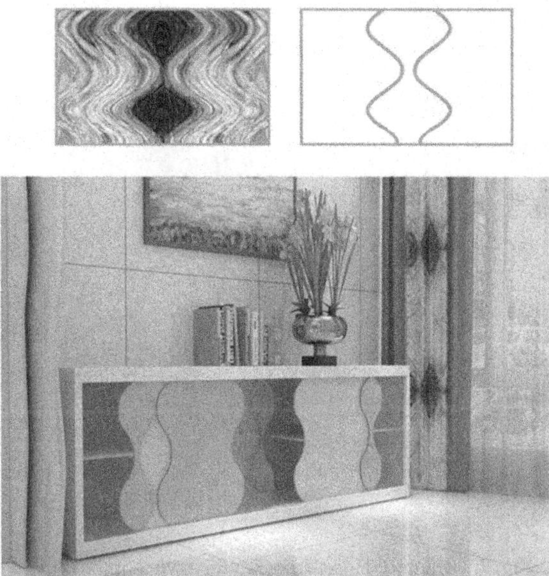

Fig. 6. Activity type and multifunctional cabinet

3.3 Turning "Art Work" into "Interior Design" from the Inner-Level

When product safety and comfort have been satisfied, emphasis can shift toward the decorative, emotional, and symbolic attributes of design (Crilly et al. 2004).

The successful product design meets or exceeds the emotional needs of users beyond utility and quality. Incorporating "feeling" into product design to present the emotional communication of user experiences has become a design trend of the twenty first century, according to McLoone et al. (2012).

If the "outer-level" is the direct experience and performance, "performance level" is a function of the use and effectiveness, and therefore, "spiritual level" is a profound meaning and emotion. When the soul level converses, it pays more attention to contextual sense, story, moral, cultural traits, and feelings that carry other attributes. The implementation phase is shown in Fig. 7. Although the idea expressed the structure of Idyllic Style composition, it was too complicated to express the inner meaning of Idyllic Style composition. Through the analysis of "Reflected sunlight and cloud shadow lingered over and over", a mirror material was chosen to simulate the skylight and surface reflection, in order to increase and highlight the artistic conception of "Reflected sunlight and cloud shadow lingered over and over". For the user who likes to collect arts and crafts, the open cabinets serve as display as well as storage. The final "Memory" closet is shown in Fig. 7.

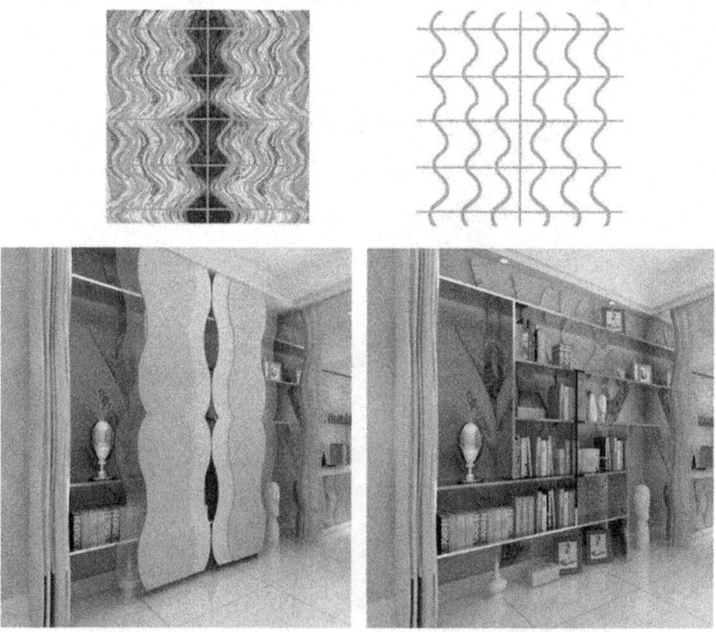

Fig. 7. Memory closet from Idyllic style composition

4 Summary

With the development of society and the improvement of living standards, cultural and creative industries have developed well in recent years. How to turn "Arts" into "Business" for "Creativity" and "Design", and E-business for creative industries are important research issues. Those issues have not been well covered until now. Therefore, based on the e-business, this paper proposes a research framework for illustrating how to transform “artwork” into “e-business”, and “Idyllic Style” into “Interior Design”, and design these aesthetic features into modern products to reinforce their business value. The most important part of this framework is of value for designers because it can help to design “art elements” and “art Style” into aesthetic design.

In the study of methods and tools, Idyllic style converses the design methods and models by using qualitative analysis to investigate the conversion process of literature theory and case study analysis. Through the case study, firstly, to understanding the poetic literature and paintings express of cultural background, provide model and theory for the design; secondly, the establishment of solid steps to convert the design to provide the actual conversion cases, this is to further improve the transformation of “Idyllic Style” space into the possibilities of the business model design. The third, case-by-case basis – to establish “Idyllic Style” space design conversion mode, from cultural creation poetry to paintings in living interior design, is to extend beyond the purposes and contexts of “Idyllic Style” in time and space value within this research.

For future studies, we need a better understanding of the local culture and design where changes in consumer perception regarding aesthetics are also important in design. We also need a better understanding of user need in the global market. Therefore, how to establish a local culture into the business model and artistic transformation becomes a key issue in cultural product design and creative industry and worthy of further in-depth study.

Acknowledgements. The authors gratefully acknowledge the support for this research provided by the TOFF Group, P.R. China. The author also wishes to thank Professor Rungtai Lin for directing this study, and special thanks to Sandy Lin for authorizing the use of her paintings in this study.

References

Chen, S.J., Lin, C.L., Lin. R.: A cognition study of turning poetry into abstract painting. In: 5th Asian Conference on Cultural Studies (ACCS 2015), Kobe, Japan, May 2015

Chen, S.J., Lin, C.L., Lin. R.: The study of match degree evaluation between poetry and paint. In: The 5th Asian Conference on the Arts and Humanities (ACAH 2014), Osaka, Japan, April 2014

Crilly, N., Moultrie, J., Clarkson, P.J.: Seeing things: consumer response to the visual domain in product design. Des. Stud. **25**(6), 547–577 (2004)

Chang, S.H., Hsu, C.H., Lin, R.: Design thinking of the local culture and the global market (2013)

Fiske, S.T.: Social Cognition: From Brains to Culture. Sage, Thousand Oaks (2013)

Faiola, A., Matei, S.A.: Cultural cognitive style and web design: beyond a behavioral inquiry into computer-mediated communication. J. Comput.-Mediat. Commun. **11**(1), 375–394 (2005)

Lin, R., Sun, M.-X., Chang, Y.-P., Chan, Y.-C., Hsieh, Y.-C., Huang, Y.-C.: Designing “culture” into modern product: a case study of cultural product design. In: Aykin, N. (ed.) HCII 2007. LNCS, vol. 4559, pp. 146–153. Springer, Heidelberg (2007a)

Lin, R.: Transforming Taiwan aboriginal cultural features into modern product design-a case study of cross cultural product design model. Int. J. Des. **1**(2), 45–53 (2007)

Lin, R., Chen, C.T.: A discourse on the construction of a service innovation model: focus on the cultural and creative industry park. In: Ifinedo, P. (ed.) EBUSINESS – Application and Global Acceptance, pp. 119–136. Croatia, InTech (2012)

Lin, R.: From service innovation to qualia product design. J. Des. Sci. Spec. Issue **14**, 13–31 (2011)

Lin, R.: Designing friendship into modern products. In: Toller, J.C. (ed.) Friendships: Types, Cultural, Psychological and Social, pp. 1–23. Nova Science Publishers, New York (2009)

Lin, R., Cheng, R., Sun, M.-X.: Digital archive database for cultural product design. In: Aykin, N. (ed.) HCII 2007. LNCS, vol. 4559, pp. 154–163. Springer, Heidelberg (2007b)

Lin, R., Lin, C.L.: From digital archive to e-business: a case study of turning "art" to "e-business". In: 2010 International Conference on E-Business, Athens, Greece, 26–28 July 2010

Lin, R., Lin, P.-H., Shiao, W.-S., Lin, S.-H.: Cultural aspect of interaction design beyond human-computer interaction. In: Aykin, N. (ed.) IDGD 2009. LNCS, vol. 5623, pp. 49–58. Springer, Heidelberg (2009)

Lin, C.L., Chen, J.L., Chen, S.J., Lin, R.: The cognition of turning poetry into painting. US-China Educ. Rev. **5**(8), 471–487 (2015)

Monk, A., Lelos, K.: Changing only the aesthetic features of a product can affect its apparent usability. In: Monk, A., Lelos, K. (eds.) IFIP TC 9, WG 9.3 HOIT 2007. IFIP, vol. 241, pp. 221–233. Springer, Heidelberg (2007)

McLoone, H., Jacobson, M., Goonetilleke, R.S., Kleiss, J., Liu, Y., Schütte, S.: Product design and emotion: frameworks, methods, and case studies. In: Proceedings of Human Factors and Ergonomics Society Annual Meeting, vol. 56, no. 1, pp. 1940–1941. SAGE Publications, September 2012

Norman, D.A.: Emotional Design: Why We Love (or Hate) Everyday Things. Basic Books, New York (2004)

Smyth, S.N., Wallace, D.R.: Towards the synthesis of aesthetic product form. In: Proceedings of DETC2000/DTM-14554, ASME, New York (2000)

Xu, Y.: Classical Chinese Poetry and Prose – Golden Treasury of Song, Yuan, Ming and Qing. Peking University Press, Beijing (1997)

Yeh, M.L., Lin, P.H.: Beyond claims of truth. J. Arts Humanit. **3**(1), 98–109 (2014)

Yeh, M.L., Lin, R., Wang, M.S., Lin, P.H.: Transforming the hair color design industry by using paintings: from art to e-business. Int. J. E-Bus. Dev. **4**(1), 12–20 (2014)

Cultural Ergonomics Beyond Culture - The Collector as Consumer in Cultural Product Design

John Kreifeldt[1], Yuma Taru[2], Ming-Xean Sun[3], and Rungtai Lin[2(✉)]

[1] Tufts University, Medford, MA, USA
john.Kreifeldt@tufts.edu

[2] Graduate School of Creative Industry Design, National Taiwan University of Arts, Ban Ciao City, Taipei 22058, Taiwan
lihan.workshop@gmail.com, rtlin@mail.ntua.edu.tw

[3] Institute of Applied Arts, National Chiao Tung University, Hsinchu 300, Taiwan
buddasfox@gmail.com

Abstract. The purpose of this study is to explore the meaning of cultural objects and to extract their cultural features from Taiwan's aboriginal culture. This paper attempts to illustrate how by enhancing the original meaning and images of Taiwan aboriginal culture features and by taking advantage of new production technology, they may be transformed into modern products and so fulfill the needs of the contemporary consumer market. The gungu, literally "weaving box", in the Atayal aboriginal language, was chosen as the cultural object for this study. The paper focuses on and analyzes the weaving box's appearance, usability, cultural meaning, operational interface, and the scenario in which it is used. Then, this article intends to create an interface for examining the way designers communicate across cultures as well as the interwoven experience of design and culture in the design process.

Keywords: Cultural ergonomics · Weaving box · Cross cultural design · Taiwan aboriginal culture

1 Introduction

Designing local features into products appears to be more and more important in the global market where products are losing their identity because of similarities in technology, function, and form. Cultural features then are considered to be unique characters to embed into a product both for the enhancement of its identity in the global market and for the fulfilment of the individual consumer's experiences (Hsu et al. 2013). Using local features in design fields as a strategy to create product identity in the global market, the designer has noted the importance of associating products with cultural features in order to enhance product value (Lin 2009). At this point, the field of Industrial Design has played an important role in embedding cultural elements into products and in increasing cultural value in the global competitive product market. Therefore, designing a product with local features in order to emphasize its cultural value has become a critical issue in the design process (Hsu et al. 2011).

P.-L.P. Rau (Ed.): CCD 2016, LNCS 9741, pp. 355–364, 2016.
DOI: 10.1007/978-3-319-40093-8_36

Culture plays an important role in the design field, and cross-cultural design will be a key design evaluation point in the future. Designing "culture" into products will be a design trend in the global market. Obviously, we need a better understanding of cross-cultural communications not only for the global market, but also for local design. While cross-cultural issues become important for product design in the global economy, the intersection of design and culture becomes a key issue making both local design and the global market worthy of further in-depth study (Lin et al. 2009). The importance of studying culture is shown repeatedly in several studies in all areas of technology design.

In the global market - local design era, connections between culture and design have become increasingly close. For design, cultural value-adding creates the core of product value. It's the same for culture; design is the motivation for pushing cultural development forward. Therefore, based on the "Taiwan Experience", the purpose of this paper is to study how to transfer "cultural features" to design elements, and design "cross culture" into cultural products to reinforce their design value (Lin and Lin 2010). This paper has established a cross-cultural design model to provide designers with a valuable reference for designing a successful cultural product. Results presented herein create an interface for examining the way designers communicate across cultures as well as the interwoven experience of design and culture in the design process (Lin 2007).

2 The Collector as a Consumer

A successful consumer product is perhaps the most difficult of human use products to design. A successful product means that enough are purchased and at a price to return a sufficient and timely profit to its manufacturer. Unlike the bespoke tailor or shoemaker who designs for a particular person, the consumer product designer is greatly handicapped by knowing little about the users for whom he is designing (and will likely never see) except perhaps in a statistical way. And any consumer statistic varies greatly among potential users especially in the international market.

Furthermore, unlike designing for users of industrial, military, aviation, or medical products, the designer of a consumer product faces perhaps the ultimate challenge: the consumer has the option of choice especially in a competitive market. A consumer need not purchase the designer's product. And even if purchased, the product need not be used resulting in lack of repurchase sales or bad word-of-mouth publicity. And even if used it may not be used correctly nor safely, nor maintained correctly or at all if such is required, etc., all with similar negative impacts on future sales.

The basic anthropometric and physiological variables determine the goodness of "fit" of the product to the user or the ability to use it "correctly" (i.e., safely and functionally as the designer intended). The human body has definite limitations in sizes, ranges, preferred direction of motions, etc. The magnitude of the difficulty in designing a successful consumer product becomes clearer as consumer variation in those psychological and aesthetic factors which critically affect purchase are added to the "goodness of fit" variables (Lin and Kreifeldt 2001).

The architect Louis Sullivan's dictum that "form follows function" is largely true if "function" is carefully determined and "form" implemented thoughtfully to "fit" the body.

The form can then be both physically and to some extent aesthetically pleasing because it conforms to the human body rather than depending upon the body to conform to it (Moore 1992). The well-known adaptability of the human is both a benefit and drawback in design in as much as it may be depended upon too much by the designer. Likewise, the early Industrial Designer Dreyfuss (1984, 2012) rejected the speculative design of external form alone as irrelevant. He believed that fitting machines to the users would be most efficient. Focus groups, interviews, questionnaires and such are techniques for trying to determine consumer likes/dislikes and preferences. Psycho-statistical techniques such as Multidimensional Scaling (MDS) and its relatives are further aides (Lutz and Ramsey 1974). While these have proven to be of help, it is rare that consumers can articulate their aesthetic preferences in a way useful for designers.

Consumers are usually unable to verbalize the correct reasons why they like and dislike a product which can then easily lead the designer astray. For example, the user swinging golf clubs to test them may have a strong preference for the "feel" of one versus the others or may want "more" of that particular "feel". The designer must deal with its physical attributes but the user is largely unable to verbalize what he means by "feel" or what the preferred one has that the others do not in words helpful to the designer. This is because the "feel" of the club is strongly related to its moment-of-inertia (I) which, although clearly perceptible, is a term and even concept unknown to users and even to some designers (Kreifeldt et al. 2011).

The aesthetic response of potential consumers has become a driving factor in product design. However, designers are even more handicapped because of the consumers' inability to verbalize their aesthetic preferences clearly and in design useful manner (Norman 2004). In terms of paint, canvas, frame and labour, a painting as a product would cost little. Yet a collector is willing to pay an amount for it that far exceeds its nominal value. So the design question becomes: why? The collector as consumer may provide design useful insights into purposeful aesthetic design (Kreifeldt et al. 2011; Kaplan 2004). Towards this end, aesthetic response is explored here via a particular Western person's reaction to a seemingly simple user "product" – a gungu - designed

Fig. 1. A gungu designed as a weaving as practice tool (Lin and Kreifeldt 2014)

long ago for the art of weaving as practiced by Taiwan's aboriginal Atayal weavers as shown in Fig. 1.

3 What Do You See in that Old Thing?

The Atayal weaver used a primitive type of loom sometimes called a "backstrap" or "back tension" loom. This apparatus is a type also found in many cultures particularly in South East Asian countries like Malaysia and Indonesia. Although "primitive", it permitted complex patterns of considerable beauty to be woven (Varutti 2015).

To use the loom, the weaver braced her feet against the gungu around which the continuous warp threads passed completing their circuit around the breast beam held near her body by a strap fastened at each end and passing behind her back: hence the name "backstrap". The weaver would alternately tighten and loosen the warp threads as part of the weaving process. She did this by pushing with her feet against the box creating a strain against the strap against her back to tighten the thread tension as she "beat" a new weft (cross) thread down and then relaxed to loosen the tension so that she could insert the next weft thread as shown in Fig. 2. She continued this basic process until the weaving was completed (Chang et al. 2008).

Fig. 2. Backstrap used in weaving process (Lin and Kreifeldt 2014)

The first view the collector had of such a box or even knew of its existence or purpose was in a small village town in Taiwan. The box was sitting on the floor of a modern Atayal weaver's shop and the collector described it as "leaping up" and speaking directly to his collector's soul. It appeared to him as a sculptural object with a rich golden, honey-brown patina from generations of bare feet pressing and rubbing against it.

To a collector, "weaving box" hardly gives an adequate picture of that object. In cold technical terms it was of wood and about 1½ shoulder widths wide with a sort of triangular cross section having smoothly rounded corners to facilitate the passage of the warp threads around it. The base was about 12" wide and tapered upward perhaps 14" to a smoothly rounded top which had a slit opening wide enough to admit the various sticks, shuttle, beater, backstrap and other weaving apparatus for storage as well as the weaving in progress (See Fig. 2). The hollow construction with the slit in the top made it also function as a resonant cavity. In the old days of head-taking the gungu was beat like a drum to raise an alarm or when a man brought a head back to the village to bring good fortune after some unwanted occurrence such as crop failure (Chang et al. 2008).

The weaver did not want to sell the box because it was part of her family heirlooms which was perfectly understandable and correct. Too many cultural items – material manifestations of the culture and examples by which it may be studied - have been lost or left their homes into museums and private collections. The only arguments collectors can offer are that such objects will be cherished, cared for, and preserved against the very real possibility that left in situ they might be forever lost. Moreover, such objects can foster wider interest in cultures which may be losing the fight against the transforming forces and pressures of societal evolution toward a secular rather than a spiritual society (Varutti 2015).

A wise man of the famous Iban weaving people in Borneo said that a society which is moving forward without spiritual fulfilment is paving the way for its own self-destruction and extinction. The artifacts of a culture are its external expression. Modern products need a connection with a spiritual foundation. And a culture must find its spiritual foundation (Lin et al. 2016).

4 Implications for Cultural Product Design

The extrinsic or manifest properties of the weaving box could serve as models for cultural product designs. Superficial function and appearance are important in product design. They can make the consumer/viewer respond: "that really appeals to me" or "that's interesting". But more is needed to gain real attraction to the consumer/viewer. Those are the intrinsic properties of culture which speak directly to the interior feelings or soul of the viewer. By incorporating these, the viewer may well say not just that the product is attractive but that he really desires it (Lin et al. 2015). That is, he may respond as a collector does in his desire to possess something because it touches his heart and soul and consequently be willing to spend considerable money to possess it. A common question asked of a collector who prizes a simple looking artifice such as the gungu is: What do you see in that old thing? "See" is a very short word standing for a very complex emotional reaction from seeing as well as an experiencing an actual and virtual haptic sensation of tactile feeling (Lin and Kreifeldt 2014).

The first response is to the box's extrinsic surface appearances: the sculptural qualities of size, form and shape; the color; the wonderful patina; the surface qualities of smoothness as well as the pleasing irregularities of a lovingly handmade object. The eye can partially detect these for the mind which can be additionally pleased by the virtual haptic sensations the eye sets up. Looking at an object arouses virtual sensations of tactile feel if attention is paid. The art connoisseur Bernard Berenson said that he experienced "ideated sensations" in front of paintings which stimulated his tactile sense and changed the tonus of his muscles. But the hand passed over the surface of the gungu is pleased beyond what the eye can detect and induce. Here the regular and irregular textures, the smooths and the roughs, the curves and the planes, the solidity and much more are directly felt and enjoyed. "Don't Touch" is a cruel prohibition to the haptic aesthetic sensibilities (Lin and Kreifeldt 2014). It is the equivalent of posting "Don't Look" beside the Mona Lisa. And even the ear is pleased by the sound from thumping the box and perhaps images come to mind knowing the history of its use as a drum. These are all satisfactions arising from sensory impressions and to some extent might be judged to be superficial.

But secondly, at a deeper and emotional level, a sensitive observer may "see", "feel" or even "hear" as though he were actually there the sharp clack-clack of the beaters of generations of women as they press against that box and perhaps sing as they loom cloth to clothe their children and menfolk and their spiritual times when weaving the now nearly lost powerful patterns of spiritual protection, ritual use, and cultural meaning (Kring et al. 2006). Such a collector is in contact with people of long ago and far away and there is both joy and sadness in that old weaving box. That is what one can "see" in that old thing (Lin and Kreifeldt 2014).

To a sensitive observer, the weavings made on such looms of the aboriginal peoples are also appealing as is nearly anything handmade in which the passion and "soul" of the artist as well as the technique can be perceived. Unfortunately, all the old authentic weavings seem to exist only in museums, collections and/or as fragments. In so many native cultures around the world the knowledge and necessity for their arts and crafts and spirituality have either vanished or are vanishing. Sadly, this is also true for Taiwan's aboriginals (Lin and Kreifeldt 2014). But for those who lament this fact, let them simply pay the aboriginal artists the price for their art and it will flourish as never before.

However, one must be discerning in what is purchased. If only the best is accepted, only the best will be produced. The old axiom: "bad money drives out good money" is equally true in that accepting inferior work drives out better work. It is amazing that the aboriginal women carried information for weaving complicated patterns in their memories and were able to execute it on their backstrap looms. Such knowledge needed to be carefully passed down from mother to daughter by example and instruction. Once that chain is broken, and without the means of recording the weaving instructions, a pattern could be lost to posterity.

Taiwan however is very fortunate that through the painstaking and loving work over many years by Professor Yu-Shan Tsai at Fu Jen Catholic University and of Mrs. Yuma Taru in Miaoli County, many of the aboriginal patterns which would otherwise be lost have now been preserved in modern weavers' notation so that they can be woven again. The world owes a great deal to such women.

The old authentic pieces were woven on a backstrap loom and made of hand spun material such as ramie. Before commercial dyes with their bright and wide range of colors became available, the threads were colored with native dyes. Although old patterns may be copied, modern pieces are now often woven of commercial cotton threads using commercial dyes and on a modern floor loom. Moreover, the "authentic" pieces were woven within a definite spiritual and cultural ethic (Lee 2000; Lin and Kreifeldt 2014).

Does a modern weaving suffer for these reasons against the authentic? To a collector; yes - to some extent. Clothiers appraising a fabric speak of its "hand" meaning its "feel" (Kreifeldt et al. 2011). The "feel" of a product can be as important as its "look" in terms of satisfaction. (In some cases, such as a razor or toothbrush, "feel" is more important than "look".) The beauty of a pattern, identical in a modern and in an old weaving, may be the same. However the "feel" to the fingers of a modern weaving with its uniform, smooth, commercial cotton threads differs greatly from that of an old weaving with its rougher threads of irregularly hand spun ramie. This difference is also apparent on close visual inspection. And of course, the history of the two pieces is importantly different.

Collectors of tribal art generally prefer the "authentic". They even attribute to it that important aspect of "honesty" of a work made for use within a particular ethnic culture. In fact, some collectors will accept only objects showing signs of tribal wear as an indication of its being "authentic" as long as the wear itself is "authentic". Wear tells its own stories about a tribal piece.

5 Framework for Hand Held Products

Because of their conservative natures "primitive" cultures have much to teach about modern product design. Such cultures have generally slowly and cleverly improved their tools. An example is the paddy cutting knife carved from a deer antler by an Iban man of Borneo as shown in Fig. 3. Although serving only as knife to cut the ripe rice stalks several features may be noted. Firstly, although a humble utilitarian tool it is beautifully carved with figures. In fact its beauty attracted its collector. The carved figures are not necessary for performing its physical function but have great spiritual symbolism to these people. They are also suggestive of the human need for beauty as shown in Fig. 3 (Kreifeldt and Hill 1974; Liu 2007; Lin et al. 2016).

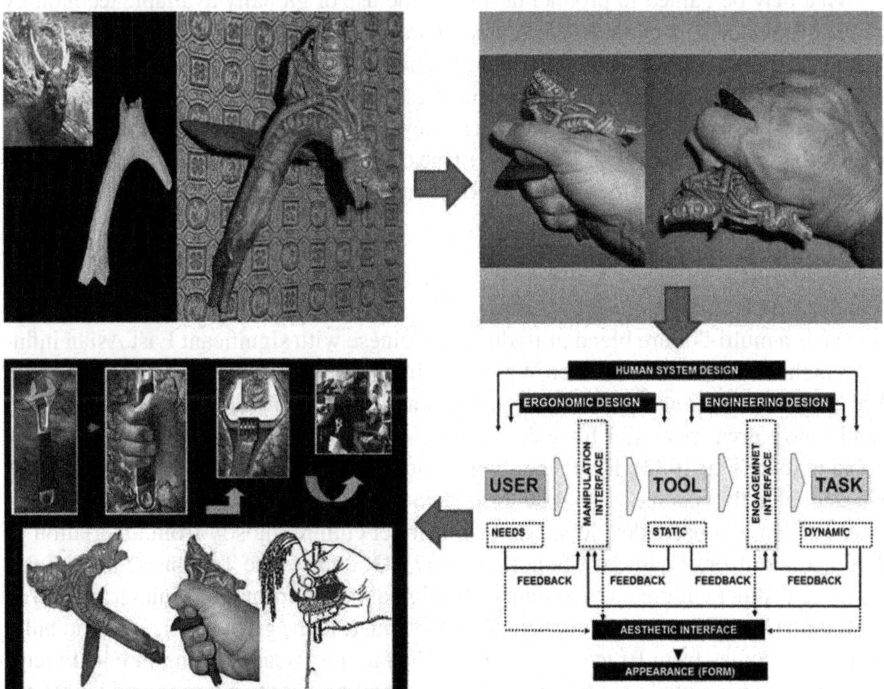

Fig. 3. Framework for Hand held products (Lin and Kreifeldt 2014)

Secondly, its design form permits gathering and cutting the rice stalk easily and naturally with one hand (one hand operation). Thirdly, and importantly for product designers, the "product designer" had taken advantage of the pronged shape of the antler so that the tool naturally conforms to the hand which has the effect of the tool holding the hand rather than the hand holding the tool. That frees up the fingers of the hand to perform the tool's function rather than being devoted to holding the tool. An examination of such simple tools or products of other cultures can readily suggest design principles (Kreifeldt and Hill 1974; Lin et al. 2016).

The "preference for the primitive" exists in every culture and every age. The "old ways" seem better than the "new ways". There is the feeling that older and less "sophisticated" works are morally and aesthetically superior to modern ones. Even the ancient Greeks looked to their past as being better. An Iban grandmother in Borneo complained that her granddaughters having been to school are now quite useless because now they "can't cook, can't mind babies, and can't even make a mat" (Lin and Kreifeldt 2014). This simple statement emphasis that "education" is a double edged sword or perhaps a sword without a grasping handle: dangerous to both user and foe. Where and how did this particular attractiveness of earlier products arise? They were generally made for a particular person, or for one's God or king. The desire was to please by all the perfection and ingenuity of which the maker was capable believing that the recipient would take no less (Kreifeldt and Hill 1974; Lin et al. 2016).

What may be gained in product design by the use of globally available technology can also produce a profound lost as that characterless technology replaces the local cultural underpinnings that create a unique character. This leads to products with an "international" design lacking any particular, pleasingly, and identifiable cultural identity. As a result they may be valued for the money paid for them but they are not treasured or cherished because they do not "speak" to the owner. They are quickly discarded when an "improved" version comes to market (Lin and Kreifeldt 2014).

6 Summary

Taiwan is a multi-culture blend of traditional Chinese with significant East Asian influences including Japanese and such Western influences as American, Spanish and Dutch. With their beautiful and primitive visual arts and crafts, Taiwan's aboriginal cultures should have great potential for enhancing design value and being recognized in the global market (Lee 1982). Evidence shows that the prospect of Taiwan's local cultures will undoubtedly become crucial cultural elements in future design applications. Over time, Taiwan gradually developed its own distinct culture, mostly from a variation of Hoklo culture from Southern China (Lee 1997). Of course, the Taiwanese aboriginals also have distinct cultures. For example, aboriginal music from the Bunun tribe played at the 1996 Olympic Games brought that form of music to the global arena. Additionally, martial art movies from Bruce Lee to Jacky Chan to the Oscar-winning movie director Ang Lee have promoted recognition of Taiwanese culture at the international level (Wu et al. 2004, 2005).

The increasing emphasis on localized cultural development in Taiwan demonstrates an ambition to promote the Taiwanese style in the global economic market. Current design philosophy and practice in Taiwan is directed to producing products with cultural significance to compete in the global market. Then a product may be produced which the consumer not only values for the money paid for it but is also treasured and cherished (Hsu et al. 2013).

Acknowledgements. The authors gratefully acknowledge the support for this research provided by the Ministry of Science and Technology, Taiwan under Grants 103-2221-E-144-001-MY2 and 103-2410-H-144-003-MY2. The authors also wish to thank those who contributed to the research.

References

Chang, J., Wall, G., Chang, C.L.: Perception of the authenticity of Atayal woven handicrafts in Wulai, Taiwan. J. Hosp. Leisure Mark. **16**(4), 385–409 (2008)

Dreyfuss, H.: Symbol Sourcebook: An Authoritative Guide to International Graphic Symbols. Wiley, Hoboken (1984, 2012)

Hsu, C.-H., Lin, C.-L., Lin, R.: A study of framework and process development for cultural product design. In: Rau, P. (ed.) IDGD 2011. LNCS, vol. 6775, pp. 55–64. Springer, Heidelberg (2011)

Hsu, C.-H., Chang, S.-H., Lin, R.: A design strategy for turning local culture into global market products. Int. J. Aff. Eng. **12**, 275–283 (2013)

Kaplan, M.: Introduction: adding a cultural dimension to human factors. In: Advances in Human Performance and Cognitive Engineering Research, vol. 4, pp. XI–XVII (2004)

Kreifeldt, J.G., Hill, P.H.: Toward a theory of man-tool system design applications to the consumer product area. In: Proceedings of Human Factors and Ergonomics Society Annual Meeting (1974)

Kreifeldt, J., Lin, R., Chuang, M.-C.: The importance of "feel" in product design feel: the neglected aesthetic "Do Not Touch". In: Rau, P. (ed.) IDGD 2011. LNCS, vol. 6775, pp. 312–321. Springer, Heidelberg (2011)

Kring, J.B.B., Morgan, J., Kaplan, M.: Cultural ergonomics. In: Karwowski, W. (ed.) International Encyclopedia of Ergonomics and Human Factors, vol. 3, 2nd edn. CRC Press, Boca Raton (2006)

Lin, C.L., Chen, S.J., Hsiao, W.H., Lin, R.: Cultural ergonomics in interactional and experiential design: conceptual framework and case study of the Taiwanese twin cup. Appl. Ergon. **52**, 242–252 (2016)

Lin, R., Kreifeldt, J.: Do Not Touch – A Conversation Between Dechnology to Humart. NTUA, New Taipei City (2014)

Lin, R., Kreifeldt, J., Hung, P.-H., Chen, J.-L.: From dechnology to humart – a case study of Taiwan design development. In: Rau, P. (ed.) CCD 2015. LNCS, vol. 9181, pp. 263–273. Springer, Heidelberg (2015)

Lin, R., Kreifeldt, J.G.: Ergonomics in wearable computer design. Int. J. Ind. Ergon. **27**, 259–269 (2001)

Lee, R.K.: The Immigration of Taiwan Southern Island Tribes. Charng-Ming Culture, Taipei (1997)

Lee, S.L.: Garments culture of Taiwan aborigines. Hist. Objects **87**, 14–28 (2000)

Lee, Y.Y.: Taiwan Aboriginal Society and Culture. Linking Book, Taipei (1982)

Lin, R.: Transforming Taiwan aboriginal cultural features into modern product design: a case study of a cross-cultural product design model. Int. J. Des. **1**, 45–53 (2007)

Lin, R.: Designing friendship into modern products. In: Toller, J.C. (ed.) Friendships: Types, Cultural, Psychological and Social, pp. 1–24. Nova Science Publishers, New York (2009)

Lin, R., Lin, P.-H., Shiao, W.-S., Lin, S.-H.: Cultural aspect of interaction design beyond human-computer interaction. In: Aykin, N. (ed.) IDGD 2009. LNCS, vol. 5623, pp. 49–58. Springer, Heidelberg (2009)

Lin, R., Lin, C.-L.: From digital archive to e-business: a case study of turning "art" to "e-business". In: Proceedings of 2010 International Conference on E-Business (2010)

Liu, C.W.: Culture and Art of the Formosan Aboriginal. Hsiung-Shih Art Book, Taipei (2007)

Lutz, F.W., Ramsey, M.A.: The use of anthropological field methods in education. Educ. Res. **3**(10), 5–9 (1974)

Moore, J.D.: Pattern and meaning in prehistoric Peruvian architecture: the architecture of social control in the Chimu state. Latin Am. Antiq. **3**, 95–113 (1992)

Norman, D.A.: Emotional Design: Why We Love (or Hate) Everyday Things. Basic Books, New York (2004)

Varutti, M.: Crafting heritage: artisans and the making of Indigenous heritage in contemporary Taiwan. Int. J. Herit. Stud. **21**(10), 1036–1049 (2015)

Wu, T.Y., Hsu, C.H., Lin, R.: A study of Taiwan aboriginal culture on product design. In: Proceedings of Design Research Society International Conference – Futureground (2004)

Wu, T.Y., Cheng, H., Lin, R.: A study of cultural interface in the Taiwan aboriginal twin-cup. In: Salvendy, G. (ed.) Proceedings of the 11th International Conference on Human-Computer Interaction, Lawrence Erlbaum Associates, Las Vegas, Nevada, Mahwah, New Jersey, USA (2005)

From Ideality to Reality- a Case Study of Mondrian Style

Rungtai Lin[1(✉)], Hui-Yueh Hsieh[2], Ming-Xean Sun[3], and Ya-Juan Gao[4]

[1] Graduate School of Creative Industry Design, National Taiwan University of Arts, New Taipei City 22058, Taiwan
rtlin@mail.ntua.edu.tw

[2] Visual Communication Design Department, Ming Chi University of Technology, New Taipei City 24306, Taiwan
huiyueh@gmail.com

[3] Institute of Applied Arts, National Chiao Tung University, Hsinchu 300, Taiwan
buddasfox@gmail.com

[4] Academy of Art and Design, Wuhan Technology and Business University, Wuhan 430065, People's Republic of China
78343821@qq.com

Abstract. Ideality describes the arts striving toward perfection, beauty and refinement in all aspects of life. For reality, the product should also fit into a context of use and meet user requirements. Transforming "ideality" into "reality" involves more than considering the product design itself. It remains a challenge to represent use contexts and user needs in a way that designers with technical backgrounds are able to make direct use of them. When designing "arts" into "business", we need a better understanding of human-art interaction not just for taking part in the humanity context, but also for developing the interactive experience of arts. Therefore, we propose a general framework for aesthetic design that applies to representing human-art interactions and translating aesthetics into user requirements in real product design cases. The intended purpose of this paper is to provide a framework for examining the way designers interact across the art and the interactive experiences of users in the design process.

Keywords: User experience · Cultural product design · Mondrian style · Aesthetics

1 Introduction

We now live in a small world with a large global market. While the market heads toward "globalization", design tends toward "localization." So we must "think globally" for the market, but "act locally" for design (Lin 2011). In the global market - local design era, connections between arts and aesthetic design have become increasingly close. For local design, culture and arts value-adding creates the core of local design value. It's the same for the global market; local design is the motivation for pushing culture and arts forward in global market development (Lin and Chen 2012). Recently, creative industries are constantly emerging in culture and arts and can become a key trend in aesthetic design (Monk and Lelos 2007). While aesthetic design is under tough competitive pressure

P.-L.P. Rau (Ed.): CCD 2016, LNCS 9741, pp. 365–376, 2016.
DOI: 10.1007/978-3-319-40093-8_37

from the developing global market, it seems that the local design should be focused on "culture and arts" for designing "aesthetics" into modern products (Smyth and Wallace 2000).

Culture and arts play an important roles in the design field, and will be a key design factors in the local design. Thus, designing culture and arts into products will be a design trend in the global market (Lin 2007). In today's competitive market, "innovation" serves as a competitive advantage allowing companies to dominate particular market segments. With respect to corporate strategy, innovation is the key not only to extending market share, but also to increasing commercial gains (Lin and Chen 2012). With the development of industrial tendencies, most companies gradually realize that the keys to product innovation are not only market and technology aspects but also aesthetic design (Smyth and Wallace 2000). Recently, there is a shift from technological innovation to aesthetics that is based on discovering new opportunities in the marketplace. Companies are more focused on adapting new technologies and combining them in ways that create new experiences and values for customers. Cultural product design has received increased attention in the academic and business communities over the past decade. Both academics and practitioners had emphasized that the role of service design in innovative product development relates not only to aesthetics, but also to aspects such as ergonomics, user-friendliness, efficient use of materials, functional performance, and so on (Lin and Chang 2004).

The importance of studying aesthetic design is shown repeatedly in several studies in all areas of design field (Crilly et al. 2004). Despite the recognized importance of aesthetic design in cultural and creative design industries, they lack a systematic approach to it (Monk and Lelos 2007). Obviously, we need a better understanding of human-arts communications not only for the global market, but also for local design. While cross-cultural issues become important for product design in the global economy, the intersection of design and culture becomes a key issue making both local design and the global market worthy of further in-depth study (Lin and Lin 2010). Therefore, this study focuses on the analysis of art works in which the aesthetic elements are used. Then, a framework is proposed to provide designers with a valuable reference for designing a successful cultural product (Smyth and Wallace 2000). Results presented herein create an interface for examining the way designers communicate across art work as well as the interwoven experience of incorporating design and aesthetics into the design process.

2 Framework for Designing Art into Reality

According to communication theory, an art work must reach three functions to express its significance through the communication system. (1) Signification: the art work can express a kind of significance; that is, the artist's intentions can indeed be expressed through the art work. (2) Expression: the art work may represent the artist's and feelings; that is, through the art works, the artist's imaginations thoughts and feelings can be reproduced. (3) Communication: the art works of signification and expression can be sent to the audience only when the artist's thoughts are identical to the audience (Fiske 2013; Norman 2004).

Based on previous studies (Lin 2007, 2009, 2011; Lin and Chen 2012; Lin and Lin 2010; Lin et al. 2007, 2009), a research framework combining communication theory with a design model was proposed to explore the issue of turing arts into reality as shown in Fig. 1. Taking Mondrian's art works as an example, the research framework consists of three main phases: art paradigm, paradigm shift model, and cultural products. The art paradigm concerns selecting appropriate art works for the paradigm shift. The paradigm shift model focuses on how to extract artistic features from art works and then transfer these art elements to design practice. The design practice is composed of three phase; identification, translation and implementation, to finally design a creative product.

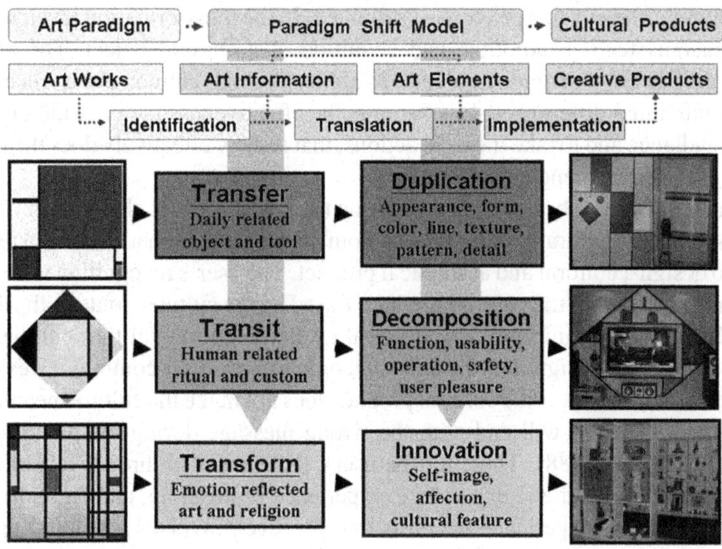

Fig. 1. The research framework for turning arts into reality

In the identification phase, art features are identified from an original art work including the outer level of colors, texture, and pattern; the mid level of function, usability, and safety, and the inner level of emotion, symbolic meaning, and stories. The designer uses the scientific method and other methods of inquiry and hence is able to obtain, evaluate, and utilize art information from the art work (Lin 2007). The translation phase translates the art information to art features within a chosen art work. The designer achieves some depth and experience of practice in these art features and at the same time is able to relate the art elements to design problems in modern society. This produces an appreciation for the interaction between arts, technology, and society (Lin 2007). Finally, the implementation phase expresses the art elements associated with the artistic features, the meaning of the chosen art work, an aesthetic sensibility, and the flexibility to adapt to various designs. At this time, the designer gains knowledge of an art work and an understanding of the spectrum of symbolic meaning and value related to it. The designer combines this symbolic meaning with his strong sense of art knowledge to deal with design issues and to employ all of the art features in designing a cultural product (Lin 2007).

For design practices of the paradgim shift model, three levels are identified as: transfer, transit and transformation, which can be mapped into three levels of design features: visceral design, behavioral design and reflective design (Norman 2004). The key factor in the transfer level is duplication which concerns the appearance of an art work and transfers its form, textures, and pattern into a new product. The visceral design feature becomes important where appearance matters and first impressions are formed. The transit level which is behavioral design concerns how to transit the use, function, performance and usability from an art work. Based on the decomposition, the behavioral design feature is the key to a product's usefulness. In the transformation level, reflective design concerns feeling, emotion, and cognition of a cultural object. The reflective design feature is the most vulnerable to variability through culture, experience, education, and individual differences. Innovaton is the effectiveness factor, which is how to touch the audience and to take the right actions; that is, how effectively does the received meaning affect the audience.

For the framework, the designer focuses on the analysis of art elements in which the art work was used. Cultural product results from the art features that have been redefined in order to design a cultural and aesthetical product. The user's recognition is developed through interaction with the cultural product. Based on the cultural context, the designer expects the user's recognition to be identical to the design model through the culture aspect of interaction design. For the user's recognition, the user communicates directly with the cultural product. If the cultural product does not make the culture meaning clear and attractive, then use will end with the wrong message during the human-product interaction (Norman 1988). Thus, for the users, there are also three levels of human-product interaction: aesthetic experience, experience of meaning, and emotional experience. The aesthetic experience which is transfer level, involves a cultural product's form, color, texture, etc., to delight the user's sensory modalities (Crilly et al. 2004). The experience of meaning which is transit level, involves the user's ability including operation, safety, etc., to assign the design features and assess user pleasure with the cultural product (Desmet and Hekkert 2007). The emotional experience which is transformation level, involves user emotion including self-image, personal satisfaction, memories, etc., which are elicited by the art works and designed into the cultural product (Bermond 2008).

3 A Case Study of Turning "Mondrian" into "Interior"

The Piet Mondrian (1872–1944) was an important contributor to the De Stijl art movement and group (Warncke 1991). He created a characteristic and immediately recognizable style of painting and evolved a non-representational form which he termed Neo-plasticism. His most famous compositions consisted of arrangements of colored fields and black lines over a white background, upon which was painted a grid of vertical and horizontal black lines and the three primary colors (Locher et al. 2005; Taft 1997). Some of the earliest experiments in computer graphics-based art mimicked some of

Mondrian's compositions, because its surface features are easily reproduced with computer algorithms (Noll 1995, 1966). Based on the research framework as shown in Fig. 1, the features of Mondrian's compositions would appear to be a good basis for reality visualization. The use of recognizable style and three distinguishable colors together with geometrical form seemed a good paradigm for turning "Mondrian" into "Interior" (Mondrian 1995, 2008).

Developing an aesthetic product involves more than considering the "culture" or "art work." Based on the art work, the aesthetic product should also fit into a context of "art work" or cultural meaning in use and meet user requirements (Dan 2013; Kujala et al. 2001). It remains a challenge to represent use contexts and user needs in a way that designers with art work backgrounds are able to make direct use of them. Using the framework as an approach, this paper explored Mondrian's art work, translating it into user needs and user requirements in aesthetic product design cases.

3.1 Turning "Mondrian" into "Interior" from the Outer Level

The design features derived from the outer level, which is visceral design concerning physical and material elements, focuses on Mondrian's composition that if color represents meaning and expression it has to be a universal, general meaning formulated in every separated color and specified in the relation unity of image which is associated with material, colors, texture, and pattern. Mondrian expressed that Unity and relationship are the determinants in the roots of the meaning in colors (Dan 2013; Locher et al. 2005; Taft 1997).

The identification phase attempts to determine user needs. Considering the situation in Taiwan's apartments, there are many utility meters, such as water, electricity, gas as shown in on left of Fig. 2, which make disorder and a mess along a long narrow passage. Furthermore, the hydrant that supplies water to extinguish fires is very important for safety. The hydrant must be visible during a fire as shown in the left of Fig. 3, but may be invisible otherwise.

Fig. 2. Storage for utility meters

Fig. 3. Storage for hydrant

In the translation phase: the analysis of the color and form could provide the designer with an idea of how to transfer the Mondrian's work into interior design. There considerable graphic documentation about Mondrian's Post-Impressionist period, especially in form and color. For example, his painting *Avond* (1908) shows a color palette consisting almost fully red, yellow and blue colors (Barriga 2011). It was the first Mondrian's work that emphasized only the use of primary colors. In this way, Mondrian eliminated all what was formal in pictorial image. He expressed that modern painting did not have to be figurative and it did not have to be implicated in representation of apparently real objects; but that painting had to be a searching of what is absolute, and that is found hidden behind real forms. In summary, his aesthetic thought was based on the searching of a pure art. Furthermore, Mondrian's art work emphasizes the meaning of harmony and order in reality.

In the implementation Phase: From a usability point of view, the designer used Mondrian's color and form for rearranging the utility storage as shown in the Fig. 2. Figure 3 shows the idea that derives from Mondrian's art work to show he meaning of harmony and order in the hydrant storage.

3.2 Turning "Mondrian" into "Interior" from the Mid-Level

The mid-level which is behavioral design focuses on the behavioral level including function, usability, and the scenarios in which people would use the "Mondrian" on different occasions. For example, Holmquist and Skog (2003) found the Mondrian's compositions to be a good basis for abstract information visualization. The use of three easily distinguishable colors together with geometrical shapes seemed ideal to visualize dynamic data concerning e-mail traffic, current weather, weather forecasts, and most recently bus departure times. These are typical examples of turning "Mondrian" into "visualization" in that data has been mapped to the size, position, and color of the fields in a composition. From the usability point of view, the "Mondrian" is a special interface used in the ambient information visualization (Holmquist and Skog 2003). Therefore, the design features on the middle level of the "Mondrian" should be focused on how to express its function based on ergonomics.

In the identification phase: What are the user needs? We need storage room in our living space, such as TV case, book shelf, cabinet, closet etc.; In addition, the user needs a projection screen and a whiteboard for teaching and writing. Therefore, the method of turning "Mondrian" into "Interior" from "ideality" to "reality" becomes an important issue at mid -level.

In the translation phase: taking Mondrian's compositions series 1917–1940 as an example, the composition series also called "Neo-plasticism" (Troy 1979) which want to emphasize the art meaning that artists want to express, but tries to balance the relationship between the form and the art meaning (Fendelman and Taylor 1999). In that time, it is necessary to emphasize the appearance because the appearance that will tell audience whether a work actually expresses a pure plasticism of the universal. Execution in ideality is to art what action in reality is to life. It is noted that people from different cultures use different ways to understand Mondrian's composition representing different cultural meanings. Within these cultures, they may share some differences and similarities in turning "ideality of Mondrian" into "reality of interior" either the form or the art meaning. "Ideality" and "reality" between the form and the art meaning are the crucial elements for the core value of the Mondrian's composition.

In the implementation phase: for the mid-level in Neo-plasticism appearance, the most external means for the expression of form and natural color are internalized and thus rendered equivalent to the pure plastic means of essence. The essence of Neo-plasticism is more important than external appearance. For example, Mondrian's "Composition 2" (1922) (Locher et al. 2005) is composed of rectangular form with colors as shown in Fig. 4. These rectangular color planes express harmony which is the nature of Neo-plasticism. Based on "Composition 2," Fig. 5 shows how to turn "Composition 2" into "reality" as a projection screen or a whiteboard for writing. Consequently, Fig. 5 shows how to combine Mondrian's art works – Tableau No. IV: Lozenge Composition with Red, Gray, Blue, Yellow, and Black (1924/1925), with "Composition With gray and Light brown 1" to design a TV case and book shelf together (McManus et al. 1993).

Fig. 4. TV case and book shelf from Mondrian's "Composition 2"

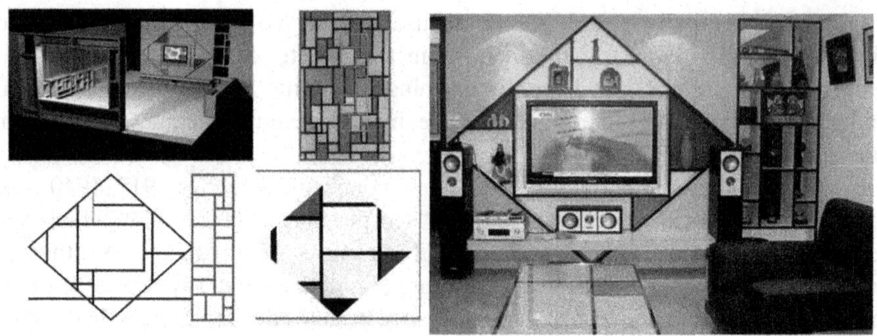

Fig. 5. TV case and book shelf from Mondrian's "Tableau No. IV"

3.3 Turning "Mondrian" into "Interior" from the Inner-Level

The inner-level which is reflective design contains special content such as stories, emotion, and cultural features, and focuses on the symbolic meaning of the Mondrian. In general, the Inner-level interface of the Mondrian is derived from the symbolic meaning of color. The reflective design focuses on the Mondrian's work that is closely linked to a spiritual and philosophical interest. His art was linked to the theosophical movement (Blavatsky 2012) which studied reality on the basis of mysticism.

The identification phase asks: What are the user needs? The author traveled all over the world and collected many souvenirs and other collections representing their memories in different countries. So, the user needs a space for keep these materials not only for display but also for memory. Mondrian was interested in esthetic and theoretical thinking that creating happiness and harmony in the inner and the outer of his works. He found a theoretical support for the development of his plastic activity, and knew a different kind of beauty: one that he creates himself, and that in nature appears only under a veil (Barriga 2011; Dan 2013).

In the translation phase, Mondrian expressed that if color represents meaning and expression, it has to be a universal meaning and formulated in every separated color and specified in the relational unity of image (Fendelman and Taylor 1999). For instance, unity and relationship are the determinants in the roots of the meaning in color. Mondrian offered no opinion on the question of whether color carries an inner meaning of its own. He needed to make the universal visible which forced him to keep available the possibilities of the pure and saturated color. Then, Mondrian used the concept in all of his works. From the beginning of the twentieth century, the esthetic-semiotic thinking currents started to be interested in language pictorial representation, by means of symbols and signs, both in abstract and figurative painting, design and architecture. Although arts are based on communicative elements, they cannot be studied exclusively through aesthetic or semiotic cases (Barriga 2011). Though Mondrian was not interested in symbology of form, his philosophical studies were based on geometric abstraction looking for the basic structure of universe. The main concept that tries to represent simplicity and harmony with the white background crossed by a lines grid of black color and the blocks of primary colors were considered by Mondrian as the basic colors of the universe (Taft 1997). For examples, Mondrian's art works Composition London (1940), Composition 8 (1939), Composition with black yellow and red (1939), and Composition in Blue (1937) are shown in Fig. 6 (Locher et al. 2005; McManus et al. 1993).

Fig. 6. Memory closet from Mondrian's "Composition 2"

In implementation phase, based on the previous composition, the original idea showed at the left of Fig. 6. Although the idea expressed the structure of Mondrian's composition, it was too complicated to express the inner meaning of Mondrian's composition. After modifying, the final "Memory" closet is shown at the right of Fig. 6.

3.4 Designing "Arts" into "Product Design"

Designing "Arts" into "Product Design" will be a design trend in the global market. This is not a new idea; for example, Rietveld founded his own furniture factory in 1918. He involved the current scientific theory, mechanical production, modern city rhythms and Stijl moment's theories, in a conceptual development of form. In 1918, he designed *the red and blue chair*, considered as a true art work by generations of designers, and a product design paradigm. (Billinghurst et al. 2001; Van Zijl 1999). On the other hand, E-business is considered to be one of the pivotal components in cultural and creative design industries which have a significant impact on consumer perception of innovation. Lin (2009) proposed an ABCDE business model for turning "Aesthetics" into "Business": we need "Creativity" and "Design," then put the results of ABCD in E-business. It is a new approach that integrates design, culture, artistic craftsmanship, creativities and service innovation design in cultural and creative design industries.

For the local design, Qualia has gained popularity and broad application in product design. "Qualia" is a Latin adjective that refers to quality and comprises five elements: attractiveness, beauty, creativity, delicacy, and engineering. The sense of difference lies in quality, which includes attractiveness, beauty, and creativity, in which content renders the product surface (Yen et al. 2013). Attractiveness, beauty, and creativity belong to the emotional condition of the product "psychology"; delicacy and engineering belong to the rational condition of the product "physiology." Thus, qualia products involve rational conditions for consumer use but do not neglect emotional appeal (Mandler 2005; Bermond 2008). Taking Mondrian's art works as an example, the author turned them into "real products." including Dining Table, Coffee Table, and Corner Table as shown in Fig. 7 from left to right.

Fig. 7. Examples of turning "arts" into "product design"

4 Summary

Understanding how to turn "Arts" into "Business" for "Creativity" and "Design", and E-business for creative industries are important research issues. Those issues are not so well covered until now. Therefore, based on the e-business, this paper proposes a research framework for illustrating how to transform "art" into "e-business", and design these aesthetic features into modern products to reinforce their business value. The framework of human-arts interaction provides a different way of thinking about interactive experiences with aesthetics. The most important part of this process is the user experience added into the cultural product design process and involved aesthetic design considerations. The framework is of value for designers because it can help to design "art elements" into aesthetic design, as well as provide users with a valuable reference for understanding aesthetic meaning. Results presented herein create an interface for looking at the way arts crosses over into product design, as well as illustrating the interwoven experience of arts and creativity in the innovation design process.

Along with Information Technology progress, e-business is becoming the most common concept in the Internet and electronic commerce world. However, in today's intensely competitive business climate, innovative products become central in e-business development. To be successful, innovative products must have a clear and significant difference that is responding to a marketplace needs. Furthermore, changes in consumer perception regarding aesthetics are also important in product design. For future studies, we need a better understanding of the acculturation process not only for the aesthetic in local design, but also for the user needs in the global market. While aesthetic features become important issues in the interactive experiences of users, the acculturation process between human and arts becomes a key issue in the cultural product design and are worthy of further in-depth study.

Acknowledgements. The authors gratefully acknowledges the support for this research provided by the Ministry of Science and Technology, Taiwan. Under Grants 103-2221-E-144 -001 -MY2 and 103-2410-H-144 -003 -MY2. The author also wishes to thank Dr. J.G. Kreifeldt.

References

Barriga, J.A.: Piet Mondrian, Plastic vision and esthetic emotion. El Artista **8**, 109–134 (2011)

Bermond, B.: The emotional feeling as a combination of two qualia: a neurophilosophical-based emotion theory. Cogn. Emot. **22**, 897–930 (2008)

Billinghurst, M., Kato, H., Poupyrev, I.: The MagicBook: a transitional AR interface. Comput. Graph. **25**(5), 745–753 (2001)

Blavatsky, H.P.: Isis Unveiled: A Master-Key to the Mysteries of Ancient and Modern Science and Theology, vol. 2. Cambridge University Press, Cambridge (2012)

Crilly, N., Moultrie, J., Clarkson, P.J.: Seeing things: consumer response to the visual domain in product design. Des. Stud. **25**(6), 547–577 (2004)

Dan, M.B.: Interwar Architecture with Reinforced Concrete Structure Exposed to Multihazard in European Context: Intervention in the Romanian and Italian Context, vol. 11. LIT Verlag Münster, Münster (2013)

Desmet, P.M.A., Hekkert, P.: Framework of product experience. Int. J. Des. **1**(1), 57–66 (2007)

Fendelman, H.W., Taylor, J.B.: Tramp Art: A Folk Art Phenomenon. Tabori & Chang, Stewart (1999)

Fiske, S.T.: Social Cognition: From Brains to Culture. Sage, Beverly Hills (2013)

Holmquist, L.E., Skog, T.: Informative art: information visualization in everyday environments. In: Proceedings of the 1st International Conference on Computer Graphics and Interactive Techniques in Australasia and South East Asia, pp. 229–235. ACM (2003)

Kujala, S., Kauppinen, M., & Rekola, S.: Bridging the gap between user needs and user requirements. In: Advances in Human-Computer Interaction I (Proceedings of the Panhellenic Conference with International Participation in Human-Computer Interaction PC-HCI 2001). Typorama Publications, pp. 45–50 (2001)

Lin, R.: From service innovation to qualia product design. J Des. Sci. Spec. Issue, 13–31 (2011)

Lin, R.: Designing friendship into modern products. In: Friendships: Types, Cultural, Psychological and Social Chapter 3, pp. 1–24. Nova Science (2009)

Lin, R.: Transforming Taiwan aboriginal cultural features into modern product design-a case study of cross cultural product design model. Int. J. Des. **1**(2), 45–53 (2007)

Lin, R., Chen, C.T.: A discourse on the construction of a service innovation model: focus on the cultural and creative industry park. In E-BUSINESS – Application and Global Acceptance, editer Princely Ifinedo, pp. 119–136. InTech, Croatia (2012)

Lin, R., Lin, C.L.: From digital archive to e-business: a case study of turning "art" to "e-business". In: 2010 International Conference on E-Business, 26–28 July 2010, Athens, Greece (2010)

Lin, R., Lin, P.H., Shiao, W.S., Lin, S.H.: Cultural aspect of interaction design beyond human-computer interaction. HCI **14**(2009), 49–58 (2009)

Lin, R., Cheng, R., Sun, M.-X.: Digital archive database for cultural product design. In: Aykin, N. (ed.) HCII 2007. LNCS, vol. 4559, pp. 154–163. Springer, Heidelberg (2007). ISBN 978-3-540-73286-0

Lin, R., Chang, C.L.: A study of consumer perception in innovative product. In: International Conference, Australia, 17–21 November 2004

Locher, P., Overbeeke, K., Stappers, P.J.: Spatial balance of color triads in the abstract art of Piet Mondrian. Percep.-Lond. **34**(2), 169–190 (2005)

Mandler, G.: The consciousness continuum: from "qualia" to "free will". Psychol. Res. **69**(5–6), 330–337 (2005)

McManus, I.C., Cheema, B., Stoker, J.: The aesthetics of composition: a study of Mondrian. Empirical Stud. Arts **11**(2), 83–94 (1993)

Mondrian, P.: Plastic Art and Pure Plastic Art, 1937, and Other Essays, 1941-1943, vol. 2. Alan Wofsy Fine Arts, San Francisco (2008)

Mondrian, P.: Natural Reality and Abstract Reality: An Essay in Trialogue Form (1919-1920). George Braziller, New York (1995)

Monk, A., Lelos, K.: Changing only the aesthetic features of a product can affect its apparent usability. In: Venkatesh, A., Gonzalvez, T., Monk, A., Buckner, B. (eds.) Home Informatics and Telematics: ICT for The Next Billion. IFIP — The International Federation for Information Processing, pp. 221–233. Springer, US (2007)

Noll, A.M.: The beginning of computer art in the United States: a memoir. Comput. Graph. **19**(4), 495–503 (1995)

Noll, A.M.: Human or machine: a subjective comparison of Piet Mondrian's "Composition With Lines" (1917) and a computer-generated picture. Psychol. Rec. **16**, 1–10 (1966)

Norman, D.A.: The Psychology of Everyday Things. Basic Books, New York (1988)

Norman, D.A.: Emotional Design. Basic Books, New York (2004)

Smyth, S.N., Wallace, D.R.: Towards the synthesis of aesthetic product form. In: Proceedings of DETC2000/DTM-14554, ASME, New York (2000)

Taft, C.: Color meaning and context: comparisons of semantic ratings of colors on samples and objects. Color Res. Appl. **22**(1), 40–50 (1997)

Troy, N.J.: Mondrian and Neo-plasticism in America. Yale University Art Gallery, New Haven (1979)

Van Zijl, I.: The Rietveld Schroder House. Princeton Architectural Press, Princeton (1999). Rietveld, G.T. (ed.)

Warncke, C.P.: De Stijl, 1917-1931. Hacker Art Books, New York (1991)

Yen, H.-Y., Lin, C., Lin, R.: A study of applying qualia to business model of creative industries. In: Rau, P. (ed.) HCII 2013 and CCD 2013, Part I. LNCS, vol. 8023, pp. 148–156. Springer, Heidelberg (2013)

Thoughts on Studying Cultural Ergonomics for the Atayal Loom

Yuma Taru[1], John Kreifeldt[2], Ming-Xean Sun[3], and Rungtai Lin[1](✉)

[1] Graduate School of Creative Industry Design, National Taiwan University of Arts, Ban Ciao City, Taipei 22058, Taiwan
lihan.workshop@gmail.com, rtlin@mail.ntua.edu.tw

[2] Tufts University, Medford, MA, USA
john.Kreifeldt@tufts.edu

[3] Institute of Applied Arts, National Chiao Tung University, Hsinchu 300, Taiwan
buddasfox@gmail.com

Abstract. The purpose of this study is to explore the meaning of cultural objects and to extract their cultural features from Taiwanese aboriginal culture. Atayal is a tribe of Taiwanese aborigines whose culture is disappearing rapidly due to a hundred years of colonization. The weaving box, a cultural object, unique to the Atayal loom, is the subject of this study. Based on the previous studies, this study proposes a cultural ergonomic research model to provide designers with a valuable reference for designing a successful cross-cultural product as well as the interwoven experience of design and culture in the design process. This study attempts to illustrate how by enhancing the original meaning and images of Taiwan aboriginal culture features they may be transformed into modern products by taking advantage of new production technology and so fulfill the needs of the contemporary consumer market.

Keywords: Ergonomics · Cultural ergonomics · Atayal loom · Taiwan aboriginal culture

1 Introduction

Cultural ergonomics extends our understanding of cultural meaning and our ability to utilize such understanding for design and evaluating everyday products (Kaplan 2004). Designers need to develop a better understanding of cultural ergonomics not just to participate in cultural contexts but also to develop interactive experiences for users. Thus, cultural ergonomics is an approach that considers interaction and experience-based variations among cultures in cultural product design (Lin et al. 2016). Hence, cultural products can extend the heritage and traditional values of different cultures to the consumer and increase the sense of spiritual essence in human life (Varutti 2015; Guttentag 2009). Perhaps the best way to extend a unique culture, as for example when we talk about the impressions of different culture garments, crafts, decorations, utensils, furniture, ornaments, packages, etc., is to promote it to users' daily lives through product usage (Lin 2007, 2009). Culture plays an important role in the design field,

P.-L.P. Rau (Ed.): CCD 2016, LNCS 9741, pp. 377–388, 2016.
DOI: 10.1007/978-3-319-40093-8_38

and cross-cultural design will be a key design evaluation point in the future. Designing "culture" into products will be a design trend in the global market. Obviously, we need a better understanding of cross-cultural communications not only for the global market, but also for local design. While cross-cultural issues become important for product design in the global economy, the intersection of design and culture becomes a key issue making both local design and the global market worthy of further in-depth study (Lin et al. 2009). The importance of studying culture is shown repeatedly in several studies in all areas of technology design.

Taiwan is a multi-culture fusion of traditional Chinese with significant East Asian influences. Over time, Taiwan gradually developed its own distinct culture, mostly from a variation of Southern China culture (Lin 2007). Evidence shows that the prospect of Taiwan's local cultures will undoubtedly become crucial cultural elements in future design applications (Lin 2009). Of course, the Taiwanese aboriginals also have distinct and abundant cultures. With their beautiful, primitive, and spiritually motived visual arts and crafts, Taiwan's aboriginal cultures should have great potential for enhancing design value, and being recognized in the global market (Hsu et al. 2013).

For example, the Atayal tribe which is composed of several subgroups is one of the best weaving tribes in Taiwan. In their traditional society, Atayal men did the hunting, fighting, farming and house building, while Atayal women were known for the artistry of their handwoven artifacts (Chang et al. 2008). Having suffered from their traditions being nearly extinguished in the past colonial periods, the Atayal tribe members are now trying to retrieve their textile traditions and they have already achieved fruitful innovations rooted in their ancestors' wisdom (Yoshimura and Wall 2014). For example, the first author has spent years "reverse engineering" many old woven tribal patterns to preserve the knowledge of how to weave them, a knowledge that was formerly passed from mother to daughter. She also runs and is trying to improve a school for the children of a poor village in the hills above Miaoli, has built a cultural center called lihang workshop and promotes interest in their culture (https://www.facebook.com/lihangworkshop).

The weaving art of the Atayal in Taiwan has developed rapidly over the past decade. Women's weavings have performed outstandingly in various textiles exhibitions through combining traditional textiles with modern weaving techniques. For example, Yuli Taki is also trying to preserve cultural patterns by commercializing use of them (Lin and Kreifeldt 2014). The Truku used to be one of the several subgroupings of the Atayal peoples but are now officially recognized as an independent group. (The aboriginal groups seem to be fractioning at a great rate.) However, while Truku weaving has much in common with other Atayal peoples, Truku textiles are distinguished by their light weight, thinness, quiet color and patterns mostly of single lozenges (https://www.facebook.com/yuli.taki/). Among some Atayal peoples such as the Malikuowan, these seemingly simple lozenge shapes are called "eyes" and stand for the blessings of countless ancestors. With those blessings the people could enter the land of happiness and join their ancestors forever.

Such spirituality characterizes much tribal design giving it an immediacy which even outsiders can feel deeply and respond to without knowing much, if anything, about the culture of the peoples who produced it. Such feeling can transcend cultural differences. An outsider may say that certain primitive art "speaks" to him which is more than just an expression.

By using a cultural ergonomic approach, the gungu, literally "weaving box" in the Atayal aboriginal language, was chosen as the cultural object for discussion in this study. A framework will be proposed for examining the way designers communicate across cultures as well as the interwoven experience of ergonomic design and culture meaning in the design process. Using the framework, this study attempts to illustrate how, by enhancing the original meaning and images of Taiwan aboriginal culture features, and taking advantage of new production technology, they may be transformed into modern products and so fulfill the needs of the contemporary consumer market (Lin 2007, 2009).

2 Cultural Object of Atayal Loom

Although the date of the first loom or even what it looked like is unknown. As a weaving tool in one form or another it dates back at least to the ancient Egyptians and Greeks (Roth 1913, 1918). Three main types of loom were used in the ancient world: the horizontal ground loom, the vertical loom with upper and lower beams around which the warp threads are wound, and the vertical loom with warp weights. The warp is the stationary threads across which the weft threads are woven in and out. The horizontal ground loom is the older of the looms of Ancient Egypt (Crowfoot 1937; Faxon 1932).

The Atayal woven crafts played a large role in the tribe's social customs and organization. These crafts were woven on a type of loom called a "backstrap" loom which is the subject of this study. "Backstrap" refers to the strap behind the weaver's back as in Fig. 1 and Table 1. The Atayal loom is one of the original types of simple movable backstrap-type looms (Broudy 1979). The earliest example (201 B.C.–8 A.D.) of a backstrap loom in eastern Asia is found at a site in Shizhaishan, Yunnan Province (Broudy 1979). It was similar in principle to the Atayal loom in being "foot braced". That is, the weaver controlled the tension of the warp threads by pushing with her feet against a brace. The foot brace could be a simple bar but in the Atayal loom it is the culturally important "box" By changing the arrangement of the warping bench and one's way of weaving, simple even weaves to Atayal's own characteristic complex patterns can be woven.

Traditional Atayal looms were composed of many parts, with one of the most important being the Weaving Box, made of tough woods like beech and Formosan michelia. The weaving box was not only an important part, but could also be used for storage when weaving wasn't taking place (Broudy 1979). In the days long ago when head hunting was practiced, the hollow box could be struck to make a loud drum sound as a signal to the village that a warrior had returned with a head. For a clear understanding of the Atayal loom, the features of all parts of the Atayal loom must be understood. Diagrams of their parts are therefore included in Fig. 1 and Table 1.

The threads in Fig. 1 are called the "warp". Weaving consists of lacing a "weft" thread over and under selected warp threads as it goes from one side of the warp to the other and then reverses direction and repeats lacing and so on until finished. The "art"

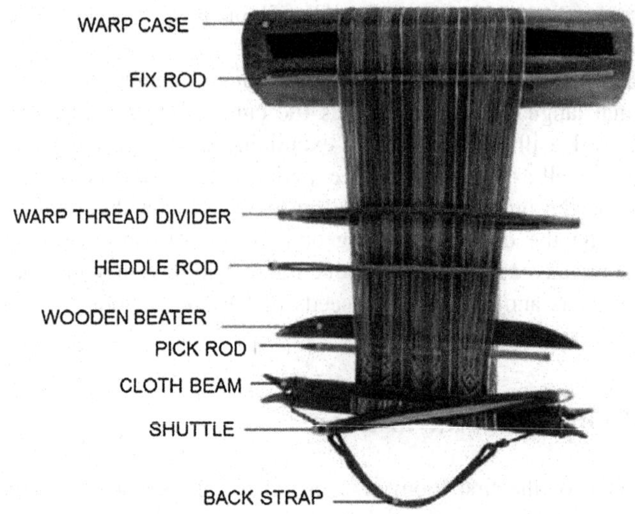

Fig. 1. Atayal Backstrap Loom (Color figure online)

consists of choosing the colors for the warp threads and the complexity of the lacing of the weft thread (which also may change colors) as it goes over some warp threads and under others. It is the particular lacing plan in combination with the coloring of the warp threads which makes the pattern. Practically infinite combinations of colors and lacings (i.e., patterns) exist. Creativity comes in designing aesthetically pleasing combinations. In tribal days before writing and modern means of recording such information existed, these highly complex combinations had to be committed to memory and passed as instructions from mother to daughter - prodigious feats of memory. Sadly, once that mother to daughter chain was broken, as by outside disruptions, this information was lost. It takes modern "reverse engineering", special coded weaving annotation, and great dedication, to reconstruct these instructions from careful examination of existing examples and record them permanently for posterity. Lest it be thought that weaving is somehow inferior to the other arts because it can be described in this mechanical sounding fashion, it is also true that making piano or organ music can be described (as Bach did) as just pressing the right keys down at the right time and the music makes itself.

The weaves used by the Atayal and patterns produced with them are technically interesting and aesthetically pleasing (Lin and Kreifeldt 2014). In the past, each tribe could be distinguished by the unique types and patterns of its weavings. Recently, with the rapidly changing social trends and progress in technology, tribes or individual studios weaving textiles hope to see this field embracing both tradition and originality in order to create different possibilities for future development (Yoshimura and Wall 2014). Furthermore, the new Atayal weavers work closely with tourism marketing channels to balance the production and marketing of textiles. Therefore, the future of weaving art is full of hope and potential. The Atayal loom is apparently unique and deserves in-depth study (Nettleship 1970).

Table 1. All parts of the Atayal Backstrap loom

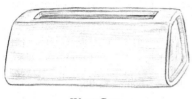

Warp Case

There are "large" and "small" sizes for warp cases, which could have the length of 90cm or 60cm, depending on the need of a weaver or the custom of a tribe. Usually it is sized to meet special physical needs of the weaver. The wooden materials usually are selected from trees that possess properties of sturdiness and firmness such as camphor tree, beech tree, Formosan Michelia tree and so on.

Fix Rod

The Fix Rod is made of straighter and longer Yushania bamboo internode. The diameter of a fix rod should be 0.6cm to 1.3cm and the required length of a rod is usually based on the width of the demanded fabric, thus several different fix rods with different sizes should be prepared in advance.

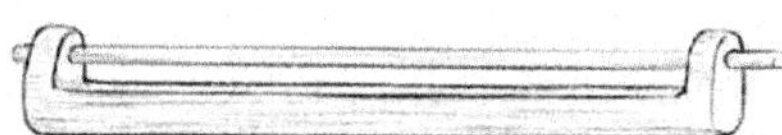

Type 1 Warp Thread Divider

Type 2 Warp Thread Divider

The length of a warp thread divider is determined by the width of the piece of weaving fabric, which could be 50cm or 35cm wide. Wood or Yushania bamboo is the selected material for making it. There are 2 different types of warp thread dividers. The first type is widely used in most of the Atayal people's areas, whilst the second type of warp thread divider is especially used in the catchment area of Ta'an river and also it's used especially for pick-up pattern weaving techniques.

Type 1 Heddle Rod

Type 2 Heddle Rod

The length of a heddle bar is around 35cm long, determined by different fabric widths. Wood or Yushania bamboo material is selected for making heddle rods. There're two types of them. The first type is made of thin and long Yushania bamboo and will get wound around with warp-tying yardage. The second type is a hairpin-shaped rod, which is made of twig wood and is widely used in the catchment area of Ta'an River. Both prongs of the hairpin-shaped rod are drilled with small eyes for fine threads to string through and get ready for sealing this part after warp threads are fixed into the oblong slot. The sealing ~~can~~ secures the warp threads from sliding off while weaving.

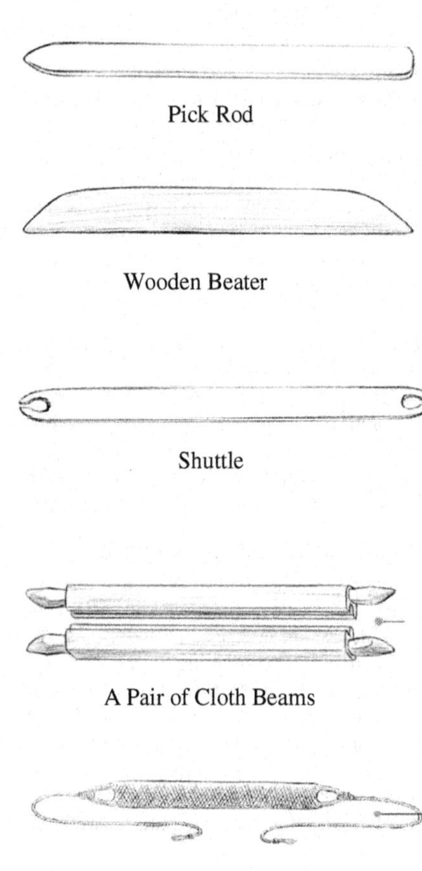

Pick rods are made of Makino bamboo or wood materials, and usually will be prepared in many different sizes for making fabrics of different widths.

A wooden beater is made of sturdy hardwood material. The blade should be thicker at the upper part and get thinned towards the lower edge. It is typically 60cm in length and 5-6cm in width.

A Shuttle is a tool designed to neatly and compactly store the weft thread and carry it across the warp yarn while weaving. Shuttles are thrown or passed back and forth through the shed – an opening made between the threads of the warp - in order to weave in the weft.

Cloth beams are made of sturdy wood material from the elm tree, camphor tree or Formosan Michelia tree. A tongue and a matching groove are cut into a pair of the cloth beams respectively for fastening the finished fabric tightly between them. The length of each beam is about 50 to 60cm.

The Back Strap is woven out of rottan material or made of ramie through the bow weaving technique. The usual length is 50cm and width is about 50cm. Extra binding strings can be made based on a weaver's need.

3 A Framework for Studying Cultural Ergonomics

Piegorsch (2009) described how an ergonomic bench was designed for indigenous weavers in Guatemala that is a typical example of cultural ergonomics. The ergonomic bench helps weavers enhanced their productivity and improved textile quality, while also preventing cumulative trauma to their health. The bench focused on user-centered ergonomic design and also stimulated self-awareness in traditional weaving. The benefits of cultural ergonomics can be represented as a cycle with five stages: health, productivity, quality, culture and self-esteem (Piegorsch 2009). It is likely to be a never-ending process and can be applied universally, strengthening the connection between the designers and their cultural heritage as shown as the outer circular factors in Fig. 2.

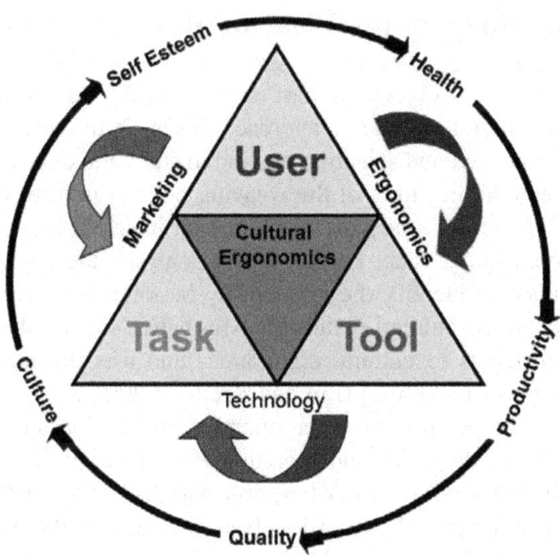

Fig. 2. A framework for studying cultural ergonomics

For the human system design, Kreifeldt and Hill (1974) proposed a user-tool-task system design model that integrates ergonomics into product design for producing aesthetically pleasing and functionally superior products. Base on the user-tool-task model, Lin et al. (2016) proposed a framework for combining cultural features with ergonomic design which facilitating an understanding of cultural ergonomics in product design shown as the inner triangular factors in Fig. 2.

For the cultural ergonomics approach (Kring et al. 2006), the framework consists of two main parts that function to explore the cultural ergonomics issues of the cultural object and to study problems related to human factors. To accomplish the outer circular factors: health, productivity, quality, culture and self-esteem, the inner triangular factors must be considered in practical ergonomic design (Piegorsch 2009). Thus, Fig. 2 details the various influences and interactions in a user-tool system and emphasizes the threefold nature of the design: user, tool (product), and task. Among the user-tool-task, there are the two interfaces of the user-tool manipulation interface (ergonomics) and the tool-task engagement interface (technology); and the various interactions between user needs and design requirements in the practical design process (marketing).

The user-tool-task model is designed to solve the problem of completing a task with a tool; it focuses first on the manipulation interface between the user and the tool and then on the engagement interface between the tool and the task. Finally, for the global market, adding a cultural dimension to ergonomics has become an important issue for exploring interaction and experience in product design (Lin et al. 2016). Along with technological progress, while product design has been transferred from being manufacturing-based to marketing driven to user centered for some time, there is now greater emphasis specifically on user experience, with ergonomics being increasingly considered in interactional design for marketing.

4 Thoughts on Studying the Weaving Box

The weaving box, a cultural object and part of the Atayal loom, is the subject of this study. Based on the cultural ergonomic approach in Fig. 2, the weaving box could be employed for a systematized and scientific method to study the three aspects of cultural ergonomics. First, ergonomic study of the weaving box across user operational situations needs to be analyzed to study the manipulation interface (ergonomics) between users and the weaving box. Then, based on that analysis, the engagement interface (technology) is studied to identify the relationship between the weaving box and the task. Finally, based on the cultural-feature transformation model, the weaving box is identified with three levels of cultural ergonomics and used to demonstrate how to design cultural products (marketing) (Lin and Kreifeldt 2001).

Considered from the perspective of ergonomics, to develop an ideal loom in the form of the weaving box, the social and operational interfaces of the weaving box both need to be well designed using a user-tool-task approach. Especially, many studies were made to evaluate the prevalence of low back pain among the handloom weavers (Chaman et al. 2015; Durlov et al. 2014; Montamedzade et al. 2014). These studies suggested the need for further research regarding the postural strain of weavers and also emphasized the implementation of ergonomic design into the weaver's loom. For a good example, the ergonomic bench in Piegorsch's research (2009) provides a culturally, environmentally, and economically viable alternative to traditional methods of working with the backstrap loom.

Considered from the perspective of technology, many tools were needed in traditional Atayal weaving as shown in Table 1. Women produced beautiful cloth relying on their professional and aboriginal weaving skills (Wu 1998) but their tools are inconvenient for fetching due to their overweight and numbers, and the tradition of weaving while sitting on the ground. In recent years Atayal people has been seeking creative and alternative ways. A new type of loom called a desktop inkle loom has been devised. Inkle weaving is a type of warp-faced weaving where the shed is created by manually raising or lowering the warp yarns (Patrick 2010), some of which are held in place by fixed heddles on a loom known as an inkle loom (https://en.wikipedia.org/wiki/Inkle_weaving).

Considered from the perspective of marketing, aboriginal cultural products that tourists purchase as souvenirs are often actually imitations of the original products, and sold without authorization from the aboriginal group (Guttentag 2009). Atayal textiles are now handwoven by some aboriginal women in Wulai who weave primarily for the Wulai Atayal Museum. Weaving exhibitions are the main purpose of the Wulai Atayal museum since it opened in 2005. Other than displaying materials, techniques and final works, the museum arranges to have weavers do live demonstrations on weekends to attract tourism. The museum also sells the works by the members in the weaving association and invites them to be the seed teachers to design promotional activities such as do-it-yourself for user experience, and promote traditional weaving through the flourishing tourism (Varutti 2015). Meanwhile, the reintroduction of weaving not only required the Atayal weavers to retrace their weaving history and to reconstruct and revive lost skills but also opened up a new opportunity to create new motifs with the Atayal loom (Chang et al. 2008; Yoshimura and Wall 2014).

5 Summary

Based on a previous discussion (Lin et al. 2016), this study proposes a cultural ergonomic research model to provide designers with a valuable reference for designing a successful cross-cultural product as shown in Fig. 3. The model consists of four main parts: conceptual model, research method, human system design, and cultural ergonomic approach. The conceptual model focuses on how to extract cultural features from cultural ergonomics and then transfer those features to the design transformation model to design cultural products.

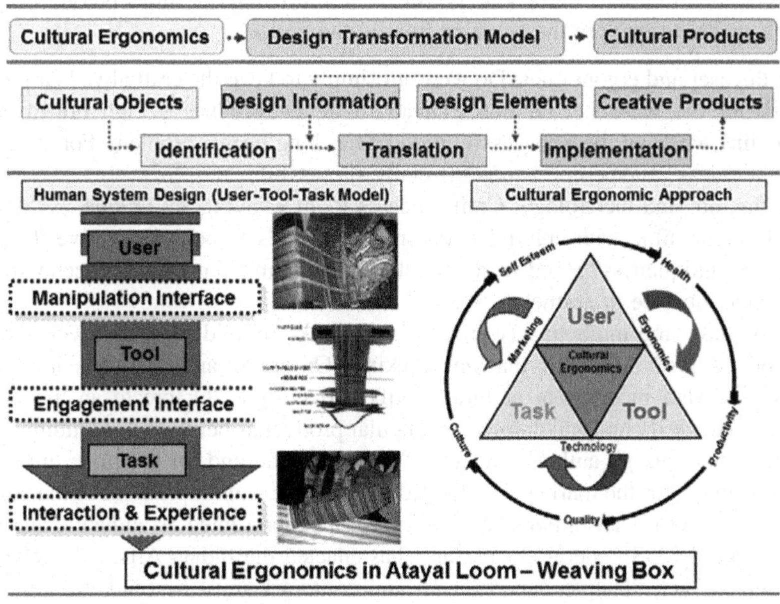

Fig. 3. A cultural ergonomic research model in Atayal loom

The research method consists of four steps: from cultural object to design information, then to design elements, finally to creative products; and three stages: (1) extracting cultural features from original cultural objects (identification), (2) translating these features into design information and design elements (translation), and (3) designing a cultural product (implementation).

The purpose of human system design research focuses on and analyzes the weaving box's appearance, usability, cultural meaning, operational interface, and the scenario in which it is used. There are social meanings, ergonomic concerns and the functional achievement associated with this cultural object. To develop an ideal loom, both the cultural and operational interfaces of the "weaning box" need to be well-studied using a user-tool-task approach (Lin and Kreifeldt 2001).

Recently, the reintroduction of weaving has had multiple effects on the Atayal community. Now the Atayal proudly claim their weaving culture as a part of their ethnic identity. The meaning of weaving has changed from the representation of the Atayal women's gender identity alone to the representation of the Atayal's collective ethnic identity as a whole (Yoshimura 2007). It has become an ethnic symbol and a tourism product. However, the Atayal tribe, especially the residents of Wulai, are now barely involved directly with tourism business although symbols of their identity are used to promote tourism (Yoshimura 2007; Yoshimura and Wall 2014). As an example of reviving tribal arts, a "carved, blackware pottery jar" recently made by Tammy Garcia of the Santa Clara pueblo tribal people in the US state of New Mexico sold at auction for $47,500. It expressed feelings of modernity but in the tradition of her people (Johnson et al. 2015).

Having this in mind, we need to consider the following questions before using the research model to explore the weaving box of Atayal loom.

1. For the user and ergonomics: Do we want simply to keep the craft alive? Or provide work for the weavers? Or make an art of it? Or produce a high priced artist? Deciding what will be a successful product has long been a problem. For every 100 "great" ideas, maybe one is commercially successful.
2. For the tool and technology: Crafts such as loom weaving are unique. Is "design" really compatible with cultural tradition which tends to be conservative if it is to retain its uniqueness? Hand work will always be a limited production technique. So its value must be in aesthetics.
3. For the task and marketing (works): Maybe make individual design works which would be prohibitive for machine making. Or create an artist weaving maker demand. Also incorporate cultural motifs and designs. Or create an association which will verify and can enforce a particular product as being of that culture. When there is not enough authentic art to meet the demand and for the price, imitations will be made for the market. The United States has a similar problem of the cultural arts of the American Indians being imitated, misrepresented as authentic and sold. Therefore the US Federal Government has enacted the Indian Arts and Crafts Act. Under this act: "Native American art and craftwork must be marketed truthfully regarding the Native American heritage and Tribal affiliation of the producer." (www.iacb.doi.gov).

There are many parallels to these questions and problems everywhere that native cultures are disappearing and their arts and crafts along with them. It is strange that as these cultures diminish or vanish altogether, their old traditional art pieces become more and more sought by museums and private collectors and consequently become more and more valuable. Beauty is the soul of the artist expressed in her art. Being based in strong religious beliefs, tribal arts express that soul very strongly. It is a mystery how tribal arts can speak to someone even across cultural oceans if not for soul-to-soul communication. As others begin to see the beauty of the art and are moved by it, they wish to possess it even without understanding or even knowing the culture behind the art. That is the passion of the collector. Such cross cultural attraction with consequent desire for possession is what designers of products for the international market should hope to have their products evoke.

Continuing studies of what makes tribal arts such as the weavings of the Atayal, or even a "tool" like the weaving box, so attractive cross culturally can definitely aid in designing successful cross cultural products.

Acknowledgements. The authors gratefully acknowledge the support for this research provided by the Ministry of Science and Technology, Taiwan under Grants 103-2221-E-144 -001 -MY2 and 103-2410-H-144 -003 -MY2. The authors also wish to thank those who contributed to the research.

References

Broudy, E.: The Book of Looms: A History of the Handloom from Ancient Times to the Present. UPNE, New York (1979)

Chang, J., Wall, G., Chang, C.L.: Perception of the authenticity of Atayal woven handicrafts in Wulai, Taiwan. J. Hospitality Leisure Mark. **16**(4), 385–409 (2008)

Chaman, R., Aliyari, R., Sadeghian, F., Shoaa, J.V., Masoudi, M., Zahedi, S., Bakhshi, M.A.: Psychosocial factors and musculoskeletal pain among rural hand-woven carpet weavers in Iran. Saf. Health Work **6**(2), 120–127 (2015)

Crowfoot, G.M.: Of the warp-weighted loom. Annu. Brit. Sch. Athens **37**, 36–47 (1937)

Durlov, S., Chakrabarty, S., Chatterjee, A., Das, T., Dev, S., Gangopadhyay, S., Sahu, S.: Prevalence of low back pain among handloom weavers in West Bengal, India. Int. J. Occup. Environ. Health **20**(4), 333–339 (2014)

Faxon, H.: A model of an ancient Greek loom. Bull. Metrop. Mus. Art **27**, 70–71 (1932)

Guttentag, D.: The legal protection of indigenous souvenir products. Tourism Recreation Res. **34** (1), 23–34 (2009)

Johnson, H.: Reflections on 40 years. Part 3. American Indian Art Magazine, vol. 40, no. 3, p. 23, Summer (2015)

Hsu, C.-H., Chang, S.-H., Lin, R.: A design strategy for turning local culture into global market products. Int. J. Affect. Eng. **12**, 275–283 (2013)

Kaplan, M.: Introduction: Adding a Cultural Dimension to Human Factors. Advances in Human Performance and Cognitive Engineering Research, vol. 4, pp. XI–XVII. Emerald Group Publishing Limited, Bradford (2004)

Kreifeldt, J.G., Hill, P.H.: Toward a theory of man-tool system design applications to the consumer product area. In: Proceedings of the Human Factors and Ergonomics Society Annual Meeting (1974)

Kring, J.B., Morgan, J.B., Kaplan, M.: Cultural ergonomics. In: Karwowski, W. (ed.) International Encyclopedia of Ergonomics and Human Factors, vol. 3, Second edn. CRC Press, Boca Raton (2006)

Lin, C.L., Chen, S.J., Hsiao, W.H., Lin, R.: Cultural ergonomics in interactional and experiential design: Conceptual framework and case study of the Taiwanese twin cup. Appl. Ergon. **52**, 242–252 (2016)

Lin, R., Kreifeldt, J.: Do Not Touch – A Conversation Between Dechnology to Humart. NTUA, New Taipei City (2014)

Lin, R., Kreifeldt, J.G.: Ergonomics in wearable computer design. Int. J. Ind. Ergon. **27**, 259–269 (2001)

Lin, R.: Transforming Taiwan aboriginal cultural features into modern product design: a case study of a cross-cultural product design model. Int. J. Des. **1**, 45–53 (2007)

Lin, R.: Designing friendship into modern products. In: Toller, J.C. (ed.) Friendships: Types, Cultural, Psychological and Social, pp. 1–24. Nova Science Publishers, New York (2009)

Motamedzade, M., Afshari, D., Soltanian, A.: The impact of ergonomically designed workstations on shoulder EMG activity during carpet weaving. Health Promot. Perspect. **4** (2), 144–150 (2014)

Nettleship, M.A.: A unique South-East Asian loom. Man **5**, 686–698 (1970)

Patrick, J.: The Weaver's Idea Book: Creative Cloth on a Rigid Heddle Loom. F+W Media Inc., Blue Ash (2010)

Piegorsch, K.: An ergonomic bench for indigenous weavers. Ergon. Des. Q. Hum. Fact. Appl. **17** (4), 7–11 (2009)

Roth, H.L.: Ancient Egyptian and Greek Looms. Library of Alexandria, Egypt (1913)

Roth, H.L.: Studies in primitive looms. J. Anthropol. Inst. Great Brit. Irel. **48**, 103–144 (1918)

Varutti, M.: Crafting heritage: artisans and the making of Indigenous heritage in contemporary Taiwan. Int. J. Heritage Stud. **21**(10), 1036–1049 (2015)

Wu, S.H.: The characteristics of Taiyal weaving as an art form. Doctoral dissertation, Durham University, UK (1998). http://etheses.dur.ac.uk/5054/

Yoshimura, M.: Weaving and identity of the Atayal in Wulai, Taiwan. Master thesis, University of Waterloo, Canada (2007)

Yoshimura, M., Wall, G.: Weaving as an identity marker: Atayal women in Wulai, Taiwan. J. Res. Gend. Stud. **2**, 171–182 (2014)

Approaching a Chinese Cultural Transferring Design Model Through Analysis of Culturally Oriented Design and Its Context

Wenjin Yao(✉) and Gang Lu

School of Design, Hunan University, Shenzhen, China
wenjin.yao@network.rca.ac.uk, gang.lu@mlab.cn

Abstract. This paper deals with the case studies and criteria applied to them in terms of Chinese culturally orientated design, in order to test the author's hypotheses about cultural reflections. It develops a three-layer design model reflects Chinese cultural elements into design in terms of symbolic, behavioural and political/philosophical, through methods and analysis of values in practice. Additionally, for the readers sympathetic with a systematic design approach or cultural identitarianism, this work addresses a view of critical understanding for facing Chinese culture in design.

Keywords: Chineseness · Cultural transfer design · Symbolic transfer · Behavioural transfer · Philosophical transfer

1 Introduction

This paper comprises four sections. Section one deals with the relevant concepts around culture, through short criteria of relevant concepts such as technology, globalisation, and some of the general definitions of culture. This section aims to generate a characterization of culture, subsequently searching what Chineseness is. The second section introduces the core hypothesis in this paper - 'Chineseness' - by comparing it to the form "Chinoiserie". The third section depicts three aspects in terms of Chinese cultural transferring design: symbolic, behavioural, and philosophical/political. Then, in Sect. 4, it forms a three-layer cultural transfer design model, which explores a systematic approach to reflecting Chineseness from various cultural angles. These four sections in paper include sources that evidence particular points of view about Chinese culture and design. Additionally they throw up some specific challenges:

How can we characterise local culture that feeds into its social context and design needs?

How can we manifest the cultural elements in design through design methods?

2 A Criteria of the Relevant Concepts Around 'Culture'

What is culture? There are thousands of definitions of culture. Matthew Arnold defined culture as 'a pursuit of our total perfection by means of getting to know, on all the matters

P.-L.P. Rau (Ed.): CCD 2016, LNCS 9741, pp. 389–396, 2016.
DOI: 10.1007/978-3-319-40093-8_39

which most concern us', 'the best which has been thought and said in the world', and through this knowledge, 'turning a stream of fresh and free thought upon our stock notions and habits, which we now follow staunchly but mechanically' [1]. Whereas the view of aspiration towards cultural perfection may not resonate completely today, the sense of culture being very broadly interpreted is one the author can identify with as a designer's 'fresh and free thought', applicable to individual contexts. In another words, culture is an empty vase, a vehicle, which takes the input and output of individuals and groups of people within their surrounding environment and context. Thus, through the criteria of the concepts above, considering the flexibility and trick of it that feeds into different design contexts, rather than define Chinese culture in any one overriding sense, the author attempt to explore a thinking process that is constructed on the understanding of Chineseness within specific design contexts.

2.1 Technology

What is technology? Where should one draw the line when defining hi-tech products? There are no standard answers to these questions. Design researcher Klaus Krippendorff asserts that every action system beyond the basic apparatus of the body is a technology [2]. Through various points in history and the development of human society, technological artefacts/products become moving targets [3]. In the way that ceramics, sculptural tools, and printmaking apparatus were state-of-the-art products thousands of years ago, more recently, films, and electrical goods were considered high-tech. Now, however, when people talk about high-tech products, we are not talking about these technologies. Most of the time, we are talking about our imagination of technology rather than a technology. The forms of high-tech devices are not derived from how they are produced and what they do, but from their users' ability to conceptualize and handle them, which we called the interface. Therefore, we noticed that sometimes, as most of the users hardly know the core technique or manufacture of a product, what they directly connect with the product is through its interface, rather than through the inner workings.

Tracing back to the first Mac, which brought together a number of technical threads in the computer that developed in the 1960s and 1970s, sparking new movements in computing, which is as we know today 'user leads' design thinking. As one of its designers, Jef Raskin remembered:

There were to be no peripheral slots so that customers never had to see the inside of the machine (although external ports would be provided); there was a fixed memory size so that all applications would run on all Macintoshes; the screen, keyboard, and mass storage device (and, we hoped, a printer) were to be built in so that the customer got a truly complete system, and so that we could control the appearance of characters and graphics [4].

On this point, hi-tech is just an inner design element, which needs to be 'well-packed', to be considered comprehensively by designers, and then expressed through an interface or interaction design in the purpose of commercial attraction. For a designer, there should be no good or bad technology, but only better or worse design choices. Moreover, for dealing with local cultural related design, it is about how to represent interfaces or interactions to users, with both 'well-packaged' technology and local cultural consideration within.

2.2 Globalisation, Localisation and Glocalisation

We cannot ignore the fact that there are billions of the world's people living in different social and cultural contexts who are quick to passively accept the exports that are full of western axiology. Today, no matter whether in terms of the image of hi-tech or the way of producing it, innovative design is taking centre-stage in the Western-World standards. Maybe from the Western side, globalisation indicates jumping out of the western culture and understanding others. However, from a non-western, for instance, the Chinese side, it means more to consider the western way, as the western world is the one outside Chinese and which leads the mainstream global market today. China has a population of 1.4-billion and a huge number of individual local cultures on top of the usual diversities of gender, age, area, education and so on. However, there exist common influences from globalisation/westernisation in today's Chinese generations as well: the people inherit specific Chinese characteristics such as strong consciousness of family, high respect for the older intelligence, etc., yet have experienced huge changes during the last thirty years; their lifestyles have shifted and they have had to accept western designs as well as western ways of life in a very short time. Thus, they advocate western technology as well as maintaining pride in Chinese traditions. These global influences comprise the Chinese culture today and are also the causes of estrangement.

We could argue that globalisation causes cultural homogeneity and destroys cultural diversity/heterogeneity in the process, by denying or ignoring cultural identity, or abstracting the cultural identity into a universal. A typical example is the similarity of products and shops in different countries of international brands to suit the purposes of global branding strategy. However, simultaneously, we cannot ignore the fact that globalisation has also fragmented the world landscapes into smaller cultural unites [5], and made culture the most important asset to work with in design's sphere [6], For instance, glocalism in design is a result and part of globalisation. It promotes local identity and highlights cultural values. This occurs maybe because of local designers attempts to save the national identity of products from the homogeneity of the global market; or alternatively, for the local users' better adaption. This trend also leads back via the abstractions of localisation into the global market, in order to increase and attract the global users' interests and curiosities in local culture.

2.3 Chinoiserie and Chineseness

Chinoiserie was a visual and aesthetic reflection of Chinese culture into design from a western perspective, as well as a westerners' Chinese cultural transfer in terms of symbolic aspects: both the decoration of 18th century and contemporary luxury design are characterised by the use of fanciful imagery of an imaginary China. It is a French term, referring to a recurring theme in European artistic styles from the 17th century, since when European design, especially the luxury end, was influenced by Chinese aesthetics and designed through Chinese cultural transfer by European methods of the crafts people. "Chinoiserie is a technical sophistication of Chinese traditional pattern" [7]. Chinoiserie satisfied the western curiosity about Chinese traditional cultural stereotypes. It is a quite visually symbolic format with whimsical contrasts of scale, and by the imitation of Chinese porcelain and the use of lacquer-like materials and decoration, e.g. a fairyland in fanciful mountainous, landscapes with cobweb bridges, carrying flower parasols, lolling in flimsy bamboo pavilions, dragons and phoenixes, etc. [7].

Today, Chinoiserie is still evident in western luxury products for its Chinese and oriental allure. Local designers in China explore Chinoiserie as well, being even much more fascinated with it than in the west. This kind of designing Chinoiserie can be regarded as a cultural symbolic transfer. The new Chinoiserie in China today is also a part of Chineseness in design as well, in terms of catering to people's impression about Chinese culture. However, Chineseness relates to or reflects Chinese cultural characters rather more than visual symbols, in terms of both an outlook of design and reflection of its cultural intelligence and wealth. If we look into our immersed culture now, firstly, today's China sees today's politics, social status, philosophy, and behaviours influenced deeply by both multiple historical and other factors of globalisation. Chineseness today both inherits the traditions, as well as maintaining a great difference from what it was centuries before. For instance, we all know that the Cultural Revolution in the 1960s and 1970s left a disjuncture among the scholarship and scholar class. That means the emphasis of the Chinese traditional philosophies is much weaker than how it was at the much older time. Yet after the turmoil of the Cultural Revolution, starting from the end of the 1970s, globalisation brought western ways and values to Chinese people's lives. Some of the traditional Chinese elements have turned out to be little more than stereotypes, rather than the genuine Chineseness manifest today. On the other hand, it is not surprising to find some of the original and strongest elements of Chinese cultural elements, such as Taoist harmony with nature, the wisdom of Buddhism, Zen, and Confucianism, etc. that exported from China and into the world, represented as much better designs in Japan rather than in China. The periphery of a cultural character and icon tends much more ambiguous with the cultural transmission.

3 Chinese Cultural Transferring Design

3.1 Chinese Symbolic Transfer into Design

Cultural symbolic transfer can be a good way to define products in the homogeneous global market. Its importance is not to pursue how much the design reflects the cultural elements, but to find valuable cultural elements that make the design different or reflect back the users' images about Chineseness. On this point, designers transfer cultural elements into product design to distinguish it, adding commercial allure (Fig. 1).

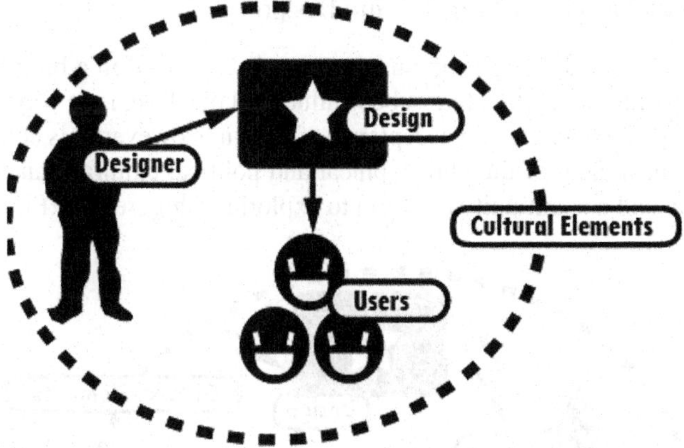

Fig. 1. The relationship of designer, design, users and cultural elements in terms of symbolic transfer.

3.2 Chinese Behavioural Transfer into Design

If we look from the perspective of users' experiences, and see products in terms of technological mediation, design evolves through users' experiences and users' interaction with design. In this way, Chinese cultural transfer into design should be considered on the level of users' behaviour. On this aspect, design focuses on reflecting and extending the thinking around Chinese behavioural transfer into and how it can be better adapted by Chinese users. To integrate the user's behaviour with design, the designers should research through user experience, search and abstract the relevant cultural elements surrounding users and then accommodate those into a design, with the ultimate goal of users' better acceptance of products (Fig. 2).

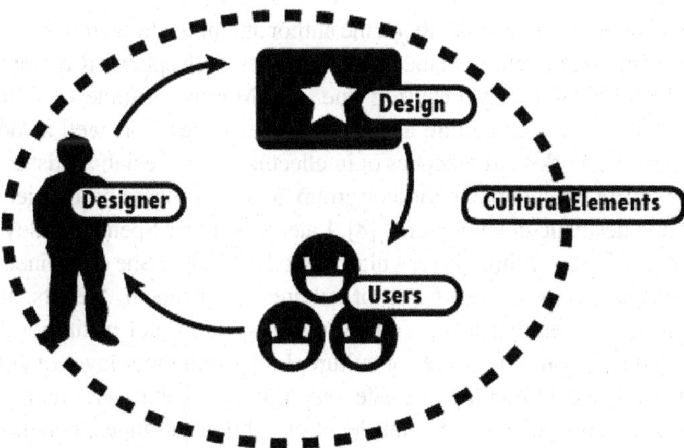

Fig. 2. The relationship of designer, design, users and cultural elements in terms of behavioural transfer.

3.3 Chinese Philosophical Transfer into Design

Moreover, the designers, designs and users were all immersed in a big philosophical/political mix of different factors that subtly influenced the designer's way of creativity, or the people's understanding and acceptance of design. However, this complexity also contributes to the wealth of the philosophical and political cultural transfer as design communication and a community platform to exploring Chineseness (Fig. 3).

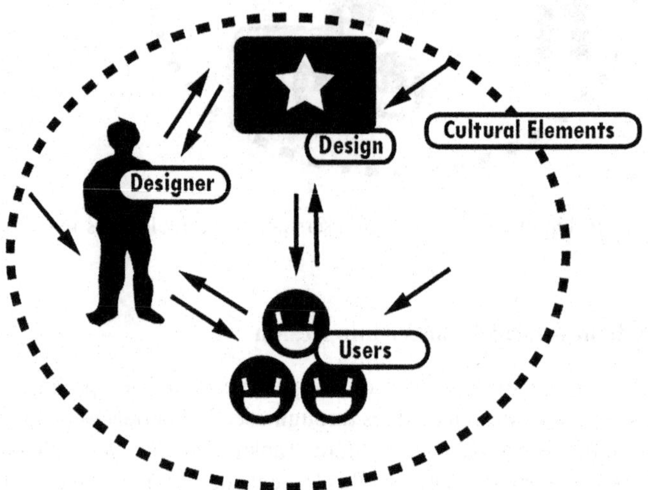

Fig. 3. The relationship of designer, design, users and cultural elements in terms of political/philosophical transfer.

4 An Emerging Model of Chineseness

Simultaneously, in order to structure them, the author attempted to search the models of the classification/definition of culture in the sociological research sphere. Raymond Williams' social cultural theory is a very inspiring one. His Marxist critique of culture studies (cultural materialism) viewed culture as a 'productive process', as well as defined three terms of culture: "the works and practices of intellectual and especially artistic activity, the particular way of life of a people, period or group, and the process of a society's intellectual, spiritual and aesthetic development" [8]. Later researcher Spencer-Oatey's extended the concept of culture as a three-layer cultural model (2000). She combined both basic assumptions and values in one 'segment' of culture. In her model, 'beliefs, attitudes and conventions' influence another layer, consisting of "systems and institutions", which in turn are encircled by a split outer layer of culture. In the split outer layer of culture, "artefacts & products" is located on the one side and "rituals & behaviour" on the other side. The model also contains another 'mental' level of culture: 'attitudes, beliefs and behavioural conventions', which makes a useful distinction between values on the one hand, and their expression in a more precise, but at a non-implemented level on the other [9]. This can be regarded as the extension of Williams' theory. Dahl reviewed Spencer-Oatey's model that it 'describes culture as a shared set of basic assumptions and values, making the level of culture more practical'. As well as, it is the combination of a number of 'additional factors that apart from values and resultant behaviour and artefacts, including a description of the functions that culture performs' [10].

In addition, in design research area, Lin and Leong defined three cultural levels for their culture-oriented design model:

- Physical or material culture
- Social or behavioural culture, including human relationships and social organization
- Spiritual culture—including art and religion [11].

Hence, inspired by Williams, Spencer-Oatey and Lin's work, the author located 'how to manifest Chineseness into design' as the following three-layer structure: symbolic layer, behavioural layer, and philosophical/political layer. This structure is a view to characterise Chineseness in terms of design practice. This also offers a platform to combine the fuzzy set of culturally oriented design concepts with a number of additional relevant research/design methods and knowledge.

This framework is a hybrid and culmination of research through design. Through analysing, combining, simplifying and structuring the ideas that arise from the previous chapters, this interpretive framework clarifies the different statuses of designing Chineseness into three layers: symbolic, behavioural and philosophical/political. It performs as a platform bringing a category of different discursive considerations of design, theories and methods to the research, in order to raise more possibilities within design practices. It also identifies a theoretical thread that divides culture into different layers, representing open-ended and ongoing inquiries, posing relevant questions about culturally orientated design (Fig. 4).

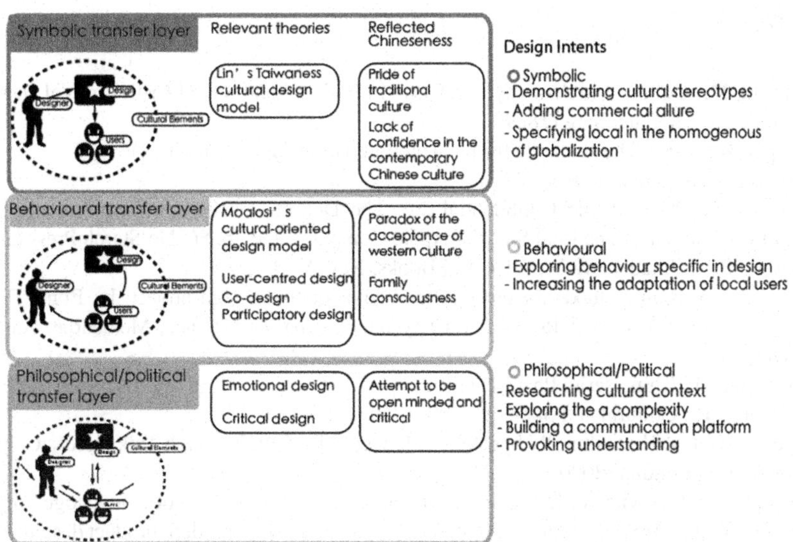

Fig. 4. Three-layer structure for culture-transfer design

This analytic framework can be dynamic, less of a hierarchical method. For design practical work always brings out more questions about the Chinese cultural and behavioural complexity, as well as broadens the research file. This method explores the manifestation of Chineseness into a structural manner (a system) that enables more apposite design methods.

5 Conclusion

This paper describes three ways of exploring the transfer of Chinese culture into design: symbolic, behavioural and political/philosophical. They culminate in an enabling developmental structure through which designers can deal with Chinese cultural complexity in design. This is for designers investigating relations between culture and design through an experiential perspective of Chinese culture in terms of developing a new understanding of 'Chineseness'. Designers in practices can manifest their own understanding of Chineseness through design, for adding special values for design from the perspectives of regarding the different kinds of relationship between the four factors: designer, design, users and cultural elements. 'Chineseness' in this work, can be re-mapped as a form of communication that deals with Chinese culture in design. It is not just along with historical stereotypes, nor a remote copy of other countries' successful cultural transfers, but rather should be inseparable from the radical social phenomena and design culture already emerging within contemporary China. The author's work is ultimately allowing Chineseness to be less implied and instead, to be made manifest, in terms of what behaviours over symbolism and decoration. This paper also remarks some stereotypes, generalisations and categorisations when designers deal with cross-cultural design from both non-Chinese and Chinese angles.

References

1. Arnold, M.: Culture and Anarchy: An Essay in Political and Social Criticism, vol. 7, p. 50. Oxford Project Gutenberg (1869)
2. Krippendorff, K.: The semantic turn: a new foundation for design (2004)
3. Wilson, S.: Information arts (2002)
4. Linzmayer, O.W.: Apple Confidential 2.0: The Definitive History of the World's Most Colorful Company: The Real Story of Apple Computer, Inc., p. 86. No Starch Press (2004)
5. Barber, B.R.: Jihad vs McWorld. Corgi Books, New York (2011)
6. Lee, K.L.: Design methods for cross-cultural collaborative design project. In: Bono, D.A.D. (ed.) Redmond in Design Research Society International Conference, Melbourne, Australia (2004)
7. Jacobson, D.: Chinoiserie. Phaidon (1999)
8. Williams, R.: Cultural and Society: 1780–1950 (1958)
9. Spencer-Oatey, H.: Culturally Speaking: Managing Rapport Through Talk Across Cultures. Continuum, London (2000)
10. Dahl, S.: An Overview of Intercultural Research: The Current State of Knowledge (2004)
11. Lin, R.: Transforming Taiwan aboriginal cultural features into modern product design: a case study of a cross-cultural product design model. Int. J. Des. **1**(2), 9 (2007)

Design and Application of the Illustrations of *Zhuangzi*

Mo-Li Yeh[1(✉)], Yuan-Qian Liu[1], and Po-Hsien Lin[2]

[1] Graduate School of Product and Media Design, Fo Guang University, Jiaosi, Yilan County 26247, Taiwan
1101moli@gmail.com, 316396246@qq.com
[2] Graduate School of Creative Industry Design, National Taiwan University of Arts, Banqiao District, New Taipei City 22058, Taiwan
t0131@mail.ntua.edu.tw

Abstract. *Zhuangzi* is a Chinese cultural treasure. *Zhuangzi* is of inestimable value due to its preservation of ancient mythological material, its literary and philosophical innovation, its eccentric imagery and rich creativity, and the strong narrative quality of its many allegories. It was often the subject of illustrations in classical works. Efforts to preserve the messages of *Zhuangzi*, to transform its abstract ideas into tangible forms as illustrations, and to excavate its treasures have proven to be a great struggle. The present study uses the notion of "Poetic techniques of shape-spirit transformation" proposed by Yeh et al. (2011) as its primary reference point. In her theory of the form and essence of traditional Chinese paintings, she first takes inventory to conduct a comparative analysis of modern illustrations derived from *Zhuangzi*, and then advances a further step toward creating a design model for transforming the artistry of *Zhuangzi* into illustrations.

Keywords: *Zhuangzi* · Transformation · Application · Animation · Illustrations

1 Introduction

Zhuangzi has had a profound influence on Chinese culture. Familiar proverbs such as "a mantis attempting to stop a chariot", "Zhuang Zhou dreams of a butterfly", and "abandoning the sacrificial vessels for the saucepans", among others, all originated from Zhuangzi, and there is no shortage of similar examples. However, due to the length of years, its difficult classical language is an obstacle even for many native Chinese speakers, giving rise to commentaries, references, and adaptations. Among the commentaries are *Zhuangzi Commentary* by Guo Xiang of the Western Jin Dynasty, *Commentary on True Scripture of Southern Florescence* by Cheng Xuanying of the Tang Dynasty, and *Zhuangzi Modern Annotated Edition and Translation* by Chen Guying in modern times. Zhuangzi has been referenced countless times. For example, the line "The immortals leave the world and do not look back, but in the world, life and death are like morning and night" from "Comments from a Visit to the City of

P.-L.P. Rau (Ed.): CCD 2016, LNCS 9741, pp. 397–405, 2016.
DOI: 10.1007/978-3-319-40093-8_40

Immortals" by Su Dongpo derives from the phrase "life and death are day and night" from "The Great Original Teacher" chapter of *Zhuangzi*. Similarly, the phrase "Who wakes up first from the great dream?" from *Romance of the Three Kingdoms* references the phrase "There will be a great awakening, and afterward it will be known that all was a great dream" from the "Making All Things Even" chapter of Zhuangzi. The story "Zhuang Zhou Drums on a Bowl and Attains the Great Dao" in Feng Menglong's Stories to Caution the World is an adaptation of the line "beating on a drum and singing" from *Zhuangzi*. This story was later turned into numerous plays and movies.

However, in this age of digital multimedia, the cultural resources of a wide-ranging, profound, diverse, conceptually rich, and idiosyncratic work like Zhuangzi have yet to be fully tapped. Under these conditions, retracing how the abstract artistic elements of Zhuangzi have been transformed into concrete illustrations, and then into outstanding cultural products such as cartoon animation, is a path of inquiry worth pursuing.

At present, animated versions of Zhuangzi are relatively few. The best-known are Tsai Chih Chung's *Zhuangzi Says* from 2004, the corporate anime xxxHOLiC: Shunmuki from 2010, and Zhuang Zhou Dreams of a Butterfly by the China Central Academy of Fine Arts from 2015. In general, the screen adaptations of the artistry of Zhuangzi have not yet reached their full potential. The present study employs the design model of "Poetic techniques of shape-spirit Transformation" proposed by Mo-Li Yeh in 2011 as its standard of judgment, undertaking a multi-faceted comparison of the successes and failures of these three two-dimensional (2D) works (illustrations). Based on an analysis of the successes and failures of the three works, the present study assembles a theory and produces a model for adapting the artistry of Zhuangzi featuring four ideal illustrations.

2 Zhuangzi and Related Visual Works

Zhuangzi's surname was Zhou, and his courtesy name was Zixiu. He lived in the town of Meng in the state of Song. His year of birth is not known, but he probably lived at the same time as Mencius (372–289 BC), and worked as a supervisor of lacquer work in Meng. He lived in poverty, and made shoes in exchange for rice when he lacked money. In fact, he looked down on wealth, social status, fame, and power. The *Historical Records* state that King Wei of Chu once asked Zhuang Zhou to become a minister, but Zhuang Zhou replied: "I would rather amuse myself in a filthy ditch than be subject to the rules of the leader of a state. I will never take office, and will continue to enjoy my freedom." He did his best to protect himself in turbulent times, to attain release, and to pursue spiritual freedom and ease. The *dao* that is ever-present in Zhuangzi's philosophy represents the origin of the world and its essence, and also refers to the highest ideal in life. It is generally thought that Zhuangzi developed and innovated upon the philosophy of Laozi. However, Ch'ien Mu and Feng Youlan believe that in terms of the history of philosophy, Zhuangzi came before Laozi, and that he formed a critical link between pre-Qin philosophers and Daoists. The 33 chapters in his work *Zhuangzi* are separated into inner, outer, and miscellaneous chapters. It is generally believed that the inner chapters are the work of Zhuangzi, whereas the outer and miscellaneous chapters were written by disciples. Throughout *Zhuangzi*, allegories are abundant, which is why the work professes to be "nine-tenths allegory" in "Allegories". Although there are relatively few animated versions of *Zhuangzi*, their number is considerable in comparison with those of other classical works, and the quality is high. Among these are comic books that have been adapted into works of animation, for instance, the adaptation of Tsai Chih Chung's comic book *Zhuangzi Says* (2004), the adaptation of *xxxHOLiC: Shunmuki* by Japanese manga studio Clamp, and *Xia Chong Guo* by the studio Ink Man. There are also animated adaptations that are not based on comics, such as *Zhuang Zhou Dreams of a Butterfly* by the China Central Academy of Fine Arts and *The Cowboy's Flute* by Shanghai Animation Film Studio. These works have all been widely praised. *Zhuangzi Says* in particular was appreciated by old and young alike, and turned into a three-dimensional (3D) version in 2010.

3 Poetic Techniques of Shape-Spirit Transformation

In the chapter "The World", Zhuangzi says in his own work *Zhuangzi* that it "employs words to offer constant insight, with important quotations to communicate the truth, and an abundance of allegories." As can be seen here, allegories occupy a key position in the artistry of Zhuangzi. Zhuangzi's allegories display a magnanimous, peculiar imagination and a style of "wild ideas and an eccentric flow of thought" which is described in *Generalization of Art/Generalization of Prose* by Liu Xizai. The mysterious philosophy behind the allegories, while constituting an advantage for adaptations, also presents numerous challenges for the creation of a perfect adaptation. Chen et al. (2012) proposes investigating the sensory characteristics of "emotions," "reason," "events," and "scenes" in the imagery and ideas of poetry, and using the attributes of sensory products to analyze four ideally designed products whose design concepts are based on said poetry. Although this model is highly reliable, and some aspects of it are praiseworthy, if used to adapt an expansive, unbridled work of classical Chinese prose such as *Zhuangzi*, the amount of work involved would be extraordinary. Comparatively speaking, the design model of "Poetic techniques of shape-spirit transformation", which is present as "adapting the form and essence of poetry for design" in this paper, constructed by Yeh et al. (2011) in *Applying Poetic Techniques of Shape-Spirit Transformation in Cultural Creative Design* proves easier to use when applied to animated adaptations of the artistry of *Zhuangzi*. "Poetic techniques of shape-spirit transformation" are based on the poet's state of mind as expressed through the poetry, and involve an investigation of the "compositional approach" and an integration of visual sensory activity and imagination as a designer would undertake to deeply penetrate the interior essence of the subject of analysis and assimilate the results, that is, to conduct an "analysis of the structure of meaning." Then comes the process of "putting pen to paper," as a method of specifically applying design adaptations, and "adapting the external forms and internal meanings of poetry," as a method of actually determining related elements such as imagery, material quality, functions, emotions, etc. Finally, the design is put into practice in a "poetic cultural product." This model can be separated into four concrete forms based on cause and effect, namely, "using form to depict form," "using form to depict essence," "attaining essence to depict form," and "depending on essence and emitting essence," that is, the four main models of "using concrete images to depict concrete images," "transforming abstract images into concrete images," "transforming concrete images into abstract images," and "using abstract images to depict abstract images." Although there are four main models, there are only two main elements, "form" and "essence." When adapting the surface "things" in *Zhuangzi* as well as the "situations" behind them from text into imagery, simplifying the four main elements of "emotions," "reason," "events," and "scenes" into the two main elements of "form" and "essence" not only reduces the number of complex procedures but also makes the train of thought easier to follow and puts greater stress on the focal points.

4 An Analysis of the 2D Structure of Current *Zhuangzi* Illustrations in Works of Animation

There is an extremely wide range of different illustrations in *Zhuangzi*, covering nearly every category of literary and commercial illustrations. Works of commercial illustration include animation storyboards, comic book design, and so on; this is the main multimedia area in which illustrations are applied. The Chinese word for "animation" is derived from the same word in English. In Latin, the word "animate" means "to make something become active." All animation achieves the effect of movement by displaying static pictures in succession. Moreover, the word "cartoon" is generally used for humorous or satirical works adapted from political caricatures, and its original meaning refers to a type of 2D drawing technique. In the broad sense, animation includes film cartoons as well as animated films, and both adapt still pictures into moving pictures through a process of static images in motion.

Animation generally uses exaggeration and richly creative activity and language to win the audience's appreciation. It does not rely on pure acting skill to brilliantly depict fantastical characters, and such a format seems more compatible with the stories of Zhuangzi than live-action film. In addition to this high degree of appropriateness, animation is also unique in that it has a consistent visual style, a rich array of colors, and a high degree of completeness. Therefore, the present study focuses on the 2D illustrated portions of the works of animation derived from three Zhuangzi stories, using the animation structure category chart in *Application of Chuang-tzu 2D animation* by Liu and Yeh (2015). Specifically, there are five main types of animation structures: theme and story, animation style, sound structure, static picture structure, and dynamic techniques. These models are used to conduct a comparative investigation of similarities, differences, successes, and failures in the current adaptation processes of the artistry of Zhuangzi. To put emphasis on key points, the present study deconstructs and analyzes three works of animation in detail, that is, the adaptation of Tsai Chih Chung's comic *Zhuangzi Says*, the OVA adaptation of Clamp's manga *xxxHOLiC: Shunmuki*, and the ink painting animation *Zhuang Zhou Dreams of a Butterfly* by the

Illustration title		Zhuangzi Says	xxxHOLiC: Shunmuki	Zhuang Zhou Dreams of a Butterfly
Style			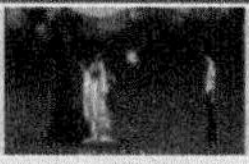	
Original text		Once upon a time, I, Zhuang Zhou, dreamt that I was a butterfly, fluttering here and there, a veritable butterfly enjoying itself to the fullest. I was not aware that I was Zhuang Zhou. Before long, I awoke, and found that I was back to myself again. Now I do not know whether I had dreamt that I was a butterfly, or whether I am now a butterfly dreaming that I am a man. There must be a difference between a man and a butterfly. The transition is called the transformation of things.		
Theme and story	Theme	Zhuang Zhou dreams that he is a butterfly	Following a dream	Zhuang Zhou dreams that he is a butterfly
	Story overview	Zhuang Zhou transforms into a butterfly and cannot tell whether he is Zhuang Zhou or the butterfly. He awakens to the theory of the transformation of things.	A boy with a strange physique works for a mysterious shopkeeper. Someone invites the boy to go off and search for treasure, and the boy finds out that the dream world is interwoven with realistic elements. At last, the boy is taken into the dream world.	Zhuang Zhou dreams that he has transformed into a butterfly, and after waking up he invents a beautiful literary world.
	Characters	Zhuang Zhou is a free and easy-going recluse who narrates the film.	Watanuki Kimihiro witnesses the boy involved in a strange incident. Yuko Ichihara, the beautiful and mysterious shopkeeper, has already died, but she survives in the dream world, where time has stopped.	Zhuang Zhou is a scholar in a landscape painting.
Narrative structure		Non-dramatic narrative	Dramatic narrative	Non-dramatic narrative
Illustration style	2D	Cartoon	Manga	Ink painting
Static picture structure	Setting	Mainly set in a traditional Chinese painting-style setting with mountains, trees, and nature, with a relatively reasonable perspective.	Close shots of cherry trees and empty backgrounds, with a reasonable perspective.	Alternates between ink painting backgrounds and a layer of flowers and birds painted in ink. Ink paintings are used to join images in multiple perspectives.
	Colors	Blue-tinted gray tones, relatively vivid colors, relatively consistent tones.	The interwoven dream world images are relatively dark, tending toward purple hues. The colors are relatively simple and consistent.	Rich coloration, but the tones are relatively consistent. The main color is grayish green. The colors are faded.
	Light	Essentially no light.	Manga style, emphasizing blocks of light on the border between light and shadow as well as diffuse lighting.	A small amount of diffuse lighting.
	Composition	Mid- to close-range perspective, with golden composition, although the composition is not well-defined.	Golden ratio composition, triangular composition, with the composition well-defined.	Scroll-style composition, golden ratio, with the composition relatively well-defined.
	Character models	Characters are simple and exaggerated, and lines are elegant and neat. Characters are flamboyant, but the simplistic design reduces the degree of personality. A skillful adaptation of Cai Zhizhong`s comic book.	The weman has white kimono, long black hair, and butterfly wings. The man is dressed as students. The characters are exaggerated and slender, the lines are elegant, and the designs are simple. As an adaptation of the story, the characters have individuality, and the work appears fresh and lively.	Characters have white clothes, no hair, with beards, like Zen or Daoist ascetics, resembling images of hermits from traditional Chinese paintings. Characters are exaggerated and drawn in freehand in a traditional ink and brush style. Lines are clearly distinguished between thick and thin, but look relatively stiff.

Fig. 1. An analysis of the 2D structure of Zhuangzi animations (Yeh and Liu 2015)

China Central Academy of Fine Arts. We have not analyzed the sound structure or dynamic techniques of three works of animation; we mainly analyzed the 2D illustration portions, specifically the theme and story, the illustration style, the static picture structure, and the appropriateness of the format for adapting stories from Zhuangzi. The study materials is the specific parts from three animations with the same subject that Zhuang Zhou dreams of a butterfly. The process of analysis is shown in Fig. 1.

5 Investigation of Application to Illustrations

Through an analysis of the illustrations above, we can first identify some commonalities in the approaches of the three illustrations to adapt the spirit of Zhuangzi. First, there is a degree of elegance and ease in the lines of the character designs in every case, which serves to adapt the free and easy-going nature of Zhuangzi's spiritual pursuits and his flamboyantly expansive writing style. Next, the characters are exaggerated and the designs are relatively simple: this is appropriate for a work of animation and is also in accordance with the eccentric, outlandish imagery of *Zhuangzi*. Additionally, in terms of composition, mid- to close-range perspectives are prevalent, and the compositions mainly use the golden ratio. The colors are relatively consistent, which serves to preserve the harmony of the images. Finally, when presenting conversations and philosophical details, the backgrounds tend to be empty or drawn in freehand, and such settings are used to place emphasis upon the storyline and the characters, or perhaps to express the fictional nature of the allegories.

The weakness of these generally successful attempts is that despite their capture of Zhuangzi's free and easy-going nature, they overlook his magnificent prose and jocular style. The use of fixed settings to place limits on time and space represents the essence of Zhuangzi but neglects the form. In their attempts to represent the spirit of Zhuangzi's Daoism, they neglected to represent the eccentricity and wildness of the Zhuangzi School.

The present study attempts to carry on the free and easy-going character of the 2D composition of these illustrations, as well as their temporal twists and turns and bold usage of composition, by applying Mo-Li Yeh's design model of "Poetic Techniques of Shape-Spirit Transformation", which adapts the "form" and "essence" of poetry, to some of the words and implications of *Zhuangzi* to create illustrations. Specifically, we aim to construct a more complete conceptual model of adapting the spirit of Zhuangzi by (1) adapting the original text of *Zhuangzi* using the four concrete methods of "using form to depict form," "using form to depict essence," "attaining essence to depict form," and "depending on essence and emitting essence," and (2) undergoing the two adaptation stages of "analysis of the structure of meaning" and "adapting the external forms and internal meanings of poetry" in each method to create illustrations. The process is shown in Fig. 2.

	Original text	Analysis of meaning	Adaptation of meaning		Draft
Using form to depict form	In the northern darkness, there is a fish, and its name is Kun. It is enormous, measuring I don't know how many miles across. It also turns into a bird, and its name is Peng. Peng measures I don't know how many miles across. When it rises in the air, its wings are like the clouds of heaven.	The transformation between Kun and Peng is a transition of sounds, and also a mythological transition. Its main significance lies in the contrasting notions that "Kun and Peng rely upon each other" and that "freedom relies on nothing."	[Form] Kun: Originally refers to fish roe. Here it is used to refer to a large fish. [Form] Peng: An ancient version of the character of "phoenix," here used to refer to a large bird. [Action] Transformation.	[Form] Select the moment that Kun transforms into Peng, when the upper part of its body has already changed into Peng and begun to fly, but its lower part is still the fish tail of Kun, which rises up from the water.	
Using form to depict essence	The lord of the south sea was Shu. The lord of the north sea was Hu. The lord of the center was Chaos...... "Every person has seven orifices from which to see, hear, eat, and breathe. Chaos does not have these. Let's bore some holes into him." Every day they bored a hole into Chaos, but on the seventh day, Chaos died.	"Shu" and "Hu" refer to a state of hurry, and "Chaos" refers to a state of integration. Seven holes were bored into Chaos, at which point he lost his essence and died. the story shows that the selfish human behavior violates nature and the necessity of the respect for the essence of nature.	[Form] The lord of the south sea, Shu. [Form] The lord of the north sea, Hu. [Form] The lord of the center, Chaos. [Action] Boring seven holes.	[Essence] The "hurried" feeling is mainly expressed by a sense of drifting, with a combination of black, white, and red colors, which are simple and stand in strong and surprising contrast. This represents a person being tempted and losing sight of their true nature.	
attaining essence to depict form	That is why it is said that this and that are created by each other. Compare life with death, compare death with life.	Zhuangzi employs three sets of instantaneous transformation to demonstrate that opposing aspects of things rely on each other for their existence.	[Essence] Death and life rely on each other for their existence and each transforms into the other.	[Form] Growing branches and leaves represent life, and withered branches and leaves represent death, and people in a tangled, yin-yang-like state represent mutual reliance and transformation.	
depending on essence and emitting essence	I left today for Yue and arrived yesterday.	"today" and "yesterday" are relative terms. The yesterday of today is the today of yesterday; the today of today is the yesterday of tomorrow.	[Essence] The relative nature of today and yesterday. Today can be called yesterday, and yesterday can be called today.	[Essence] Abstract pictures and text indicating time give a sense of temporal and spatial dislocation.	

Fig. 2. The progress of adapting Zhuangzi to create illustrations (Yeh and Liu 2016)

6 Conclusion

Qian Mu also states in his *Comprehensive Study of Zhuangzi and Laozi* that Zhuangzi's prose "is just like a cup of water" and that "it is always flowing." "But it is as if this cup of water is always changing. It takes on every sort of strange flavor, but still you can't help but enjoy drinking it…" *Zhuangzi* is a fascinating piece of work that is greatly eccentric with a consistent vision. The present study has been guided by the design model of "Poetic techniques of shape-spirit transformation," creating a series of illustrations derived from the text in an attempt to improve the currently existing illustrations. This study also has some limitations. Simple extractions of 2D illustrated images from works of animation take these images out of context, making it difficult to appreciate the 2D characteristics of the work of animation as a whole. However, to shed light on the themes in question, this study has tentatively extracted representative images, undertaking a general analysis of their composition as static pictures and discussing visual adaptations of *Zhuangzi* from the perspective of essence and form. In so doing, this study has presented an optimal point of view.

References

Chang, Y.: The study of narrative and animation languages for the surrealism anime-"naruto". J. Nat. Taiwan Coll. **85**, 57–80 (2009)

Chen, G.: Zhuangzi Modern Annotated Edition and Translation. Zhonghua Book Company, Beijing (2009)

Chen, C.: "Liberate", "The tracing" serial works the study and creation of surrealism and image in 3D computer animation. Master's thesis. Available from Airiti Library (2004)

Chen, S., Hsu, C., Lin, C.: The transformation of song Ci poetry image in qualia product design. Collected Pap. Arts Res. **19**, 99–117 (2012)

Chen, W.Q.: Creation description of short film "let go" and a study of graphic design and digital techniques. Master's thesis. Available from Airiti Library (2013)

Ch'ien, M.: Comprehensive Study of Zhuangzi and Laozi. Shenghuo, Dushu, Xinzhi Joint Publishing, Beijing (2005)

Feng, M.: Stories to Caution the World. People's Literature Publishing House, Beijing (1994)

Feng, Y.L.: A Short History of Chinese Philosoph. East China Normal University Press, Shanghai (2011)

Feng, Y.L.: A History of Chinese Philosophy. Peking University Press, Beijing (2013)

Guo, X., Cheng, X.: Commentary on True Scripture of Southern Florescence. Zhonghua Book Company, Beijing (1998)

Hu, X.: Tao and art - "ZhuangZi" philosophy, aesthetics and literary arts. Doctoral dissertation, Fudan Universit, Shanghai (2003)

Huang, Y., Yu, W.: Discussion of the First Animated Film. YLib, Taipei (1997)

Jingwei Media: Zhuang Zhou Dreams of Being a Butterfly (animated work), Beijing, China
Central Academy of Fine Arts Urban Design Institute Film Workshop (2015)

Kang, S.S.: Zhuangzi Speaks (animated work). Asia Animation Ltd., Taiwan (2004)

Liu, X.: Generalization of Art. Shanghai Guji Press, Shanghai (1978)

Liu, Y.Q., Yeh, M.L.: Application of Chuang-tzu 2D animation. 2015 Forum and Conference on Basic Design and Art, Kun Shan University No. 2 Creative Media Institute Film and Sound Study Center, December 2015

Luo, Y., Zhang, P.: A History of Chinese Philosophy. Fudan University Pres, Shanghai (2005)

Nie, X.: Cartoon. Fudan University Press, Shanghai (2014)

Sun, L., Bai, Y.: The road of originality in Chinese Animation. Zhongguancun **5**, 32–33 (2009)

Tang, B.H.: Xia Chong Guo (animated work). Ink Man, Beijing (2013)

Tsai, H.W.: The research and creation of blended animation by 2D handy-sketched animation and 3D computer animation. Master's thesis. Available from Airiti Library (2008)

Tsai, C.C.: Zhuangzi Speaks: The Music of Nature. Xiandai Press, Beijing (2013)

Mizushima, T.: xxxHOLiC: Shunmuki (animated work). Production I.G., Japan (2009)

Wang, J.: Foundations of Animation Art. Hunan Normal University Press, Changsha (2008)

Wang, S.S.: Animation and Comics Design I. Artist, Taipei (2009)

Wei, T.: The Cowboy's Flute (animated work). Shanghai Animation Film Studio, Shanghai (1963)

Wen, Y.D.: The Complete Wen Yiduo. Hubei People's Press, Changsha (2004)

Wu, P.F.: The timing principle construction in 3D cartoon character animation visual language–a study exemplified by "toy story". Master's thesis. Available from Airiti Library (2002)

Wu, Z.: Aesthetics and experience in creative cultural industry–the exploratory study of hollywood films. Master's thesis. Available from Airiti Library (2004)

Ye, L.: The Outline of Chinese Aesthetic History. Shanghai People's Press, Shanghai (2014)

Yeh, M.L., Lin, P., Hsu, C.: Applying poetic techniques of shape-spirit transformation in cultural creative design. J. Des. **16**, 91–105 (2011)

Yuan, X.: A History of Chinese Literature. Higher Education Press, Beijing (1999)

Culture and Mobile Interaction

Mobile User Interaction Development for Low-Literacy Trends and Recurrent Design Problems: A Perspective from Designers in Developing Country

Elefelious G. Belay[1(✉)], D. Scott McCrickard[2], and Solomon A. Besufekad[3]

[1] IT PhD Program, Addis Ababa University, Addis Ababa, Ethiopia
elefelious@bdu.edu.et

[2] Center for HCI and Department of Computer Science, Virginia Tech, Blacksburg, VA, USA
mccricks@cs.vt.edu

[3] Center for IT Research and Innovation, IT PhD Program, AAU, Addis Ababa, Ethiopia
solomon.atnafu@aau.edu.et

Abstract. This paper identifies factors important in low-literacy mobile user interaction design and development. It explains the limitations and recurrent design problems from developing countries, focusing on Ethiopia as a primary case study, with special consideration for the designer perspective. This exploratory research effort examines the match and mismatch in usability design guidelines for mobile interaction in developing countries. It also identifies the design and usability factors that affect mobile service (m-service) delivery in developing countries: context gaps, designer gaps, and technology gaps. Further, the paper examines the designer perception towards design guidance requirement and application. In so doing, it seeks to provide input for design guidance development in a generic way such that mobile user interface designer understanding will be enhanced and m-service delivery in developing countries will be more usable.

Keywords: Mobile user interaction · Low-Literacy · Recurrent design problems

1 Introduction

According to a report of the International Telecommunication Union, by the end of 2015, the mobile cellular subscription was projected to reach 91.8 and 73.5 per 100 inhabitants of developing countries and of Africa, respectively [1]. The numbers have been growing fast each year. The number of mobile subscriptions, deployment of extensive mobile infrastructure, and prevalence of low-cost mobile devices reflect great promise toward addressing the gaps in delivering different social (such as health care and agriculture) and economic (such as financial and banking) services. Despite the

P.-L.P. Rau (Ed.): CCD 2016, LNCS 9741, pp. 409–417, 2016.
DOI: 10.1007/978-3-319-40093-8_41

overwhelming number of mobile users (mobile subscribers) their mobile service adoption (use pattern) has received little consideration within the many efforts of researchers addressing technology impact in developing society [2]. It is thus essential to examine these ever-growing resources and focus on better service adoption and diffusion of mobile services to meet the promise.

In general, designing mobile solutions for developing countries has unique challenges: power, device capability, privacy/security, and uncertain network communication are only a few [3–5]. Beyond these technological inefficiencies there are also limitations in terms of computing experience (most users have never used computing devices) and literacy. In most developing countries about half of the society is illiterate [3] (including for the country considered in this paper, Ethiopia [6]). Other factors like language and social value differences are additional challenges that hinder good provision of m-services in the region.

While a large percentage of users whose primary platform for accessing information and communication is the mobile phone, the previously mentioned challenges and limitations affect mobile user interface design. For instance power and device capability are related to the size and type of interface (multimedia application require a better device capability, including more power and space consumption). Thus, exploring mobile user interface usability that helps overcome these challenges is paramount and is an important element for mobile services adoption and diffusion.

In an effort to address these challenges, one of the suggested solutions is to document and codify the design knowledge of human-mobile interaction for mobile devices in developing nations [7]. This is part of work to lay down a foundation for building mobile user interface design knowledge for low-literacy. Other researches pointed out instead of redeploying technologies for developing countries that are meant to industrialized countries, human-computer interaction methods should focus on designing technologies that addresses the local contexts [3, 5].

The work reported here represents one component of the effort to support mobile user interface designer for low-literacy: providing concrete design guidance. We believe that good design guidance facilitates communication with the designer and can have great impact on mobile interface design for low-literacy. Since it is rare to find applications (and application designers) centered on rich experience and well-founded knowledge, extracting design guidance for this user group is difficult. Hence, it is essential that the development of effective design guidance should be supported by analysis of the context of use and user and also the local designer practices [8].

To capture knowledge of the current practices and recurrent design problem, we developed interview guides and interviewed a number of local designers in two stages. The first was informal interviews which were not recorded to get a sense of general design practices for mobile software developers in Ethiopia. The second phase is formal semi-structured interview to learn about specific, common design practices that should be shared across the community. The interviews of the designers focused on their design experience and recurrent design problems in designing mobile user interfaces for low-literacy situations.

2 Related Work

Despite the significant progress of user interface design [9, 10], advances specific to low-literacy mobile user interface are not yet comprehensively addressed [9]. Most low-literacy users from developing regions (that have high illiteracy rate [6]) encountered difficulties in using the most basic features of both mobile and other computing interfaces (such as making phone call, clicks) are not intuitive to them [11]. In recent years, a number of efforts in designing interfaces considered the skill, knowledge and experience of this user group [12–15].

Most literatures in this progress agree mobile user interface design for low-literacy user group should be different from those of the literate one (which can be communicated through textual description) [12–14, 16]. Nonetheless, there are also claims that highlight the challenges of textual interface for literate novice users [15]. Most of these efforts are based on of ethnographic research [12, 15, 16, 20] and presented the usability barrier of low-literacy and provide suggestion of design ideas in the form of general design recommendations and also features that contributed towards the successful low-literacy design.

Many researchers have made contributions in the area of interface design for low-literacy. Huenernfauth [18] outlined design guidelines to design user interface for illiterate users. Medhi et al. [15] studied and identified mobile interface usability challenges of low-literacy and novice mobile users; the work also further suggested design advices suitable for this user group, which improve the identified usability barriers. Chaudry et al. [14] conduct usability evaluation of non-text based graphical widgets focused on low-literacy user group, and based on the result of the evaluation some design recommendations are provided. Medhi et al. [12] suggested and tested text-free user interface design for low-literacy user to access employment information. Parikh et al. [19] presented the key user interface design features that are important for low-literacy user and success of managing financial institution in rural India. Gitau et al. [16] explored prospect and challenges of first-time mobile-only internet users who are low-literate and have no experience in other computing devices. Medhi et al. [15, 20] focused on evaluating and comparing non-literate and semi-literate users using three design artifacts.

In all, these contributions present usability challenges of low-literacy (such as visibility of functions, menu navigation, scroll bars, textual presentation) and provide design recommendation (regarding graphical representations, voice interfaces, avoiding textual input, minimizing navigation) [12, 14–16, 18–20]. Beyond contextual factors and generalizability of the research approach, most of these work share notions both in terms of usability challenges and design recommendations.

3 Methodology

Our goal in this paper is to gain a deeper understanding of the local mobile user interface designer practices, thoughts, and experiences. We also sought to get this information in the context of their actual situations, making interview and focused group discussion an attractive and fruitful methodology that provides a detailed account of their practice and experience. The interview was made in two phases: one was informal and focused on general design practice and issues, and the other was formal semi-structured interviews with more detail. The mobile application developers (user interface designers) and companies were selected by consulting the Ministry of Communication and Information Technology, who has up-to-date information of the industry. This information shows there exist only few mobile application developer and companies in the country. As it is a qualitative research we have sought an adequate number of samples to better enlighten and understand the approaches under consideration.

All interviews were conducted by one interviewer; an interview took an average of fifty-five minutes (ranging from forty minutes to an hour and half). In an individual interview consisting of fourteen participants, eleven were male and three were female with an average age of twenty seven. Participants' educational background also ranges from information technology first degrees to PhDs (nine BSc., four MSc., one PhD). Their experience in mobile application development ranges from one year to six years of experience.

For the two group discussions, one had 6 (1 female, 5 males) and the other had 7 (2 females, 5 males) participants. The two discussions took a total of three hours and twenty minutes. Three of the participants in the group discussion have a Master's degree and all the rest have bachelor degree. Their experience in mobile application development also ranges from one to six years.

4 Findings and Discussions

Both the formal and informal interviews and the focus group discussions generally draw a large amount of qualitative data, on the different issues of the current mobile user interface design trend and the recurrent design problems. Moreover, it also unearths the experience and attitude towards the application of design guidance in their design. This paper summarizes the salient findings of the current mobile user interface design trends and their implication for how we can best support the design guidance development process and product that will help both the Ethiopian low-literate mobile user and designer.

Based on our research interest, the following four main themes emerged as results of the analysis: current mobile user interface design practice, classification of mobile users, recurrent design problems in low-literacy mobile user interface design, and source of design knowledge and its relevance.

4.1 Current Mobile User Interface Design Practice

The interviews and group discussions demonstrated that mobile user interface design is considered part and parcel of the implementation process, not as independent process to pursue. No particular emphasis is given for designing the user interface early in the development and also later in the testing stage. Only one participant mentioned a different practice than the others, his experience is described as:

'I usually try to sketch the user interface on the paper before I start the implementation process.' [Participant 3]

The result of the analysis also revealed user interface design is neither a component of the process nor obtain reasonable attention in development of mobile application. Designers tend to focus more on the internal implementation aspects of the system. However, participants from one mobile device manufacturer affiliated application development company mentioned that they only develop for a target device and test the completed application, no special focus is given for the interface.

'Mobile Application development is not widely practiced as you know. Thus for the application we develop we only focus on the functionality of the apps rather than the interface.' [Participant 6]

'Our mobile application are tested by both internal and external users and we don't have a special interface evaluation test rather we run test on the final application.' [Participant 8]

Participants consistently expressed the current mobile user interface design trend follows traditional application development processes. It is also neglecting people who have issues as a result of various technical (such as bandwidth limitation, unreliable connection) and economic (such as device capability, cost of connection) reasons. Even most typical applications of m-services are based on short message and Unstructured Supplementary Service Data (USSD) that is practically of no use to low-literacy user group.

'Most of the application we developed are not focused on certain user group and did not give a special attention neither for low-literacy nor rural users unless and otherwise a specific application are requested by a certain organization.' [Participant 10]

'Many mobile applications such as bank application uses USSD which is pretty much difficult for low-literate user group.' [Participant 3]

Participants felt that the available choice of mobile infrastructure and communication technologies are limited and pose a big challenge in application development. For example, participants argued that a result of communication bandwidth could potentially be a problem for not designing either audio or multimedia applications for the low-literate user group.

'Most low-literacy mobile users are living in rural area where there is inadequate infrastructure, such as 2G mobile network and it is very difficult to design a multimedia interface having this technology.' [Participant 5]

All participants somehow highlighted the challenges of designing for diverse mobile devices that have various features, type and size (screen size), capability (internal/hardware capability of the device), input methods (touch, keypad). In line with this, they also highlighted the need for local language (such as Amharic soft keypad) input mechanism standardization.

'There is no hard keyboard for Amharic language but there are various soft keyboard which are diverse and difficult to use that require common standard.' [Participant 12]

4.2 Classification of Mobile Users

According to the UNESCO report literacy rate in Ethiopia among the population aged 15 years and older (which is considered as adult) is 49.1 percent - nearly half of the population [6]. And more than 80 percent of the population of Ethiopia lives in rural area with low resource setting.

Low-literacy in most mobile interaction design research is defined only from the educational perspective [12, 14, 18]. Our research considers education as one parameter and claims other parameters (such as computing literacy, technology exposure, level of assistance required) to be considered for mobile user classification. Based on this we characterize users in three groups (m-illiterate, m-semi-literate, m-literate) [11]; the former two are also considered as part of the low-literacy mobile user group. How each of the additional parameters influence and impact the mobile interaction design has been assessed in this research.

While participants agreed on the concept of classifying mobile user groups, they were also initially thinking the conventional definition of literacy/illiteracy. After we presented the definition they also reflect their ideas towards additional parameters.

> *'Even people who has moderate education such as high school and haven't use any computing device are always encounter in using even the most common functionalities of the mobile.' [Participant 2]*

Participants also argued people who have moderate experience have to be considered differently in user interface design.

The designers also strongly argued that people who have moderate experience have to be considered differently in user interface design; however one participant reflected his view which is a bit different from the others – he argued that the difference between m-semi-literate and m-literate is a matter of experience and did not require a different design for this user group:

> *'It only requires training to use a mobile phone but not required a different design to accommodate their needs'. [Participant 5]*

In all, the result of the analysis highlighted that the different parameters we identified can prove useful for the classification of mobile user groups, and each characteristic along with the user group lead to informed discussion. The refined version of the result is shown in Table 1.

Table 1. Characteristics of different mobile users group

Characteristics	M-illiterate	M-semi-literate	M-literate
Education	No	Yes/No	Yes
Computing literacy	No	Rare/fair	Yes
Technology exposure	No	Rare/fair	Yes
Level of assistance required	Yes	Somehow	No

4.3 Recurrent Design Problems in Low-Literacy Mobile User Interface Design

There has been a good deal of discussion about the benefits of designing user interfaces for low-literacy groups, including research and results from the Microsoft India research group [12, 17, 20]. This research is part of an ongoing effort to provide plausible design guidance for designers of low-literacy mobile user groups. In our interviews and focus group discussion, we explore the recurrent design problems that are important for designing mobile user interface for low-literacy user groups in the Ethiopian situations.

Generally, the results of the research led us to propose the recurrent design problems specific to low-literacy mobile user interface design. Some of the recurrent design problems that emerged from the analysis of data are summarized and presented in Table 2. The general and specific recurrent design problems described by the designer are intended to supplement the design guidance development process and results. This analysis provides design insights by highlighting possible solutions.

Table 2. Identified low-literacy mobile user interface recurrent design problems

General problem	Specific problem	Description
- Language barrier	- Various local language (Localization) - No standard for local font and alphabet - Diverse presentation of alphabet in the keypad	- English is not local language (which most mobile applications are being implemented) - Font and alphabet are different and has no standard
- Limited device capability	- Limited memory/storage - Slow processing speed	- Most low-literate users have low-cost device with lower capacity
- Text-based application	- Unstructured Supplementary Service Data - Short message (Difficult for both input and output interaction)	- Difficult to read and write - Limited (fewer) description availability
- Menu hierarchy	- Difficulty in navigation - Tough to figure out (guiding)	- Not able to traverse simple hierarchies
- Mobile network connection	- Low quality connection - 2G mobile network capacity	- Bandwidth requirements for multimedia (for graphical representation)
- Error feedback	- Error response - Error correction mechanism	- Require ways to correct and communicate errors

4.4 Source of Design Knowledge and Its Relevance

In this section we have explored the designers' requirements for proven solution and their current source of design principle and guidance. Participants are not aware of the availability of any mobile design guidance. Most of the designers' inspiration comes from their intuition and web search. Few of the participants describe general design advice like is found in an android guidebook or web site.

Some did mention browsing the web to see how to implement design features. Some describe mixed approaches that tend to be incremental; design and implementation approaches together. No clear distinction between design and implementation seemed to emerge from discussions; e.g., *'I haven't used any design guidance in my design, what I usually did is browse a similar application when I started to implement.' [Participant 6]* Participants are not aware of design structures like interaction patterns. Some identified software design patterns but not interaction design patterns.

5 Conclusion

This paper presented the designer perspective toward mobile interaction design for low-literacy situations. We described current mobile user interface design trends and some resulting recurrent design problems that emerged from the analysis of local designers' perception. We envisage that these recurrent design problems are considered and will be leveraged in design structure development for mobile interaction design for low-literacy.

The paper also describes the feasible and essential parameters that help to characterize the mobile user group. Moreover the paper briefly presented how these local designers perceived and make use of design guidance and principle. We are hopeful that the results of this paper will provide initial insights to the development of effective and formal design guidance that is useful (and used) by designers.

Our future work will combine the results of these findings, analysis of the context of use and user with theoretical and practical rationale to propose design patterns for mobile low-literacy. More broadly, we plan to pursue ways to support designers in crafting mobile technologies to support health, agriculture, and business [11, 21, 22].

References

1. International Telecommunication Union. ICT Facts and Figures (2015). Internet: http://www.itu.int/en/ITU-D/Statistics/Documents/facts/ICTFactsFigures2015.pdf
2. Donner, J.: Research approaches to mobile use in the developing world: a review of the literature. Inf. Soc. **24**(3), 140–159 (2008)
3. Brewer, E., Demmer, M., Ho, M., Honicky, R.J., Pal, J., Surana, S.: The challenges of technology research for developing regions. IEEE Pervasive Comput. **2**, 15–23 (2006)
4. Wyche, S.P., Murphy, L.L.: Dead China-make phones off the grid: investigating and designing for mobile phone use in rural Africa. In: Proceedings of the Designing Interactive Systems Conference, pp. 186–195 (2012)

5. Brewer, E., Demmer, M., Du, B., Ho, M., Kam, M., Nedevschi, S., Pal, J., Patra, R., Surana, S., Fall, K.: The case for technology in developing regions. Computer **38**(6), 25–38 (2005)
6. UNESCO: Adult and Youth Literacy, 1990–2015 Analysis of data for 41 selected countries (2012)
7. Ho, M.R., Smyth, T.N., Kam, M., Dearden, A.: Human-computer interaction for development: the past, present, and future. Inf. Technol. Int. Dev. **5**(4), 1 (2009)
8. Kunert, T.: User-Centered Interaction Design Patterns for Interactive Digital Television Applications. Springer Science & Business Media, Heidelberg (2009)
9. Shneiderman, B.: Designing the user interface, Pearson Education India, Gurgaon (2003)
10. Tidwell, J.: Designing Interfaces. O'Reilly Media, Inc., Sebastopol (2010)
11. Belay, E.G., McCrickard, D.S.: Comparing literature claims and user claims for mobile user interface design: a case study. In: Proceedings of the IEEE Conference on Collaboration Technologies and Systems (CTS 2015), pp. 418–425, Atlanta, GA (2015)
12. Medhi, I., Sager A., Toyama, K.: Text-free user interfaces for illiterate and semi-literate users. In: International Conference on Information and Communication Technologies and Development, ICTD 2006. IEEE (2006)
13. Ghosh, K., Parikh, T.S., Chavan, A.L.: Design considerations for a financial management system for rural, semi-literate users. In: CHI 2003 Extended Abstracts on Human Factors in Computing Systems. ACM (2003)
14. Chaudry, B.M., Connelly, K.H., Siek, K.A., Welch, J.L.: Mobile interface design for low-literacy populations. In: Proceedings of the 2nd ACM SIGHIT International Health Informatics Symposium, pp. 91–100 (2012)
15. Medhi, I., Patnaik, S., Brunskill, E., Gautama, S.N., Thies, W., Toyama, K.: Designing mobile interfaces for novice and low-literacy users. ACM Trans. Comput.-Hum. Interact. (TOCHI) **18**(1), 2 (2011)
16. Gitau, S., Marsden, G., Donner, J.: After access—challenges facing mobile-only Internet users in the developing world. In: Fitzpatrick, G., Hudson, S. (eds.) Proceedings of the 28th International Conference on Human Factors in Computing Systems (CHI 2010), pp. 2603–2606. ACM, New York (2010). doi:10.1145/1753326.1753720
17. Medhi, I., Kuriyan R.: Text-free UI: prospects and challenges for ICT access. In: Proceedings of the 9th International Conference on Social Implications of Computers in Developing Countries, Sao Paulo, Brazil (2007)
18. Huenerfauth, M.P.: Design approaches for developing user-interfaces accessible to illiterate users. University College Dublin, Ireland (2002)
19. Parikh, T., Ghosh, K., Chavan, A.: Design studies for a financial management system for micro-credit groups in rural India. In: ACM Conference on Universal Usability, pp. 15–22. ACM Press, New York (2003)
20. Medhi, I., Gautama, S.N., Toyama, K.: A comparison of mobile money-transfer UIs for non-literate and semi-literate users. In: Proceedings of the SIGCHI Conference on Human Factors in Computing Systems, pp. 1741–1750 (2009)
21. Blackman, K.C.A., Zoellner, J., Kadir, A., Dockery, B., Johnson, S.B., Almeida, F.A., McCrickard, D.S., Hill, J.L., You, W., Estabrooks, P.: Examining the feasibility of smartphone game applications for physical activity promotion in middle school students. Games Health J. **4**(5), 409–419 (2015)
22. Seyam, M., McCrickard, D.S.: Collaborating on mobile app design through pair programming: a practice-oriented approach, overview, and expert review. In: Proceedings of the IEEE Conference on Collaboration Technologies and Systems, pp. 124–131 (2015)

Exploration of Smart Phone Knowledge Management Application Design for Nomadic Maintenance Workers

Ziyang Li, Pei-Luen Patrick Rau(✉), Nan Qie, and Man Wu

Institute of Human Factors and Ergonomics, Department of Industrial Engineering, Tsinghua University, Beijing 100084, China
rpl@mail.tsinghua.edu.cn

Abstract. Knowledge management systems are built to organized knowledge for certain companies or organizations. This study investigates an experience sharing application on the smart phone to help manage the experience of elevator maintenance workers. Results indicate that the training mechanism (one master teaches one apprentice) and nomadic property of maintenance work contribute to the design and usage of the application. Besides, the potential use cases of the application include search, ask and share experience. The experience sharing application will help improve workers' expertise and guarantee their job safety.

Keywords: Knowledge management · Maintenance worker · Experience sharing application

1 Introduction

Knowledge is a key resource for companies but how to find and leverage the knowledge within the company and the staff is a problem. Under the background of Industrial 4.0, companies pay lots efforts to build Smart Factory to provide assistance to people and machines to execute tasks [1, 2]. This is achieved by systems taking considerations of context aware information. Corporations in software engineering or consulting have developed knowledge management systems to share experience among teams in an organization. But as far as we know few study investigates the knowledge management systems to the blue-collar worker, especially maintenance workers, and maintenance companies are in desperate need of knowledge management systems.

Take the elevator industry as an example, by the end of 2014, total number of elevators in China reaches 3.6 million, ranking first in the world and grows with the speed of 20 % annually [3]. However, due to the lack of effective maintenance, elevator entrapment failure and fatal accidents occur frequently. For example, on average forty trapped people are rescued in elevators in Guangzhou city every day [3]. At the same time, elevator companies experience a serious shortage of elevator maintenance workers, especially the experienced ones. The inadequacy of individual experience not only reduces the maintenance efficiency but also threatens the safety of workers. Influenced by the nomadic property of maintenance work (i.e. workers go to various equipment locations to complete repair missions with one partner) and the educational level of the workers, knowledge management is a big problem for maintenance workers.

P.-L.P. Rau (Ed.): CCD 2016, LNCS 9741, pp. 418–425, 2016.
DOI: 10.1007/978-3-319-40093-8_42

The web-based community provide good directions for the companies' knowledge management [4, 5]. Moreover, the development of mobile internet and the popularity of smart phones promote the applications of social networks used during the work. The paper aims to explore the nature of maintenance work and provide directions for the design of the maintenance knowledge management application for maintenance workers.

2 Literature Review

2.1 Maintenance Work and Maintenance Knowledge

Maintenance ensures proper operations and keep the product' life cycle down through regularly maintenance interventions (corrective, preventive, conditions based, etc.) [4]. Intervention measures depend on the model and the condition of maintenance equipment, which puts forward high requests to maintenance workers' skills. Waeyenbergh and Pintelon [4] proposed that the maintenance knowledge (know-how) was acquired through work itself rather than books. Maintenance workers need to reach the locations of equipment to be repaired. Sharing knowledge and learning from each other become difficult for geographically dispersed workers.

In conclusion, user-centered product design needs to consider the characteristics of nomadic maintenance work to better develop the experience sharing application.

2.2 Factors Effect Knowledge Management

The design of knowledge management application will be affected by various factor. De Long and Fehey [8] pointed out that "Investment in information technology would not change the culture by itself." Thus, knowledge management must align with culture norms of the company if they are to be achieved. Companies' culture norms dictate and distinguish the knowledge belongs to organization or individual, we need to understand the culture of organization before knowledge management.

Besides, characteristics of web systems determine the effect of knowledge management. The collaborative learning systems can be generally categorized into two types: Wiki and Community Question Answering (CQA) system. Wiki is an editable website allow people to build up knowledge collaboratively [9] and considered as one of best examples of collective intelligence and a structured way to record knowledge, but most experience of maintenance workers are unstructured. Cole [10] has described a failed experiment to use Wiki technology in higher education for not considering the actual condition of target users, so Wiki may not be a good tool for maintenance workers to share experiences. On the contrary, CQA system is a service where people can ask questions and share knowledge by providing answers to questions asked by other users [10] and Srba and Bieliková [11] described an potential of CQA systems to be applied in educational environment. Thus CQA systems are suitable to answer subjective, non-factual and context-aware queries which might be more suitable for experience sharing. Moreover, users' knowledge acquisition scenarios of should be combined with the system design [11]. It is important to explore the character of users and using scenarios before the knowledge management application development.

The main goal of this paper is to explore the design of experience sharing application for elevator maintenance workers, specifically the nature of maintenance work and potential use scenarios of systems. With the help of the smart phone application, maintenance companies could effectively manage maintenance knowledge to improve workers' expertise and guarantee their job safety.

3 Methodology

This study used the observation method and the focus group interviews to understand the the characteristics of the elevator maintenance work. The observation method was conducted to understand maintenance workers' workflow and tools during the work. Since workers with different expertise may have different experience in knowledge management, the focus groups interviews were carried out for the experienced workers' group and the new coming workers' group separately to gain their idea.

3.1 Participants

Six elevator maintenance workers (male) were recruited and classified into two groups according to their level of expertise in elevator maintenance. Three younger workers (ages 28–30) who had less than five-year experience were assigned in the new coming workers group. Three experienced workers (ages 43–49) who had more than twenty-year experience were assigned in the experienced workers group. Participants are from the same elevator company. Since most elevator maintenance workers were male, this study just invited male workers.

3.2 Procedure

The experiment was conducted in the Training Building of the elevator company. First, the on-site work observation was at the elevator machine room. One experienced worker (29-year experience) demonstrated the basic maintenance process of elevator machine room and introduced the tools used during the work. Two instructors observed the whole maintenance process and asked questions when they did not understand. The whole process was recorded by video camera.

Second, the focus interview was conducted for two groups separately in meeting room and the whole process was recorded by the voice recorder. Two instructors interviewed maintenance workers in three aspects:

1. work condition (e.g., "Can you describe your typical working day?"; "How the maintenance work is allocated?"; "How is your workload?"; "What tools are used during the work?"; "How often do you see your co-workers and in what ways?"; "How do you get in touch with your co-workers?");
2. maintenance knowledge and knowledge management (e.g., "What is the training procedure?"; "Describe your experience in being a master or an apprentice." "How

do you solve your problems encountered during the work"'; "Do you have experience in asking co-workers for help and how often do this kind of things happen?" "Will you share your experience in solving problems to others and how?")
3. attitude toward the experience sharing application (e.g., "What do you usually use your smart phone for?"; "What is your attitude toward experience sharing among workers?", "What do you think if there is an experience sharing application that could help you share experience or learn something?").

4 Results

From the on-site observation and focus interview, this study gained some insights into the nature of nomadic maintenance and maintenance workers' characteristic. This study organized our findings in the following sections:

4.1 Nature of Nomadic Maintenance Work

Different from office staff work in the office, the maintenance workers went to around four designed locations to complete their repair missions everyday. Besides, the work was planned to carry out regularly alone or with a partner. This nomadic characteristic of maintenance work made it hard for workers to communicate face-to-face. Thus smart phone became an important tool to their work. All of them had smart phones and had habits in using social applications.

In the management level, the maintenance workers were organized in teams (around nine workers) which were responsible for regional elevator maintenance work. In each team, tasks were assigned by the team leader through smart phones. Workers used the instant message, like We-Chat (Chinese popular mobile text and voice messaging communication service), for communication. Besides, workers' hands were full of oil when they were working, so voice messaging of We-Chat made communications easier. They also needed instant message to send pictures to the team leader if they need to order parts.

If a part of the elevator is broken, I need to send the leader the photo of the part by We-Chat to order it. We also have the We-Chat group for group communicate. But too many people are in it, and it is hard to find the history message or get the feedback immediately. (29, 3-year experience)

Maintenance workers used phone calls and social applications for work communicate, and it was the only way for them to contact to the outside.

4.2 Maintenance Knowledge

Because maintenance workers were exposed to dangerous conditions during repair work, workers wore professional cloth with a bag of professional equipment and the maintenance work follows standard procedures. The rules of the maintenance work were that problem solving went first and followed the regular inspection routine. The experience was precious and extremely useful in troubleshooting, because problems were various, which needed the workers knew a wide range models of machine. Moreover, workers needed to use sensory perception such as visual check, sound listening and the sense of touch to diagnose troubles. Aristotle (1978) suggested experience emanated from sensory perception. This kind experience was hard to explain. The maintenance knowledge was accumulated during practical working, so the longer the worker worked, the more experienced the workers were. Due to the nomadic characteristics of maintenance work, it was hard to share their own experience to others by traditional communication.

4.3 Current Knowledge Sharing Mechanism

As with most blue-collar workers, new coming workers learned most skills during the apprenticeship. The new comer would work with the experienced master who was in the same organization for some time and after that he needed to work alone. The diagnostic process and competence of maintenance was experience-guided [15]. With limited experience, new comers spent more time to complete the task and sometimes called others for help when they worked alone. Two expertise groups had different attitudes in knowledge sharing. New comers mentioned following words about asking for help:

> *I prefer to solve problems myself, which made me proud of myself. If I can not solve problems, I will call experienced peers for help first and then the senior workers because I do not want to loose my face in front of the master. (30, 2-year experience)*

New comers preferred to solve problems alone but they do not have much choice to learn from each other. Phone calls or instant message (like We-Chat) were main ways for experience exchanging. For experienced maintenance workers, they felt pleased to help others. However, the experience sharing process was a disturbance to the experienced workers' work. One participant expressed his experience in helping others:

> *I usually answer workers' phone calls. Just yesterday, a young worker called me for help. After his description, I told him the solution immediately. And after solving it, he called back again to praise me and thank to me, but I do not have much time to talk to him. I was working as well. (47, 25-year experience)*

The ability to help others is the reflection of one's knowledge and workers are proud of their skills. Even the experienced workers would also ask workers who is senior to them for help.

> *I have been in maintenance industry for more than 20 years and I still need to ask the senior workers who are older than me for help if I can not solve the problem. It is common in our industry. (43, 23-year experience)*

This dedicated that all the maintenance workers had the requirement for asking questions and sharing experience to share. Current ways could only share knowledge within a small scope and this process could not be recorded.

5 Discussion

During the interview, workers showed positive attitude toward the concept of smart phone application which could manage maintenance knowledge. Young workers advised "the application should help learn some experience" (28, 1 year-experience). Also, experienced workers suggested that "workers could share experience on the application and search for certain question on it" (49, 29 year-experience). Therefore, the experience sharing application should take advantage of the CQA system to manage workers experience and provide context-aware assistance to workers. Workers could ask questions, share experience and search for problems on this application.

Potential use cases are generated from the knowledge sharing problems faced by maintenance workers. The use cases can be categorized into four kinds: (1) search and ask question; (2) remote assistance by answering other questions or sharing experience; (3) capture experience by others' sharing; (4) connect intra-organizational wide workers. In this way workers could try to solve problems by themselves with this mobile database. The application could reduce experienced workers' workload to answer same questions over and over again, and provide new comers good learning opportunities. New comers could capture the experience besides on-site working with the mentor. What's more, this platform could connect the intra-organizational maintenance workers. The design guidelines on the design of maintenance knowledge management application are summarized in the Table 1.

Table 1. Design guidelines for the maintenance knowledge management application

Potential use cases	Design guidelines	Solved current problems
Search	Support keyword search and question-asking	Phone calls are in-efficient and endangering on-site work safety
Support	Knowledge can be shared in the form of answers to the questions or experience	Experience sharing is limited in a small scope (e.g. team, master-apprentice) and the process can not be recorded
Discover	Knowledge shared by other workers' can be shown on the interface	Workers' ability depends on whether they encountered the problems before
Connect	Connect company wide workers, provide personal information interface	Nomadic nature of maintenance work hinders learning and communication between workers

The experience sharing application is to design to manage organizational wide knowledge, so the norm of the industry or company must be considered during the application design. Current training mechanism (i.e., newcomers learn skills by following the master) of maintenance workers cultivates their willingness to share their knowledge. Then this norm will influence users' behavior in online community [12]. Moving experience sharing process to the smart phone application not only improves the efficiency but also guarantees workers' job safety by avoiding disturbances.

Moreover, the usage of technology needs to support the pre-existing behavior of the users [10]. The nomadic nature of maintenance work makes social applications a necessary tool during the work, so the smart phone application used under experience-sharing context would be useful. The application could connect the geographically dispersed maintenance workers, but different from instant message, this application aims to exchange professional knowledge and all the records would be well stored and easily retrieved.

6 Conclusion

This study explores the design of experience sharing application for elevator maintenance workers. Results indicate that the application should take advantage of the CQA system and the potential use cases include "Search", "Support", "Connect" and "Discover".

Besides, the current training mechanism and nomadic property of the maintenance are found contribute to the application usage. Further studies can be done to design the interface and detailed functions of the experience sharing application and test the usability of the application.

Acknowledgments. This study was funded by United Technologies Corporation. We are grateful to the employees whom we have worked with for providing their advice in our research.

References

1. Hermann, M., Pentek, T., Otto, B.: Design principles for industrie 4.0 scenarios: a literature review. Working Paper No. 01 (2015)
2. Lucke, D., Constantinescu, C., Westkämper, E.: Smart factory-a step towards the next generation of manufacturing. In: Mitsuishi, M., Ueda, K., Kimura, F. (eds.) Manufacturing Systems and Technologies for the New Frontier, pp. 115–118. Springer, London (2008)
3. General Administration of Quality Supervision, Inspection and Quarantine of the People's Republic of China. http://www.aqsiq.gov.cn/
4. Ackerman, M.S., Wulf, V., Pipek, V.: Sharing Expertise: Beyond Knowledge Management. MIT Press, Cambridge (2002)
5. Zhang, J., Ackerman, M.S.: Searching for expertise in social networks: a simulation of potential strategies. In: Proceedings of the 2005 International ACM SIGGROUP Conference on Supporting Group Work, pp. 71–80. ACM (2005)
6. Waeyenbergh, G., Pintelon, L.: A framework for maintenance concept development. Int. J. Prod. Econ. **77**, 299–313 (2002)
7. Pintelon, L., Waeyenbergh, G.: A practical approach to maintenance modelling. In: Ashayeri, J., Sullivan, W.G., Ahmad, M.M. (eds.) Flexible Automation and Intelligent Manufacturing, pp. 1109–1119. Begell House, New York (1999)
8. De Long, D., Fehey, L.: Diagnosing cultural barriers to knowledge management. Acad. Manag. Executive **14**(4), 113–127 (2000)
9. Franklin, T., Van Harmelen, M.: Web 2.0 for content for Learning and Teaching in Higher Education. JISC (2007). www.jisc.ac.uk/media/documents/programmes/digitalrepositories/web2-contentlearningand-teaching.pdf

10. Cole, M.: Using Wiki technology to support student engagement: lessons from the trenches. Comput. Educ. **52**(1), 141–146 (2009)
11. Srba, I., Bieliková. M.: Discovering Educational Potential Embedded in Community Question Answering. Proc. EKM (2014)
12. Fischer, M., Römmermann, E., Benckert, H.: The design of technical artifacts with regard to work experience. the development of an experience-based documentation system for maintenance workers. AI Soc. **10**(1), 39–50 (1996)

Discovery of Smartphone User Group Profiling Based on User's Motivations and Usage Behaviors Through Focus Group Interviews

Jimin Rhim, Seul Lee, and Young Yim Doh(✉)

Graduate School of Culture & Technology, KAIST,
291 Daehak-ro (373-1 Guseung-dong),
Yuseong-gu, Daejeon, Republic of Korea
{kingjimin,ardet,yydoh}@kaist.ac.kr

Abstract. Smartphone overuse is a growing social concern especially for adolescents and young adults. There has been attempts to mitigate smartphone overuse, however these trials mainly focused on curtailing usage time, disregarding users' various usage contexts. The objective of this research is to profile smartphone users by understanding their needs and goals of smartphone usages to suggest personalized guidelines to help develop healthy smartphone usage habits. Focus- group interviews were conducted on twenty (13 male, 7 female, M = 28.4, *SD* = 2.7) young adults. Five smartphone usage behavior indexes conveying users' needs and motivations (communication, entertainment, functional tool, information search, and life logging) were used as criteria for profiling user groups. As a result, three groups (Social Fun Seeking, Leisure Activity Seeking, and Information Seeking) were classified. Problematic smartphone usage behaviors for each group are defined and preventive guidelines for healthy smartphone usage are suggested.

Keywords: Smartphone · User profiling · FGI · Personlaized intervention strategies

1 Introduction

Smartphone, which is defined as handheld personal computer, is one of distinguishing evolutions of portable information and communication technologies [1]. Diffusion of smartphones in the US was 25 % and 14 % worldwide in 2009 [2]. According to "U. S. Smartphone Use in 2015" by Pew Research Center, 64 % of American adults own a smartphone and this phenomenon is especially high among young adults [3]. Another report shows that smartphone penetration was nearly 90 % in age between 18–34 in the U.S. [4]. Smartphone ownership has rapidly diffused in South Korea. Smart media penetration rate in Korea had increased from 31.3 % in 2011 to 78.6 % in 2014 [5]. According to Pew Research report in 2016, smartphone ownership rate in South Korea was 88 % in 2015, which was the highest among 40 countries [6]. In particular, the ownership rate was 100 % in the age between 18 and 34 [6]. Therefore, high rate of smartphone diffusion in adolescents and young adults created various social concerns in South Korea.

P.-L.P. Rau (Ed.): CCD 2016, LNCS 9741, pp. 426–435, 2016.
DOI: 10.1007/978-3-319-40093-8_43

Defining characteristics of smartphone is that it is a portable device, which allows persistent network connectivity and installation of various applications. It allows users to surf the Internet, watch videos, take pictures, and listen to music in addition to making phone calls and sending text messages. Because of these diverse functions, smartphones have the potential to produce various usage patterns among different users [1]. Due to these characteristics, many people rely on smartphones for various activities, thus smartphone overuse became a growing social concern especially for adolescents and young adults [1]. According to some researchers, possible problematic consequences of smartphone overuse include individual mental and physical health issues and social conflicts. Dried eyes, sleep pattern disturbance, carpal tunnel [7], musculoskeletal symptoms [8, 9] and forward head posture [10] are some typical symptoms due to smartphone overuse. Furthermore, one of distinguishing social problems caused by smartphone overuse is creation of interpersonal conflicts when it becomes a barrier to face-to-face interactions [11].

In order to determine smartphone addiction, Smartphone Addiction Proneness Scale (SAPS) was developed in South Korea to diagnose smartphone addiction levels. This scale is composed of four subdomains (disturbance of adaptive functions, virtual life orientation, withdrawal, and tolerance) [12]. However, since this questionnaire was developed based on scales that were used to diagnose Internet and mobile phone addiction before diffusion of smartphones, the scale may not completely reflect smartphone usage phenomenon nor include specific smartphone usage patterns. Another Smartphone Addiction Proneness Scale (SAPS), Kwon et al. developed the Smartphone Addiction Scale (SAS) in 2013 [13]. The scale is composed of six main factors (daily-life disturbance, positive anticipation, withdrawal, cyberspace-oriented relationship, overuse, and tolerance). Furthermore, they made a shorter version of SAS for young children with ten questions from the original scale [12]. Some of shortcomings of these scales are that they evaluate users' addiction levels with uniform criteria which is composed of questions about usage time and phenomenological index of smartphone overuse. This does not concern psychological mechanism of smartphone overuse which include users' diverse needs and motivations. National Information Society Agency (NIA) in South Korea developed a 'Smart Media Addiction Prediction Index' which is consisted of questions about smart media burden index (usage time, used contents, user motivations) and smart media risk factors (social and psychological factors such as anxiety, loneliness, impulsivity and family interaction). This was a meaningful attempt that includes questions about individual risk factors and social context related to media addiction to subdivide the user groups and identify the subjects of smart media addiction prevention [14]. However, they did not concern how these different factors contribute to make a complex behavior patterns of individual users and how the user groups are subdivided by their usage characteristics. The limitation of this approach is that instead of considering diverse patterns of user groups and inventing personalized intervention strategies, they only identified the levels of severity in addiction level such as general group, potential risk group and high-risk group.

There have been several attempts to help those who are diagnosed as high-risk group of smartphone addiction. Although the media reports that rate of high-risk group is constantly increasing, it is still about 10 % of the entire smartphone user population [15]. Rather than trying to reduce the level of excessive user rate of smartphone use on those who are already diagnosed as high-risk group, preventive intervention strategies should be available for broader user population to reduce overall problematic smartphone use. Such preventive attempts include educational programs in schools [15–17] and smartphone applications [18–21] that help people manage their smartphone usage times. Most of these applications record and show the names of smartphone applications that were used, and time spent on using those applications. Furthermore, some applications deny access of smartphones for certain period of time when ones usage time exceed the preset time limits. However, these applications does not consider individual user's complex usage contexts when providing preventive interventions. For preventive interventions of smartphone overuse to be more effective, instead of focusing on reducing absolute usage time, incorporating various usage patterns, needs, and motivations of users are necessary. Based on these interpretations, it is possible to construct personalized prevention strategies for different user groups.

2 Research Method

This study was designed to obtain qualitative feedbacks from users' smartphone usage patterns and motivations. The primary goal was to categorize distinctive user groups based on smartphone usage motivations and behaviors then characteristics for each user profile.

2.1 Study Design

We have conducted focus group interview to gather qualitative research data collection. Prior to the interviews, participants conducted an online questionnaire that examined levels of smart phone addiction using SAPS [12]. Questionnaire results were used as reference to evenly distribute participants with varying smartphone addiction levels into groups. One moderator led the interview sessions while the other researcher transcribed conversations, and the entire process took about 90 min. Each participant was rewarded with about US$15 gift certificate.

2.2 Participants

Possibly excessive use of the Internet or smartphone is more prevalent among university students, because often, they are highly Internet literate and use smartphones for many purposes; they have flexible schedules with little external control over their Internet or smartphone use [22]. A total of twenty university students (13 male, 7 female; average age = 28.4, SD = 2.7) participated in the focus group interviews. Five sessions of focus group interview consisting of four mixed gender participants were conducted. All participants were graduate school students of various majors including industrial design, computer science, psychology, biology and others. All the participants used computers and smartphones almost every day and owned their own smartphones. They rated their skill of using computers and smartphones as advanced.

2.3 Interview Questions

Researchers defined five smartphone usage behavior indexes (communication, entertainment, functional tool, information search, and life-logging) based on most distinctive smartphone usage activities as criteria for semi-structured interview. Interview session consisted of questions that seek users' general smartphone usage behavior related information (e.g., How long have you used smartphone? Which function do you consider as the most important when purchasing a smartphone?), communication activities (e.g., What kind of communication activities do you do with smartphone? How often and how long do you use smartphone for communication activities?), entertainment activities (e.g., What kind of entertainment activities do you do with smartphone? How often and how long do you use smartphone for entertainment activities?), functional tool usages (e.g., What kind of functional tools do you use with smart phone? How often and how long do you use a smartphone for functional tools?), information search activities (e.g., What kind of information search activities do you do with smartphone? How often and how long do you use a smartphone for information search activities?), and life-logging related activities (e.g., What kind of life-logging activities do you do with smartphone? How often and how long do you use smartphone for life-logging activities?). After discussing these questions above, each participant was asked to rank the five usage behavior indexes that he or she most frequently used, and then rank them in the order of personal importance.

3 Results

Three researchers analyzed self-reported answers from participants to gain further insight of how participants use such functions and perceive them using affinity diagram method. This method is effective in organizing large amount of qualitative data into sub-groups with similarities [23].

3.1 Smartphone Usage Behavior Indexes

Findings from participants' answers for each behavior index (Communication, Entertainment, Functional tool, Information search, and Life-logging) are described in the tables below. Descriptions are categorized into Main Activities, Reasons for Usage, Usefulness, and Potential Consequences of Overuse. Findings describe general characteristics of each behavior index. Table 1 describes details of Smartphone Usage Behavior Index for Communication. Table 2 describes details of Usage Behavior Index for Entertainment. Table 3 describes details of Smartphone Usage Behavior Index for Functional Tool. Table 4 describes details of Smartphone Usage Behavior Index for Information Search. And Table 5 describes details of Smartphone Usage Behavior Index for Life-logging.

Table 1. Smartphone usage behavior index: communication

Descriptions	
Main activities	KakaoTalk [24], SNS (e.g., Facebook, Instagram, Twitter), Blogs, Telephone, Text, Messenger, LinkedIn [25]
Reasons for usage	Because many people including family members and close friends use communication applications; The characteristics of digital media allows convenient and frequent communication
Usefulness	Allows quick, convenient, and economical communication
Potential consequences of overuse	Frequent notification checks (from SNS, applications etc.) reduce concentration level and inhibit workflow, and overuse may lead to unintentional time consumption. Furthermore, ease of communication tends to result in frequent usages and people sometimes feel pressure to promptly reply to the others. This may lead to reduction of frequency of face-to-face communication
Findings	Communication is most frequently used function and many users have experienced unintentional overuse at certain points of smartphone usage

Table 2. Smartphone usage behavior index: entertainment

Descriptions	
Main activities	Games, movies, TV, music, web-cartoon, e-book, shopping, web surfing, internet radio, user created contents (e.g., taking pictures, videos, producing music, drawing)
Reasons for usage	Provides convenient usage with less constraints in time, space and money for fun (e.g., killing time, use while commuting)
Usefulness	Fun, accomplishment, immersion, effective use of spare time, able to share links with friends, reduces stress and sense of loneliness
Potential consequences of overuse	Participants often spend more time on entertainment related functions than intended. Sometimes unnecessary monetary spending occurs due to immersion in certain contents such as mobile social games. Long hours of smartphone usage may cause health problems such as sleep disturbance, sore eyes, wrist-ache, and backache
Findings	Using entertainment related activities more than intended was core problem for many users

Table 3. Smartphone usage behavior index: functional tool

Descriptions	
Main activities	Camera, alarm, phone, memo, banking, calendar, record, dictionary, map, calculator, cloud services (e.g., google drive, drop box), e-mail, remote controller, to do list
Reasons for usage	To accomplish practical and functional tasks; various tasks can be done within one device

(*Continued*)

Table 3. (*Continued*)

Descriptions	
Usefulness	Do not have to carry many different devices because smartphone integrates many functional devices
Potential consequences of overuse	Using Functional Tool related functions itself is not threat for over usage nor have severe negative impacts
Findings	Since Functional Tool related functions are practical or productive, using such functions are not perceived as problematic in general. However, results from Functional Tool use can be lead into other smartphone activities with potential of overuse (e.g., after taking pictures and then uploading them into SNS)

Table 4. Smartphone usage behavior index: information search

Descriptions	
Main activities	Search daily information (e.g., path finding, job search, weather), web surfing (e.g., information, news, shopping information, scholar, dictionary), make reservations etc.
Reasons for usage	Characteristics of smartphone allow quick and easy search with minimal constraints in time, space and money
Usefulness	Searching for daily information including weather, bus time, directions and so on are convenient
Potential consequences of overuse	Information Search Function itself is practical, yet when spending too much time searching unrelated issues or when searching certain information leads into other unexpected activities may become problematic. Due to frequent searching, thinking process can be simplified or users may over rely on the searching devices
Findings	Many people use smartphones for simple information search in daily bases. Sometimes, when using portal sites, searching activities unintentionally leads to entertainment related activities

Table 5. Smartphone usage behavior index: life-logging

Descriptions	
Main activities	Taking pictures/videos, memo (e.g., ideas, gas ledger, household ledger, grocery-list), SNS (e.g., Instagram, Twitter, Facebook), health related recording (e.g., wearable devices, work out logging, sleeping cycle, menstrual phase calendar)
Reasons for usage	To check one's daily life cycles; To quickly record specific information (e.g., car repair record)
Usefulness	Digitalized logging information clearly shows accumulated data; Using smartphone allows easy sharing, automatic location recording, and convenient data logging using specialized applications

(*Continued*)

Table 5. (*Continued*)

Descriptions	
Potential consequences of overuse	Using smartphone applications for life-logging purpose itself is not perceived as a serious threat for over usage. However, excessively logging data without clear purposes can be a waste of time and cellular data
Findings	Smartphone allows quick and convenient life-logging. Using such function itself hardly leads to prolonged smartphone usage. However, results from life-logging can lead to other smartphone activities with potential of overuse (e.g., recording exercise logs and then uploading them into SNS)

3.2 Smartphone User Group Profiling

Participants (two participants who did not show significant patterns were excluded) were categorized into three Smartphone User Groups (Social Fun Seeking Group, Leisure Activity Seeking Group, Information Seeking Group) from self-reported smartphone usage patterns based on the answers from the focus group interview sessions. General descriptions and characteristics of each group are described below. The solid line is the average rank of frequency of each behavior index, and the dotted line is the average rank of evaluated importance of each behavior index in Fig. 1.

Social Fun Seeking Group. Six participants were categorized into Social Fun Seeking Group. Figure 1 shows general pattern of smartphone usage behavior of this group. Relative usage frequency of communication appeared to be the highest, and users in this group tended to use communication functions more than they considered it to be important. One of favored forms of communication activities for this group is talking with friends over social casual games, which also leads into conversations on SNS and communicative applications on the smartphone.

Leisure Activity Seeking Group. Seven participants were categorized into Leisure Activity Seeking Group. Figure 1 shows general pattern of smartphone usage behavior of this group. Relative usage time of entertainment function appeared to be the highest, yet users in this group tended to use entertainment functions more than they considered it to be important. Prominently used forms of entertainment activities are game, radio and YouTube. Participants in this group preferred to enjoy leisurely activities using smartphones by themselves to reduce stress.

Information Seeking Group. Five participants were categorized into Information Seeking Group. Figure 1 shows general pattern of smartphone usage behavior of this group. Relative usage frequency of information searching appeared to be the highest and participants in this group considered information searching to be most important. Search engines are frequently accessed for information searching. Participants searched simple information such as path finding, spell checks, timetable for transportation, and hobby related information using a smartphone. Participants in this group did not frequently use nor considered entertainment function to be important (Table 6).

Table 6. Smartphone user group profiling

Group name	Participant number (%)	Characteristics
Social Fun Seeking Group	6 (33.3 %)	Use Communication function the most and enjoy social activities with digital media
Leisure Activity Seeking Group	7 (38.9 %)	Use Entertainment function the most to reduce stress
Information Seeking Group	5 (27.8 %)	Find the importance of Information Searching function more than any other groups

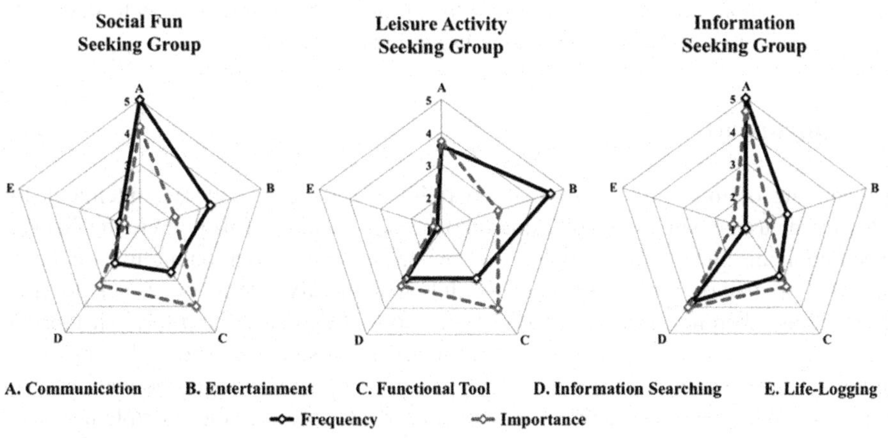

Fig. 1. Comparisons of smartphone user groups

4 Discussion

This paper presented categorization of smartphone user groups based on users' smartphone usage behaviors and motivations to gain further insights of specific user groups. Figure 1 shows comparisons of distinctive features of three smartphone user groups (Social Fun Seeking Group, Leisure Activity Seeking Group and Information Seeking Group). Discrepancies between actual usage frequency and considered importance can be observed. It can be inferred that different smartphone users have varying motivations and goals for smartphone usages with different smartphone usage patterns. This indicates that considering smartphone usage time without regarding usage contexts to determine smartphone overuse could be misleading. Ultimately, the findings of this study can be the starting point for further research on excessive problematic smartphone use prevention by providing practical recommendations for differing user groups. Despite exploring specific user motivations and usage behaviors or specific smartphone index and then profile different smartphone user groups with distinctive characteristics, some limitations should be noted. First, only South Korean students participated in this study. Therefore the study finding may not be generalized to other cultural, age, or education-level groups. Second, this study was conducted in the form of self-report assessment. Therefore discrepancies between participants' actual and perceived smartphone usage behavior may exist. Third, the questionnaires covered participants' smartphone usage behaviors without specific duration nor particular contexts. In the future, more specific user contexts should be defined to gain understandings to form more robust user groups. Furthermore, based on user group's characteristics, differing mediation guidelines that are more specific to the user profile can be applied to form sustainable healthy smartphone usage habits. In the future, smartphone usage log data and comprehensive usage contexts should be integrated into software for more accurate and objective user profiling for instantaneous feedbacks to the users for more effective smartphone usage habit formation.

5 Conclusion

The finding of this study show that smartphone users have different intentions for smartphone usage with distinctive smartphone usage patterns. This point to the fact that when applying intervention strategies to prevent excessive smartphone uses, a single intervention method is not sufficient enough to help modify smartphone usage patterns. The findings therefore provide support to the core ideas that to help form sustainable healthy smartphone usage habits, different intervention strategies should be applied to different smartphone user group by considering specific usage motivations and behaviors. With the growing prevalence of concerns for problematic smartphone usage, it is imperative that more research on this topic is conducted. Furthermore, prevention techniques that are more specific to the user should be considered by institutions such as schools or universities to establish broader prevention.

Acknowledgements. This study is supported by the project "Digital Overuse and Addiction Prevention Technology Research" of KAIST in 2014.

References

1. Oulasvirta, A., Rattenbury, T., Ma, L., Raita, E.: Habits make smartphone use more pervasive. Pers. Ubiquit. Comput. **16**(1), 105–114 (2012)
2. Falaki, H., Lymberopoulos, D., Mahajan, R., Kandula, S., Estrin, D.: A first look at traffic on smartphones. In: Proceedings of the 10th ACM SIGCOMM Conference on Internet Measurement, pp. 281–287. ACM (2010)
3. Smith, A.: U.S. Smartphone Use in 2015. Pew Research Center, Washington DC (2015)
4. Lipsman, A.: Teens and Older Demos Driving Gains in U.S. Smartphone Penetration. comScore Inc., Reston (2011)
5. Korean National Information Society Agency: A Survey on Internet Addiction. Ministry of Science, ICT and Future Planning (2014)

6. Poushter, J.: Smartphone Ownership and Internet Usage Continues to Climb in Emerging Economies. Pew Research Center, Washington DC (2016)
7. Shim, J.M.: The effect of carpal tunnel changes on smartphone users. J. Phys. Ther. Sci. **24**(12), 1251–1253 (2012)
8. Kim, G.Y., Ahn, C.S., Jeon, H.W., Lee, C.R.: Effects of the use of smartphones on pain and muscle fatigue in the upper extremity. J. Phys. Ther. Sci. **24**(12), 1255–1258 (2012)
9. Eom, S.H., Choi, S.Y., Park, D.H.: An empirical study on relationship between symptoms of musculoskeletal disorders and amount of smartphone usage. J. Korea Saf. Manag. Sci. **15**(2), 113–120 (2013)
10. Is, W.I.: Modern Life Alert: Forward Head Posture Can Damage Your Health (2014). http://www.foundationpilates.com/modern-life-alert-forward-head-posture-can-damage-health/
11. Tertadian, E.: The Smart Phone as a Conflicting Third Party in Interpersonal Relationships. Communication Studies Undergraduate Publications, Presentations and Projects, paper 14. University of Portland, Portland (2012)
12. Shin, K.W., Kim, D.I., Jung, Y.J.: Development of Korean smart phone addiction proneness scale for youth and adults. Korean National Information Society Agency, Seoul (2011)
13. Kwon, M., Lee, J.Y., Won, W.Y., Park, J.W., Min, J.A., Hahn, C., Kim, D.J.: Development and validation of a smartphone addiction scale (SAS). PLoS ONE **8**(2), e56936 (2013)
14. National Information Society Agency: Study of Internet Addiction Prediction Index Development. Korean National Information Society Agency, Seoul (2013)
15. Internet Addiction Prevention Center, 7 March 2016. http://www.iapc.or.kr/prev/guide/showPrevGuideDetail.do
16. Financial News: "Preventing adolescents' smartphone addiction with 'practice notebook'", 23 December 2015. http://www.fnnews.com/news/201512231351289893. Accessed 7 Mar 2016
17. Internet Addiction Prevention Center, 7 March 2016. http://www.iapc.or.kr/prev/guide/showPrevGuideMentoDetail.do
18. Application: "My Mobile Day", 7 March 2016. https://play.google.com/store/apps/details?id=com.mymobileday
19. Application: "BreakFree", 7 March 2016. https://play.google.com/store/apps/details?id=mrigapps.andriod.breakfree.deux
20. Application: "UBhind (How much time do you spend with your smartphone a day?)", 7 March 2016. http://www.rinasoftglobal.com
21. Application: "PhoneStop", 7 March 2016. https://play.google.com/store/apps/details?id=com.forple.phonestopexamversion
22. Turel, O., Mouttapa, M., Donato, E.: Preventing problematic Internet use through video-based interventions: a theoretical model and empirical test. Behav. Inf. Technol. **34**(4), 349–362 (2015)
23. Cohen, L., Cohen, L.: Quality Function Deployment: How to Make QFD Work for You. Addison-Wesley, Reading (1995)
24. "KakaoTalk." Wikipedia. Wikimedia Foundation, April 2012. Web 05 February 2015. http://en.wikipedia.org/wiki/KakaoTalk. Accessed 7 Mar 2016
25. "LinkedIn." Wikipedia. Wikimedia Foundation, 4 February 2015. Web 05 February 2015. http://en.wikipedia.org/wiki/LinkedIn. Accessed 7 Mar 2016

User Requirements of Wearable Technology for Activity Tracking

A Comparison Between German and Chinese Users

Liuxing Tsao[1], Lukas Haferkamp[1,2], and Liang Ma[1(✉)]

[1] Department of Industrial Engineering, Tsinghua University, Beijing 100084, China
clxl4@mails.tsinghua.edu.cn, Lukas.haferkamp@rwth-aachen.de, liangma@tsinghua.edu.cn

[2] RWTH Aachen University, Aachen 52056, Germany

Abstract. Wearable technology has been enjoying a growth of market since it first caught attention of the public in 2010. More than 400 wearable devices have been developed and 60 % of them are activity trackers. China has a great market potential for wearable devices due to the high acceptance of wearable technology in Chinese users. It is important and necessary for designers to understand the specific user requirements and preferences of wearable devices for activity tracking and specify the different preferences among China and other countries. In this study, we collected both qualitative and quantitative user requirements of Chinese and Germans then compared the result to elicit practical design instructions. Semi-structured interviews were conducted firstly on ten Germans and ten Chinese to obtain qualitative requirements. A quantitative questionnaire was designed based on the findings of the interviews and a total of 158 respondents participated the survey (52 from Germany, 97 from China and 9 from other countries). Descriptive statistics were summarized and non-parametric tests were used to compare the requirements between Chinese users and German users.

Keywords: Wearable technology · User requirements · Cultural differences · Activity tracker

1 Introduction

Wearable technology has been enjoying a growth of market since it first caught attention of the public in 2010. It was estimated that the Compound Annual Growth Rate would vary between 24.56 % [1] up to as high as 154 % [2] from 2013 until 2017, which would increase the market size to up to $50 billion in 2018 [3].

Wearable devices referred to electronic devices attached and/or embedded in clothes and accessories, which could be worn comfortably on the body [4]. As defined by [5], three distinct characteristics should be included in wearable devices: (1) they integrate seamlessly with the user's fit; (2) they allow for sensory input; and (3) they

P.-L.P. Rau (Ed.): CCD 2016, LNCS 9741, pp. 436–447, 2016.
DOI: 10.1007/978-3-319-40093-8_44

are connected with other devices. More than 400 wearable devices have been developed by worldwide corporations as well as startups [6], among which 193 devices are capable for fitness use and 253 devices are related with lifestyle. These activity trackers were proven to be the most successful among all the wearable devices and accounted for over 60 % of all wearables on the market [5, 7].

Though few studies addressed user requirements for activity trackers, studies revealed how users accepted mobile/wearable technologies. A series of four studies in University of Illinois revealed that (1) there was a strong influence of the perceived maturity of a technology on the adaption. At the same time, the familiarity of the technology impacted the user perceived ease of use [8]; (2) functionality, portability, performance, usability and network were five important features during design of wearable devices [9]; (3) the mobility of a mobile technology was not necessarily geographical moveable but the devices should "roam freely" among different user scenarios [9].

Specifically, preliminary experimental studies pointed out several requirements of wearable devices. In [10], 26 participants used wearable devices in their daily life and indicated two key concerns: (1) data capture and analysis of current technology need to be improved; and (2) privacy problems should be carefully handled. Privacy concerns were also discovered in [11, 12]. "Persistent identity" which meant to identify the identity of a specific user was appealing to users [2, 13]. Other key characteristics of wearable devices included data accuracy, appealing design, ease of use and independency from smartphone. Furthermore, sensor analytics and mobile payments were two promising applications for wearable devices [2].

It is believed that China would become a great market potential for wearable devices with a growth from 420 million to 1 billion in 2015 [14]. Chinese might contribute a significant higher share than western countries based on the results of an online survey with 24,000 respondents in 2014 [15]. Cultural differences between Chinese users and the worldwide designers [16] might challenge the adoption of the designed wearable devices (specially, the activity trackers). It is important and necessary for designers to understand the specific user requirements and preferences of wearable devices of activity tracking and specify the different preferences among China and other countries.

Aimed at figuring out the specific requirements of wearable devices for activity tracking of Chinese users and comparing the findings with those of western countries (German as a representative), preliminary interviews and semi-structured interviews were conducted to collect qualitative requirements. A quantitative questionnaire was designed based on the findings and a total of 158 respondents participated the survey (52 from Germany, 97 from China and 9 from other countries) answered the 39-question survey. Descriptive statistics were summarized and non-parametric tests were used to compare the requirements between Chinese users and German users.

2 Method

2.1 Qualitative Interviews and Findings

The first step of the study were qualitative requirements elicitation interviews. Five preliminary interviews were conducted to understand attitudes towards using wearable devices for activity tracking. Then semi-structured interviews were conducted with ten German and ten Chinese participants to collect information for questionnaire design. The interview consisted of six sections: (1) "previous experience with wearable devices"; (2) "functional requirements"; (3) "physical appearance"; (4) "battery"; (5) "robustness"; and (6) "data".

The main findings of qualitative requirement elicitation were summarized below. These functions and attributes were used to design the user survey questionnaire.

- A **long battery life** (mentioned by all the 20 participants) was expected though not exact duration could be concluded.
- The preferred **location** of wearing the devices were head and wrist.
- Users thought the **interaction between the wearables and other devices** were important and all of the interviewees agreed the connection to smartphones.
- **Upload activity data** to social network caught interests of the respondents and they expected to gain motivation from the activity share.
- The **privacy and data security** should be guaranteed, especially for the German users (7 out of 10 mentioned the concern).
- Every participant described **desired appearance** of a wearable activity tracker. Frequently mentioned styles included: (1) a conventional watch; (2) jewelry; (3) designs that were outstanding/technical/futuristic; (4) simple design.
- More than two third participants expected a **waterproof** wearable device.
- The **functions** of a wearable devices for activity tracking should include step count, GPS tracking, sleep monitoring, calories burned, cellphone handling capability, conventional watch functionality, and biodata monitoring.

2.2 Requirements Elicitation Survey

The user requirement elicitation surveys were designed based on the results of the interviews. The questionnaire was made up by three sections. The first (1) section was "the participant's personal information". This section comprised the participant's age, their nationality and the familiarity of the user with wearable devices. The second (2) section was "general preferences for wearable devices for activity tracking". In this section, we asked the preferred location of the wearable device, preferred method to unlock the wearable device and preferred appearance of the wearable device. For these three categories, participants could check as many options as they thought appropriate. Multiple choices questions collected the expected battery lifetime, data display, independence of the device and the extent connected to social networks. Then seven items regarding the characteristics of wearable activity trackers were rated using 7-point scale ("1: very important" to "7: not important"). The last section (3) contained 21 functions collected from market research and interview results. Using a 7-point scale, participants rated their perceived usefulness of the functions ("1: Must have" to "7: useless").

The questionnaire was designed in English to avoid misunderstanding caused by interpretation. Online questionnaires were distributed on campus of Tsinghua University.

Descriptive statics were summarized, Mann-Whitney independent non-parametric tests were used to compare the requirements of Chinese and Germany users.

3 Results

3.1 Participants

The questionnaire was answered by 158 respondents (Male = 93, Female = 65), in which 52 were Germany, 97 were Chinese and 9 were from other countries. The age distribution is listed in Table 1. Regarding the previous experience of using wearable devices, up to 54.43 % (86 respondents) did not use wearable devices, 22.78 % (36 respondents) wore the devices sometimes, 7.59 % (12 respondents) wore the devices more than three days a week, 8.86 % (14 respondents) used the devices every daytime and the remaining 6.32 % always wore a wearable device.

Table 1. Age distribution of the participants

Age (years)	<18	18–25	26–30	31–35	41–50	51–55	56–60
Count	1	134	16	2	2	2	1
%	0.63 %	84.81 %	10.13 %	1.27 %	1.27 %	1.27 %	0.63 %

3.2 Location of Wearing the Devices

As illustrated in Fig. 1, the “wrist” was chosen as preferred location by more than 40 % (43.67 %) respondents, regardless of the culture background of the users. The second and third preferred locations were “arms” and “fingers”, chosen by 37.34 % and 29.11 % participants, respectively. “Chest”, “torso”, “legs” and “feet” were only preferred by around 15 % or less respondents, which suggested the designers to avoid these positions.

Comparing the preference between Germans and Chinese, we found that although “fingers” seemed to be a good position, the percentage of Chinese who preferred “fingers” was as twice as that of Germans. Another position that Chinese respondents liked more was “waist”, but we thought this difference was caused by the misread on the word “waist” as “wrist”. Positions that Germans preferred more than Chinese were “feet”, “torso”, and “chest”, but they were not popular choices for all the participants.

3.3 Unlock Mechanism

As shown in Fig. 2, unlock the wearable devices by fingerprint was the most popular choice (overall percentage 58.23 %). PIN was preferred by nearly 40 % (39.87 %) respondents, which came as the second popular unlock mechanism. An interesting point to notice was that fingerprint was preferred by 65.98 % Chinese while only 46.15 % Germans checked this mechanism. Inverse result occurred in PIN, 55.77 %

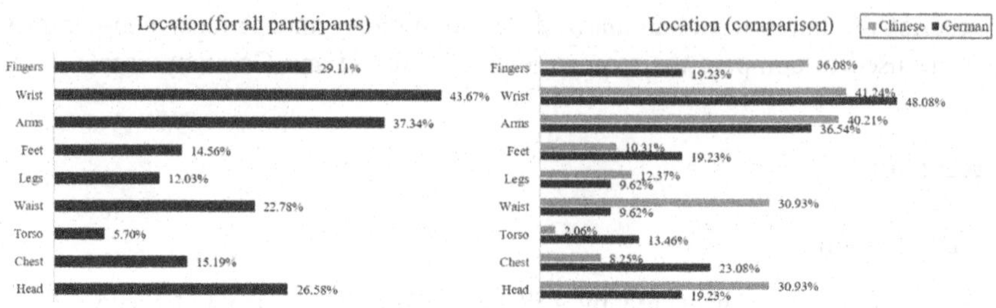

Fig. 1. Preferred location of wearing the devices

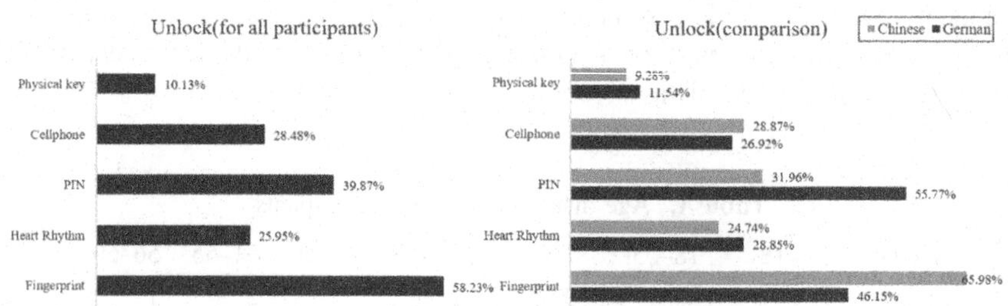

Fig. 2. Preferred unlock mechanism for the devices

Germans chose this option while only 31.96 % Chinese checked the item. We inferred that there was a difference in the preferred unlock mechanism between Chinese and Germans, and suggested unlock by fingerprint for Chinese and by PIN for the Germans.

3.4 Appearance

The top 2 chosen design styles for the wearable devices were "simple design" (60.13 %) and "as a conventional watch" (47.47 %) (See Fig. 3). But "simple design" was much more popular in German users than in Chinese users with a great gap between the percentages (German: 75.00 %, Chinese: 51.55 %). This difference was consistent with the finding that Chinese users enjoyed "outstanding (20.62 %)" and "futuristic (28.87 %)" appearance more, compared with a relatively low preference on these two styles in German users ("outstanding": 5.77 %, "futuristic": 17.31 %). We inferred that although simple design was preferred by most users, the designers also need to integrate outstanding and futuristic features to the devices for the Chinese users.

3.5 Battery Lifetime

The distribution of expected minimal battery lifetime had two peaks (See Fig. 4). More than half participants stated their minimal battery lifetime to be either 1 or 3 days. Due to a relative high selection frequency on the duration "1 week", we would suggest a

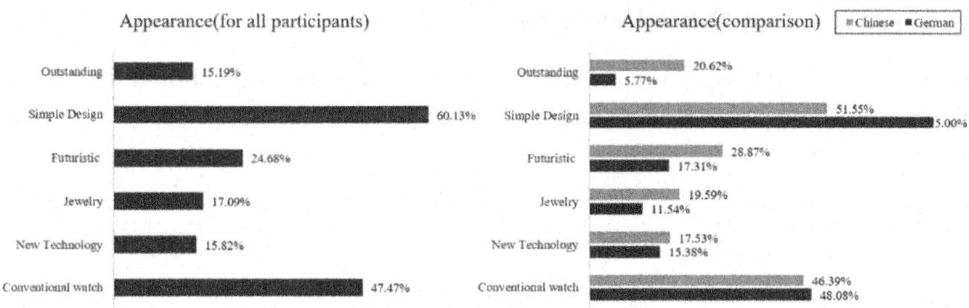

Fig. 3. Preferred appearance of the devices

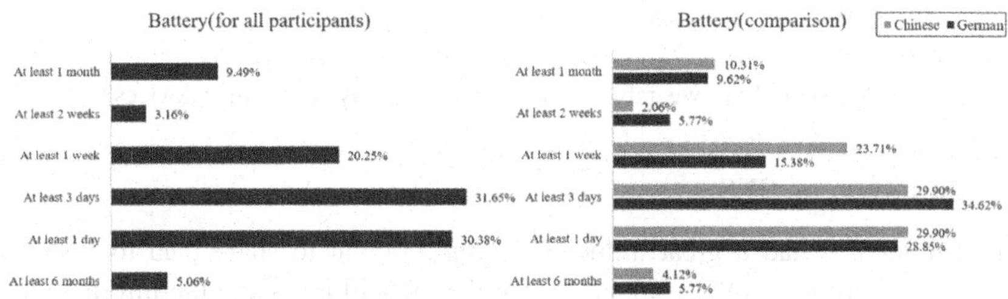

Fig. 4. Minimal battery lifetime of the devices

1-day to 7-day battery lifetime. There was little influence of the culture on the preferred battery lifetime.

3.6 Display

The answer of whether to include a display was demonstrated in Fig. 5. No significant difference was recognized between the Chinese and German respondents. Because more than half respondents (52.53 %) chose to have a display in their wearable devices for activity tracking, we suggested that the device for activity tracking should have a display.

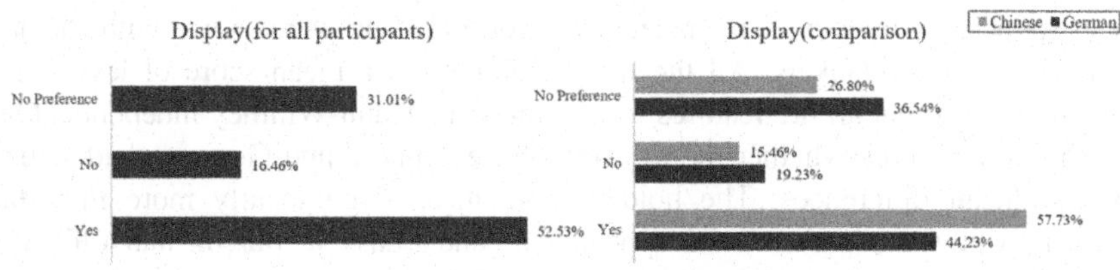

Fig. 5. Should the wearable have a display?

3.7 Dependency on Other Devices

More than 60 % (60.76 %) participants thought their devices should be partially dependent on their smartphones, and cultural difference did not influence the results much (See Fig. 6).

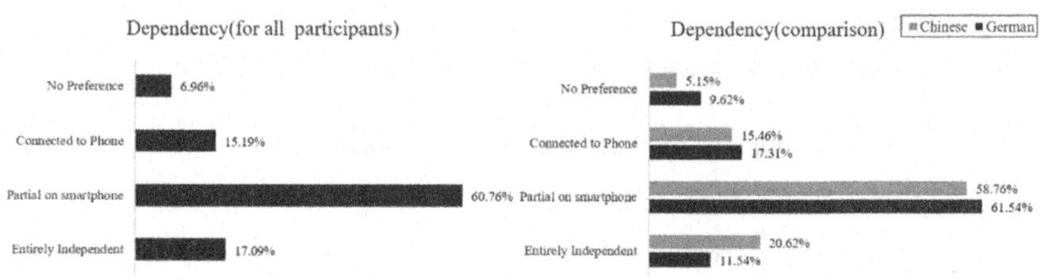

Fig. 6. Should the wearable be used independently from other devices?

3.8 Share Data on SNS

Cultural difference had a great influence on the opinion to share data to SNS (See Fig. 7). Most Germans (69.23 %) stated that they would not share the information on SNS (69.23 %). However, Chinese preferred to share the data (37.11 %) or held a neutral opinion (48.15 %) on whether to share the data to SNS.

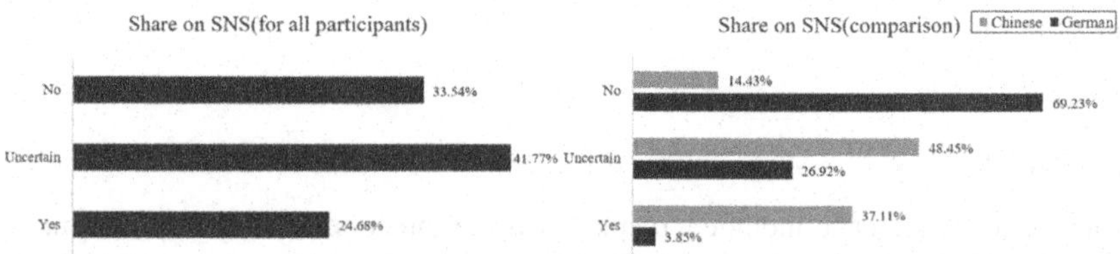

Fig. 7. Would you like to share the data from the wearable in social network?

3.9 Attributes and Features

In Table 2, we listed the importance scores for seven design features of wearable devices for activity tracking. The mean scores for each item were shown with standard deviations given in blankets. All the listed features got a mean score of less than 3 points, indicating that all the features were important. Mann-Whitney independent test was used to determine whether the answers of the Chinese and Germans had statistically significant differences. The bolded score meant significantly more important (significantly lower score). “Good appearance” and “Easy to put on and off” were regarded more important for the Chinese while “Physical robustness” was rated more important for the Germans.

Table 2. The importance of the attributes (1: very important to 7: not important)

	Attributes	All (N = 158)	German (n = 52)	Chinese (n = 97)	p-value
A01	Good appearance	2.36(1.4)	2.85(1.65)	**2.09(1.22)**	<0.01
A02	Easy to put on and off	1.80(1.15)	1.98(1.08)	**1.7(1.18)**	<0.05
A03	Small size	2.22(1.13)	2.1(0.93)	2.25(1.23)	
A04	Low weight	1.86(1.14)	1.96(0.97)	1.79(1.26)	
A05	Device is waterproof	2.08(1.39)	1.88(1.17)	2.14(1.51)	
A06	Physical robustness (e.g. shatterproof)	2.01(1.12)	**1.65(0.9)**	2.22(1.19)	<0.01
A07	Privacy and data security	1.85(1.29)	1.67(0.98)	1.91(1.42)	

3.10 Functions

In Table 3, we listed the mean score and standard deviation (in blankets) for 21 functions. A less than 3.5 point meant that the function was useful. From a comparison of the ratings using Mann-Whitney test, we concluded that the preferences varied between Chinese and Germans. The significantly more useful (lower score) were bolded.

Useful functions selected by both cultures were: GPS tracking, alarm clock, intelligent alarm, sleep monitoring, calories burned, watch, blood pressure measurement, find the device, charging by induction, and inform the incoming call.

Some functions were thought as useful only by the Chinese: mobile payment, wireless key, step count, activity identification, and temperature measurement, monitoring audio data, illness detection, calendar, voice control, and display test message. Mann-Whitney test results showed that except for the "monitoring audio" function, all the differences between the Chinese and Germans were significant at 95 confidence level.

Table 3. The usefulness of the functions (1: must have to 7: useless)

	Functions	All (N = 158)	German (n = 52)	Chinese (n = 97)	p-value
F01	Mobile payment (ability to pay with the wearable device)	3.86(1.82)	4.71(1.82)	**3.38(1.69)**	<0.001
F02	Wireless key (opens car/house doors wirelessly, unlocks the cellphone, etc.)	3.33(1.7)	4.02(1.82)	**2.92(1.55)**	<0.001
F03	Step count (calculates the steps taken every day)	2.99(1.69)	3.67(1.99)	**2.62(1.42)**	<0.01
F04	GPS tracking	2.37(1.35)	2.46(1.49)	2.28(1.29)	
F05	Alarm clock	2.83(1.54)	3.10(1.61)	2.72(1.52)	

(*Continued*)

Table 3. (*Continued*)

	Functions	All (N = 158)	German (n = 52)	Chinese (n = 97)	p-value
F06	Intelligent alarm clock (wakes the user up in phases of light sleep within a preset timeframe. This improves the users sleep quality)	2.80(1.58)	3.27(1.83)	**2.56(1.41)**	<0.05
F07	Sleep monitoring (keeps track of the time slept and deep sleep periods)	2.90(1.64)	3.35(1.84)	**2.66(1.46)**	<0.05
F08	Device calculates the calories burned	2.84(1.73)	3.48(2.04)	**2.45(1.43)**	<0.01
F09	Substitutes a watch, (i.e. displays time conveniently)	2.40(1.27)	2.42(1.41)	2.31(1.13)	
F10	Activity identification (the device can tell, which activity is performed, e.g. tennis, football, office work, driving a car.)	3.27(1.74)	3.94(1.95)	**2.91(1.58)**	<0.01
F11	Blood pressure measurement	2.92(1.45)	2.98(1.43)	2.78(1.42)	
F12	Body temperature measurement	3.09(1.46)	3.52(1.61)	**2.8(1.32)**	<0.01
F13	Monitoring of audio data	3.53(1.77)	3.9(1.98)	3.29(1.63)	
F14	Monitoring of video data	4.00(1.74)	4.83(1.72)	**3.57(1.6)**	<0.001
F15	"Find the device function" (wearable device can be found by with the user's cellphone or personal computer)	2.42(1.33)	2.88(1.49)	**2.12(1.18)**	<0.01
F16	Illness detection (the device detects the health status of the user)	2.99(1.72)	3.75(1.74)	**2.56(1.58)**	<0.001
F17	Induction charging (the device can be charged by induction)	2.59(1.35)	2.85(1.49)	2.45(1.29)	
F18	The device includes a calendar	3.31(1.67)	3.73(1.73)	**3.08(1.64)**	<0.05
F19	Voice control (the device can be controlled by voice commands)	3.18(1.78)	3.85(1.98)	**2.77(1.56)**	<0.01
F20	Display of text messages from smartphone	3.22(1.77)	3.67(1.91)	**2.96(1.68)**	<0.05
F21	Inform user about incoming call	2.81(1.68)	3.15(1.97)	2.58(1.47)	

4 Discussion

Among all the features and functions rated in the questionnaire, we found the biggest difference between Germans and Chinese was on whether to share the activity data to the social networks. Chinese users supported the opinion to share data to SNS while most Germans denied this idea. The different preference regarding the connection to social networks was also reflected in the results of the semi-structured interviews.

This difference could be partially explained by the different use patterns of social networking services [17]. Chinese had a share of 61.6 % of mobile users amongst the users of social networking services [18]. A survey in Germany on the other hand revealed that in 2013 only 18 % of German participants regularly used their mobile devices to access social network services [19]. The difference in behavior did also manifest in the spread of different types of social networking services in China and Germany. In 2014 Facebook had a market share of 71 % in Germany [20], while the social networking services in China did focus more on mobile use, as for example WeChat, which was used by 73 % of the Chinese online population [21].

Another noticeable item was "mobile payment". It was rated second highest (second important) by German participants (4.71, not important) as well as Chinese (3.38, a bit important) with an average rating for all participants of 3.86 (not important). The result was not in conformity to previous surveys [2] which stated that mobile payment was one of the "killer features" of wearable technology. One of the causes was a perceived security risk of mobile payment from the users. Consumers were also concerned about the device and the network reliability. Furthermore, users feared of too complex data input formats, codes and service numbers, complex registration procedures, and management of separate accounts [22].

The above findings suggested that wearable devices designed for Chinese should include the data sharing function but had to exclude this function when designed for Germans. Security of data privacy and simplification of payment procedure need to be carefully considered and guaranteed.

There were limitations to the results of this paper. Firstly, only 158 participants took part in the survey and they were mainly college students recruited on the campus of Tsinghua University. The college students did not represent the potential users of wearable devices. Secondly, the survey and the interviews were conducted in English to minimize the translation errors of responses but none of the participants was a native English speaker. This might negatively affect the results due to the misunderstanding of the questions. Lastly, cultural differences in response style might lead to a bias of the results. A more extreme response style (ERS) of the Germans and a more acquiescence response style (ARS) by the Chinese might influence the comparison of the answers between two countries.

5 Conclusion

In this paper, we collected the user requirements of wearable devices for activity tracking and compared the results between Germans and Chinese to address the influence of cultural difference. The requirements and differences on user requirements would guide the development of wearable devices for activity tracking. The different preferences between Chinese respondents and Germany respondents suggested the designers to include different functions and features in wearable devices for activity tracking.

Acknowledgements. This study was supported by the National Natural Science Foundation of China (NSFC, Grant Number 71101079 and Grant Number 71471095). This study was also supported by Tsinghua University Initiative Scientific Research Program under Grant Number: 20131089234.

References

1. Markets and Markets. Wearable Electronics and Technology Market worth $11.61 Billion by 2020 (2014). http://www.marketsandmarkets.com/PressReleases/wearable-electronics.asp
2. Huberty, K.L., Meunier, F., Faucette, J., Weiss, K., Kim, S., Ono, M., Almerud, M., et al.: Wearable Devices: The Internet of Things Becomes Personal (2014). Morgen Stanley Research Global
3. Ford, A.: What needs to happen for wearable devices to improve people's health? (2015). http://scopeblog.stanford.edu/2015/01/20/what-needs-to-happen-for-wearable-devices-to-improve-peoples-health/
4. Tehrani, K., Michael, A.: Wearable Technology and Wearable Devices: Everything You Need to Know (2014). http://www.wearabledevices.com/what-is-a-wearable-device/
5. Berghaus, S., Back, A.: Requirements elicitation and utilization scenarios for in-car use of wearable devices. In: 48th Hawaii International Conference on System Sciences, pp. 1028–1037 (2015)
6. Vandrico Solutions Inc.: Wearable Technology Database (2015). http://vandrico.com/database
7. Allied Business Intelligence, Inc.: Wearable Computing Devices, Like Apple's iWatch, Will Exceed 485 Million Annual Shipments by 2018 (2013) https://www.abiresearch.com/press/wearable-computing-devices-like-apples-iwatch-will
8. Gebauer, J., Shaw, M.J., Subramanyam, R.: Once Built Well, They Might Come: An Empirical Study of Mobile E-Mail (2007). http://www.business.uiuc.edu/Working_Papers/papers/07-0117.pdf
9. Gebauer, J., Tang, Y., Baimai, C.: User requirements of mobile technology: results from a content analysis of user reviews. Inf. Syst. e-Bus. Manag. **6**(4), 361–384 (2008)
10. Brauer, C., Barth, J.: The Human Cloud: Wearable Technology from Novelty to Production (2013). http://www.rackspace.co.uk/sites/default/files/whitepapers/The_Human_Cloud_-_June_2013.pdf
11. Starner, T.: The challenges of wearable computing: part 1. IEEE Micro **21**(4), 44–52 (2001). doi:10.1109/40.946681
12. Motti, V.G., Caine, K.: Users' privacy concerns about wearables: impact of form factor, sensors and type of data collected. In: Brenner, M., Christin, N., Johnson, B., Rohloff, K. (eds.) Financial Cryptography and Data Security. LNCS, vol. 8976, pp. 231–244. Springer, Heidelberg (2014)
13. Jackson, B.: Bionym releases developer hardware in pursuit of 'persistent identity' (2014). http://www.itbusiness.ca/news/bionym-releases-developer-hardware-in-pursuit-of-persistent-identity/51536

14. CCTV. Huge market potential for wearable devices in China (2015). http://english.cntv.cn/2014/08/24/VIDE1408826279064372.shtml
15. Xinhua. Wearable devices have bright future in China: survey (2015). http://news.xinhuanet.com/english/china/2015-01/17/c_133926120.htm
16. Hofstede, G.H., Hofstede, G.J., Minkov, M.: Cultures and Organizations: Software of the Mind: Intercultural Cooperation and its Importance for Survival (Rev. and Expanded), 3rd edn. McGraw-Hill, New York (2010)
17. Wang, Y., Norice, G., Cranor, L.F.: Who is concerned about what? A study of American, Chinese and Indian users' privacy concerns on social network sites. In: McCune, J.M., Balacheff, B., Perrig, A., Sadeghi, A.-R., Sasse, A., Beres, Y. (eds.) Trust 2011. LNCS, vol. 6740, pp. 146–153. Springer, Heidelberg (2011)
18. Statista Inc.: Facts and statistics about Social Networks in China (2015). http://www.statista.com/topics/1170/social-networks-in-china/
19. Bundesverband Informationswirtschaft, Telekommunikation und neue Medien e.V. Mobile Nutzung sozialer Netzwerke voll im Trend (2013)
20. Bloching, B., Hennig-Thurau, T., Kiene, R., vor dem Esche, J., Wege, E.: German digitalization Consumer Report (2014). http://www.rolandberger.com/media/pdf/Roland_Berger_German_Digitalization_Consumer_Report_20140718.pdf
21. Rao, R.: Chinese messaging app WeChat poised to conquer India, the world (2015). http://www.zdnet.com/blog/new-india/
22. Mallat, N.: Exploring consumer adoption of mobile payments - a qualitative study. J. Strateg. Inf. Syst. **16**, 413–432 (2007)

Rediscover Herbal Lane- Enhancing the Tourist Experience Through Mobile Applications

Fang-Wu Tung(✉) and Min Wu

Department of Industrial and Commercial Design, National Taiwan University of Science and Technology, 43, Sec. 4, Keelung Rd., Taipei 106, Taiwan
fwtung@mail.ntust.edu.tw, palwm@hotmail.com

Abstract. This study explores how to use a mobile service to improve tourists' experiences when visiting Herbal Lane's business district in Taipei. In Taiwan, mobile broadband Internet access is very popular, and it can thus support mobile applications to provide visitors with better tourism experiences. We approached the research by conducting a design project. This study developed a mobile application by integrating professional fields including design, information engineering, and traditional Chinese medicine. This study delivered a workable prototype—a mobile application for visiting Herbal Lane. With the workable prototype, we further carried out a user-testing study to understand whether the mobile application can improve visitors' experience in Herbal Lane district. A total of 114 visitors (61 male and 53 female) were recruited to participate in the user-testing study. The results indicated that the mobile application could improve visitors' tourism experiences more than those without the mobile application. The mobile application significantly enhanced the visitors' tourism experience on the four dimensions: enjoyment, novelty, local culture, and involvement. The findings and implications are further discussed in this paper.

Keywords: Mobile application · Tourism experience · Design

1 Introduction

This study explores how to use a mobile service to improve visitors' tourism experience when visiting Herbal Lane's business district in Taipei. Herbal Lane, which is the largest business cluster of herbal business in northern Taiwan, is one of the many regions in Taipei that is worth marketing and promoting (see Fig. 1). This is because its long history of herbal culture makes it a very unique tourist attraction in Taipei. Herbal Lane is an ancient street that has experienced urban periphery problems, but owing to the changing population and urban development over time, it has gradually transformed into a tourist attraction for health, wellbeing, and cultural tours. The buying and selling activities in Herbal Lane are rare and novel for visitors and thus easily attract people's attention. In order to develop the tourism resources of Herbal Lane, the city's municipalities have displayed wooden plaques at each intersection. However, despite these attracting some visitors to the area, the visitors often fail to understand the special characteristics of the

P.-L.P. Rau (Ed.): CCD 2016, LNCS 9741, pp. 448–458, 2016.
DOI: 10.1007/978-3-319-40093-8_45

herbal industry. Reforming the street and the region can promote Herbal Lane to make it well-known, but it cannot expand the market or attract younger generations to continue the culture of the herbal industry. While the government is focusing in promoting the Herbal Lane business district, it is limited to using traditional forms of landscape transformation, without considering the herbal industry and its unique culture of herbal health and wellbeing. This means that visitors are unable to develop an understanding of the long and profound herbal culture, and new customers cannot be developed in order to continue the culture of the industry.

Fig. 1. Herbal Lane's business district in Taipei

In recent years, business owners in the Herbal Lane business district have tried to use digital marketing to develop the market and attract new customers. Some shops have already carried out promotional activities such as QR-code scanning or Facebook check-in, indicating that business owners in Herbal Lane are actively seeking new media exposure and promotional methods to gain acceptance of the herbal industry from a larger population. While the business district is a component of a city, the development of a city's business district is closely related to urban prosperity, and thus district transformation is an import part of urban promotion. Kotler et al. [1] proposed the concept of place marketing and regarded a region as a corporate body. Driven by market demand and by combining the local advantages and characteristics, the region can be actively developed into an attractive product to promote the development of the local economy, tourism, and investment. As a result, when promoting a business district, the different characteristics will often require different strategies for promotion [2].

Mobile service can be used to strengthen the business district and tourism industry. In Taiwan, mobile broadband Internet access is very popular, and it can thus support mobile applications to promote regions. This study attempts to promote regional marketing by integrating designs with mobile service. Herbal Lane's business district is currently going through a transition to open the market to new customers. Therefore, by incorporating new methods of design and mobile service, Herbal Lane's business district could provide consumers and visitors with a profound experience, thus improving the image of the region. For this reason, our study uses Herbal Lane as the research field. We approach the research by conducting a real design project. Design is an approach of inquiry and action used by humans to engage with the world. Cross [3] coined the term "designerly ways of knowing" to highlight the uniqueness of design knowledge, and he argued that part of design knowledge is inherent in the activity of designing, gained by engaging in and reflecting on activities through the design process. Thus, we carried out a design project by focusing on the design of a mobile service to enhance the tourism experiences in Herbal Lane. The design outcomes created through this study served as answers to the design inquiry and sources of design topics [4, 5]. Further, the design outcome was used as a workable prototype to conduct a field study to gain insight into the effects of the design outcome on visitors' experiences of Herbal Lane.

2 Tourism Experience

Tourism experience forms the core of tourism activities and affects visitors' psychological factors or travel behaviors during their journeys. People visit various places and seek various entertainment and recreations because they are bored with their bland lifestyle and they wish to pursue something that they cannot usually grasp [6]. Otto and Ritchie [7] concluded that people who travel possess a subjective state of mind based on the following types of experiences. First, the external environment stimulates the visitors' senses. The visitor feels and interprets the information received based on their individual knowledge and previous experiences. The information is integrated and stored in their memories. The series of processes constitutes the tourism experience. Therefore, tourism experience is a process. Even when the process ends, the feelings that people experienced stay in their memories, and the souvenirs they purchased bring them unforgettable memories. Ooi [8] proposed that the visitors' backgrounds and interests could affect their tourism experiences. For example, two travelers doing the same thing at the same location can have very different travel experiences depending on their feelings and emotions at a particular time. Kim et al. [9] proposed seven factors of memorable tourism experiences (MTE): (a) hedonism, (b) meaningfulness, (c) involvement, (d) local culture, (e) knowledge, (f) novelty, and (h) refreshment. Sthapit [10] used the MTE scale was to investigate the impact of each factor on visitors' tourism experiences in Rovaniem city. The results showed that "local culture" and "novelty" have the most significant impacts on visitors' tourism experiences. Research on tourism experience has gradually changed from focusing on physical objects to studying visitors' subjective perceptions [11]. Tourism service providers should comprehensively weigh the proportion of each factor of memorable tourism experiences to better tourists' experiences.

3 Mobile Applications

Nowadays, the constantly evolving information technology can allow visitors to a location to rapidly understand the area, and many suitable services and products have been developed to meet consumer requirements [12]. After the rapid development in recent years, mobile phones have become the most convenient mobile device, evolving from feature phones to the current mainstream smart phones with the expansion features for third party programs. Because phones support the functional expansion of countless mobile applications, mobile phones have become mobile service-providing centers. Henseler et al. [13] stated that mobile services have become increasingly important because of improved access to the Internet and the large amount of add-on functions on newer models. People's acceptance of mobile services has risen due to the popularity of smart phones and the functions of the available applications.

Owing to this increased acceptance of smart phones, carrying out marketing campaigns using the Internet and smart phones has become an effective promotion strategy. Shankar and Balasubramanian [14] stated that mobile marketing between the business and the consumer could be regarded as using mobile media, equipment, or technology to perform a wide range of interactions and promotions. The smart phone can be used at anytime and anywhere, and its interactive function makes it easy for users to rapidly share and spread their travel experiences through social network platforms. With the mobile content, we can combine the visitors' virtual experience with their real experiences on site to effectively promote and market the region and bring a different experience to the visitors. For example, because almost every attraction in London has a long history and cultural background, an application called Street Museum was developed, which enables visitors to see how the streets where they are standing looked in the past. Another example is the Ubiquitous Art Tour in Tokyo, which offers visitors "Ubiquitous Communicators" to guide them to respective art works in Tokyo's Midtown area. As the visitors stand in front of each artwork, they can access information about the art and the artists with images that introduce the creative process.

The functions of smart mobile devices are becoming more powerful. The involvement of information technology in marketing is no longer limited to providing a functional user interface. Using technology, we can establish an environment that combines the real world with the virtual world, based on the existing service, and provide a valued and innovative service. The concept of integrating O2O (Online to Offline) has been increasingly accepted by consumers. Using information technology, we can create interactive experiences between the people and the location, which contributes to regional marketing and promotions. This study uses Herbal Lane as the research field. By implementing and verifying our design project, we explore how to develop a mobile application to market the business district and improve the travel experience of visitors.

4 Design Project

This study focuses on the business district in Herbal Lane and explores how to improve visitors' experience of the business district using a mobile application. We formed a multidisciplinary team that consisted of design and computer science students who collaborated with a traditional Chinese medicine (TCM) practitioner on the approach for this design project over nine months to develop a mobile application for Herbal Lane.

4.1 Problem Finding

First, we started with interviewing business owners in Herbal lane to understand the development and challenges of Herbal Lane's business district. We then observed the visitors' behaviors and interviewed the visitors to understand their travel experiences. From the interviews and observations, we learned that the younger travelers are unfamiliar with and lack interest in the herbs and their efficacy despite the benefits to their health and wellbeing, which prevents them from enjoying their experiences in Herbal Lane fully. We therefore aimed to design a solution that would trigger the visitors' interest in the herbs in Herbal Lane. In order to achieve effective marketing results, the marketing content needed to be relevant to the consumers, containing compelling and contextual factors that would entertain the consumers sufficiently for them to share the products with others.

4.2 Solution

Based on the problem we discovered above and to promote the business district in Herbal Lane, we aimed to propose a solution that can establish connections with the visitors and the Herbal Lane by providing them with a novel way to experience the Herbal Lane. This study developed a mobile application to allow visitors to understand the properties of herbs in Herbal Lane based on their individual needs, thereby motivating them to explore Herbal Lane. This project developed a mobile application that can determine user body constitution by asking him/her questions and was inspired by the ten questions used for the TCM diagnosis from which a TCM practitioner learns about patient body constitution. The mobile application then recommends a suitable herb to the user according to the body constitution of the user. This creates connections between the visitors and the herbs in Herbal Lane, and guides them to Herbal Lane to search the recommended herbs. Icon tags are displayed on the herb containers so that visitors can use the pattern recognition feature in their mobile phones to ensure they find the correct herb that was recommended to them, thereby allowing visitors find the suitable herb for their health and wellbeing. With the mobile application, the new tourism experience in Herbal Lane is described below.

4.3 New Tourism Experience in Herbal Lane

Understanding Your Body Constitution. To build connections with the visitors and spark their interest, we invited business owners from Herbal Lane and senior TCM practitioners to participate in discussions and develop a database for "question-body constitution -herb." By asking a series of questions, the body constitution of the visitor can be estimated and the suitable herb for the health and wellbeing of the visitor can be recommended. Once they finish answering the questions, they are notified of their body constitution and the recommended herbs.

Finding Your Herb. After answering the questions, the application recommends suitable herbs to the visitors by displaying pictures and icons of the recommended herbs.

The visitors are then invited to go to Herbal Lane to find the herbs. The pictures or icons of the herbs help visitors to find the recommended herbs, and the icon on the herb container can be scanned using the camera on the mobile phone to obtain information about the herb. When the phone camera is held close to the tag of the herb, based on pattern recognition, the application can automatically identify the type of the herb and notify the visitors if they have found the correct herb (see Fig. 2).

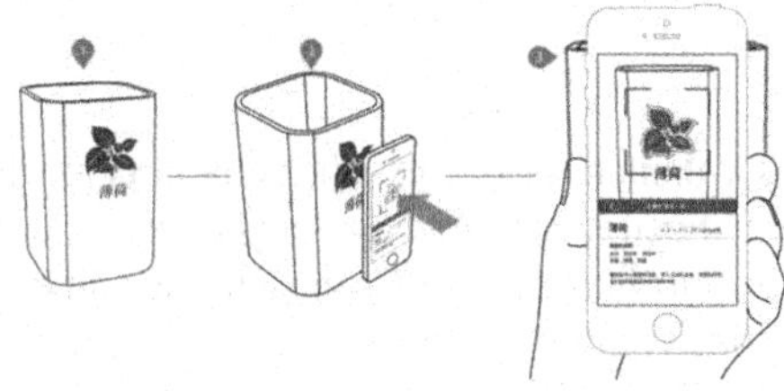

Fig. 2. One kernel at *xs* (*dotted kernel*) or two kernels at *xi* and *xj*

Share Your Finding. When the visitor has found the correct herb, the system will introduce the preparation method and efficacy of the herb. Once the system has obtained consent from the user, the herb information will be automatically uploaded to social media platforms.

4.4 User-Testing Study

In order to understand whether the mobile application proposed in the study can improve visitors' experience when they go to Herbal Lane, we obtained permission from the shops in Herbal Lane to perform a user-testing study. We recruited 114 visitors (61 male and 53 female) to participate in the study. The participants, aged between 20 and 35, were divided into two groups randomly; 55 participants used the application while the other 59 did not use the application. The application could be downloaded via the QR code on the site. The two groups were similar in sex distribution and age. Once the participants had completed their tour of Herbal Lane, we asked them to fill out a questionnaire. The participants were thanked and offered a gift certificate worth $8.

4.5 Measurement Tools

The tourism experience questionnaire was modified from a version of the MTE scale proposed by Kim et al. and focused on four factors of tourism experience: hedonism, novelty, local culture, and involvement.

The hedonism factor consisted of four items: (1) Visiting Herbal Lane was pleasurable, (2) I indulged in the activities in Herbal Lane, (3) I really enjoyed this tourism experience, and (4) Visiting Herbal Lane was exciting. The novelty factor consisted of three items: (1) Visiting Herbal Lane was unique, (2) Visiting Herbal Lane was different from previous experiences, and (3) I experienced something new at Herbal Lane. The local culture factor comprised two items: (1) I have a good impression of the local people and (2) I closely experienced the local culture. The involvement factor contained three items: (1) I visited a place where I really wanted to go, (2) I enjoyed the activities that I really wanted to do, and (3) I was interested in the main activities of this tourism experience. The scales were measured using a set of paper-and-pencil questionnaires, and each item was scored using a 7-point Likert scale ranging from 1 (very strongly disagree) to 7 (very strongly agree).

5 Results

Internal consistency was calculated to assess the reliability of the scales. Cronbach's alphas for the four factors of hedonism, novelty, local culture, and involvement were all higher than 0.7. According to Nunnally, a Cronbach's α value of 0.7 is adequate for internal consistency reliability; therefore, the measures used in this study demonstrated adequate reliability. Table 1 shows the mean scores of hedonism, novelty, local culture, and involvement rated by the participants. A t-test was performed to examine whether the use of mobile application affected the visitors' tourism experience regarding hedonism, novelty, local culture, and involvement. The results showed that the mobile application developed in this study significantly enhanced the visitors' tourism experience on the four dimensions.

Table 1. The results of the user-testing study

Independent variable	Condition	N	Mean (SD)	t
Hedonism	With app	55	5.42 (0.86)	5.14***
	Without app	59	4.53 (1.00)	
Novelty	With app	55	5.92 (0.86)	4.89***
	Without app	59	5.06 (0.99)	
Local culture	With app	55	5.50 (1.16)	3.16**
	Without app	59	4.86 (0.98)	
Involvement	With app	55	5.39 (0.93)	4.71***
	Without app	59	4.52 (1.04)	

** $p < 0.01$; *** $p < 0.001$ (2-tailed)

5.1 Hedonism

The mean of hedonism rated by the participants who used the mobile application was 5.42 (0.86) and by those who did not use mobile application was 4.53 (1.00). The differences were statistically significant at $p < .001$ by independent t-test. Based on the survey results, participants using the mobile application had higher scores than those without a mobile application when answering, "I indulged in the activities in Herbal Lane" and "Visiting Herbal Lane was exciting." The participants who used the mobile application found the experience of visiting Herbal Lane pleasant; they enjoyed visiting Herbal Lane and participating in the activities.

5.2 Novelty

The mean of novelty rated by the participants who used the mobile application was 5.92 and by those who did not use mobile application was 5.06. The differences were statistically significant at $p < .001$ by independent t-test. Participants without the application found the herbs being sold at the shops in Herbal Lane very novel. Their travel experiences were completely different to their experiences of previous attractions. The participants with the application also felt the novelty of the Herbal Lane experience, expressing it as a new and interesting experience to use the application to not only guide their visit to Herbal Lane but also gain a more in-depth understanding of the herbs for health and wellbeing. The results show that using a mobile application in a unique business district such as Herbal Lane can improve the sense of novelty for visitors in regards to their tourism experience.

5.3 Local Culture

The mean of local culture rated by the participants who used the mobile application was 5.50 and by those who did not use mobile application was 4.82. The differences were statistically significant at $p < .01$ by independent t-test. When the participants without the application visited Herbal Lane, they could understand the history of Herbal Lane through the introduction at the entrance of Herbal Lane. By contrast, the participants who used the application while visiting Herbal Lane used the mobile application to participate in the herb searching activities and develop an understanding of the herbs on Herbal Lane. They could also understand related knowledge about the herbs through the application. The information provided by the mobile application allowed the visitors to acquire basic information about the herbs, encouraging them to inquire further about the efficacy of the herbs and how to consume the herbs. The visitors therefore gained a deeper impression of the cultural environment of Herbal Lane than those without the application.

5.4 Involvement

The mean of involvement rated by the participants who used the mobile application was 5.39 and by those who did not use mobile application was 4.52. The differences were statistically significant at $p < .001$ by independent t-test. The results from the survey showed that the participants with the application were significantly more involved than those without the application while they were visiting Herbal Lane. They gave high scores in their feedback for 5.40 (1.13) and 5.78 (1.01) stating, "I enjoyed the activities that I really wanted to do" and "I was interested in the main activities of this tourism experience." This shows that the visitors believed that the mobile application proposed in our study can help visitors to enjoy participating in activities in Herbal Lane, and hence improve their degree of involvement while visiting Herbal Lane.

6 Conclusion

This study developed a mobile application to promote Herbal Lane's business district by integrating professional fields including design, computer science, and TCM. It is hoped that the application will improve the tourism experience for visitors and help them understand more about the herbs in Herbal Lane so that they can become potential consumers. This study conducted a design project to approach this topic and delivered a workable prototype—a mobile application for visiting Herbal Lane. With the workable prototype, we carried out a user-testing study to understand whether the mobile application would enhance a visitor's tourism experience. The results indicated that the mobile application could improve visitors' tourism experiences comparing to those without the mobile application. Based on the findings of this study, further discussions follow.

6.1 Enhance the Tourism Experience with Mobile Application

The mobile application proposed in this study can improve the visitors' tourism experiences while visiting Herbal Lane. It is therefore feasible to use the mobile application for regional promotion from the aspect of enhancing visitors' travel experiences. The application not only allows users to perceive a sense of joy and novelty, but can also promote the local culture to the visitors and increase their willingness to participate during the visit. The mobile application proposed in this study provides a new channel for visitors to encounter Herbal Lane and the local shops, and to understand the culture of Herbal Lane. As a result, visitors are not merely walking past attractions quickly, but can instead gain a deeper understanding of Herbal Lane's culture and learn about the herbs. The practical experiments showed that the application helped the visitors to become more involved in the activities at Herbal Lane. In addition to enjoying various herbs, they were also more willing to ask the shop assistants about the effects of those herbs, thus forming an interaction between the shop assistants and the visitors. In addition, by the end of the tour, since visitors gained an initial understanding of Herbal Lane, they experienced Herbal Lane from another perspective and demonstrated a stronger desire to make a purchase.

6.2 Increase the Touch Points

A destination 'touch point' is any point of contact that a visitor uses to find out about a product or service, or to make a purchase. Using a mobile application to enhance visitors' tourism experiences can increase the touch points between the visitors and the place they are visiting so that the visitors can actively interact with the people, objects, and environment of the location. In our study, the visitors who used the application to visit Herbal Lane gave positive feedback about the built-in interactive sections of the application, including the herb searching activity, which guides visitors to actively search for the herbs that are suitable for their body constitutions. Through the pattern recognition feature, visitors can obtain information about the herbs in Herbal Lane. The design of the activity is exploratory, and can thus stimulate the visitors' curiosity while increasing the touch points of Herbal Lane. Once the visitors have completed the herb searching activity, the mobile application provides herb information, thus allowing the visitors to upload the information to social media channels and share it with their friends. This public exposure can attract more visitors in the future. Promoting cultural marketplaces, such as Herbal Lane, by designing a mobile application that aims to increase the touch points of the attraction increases the chances for visitors to encounter the local culture. This is a sustainable strategy for tourist attraction sites to attract more visitors long term.

6.3 Suggestions for Future Modifications

Based on the participants' feedback, we outline three suggestions to modify the mobile application. The first modification is to offer more information about Herbal Lane. When visitors enter an unfamiliar place, they have an urge to find out more about the place. The mobile application can rapidly provide information in many forms. Our study results show that a useful and easy-to-use application is essential for visitors' travel experiences. While the application in our study provided an experience for exploring herbs, the participants expressed that basic information about attractions could be included and introduced when appropriate so that the visitors could know more about the places they visited. Another user requirement is the inclusion of a reasonable navigation route. In our study, herb-searching activity was used to guide the visitors to Herbal Lane to explore the herbs. Some users stated that in subsequent versions, the navigation function of the application could be enhanced by adding a location-based service (LBS) to provide guidance during the exploration process and to make the experience more interesting. The third requirement is to combine multiple modalities for the interface design. A good interface design can significantly enhance the usability and reduce the operation burden on the users; it can also indirectly improve the quality of the user experience. The participants stated that the interface design of the application in this research was simple and refreshing, which reflects the actual atmosphere of Herbal Lane. Regrettably, the operating interface designed for this study focused on the presentation of the visual arrangement; however, the participants stated that audio feedback and presentation would enhance the usability. Subsequent designs should therefore use an improved visual interface and audio feedback to enhance users' interest in the exploratory game and the guidance provided by the interface.

Acknowledgments. This material is based upon work supported by the Ministry of Science and technology of the Republic of China under grant MOST 102-2218-E-011-018- and MOST 104-2410-H-011-026-.

References

1. Kotler, P., Haider, D.H., Rein, I.: Marketing Places. The Free Press, New York (1993)
2. Wu, F.: Place promotion in Shanghai, PRC. Cities **17**(5), 349–361 (2000)
3. Cross, N.: Designerly ways of knowing: design discipline versus design science. Des. Issues **17**(3), 49–55 (2001)

4. Biggs, M.: The role of the artefact in art and design research. Int. J. Des. Sci. Technol. **10**(2), 19–24 (2002)
5. Mäkelä, M.: Knowing through making: the role of the artefact in practice-led research. Knowl. Technol. Policy **20**(3), 157–163 (2007)
6. Feifer, M.: Going Places. The Ways of the Tourist from Imperial Rome to the Present Day. MacMillan London Limited, London (1985)
7. Otto, J.E., Ritchie, J.R.: The service experience in tourism. Tourism Manag. **17**(3), 165–174 (1996)
8. Ooi, C.S.: A theory of tourism experiences. In: Experiencescapes: Tourism, Culture and Economy, pp. 53–68 (2005)
9. Kim, J.H., Ritchie, J.B., McCormick, B.: Development of a scale to measure memorable tourism experiences. J. Travel Res. 13–25 (2010)
10. Sthapit, E.: Tourists' Perceptions of Memorable Experience. Testing the Memorable Tourism Scale (M.T.Es) AmongTourists to Rovaniemi, Lapland Pro gradu thesis Tourism Research, EMACIM Studies (2013)
11. Uriely, N.: The tourist experience: conceptual developments. Ann. Tourism Res. **32**(1), 199–216 (2005)
12. Castells, M.: The information age: economy, society, and culture. Volume I: The Rise of the Network Society (1996)
13. Henseler, J., Ringle, C., Sinkovics, R.: The use of partial least squares path modeling in international marketing. Adv. Int. Mark. (AIM) **20**, 277–320 (2009)
14. Shankar, V., Balasubramanian, S.: Mobile marketing: a synthesis and prognosis. J. Interact. Mark. **23**(2), 118–129 (2009)

Assessing the Effects of Mobile Service Quality on Customer Satisfaction and the Continued Usage Intention of Mobile Service: A Study of Non-gaming Mobile Apps

Wei-Tsong Wang[1(✉)] and Wen-Yin Chen[2]

[1] Department of Industrial and Information Management, National Cheng Kung University, Tainan, Taiwan
wtwang@mail.ncku.edu.tw

[2] Institute of Information Management, National Cheng Kung University, Tainan, Taiwan
wenying30@gmail.com

Abstract. Research indicates that one of the key drivers of the development of m-commerce is the provision of various types of high-quality mobile applications/services (apps). Business managers have thus been devoting themselves into not only attracting new customers but also retaining existing customers. Despite the considerable amount of studies on mobile apps, there are few studies that specifically investigate the effects of mobile-service-related quality factors on m-commerce consumers' continuance intention regarding specific mobile apps. This study thus develops a research model that describe the relationships among mobile-service-quality factors (interaction quality, environment quality, and outcome quality), customer satisfaction, and the mobile-apps users' continuance intention. The proposed research model was empirically validated using data collected from the users of mobile apps in Taiwan. The research results indicate that the three quality factors were key determinants of customer satisfaction and continuance intention. Theoretical and practical implications are subsequently discussed.

Keywords: Mobile apps · Mobile service quality · Customer satisfaction · Continuance intention

1 Introduction

Because of the increasing popularity of mobile devices, including smart phones and tablets, the market potential of mobile commerce (m-commerce) has been growing all over the world. The emergence of the m-commerce era and the prosperous development of mobile technologies enable the mobile devices to serve as not only communication devices but also multi-functional personal digital assistants in people's daily lives. Research indicates that one of the key drivers of the development of m-commerce is the provision of various types of high-quality mobile applications/services (mobile apps).

P.-L.P. Rau (Ed.): CCD 2016, LNCS 9741, pp. 459–467, 2016.
DOI: 10.1007/978-3-319-40093-8_46

Compared to the conventional electronic commerce (e-commerce) services, mobile apps has the unique characteristics, including location-awareness, conditions of usage, adaptivity, ubiquity, personalization, and broadcasting, which allow customers to use mobile applications/services anytime and anywhere. Because the current mobile application/service market is highly competitive, business managers have thus been devoting themselves into not only attracting new customers but also retaining existing customers. Additionally, research indicates that the unit cost of acquiring a new customer is much higher than that of retaining an existing customer, enhancing customers' continuance intention is critical to mobile application providers in terms of cost saving and business expansion. Consequently, there have been many studies that investigate critical factors influencing the intention of the users of mobile apps to continue to use those applications in order to provide managers of corporations with guidelines regarding the establishment of favorable long-term relationships with their customers in order to acquire sustainable competitive advantages.

Although a considerable amount of the mobile apps are provided to m-commerce consumers for free, those consumers tend to consider carefully regarding the use of a specific mobile application/service in terms of whether the use of a particular mobile app would satisfy their specifics needs the most before downloading them because of the concern regarding the relatively limited storage space and operating capabilities of their mobile devices. Therefore, good service quality of mobile apps can enhance customers' satisfaction regarding their use experience of those mobile apps, which, in turn, decrease customers' intentions to switch to competing mobile apps. However, there are few studies that specifically investigate the effects of mobile-service-related quality factors on m-commerce consumers' continuance intention regarding specific mobile apps. It is thus difficult for us to identify the key success factors that significantly influence the variation of customer loyalty to a specific mobile app. Consequently, how to strengthen m-commerce users' intention to continue to use specific mobile apps via improving mobile service quality is considered to be an important issue that deserves extra research efforts.

Based on the discussion of our research background and motivations represented above, the purpose of this study is to investigate the relationships among mobile services quality, customer satisfaction, and customers' continuance intention from the viewpoint of mobile service quality. This study thus proposes a research model that depicts how the three mobile-service-related quality constructs, including interaction quality, environment quality, and outcome quality, affect customer satisfaction and customers' continuance intention regarding a specific mobile app.

2 Literature Review

In this section, we introduce the development of mobile services and mobile applications. Then, we discuss service quality from the perspective of m-commerce to find out the key quality factors that may affect customer satisfaction and continuance intention of mobile apps' users. Finally, a research model is proposed to investigate the effects of the key quality factors on the customer satisfaction and continuance intention.

2.1 Mobile Applications/Services

Because of the exceptional development of mobile devices, the major form of mobile services is mobile apps in the current mobile commerce market. Taylor et al. [1] define mobile apps as small programs that run on mobile devices and perform missions such as internet banking, gaming, or web page browsing. In 2012, 54.9 % of cell phone users in the U.S. use smartphones as a result of the popularity of mobile apps. Nielsen reports that from 2011 to the second quarter of 2012, the average number of apps installed on a smartphone has increased from 32 to 41.

However, because the number of mobile apps in the market is increasing rapidly, mobile service providers are encountering fierce competition in the marketplace. Consequently, it is critical for mobile service providers to find out the critical success factors of enhancing customers' continuance intention. Many studies have been focusing on this issue and most of them highlight the importance of the construct of service quality in the information systems success model proposed by DeLone and McLean [2] in understanding the success of mobile apps. Although many academics consider m-commerce as an extension of e-commerce, m-commerce services are quite different from traditional e-commerce services because of their unique service attributes and industry features. Consequently, the evaluation of service quality of mobile services should be based on the service quality evaluation models that take into considerations of the unique features of m-commerce.

2.2 Mobile Service Quality

Previous research of customer satisfaction has indicated that service quality is an important evaluation index [3]. Service quality plays a key role in helping different industries evaluate if they clearly understand customers' needs in traditional business environment. At the era of Internet, service still plays an influential role in electronic commerce and mobile commerce [4, 5]. However, many corporations simply use web sites and mobile services as new tools of posting static company information on the Internet, but do not appropriately take advantage of web sites and mobile services for boosting companies' businesses. When users reply more and more heavily on various web-based applications in their daily lives, how to provide them with better services to attract customers and how to evaluate the service quality of mobile services have become a major concern to corporations.

The arrival of mobile commerce era motivates mobile service providers to develop methods that help them appropriately evaluate the perceived mobile service quality of customers in order to achieve higher customer satisfaction and to increase the value of services in the extremely competitive environment of mobile services [6–8]. A review of the literature regarding the evaluation of the mobile service quality reveals that most of the existing studies focus on the viewpoint of customer satisfaction. For example, Kim et al. [6] use summarize the findings of prior literature [9–11] to develop a theoretical framework to define the six dimensions of mobile service quality, including call quality, value-added services, customer support, loss cost, move-in cost, and interpersonal relationship. Brady and Cronin [3] also propose a framework that incorporates three primary dimensions of mobile service quality (interaction quality, physical environment quality and outcome quality). However, the dimensions of service quality proposed by Brady and Cronin [3] are limited to the measurement of service quality in traditional service contexts. The sub-dimensions, for example, ambient condition/social factors, are not applicable in measuring the service quality of virtual services. Therefore, Lu et al. [8] refine Brady and Cronin's [3] framework and propose a model of mobile service quality. Their model consists of three primary dimensions: interaction quality, environment quality, and outcome quality. Thus, this study chooses mobile applications as the main research subject from various mobile services and adopts Lu et al.'s [8] mobile service quality model for our investigations. This framework of mobile service quality includes three primary dimensions. First, interaction quality refers to quality of a customer's interaction with the mobile service provider during the service delivery. Additionally, environment quality refers to quality evaluation of customers toward utility equipment, interface design, and the appropriateness of provided contents. Finally, outcome quality refers to the service experience that customers perceive during the service delivery process and what customers are left with when the service procedure is finished.

3 Research Model and Research Hypotheses

Based on the results of our literature review, a theoretical model to assess the consumers' satisfaction and continuance intention with regard to mobile applications is developed, as presented in Fig. 1. In the remaining part of this section, the development of our research hypotheses will be discussed in details.

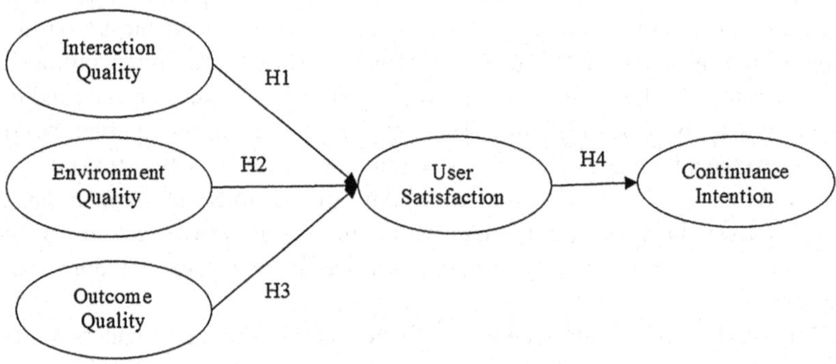

Fig. 1. The research model

The effects of service quality on user satisfaction have been discussed in many studies [2, 3, 12, 13]. A lot of investigations have also been made in the existing marketing literature of mobile business [8, 14, 15].

Chae et al. [16] argue that connection quality, content quality, interaction quality, and contextual quality will affect user satisfaction. Connection quality and content quality refer to the stability and the usefulness of the information of mobile services, which are believed to affect user satisfaction. In this study, these two qualities are classified into environment quality. Interaction quality refers to the interactive relationship with service providers, including the most used positioning and navigation functions. Finally, contextual quality belongs to one of the sub-dimensions of the outcome quality. To mobile application customers, the user satisfaction would be enhanced when service providers provide the required services at the right time. Chiou and Droge [17] also indicate that interactive service quality plays a key role in forming user satisfaction, because it affects how customers perceive the service quality. Kuo et al. [18] point out that factors including interface design, system reliability, connection stability (i.e., environment quality) can significantly influence the user satisfaction of mobile services. Finally, Dabholkar and Overby [19] investigate real estate agents and find out that outcome quality is closely connected to customer satisfaction. However, Zhao et al. [15] indicate that even though that the service quality is high, the negative WOM of outcome quality for services or commodities will create unpleasant shopping experiences to customers and the degree of customer satisfaction would be low. Based on the discussion above, the following hypotheses are developed.

H1: Interaction quality positively influences user satisfaction regarding a mobile application.

H2: Environment quality positively influences user satisfaction regarding a mobile application.

H3: Outcome quality positively influences user satisfaction regarding a mobile application.

From the viewpoint of mobile service providers, the purpose for providing satisfied services is to attract customers to continually use their mobile services, and thus to increase customers' adhesion of services for acquiring more commercial benefits. In the e-commerce field, Bhattacherjee [20] points out that satisfaction is a key predictor of users' continuance use intention. Additionally, Riel et al. [21] find out that satisfaction positively influenced customers' continuance use intention of portal sites. The above literature have proved that customers' satisfaction with products or services will directly or indirectly affect their willingness to repurchase or reuse [22–24]. In summary, user satisfaction and continuance use intention usually have a positive relationship. Therefore, the following hypothesis is proposed.

H4: User satisfaction positively influences users' continuance intention regarding a mobile application.

4 Data Collection and Analysis

4.1 Instrument Development

To develop an effective survey, 47 items relevant to the five constructs of the research model were adapted from the existing literature and refined based on the specific topic of this study. All of the survey items were pilot-tested with 34 individuals who had experience in using mobile applications on a daily basis. The internal consistency and reliability were examined using Cronbach's alpha coefficient analysis. The questionnaire was further refined based on the results and feedback from the pilot test. The final questionnaire consisted of 42 items. Items included in the final revised questionnaire were considered highly reliable because the individual Cronbach's alpha coefficients of all the first-order constructs reached the recommended level of 0.7 (ranging from 0.77 to 0.90). The items in the survey were measured using a seven-point Likert scale ranging from (1) strongly disagree to (7) strongly agree.

4.2 Data Collection and Analysis

The data for this study were collected using an online questionnaire to survey consumers who had experience in using mobile applications on a daily basis in Taiwan. The most popular online bulletin board system (i.e., the PTT) were selected as the survey distribution channels. Of the 367 questionnaires received, 72 incomplete or problematic responses were later removed, yielding 295 valid responses and a rate of useful response of 80.4 %.

The technique of the component-based structural equation modeling (SEM), namely the partial least squares (PLS), was adopted for the data analysis procedure of this study. The reliability of the measures for each of the five latent constructs was first tested by examining the individual Cronbach's alpha coefficients. For the five constructs investigated, all of these were greater than the recommended level of 0.7 or higher (ranging from 0.70 to 0.90). Then, using the SPSS and SmartPLS 2.0 software packages, the psychometric properties (i.e., construct validity) of the measurement model were assessed in terms of convergent and discriminant validity [25, 26].

Three primary measures were used to evaluate the convergent validity of the measurement model: (a) the factor loadings of the indicators, which must be statistically significant with values greater than 0.6; (b) composite reliability (CR), with values greater than 0.6; and (c) average variance extracted (AVE) estimates, with values greater than 0.5. The results of our analysis indicate that all factor loadings (ranging from 0.67 to 0.93) of the measures used were statistically significant, and all were larger than the restrictive criterion of 0.6. Additionally, all CR values (ranging from 0.82 to 0.92) were higher than 0.6, indicating a reliable measurement model. Finally, the AVE values ranged from 0.60 to 0.65, indicating that each construct was strongly related to its respective indicators. Overall, the measurement model exhibited adequate convergent validity. Finally, the discriminant validity of the measurement model was determined to be satisfactory, since the squared correlations between constructs were smaller than the corresponding AVE estimates [25]. To conclude, the measurement model was adequate.

By adopting the PLS technique using the bootstrapping procedure, the structural model was evaluated for hypotheses testing. Bootstrapping of the 295 cases (the same as the original sample size) was conducted with 1000 samples to evaluate the significance of the proposed research hypotheses. Figure 2 presents the standardized path coefficients and t values, the significance of the paths, and the coefficients of determination (R^2) for each endogenous construct. As shown in Fig. 2, all the hypotheses were supported by the data.

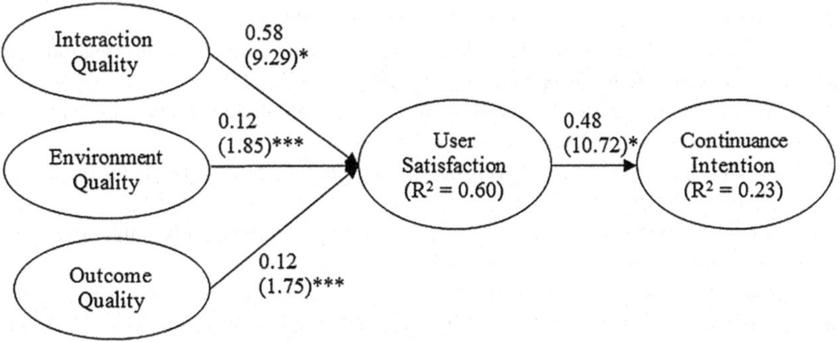

Note 1: Standardized path coefficients are reported (*t* value in parentheses)
Note 2: * $p < 0.01$; ** $p < 0.05$; *** $p < 0.1$.

Fig. 2. The hypothesis testing results

5 Discussion and Conclusion

This study has developed and validated a research model for explaining the satisfaction and continuance intentions of mobile application/service users by adopting the perspective of mobile service quality. Interaction quality, environment quality, and outcome quality were all found to be significant factors in determining user satisfaction and continuance intentions regarding mobile applications/services. The research findings can thus provide mobile service providers with significant insights into how factors of mobile service quality may impact the continuous adoption of mobile applications/services. Additionally, the validation of the proposed research model has provided support of simultaneously adoption of interaction quality, environment quality, and outcome quality as key factors influencing users' continuance intentions in the context of the use of mobile applications/services. To further extend the contribution of this study, more research that aims to examine the proposed research model using a variety of samples that have a higher degree of representativeness in similar and different contexts is thus needed to further validate it, or refine it by identifying additional variables which can enhance the ability of the proposed research model to explain and predict the satisfaction and continuance intentions of the users of mobile applications/services, such as different dimensions of users' trust in the mobile service providers (as the reflection of the influence of mobile service quality), habit of mobile service users, and other key mobile service quality factors.

References

1. Taylor, D.G., Voelker, T., Pentina, I.: Mobile application adoption by young adults: a social network perspective. Int. J. Mob. Mark. **6**(2), 60–70 (2011)
2. DeLone, W.H., McLean, E.R.: The DeLone and McLean model of information systems success: a ten-year update. J. Manag. Inf. Syst. **19**(4), 9–30 (2003)
3. Brady, M.K., Cronin, J.J.: Some new thoughts on conceptualizing perceived service quality: a hierarchical approach. J. Mark. **65**(3), 34–49 (2001)
4. Li, Y.N., Tan, K.C., Xie, M.: Measuring web-based service quality. Total Qual. Manag. **13**(5), 685–700 (2002)
5. Parasuraman, A., Grewal, D.: The impact of technology on the quality-value-loyalty chain: a research agenda. J. Acad. Mark. Sci. **28**(1), 168–174 (2000)
6. Kim, M.K., Park, M.C., Jeong, D.H.: The effects of customer satisfaction and switching barrier on customer loyalty in Korean mobile telecommunication services. Telecommun. Policy **28**, 145–159 (2004)
7. Lai, F., Griffin, M., Babin, B.J.: How quality, value, image, and satisfaction create loyalty at a Chinese telecom. J. Bus. Res. **62**, 980–986 (2009)
8. Lu, Y., Zhang, L., Wang, B.: A multidimensional and hierarchical model of mobile service quality. Electron. Commer. Res. Appl. **8**, 228–240 (2009)
9. Dick, A.S., Basu, K.: Customer loyalty: toward an integrated conceptual framework. J. Acad. Mark. Sci. **22**(2), 99–113 (1994)
10. Gerpott, T.J., Rams, W., Schindler, A.: Customer retention, loyalty, and satisfaction in the german mobile cellular telecommunications market. Telecommun. Policy **25**, 249–269 (2001)
11. Lee, J., Lee, J., Feick, L.: The impact of switching costs on the customer satisfaction-loyalty link: mobile phone service in France. J. Serv. Mark. **15**(1), 35–48 (2001)
12. Caro, L.M., Garcia, J.A.M.: Developing a multidimensional and hierarchical service quality model for the travel agency industry. Tour. Manag. **29**, 706–720 (2008)
13. Pitt, L.F., Watson, R.T., Kavan, B.: Service quality: a measure of information systems effectiveness. MIS Q. **19**(2), 173–187 (1995)
14. Turel, O., Serenko, A.: Satisfaction with mobile services in Canada: an empirical investigation. Telecommun. Policy **30**, 314–331 (2006)
15. Zhao, L., Lu, Y., Zhang, L., Chau, P.Y.K.: Assessing the effects of service quality and justice on customer satisfaction and the continuance intention of mobile value-added services: an empirical test of a multidimensional model. Decis. Support Syst. **52**, 645–656 (2012)
16. Chae, M., Kim, J., Kim, H., Ryu, H.: Information 245quality for mobile internet services: a theoretical model with empirical validation. Electron. Market **12**(1), 38–46 (2002)
17. Chiou, J.S., Droge, C.: Service quality, trust, specific asset investment, and expertise: direct and indirect effects in a satisfaction-loyalty framework. J. Acad. Mark. Sci. **34**(4), 613–627 (2006)
18. Kuo, Y.F., Wu, C.M., Deng, W.J.: The relationships among service quality, perceived value, customer satisfaction, and post-purchase intention in mobile value-added services. Comput. Hum. Behav. **25**(4), 887–896 (2009)
19. Dabholkar, P.A., Overby, J.W.: Linking process and outcome to service quality and customer satisfaction evaluations: an investigation of real estate agent service. Int. J. Serv. Ind. Manag. **16**(1), 10–27 (2005)
20. Bhattacherjee, A.: Understanding information systems continuance: an expectation confirmation model. MIS Q. **25**(3), 351–370 (2001)

21. Riel, A.C.R.V., Liljander, V., Jurriens, P.: Exploring consumer evaluations of e-services: a portal site. Int. J. Serv. Ind. Manag. **12**(4), 359–377 (2001)
22. Bhattacherjee, A.: An empirical analysis of the antecedents of electronic commerce service continuance. Decis. Support Syst. **32**(2), 201–214 (2001)
23. Bhattacherjee, A., Perols, J., Sanford, C.: Information technology continuance: a theoretical extension and empirical test. J. Comput. Inf. Syst. **49**(1), 17–26 (2008)
24. Chen, S.C., Chen, H.H., Chen, M.F.: Determinants of satisfaction and continuance intention towards self-service technologies. Ind. Manag. Data Syst. **109**(9), 1248–1263 (2009)
25. Fornell, C.R., Larcker, D.F.: Evaluating suctural equation models with unobservable variables and measurement error. J. Mark. Res. **18**(1), 39–50 (1981)
26. Hair, J.F., Black, W.C., Babin, B.J., Anderson, R.E.: Multivariate Data Analysis: A Global Perspective, 7th edn. Pearson Education, Upper Saddle River (2010)

Research on the Impact of Menu Structure of Smart Phones on Dual Task Performance

Huining Xing(✉), Hua Qin, and Dingding Wang

Department of Industrial Engineering, School of Mechanical-Electronic and Automobile Engineering, Beijing University of Civil Engineering and Architecture, Beijing 100044, China
1259183822@qq.com

Abstract. The purpose of this paper is to study the influence of smartphone application arrangement on user performance of completing a sub-task and satisfaction in the course of telephoning. Base on simulated smartphone interface, three kinds of application arrangement are designed for the experiment. Participants begin to conduct another application in a kind of application arrangement while telephoning. The results show that the user's operation time is the shortest and satisfaction is the best while frequent applications arranged on the telephoning interface. And the followed is the applied application arranged on the telephoning interface.

Keywords: Smart phone · Menu structure · Application arrangement

1 Introduction

With the emergence of smart phones, applications which with varieties of functions have been appearing, these applications can be used in playing games, navigation, taking photos, learning and so on, in 2015, there are about 1,400,000 kinds of applications for apple smart phone and about 1,830,000 kinds of applications for android mobile phone [1], in which the apple mobile users' download has reached 1 billion times. But due to the limited screen size and too many applications have been downloading, the users' needs to organize them on the mobile phone interface according to the certain way.

The early mobile phone menu organization form is mostly static form, mainly including scrolling menu and hierarchy menu etc., studies have shown that scrolling menu will lower the efficiency of operation [2, 3], but the deeper of hierarchy menu level, the more time users need to spend to learn, and the more wrong choice made on possible paths [3, 4], compared the operation performance of hierarchy menu with the scrolling menu on the small screen, it is found that the operation performance of hierarchy menu is superior to scrolling menu [5].

For smartphone users who need to install new applications and delete old applications constantly, if these applications presented by static way, obviously that can cause trouble to the user. Method applied at present is mainly hierarchical management which is classifying the application or paging in sequence [6, 7], the study also considered that using adaptive user interface can also solve this problem [8, 9], an adaptive

P.-L.P. Rau (Ed.): CCD 2016, LNCS 9741, pp. 468–476, 2016.
DOI: 10.1007/978-3-319-40093-8_47

user interface can change its layout, function, structure elements according to user's behavior [10–12], Mitchell and Shneiderman order the arrangement of menu items from high to low according to the usage frequency of menu item. Results showed that this method did not improve the operation performance, users prefer traditional static menus. Due to this method has changed the original structure of the interface, thus undermining the user's mental model [13]. While someone improved the operation performance with this method [14]. At present, for the adaptive menu interface of mobile phone, there are some research started to study in the aspects of situation awareness, shortcuts, etc. [15, 16].

With the continuous expansion of the functions of programs, there is a growing need for the use of other functions while people using a certain function of one application in mobile phone, which namely is that don't turn off one function which is used, at the same time using another or several functions, for example, someone finds the map while telephoning. For such a large screen of computer and it can present multiple applications on the same interface, whereas it's usually difficult to present two or more application interfaces on the same interface, and small size screen will make it hard for users to form mental model on the menu structure, and beyond the capacity of short-term memory [17]. If the user needs to open another one at the same time, which way that the organization of these applications will be presented and makes higher operation performance and better satisfaction is particularly important.

Due to the different navigation effect of different application arrangements on users, therefore, the purpose of this study is to explore the effect of smartphone application arrangement on the operation performance and users' subjective satisfaction of completing sub-task under the conditions of the implementation of the main tasks.

2 Experimental Design

In order to study the influence of the application arrangement of the adaptive menu structure on the operation performance and the subjective satisfaction of users who complete the sub-tasks, the Flash software was used to simulate the mobile phone interface so that participants are able to test by it. Firstly, three kinds of application arrangement are designed, and the participants can complete the main task of the calling under a menu structure in an application arrangement, at the same time they need to complete a sub-task of another application.

2.1 The Application Arrangement of the Menu and Simulation Interface

There are three kinds of application arrangement in the experiment:

Common menu, according to the using frequency of the menu items, the six most frequent items will be presented on the main task interface. If you need other items, you should click on the "home" button and then return to the main interface to find necessary menu items.

History menu, according to the time sequence, which means the used items nearer to the current time then the items presented more ahead. The used items will be presented on the main task interface. If you need the unused ones, you should click on the "home" button and then return to the main interface to find necessary menu items.

Hierarchy menu, the first level of the items will be presented on the main task interface, and the following sub menu items will be presented after clicking the first level menu item.

According to the three kinds of application arrangement, the experiment has five simulation interfaces. The interface 1 is the main interface, rendering all the application icons, establishing the link relations to the "home" button on interface 2–4. The main interface has two pages, with a total of 34 application icons. The icons are divided into two types– the task icons and the common icons. The first page has 20 application icons, including 4 task icons and the 16 common icons. There are 14 application icons on the second page, including 2 task icons and 12 common icons. The task icons are the ones which are chosen by the participants in the process of the experiment tasks.

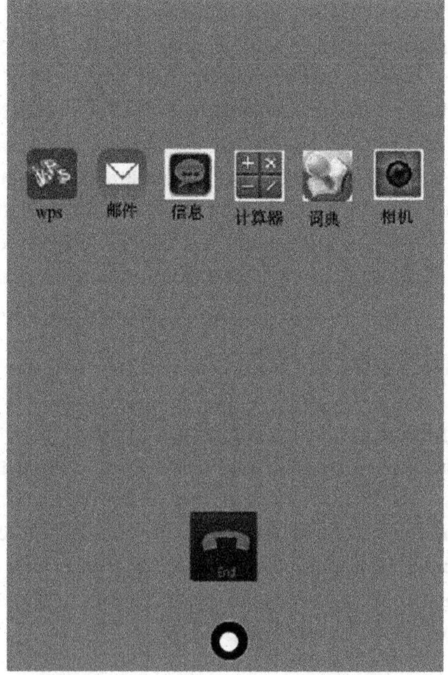

Fig. 1. The interface of common menu

The interface 2 simulates the common menu; the interface function elements include the telephone icon and six commonly used function icons, and a "home" button (Fig. 1).

The interface 3 simulates the history menu; the interface function elements include the phone icon and used application icons. The used application icons can be viewed by sliding around the button, and the icons will be presented at the bottom of the interface (Fig. 2).

Fig. 2. The interface of history menu

The interface 4 simulates the Hierarchy menu; all the applications are presented by two levels. The four classifications in the first level are presented by four icons and the applications in the second level are categorized into the four types. Clicking on the icons in the first level all the applications contained will appear; and these four categories are “life”, “entertainment”, “social”, “system”, respectively (Fig. 3).

The interface 5 is the ending interface.

The experiment simulates the mode of touch interaction interface of mobile phones; the size of the simulation interface is 7.9 * 5.8 cm, and the icon size is 1.3 * 1.3 cm with the menu name placed right under the icon; the font is song typeface and the font size is 9 pt.

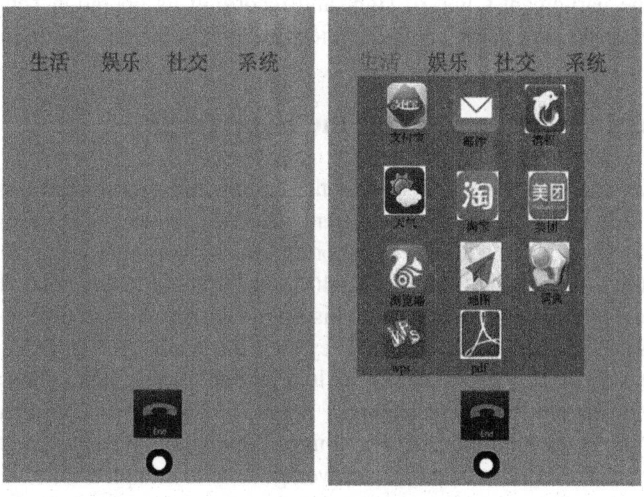

Fig. 3. The interface of hierarchy menu

2.2 Experiment Tasks and Processes

There are 18 people tested in the experiment; the age range is about 20 to 30 years old, with an average age of 24. Their using time of mobile phone is more than 3 years. The participants are grouped into three groups by random. The participants in each group only use one kind of menu organization in the experiment. Each participant will complete four different tasks:

Task 1: when you are chatting with your friend on the phone, he/she sends you an email, and this email is very important, which need you to find this email right now.
Task 2: now you are chatting with your friend on the phone, at this moment your WeChat ringing; you receive a WeChat message, and you want to view the contents of this message right now.
Task 3: now you are chatting with your friend on the phone, at this moment you find the roadside scenery is very beautiful; you want to take photo by the cell phones.
Task 4: now you are on the phone with your friends, and your friend is telling you how to reach the destination, but you can't find the right direction, so you need to use a compass application in the cell phone to determine the azimuth.

Before the start of the experiment, the participants should understand the research purpose of the experiment by the introduction of the experiment, sign the "informed consent", and fill in the tables of personal basic information and mobile phone usage information. Then they need to be introduced the experimental simulation interface, and practice until the participants believe that they have already been familiar with the interface.

In official experiment, the simulation interface of mobile phone will be displayed on the screen of computer; participants start the tasks as soon as they heard "start" and timing begins, after the participants found the target icon, the interface prompts into work and end time. In the process of implementing the task, the TobiiStudio eye tracker will record the participant's line of sight and recording its operation behavior. After completing all tasks, the participants need to fill the satisfaction questionnaire.

3 The Results and Analysis of the Experiment

Table 1 shows the mean and variance of the completion time of the task under the condition of different application arrangement. The data shows that the average time to complete task 3 is 2.31(s), which is the shortest one for common menu. In this menu, the average time to complete task 4 is 8.44(s), which is the longest one. The average time to complete all task is 4.48(s). About history menu, the average time to completing task 2 and task 4 are shorter than others. They are 1.57(s) and 1.90(s). The average time to complete task 3 is 25.62(s), which is the longest one. In this menu, the average time to complete all task is 8.41(s). For hierarchy menu, the average time to complete task 2 is 3.93(s) which is the shortest one. The longest time is the average time to complete task 1 which is 12.10(s). In this menu the average time to complete all task is 10.43(s).

Thus, the operating time for common menu is the shortest. Figure 1 present the average time to complete tasks in different application arrangement intuitively.

Table 2 shows the mean and variance of the focuses in the process of the task under the condition of different application arrangement. For common menu, the data shows that the average focuses in the process of task 3 are 30.50, which is the least quantity; the focuses in the process of task 4 are 52.17, which is the most quantity. The average focuses in the process of all tasks are 36.96. About history menu, the average focuses in the process of task 2 and task 4 are less than others'. They are 19.67 and 28.50. The average focuses in the process of task 3 are 92.67, which is the most quantity. In this menu, the average focuses in the process of all task are 46.75. For hierarchy menu, the average focuses in the process of task 2 are 26.67, which is the least quantity. The most focuses are the average focuses in the process of task 1 which are 76.67. In this menu the average focuses in the process of all task are 43.96. Thus, the quantity of focuses for common menu is the least. Figure 2 present the average focuses in the process of tasks in different menu organization form intuitively.

Table 1. Descriptive statistics of time.

Variables	Common menu		History menu		Hierarchy menu	
	Average value(s)	Standard deviation	Average value(s)	Standard deviation	Average value(s)	Standard deviation
Task 1	3.54	1.70	4.55	1.99	22.97	12.10
Task 2	3.64	1.48	1.57	0.36	3.93	1.46
Task 3	2.31	0.60	25.62	12.27	5.60	3.50
Task 4	8.44	8.24	1.90	0.90	9.22	4.25
Total	4.48	4.66	8.41	11.75	10.43	9.87

Table 2. Descriptive statistics of number of fixation

Variables	Common		History		Hierarchy	
	Average value	Standard deviation	Average value	Standard deviation	Average value	Atandard deviation
Task 1	31.33	11.00	46.17	20.89	76.67	22.33
Task 2	33.83	11.22	28.50	4.14	26.67	13.08
Task 3	30.50	9.73	92.67	32.23	33.83	22.12
Task 4	52.17	22.87	19.67	8.24	38.67	23.98
Total	36.96	16.43	46.75	34.17	43.96	27.72

Table 3 shows the mean and variance of the participants' satisfaction under the condition of different application arrangement. The average participants' satisfaction about common menu is 6.35, 5.35 for history menu and 4.90 for hierarchy menu. So the most popular menu is the common menu. The history menu is worst (Figs. 4 and 5).

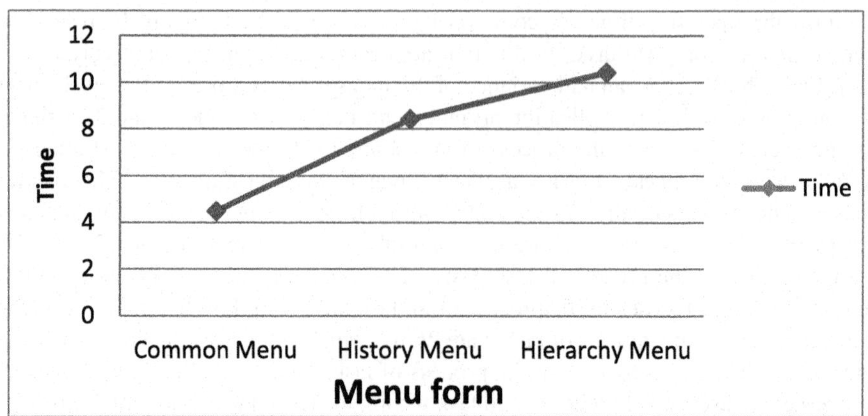

Fig. 4. Mean time on different menu construction

Table 3. Descriptive statistics of Satisfaction

Variables	Average value	Standard deviation
Common menu	6.35	0.73
History menu	5.85	0.90
Hierarchy menu	4.90	1.29
Total	5.70	1.16

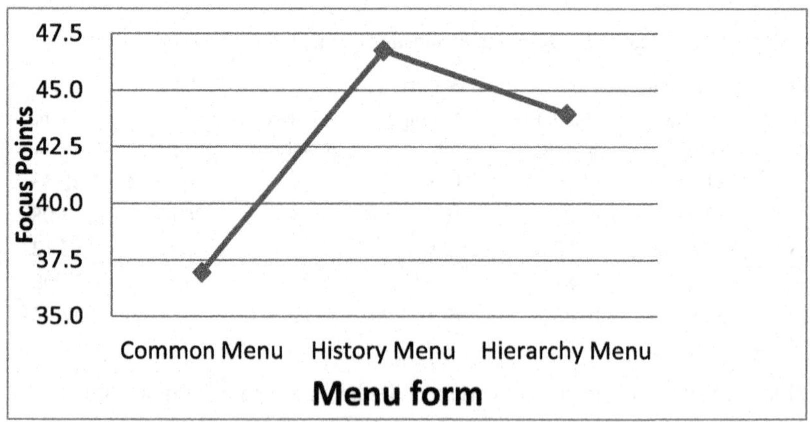

Fig. 5. Mean number of fixation on different menu construction

4 Conclusions

The purpose of this study is to explore the impact of the organization form of mobile phone applications on the operation performance of completing sub-task and subjective satisfaction of users under the implementation of the main task. Experimental results show that the operation time and subjective satisfaction of the users under the common menu are significantly better than the history menu and hierarchy menu, following by history menu.

Despite the fact that the screen of smartphone only presents a single interface of the application when the current users in the operation of an application, but with the increasing of functions of smartphone applications, there are more and more demands to operate two or more applications at the same time, for the small screen, how to improve its operation performance and satisfaction while users in the operation of a function of an application and easy to find other applications at the same time, which are closely related with the application arrangement.

Acknowledgement. The research project presented in this paper is a part of the Project "Research on Technology and Standards of Information Presentation Density of Information Display Interface and Menu Dialog Ergonomics Design", which was supported by the China National Institute of Standardization. The authors would like to acknowledge the support of the China National Institute of Standardization for this project (2014BAK01B01-2).

References

1. Wikipedia. http://is.gd/pzjWb6
2. Dillon, A., Richardson, J., McKnight, C.: The effects of display size and text splitting on reading lengthy text from screen. Behav. Inf. Technol. **9**(3), 215–227 (1990)
3. Jones, M., Marsden, G., Mohd-Nasir, N., Boone, K., Buchanan, G.: Improving web interaction on small displays. Comput. Netw. **31**, 1129–1137 (1999)
4. Tang, K.: Menu design with visual momentum for compact smart products. J. Hum. Factors Ergon. Soc. **43**(2), 267–277 (2001)
5. Wang, A.H., Lai, Y.Y., Sun, C.T.: Effect of PDA scrolling- and hierarchy-menu design on users' operating performance. Displays **25**, 109–114 (2004)
6. Bohmer, M., Bauer, G.: Exploiting the icon arrangement on mobile devices as information source for context-awareness. In: Proceeding of Mobile HCI (2010)
7. Huhtala, J., Mäntyjärvi, J., Ahtinen, A., Ventä, L., Isomursu, M.: Animated transitions for adaptive small size mobile menus. In: Gross, T., Gulliksen, J., Kotzé, P., Oestreicher, L., Palanque, P., Prates, R.O., Winckler, M. (eds.) INTERACT 2009. LNCS, vol. 5726, pp. 772–781. Springer, Heidelberg (2009)
8. Benyon, D.: Adaptive systems: a solution to usability problems. User Model. User-Adap. Inter. **3**(1), 65–87 (1993)
9. Weld, D.S., Anderson, C., Domingos, P., Etzioni, O., Gajos, K., Lau, T., Wolfman, S.: Automatically personalizing user interfaces. In: Proceedings of the 18th International Joint Conference on Artificial Intelligence (2003)

10. Van Velsen, L., Van der Geest, T., Klaassen, R., Steehouder, M.: User-centered evaluation of adaptive and adaptable systems: a literature review. Knowl. Eng. Rev. **23**(03), 261–281 (2008)
11. Verkasalo, H.: Contextual patterns in mobile service usage. Pers. Ubiquit. Comput. **13**(5), 331–342 (2009)
12. Do, T.M.T., Perez, D.G.: By their apps you shall understand them: mining large-scale patterns of mobile phone usage. In: Proceeding of the 9th International Conference on Mobile and Ubiquitous Multimedia (2010)
13. Mitchell, J., Shneiderman, B.: Dynamic versus static menus: an exploratory comparison. SIGCHI Bull. **20**(4), 33–37 (1989)
14. Park, J., Han, S.H., Park, Y.S., Cho, Y.A.: Adaptable versus adaptive menus on the desktop: performance and user satisfaction. Int. J. Ind. Ergon. **37**(8), 675–684 (2007)
15. Bridle, R., McCreath, E.: Inducing shortcuts on a mobile phone interface. In: Proceeding of the 11th International Conference on Intelligent User Interface, pp. 327–329 (2006)
16. Vetek, A., Flanagan, J.A., Colley, A., Keränen, T.: SmartActions: context-aware mobile phone shortcuts. In: Gross, T., Gulliksen, J., Kotzé, P., Oestreicher, L., Palanque, P., Prates, R.O., Winckler, M. (eds.) INTERACT 2009. LNCS, vol. 5726, pp. 796–799. Springer, Heidelberg (2009)
17. Albers, M., Kim, L.: Information design for the small-screen interface: an overview of web design issues for personal digital assistants. Tech. Commun. **49**(1), 45–60 (2002)

Proposal of Chinese Tourist Support System to Enjoy the Holy Land Pilgrimage in Japan

Ni Zhang(✉) and Katsuhiko Ogawa

Graduate School of Media and Governance, Keio University, Fujisawa, Kanagawa, Japan
{ni9zhang,ogw}@sfc.keio.ac.jp

Abstract. Many Chinese get familiar with Japan via comics, animations, movies or dramas; especially some scenes in these works were actually drawn on real life. Recently, touring to these places is an on-going new reason for visiting Japan. However, finding the scenes from the real world without a guide is very difficult, and collecting the information about the location of scenes always cost plenty of time on Internet. This paper clarifies the conditions of designing a new media system to raise Chinese tourists' joyfulness out of the holy pilgrimage trip, and proposes a new media system to support them to record and share distinct routes for location of scenes.

Keywords: Chinese tourist · Seichi Junrei · Japanese culture · Holy land · Pilgrimage · Record · Location of scenes

1 Introduction

Seichi Junrei, a Japanese word, which describes this phenomenon, is accepted by Japanese popular culture that means pilgrimage to sacred places of Japanese animations, dramas and movies. It is also called contents tourism. To most Chinese, Japan is not only an exquisite neighboring country, but also has unique and precious culture that fascinates them. Chinese tourists who are deeply impressed by Japanese comics, animation, movies and dramas start to seek and visit the location of scenes in Japan. The best example is *Slam Dunk*, the most popular Japanese animation in China, when broadcasted in late 1990s that turns almost every teenager a super-fan to it. Nonetheless after around 15 years, those teenage audiences are in their late 20s and early 30s, but the topics of *Slam Dunk* are still quite popular in all Chinese social medias. Moreover, most of them are not aware of that all scenes in *Slam Dunk* are existed in real life until the emergence of Internet and social media, for example the main anime set was originated from Kanagawa. Although there are lots of Japanese smartphone applications or websites are designed to promote Seichi Junrei and to inform users the locations of some important scenes, it is not user-friendly to those foreigners who do not speak Japanese or even do not know the existence of certain products but have strong interest of Seichi Junrei. In addition, searching information before the visit is quite time consuming, and some potential visitors may lose interests over complications. Find a trustful guide is a good alternative, but the cost may scare some low-budget travellers away. Moreover, the information about the movie sets is quite dispersed on Internet thus hard to be collected,

P.-L.P. Rau (Ed.): CCD 2016, LNCS 9741, pp. 477–487, 2016.
DOI: 10.1007/978-3-319-40093-8_48

which further led to many travellers had to choose a package tour or group tour to meet their demand.

Weibo, a China-based micro-blogging service, was launched in 2009 and became one of the most popular social media platforms in China. Attributes to the prosperous development of Internet infrastructure and independence from big social-media players, the Chinese Internet environment offers fertile soil for Weibo, whom has gained 220 million monthly active users as to Sep 2015 [1]. Not long ago, the only channel to obtain information about Japanese comics, animation, movies and dramas was mass media. Nowadays people can search in social media and investigate what other users just post immediately, and even find new friends who share common topics, such as Japan. In China, the use of Internet has reached 90.3 % user coverage and far exceeded the use of television and newspapers to get latest information and news that are related to Japan [2]. According to the interviews conducted by Zhou [3], 39 Japanese local governments have opened their official Weibo accounts in order to promote their cities and attract more Chinese tourist. The popularity of Weibo began to change the behavior of both Chinese tourists and Japanese tourism organizations.

This papers aims to find a way to support holy pilgrimage trip for Chinese. Regarding the difficulties of Chinese free tour in Japan, this paper proposes a new media tool to support tourists to find, record and share distinct routes for location of scenes. The later part will conduct as follows: First, analyze the behavior of Chinese tourists in Japan, followed with description of the concept of the media tool. Secondly, present analyses of five experiments of *Slam Dunk* pilgrimage, by consulting my contents in a reality recording system designed by Utsumi [4]. In the last section, the results and future work will be explained.

2 Analysis of Chinese Tourist Behavior in Japan

For deeper understanding of how to assist Chinese tourists to enjoy the contents tourism, this study conducts three different surveys and interviews to understand why Chinese tourists are traveling in Japan, what are their wishes and expectations. The details are as follows:

2.1 Demographical Analysis

The first survey was conducted during June 12th, 2015 to June 22th, 2015. The number of participants is 42. The study shows that most Chinese chose participating the group-tour as their first tour in Japan. Before their trips, they searched on Weibo or consulted friends who have been to Japan before. For the reason why traveling to Japan, 50 % of them claimed the short distance and the other 30 % were attracted by Japanese animations, dramas, movies. Moreover, 80 % of them expressed that they want to have a look about the locations of scenes.

It shows that most group-tour tourists were also looking forward visiting the locations of scenes, which were excluded from the pre-designed itinerary. Thus, Seichi Junrei will have strong potential among Chinese free independent tourists.

2.2 Behavior Analysis

In order to figure out the motivation and behavior of Chinese free tourists, we conducted the following interview and experiment.

Interview in Kawagoe. Kawagoe is a small city in Saitama Prefecture, and local residents prefer to call it "The Little Edo", because most of its architectures are remained in Edo-time style. Chinese tourists are not common there because this city is not in a typical Chinese group-tour's itinerary. However, with the broadcasting of Japanese animation, *Kamisama Kiss*, younger generation starts to notice it (Fig. 1). We managed to interview 10 Chinese tourists there. Two young people are attracted to Kawagoe because of this animation. Even though they understand their trip is alike Seichi Junrei, there was not a Chinese tool could help them to get information, thus they spent a lot of time on searching online and planning, all by themselves.

Fig. 1. The animation and the real location of the scene in Kawagoe

In contrast, the other eight middle-aged participants who were brought there by friends, knowing no more information other than "it is a traditional city". They heavily relied on their friends as tourist guide and interpreter because they do not speak Japanese and manage simple English thus they also have not derived any information from foreign websites in advance.

From our perspective, the lack of a systemized tool in Chinese is inconvenient for most Chinese who wish to have a free trip, not to mention Seichi Junrei.

Experiment in Holy Land Pilgrimage. In China, *Paradise Kiss, Shitsuren Chocolatier*, and *Lost in Translation* are three well-known movies and dramas about Japan and each of them has numerous fans on Weibo. We requested two groups to have a Seichi Junrei about the three movies and dramas on October 21th, 2015. The Weibo group can search the three mentioned works on Weibo during the progress while the comparison group did not prepare in advance but just visiting some locations of scenes. The result shows that the Weibo group created more topics, took more photos, located more original shooting locations and enjoyed the experiment more than the comparison group.

With the help of Weibo, Chinese tourists could easily recall storyline and original scenes continuously and enjoy recording photos and instant experiences. Regarding the interview and the experiment above, a systemized Chinese media tool that provides great information about Japanese animations and dramas is extremely necessary to Chinese free trip tourists.

3 System Concept

According to the survey of Chinese Tourist above, as a media for supporting holy land trip of Chinese, the following conditions were found to be necessary:

1. A Chinese system;
2. Quoting from Weibo;
3. Recording photograph.

Thus, we propose a media tool for Chinese pilgrims that can record pictures and experiences of the special location in reality, while at the same time can show the virtual world and topics of the same location via Weibo.

The main feature of the tool is, firstly, in order to ensure that Chinese tourists could immerse into a Seichi Junrei journey, a platform with attractive content and rich topics is very important. And Weibo can play such role. As the previous experiment implies, that if a tourist refreshes a topic about certain animation when who is travelling at the locations, he/she will receive fertile resources of that animation. Forms of those resources could be photographs, video clips, screenshots or texts that could evoke his/her memories of the animation and be better immersed into the joyfulness of Seichi Junrei.

Secondly, we use Whispath, a recording media related to locations, designed by Utsumi. It is different from other social medias due to its unique function of adding location information under the texts and the posts are displayed directly on the Google map. Every user would see all other users even if they have not 'added' or 'followed' the other. We use the system to support Chinese pilgrims to record photos and texts of their familiar scenes (Fig. 2). The tourists could take advantages of pioneers' recordings when visiting holy land pilgrimages. The photos and texts previous recorders that are showed on the map will guide them to movies sets or original animation scenes when they approaching the right spot.

Every time when users upload photos and texts, they need to type a name of the route and record a Seichi Junrei on the interface. Then they can review theirs or others' paths by selecting the name.

The objects that are recorded by pilgrims could be an ordinary school or even a crossroad, other than general understanding of a tourist 'attraction'. Because those objects are junctions of virtual and actual worlds, and from general tourists' perspective it is meaningless and they would not record them. However the Seichi Junrei recording is taking impressions of a work as a reference to understanding and marking an actual

Fig. 2. Whispath

place. General tourists are motivated by online posts of attracting sceneries or recommendations of previous tourists, but pilgrims track clues from virtual worlds and connect to real world or follow previous pilgrims' experiences.

4 Experiment

According to the user-centered design stories [5], in order to know the record preferences and conventions of Chinese tourists when they are having a holy land pilgrimage, it is important to conduct an experiment with typical users in a real-world environment in the design process.

4.1 Methods

As one of the most influential animations and comics, *Slam Dunk* (a story about some basketball teams in different high schools) is a typical work that suits for this test. Thus, Enoshima, where is the location of *Slam Dunk* in Kanagawa is chosen to be the test place. This media is designed for Chinese tourists, therefore the test subjects must be the Chinese who have watched *Slam Dunk* before and are interested in visiting the real location. The Experiments were conducted in December 2015 and January 2016 in Enoshima, Kanagawa, Japan, and five Chinese participants were involved excluding me. The experiment was mainly aimed at the following pilgrims [6]. We created the first recording of *Slam Dunk* in the prototype. The first participant referred on our contents, and the second participant referred on both the first participant's recording and ours. The latter ones referred on all the previous contents. All of them uploaded their own records in the system as they consulted from the existing information.

4.2 Supporting System

From the three supporting conditions (A Chinese system, the consultation of Weibo and the picture recording), which are previously identified in the concept we've selected picture recording as the main subject of this experiment. By utilizing Whispath, the experiment aim to discover the subject's problems and effectiveness when being used in the Chinese holy land pilgrimage.

4.3 Contents

All of the participants took Enoden (i.e. the Enoshima Electric Railway) as the only transport vehicle, which is also an important element in *Slam Dunk*. Experiments started from the departure station of Enoden, Fujisawa Station. As the initiate recorder, we checked a lot of information about location and station on Weibo and blogs in advance. Also we took some screenshots from the scenes that are related to Enoshima. We were consulting the prepared information, screenshots and Weibo as we were seeking for the right positions in the progress of Seichi Junrei. When we matched the virtual scenes and actual place, the photos and texts were updated to the system. Took our recordings as reference, the system of experiments was ready. Five participants followed contents to start recording their Seichi Junrei.

4.4 Results

All of the details of record locations are as below (Table 1). The reference locations come from our recording.

Note: The first five locations were recorded in the pioneers' recordings.

Two participants, first and third recorded less than ours. The second, the forth and the last participants mark more different locations than those. Especially the second and the fifth subjects, they not only recorded *Slam Dunk*, but also marked *TariTari* and *Tsuritama*, two animations that also take Enoshima as the background.

The first participant said if this tool will be available in near future, she would not spend any time for preparing a Seichi Junrei trip any more. However, she mentioned even though she found pieces of recordings uploaded by pioneer pilgrim about *Slam Dunk* at the right spot, it is still difficult to match. Moreover, she complained that she had to re-type the user name and path name every time when updating new recording.

The second subject was not only a following pilgrim to *Slam Dunk*, but also a pioneering pilgrim to the other two animations in Enoshima. At beginning, she was upset because no consulting pictures about the two animations (*TariTari* and *Tsuritama*). Then she searched lots of screenshots as consultations and took pictures together with the virtual screenshots and real photos.

When the third recorder re-entered the name of the path to upload more pictures, he miss-spelled it and some recordings were showed under another path, without his notice. Resulted to an uncompleted path of Seichi Junrei. Also she mentioned that the user interface does not match smartphone application and not easy to use.

Some subjects felt more easily to find the locations of scenes with the help of the system, but they also experienced inaccurate marking location due to imprecise navigation.

5 Behavioral Analysis

As a unique feature of Japanese culture, ACG (animation, comic and game) absolutely becomes one of the best selling points to attract people from all over the world, especially Asian youngsters who prefer free tour than package tour. From the research of Benjamin [7], many Hong Kong youth care more about pop-culture tourism than heritage tourism or nature tourism. They may visit Tokyo University or small infamous shrine or *Koshien* (a baseball game) that relate to animations or comics, instead of visiting any traditional tourist attractions. According the behavior of the five Chinese participants, we picked up the typical three of them to analyze.

- The tourist who has never been to Enoshima

The first participant, she had never been to Japan but still chose the free tour. She did not do any preparation in advance and only accounted on the recordings that were created by me. She got off at the Kamakurakokomae Station where is the spot of Ryonan High School Station in *Slam Dunk*. Nonetheless the appearance of the real station was exactly reproduced in the animation, however, she did not recognize the scene in the real world until she found the comic pictures updated by us was right in there. When she suddenly realized what in front of her is the scene that she has watched numerous times in the animation, the tone of her comments are with amazement as dream come true. 'I could not believe I am at the crossing!' 'That is the legendary Ryonan high school!' She was so happy to be enlightened with the comparisons of comic picture and the real scene. After she checked all the previous location recording there, she chose to take pictures of the station, the railway crossing and Kamakura high school that the three most presented scenes on Weibo (Fig. 3). In early 2000s, Internet assisted spreading digital production and sharing contents to the mass [8, 9]. Here the media plays a prominent role in leading pilgrims. Especially with the prosperous development of social media, personal contributed information possesses vital referencing value. The previous recording left by us recalled her some scenes of *Slam Dunk*. In addition, information on Weibo also has a significant impact on Chinese tourists' behaviors of Seichi Junrei marking.

- The tourist who has been Enoshima many times

The Second recorder is a big fan of many animations and comics. This was not her first time visiting the locations of *Slam Dunk*; nevertheless, she still wanted to take pictures on the railway crossing which always appeared in opening theme song (Fig. 4). She commented with strong emotion, 'Not every Enoden met Hanamichi Sakuragi (the main character of *Slam Dunk*) is the green train', shows her high request of details in Seichi Junrei. Different with those who were first time there, because she had been many times there, she did not focus on finding out the exact location but devoting to maximize reforming the scenes in reality. The differences of her pictures and comments from others' also verify her special request that she wants her path to be separated from

Fig. 3. The first recording

'normal' recordings. However, as she had been there many times, she lost the fresh feeling and did not record all the scenes marked by prior participants. Because of the imprecise navigation results to incorrect location mark, and the repetition of re-entering user name and path name, both affect the entire experience of Seichi Junrei and reduce her impetus to record. She only recorded typical two scenes that had deep impressed her and less motivated to record more. As a chance went to Enoshima again, she is absolutely not just satisfied with *Slam Dunk* tourism. Some landmarks reminded her of the other two animations that also took Enoshima as a background. Thus she began to enjoy another Seichi Junrei and continued to make notes in the system after she finished all her recording about *Slam Dunk*. To a certain extent, she was also a pioneering pilgrim [6] and became the reference to the last participant.

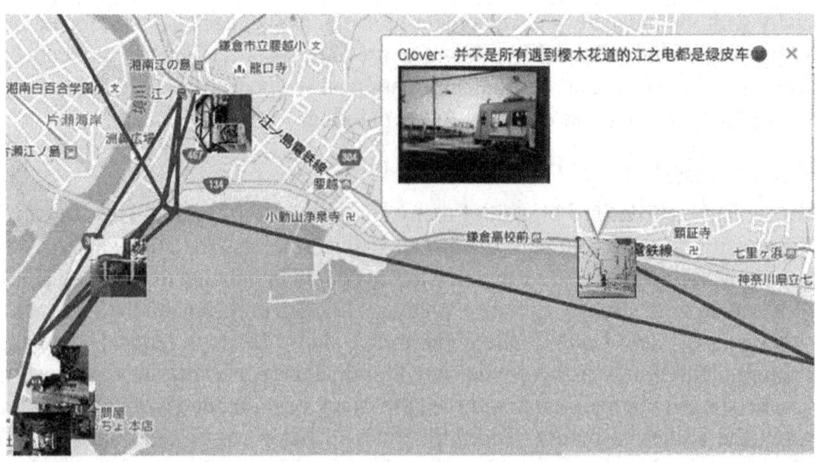

Fig. 4. The second recording

- The tourist who likes Seichi Junrei

The fifth participant has rich experience of Seichi Junrei and has been following several blogs which updating notes and commendations of holy land trip regularly. He is familiar with getting information solely from blogs thus we spent a long time to explain the functions of Whispath, the study cost and switch cost is for experienced pilgrims are significant. What he marked for *Slam Dunk* is as same as the first participant did. He commented of the gate is 'I really want to see the school's basketball stadium, whether it is the same as that in the comic.' But Kamakura high school prohibits entry of travellers, thus we can see that even though his comment is under the picture of the school's gate, it is actually related to the gym, and none of other participants ever mentioned that. Without other referencing contents of *Slam Dunk* for him to explore, he found the third participant's sharing of *Taritari* and *Tsuritama*, and decided to follow her. He also experienced imprecise navigation issue, resulting in incorrect locating information of his marks (Fig. 5). It is clearly to see that his photos are deviated from the third participant's marks nevertheless they recorded at the same location.

Fig. 5. The fifth recording

To the tourist who has never been to Enoshima, she could find out the scenes by utilizing the supporting system. It combined the image with the location information rather than a mere description of the location. Media and film provide a wealth of real or imagined meaning to signify the attraction of a place where is made to be more attractive, through constructing or reinforcing particular images of those places, and acting as 'markers' [10, 11]. From the details of Table 1, one can easily identifies the railway crossing and Kamakura high school are the only two locations that have been taken photos or recorded texts by all participants. They considered these two places as main elements of the animation that appeared too many times in the animation. The first participant told that she could recall plenty of scenarios while seeing the typical two places. Thus these two places are the most emotional for people-place bonding. The other explanation attributes to the influence of media. Contents tourism is of particular use in an age of 'multi-use' or the 'media mix' [9]. Yamamura summarized three periods. The first is in the 1990s, when multi-use started to grow among comics, animations and games; second is in early 2000s when internet assisted spreading digital production and sharing contents to the mass [8]. These two locations are the most commented, reviewed and forwarded *Slam Dunk* topics on Chinese media. The supporting system provided both comic scenes and real photos as a consultation. As the combination of virtual world and real world, the participant could recognize the scenes easily.

Table 1. Location details

Location / Testing Subject	Fujisawa Station	Kamakurakokomae Station	Railway Crossing	Shonan Beach	Sloping Road	Kamakura High School	Others	Others	Others	Others
1		●	●			●				
2	●		●			●	Enoshima Station (Tsuritama)	Enoshima Landmark (Tsuritama)	The Gate of Enoshima Shrin (Tsuritama)	Downhill Path (Taritari)
3			●			●				
4		●	●	●	●	●	Enoshima Station	Uniform and Tram (In Enoden)	Students of Community Activities (At the Gate of School)	Gym
5		●	●			●		Enoshima Landmark (Tsuritama)	The Gate of Enoshima Shrin (Tsuritama)	Lighthouse (Tsuritama)

- The problems occurred in Whispath

However, it is also obviously that there are many problems in Whispath when it is used in Chinese holy land pilgrimage. The first one is that the system, especially it is in English and Japanese, confused some participants. Since we explained a lot about how to utilize it, some Chinese subject has felt upset and bother. Second, since Whispath needs to re-enter user name and path name when users want to update a photo or comment, it gives the bad influence to the experience of Chinese Seichi Junrei, and reduces the motivation of recording. Even some users miss-spelled the path name, it results the records were separated. Third, the imprecise navigation has to be fixed; otherwise the supporting system could not have effectiveness because of the incorrect location mark.

6 Conclusion

This paper introduced the Japanese pop culture's influence to young Chinese tourists, and clarify Weibo can motivate them to participate Seichi Junrei. There is substantial evidence, expanded in this paper, which the great potential of Seichi Junrei in Chinese tourism market and the deficiency of a Chinese Seichi Junrei tool. We clarified the concept of the proposed media tool. We also identify issues from the result if the experiment of Chinese holy land trip.

According to the experiment of Chinese young pilgrims by utilizing the supporting system, we analyzed their behavior and found the some effectiveness and problems of the system, which is based on Whispath. The combination of image and location information could help Chinese tourists recognize the scenes more easily and provide them many references of Seichi Junrei from other previous recorders. However, the imprecise navigation and re-typing also has great negative impact on their entire experience and recording desire.

Enlarging the experiment, there are several promising avenues for further research. We must fix the problems that influence the experience of Chinese holy land pilgrimage. And if it is possible to receive copyright authorization of certain work and sends original pictures to travellers automatically when they approaching a location, we also want to test it would help travellers to match the virtual with the actual or not. For those Chinese fans that lack of Japanese official information channel, If Japanese works related Weibo API could be used in our record system, we wonder users would be motivated to find out more actual scenes in their memories or not. In addition, in order to make system user-friendlier to Chinese, it is necessary to keep on working on the user interface. A simple user interface in Chinese is necessary. Moreover, it should make more Chinese tourists to test the system and adjust the design is ok or not.

References

1. Ir.weibo.com: Weibo Corp - Investor Relations - Press Releases. http://ir.weibo.com/phoenix.zhtml?c=253076&p=irol-newsArticle&ID=2113781
2. Hokkaido University: Emergency investigation report related to Hokkaido tourism industry (2011). 北海道観光産業に関わる緊急調査報告書, 東日本大震災に関わる調査研究プロジェクト
3. Zhou, F.: Internet and Chinese tourists visiting Hokkaido: towards a qualitative internet research on tourism studies. Res. J. Graduate Students Lett. **12**, 85–102 (2012). インターネットと北海道への中国人観光者:観光研究における質的オンライン研究の応用について
4. Utsumi, S., Ogawa, K.: Proposal of whisper media "Whispot" to relate to location. The 77 National Convention of IPSJ, 01, 317–319 (2015). 場所つながりのささやきメディア "Whispot"の提案
5. Righi, C., James, J.: User-Centered Design Stories. Elsevier/Morgan Kaufman, Amsterdam (2007)
6. Okamoto, T.: Tourism sociological study on the characteristics of the travelers in the information society. Hokkaido University (2012). 情報社会における旅行者の特徴に関する観光社会学的研究
7. Ng, B.: Hong Kong young people and cultural pilgrimage to Japan: The role of Japanese popular culture in Asian tourism. Asian tourism: growth and change, pp. 183–192 (2008)
8. Seaton, P., Yamamura, T.: Japanese popular culture and contents tourism – introduction. Japan Forum **27**(1), 1–11 (2014)
9. Yamamura, T.: Anime manga de chiiki shinko. Tokyohoreishuppan, Tokyo (2011)
10. Beeton, S.: Film-Induced Tourism. Channel View Publications, Clevedon (2005)
11. Heilman, S., MacCannell, D.: The tourist: a new theory of the leisure class. Soc. Forces **55**(4), 1104 (1977)

Culture in Smart Environments

Crossing Disciplinary Borders Through Studying Walkability

Stefania Bandini[1,2], Andrea Gorrini[1(✉)], and Katsuhiro Nishinari[2]

[1] Department of Informatics, Systems and Communication, CSAI-Complex Systems and Artificial Intelligence Research Center, University of Milano-Bicocca, Viale Sarca 336 - Edificio U14, 20126 Milano, Italy
stefania.bandini@disco.unimib.it, andrea.gorrini@unimib.it
[2] RCAST-Research Center for Advance Science and Technology, The University of Tokyo, 4-6-1 Komaba, Meguro-ku, Tokyo 153-8904, Japan
tknishi@mail.ecc.u-tokyo.ac.jp

Abstract. Computer-based simulations of pedestrian dynamics are aimed at improving the walkability of urban crowded scenarios, considering the pedestrians' comfort and safety. The validation of the developed models requires a cross-disciplinary approach, and the acquisition of empirical evidences about human behavior is mandatory. The main purpose of this work is to report two case studies which allowed to perform simulations and validate the `ELIAS38` agent-based computational model: (*i*) the naturalistic observation of pedestrian dynamics in an urban commercial-touristic walkway, focused on the impact of grouping and ageing on speed; (*ii*) the controlled experiment of pedestrian spatial behavior, focused on the impact of speed and cultural differences on personal space.

Keywords: Pedestrian · Walkability · Groups · Age · Culture · Proxemics

1 Introduction

Progressive urbanization is a global tendency and it is estimated that by 2025 the 58 % of the world population will live in large urban agglomerates [17]. Many cities around the world are developing advanced and integrated solutions comprising sustainable mobility strategies to meet the citizens' needs and to increase their quality of life [25]. Facing this trend, advanced urban planning activities are shifting toward a focus on *walkability*, namely how conducive and friendly the urban environment is for walking (e.g., quality of sidewalks, route navigation, pedestrian-vehicular interaction) [1]. Moreover, the European Charter of Pedestrians' Rights[1] (1988) highlighted the need to ensure the comfort and safety of pedestrians in urban areas, including the elderlies and people with impaired mobility (i.e. *pedestrian-friendly cities*).

[1] http://goo.gl/7J8xij.

P.-L.P. Rau (Ed.): CCD 2016, LNCS 9741, pp. 491–503, 2016.
DOI: 10.1007/978-3-319-40093-8_49

The evaluation of the walkability degree of urban areas requires the involvement of many actors, skills, and disciplines, in a global scenario: the strategic and practical solutions which will emerge will be not just a mere sum of pieces of knowledge, and only cross-disciplinary attitudes in the creation of innovative approaches will increase the possibility to succeed for the future of our style of life in the cities (e.g., urban planning, traffic engineering, health science, social science, computer science).

Within this scenario, the role of advanced computer-based systems for the simulation of the dynamical behavior of pedestrians [11] is becoming a consolidated and successful field of research and application, thanks to the possibility to test the efficacy of alternative spatial layouts focusing on pedestrian dynamics and walkability assessment. The development of validated and realistic simulation systems also requires a cross-disciplinary approach, involving not only heterogeneous knowledge to be incorporated in the computational models, but also diverse methodological approaches to collect, validate and test the model itself and the related simulation results in order to support at best decision makers and planners.

The main purpose of this paper is to introduce some results of a cross-disciplinary methodological framework aimed at collecting empirical data about human locomotion and spatial behavior through naturalistic observations (*in vivo*), controlled experiments (*in vitro*) and agent-based simulations (*in silico*). This methodological framework contributes to the study of walkability through the theoretical definition and the empirical study of three main factors which drive pedestrian behavior in terms of speed profiles and stress-response to density in urban crowded scenarios: group-driven, age-driven and cultural-driven pedestrian behavior.

Section 2 briefly introduces such factors as distinctive of the proposed approach, while the proposed methodology is presented in Sect. 3, with reference to the design and execution of naturalistic observations and controlled experiments, providing data to feed the agent-based simulation system `ELIAS38` [2]. Case studies are presented in Sect. 4, focusing on the empirical investigation of the impact of grouping, ageing and cross-cultural differences on pedestrian locomotion and spatial behavior. Final remarks about results and their employment for assessing the quality of simulation results (heterogenous group and age-driven speed profiles), as well as ongoing works about the assessment of walkability in urban critical scenarios are presented in Sect. 5.

2 Modeling Group, Age and Cultural-Driven Pedestrian Behavior

The development of computer-based models and systems to simulate the dynamical behavior of crowds and pedestrians is challenged in facing three main factors characterizing the reality of the collective walking: groups, age and culture. Speed profiles and stress-response to density in urban crowded scenarios highly depend on these factors, contributing to the definition of assessment issues for walkability.

- **Group-driven pedestrian behavior**: recent empirical contributions [13,22] clearly showed that pedestrian flows in urban crowded scenarios are characterized by the preponderant presence of groups, with the prevalence of *dyads* in the related granulometric distribution. This phenomenon is largely determined by the motivation by which people are gathered or move through a certain environment, and/or by the type of event they are participating to [6]. For example, train stations are mainly characterized by the presence of fast moving single commuters, while other collective venues are more often characterized by the presence of informal and/or structured groups of visitors, generally moving slower than the former type of pedestrian. Analyses of pedestrian dynamics not considering the impact of groups have a reduced accuracy, since grouping was found to negatively impact flow rate, speed and evacuation time [30]. This is due to the difficulty of group members in coordinating their movement depending on (*i*) the environmental level of density [7,21], (*ii*) the need to maintain spatial cohesion to communicate while walking (i.e. *proxemic behavior*) [15] and (*iii*) the urgency to evacuate together in case of emergency (i.e. *affiliative behavior*) [20].
- **Age-driven pedestrian behavior**: the notion of *Age-friendly Cities*, introduced by the World Health Organization [24], offers a framework for the development of urban contexts encouraging inclusion and active ageing of the citizens. It contains guidelines and policies for assess and increase the accessibility of urban facilities and services for the elderly. Moreover, the mobility of aged people is a key factor for maintaining an active and productive status, in spite of the progressive decline of cognitive and locomotion skills linked to ageing [27]. Compared to adult pedestrians, elderlies are characterized by lower speed and larger interpersonal distances while walking. This is strongly conditioned by the progressive decline in the operation of (*i*) perceptive sensors (e.g. limited perception of light and colors) and (*ii*) locomotor-cognitive skills (e.g., reduced range of motion, loss of muscle strength and coordination, changes in posture, diminished attention and reaction time, spatial disorientation) [31]. All these bodily changes lead to a subjective perception of physical vulnerability and a sense of fragility at the psychological level [32]. This is the reason why aged people are more provident in the space, and they move more slowly keeping more space around themselves.
- **Culture-driven pedestrian behavior**: social and spatial interactions of pedestrians in urban crowded scenarios depend on several socio-psychological factors related to the variability among subjects' culture (i.e. *crowd profiling*) [6]. In particular, cross-cultural differences has an impact on human response to the physical condition of density by itself. The need of optimal reciprocal distances with other people is driven by psychological factors and social norms related to the notion of *personal space* [16]: the area immediately surrounding individuals, into which strangers cannot intrude without arousing discomfort and stress (i.e. *crowding*) [4]. In high-contact cultures (e.g., the Mediterranean, Arabic, Hispanic cultures) people exhibit closer distances compared to no-contact cultures (e.g., Northern European, Caucasian American cultures) [15]. The Japanese culture is characterized by a scarce acceptance for

spatial proximity during face to face social interaction, but an high tolerance for spatial intrusion in situation of high density in public spaces [19]. Lastly, the intensity of sensory inputs and physical contact in high density situations can be labeled either positively or negatively, depending on contexts of social interaction [26].

3 Methodological Framework

As previously mentioned, providing methodological and technological supports to decision makers through new generations of simulation systems for walkability assessment means providing realistic models and accurate data collection. The here proposed approach is based on the integration of data collection methodologies from social sciences through naturalistic observations and experiments of pedestrians' behavior (i.e. *analysis*), and the related activity of agent-based modeling and simulation of pedestrians dynamics (i.e. *synthesis*) [3].

3.1 In Vivo Observation

Unobtrusive naturalistic observations, *in vivo* (from Latin, living), allow to collect empirical data about pedestrians' behavior, considering the physical and social features of the environment in which the subjects are situated (subjects are not aware to be observed, the observer does not intrude the stage) [10]. This method is characterized by the possibility to exert a limited amount of control over the environment, but by an higher possibility to generalize results (i.e. *external validity*) [12].

Design and perform naturalistic observations in urban scenarios requires to systematically consider several practical elements (e.g., features of the scenario, duration time, staff members, equipment for data collection, authorization, ethical restrictions). In particular, the issue about the privacy of the people participating the study represents a crucial aspect, due to the difficulty to obtain their informed consent beforehand [33].

The information collected during the survey (e.g., notes, video footages) are analyzed by using quantitate techniques and statistics, focused on the occurrence and modalities of specific behavioral indicators (e.g., level of density, trajectories, speed, grouping, pedestrian profiling, habits). It is also highly recommended to cross-check results by means of two or more observers, who analyze data by using a shared taxonomy for the definition of the observed phenomenon.

3.2 In Vitro Experiment

Controlled experiments, *in vitro* (test tube), allow to systematically measure the impact of a manipulated stimulus event (i.e. *independent variable*) on pedestrians' behavior (e.g., crowding stress reaction to density, speed, spatial behavior) [10]. Contrary to naturalistic observations, experiments are performed in laboratory settings in order to exert the maximum amount of control over the environment (i.e. *internal validity*). The most critical aspect is the limited possibility to extend the results achieved in an artificial setting to natural contexts, considering also that the merely presence of the experimenter has an impact on subjects' behavior in terms of performance and social interaction (i.e. *Hawthorne effect*) [10].

Experiments are aimed at verifying the validity of a priori hypotheses by means of standard and replicable procedures, typically following the protocol of clinical trials [12]: participants are randomly assigned to the treatment condition or control condition (no treatment), in order to compare results (i.e. *between subjects*). Alternatively, all participants are assigned to the treatment condition, in order to compare results among pre-test and post-test measurements (i.e. *within subjects*). Since experiments on human behavior potentially includes stressful or harmful factors related to the procedure by itself, it is required to obtain the authorization of the ethic committee of the institution that promotes the survey and the informed consent of participants [33].

3.3 In Silico Simulation

Although there are some objections about the simplified level of correspondence between computer-based simulations and complex social systems [11], this methodology, *in silico* (on the computer) allows to envision those phenomena that are difficult to be directly observed in real scenarios, testing alternative conditions and courses of action (i.e. *what-if scenarios*). The issue of defining formal computational models about pedestrian dynamics has been tackled from different perspectives:

- *Physical* approach [18] represents pedestrians as particles subject to forces (e.g., attraction and repulsive forces), in analogy with fluid dynamics;
- *Cellular Automata* approach [23] represents pedestrians as occupied states of the cells. Pedestrian interactions are based on the *floor field* method: a virtual traces that influence pedestrian transitions and movements;
- *Agent-based* approach [8] represents pedestrians as heterogeneous, autonomous and situated entities moving according to behavioral rules and specifications.

`ELIAS38` (the name is in memory of Elias Canetti [5] who studied the behavior of crowd for thirty-eight years) is an agent-based simulation systems whose core computational model allows the explicit representation of groups of agents, interacting through proxemics rules [2,3]. Agents are characterized by (*i*) perceptive and behavioral specifications (e.g., perceive and avoid obstacles, follow paths, perceive other agents) and the (*ii*) capability to communicate in order to achieve some individual or shared goals (e.g., every group is driven by the tendency to maintain spatial cohesion during locomotion). Data coming from the quantitative analysis of *in vivo* and *in vitro* studies allow the calibration and the validation of the simulation tool, in order to apply analytical tools (e.g., Fruin's Walkway Level of Service Criteria (LOS) metrics [9]) on what-if sessions at different conditions. Within this computational framework, it is possible to perform walkability assessments in terms of the above-mentioned speed profiles and stress-response to density in presence of groups, heterogeneous ages and cultural proxemics specifications.

4 Case Studies

This Section presents two empirical studies based on (*i*) the observation of small size group behavior (i.e. *dyads*) walking in situation of irregular density, considering also the impact of age, (*ii*) the experimental investigation of personal space in dynamics setting.

4.1 Observation of Pedestrian Circulation Dynamics

The survey was performed on November 24th 2012, and it consisted of the unobtrusive video-recorded observation of pedestrian circulation dynamics at the Vittorio Emanuele II gallery (Milan, Italy). The gallery is a popular touristic-commercial walkway, exclusively intended for pedestrians and characterized by heterogeneous pedestrian profiles (tourists, shoppers, strollers and inhabitants) and group granulometric distribution [13].

Data analysis was focused on estimating the environmental level of density and the speed of a sample of singletons and dyads composed of adult and elderly pedestrians. The detection of dyads and elderly pedestrians (approximately 70 y.o.) was supported by an *ad hoc* designed checklist, comprising a set of locomotion, communication and physical indicators. No.62 pedestrians were tracked by using the open source software *Tracker Video Analysis and Modelling Tool* (www.cabrillo.edu).

Level of Density. The average level of density was 0.22 people/squared meter. The average flow rate was 7.78 pedestrian/minute/meter. Results (see Fig. 1) were compared according to the Walkway Level of Service Criteria (LOS) [9]: a range of values that standardly describe the impact of contextual situations of density on pedestrian circulation dynamics (from LOS A-pedestrian free flow, to LOS F-extremely difficulty in walking movements). The average level of density and flow rate corresponded to LOS B, that is associated with minor conflicts under low-medium density condition.

Speed and Trajectories. The sample[2] was composed of: 15 adult singles (AS), 16 adult dyad members (AD), 15 elderly singles (ES), 16 elderly dyad members (ED). Results about speed and trajectories are presented in Fig. 2 and Table 1.

[2] 60 % single males and 40 % single females. 25 % male-male dyads, 25 % female-female dyads, 50 % mixed gender. 58 % pedestrians from South to North, 42 % from North to South. Pedestrians who stopped were not tracked, as well as mixed age dyads.

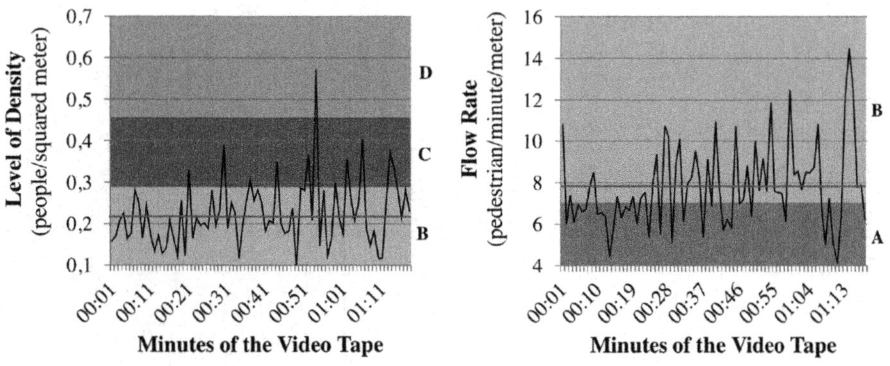

Fig. 1. Results about level of density, flow rate and LOS.

A two-factor analysis of variance[3] showed a significant main effect for the *group* factor on speed [$F(1,58) = 28.61$, $p < 0.0001$], and a significant main effect for the *age* factor on speed [$F(1,58) = 105.97$, $p < 0.0001$]. Finally, results showed that the interaction between the *group* and *age* factors on speed was significant [$F(1,58) = 13.58$, $p < 0.001$]. A series of independent-samples t-tests showed a significant difference between the speed of: AS and AD, $t(29) = 2.05$, $p < 0.0001$; AS and ES, $t(28) = 2.05$, $p < 0.0001$; AS and ED, $t(29) = 2.05$, $p < 0.0001$; AD and ES, $t(29) = 2.05$, $p < 0.001$; AD and ED $t(30) = 2.04$, $p < 0.0001$. There was not a significant difference between the walking speed of ES and ED, $t(29) = 2.05$, $p = 0.21$.

Results showed that at LOS B dyads walked 30 % slower than singles, and that elderly walked 40 % slower than adults. Further analysis showed that pedestrians' trajectories, gender and direction of movements had no significant effect on speed.

4.2 Experiment of Pedestrian Personal Space

The experiment was performed on June 8th 2013, at Research Center for Advance Science and Technology-RCAST of The University of Tokyo (Japan) [14]. It was aimed at measuring personal space in static and dynamic settings, taking into account the impact of speed and cross-cultural differences. In particular, the front zone of pedestrian personal space was assumed to be larger than the one in static settings and linearly speed-dependent. This is due to the need of an additional margin projected towards the direction of movement to anticipate the spatial intrusion of oncoming pedestrians.

The sample was composed of No.20 male subjects (from 18 to 25 y.o., with sufficient visual capacity, 17 Japanese, 2 Vietnamese and 1 Chinese). The subject's *state of movement* and *speed* were defined as independent variables. The size of personal space was deduced from the effects of discomfort caused by

[3] All statistics hereby presented were conducted at the $p < .01$ level.

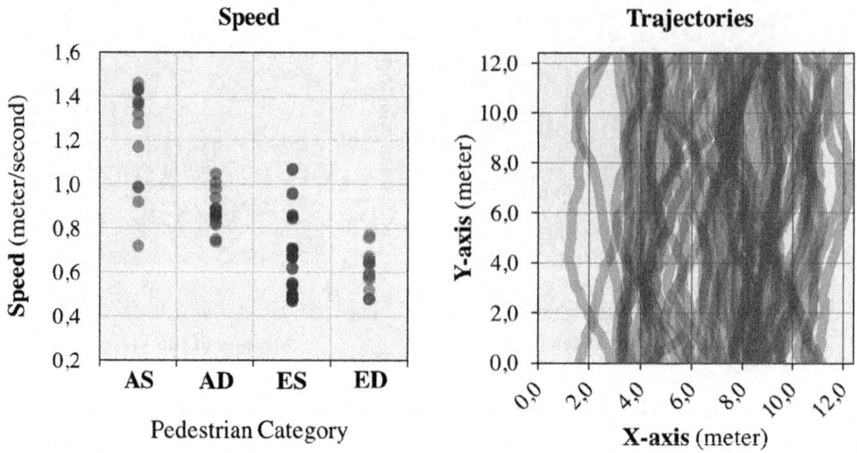

Fig. 2. Results about speed and trajectories.

Table 1. Results about speed and trajectories.

	Adult singles	Adult dyads	Elderly singles	Elderly dyads
Speed	1.25 m/s ± 0.23	0.88 m/s ± 0.08	0.68 m/s ± 0.19	0.61 m/s ± 0.09
Trajectories	13.01 m ± 0.56	12.86 m ± 0.49	12.80 m ± 0.34	12.84 m ± 0.34

spatial invasion. The experiments comprised three procedures performed within subjects (see Fig. 3):

(A) Stop-distance procedure (static setting): participant had to stop the approach of the confederate (who walked straight from a distance of 5 m), when he felt uncomfortable about spatial nearness; the distance between them was measured as the size of the front zone of participant's personal space;

(B) Approach-distance procedure (dynamic setting): participant walked towards the stationary confederate and stopped the approach when he felt uncomfortable;

(C) Locomotion-distance procedure (dynamic setting): participants walked towards the oncoming confederate and stopped the approach when he felt uncomfortable (the confederate had to stop immediately after).

Each procedure was repeated three times according to the modalities of the variable *speed* (low, medium, high speed). Participants were asked to walk following foot markers drawn on the floor, and to synchronize their gait to digital-metronome background sounds: low speed (70 bpm, 0.93 m/s), medium speed (90 bpm, 1.23 m/s), high speed (110 bpm, 1.46 m/s). Results are presented in Fig. 4 and Table 2.

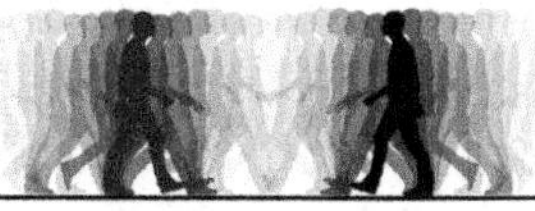

Fig. 3. The experimental procedures (participant is highlighted with red color). (Color figure online)

Table 2. Results about personal space among the different procedures.

Speed	0.93 m/s	1.23 m/s	1.46 m/s
(A) Stop-distance	72.15 cm ± 25.71	94.40 cm ± 22.12	96.00 cm ± 29.16
(B) Approach-distance	70.10 cm ± 22.96	71.70 cm ± 20.29	68.45 cm ± 23.09
(C) Locomotion-distance	71.45 cm ± 21.78	68.90 cm ± 24.02	91.10 cm ± 30.30
A/B/C Procedures	71.23 cm ± 23.16	78.33 cm ± 24.25	85.18 cm ± 30.01

Stop-Distance. A one-factor analysis of variance showed a significant effect for the *speed* factor on subjects' personal space when approached by the confederate [$F(1,57) = 5.32$, $p < 0.01$]. A series of two-tails paired-samples t-tests showed a significant difference between the size of personal space at low and medium speed approach, $t(19) = 2.86$, $p < 0.01$; low and high speed approach, $t(19) = 2.86$, $p < 0.001$. There was not a significant difference comparing medium and high speed approach, $t(19) = 2.86$, $p = 0.79$. In conclusion, results showed that the size of the front zone of subjects' personal space in static settings is affected by walking speed of the approaching confederate.

Approach-Distance. A one-factor analysis of variance showed no significant effect for the *speed* factor on subjects' personal space when approaching the static confederate [$F(1,57) = 4.99$, $p = 0.89$]. A series of two-tails paired-samples t-tests showed no significant difference between results and the size of personal space in static setting (stop-distance procedure at low speed). In conclusion, results showed that the size of the front zone of subjects' personal space when moving towards a stationary person is not affected by speed, and it is similar to personal space in static situations.

Locomotion-Distance. A one-factor analysis of variance showed a slight significant effect for the *speed* factor on subjects' personal space when approaching the oncoming confederate [$F(1,57) = 4.99$, $p = 0.0154$]. A series of two-tails paired-samples t-tests showed a slight significant difference between the size of personal space at low and high speed reciprocal approach, $t(19) = 2.86$, $p = 0.011$; medium and high speed approach, $t(19) = 2.86$, $p < 0.01$. There was not a significant difference comparing low and medium speed reciprocal approach, $t(19) = 2.86$, $p = 0.60$. A two-tails paired-samples t-test showed a slight significant difference between personal space in dynamic setting (high speed reciprocal

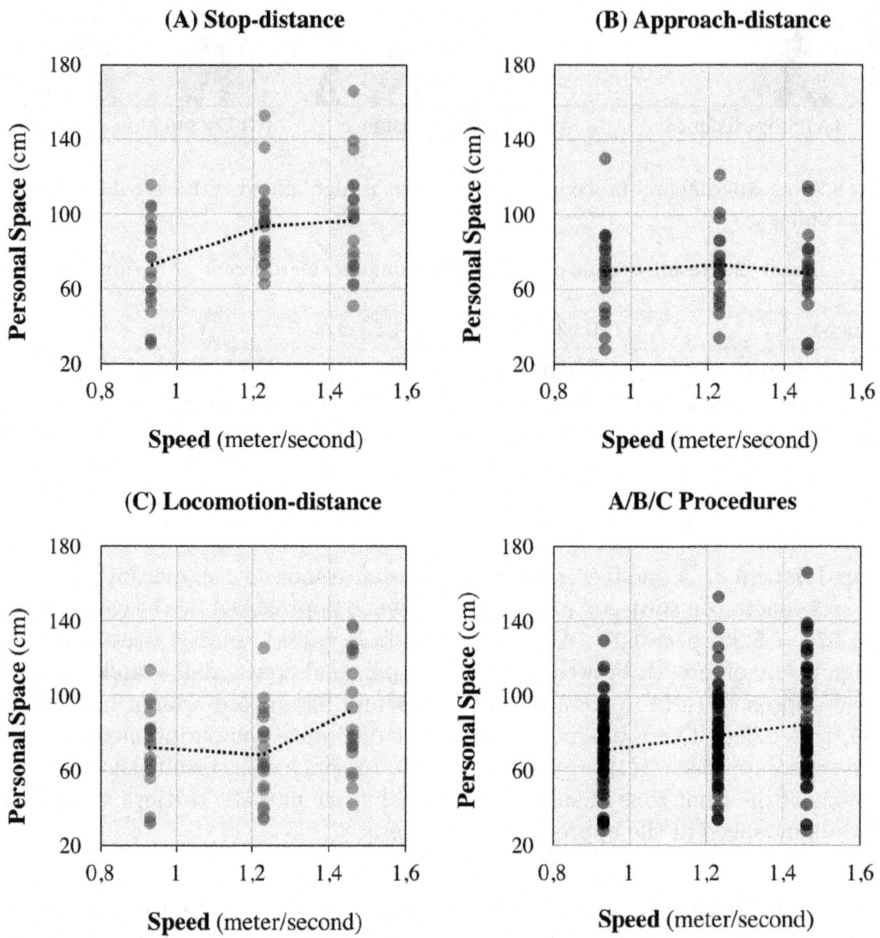

Fig. 4. Results about personal space among the different procedures.

approach) and personal space in static setting (stop-distance procedure at low speed), $t(19) = 2.86$, $p < 0.05$. In conclusion, results showed that the size of the front zone of subjects' personal space when approaching the oncoming confederate is affected by speed and that it is larger than the one in static settings.

Comparing the Impact of Speed. A linear regression was conducted to test the effect of speed on personal space among A, B and C procedures, which was significant [$F(1,179) = 8.62$, $p < 0.01$]. Results demonstrated that the size of the front zone of personal space is linearly speed-dependent, considering both static and dynamic settings.

5 Final Remarks

The current work has proposed a cross-disciplinary methodology for studying pedestrian locomotion and spatial behavior by means of empirical investigations and pedestrian computer-based simulations to support walkability assessments. The first case study was aimed at testing the impact of grouping and ageing on pedestrian behavior in an urban crowded scenario. Results showed that in situation of irregular flows age significantly reduced the speed due to locomotion skills decrease, and that dyads walked much slower than singles due to the need to maintain spatial cohesion to communicate.

The second case study was based on the experimental investigation of pedestrian personal space, taking into account the impact of speed and cross-cultural differences. Results showed that the front zone of pedestrian personal space is larger then the one in static settings (low speed approach), and that its size is linear speed-dependent. Considering the socio-demographic characteristics of participants (almost Japanese male students), results confirmed that static personal space in Japanese culture is larger than Caucasian-American culture [16].

According to the proposed methodological approach (see Sect. 3), a simulation campaign was executed to test the efficacy of the computational model incorporated in `ELIAS38` in representing group-driven heterogenous speed profiles at irregular condition of density, comparing results with the gathered empirical data [2]. Results showed that the model is consistent with the collected empirical data, representing a promising step for the improvement of the tool. In particular, the model has been able to reproduce results similar to single pedestrians' speed, but it showed a decrease in the velocity of group members lower than the observed one. However, the achieved results must be evaluated considering the adopted model configuration: all the agents have the same desired speed (1.30 m/s). This is based on the empirically observed velocity of pedestrians traveling for business purpose in an airport terminal [28], which is different from the leisure scenario observed at the gallery.

At this stage, the software has been already employed towards the simulation of real case scenarios, supporting the design of practical solutions for managing pedestrian circulation dynamics in urban contexts (e.g., designing the spatial layout of organized queue areas and access ramps in public transport stations).

In conclusion, the presented cross-disciplinary approach could be of notable interest for those attempting to properly plan and design the spatial layout of urban environments to enhance pedestrian mobility and walkability. On-going works are aimed at: (*i*) calibrating agents' speed according to the features of different simulated scenarios, as well as age-driven desired speed [29]; (*ii*) defining a proximity-based measure of density relying on the notion of pedestrian personal space and collision avoidance dynamics; (*iii*) assessing the walkability of a critical area in the city of Milan, characterized by the massive presence of elderly inhabitants and pedestrian-car risky interactions.

Acknowledgments. The Italian law was complied with respect to the privacy of the people recorded during the *in vivo* observation. The experiment *in vitro* was performed within the authorization of The University of Tokyo and it was founded by the Japan Society for the Promotion of Science (JSPS). The authors thank Giuseppe Vizzari, Luca Crociani and Kenichiro Shimura for their valuable contributions.

References

1. Abley, S.: Walkability scoping paper. Charted Traffic Transp. Eng. **4**, 2011 (2005)
2. Bandini, S., Crociani, L., Gorrini, A., Vizzari, G.: An agent-based model of pedestrian dynamics considering groups: a real world case study. In: 2014 IEEE 17th International Conference on Intelligent Transportation Systems (ITSC), pp. 572–577. IEEE (2014)
3. Bandini, S., Gorrini, A., Vizzari, G.: Towards an integrated approach to crowd analysis and crowd synthesis: a case study and first results. Pattern Recogn. Lett. **44**, 16–29 (2014)
4. Baum, A., Paulus, P.: Crowding. In: Stokols, D., Altman, I. (eds.) Handbook of Environmental Psychology, pp. 533–570. Wiley, New York (1987)
5. Canetti, E.: Crowds and Power: Masse und Macht. Viking Press, New York (1962)
6. Challenger, W., Clegg, W., Robinson, A.: Understanding Crowd Behaviours: Guidance and Lessons Identified. UK Cabinet Office, London (2009)
7. Costa, M.: Interpersonal distances in group walking. J. Nonverbal Behav. **34**(1), 15–26 (2010)
8. Ferber, J.: Multi-agent Systems: An Introduction to Distributed Artificial Intelligence. Addison-Wesley Reading, Boston (1999)
9. Fruin, J.J.: Pedestrian Planning and Design. Metropolitan Association of Urban Designers and Environmental Planners, New York (1971)
10. Gifford, R.: Research Methods for Environmental Psychology. Wiley Blackwell & Sons, Oxford (2016)
11. Gilbert, N., Troitzsch, K.G.: Simulation for the Social Scientist. McGraw-Hill, London (2005)
12. Goodwin, C.J.: Research in Psychology: Methods and Design. Wiley, New Jersey (2009)
13. Gorrini, A., Bandini, S., Vizzari, G.: Empirical investigation on pedestrian crowd dynamics and grouping. In: Chraibi, M., Boltes, M., Schadschneider, A., Seyfried, A. (eds.) Traffic and Granular Flow'13, pp. 83–91. Springer, Switzerland (2015)
14. Gorrini, A., Shimura, K., Bandini, S., Ohtsuka, K., Nishinari, K.: Experimental investigation of pedestrian personal space: toward modeling and simulation of pedestrian crowd dynamics. J. Transp. Res. B **2421**, 57–63 (2014)
15. Hall, E.: The Hidden Dimension. Doubleday, New York (1966)
16. Hayduk, L.A.: Personal space: where we now stand? Psychol. Bull. **94**(2), 293–335 (1983)
17. Heilig, G.K.: World urbanization prospects: the 2011 revision. United Nations, Department of Economic and Social Affairs (DESA), Population Division, Population Estimates and Projections Section, New York (2012)
18. Helbing, D.: Traffic and related self-driven many-particle systems. Rev. Mod. Phys. **73**(4), 1067 (2001)
19. Iwata, O.: Crowding and behavior in japanese public spaces: some observations and speculations. Soc. Behav. Pers. Int. J. **20**(1), 57–70 (1992)
20. Mawson, A.R.: Mass panic and social attachment: the dynamics of human behavior. Ashgate Publishing Company, Burlington (2007)

21. Moussaïd, M., Perozo, N., Garnier, S., Helbing, D., Theraulaz, G.: The walking behaviour of pedestrian social groups and its impact on crowd dynamics. PloS ONE **5**(4), e10047 (2010)
22. Musso, A., Nuzzolo, A., Crisalli, U., Longo, G.: Transportation Research Procedia, vol. 5. Elsevier, Japan (2015)
23. Nishinari, K., Kirchner, A., Namazi, A., Schadschneider, A.: Extended floor field CA model for evacuation dynamics. IEICE Trans. Inf. Syst. **87**(3), 726–732 (2004)
24. World Health Organization: Global age-friendly cities: a guide. World Health Organization (2007)
25. World Health Organization, et al.: Pedestrian safety: a road safety manual for decision-makers and practitioners. World Health Organization (2013)
26. Patterson, M.L.: An arousal model of interpersonal intimacy. Psychol. Rev. **83**(3), 235–45 (1976)
27. Schaie, K.W., Willis, S.L.: Handbook of the Psychology of Aging. Academic Press, New York (2010)
28. Schultz, M., Schulz, C., Fricke, H.: Passenger dynamics at airport terminal environment. In: Rogsch, C., Klingsch, W., Schadschneider, A. (eds.) Pedestrian and Evacuation Dynamics 2008, pp. 381–396. Springer, Heidelberg (2010)
29. Shimura, K., Ohtsuka, K., Vizzari, G., Nishinari, K., Bandini, S.: Mobility analysis of the aged pedestrians by experiment and simulation. Pattern Recogn. Lett. **44**, 58–63 (2014)
30. Templeton, A., Drury, J., Philippides, A.: From mindless masses to small groups: conceptualizing collective behavior in crowd modeling. Rev. Gen. Psychol. **19**, 215–229 (2015)
31. Webb, J.D., Weber, M.J.: Influence of sensory abilities on the interpersonal distance of the elderly. Environ. Behav. **35**(5), 695–711 (2003)
32. Winogrond, I.R.: A comparison of interpersonal distancing behavior in young and elderly adults. Int. J. Aging Hum. Dev. **13**(1), 53–60 (1981)
33. World Medical Association. World medical association declaration of helsinki: ethical principles for medical research involving human subjects. Int. J. Bioeth., **15**(1), 124 (2004)

Optimized Environment Designing of Nanjing South Railway Station Based on Pedestrian Simulation

Ying Cao(✉), Qijun Duan, and Ning Zhang

School of Design Arts and Media, Nanjing University of Science and Technology, 200, Xiaolingwei Street, Nanjing 210094, Jiangsu, China
caoying6916@163.com, pylduan@aliyun.com, znn1224@126.com

Abstract. The rapid development of China urbanization and smart transportation has promoted the optimized environment design research of Chinese railway station, while earlier rapidity construction and changing commerce operation based on original railway station have posed various contradictions of function, business and culture. This paper aims at proposing optimized environment design solutions based on pedestrian simulation as exemplified Nanjing South Railway Station, which is the largest railway junction station in Asia. In this paper, simulation experiment of passenger traffic is implemented to diagnose environmental problems, which is based on passengers' behavioral patterns. Then, five kinds of optimized design solutions are proposed pointedly according to quantized conclusion of the simulation. In addition, a special 'Optimized Simulation Sample' System (a.k.a. OSS) of passenger traffic is established, for evaluating whether expected effects have been realized by using the framework of AnyLogic 7.0. In the end, the optimized environment designing is implemented based on pedestrian simulation. In this way, the existing environment problems of railway station can be identified precisely and optimized design solutions can be more effective.

Keywords: Pedestrian simulation · Environment design · Passenger behavior · Nanjing South Railway Station

1 Introduction

The rapid development of China urbanization and smart transportation has promoted the optimized environment design research of Chinese railway station. The railway station displays regional culture as a city landmark, while earlier rapidity construction and commerce operation based on original railway station have posed various contradictions, which need to be solved urgently. Most of environment design research was related to passenger sensory experience rather than behavioral data analysis, which leads to the ignorance of passengers' potential demands.

Under the circumstances, the optimized environment designing project of Nanjing South Railway Station, which is the largest railway junction station in Asia, is commissioned to our design team by Shanghai Railway Bureau of China, for solving the

P.-L.P. Rau (Ed.): CCD 2016, LNCS 9741, pp. 504–515, 2016.
DOI: 10.1007/978-3-319-40093-8_50

existing environment problems and improving passengers' experience on the waiting floor based on analysis of pedestrian simulation, which is one most effective ways to establish the scientific relationship between human behavior and environmental space of railway station.

The location of Nanjing is in the confluence of the Yangtze River and Beijing-Shanghai railway (Fig. 1). Nanjing South Railway Station connects five high-grade railway lines as the national principal railway station. And its location is on the main axis of Nanjing city (Fig. 2). The gross area of Nanjing South Railway Station is approximately 458000 m^2, the daily passengers traffic is more than a hundred thousand passengers. It has been operated in 2011.

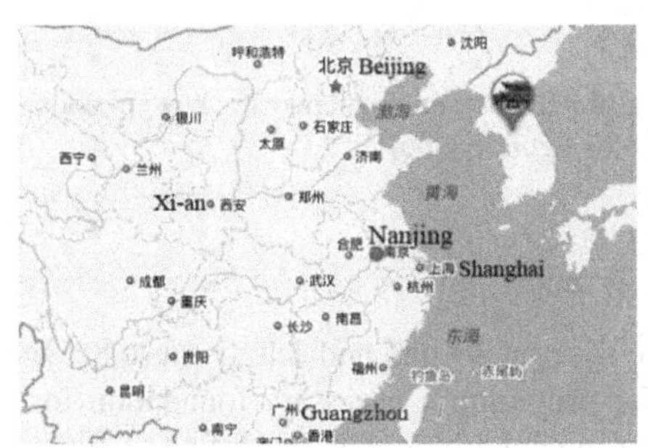

Fig. 1. Nanjing location

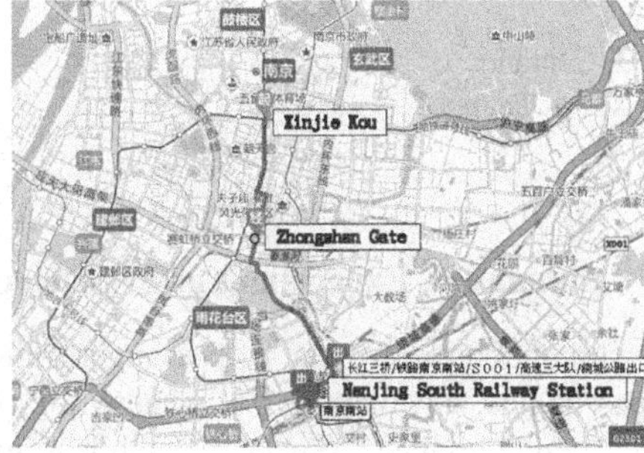

Fig. 2. Nanjing South Railway Station location

2 Diagnosis of Environmental Problems

2.1 Passengers' Behavioral Patterns in Key Periods

A database of 250 passengers' behaviors based on on-site observing and video tracking is quantified for recording their behavioral patterns and active time. The conclusion consists of three parts:

(1) Duration of stay. 10 % of passengers stay within 15 min. 32 % of passengers stay between 15 and 30 min. 44 % of passengers stay between 30 min and 1 h. 14 % of passengers stay more than 1 h (Fig. 3).
(2) Behavioral pattern. 46 % of passengers are only waiting for the trains. 24 % of passengers have a meal before getting on trains. 13 % of passengers are shopping during the waiting. 7 % of passengers consult information from the staff or service facilities. 6 % of passengers need necessary service, including travel help for disabled passengers, care services for maternal and child and emergency care of elderly passengers. 2 % of passengers store their luggage. 2 % of passengers have other behaviors (Fig. 4).
(3) Passengers' behavioral patterns in key periods. Passengers who stayed within 15 min are just waiting for the trains. Passengers who stayed between 15 and 30 min have a meal. Passengers who stayed between 30 min and 1 h have a meal

and go shopping. Passengers who stayed more than 1 h need to store luggage, station services, or querying besides above-mentioned behavior patterns (Fig. 5).

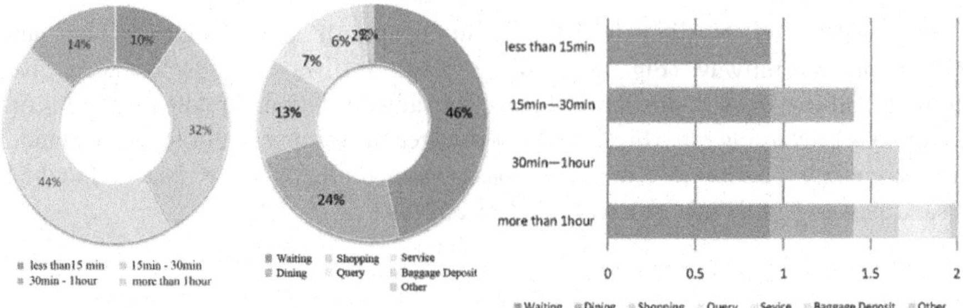

Fig. 3. Duration of stay (Color figure online)

Fig. 4. Behavioral patterns (Color figure online)

Fig. 5. Behavioral patterns in key periods (Color figure online)

2.2 Simulation Experiment of Passenger Traffic

The simulation experiment of passenger traffic is set at 30 min and 1 h, because 86 % of passengers stay within 1 h. Meanwhile, for providing a necessary foundation for experimental analysis, our team establish environmental base map according to functional zones, facilities distribution and detailed dimension of waiting floor. Then, passengers' traffic density and active chain is simulated by using the framework of AnyLogic 7.0. Analytical drawings are shown in Figs. 6 and 7.

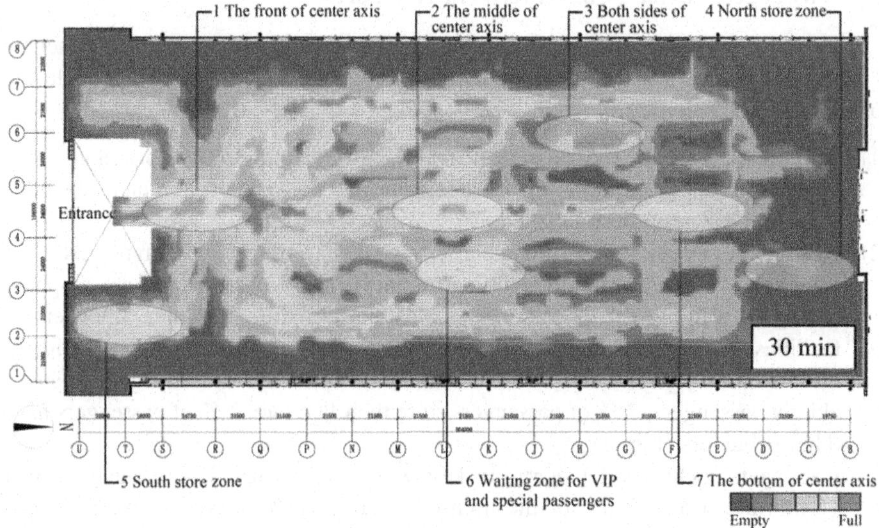

Fig. 6. Simulation of passenger traffic at 30 min (Color figure online)

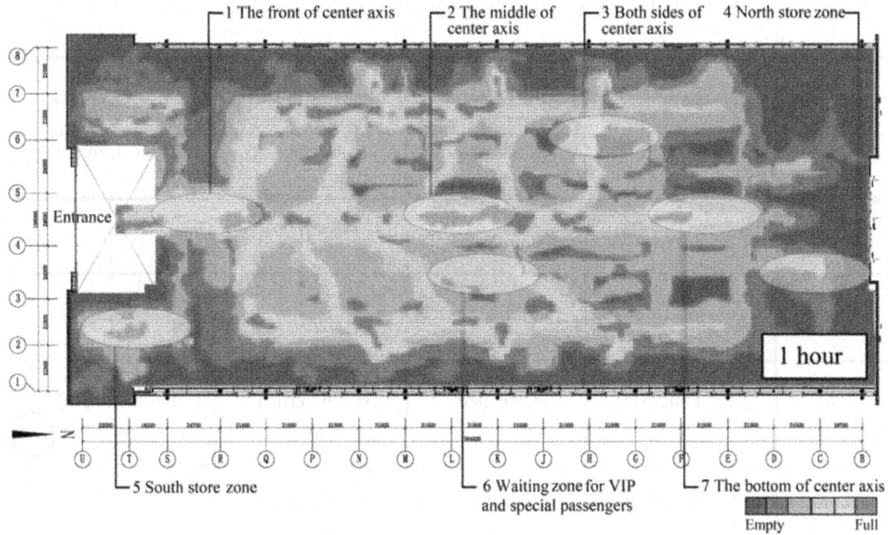

Fig. 7. Simulation of passenger traffic at 1 h (Color figure online)

The conclusions are as follows: The blue zones on the outer edge represent less passenger traffic. The green zones at the center of floor mean steady traffic. The yellow zones in the front and the middle of waiting floor indicate concentrated passenger traffic. The red zones at the center axis and waiting zone mean congested traffic.

2.3 Simulation Sample System of Passenger Traffic

For obtaining quantized conclusion of the simulation experiment, a special 'Simulation Sample System of Passenger Traffic' is established. The procedure is divided into three steps:

(1) Selecting simulation samples. To choose 7 key locations in the environmental base map as the target samples such as the front of center axis, the middle of center axis, both sides of center axis, north store zone, south store zone, waiting zone for VIP and special passengers and the bottom of center axis.
(2) Analyzing the changes of passengers' traffic density and comparing traffic density of these samples at 30 min and 1 h.
(3) Establishing simulation sample system of passenger traffic. The quantized conclusions are as follows: The traffic in the front of center axis is very congested. The traffic in the middle of center axis is crowded. Both sides of center axis have huge vertical traffic. The north store zone is lack of shopping passengers. The south store zone has appropriate density. The traffic of the waiting zone for VIP and special passengers occur the route intersection with revenue passenger. The passengers at the bottom of center axis stay for a while (shown in Table 1).

Table 1. Simulation samples of passenger traffic

Sample	Test sample 1		Test sample 2		Test sample 3		Test sample 4	
Location	The front of center axis		The middle of center axis		Both sides of center axis		North store zone	
Period	30 min	1 hour	30 min	1 hour	30 min	1 hour	30 min	1 hour
Drawing								
Condition	Very congested		Crowded		Huge vertical traffic		Less shopping traffic	
Sample	Test sample 5		Test sample 6		Test sample 7			
Location	South store zone		Waiting zone for VIP and special passengers		The bottom of center axis			
Period	30 min	1 hour	30 min	1 hour	30 min	1 hour		
Drawing								
Condition	Appropriate traffic		Route intersection		Passengers stay			

2.4 Analysis of Environmental Problems

The environmental problems on the waiting floor of Nanjing South Railway Station contain five parts according to simulation conclusion:

(1) **The location of the waiting zone for VIP and special passengers is unreasonable** (Fig. 8: Blue zones). The routes of different passengers, including revenue passengers and VIP and special passengers interfere with each other. The special passengers' route is not convenient and VIP passengers are lack of privacy.

(2) **The number of inquiry desk is not enough and its functions need to be separated.** It only has one inquiry desk in the middle of center axis to take three functions such as enquiry, service and medical aid. Its utilization rate cannot satisfy passengers' requirements due to the over long route (Fig. 8: Red zone).

(3) **Service facilities need to be improved.** The shortage of information equipments cause passengers waiting for a long time. Baggage deposit at the bottom of center axis is too far (Fig. 8: Green zones). And public facilities for children are missing.
(4) **Scattered shops are lack of unified design** (Fig. 8: Yellow zones). The business of stores is unsatisfactory except food shops, especially in north store zone because its location is far away from waiting zone.
(5) **Local culture characteristics are not obvious.** Passengers have no idea which city they stay and what is the spirit of this station.

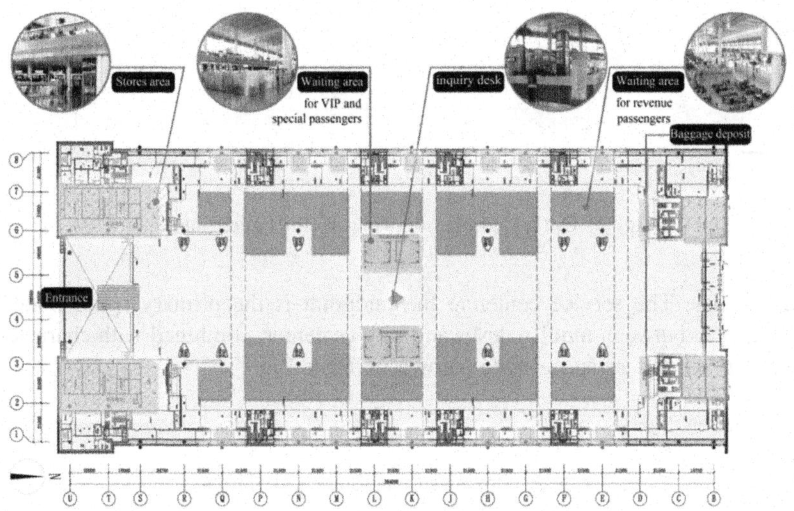

Fig. 8. Plan drawing (Color figure online)

3 Optimized Design Solutions

3.1 Separation of Different Passengers

In order to shorten distance and avoiding interference, the waiting zone for VIP and special passengers is removed to east side of entrance so that their route can be separated from revenue passengers (Fig. 9: Blue zone).And the waiting zone for revenue passengers is arranged symmetrically in both sides of center axis (Fig. 9: Gray zones).

3.2 Improvement of Center Zone

For emphasizing central axis and creating space sequence, a center zone is established along with the central axis of waiting floor, which is arranged multiple space nodes, including inquiry desk, service center, cultural display and characteristic landscape (Fig. 9: Red zones). The inquiry desks in both ends of center zone are the start and end

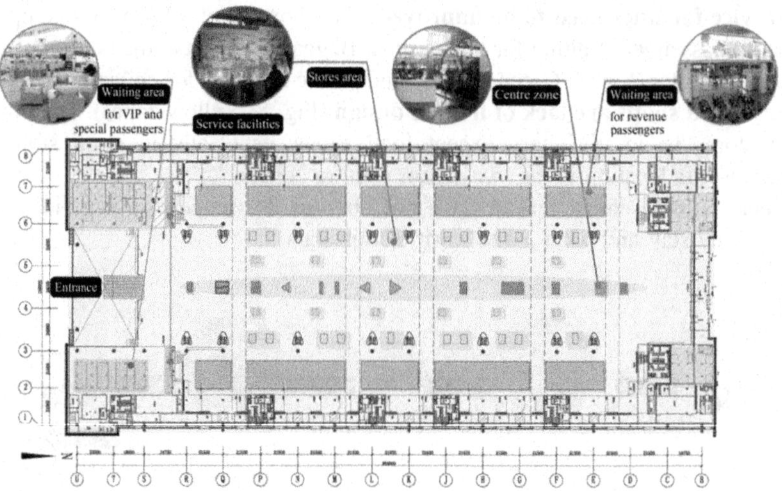

Fig. 9. Optimized plan drawing (Color figure online)

of space nodes. The service center in the midpoint is the primary space node. The cultural display between inquiry desks and service center, combined with characteristic landscape, is secondary space node (shown in Table 2).

Table 2. Optimized environment designing

Vertical section drawing of the waiting floor			
Inquiry desk	Center axis	Cultural display	Store zone
Medical aid station	Center axis	Cultural display	Store zone

3.3 Addition of Service Facilities

Two service facilities zones are established in both sides of entrance (Fig. 9: Green zones) in order to integrate these functions of baggage deposit, information query and cash withdrawal, etc. In addition, for providing medical emergency, a medical aid station is arranged in the west side of center axis. Public facilities for children and the disabled are added in public lavatory and waiting zone for special passengers.

3.4 Redesign of Store Zone

For avoiding interference of shopping route, service route and sightseeing route. Four-row store zone is unified designed in both sides of center axis to sell foods, magazines, costumes and digital products near the waiting zone for revenue passengers (Fig. 9: Yellow zones). Then, food shops are removed to the west side of the entrance so as to meet passengers' dining requirements in a shortest route. In addition, the enclosed north stores are replaced by open type stores to attract more passengers.

3.5 Promotion of Regional Culture

The regional culture is inherited and remodeled. The center axis is the emblem of main axis in Nanjing city. Many unique structure elements in traditional Chinese architecture are used such as Tianjing, Dougong and Louchuang, etc.

Study on the regional culture elements of south Jiangsu. The circle portal of inquiry wall is printed by Pixie pattern, which is the emblem of Nanjing city. The lamps in cultural booths are printed by plum pattern, which is the flower of Nanjing city. The ceramic store applies symbolic architectures of South Jiangsu to demonstrate characteristic topics.

4 Evaluation of Optimized Environment Designing

4.1 Optimized Simulation Experiment

For determining the optimized expected effects have been intuitively realized, the optimized simulation experiment of passenger traffic is also set at 30 min and 1 h by using AnyLogic 7.0. And analytical drawings are shown in Figs. 10 and 11.

Comparing optimized traffic density with present situation, the optimized conclusions of simulation experiment are as follows: The blue zones reduce in a small range, especially at the bottom of waiting floor. It means that the passenger traffic of north stores is improved. The proportion of green zones is increased significantly so as to most of passenger traffic is evenly distributed. The decreased yellow zones in the middle of waiting floor show that passengers' partition is very effective. The area of red zones has a huge decrease so that congestion situation is improved properly.

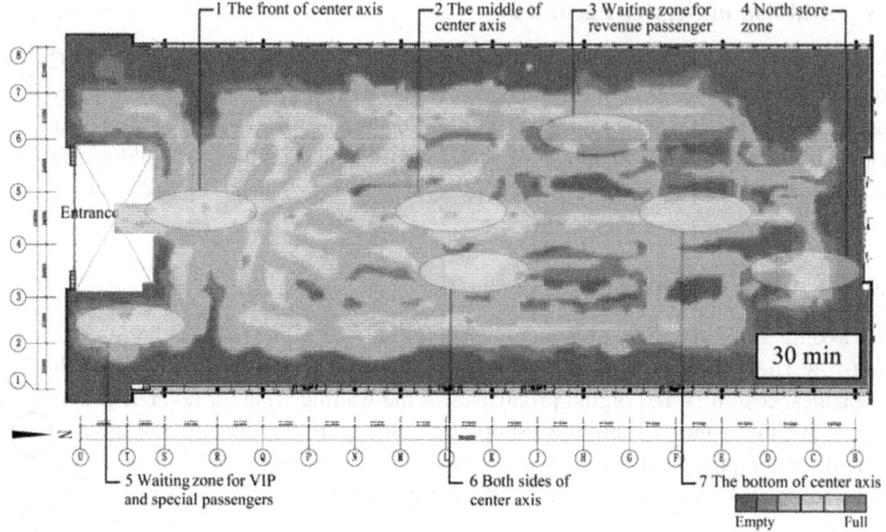

Fig. 10. Optimized simulation of passenger traffic at 30 min (Color figure online)

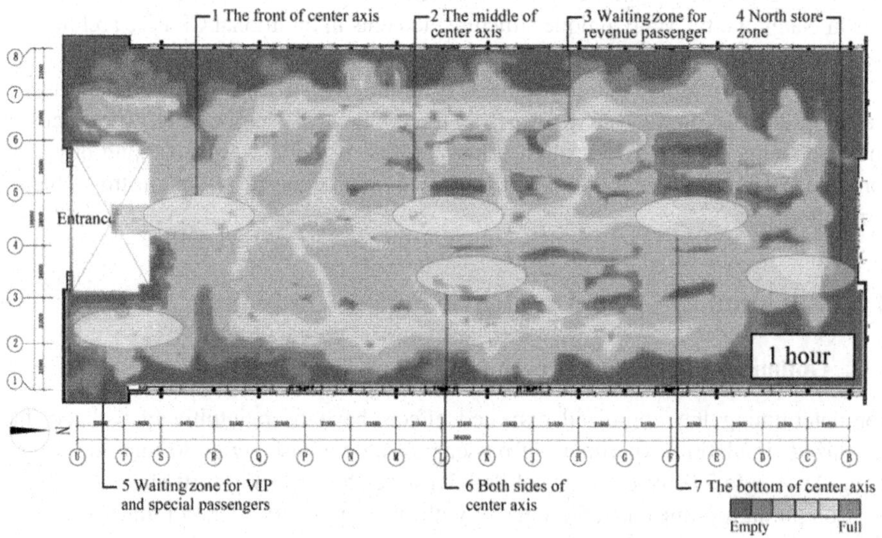

Fig. 11. Optimized simulation of passenger traffic at 1 h (Color figure online)

4.2 Optimized Simulation Sample System

For obtaining quantized conclusion of optimized simulation, a special 'Optimized Simulation Sample' system (a.k.a. OSS) of passenger traffic is established. All the target samples are the same as before. The result comes out after comparing the improvement of optimized traffic density at 30 min and 1 h: The traffic in the front of center axis is effectively separated. The congestion in the middle of center axis is improved significantly. The traffic of the waiting zone for revenue passengers is evenly distributed. The shopping traffic of north store zone is increasing. The traffic of the waiting zone for VIP and special passengers has appropriate density. Both sides of center axis have steady shopping passengers. The traffic at the bottom of center axis is evenly distributed (shown in Table 3).

Table 3. Optimized simulation samples of passenger traffic

Sample	Test sample 1		Test sample 2		Test sample 3		Test sample 4	
Location	The front of center axis		The middle of center axis		Waiting zone for revenue passengers		North store zone	
Period	30 min	1 hour	30 min	1 hour	30 min	1 hour	30 min	1 hour
Drawing	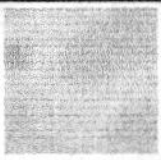							
Condition	Effectively separated		Congestion improved		Evenly distributed		Shopping traffic increasing.	
Sample	Test sample 5		Test sample 6		Test sample 7			
Location	Waiting zone for VIP and special passengers		Both sides of center axis		The bottom of center axis			
Period	30 min	1 hour	30 min	1 hour	30 min	1 hour		
Drawing								
Condition	Appropriate traffic		Steady shopping traffic		Evenly distributed			

5 Implementation of Optimized Environment Designing

Our design team confirms that the above-mentioned five design solutions are very effective to solve these contradictions of function, business and culture on the waiting floor of Nanjing South Railway Station. And expected effects have been realized based on optimized simulation outcome. Then, Shanghai Railway Bureau of China passed our optimized environment designing after three rounds of design presentation, plan modification and achievement demonstration. In the end, the optimized environment designing is implemented. Finished photos are shown in Table 4.

Table 4. Finished photos

 Inquiry desk	 Cultural display	 Waiting zone	 Store zone

Medical aid station	Cultural display	Service center	Store zone

6 Conclusion

From the perspective of environment design, this paper aims at proposing optimized design solutions based on pedestrian simulation as exemplified the waiting floor of Nanjing South Railway Station. The purpose of optimized design is to improve the facilities and functions of Nanjing South Railway Station, and to enhance the city's culture characteristics.

Depending on the thought of pedestrian simulation, the simulation experiment of passenger traffic is implemented to diagnose environmental problems, which is based on passengers' behavioral patterns. In addition, a special 'Optimized Simulation Sample' System (a.k.a. OSS) of passenger traffic is established, for evaluating whether expected effects have been realized. In the end, five kinds of optimized design solutions are proposed and implemented according to the quantized conclusion of the simulation.

In this way, pedestrian simulation can provide more effective technical supports for optimized environment design. Therefore, the existing problems can be identified precisely and the optimized design solutions can be pointedly proposed.

Acknlowledgment. This research is supported by "the Social Science Foundation of Jiangsu Province" (Grant No. 15ZHD001), and funded by "2013 Research Initiation Project of Nanjing University of Science and Technology".

References

1. Zhang, G., Chen, Y., Li, P., Fibbe, S., Brayne, C.: Study on evaluation indicators system of crowd management for transfer stations based on pedestrian simulation. Int. J. Comput. Intell. Syst. **4**(6), 1375–1382 (2011)
2. Hu, Q.Z., Deng, W.: Optimization Models and Rating Methods of Urban Public Transport. Science Press, Beijing (2009)
3. Ekmekcioğlu, M., Kutlu, A.C., Kahraman, C.: A fuzzy multi-criteria swot analysis: an application to nuclear power plant site selection. Int. J. Comput. Intell. Syst. **4**(4), 583–595 (2011)

Observations on Global Urban Millennials' Social and Civic- Interactions Mediated by New Technologies

Suruchi Dumpawar, Vicky Zeamer(✉), Anika Gupta, Blanca Abramek, and Federico Casalegno

MIT Mobile Experience Lab, Massachusetts Institute of Technology, Cambridge, MA, USA
vzeamer@mit.edu

Abstract. Researchers and city visionaries have focused a lot of attention on the "smart" city of the future. In this paper, we propose a qualitative research methodology that grounds the proposed future city in the actual experiences and expectations of these cities' most rapidly-growing population group: Millennials, or those currently between the ages of 18 and 35. Based on our findings, we describe several key trends in Millennials' urban behavior, and link these trends to developments in urban infrastructure and connectedness. Finally, we use these trends as the basis for a proposed *Networked city,* a city characterized by open information, linked digital and physical infrastructure, and a focus on sociability and interaction.

Keywords: User study · Social interaction · Field study · Social network · Community · Physical environment · Civic engagement · Ethnography · Urban design · Millennials

1 Introduction

Today's cities are radically changing - creating unprecedented change in our lifestyles. These lifestyle changes, in turn, feed back into how cities evolve. The digital information era offers new opportunities for connectedness, allowing cities to become more like intelligent organisms that can make coordinated responses to changing urban conditions and needs. The cities of the future will indeed be smarter, in the sense that they will leverage the expanding potential of communications technologies to enhance urban environment. In his seminal work *City of Bits: Space, Place, and the Infobahn,* designer and technologist William J. Mitchell described this feedback process as follows:

> "[The environment of the city] matters because the emerging civic structures and spatial arrangements of the digital era will profoundly affect our access to economic opportunities and public services, the character and content of public discourse, the forms of cultural activity, the inaction of power, and the experiences that give shape and texture to our daily routines." [1].

Mitchell argued that understanding the relationship between emerging technologies and urban design is crucial, as this relationship is one that can be leveraged to build a city that supports the kind of life its citizens desire.

The promise embodied in Mitchell's work is what fueled our research. Our goal was to explore how cities grow and take on new technological and infrastructure changes in

P.-L.P. Rau (Ed.): CCD 2016, LNCS 9741, pp. 516–526, 2016.
DOI: 10.1007/978-3-319-40093-8_51

response to their citizens, and how citizens are impacting what sorts of technologies are becoming widely adopted in their own cities. Cities will especially need to address the human needs and expectations of an increasingly influential cohort of residents – the Millennials, who are the subject of this research.

Millennials are early adopters of new technology. They are also flocking to cities in increasing numbers.

Our research asked two main questions:

1. What do Millennials expect from cities?
2. What are the characteristics of a city that responds to Millennials' expectations?

In this paper, we will focus on how Millennials social and civic experiences in cities are mediated by emerging networked technologies. This focus is just a portion of a much larger lifestyle observatory project focused on Millennials and urban transformation.

2 Methodology

Our goal was to explore Millennials' experiences in cities, and we drew on a mixed, interdisciplinary variety of qualitative methods in order to approach our questions. We also chose ten global cities as the focal points for our observation. Our project area was focused on Europe and the Americas, and we deliberately included acknowledged mega-cities as well cities that are still developing. Our project cities were: Barcelona, Berlin, Boston, Detroit, Glasgow, Istanbul, Lima, New York City, Paris, and Saõ Paulo. These cities were chosen because as urban centers they continue to attract Millennials, and together they offer a multi-faceted perspective on how to adapt and respond to the needs and expectations of young residents. **The motivation behind selecting a diverse sample of cities, with particular opportunities and challenges, was to glean insights specific to the context of one city and also extract findings that cut across multiple cities.** It is also important to note that although the Millennial experience from city to city is unique, several common themes and trends emerged.

The research problem involved gaining a deep and experiential understanding of experiences in these cities. The research methodology combined immersion, visual ethnography, and extensive semi-structured interviews with Millennial residents and experts. The Millennial interviews were structured around similar themes: researchers aimed to sample a variety of opinions on key urban issues, like housing, mobility, culture, health and civic participation.

In each project city researchers interviewed ten Millennial participants, who were recruited through a combination of methods - reaching out to the professional network and social network of the MIT Mobile Experience Lab researchers, contacting Millennials with influential blogs, and snowball sampling. To substantiate findings and insights from our Millennial interviews, we spoke with thought leaders from diverse fields, including urban design and planning, architecture, civic technology, housing, and mobility. Visual ethnography then supplied pictures of the research cities, both through the eyes of participants and through the eyes of immersed researchers.

By combining varied research methods, the research team was able to produce a multi-faceted but deeply grounded picture of how Millennials interact with their urban environment, and how they would like these interactions to evolve in future.

3 Results

Our research is organized around specific trends that reflect issues of great importance to Millennials living in cities. These **findings reveal a gap between emerging behavior and the traditional opportunities for social connectivity and civic engagement offered by existing systems.** Based on our observations we propose a prototypical *Networked City* – a city where urban systems are designed to address the emerging civic and social behavior and expectations of Millenials. We further outline two critical aspects of how the *Networked City* functions: harnessing urban data and enabling social connections.

3.1 Living Digitally

Millennials live their lives digitally. This sentiment was echoed multiple times by study participants, regardless of where in the world they live. This expectation has already wrought big changes in how cities interact with citizens, and the trend shows no sign of abating. Millennials have become used to constant connectivity, and their mobile devices are deeply incorporated into how they experience the cities in which they live.

A 23-year-old student in São Paulo, Brazil speaks of her iPhone as if it were a bodily appendage, revealing how the phone's affordances shape her interactions with the city in a method that they controls:

> "Both in the gym and in the park, I have music with me. And I always use apps to monitor bodily functions. I check on myself step by step…"

A Millennial's City Life is a Never-Ending Combination of the Digital and the Physical. The expectation of digital interaction with a city does not stop at municipal authorities, or even with municipal facilities. Everything from organizing a political protest to finding a new band to meeting a romantic partner has manifested in the digital realm. Millennials around the globe expect to interact with the whole of the physical infrastructure of their cities – from accessing transit schedules and tracking the actual locations and expected arrival times of buses and metros, to knowing where the nearest bike-sharing station might be. Millennials have also been shaped by social technology that enables constant connectedness. Their communities exist both physically and digitally, and they expect cities to have online spaces where residents can share ideas and passions that reinforce their physical lives.

3.2 Emerging Online Civic Space

Social media offer spaces where Millennials create and define themselves, and by extension their social spheres and relationships. One of the most striking aspects of

Millennials' use of social media is how it enables new civic possibility in the city. Social media create a new gathering place for citizens to interact, one that many of our participants reported entering. Sociologist Ray Oldenburg has described the importance of having urban spaces where people can come together in his book *The Great Good Place (Third Places)*:

> "In order for the city and its neighborhoods to offer the rich and varied association that is their promise and potential, there must be neutral ground upon which people may gather. There must be places where individuals may come and go as they please, in which no one is required to play host, and in which we all feel at home and comfortable." [2]

These Third Spaces, Oldenburg argues, are spaces between the workplace and an intimate home, and therefore, allow for a neutrality that is not often afforded to those other locations. Third Spaces, therefore, offer a unique freedom. [2] Social media, and more broadly the Internet, have emerged as a powerful space for civic issues in part because they aren't associated with any official civic authority.

Several young people we spoke with were deeply familiar with using social media for civic organizing. Some shared their experiences with digitally enabled protest movements. In Istanbul, Millennials talked about how Facebook had been a central part of organizing the Gezi Park protest movement, a series of demonstrations across Turkey in 2013 demanding greater personal and press freedoms. A 29-year-old architecture and design researcher in Istanbul said:

> "as the public space started to become abstract, we started to live that space in social media … Those [young] people connect more on social media and it affects the way in which that part of the city changes."

Her statement suggests a feedback loop that encompasses the lived digital and lived physical experience. Rather than existing separately, these two spaces are in constant conversation with each other, and what happens in one affects the other. Sometimes, these conversations involve the local municipal authority:

> "The Kadıköy municipality makes effective use of Twitter. Some of the tweets are really humorous and young people definitely respond to that. Some times they interact with the municipality just to get a humorous response from them."

By participating in this feedback loop of conversation, the authorities in the Kadıköy neighborhood became a rich part of their residents' emotional lives, possibly even making the city a more attractive place to live.

Among Millennials in São Paulo, Facebook often entirely substitutes for functions usually provided by the community or the city, determining relationships, information and possible participation. This happens so much that the lifestyle of individuals overlaps seamlessly with available communication infrastructure in a kind of "reflection" that seems to design and put together a parallel city, a "second city." One interviewee suggested the existence of this second city:

> "The city hardly offers anything for this [cultural outreach]… [there is] only Facebook, even when I communicate and advertise my shows. This is the only way to reach people who are really interested."

Ubiquitous connectivity in the hands of Millennials is transforming the relationship between city dwellers and their governments. As Millennials exert greater influence on digital channels it shapes the ways in which they perceive the role of civic authorities in cities, and their own civic responsibilities. This collaboration between civic authorities and Millennials happens through both informal and formal systems.

The past few years have seen a shift in the way governance at the city level functions. This shift can be seen in the growing influence and impact globally of open government data, a practice in which governments release to the public government data in a machine-readable and freely accessible format. For many city governments, the goal is to engage tech-savvy individuals in collaboration with the city to find solutions to civic problems. **Through websites such as** Challenge.gov**, government agencies actively seek and reward innovative solutions to problems too complex or time consuming for them to address on their own.** Websites such as *SeeClickFix* make it easier for citizens to report non-emergency issues in their neighborhoods, encouraging active citizenship. Apps such as *Adopt-a-Hydrant* allow citizens to take temporary responsibility for city infrastructure. "Towards Data Driven Cities," a study by *La Fabrique de la Cité* that puts a spotlight on many such initiatives in American cities, highlights the role urban data and digital tools can play in collaborative approaches towards governance [3].

What we see more and more is that cities are moving from a top-down approach to governance to a more collaborative one by supporting practices and approaches that allow citizens to show more agency and leverage new technologies. According to a survey by the Pew Research Center, the Millennial age group is much more likely to be politically active through social media (57 percent use social media to participate in political activity and conversations) [4]. Organizations such as *Code for America* place young technologists and developers at the city government level to improve the ways cities function. These types of organizations have become key links between young civic hackers and city governments in the United States. Similar organizations now exist in many countries around the world.

3.3 The Changing Nature of Ownership (from Physical to Digital)

In addition to migrating social and civic interactions onto a digital landscape, the Internet and cloud computing have moved many items from the physical to the digital world and changed the ways in which Millennials understand what it means to own an item. These changes in ownership patterns have allowed Millennials to more efficiency use limited (and expensive) urban resources like space and transportation.

Compared to previous generations, **Millennials' physical items are more compact or they exist entirely digitally.** This new ownership has serious implications for housing and community spaces.

A lack of physical presence extends to other physical items that are fast becoming obsolete. No longer does the Millennial need a drawer in the kitchen to stash a horde of paper take-out menus, as they all exist within a smartphone app or on a website. Nor do Millennials typically print out documents or even photos, freeing up the space required by file cabinets or large bookshelves. Even the heaviest tomes can be kept on an iPad, Kindle, or other eReader.

As Grace Ehlers of the retail industry website *The Robin Report*, explains, "Even owning the latest album of your favorite band feels a lot less appealing when you can stream it immediately on and offline with a Spotify pro membership, without taking up any space on your hard drive [5]."

Closets, too, are shrinking as it becomes easier to buy, sell, and rent clothing and fashion accessories. **Millennials are engaging in a new type of material wealth ecosystem that favors reselling, renting, and reusing physical items.** Startups such *Rent the Runway*, *Le Tote*, and *Birchbox* are major players in changing the way consumers shop for beauty and fashion items. *Birchbox* is a beauty product subscription box service that allows customers to customize what type of products they are interested in, such as "trendy," "classic," or "adventurous." For $10 a month, *Birchbox* ships the customer a box of sample-size beauty products to try out – each specially curated for the recipient, and requiring no large upfront investment in a product. These services offer the joy of consumption, without the lingering material artifacts. *Rent the Runway* is a clothing service that allows costumers to rent high-fashion dresses for a fraction of the purchase cost simply by choosing the dress online and then having it shipped. *Rent the Runway* addresses two major issues: (1) limited space in urban closets, especially for formal items that are less frequently worn and (2) the rise of social media, which means that a picture of a dress can live online eternally in photos. *Rent the Runway* is one of several companies that aims to offer Millennials a plethora of choices, without adding to the physical items they will have to store and move. The existence of these services feeds back into city infrastructure. Millennials can change residences more readily because they own fewer things, leading to a greater tolerance for physical transience and a greater ability to travel large distances for work or pleasure.

The changing nature of physical space, both as a resource and as an obstacle, leads Millennials to view the utilization of assets in a distinct way.

3.4 Optimizing Resources with a Human Touch

Millennials do not always view sharing as a purely economic transaction. While sharing lends itself to more efficient utilization of resources, **Millennials also care about the human dimension of sharing, and appreciate the ability to connect and interact with strangers in the process of using shared systems in the city**. According to a study by the consulting firm PricewaterhouseCoopers, trust and a sense of community contribute to adoption of the sharing economy - a sentiment echoed by some of our participants. [6] Explaining his motivation for using long-distance ride sharing apps, a 24 year old artist and designer from Detroit noted, "There is definitely a community and social aspect to it [ridesharing] … Even if you are driving somewhere, I would rather be driving there with someone than being alone." A 24 year old MBA student from Paris compared the experience of using *Uber* in Paris and in Boston. He framed his decision-making process in terms of the kind of relationship he formed with *Uber* drivers:

> "… I use [Uber] in Boston and not in Paris. In Boston I'd say that they are not professional drivers. In Boston, they are students or people who want to support themselves. In Paris, it is different. In Europe there is regulation that they are trying to impose on the drivers. So, they will be professionals and you don't form the same relationship. So, it is not the same."

These comments illustrate that mobility for Millennials transcends the purely physical provision of "transit" or "transport" to include social and digital components, and is defined by access and experience rather than ownership. **Rather than creating new hard physical assets, governments should focus on optimizing and maximizing the use of existing assets.** Such an approach can turn disconnected parts of the city into accessible resources, without requiring the heavy capital investment that constructing new transit would require. Creating mobility, therefore, becomes a problem of unlocking existing potential.

Greg Lindsay, a journalist and urbanist, told our research team: "With new mobility comes the notion that there are assets everywhere that are in public and private and community sectors, and it is all really an issue of how you bring together existing assets. You can solve for networked assets." At the same time policy makers should rethink and reimagine existing systems to adapt to the emerging models of ownership. Some shared systems, such as *Uber* and *Airbnb,* have seen considerable backlash in cities. Rather than confronting or shutting down these services, governments should work to create regulatory frameworks that make sharing work well with already existing civic systems and goals. How can cities create legal, social, and economic platforms for sharing?

3.5 Curating Authentic Local Experiences

Millennials' desire for greater richness and variation in their experiences seems to trump owning things for many Millennials. The sharing economy makes owning physical assets not as attractive, from both a financial and social perspective, so Millennials instead crave a different type of "thing" to acquire. Monique Dagnaud, a Paris-based sociologist of Internet and youth culture, told us that Millennials gravitate towards new experiences and sensations. This is not just about traditional cultural events, but also includes experiences in retail, food, travel, and hospitality. **Millennials are watching the increased homogenization of spaces (through the rise of strip malls and chains), which strips urban experiences of their uniqueness and diminishes why Millennials flock to cities in the first place.** But rather than just bemoan the ubiquity of big supermarket chains, coffee shop franchises, and restaurants such as Tesco or Starbucks, **Millennials are looking for ways to fill the niche with more local, nuanced, and authentic experiences.** For instance, a Berlin Millennial describes his quest for unique experiences in the city. He says:

> "There are a lot of houses and buildings from 20 years ago, and punk people kinda took charge of these houses. The police tried to get them houses but they couldn't. To stabilize their living conditions, they have parties there on the weekends. That's where I like to go. I don't like to go the big clubs, where it's just about dancing and drinking. I like the more honest spaces."

Of course, in every generation there is discontent about monopolies, whether these monopolies are of the military, political, or economic variety. **What is different today is that Millennials have the tools to invent valid alternatives.** In their research on online networks and individual agency, Lee Rainie and Barry Wellman argue:

> "A different social order has emerged around social networks that are more diverse and less overlapping than those [of] previous [generations]. The networked operating system [that is composed of other loosely but more broadly connected individuals] gives people new ways to solve problems and meet social needs. It offers room to maneuver and more capacity to act [on one's own]." [7]

This is to say that networked connectivity, technologically and socially, has given Millennials a unique amount of power to create their own experiences. Millennials can work from anywhere, set up a website in minutes, connect to a payment system such as *PayPal* or *Venmo*, and start advertising on *Facebook* and *Twitter* in a matter of seconds. Technologically savvy and geographically mobile, Millennials are on the hunt for unique experiences and they put their skills and street-smarts to work creating or obtaining products and services that are not generic and uniform. They invent new ways not only of accessing and organizing cultural events but also spreading the word about them. Much of this conversation happens on digital platforms, where Millennials can form niche communities focused on like-mindedness. The unusual and serendipitous is always an attractor. One young person in Detroit told us,

> "I've gone to micro music festivals and concerts and the only way you find out about them is on Instagram… It's really nontraditional; I've been to book signings with kegs. That Instagram concert was in a community space next to this little bodega market in the villages and the only way you were going to know about it is if you were following that market [on social media]."

And many such experiences are for sale: a cooking class with a top Michelin-rated chef; a street tour with a Brooklyn graffiti artist; or an excursion into New York City's Central Park at dusk to try out urban foraging. An *Eventbrite* sponsored research on American Millennials suggests that Millennials value meaningful experiences over accumulating possessions, and increasingly spend more time and money in seeking out unique experiences [8]. According to the study, 69 % of Millennial participants felt that attending live events helped them feel connected to "other people, the community, and the world." [9]

In relation to urban planning and design, this means that Millennials value the experiential aspects of a city along with its functional aspects. Many of the experts with whom we spoke encourage a more experience-centric view that seems to correspond with Millennials' interest in experiencing and discovering the city. Experts have observed how the transit system in cities can transform the experience of moving around. Georges Amar, a futurist and mobility specialist, told the research team: "[in] the evolution of the buses in the last 50 years you see that the windows have become bigger and bigger," to enhance the visual experience of moving around in the city. Supporting this view, a young Parisian remarked, "I love to take the bus when I can, because I love to see the city." A few Millennials we spoke with in Paris and Istanbul expressed their preference for particular modes of navigating the city because of the ways in which it allowed them to experience the city visually and make new discoveries.

Millennials wish to discover new things and meet new people in the process of moving around in the city. Millennials are not unique in this desire, but connectedness offers new opportunities to leverage their desire to explore. Location-aware apps such as *Foursquare* have gamified the process of discovering places of interest in the city through personalized recommendations and social connections. The growing popularity of geocaching and alternative reality games, which mix the physical and digital worlds, encourage players to discover clues, locations, and trails hidden in the physical environment. These games suggest that this self-directed, digitally-guided progress through a city can be a means by which to uncover its mysteries. Substantiating this view, a young man in Detroit described his perfect commute. "I like to explore the city and not go straight to the destination," he said. "I like to find some cool spots … That would be my perfect commute, meeting people and finding new things in the midst of going somewhere."

This sort of drifting in the city is reminiscent of psychogeography, which emphasized playful movements in urban environments to discover the city.

4 A Proposal for the Networked City: Seamless Connection Between People, Places and Things

In the city of tomorrow, networked devices will be even more inexpensive and ubiquitous, and deeply incorporated into the fabric of our cities. In what we are referring to as the *Networked City*, Millennials are able to effortlessly connect with people, places, things, and experiences. Systems are well-integrated, seamless, and intuitive; paying for a parking ticket is as effortless as calling an *Uber* and requesting a city service is as seamless as ordering something on *Amazon*. These new civic services make use of the digital features that Millennials increasingly expect in their day-to-day transactions. The *Networked City* actively engineers social connections by creating spaces that make it easier to meet people who share a common interest, profession or passion. These opportunities for physical connection operate like social networks do online. In the following paragraphs we outline two key aspects of the Networked City.

4.1 Urban Data

Cities are increasingly combining and analyzing data from multiple sources to understand various city functions (like mobility and public safety), ultimately influencing the design and planning of cities. Through the installation of networked objects, cities have begun to harness and interpret the data generated by mobile devices and social networks. These data describe the urban environment, as well as the city's day-to-day operations. Some of these data have been released for public use through open data portals, allowing services, apps, and websites to access and incorporate more detailed urban information. In the *Networked City,* urban data are interlinked, open, easily accessible, and understandable. Millennials have access to not only their own data but also their city's, and can track, utilize, and gain insights from urban data like they do from their personal fitness data.

4.2 Sociable Spaces

Millennials are used to forming social ties in the digital world, and expect urban space in cities to enable similar connections. In our interviews and observations, we found that

Millennials are attracted to cities and neighborhoods with a high potential for social interaction. Because social networks are much more diffused than they were when Generation X members were in their twenties, Millennials place great value on places where they can serendipitously meet people who share their interests and values. Socializing has always been important for young people, but today the line between socializing and networking has blurred. In the economy of freelance gigs, internships, part-time jobs, micro-entrepreneurship, co-working, and working from home, with a deregulated and fluid job market, social encounters in cities have become a source of work and livelihood for many Millennials. The *Networked City* brings different people together digitally and physically, and supports the formation of bottom-up communities through deliberate design of space.

5 Conclusion

The past several years have seen an influx of new – and younger – residents into cities. These residents, known as Millennials, have been the focus of intensive research, but much of this research has focused on their individual preferences and consumption patterns. In this project, we attempted to use a multi-sited, multi-disciplinary approach to better understand how these individual preferences can be shaped into a more responsive, more connected, more communal urban environment. We linked together Millennials' love of online subscription apps, for example, and their increased transience within urban centres. We linked urban data to personal fitness data, and online Facebook groups to physical meetups.

Through detailed observation of Millennials' behavior in cities, as well as their reported preferences, we were able to isolate several key ideas that will be essential to city planners who want to design the cities of the future. These future cities, which we describe as the prototypical *Networked City,* will be characterized by open feedback loops, conversation between urban environments and residents, and expanded sociability. Civic officials will rebrand cities to focus on experience, rather than ownership, and will work with Millennials to develop technology-focused urban 'hacks' that will improve quality of life from the bottom up.

Millennials represent an enormous resource for urban governments. These residents are young, technology-focused and passionate about urban space. Their dreams encompass the best of what technology can create, and their desire to participate digitally and physically – in partnership with urban infrastructure - can transform the cities of the past into the smart, connected cities of the future.

Acknowledgements. We would like to thank our sponsors La Fabrique de la Cité, and Millennials and experts, who participated in this project. This research would not have been possible without their thoughts and insights.

References

1. Mitchell, W.J.: City of Bits: Space, Place, and the Infobahn (1996). Chapter 1
2. Oldenburg, R.: The Great Good Place (Third Places). Part I: The Character of Third Places (1989)
3. La Fabrique de la Cité: Towards data-driven cities? (2015). http://www.thecityfactory.com/fabrique-de-la-cite/data.nsf/951F68AEB0B75B1CC1257E0F003225D2/$file/etude_ud_en_9juin.pdf. Accessed 15 Aug 2015
4. Pew: Civic Engagement in the Digital Age
5. Ehlers, G.: The Robin Report: Who Will Buy? http://therobinreport.com/who-will-buy/. Accessed 5 May 2015
6. PricewaterhouseCoopers: The Sharing Economy. www.pwc.com/CISsharing. Accessed 24 July 2015
7. Rainie, L., Wellman, B.: Networked: The New Social Operating System of Networked Individualism. MIT Press, Cambridge (2012)
8. Eventbrite: Fueling the Experience Economy
9. Eventbrite

Constructing the Research Model of Beijing Neighborhood Through the Living Lab Method

Zhiyong Fu(✉) and Yaohua Bu

Tsinghua University, Beijing 100084, China
fuzhiyong@tsinghua.edu.cn, byh15@mails.tsinghua.edu.cn

Abstract. Urban regeneration has become the new direction for smart city development since the rise and expansion of mass new urban information and communication technologies (ICTs), and the living lab method is now widely used in participatory design and research to deep dig the urban lifestyle in the context of regenerating urban sustainability. In this paper, we aim to build a multi-dimensional community research model to describe the Beijing Hutong life by living lab process. There are three layers in this model, i.e. infrastructure, activity and information layer. The infrastructure layer includes the physical living environment and public facilities in Hutong; the activity layer is about how citizen live in their home and communicate with their neighbors; and the information layer describes the culture, organization and policy related to Hutong life. This model is used in a collaborative project in Dashila, Beijing. The final prototypes and deliverables include the Traffic Caution Light Device, Energy Efficiency Smart-Bill and RFID tag. The model & tools developed in this project will be used to support the further urban regeneration research.

Keywords: Living lab · Design research · Urban regeneration · Smart community · Beijing Hutong

1 Introduction

In the current smart city construction, the urban regeneration and smart community has become the new trend of technology-driven solution. The living lab and participatory design method was originally developed in Europe, and there has been much experience that could be borrowed to solve the China problems. In A collaborative class hosted by Tsinghua University, Stanford University and Cinnovate Center, a NGO incubated by Intel, we try to establish a multi-dimensional community research model, in which we combine the Living lab and participatory design methods, to demonstrate the current situation of the Hutong, to discover the design needs of community users, to deal with and to carry on the urban sustainability research and the smart community construction.

New digital technology is opening a wave of urban regeneration. The Internet of things connects the city infrastructure with other public facilities and citizens [1]. Collaborative technology is facilitating the transformation of function of the community, and digital technology can help the city decision-makers in managing the integration of city resources, public service and policy more intelligently through the use of big data

P.-L.P. Rau (Ed.): CCD 2016, LNCS 9741, pp. 527–539, 2016.
DOI: 10.1007/978-3-319-40093-8_52

technology, which also enhance the public's ability to solve problems directly and tend to shape the new "sharing economy". Sharing economy [2] is changing both what we can do together across neighborhoods and how we think about sharing our time, materials and skills. It is possible to design to boost resource management, economic well-being and social resilience by fostering sharing practices. In order to take advantage of these opportunities, we are trying to pave the way to new forms of usage and introduce novel interaction between several devices.

2 Smart City Platform and the Model of Hutong

2.1 The Directions of Smart City

"Smart City" is a slippery term applied to everything from urban design to higher education policy. But the most universal definition is the use of information technology to attack urban problems [3]. There are usually two directions [4]:

First is technology-intensive city, where sensors are everywhere and public services are provided in a very efficient manner. The International Telecommunication Union (ITU) gives its own definition and interpretation "A smart sustainable city is an innovative city that uses information and communication technologies (ICTs) and other means to improve quality of life, efficiency of urban operation and services, and competitiveness, while ensuring that it meets the needs of present and future generations with respect to economic, social and environmental aspects" [5].

Second is smart citizens, a better relationship between citizens and governments leveraged by technology. The common characteristic is embarking from the reality of the community needs, using the new techniques of digital tools, through participatory design so that the public participate in the maintenance of the new community building activities [6]. It increases both mobility and accessibility, allowing people to get access to a great amount of local information and interact with others anytime and anywhere.

2.2 Build the People Oriented Smart City

To build the smart city, we will create methodologies, frameworks, and approaches to enable the Smart Cities, a global network of smart cities and their applications that securely and collaboratively work together to improve the quality of life of their citizens, as well as greatly improve cost and energy efficiency of city operation and infrastructure [7]. To truly develop Smart Cities, a combination of multimedia, human factors, and user-centered systems methodology and design principles will have to be applied [8]. The introduction of broader participation to include such as the NGOs to improve the quality of life in old cities and to form a good environment of the platform has important significance [9].

A lot of smart city projects have been created taking advantages of the development of mobile devices [11]. Urban Mechanics New office and Boston University's research and development of the application of Street Bump—Boston is a typical case. When the driver encounters turbulence, the software will use the phone's accelerometer to detect the data which is later returned to the municipal government [10]. Nairobi [12] is one of the fastest growing metropolitan cities in Africa. Based on the survey's findings, the design team develops a mobile crowdsourcing application, called CommuniSense, to collect road quality data. The application serves as a tool for users to locate, describe, and photograph road hazards. Through "I love Beijing" [10] appliance reported to the municipal government in China, the application can also find a map of the city market. Through crowdsourcing data people can use low cost sensor to measure and create environment of crowdsourcing map; city government can use crowdsourcing data from social media sites and smart phone sensors as a supplement to the urban network.

The Baitasi is an old neighborhood near the White Dagoba Temple with low-rise residential housings and building districts that need regeneration. The Baitasi regeneration plan is part of the 2015 Beijing international design week. The project explores another urban renewal and community reconstruction through the design. Setting the context in The White Pagoda Temple region, the project is themed around "connection and symbiosis" and explores how to use culture as clues to the past relationship groups within the community integration and today's Internet and smart hardware, The Baitasi regeneration plan include physical space update, basic energy transformation, public environmental reconstruction and the overall region revitalization, while maintain the unique culture of the neighborhood.

2.3 The Model of Hutong

But the building of new form of the Hutong community also encountered some problems. First of all, although a lot of Hutongs are located in the historical and cultural protection zone, they are not in good conditions. Secondly, Hutong tourism planning and tourist routes for especially foreign visitors are not well-developed, which need to be improved. Thirdly, while Hutong path can play a significant role in urban traffic system, it is a difficult task to find a balance between modern transportation planning and the original atmosphere maintaining. Fourthly, life quality of Hutong residents has not been improved; some residents are reluctant to change the traditional way of using coal for heating [13]. Although there are continuous explorations in this area, the policy measures, regulations and other implementation of the test is lacking. Therefore, we attempt to use the method of living lab to build a multidimensional research model, to encourage residents' participation in the design and plan of their neighborhood, to meet the needs of both Hutong revitalization and the residents' life quality improvement.

3 Living Lab Method and Multidimensional Research Model

3.1 Living Lab Method

Living lab research method was originally proposed by an MIT professor William Mitchell. It considers "living lab is a research method, in the diversity and evolution of the actual living environment through perception, prototype, verify and improve all kinds of complex solution", laboratory environment brings the user to real life to verify whether the demo is valid or not.

Living lab is a kind of innovative research tool, used to improve the program to develop the innovative products and services, through the actual application of the test to enhance the applicability of products in the future market. Employment of user-driven, open innovation pattern enables users to also become innovators. In the open living laboratory, we aim to make the cycle of new product life endless and achieve continuous improvement of the new products and services research development.

Living lab researchers advocate methods that facilitate co-operation in teams with mixed expertise. These participatory methods provide a "third space" [14] for designers and users to meet in. Artifacts or representations [15] that make sense to everybody facilitate cooperative work; they further promote mutual understanding and help making implicit knowledge explicit in the process [16] (Figs. 1 and 2).

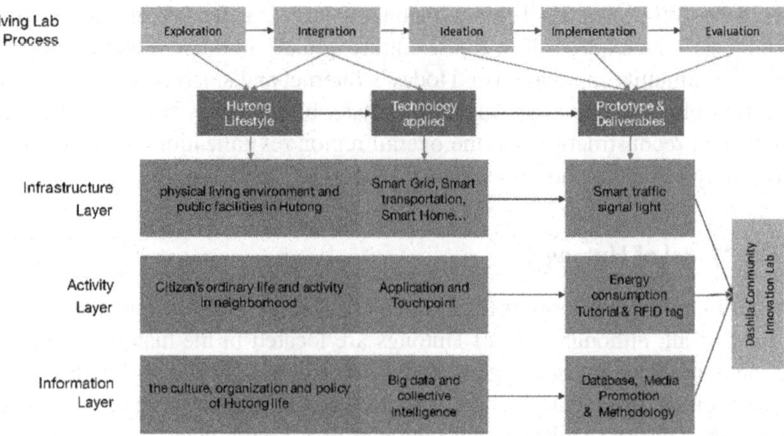

Fig. 1. Living lab research process

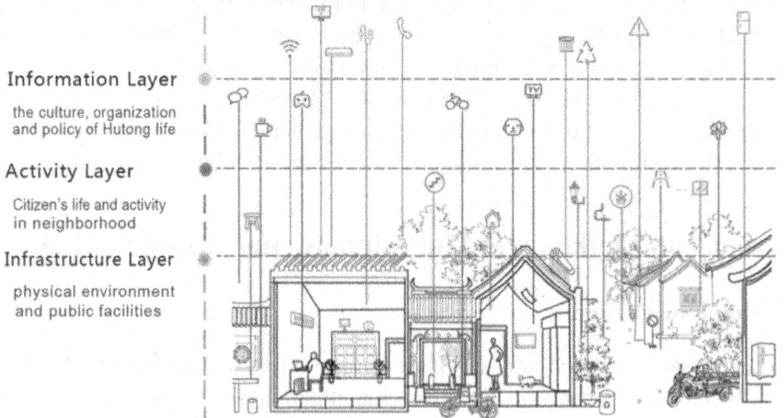

Fig. 2. Multi-dimensional community research model

3.2 Multidimensional Research Model for Hutong

Beijing Hutong is a place with rich history and culture. What we wish to do is to conduct an in-depth research based on Multidimensional research model to construct new forms of community. To focus on our research, the program is narrowed down to the TieShu byway whose environment layer, activity layer and information layer is our main attention. Through the development process of the city development model, we design the model of Hutong focused on research direction from "bottom to top ". At the same time, multi-dimensional research model is a problem-oriented model owing to the growing complexity and uncertainty of the city. To launch our design, we invite experts, research teams, user groups, and the investors to participate in the whole design process.

Environmental Layer. Hutong of the environmental layer, including the physical living environment and public facilities. In this layer we will use more research methods to study the morphology, ecological system and social environment of space. Due to the drawbacks of infrastructure, some problems such as Hutong road traffic jam is likely to occur. However, there are positive cases, such as Hutong nameplate indicating system, which is not only a part of a sense of the Hutong resident self-identity, but also helps Hutong visitors with valid travel route indication information. Hutong has its own unique environment, Beijing quadrangle is semi-closed house, the gate of the quadrangle has a high threshold, so the car can't be parked in the courtyard. In the past, the narrow roads were not an issue as most people used to travel around by walking or cycling. However, as more people switch to cars and electric bikes, it poses more transportation problems. Some of the roads are simply too narrow for cars to pass through causing jams. Whether the original shape of the Hutong is to be fully retained and how to solve the history building problem, we need to consider profoundly.

Activity Layer. In order to understand the current situation of the life of the people in the Hutong, we need to visit the family environment of the residents in the Hutong. We divided user activity layer into two parts including "citizen's ordinary life and communicate with neighborhood" and "application and touchpoint". As a traditional way of life in the community, the people living pace is slower, their entertainment and leisure style is more traditional, and the interaction between the neighborhoods is more close. For example, the residents of the Hutong at home like watching TV, some residents still maintain the habit of listening to the radio. Quiet and leisurely lifestyle in Hutong reflects the citizen are mostly senior citizens and they are not used to accepting new things. What we need to do is to understand the core Hutong community culture, respect the local resident lifestyle. So our design should also be maintained as part of the Hutong emotion.

Information Layer. The use of cultural communication, government policy and technical means facilitates the association of the physical world and the virtual world. Construction of the city's information technology development is inseparable from the wisdom of the community. The construction of intelligent community utilizes the new generation of information technology such as the Internet of things, cloud computing, mobile Internet, intelligent terminal information and automatically perceive, timely transfer and timely publish all kinds information closely related to people's life to achieve community "management, education services," organic integration, to improve community functions and to strengthen community service [17]. In information management, the government through the promulgation of policies, regulations influence on the impact of the community. For example, by the end of August 2014, all Hutong residents had started to use electric heating. So the government gave Hutong citizen special subsidies for "coal to electricity" project. Support from the government gradually helps the Hutong residents adapt to the new energy policy.

4 Living Lab Research Process

In order to carry out the problems and solutions for Hutong, we obtained skills from our Living lab participatory process. We use different design methods do Living lab research and the following mainly takes Hutong traffic problems as an example (Fig. 3).

Focus point		The user pain points	Design methods	Layers	Solution
Outside	Traffic jam in Hutong	Traffic jams often occurs	Observing	Information Layer Environment Layer	Traffic Caution Light Device
		Narrow road in the Hutong	Measuring		
		A lot of cars in Hutong	Counting		
		Road bearing capacity is small	Interview		
		Impact on pedestrian safety	Workshop		
Indoor	Hutong energy	Energy bill's information is limited	Observing	Information Layer Activity Layer	Energy efficiency Smart-Bill & Stickers
		Some of residents don't pay attention to the ennergy bill	Interview		
		Energy bills difficult to keep tidy	Observing		
		Energy saving consciousness	Workshop		

Fig. 3. Living lab research process summary

Observations. Observation [18] will also help us to understand users' context, establish common ground, and identify important terminology for better communication. From our observation, even though there are only 2 lanes in the area, the roads do not jam up often. This could be due to the fact that there are a larger percentage of people choosing to walk instead of drive.

We can observe from this map that the width of the Hutong is inconsistent. The inconsistency especially troubles new drivers as they are unfamiliar with the roads. If they were to drive into a narrow road, they might not be able to proceed. Also we noticed that there were several cars parking along the roadside permanently. Considering how narrow the roads in the Hutongs are, car parked along the Hutong will only make it narrower and inconvenient for drivers and other road users.

Interview. The Tsinghua group made several trips to Dashilar Hutong to conduct the interviews. For interviews that were conducted in the residences, they were arranged by student representatives and the community partners. With the help of our community partners, we were able to arrange interviews with residents of the Hutong and even conducted interviews in their houses. These interviews generally lasted an hour as we went in depth asking about their lifestyle in the Hutong. Other than that, we also approached store owners by buying a drink from them and pedestrians in the Hutong with a short interview. In total, we conducted interviews with about 40–50 people.

Measuring and Counting. During one of the site visit to Dashilar, the Tsinghua group decided to measure the width of the alley without the use of professional tools. Instead, we measured them using our arm span. Every member linked arms and we calculated the width of the alley according to the number arm span needed to reach from one end to another end. With that, we made a map indicating the width of the Hutong.

Workshop. We test whether our ideas are feasible with a large population of Hutong citizens from two groups: The first group are 20 young people, the other group are 20 middle-aged citizens. By introducing participatory workshop, these ambiguities are welcome: they invite participants to ponder advantages and drawbacks of each interpretation and form an opinion about what they saw. This is a way to engage them to become designers. For example, the young group of participants hold that solving the problem of traffic jam requires that there are more parking lot and increase parking capacity. The middle-aged group of participants believe that the problem is because many residents are more willing to park the car near their house. One possible solution to this would be to fine people who parked on the street at a rate that is higher than the rate of parking lots close. Thus to disincentive people from parking there.

Data Monitor. We use map navigation app with GPS navigation function. The observation was focused on the Beijing Dashilan road, based on the monitoring data of map navigation tools, we can use Hutong road congestion data for quantitative analysis and know when the rush hour of the day. But the disadvantage of this method is, nearly most of map navigation app only collect the road congestion data of width more than 7 m in Hutong. So a number of narrow lane road congestion data remain sparse.

5 Findings in Different Layers

5.1 Reasons for Prototype Generation

Transportation Problems that Arises Daily in Tieshu Byway. According to Living Lab design, we find the main cause of traffic jam turns out to be an illegal parking on the limited byway. Most of alleyways near Tieshu byway are measured from 5 m to 7 m^2. The heavy traffic jam happens if the cars come from both directions into one alley, blocked by parked cars. In this situation, car drivers are stuck on the street as long as they enter the jammed area since other drivers come into the area back to back. We need technological prototypes to help us explore how to deal with traffic jam. Therefore, we felt it necessary to come up with a solution to ease the traffic situation. This is also the problem belonging to the environment lever in Hutong.

Lack of Information on the Energy Bill. The investigation of real energy bills of the respondents validates that the current energy bills could be improved to be more user friendly. Considering that the energy users in the Hutong are the low income old Beijing citizens, the visualizing information would be readable for them. Also, since the existent bills did not contain safety tips and ways to save energy, the inclusion of those advice on the new smart bills will be the most effect way to encourage household to economize on energy.

6 Prototype and Demo Presentation

6.1 Demo: Energy Efficiency Smart-Bill and Stickers

Based on the original electricity bills which is difficult to understand, we made a visualization improvement for the Hutong residents. Firstly, there is a clip at the top right corner. It is cut into a "U" shape which can help users to carry bills. Secondly, with the content of the bill, residents can compare the recently electricity cost and the cost in former years through the bill, so that they can have the idea of when they use most visually. At the same time, the residents' electric bills would be compared with their neighbors. Residents would know if their energy use is higher than the average level or not, which could help them save energy. Thirdly, It is designed to be a label that can be pasted in the form of two-dimensional code or used FRID technology, users can scan through the phone to get more abundant information. In addition, the households can attach the stickers on their appliances, such as fridge, air conditioner, heater, and TV. Residents could paste them on the appliances so that people would know which kind of appliance costs more electricity, and which kind of appliances may be ignored. Moreover, considering stakeholders including power suppliers and advertisers, there is an advertising area on the bill to improve the feasibility of the bill design. We also encourage residents to pay the electricity bills online, by which residents could receive online electricity bills containing even more information than those papery. The form of label allows the user to see the information more clearly and obviously.

6.2 Traffic Congestion Traffic-Caution Light Device

From the interview result and our field observation, traffic congestion problem was very serious in Hutong. Congestion usually happened in the main street, when people went to work and went home. By measuring the width of streets and analyzing the shapes of Hutong, we found that traffic congestion was mainly caused by a strong need of parking area, the narrow streets, and the large vehicle flow (Fig. 4).

So we design the traffic caution light device focused on the Hutong road's width less than 7 m. When traffic congestion happens and lasts more than 5 min, the traffic caution light will turn yellow. It means there was a traffic jam but just lasted for a little while. But when the light turns red it means that the traffic jam was last more than 10 min so

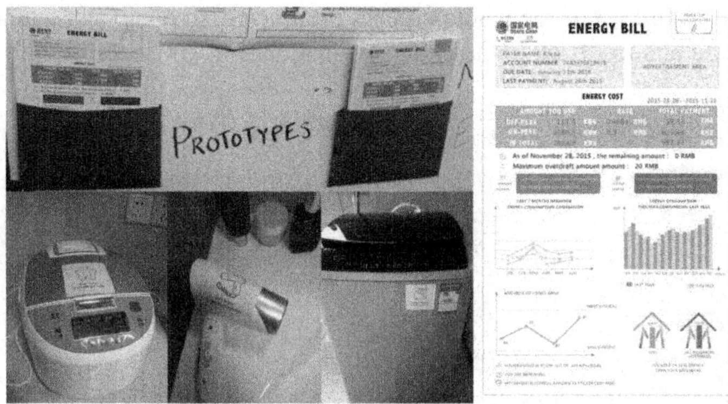

Fig. 4. Energy efficiency smart-bill and stickers demo

we do not recommend you to drive through this road. In this way, we could remind the drivers, if there's traffic congestion, drivers are advised to take a turn or stop their cars in advance. The traffic light demo was made by Arduino Electronic component and it includes a number of Infrared sensors. While it will also bring some problems. For example, we need so many Infrared sensors set every few meters on the road. Obviously, it will cost a lot of money. At the same time, the Infrared sensor to identify the accuracy of road congestion is not very high, because the temporary stop of the vehicle blocking the side of thee roads will cause the signal's error. So it is still a simple demo, we hope it can be further improved, using NFC technology to identify the running condition of the car on the road and judging the road congestion more accurately (Fig. 5).

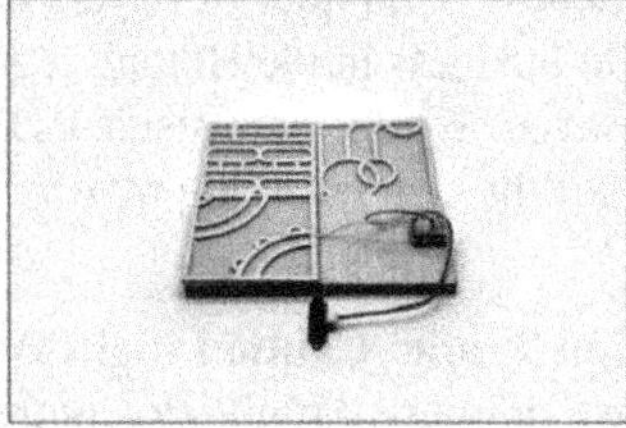

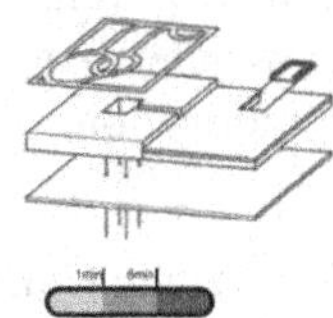

Fig. 5. Traffic light device demo

6.3 Evaluation

There are various modes of approaches to measure demo effects. Traditionally, there are two methods including using questionnaires administered after an experience, which asks the user to rate his/her feelings about what happened, and analysis of videotaped sessions with users that typically combine interpretation of think-aloud commentary with deciphering of other cues of emotion (smiling, gestures and the like) to develop an impression of user's effective reactions [19]. In the design process, we ensure that the participatory evaluation of the whole process is sufficient to open, and maintain interactive response and feedback to the public evaluation (Fig. 6).

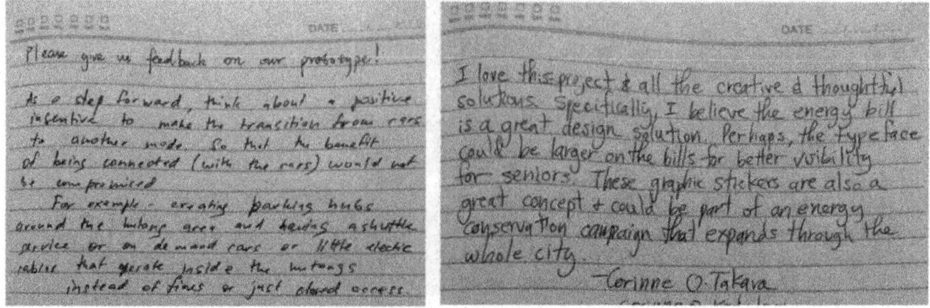

Fig. 6. Audiences' comments in the project exhibition

6.3.1 Energy Efficiency Smart-Bill and Stickers Evaluation

So we participate in design method to evaluate our design demo, we give energy efficiency Smart-Bill & stickers to 50 citizens who live in Hutong, recording user's behaviors when they receive bill's (including facial expressions and body languages). Ask users about differences between the old bill and the efficiency Smart-Bill Energy and let us be informed of whether differences are important to or offensive to users. We focus on the behaviors when they receive stickers, for instance, whether user will paste stickers immediately on household appliances, or drop it directly. We ask the users whether they like this design, whether they think it is useful and able to enhance their awareness of environmental protection, and other related issues.

According to the feedback: A number of payers do not concern with their energy bills; Some payers who do business in the Hutong regard the utilities as the fixed cost, which is inflexible to be saved. While some residents consent that current bill provides little information, so we still have areas to improve.

6.3.2 Traffic Congestion Traffic-Caution Light Device Evaluation

In user testing, because we only use Arduino to complete a demo, not in the real road in the Hutong erecting sensor monitoring road congestion. So we built a simulated Hutong crossroad experiment scene, inviting Hutong citizens (each citizens can control in the hands of the toy car, the simulation Hutong's "driver"). We set up demo at one of the intersection. We put the device to test whether the drivers were able to make the corresponding reflection including making timely feedback and congestion avoidance behavior when they saw the light. By testing 30 drivers, we watch user behaviors to prove that the analysis of the design of our program is able to play the role of traffic congestion warning indication. According to the results of the experiments, we found that 30 drivers would pass through the road directly when they saw the green light. When the light turned yellow, 15 drivers would stop and observed the road condition. While only when the light turned red, there would be more than half of the drivers to stop and look, paying attention to light meaning, and made corresponding reaction such as stopping or turning to another intersection. The experiment reflected that our designed devise confused the drivers, so the recognition was not strong.

Through prototype testing, we provide a reliable direction for future improvements based on the feedback from the user. The challenges about Caution Light Device Traffic: Some of the drivers may not be bothered with the device; The drivers cannot detour or u-turn once they are in the lanes in the Hutong. What the design can borrow ideas from are as follows: One of the reasons for traffic jam in Hutong is that the drivers do not know this road has been blocked and continue to go inside; There are a large number of the users hoping there is a traffic jam early warning function combined with existing mobile map navigation, so it can design a suitable route to avoid congestion ahead of time.

7 Discussion and Next Steps

A suitable model helps us to better perceive the problems we study, to find relevant answers. Model is the basis of our understanding. Through the model we can describe the multidimensional level of the Hutong, to help us to understand the culture of the Hutong and the real needs of the residents. We develop design tools to help users to better participate in our project, better explore and define the user requirements, more effectively get useful information and data. The project has completed the first iteration process from research to evaluation, in which we validated the first major assumption about the needs of local citizen. Next challenge is how to expand this project to the broader community [20]. Move toward the goal of converting our project into a sustainable activity to revitalize the local community.

New technologies will be the good way to collect the data, and record people's activities in the Hutong, but we need to think more about how to embed it in people's daily life in an unobtrusive manner. We will look for the opportunities to establish a sustainable mechanism and ecosystem. In the case of Hutong, we will co-build the community innovation lab with Cinnovate Center to promote community residents' participation in their own initiative, and to form the effective mechanism among the community residents, the changemakers, NGOs the neighborhood committee and local government.

8 Conclusion

Living lab as an innovation method has been widely applied in the Europe, but in China it is just at the very beginning stage. In this paper, we use it to construct new forms of the Beijing Hutong. We designed Energy Efficiency Smart-Bill and RFID tag, which is used as the guide and instruction manual to carry out the experiment. For congestion in Hutong, we do technical prototype to demonstrate a Traffic Caution Light Device, which can indicate road congestion in the Hutong and also act as one of the Hutong's geotag. These tentative prototypes supported the further researches in the infrastructure level, activity level and information levels of Hutong. The model combined with the Living lab methods assist us to demonstrate the state of the Hutong, to discover the design needs of community residents, to carry on the sustainable urban development and to construct the smart community in the future.

Acknowledgments. Many thanks to Deland Chan and Kevin Hsu at Stanford University and Lan Li at Tsinghua University co-conduct the class, and the project related students including Yinshuai Zhang, Ellena Jang, Taoran Tang, Adelbert Tan, Cindy Lin, Karen Lee, Julianne Dones, Alicia Menendez, Daphne Gan, Dongda Wang, Zhijia Chen, Yingqi Wang. We express the sincere thanks to their contributions.

References

1. Wirtz, H., Rüth, J., Serror, M., Bitsch Link, J.Á., Wehrle, K.: Opportunistic interaction in the challenged internet of things. In: CHANTS 2014: Proceedings of the 9th ACM MobiCom Workshop on Challenged Networks, pp. 7–12. ACM (2014)
2. Malmborg, L., Light, A., Fitzpatrick, G., Bellotti, V., Brereton, M.: Designing for sharing in local communities. In: CHI EA 2015: Proceedings of the 33rd Annual ACM Conference Extended Abstracts on Human Factors in Computing Systems, pp. 2357–2360. ACM (2015)
3. Johnson, D.: Smart city development in China. China Bus. Rev. (2014). http://www.chinabusinessreview.com/smart-citydevelopment-in-china/
4. Arturo M.-K., Victor M.: Building smarter cities, co-authored by (from the IC4D blog) (2015). http://www.worldbank.org/en/topic/ict/brief/smart-cities
5. The International Telecommunication Union: Sustainable Smart Cities: From Vision to Reality (2014). http://www.itu.int/en/ITU-T/Workshops-and-Seminars/Pages/2014/14-oct.aspx
6. Portmann, E.: Cities: big data smart, hackers civic, the quest and for a new Utopia. In: Portmann, E., Finger, M. (eds.) HMD Praxis der Wirtschaftsinformatik, vol. 52, pp. 470–481. Springer, Heidelberg (2015)
7. Schleicher, J.M., Vögler, M., Inzinger, C., Dustdar, S.: Towards the internet of cities: a research roadmap for next-generation smart cities. In: UCUI 2015: Proceedings of the ACM First International Workshop on Understanding the City with Urban Informatics, vol. 15, pp. 3–6. ACM, Austria (2015)
8. Amaba, B.A.: Industrial and business systems for smart cities. In: EMASC 2014: Proceedings of the 1st International Workshop on Emerging Multimedia Applications and Services for Smart Cities, pp. 21–22. ACM (2014)
9. Kusano, O., Ohno, T., Kohtake, N.: Participatory design process to solve social issues in local community: a use case. In: PDC 2014: Proceedings of the 13th Participatory Design Conference: Short Papers, Industry Cases, Workshop Descriptions, Doctoral Consortium Papers, and Keynote Abstracts, vol. 2, pp. 123–126. ACM (2014)
10. Intel (China) Co. Ltd, The United Kingdom National Science and Art Foundation, The United Nations Development Program: The core of the world's social innovation center: to re-create the wisdom of the city
11. Geser, H: Towards a Sociological Theory of the Mobile Phone (2004). http://socio.ch/mobile/t_geser1.htm
12. Santani, D., Njuguna, J., Bills, T., Bryant, A.W., Bryant, R., Ledgard, J.: CommuniSense: crowdsourcing road Hazards in Nairobi, MobileHCI 2015: Proceedings of the 17th International Conference on Human-Computer Interaction with Mobile Devices and Services, pp. 445–456. ACM (2015)
13. Lee, L., Feng, P., Tang, Y.: Investigation report on the current situation of old town in Beijing, Beijing Plan. Rev. **4** (2007)

14. Muller, M.J.: Participatory design: the third space in HCI. In: Sears, A., Jacko, J.A. (eds.) The Human-Computer Interaction Handbook, pp. 1051–1068. Lawrence Erlbaum, Mahwah (2003)
15. Wall, P., Mosher, A.: Representations of work: bringing designers and users together. In: PDC 1994, pp. 87–98 (1994)
16. Hecht, M.K., Maass, S.: Teaching participatory design. In: PDC 2008: Proceedings of the 10th Anniversary Conference on Participatory Design 2008, pp. 166–169. ACM (2008)
17. Wu, C., Zhou, B., Zhu, L.: Research on the construction of community management platform for Intelligent Community, countermeasure and suggestion (3) (2013)
18. Landgren, J., Nulden, U.: A study of emergency response work patterns of mobile phone interaction. In: CHI 2007: Proceedings of the SIGCHI Conference on Human Factors in Computing Systems, pp. 1323–1332. ACM (2007)
19. Isbister, K., Höök, K., Sharp, M., Laaksolahti, J.: The sensual evaluation instrument: developing an affective evaluation tool. In: CHI 2006: Proceedings of the SIGCHI Conference on Human Factors in Computing Systems, pp. 1163–1172. ACM (2006)
20. Kusano, K., Ohno, T., Kohtake, N.: Participatory design process to solve social issues in local community: a use case. In: PDC 2014: Proceedings of the 13th Participatory Design Conference: Short Papers, Industry Cases, Workshop Descriptions, Doctoral Consortium papers, and Keynote abstracts, vol. 2, pp. 123–126 (2014)

The Creative City: An Innovative Digital Leadership Program for City Decision Makers

Christopher G. Kirwan[1(✉)], Dan Yao[2], and Wanni Dong[2]

[1] Henley Business School, Reading RG6 6UD, UK
christopher.g.kirwan@gmail.com
[2] Tsinghua University, Beijing 100084, China
yaod14@mails.tsinghua.edu.cn, dawn0311@gmail.com

Abstract. As cities have become more advanced through the emergence of new technologies and Smart Cities solutions, there is a greater necessity to unlock the true potential of cities based not only on the technological dimensions, but on a more holistic approach incorporating strategies embodying design thinking, resource optimization, system integration and stakeholder engagement, enhanced via new technologies, fundamental to harnessing the creative potential of cities. This paper seeks to outline and define the key theoretical concepts and methodology of the Creative City Digital Leadership Program, a joint initiative between Tsinghua University's Service Design Institute, Henley Business School's Informatics Lab and Parsons Institute for Information Mapping established to provide a new digital platform for training city leaders and managers seeking alternative approaches.

Keywords: Digital leadership · Smart cities · Urban ecosystems · Resource optimization · System integration · Stakeholder engagement · Design thinking · City DNA · Urban branding · Urban interface · User experience

1 Introduction

With a rapid urbanization across the developing countries in Asia, Africa, the Middle East, and Latin America and a slower but continuing urban growth in the developed world, 2.5 billion people worldwide are poised to become urban dwellers in the next three decades. As populations swell, some of these cities will grow as great centers of wealth creation while others are likely to fail due to the lack of a clear vision and development strategy [1]. The concentration of activity in cities has led to a fierce competition to attract human capital and manage resources. In China alone, there are 300 cities designated as pilot Smart Cities competing for government support, global resources, and technology innovation. Each of these cities is seeking a unique identity and innovative strategy to attract new talent, improve quality of life and advance its position in the national and international marketplace. In order to achieve these goals, a new breed of digitally savvy city leaders and managers will be required to understand the potential of new technologies and how these can unlock the value proposition of Creative Cities.

P.-L.P. Rau (Ed.): CCD 2016, LNCS 9741, pp. 540–550, 2016.
DOI: 10.1007/978-3-319-40093-8_53

2 The Creative City

2.1 Overview

As cities are now competing more than ever for global recognition, there is a need to unlock the true potential of cities based on a more holistic approach incorporating strategies embodying design thinking, resource optimization, system integration and stakeholder engagement, enhanced via new technologies, fundamental to harnessing the creative potential of cities. This issue is indeed one of the most challenging to define, as it is a combination of hard and soft assets that make up the creative composition of cities. This paper seeks to provide a brief overview of the notion of Creative Cities and how through the process of defining the potential of each city, leaders and managers can gain insight into the ways that Creative City methodology can be applied to their city; to have an ultimate impact on the growth, quality of life and sustainability and to better understand how new technologies can achieve these goals.

2.2 The Unique Identity of Cities – Macro

Throughout the world, cities have been competing on many levels to attract trade, labor and other resources while at the same time defining their unique identities. The Creative City is based on many factors that must be incorporated to establish a unique position based on a combination of identity, positioning and resource allocation that each city offers within local and global markets. The Creative City concept is based on the principle that in order for a city to reach its full potential, these elements must be identified and optimized. These multi-facets are represented in The Cities of Opportunity 2015 Report published by PwC ranking cities based on multiple indices that provide a wide spectrum of criteria to measure the success of cities. The report analyzes the trajectory of 30 major cities, all capitals of finance, commerce, and culture through their current performance criteria and what makes these cities function better [2]. As defined in the PwC report, technology, intellectual capital and openness to the world through telecommunication access are some of the key drivers of the growth and prosperity of cities. When defining the key drivers, technology quickly bridges to innovation and creativity.

Today cities around the world are being revitalized through many different strategies. For example, the regeneration of historical districts in Shanghai, government green design policies in Berlin, and the re-branding of Florence, Italy to call attention to its exceptional cultural legacy, efforts in each case that were planned to capitalize on the unique consumer appeal of each destination. The Creative Cities concept can be used to facilitate this renewal process by developing strategies that capture the inherent characteristics of a city or region, employing various strategies to channel these assets into a comprehensive, integrated approach to reflect the city as a desirable place to live, work, play and invest and to inform city leaders how to unlock the true potential of their city. As part of this movement, many cities have finally realized the importance of soft resources and have invested in the creation and development of major business and cultural events in the form of expos, trade fairs, industry forums, film and fashion festivals, with each city looking to be differentiated in the global market by these venues.

Cities around the world like London, Beijing and New York have established major cultural events that have indeed created highly significant global recognition and economic benefits.

2.3 Innovation Districts - Geographic

According to the Brookings paper "The Rise of Innovation Districts: A New Geography of Innovation in America," new districts are emerging, where "leading-edge anchor institutions and companies cluster and connect with start-ups, business incubators and accelerators." Featured as "physically compact, transit-accessible, and technically-wired," these new urban zones as "innovative districts," are supporting mixed-use development and have been considered to be a new model for economic growth.

At a time when stagnant growth, rising social inequality and increasing environmental degradation are posing great challenges to the cities, the emergence of innovation districts can play a unique role in stimulating local economies by encouraging and facilitating co-invention and co-production across sectors and disciplines, in reducing inequality with its capacity to include more disadvantaged population in the growth, and in rehabilitating the environment through more efficient and friendly use of land [3].

Similar to industrial districts and suburban science parks, innovation districts are also manifesting as well as changing the preferences of people and industry in current technology driven activities, creating new models that connect the forging of economy, the management of place, and the building of network [3].

2.4 Building Capacity and Improved Decision-Making – Integrated Approaches to Policy and Leadership

An integrated assessment for urban sustainability and development, as Dawson and colleagues point out, is "much more than an exercise in modeling and data analysis." Rather, it must consider and connect both the hard and soft systems, focusing on the interaction between and involvement of researchers and stakeholders. The integrated approach distinguishes itself in its great emphasis on the "explicit and transparent" reflection and learning process in urban planning and management [4].

The first element of an integrated approach is to engage the end users in defining policy questions and drivers, in order to set a practical goal and scope of the assessment. In this way not only the relevance of research is justified in a policy context, but also the decision makers will be inspired to engage in the process as it progresses, which is "particularly important in an evolving policy landscape" [4]. Moreover, it is important that the integrated assessment participates in a wider "dialogue," an interaction with the urban area, i.e., no matter being carefully designed or coincidently happened, the approach can be a monitor and displayer of urban changes through its regular reviews and updates.

In addition to direct economic costs and benefits which are easier to capture, it is also vital to employ a more complex and sophisticated approach in the evaluation of long-term urban sustainability delivering, since issues such as amenity, social benefits, political costs can hardly be measured in a tangible way. Therefore, "non-monetary approaches" must be considered and developed in mainstream decision-making and methods such as multi-criteria analysis will help the decision makers understand the impacts of different choices.

3 Theory and Methodology of Creative Cities - Digital Leadership

3.1 Purpose

The Creative City concept must define an innovative approach that optimizes the unique identity and specific resources of each city. With the emergence of new Smart City models currently being applied across major cities throughout the developed and developing world, there has been an increased need to train city leaders about the complex systems and strategies related to the innovative management of cities. The Creative City Digital Leadership Program is a new initiative to fill this void by enabling city leaders to be exposed to global best practices in the planning, design, implementation and operation of a new generation of digitally based tools to optimize the functions of cities. The ultimate purpose is to improve quality of life for its citizens, stimulate economic growth while preserving and protecting the natural environment.

However, innovation is an ambiguous word that can have many meanings and applications as seen through the multifarious interpretations of the recent explosion of this term applied to companies and cities. Innovation primarily derives from the technology sector and has been a means to unlock potential at different scales from people, companies, cities and nations. In some cases, Innovation has now been equated with the potential of global economies as the primary driver of change and future growth. In the knowledge economy, innovation is what underpins the creation and management of IP linked to research and development of new technologies. In fact in some countries where manufacturing has been replaced by the knowledge economy, as in the case with the UK, innovation and the development of IP has become a critical part of the GDP and may be one of the most defining factors in economic growth and sustainability.

The Creative City concept builds on the unique drivers of each city to explore, augment and perpetuate greater soft power in cities made possible by advancements in new technologies, digital systems, media, big data and behavioral analytics including smart cities and innovative approaches to city management. The Creative City methodology explores the key factors that allow cities to stimulate and support innovative in order to unlock their creative potential. These elements can be in the form of important research, pilot projects and the establishment of applications that provide the exploratory functions to unearth potential innovation at different scales from community-based projects to large-scale citywide development.

3.2 Methodology: Macro City DNA – Defining the Unique Strengths/Assets

Each city has its own unique DNA that combines geographic location, physical layout, socio-demographic composition, cultural and physical resources, including workforce, and industry sectors. Professor Michael Porter from Harvard University focuses on how to optimize these resources to achieve competitive advantages [5, 6]. Building on

Porter's model, each city needs to understand its unique DNA to achieve its maximum potential. The CITY DNA model allows cites to develop a strategy based on the creative and cultural assets in order to identify a core DNA. From this base, a theoretical and practical methodology can be developed that proposes a combination of City Branding, Media Architecture and Cultural Programming to represent and express the unique DNA of each city (Fig. 1).

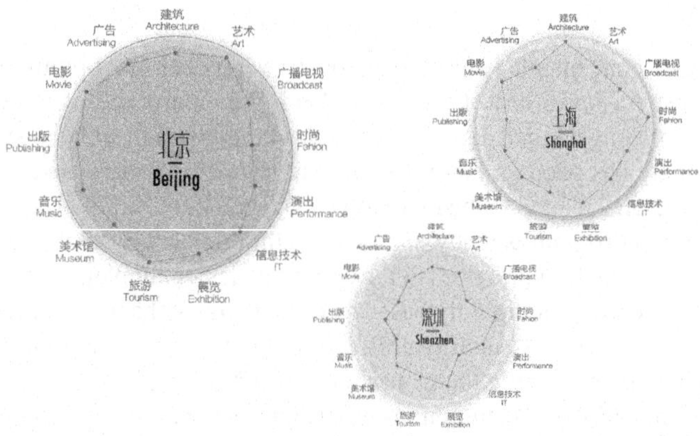

Fig. 1. Mapping the creative industries in China's leading cities

The Creative City Leadership Program builds on these elements to develop a training program to help city leaders understand how to map and visualize a strategy that connects physical and virtual urban systems from unique stakeholders' points of view based on the CITY DNA perspective. To partially illustrate this process of differentiation, a comparative study was conducted by Kirwan/Fu Information Architecture class at Tsinghua University to map the creative industries within leading cities in China with the result of better understanding the competitive strengths of these cities.

3.3 Methodology: Design Thinking - Strategies for Broader Applications

Across multiple business lines, cities are now looking at new innovative models derived from tech culture - *body storming, hackathons, start-ups incubators* - while simultaneously introducing interdisciplinary approaches and borrowing methodologies from outside fields including design where companies such as IDEO, FROG and others have brought a more holistic approach to innovation. Design thinking plays a key role in establishing an open source, iterative process that allows for ideas and collaboration to stimulate interdisciplinary solutions. This is due to the inherent nature of the design process to identify gaps and propose comprehensive solutions. Unlike many other disciplines, design is able to adapt itself to each context and to form a language inherently connected or drawn from that unique combination of factors. Therefore, design thinking requires an open-ended approach that the design process is capable of facilitating. Creative City Digital Leadership Program draws from the key strategies of Design thinking to unearth the potential concepts that can define the programming of cities (Fig. 2).

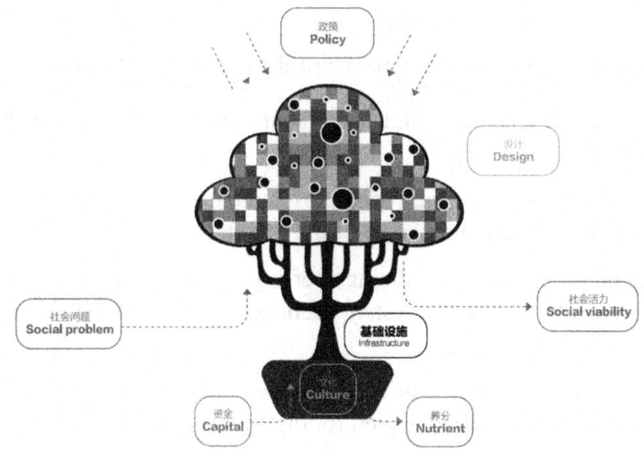

Design Thinking draws from multiple factors processed through a holistic approach

Fig. 2. Design thinking tree

3.4 Methodology: The Practice of Convergence (Interdisciplinary Approach)

The convergence of design thinking, advanced computation and business innovation is now at the core of new educational models and has led to the emergence of hybrid professional fields and careers such as *Information Architecture, User Experience, Data Visualization* and other new media related fields that have drawn from diverse areas of knowledge and are now influencing the nature of how cities are rethinking their approach [7]. The Creative City Digital Leadership Program develops a comprehensive planning methodology that draws from the key strategies across different disciplines including economics, urban planning, sustainable design, ecology, sociology and behavioral sciences, computer programming, media and interactive design. This process examines both macro and micro aspects and develops urban strategies to provide a broader conceptual understanding of how and why these applications serve to enhance the experience of cities [8].

3.5 Methodology: Collective Intelligence

The Creative City Digital Leadership Program utilizes theories and applications of *collective intelligence* to visualize and model patterns and trends of cities [9]. Data visualizations of the 'urban pulse' provide insights into urban behavior and lifestyle trends to better understand how cities work, enabling city leaders to gain valuable insights for the planning and design of their cities. A key aspect of the application of collective intelligence is to create urban-scale, multi-sector datasets to deliver comprehensive urban simulations [10]. By collecting data and visualizing information across multiple urban functions, it is possible to understand how the interdependencies of urban functions, both physical and virtual, may be optimized through the planning and design of innovative interventions to achieve the creative potential of cities.

3.6 Four Levels of the Creative City Digital Leadership Program Development

Systems: Comparative analysis of urban systems and the relationship of physical and digital/media layers.

Typologies: Codifying emerging typologies and patterns in urban systems by representing the hierarchy and components of the system.

Navigation and Interface: Visualizing user experience of the system and how users dynamically interact within the system architecture including both physical digital realms.

Interventions: Developing a comprehensive plan that identifies gaps in existing urban systems where there is a potential need for digital/smart solutions (Fig. 3).

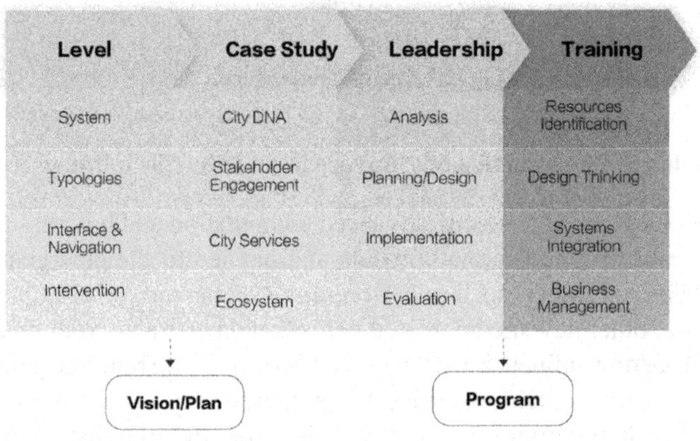

Fig. 3. Creative city Digital Leadership Program matrix

4 The Creative City Innovation Alliance

Three institutes will form one new entity representing the new Creative Cities Innovation Alliance that will serve as a collective think-tank as well as the founding contributors of the Creative Cities Digital Leadership Program:

Service Design Institute, Academy of Arts and Design, Tsinghua University. As a new integrated discipline, service design combines theory and methodologies from multiple fields bridging academia, industry and government to provide real solutions and applications to the complex problems facing the advancement of our society, environment and the global economy. In order to achieve China's vision to progress from a nation of manufacturing to knowledge industry and to become a pioneer in design and technology innovation, the Chinese government has initiated national plans based on the integration of the IT industry with traditional industries and university-industry collaborative innovation programs across China and linking to the world. Design and the fusion of culture and technology are the core impetuses for this industry reform. The role of the Service Design Institute at Tsinghua University is to develop innovation models to promote and advance the new category of service design while stimulating business innovation in China. Based on an international platform, collaborative format and shared research, the Service Design Institute focuses on the creation, education, promotion, and connection of a new Service Design framework. There are two new opportunities in China for Service Design in the context of Smart Cities: "New Lifestyle Design" and "Design for People" rethinking and redesigning the urban experience via infrastructure, mobility, healthcare, retail, recreation, and to create new opportunities for the private sector shaping the new lifestyle for today and future citizens.

Design Beijing Lab, Academy of Arts and Design, Tsinghua University. Within the Service Design Institute, Design Beijing Lab utilizes design thinking to actively develop projects for the economic, social and environmental benefit of Beijing. The lab has worked on many Smart City applications and has participated in Beijing Design Week and Beijing Smart City Expo for the past 6 years bringing new ideas related to the interface between humans, computer and cities. The lab functions as a platform for research, planning, design and experimentation for new media applications. Multi-disciplinary teams conduct analysis of urban activity in both the physical and the virtual realms and the patterns of citizen interaction, providing valuable data for the identification of key trends and opportunities for new urban lifestyle applications. As a result, cities, companies and individuals are enabled to better adapt and improve, creating solutions for the public future wellbeing and quality of life.

Henley Business School Informatics Research Center. Part of Henley Business School at the University of Reading, the Informatics Research Center (IRC) provides a center for interdisciplinary and collaborative research in Informatics. Benefiting from input of knowledge and expertise from various subject fields, including Biodiversity, Business Management, Economics, Information acquisition and assimilation, Intelligent Pervasive Spaces, Computer Science, Cognitive Science and Systems Engineering, across a number of Schools and beyond, the IRC aims to construct digital infrastructures for innovations in domains of business and management, IT for strategic management, enterprise information systems, financial modeling and prognostics, bio-computing, construction management, intelligent buildings, pervasive intelligent spaces, and IT supported collaborative work. The role of digital infrastructures construction is to boost ICT capacities for both decision-makers and the city operation systems, facilitating the implementation of creative city plans [11].

Digital Leadership Program – Henley Business School, University of Reading. While the development of digital technologies such as social media, mobility, analytics, cloud computing and the Internet of Things are creating innovation opportunities and competitive advantage for cities that embrace it, challenge is also posed to the efficient and effective operation of a much more complex urban systems, requiring a new generation of digital leaders who can critically think about the ways in which digital technologies can be utilized, to creatively manage the resources and to coordinate among the stakeholders. As a collaborative network platform set up by Henley Business School, the Digital Leadership Program aims to close the gap between supply and demand of digital leadership skills required in driving business and public sector innovations [12]. Incorporating a series of research and knowledge transfer projects, the program is designed to explore the strategic role of leadership in the digital economy, to exchange research findings, practices, policies and programs in digital leadership, and to enhance leaders' competencies in technology-enabled decision-making.

Parsons MFA in Design and Technology. Today's designer faces two fundamental challenges: the expanding influence of design within society and the growing role of technology within design. The MFA in Design and Technology (MFA DT) provides students with a lively and dynamic environment in which to use design research, process, applied theory, and writing to address these challenges. Students push their experimentation beyond the visual: Design is seen as a mechanism for developing strategies, knowledge organization, business structures, and social consciousness. Areas of study include Interaction (mobile, games, Web, and installation), Physical Computing (programming code and chip-based applications such as toys, fashion, media in architecture, and performance technology), 2D and 3D Animation, Motion Graphics, and Digital Filmmaking.

Parsons Institute for Information Mapping. Parsons Institute for Information Mapping (PIIM) is a Research, Development and Professional facility within The New School and located in New York City. PIIM's mission is to advance the field of Knowledge Visualization through academic and commercial pursuits. PIIM researchers and staff disseminate their expertise in information categorization, knowledge representation, information taxonomy development, information logic and ranking/scoring, knowledge visualization, and Graphic User Interface (GUI) and User Experience Design (UXD) by developing powerful tools and methods for decision makers and analysts. PIIM's work seeks to increase decision maker and analyst cognition of complex data sets via efficient experiences and visualizations. In both its own research and in its engagements with government agencies, corporations and other organizations, PIIM pushes the boundaries of information, engineering and visual design to develop new ways of thinking about information — and to build and deliver corresponding real world solutions [13].

5 The Creative City Research Projects

Creative Cities Innovation Alliance incubates academic research and projects that support the development of cities as centers of innovation. An example of a past project from Prof. Fu/Kirwan at Tsinghua University's Design Beijing Lab includes InnoZone, part of Beijing Smart City Expo (Fig. 4).

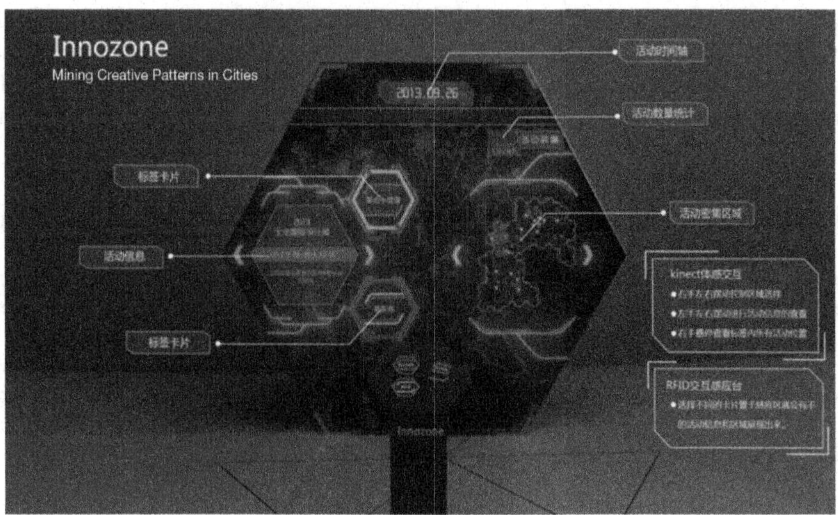

InnoZone maps patterns of human aspirations within the Creative City

Fig. 4. InnoZone interface

InnoZone. Innozone data mines and visualizes patterns of innovation in the city - an interactive visualization project aimed at users that want to enhance their understanding and ability to engage in cultural activities within the city based on their individual profile and personal interests. By sourcing all types of activities in Beijing via the Internet, both men and women and people at different stages of life can pursue self-realization and life long learning by identifying and participating in appropriate activities including lectures, exhibitions and salons based on geographic location and accessibility. In addition to serving individual users, the InnoZone system, built using Arduino, mines and composites data collected over time and maps this information on a central citywide visualization illustrating emerging patterns of cultural activity within Beijing. The project was debuted at during Beijing Design Week's Smart City Expo.

6 Conclusion

The Creative City Innovation Alliance, with participants: Tsinghua University, Henley Business School and Parsons/New School University, has been formed to create a global partnership with the goal of training city leaders in identifying the unique cultural resources of their cities and finding ways to unleash their potential as Centers of Innovation. By establishing research bases in Beijing, London and New York, this alliance will take advantage of being situated in the leading centers of growth, technological advancement and mega-trends.

The Alliance plans to offer the Creative City Digital Leadership Program, an online platform combining executive education training modules and a digital dashboard for city leaders supplemented with on-location workshops in Beijing, London/Reading and New York utilizing the highly experienced personnel and unique resources at each university to assist participating city leaders in creating the necessary framework for Innovation Districts and to train them in using the latest digital technologies in the planning and management of their communities.

Acknowledgments. We are pleased to recognize contributions to this paper made by the following colleagues: Academic Research and Collaboration – Prof. Zhiyong Fu, Academy of Arts and Design and co-founder of Design Beijing Lab, Tsinghua University, Beijing, China; Sven Travis, Faculty Parsons School of Design, New York, USA; Prof. Kecheng Liu, Dr. Weizi Li, Henley Business School, University of Reading, England; Dr. Biyu Wan, National Smart City Joint Lab, Beijing, China. Design Beijing Lab, School of Art and Design Tsinghua University Student Projects: InnoZone – Yiming Wei, Xue Dong and Shukai Wang, Beijing, China. Editorial Support – Ernest E. Kirwan, AIA, retired architect/planner and faculty member, Harvard Graduate School of Design, Cambridge, Massachusetts, USA.

References

1. PwC Real Estate 2020, Building the Future. www.pwc.com/realestate
2. PwC: Cities of Opportunities 6 (2015)
3. Katz, B., Wagner, J.: The Rise of Innovation Districts: A New Geography of Innovation in America. Brookings, Washington (2014)
4. Dawson, R.J., Wyckmans, A., Heidrich, O., Köhler, J., Dobson, S., Feliu, E.: Understanding Cities: Advances in Integrated Assessment of Urban Sustainability. Centre for Earth Systems Engineering Research (CESER), Newcastle (2014)
5. Porter, M.: The competitive advantage of nations. Harvard Bus. Rev. (1990)
6. Porter, M.: The competitive advantage of the inner city. Harvard Bus. Rev. (1995)
7. Lima, M.: Visual Complexity: Displaying Complex Networks and Data Sets. Princeton Press, Princeton (2011)
8. Kirwan, C.: Urban media: a design process for the development of sustainable applications for ubiquitous computing for livable cities. In: Proceedings of the 2011 ACM Symposium on the Role of Design in UbiComp Research and Practice. ACM (2011)
9. Kirwan, C.: Cybernetics revisited: toward a collective intelligence. In: Visual Complexity Mapping Patterns of Information, pp. 252–254 (2011)
10. Kirwan, C.G.: Defining the middle ground: a comprehensive approach to the planning, design and implementation of smart city operating systems. In: Rau, P. (ed.) CCD 2015. LNCS, vol. 9180, pp. 316–327. Springer, Heidelberg (2015)
11. Liu, K., Li, W.: Organizational Semiotics for Business Informatics. Routledge, Abingdon (2015)
12. The Digital Leadership Forum at Henley. http://www.henley.ac.uk/digital-leader-ship/forum
13. Kirwan, C., Travis, S.: Urban media: new complexities, new possibilities – a manifesto. In: Foth, M., Forlano, L., Satchell, C., Gibbs, M. (eds.) From Social Butterfly to Engaged Citizen, pp. 235–252. The MIT Press, Cambridge (2011)
14. New Cities Foundation. http://www.newcitiesfoundation.org

Co-design, Co-creation, and Co-production of Smart Mobility System

Hiroko Kudo(✉)

Faculty of Law, Chuo University, Hachioji, Tokyo, Japan
hirokokd@tamacc.chuo-u.ac.jp

Abstract. Smart Cities with their mobility system are assumed to be based on smart technology, smart people or smart collaboration, assigning citizens significant roles. While some argue that ICT will enhance democratic debate and empower citizens, others concern about the development of Smart Cities "without critical discussions and politics". Japanese Ministry of Economy, Trade and Industry (METI) launched its Smart City project in 2010, setting specific criteria to ensure the "participation of all the stakeholders"; however, drawing on analysis of official documents as well as on interviews with each of the four Smart Communities' stakeholders, the paper explains that very little input is expected from Japanese citizens. Instead, ICTs are used by municipalities and electric utilities to steer project participants and to change their behaviour. The objective of these experiments would not be to involve citizens in city governance, but rather to make them participate in the co-production of public services.

Keywords: Co-design · Co-creation · Co-production · Citizen participation · Pedestrian involvement · Mobility system

1 Introduction

Establishment and management of better mobility system has become an essential part of smart cities because of its importance for smarter environment. Participation of pedestrians and drivers is indispensable to design and deliver smart mobility system; however these co-creation processes are not yet theoretically developed and are difficult to implement in practice. The paper thus tries to understand these mechanisms from similar processes of Smart Cities and draw lessons from those cases.

Japan has been facing three main challenges concerning ecological issues as many other countries: reducing CO_2 emissions in order to mitigate climate change; ensuring its energy independence and security (renewable energy, energy conservation and efficiency improvements); revitalizing its economy by strengthening its competitiveness and becoming a leader in future "green" markets. To deal with these issues, the Japanese Government has been implementing various initiatives, among which regulations and subsidies, but also schemes such as a feed-in-tariff for renewable energy and eco-cities' experimentations since the Eco-Town program launched in 1997.

More recently, in 2010, the Ministry of Economy, Trade and Industry (METI) selected four Smart Communities – Keihanna Science City, Kitakyushu Smart

P.-L.P. Rau (Ed.): CCD 2016, LNCS 9741, pp. 551–562, 2016.
DOI: 10.1007/978-3-319-40093-8_54

Community, Toyota Smart Melit (Mobility & Energy Life in Toyota City), and Yokohama Smart City – within the "Demonstration of Next Generation Energy and Social Systems" project. Although only one of these is officially entitled "smart city", the New Energy Promotion Council (NEPC), a METI agency, defines these projects as "smart cities [which] are a new style of city providing sustainable growth and designed to encourage healthy economic activities that reduce the burden on the environment while improving QoL (Quality of Life)".

Smart Communities are based on smart grid technologies, which associate information flows to energy flows in order to optimizing the energy production and distribution, introducing safely as much renewable energy as possible and achieving peak shift through dynamic pricing or demand response schemes. However, Smart Communities aim at going further and beyond the mere smart grid, focusing not just on energy issues but also on the involvement of all the stakeholders. Another objective is to make "smart" not only the grid, but also industry, commerce, business and households' behaviours, including mobility issues. According to METI's call for projects and Smart Communities' master plans, a very innovative feature of Smart Communities is the participation of all the stakeholder among which the citizens, and the behavioural change through lifestyle innovation.

The paper thus investigates the citizen participation system and effectiveness in Japanese Smart Communities, as it has been pointed out as a crucial factor of success for eco and smart cities [1], especially when energy infrastructure and natural resources management are involved [2, 3]. However, the "participation" quoted in the call for projects and Master Plans do not seem to have been implemented on a large scale. Although the time period for application was rather short (one year) and did not allow the citizens to participate in the process of building the project, documents and interviews with the four Smart Communities stakeholders revealed that few significant participatory systems such as deliberating workshops or civic forum were neither embedded into the master plan, nor organized since the beginning of the implementation.

Indeed while observing Japanese Smart Communities it appears that citizen participation does not really take place but also was not actually part of the objectives. Therefore, the research also seeks to explain this gap between claimed and actual citizen participation. Numerous social studies have highlighted serious acceptance problems encountered by energy infrastructure [3–5] and especially smart grid-based projects [6, 7]. These studies consider participation of citizen as well as their mere consultation or feedback request as key factors to their acceptance of the project. Furthermore, behaviour change policies in the field of energy consumption are considered to have resulted in a series of failures for many years [8–10], and recent studies in social psychology and behavioural economics have been promoting new tools in order to overcome behaviour change obstacles [11–14].

Interviews with local governments and private sector stakeholders revealed that each Smart Community focuses on changing participants' behaviours rather than on promoting their participation as citizens. Thus, the paper intends to analyse the policy tools implemented in order to promote citizen acceptance and behaviour change in Japanese Smart Communities, and to understand what kinds of knowledge are mobilized. Furthermore, the issue of citizen participation as a policy instrument promoting acceptance and behaviour chance rather than participation in policy and decision making will be discussed. The paper examines the questions through document analysis and interviews with the stakeholders of the projects.

The paper begins by exploring theories of participation to see how it has been transformed under New Public Management (NPM) and later with the introduction of New Public Governance (NPG). As Smart Communities use information and communication technology (ICT), the potential impact of ICT on participation will also be investigated. The paper then introduces Japanese Smart Communities and the research methodology. It then examines the questions through document analysis and interviews with the stakeholders of the projects. Although the authors conducted interviews within each of the four initiatives, the paper focuses on Kitakyushu's case as an illustration of Smart Communities' rationale. Kitakyushu has the advantage of exhibiting the same participatory mechanisms but with a more pro-active approach. While the other cases give very little additional insights about public participation in smart cities, Kitakyushu's case allows us for more substantial investigation and analysis.

The paper tries to identify the importance of participation in co-designing and co-production of Smart City through literature review as well as a Japanese case study and understand the role of the citizen.

2 Literature Review

2.1 New Public Management (NPM) and ICT

New Public Management (NPM) was introduced into the traditional form of public administration and changed its managerial style through a series of techniques imported from business management [15]. Besides efficiency, effectiveness, and accountability, customer-oriented and/or outcome-oriented thinking has been introduced in policy making and implementation processes [16]. Reform in public service delivery, influenced by these orientations, forced public sector organisations to outsource some functions, privatize enterprises, and revise the role of government in accordance with the role of private sector and civil society. Public and Private Partnership (PPP), the Private Finance Initiative (PFI), and other forms of collaborations became alternatives to traditional government restructuring. This trend has evolved into the public governance model, with greater emphasis on integrating politics and management rather than relying merely on the introduction of new management techniques.

With the introduction of NPM, markets, managers and measurement were introduced [17]. Some of the characteristics of NPM were represented as decentralisation, management by objectives, contracting out, competition within government, and customer orientation [18]. NPM also brought ICT into public administration and promoted e-Government. Renewal of public management and public service delivery has then become an important trend in recent public sector reform.

Introduction and use of ICT to improve managerial processes and to enhance communication to and with the citizens is a key factor for a successful e-Government policy. It first developed as a tool for better governance in terms of efficiency in office work/administrative systems/tasks, data processing and dissemination. However, it is now recognized as an important tool of communication between government and its stakeholders, providing an interface between them. E-Government has become one of the most important elements in public sector reform, as it offers transparency, accountability, interface with citizens, access to information, and good governance, including prevention of corruption. When there is high demand for accountability and transparency, introduction of e-Government is a common strategy [19].

2.2 Public Service Delivery Under NPM and Public Governance

Many authors have focused their research efforts on the analysis of decentralisation processes, following the public governance approach. Following the implementation of public sector reform based on NPM, the dimension of public administrations, especially at the local level, has prompted renewed both practical and academic interest. The dimension of local governments has become very important for two main reasons: regional competitiveness and capacity to provide public services.

In terms of public services, it is important to highlight the impact of the decentralisation process especially on public administrations at the local level [20]. First, the number of public services provided by local governments has increased. Secondly, the decentralisation process has influenced local governments funding system, which has changed from an indirect to a direct system, that is to say, local governments are increasingly financed by their citizens. As a consequence, many local governments do not have sufficient financial resources to fund the provision of the services needed. These changes are also accompanied by demands for increasingly complex public services, which are difficult for a single local government to provide. These administrations therefore need new strategies to exploit their financial, material and human resources more efficiently, with the aim of satisfying citizens' demand for increasingly complex services.

The decentralisation process has confirmed new interests in institutional models of governance among public administrations operating at different levels and at the same level. All this interest has grown within a theoretical framework known as "Public Governance" [16, 17]. At citizen-related level, the most important objective stemming from decentralisation is to have public services, which reflect different needs and requirements of the citizens, of a higher quality at lower cost [18]. These interests have led to the network governance approach as well as participatory discourse.

2.3 Citizen as Stakeholder Under New Public Governance

Attentions on public service delivery and the role of citizens and social sector in its process lead to New Public Governance (NPG). It was also proposed as critiques to NPM, which merely stressed efficiency, effectiveness and managerial techniques.

Some authors, in particular Osborne, ironically defined NPM as "a transitory stage in the evolution towards New Public Governance" [12]. Not only public service delivery, but also the policy making process became key features of NPG. Bovaird pointed out that "radical reinterpretation of policy making and service delivery in the public domain resulting in Public Governance" [21].

Indeed, NPG has adopted citizen-centric approach and tries to guarantee participation of stakeholders, including social sector. It is based on network governance and focuses on joined-up governance and co-production. Since the public service delivery was the critical issue, which made NPM shift to NPG, it is considered as synonym of New Public Service (NPS). NPG stresses the importance of democratic decision-making and has evolved on changing characteristics of accountability.

Pestoff pointed out that under NPG, "central role attributed to citizen co-production and third sector provision of public services" [22], while Osborne defined NPG as "it posits both a plural state where multiple interdependent actors contribute to the delivery of public services and a pluralist state, where multiple processes inform the public policy making system" [12].

Stakeholder in network is a crucial element in NPG. Bovaird pointed out that governance provides a set of balancing mechanisms in a network society and defined NPG as the ways in which stakeholders interact with each other in order to influence the outcomes of public policies. NPG "seriously questions the relevance of the basic assumptions of NPM that service delivery can be separated from service design, since service users now play key roles in both service design and delivery". And "service users and professionals develop a mutual and interdependent relationship in which both parties take risks and need to trust each other" [21]. Trust has thus become an important issue under NPG.

Another keyword that many authors pointed out to describe the characteristics of NPG has been negotiation. Bovaird wrote that "policy making is no longer seen as a purely top-down process but rather as negotiation among many interacting policy systems" and that "services are no longer simply delivered by professional and managerial staff in public agencies, but they are co-produced by users and communities" [21]. He pointed out "emerging role of user and community co-production.

It is clear, at least from the literatures, that NPM and then NPG both pointed out the importance of participation, among others, while promoted e-Government. Smart City projects are locally promoted ICT strategy, focusing mostly on the better use of energy in the community, through incentives as well as disincentives and thus trying to change the behaviour of the residents. Thus they could be good case to examine the NPG model.

2.4 ICT Potential for Participation

Some scholars consider ICT to be a powerful means to promote and improve public participation [23, 24]. ICT may reduce participation costs by enabling citizens to participate through their mobile devices at any time and place [25]. The modes of expression and communication provided by ICT also allow new publics to have interest and legitimacy in participating in public affairs [26]. Not only would ICT widen the public of participation; it also has the potential to enrich the content of citizens' input that would no longer be solely in a discursive form [24]. Collaborative tools such as citizen sensing and other interactive applications [27] have the potential to enhance democratic debates, while information aggregators may facilitate citizen engagement [28].

E-participation, which mobilises ICT for participatory process, aims to increase citizens' abilities to participate in the political process [29]. This can go beyond by not only supplying citizens with information on public policies, but also giving them an opportunity to co-create them. Interactions between governments and citizens consist of provision of information, consultation and active participation of citizens on political decision-making [30]. ICT supports these interactions [31], and is believed to renew the trust in government [32]. In the electronic environment, citizens can interact with public officials in a more informal way and the nature of interactions would therefore become more horizontal and egalitarian [33].

Furthermore, it is worth noting that given the peculiarities of Japanese society, scholars argue that more than elsewhere, ICT could greatly boost citizen participation in Japan: for Ishikawa, "Internet is an ideal tool for jump-starting deliberative democracy in Japan" [23]. Moreover, reflected by Sabouret who qualifies Japanese as "homo technophilus" [24], many scholars consider that Japanese people are keen to use new technology. However, the possibility of ICT to stimulate public participation is subject to criticisms. First, the promises of increased social inclusion may be counterbalanced by new forms of exclusion, regarding the elderly in particular [34]. This caution is especially relevant with regard to Japanese society since in 2014, 26 % of the population is over 65 years of age. Second, although ICT allows for new forms of expression and creativity, it also favours individualised patterns of participation at the expense of collective patterns based on open discussion [35].

The paper takes Smart Community Projects as an example to examine the citizen participation in Japanese NPM as well as NPG, which could reflect on the co-design, co-creation, and co-production of mobility system.

3 Case Study

3.1 Methodology

This research is based on qualitative analysis and uses the following analytical tools: research on primary documents, semi-directive interviews and field observation. It first examined documents of METI and Smart Community cases, including their Master Plans as well as press release and communication materials. Other related documents were received directly from the institutions during the field survey. This first step aimed to understand the extent of public participation, and to identify the nature of its mechanisms.

Second, semi-structured interviews were conducted with METI, the local governments and private actors involved in each project, as well as with Smart Communities' inhabitants, from February to July 2014. In total, thirty-four interviews were carried out with the main stakeholders.

Third, in the case of Kitakyushu, besides the interviews with two dozen of residents, a field observation was carried out. The author attended to one of the regularly scheduled meetings of all stakeholders, including a representative of the citizens, and participated in the Higashida Share Festival, held on 17–18 May, 2014, during which the author talked with the residents on an informal basis.

3.2 Kitakyushu Smart Community

This project was proposed by Kitakyushu City Government, Nippon Steel, IBM Japan, and Fuji Electric Systems.

Kitakyushu City is located in an historical industry area and an historical company town. It has hosted since 1901 the very first Japanese steel works (Yawata Steel Works was a public company, then became Nippon Steel), on which the city relies its development. After the successful overcome of the territory from typical pollution and issues related to coal mining, fossil-fuel power station, and steel works, the territory launched eco-friendly, eco-driven, eco-related, and ecological industries. It became one of the first cities to host landfill sites as well as factories for the recycling of consumer electronics. The city used to rely on heavy industry, however has been successfully converting into green economy. In the Higashida area of Yahata-Higashi ward, the site of the operational experiments and of the Yawata Steel Works, the city is proceeding with the development of a new city district on unused land. In the new district, the City is pushing ahead with the establishment of a variety of new energy distribution infrastructure, for example, for the supply of energy produced by natural gas cogeneration by means of the steelworks' transmission network, and the supply of hydrogen produced by the steelworks by pipeline to areas within the district.

Sketching a vision of the optimum form for community energy management, the project seeks to create the appropriate social structures for a low-carbon society by innovating lifestyles, business styles, and urban planning. By means of the establishment and operation of a customer energy management system called Smart Community Centre, the project aims to establish mechanisms for citizens and companies to think about and participate in the process of energy distribution. The city believes that making energy use visible can encourage change in lifestyles and business. In addition, other initiatives include preparation for the large-scale introduction of next-generation vehicles and their linkage with public transport.

Due to factors including the establishment of environmental facilities and the introduction of a range of new energy sources, the Higashida area in Yahata-Higashi ward of the City already emits 30 % less CO_2 than other areas in the city. This trial aims, by means of initiatives including further introduction of new energies, the use of community energy management, and the establishment of new transport systems, to achieve a further 20 % reduction, reducing CO_2 emissions to more than 50 % less than other areas in the city. In order to achieve these goals, a Smart Community, which provides advanced energy control and optimizes total energy distribution, encompassing electric vehicles (EV) is established and in parallel with the establishment of charging infrastructure to facilitate large-scale introduction of EV, the construction of next-generation traffic systems linking bicycles and public transport.

It is clear that the city had concentrated its attention on energy, not necessary on ICT driven services, although the very first intention of METI was the smart gird, the smart community, and the smart city in terms of ICT use. This is not because the city has strong interests in environmental industry, but can be observed in other projects as well. It is, however, not clear, if the city had really considered the project in terms of creating smart city using ICT as major driver. From the official materials of the municipality and interviews conducted among the public servants in the municipality, it emerges that the main focus of the municipality has been the energy issue, and not the community planning and/or citizen services.

The residents were rather passive during these events, letting the local authorities and the industrial actors decide for them and following their decisions. This tendency can be observed in cities and territories, where there used to be dominant economic actor. The citizen participation looks weak in both areas, not because residents are not interested in their cities, but because they have strong trust in established institutions and let them decide on their behalf.

3.3 Analysis: Co-design, Co-creation, and Co-production?

The private companies involved in the project had collaborated with the municipality from a very early stage of the project, prior to the official call of METI. They created a secretariat for the project within the municipality, dispatching their staff to it. They agree that in this way, they were able to gain trust from the residents in the planned area. This is confirmed from the citizens as well. They agree to the fact that the major industrial actors have been "the authority" together with the municipality in the territory.

The citizen participation is guaranteed in two processes; one is residents briefing before initiating the project involving residents and the other is feedback meetings during the project implementation. During the first, consensus building, especially for privacy issue, was achieved. Since some experiments, including Dynamic Pricing, required data gathering of private households, consensus of residents were needed. Most of the residents in the area participated actively in the area, although there was no direct "participation" during the designing process of the project. This sounds a bit contradictory; indeed, most residents agreed to participate in the project and gave consensus of gathering and using their household energy consumption data by the smart community consortium, without strong concern and/or specific request to the project. During the feedback meetings, the project team gathered information, opinions, and suggestions of the residents. In these meetings, residents were asked to answer the questioner and express their opinions. Besides some suggestions regarding the tariff differences, few opinions were gathered. This is not an isolated case in Japan; it is rather common that these town meetings and feedback meetings get few feedbacks.

Many private companies actively participated in the project, since they have various interests of their own; however there had been a clear hierarchy among them. They say that it has been not a trouble, since the organization has functioned well. This view is confirmed by the municipality, which explained this tendency as trust to "the authority".

The municipality has been the major actor together with a small number of private companies. The city actively invested in the project in advance, following its environmental as well as industrial strategies. It has promoted Eco-town projects among others. Their strategies have enjoyed strong support by the citizen and thus the smart city project has also enjoyed strong support.

The project team, however, pointed out one interesting feature; changing behaviours of the residents in terms of their energy consumption. Since the households get information about the details of their energy consumption, they now try to "save" energy in peak times, rationalising their consumption. This means that the dynamic pricing made the residents aware of their consumption patterns, made them consume rationally, and thus made them "save" energy at the same time.

Like in other Smart Communities Projects, also in Kitakyushu case, it appears that citizen participation does not really take place but also was not actually part of the objectives. Citizen participation was formally designed in the process, but it has never actively implemented.

The results of interview also reminds us to consider the trust factor in this case, since trust has been noted by various actors as well as trust is one of the new key elements under NPG.

4 Findings and Implications

NPM had introduced collaborative government and co-production in public service delivery. NPG concepts explain the conditions of the stakeholders involved in these processes.

From the description above mentioned of projects under Smart City and Smart Community, and of the Japanese e-Government policy and strategy, it is possible to draw various observations.

First, the current Smart City and Smart Community projects are still in a too early stage to understand the very intention of the government as well as municipalities. However, from the materials of METI, it is rather clear that the original policy of Smart City and Smart Community is the economic stimuli, considering that the investment related to the projects might boost industrial activities in the territories. The fact, that the private companies in the territories, and major energy, telecom, and IT companies are involved from the very early stage of the projects, means that the Ministry was mostly keen on the creation of new industry through the projects. This process has been typical to the Ministry; it is well known that the high-tech industry had benefited mostly from these policies [36].

Second, the major part of the current projects regards on energy, especially on energy saving and creation of new energy sources. City planning and building management are part of this energy saving strategy. The latter was launched before these projects, mostly by local governments. Building energy management was sought to save urban energy consumption, at least to rationalise it. At territorial level, energy saving strategy was introduced by private companies, including developers and building companies. However these projects remained isolated ones, without broader strategy for the community. Then the Smart City and Smart Community projects included these experiences into its policy and have been successfully applied in many foreign projects. After the Earthquake, this tendency became more evident, although projects in the area of earthquake have little to do with energy saving.

Third, in terms of ICT use in the territory, the Smart City and Smart Community projects have realised little until now. They included intelligent traffic management system and EVs in the original projects; however these are only on a very early stage.

Forth, it is interesting to note that the various projects related to ICT have initiated by different ministries and have been poorly coordinated. Major ICT projects in central and local governments have been promoted by MIC (Ministry of Internal Affairs and Communications); meanwhile ICT industry related projects have been promoted by METI. They were independently initiated and although many projects had similar characteristics, they are not coordinated among themselves. It is possible to observe typical sectionalism among ministries, which is one of the obstacles for integrated ICT policy development in Japan.

Lastly, the Smart Community in Kitakyushu, in particular, has revealed interesting features: behaviour change of the residents in energy consumption, while they show little participation. The case, given the historical peculiarity of the territory, could be an interesting case to study trust among institutions and its impact on participation and behaviour change.

The pattern of participation can be explained by the focus of Japanese smart cities on energy issues, and by Japanese society's traditional characteristics that seem to be favourable to co-production of public services. However, since the experimentation only started in 2012, it is still unclear whether these practices will be maintained in the long term. Furthermore, the limitation of the area, the number of residents involved and the peculiarity of Kitakyushu city do not enable to contend that citizens would be that much cooperative in other contexts. Nevertheless, although this article does not aim at providing generalisable conclusions about participation in smart cities, the fact that citizen involvement shows similar characteristics in other Smart Communities as well support the idea that Kitakyushu's case is far for being unique. Accordingly, other smart city projects may dram lessons from Kitakyushu Smart Community. Especially, it underlines the importance of the trust factor, which is precisely one of the new key elements under NPG, for the participation of citizens to the energy management co-production.

Furthermore, another ambition of this article is to highlight that it is better to be cautious with "citizen participation" claims when it comes to smart cities. The smart grid technologies Smart Communities rely on are at the core of smart city projects throughout the world. Therefore, the fact that smart cities may mobilise ICT to steer citizens rather than to catalyse public participation calls for further research. Indeed, the Japanese case suggests an interlocking between the rise of smartness and the emergence of a "behaviour change agenda" based on the use of behavioural sciences and big data. In this regard, citizen involvement in smart cities may be considered as a disciplinary strategy [37] and seen as a means rather than as an end in itself; in other words, as a policy instruments aiming at improving efficiency rather than deepening democracy. Although already underlined by the literature [21], the ambiguous relation between co-production and governmental approaches to behaviour change would deserve further analysis when ICT is at stake.

Since the characteristics of co-design, co-creation, and co-production with citizen in Smart Cities are similar to those of mobility system, the involvement of pedestrians and drivers are essential as well as inevitable, although there are theoretical as well as practical difficulties. The implication to mobility system needs to be analysed through case studies.

References

1. Carabias, V., Moser, C., Wilherlmer, D., Kubeczko, K., Ruben, N.: The importance of participatory foresight on the way towards smart cities. IFA Academic Seminar 2013 (2013)
2. Simard, L.: Repenser la démocratie participative dans le secteur de l'énergie, Mémoire déposé dans le cadre de la commission sur les enjeux énergétique du Québec (2013)
3. Maruyama, Y., Nishikodo, M., Iida, T.: The rise of community wind power in Japan: enhanced acceptance through social innovation. Energy Policy **35**, 2761–2769 (2007)
4. Fortin, M.-J., Fournis, Y.: L'acceptabilité sociale de projets énergétiques au Québec: la difficile construction par l'action publique, Symposium Territoire et Environnement: des représentations à l'action, Tours, 8–9 December 2011
5. Wüstenhagen, R., Wolsink, M., Burer, M.J.: Social acceptance of renewable energy innovation: an introduction to the concept. Energy Policy **35**, 2683–2691 (2007)
6. Karlin B.: Public acceptance of smart meters: integrating psychology and practice. In: ACEEE Summer Study on Energy Efficiency in Buildings, pp. 102–113 (2012)
7. Wolsink, M.: The research agenda on social acceptance of distributed generation in smartgrids: renewable as common pool resources. Renew. Sustain. Energy Rev. **16**, 822–835 (2012)
8. Maréchal, K.: Not irrational but habitual: the importance of "behavioural lock-in" in energy consumption. Ecol. Econ. **69**(5), 1104–1114 (2010)
9. Steg, L.: Promoting household energy conservation. Energy Policy **36**, 4449–4453 (2008)
10. Sanne, C.: Willing consumers or locked-in? Policies for a sustainable consumption. Ecol. Econ. **42**, 273–287 (2002)
11. Ito, K., Ida, T., Tanaka, M.: Using dynamic electricity pricing to address energy crises evidence from randomized field experiments. Mimeo (2013)
12. Osborne, S.: The new public governance? Publ. Manag. Rev. **8**(3), 377–387 (2006)
13. Marres, N.: The cost of public involvement: everyday devices of carbon accounting and the materialization of participation. Econ. Soc. **40**, 510–533 (2011)
14. Thaler, R.H., Sunstein, C.R.: Nudge. Improving Decisions About Health, Wealth, and Happiness. Yale University Press, New Haven (2008)
15. Olson, O., Guthrie, J., Humphrey, C.: Global Warning! Debating International Developments in New Public Financial Management. Cappelen Akademisk Forlag, Oslo (1998)
16. Kettl, D.F.: The transformation of governance: globalization, devolution and the role of government. Publ. Adm. Rev. **60**(6), 488–497 (2000)
17. Ferlie, E., Ashburner, L., Fitzgerald, L., Pettinngrew, A.: New Public Management in Action. Oxford University Press, Oxford (1996)
18. OECD: Managing Decentralisation: A New Role for Labour Market Policy, Organisation for Economic Co-operation and Development. OECD Publishing, Paris (2003)
19. Kudo, H.: E-governance as strategy of public sector reform: peculiarity of Japanese IT policy and its institutional origin. Financ. Account. Manag. **26**(1), 65–84 (2010)
20. Fedele, P., Ongaro, E.: A common trend, different houses: devolution in Italy, Spain and the UK. Publ. Money Manag. **28**(2), 85–92 (2008)
21. Bovaird, T.: Beyond engagement & participation: user & community co-production of public services. Publ. Adm. Rev. **67**(5), 846–860 (2007)
22. Pestoff, V.: New public governance and accountability: some jewels in a treasure chest. In: CIES Centro de Investigación de Economía y Sociedad, N. 91 (2011)
23. Ishikawa, Y.: Calls for deliberative democracy in Japan. Rhetor. Publ. Aff. **5**(2), 331–345 (2002)

24. Sabouret, J.-F.: L'Empire de l'intelligence. Politiques scientifiques et technologiques du Japon depuis 1945. CNRS Editions, Paris (2007)
25. Marres, N.: Material Participation: Technology, The Environment and Everyday Publics. Palgrave Macmillan, London (2012)
26. Muhlberger, P., Stromer-Galley, J., Webb, N.: Public policy and obstacles to the virtual agora: insights from the deliberative e-rulemaking project. Inf. Polity **16**(3), 197–214 (2011)
27. Gutiérrez, V., Galache, J.A., Sánchez, L., Muñoz, L., Hernández-Muñoz, J.M., Fernandes, J., Presser, M.: SmartSantander: internet of things research and innovation through citizen participation. In: Galis, A., Gavras, A. (eds.) FIA 2013. LNCS, vol. 7858, pp. 173–186. Springer, Heidelberg (2013)
28. Kavanaugh, A., Krishnan, S., Pérez-Quiñones, M., Tedesco, J., Madondo, K., Ahju, A.: Encouraging civic participation through local news aggregation. Inf. Polity **19**(1–2), 35–56 (2014)
29. Sanford, C., Rose, J.: Characterizing eParticipation. Int. J. Inf. Manag. **27**(6), 406–421 (2007)
30. Gramberger, M.R.: Citizens as Partners: OECD Handbook on Information, Consultation and Public Participation in Policy-Making. OECD, Paris (2001)
31. Akrivopoulou, C.M.: Digital Democracy and the Impact of Technology on Governance and Politics: New Globalized Practices. IGI Global, Hershey (2013)
32. Hague, B.M., Loader, B.: Digital Democracy: Discourse and Decision Making in the Information Age. Routledge, New York (1999)
33. Macintosh, A., Coleman, S., Schneeberger, A.: eParticipation: the research gaps. Electron. Particip. **5694**, 1–11 (2009)
34. Millward, P.: The "grey digital divide": perception, exclusion and barrier of access to the internet for older people. First Monday **8**(7) (2003)
35. Mabi, C., Sa Vilas Boas, M.-H., Nonjon, M.: Comprendre la signification politique des technologies. In: De Biase, A., Ottaviano, N., Zaza, O. (eds.) Digital Polis. La ville face au numérique
36. Okimoto, D.I.: Between MITI and the Market: Japanese Industrial Policy for High Technology. Stanford University Press, Stanford (1989)
37. Vanolo, A.: Smartmentality: the Smart City as disciplinary strategy. Urban Stud. **51**(5), 883–998 (2014)

Towards the Development of an EIT-based Stretchable Sensor for Multi-Touch Industrial Human-Computer Interaction Systems

Stefania Russo[1(✉)], Samia-Nefti Meziani[1], Tauseef Gulrez[1], Nicola Carbonaro[2], and Alessandro Tognetti[2]

[1] Autonomous System and Robotics Research Centre, University of Salford, Manchester, UK
{s.russo1,s.nefti-meziani,T.Gulrez}@salford.ac.uk
[2] Research Centre E. Piaggio, University of Pisa, Pisa, Italy
{nicola.carbonaro,a.tognetti}@centropiaggio.unipi.it

Abstract. In human-computer interaction studies, an interaction is often considered as a kind of information or discrete internal states of an individual that can be transmitted in a loss-free manner from people to computing interfaces (or robotic interfaces) and vice-versa [5,17].

This project aims to investigate processes capable of communicating and cooperating by adjusting their schedules to match the evolving execution circumstances, in a way that maximise the quality of their joint activities. By enabling human-computer interactions, the process will emerge as a framework based on the concept of expectancy, demand, and need of the human and computer together, for understanding the interplay between people and computers.

The idea of this work is to utilise touch feedback from humans as a channel for communication thanks to an artificial sensitive skin made of a thin, flexible, and stretchable material acting as transducer. As a proof of concept, we demonstrate that the first prototype of our artificial sensitive skin can detect surface contacts and show their locations with an image reconstructing the internal electrical conductivity of the sensor.

1 Introduction

Over the last two decades, touch screen technologies used as industrial control panels have gained considerable interest with the evolution of smart materials and digital products. The drawback is that this scenario is emphasising the separateness between human and computer by treating them as disassociated entities. For example, capacitive touch screens do not work unless the user is working with bare hands or with particular gloves with a conductive yarn that allows an electric charge. Consequently, the challenges of having a portable touch screen which resolves the problem of the costs, hand occupation, and productivity, are still hounding the industries. For these reasons, the demand for effective human-computer interaction technology has increased.

P.-L.P. Rau (Ed.): CCD 2016, LNCS 9741, pp. 563–573, 2016.
DOI: 10.1007/978-3-319-40093-8_55

Humanistic Intelligence theory states that the user and the computer are not two separate entities but they work together having the human in the feedback loop of the computational process. In this case, the user takes advantage of the augmented sensing modalities and additional senses offered by the computer [14] which is a continuously running and always-ready interface. It is then clear that sensing elements are key factors in human-computer interaction. They significantly improve the performance of the system which is expected to intelligently perform in changing surroundings and to be more responsive to human commands. Such way of implementing a new type of man and sensory-machine interface technology has facilitated and opened up an interaction that can be easily accessed by the user. This is going to be beneficial and leading to a new form of synergy between human and computer when compared to the hand-held devices [13] usually used in industrial scenarios.

One solution for smart sensing in HCI which has recently been addressed, is the use of small sensor accessories as wearable technologies [15], monitoring physiological, environmental and activity parameters of people as well for rehabilitation, sport [6,12,19], etc. The meaning of this rise is that there is the need for sensors to be functional, ergonomic, stretchable and operative at high strains without being obstructive. Previous approaches in stretchable sensors include, for example, a soft sensor flesh for whole body tactile sensor system [24], or serpentine-like channels within an elastomeric matrix forming a network that is used like a keypad [10]. These devices are flexible but suffer from fragility, because they are made of rigid sensing materials embedded in a soft substrate creating stiffness and risking the material failure. Furthermore, they present wires within the active sensing area that limits the overall deformation and cannot guarantee that the sensor itself is going to take the shape of the support where it is mounted on. These critical limitations hinder their integration for artificial skin purposes.

To address these limits, in this paper we explore how an Electrical Impedance Tomography (EIT) based stretchable pressure sensor can be utilised as a multi-touch screen interfacing system for industrial control applications. The sensor is flexible and stretchable, capable of covering natural curved or flat shapes and it is used to measure forces applied by dragging or pinching interactions. If mounted on the forearm of a wearer, the output of the sensor can be used to generate a feedback in order to connect by local communication the machine systems and the users in an industrial environment, improving the productivity and flexibility of the worker and decreasing pressure towards automation. The sensing method employed is based on our observation that EIT can be used to measure the changes in electrical resistivity inside a stretchable and electrical conductive material; this is done by injecting several small currents and measuring the resulting voltage at the boundary of the conductive medium [18] as shown in Fig. 1. The injection and the measurement is repeated until every electrode has received a current injection; in this way, by scanning around various driving electrode pairs, the measured voltage data are then processed applying an imaging technique, and an image of the conductivity inside the domain is

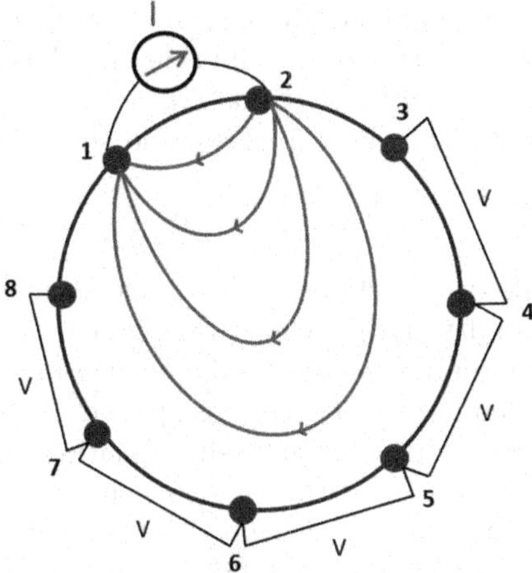

Fig. 1. Representation of the first current injection and voltage measurement set. The red lines represent the current paths inside the conductive medium when a current is injected between electrodes 1 and 2. (Color figure online)

showed through an inverse solution of Maxwell's equations. With an electrical conductive, homogeneous, and stretchable material as a conductive medium, an intuitive and wearable interface can be achieved and used as an industrial controller without altering the original shape of the object where it is placed. Other applications cover the majority of the domains where a soft and stretchable pressure sensor is required, e.g. robotics, capturing human kinematics, pressure-sore prevention [7,9], industrial automation and manufacturing. This will bring to the development of an unobtrusive device that does not interfere with the users, and helps them to become familiar with the task and accomplish intended goals on the target application. The remainder of the paper will be organized describing an overview of tactile sensors and EIT-based systems. Then a specific section will describe the experimental set-up, data acquisition and reconstruction technique. Discussion and conclusions will be presented in the last sections.

2 Sensitive Skin Based on EIT

2.1 Inverse Solution and Image Reconstruction

EIT works minimising the difference between experimentally measured boundary voltages and an analytical forward operator that predicts these boundary voltages simulating the same injection and measurement process that produced them [20]. The approach used is the output least squares, that minimises the sum of squares error:

$$min(||V_m - F(\sigma)||^2), \tag{1}$$

where V_m is a vector of experimentally measured voltages, $F(.)$ is the forward operator, and σ is the conductivity distribution that has to be reconstructed. This is done considering an initial estimation of the conductivity σ_0 and by linearising F with the Taylor series expansion and substituting in (1):

$$\partial(V) \approx J\partial\sigma + w. \tag{2}$$

The term ∂V is the difference between two voltage set measurements, w is the noise, and J is a sensitivity matrix called Jacobian which represents how the voltage across the electrodes is related to the change in electrical conductivity within the conductive medium when current is applied. For solving this equation, the EIT system is expressed trough Maxwell's equations for electromagnetism, assuming for simplicity that we are using a direct current or at a sufficiently low frequency so the magnetic field can be neglected. Our system Ω is modelled with conductivity σ and a smooth (or smooth enough) boundary $\partial\Omega$ and completed with the boundary equations. Different types of models which can be used; in this work we applied the complete electrode model [7]:

$$\sigma\nabla\phi \cdot \boldsymbol{n} = \frac{1}{z_l}(V_l - \phi) \tag{3}$$

$$\int \sigma\nabla\phi \cdot \boldsymbol{n}\ \partial\Omega = 0, \tag{4}$$

where the unicity of the solution is provided considering the conservation of charge theorem, assuming a voltage drop due to contact impedance between the electrodes and Ω, and the total current through the electrodes which is zero. Our model is then transformed from its continuous form into a discrete approximation by finite elements with the Finite Element Method. In this way, knowing the applied current and the conductivity distribution, the resulting boundary potentials of the object can be simulated. The Jacobian J is then found by perturbing the conductivity of the elements of the mesh and then calculating the changes in potential at the electrodes.

For the nature of the calculation, some terms in the Jacobian matrix will have small values. This becomes an ill-conditioned problem as the solution will show an undesired tendency of amplifying noise, being very sensitive to small changes in the measured potentials. This problem is solved by approximating the solution through regularisation. In this work, the Tikhonov regularisation method is shown but other approaches based on the singular value decomposition (SVD) exist. In the Tikhonov regularisation, the ill-posed problem is solved through minimisation of the least-square function, as explained in [11]:

Trough regularisation, the dynamic time-varying distribution of conductivity changes as:

$$\delta\sigma = (J^T J + \alpha^2 Q)^{-1}(J^T) \tag{5}$$

where α is a scalar hyperparameter that controls the amount of regularisation (e.g. the smaller is α, the more the solution tends to be ill-posed) and Q is found from a regularisation matrix that controls the assumption of smoothness of the reconstructed σ. The regularisation matrix is commonly chosen between different regularisation methods [18], while the hyperparameter α is usually chosen heuristically. When the system is modelled, the Jacobian and the parameters needed for its solution are computed only once and off-line. Then, the current injection starts and, at every step, two different sets of measured boundary voltages are compared for the difference imaging. This is done in a loop that allows real-time implementation of the system. High reconstruction rates are reported in literature [21–23].

2.2 Artificial Sensitive Skin Fabrication

The electrical conductive material used in EIT techniques is one of the main component of this method. Different materials have been used in previous works. In [8,20] the authors have used polymers/rubbers with conductive micro-fillers, but the results are very dependent on the current path formed by the nanofillers inside the flexible matrix when the material is stretched or compressed, thus creating a non-homogeneous conductivity distribution. In [16], a knit fabric sprayed with a water-based carbonic paint is presented with conductivity changes in the horizontal plane due to stretching. Chossat et al. [3] developed a tactile sensor by using a silicone rubber containing microchannels filled with conductive ionic liquid. The experimental results showed that in their prototype the spatial resolution depends on the density of the conductive channel in the soft matrix. In [2] two different layers of conductive fabric are used. The materials responds in different ways to stretching and pressure thus eliminating changes in conductivity due to one of the two stimuli.

We decided to choose a Medtex 130 conductive knit fabric, with the aim of using it as a wearable touch sensor. It is a silver-plated highly conductive nylon that is stretchable in both directions; this material is light-weight, low cost, and with homogeneous conductivity and surface resistivity $\leq$1 ohm/sq. Unfortunately, the material also gives changes in its conductivity due to stretching while the main idea of this work is to have a pressure sensor. Being this study a proof of concept we will focalise more on the experimental setup itself and on the first simulation and experimental results, while leaving the study of different materials to future works. As we are working with difference imaging, the changes in conductivity due to the pre-stretching of the conductive textile are not considered. The material was cut in a circular shape with a diameter of 10 cm. The calculated surface resistance was around 40 Ω. Stainless Steel circular button electrodes were pierced into the sample with a 3.5 cm gap in between as shown in Fig. 2. The single layer sample was then placed on a soft foam support to decrease the sensitivity to stretching in the vertical axis when pressure is applied.

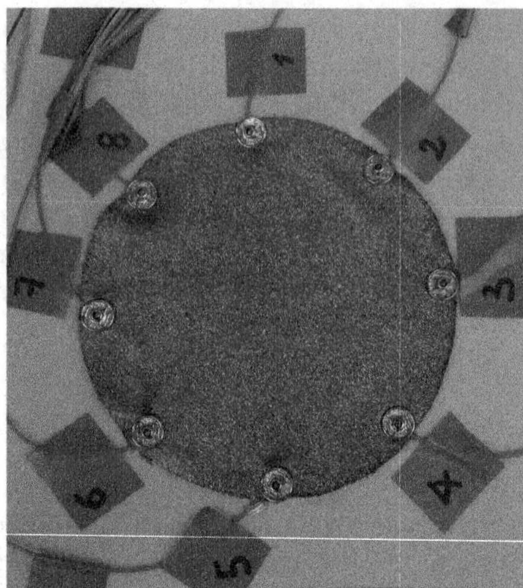

Fig. 2. Conductive material Medtex 130 knit fabric with 8 stainless steel circular button electrodes, placed on a soft foam support.

3 Proposed Electrical Impedance Tomography Method

The conductive medium requires a constant DC current generator capable of producing a constant current independent of the load to which it is connected. The circuit is supplied with 5 V for the portability of the system. Considering the resistivity of the sample material, the circuit is able to supply a constant current of 14–16 mA without saturation of the used Op-Amp with a maximum allowed connected load of 100 Ω. For the multiplexed voltage readings, the National Instruments PCI6071E data acquisition (DAQ) board has been used. This is a multifunction E Series card and, for input signal ranges between 0 to +200 mV as in our case, the precision in the measurement is 48.8 µV. The DAQ has been used in differential mode using two analog input lines. One line connects to the positive input of the device programmable gain instrumentation amplifier (PGIA), and the other connects to the negative input of the PGIA, with low settling times at all gains, ensuring to use the maximum resolution of the ADC. Differently from previous works [4], we did not use two multiplexers for the voltage readings, thus decreasing the electrical noise and the settling time. For the control of the current supply we mounted two 8-channels Analog Devices multiplexers. One of the two multiplexers was used for connecting one electrode to the current source, while the other one was used to connect the second electrode to the ground during the current injection process. With 8 channels, we used 3 control variables plus an enabling variable for every multiplexer, all controlled by the National Instrument PCI 6704 board that generates the control variables as output voltages, and the supply voltage for the multiplexers and the constant current generator. A voltage of 5 V was used as power supply in order to bring

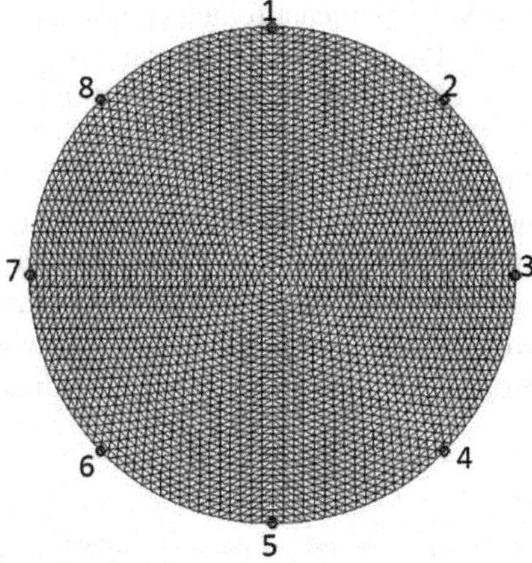

Fig. 3. FE model of the conductive medium showing the boundary electrodes and a uniform mesh density.

this first prototype as a portable system in future studies. For the management of the control and acquisition card we have used a Simulink platform to create a verification algorithm and synchronization of the inputs and outputs. In Simulink, we used Real Time Windows Target that provides a real-time kernel for executing the model; we chose a sample time for the voltage readings of 200 Hz and selected the input and output channels for the current injection. The first tests were conducted using the adjacent stimulation method for the current injection and measurement pattern due to its well-known use in EIT literature. Voltage measurements were acquired also from the drive electrodes, but then removed via software for eliminating most of the noise and errors due to contact impedance mismatch. The voltage measurement were then sent to EIDORS software [1] for the image reconstruction. This software platform is available under a General Public License and is used for the forward and inverse modelling of EIT. It also creates a FE model of the conductive medium (Fig. 3), and trough an inverse analysis it reconstructs the image of the internal conductivity of the material, assigning a value of the changes in conductivity for every node of the FE model. This is done based on the voltage dataset acquired once a complete set of currents has been injected.

4 Results and Discussion

4.1 Simulation Studies

Before conducting the experiments a simulation of the expected results was carried out in EIDORS. The FE mesh is constructed using the Medtex 130 physical sample as a reference. A uniform mesh density function was chosen and eight electrodes were selected and modelled to coincide with the physical setup.

The current injection and voltage measurement patterns were defined as well as the current amplitude. A value for the hyperparameter α of 0.5 was chosen for controlling the smoothness of the solution and the regularisation matrix was also selected at this stage. As illustrated in Fig. 4, a mesh of our conductive material was constructed and a simulated load was applied in the central area of the mesh through a change in conductivity, in order to generate the expected reconstructed image. This is done by setting up via software the current stimulation pattern and calculating the resulting voltage on each element of the mesh through a forward solver. Based on this, EIDORS recreates the conductivity of the elements in the mesh and generates an image of the reconstructed conductivity.

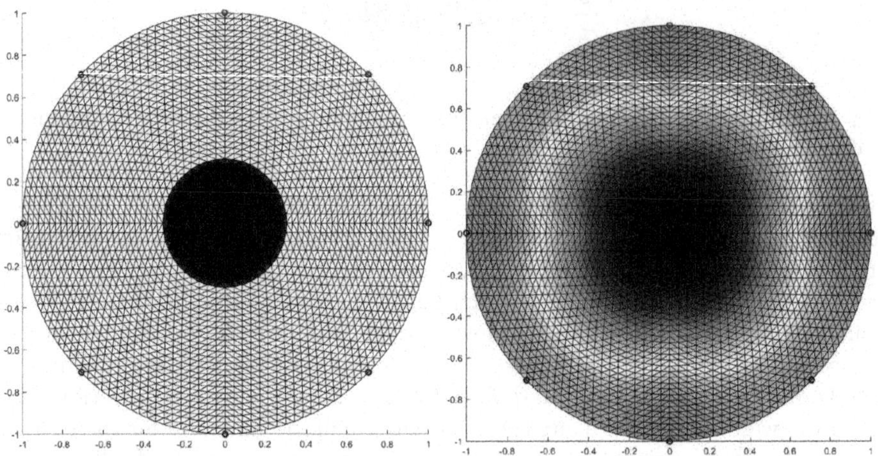

Fig. 4. Figure: On the left, a 3 cm diameter change in conductivity is simulated in the centre of the EIT model and the reconstructed image is shown on the right. It is visible that the simulated applied pressure has an influence on the conductivity changes in the pressure area and its proximity.

4.2 Experimental Results: Contact Location and Image Reconstruction

A conductive 250gr load (2.5 N) of 3 cm diameter was placed over the pressure sensitive sensor to see the results of the applied pressure. Differential voltage readings of about 100 mV were acquired with the DAQ card and sent to EIDORS for the image reconstruction. Voltage measurements taken from the electrodes carrying current were then removed via software. As shown in Fig. 5, the sensor was able to recognise the applied load through a change in the conductivity. The reconstructed image presents a blurred area near the area of pressure: this is due to the chosen material that has high hysteresis and high response to stretching, as expected. Also, the accuracy and resolution of the reconstructed image depend

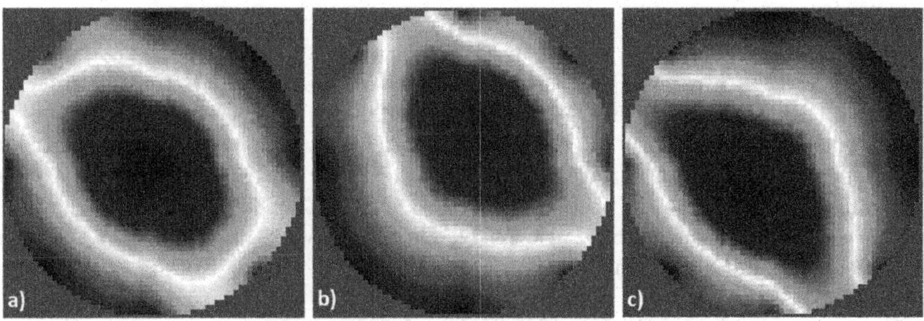

Fig. 5. Experimental results show how the stretchable sensor can detect pressure and contact location. In (a) a conductive load of 250gr was placed in the centre of the sensor, while in (b) and (c) the load was placed near electrodes 2–3 and 6–7 respectively.

on the regularisation methods, the choice of the hyperparameter, the accuracy of the electrode placement, and the presence of the electrical noise. Furthermore, by increasing the number of electrodes the resolution can be improved, as already explained in [18].

5 Conclusion

The goal of this paper was to develop the proof-of-concept of an EIT-based stretchable sensor for wearable touch screens which can be a key feature for enabling safe and effective human-computer interaction in industrial applications. We introduced the EIT technique to estimate the internal conductivity of a conductive stretchable medium based on the voltage data acquired from its boundary. The complete absence of wires inside the internal structure of the sensor allows it to be stretchable and easily placed on 3D shaped surfaces. Also, as we have used a difference imaging method, only the conductivity changes with respect to an initial baseline are shown, meaning that the initial changes due to the pre-stretching are not crucial in the application of the sensor. We have developed an experimental set-up with a constant 14 mA DC current generator, two multiplexers for the current injection and a DAQ card for the voltage readings. Experimental results shown herein demonstrate a good match with the simulation studies conducted in EIDORS. Future studies will focus on the development of a real-time setup and on the study of different materials and different types of current injection and voltage measurements for the integration of the sensor in a portable and wearable pressure-sensitive touch screen.

Acknowledgment. The research leading to these results has received funding from the People Programme (Marie Curie Actions) of the European Unions Seventh Framework Programme FP7/2007-2013/ under REA grant agreement number 608022.

References

1. Adler, A., Lionheart, W.R.B.: Uses and abuses of EIDORS: an extensible software base for EIT. Physiol. Meas. **27**(5), S25–S42 (2006)
2. Alirezaei, H., Nagakubo, A., Kuniyoshi, Y.: A highly stretchable tactile distribution sensor for smooth surfaced humanoids. In: 2007 7th IEEE-RAS International Conference on Humanoid Robots, pp. 167–173. IEEE (2007)
3. Chossat, J.-B., Shin, H.-S., Park, Y.-L., Duchaine, V.: Soft tactile skin using an embedded ionic liquid and tomographic imaging. J. Mech. Robot. **7**(2), 021008 (2015)
4. Gani, A., Salami, M.J.E.: A LabVIEW based data acquisition system for vibration monitoring and analysis. In: Student Conference on Research and Development, SCOReD 2002, pp. 62–65. IEEE (2002)
5. Gulrez, T.: Role of haptic interfaces in robot-assisted minimally invasive surgery. Int. J. Swarm Intell. Evol. Comput. (2014)
6. Gulrez, T., Tognetti, A.: A sensorized garment controlled virtual robotic wheelchair. J. Intell. Robot. Syst. **74**, 847–868 (2013)
7. Holder, D.S.: Electrical Impedance Tomography Methods, History and Applications. Series in Medical Physics and Biomedical Engineering. CRC Press, Boca Raton (2004)
8. Kato, Y., Mukai, T., Hayakawa, T., Shibata, T.: Tactile sensor without wire and sensing element in the tactile region based on EIT method. In: IEEE Sensors 2007, pp. 792–795. IEEE (2007)
9. Knight, R.A., Lipczynski, R.T.: The use of EIT techniques to measure interface pressure. In: Annual International Conference of the IEEE Engineering in Medicine and Biology Society, pp. 2307–2308 (1990)
10. Kramer, R.K., Majidi, C., Wood, R.J.: Wearable tactile keypad with stretchable artificial skin. In: 2011 IEEE International Conference on Robotics and Automation (ICRA), pp. 1103–1107, May 2011
11. Lionheart, W.R.: EIT reconstruction algorithms: pitfalls, challenges and recent developments. Physiol. Meas. **25**(1), 125–142 (2004)
12. Lorussi, F., Rocchia, W., Scilingo, E.P., Tognetti, A., De Rossi, D.: Wearable, redundant fabric-based sensor arrays for reconstruction of body segment posture. IEEE Sens. J. **4**(6), 807–818 (2004)
13. Mann, S.: Wearable computing: a first step toward personal imaging. Computer **30**(2), 25–32 (1997)
14. Mann, S.: Wearable computing: toward humanistic intelligence. IEEE Intell. Syst. **16**(3), 10–15 (2001)
15. Meyer, J., Lukowicz, P., Troster, G.: Textile pressure sensor for muscle activity and motion detection. In: 2006 10th IEEE International Symposium on Wearable Computers, pp. 69–72, October 2006
16. Nagakubo, A., Alirezaei, H., Kuniyoshi, Y.: A deformable and deformation sensitive tactile distribution sensor. In: IEEE International Conference on Robotics and Biomimetics, pp. 1301–1308 (2007)
17. Pour, P.A., Gulrez, T., AlZoubi, O., Gargiulo, G., Calvo, R.A.: Brain-computer interface: next generation thought controlled distributed video game development platform. In: IEEE Symposium On Computational Intelligence and Games, pp. 251–257, December 2008
18. Silvera-Tawil, D., Rye, D., Soleimani, M., Velonaki, M.: Electrical impedance tomography for artificial sensitive robotic skin: a review. IEEE Sens. J. **15**(4), 2001–2016 (2015)

19. Stoppa, M., Chiolerio, A.: Wearable electronics and smart textiles: a critical review. Sensors **14**(7), 11957 (2014)
20. Tallman, T.N., Gungor, S., Wang, K.W., Bakis, C.E.: Damage detection and conductivity evolution in carbon nanofiber epoxy via electrical impedance tomography. Smart Mater. Struct. **23**(4), 045034 (2014)
21. Tawil, D.S.: Artificial skin and the interpretation of touch for human-robot interaction. Ph.D. dissertation, School Aerosp., Mech. Mechatron. Eng., Univ. Sydney, New South Wales, Australia (2012)
22. Tawil, D.S., Rye, D., Velonaki, M.: Interpretation of the modality of touch on an artificial arm covered with an EIT-based sensitive skin. Int. J. Robot. Res. **31**(13), 1627–1641 (2012)
23. Wilkinson, A.J., Randall, E.W., Cilliers, J.J., Durrett, D.R., Naidoo, T., Long, T.: A 1000-measurement frames/second ERT data capture system with real-time visualization. IEEE Sens. J. **5**(2), 300–307 (2005)
24. Yoshikai, T., Hayashi, M., Ishizaka, Y., Fukushima, H., Kadowaki, A., Sagisaka, T., Kobayashi, K., Kumagai, I., Inaba, M.: Development of robots with soft sensor flesh for achieving close interaction behavior. Adv. Artif. Intell. **12**, 27 (2012)

Kansei Robotics for Safe and Stress-Free Livesphere

Understanding Personal Preferences from Behavior Patterns

Takashi Sakamoto[1(✉)], Toru Nakata[1], and Toshikazu Kato[2]

[1] National Institute of Advanced Industrial Science and Technology (AIST), Tokyo, Japan
{takashi-sakamoto, toru-nakata}@aist.go.jp
[2] Chuo University, Tokyo, Japan
kato@indsys.chuo-u.ac.jp

Abstract. Each person has his own personal feature which includes physical, physiological, psychological and cognitive characteristics. Kansei, i.e., affection, is a mechanism which characterizes each person's mental and behavioral processes interacting with the world. In this mechanism, multimedia and multimodal information from other people, objects and environment are received physically and physiologically through the five senses related to his age, gender and body conditions. The information is interpreted subjectively to its psychological and cognitive images associated with his personal preference, experiences, knowledge and cultural background. Some decisions are made based on his purpose of actions and his lifestyle. Then, specific behaviors, such as verbal and non-verbal responses, are activated and shown to the other people, objects and environment. "Kansei" is an important perspective for understanding personal preferences and giving suitable assistance to each person. This perspective is supported by the human-centered science and technology of "kansei engineering." This paper proposes the framework of Kansei modeling through unconscious behavior in interaction in living space to provide safe and stress-free living space.

Keywords: Kansei engineering · Affective engineering · Kansei modeling · Behavior log and analysis · Safe and stress-free livesphere

1 Introduction

Ubiquitous, mobile and wearable networks unified on the internet are rapidly embedded into our daily living sphere. That means people, unfamiliar to information technology and human computer interaction issue, are becoming a large part of the users of the unified information environment. Thus we need a new concept of information environment design which does not force a person to have and use any computer skills to manage his living space in safe and stress-free. Such an information

P.-L.P. Rau (Ed.): CCD 2016, LNCS 9741, pp. 574–583, 2016.
DOI: 10.1007/978-3-319-40093-8_56

environment would provide modest and human friendly manner for users including elderly people.

Information assistance services are mostly based on social recommendation by collaborative filtering of huge number of logs of many consumers, which do not cover the differences of personal taste of each consumer. To perform personalized information assistance we need effective method for collecting decision-making data of each person with various kinds of objects without forcing prompted interactions with electronic gadgets.

This paper introduces a concept of Kansei mechanism and its modeling method through unconscious interaction with unified information environment.

2 Kansei Modeling

Subjective feature of each user's requirement in information service can be schematically summarized as following [1];

(1) Intuitive perception process: A user may receive some impressions viewing objects. We assume such a process as physical, physiological, psychological and cognitive levels of interpretation. In this process, a portion of the graphical features of an object, such as its colors and their combination, textures and shape, is a dominant factor in his intuitive perception. We can statistically model these relationships between some graphical features of objects and their interpretations [2, 3].

(2) Subjective interpretation of situations: A user may show his intentional choice of assistance services according to his situation, such as time, place and occasion. Even if people physically sharing the same time, place, and occasion, each of them may feel different impression and may expect to receive different assist according to his life style and physical conditions. We assume such a process as physical, bottom-up multiple interpretation and top-down assistance-based levels of interpretation. We can model these relationships by statistical behavior log analysis.

(3) Knowledge structure of service domain: Novice users may only have restricted knowledge on a service domain, while the others have much and well organized. Such a difference means each user is expecting his own answer according to his knowledge base in his mind. We can formalize this kind of knowledge structure as ontology. We are also relating subjective concepts on feeling with some graphical features of objects.

(4) Feature of behavior pattern: A user often shows some specific behavior unconsciously according to his interest (or stress) on something; for instance, if he is interested in some goods, he often watches, touches and grasps them unconsciously to have a closer look at them. Thus, we can statistically analyze a degree of interest on objects by each person's behavior log [4–6].

(5) Tendency of decision making process: A person often makes his own decision pattern according to his view of life, which is originate from his intuitive perception process of objects and subjective interpretation process of situations,

which is compared with his knowledge base in his mind, and which cause the difference in his behavior pattern in taking an action.

We can schematically summarize such relationships as shown in Fig. 1.

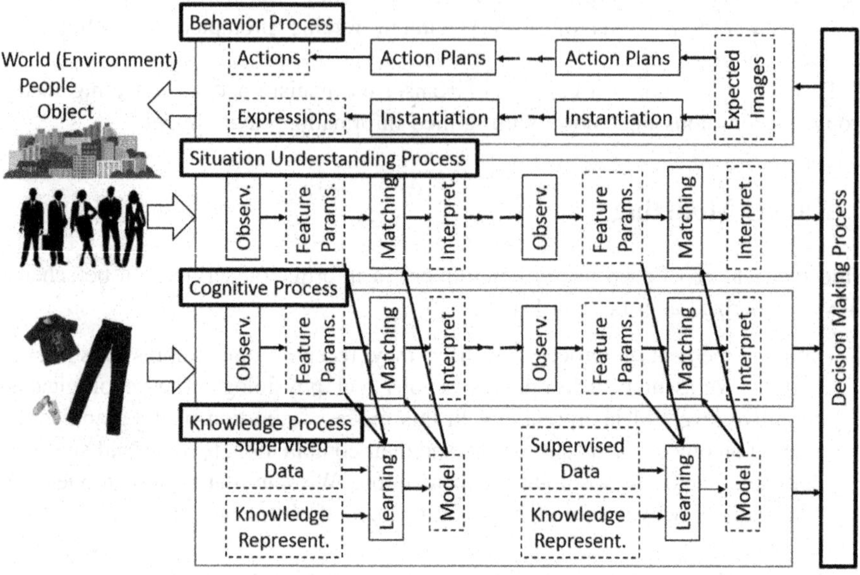

Fig. 1. Schematic model of Kansei [1]

Fig. 2. Micro, mezzo and macroscopic views

3 Personal Assistance Service Using Ubiquitous Environment

3.1 Kansei Modeling on Personal Preferences: Smart Sphere

Information assistance services, e.g., recommendation services, are mostly based on social recommendation by collaborative filtering of huge number of shopping logs of many consumers, which do not cover the differences of personal taste of each consumer. Otherwise a user has to register his preferring items which are referred as a template of the user's model. Such systems force their users to answer a huge number of questionnaires to describe the individual preferences. These make users feel much stress in information assistance service.

Our basic ideas are (1) to find user's interested and/or preferred items through observation on his behaviors in ubiquitous information environment, (2) to automatically build his preference model, and (3) to apply the model to provide suitable information service in the real world [9].

3.2 Micro, Mezzo and Macroscopic Observation

Utilizing ubiquitous sensors, we apply three observation methods to modeling each user's preferences, which are micro, mezzo and macroscopic observation methods as shown in Fig. 2.

(A) Microscopic view identifies a user by his ID tag as well as detects eye tracks by his facial image and some handling motions on some item by locally equipped cameras.
(B) Macroscopic view covers a location of each person in a room by a matrix of global view cameras equipped on the ceiling. It also covers the overall spatial allocation and density of the people as well as the items in the room.
(C) Mezzoscopic view extracts and traces each person's locations and behaviors as time series data both from microscopic and macroscopic views. It also manages personal behavior log database.

3.3 Indirect Interaction in Active Observation

To enforce answering a huge number of questionnaires on users is a bottleneck in modeling personal preferences. One idea is just taking their behavior log via ubiquitous sensors without asking them, and mining some specific features by statistical analysis. Such a method is called passive observation. The problem of this method is to require long time and huge personal log to cover enough behavior data.

Our idea is to show several messages to each user, i.e., applying active observation, without expecting direct answers. If a message is informative and interesting to a user, he may pay attention, gaze, and follow the suggestion according to the message. In this process he is freely behaving by his intention without feeling any enforcement to answer to the system. In this case, monitoring each user's behavior, i.e., responses to the messages, via ubiquitous sensors enables to attain enough behavior data effectively. This method corresponds to indirect interaction in active observation. The system can throw suitable and controlled messages to a user to build up his precise preference model without putting any stress on him. Thus, the system can statistically analyze a degree of interest on objects by each person's behavior log effectively without a huge number of questionnaires.

4 Experimental Prototype: Smart Shop

In the business field, finding consumers' preferences is an important issue. Point of sales systems are popularly used to detect the current consumers' preferences as well as store management.

We have been developing an experimental prototype system, Smart Shop, as typical application of personal information assistance in shopping context [7].

(1) Microscopic view devices: Each shelf is equipped with (a) an RFID tag reader to identify each consumer around there, (b) a facial camera to detect his face direction, (c) several item cameras to detect his behaviors related to the items, such as touching, grasping and wearing, and (d) several LCD monitors to show personal messages to him as well as to show public messages to the consumers.
(2) Macroscopic view devices: The ceiling of the shop is equipped with camera array to cover whole area without occlusion to detect a location of each consumer at each time slice.
(3) Smart shop servers: We have three types of database servers; which are (a) microscopic information servers to detect each behavior of the customer by image processing with his customer-ID by an RFID reader at each shelf, (b) a macroscopic server to integrate location data of consumers' from camera array by image processing at each time slice, (c) a mezzoscopic server to integrate personal behavior log data from microscopic servers and macroscopic server and to manage the behavior log database, (d) a preference model server to statistically analyze each customer's preferences from each of his behavior logs and to manage preference model database, and (e) a recommendation server to assist a customer in shopping.

We can expect that the consumer's preference may appear his behavior; for instance, the order "grasp > touch > watch > ignore" shows his interest. Our assumption is that we can construct his preference model on items by behavior analysis.

Nevertheless we should note that we cannot directly estimate consumer's preference form a single behavior itself. It should be evaluated all through his behavior log. It is because "shopping style" is roughly classified into two types; direct shopping type and survey type. For the former type, even a single touch shows a strong interest, while for the latter, a single touch is just one of them.

The system functions are as following;

(1) If a customer comes to a shelf, its microscopic server is activated and senses his RFID to identify.
(2) If he is interested in an item, he may stay there for a while to watch. If he is more interested in it, he may also touch and grasp it to have a closer look at it. Such a sequence can be detected by the ubiquitous cameras in the space. Thus, his personal behavior log is accumulated into the smart shop personal behavior log database.

(3) By statistical analysis on the frequency and total elapsed time of watch, touch and grasp of each item, we can judge the shopping style and finally estimate the preference of the consumer on the items in the shop.

Through this process and iteration, the system can build up and update each customer's preference model without forcing him to answer huge questionnaires.

5 Experiments for Kansei Modeling

5.1 Estimation of Dominant Attributes

We adopt conjoint analysis as to find the dominant attributes [8]. The sample products for the method are provided based on an orthogonal array. We analyze these products with quantification methods 1. The explanatory variables are the product attributes and the response variables are the degree of taste to the products estimated by the Smart Shop. As the result of the multiple regression analysis, the maximum $|t|$ value of each attributes are considered as the degree of dominant attributes and the maximum degree is considered as the best dominant attribute.

5.2 Method of Recommendation Considering Dominant Attributes

The Smart Shop recommends products based on each customer's taste when they stand in front of a digital signage device. They are recommended by order having high score as follows:

$$Score_p = \sum_{(a,v) \in p} \frac{V_a \times S_v \times D_a}{S \times N_v},$$

where p, a, and v are a product, an attribute, and an attribute value. V_a is a number of total attribute values the attribute a has. S_v is a number of times a customer chose products which has the attribute value v. D_a is a degree of dominant attributes of the attribute a. S is a total number of times a customer chose products. N_v is a number of products which have attribute value v. The taste degrees of each attribute value are obtained by D_a and the number of times a customer chose v. The scores of each product p are obtained by the total of the taste degree of each attribute falling under p.

We conducted an experiment to compare our implicit method by Smart Shop and previous explicit one by questionnaire. Subjects were 4 male students. The process is as follows:

1. A subject did shopping in Smart Shop. The products were 18 t-shirts selected randomly. The Smart Shop analyzed the subject's action data and estimated a formula of subject's action pattern.
2. The subject also did shopping in the Smart Shop. However the products were 18 t-shirts selected based on an orthogonal table. The Smart Shop estimated the taste degree of products and the degree of dominant attributes based on the action pattern formula.

3. The subject answered survey questions to evaluate the preference to the products with five phases (+2, +1, 0, −1, −2). We also estimated the degree of dominant attributes based on the answer.
4. Each recommendation products of the Smart Shop and the questionnaire data obtained by the degree of dominant attributes. Digital signage devices showed five of them based on the subject action for products. The subject evaluated the preference to the five recommendation products with five phases. This recommendation step was repeated 3 times and we got 15 product evaluations in total.

5.3 Active Observation for Quick Modeling of Dominant Attributes

In order to adopt active observation, we need stepwise estimation of preferred attributes through the temporal behavior log. In our experiment, we have simply applied rough set analysis to figure out the common attributes with column score and column index among items rather strongly interacted as "look," "touch" and "take" actions.

According to the highest attributes at each step, the system shows explanation message through a digital signage concerning the interacting item at the moment. If some attribute is important to the specific customer, such an attribute and its value enables him to decide the value for him, which strengthen the user's model. Otherwise the system reduces the score and index values of the attribute and its value for him.

6 Current Results and Discussions

6.1 Evaluation of Recommendation Method Considering Dominant Attributes

Table 1 shows the rates which evaluations estimated by Smart Shop have matched with user-given estimated values in questionnaire. The evaluations were divided into likes and dislikes. We separated into two cases; "like" and "dislike". Here, the estimation value 0 in the answer to a questionnaire may differ for each user. The estimation accuracies of subject A and B were more than 61 % in both case, however, it of subject C and D were less than 50 % in case that 0 is likes.

Table 2 shows the degree of dominant attributes estimated by Smart Shop or with questionnaire. The dominant attribute estimated by Smart Shop were matched with another estimated with questionnaire about subject A and B. Particularly about subject A, the order of dominance were also matched with another. The decimal place's difference about subject B suggests that Smart Shop can estimate the degree of dominant attributes more correctly than questionnaire. However, the dominant attributes of 2 methods were matched about subject C and D. These results may be caused by Smart Shop's estimation or questionnaire.

Table 3 shows the ratio which subjects liked the recommended products. All subject's results were more than 60 %. The results suggest Smart Shop with this study's method can provide stable satisfaction to each subject.

Recommended Products for subject A and B by Smart Shop were the same as another by questionnaire because both estimated dominant attributes were the same. On the other hand, those for subject C and D were not the same as another. Subject C rated the products recommended by Smart Shop less by 30 % than another although subject D rated them more by 6.7 %. These results indicate the need for review of the action pattern formula by Smart Shop.

Therefore we reviewed and optimized the action pattern formula of all subjects to maximize adjusted R-square. Some of the formulas have had unnecessary variables.

Table 4 shows the degree of dominant attributes estimated with optimized formulas

Table 1. Estimated rate of taste by Smart Shop's behavior observation

Subject	Like: +2 ~ 0 Dislike: −1 ~ −2	Like: +2 ~ +1 Dislike: 0 ~ −2
A	0.722	0.722
B	0.611	0.833
C	0.389	0.667
D	0.500	0.833
Average	0.556	0.764

Table 2. Dominant attribute rates of each subject ($|t|$ value)

Subject	Method	Color	Design	Shape
A	Smart Shop	0.434	**2.288**	1.929
	Questionnaire	0.569	**3.128**	2.560
B	Smart Shop	1.691	**2.938**	1.756
	Questionnaire	3.232	**3.555**	3.232
C	Smart Shop	**2.084**	0.849	1.443
	Questionnaire	2.410	2.410	**8.677**
D	Smart Shop	2.932	**4.962**	2.039
	Questionnaire	6.978	3.806	**8.881**

Table 3. Good evaluation rate in the recommendation

Subject	Smart Shop	Questionnaire
A	0.800	0.800
B	0.667	0.667
C	0.333	0.600
D	0.667	0.600

of Smart Shop. The optimized formula of subject C made his dominant attributes, estimated by Smart Shop, agree with another by questionnaire. Those of subject A, B

Table 4. Dominant attribute rates of each subject (re-estimate)

Subject	Method	Color	Design	Shape
A	Smart Shop	0.283	**1.794**	**1.794**
	Questionnaire	0.569	**3.128**	2.560
B	Smart Shop	1.693	**3.093**	1.685
	Questionnaire	3.232	**3.555**	3.232
C	Smart Shop	1.659	0.857	**1.671**
	Questionnaire	2.410	2.410	**8.677**
D	Smart Shop	2.932	**4.962**	2.039
	Questionnaire	6.978	3.806	**8.881**

and D were not changed. We can consider the product recommendation by Smart Shop is able to satisfy subject C well as another by questionnaire.

Finally, these results presented Smart Shop with our method attained implicit estimation of dominant attributes in 3 of 4 subjects. These also presented that, in the case of estimated dominant attributes by Smart Shop and another by questionnaire did not fit, it satisfied a subject better than modeling by questionnaire.

6.2 Evaluation of Active Observation for Quick Modeling of Dominant Attributes

In our current experiment in order to simplify the experiment process, the importance values of each item is directly assigned by the user. Step by step, the system updates estimated importance of attribute and its value and shows explanatory information on the display.

By the passive observation method, we needed randomly selected 200 items to build each user's preference model on attribute and its value in 80 % precision. By adopting active observation, we needed randomly selected only 60 items to build the same precision model. That shows the efficiency of the active observation. If the method is adopted with the passive observation mechanism in Smart Shop, it reduces the user's stress during behavior log acquisition and information recommendation as well.

7 Concluding Remarks

This paper proposed a concept of KANSEI modeling from the aspects of users' needs in information service. The key issue is to computationally describe human information processing process from these aspects; (1) intuitive perception process, (2) subjective interpretation of their situations, (3) knowledge structure of service domain, (4) feature of behavior pattern, and (5) decision making process. We should notice that these aspects are in the same framework of modeling in robotics field.

As a typical example of this idea, we had shown the estimation method of product dominant attributes for each customer through behavior observation in a retail store.

Also, we implemented the product recommendation system for experiments which recommends products based on each customer's dominant attribute estimated using Smart Shop.

Acknowledgment. The series of these studies are supported by KAKENHI, Japan Society for the Promotion of Science (JSPS), Grant-in-Aid for Scientific Research (S) 19100004, (A) 25240043, and are also supported by Kansei Robotics Research Center, Institute of Science and Engineering, Chuo University.

References

1. Kato, T.: KANSEI robotics: measurement and modeling of KANSEI from robotics aspect. J. JSAI **21**(2), 183–188 (2006). (in Japanese)
2. Kato, T.: Trans-category retrieval based on subjective perception process models. In: Proceedings of IEEE International Conference on Multimedia and EXPO, ICME 2004, June 2004
3. Takeda, Y., Kato, T.: Computational modeling of visual perception and its application to image enhancement. In: Proceedings of KEER 2010 (International Conference on Kansei Engineering and Emotion Research 2010), pp. 1763–1777, March 2010
4. Sea-Ueng, S., Pinyapong, S., Ogino, A., Kato, T.: Prediction of consumer's intention through their behavior observation in ubiquitous shop space. Kansei Eng. **7**(2), 189–195 (2008)
5. Imamura, N., Suzuki, H., Nagayasu, K., Ogino, A., Kato, T.: Modeling customer preferences for commodities by behavior log analysis with ubiquitous sensing. In: Proceedings of KEER 2010, pp. 1200–1213, March 2010
6. Ogino, A., Imamura, N., Kato, T.: Modeling of human interest in products by observing behaviors of customer in a store. In: Proceedings of KEER 2010, pp. 2072–2081, March 2010
7. Kato, T.: User modeling through unconscious interaction with smart shop. In: Stephanidis, C. (ed.) Universal Access in HCI, Part II, HCII 2011. LNCS, vol. 6766, pp. 61–68. Springer, Heidelberg (2011)
8. Yomo, A. et al: Estimation of important attributes of items in purchase process for personalized recommendation service. IPSJ SIG Technical reports 2012-HCI-147 (20), pp. 1–8 (2012) (in Japanese)
9. Tajima, T., Iida, Y., Kato, T.: Modeling preferences for commodities by active observation with unforced natural behavior of customers. In: Proceedings of HCI International 2013, pp. 466–474 (2013)

Connected and Open Platform-Based Approaches for Smart Car Service Design

Xiaohua Sun(✉), Tong Li, and Zexi Feng

College of Design and Innovation, Tongji University, 281 Fuxin Road, Shanghai, China
xsun@tongji.edu.cn, tjlittle@126.com, evan.work@icloud.com

Abstract. Smart Car Services refer to a rich variety of services for drivers or passengers that are brought to people in recent years through mobile Internet, car-to-car network, IOT, big data, and other technologies. Because of their relationship with cutting-edge technology, most of them are original by nature, and there lacks clear approaches for the design of this type of services. Based on the study of existing services and our own design practices, we propose in this paper two general approaches that together covers the majority of the space of smart car service innovation. We further proposed three perspectives to look at smart car services along with corresponding design methods for each of them. We also exemplify in detail the approaches and methods using our own design cases.

Keywords: Smart car service · Connected · Open platform

1 Introduction

With the development of digital technology, cars are acquiring more and more functionalities of mobile electronic devices rather than only as a tool for transportation. More and more services can now be developed to bring convenience to people's driving or riding of cars. We call in this paper this type of services brought to us by new technologies as smart car services. Currently, most of the efforts in smart car service design are either falling into individual application directions, such as car rental [3, 8, 10], or focused on the utilization of a specific technology, such as OBD [1, 4, 9]. There lacks an overall framework to help designers envision varieties of innovative services. We thus propose in this paper the Connected and Open Platform-Based approaches, which together construct a 3D coordinates for exploring different possibilities in smart car service innovation. We will introduce in detail in the following sessions: (1) the 3D framework formed by the two approaches, (2) three perspectives to interpret the concept of Connected, and (3) how each of them could be further augmented through opening up the data and control accessibility of a car to different services. We also use three of our design cases as examples to show how these approaches and associated methods could help with the initiation of new services.

P.-L.P. Rau (Ed.): CCD 2016, LNCS 9741, pp. 584–591, 2016.
DOI: 10.1007/978-3-319-40093-8_57

2 Connected and Open Platform-Based Approaches

People, Car, and Environment are three key components for constructing car services. For smart car service, the People component can be further expanded to people's digital life, and the Environment component can include not only the physical but also the digital environment encompassing people and cars. While delineating new car services, one could think from the direction of linking cars with each other, linking cars with people's digital life, and linking cars with rich services and data available in the digital environment. As illustrated in Fig. 1, this approach of connecting the key components with each other helps to form a plane that could cover all the potential relationships. On the other hand, for a specific car in the network, there are data at different levels of availability for the plane of service (e.g. entertainment information, environmental data, driver data, car position, interior and ambient setting, vehicle status, driving control, etc.). This could thus form another dimension perpendicular to the service plane and suggest potential features based on the property of data at different levels in sensing and controlling a car. Together, these two dimensions cover an innovation space with both the broadness of linking a car to all other types of components and the depth of sensing and controlling a car at different levels.

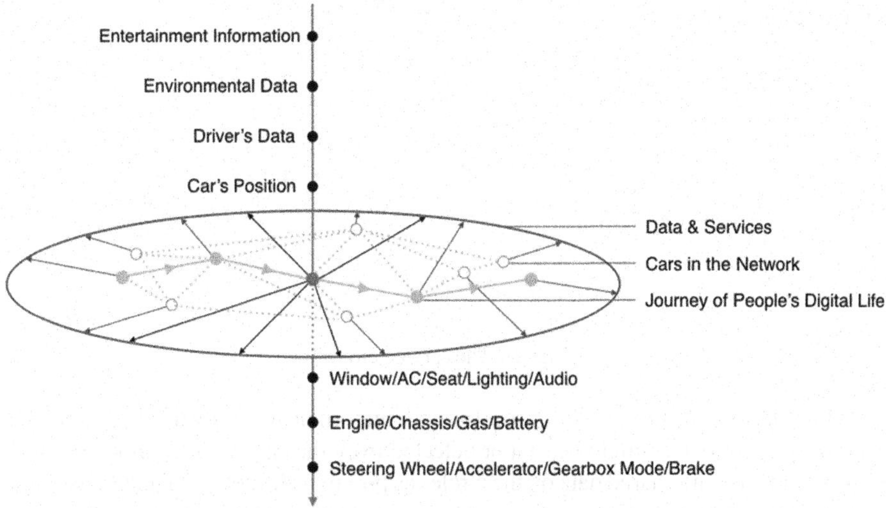

Fig. 1. The connected and open platform-based approaches

We here define those three types of linking a car to other components as the "Connected" approach and will explain in detail the characteristics and design methods of each type. For accessing the data and control of a car, it is normally through the "Open Platform-Based" approach, in which car companies develop an open platform through which third-party applications can sense and control a car to certain level. We will explain in later session how this possibility of in-depth accessing of a car can augment the possibilities brought by the "Connected" approach.

3 Three Perspectives for Interpreting the "Connected" Concept

The three ways of linking a car to other components in smart car service construction are indeed three perspectives for interpreting the same trend of connecting. There are thus overlaps in service features designed through each of them. However, they each bring to us a unique entry point to tackle the same problem. A set of methods can also be derived out corresponding to the characteristics of each of them.

3.1 Service Circle

When thinking from the angle of connecting a car to services and data available in the digital environment, one could resort to a circular structure (as shown in Fig. 2) with the car residing in the center and surrounded by the circles of services and shared data. The construction process could start from the car, either as an active request for service sent from the driver/passenger or as trigger for certain services based on information of the car or the driver detected by the system. When the request or trigger hit the circle of services, there could be one service respond to it (Fig. 2(b)), or multiple related services respond in synergy (Fig. 2(c)). It is also possible that one service would resort to data shared by other services and return to the user a more comprehensive and customized service feature.

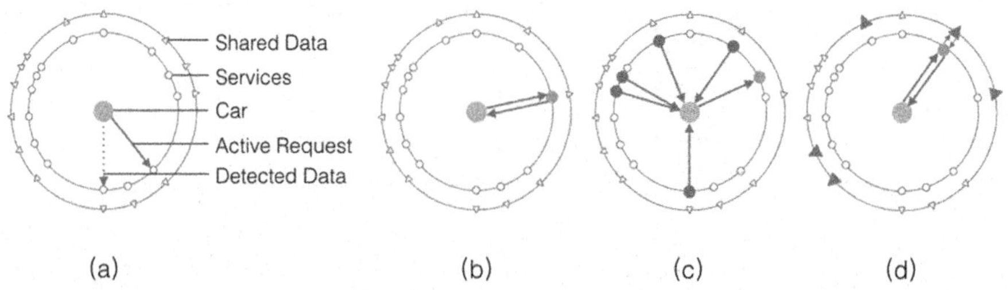

Fig. 2. The service circle

While designing through this process, it is important to go over all the possible requests or triggers that could be sent or detected from the car, and then link them with as many services and shared data on the circles as possible. After the driver or passenger receives the feedback, this procedure could be repeated for requests or triggers in the next steps. For example, when the driver or passenger in a car sends out the request to look for a restaurant for lunch, we can connect it with one or multiple on-line restaurant recommendation platforms, which could provide recommendations based on the car's location and the driver's former preferences. They can also resort to allergic information and dietary suggestion of the user shared by health-related platforms. After the restaurant is decided from the user side, this information would further trigger more services such as restaurant reservation, parking reservation, and recommendations for shopping in the adjacent areas.

3.2 Service Line

With its ever increasing level of smartness, the car is no longer only a driving tool for people, but is becoming a more and more important element in people's digital life. People may set the destination and turn on the AC of a car while at home, and may be advised to adjust their route based on activities in their to-do-list. It is also possible to have the AC at home turned on from the car on the driver's way back home.

In order to help better sort out the service potentials in this context of digital life, we propose to use a Service Line structure as coordinate to locate service features. As shown in Fig. 3, the structure includes a Service Line, an Action Line, and a Location Line. Since it is about people's digital life, the design process starts from defining the customer journey map by scenario, such as daily activities during weekdays or activities before, during and after traveling. For example, the journey map for daily activities may include getting up, going to work, grabbing lunch and stopping by the grocery store after work, etc. All the actions are then plotted on the Action Line by time. Considering of the fact that cars are directly associated with journey in the physical world, for the design of car services, a sequence of locations corresponding to the actions are further derived out and plotted on the Location Line (Those at which people is in the car are plotted as filled dots and those at which people is not with the car are plotted as circles). This Location Line is then used as coordinate for the identification of service features. Besides designing services by directly associating with a key location (such as home, office, restaurant, etc.), one could also consider the adjacent area of a key location (such as the surrounding area of a shopping mall) and derive related services (such as parking space reservation) when driving near the destination. It is also possible to identify on the Location Line city districts passed through which have rich service potentials (such as commercial districts) and define information push type of services that are not initiated from the user action.

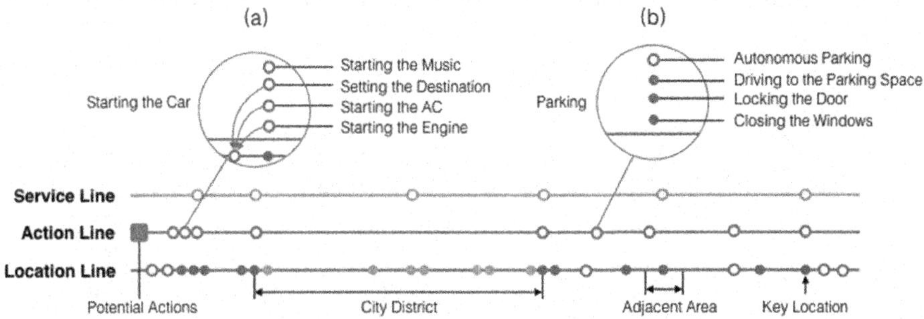

Fig. 3. The service line

Besides actions that could be plotted on the Action Line, there are also actions just put on a to-do-list by the user. Those are considered as potential actions that don't have specific locations to associate with. When deriving service features, these potential actions could be brought up at each location to see whether and how they could be associated with the location under consideration. For example, if the user has added the action of purchasing milk to his/her to-do-list, we may add to the service the function of reminding the user of the milk-purchasing task when he/she gets to a location with a grocery store in the adjacent area.

3.3 Service Network

Connecting cars with each other is similar to the process of forming a social network among them. We could thus carry out service design in this direction from in-depth study of nodes on the network and from thorough analysis of relationships that could be formed among them.

For the design of services, the node of a car could be looked at as a car by itself, or from the point of view of the driver or passengers in the car. Further study could be carried out over the information a car could provide and receive, the needs and behavior of the driver and passengers, etc. This information can then serve as the starting point for the construction of the service network. As shown in Fig. 4(a) connections could be formed between cars, drivers, passengers, and even between a car and the driver or passengers in another car. Designers could take social relationship (such as sharing, collaborating, game playing, etc.) for reference when coming up with possible types of relations to form the network. For example, cars could share sensorial data with each other for driving assistant purpose, they could also collaboratively collect, report, and form maps of road condition, traffic condition, etc. Drivers could share entertainment materials, sceneries, and traffic information with each other, they could seek help in the network when there are emergencies, they could also form a temporary chatting group with near cars when there is a heavy traffic jam. For passengers or even drivers, multi-player game, especially those associated with traveling environment or driving history, could be envisioned to make the driving experience more engaging. Designers could also take the social norms concept and apply it to the "society" of cars. For example, the car of a driver with bad driving behavior record may send out alert messages to near by cars (for ADAS or autonomous driving) or drivers (Fig. 4).

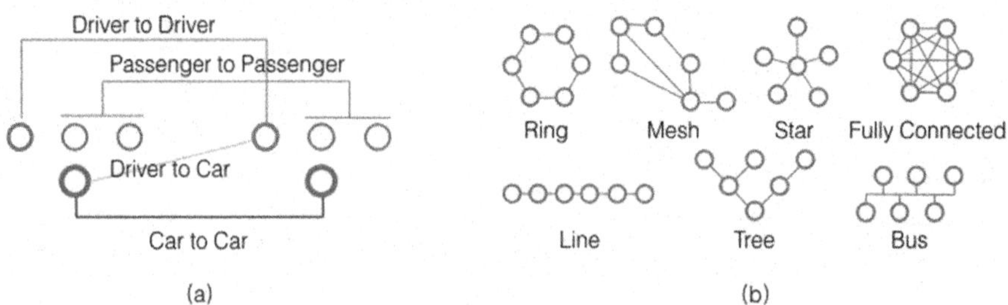

Fig. 4. Service network (mark the relationship)

Besides taking social network for reference semantically, during the construction of the network, the seven main topologies for computer networks (Fig. 4(b)) could also be taken as syntactic reference. They can help the designers to get a clear understanding of the characteristics of each type of topology and organize the network more systematically.

4 Augmenting the Service Through "Open Platform"

Encouraging and supporting users or third party developers to participate in the design and development of applications satisfying people's everyday needs for car services is a meaningful direction to go in order to bring to car applications the same level of richness as mobile apps. Many car companies build their Open Platform to support users to develop applications using the platform API and sense/control cars of their brand through the Open Platform. There are also public platforms, such as OpenXC [7] and CARGO [2], aiming at achieving the Apple Store effect in an even bigger scope. By installing their products, they enable users and developers to monitor data collected through on-board sensors and to develop applications through their platforms. Of course, for public platforms, to unlock hardware data, support and participation from automakers is very important. There are already platforms focusing on facilitating such collaborations. The Open Automotive Alliance (OAA) [5] comprised of leading automakers and technology companies has the aim of creating in collaboration opportunities for developers to deliver a more safe, intuitive, and seamless driving experience to users. OpenCar [6] offers API, toolset, and simulator for automakers, system integrators, and software developers to build apps on a uniformed platform.

Both the efforts by car manufactures and that by public platforms help to make vehicle data accessible for third-party developers and enable the delivery of services that would not be possible previously. People are now able to control car window, air conditioner, lighting, audio system, and even car engine remotely. It is also possible to intervening a car's speed and direction under different service conditions. For services designed through the three types of "Connected" approaches introduced in the above session, this Open Platform-Based approach could help to expand or augment them to a broader scope and to a deeper level.

While designing through the Service Circle approach, from one side, there are more types of data could be detected from the car, from the other side, the services we linked to on the circle are now empowered with the capability to control the car. They can now provide to the car functions not only in the form of information but also as actions taken over the car. For example, designers can now envision the function of linking the recent health data of a driver with the sensorial data of his/her current condition in the car and alert the driver, surrounding passengers, and even the health service providers when there are serious health conditions detected. The service can even stop the car remotely if necessary.

When working with the Service Line structure, what was considered as one action previously is now able to be split into multiple segments. Some of them, such as the parking part in Fig. 3(b), can be conducted autonomously and others still under the drivers' control if they wish. Also, after splitting a combo action into small segments, they can be linked to different points on the Location Line. As shown in Fig. 3(a), setting the destination, starting the AC, starting the engine, these three actions which are previously part of the action of starting a car, are now able to take place when people are still in their house.

For the Service Network of cars, when more data of a car are made available, the communication among them could reach a deeper level. Services previously made up of car-to-car information sharing can also be expanded to include emergency alert or other functions based on vehicle status data.

5 Design Cases

In a service system design project for recreational vehicles (RV), we followed the approaches and methods introduced above explicitly, and achieved a system with functions of rich varieties and covering many dimensions. For recreational vehicles that are supporting people's touring, the perspective of linking a car to useful services and data is an important direction to go. During the construction of the system, we first integrated Ma Feng Wo, a web platform for touring, to let users benefit from all the touring services it provides (touristic attractions, travel guide, travel program, hotels, ticket booking, tourism product) in one stop. We also bring to users information and services unique for traveling by recreational vehicles, such as information about the camping site, supply station, and rescue team, and services for customized navigation, themed route planning, route recommendation, RV community platform, and even RV radio station.

The perspective of linking cars with cars from their potential relationships also played an important role in helping us constructing the social community and especially the fleet touring part of the system. Users could form teams before departure through online platforms. One RV could also join a fleet close by on their way of heading towards the same destination. Different vehicles in a fleet can choose to play different roles in a team collaboration, e.g. head vehicle, tail vehicle, vehicle responsible to repairing, and vehicle providing nursing service. The head vehicle can share with others road conditions or front view of the sceneries. The system could support mutual chatting among all the vehicles in the fleet and support passengers from different vehicles to play games together with each other.

The Open Platform-Based approach also inspired us to introduce to the system a set of functions supporting the top-down management of all the vehicles belong to the platform. For example, the system could monitor hardware conditions of the vehicles, remind the driver timely when there is any abnormal vehicle status detected, and contact the nearest repairing and rescue site correspondingly. The system could also stop the vehicle when they are detected getting close to dangerous zones or getting too far away from the route they are suppose to take according to the rental contract.

Different from the top-down utilization of Open Platform in the example above, we experimented in another project the approach of assisting end users to make the most out of this mechanism. We developed an App using the API provided by the Open Platform of PSA to allow users to add IFTTT type of customized scenarios, e.g. turning the air conditioner on when the temperature in the car is above 25 degree, turning on the heater when temperature in the car is below 18 degree, switch the mode of ambient light, music, and fragrance according to the weather outside and the time of the day, etc.

The perspective of connecting the car with one's daily activities also inspired us in inventing another smart service providing scenario-based automatic setting adjustment. After the user synchronizes his/her personal schedule into the system, a sequence of scenario key points will be generated along with appropriate settings of air conditioning, music, lighting etc. according to the user's previous preference. All the settings will be executed over the journey to provide the user with a considering experience with smooth transitions.

6 Conclusions

We propose in this paper the connected and open platform-based approaches in the design of smart service for cars. Hope the analysis of the smart car services from the three main perspectives and their corresponding methods of design could be helpful for the invention of more innovative services. With the development of the technology, there will be more tools help to connect a car with other cars and with diverse data and services. More possibilities may also emerge in opening the data and control accessibility of a car to third-party applications, especially in the stage of autonomous or half-autonomous driving. However, the Open aspect would worth further research regarding driving safety, data security and many other issues. We will set this as the subject to focus on as the next step, studying the level to which people would like to open the data of their cars, under what conditions, and with what kind of expectation for return. This could help delineate the balance line in inventing open platform-based services.

References

1. Al-Taee, M.A., Khader, O.B., Al-Saber, N.A.: Remote monitoring of vehicle diagnostics and location using a smart box with global positioning system and general packet radio service. In: IEEE/ACS International Conference on Computer Systems and Applications. AICCSA 2007. IEEE (2007)
2. Cargo. http://www.cargo.ai
3. Ekiz, E.H., Bavik, A.: Scale development process: service quality in car rental services. Electron. J. Bus. Res. Methods **6**(2), 133–145 (2008)
4. Kim, M., Nam, J.-H., Jang, J.-W.: Implementation of smart car infotainment system including black box and self-diagnosis function. Int. J. Softw. Eng. Appl. **18**, 267–274 (2014)
5. Open Automotive Alliance (OAA). http://www.openautoalliance.net
6. OpenCar. http://www.opencar.com/about-us/
7. OpenXC. http://openxcplatform.com
8. Pachon, J., Iakovou, E., Chi, I.: Vehicle fleet planning in the car rental industry. J. Revenue Pricing Manag. **5**(3), 221–236 (2006)
9. Siegel, J., et al.: Vehicular engine oil service life characterization using On-Board Diagnostic (OBD) sensor data. In: IEEE SENSORS 2014, IEEE (2014)
10. Yang, Y., Jin, W., Hao, X.: Car rental logistics problem: a review of literature. In: IEEE International Conference on Service Operations and Logistics, and Informatics, IEEE/SOLI 2008, vol. 2. IEEE (2008)

Environment-Specific Smart Service System Design

Xiaohua Sun(✉) and Jintian Shi

College of Design and Innovation, Tongji University, 281 Fuxin Road, Shanghai, China
xsun@tongji.edu.cn, shijintian1017@126.com

Abstract. Specific environment provides a certain type of functional services, if we organize them in service design thinking, the services would be more systematic, comprehensive and reasonable. This paper puts forward ESSD that puts "Service" as core and essential mindset to construct the relationship among components in the whole system. The concept of ESSD will be elaborated in this paper in four steps: (1) Definition of ESSD; (2) What ESSD could do and how does it work; (3) Differences with PSSD (Product Service System Design) and its characteristics; (4) Characteristics of SESSD (Smart Environment Service System Design) where "Smart" is both augmentation and new approach to design.

Keywords: Environment · Smart service · Service system design · IOT · Big data

1 Introduction

Different types of environments have their core functional services. When designing architecture or space, designers usually take account of functions of the environment while not apply systematic design and construction to the service itself [1]. If it were possible for designers to design the functional services offered by specific environment from the perspective of service system, such as regarding hospital as a system for medical and doctoring services, we would establish an overall and optimized service system for different stakeholders involved [2]. To get systematic environment-specific service design approaches and mindset, in this paper we mainly put forward the concept of ESSD (Environment Service System Design) that is designing systematically and comprehensively for certain functional services in a specific space, holding the essential mindset of Service System Design, the process of ESSD. We also discuss about the differences between ESSD and PSSD (Product Service System Design), unique characteristics of ESSD, features of SESSD (Smart Service System Design) and their construction thinking which is capable of rationalizing relationships among services in a specific environment.

2 Working Principles of ESSD

ESSD is highly capable of helping effectively organize and coherently sort out related services of a specific environment. Usually a certain space is designed to arm with some conditions so that to create functional services for meeting our needs; ESSD could help

P.-L.P. Rau (Ed.): CCD 2016, LNCS 9741, pp. 592–599, 2016.
DOI: 10.1007/978-3-319-40093-8_58

us arrange all service components from fragments into a comprehensive entity in the mindset of service design, and further establish a rational environment-specific service system.

From the perspective of service design, ESSD takes overall account of each component in it: Firstly, ESSD makes several outlook visions for final service with some tools (e.g. mood board, positioning map, personas, etc.); then it settles down explicit service scenarios, puts forward offerings as many as possible and as detailed as possible, marks out relevant stakeholders and touch points for corresponding offerings. All offerings could be arranged into different sub-systems. The division could be according to management department, service type, property affiliation or other aspects. In each sub-system map, stakeholders could be connected with main touch points by offerings in form of various flow (information flow, material flow, financial flow, staff flow, etc.), which makes relationship more understandable. Finally, a comprehensive system map elaborates the overall structure, as well as user journey map developed by timeline could clearly illustrates continuous service procedure and involved touch points [3]. Additionally, the functional services in specific environment are supposed to link pre-service, in-service with post-service into a closed loop.

As shown in Fig. 1, some design tools and methodologies for ESSD are referenced from PSSD (Product Service System Design). PSSD develops a certain project by focusing on "Service" and then extending relevant network step by step, the same dose ESSD. Thus some tools for PSSD could be instructive to ESSD; while some of methodologies based on PSSD vary for ESSD.

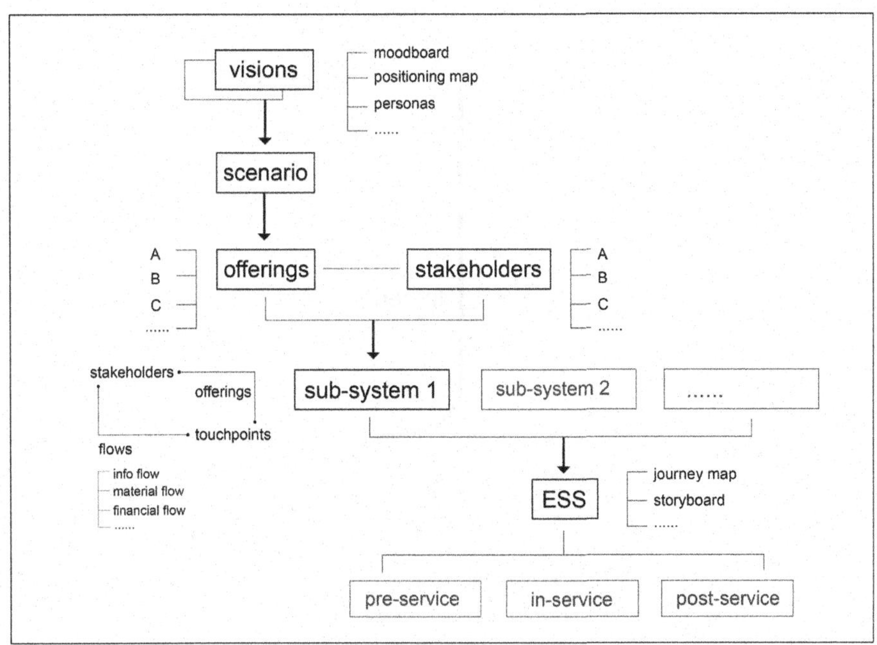

Fig. 1. Main procedure and design methodologies of ESSD

3 Characteristics of ESSD

As stated above, PSSD has provided much reference values for ESSD, while the latter also has its own unique features comparing with PSSD.

(1) The Social Tie Among Stakeholders in ESSD Gets Easier to be Strengthened. Since environment has bigger capacity both physically and virtually compared with products, more kinds of relationship could be created among different stakeholders in ESSD. Environment supplies people in it with diverse means to create diverse social relationship, like collaboration, temporary teambuilding, random competition, or one by one PK. The larger capacity of the environment also brings about more possibilities for design. In an environment, it is possible for numbers of people to simultaneously interact then connect with one specific space or an object in it. The mutual contagiousness between people and physical location gets to be stronger, a specific physical environment is capable of producing more implications for people's behaviors meanwhile people possess more reforming force to it.

As the above service system design for Imperial Street in Hangzhou in Figs. 2 and 3 developed by CDI (Center for Digital Innovation, Tongji University), the whole journey was connected with interlocking games or activities: for fulfilling game mission, a visitor has to collaborate with others to Cos-play; to get a coupon, visitors need to take active part in store games with retailers. Various kinds of positive interaction are helpful for strengthening social ties among stakeholders.

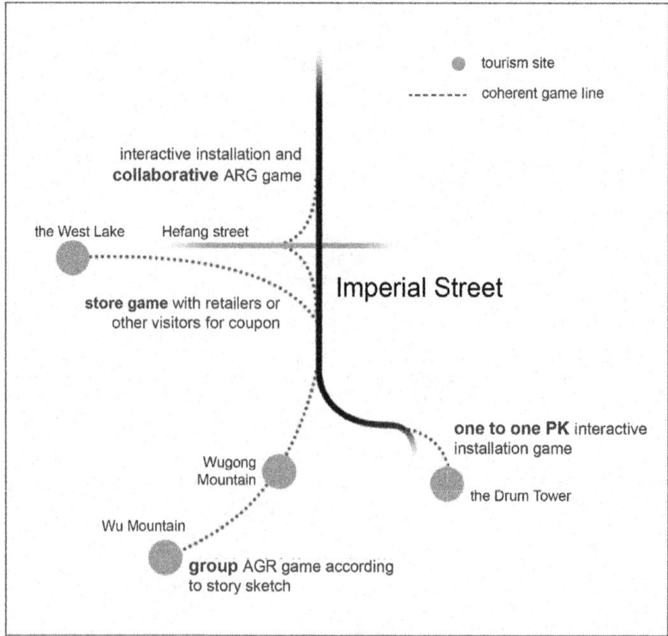

Fig. 2. Various types of social tie created by games of imperial street

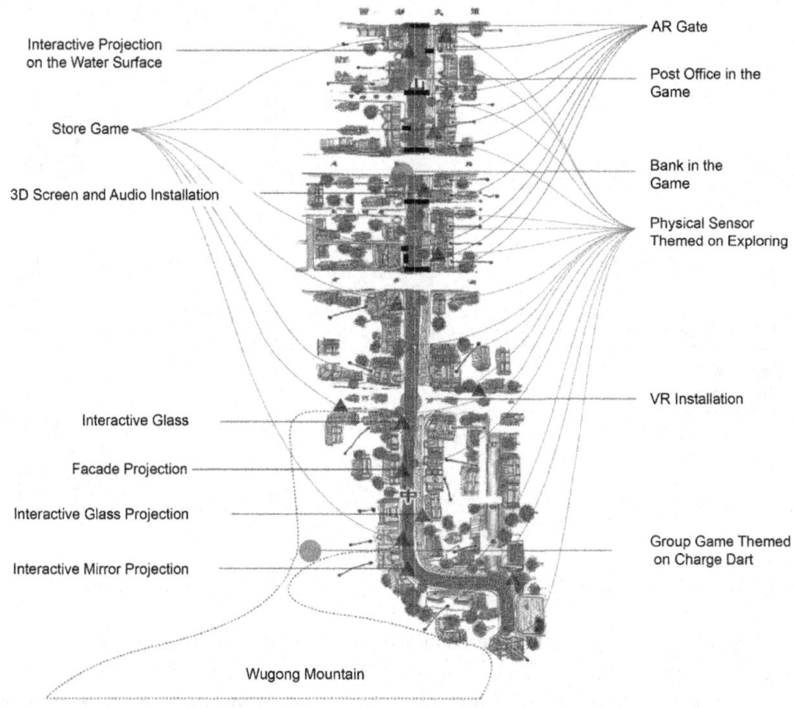

Fig. 3. Various forms of games designed in imperial street

(2) ESSD Holds Larger Base for Variation in the Environment. A specific environment could both enhance major functions and satisfy minor needs. It could hold a variety of touch points to give people more activity choices and more support to individual differences.

As illustrated in Fig. 4, Smart Lanxi designed by CDI offered citizens multiple activities in one environment at the same time: interactive screen tower made people enjoy visual amazement brought by new technology; LBS-social game helped youngsters make acquaintance with new friends efficiently; media theater provided the old with metrical local folk; stores organized various activities and customized information push to involve citizens on site. Many needs of citizens could be satisfied in one place.

(3) Long-Term Relationship with Users Gets Harder to Maintain. Due to high portability of product, once the relationship between users with products is established, this long-lasting and stable relationship begun to form, and even gradually has strengthened. While confined to space limitation, the relationship between users with a certain space weakens or even disappears with their leave, which requires ESSD to resort to various measures to build up and maintain long term relationship with users, such as member system, or community. In ESSD for Imperial Street, membership system is helpful for retailers and operators to keep in close touch with customers. The shipping

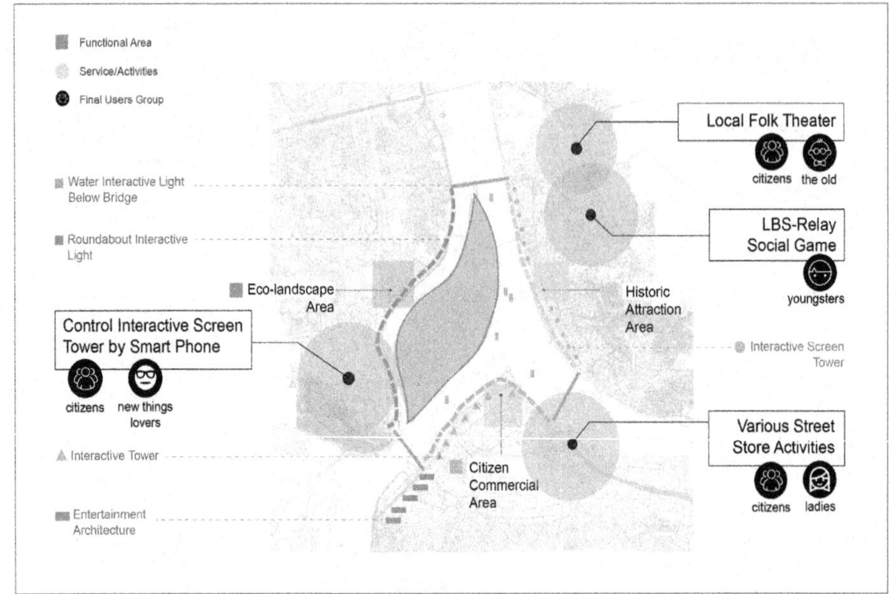

Fig. 4. Multiple activities offered in one place simultaneously in smart Lanxi

service, sales deputy, merchandise info push and game community all help to increase user agglutinant exceedingly.

(4) Effectiveness of Self-explanatory for Environment Need to be Enhanced. Unlike products which usually containing clear implications for their functions, services and values, environment is much insufficient in self-expressiveness. Therefore, ESSD has more needs for touch points to help people make the most of the space for their intentional services. In smart service system design for Shanghai No.10 People's Hospital by CDI, an AR digital way-finding system with HIS information integrated helps to provide doctoring service procedure, paths and destination info conveniently.

4 SESSD

With the radical breakthrough brought by new technologies, the role of digital technologies in ESSD has become more and more significant, and ESSD has gradually updated into SESSD (Smart Environment Service System Design). This requires us to pay attention to various context ingredients while treating and utilizing "Smart". The "Smart" in SESSD mainly refers to breakthrough advance created by new digital technologies, such as mobile Internet, IOT (Internet of Things), big data and so on. Additionally, "Smart" for SESSD in not only an enhancement but also a new dimension of design. SESSD has the following three "Connection"s as its characteristics that are also the entry points for design.

(1) Connecting Different Stakeholders Through Smart Touch Points. Touch points in ESSD refer to the points of certain service system users could contact, as well as key components providing the core services to users and making the whole system function. Mobile Internet, sensors, digital interactive installation or other smart touch points in SESSD act a vital role in communication between systems with their users. With its capability in information processing, the smart touch points could serve as linkage points in the formation of a rich network among various stakeholders. Users could keep in touch with others anywhere in anytime; operators could supply users more customized info push or services; collaborators could manage the system and communicate with each other more conveniently. Intercommunication network among different stakeholders keeps open, and this interconnection expands in more and more directions with the advancement of touch points.

In the SESSD case for an exhibition hall designed by CDI, as Fig. 5 below illustrates, as an important smart touch point, the smart phone App could effectively help visitors check event info, book tickets, submit feedback, communicate with exhibitors or 3rd party partner, and share visiting experience with other visitors. Other stakeholders (e.g. The management with exhibitors, or collaborators) could also build up direct communication more conveniently with the App.

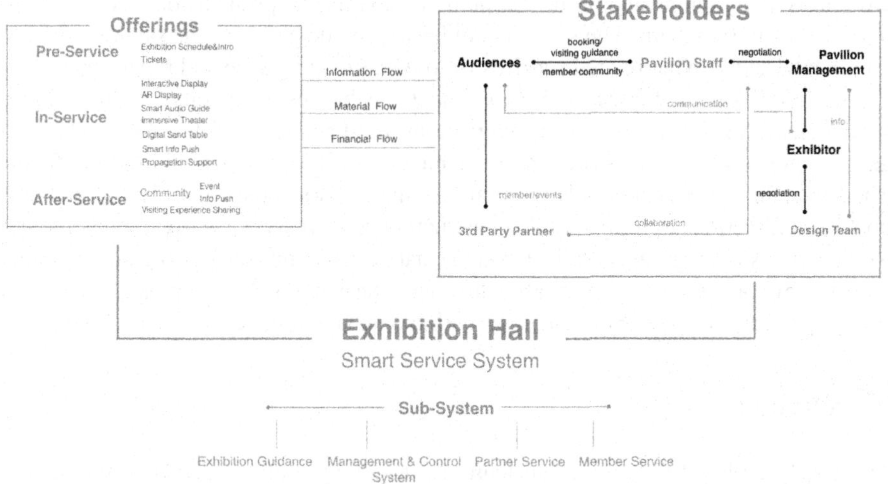

Fig. 5. Easier to connects different stakeholders about the hall by smart phone app

(2) Connecting the Physical with the Virtual through IOT. As important transfer flow, material flow and information flow individually stream as service carrier in ESSD. IOT (Internet of Things) could innovate in the form of flows—connect material flow with information flow, making every physical entity in SESSD be traceable and get informed of its own "story" in this digital information era.

Vegetables from smart farms [4] with IOT technology makes it possible for customers to be informed of their "personal ID", such as their hometown, age, "parents" (farmers) or health condition. Plantation and production procedure of the vegetables becomes transparent, accurate and evident. The connection of the physical and the virtual helps to form flows with dual properties and enhance the quality of the service in SESSD.

(3) Connecting the System with the Outside Information and Service Through Big Data. In ESSD, information flow is helpful to connect the internal system, linking various stakeholders, offerings, and sub-systems with each other. With the support of big data platform, information in ESSD could be further connected with the information and services out of the system, and enhance the quality of the services both in depth and in diversities.

CDI Soul, an office management and control system designed by CDI, makes the most of big data to provide users with quantities of "considerable and understanding" services. Once the platform got one user's data, this would not only open up his/her personal information channel, but also connect with more info resource from big data platform to optimize the service, e.g. when a VIP user getting close to the office building, the system would control the window, door, light, and air conditioner system to supply the user with the most decent indoor condition, according to the information combining personal preferences, schedules, health data, and external environment conditions from big data platform.

In a smart shopping service system designed by CDI, big data platform helps to get customers' daily online and offline shopping behaviors and push customized merchandise information to them. The system could also provide prices of the same product in other malls and provide related services for product maintenance and repairing.

New digital technology as a "Smart" impetus enhances the quality and diversity of services in SESSD, also opens up new directions for SESSD in the future; it is far beyond an intelligent tool, but is already an inevitable context for designers in different fields. The above three aspects not only illustrate the main characteristics of SESSD, but also points out directions to follow while constructing a smart service system: constructing a rich network among stakeholders through smart touch points; increasing quality of the offerings by connecting the information flow with the material flow; expanding the depth and scope of the services by connecting with the outside information and services.

5 Summary

This paper explored the definition, features, designing tools of ESSD (Environment Service System Design) and characteristics of SESSD (Smart Environment Service System Design) through four coherent steps. One of the goals of this research is how to show the importance of converting from design for a specific environment in material logic to design for a specific functional service in behavior logic for ESSD. We also aim at exploring the ways to apply potentials of new technologies on SESSD to enhance the overall quality of the services in design of the digital era. We hope our findings and design approaches could inspire more new forms of innovation in service system design.

References

Bieberstein, N., Bose, S., Fiammante, M., Jones, K., Shah, R.: Service-Oriented Architecture Compass: Business Value Planning, and Enterprise Roadmap. Prentice Hall, Upper Saddle River (2005)

Vezzoli, C.: Product-Service System Design for Sustainability, pp. 147–159 (2011)

Service Design Methodologies. http://www.servicedesigntools.org/

Smart Farming. http://www.hesitan.com/cc?ID=rdsf_02,29890&url=_print

Older Drivers' Acceptance of Vehicle Warning Functions and the Influence of Driving Experience

Lin Wang(✉)

Department of Library and Information Science,
Incheon National University, Incheon, South Korea
wanglin@inu.ac.kr

Abstract. Warning functions in vehicles can be very useful to older drivers for avoiding crashes due to failure to perceive the danger of a situation. This study investigated older drivers' acceptance of vehicle warning functions and the influence of driving experience. The results indicated that, in general, the perceived importance of external environment warnings is significantly higher than the perceived importance of car status warnings and driver condition warnings to older drivers. However, driving experience significantly influences the perceived importance of warning functions. With increasing driving experience, both the perceived importance of external environment warnings and the perceived importance of car status warnings significantly decrease. There is no decrease in the perceived importance of driver condition warning functions.

Keywords: Older drivers · Driving experience · Vehicle warning functions

1 Introduction

It was estimated that if the current traffic fatality rate for older people continues, especially as baby boomers reach their golden years, the number of older-occupant fatalities could approach nearly 20,000 per year in the U.S. in the near future. This is almost equal to the annual number of deaths caused by drunk driving on the nation's highways [1]. Declines in both physical and cognitive abilities due to aging create several problems for older drivers while driving. It was found that 60 % of the crashes involving older drivers were due to "informational" causes, such as failure to perceive the danger of a situation or failure to respond appropriately to a dangerous situation [2]. With the developments in sensing and information technologies, warning functions in vehicles can be very useful to provide full-scale information about the external environment, vehicles, and even drivers themselves. The warning messages would help older drivers perceive the danger of a situation.

This research studied older drivers' perceived importance of the vehicle warning functions and investigated the correlation between driving experience and the perceived importance of the warning functions. The research findings are expected to be useful to designers and researchers investigating older drivers.

P.-L.P. Rau (Ed.): CCD 2016, LNCS 9741, pp. 600–607, 2016.
DOI: 10.1007/978-3-319-40093-8_59

2 Literature Review

Because of aging effects, older adults often experience many difficulties while driving. Vision impairment is one of the most important causes of driving difficulties of older adults [3]. The types of vision problems of older drivers reported include reduced visual field, reduced vision at night or in dim light, and reduced ability to visually define and separate objects [4]. Reduced muscle strength, endurance, flexibility, and motor speed also influence driving abilities [5]. For example, reduced neck rotation may impair the driver's ability to turn their head to see relevant stimuli in their periphery, which is necessary for safe driving in complex traffic situations and when changing lanes [5]. Besides the physical aging effects mentioned above, cognitive aging effects also influence driving abilities significantly. For example, older drivers often have difficulty dealing with unexpected situations due to the decrease in perceptual speed and reaction time [6]. A few aging effects and their influence on driving abilities are summarized in Table 1.

Table 1. Aging effects and their influence on driving ability

Aging effects	Influence on driving ability
Reduction in visual acuity and contrast sensitivity [7, 8]	Reduced ability to visually define and separate objects [4, 9–11]
Reduced ability to see at night [12, 13]	Reduced ability to see objects at night, dusk, or in dim light [4, 14]
Increased glare sensitivity [7]	Difficulty when driving into the sun or other glare [14]
Reduced visual field [4, 15, 16]	Higher accident rate in situations involving left turns, intersections, and overtaking [17]
More susceptible to fatigue [18]	Not suitable for long-distance driving or driving in very hot or cold weather [19]
Reduction in muscle strength, endurance, flexibility, and motor speed [5, 20, 21]	Reduced neck rotation may impair the ability of the driver to turn their head to see relevant stimuli in their periphery, necessary for safe driving in complex traffic situations and when changing lanes [5]
Decrease in perceptual speed and reaction time [6, 22, 23]	The speed at which visual information is processed is an important factor for successfully negotiating difficult or dangerous traffic situations [5]
Spatial ability loss [24, 25]	At risk of multiple-vehicle involvement at intersections [4]
Executive ability loss [26]	Difficulties occur at the level of executive function given that the types of crashes in which older adults are involved often occur in complex traffic situations [5]

Vehicle warning functions can be useful to older drivers whose perception abilities have declined because of aging. Vehicular crashes are often influenced by three factors —the environment, the vehicle, and the driver [27]. Warning functions can also be divided into external environment warnings, driver condition warnings, and car status warnings. External environment warnings include warnings of dangers outside the vehicle such as forward collision warning and pedestrian warning. Driver condition warnings are warnings about the drivers themselves such as fatigue warning systems. Car status warnings are warnings of vehicles such as car status check systems. This study sought to determine the type of warning function that was perceived to be the most important by older drivers. The study also investigated whether driving experience would influence the perceived importance of the warning functions. There were two research questions in this study:

Research question 1: How do older drivers rate the three types of warning functions?

Research question 2: Would their driving experience have an influence on their rating?

3 Method

A survey was used as the research method to investigate older drivers' rating of the three types of warning functions and the relation between their driving experience and acceptance of different warning functions. The seven-point Likert scale was used to measure the perceived importance of each warning function.

3.1 Questionnaire Preparation

The questionnaire consisted of two parts. The first part collected the demographic and driving experience information of the subjects. The information pertaining to demographics included subjects' age, gender, education level, current occupation, driving experience, and frequency of driving. The second part investigated the perceived importance of the warning functions. The subjects were asked to rate the extent to which they agreed with the statements that followed.

Statements of external environment warning functions:

- Danger warning system is important to me.
- Pedestrian warning and braking system is important to me.

Statement of driver condition warning functions:

- Fatigue warning system is important to me.
- Driver condition warning system is important to me.

Statement of car status warning functions:

- Car status warning system is important to me.
- Lane departure warning system is important to me.

3.2 Subjects and Survey Details

Older drivers between 55 and 75 years of age who had a driving experience of more than one year could participate in the survey. A total of 163 subjects participated in the study including 118 males and 45 females. The average age of the subjects was 60.9 y (SD = 5.4 y). The average driving experience was 27.6 y (SD = 10.3 y). 107 subjects drove their cars almost every day, 36 subjects two to three times per week, and 20 subjects less then or approximately once per week. 118 subjects had high school or secondary school education, 43 subjects had bachelor or college degrees, and 2 subjects had masters or higher degrees.

3.3 Survey Conduction

The survey was conducted at transportation centers, taxi companies, and senior centers. Paper-based questionnaires were distributed in person by a research assistant. First, the research assistant provided a brief description of the research. Then, if the older drivers agreed to participate in the study, they were asked to sign an informed consent form and fill the questionnaire. After they finished the questionnaire, they could receive a token compensation worth $5 such as bread and milk.

4 Result

The ANOVA test was used to investigate the differences of the perceived importance of different types of warning functions to older drivers. The testing results showed that there was a significant difference between the ratings for external environment warnings and those for driver condition warnings. Moreover, there was a significant difference between the ratings for external environment warnings and those for car status warnings. The perceived importance of external environment warnings was 7.1 % and 5.3 % higher than that of driver condition warnings and car status warnings, respectively. Detailed data and p values are shown in Table 2.

Table 2. Comparison of the importance of external environment warning, driver condition warning, and car status warning to older drivers.

Variable 1	Variable 2	P value
External environment warning Mean = 6.0 SD = 1.01	Driver condition warning Mean = 5.6 SD = 1.19	0.002*
External environment warning Mean = 6.0 SD = 1.01	Car status warning Mean = 5.7 SD = 1.08	0.022*
Driver condition warning Mean = 5.6 SD = 1.19	Car status warning Mean = 5.7 SD = 1.08	0.377

Further, the influence of driving experience on the perceived importance of different types of warning functions was investigated. Correlation analysis was used to study the relationship between driving experience and the perceived importance of the warning functions. First, correlation analysis was used to test the relationship between driving experience and the perceived importance of external environment warnings. The testing result found a significant negative correlation (Pearson correlation = −0.216, p = 0.007). It meant that the perceived importance of external environment warnings significantly decreased with increasing driving experience. Further, there was a significant negative correlation between driving experience and the perceived importance of car status warnings (Pearson correlation = −0.207, p = 0.009), which meant that the perceived importance of car status warnings significantly decreased with increasing driving experience. There was no significant correlation between driving experience and the perceived importance of driver condition warnings (Pearson correlation = 0.017, p = 0.830).

In order to have an intuitive understanding of how these three variables changed with driving experience, linear regression was performed between these variables and driving experience. As shown in Fig. 1, with increasing driving experience, the perceived importance of external environment warnings and car status warnings significantly decreased. It meant that for experienced older drivers, the perceived importance of external environment warnings and car status warnings was not as important as for relatively inexperienced older drivers. On the contrary, there was no significant decrease in the perceived importance of driver condition warnings with increasing driver experience. This meant that for older drivers with different amounts of driving experience, driver condition warnings were equally important. For relatively inexperienced older drivers, the driver condition warning was still significantly less important than external environment warnings and car status warnings; however, with increasing driving experience, the driver condition warning was as important as the other two types of warnings.

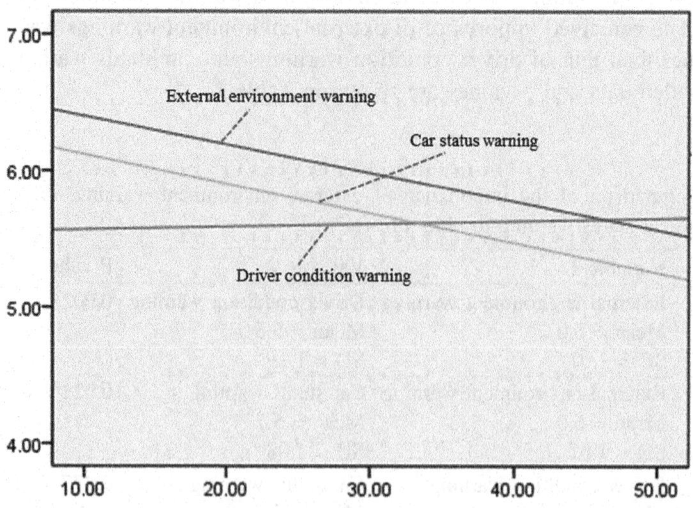

Fig. 1. Output graph of linear regression between the scores of warning functions and older drivers' driving experience.

5 Discussion

This study investigated older adults' acceptance of different vehicle warning functions and the influence of driving experience on the acceptance. The study results indicated that, in general, the perceived importance of external environment warnings is significantly higher than the perceived importance of car status warnings and driver condition warnings to older adults. Owing to declines in perceptive abilities and speed, the external environment warning is very important for them. About 60 % of crashes involving older drivers were due to "informational" causes such as failure to perceive the danger of a situation or failure to make an appropriate response to a dangerous situation [2]. It is essential to ensure information accuracy as older drivers' perception of the external environment is very important.

Also, the results indicated that driving experience significantly influences the perceived importance of warning functions. With increasing driving experience, both the perceived importance of external environment warnings and perceived importance of car status warnings significantly decreased. However, there was no decrease in the perceived importance of driver condition warning functions. The literature suggested that with practice, drivers learn where to search for relevant information and respond to it more quickly [28, 29]. Experienced drivers look at the road farther ahead than novices [30]. For experienced older drivers, the perceived importance of external environment warnings and car status warnings were found to be lower than that for relatively inexperienced older drivers. However, the importance of driver condition warnings does not change for both experienced and novice older drivers. Recently, researchers have begun to investigate and develop technologies to monitor the vital signs of older drivers. For example, Walter et al. investigated embedded measurement techniques for non-contact monitoring of vital signs, including capacitive electrocardiogram monitoring (cECG), mechanical movement analysis (ballistocardiogram, BCG) using piezo-foils, and inductive impedance monitoring [31]. Older drivers may be easily tired and may feel sleepy owing to the effects of medication. Moreover, their health condition may suddenly deteriorate owing to health problems such as hypertension and heart disease. Monitoring of driver function and driver condition warnings could help prevent crashes to some extent.

The subjects' past exposure to the warning functions, which may have had an influence on their ratings, was not investigated; this is a limitation of this study. In future studies, more warning functions should be studied with a more detailed description of each function.

References

1. Burkhardt, J.E., Berger, A.M., Creedon, M.: Mobility and Independence: Changes and Challenges for Older Drivers. Ecosometrics, Bethesda (1998)
2. Fell, J.C.: A motor vehicle accident causal system: the human element. Hum. Factors: J. Hum. Factors Ergon. Soc. **18**, 85–94 (1976)

3. Owsley, C., Ball, K., Sloane, M.E., Roenker, D.L., Bruni, J.R.: Visual/cognitive correlates of vehicle accidents in older drivers. Psychol. Aging **6**(3), 403 (1991)
4. Preusser, D.F., Williams, A.F., Ferguson, S.A., Ulmer, R.G., Weinstein, H.B.: Fatal crash risk for older drivers at intersections. Accid. Anal. Prev. **30**(2), 151–159 (1998)
5. Anstey, K.J., Wood, J., Lord, S., Walker, J.G.: Cognitive, sensory and physical factors enabling driving safety in older adults. Clin. Psychol. Rev. **25**(1), 45–65 (2005)
6. Salthouse, T.A.: The processing-speed theory of adult age differences in cognition. Psychol. Rev. **103**(3), 403 (1996)
7. Haegerstrom-Portnoy, G., Schneck, M.E., Brabyn, J.A.: Seeing into old age: vision function beyond acuity. Optom. Vis. Sci. **76**(3), 141–158 (1999)
8. Wang, L., Sato, H., Rau, P.L.P., Fujimura, K., Gao, Q., Asano, Y.: Chinese text spacing on mobile phones for senior citizens. Educ. Gerontol. **35**(1), 77–90 (2008)
9. Wang, L., Rau, P.L.P., Salvendy, G.: Older adults' acceptance of information technology. Educ. Gerontol. **37**(12), 1081–1099 (2011)
10. Wang, L., Rau, P.L.P., Salvendy, G.: A cross-culture study on older adults' information technology acceptance. Int. J. Mobile Commun. **9**(5), 421–440 (2011)
11. Li, H., Rau, P.L.P., Fujimura, K., Gao, Q., Wang, L.: Designing effective web forms for older web users. Educ. Gerontol. **38**(4), 271–281 (2012)
12. Rubin, G.S., Roche, K.B., Prasada-Rao, P., Fried, L.P.: Visual impairment and disability in older adults. Optom. Vis. Sci. **71**(12), 750–760 (1994)
13. Freeman, E.E., Munoz, B., Turano, K.A., West, S.K.: Measures of visual function and their association with driving modification in older adults. Invest. Ophthalmol. Vis. Sci. **47**(2), 514–520 (2006)
14. Wood, J.M., Lacherez, P.F., Anstey, K.J.: Not all older adults have insight into their driving abilities: evidence from an on-road assessment and implications for policy. J. Gerontol. Series A: Biol. Sci. Med. Sci. **68**, 559–566 (2013)
15. Asano, Y., Saito, H., Sato, H., Wang, L., Gao, Q., Rau, P.L.P.: Tips for designing mobile phone web pages for the elderly. In: Jacko, J.A. (ed.) Human-Computer Interaction. Interaction Design and Usability, pp. 675–680. Springer, Heidelberg (2007)
16. Ball, K., Rebok, G.: Evaluating the driving ability of older adults. J. Appl. Gerontol. **13**(1), 20–38 (1994)
17. Stalvey, B.T., Owsley, C.: Self-perceptions and current practices of high-risk older drivers: implications for driver safety interventions. J. Health Psychol. **5**(4), 441–456 (2000)
18. Summala, H., Mikkola, T.: Fatal accidents among car and truck drivers: effects of fatigue, age, and alcohol consumption. Hum. Factors: J. Hum. Factors Ergon. Soc. **36**(2), 315–326 (1994)
19. Brenton, M.: The Older Person's Guide to Safe Driving. Public Affairs Pamphlet No. 641. AAA Foundation for Traffic Safety, Falls Church (1986)
20. Hawthorn, D.: Interface design and engagement with older people. Behav. Inf. Technol. **26** (4), 333–341 (2007)
21. Hawthorn, D.: Possible implications of aging for interface designers. Interact. Comput. **12** (5), 507–528 (2000)
22. Wang, L., Sato, H., Jin, L., Rau, P.L.P., Asano, Y.: Perception of movements and transformations in flash animations of older adults. In: Jacko, J.A. (ed.) Human-Computer Interaction. Interaction Design and Usability, pp. 966–975. Springer, Heidelberg (2007)
23. Sato, H., Fujimura, K., Wang, L., Jin, L., Asano, Y., Watanabe, M., Rau, P.L.P.: The impact of moving around and zooming of objects on users' performance in web pages: a cross-generation study. In: Jacko, J.A. (ed.) Human-Computer Interaction Interaction Design and Usability, pp. 921–928. Springer, Heidelberg (2007)

24. Myerson, J., Hale, S., Rhee, S.H., Jenkins, L.: Selective interference with verbal and spatial working memory in young and older adults. J. Gerontol. Series B: Psychol. Sci. Soc. Sci. **54** (3), P161–P164 (1999)
25. Schaie, K.W., Willis, S.L.: Psychometric intelligence and aging. In: Perspectives on Cognitive Change in Adulthood and Aging, pp. 293–322. McGraw Hill, New York (1996)
26. Bryan, J., Luszcz, M.A.: Measurement of executive function: considerations for detecting adult age differences. J. Clin. Exp. Neuropsychol. **22**(1), 40–55 (2000)
27. Marshburn, E.G.: Beyond human factors: examining the underlying determinants of recreational boating accidents with spatial analysis and modeling (2014)
28. Summala, H., Lamble, D., Laakso, M.: Driving experience and perception of the lead car's braking when looking at in-car targets. Accid. Anal. Prev. **30**(4), 401–407 (1998)
29. Theeuwes, J., Hagenzieker, M.P.: Visual search of traffic scenes: on the effect of location expectations. Vis. Veh. **4**, 149–158 (1993)
30. Mourant, R.R., Rockwell, T.H.: Strategies of visual search by novice and experienced drivers. Hum. Factors: J. Hum. Factors Ergon. Soc. **14**(4), 325–335 (1972)
31. Wartzek, T., Eilebrecht, B., Lem, J., Lindner, H.J., Leonhardt, S., Walter, M.: ECG on the road: robust and unobtrusive estimation of heart rate. IEEE Trans. Biomed. Eng. **58**(11), 3112–3120 (2011)

Services, Appearances and Psychological Factors in Intelligent Home Service Robots

Hsiu-Ping Yueh[1,2] and Weijane Lin[1,2(✉)]

[1] Department of Bio-Industry Communication and Development, National Taiwan University, No. 1, Sec. 4, Roosevelt Road, Daan District, Taipei 10617, Taiwan, ROC
yueh@ntu.edu.tw

[2] Department of Library and Information Science, National Taiwan University, No. 1, Sec. 4, Roosevelt Road, Daan District, Taipei 10617, Taiwan, ROC

Abstract. This study conducted a questionnaire survey to investigate the requirements and preferences toward the services and appearance of home service robot. And the psychological factors regarding human robot interaction, including likability, sincerity, trust and privacy were explored and discussed. The preliminary results show that functions of house chores, security and emergency detecting were highly expected and preferred by 267 participants. While the social and caretaking/nursing functions were not preferred as expected. The participants liked medium size robots without too many facial features. Hands and arms that extended human reach were more valued than legs and wheels that substitute human movement. Participants also valued the interface of response and information, such as the body screen on the robot. Psychological factors of likability, sincerity, trust and privacy correlated with each other significantly, and were also related to the preference of robot appearance. This study takes a clear profile of the users' expectation on future home intelligent service robots.

Keywords: Intelligent service robot · Human-robot interaction · Home service robot

1 Introduction

The rapid development of robots has not only speed up the implementations in industries but also in our daily life environment. Features of autonomous systems intelligence, social systems intelligence and augmentation of human beings have gained much attention in the design and development of intelligent service robot [1, 2]. However, technological use and affordance today have changed and transformed in a significant way, and the perspective toward the intelligent service robots in home environment are different. Therefore, this study aims to investigate users' attitude towards the home intelligent service robots, including the services, outfits and the psychological factors in human robot interaction. And the necessary requirements of home service robots are constructed. Through the multidimensional investigation, users' needs and the relationship of HRI factors with the robots appearance are discovered for designing attractive and trustable robots.

P.-L.P. Rau (Ed.): CCD 2016, LNCS 9741, pp. 608–615, 2016.
DOI: 10.1007/978-3-319-40093-8_60

2 Research Design

The survey plans to figure the attitudes and expectations toward home ISRs in services, appearances, and human robot interactions (HRIs). Questionnaire was designed into 6 parts according to the three aspects of expectations and one portion of personal information. Part 1 was the personal information. It included the surveyors' nationality, age, gender, major, and buying behavior. In the buying behavior, we investigated their buying tendency (how long would you buy new products after they had been sold), having any home ISR and the satisfaction about it, and the willingness to own any home ISR in the future. While users' background and direct using experiences might affect their attitude toward intelligent service robots, indirect experiences such as users' buying intensions and use of homogeneous products may also affect their perspectives toward home service robots. The second part of the survey investigated the requirement about the services carried out by intelligent service robots at home. Six-points scale was used to evaluate 18 services in each. The higher score was the higher requirement for that service, and participants' perceived importance of each function was collected and analyzed.

The third part of the survey investigated the style traits, body structures, and size about the appearance of intelligent service robots. In style traits, 8 questions of semantic differential scale were used to collect participants' opinions about how the intelligent service robots should look like. The participants also expressed how comfortable they would feel toward different types of service robots with a seven-points scale. Six kinds of body structures were asked through two alternative responses method. In each question, participants chose one kind of structures they liked. Finally, they were asked to circle the favorite size of robots.

The survey also collected participants' opinions of human robot interaction, likability, sincerity, and trust and privacy in specific. Six points scale was used to evaluate the degree of agreeableness. The higher score was the higher agreeableness. Likability is a positive emotion toward a personal attractive trait. In order to figure out how the robot should be in their attractiveness, the scale we used was modified from Rau's in 2009 [3]. The calculated Cronbach's α for likability in our study is 0.88. Sincerity represents the true heart in a human interaction. We developed 11 questions in the sincerity factor and Cronbach's α is 0.90. The trust and privacy was evaluated whether the robot was believable and trustworthy. The scale also referred from Rau's report [3]. In this study, the Cronbach's α for trust and privacy is 0.86. The more likability, the more sincerity and trustee would be assessed. The three HRI components should highly correlate to each other.

The final part of the survey investigated participants' acceptance toward the intelligent service robots in the future. We asked the participants to prioritize their preferences among entertainment robots, assistant/servant robots, social companion robots, caretakers/nurse robots, labor service robots, safety/security robots, information providing robots and remotely accessed robots. We also asked how much money would you spend on purchasing robots and when will you purchase it. One open question was addressed to describe the other ideas about home intelligent service robots.

3 Preliminary Findings

By ruling out the missing responses, 267 valid responses were used for further analysis. The following session reported the preliminary findings including the descriptive statistics of participants' preferences of intelligent service robots, and the relationship between participants' features and their attitudes toward the service robots.

3.1 Participants' Expectation Toward the Services of Home Robots

Among the 267 participants, 54 % were females and 46 % were males. And their ages ranged from 18 to 35 years old. The portions of age under 18 was 17 %, 19 to 25 was 79 % and 26 to 35 was 3 %. Most of the participants did not have any home intelligent service robots (98 %). The buying tendency for new products, 20 % would buy them after they sold in several months, 65 % was after one year and 15 % was above 2 years. When we asked the willingness to own any home service robots, 57 % said they will and 36 % were not sure.

The services which were thought as needed for a home service robot, with the average score above 5, were house chore related function, security function and detecting emergency phenomenon such as earthquake and typhoon. The social factors such as companion, chatting, interpersonal communication and connections were evaluated somewhat not necessary with the average around 3. The details of the service assessment were shown as Fig. 1.

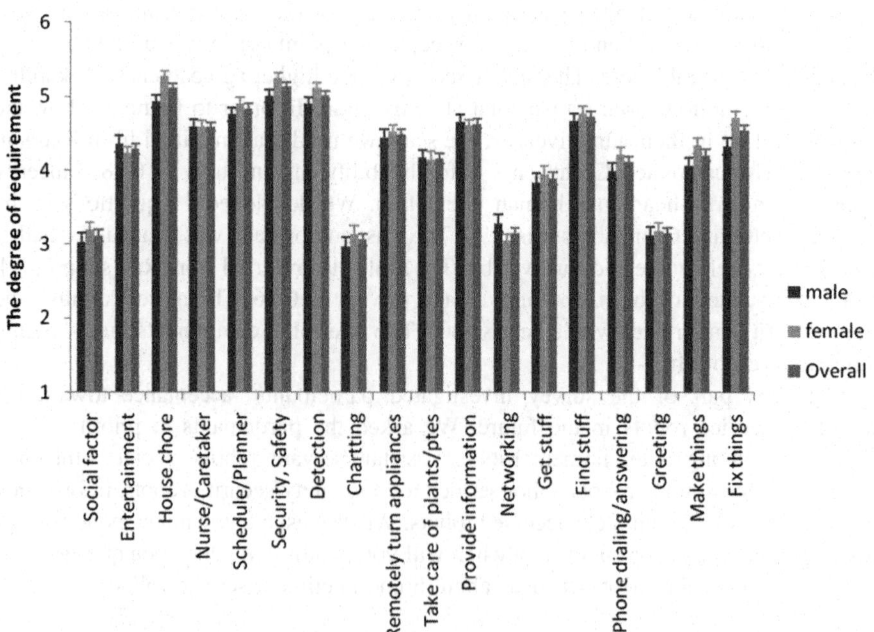

Fig. 1. Participants' requirements of services provided by home ISRs (Color figure online)

The general pattern of requirements in each service was the same between overall data and each gender. However, there were some different opinions between male and female participants regarding home assistance tasks. As shown in Fig. 1, it was found that female participants emphasized more on house chore ($t(265) = -2.86$, $p < .01$), security/safety ($t(265) = -2.30$, $p < .05$) and fix things ($t(265) = -2.60$, $p < .01$) than male participants.

One way ANOVA was conducted to compare the three buying tendencies: buying new products in several months, after one year and above two years. Once the ANOVA was significant, LSD was used for post hoc analysis. We only found significant difference in fix things service ($F(2,264) = 4.52$, $p < .05$). Post hoc showed the average score of buying after one year was significant higher than above two years ($p < .05$).

3.2 Participants' Preferences of the Robot Appearance and Body Feature

For the appearance of the home service robots, the participants were more comfortable in associating home ISRs with futuristic, machine-like, simple, female figure, brighter color, light weighted, organic and low character. However, the average scores we got were all closing to the middle score 4. Only exception was the color trait. It must be bright not dark (Fig. 2).

For the body structures of the home service robots, chi-square analysis was conducted to examine the proportion differences in each item related to body structure. And the results suggested significant preferences on fingers instead of palms

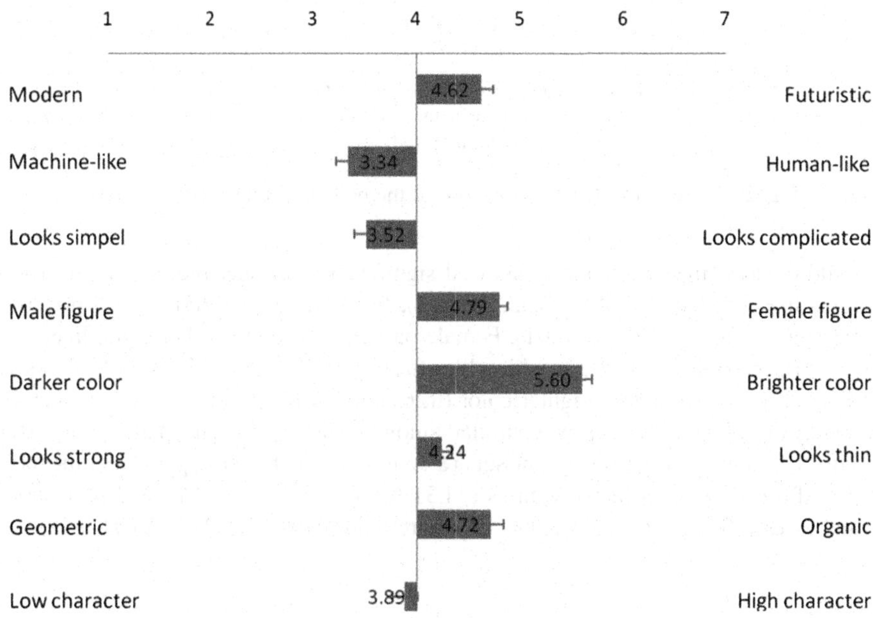

Fig. 2. Participants' expectations of the style traits of the home ISRs

($\chi 2 = 78.75$, $p < .01$), and on less facial features ($\chi 2 = 29.67$, $p < .01$) with abstract instead of concrete faces ($\chi 2 = 21.07$, $p < .01$). Also the participants expected the home service robots to have arms ($\chi 2 = 228.50$, $p < .01$) and a body screen in the front ($\chi 2 = 117.34$, $p <.01$). Generally the participants liked home service robots to have finger (77.15 %), no facial feature (66.67 %), virtual face (64.04 %), arm (96.25 %) and body screen (83.15 %). And they preferred home service robots of medium size ($\chi 2 = 262.39$, $p < .01$). Other body features including wheels (54.68 %) or feet (45.32 %) was not significantly different ($\chi 2 = 2.341$, $p = .13$) (Fig. 3).

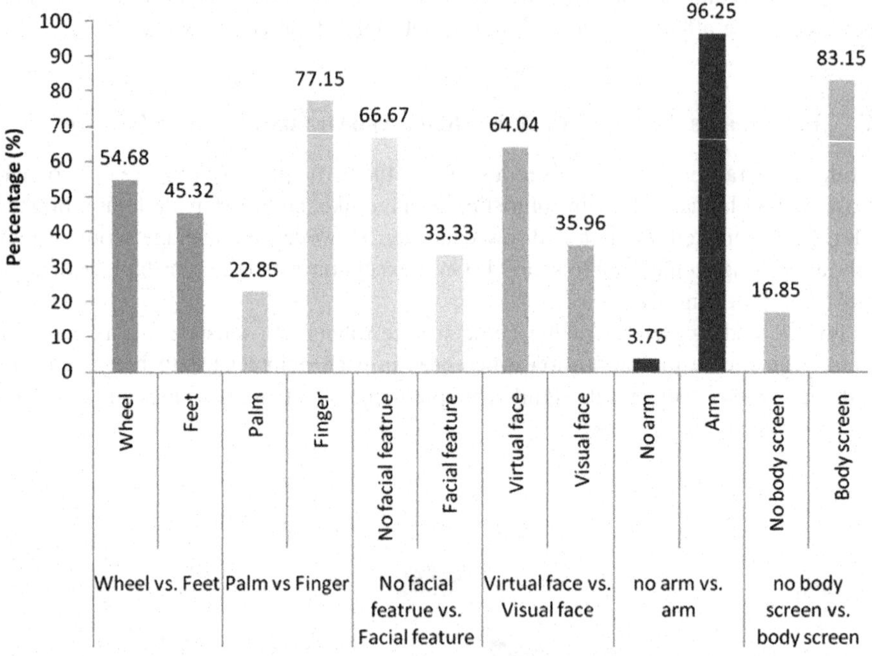

Fig. 3. Participants' expectations toward the body structures of home ISRs

Additionally, male participants showed significantly stronger preferences over the features like futuristic ($t(265) = 2.53$, $p < .05$), female figure ($t(265) = 2.17$, $p < .05$) and organic ($t(265) = 5.03$, $p < .01$). Female participants, on the other hand, liked the home service robots of more machine-like ($t(265) = 3.77$, $p < .01$), simple looks ($t(265) = 5.01$, $p < .01$), and brighter color ($t(265) = -3.10$, $p < .01$). The tendency in choosing the body structures was similar among male and female participants. But based on further comparison by chi square analysis, female participants significantly preferred robots without facial features (74.31 %; $\chi^2 = 8.21$, $p < .01$), and of abstract virtual faces (70.38 %$\chi^2 = 5.04$, $p < .05$) more than males (57.72 %; 56.91 %).

3.3 Participants' Perceived Importance of the HRI Factors

A correlation analysis was conducted on the three HRI dimensions. The results suggested that the participants viewed the trust and privacy (5.01/6) as the most important aspects for them to interact with home service robots, followed by the likability (4.65/6) of the robot, and the last issue is the sincerity of the robot. It was also found that the likability of robots possibly affected the trustworthy to robots in interaction, and vice versa (Table 1).

Table 1. Analysis of Correlation between Likability, Sincerity, Trust and Privacy

HRI factors	Mean	SD	Likability	Sincerity	Trust and Privacy
Likability	4.65	0.77	1.00		
Sincerity	4.42	0.85	0.69**	1.00	
Trust and Privacy	5.01	0.72	0.70**	0.66**	1.00

** Result is significant at 0.01 level (2-tailed)

Echoing the perceived importance reported by the participants, the comparison of participants of different buying tendency also found that those who tended to buy things later in one year, viewed sincerity as the least important for home service robots, their scores were significantly lower than the participants who bought things in several months, and those who bought in more than two years ($p < .05$).

3.4 Participants' Preference of the Robot Types

Among the eight major types of robots, most participants thought the most popular robot was labor service robot in the future. The second was the safety/security robot. The following sequence was remotely accessed robot, assistant/servant robot, information providing robot, caretakers/nurse robot, and entertainment robot. The last one was social companion robot. The participants estimated time to have a robot at home is within 10 years (43 %). And the average price they would afford was 175,292 NT dollars (about $5,200), which equaled to the costs of 4 refrigerators or 2 motorbikes. The results reflected the participants' stereotypes of expensive robots (Fig. 4).

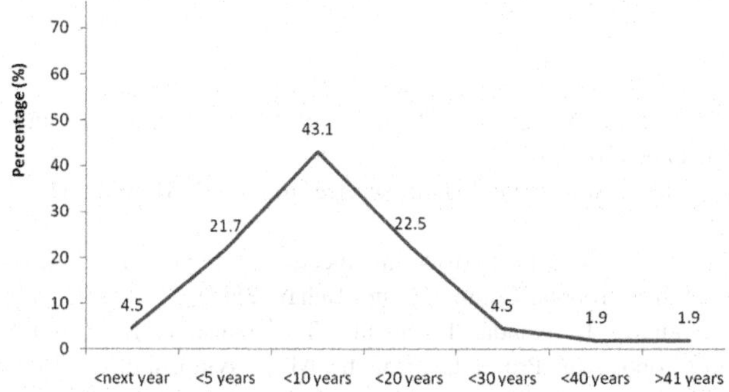

Fig. 4. Participants' estimated time to purchase a home ISR

4 Discussion and Conclusion

These results showed that the services of home ISRs were preferred in the order of house chore related function, security function and detecting emergency function. If designing involved gender preferences, the house chore, security/safety and fix things functions would be more important for female users. By comparing the participants of different buying tendencies, it was found that late buyers (after one year) valued the practical function, such as fixing things, of the home service robots. While the results of this study suggested that the local requirements of service robot in Taiwan were similar to the worldwide societies [4–7], the participants in this study emphasized the practical functions than the previous studies. Our participants expected the home ISRs to provide services in labor, secure, servant or information providing dimensions first. And viewed the social functions and features, such as caretaking and nursing as least necessary.

For the outlooks of the home ISRs, the results suggested a preferable robot of a human-like physical structure, but without an actual face and face features. Abstract representation of virtual faces is more acceptable among all participants, and specifically valued by female participants. The limbs of robots must have arms and hands for reaching out. Mobility was regarded as necessary for home ISRs, but it did not matter whether the robots moved by wheels or feet. Also the participants expected a body screen on the robots. Participants' preferences toward the appearances and functions of home service robots suggested that they perceived home ISRs as more like a machine than an agent. With the correlation analysis of robot outlooks and the HRI factors, the results clearly showed that once the appearance of the home ISRs is suitable for users, the likability and trustworthy could also be enhanced.

This study conducted a multidimensional development of home ISRs through the survey. The preliminary findings of the study answered the questions about what robots can do, how they look like and how the interaction between human and robots. To figure out the demanding differences in gender and buying tendency, the comparisons were also conducted and found out some interesting results. The designers in the future can consider the differences in different groups to design more favorable and useable home ISRs for each possible owner.

References

1. Numao, M., Kuniyoshi, Y.: 50-Year Outlook of Robot Technology Future Vision and Technical Challenges (2008)
2. Khan, Z.: Attitudes towards intelligent service robots. NADA KTH Technical report, Stockholm (1998)
3. Rau, P.L.P., Li, Y., Li, D.: Effects of communication style and culture on ability to accept recommendations from robots. Comput. Hum. Behav. **25**(2), 587–595 (2009)
4. Bartneck, C., Nomura, T., Kanda, T., Suzuki, T., Kennsuke, K.: Cultural differences in attitudes towards robots. In: Proceedings of the AISB Symposium on Robot Companions: Hard Problems and Open Challenges in Human-Robot Interaction, pp. 1–4 (2005)

5. Dunn, J., Schweitzer, M.: Feeling and believing: the influence of emotion on trust. J. Pers. Soc. Psychol. **88**(5), 736–748 (2005)
6. Nomura, T., Kanda, T., Suzuki, T., Yamada, S., Kato, K.: Influences of concerns toward emotional interaction into social acceptability of robots. In: Proceedings of 4th ACM/IEEE International Conference on Human-Robot Interaction (2009)
7. Norman, D.A.: The design of future things. Basic Books, New York (2007)

Design of User Interface for Elderly Care Supervision System Based on Sensor Network

Yi-Chong Zeng(✉), Yu-Ling Hsu, Te Yu Liu, Yen-Chieh Cheng, Huan-Chung Li, Grace Lin, and Wen-Tsung Chang

Data Analytics Technology and Applications Research Institute, Institute for Information Industry, Taipei, Taiwan, ROC
{yichongzeng,ylhsu,arderliu,yccheng,wiselyli, gracelin,wtchang}@iii.org.tw

Abstract. The world trends toward aging society because of low total fertility rate and long human life, and we have to face the issue that youth in the feature will have heavier load to take care of the elderly living than that at present. In order to solve such problem, cyber physical system is implemented, which is a collaborating system by integrating computational elements and physical entities. In this work, we develop the framework of the elderly care supervision system based on sensor network, and it is verified in a long-term caring facility for dementia caring. Moreover, user interface runs the developed software. Caregiver, family member, and system manager can manipulate the friendly user interface to obtain information of the elderly activity and the anomaly. The resultants will demonstrate that how activity recognition and elderly living analysis are implemented by application program runs on mobile device.

Keywords: Cyber physical system · Elderly care · Human-computer interaction · Sensor network · Activity analysis

1 Introduction

Facing the issues of total fertility rate (TFR) of the world declining and population aging, it implies that an aging society is coming. According to the reports [1, 2], TFR of the world declines from 4.85 in 1970 to 2.63 in 2015. Additionally, regions with the lowest five TFRs of world were in Asia in 2015, they were South Korea, Hong Kong, Taiwan, Macau, and Singapore. Low TFR means that youth will have heavy load in the elderly care in the future due to the ratio of elder to youth increases year by year. In [3], the report reveals that caregiver support ratio is 7 in 2010 in America, and it will drop to 3 in 2050. Therefore, how to manage manpower efficiently in the elderly care is an important task now.

Cyber physical system (CPS) is a collaborating system by integrating computational elements and physical entities. In the past, researchers investigated approaches based on CPS to take care of people living in smart home. For physical entities of CPS, diverse sensors are deployed in building, including, temperature sensor, humidity sensor, ambient light sensor, current sensor, positioning sensor, passive infrared motion sensor,

P.-L.P. Rau (Ed.): CCD 2016, LNCS 9741, pp. 616–627, 2016.
DOI: 10.1007/978-3-319-40093-8_61

and depth camera, etc. Moreover, sensors on wearable devices are capable of collecting vital signs and people action, such as, accelerometer, gyroscope, heart rate variability, body temperature. In the literature [4–7], the applications based on CPS were presented, including, activity analysis/recognition, anomaly detection, home energy saving, and preference estimation, etc. In [4, 5], Weng et al. analyzed human activity in home for determination of energy-saving service. Their improved method was performed on multi-resident environment. In [6], Gu et al. used data mining instead of machine learning for recognition of 25 daily activities.

A common management technology is applied to those sensors and transmits sensing data to cloud server through Internet. Cyber layer subscribes data from cloud server. Subsequently, analysis technologies are applied to sensing data, such as activity recognition (AR) and anomaly detection (AD). The objectives of AR are to recognize the elderly activity as well as to generate activities of daily living (ADL). The objective of AD is to detect abnormal activity/behavior by analyzing recognized results, and then warning sign is activated. In the previous work [7], we proposed a scheme to analyze sensing data as well as to recognize people activity. The analyzed data were mono-type sensing data collected in the single-woman home [8]. Our scheme can recognize activity, detect anomaly, generate ADL, and estimate personal preference in activity habit.

In this work, we develop the framework of the elderly care supervision system based on sensor network, and it is verified in a long-term caring facility for dementia caring. The user interface displayed information of deployed sensors, elder's activity and anomaly is designed for caregiver, family member, and system manager. The elderly ADL recognized by analyzing ambient sensing data and body sensing data are stored in cloud server; moreover, the system detects the elderly anomaly and then lights up a bulb for warning. Caregiver can obtain information of elder's activity and abnormal event informed by the portable device. Family member can remotely look over his/her grandparent's health status shown on the portable device. For system managers, they operate the portable device to monitor connection status of ambient sensors. The rest of this paper is organized as follows: the interview to the long-term caring facility and the scenarios for the elderly care are described in Sect. 2. Sensor deployment and architecture are, respectively, introduced in Sects. 3 and 4. Activity analysis is presented in Sect. 5. The user interface and functions will be shown in Sect. 6, and the concluding remarks will be drawn in Sect. 7.

2 Interview and Scenario Design

In order to understand trend of elder care in upcoming aging society and requirement of caring facility, we visited and interviewed health professionals, doctors, and caregivers. Table 1 lists the interview summary with respect to four major aspects, namely, safety, health, caregiver load, and quality of care. According to the insights gained from the interviews mentioned above, we proposed three scenarios in our design, namely, straying detection, sleep pattern detection, and night-time bed-leaving detection.

Table 1. Interview summary with respect to four major aspects

Major aspects	Sample issues
Safety	• Safety First! It's important to provide immediate notification for falling accidents • Need information and communication technology (ICT) to help or prevent straying and to detect night-time bed-leaving for the elderly
Health	• It is important to help the elderly to establish regular life activities patterns • Healthy life styles are helpful, e.g., exercises, enough sleep, healthy diet
Caregiver load	• There exists shortage of caregiver in most elderly care facilities • Paper work is time-consuming, ICT could improve efficiency in caring tasks
Quality of care	• With sensor network, caring process could be personalized and optimized • User interface design could help caregiver/medical professionals to quickly understand the elderly health and care condition

2.1 Scenario 1: Stray Detection

Wandering behaviors and getting disoriented situations are commonly seen in the elderly with dementia. Therefore, in this scenario, beacon sensors first collect the position and the time data of the elderly as shown in Fig. 1(a). Then, with the forbidden area detection, the proposed system could notify caregiver immediately to find the elder as well as to offer in-time assistance.

2.2 Scenario 2: Sleep Pattern Detection

Dementia and sleep are closely related with one another. The elderly with dementia tends to have irregular sleep pattern, and lack of sleep increases the risk of dementia later in life. Thus, in our design shown in Fig. 1(b), motion sensor detects elder's action automatically when he/she sleeps on the bed. The duration of activity between two active signs of motion sensor is analyzed for estimation of sleep pattern. Moreover, through sleep pattern and anomaly detection, our system could actively notify caregiver to pay attention to elder's sleep.

2.3 Scenario 3: Night-Time Bed-Leaving Detection

Caring facility concerns the issue of the elderly safety during night time. It is high possibility that elder falls when he/she gets out of bed at night. Therefore, sensor deployed on bedside detects incident of night-time bed-leaving. In addition, the system activates night light near the bed, so that it is helpful to decrease the risk of falling. Meanwhile, the system turns on the bulbs in nursing station, and it notifies caregiver to take care of the elderly immediately. Figure 1(c) shows the flowchart of the scenario 3.

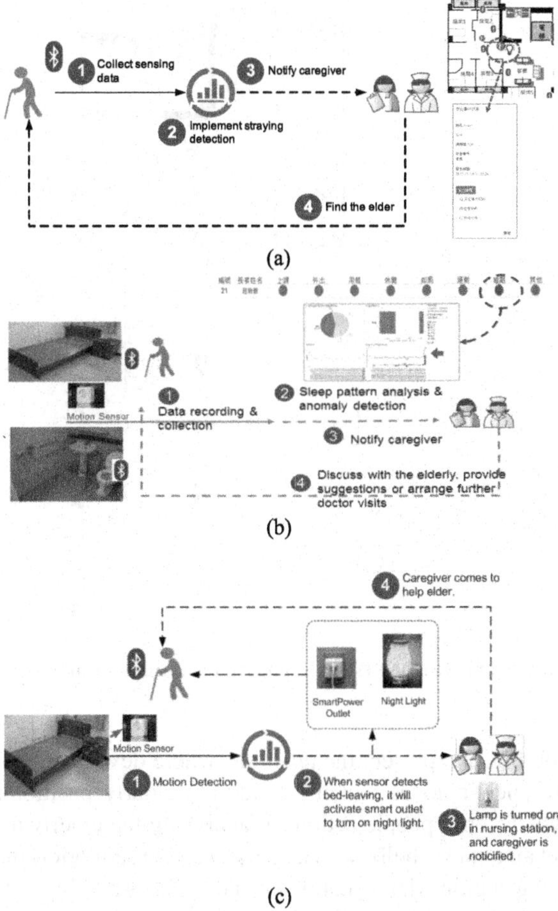

Fig. 1. Flowcharts of three scenarios, including (a) straying detection, (b) sleep pattern detection, and (c) night-time bed-leaving detection.

3 Deployment

The issue of deployment is divided into three major topics, including, space field, devices, and subjects. Figure 2 portrays two floors of the institution for dementia caring facility, where Fig. 2(a) indicates the first floor of institution including the entrance and a larger space of rehabilitation room as well as Fig. 2(b) represents the third floor of institution accommodates nine rooms including toilets, a living room, a nursing station, a dining room, a yard, and a activity room.

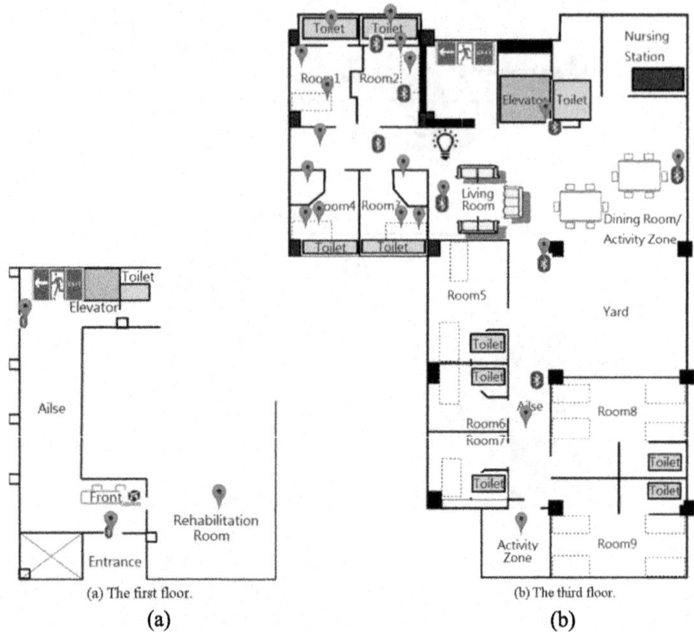

Fig. 2. Sensor deployment in (a) the first floor, and (b) the third floor in the caring facility (Color figure online)

The red pins on Fig. 2 represent the positions where devices/sensors are deployed. These devices are anchor nodes which provide the elderly positioning information; motion sensors which sense people action for analyzing the elderly activity status; air mentors that detect air quality; bulbs which adjust the light saturation and colors to alarm caregivers in nursing station what situation is; and badges (mobile nodes) are wearable devices which send signal periodically to anchor nodes in order to track the elderly position. In the experimental environment, the tested elders' ages range from 70 to 80 years old and live in Room 1, Room 2, Room 3, and Room 4 on the third floor as shown in Fig. 2(b). They wear badges, and their families accept the agreement for personal positioning owing to privacy.

4 System Architecture

We push messages to data bus and send messages to all subscribers which interested in our channel. Therefore, subscribers receive only topics of the interest without receiving all information from data bus, so applications can easily obtain accurate information on the desired system to supervise. The abilities of multi-channel data bus have three: (1) pub/sub: publish and subscribe message for data bus by topic; (2) cross-platform: supports message passing for different platform and virtual machines; and (3) immediacy: instant information delivered to the data bus and various services instantly receive data.

In order to allow that CPS integrates every type of device, CPS has a service model for data normalization, so that the system can obtain information in a variety of environments, such as medical, home. In addition, the information is converted into a unified format. In this work, the system supports the health and environmental equipments, it integrates data formats and units from various manufacturers, so that we can collect messages and control devices through Internet. Figure 3 shows the diagram of devices and equipments connection in this work. It is established for intelligent health care system, and it is helpful to improve quality of personal health management.

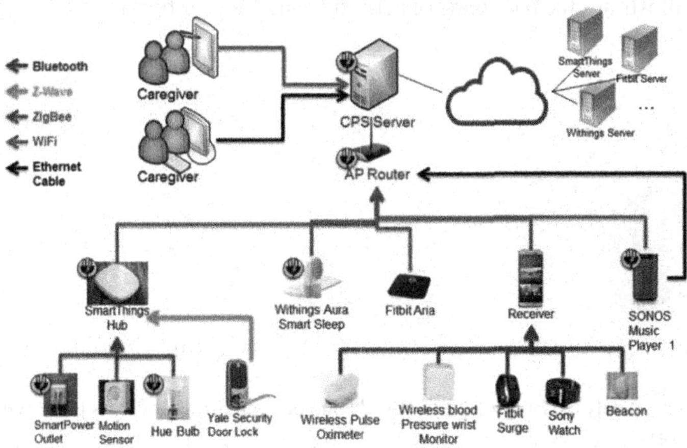

Fig. 3. Diagram of devices and equipments connection (Color figure online)

5 Activity Analysis

According to the interview summary mentioned in Sect. 2, caregivers in caring facility concern elders' position and their states. There are two ways to obtain people's position in this work. Tracking people using wearable devices, such as, beacon sensor, smart watch, and smart phone, is a direct method. Meanwhile, some wearable devices provide more functions to measure vital signs and then are capable of transmitting data to cloud server via wireless communication. However, in some situations people feel uncomfortable by wearing device, such as the elderly with dementia. Position tracking will be failed as people take off the devices. The other method is to analyze sensing data derived from ambient sensors, such as passive infrared motion sensor. While people appear in room, sensors deployed around the room will be activated. The objective of activity analysis is to mine useful information by analyzing sensing data. In the previous work [7], we proposed methods to recognize people activity with respect to his/her position. There are eight daily activities recognized, and those activities are highly related to functions in rooms. In this work, we emphasize on three types of activity analysis, and the details are described as follows.

5.1 Activity of Daily Living

In the elderly caring facility, eight activities are recognized, including, "Sleep", "Relaxing", "Eating", "Toilet", "Go out", "Exercise", "Attend Class", and "Others". The elderly wears a badge which is a positioning sensor in order to acquire his/her position immediately. Furthermore, passive infrared motion sensors are deployed on bedside and on ceiling above bed. The objective of deploying motion sensors is to detect sleep status and incident of night-time bed-leaving. Figure 4(a) shows the pie chart of ADL one day, and the area of pie represents the ratio of total hours of activity to 24 h. Figure 4(b) illustrates the bar charts of activities one day, the bar size represents duration of activity.

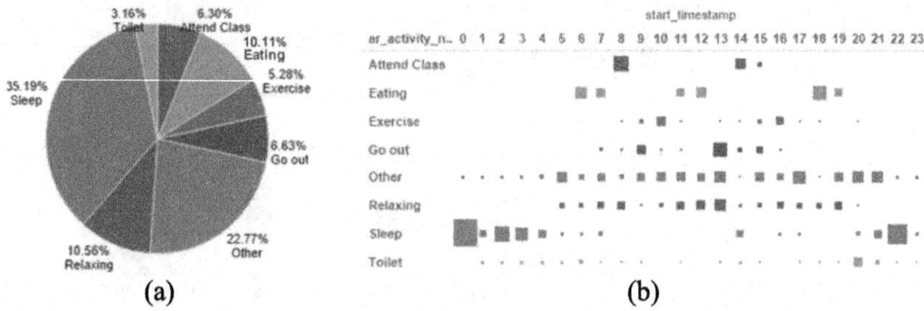

Fig. 4. Activity Analysis: (a) pie chart of ADL one day, and (b) bar charts of activities one day (Color figure online)

5.2 Preference in Duration of Activity

Everyone spends time in activity is different to another does. However, his/her preference in duration of activity is not change violently. Referred to [7], durations of all activities are collected and cumulative distribution functions (CDF) of scaled-durations of activities are computed. The CDF of scaled-duration of activity is approximate to that of normal distribution. Therefore, the 95 % confidence interval of normal distribution is a criterion to estimate duration of activity. For example, Fig. 5 shows two CDFs

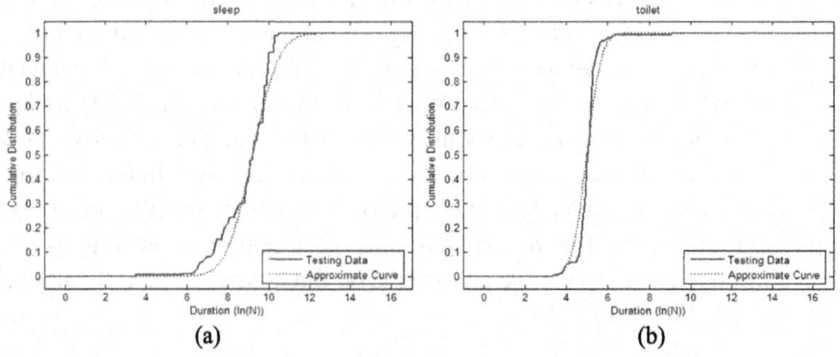

Fig. 5. Cumulative density functions of (a) "Sleep", and (b) "Toilet"

corresponding to "Sleep" with the duration of 29,732 s and "Toilet" with the duration of 270 s.

5.3 Anomaly Detection

Three kinds of conditions are concerned as anomaly in caring facility, i.e., falling down, abnormal behavior, and straying. Wearable devices (such as, smart phone and smart watch) embedded accelerometer and gyroscope are helpful for detection of the elderly falling immediately. Furthermore, the factors that lead to the elderly falling after he/she gets out of bed are unsafe environment (such as, dimly-lit room) and un-awakened consciousness. In order to prevent accident, passive infrared motion sensor deployed at bedside is employed to detect incident of night-time bed-leaving.

While the elderly spends more time in activity than usual, the situation is considered as abnormal behavior. For instance, someone spends more time in the toilet, it is highly possible that people has fallen or fainted a period of time. Therefore, the estimated duration of activity (mentioned in Sect. 5.2) is employed to determine when abnormal behavior begins.

For straying, it is an emergency that the elderly with dementia leaves caring facility without any caregiver notifies it. To solve such problem, the elderly wears a badge embedded with positioning sensor. The system detects whether people locates in forbidden area, such as, front gate. If elder enters the forbidden area, the system sends warning message to notify caregiver.

6 User Interface and Functions

We develop framework of elderly supervision system based sensor network. Figure 6 shows the diagram of the proposed system, and it is verified in the caring facility. Caregiver, family member, and system manager can browse information via the designed user interface performed on portable device. The details of functions of user interface are introduced as follows.

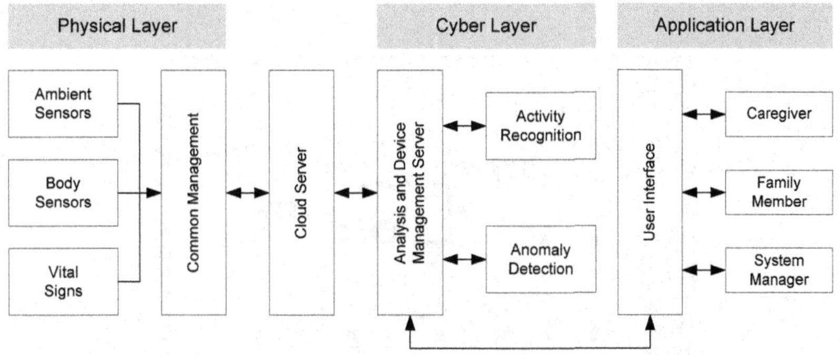

Fig. 6. The diagram of elderly care supervision system

6.1 Main Page

Figure 7 shows the main page of the designed user interface, where three buttons placed on for caregiver, family member, and system manager. Caregiver monitors elder's activity and abnormal event. Family member can remotely look over his/her elderly member's health status. For system managers, they monitor connection status of sensors deployed in the facility.

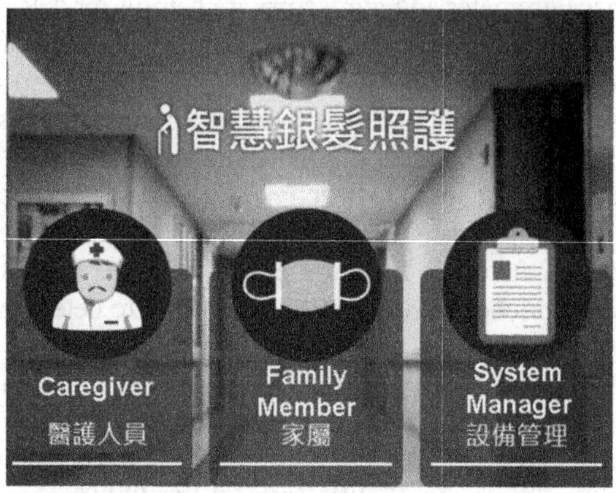

Fig. 7. Main page of the designed user interface

6.2 Descriptions of Functions

Caregiver can browse four kinds of information by pressing left-hand side buttons on page as shown in Fig. 8, including, real-time monitoring, safety incident, activity of daily living, and information of vital sign. For real-time monitoring, Fig. 8 shows four elders' positions with different icons. The green-circle represents the No. 19 elder is normal. The red-icons are warning signs. The red-triangle, the red-rectangle, the red-star represent the anomalies of night-time bed-leaving, straying, and falling, respectively.

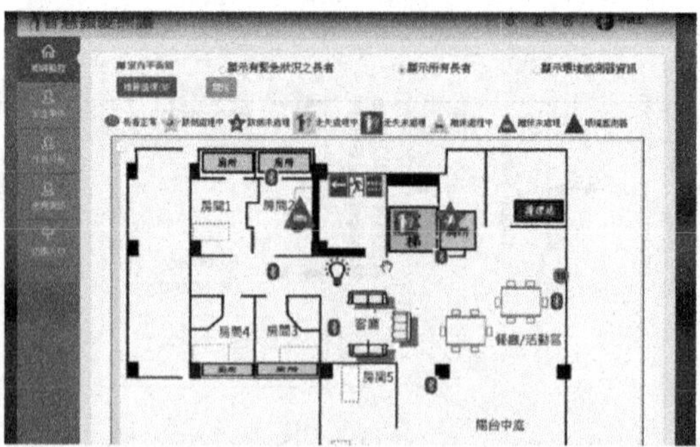

Fig. 8. Interface of real-time monitoring (Color figure online)

Pressing the red-icon or the button of safety incident, caregiver obtains the 3-min history trajectory of unsafe incident. For example, Fig. 9 displays the history trajectory of the elderly straying.

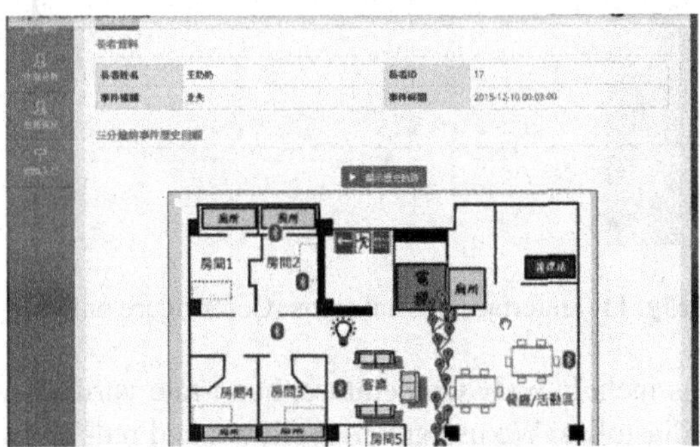

Fig. 9. Interface of safety incident (Color figure online)

The function of ADL is to reveal the elderly activity status. The first function is to list the summaries of the eight activities as shown in Fig. 10(a). Green-circle and red-circle represent normal status and abnormal status yesterday, respectively. Pressing the elder's name, the user interface displays four charts of the elderly ADL as shown in Fig. 10(b), including, the percentages of eight activities per day (top-left), ADL per day (top-right), normal/abnormal activities per month (bottom-left), and difference between normal ADL and recognized ADL (bottom-right). The top two charts are generated base on activity recognition mentioned in Sect. 5.1. The chart of normal/abnormal activities per month summarizes the results of anomaly detection mentioned in Sect. 5.3. In order to observe whether the elderly activity changes violently or not, the bottom-right chart illustrates the difference between normal ADL and recognized ADL. The normal ADL is computed by averaging 7-day ADL prior to the observational day. Caregiver and family member are authorized to monitor the elderly health status by pressing the button of information of vital sign, which is shown in Fig. 11.

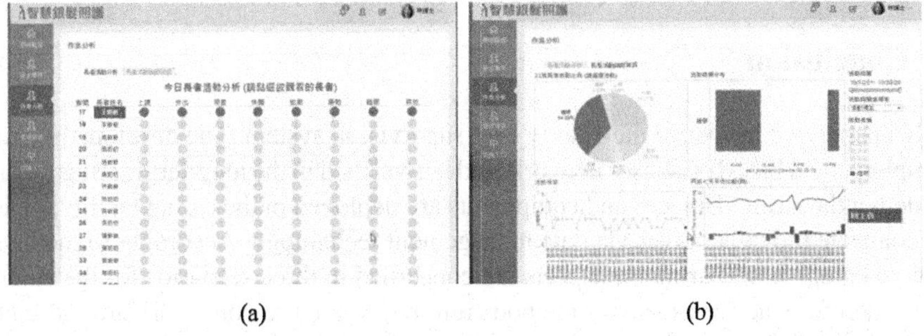

(a) (b)

Fig. 10. Interfaces of the elderly (a) activity status yesterday, and (b) activity of daily living (Color figure online)

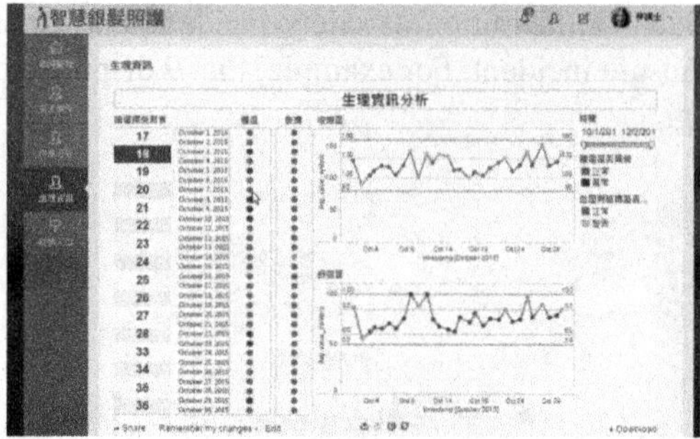

Fig. 11. Interface of vital signs (Color figure online)

Those vital signs include body temperature, heart rate variability, and blood pressures (systolic and diastolic). We use green-, yellow-, and red- icons represent normal status, warning, and abnormal status, respectively.

System manager can remotely monitor sensors via user interface after pressing the button of device management on the main page. Figure 12 lists details of sensors deployed in the caring facility, including numbers of active sensors and inactive sensors, sensor type, sensor position, sensor status, interfacing type, and device manufacturers.

[illegible]	[illegible]	[illegible]	[illegible]
[illegible]	222	71	50
[illegible]	11	5	8
[illegible]	211	66	42

No.	[illegible]	[illegible]	[illegible]	[illegible]	[illegible]	[illegible]	[illegible]	[illegible]
1	Philips	HUE	[illegible]	Bulb	3	T1,T2	on	[illegible]
2	Philips	HUE Hub	[illegible]	Color Control	1	T1,T2	on	[illegible]
[illegible]	[illegible]	Switch	[illegible]	Outlet	1	T1	on	[illegible]
4	SmartThings	Motion Sensor	Motion[illegible]	Motion	1	T1	on	[illegible]
5	SmartXLab	Motion sensor	Motion[illegible]	Motion	20	T1,T2,T3	on	[illegible]
6	SmartXLab	Anchor with Motion sensor	[illegible] & Motion[illegible]	Location	20	T1,T2,T3	on	[illegible]
7	SmartXLab	Mobile Node	[illegible]	Location	4	T1,T2,T3	on	[illegible]
8	SmartXLab	Gateway	[illegible]	Location	2	T1,T2,T3	on	[illegible]
9	[illegible]EBM	Ear thermometer	[illegible]	Thermometer	1	T1	on	[illegible]
10	[illegible]EBM	Blood Pressure	[illegible]	Blood Pressure	2	T1	on	[illegible]
11	CoAsia	Air Mentor Pro	[illegible]	Air Quality	1	T1	on	[illegible]

Fig. 12. Interface of device management

7 Conclusion

In this paper, we introduce the elderly care supervision system. The developed system is implemented based on sensor network, and it is verified in the long-term caring facility for dementia caring. Devices and equipments are deployed in the caring facility, which are connected to cyber layer via data management technology. According to the interview to caregivers, four major aspects are concerned in three scenarios for the elderly care. Therefore, activity analysis methods referred to the previous work are presented for detections of elders' activity statuses and anomaly. Finally, caregiver and family member can browse the elderly activities via the designed user interface. System managers can monitor connection status of sensors via the user interface as well.

References

1. United Nations, World Population Prospects: The 2012 Revision, Population Division (2013). http://esa.un.org/unpd/wpp/Excel-Data/EXCEL_FILES/2_Fertility/WPP2012_FERT_F04_TOTAL_FERTILITY.XLS
2. CIA World Factbook: Total Fertility Rate Country Comparison to the World. https://www.cia.gov/library/publications/the-world-factbook/rankorder/2127rank.html
3. Redfoot, D., Feinberg, L., Houser, A.: The aging of the baby boom and the growing care gap: a look at future declines in the availability of family caregivers. AARP Public Policy Institute, Washington (2013). http://www.aarp.org/content/dam/aarp/research/public_policy_institute/ltc/2013/baby-boom-and-the-growing-care-gap-insight-AARP-ppi-ltc.pdf
4. Weng, M.-Y., Wu, C.-L., Lu, C.-H., Yeh, H.-W., Fu, L.-C.: Content-aware home energy saving based on energy-prone context. In: 2012 IEEE/RSJ International Conference on Intelligent Robots and Systems (IROS), pp. 5233–5238 (2012)
5. Lu, C.-H., Wu, C.-L., Yang, T.-H., Yeh, H.-W., Weng, M.-Y., Fu, L.-C., Tai, T.Y.C.: Energy-responsive aggregate context for energy saving in a multi-resident environment. IEEE Trans. Autom. Sci. Eng. **11**(3), 715–729 (2014)
6. Gu, T., Wu, Z., Tao, X., Pung, H. K., Lu. J.: epSICAR: an emerging patterns based approach to sequential, interleaved and concurrent activity recognition, In: Proceedings of the 7th Annual IEEE International Conference on Pervasive Computing and Communications (Percom 2009), pp. 1–9, March 2009
7. Zeng, Y.-C., Chiu, Y.-S.,Chang, W.-T.,: Activity recognition and its applications for elder care based on mono-type sensor network. In: 2015 IEEE 4th Global Conference on Consumer Electronics (GCCE), pp. 44–47, October 2015
8. WSU CASAS Datasets. http://ailab.wsu.edu/casas/datasets.htm

A Framework for Integrating Industrial Product-Service Systems and Cyber-Physical Systems

Maokuan Zheng[1], Wenyan Song[2(✉)], and Xinguo Ming[1]

[1] School of Mechanical Engineering, Shanghai Jiao Tong University, Shanghai, China
zhengmaokuan@163.com, xgming@sjtu.edu.cn
[2] School of Economics and Management, Beihang University, Beijing, China
songwenyan@buaa.edu.cn

Abstract. The transformation to service economy calls for the development of Industrial Product Service Systems (IPS2), which has changed traditional business models greatly. In recent years, there are trends and needs from the industry to further develop IPS2 by integrating advanced information technologies. While the emergence of Cyber-Physical Systems (CPS) provides whole new viewpoints and approaches for IPS2 construction, there are still no public recognized systematic solutions. To solve this problem, the concept of intelligent IPS2 and a framework integrating IPS2 with CPS is proposed in this work. The system decomposition and intellectualization process of intelligent IPS2 are analyzed, trying to figure out the interaction mechanisms between IPS2 and CPS. Then A general architecture of CPS supported intellectualization of IPS2 is developed, which is constructed by five layers. The model for intelligent IPS2 is put forward based on industry investigation, trying to offer possible guidelines and roadmap for those service transforming companies.

Keywords: Industrial Product Service Systems (IPS2) · Intelligent IPS2, Cyber-Physical System (CPS) · Business model · Value co-creation

1 Introduction

As the society developing towards service economy, researches on Industrial Product Service Systems (IPS2) have received great attention from both academia and industries [1]. Advantages of the development of IPS2 are widely discussed. New business models based on service logic have been showing significant power in achieving sustainable economy [2]. IPS2 is integration of industrial product and service shares, which represents a new solution-oriented approach for delivering value in use to the customer during the whole life cycle of a product [3]. However, the present researches about IPS2 are mainly focused on basic concepts, business models, value chain and operational scheme design of IPS2 [4–6]. How to connect these theories with the real operations in industry is still not be solved.

Recent years, the fast development of communication technologies, Internet of information, Internet of things, cloud computing and big data analytics have changed

P.-L.P. Rau (Ed.): CCD 2016, LNCS 9741, pp. 628–637, 2016.
DOI: 10.1007/978-3-319-40093-8_62

the objective internal and external environment for IPS2 development. There is a trend for integration of products, services, sensors, and the Internet, which has already been discussed as Cyber-Physical Systems (CPS) [7, 8]. CPS may bring a breakthrough in the development of IPS2.

This work is based on systematic investigation during project cooperation with three typical IPS2 companies in three different industries (construction machinery, elevator and power equipment) in eastern China, including. Those companies are trying to establish intellectualized industrial product service systems by integrating CPS, which are defined as intelligent IPS2 in this work. The research is trying to figure out a general framework and maturity model for intelligent IPS2.

Contents of this work are organized as follows. An introduction and a brief review of present work about IPS2 and CPS are carried out to clarify related concepts and depict state of the art in Sects. 1 and 2. Then a framework of CPS integrated intelligent IPS2 is proposed in Sects. 3 and 4, which contains three procedures, including system decomposition of intelligent IPS2, intellectualization process of IPS2 by integrating CPS, and then a general architecture of CPS supporting Intellectualization of IPS2. Last, the discussions and conclusions are offered in Sect. 6.

2 Related Work About CPS

A CPS is a system of collaborating computational elements controlling physical entities. Embedded computers and networks monitor and control the physical processes, usually with feedback loops where physical processes affect computations and vice versa [9]. The notion is closely tied to concepts of robotics and sensor networks with intelligence mechanisms proper of computational intelligence leading the pathway. Ongoing advances in science and engineering will improve the link between computational and physical elements by means of intelligent mechanisms, dramatically increasing the adaptability, autonomy, efficiency, functionality, reliability, safety, and usability of cyber-physical systems [10]. Today, a precursor generation of CPS can be found in areas as diverse as aerospace, automotive, chemical processes, civil infrastructure, energy, healthcare, manufacturing, transportation, entertainment, and consumer appliances.

The emergence of CPS provides whole new viewpoints and approaches for IPS2 construction. The improvements of information, automation, sensing and artificial intelligent technologies have changed the way of contacting, interacting and problem solving. And now, it's also beginning to change traditional business models. As mentioned above, while CPS has been widely applied in improving product design, manufacturing intelligence and other areas, CPS is rarely studied to support IPS2 intelligence.

Technologies will offer new opportunities for companies to provide novel products and services [11]. We believe the advent of CPS will enhance and accelerate the process [12]. So far, there have been some researches using information technologies to help improve the operational performance of service tasks. Zhu et al. [13] proposed a web-based product service system for aerospace maintenance, repair and overhaul services. Zhang et al. [14] offered a framework for design knowledge management and reuse for product service systems in construction machinery industry. Teixeira et al. [15] tried to figure out a novel framework linking prognostics and health Management and product–service systems using online simulation. Selak et al. [16] presented a condition monitoring and fault diagnostics (CMFD) system for hydropower plants (HPP). Though those researches about information technology applications in supporting product service systems have been conducted, none of them have given a systematic framework of how information technologies, especially CPS, can be integrated with IPS2.

3 Framework Decomposition of Intelligent IPS2

An intelligent IPS2 firstly should be a product service system, which means that the basic value co-creation network should be built up according to the IPS2 business model. Based on the summary of investigation in several different industries and literature review, a framework of intelligent IPS2 is proposed, as shown in Fig. 1. The framework consists of seven parts, namely customer needs centered product lifecycle, stakeholders, service abilities, business models, cyber physical system, supporting

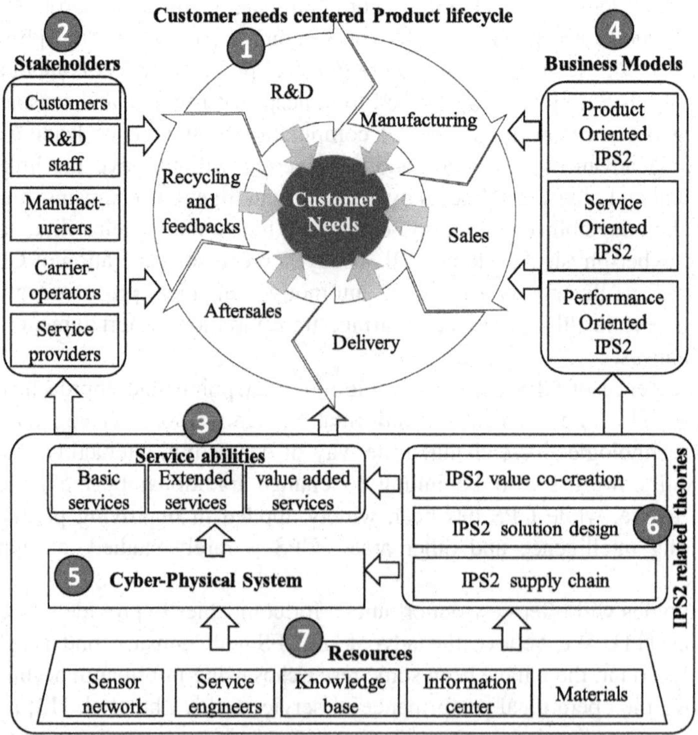

Fig. 1. The proposed framework of Intelligent IPS2 integrating CPS

theories and resources. The coordination of these modules is the basis for the construction and normal operation of intelligent IPS2.

Customer Needs Centered Product Lifecycle Under Service-Dominant Logic. Traditional understanding of IPS2 value chain mainly focuses on the after sales procedures. In this paper, based on the work of Aurich et al. [17, 18], Takata and Umeda [19], it is extended to the whole lifecycle of products with customers participated in every stage, including product R&D, manufacturing, sales, delivery, after sales and recycling. Characters and requirements in other procedures of the product lifecycle are also developed, which could be found in Table 1.

Table 1. Service characters and requirements in the full product lifecycle

Product lifecycle	Requirements in service-dominant logic
R&D	Module design for manufacturing and after sales services
	Standard interface and port for upgrading and expand
	Interaction module for service request and feedback
	Systems and tools allowing customer participated design
Manufacturing	On-demand personalized manufacturing
	Customer participated manufacturing
	Manufacturing to service orders
Sales	Customer behavior and needs based on market segmentation
	New contract modes: Leasing, performance contracting, etc.
	Products and services trial experience and direct selling
	Configurable purchase scheme
	Online to offline sales mode
Delivery	Shared supply network
	Visualized delivery information
	controllable delivery process
After sales	Product maintenance, repair, etc.
	Product upgrading, reforming, etc.
	Remote monitoring, fault alarm, etc.
	Financial leasing, project consulting, data service, etc.
Recycling & feedbacks	Direct feedbacks from customers or users
	Harmless treatment
	Product recycling tracing
	Remanufacturing

Stakeholders. In an intelligent IPS2, stakeholders generally include customers (or users), R&D staff, manufacturers, carrier operators, all kinds of service providers and other related roles participating throughout the lifecycle of products. Different industries may have different stakeholder constitution. But under the notion of IPS2, all stakeholders are supposed to cooperate as a network for value co-creation. Value co-creation is realized through work flow reconfiguration and business model innovation other than simple transaction and compromise.

Service Abilities. With all the resources integrated and CPS supporting, three categories of service packages or service abilities, including basic services, extended services and value added services, can be configured and provided according to specific needs of different customers. Basic services are the core of IPS2, then follows extended services in the middle layer, and value added services in the outermost layer. Characters and examples of different service categories are offered in Table 2.

Table 2. Three layers of service category

Service category	Characters	Examples
Basic services	Services offered to ensure the normal operation or quality of products	Product maintenance, spare parts replacement, etc.
Extended services	Services offered to extend or upgrade basic functions or structure of products	Remote monitoring, fault alarm, software updating, hardware reforming, etc.
Value added services	Senior services offered to help customer extend ability or business scope	Finance leasing, project consulting, data service, etc.

IPS2 Business Models. Generally, existing business models of IPS2 basically can be summarized into three categories [4, 20], which are product oriented IPS2, use oriented IPS2 and performance oriented IPS2, which are explained in detail in Table 3. In the paradigm of service-dominant logic and CPS integration, service and performance oriented IPS2 are becoming much more popular. The supporting of CPS accelerates the evolvement of the transformation from product based business models to service based business models.

Table 3. Three basic business models of IPS2

Business model	Characters	Examples
Product oriented IPS2	The manufacturers provide products and related services to the consumers who have the ownership of products	Maintenance, repair, distribution, reuse, recycling, training and consulting
Use oriented IPS2	Manufacturers who have the ownership of products provide customers with the usage and function of products	Product rental, leasing or sharing of passenger cars, air conditioner, construction machinery
Performance oriented IPS2	Manufacturers offer a customized mix of services to guarantee a certain result or capability instead of a product and the customers pay only for the performance	Energy performance contracting, Compressed air supplying contract, all-inclusive printing service, etc.

Cyber Physical System. CPS is the key factor in the intellectualization process of IPS2. CPS integrates all kinds of resources and packages them as services and release them automatically or autonomously. Detailed research about how CPS interacts with IPS2 and structure of CPS will be introduced in the following Sect. 4.

Related Supporting Theories. Apart from CPS, theories about directing the transformation of traditional companies to service based business models should be proposed and developed. Those theories can be categorized from three dimensions. The first are theories about helping figure out the mechanism of value network and value creation in IPS2. The second are those supporting IPS2 scheme design to meet customer needs as far as possible. The third are from the operational layer that direct IPS2 supply chain in order to improve the efficiency of service supplying and cut down the costs. All those theories should be combined together forming a theoretical system to support service ability fostering, service modes innovation, service workflow optimization and finally value co-creation.

Service Resources. Service resources are basic support for the operation of intelligent manufacturing. Service resources can be divided into two kinds, which are physical resources and virtual resources. Different from traditional IPS2, physical resources get upgraded and are able to be connected to the network via the embedded intelligent modules, including bar codes, chips, RF wireless module or other sensors. With the intelligent module, these physical resources are packaged as virtual resources, which can be perceived, managed, dispatch and even controlled remotely through the CPS. The virtual cyber system and the real physical system will be operated in two parallel spaces with precise synchronization.

4 Intellectualization Process of IPS2 by Integrating CPS

CPS helps IPS2 to enhance the loose relationships between stakeholders and resources, and to be closed integrated network connections. The purpose of integrating IPS2 with CPS is to improve the operational efficiency and accelerate the process of value co-creation in following ways:

Service Process Automation. With CPS integrated, customer needs and product usage data can be obtained directly. Service needs can be fast responded automatically. Meanwhile, orders from customers and pre-services forecasted from data statistics are able to be processed automatically. Proactive services become a mainstream that customer needs can be satisfied just at the right time instead of passive service offered after serious problems occur with customer complains.

Service Activity Autonomy. Both users and products can be served by themselves with CPS supporting. Products can upgrade their software automatically, or even self-diagnosis and self-healing when hardware failure or software crash occur. Users can learn new skills and get technical support with the help of embedded interactive guide software. Fast developing artificial intelligence will enhance and accelerate this trend of CPS application in intelligent IPS2 significantly.

Service Resource Integration. Under the circumstances of Internet of information and things, those supportive virtual and physical resources can be distributed in a more efficient way. Information of service needs, resource allocation and amounts gets integrated seamlessly. And meanwhile, physical resources are shared and planed with centralized management, so that the inventory, risks, costs and wastes can be minimized towards stable and sustainable operation.

5 Architecture for CPS Supported Intellectualization of IPS2

A general architecture of CPS supported intellectualization of IPS2 is proposed as depicted in Fig. 2, which is constructed by 5 layers. Descriptions of organization and function in each layer from bottom to top are as follows.

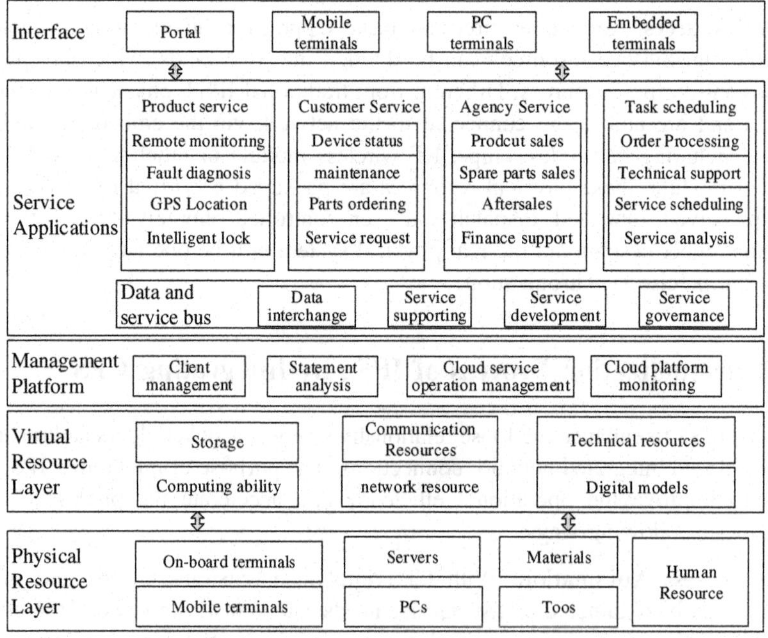

Fig. 2. A general architecture for CPS supported intellectualization of IPS2

(a) Physical resource layer: With the support of embedded cloud terminal technology and Internet of things, physical resources, including equipment, tools, materials, engineers and so on, are able to be connected to the network. Meanwhile, connection interfaces for cloud services virtual resource packaging and invocation are also provided in this layer.

(b) Virtual resource layer: In this layer, service resources connected to the network are collected as virtual service resources. Then, they would be packaged as cloud service using tools of cloud service defining and virtualization, and released to cloud service center through cloud management platform. This layer provides functions and virtual resources including storage ability, techniques base, computing ability, communication resources, network resources, digital model library and so on.
(c) Management platform: As the console of cloud service, management platform is an important support for management staff to monitor, supervise, analyze and optimize cloud services. Cloud basic management covers the function of platform service scheduling and distributing. Cloud platform monitoring is for the real-time management of platform performance indicators. Cloud platform operation management is developed for supporting resource distribution and tasks assignment.
(d) Service layer: This layer integrates data and service bus of the cloud platform and core service packages. Comprehensive intelligence service for customers, distribute agents, equipment operators, service engineers are provided from this layer.
(e) Interface layer: Base on cloud service platform, users can login through multiple log modes and terminals, while experiencing the same service applications. Services can be invoked form portal website, on-board terminals, mobile terminals, PC terminals and other approaches.

6 Discussions and Conclusions

The servitization trend of manufacturing industry is irreversible. Under this circumstance, the integration of CPS in IPS2 have been proved to be effective in improving service efficiency and reducing service costs. Based on the summary of investigation of several typical servitization industry, we found that companies in these industries are trying to build their own smart Industrial Product Service Systems by integrating CPS.

A general framework of intelligent IPS2 including 7 basic modules is proposed to guide the service transformation for manufacturing companies. We consider that the intellectualization of IPS2 by integrating CPS can be realized with three approaches, which are service process automation, service activity autonomy and service resource integration, respectively. In the meantime, the general five-layer architecture of CPS supporting intelligent IPS2 is also presented. Companies can make a customized version based on this proposed general architecture according to their own characteristics and particularities.

Those main findings presented in this work, have been validated with several cooperation projects. However, the research in this paper still needs improvements. Achievements of this work are studied from large groups or companies, so how these approaches can be applied to small and medium sized companies will be a new direction for future research.

Acknowledgements. The work described in this paper was supported by the fundamental Research Funds for the Central Universities, Shanghai Institute of Producer Service Development (SIPSD) and Shanghai Research Centre for industrial Informatics (SRCI2); and a grant from the National Science Foundation of China (Grant No. 71501006).

References

1. Lusch, R.F.: Service-dominant logic: reactions, reflections and refinements. Marketing Theory **6**(3), 281–288 (2006)
2. Mont, O.K.: Clarifying the concept of product–service system. J. Clean. Prod. **10**(2002), 237–245 (2001)
3. Meier, H., Völker, O., Funke, B.: Industrial product-service systems (IPS2). Int. J. Adv. Manufact. Technol. **52**(9–12), 1175–1191 (2010)
4. Wang, P.P., Ming, X.G., Li, D., Kong, F.B., Wang, L., Wu, Z.Y.: Status review and research strategies on product-service systems. Int. J. Prod. Res. **49**(22), 6863–6883 (2011)
5. Vasantha, G.V.A., Roy, R., Lelah, A., Brissaud, D.: A review of product–service systems design methodologies. J. Eng. Des. **23**(9), 635–659 (2012)
6. Wilson, H., Walton, I.M., Tranfield, D., Michele, P., Martinez, V., Lockett, H., Kingston, J., Johnson, M., Irving, P., Cousens, A., Bastl, M., Angus, J.P., Alcock, J.R., Tiwari, A., Braganza, A., Shehab, E., Roy, R., Peppard, J., Greenough, R., Neely, A., Evans, S., Lightfoot, H.W., Baines, T.S.: State-of-the-art in product-service systems. Proc. Inst. Mech. Eng., Part B: J. Eng. Manufact. **221**(10), 1543–1552 (2007)
7. Sha, L., Gopalakrishnan, S., Liu, X., Wang, Q.: Cyber-physical systems: a new frontier. In: Yu, P.S., Tsai, J.J.P. (eds.) Machine Learning in Cyber Trust, pp. 3–13. Springer, Ney York (2009)
8. Broy, M., Cengarle, M.V., Geisberger, E.: Cyber-physical systems: imminent challenges. In: Calinescu, R., Garlan, D. (eds.) Monterey Workshop 2012. LNCS, vol. 7539, pp. 1–28. Springer, Heidelberg (2012)
9. Lee, E.A.: Cyber-physical systems-are computing foundations adequate. In: Position Paper for NSF Workshop on Cyber-Physical Systems: Research Motivation, Techniques and Roadmap. Citeseer (2006)
10. Alippi, C.: Intelligence for Embedded Systems. Springer, Switzerland (2014)
11. Sztipanovits, J.: Cyber physical systems—convergence of physical and information sciences. it-Information Technology Methoden und innovative Anwendungen der Informatik und Informationstechnik **54**(6), 257–265 (2012)
12. Boehm, M., Thomas, O.: Looking beyond the rim of one's teacup: a multidisciplinary literature review of product-service systems in information systems, business management, and engineering & design. J. Clean. Prod. **51**, 245–260 (2013)
13. Zhu, H., Gao, J., Li, D., Tang, D.: A web-based product service system for aerospace maintenance, repair and overhaul services. Comput. Ind. **63**(4), 338–348 (2012)
14. Zhang, D., Hu, D., Xu, Y., Zhang, H.: A framework for design knowledge management and reuse for product-service systems in construction machinery industry. Comput. Ind. **63**(4), 328–337 (2012)
15. Teixeira, E.L.S., Tjahjono, B., Alfaro, S.C.A.: A novel framework to link prognostics and health management and product-service systems using online simulation. Comput. Ind. **63** (7), 669–679 (2012)
16. Selak, L., Butala, P., Sluga, A.: Condition monitoring and fault diagnostics for hydropower plants. Comput. Ind. **65**(6), 924–936 (2014)
17. Aurich, J., Schweitzer, E., Fuchs, C.: Life cycle management of industrial product-service systems. In: Takata, S., Umeda, Y. (eds.) Advances in Life Cycle Engineering for Sustainable Manufacturing Businesses, pp. 171–176. Springer, London (2007)

18. Aurich, J., Fuchs, C., DeVries, M.: An approach to life cycle oriented technical service design. CIRP Ann. Manufact. Technol. **53**(1), 151–154 (2004)
19. Takata, S., Umeda, Y.: Advances in Life Cycle Engineering for Sustainable Manufacturing Businesses: Proceedings of the 14th CIRP Conference on Life Cycle Engineering, Waseda University, Tokyo, Japan, 11–13 June 2007. Springer, London (2007)
20. Tukker, A.: Eight types of product–service system: eight ways to sustainability? Experiences from SusProNet. Bus.Strateg. Environ. **13**(4), 246–260 (2004)

Design Research on Urban Public Space Share Interactive Mode Under the Background of Internet Plus

Ping Zhou[1] and Zhiyong Fu[2(✉)]

[1] School of Architecture and Art, Central South University, Changsha 41000, Hunan, People's Republic of China
zhouping_322@126.com

[2] Academy of Art and Design, Tsinghua University, Beijing, China
fuzhiyong@tsinghua.edu.cn

Abstract. In terms of travel, social networking, consumer and other aspects, internet changes human behavior and urban public space. Location Big Data, Socially Aware Computing and PSPL Survey provide a basis for research and guidelines for the city's public spaces design of Internet plus. From the perspective of the Internet plus, combined with the location of Location Big Data, Socially Aware Computing and PSPL Survey, this article explains the interactive behavior between people, the innovative behavior between people and the environment, the interactions behavior between people and the objects, discusses the integration of "Urban Public Space Design" and "interaction design" in the future, explore the vitality, networking, dynamic, sharing, of urban public spaces. This article aims to construct a design patterns in sharing interactive of urban public space from Internet plus interactive for urban residents, to provide a spatial form of more experienced, participatory and dynamic, so as to enrich the innovative ideas of human urban design under the back ground of internet new context.

Keywords: Urban public spaces · Internet plus · Interactivity · Interactive mode · Design research · Location big data · Socially aware computing · PSPL survey

1 Introduction

Internet is a vast network waved by various networks through a set of common protocol, single and international logically [1]. "Internet plus" represents a new economic form [2], which means relying on the Internet information technology to realize the combination of the Internet and traditional industries, so as to to optimize the production factors, update the business system, and reconstruct business model to complete the economic transformation and upgrade. "Internet plus" program aims to give full play to the advantages of the Internet, make an in-depth integration of the Internet and traditional industries, to promotion economic productivity by industrial upgrading, and finally realize the increase of social wealth [3]. "Internet plus" is a new format of development of China in the situation of Innovation 2.0, new format of economic and social development in term of evolution and drive of Internet form pushed by Knowledge-based society and Innovation 2.0. Internet plus is a further practical achievement of Internet

P.-L.P. Rau (Ed.): CCD 2016, LNCS 9741, pp. 638–646, 2016.
DOI: 10.1007/978-3-319-40093-8_63

thinking, representing an advanced production power, promoting continuous evolution in economic form and further leading to vitality of social economic entity, providing a broad network platform for reform, innovation and development [4].

Urban public space refers to open space volume existing between building entities in a city or groups of cities, open places for urban residents to carry out public communication activities, serving most people; meanwhile, it is also important places for human and nature in material communication, energy exchanges and exchange of information, playing a significant role of reflecting the city's image. It is also called living room' and 'show window' of a city [5].

Urban public space is an important part of urban space with physical attribute of the built environment and social attribute on the background of politics, economy and culture while the later is the determinant of the former and the former carrier and presentation of the later. Only physical attribute is focused initially rather than social attribute in the definition of public space which is regarded same with that of open space and external space, etc. Carr (1992) defined public space in Urban space—public space as, "public places where people carry out functional activities or ceremony activities no matter in daily life or seasonal festivals, making people make up society." Physically public space and socially public space are an integral whole according to development of social history.

2 Support of Research on Urban Public Space Form Relevant Technical Method

With development of times, multi-side dialogue between various fields has been a new tendency of innovation and the alternative relationship between disciplines is increased year after year gradually, in addition, crossover design method has been a new design strategy in the current design field. Urban design is of integration, the connotations of which is gradually developed and redefined under the background of Internet. Kevin Linch set vitality as primary index for evaluating the quality of space form in book The Good City Form. He defined vitality in this way: the support degree of inhabitation mode for vital functions, ecological requirements and human capacity. With development of technology, Internet changes human behaviors in aspects of travel, social communication, consumption and housing and so on, making increasingly strong and dynamic subject consciousness in the creative process of urban public space design. Design disciplines are undergoing social turns as objects of design research change from forms to behaviors in interpersonal communication while the focus is gradually changed into human social demands [6]. Technology in social computation such as location big data and socially aware computing provides the studying foundation for urban public space design under the background of Internet plus while PSPL Survey is used as the main one in guiding urban public space design.

2.1 Location Big Data

Big data refers to polymerization of large and complex data sets. Scale and complexity of these data sets are often beyond the ability of the current database management software and data processing techniques in obtaining, management, retrieval, analysis, excavation and visualization within acceptable time. Location big data, LBD is an important part of big data. One key point for smart cities is to establish a ubiquitous urban computing system, which involves three major aspects of ubiquitous mapping, location big data analysis and service providing. Therefore, analytic processing and assistant decision of big data have become the key issues in smart cities implementation and urban geographic situation analysis [7].

2.2 Social Perception Computation and Design Research

Socially aware computing is aimed at carrying out real-time awareness and identification of social individual behaviors, analyzing, mining characteristics and rules of social interaction, assisting individual social behaviors and supporting the interaction, communication and cooperation of the community by large scale multi-type sensor devices increasingly deployed in human living space [8].

Social aware computing focused on using advanced computer science and technology to be aware of individual behaviors and group interaction in reality, understand the activity patterns of human society and provide intelligent assistant and support for individual and group interaction. Social internet analysis, machine learning, data mining and other methods are adopted to analyze group social interaction; socially aware computing is applied in aspects of urban social interwork, intelligent transport management, urban planning and development and so on.

2.3 Assessment Guidelines – PSPL

"Public Space - Public Life" survey method (PSPL Survey) is the main one adopted by Jan Gehl in his research on "the relationship between public space and public life" and later guidance in design. The method is aimed at providing basis for design and transformation of public space and further creating public space with high quality, meeting the demands of citizens in their developing public life by effectively understanding and grasping human activities and characteristics of their behaviors in public space based on results of analysis combining the quantitative and the qualitative [9].

As an assessment method of quality and citizens' living conditions in term of urban public space, this method is popular and easy to understand, evaluating public space quality and public living conditions to great extent. People are studied in their daily public life and usage of public space to discover the relationship between public space and life while data collection, processing and analysis are carried out for final usage through observation, interview and record of people in their activities and state of activity. This method is adopted in public space transformation project in New York and nine planning countermeasures and suggestions are proposed after research and analysis with a result of twofold increment in bicycle path and significant contribution in environmental protection of New York.

3 Research on Sharing Interactive Mode of Urban Public Space

3.1 The Design Framework of the Sharing Interactive Patterns of Urban Public Space

Design research on urban public space focuses on the interactive form of human experiences and participation by modern tech means under the background of information society and Internet plus. It is of characteristics of interactivity, participatory, science and technology. It is necessary to carry out deep researches on some core conceptions and theories from perspective of urban design, architectural planning theory, sociology, computer science and psychology and so on.

From the perspective of design research, analysis is made of interactive relationship between human, human and environment, human and objects in urban public space design based on direct support from such computer science as location big data and social perception, basis for implementation of usage of public space. PSPL Survey is an assessment method mainly for public life and public space, putting the space to good use and meeting the relevant demands of citizens in better harmony with the people-oriented design conception. The design framework of sharing interactive modes of urban public space and its content are as follows in Table 1.

Table 1. The design framework of interactive patterns in sharing urban public space and its content.

Conception	Interactive behavior	Innovative behavior	Inter-behavior
Relationship	Between human	Between human and environment	Between human and machine
Characteristic	Energetic	No-linear	Interactivity
Location big data	Data and information gathering, sharing, analysis and feedback	Platform for information sharing, exchange and gathering	Implementation of carrier, operation and application
Social perception	Human's participation and cooperation are necessary	Public space situation	Interactive pattern and information feedback
PSPL survey	Evaluating the space life	Evaluating space life and quality	Evaluating the space life

Detailed description and illustration of public space application will be carried out in the following from perspective of interactive behaviors, innovative behaviors and inter-behavior in the following based on the above research framework after practice, verification and improvement through specific projects.

3.2 Public Space Application Based on Interactive Behaviors

The value of public space is realized in people's participation and interaction and urban public space design under the background of Internet plus is design of people's lifestyle in the information age in fact. In term of interaction between people, urban public space design focuses on generation of information content, collection, share and feedback of data, in which people's participation and cooperation are necessary. At present, more and more design research begins to focus on mobile internet and the new way it provides for urban public space design. According to the current research, that obtaining the public's interaction and feedback as well as the way of applying the public data effectively is to be addressed urgently.

For example, I Love Beijing—online map and mobile app, it is used by urban maintenance personnel to cover such urban problems as road depression and lamp breakage, etc. Beijing Chengguan create I Love Beijing, city administration map public service platform based on theory of Innovation 2.0 and People's city, people manage while my territory, I control. At present, I Love Beijing has four functions: firstly, tip-offs, complaints, counsels, suggestions can be carried out directly through our website, city administration map as well as telephones, mail multi-channel accesses. Secondly, services of combination between dredging and blocking. The one proposed is convenience vegetable markets as more than 600 vegetable markets in Beijing are covered on the app. These markets are irregular and it is hard for the municipal government to trace their market hours, vegetable varieties and other information. Beijing residents are able to make scores and comments on market, correct error contents and add new ones, for example, information on market hours, through I Love Beijing. Thirdly, government affair maintenance and compilation system, through which the public are able to carry out compilations of the policies we upload, including giving policy suggestions. Fourthly, open data. We upload such data online as information on vegetable market to it and the data involved is original. Figure 1 is "I Love Beijing" for Smart City Administration: Cloud – Terminal Supporting Platform. Figure 2 is "I Love Beijing" for iPhone and Android: Mobile Public Service APP.

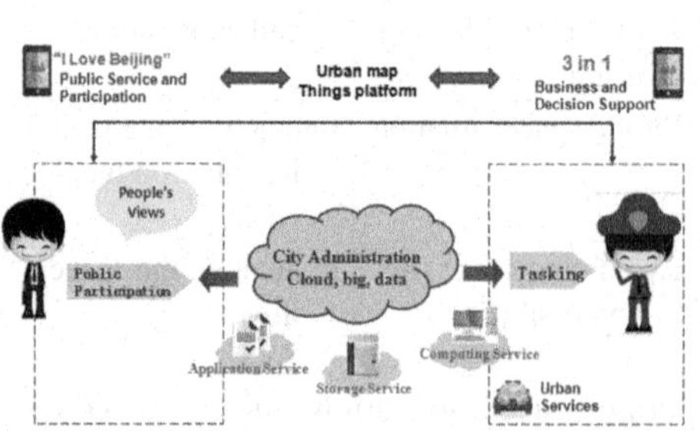

Fig. 1. "I Love Beijing" for smart city administration: cloud – terminal supporting platform.

Fig. 2. "I Love Beijing" for iPhone and Android: mobile public service APP.

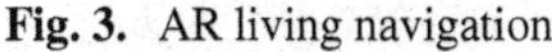
Fig. 3. AR living navigation

Fig. 4. Function interface

3.3 Public Space Application Based on Innovative Behaviors

Urban public space design must be fully people oriented, combine with environment to learn people's behavior pattern and mental tendency on one hand, and realize environment's guidance of people on the other hand. With rapid improvement of big data analysis ability and development of social media based on geographic information coding, new method and data make the effective measurement of urban street design and its attractively touchable. Innovative behaviors are requirement of city's humanization more as well as shaping experience city and dynamic city.

Such as based on geographical position and social function of application - Gaode navigation, it is an offline mobile navigation software for car-owners with distinguishing features of safety, easy to use and efficiency. Gaode map has created the best "living map" by using advanced technology for the users. That is, the design concept of human nature, rich interface reminder, clear voice guidance, beautiful interface and good navigation experience. Various depth POI points are more than 26,000,000, such as food, hotels, shopping malls and so on, and other all-round vast life information available for the search query, like clothing, living, transportation, entertainment, etc. Displaying the real road scene on the mobile phone screen by the camera, AR living navigation overlays road signs on the screen by using the navigation system, so that the users are able to experience the real scene navigation. Figure 3 is AR living navigation. Figure 4 is Function interface of Gaode.

3.4 Public Space Application Based on Inter-behavior

Inter-behavior focuses on characters and objects where the later refers to products and tangible substances in reality associated with Internet, meeting the requirements of interactive relationship establishment and building a bridge for interactions between urban spaces.

Recently, the air quality in Beijing can be described with words "bad and terrible". The hazy weather impresses people and people begin gradually to realize that air dust is harmful to their body. Therefore, people pay more and more attention to PM2.5 as these fine particles are more harmful to human body and air quality, beyond imagination.

In such a situation, mobile apps for providing officially air quality indexes appear naturally, very popular among the citizens. Some students and designers also participate in research and development of low-cost sensor devices which are available for citizens to measure air quality. Air.Air! is a convenient air quality monitor access to smartphone with display of regions with poor air quality and it will give a warning through smartphone. Pecking design students develop a air pollution monitor, the color of which changes gradually according to the degree of air pollution, making technical information more visual [10]. FLOAT smart kite designed by a designer in Beijing can measure the air quality over the city and make air quality map [11]. Figures 5 and 6 is about Air.Air!

Fig. 5. Air.Air! design model

Fig. 6. Air.Air! scenarios

4 Questions and Discussions

Location big data and socially aware computing technology applied in the sharing interactive mode of public space enable urban space design to be with more science and technology, interactivity, vitality and share, etc. In term of urban public space sustainable design, it is also necessary to focus and consider the virtual space shape and humanization. With rise of Internet plus, more and more designers and urban planners as well as audience begin to link mobile network with traditional industries in social life, active the public space design mode, enriching the audience's participation modes in public space and promoting communication between the designer and the audience. Audience's participation and feedback are required in public space under the background of internet in order to implement effectively sustainable operation of urban public space sharing interaction.

4.1 Improve Public Space Experience Based on Socially Aware Computing and PSPL Survey

The users' requirements of public space are changeable and dynamic. With internet's entrance in life, people's living habits are changed and it becomes hard for traditional public space design to meet the demands of its users. Research on public space design provides evaluations of various activities in public space and proposes design and reconstruction basis based on combination of rational cognition, perceptual experience and empirical analysis according to relevant users, group behaviors, data information and survey and analysis by combing with PSPL survey. However, it is unclear about how to establish public space quality standard and experience effects. It will be helpful to learn and analyze users, groups' behaviors and feelings, understand social activity modes of users and groups, providing intelligent auxiliary and supports and the information feedback help designers' optimization of spatial experience based on social perception computation. From perspective of design method, means of design are updated gradually and traditional means of design are sufficient to meet the demands of the current newly emerging design strategies. Urban design of integrity and establishment of platform for the sharing interactive mode of public space and solutions under the background of internet meets the demands of people in their interaction and application in spatial activities to greater extent. In addition, the design method combining social awareness and PSPL survey together is helpful for improving public spatial experience design.

4.2 Improve Public Space Innovation Based on Technology Means

Modern society has developed informational, omnidirectionally with digitization and intellectualization, marked by 'numbers' and 'net'. American scholar Negroponte always said, "the community consisting of internet users will be the tendency in daily life, the population structure will also become more and more similar with that of the world itself" [12]. It is can imaged that urban residents in future will complete their daily life through internet and changes in production and lifestyle of cities will lead to urban morphology—structure's fundamental transformation. With development of big data, transparent computation and VR technology and application of computer technology, new technology will redefine digital public space and bring unlimited space for future public space design as well and virtual space will be closer to our daily life in the future. Object images of urban space gives people subject image through their senses, that is, cities in their minds [13]. Human subject image plays significantly important role in urban public space creative design. Use new technical means to excavate psychological perception, put social perception technology to big use and promote the audience's participation in public space by catering to the audience with new interactive mode.

5 Conclusion

Research on public space design under the background of internet plus is cross-discipline involving urban design, construction planning, design research and computer science, etc. With continuous development of new technology's connotation and application, human participation will be required in future spatial structure to greater extent and the public will be the audience of space as well as participants in space design. Public space design is widened in breadth and depth based on location big data, social awareness and

PSPL Survey. The quality of public spatial from will be further improved if the technology, means and thinking of internet are integrated into traditional urban public space design. Interpretation of artificial space and space's shaping people and reflection of share interactive space applications with characteristics of participation and immersion by combining factors of technology and humanization will be another topic for public space design.

Acknowledgements. The paper received the support of the "Development Research of Hunan Animation Cultural Creative Industry" Hunan Philosophy and Social Science Fund Project, 14YBB084 in 2014, and Central South University undergraduate teaching reform project – "Digital Media Arts core curriculum optimization".

References

1. Biying network. http://www.bing.com
2. Cao, G.: "Internet+" Represents a New Economic Form by on 21st March 2015. http://tech.sina.com.cn/i/2015-03-21/163710019803.shtml
3. Huang, C., Wang, D.: What does "internet+" mean – a deep understanding of "internet+". News Writ. **5**, 5–9 (2015)
4. Baidu Baike. http://baike.baidu.com
5. Wang, P.: Systematic Construction of Urban Public Space. Southeast University Press, Nanjing (2002)
6. Fu, Z.: The design theory and research framework for pubic service in social media age. J. DMI Int. Design Manag. Conf. Thesis Collect. (Chin. version) **3**, 175–180 (2011)
7. Liu, J., Fang, Y., Guo, C., Gao, K.: Analysis, process and research development of location big data. J. Geomat. Inf. Sci. Wuhan Univ. 379–384 (2014)
8. Yu, Z., Yu, Z., Zhou, X.: Socially aware computing. J. Chin. J. Comput. 17–24 (2012)
9. Zhao, C., Yang, B., Liu, D.: PSPL survey: the evaluation method for quality of public space and public life—the study on Jan Gehl's theory and method for public space design (Part 3). J. Chin. Gard. 34–38 (2012)
10. http://www.artlinkart.com
11. http://www.demohour.com/projects/322832
12. Zhang, H.: City Space Interpersonal—Comparison and Research of Social Development in Domestic and Foreign Cities. Southeast University Press, Nanjing (2003)
13. Xia, Z., Huang, W.: Urban Space Design. Southeast University Press, Nanjing (2002)

Cross-Cultural Design for Health, Well-being and Inclusion

Can Autonomous Sensor Systems Improve the Well-being of People Living at Home with Neurodegenerative Disorders?

Tauseef Gulrez[1(✉)], Samia-Nefti Meziani[1], David Rog[2], Matthew Jones[2], and Anthony Hodgson[3]

[1] Autonomous System and Advanced Robotics Research Centre, University of Salford, Manchester, UK
{T.Gulrez,s.nefti-meziani}@salford.ac.uk
[2] Department of Neurology, Salford Royal NHS Foundation Trust, Salford, Manchester, UK
{david.rog,matthew.jones}@srft.nhs.uk
[3] Research and Development, Salford Royal NHS Foundation Trust, Salford, Manchester, UK
anthony.hodgson@srft.nhs.uk

Abstract. In this paper, we describe the development of an autonomous tracking system to be used in the home of the elderly population living with neurodegenerative disorders including dementia. The technology advancement has potential to produce low-cost solutions for elder-care in a residential setting. Our approach is based on the concept that body tracking interventional systems can be developed by utilizing low-cost technological solutions affordable to the aged population and can be deployed in the residential settings. We are exploring the usefulness of such systems in providing information that can assist with assessment of performance of activities of daily living in the periods between hospital clinic visits. Management of neurodegenerative disorders such as dementia and multiple sclerosis involve periodic review of patients at a specialist clinic. At these reviews the clinician solicits information about activities of daily living over the preceding period. This period can be a long interval of 6 to 12 months. When self-reports of activity are compared with independent objective measures, discrepancies are found in many areas of healthcare. This can cause difficulties in management of treatment. The autonomous sensor tracking systems developed here could improve care by giving clinicians objective assessments of relapses in the intervals between clinic visits. This could reduce the time spent on in- clinic examination as clinicians can use objective measures instead of semistructured interviews aimed at eliciting an accurate history. This will allow more time to spend on well-being and treatment options.

Keywords: Human body tracking · Human-computer-interaction · Kinect based interventional tracking · Activities of daily living · Medical history taking

P.-L.P. Rau (Ed.): CCD 2016, LNCS 9741, pp. 649–658, 2016.
DOI: 10.1007/978-3-319-40093-8_64

1 Introduction

Clinicians often rely on self-reporting of patients for the interval between the last hospital-visit to the present hospital-visit, for the assessment of performance of the patient to track the neurological disease progression. The self-reporting assessment system has been criticized by many clinicians and is prone to discrepancies in many areas of healthcare system. In neurological disorders such as Multiple Sclerosis (MS) and fronto-temporal dementia (FTD) personality changes occur e.g. dramatic increase in social submissiveness and introversion. There are no studies which can quantify the physical activity changes at home for such FTD or MS population. It is of paramount importance to clinicians to objectively quantify the behavioural features (over an extended period of activity in a home situation) for the accurate diagnosis of the disease. Moreover, the movement assessment of patients living with neurodegenerative disorders such as MS is an important factor for clinicians to monitor disease progression and respond for timely intervention. A low-cost, unobtrusive sensorized system capable of autonomously detecting patients behavioral state at home could help significantly improve accuracy of assessments and hence improve quality of care for these patients. In order to achieve this goal we need to develop a system which can relate the in-home physical activity to activity within the clinical test.

Wearable devices unarguably can detect the patient's living state at home, these include pedometers, specialized accelerometers, etc. [7]. However, the biggest disadvantage of wearable devices is compliance with the need to wear or carry them. There are also issues with collecting continuous sets of data as well as battery life. Environmentally mounted sensors that make passive observations of patients while at home overcome many of these deficits. Several studies have discussed the non-wearable preference of older adults [4]. Numerous researchers have looked at the use of environmentally mounted sensors, such as vibration sensors mounted on the floor [16], infrared passive sensors [15], acoustic sensors [10], and video streaming (an intrusion into privacy), including traditional cameras [9] and thermal imaging sensors [12]. Studies have found that privacy concerns of older adults to vision-based monitoring systems may be addressed by the use of appropriate privacy preserving processing techniques, such as silhouettes [3].

Early reports suggest the Kinect can identify pose [1,6,11], simple stepping movements [5] and postural control [2] in healthy adults, although some have raised concerns about the accuracy of the skeleton model estimation during unconventional body postures or when using wheelchairs or walkers [8,13]. There is also growing evidence for the use of exercise-based computer games (exergames) to retrain motor function in people with Parkinson's disease (PD) [14], although evidence of their safety and efficacy are yet to be established [11]. Exergaming as a therapeutic tool that incorporates functional, purposeful and engaging exercise in a quantifiable and reliable way that also encourages high volumes of practice and potentially improved motivation and adherence [12]. A player's movement can be recorded whilst playing a game using the Kinect, allowing clinicians to ensure the patient perform exercises correctly.

In this research paper, we demonstrate proof of concept of obtaining early stage experimental results of physical activity obtained in a domestic setting. We demonstrate an unobtrusive continuous gait monitoring system based on the Microsoft Kinect sensor that could measure the gait of older adults, in their homes, during normal daily activity. However, the output of the system, measures of in-home gait speed, stride time, stride length, etc., is not easily interpretable, as such parameters have never before been available. Thus, either a large scale study to directly relate these in-home gait parameters to health status is needed, or a methodology to relate the parameters to existing well studied and understood domains needs to be developed. For this work, the Kinect-based in-home gait system was deployed in a residential setting. While the systems were installed, the participants also completed preliminary walking assessment consisting of standard mobility test, such as a short maximum speed walk (SMSW). The SMSW test has been widely studied and shown to be a good measure of functional ability as well as an indicator of falls risk in the elderly [7,15]. As such, mapping of the residential gait data to this well understood domain would facilitate interpretation of the data by a clinician.

This paper presents a methodology for and results from estimating walk time from in-home gait data, specifically walking speed, collected by the Kinect-based systems. The purpose is not to measure SMSW time directly, but to map the in-home gait data to a domain that clinicians understand; and to assess the accuracy of the mapping with regards to what could theoretically be expected. Although this paper focuses on mapping in-home gait speed to SMSW time, the approach could be used with any data source, and any well studied domain. Section 2 of this paper discusses the materials and methodology used in the area of in-home gait and functional ability assessment. Section 3 contains the results of estimating SMSW time from in-home gait speed and compares it to estimates made using SMSW measured by a clinician at the same time. Finally, a discussion of the results and their implications is given in Sect. 4.

2 Materials and Methods

2.1 Ethics Statement

No video recordings during any task were made in this study. The Kinect sensor's numerical data was recorded that directly related to walking movements. The numerical data was de-identified, representing joint positions, were stored in the database for further analysis. Volunteers were researchers at the University of Salford, Manchester and Salford Royal NHS Foundation Trust.

2.2 Second Generation Microsoft Kinect V2 Based Sensing

The Microsoft Kinect is a camera-based sensor primarily used to directly control computer games through body movement. The Kinect tracks the position of the limbs and body without the need for handheld controllers or force platforms.

Use of a depth sensor also allows the Kinect to capture three-dimensional movement patterns. We propose that this system has the potential for remote assessment of movement symptoms in people with neurological disorders, exemplified by MS and FTD symptoms.

2.3 Data Collection

The data acquired during subject monitoring included 3-D body joint information provided by Microsoft Kinect V2 at a rate of 30 frames per second. The data acquisition was supported by an in-house developed application written in MS Visual studio 2015 C++ using the Kinect SDK v2.0. Microsoft Kinect sensor with the use of its software development kit (SDK) provides three-dimensional skeletal data on 26 joint positions over time. We chose to record the positions of four skeletal joints namely, spine-base, hip, knee and ankle center of gravity or leg movements, which are potential walking velocity indicators. With 7 joints (spine-base, left and right joints for hip, knee and ankle) and 3 floating point values (real numbers) representing the x, y, and z positions for each joint, each motion frame was expressed as a 21-element position vector. The 3D position (x, y, z) of a joint is expressed in the position coordinate system of the Kinect sensor and the units are in meters (as shown in Fig. 1). The walking speed rely on motion dynamics so our system is view-independent, i.e., there is no need to express the recorded positions in the coordinate system of the subject's body. The dynamic of each joint is computed using the variation of position of the joint over time. In the first step, each joint motion, defined by the sequence of 3D positions, is replaced by the distance between each frame particular joint that varies from $0 \ldots k$, where k is the number of frames in a performed motion.

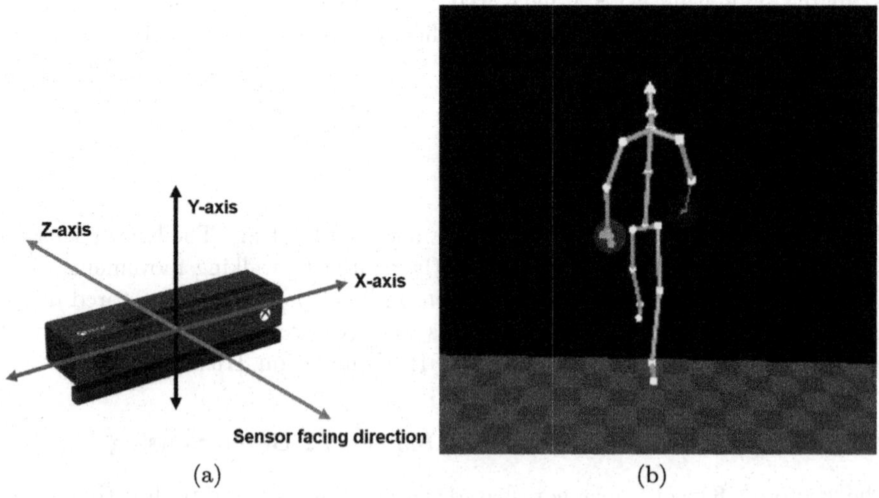

Fig. 1. Planar view of Microsoft Kinect - (a) The 3D planar view associated with Microsoft Kinect. (b) Skeletal tracking and joints in x,y - plane.

The instantaneous velocity of motion for a particular joint is calculated as the resultant of $\boldsymbol{x}$, $\boldsymbol{y}$, and $\boldsymbol{z}$ positions over all frames that represent a motion. The instantaneous velocity V_{inst} for a given 3D motion is computed as follows:

$$V_{inst} = \frac{d(x, y, z)}{dt} \quad (1)$$

$$V_{inst} = \frac{1}{T}\sqrt{(x(k) - x(k-1))^2 + (y(k) - y(k-1))^2 + (z(k) - z(k-1))^2} \quad (2)$$

where $\mathbf{T}$ is the sampling interval and equals the reciprocal of the sampling frequency $(1/30 = 0.0333)$ s and $\boldsymbol{k}$ is the number of joint data points. The subject's kinematic properties can be extracted using the value of the joint positions, and if required joint angles, angular velocities and accelerations can be calculated based on the time history of the joint positions. Moreover, to remove possible artefacts in the joint position data, a 2D moving average filter was used to smooth the data (as shown in Fig. 2).

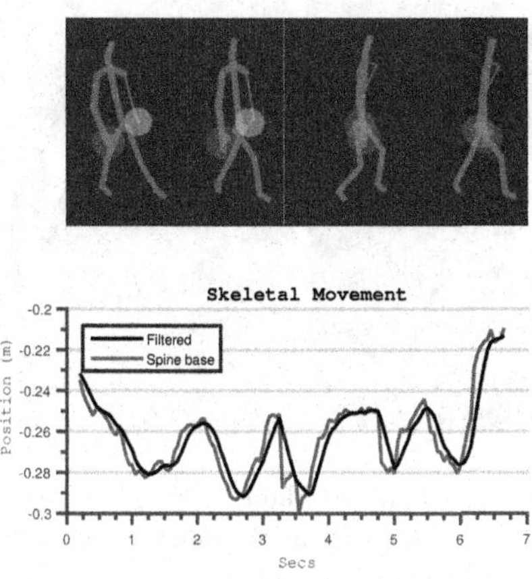

Fig. 2. Plot of correlation spine-base position data during walk; used to identify when steps occur. A moving average smoothed filter output is also shown in black. (Color figure online)

2.4 Kinect Based Short Maximum Speed Walk (SMSW) Assessment

The short maximum speed walk (SMSW) assessment at Salford Royal NHS Foundation Trust (hospital), is usually carried out in a narrow corridor. The Kinect sensor was mounted on 2.5 m height tripod at the end of the same corridor of the hospital, thereby covering a rectangular area of roughly 3.5 × 2.5 m (see Fig. 3(a)). Each subject was tested in an evenly lit environment in a single session of sequential tests as shown in the Fig. 3(a) and (b). All subjects were given the same instruction as specified in a standardized test procedure: "Walk as fast as you can towards the sensor". The starting point for walking was approximately three meters outside the detection range of the sensor. We postulated that this would allow the subject to reach maximum walking speed before reaching the measurement zone. The start was given as a voice command. An automatic computer-generated sound signalled the subject to end the experiment after leaving the opposite edge of the sensor measurement zone. Similarly, the same software was used to calculate the time taken from the initial point of start to the end point 25-foot mark. The time taken to complete a timed 25-feet walk (T25-FW) gives a quantitative mobility and leg function measure, based on a 25 feet walking distance.

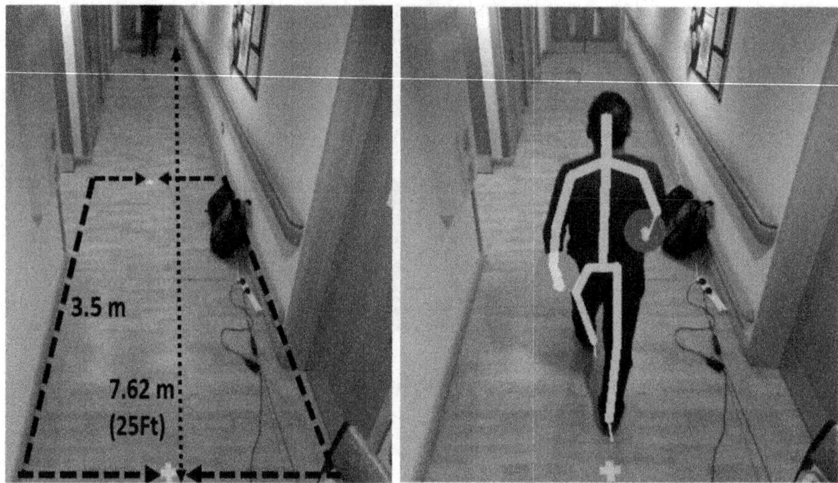

Fig. 3. Schematic system setup (in xy-plane). (a) The Kinect sensor was positioned 2.5 m above ground. Subjects walked with maximum speed towards the Kinect camera. (b) Sample screenshot of a healthy subject during the test with skeleton projection (green lines). The spine-base joint was used as the data source for analysis. (Color figure online)

2.5 Residential Autonomous Sensing System

A Microsoft Kinect sensor and computer were deployed in a residential apartment as part of a volunteer study at researchers' house. The Kinect was installed on a 2.5 m height tripod, which can easily be placed on any shelf a few inches below the ceiling (height 2.5 m), above the front door. This arrangement has proven to be unobtrusive to the residents, with most indicating that they do not notice the equipment after a short period of time. The output of the Kinect based residential autonomous systems was a dataset in which each entry corresponds to a joint position of the skeletal movement that occurred in the apartment (Fig. 4).

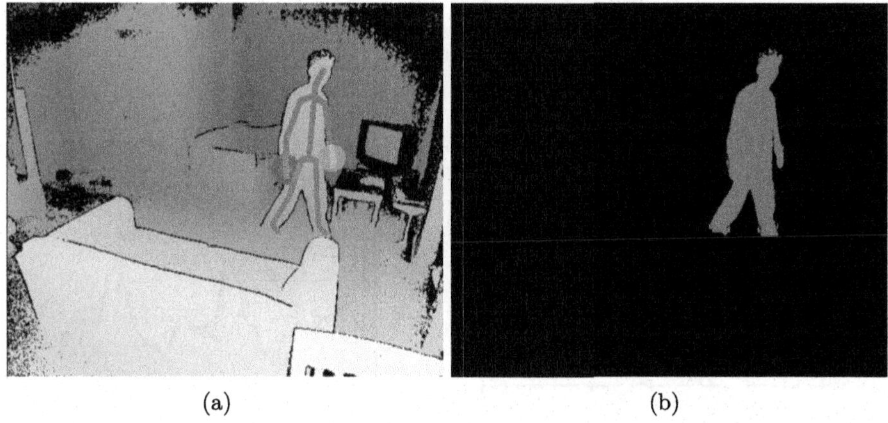

(a) (b)

Fig. 4. Kinect sensor installed in a residential setting. (a) The background is subtracted while depth silhouettes and skeletons are determined by the Kinect SDK. (b) Infra-red and depth sensing from the similar image.

3 Results

The participants performed a set of walking movements which involved spine base, hips, knee and ankle joints. Figures 2 and 5 represent the time series of spine base, hip and ankle positions (which compound the walking movement) and the root mean squared errors (RMSE) are shown in Fig. 6. Joint movements are reported in Figs. 2 and 5 represents the evolution of the walking movement where as the continuous curve is the filtered output of the each joint position. The results in Figs. 2 and 5 show the walking movement from one of the experiments using the Kinect based system during the assessment at the hospital. A correlation coefficient r and RMSE was calculated between the joint (spine-base,

Table 1. Mean RMSE (meters), Correlation (r) between the joint positions during assessment at hospital and in-home monitoring system.

Experiment	Joints	RMSE(m)	r
Subject 1	Spine-base Assessed/In-home	0.010	0.95
	Hip Assessed/In-home	0.011	0.93
	Ankle Assessed/In-home	0.010	0.91
Subject 2	Spine-base Assessed/In-home	0.011	0.94
	Hip Assessed/In-home	0.015	0.94
	Ankle Assessed/In-home	0.012	0.90
Subject 3	Spine-base Assessed/In-home	0.013	0.95
	Hip Assessed/In-home	0.015	0.94
	Ankle Assessed/In-home	0.10	0.93

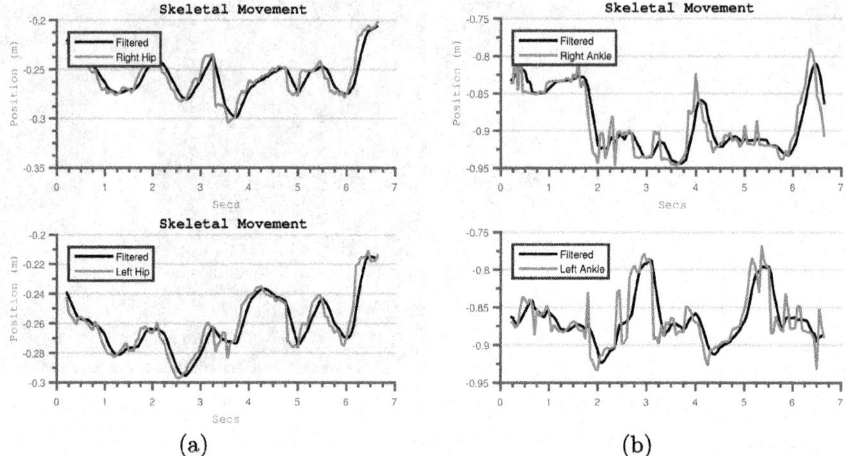

Fig. 5. Joint positions and moving average filtered output. (a) Left and right hip joint position and filtered output. (b) Left and right ankle joint position and filtered output. (Color figure online)

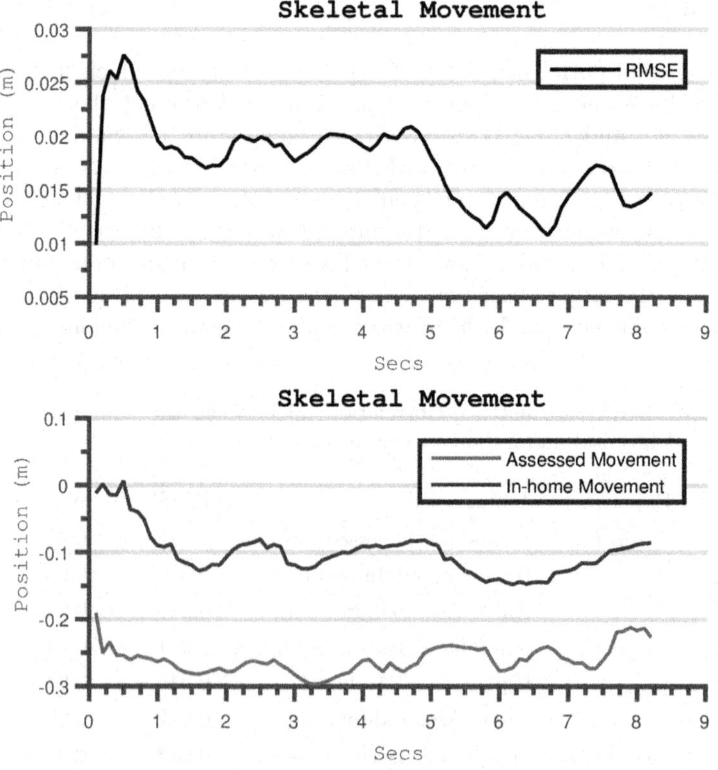

Fig. 6. Root mean squared error and correlation between the walking speeds, obtained during clinical assessment at hospital and at residential setting. (Color figure online)

hip and ankle) positions obtained during the clinical assessment and the in-house monitoring as tabulated in Table 1. On average, the RMSE was less than 0.012 for all joint positions and the correlation coefficient varied between $0.90 \leq r \geq 0.95$. Correlations between time series of walking assessment at Table 1. Mean RMSE (meters), Correlation ($\boldsymbol{r}$) between the joint positions during assessment at hospital and in-home monitoring system as tabulated in Table 1. The results obtained correspond to what we expected. Walking readings at assessment and in-home monitoring are determined by joint positions activity, which do not necessarily occur simultaneously.

4 Conclusions

In this an early stage of proof of concept study, we investigated the applicability and feasibility of Microsoft Kinect v2 assisted motion analysis during the hospital walking gait assessments and in-home monitoring. Our primary question was whether skeletal tracking data recorded by the Kinect based system would yield reliable information for clinicians to assess the walking gait from in-home monitoring system. Using the spine-base, hip and ankle joints, we established the test SMSW to analyse person's gait at maximum walking speed. The linear distance covered by the recognition area was only 3.5 m (see Fig. 1 and Table 1), and consequently only a few steps of each subject were analysed. Despite this short walking and recording time, the overall detection quality of the target hip-centre joint of the SMSW over time was excellent.

The noise from the Microsoft Kinect based system was filtered out by applying a custom-built moving average filter developed during the analysis of this experiment. After filtering the SMSW average walking speed parameter was excellent and on par with T25FW. An analysis of skeletal data from spine-base, hip and ankle joints was performed for the walking assessment in healthy subjects. Our findings show that Kinect-based motion analysis is also feasible in Multiple Sclerosis (MS) patients and can detect gait differences in comparison to healthy controls.

References

1. Chang, Y.J., Chen, S.F., Huang, J.D.: A kinect-based system for physical rehabilitation: a pilot study for young adults with motor disabilities. Res. Dev. Disabil. **32**(6), 2566–2570 (2011)
2. Clark, R.A., Pua, Y.H., Fortin, K., Ritchie, C., Webster, K.E., Denehy, L., Bryant, A.L.: Validity of the microsoft kinect for assessment of postural control. Gait Posture **36**(3), 372–377 (2012)
3. Demiris, G., Oliver, D.P., Giger, J., Skubic, M., Rantz, M.: Older adults' privacy considerations for vision based recognition methods of eldercare applications. Technol. Health Care **17**(1), 41–48 (2009)
4. Demiris, G., Rantz, M.J., Aud, M.A., Marek, K.D., Tyrer, H.W., Skubic, M., Hussam, A.A.: Older adults' attitudes towards and perceptions of smart home technologies: a pilot study. Med. Inf. Internet Med. **29**(2), 87–94 (2004)

5. Fern'ndez-Baena, A., Susin, A., Lligadas, X.: Biomechanical validation of upper-body and lower-body joint movements of kinect motion capture data for rehabilitation treatments. In: 2012 4th International Conference on Intelligent Networking and Collaborative Systems (INCoS), pp. 656–661. IEEE (2012)
6. Galna, B., Barry, G., Jackson, D., Mhiripiri, D., Olivier, P., Rochester, L.: Accuracy of the microsoft kinect sensor for measuring movement in people with parkinson's disease. Gait Posture **39**(4), 1062–1068 (2014)
7. Gosney, J.L., Scott, J.A., Snook, E.M., Motl, R.W.: Physical activity and multiple sclerosis: validity of self-report and objective measures. Fam. Commun. Health **30**(2), 144–150 (2007)
8. Gulrez, T., Tognetti, A.: A sensorized garment controlled virtual robotic wheelchair. J. Intell. Rob. Syst. **74**(3–4), 847–868 (2014)
9. Lee, T., Mihailidis, A.: An intelligent emergency response system: preliminary development and testing of automated fall detection. J. Telemedicine Telecare **11**(4), 194–198 (2005)
10. Li, Y., Zeng, Z., Popescu, M., Ho, K.: Acoustic fall detection using a circular microphone array. In: 2010 Annual International Conference of the IEEE Engineering in Medicine and Biology Society (EMBC), pp. 2242–2245. IEEE (2010)
11. Lim, D., Kim, C., Jung, H., Jung, D., Chun, K.J.: Use of the microsoft kinect system to characterize balance ability during balance training. Clin. Interv. Aging **10**, 1077–1083 (2015)
12. Mastorakis, G., Makris, D.: Fall detection system using kinect's infrared sensor. J. Real-Time Image Proc. **9**(4), 635–646 (2014)
13. Obdrzalek, S., Kurillo, G., Ofli, F., Bajcsy, R., Seto, E., Jimison, H., Pavel, M.: Accuracy and robustness of kinect pose estimation in the context of coaching of elderly population. In: 2012 Annual International Conference of the IEEE Engineering in Medicine and Biology Society (EMBC), pp. 1188–1193. IEEE (2012)
14. Padala, K.P., Padala, P.R., Burke, W.J.: Wii-fit as an adjunct for mild cognitive impairment: clinical perspectives. J. Am. Geriatr. Soc. **59**(5), 932–933 (2011)
15. Sixsmith, A., Johnson, N., Whatmore, R.: Pyroelectric ir sensor arrays for fall detection in the older population. J. de Phys. IV (Proceedings) **128**, 153–160 (2005). EDP sciences
16. Zigel, Y., Litvak, D., Gannot, I.: A method for automatic fall detection of elderly people using floor vibrations and sound-proof of concept on human mimicking doll falls. IEEE Trans. Biomed. Eng. **56**(12), 2858–2867 (2009)

Kitchen KungFu: A Match-3 Game to Explore Chinese Medical Beliefs

Shuyu Li[1,2] and Pei-Luen Patrick Rau[1,2](✉)

[1] Department of Foreign Languages and Literatures, Tsinghua University, Beijing, China
lishuyusylvia@gmail.com, rpl@mail.tsinghua.edu.cn

[2] Department of Industrial Engineering, Tsinghua University, Beijing, China

Abstract. Chinese people have their own set of medical beliefs. However, it could cause misunderstanding during cross-cultural communication, especially under clinical settings. In this case study, we designed an educational game *Kitchen KungFu*, which incorporates knowledge of Chinese medical beliefs into the rules of match-3 games like *Candy Crush Saga*. Specifically, the game presents yin-yang theory and the cold-hot foods culture. Ten international participants were recruited to play the game and give feedback. Quantitative and qualitative analyses showed that this educational game increased participants' agreement with and knowledge of Chinese medical beliefs. As an exploration of employing gamification to promote cross-cultural understanding, *Kitchen KungFu*'s design and evaluation process could provide valuable reference for future studies.

Keywords: Cross-cultural communication · Chinese medical beliefs · Gamification · Educational game

1 Introduction

1.1 Chinese Medical Beliefs

Chinese people have their unique beliefs about healthcare and medicine. These medical beliefs are shaped by various factors. Among others, Traditional Chinese Medicine (TCM) plays an important role. For example, theories of Zang-fu (viscera) and Ching-lo (meridian), and theory of Chi (energy) constitute ancient people's understanding of human's physical structure [1]. Besides TCM, religions and philosophies also bring profound influence. For example, yin-yang theory and five-element theory, which are stemmed from Taoism, shape the basic logic of traditional Chinese medical system. Fatalism, which is advocated by Buddhism, could affect patients' response to certain diseases and medical treatments [2]. And Confucianism emphasizes family values and respect to doctors [3]. Meanwhile, some social and cultural customs like Fengshui and fortune-telling also have impact on people's medical beliefs and practices [4].

1.2 Cross-Cultural Communication

Even as western medicine is globally dominant, Chinese people still, to some extent, hold to their own medical beliefs. Undoubtedly this cultural uniqueness shapes

P.-L.P. Rau (Ed.): CCD 2016, LNCS 9741, pp. 659–667, 2016.
DOI: 10.1007/978-3-319-40093-8_65

Chinese's cultural identity. However, it can also result in misunderstanding during cross-cultural communication, especially under clinical settings. For example, a western physician may not understand when his Chinese patient says he feels "numb" in his body, which is caused by inadequate "blood and energy" [5]. Or, due to Chinese's holistic view regarding body and mind as unitary, patients with mental illness like depression tend to describe their diseases as physical symptoms. In that situation, western doctors might fail to diagnose the true causes [6].

To avoid the trouble, some immigrants would choose Chinese clinicians or even return to home countries for medical treatment [5], which leads to inconvenience and further cultural isolation. Therefore, raising awareness on Chinese medical beliefs is a worthy effort to bridge the cultural gap.

Though introductory materials on Chinese medical beliefs are not rare, most of them are in the form of books and articles. On mobile platform, some applications featuring TCM are also available, for example, *Eastland Herb*, *Traditional Chinese Medicine* and *TCM Herbal Formula Library*. However, most of them are abbreviated versions of medical books or lists of diseases, cures and herbs, which lack interaction and entertainment. In order to address the gap, we designed an educational game called *Kitchen KungFu*, and evaluated its effect on changing player' level of agreement with and knowledge of Chinese medical beliefs.

2 Ideation

2.1 Theme

Among various Chinese medical beliefs, yin-yang theory is a core concept as well as the most influential one even among the highly westernized Chinese people [5]. It stems from Taoism, representing the balance between two opposite forces. In foods, yin-yang is demonstrated as their cold or hot properties. People take proper foods according to their own cold or hot "body constitution" to keep the balance [1]. Considering that food properly demonstrates the essence of Chinese medical beliefs, as well as stimulates people's interest, we employed it as our design's starting point.

2.2 Gamification

We decided to apply gamification to introduce Chinese medical beliefs because it could stimulate users' interest and convey knowledge at the same time. According to Deterding et al., gamification is using "game design elements in non-game contexts" [7]. Within the broad category of game, educational games are those designed to facilitate learning [8]. Using game elements in learning environment could increase players' incentives and interest, resulting in higher-level memorization and lasting influence [7, 9].

Among various game genres, we based our design on match-3 game, or matching tile game, whose core mechanics is to make and eliminate combos of three or more same items by swaping adjacent items. Such games include *Candy Crush Saga* and *Bejeweled*. The simplicity of match-3 game enables it to be easily played and spread across different cultures [10]. Meanwhile, its "matching" nature provides a suitable base for us to add more complicated rules and demonstrate Chinese medical philosophy.

3 *Kitchen KungFu*

3.1 Prototype

The game is named as *Kitchen KungFu*, indicating that it is about both food and Chinese culture. A cartoon panda is designed as narrator, introducing background knowledge and rules. Overall, the game content consists of two sections: 1. cold and hot foods 2. food and body interaction. Within each section, there is one warm-up exercise where related concepts and theories are introduced. In the first section warm-up, players learn about yin-yang theory and cold-hot foods, and anticipate the category of some common foods (shown in Fig. 1). In the second section, players complete a simple quiz to determine their body constitution, and then learn about the relationship between body and foods (shown in Fig. 2).

Fig. 1. Warm-up exercise in the first section

Following the warm-up exercise, there are several match-3 game levels from easy to hard. The main interactive area is a 7 * 7 grid, where various food items are randomly distributed. The goal is to eliminate enough cold or hot foods according to instructions. In the first section, a yin-yang shaped pan is designed as status bar to visualize the connection between food and medical philosophy. As players eliminate more and more target foods, the corresponding hemisphere increases from empty to full. In the second section, players are required to eliminate target foods to neutralize cold or hot types of body constitutions. The abstract body constitution is presented as ice or fire icons.

Fig. 2. Warm-up exercise in the second section

Since the whole game context is about food and Chinese culture, some power-ups are designed with cultural implications as well. For example, the "family dinner" power-up will lengthen the countdown by five seconds. It indicates Chinese people's emphasis on having meals with family (Table 1).

Table 1. Game elements

Elements	Icons	Implications
Food items		Cold foods
Food items		Hot foods
Status bar		Yin hemisphere: cold Yang hemisphere: hot
Ice and fire		Ice: cold body constitution Fire: hot body constitution
Power-up 1		Family dinner: adding five seconds
Power-up 2		Recipe: reminder of target foods
Power-up 3		Spoon: breaking up ice or putting up fire

To create an immersive playing experience, we incorporated background music loops and various sound effects into the game. As players conduct each operation, there are sounds of cheers or regrets, according to whether target or non-target foods are eliminated. In this aspect, *Kitchen KungFu* is different from common match-3 games, where positive feedback is plenty while negative feedback is limited [10]. Since an important goal of our game is to help players differentiate food categories, we used both positive and negative sounds to assist players' memorization (Fig. 3).

Fig. 3. Completing different levels

3.2 User Testing

In order to evaluate how *Kitchen KungFu* would influence non-Chinese people's agreement with and knowledge of Chinese medical beliefs, we conducted a user test. Ten participants were recruited, all international students studying in Tsinghua University. They came from different countries including Thailand, New Zealand, Brazil, Netherlands, France, Morocco, Bangladesh and Iran. They were instructed to play the game, and complete a questionnaire both before and after the game. An in-depth interview followed up to understand participants' detailed opinions on Chinese medical beliefs and the game.

The pre-game questionnaire consisted of five statements on Chinese medical beliefs. Participants chose their level of agreement with each statement on a 5-point Likert scale from "strongly disagree" to "strongly agree". The first four statements were set according to Chew's research on Chinese cultural beliefs, assessing participants' agreement with certain TCM concepts and practices [11]. The fifth statement measures participants' willingness to consult TCM for themselves (shown in Table 2). The post-game questionnaire included the same five statements and four questions assessing players' memorization of related knowledge. They were all multiple-choice questions, asking about the categories each food belongs to and medical solutions to specific scenarios, all of which are explicitly demonstrated in the game.

Table 2. Average answer to each statement before and after the game

Statements	Before	After
1. Certain diseases are caused by 'too much heat' or 'too much coldness' in the body (disruption of yin-yang balance)	3.8	4.2
2. Fever is due to excessive heat inside the body	3.0	3.6
3. After childbirth, the woman should take 'hot' foods like ginger and red wine to expel the 'coldness' in body	2.8	3.8
4. Traditional Chinese herbal medicine has fewer side effects than Western medicine	3.6	3.9
5. I will consider seeking TCM when I am sick	3.0	3.6

4 Results and Analysis

4.1 Data Interpretation

We calculated each participant's level of agreement with Chinese medical beliefs by averaging their answers to the first five statements. Before the game, the mean of the ten participants' agreement level is 3.24 (SD = 0.68). After the game, the mean is 3.82 (SD = 0.58). A paired t-test was conducted to measure the difference of agreement before and after the game (p = 0.056) (shown in Table 3). Considering that the number of participants is limited, the actual agreement level change was more significant than the p-value indicated. While most participants' rated higher after the game, three persons' answers remained the same. Abdellah, a player from Morocco, rated low on the second and third statements both before and after the game. During the interview, he explained he disagreed with the cause of fever and the childbirth practice, and since the game did not explain those aspects, his answers did not change after it. Shaya was familiar with Chinese medical beliefs before the game. She specially mentioned that the interval between two questionnaires was too short that for a person who already agreed with Chinese medical beliefs, the change could be insignificant.

Table 3. Average answer of each player before and after the game

Participants	Before	After
Shanto (Bangladesh)	1.8	3.4
Vincent (France)	3.4	4.0
Peter (Netherlands)	3.2	4.4
Yvonne (Netherlands)	3.4	3.6
Cheng (New Zealand)	4.0	4.6
Nittita (Thailand)	3.4	4.0
Rafael (Brazil)	3.0	4.0
Wildiner (Brazil)	3.4	3.4
Abdellah (Morocco)	2.6	2.6
Shaya (Iran)	4.2	4.2
Average	3.24	3.82

We also found that in certain cases, participants' agreement with the statements might not reflect their agreement with Chinese medical beliefs. For example, Vincent from France chose 2 to the statement "fever is due to excessive heat inside the body" before the game and 1 after it. He explained that since playing sports and warming up the body will help relive the fever, the fever was instead caused by too much coldness. As a result, though Vincent believed in yin-yang theory, he used it to reach an opposite conclusion.

As to the memorization of knowledge, the last four questions have an average accuracy of 82 %, 70 %, 80 % and 70 % respectively. According to the interview, most participants did not know about cold-hot food culture nor had related knowledge before, though many of them had heard of yin-yang theory. Thus the result indicates that the game was effective in imparting knowledge and helping players develop a short-time memorization.

However, there are limitations on the sample's number and representativeness. All participants are students in Tsinghua University, from bachelor to PhD degrees. Most of them are from Asian and European countries, which could not comprehensively reflect international players' situations.

4.2 Educational Game

Overall, each player took an average of 25 min to finish *Kitchen KungFu*. Though they were told in advance that they could have certain difficult levels skipped, many insisted on finishing the whole game independently and enjoyed meeting the challenge. After the game, most participants expressed strong interest in the concept of educational game. They liked to learn while having fun, and were ready to know more about Chinese medical beliefs. One participant remarked that *Kitchen KungFu* was different from ordinary match-3 games like *Candy Crush Saga*, "Besides speed and observation, it adds another dimension. You need to remember the knowledge presented before to better pass each level."

Meanwhile, the interview provided insights into the balance of entertainment and learning in an educational game. One participant commented that he did not strive to memorize specific hot or cold foods once he found that eliminating non-target items would not reduce scores. This might suggest that the ratio of positive and negative feedback should be given more consideration.

Other factors also influence participants' interest and learning results. For example, players' technological familiarity and previous experience with match-3 games largely determined their initial inclination towards *Kitchen KungFu*. Those who were already fans of match-3 games, or those confident that they would quickly learn the game expressed a higher morale. But two participants expressed worries before the game for they seldom played mobile games before. One of them failed several levels and became a bit depressed, while the other gradually gathered confidence and passion as he became familiar with various operations.

Some usability issues, like the device's slow response and certain levels' high degree of difficulty, also had negative affect on players. Such observations and feedback provide direction for the game's future improvement.

4.3 Cultural Diversity

Though western medicine is prevalent across the world, the interview reveals participants' notion of medical diversity. Instead of taking western medicine as the only cure, many participants were open to solutions from other cultures, including TCM and traditional medicine from their own countries. Several participants expressed their preference to herbal medicine over western medicine, because herbs were more "natural" and would cause fewer side effects. A participant from Iran noted that recently in her country, instead of seeking only western healthcare, people and government were placing more emphasis on traditional medicine industry.

Traditional and modern medicine's efficacy is still a topic under heated discussion, but it is not our focus in this study. However, as medical beliefs are a facet of culture, this conveys an encouraging message that these players are, to some extent, embracing cultural diversity.

5 Conclusion

Kitchen KungFu is an exploration to present cultural values through gamification. By designing a game that incorporates Chinese medical beliefs and conducting a user test after the game, our study provides valuable reference to gamification's potential for improving cross-cultural communication.

In future study, we will refine the game's visual design and improve its usability. We will also expand its educational content from yin-yang theory to more comprehensive themes like five-element theory, nutrition diet and Chinese cuisine. Meanwhile, we hope to add more variety to the game mechanics.

Acknowledgements. This study was funded by a Natural Science Foundation China grant 71188001 and State Key Lab Automobile Safety and Energy.

References

1. Ni, M.: The Yellow Emperor's Classic of Medicine. Shambhala Publications, Boston (1995)
2. Heiniger, L.E., Sherman, K.A., Shaw, L.K.E., Costa, D.: Fatalism and health promoting behaviors in Chinese and Korean immigrants and caucasians. J. Immigr. Minor. Health **17**(1), 165–171 (2013)
3. Yeo, S.S., Meiser, B., Barlow-Stewart, K., Goldstein, D., Tucker, K., Eisenbruch, M.: Understanding community beliefs of Chinese-Australians about cancer: initial insights using an ethnographic approach. Psycho-Oncology **14**(3), 174–186 (2005)
4. Yip, K.S.: Traditional Chinese religious beliefs and superstitions in delusions and hallucinations of Chinese schizophrenic patients. Int. J. Soc. Psychiatry **49**(2), 97–111 (2003)
5. Green, G., Bradby, H., Chan, A., Lee, M.: "We are not completely Westernised": dual medical systems and pathways to health care among Chinese migrant women in England. Soc. Sci. Med. **62**(6), 1498–1509 (2006)

6. Yeung, A., Kam, R.: Illness beliefs of depressed Chinese-American patients in a primary care setting. Perspectives in cross-cultural psychiatry, pp. 21–36 (2005)
7. Deterding, S., Dixon, D., Khaled, R., Nacke, L.: From game design elements to gamefulness: defining gamification. In: Proceedings of the 15th International Academic MindTrek Conference: Envisioning Future Media Environments, pp. 9–15. ACM, September 2011
8. Dondlinger, M.J.: Educational video game design: a review of the literature. J. Appl. Educ. Technol. **4**(1), 21–31 (2007)
9. Moreno-Ger, P., Burgos, D., Martínez-Ortiz, I., Sierra, J.L., Fernández-Manjón, B.: Educational game design for online education. Comput. Hum. Behav. **24**(6), 2530–2540 (2008)
10. Juul, J.: Swap adjacent gems to make sets of three: a history of matching tile games. Artifact **1**(4), 205–216 (2007)
11. Chew, K.S., Tan, T.W., Ooi, Y.T.: Influence of Chinese cultural health beliefs among Malaysian Chinese in a suburban population: a survey. Singap. Med. J. **52**(4), 252–256 (2011)

Young and Elderly, Normal and Pathological Gait Analysis Using Frontal View Gait Video Data Based on the Statistical Registration of Spatiotemporal Relationship

Kosuke Okusa[1](✉) and Toshinari Kamakura[2]

[1] Kyushu University, Fukuoka 815-8540, Japan
okusa@design.kyushu-u.ac.jp
[2] Chuo University, Tokyo 112-8551, Japan
kamakura@indsys.chuo-u.ac.jp

Abstract. We study the problem of analyzing and classifying frontal view gait video data. In this study, we focus on the shape scale changing in the frontal view human gait, we estimate scale parameters using the statistical registration and modeling on a video data. To demonstrate the effectiveness of our method, we apply our model to young and elderly, normal and pathological gait analysis. As a result, our model shows good performance for the scale estimation and gait analysis.

Keywords: Shape analysis · Gait analysis · Scale estimation

1 Introduction

We study the problem of analyzing and classifying frontal view gait video data. A study on the human gait analysis is very important in the fields of the health/sports management, medical research, and the biometrics.

Gait analysis is mainly based on motion capture system and video data. The motion capture system can give the precise measurements of trajectories of moving objects, but it requires the laboratory environments and this system cannot be used in the field study. On the other hand, the video camera is handy to observe the gait motion in the field study.

From the standpoint of health/medical research area. Gage [3] proposed brain paralysis gait analysis using gait video data. Kadaba *et al.* [5] discussed importance of lower limb in the human gait using gait video data too. Many gait analysis have recently analyzing using video analysis software (e.g. Dartfish, Contemplas, Silicon Coach). For example, Borel *et al.* [2] and Grunt *et al.* [4] proposed infantile paralysis gait analysis using lateral view gait video data.

From the standpoint of statistics, Olshen *et al.* [11] proposed the bootstrap estimation for confidence intervals of the functional data with application to the gait cycle data observed by the motion capture system.

P.-L.P. Rau (Ed.): CCD 2016, LNCS 9741, pp. 668–678, 2016.
DOI: 10.1007/978-3-319-40093-8_66

However, most studies have not focused on frontal view gait analysis, because such data has many restrictions on analysis based on the filming conditions.

The video data filmed from the frontal view is difficult to analyze, because the subject getting close in to the camera, and data includes the scale-changing parameters [1,6]. To cope with this, Okusa *et al.* [10] and Okusa & Kamakura [7] proposed a registration for scales of moving object using the method of nonlinear least squares, but Okusa *et al.* [10] and Okusa & Kamakura [7] did not focus on the human leg swing. Okusa & Kamakura [9] focus on the gait analysis using arm and leg swing model with estimated parameters and application to the normal/pathological gait analysis. However, their models have many of parameters, and it raise calculation cost and instability of parameter estimation.

On the other hand, from the stand point of biometrics, many of this area's researchers mainly using human silhouette shape for the gait authentication. However, they did not focus on the scale registration in the frontal view gait analysis case. In this area, just normalize the human silhouette and it apply to the gait authentication. It is reasonable to suppose that the normalize of the human silhouette lost a lot of gait information.

In this study, we focus on the scale changing of human shape in the frontal view gait analysis, we estimate scale parameters using the statistical registration and modeling on a video data. To demonstrate the effectiveness of our method, we apply our model to the frontal view gait analysis. As a result, our model shows good performance for the scale estimation and gait analysis.

The organization of the rest of the paper is as follows. In Sect. 2, we discuss the advantage and problem of frontal view gait analysis. In Sect. 3, primarily, we describe archetype model proposed in Okusa & Kamakura [8]. Next, we discuss the modified model for the shape scale registration. In Sect. 4, we validate our modified model using the frontal view gait analysis. We conclude with a summary in Sect. 5.

2 Frontal View Gait Data

In this section, we describe an overview of frontal view gait data. Many of gait analysis using lateral view gait data (e.g. Borel *et al.* [2], Grunt *et al.* [4], Barnich & Droogenbroeck [1], Lee *et al.* [6]), because observed data not includes the scale-changing parameters, it is easy to detect the human gait features. In a corridor like structure, the subject is approaching a camera. Such case is difficult observe lateral view gait.

In a lateral view gait, at least two cycles or four steps are needed. For more robust estimation of the period of walking, about 8 m is recommended. To capture this movement, the camera distance required is about 9 m. Practically, having such a wide space is difficult. On the other hand, frontal view gait video is easy to observe 8 m (or more) gait steps [6].

Figure 1 is an example of frontal view gait data recorded by Fig. 2 situation. Figure 1 illustrates difficulty of frontal view gait analysis. This figure indicates the subjects getting close in to the camera and the subjects scaling is changing.

Fig. 1. Frontal view gait data

The frontal view gait analysis requires registration of scale-changing component. Figure 3 shows subject's width time-series behavior of frontal view gait data. This figure illustrates frontal view gait data contains many of time-series components.

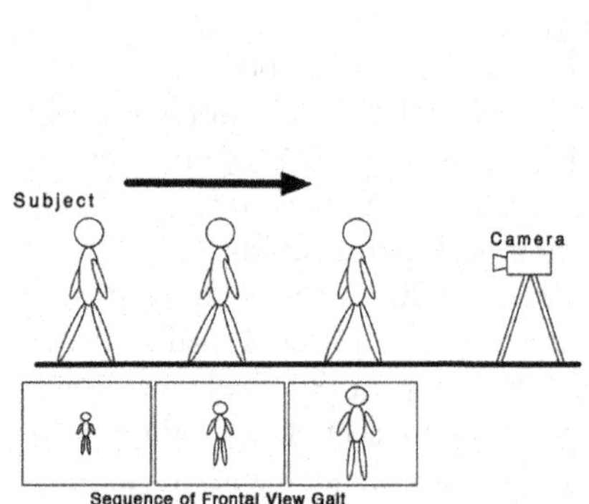

Fig. 2. Filming situation of frontal view gait data

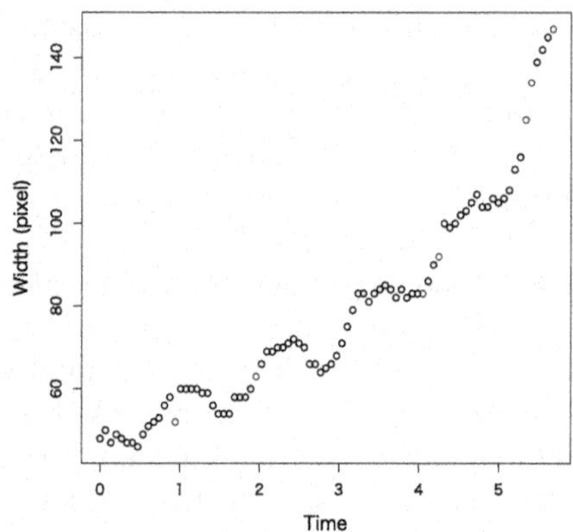

Fig. 3. Time-series behavior of frontal view subject width

3 Modeling of Frontal View Gait Data

3.1 Preprocessing

The raw video data is difficult to observe subject width and height time-series behavior, because data contains background. We separate subject from background using background subtraction method (Eq. 1).

$$\Delta^{(T)}(p,q) = |I^{(T)}(p,q) - B(p,q)|, \quad T = 1, ..., (n-1),$$
$$\Delta^{(T)}(p,q) = \begin{cases} 1 & (\Delta^{(T)}(p,q) > Th) \\ 0 & (\text{Otherwise}). \end{cases} \tag{1}$$

Here, $\Delta^{(T)}$ is an background subtraction image, $I^{(T)}, B$ are grey scaled video data image and background image at frame T respectively. (p, q) is the pixel coordinate.

Generally, this method is difficult to apply to the field study data (e.g. security camera), because the all background pixels are not static. However, in the experimental environment case, background pixels are tunable. We can assume that inter-frame subtraction method is reasonable. In the field study data, many of researchers are using "dynamic background subtraction" method (see Tamersoy [12], Zheng *et al.* [13]).

After the background subtraction, we apply the Laplacian filter to extract the subject's shape image. Figure 4 is background subtraction (left side) and Laplacian filtered image (right side) of frontal view gait data. From this figure, this preprocessing can extract the subject shape from video data. In this research, we focus on the subject's width/height. We can assume that subject's width/height as a bounding rectangle of subject's shape.

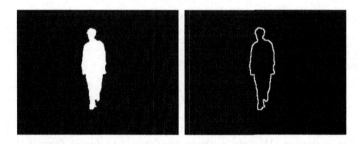

Fig. 4. Background subtraction (left side) and Laplacian filtered (right side) image of frontal view gait image.

3.2 Relationship Between Camera and Subject

In this section, we describe archetype model proposed in Okusa & Kamakura [8]. Figure 5 shows a relationship between camera and subject. From Fig. 5, width and height model has same structure. In this section, we describe the subject's width modeling. We can assume simple camera structure. We consider the virtual screen exists between observation point and subject, and we define x_i as subject width on the virtual screen at i-th frame $(i = 1, ..., n)$.

Here we define z_i, z_j as distance between observation point and subject at i-th, j-th frame, z_s as distance between observation point and virtual screen, $\theta_{x_{i1}}$, $\theta_{x_{i2}}$ as subject angle of view from observation point at i-th frame, d as distance between observation point and 1st frame, v_i as subject speed at i-th frame. Okusa *et al.* [10] defined the subject length L was constant. We assume that L has the time-series behavior and we define L_i is the subject length at i-th frame.

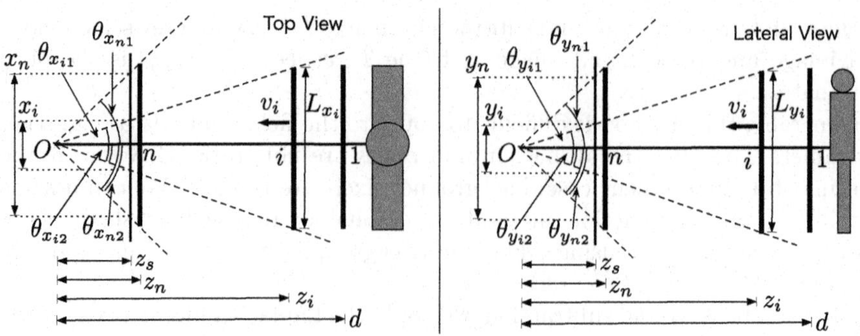

Fig. 5. Relationship between camera and subject

x_i at i-th frame depends on $\theta_{x_{i1}}$, $\theta_{x_{i2}}$ as shown in Fig. 5.

$$x_i = z_s(\tan\theta_{x_{i1}} + \tan\theta_{x_{i2}}). \tag{2}$$

Similarly, the subject length at i-th frame is

$$L_{x_i} = z_i(\tan\theta_{x_{i1}} + \tan\theta_{x_{i2}}). \tag{3}$$

From Eqs. (2), (3), ratio between x_n and x_i is

$$\frac{x_n}{x_i} = \frac{L_{x_n} z_i}{L_{x_i} z_n} \tag{4}$$

Frame interval is equally-spaced (15 fps). Okusa *et al.* [10] assumed the average speed is constant. We can assume that average speed from i-th frame is $(n - i) = (z_i - z_n)/\bar{v}$, therefore z_i is $z_i = z_n + \bar{v}(n - i)$. We substitute z_i to Eq. (4)

$$x_i = \frac{M_{x_i}\gamma}{\gamma + (n - i)} x_n + \epsilon_i, \tag{5}$$

where γ is $z_n/\bar{v}$, M_{x_i} is L_{x_i}/L_{x_n}, ϵ_i is noise. From Eq. (5), predicted value $\hat{x}_i^{(n)}$ is registration from i-th frame's scale to n-th frame's scale

$$\hat{x}_i^{(n)} = \frac{\gamma + (n - i)}{M_{x_i}\gamma} x_i. \tag{6}$$

Next, we discuss the modified model for the shape scale registration.

3.3 Modified Model for the Shape Scale Registration

Let us consider the scale of shape, it seems that subject's width and height's has same relationships.

From Eq. (5), we can define subject height as

$$y_i = \frac{M_{y_i}\gamma}{\gamma + (n - i)} y_n + \epsilon_i, \tag{7}$$

where M_{y_i} is L_{y_i}/L_{y_n}.

We can assume that subject's width and height are same scale changing components γ, we can estimate common scale parameter γ from the following nonlinear least squares equation.

$$S(\gamma, M_x, M_y) = \sum_{i=1}^{n} \left[\left\{ x_i - \frac{M_x \gamma}{\gamma + (n-1)} x_n \right\}^2 + \left\{ y_i - \frac{M_y \gamma}{\gamma + (n-1)} y_n \right\}^2 \right] \to \min .$$

We set the initial value γ as $\frac{1}{2n} \sum_{i=1}^{N} \left(\frac{x_i(n-i)}{x_i - M_x x_n} + \frac{y_i(n-i)}{y_i - M_y y_n} \right)$ where mean value of solve Eqs. (5), (7) for γ, and M_x, M_y as 1 (Okusa *et al.* [10]).

In next session, we validate the effectiveness of our model.

4 Experiments and Results

In this section, we validates our modified model using the frontal view gait authentication. To validate the effectiveness of our model, we observes frontal view walking video data (10 steps, Male, average height: 176.4 cm, sd: 3.07 cm) and apply to our proposed model.

Figure 6 is plot of the one of the 10 subjects width (pixel) time-series behavior. Here, continuous line represent fitted value of Eq. 5. Similarly, Fig. 7 is plot of subject height (pixel) time-series behavior. Here, continuous line represent fitted value of Eq. 7. From Figs. 6 and 7, proposed model is good fitting for frontal view gait data.

Figure 8 is plot of the scale-corrected result of circumscribed quadrangle of human gait silhouette based on the proposed method. Left side picture and right side picture are scale-corrected and non-corrected results, respectively. From Fig. 8, proposed model is able to correct the scale changing components. Proposed method keeps arm and leg swing components after the registration.

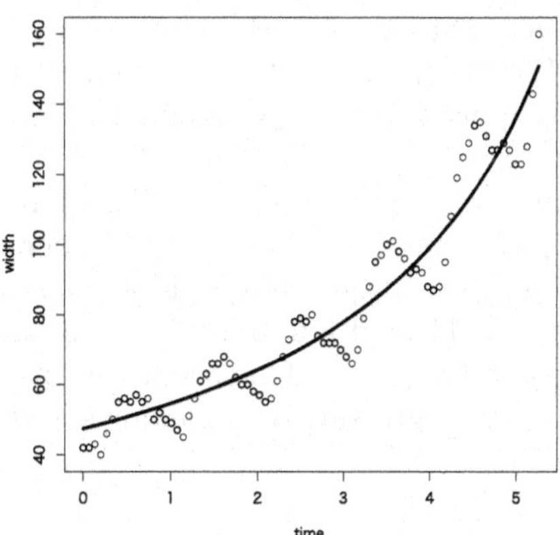

Fig. 6. Fitted value of subject's width

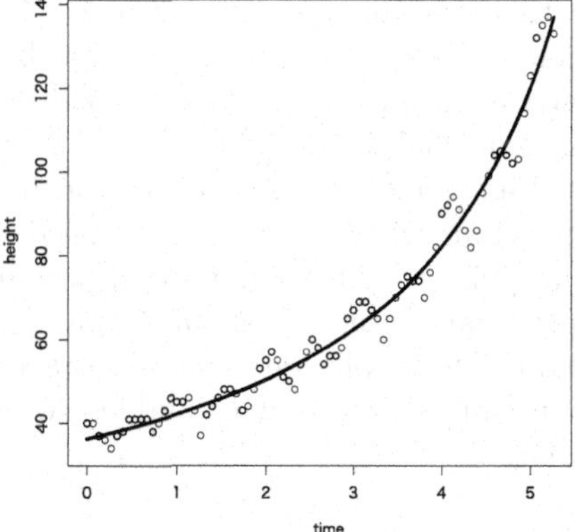

Fig. 7. Fitted value of subject's height

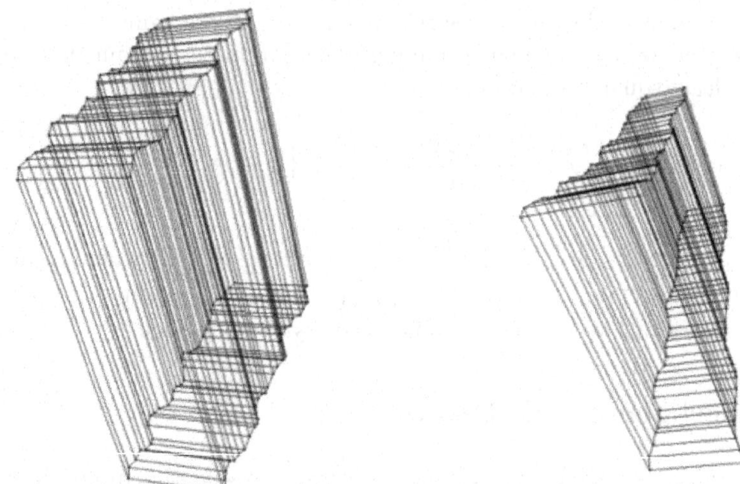

Fig. 8. Scale-corrected result of circumscribed quadrangle of human gait silhouette (left side), non-corrected result (right side)

4.1 Gait Analysis

To demonstrate the effectiveness of our method, we conducted two sets of experiments, assessing the proposed method in gait analysis for young/elderly person and pathological gait detection. We use SONY DCR-TRV70K camera. Frame rate of video data is 15 fps and resolution is 640 × 480.

In this paper, we focus on $\hat{\gamma}$ (speed parameter), $(\hat{P}_1+\hat{P}_2)/2$ (width amplitude parameter), and $\hat{b}_1$ (height amplitude parameter).

4.2 Gait Analysis: Young Person

In this experiment we took movie of 120 subjects walking video data from frontal view (10 steps, Male: 96 (average height: 173.24 cm, sd: 5.64 cm), Female: 24 (average height: 156.25 cm, sd: 3.96 cm)) and apply to our proposed method for the gait analysis.

Figure 9 is plot of speed vs width amplitude vs height amplitude. Figures 10 and 11 are width amplitude vs speed and height amplitude vs speed. The important point to note is that speed parameter $\hat{\gamma}$ is $z_n/\bar{v}$. If the subject walking fast, speed parameter $\hat{\gamma}$ is small. From Figs. 9, 10 and 11, width amplitude vs speed and height amplitude vs speed have a nonlinear relationship. This results means, if the subject's arm swing and leg swing moving strongly, subject's walking speed is fast.

4.3 Gait Analysis: Elderly Person

In this experiment we took movie of 60 subjects walking video data from frontal view (10 steps/average age: 76.97sd: 4.16/pathological gait subjects; average age:

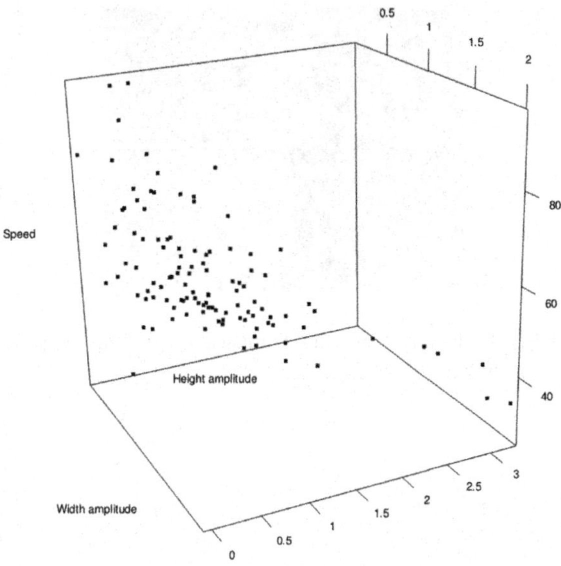

Fig. 9. Speed vs width amplitude vs height amplitude (young)

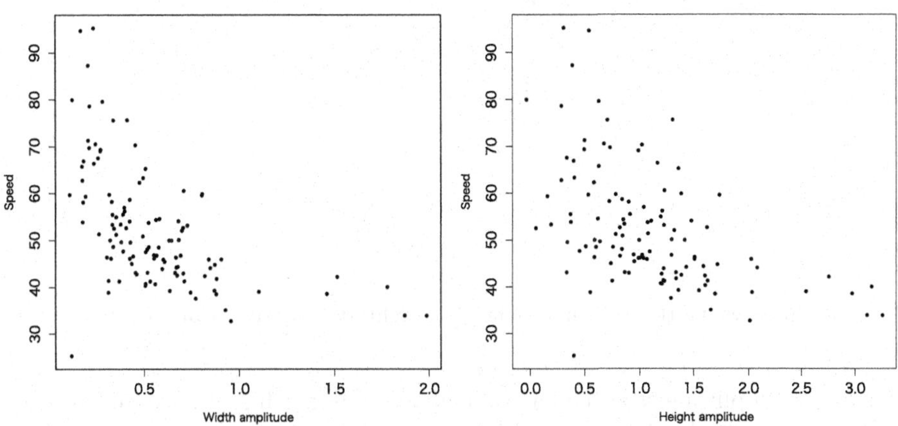

Fig. 10. Width amplitude vs speed (young)

Fig. 11. Height amplitude vs speed (young)

77.56sd: 4.35/normal gail subjects; average age: 75.37sd: 3.18) and apply to our proposed method for the gait analysis. Figure 12 is a example of elderly person's frontal view walking data.

Figure 13 is plot of speed vs width amplitude vs height amplitude. Black and red dot means normal and pathological gait subjects respectively.

Figures 14 and 15 are width amplitude vs speed and height amplitude vs speed. Black and red dot means normal and pathological gait subjects respectively. From Figs. 13, 14 and 15, normal gait subject width amplitude vs speed

Fig. 12. Elderly person's frontal view walking data

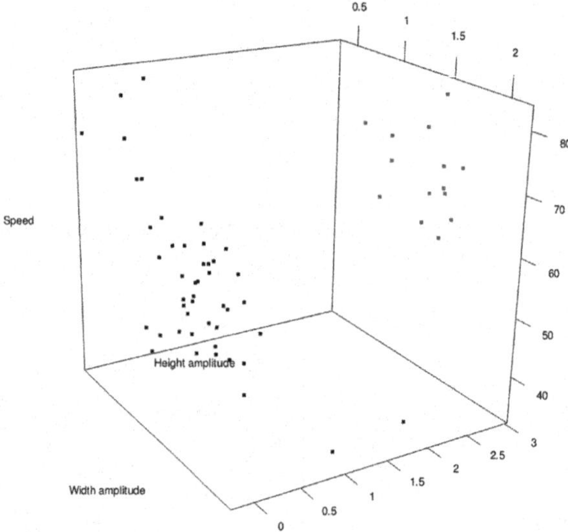

Fig. 13. Speed vs width amplitude vs height amplitude (elderly) (Color figure online)

and height amplitude vs speed have a nonlinear relationship like a young person. However, on the other hand, pathological gait subject estimated parameters does not have nonlinear relationship. These pathological gait parameters clustered in different place from normal gait subjects. The result leads to our presumption that the pathological gait subject trying to moving fast, but this effort is not effective to moving speed.

4.4 Pathological Gait Detection

In this section, we apply K-NN classifier (K=3), using the estimated parameters, to perform normal/pathological gait detect, and present results from an experiment involving 120 subjects (young person), and 60 subjects (elderly person).

To evaluate our estimated parameters, we apply these parameters to leave-one-out cross-validation test. Table 1 is average detection rate of

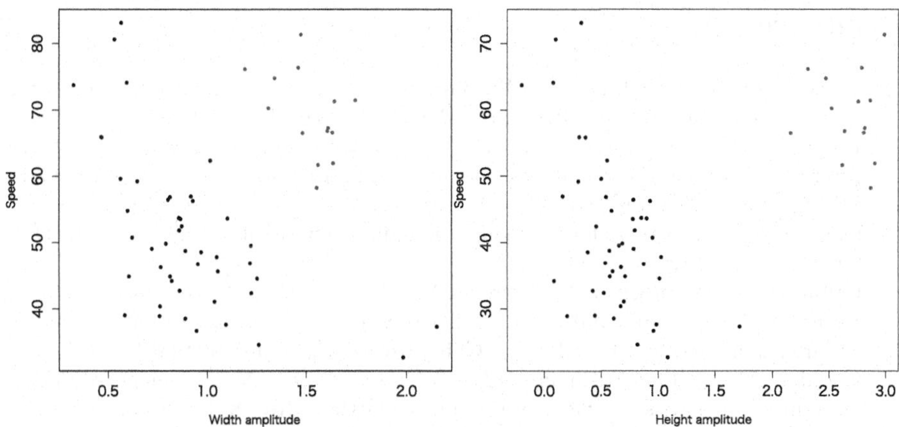

Fig. 14. Width amplitude vs speed (elderly) (Color figure online)

Fig. 15. Height amplitude vs speed (elderly) (Color figure online)

normal/pathological gait. Table 1 shows our estimated parameters may be used for the normal/pathological gait detection.

Table 1. Normal/Pathological gait average detection rate (%)

	Normal gait	Pathological gait
Normal gait	98.2	1.8
Pathological gait	0	100

5 Conclusion

In this article, we focus on the shape scale changing in the frontal view human gait, we estimate scale parameters using the statistical registration and modeling on a video data. To demonstrate the effectiveness of our method, we apply our model for the frontal view human gait analysis. As a result, we also show that our method may be used for the frontal view human gait analysis.

In next phase, we need to speed up the calculation cost of our method. Additionally, we need to implement the gait analysis system based on the proposed method and demonstrate it.

Acknowledgement. This work was supported by JSPS KAKENHI Grant Number 30636907, 40150031.

References

1. Barnich, O., Droogenbroeck, M.V.: Frontal-view gait recognition by intra-and inter-frame rectangle size distribution. Pattern Recogn. Lett. **30**, 893–901 (2009)
2. Borel, S., Schneider, P., Newman, C.J.: Video analysis software increases the inter-rater reliability of video gait assessments in children with cerebral palsy. Gait Posture **33**(4), 727–729 (2011)
3. Gage, J.R.: Gait analysis for decision-making in cerebral palsy. Bull. Hosp. Jt. Dis. Orthop. Inst. **43**(2), 147–163 (1982)
4. Grunt, S., van Kampen, P.J., Krogt, M.M., Brehm, M.A., Doorenbosch, C.A.M., Becher, J.G.: Reproducibility and validity of video screen measurements of gait in children with spastic cerebral palsy. Gait Posture **31**(4), 489–494 (2010)
5. Kadaba, M.P., Ramakrishnan, H.K., Wootten, M.E.: Measurement of lower extremity kinematics during level walking. J. Orthop. Res. **8**(3), 383–392 (1990)
6. Lee, T.K.M., Belkhatir, M., Lee, P.A.: Fronto-normal gait incorporating accurate practical looming compensation. In: Pattern Recognition (2008)
7. Okusa, K., Kamakura, T.: A statistical registration of scale changing and moving objects with application to the human gait analysis. Bull. Jpn. Soc. Comput. Statist. **24**(2) (2012) (in Japanese)
8. Okusa, K., Kamakura, T.: Fast gait parameter estimation for frontal view gait video data based on the model selection and parameter optimization approach. IAENG Int. J. Appl. Math. **43**(4), 220–225 (2013)
9. Okusa, K., Kamakura, T.: Gait parameter and speed estimation from the frontal view gait video data based on the gait motion and spatial modeling. Int. J. Appl. Math. **43**(1), 37–44 (2013)
10. Okusa, K., Kamakura, T., Murakami, H.: A statistical registration of scales of moving objects with application to walking data. Bull. Jpn. Soc. Comput. Stat. **23**(2), 94–111 (2011) (in Japanese)
11. Olshen, R.A., Biden, E.N., Wyatt, M.P., Sutherland, D.H.: Gait analysis and the bootstrap. Ann. Stat. **17**(4), 1419–1440 (1989)
12. Tamersoy, B.: Background subtraction - lecture notes (2009)
13. Zheng, S., Zhang, J., Huang, K., He, R., Tan, T.: Robust view transformation model for gait recognition. In: International Conference on Image Processing (ICIP), pp. 2073–2076 (2011)

Research on the Characteristics of Headforms and Classification of Headforms of Chinese Adults

Linghua Ran(✉), Hong Luo, Xin Zhang, Huimin Hu, Taijie Liu, and Chaoyi Zhao

Ergonomics Laboratory, China National Institute of Standardization, Beijing 100191, China
ranlh@cnis.gov.cn

Abstract. The characteristics of heads have been analyzed based on the head dimensional data of 3000 Chinese adults of different areas, ages and sexes, headforms have been classified according to the head height, breadth and length, two-dimensional distributions of head height-length indices and head breadth-length indices have been established, and headform groups and coverage rates have been provided. The research can support the production and specification setting of the head and face products, especially the head protection products.

Keywords: Characteristics of heads · Classification · Chinese adults

1 Introduction

With the development of the industrial production, the suitability of the safety protection products, such as the safety helmet and respiratory protection product, has become a big concern, since products with suitable dimensions can not only satisfy the wearing comfortableness, but also meet the requirement of protecting physical health of workers. The head data can provide bases for the designing of a series of head devices, including the headgear, safety helmet, respiratory protection mask, etc. The method for type and size classification of the protecting products and the coverage proportion both depend on the distribution of the head dimensions and the grading algorithm of the headform samples. The study on the specifications in headform distribution can provide basically guiding data for the dimensions and production quantities of head and face products, esp. head and face labor-protection products.

China formally promulgated the 'Headform Series of Chinese Adults' (GB 2428-81) in 1981, in which there are description and classification of headform characteristics of males and females respectively, with 13 headforms in total [1]. In 1988, 22,300 Chinese adults were investigated and a data base of Chinese adult human-body dimensions was established, with 7 face and head data items, which are the head full height, head sagittal arc, bitragion-coronal arc, maximum head breadth, maximum head length, head circumference and morphological facial length [2].

P.-L.P. Rau (Ed.): CCD 2016, LNCS 9741, pp. 679–685, 2016.
DOI: 10.1007/978-3-319-40093-8_67

On the basis of this, China promulgated GB/T 2428-1998 Head and Face Dimensions of Adults in 1998, after measuring 393 people as a small sample group (7 basic indexes), and calculated and established a sub-database of the corresponding head and face dimensions of the sample group of Chinese adults [3]. Individual Protection Standardization Committee established a GB/T 23461-2009 'Three-Dimensions of Male Adult Headforms' according to the three-dimensional data of 3000 male adults in 2009 [4].

GB/T 2428 takes the two-dimensional distribution of the one-dimensional feature size of the head and face as the basis for setting the specifications of head and face, and focuses on the application of two-dimensional graphic design. GB/T 23461-2009 'Three-dimensions of Male Adult Headforms' divides the three-dimensional headforms into seven types based on the two-dimensional distribution of the head breadth and head height indices, and takes the distribution of the zoom factor of physical volume as the basis for the three-dimensional headform classification, highlighting the application of the digital design of the three-dimension modeling of the head, and being more suitable for the current trend of making digital design of products. However, GB/T 23461-2009 takes the samples of males aged 16–36 as the main object of study, regardless of the middle-aged and aged male group as well as the female group. The data used in the study includes the male and female samples aged 18–65, and the head specifications of the male and female groups are classified with the method proposed in the GB/T 23461-2009, based on the analysis of the headform characteristics of the sample groups.

2 Methods

2.1 Basic Information of the Samples

The samples used in the Study come from the database of adult human-body dimensions established in 2009 by the Chinese Standardization Institute, and the database includes data of 3000 human samples, of which the male and female each accounts for 50 % respectively and the measurement points mainly include four regions of Beijing, Tianjin, Shanghai and Xi'an. The age range of the samples are from 18 to 65 years old, of which the males have their average age of 37.7 ± 13.5 and the female 38.8 ± 13.4. See the following (Table 1) for the details of the sample distribution.

Table 1. Sample distribution

Sex	Numbers	Average age	Source of sample
Male	1515	37.7 ± 13.5	Beijing, Tianjin, Shanghai and Xi'an
Female	1594	38.8 ± 13.4	Beijing, Tianjin, Shanghai and Xi'an
Total	3109		

2.2 Methods for Measurement

The Human Solution 3D Scanner was adopted for anthropometric survey. The accuracy of the scanner is 2 mm, and the scan time is less than 10 s one person. Before the start of the survey, the measurement team was trained in anthropometric techniques and was checked for consistency in their survey procedures to ensure the reliability of the anthropometric data. Head data in the survey include six items, namely head length, head breadth, head height, head sagittal arc, bitragion-coronal arc and head circumference, the definitions of which are all from GB/T 5703-2010 [5]. The dimension values obtained were categorized according to sex and age groups and abnormity data examination was conducted. The extreme outliers and unreasonable results were identified and eliminated carefully by using 3σ test, peak value test and logical value test.

3 Basic Statistics and Analysis of the Data

3.1 Relationship of Sex and Head Dimensions

Independent samples are used for inspecting and analyzing the relationship between sex and head dimensions, and the result shows that aside from head length and head circumference, there are significant differences ($P < 0.01$) in the data of the other four items, and the dimensions of head and face of the males are obviously bigger than those of the females, so the differences between male and female should be fully considered in the design of products.

3.2 Relevance Among the Head Data

The correlation coefficient r between six head dimensions were calculated to judge the intimacy ratio of the correlations between all the data. The equation of $0 < |r| < 1$ indicates that there is linear correlation to some extent between two variables. The more $|r|$ approaches 1, the closer the linear correlation between the two variables becomes. The more $|r|$ approaches 0, the weaker the linear correlation between the two variables becomes. We can classify it into three categories: $|r| < 0.4$ represents weaker linear correlation; $0.4 \leq |r| < 0.7$ represents significant linear correlation; $0.7 \leq |r| < 1$ represents closer linear correlation.

Calculate the related coefficients among the data of the head as shown in the following (Table 2).

- All of the linear correlations between the six measurements are not significant (below 0.6).
- There are comparatively closer correlations between head length and sagittal arc, and between the head breadth and bitragion arc. Head height and the bitragion arc also have comparatively closer correlations (0.4–0.6).
- The relativity (around 0.3) is low in the size of the three items, namely, the head length, head breadth and head height, showing a mutual independence of the three dimensions. In the head classification and product design, the three dimensions should all be considered.

Table 2. List of correlation coefficient (r) between the head dimensions

Items	Head height	Head breadth	Head length	Sagittal arc	Bitragion arc	Head circumference
Head height	1	.305**	.268**	.359**	.400**	.212**
Head breadth	.305**	1	.311**	.339**	.474**	.370**
Head length	.268**	.311**	1	.584**	.284**	.572**
Sagittal arc	.359**	.339**	.584**	1	.360**	.358**
Bitragion arc	.400**	.474**	.284**	.360**	1	.258**
Head circumference	.212**	.370**	.572**	.358**	.258**	1

4 Classification of Headforms

4.1 Analysis of the Head Indices

The Study was made to the purpose of practical engineering application. In the Study, we presume that the headform samples of each group are similar in shape, and adopt three linear key dimensions, i.e. head length, head breadth and head height, to show the shape information of the human head, and make classification of the headforms with the head breadth and head height coefficients.

The head breadth-length index = (maximum head breadth/maximum head length) × 100, namely, the proportion of the maximum head breadth against the maximum head length; the head height-length index = (maximum head height/maximum head length) × 100, namely, the proportion of the head height against the head length.

The three dimensions of head length, head breadth and head height in head indices are considered since the three indices can reflect the proportational relationship among various parts of the head and face, and can also show different types of head and face (Table 3).

Table 3. Dimensions of the total headform samples

Sex	Statistical value	Head height (mm)	Head breadth (mm)	Head length (mm)	Head breadth-length index	Head height-length index
Male	Mean	233	164	197	83	119
	Std. Deviation	15	8	8	4	8
	Minimum	191	134	171	66	94
	Maximum	271	187	225	100	140
Female	Mean	226	159	187	85	121
	Std. Deviation	12	7	8	5	8
	Minimum	191	131	166	69	96
	Maximum	260	192	216	105	145

4.2 Two-Dimensional Distribution of the Head Indices and Grouping of the Headform Samples

Tables 4 and 5 provide two-dimensional distributions of the head height-length indexes and the head breadth-length indexes of the adult Chinese male and female. Whether or not to produce the very model and how many related products to be produced can be determined based on the proportions of the groups covered by the various headforms in the table.

Table 4. Two-dimension distribution of the cephalic indices of the male

Head breadth-length index	Head height-length index						
	≤ 100	100–109.99	110–119.99	120–124.99	125–129.99	130–135.99	≥ 135
≤ 74.99	0.10 %	0.80 %	1.40 %	0.30 %	0.10 %	–	–
75 ~ 79.99	0.50 %	5.60 %	10.40 %	2.80 %	1.80 %	0.30 %	–
80 ~ 84.99	0.20 %	5.60 %	17.50 %	10.40 %	6.20 %	1.90 %	0.20 %
85 ~ 89.99	0.30 %	2.50 %	8.60 %	7.80 %	5.10 %	3.10 %	0.50 %
90 ~ 94.99	–	0.10 %	1.20 %	1.30 %	1.30 %	1.30 %	0.20 %
≥ 95	–	–	–	0.20 %	0.10 %	0.20 %	0.10 %

Table 5. Two-dimensional distribution of the cephalic indices of the female

Head breadth-length index	Head height-length index						
	≤ 100	100–109.99	110–119.99	120–124.99	125–129.99	130–135.99	≥ 135
≤ 74.99	0.10 %	0.30 %	0.80 %	0.30 %	0.10 %		
75 ~ 79.99	0.30 %	2.80 %	7.70 %	2.50 %	1.30 %	0.30 %	
80 ~ 84.99	0.30 %	3.10 %	17.70 %	9.40 %	3.80 %	1.50 %	0.20 %
85 ~ 89.99		1.00 %	9.50 %	10.20 %	7.30 %	3.40 %	1.10 %
90 ~ 94.99		0.10 %	2.50 %	2.60 %	3.30 %	2.50 %	1.30 %
≥ 95			0.10 %	0.90 %	0.80 %	0.70 %	0.40 %

Note: The headform groups with coverage rates less than 1 % do not generate standard headform.

4.3 Groups and Coverage Rates of Headforms

Tables 6 and 7 show that, for the males, the middle-upright type, round-upright type and round-high type account for 18.80 %, 34.70 % and 29.50 % respectively, which take a proportion of 74.3 % in the total headforms, and for the females, the middle-upright type, round-upright type and round-high type account for 12.00 %, 31.60 % and 30.70 % respectively, which take a proportion of 74.3 % in all the headforms. This shows that 70 % of the Chinese people possess round-upright type, round-high type and middle-upright type, with relatively shorter and rounder headforms indicated in the classification based on the head length-breadth indices. For the male, the five types of headforms, namely, the middle-upright type, round-upright type, round-high type, middle-high type and round-extra-high type, account for 93.7 % against all the headforms, and for the female, the five headforms, namely, the middle-upright type, round-upright type, round-high type, super-round-high type and round-extra-high type, account for 88.1 % of all the headforms, showing that there are five headforms, in each group, which can represent the main part of the group.

Table 6. Groups and coverage rate of the headforms of the male

Head breadth-length index	Head height-length index		
	≤ 119.99	≤ 129.99	≥ 130.00
≤ 79.99	18.80 % (Middle-upright type)	5.00 % (Middle-high type)	0.30 % (Middle-extra-high type)
≤ 89.99	34.70 % (Round-upright type)	29.50 % (Round-high type)	5.70 % (Round-extra-high type)
≥ 90.00	1.30 % (Super-round-upright type)	2.90 % (Super-round-high type)	1.80 % (Super-round-extra-height type)

Table 7. Groups and coverage rates of the headforms of the female

Head breadth-length index	Head height-length index		
	≤ 119.99	≤ 129.99	≥ 130.00
≤ 79.99	12.00 % (Middle-upright type)	4.20 % (Middle-high type)	0.30 % (Middle-extra-high type)
≤ 89.99	31.60 % (Round-upright type)	30.70 % (Round-high type)	6.20 % (Round-extra-high type)
≥ 90.00	2.70 % (Super-round-upright type)	7.60 % (Super-round-high type)	4.90 % (Super-round-extra-high type)

4.4 Basic Dimensions of the Main Headforms

The headforms of the Chinese male and female are focused on the three types including the middle-upright type, round-upright type and round-high type, so the groups of the three types should be mainly considered in the design of head products. See the Table 8 for the basic dimensions of the heads of the three headforms.

Table 8. Basic dimensions of the main headforms

Headforms	Statistical value	Male			Female		
		Head full-height	Head breadth	Head length	Head full-height	Head breadth	Head length
Middle-upright type	Mean	227	158	203	220	152	196
	Std. Deviation	13	6	8	11	6	6
Round-upright type	Mean	224	166	198	217	159	189
	Std. Deviation	12	7	8	10	6	7
Round-high type	Mean	242	165	194	231	159	186
	Std. Deviation	9	7	6	8	6	6

5 Conclusion and Outlook

In the Study, a classification of the headforms was made according to the head height, head breadth and head length of the Chinese male and female, and a two-dimensional distribution of the head height-length and head breadth-length indices was established.

Human head is of a very complicated three-dimensional shape, and the information of size and shape in all spatial directions should be fully considered. In the perspective of increasing the suitability of the products, the shape information among the data points of the surface of the human body should not be ignored. In the Study, we will further analyze the three-dimensional shape information of the head and face of human body and explore the new method for headform classification so as to provide bases for the improvement of the ergonomic design and for the enhancement of the suitability of the products.

Acknowledgment. This work is supported by Quality Inspection Industry Research Special Funds for Public Welfare (201510042) and National Science and Technology Basic Research (2013FY110200).

References

1. GB 2428-1981, Headform Series of Chinese Adults (1981)
2. GB 10000-1988, Human dimensions of Chinese adults (1988)
3. GB/T 2428-1998 Dimensions of head and face of adults (1998)
4. GB/T 23461-2009, Three-dimensions of Male Adult Headforms (2009)
5. GB/T 5703-2010, Basic human body measurements for technological design (2010)

Usability Evaluation of Blood Glucose Meters for Elderly Diabetic Patients

Peter Rasche[1(✉)], Pilsung Choe[2], Sabine Theis[1], Matthias Wille[1], Christina Bröhl[1], Lea Finken[1], Stefan Becker[3], Christopher M. Schlick[1], and Alexander Mertens[1]

[1] Chair and Institute of Industrial Engineering and Ergonomics of RWTH Aachen, Bergdriesch 27, Aachen, Germany
p.rasche@iaw.rwth-aachen.de
[2] Qatar University, Doha, Qatar
[3] University Hospital Essen, Essen, Germany

Abstract. In the context of this study the usability of the first blood glucose meter that is connectable to a smartphone has been investigated by the use through diabetic patients of different ages and with different technical experiences. According to DIN ISO 2028-1 the participants had to solve usability-tasks with the think-aloud-method. Additionally the cognitive load has been measured for each task. As control variables we asked for age and gender as well as technical affinity and Health Literacy. A total of 12 participants (mean age = 60.17 years) took part in this study. The results show that elderly diabetic patients are willing and able to use modern blood glucose meters. A blood glucose meter for elderly should store data for about three months and should be able to export data easily to the physician by a file type like CSV. The blood glucose testing strip should have a mark which describes the orientation and way it should be inserted into the blood glucose meter. The testing strip should also be illuminated to improve blood glucose measurements during nighttime.

Keywords: Acceptance · Elderly people · Usability · Healthcare · Mental demand

1 Introduction

The quantity of diabetic patients in Germany is increasing exponentially. The International Diabetes Foundation states that 7.6 million people had diabetes in Germany [1]. More than half of those affected are older than 65 years, and the risk to come down with diabetes increases with age [2, 3]. In the context of a therapy, an autonomous control of the blood sugar level through the patient is often necessary. For this purpose so-called glucometers are used. In the course of the increasing digitalization, glucometers have been extended by many functions so that modern devices do not only measure the blood sugar level, but, in combination with a mobile terminal, also enable to process and analyze the recorded data and give feedback to the user. Various studies showed that those systems increase treatment adherence and patient satisfaction if they are accepted by the user [4, 5]. Hence the usability is especially important because a

P.-L.P. Rau (Ed.): CCD 2016, LNCS 9741, pp. 686–694, 2016.
DOI: 10.1007/978-3-319-40093-8_68

device that is not fit for this purpose may lead to an incorrect measurement and a decreasing therapy adherence [6].

This explorative study examined the usability of a glucometer connected to a smartphone with elderly patients. For this purpose, different key aspects of performance of a modern glucometer were considered. Additionally the usability has been explored by simulated blood sugar measurements. Thus, concrete design guidelines and recommendations for the design of modern glucometers could be derived.

2 Method

In the context of this study the first blood glucose meter which is connectable to a smartphone iBG-Star has been investigated according to DIN ISO 20282-1. For this investigation different usability tasks were defined which the participant had to process independently (Table 1).

Table 1. Usability tasks corresponding to the order of processing

No.	Task
1	Unpacking out of carton
2	Unpacking out of transport bag
3	Charging glucometer
4	Connecting the glucometer to tablet
5	Inserting blood glucose monitoring strips into glucometer
6	Simulated blood sugar measurement
7	Connecting glucometer to smartphone
8	Inserting blood glucose monitoring strips into glucometer
9	Simulated blood sugar measurement

During the processing, participants were observed using the think-aloud-method [7]. Subsequent to each task the subjective mental load was evaluated using the Rating Scale of Mental Effort [8]. This method is based on a visual and linguistically encoded scale of 150 Points (Fig. 1). Subjects rated their individual mental effort.

Since the glucometer is connectable to different types of mobile terminals the usability tasks were set twice. During the first run participants used the glucometer in combination with an iPad 2, and during the second one with an iPhone 4S. Therewith should be examined if the use of a smartphone or a tablet and related advantages and disadvantages do have an impact on usability. Compared to the presentation on a smartphone or the glucometer-display itself the larger display area of a tablet could be advantageous for elderly people, whereas the size of the mobile terminals could have a negative impact. A summarizing judgement of the usability in arithmetical form has been conducted employing the Post Study Usability Questionnaire [9].

Besides the usability tasks, a semi-structured interview was conducted which was supposed to examine factors of acceptance of a modern diabetes management system. We placed special focus on aspects of data processing and data release. Furthermore

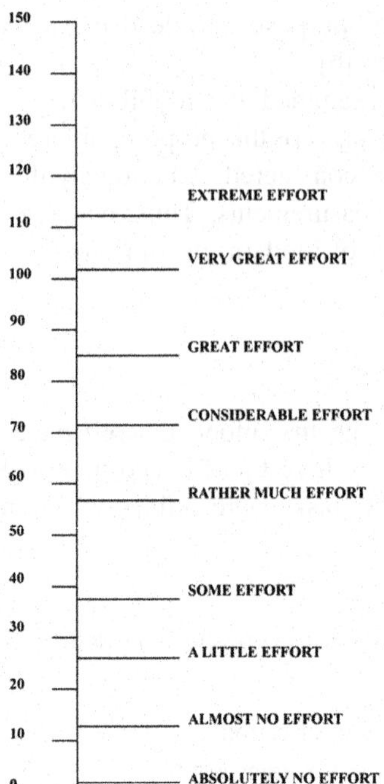

Fig. 1. Rating scale of mental effort according to Zijlstra [8]

participants were asked about their acceptance of functions that guide them and, beyond that, encourage them to lead a healthy life (Table 2).

As control variables age, gender and technical affinity were recorded. The latter one was estimated by employing a questionnaire used in previous research [10]. Using another questionnaire, the previous therapy was evaluated. For this purpose participants

Table 2. Aspects that are evaluated by using the semi-structured interview

No.	Aspect
1	System gives instructions for a healthy life
2	System saves data automatically
3	Added value of an automatic data storage
4	Added value of a development display of stored data
5	Period for storing data
6	Automatic transfer of data to the treating physician
7	Diary function to collect more data such as eating habits and amounts of carbohydrates
8	Reminder for unrealized daily goals
9	Notification of compliant behavior to the health insurance
10	Desirable functions of a modern diabetes management system
11	Advantages and disadvantages of the considered system compared to the previously used system

were asked to state which health-related data they record in the context of their therapy and where they store it. In order to comprehensively document the participants' health-related knowledge we used the Health Literacy Questionnaire [11]. This questionnaire examines in how far the participant knows important facts about the disease, its therapy and compliant behavior.

After an approval of the ethics committee of the faculty of medicine of the RWTH University (EK028/15) participants were recruited via self-help groups and postings in the Aachen area.

2.1 Participants

Overall N = 12 participants (male = 4; female = 8) participated in this study (see Table 3). The average participant age is 60.17 (SD = 15.04). All participants stated that they are diabetics for more than ten years, whereby five participants suffer from type I diabetes, six from type II diabetes and one participant from type 3c diabetes. Three out of 12 participants stated that they suffer from physical constraint as a consequence of diabetes. On average the participants perform 3.58 blood sugar measurements a day, whereby the minimum in this sample is two measurements and the maximum seven measurements a day. With regard to the therapy compliance, the amount of daily blood sugar measurements of all participants corresponded with the specifications of the treating physician. Regarding the individual therapy, the semi-structured interview revealed that all participants hand over their therapy related health data to their doctor

Table 3. Characteristics of the analyzed participants

Variable	Level	Frequency/data
Sex	Male	4
	Female	8
Age (years)		60.17 (SD = 15.04)
Highest educational qualification	Finished secondary school	2
	Finished professional education	8
	Holding a university degree	2
Type of diabetes	Type I	5
	Type II	6
	Type 3c	1
Duration of therapy (years)	<2	1
	2–10	0
	>10	11
Health literacy	Access	3.25 (SD = 0.866)
	Understand	3.22 (SD = 0.519)
	Appraise	2.71 (SD = 0.964)
	Apply	2.83 (SD = 0.536)
	Disease prevention	3.17 (SD = 0.577)
	Health promotion	2.96 (SD = 0.698)
Technical affinity		2.672 (SD = 0.406)

personally. Seven out of ten documented their data paper-based. Only three participants stated that they enter their values in digital form and that they are stored in the glucometer itself.

2.2 Experimental Apparatus

The blood glucose meter "iBG-Star" produced by AgaMatrix Inc., 7C Raymond Avenue, Salem, NH 03079, USA which is distributed in Germany by Sanofi-Aventis Deutschland GmbH, Industriepark Hoechst, K703 Brüningstr. 50, 65926 Frankfurt am Main has been investigated in the context of this study. Besides that, an iPhone 4S (16 GB) and an iPad 2 (32 GB) by Apple Inc., 1 Infinite Loop, Cupertino, CA 95014 USA were used (Fig. 2).

Fig. 2. Blood glucose meter iBG-Star (Sanofi-Aventis Deutschland GmbH, 2015)

The products tested were provided by mySugr GmbH, Schottenfeldgasse 69/3.1, 1070 Wien, Austria. The necessary Blood Testing Strips were provided by Sanofi-Aventis Deutschland GmbH, Industriepark Höchst K703, 65926 Frankfurt, Germany.

3 Procedure

After the examiners welcomed the participants, an informal interview was conducted in order to collect information about their demographics and the individual diabetes therapy. After that, participants independently completed the questionnaires on technical affinity and Health Literacy. This was followed by the independent performance of usability tasks through the participants themselves. For this purpose, participants were introduced to the concept of the Rating Scale of Mental Effort by practicing the visual and linguistically encoded scale employing five everyday examples. Following this, participants were asked to unpack the product using the think-aloud-method.

Afterwards, a simulated blood sugar measurement was conducted using the glucometer in combination with an iPad. For direct comparison a second simulated measurement was conducted in which the glucometer was connected to an iPhone. Subsequent to these tasks, participants were asked to fill in the Post Study System Questionnaire (PSSUQ) with reference to both measurements. Thus a universal evaluation of the glucometer in full operational spectrum could be ensured. This was followed by an informal interview concerning the advantages and disadvantages of each measurement in relation to the glucometer used by the participants in everyday life. Each appointment was concluded with a semi-structured interview which examined acceptance factors of modern diabetes management systems. As compensation for their effort participants received 20 euros.

4 Results

The examination of technical affinity showed that participants were rather hostile to technology since the average value across all participants is 2.672 (SD = 0.406) on a 4-Likert-scale (1 = 'I fully agree' to 4 = 'I completely disagree'). According to the Post Study System Usability Questionnaire the investigated glucometer was averagely evaluated with a value of 2.06 (SD = 1.02) on a 7-Likert-scale (1 = 'I fully agree' to 7 = 'I completely disagree') for usability. The inspection of the requested RSME-values confirms this usability evaluation (Fig. 3).

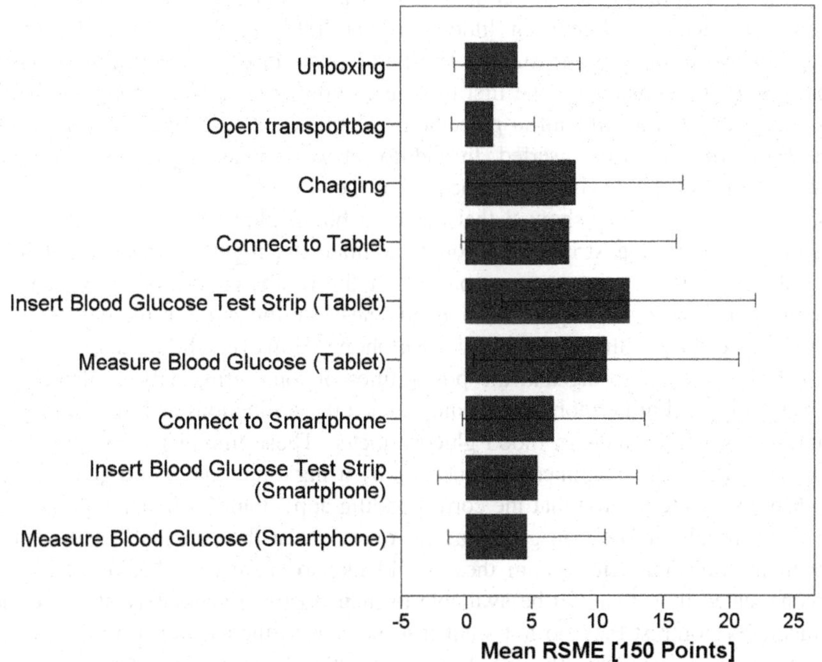

Fig. 3. Averages of the RSME values for each usability task

Furthermore participants stated that the glucometer can be used significantly better combined with the smartphone. Assumed advantages of the tablet as a result of the larger display were eliminated by disadvantages of the handling. Participants reported that the sheer size of the glucometer makes it more attractive due to the fact that it can be easily carried along in everyday life. Equally, half of the participants were convinced by the modern design of the glucometer as well as the evaluation possibilities with the aid of the app. On the other hand they considered the amount of product components that are necessary for a blood sugar measurement such as monitoring strips, lancet and charger as a disadvantage. Furthermore they criticized that the glucometer is solely compatible with apple products. They would like to have a universal port which allows applicability with mobile devices from different manufacturers.

5 Discussion

This paper presented a usability evaluation of the first blood glucose meter which is connectable to a smartphone. Elderly diabetic patients, who participated in this study, stated that they would recommend this modern glucometer. The space-saving and modern design of the evaluated glucometer was judged as beneficial and attractive.

According to the Post Study System Usability Questionnaire the blood glucose meter has a good usability as the value is around 2 points on the 7-Likert-scale. The inspection of the requested RSME-values confirms this usability evaluation. The requested values vary between 0 points and 50 points for individual participants on a 150-point scale (Fig. 1). The maximum value which was gathered of 50 points corresponds to a mental load between 'little effort' and 'relatively large effort'. The highest average mental effort was measured when participants inserted blood glucose testing strips into the glucometer for the first-time in combination with a tablet. The participants stated that it was difficult to perceive in which orientation and at which position the testing strip has to be inserted. In addition it was exhausting to insert the small testing strip into the likewise small opening of the device.

Qualitative interviews showed that the used blood glucose meter lacked an illumination of the testing strip. This would facilitate the nightly measurement in the bedroom and thereby other persons present in the room would not be wakened by someone switching on the lights. Participants clearly criticized that the device cannot be used universally with every type of smartphone. However, the participants appreciated the automatic storing and the possibilities of long-term analysis of the tested blood sugar level. Furthermore participants named these functions as basic requirement for the use of such a modern blood glucose meter. These findings correspond to the results of Valdez who examined this question by using a fictional blood glucose meter [12]. Moreover, they stated that the corresponding app should visualize a period of at least three months in order to give a useful overview of the personal health state. In reply to the question with whom they would like to share their health-related data everyone stated that it should be available to their doctor immediately after the measurement. By contrast they do not want it to be sent to their health insurance or any other external group in health care. Besides the blood sugar value, further data, for example physical activity behavior or personal nutrition, should be recorded and stored.

The only restriction that was named in this regard is that there should be the possibility of correcting data because a glucometer is a device that often is not used by only one person. This leads to the risk that the values of another person could be assigned to the patients personal health file.

Asked about their actual diabetes therapy, participants reported that their physicians in charge do often not have the appropriate system available in order to transfer the data from their blood glucose meter digitally. Furthermore, they claimed that their glucometer is not designed to transfer data in an manner other than transcribed paper form. Participants agreed that this effort should be reduced through the use of a modern glucometer and that the automatic data backup would be a fundamental requirement if they would think about buying a modern glucometer connectable to a smartphone.

In conclusion, it can be noted that digitalization of a glucometer produces clear benefits for patients and doctors and that these advantages are also advocated for by elderly diabetic patients with low technical affinity. On the other hand, a lot of work is necessary to enhance interoperability among blood glucose meters and diabetic management systems as well as between patients' and physicians' systems.

Acknowledgement. We would like to thank all participants, the company mySugr GmbH for the provision of the examined iBG-Star blood glucose meters and the Sanofi-Aventis Deutschland GmbH for the provided blood testing stripes. This publication is part of the research project 'TECH4AGE', financed by the Federal Ministry of Education and Research (BMBF, FKZ 16SV7111) and promoted by VDI/VDE Innovation + Technik GmbH.

References

1. Aguiree, F., Brown, A., Cho, N.H., Dahlquist, G., Dodd, S., Dunning, T., Hirst, M., Hwang, C., Magliano, D., Patterson, C.: IDF diabetes atlas [Online] (2013)
2. Girlich, C., Hoffmann, U., Bollheimer, C.: Behandlung des Typ-2-Diabetes beim alten Patienten. Der Internist **55**(7), 762–768 (2014). doi:10.1007/s00108-014-3466-1
3. Zeyfang, A., Bahrmann, A., Wernecke, J.: Diabetes mellitus im alter. Diabetol. Stoffwechsel **8**(S 02), S200–S206 (2013)
4. Free, C., Phillips, G., Watson, L., Galli, L., Felix, L., Edwards, P., Patel, V., Haines, A.: The effectiveness of mobile-health technologies to improve health care service delivery processes: a systematic review and meta-analysis. PLoS Med. **10**(1), e1001363 (2013)
5. Kim, H.-S., Choi, W., Baek, E.K., Kim, Y.A., Yang, S.J., Choi, I.Y., Yoon, K.-H., Cho, J.-H.: Efficacy of the smartphone-based glucose management application stratified by user satisfaction. Diabetes Metab. J. **38**(3), 204–210 (2014)
6. El-Gayar, O., Timsina, P., Nawar, N., Eid, W.: Mobile applications for diabetes self-management: status and potential. J. Diabetes Sci. Technol. **7**(1), 247–262 (2013)
7. Leck, T.: Im Erstkontakt Gewinnen Worum Es in Sekunden Geht. Springer Fachmedien, Wiesbaden (2012)
8. Zijlstra, F.: Efficiency in work behaviour: a design approach for modern tools. Ph.D. thesis, TU Delft, Delft University of Technology, Soesterberg (1993)
9. Sauro, J., Lewis, J.R.: Quantifying the User Experience: Practical Statistics for User Research. Elsevier, Philadelphia (2012)

10. Jay, G.M., Willis, S.L.: Influence of direct computer experience on older adults' attitudes toward computers. J. Gerontol. **47**(4), P250–P257 (1992)
11. Hls-Eu Consortium. Comparative report of health literacy in eight EU member states. The European Health Literacy Survey HLS-EU [Online] (2012)
12. Calero Valdez, A.: Technology acceptance and diabetes. User centered design of small screen devices for diabetes patients, 1. Aufl; Dissertationen/HCI Center der RWTH Aachen 1, Apprimus-Verl, Aachen (2014)

A Cross-Cultural Adaptation in Reporting Perinatal Safety Events

Weiying Shan[1], Chen Liang[2], Weichao Shan[1], Na Yang[1], and Yang Gong[2(✉)]

[1] Chengde Medical College, Chengde, China
chengdeuyn@163.com, 16442297@qq.com, yangna03@126.com
[2] The University of Texas Health Science Center at Houston, Houston, TX, USA
{Chen.Liang,Yang.Gong}@uth.tmc.edu

Abstract. Incident reporting enables clinicians to examine historical patient safety events and to target different levels of analysis toward actionable knowledge. The cross-cultural adaptation of reporting instruments promotes the international communication on medical errors and patient safety culture. This study initializes a translation and adaptation of the Common Formats (in US) to Chinese and a localized reporting on perinatal incidents in a Chinese hospital. The results demonstrate the validity of the cross-cultural translation and diversity in a typical perinatal incident reported by Chinese clinicians. These findings suggest (1) a comprehensive data report format is critical in the incident reporting; (2) an imperative need of cross-cultural study on incident reporting; (3) future direction of incident reporting and patient safety culture.

Keywords: Perinatal safety · Data quality · Clinical information system · Cross-cultural study

1 Introduction

Following the Institute of Medicine's (IOM) report 'To Err Is Human', patient safety reports record and communicate information relevant to patient safety events and quality problems [1]. To date, patient safety reporting has gained increasing attention because it leads to learning from the causation of previous incidents and preventing potential harms [2, 3]. It has been documented that collecting, analyzing, and communicating patient safety information play important roles in reporting [4–6]. Challenges to these aspects of reporting are recognized as (1) the difficulty of collecting data in high quality [5]; (2) the lack of effective analytics of generating actionable knowledge [4]. Most importantly, data collection is one of the cornerstones of the reporting since it enables analytics at different levels [7]. A recent study indicated that a comprehensive definition and classification of reports can facilitate information integration and the disclosure of hidden and recurring harms that point to system vulnerabilities [8, 9].

C. Liang and W. Shan contribute equally.

P.-L.P. Rau (Ed.): CCD 2016, LNCS 9741, pp. 695–703, 2016.
DOI: 10.1007/978-3-319-40093-8_69

In 2009, the Agency for Healthcare Research and Quality (AHRQ) in the US developed standardized definitions and reporting formats for patient safety events, i.e. Common Formats. The Common Formats receive and aggregate patient safety related information ranging from general concerns to frequently occurred and clinically significant events [10]. In practice, the use of the Common Formats demonstrates the capacity of enhancing information classification, error identification, and harm scaling [11–13].

When it comes to the discussion of patient safety in China, there are concerns about patient safety reporting in a wide spectrum of patient safety events [14, 15], in which cultural competence and health information technology (i.e., data exchange and system interoperability) have been recognized recently [14, 16, 17]. This paper aims to perform a field trial of utilizing the Common Formats in a perinatal safety reporting system in a Chinese Hospital. The challenges of reporting perinatal incidents reside in the quality of reported data and substantial analytical bias [18–23]. The detailed tasks include (1) translating relevant Common Formats into Chinese; (2) employing cross-cultural adaptation; (3) utilizing translated forms to report patient safety events in the Chinese hospital; (4) performing quantitative and qualitative analysis from the perspective of health informatics.

2 Background

2.1 Incident Reporting

Incident reporting is recognized as one important factor to improve to the safety culture [24]. The goal of incident reporting in a hospital is to prevent recurrence of incidents by collecting useful clinical information from documented incidents. Therefore, a reporting system as such should include a comprehensive data entry design for categorizing incidents and more importantly, the clinical information underlying the description of the incident [25]. In many countries, the structure of such categorization varies between hospitals [5, 26, 27]. The inconsistency in language has become another barrier that affects the utility of reporting [2, 28]. These problems jointly hamper the incident reporting from improvement.

In the US, incident reporting has drawn ascending attention as a nationwide patient safety program [29, 30]. Although incident reporting has been broadly implemented in US hospitals, the ever-existing question is how the reporting can advance safety efforts effectively [31, 32]. To maximize the safety efforts through reporting, US hospitals may work with AHRQ funded patient safety organizations (PSO), which provide expertise in incident reporting, to aggregate patient safety events through the existing reporting systems. In addition, the Common Formats were developed to facilitate the aggregation of patient safety information.

2.2 Perinatal Safety

Improving perinatal safety is a complex undertaking that involves multidisciplinary team care and various components of such a care. An initiative of perinatal safety is to identify problems and generate actionable knowledge to reduce future harm [33]. The use of clinical information requires effective data communication, error analysis, and clinical decision support where information technology plays an important role [34].

The Common Formats contribute to the data collection, organization, and communication in an early stage of perinatal incident reporting. In the Common Formats, a perinatal incident form is designed for event-specific information that is highly important in perinatal incidents. Information that is required, but not specific for perinatal incidents is collected through the generic formats.

2.3 Cross-Cultural Adaptation in Healthcare

The globalization of healthcare indicates a great need for cross-cultural research [35]. The clinicians and researchers need valid and reliable instruments in a diverse language and culture. Accordingly, various methodologies were established for translating, adapting, and validating healthcare instruments in the cross-cultural context. The current version of the Common Formats is designed for the US hospitals and healthcare institutes use but not for such healthcare settings abroad the US.

Table 1. Qualifications of the translators.

Task	Translator	Title	Expertise	Tenure of research
Translation	A	Associate professor	Clinical care	16
	B	Lecturer	Specialized English in nursing	3
Back-translation	C	Professor	Perinatal nursing	23
	D	Lecturer	Perinatal nursing	6
Reconciliation	E	Professor	Perinatal nursing	23
	F	Chief physician	Obstetrics and gynecology	20
	G	Lecturer	Nursing in obstetrics and gynecology	6

3 Design and Implementation

3.1 Cross-Cultural Translation and Adaptation of the Common Formats

Seven independent health care professionals were involved in the cross-cultural translation and adaptation of the Common Formats. The task includes translation, back-translation, and reconciliation as listed as follows [36–38]. (1) Five perinatal related forms were translated to Chinese, which comprise of healthcare event reporting form (HERF), patient information form (PIF), summary of initial report (SIR), Perinatal Form, and Perinatal Event Description. Translators A and B performed the translation. Items in the original Common Formats that do not fit in Chinese settings were modified or removed. (2) To maximize the equivalence of meaning between the source and target text, translators C and D performed the back-translation that translates the Chinese translation back to English. (3) In the reconciliation, translators E, F, and G compared the original text with the back-translated text for issues such as confusion, ambiguities, and errors. A reconciliation report with notes of these issues and the recommended edits and adjustments was sent to the panel of seven translators (A, B, C, D, E, F, and G) for discussion. A consolidated version of Chinese translation is formed once all issues are addressed. See Table 1 for qualifications of the seven translators.

Table 2. An example of de-identified incident description.

An adverse event of obstetrics
A female, 32 y/o, gave birth to her first fetus after cesarean section 5 years ago. She came to our hospital waiting for her second baby delivery on Sep, 18th, 2014.
She was diagnosed as Full-term pregnancy (38 + 4 weeks), second fetus, ROA. She had no vaginal bleeding, no abdominal pain, no premature rupture of fetal membranes. Because of her scarred uterus, she applied for her second caesarean. We performed uterine lower segmental cesarean to her on 19th, September 2014. The operation process was successful, the new baby's weight is 3800 g and the APGAR score is 9–10–10. But we found her new baby's right elbow eversion and felt bone friction sensation. We doubted neonate bone fracture, so an orthopedist came and suggested an X-ray examination. Later the X-ray confirmed the diagnosis of neonate right humeral fracture. Quickly the new baby was applied reduction and external fixation of fracture. Baby's other body indexes were good except the fracture. On the 11th day after neonate birth, the second X-ray showed favorable restoration and new poroma.
The mom-baby left our hospital on the same day.

3.2 Reporting and Data Collection

The Perinatal Form and Perinatal Event Description were utilized to report a perinatal incident de-identified from a Chinese hospital and written in Chinese (see Table 2). Twenty-one graduate students in the School of Nursing participated in the reporting. Table 3 shows the demographics of the participants.

The participants were instructed prior to the reporting, where the Perinatal Event Description Form was utilized for the definitions of concept/terminology. Each participant was asked to provide general information regarding education, degree, specialty, and clinical training prior to the reporting. The reporting was administered utilizing paper-based materials. We previewed the returned forms (response rate: 100 %) and found all responses were complete and adequate.

4 Results

The demographics of the participants are shown in Table 3. The Perinatal Form comprises of 20 items directly related to perinatal incidents. For a complete form, please direct to https://www.psoppc.org/web/patientsafety/version-1.2_documents, and access Perinatal Form. The discrepant responses were found in five items (25 %):

Table 3. Demographic characteristics of the participants.

Characteristics	n	%
School grade		
1st year	11	52.3
2nd year	6	28.5
3rd year	4	19.0
Previous clinical training		
Urinary surgery	2	9.5
ICU	1	4.7
Pediatrics	1	4.7
Gynecology and obstetrics	2	9.5
Surgery	1	4.7
Endocrinology	1	4.7
No previous clinical training	13	61.9
Area of research		
Nursing management	4	19.0
Surgical nursing	1	4.7
Nosocomial infection management	1	4.7
Nursing ethics	1	4.7
Psychiatric nursing	4	19.0
Aged nursing	1	4.7
Nursing of gynecology and obstetrics	1	4.7
Nursing education	4	19.0
Nursing psychology	4	19.0

The percentage is rounded to tenths.

Figure 1 shows a part of items with diverse responses. In Item 5, four participants accounted that only the neonate was affected by the event, while the rest accounted both of mother and neonate. In Item 6, 16 participants identified the outcomes to the mother as 'injury to body part or organ', whereas the rest specified 'psychological influence'. In Item 11, 19 participants chose 'Birth trauma/injury as listed under ICD-9-CM 767 or ICD-10-CM P10-P15', whereas one chose 'Five-min Apgar < 7 and birth-weight > 2500 g' and the other one chose both. In Item 16, 15 participants identified an induced labor, while five other participants identified an augmented labor, and one specified 'unknown'. In Item 19, 14 participants identified there was no instrumentation used to assist vaginal delivery, whereas the rest identified 'unknown'.

5 Discussion and Future Work

Utilizing the Common Formats in a cross-cultural study shows that some items may not be completely adapted to the reporting forms in the local Chinese hospital, even though the rigorous translation and verification process were in place. For example, in the Common Formats, a perinatal period extends from the 20th week of gestation through

5. Who was affected by the event? CHECK ALL THAT APPLY:
- a. ☐ Mother
- b. ☐ Fetus(es)
- c. ☐ Neonate(s)

6. Which adverse outcome(s) did the mother sustain? CHECK ALL THAT APPLY:
- a. ☐ Hemorrhage requiring transfusion
- b. ☐ Eclampsia
- c. ☐ Magnesium toxicity
- d. ☐ Infection → **7. Which of the following maternal infections?** CHECK ONE:
  - a. ☐ Chorioamnionitis
  - b. ☐ Endometritis
  - c. ☐ Other: PLEASE SPECIFY ______
- e. ☐ Injury to body part or organ → **8. Which body part(s) or organ(s)?** CHECK ALL THAT APPLY:
  - a. ☐ Uterine rupture
  - b. ☐ Third- or fourth-degree perineal laceration
  - c. ☐ Ureter
  - d. ☐ Bladder
  - e. ☐ Bowel
  - f. ☐ Other: PLEASE SPECIFY ______
- f. ☐ Death
- g. ☐ Other: PLEASE SPECIFY ______

11. Which adverse outcome(s) did the neonate sustain? CHECK ALL THAT APPLY:
- a. ☐ Birth trauma/injury as listed under ICD-9-CM 767 or ICD-10-CM P10-P15 → **12. Which birth trauma/injury?** CHECK ONE:
  - a. ☐ Subdural or cerebral hemorrhage
  - b. ☐ Injury to brachial plexus, including Erb's or Klumpke's paralysis
  - c. ☐ Other: PLEASE SPECIFY ______
- b. ☐ Five-minute Apgar < 7 and birthweight > 2500 grams
- c. ☐ Anoxic or hypoxic encephalopathy
- d. ☐ Seizure(s)
- e. ☐ Infection (e.g., group B strep)
- f. ☐ Unexpected death
- g. ☐ Other: PLEASE SPECIFY ______

16. Was labor induced or augmented? CHECK ONE:
- a. ☐ Yes → **17. Which one?** CHECK ONE:
  - a. ☐ Induced
  - b. ☐ Augmented
- b. ☐ No
- c. ☐ Unknown

19. Regardless of the final mode of delivery, was instrumentation used to assist vaginal (or attempted vaginal) delivery? CHECK ONE:
- a. ☐ Yes → **20. What instrumentation was used?** CHECK ONE:
  - a. ☐ Vacuum
  - b. ☐ Forceps
  - c. ☐ Vacuum followed by forceps
- b. ☐ No
- c. ☐ Unknown

Fig. 1. Items selected from the perinatal form of the common formats.

four weeks (28 days) postpartum, whereas Chinese healthcare systems use the 28th week of gestation through seven days postpartum. WHO defines a perinatal period of the 22th week of gestation through seven-day postpartum.

The diversity shown in the reports may partially depend on the understanding of the sample case and the interoperability of the report form. (1) The various understandings may be due to specialties and clinical experiences. For instance, in item six, 'Which adverse outcomes did the mother sustain?', five out of 21 participants suggested that the mother was psychologically affected by the adverse event. Three of them are specialized in nursing psychology, one is in nursing ethics, and the other one is nursing in psychiatry. As indicated in the results, reporters who received training in nursing psychology or psychiatry tend to conclude psychological influences from the report. Regulations may be developed in reporting formats to reduce such ambiguities. The responses from the other participants reflect their clinical specialty and previous training to a certain extent.

It remains unclear if the Common Formats allow reporters to include reasonable assumptions based on their clinical expertise. (2) The results from item 5 indicate a subject judgment is involved in the reporting. There were four participants out of 21 did not check that 'mother was affected by the event'. Two participants amongst the four argued there was no mention of the mother in the description, whereas the other two believed that compared to the fetal fracture mother was barely affected by the event. (3) The diverse responses to item 11 and 19 indicate a discrepant understanding of the incident due to the incompleteness of information from the report and the oversimplified items in the perinatal form.

Based on our findings, we suggest improving the perinatal safety in two aspects. First, structured data entry is recommended in the collection of the data. A number of the discrepant responses are due to the loss and ambiguity of the information. Structured data entry may reduce such vulnerability. This suggestion is in line with the advantages of the Common Formats as they provide a framework for structured data entry for patient safety events. Second, further studies should expand to the translation of all the other Common Formats, which would help a quick adaptation in using a reporting standard of patient safety events. Our findings in perinatal reporting have disclosed a pressing need of cross-cultural adaptation of perinatal incident reporting in Chinese hospitals. When it comes to the discussion of patient safety in China, there are concerns of incident reporting in a wide spectrum of medical adverse events [14, 15].

Acknowledgement. This project is in part supported by a grant on patient safety from the University of Texas System and a grant from AHRQ grant 1R01HS022895.

References

1. Kohn, L.T., Corrigan, J.M., Donaldson, M.S.: To Err Is Human: Building a Safer Health System. National Academies Press, Washington, DC (2000)
2. Mahajan, R.P.: Critical incident reporting and learning. Br. J. Anaesth. **105**, 69–75 (2010)
3. Pronovost, P.J., Thompson, D.A., Holzmueller, C.G., Lubomski, L.H., Dorman, T., Dickman, F., Fahey, M., Steinwachs, D.M., Engineer, L., Sexton, J.B., et al.: Toward learning from patient safety reporting systems. J. Crit. Care **21**, 305–315 (2006)
4. Leape, L.L., Abookire, S., World Health Organization: WHO Draft Guidelines for Adverse Event Reporting and Learning Systems: From Information to Action. World Health Organization, Geneva (2005)
5. Gong, Y.: Data consistency in a voluntary medical incident reporting system. J. Med. Syst. **35**, 609–615 (2011)
6. Gong, Y., Zhu, M., Li, J., Turley, J., Zhang, J.: Clinical communication ontology for medical errors. In: AMIA Annual Symposium Proceedings, p. 930. American Medical Informatics Association (2006)
7. Tamuz, M., Thomas, E.J., Franchois, K.E.: Defining and classifying medical error: lessons for patient safety reporting systems. Qual. Saf. Health Care **13**, 13–20 (2004)
8. Barton, A.: Patient safety and quality: an evidence-based handbook for nurses. AORN J. **90**, 601–602 (2009)
9. Battles, J.B., Kaplan, H., Van der Schaaf, T., Shea, C.: The attributes of medical event-reporting systems. Arch. Pathol. Lab. Med. **122**, 132–138 (1998)

10. Clancy, C.M.: Common formats allow uniform collection and reporting of patient safety data by patient safety organizations. Am. J. Med. Qual. **25**, 73–75 (2010)
11. Raju, T.N.K., Suresh, G., Higgins, R.D.: Patient safety in the context of neonatal intensive care: research and educational opportunities. Pediatr. Res. **70**, 109–115 (2011)
12. Lucas, J., Bulbul, T., Anumba, C.J., Messner, J.: Evaluating the role of healthcare facility information on health information technology initiatives from a patient safety perspective. American Society of Civil Engineers, pp. 720–727 (2011)
13. Williams, T., Szekendi, M., Pavkovic, S., Clevenger, W., Cerese, J.: The reliability of AHRQ common format harm scales in rating patient safety events. J. Patient Saf. **11**, 52–59 (2015)
14. Nie, Y., Mao, X., Cui, H., He, S., Li, J., Zhang, M.: Hospital survey on patient safety culture in China. BMC Health Serv. Res. **13**, 228 (2013)
15. Liu, C., Liu, W., Wang, Y., Zhang, Z., Wang, P.: Patient safety culture in China: a case study in an outpatient setting in Beijing. BMJ Qual. Saf. **23**, 556–564 (2014)
16. Zhang, M.-L., Zhou, Z.-H.: ML-KNN: A lazy learning approach to multi-label learning. Pattern Recogn. **40**, 2038–2048 (2007)
17. Saha, S., Beach, M.C., Cooper, L.A.: Patient centeredness, cultural competence and healthcare quality. J. Natl Med. Assoc. **100**, 1275 (2008)
18. MacDorman, M.F., Munson, M.L., Kirmeyer, S.: Fetal and perinatal mortality, United States, 2005. National Vital Statistics Reports, vol. 56 (2007)
19. Goldhaber, M.K.: Fetal death ratios in a prospective study compared to state fetal death certificate reporting. Am. J. Publ. Health **79**, 1268–1270 (1989)
20. Gaudino Jr., J.A., Blackmore-Prince, C., Yip, R., Rochat, R.W.: Quality assessment of fetal death records in Georgia: a method for improvement. Am. J. Publ. Health **87**, 1323–1327 (1997)
21. Martin, J.A., Hoyert, D.L.: The national fetal death file. Seminars in Perinatology, pp. 3–11 (2002)
22. Alexander, G.R.: The accurate measurement of gestational age–a critical step toward improving fetal death reporting and perinatal health. Am. J. Publ. Health **87**, 1278 (1997)
23. Greb, A.E., Pauli, R.M., Kirby, R.S.: Accuracy of fetal death reports: comparison with data from an independent stillbirth assessment program. Am. J. Publ. Health **77**, 1202–1206 (1987)
24. Singer, S.J., Gaba, D.M., Geppert, J.J., Sinaiko, A.D., Howard, S.K., Park, K.C.: The culture of safety: results of an organization-wide survey in 15 California hospitals. Qual. Saf. Health Care **12**, 112–118 (2003)
25. Runciman, B., Walton, M.: Safety and Ethics in Healthcare: A Guide to Getting It Right. Ashgate Publishing Ltd, Burlington (2007)
26. Runciman, W., Hibbert, P., Thomson, R., Van Der Schaaf, T., Sherman, H., Lewalle, P.: Towards an International classification for patient safety: key concepts and terms. Int. J. Qual. Health Care **21**, 18–26 (2009)
27. Liang, C., Gong, Y.: On building an ontological knowledge base for managing patient safety events. In: MEDINFO 2015: EHealth-Enabled Health: Proceedings of 15th World Congress on Health and Biomedical Informatics, p. 202 (2015)
28. Johnson, C.W.: How will we get the data and what will we do with it then? Issues in the reporting of adverse healthcare events. Qual. Saf. Health Care **12**, ii64–ii67 (2003)
29. Nieva, V.F., Sorra, J.: Safety culture assessment: a tool for improving patient safety in healthcare organizations. Qual. Saf. Health Care **12**, ii17–ii23 (2003)
30. Bagian, J.P., Lee, C., Gosbee, J., DeRosier, J., Stalhandske, E., Eldridge, N., Williams, R., Burkhardt, M.: Developing and deploying a patient safety program in a large health care delivery system: you can't fix what you don't know about. Jt. Comm. J. Qual. Patient Saf. **27**, 522–532 (2001)

31. Farley, D.O., Haviland, A., Champagne, S., Jain, A.K., Battles, J.B., Munier, W.B., Loeb, J.M.: Adverse-event-reporting practices by US hospitals: results of a national survey. Qual. Saf. Health Care **17**, 416–423 (2008)
32. Nucklos, T.K.: Incident reporting: more attention to the safety action feedback loop, please (2011). http://www.webmm.ahrq.gov/perspective.aspx
33. Wagner, B., Meirowitz, N., Shah, J., Nanda, D., Reggio, L., Cohen, P., Britt, K., Kaufman, L., Walia, R., Bacote, C., et al.: Comprehensive perinatal safety initiative to reduce adverse obstetric events. J. Healthcare Qual. **34**, 6–15 (2012)
34. McCartney, P.R.: Using technology to promote perinatal patient safety. J. Obstet. Gynecol. Neonatal. Nurs. **35**, 424–431 (2006)
35. Sousa, V.D., Rojjanasrirat, W.: Translation, adaptation and validation of instruments or scales for use in cross-cultural health care research: a clear and user-friendly guideline. J. Eval. Clin. Pract. **17**, 268–274 (2011)
36. Brislin, R.W.: Back-translation for cross-cultural research. J. Cross Cult. Psychol. **1**, 185–216 (1970)
37. Harkness, J.A., de Vijver, F.J.R., Mohler, P.P., Fur Umfragen, Z.: Cross-Cultural Survey Methods. Wiley, Hoboken (2003)
38. Guillemin, F., Bombardier, C., Beaton, D.: Cross-cultural adaptation of health-related quality of life measures: literature review and proposed guidelines. J. Clin. Epidemiol. **46**, 1417–1432 (1993)

Research Service Design Based on Online Public Service Platform — APP Design for Mutual Learning Through Sign Language Short Video

Youxin Wu[1(✉)], Yin Liang[2], Haiyang Sun[1], Jingxian Chen[1], Yi Liu[1], Jian Lin[1], and Binbin Li[1]

[1] Jiangnan University,
No. 1800, Lihu Road, Binhu District, Wuxi, Jiangsu, China
wuyouxin@vip.163.com,
{475811998,353773090,1075838954}@qq.com,
ianlinjl@hotmail.com, lbbwx@vip.sina.com
[2] Politecnico di Milano, Piazza Leonardo da Vinci, 32, Milan, Italy
yl401402@hotmail.com

Abstract. Deaf people is a special group whose biggest social barrier is that it is difficult for them to communicate with hearing people. Puji Public Service Net Platform has been devoted into the popularization of the sign language culture, with the convergence of all kinds of stakeholders such as volunteers, public service organizations, deaf groups and government administration department. Cooperated with Puji Public Service Net Platform, our designing team has established an ideal multiple-contact service mode through the factual and desktop research, the service designing tools such as personas and case studies etc.

The designing of "The Taste of Sign Language" APP is devoted into promoting equal communication through video communication of learning sign language between the hearing people and the deaf. Through recording the life little by little, sharing thoughts and online social scenes of the information, the short video application motivates the 'performance' desire of the users, builds the empathy, gradually improves the user stickiness and helps the users to form a habit. The development and application of the service designing has provided new trainof thought and solutions for public welfare undertakings.

Keywords: Public service net platform · Service design · User experience · Empathy · Short video application

1 Introduction

Deaf People is the disabled people with the hearing loss cause of congenital defect or human factors, hereinafter referred to as the deaf. According to the sixth National Census Data of 2010, there are around 20.75 million deaf people, among whom there are 8675 deaf people in Wuxi City including 4831 deaf males. According to the national standard, there are four grades (Grade I is the most serious) for the hearing of deaf people. Because of the congenital defect or human factors, this group cannot hear sound

P.-L.P. Rau (Ed.): CCD 2016, LNCS 9741, pp. 704–716, 2016.
DOI: 10.1007/978-3-319-40093-8_70

from the outside, so their 'talking' style and habit is different from that of hearing people. On one hand, the deaf feel inferior caused by hearing barrier and gradually reduce the communication with the outside; on the other hand, the hearing people are lack of the chances of taking care of the deaf cause of not knowing how to communicate with the deaf. Just because of the existence of the incomprehension and the communication barrier, an invisible "wall" form between the deaf and the hearing people.

Puji Public Service Net Platform has been devoted into the popularization of the sign language culture, with the convergence of all kinds of stakeholders such as volunteers, public service organizations, deaf groups and government administration departments. This organization consider the deaf as a special group, the biggest social barrier is that it is difficult for them to communicate with the hearing people. Such barrier makes their living and mental space extremely narrow and leaves the warmhearted people away from their world. Our designing team of this subject had the cooperation with Puji Public Service Net Platform, establishing the ideal multiple-contact service mode through the factual and desk research, the service designing tools such as personas and case studies etc. "The Taste of Sign Language" APP is devoted into promoting the equal communication through the video communication of learning sign language between the hearing people and the deaf. Through recording the life little by little, sharing the thoughts, the online social scenes of the information times, the short video application motifs the 'performance' desire of the users, builds the empathy, gradually improves the user stickiness and helps the user to form habit.

The development and application of the service designing has provided new train of thought and solutions for public welfare undertakings [1]. The development and application of the service designing has provided methodology and solutions for public welfare undertakings. The service design of the public service projects is not the same as the commercial project, preferring the social value to the economic maximization. With the social responsibility, the designers should reexamine the designing, pay more attention to the design for the social public benefit, which demands the designers to integrate all kinds of social resources creatively through social innovations [2]. One of the main characteristics of social innovation is satisfying the unsatisfied demand of the oppositely vulnerable group [3]. It is not only the object requirement for the designers in modern society through satisfying the demand of the vulnerable group and improving their communications with other members of society, but also the reflection of the designers' intrinsic properties as social agent [4]. The designers of 'Pushing Wall' Interesting Sign Language APP value keeping the interest of the deaf and the hearing people for the mutual learning the software tools, to push over the invisible wall between the deaf and the hearing people and then help the deaf return the society (Fig. 1).

2 Concepts and Discussions

Determining how to design the effective service procedure for the social problems creatively, there is one basic way, finding the effective cases through the investigation, then building a replicable solution on this base [5]. After the preliminary case analysis and user survey, the mutual learning style through short video on Mobile APP. Whatever iCastshow, Kuaishou, Papaqi and Weishi within China, and the Vine, Dubsmas

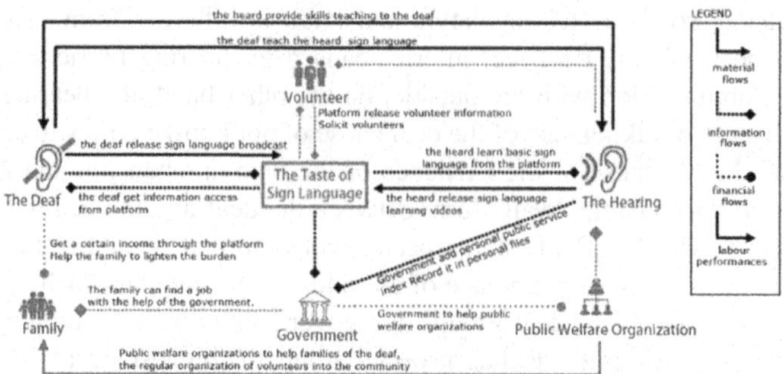

Fig. 1. Background of the project

and Instagram abroad, the short video sharing are triggering the social circles quietly. The novelty of the social contact motivates the users' power to share for the first time. With the functional and social driving force, the short video sharing also has the spirit demand of communication and feelings. The above two elements makes the necessity of its existence.

2.1 Overall Process

Service design for social innovation follows the standard procedure of service design and it is carried on iteratively throughout four steps of investigation, designing, feedback and execution [6]. Through the extensive investigation, the design team and the stakeholders built up empathy and trust relationship mutually, brought in the service strategy of the interaction among multi-dimensional different-type users in the following steps, designers integrated a series of online service function of interaction education, information sharing and weak-tie social contact etc. The team has produced several lo-fi service designing modes such as story board, customer journey and blue print etc., making the service procedure and scenes visible to the stakeholders for better understanding. At the same time, the team designed the hi-fi service modes including the sign language education APP and series of short video application, then optimized the user experience of each touchpoint to form an integrated service system through the short video and application design (Fig. 2).

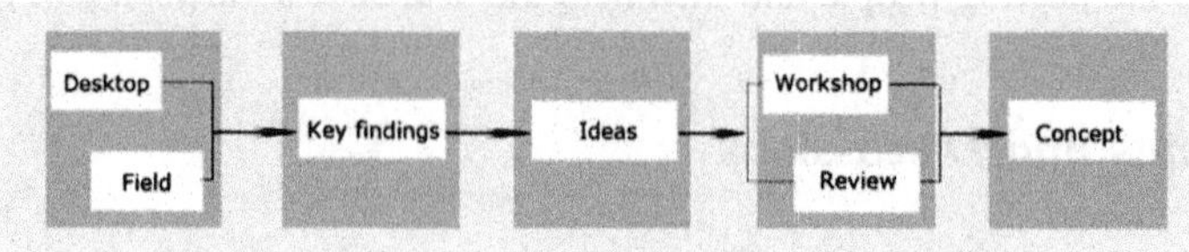

Fig. 2. Overall methodology of the project

2.2 Questionnaire and Data Processing of Empirical Research

For this research, we handed out the questionnaires to the deaf and the hearing people and finally received 209 hearing people questionnaires and 296 deaf questionnaires. If the answers of a questionnaire were nearly the same or not written seriously, the questionnaire was regarded as a waste questionnaire. There were 3 waste questionnaires of hearing people, meaning the waste questionnaire ratio was 1.4 %, while 44 waste questionnaires of deaf people, meaning the waste questionnaire ratio was 14.8 %. The work was done through SPSS17.0 software package and Excel, such as logging the questionnaire data, statistics, filing, analysis, correlation analysis and element analysis according to the data base.

Research Result I of the Empirical Research: Communication Experience Analysis of the Deaf-hearing Communication. From Fig. 3 we could see: the evaluation index of the hearing people testee is CSI (1.67–3.72)toward the deaf-hearing communication experience. The highest score of the hearing people testee is the cooperation attitude, CSI (3.72), but the sign language skill of them is the lowest (1.67). For the deaf testee, the evaluation index is CSI (3.26–3.85) toward the deaf-hearing communication experience, among all of the aspects, the lowest CSI is the sign language skill of the hearing people: 3.26, the highest CSI is their cooperation attitude: CSI (3.85). For the familiarity to the deaf people is in the middle as (3.53). Through the comparison of the two curves of the hearing people and the deaf, we could see the CSI index of the hearing people testee is lower than that of the deaf on every aspect, so generally speaking, the total experience of the hearing people is worse than that of the deaf on deaf-hearing communication. So we can conclude that the deaf and the hearing people are both enthusiastic about the communication cooperation, but can not communicate successfully with the sign language skill limit, and the same time, the low familiarity to the deaf people makes the deaf-hearing communication a sea of troubles, and leads to the big difference of the communication experience.

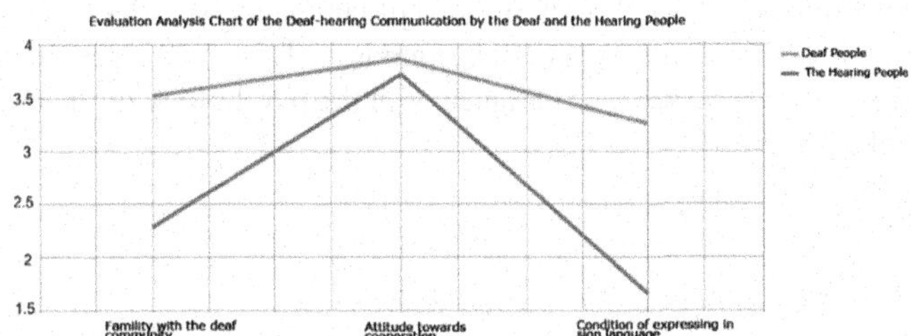

Fig. 3. Evaluation analysis chart of the deaf-hearing communication by the deaf and the hearing people (Color figure online)

Result II of the Empirical Research: Relative Experience Analysis of the Deaf-hearing Communication. From Fig. 4 we could see the cooperation attitude index curve of all age groups is CSI (3.62–3.93), apparently higher than the curve of familiarity and the curve of the sign language expression. The attitude curve reaches the peak during the testee aged 36-45: CSI 3.93. The score of the testee aged above 45 is the lowest, only (3.62).For the familiarity to the deaf, the score difference is CSI (2.42–3.37), oppositely big among the age groups. For the sign language curve, the testee score of all age groups is generally lower than that of the other curves, CSI (2.18–2.76). We could see the following information through the score of the testee of all age groups for the familiarity to the deaf, cooperation attitude and the sign language expression: The testee experience difference is the lowest above age 45, the three index difference is 0.86.

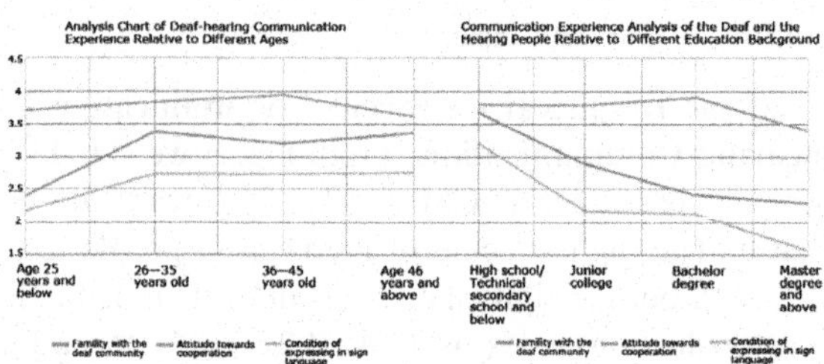

Fig. 4. Communication experience analysis of the deaf and the hearing people relative to different ages and different education background (Color figure online)

We could see according to the CSI curve, the score of the testee with and under the education background of high school/secondary technical school is generally higher than that of the other testee with other education backgrounds, while the score of the testee with and above the master degree is lower than that of the other testee with other education backgrounds, which indicates the education level is inversely proportional to the evaluation of the communication experience between the deaf and the hearing people, Through analyzing the users' cooperation attitude CSI (3.37–3.89). From the curve of the familiarity to the deaf, we could see the CSI of the testee with different education backgrounds is 2.25–3.65. For the sign language expression curve, the score of the testee with different education backgrounds is 1.56–3.20, It is means the sign language expression experience is at variance with the psychology of the user with high education level (Fig. 5).

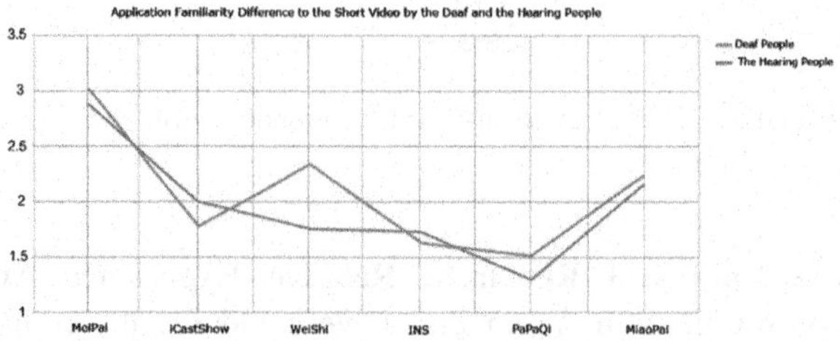

Fig. 5. Application familiarity difference to the short video by the deaf and the hearing people (Color figure online)

Result II of the Empirical Research: Experience Analysis of the Video Application of the Deaf-hearing Group. From Fig. 6 we could see: On the CSI curve, the deaf is most familiar with Meipai with SCI index 2.8 ~ 3.1, apparently higher than the application of the application of the other videos. The next is Miaopai, SCI index is above 2.2. For the familiarity to Weishi, there is big difference between the deaf and the hearing people, the deaf more familiar than the hearing people by 0.7. We could figure it out from the curve, except Weishi, both the deaf and the hearing people are similar to each other on the familiarity to the other videos. And the deaf much more prefer Weishi.

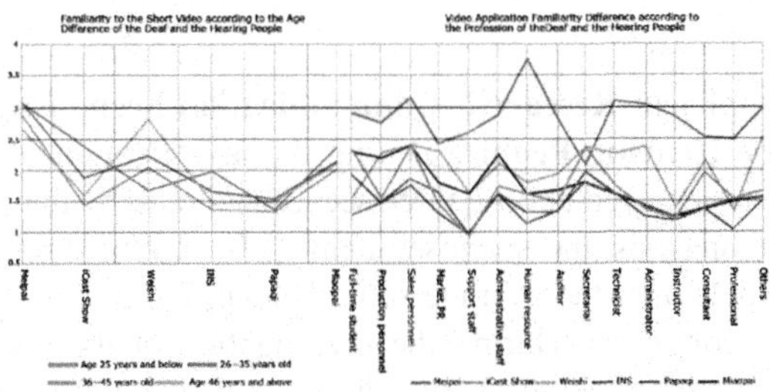

Fig. 6. Video application familiarity difference according to the age and the profession of the deaf and the hearing people (Color figure online)

Result IV of the Empirical Research: Relative Experience Analysis about the Video Application by the Deaf and the Hearing People. From Fig. 6 we could see: On the CSI curve, the deaf and the hearing people at all age groups are the most familiar with Meipai, SCI index being 2.5 ~ 3.1, apparently higher than the application of the other kinds of videos. The next is Miaopai, SCI index of all age groups beyond 2.0. Usually the school students under the age 25 are not so familiar with Weishi video software, apparently different from the other age groups. From the curve chart we could see, except Weishi Video, the SCI of all age groups are generally similar, which means the people of all age groups have the similar familiarity to the videos. In addition, young people more prefer Meipai, iCastshow and Miaopai. Except Meipai, known to all, the middle-aged people over 45 prefer the Weishi video application (Fig. 7).

We could see: On the CSI curve, except administrative staff, the people of all professions is much more familiar with Meipai than the application of the other videos with SCI index kept 2.5 ~ 3.8, among whom the main application group of Meipai is human resource, teschenitic, full-time student and sales personnel, knowing more about Meipai. Comparatively speaking, except Meipai, the people of all professions are oppositely familiar with Weishi with the SCI index 2.4 ~ 2.6, among whom the full time student, teacher and professionals know little of Weishi, with the professional index at the lowest (1.35). The familiarity to Papaqi of the people of all professions is below 2.0, among whom the support staff knows the least with the lowest index (1.02), which means most of the people are not familiar with this software and rarely use it.

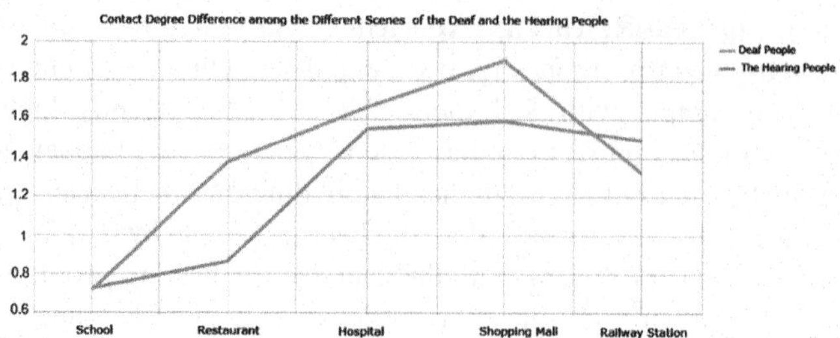

Fig. 7. Contact degree difference among the different scenes of the deaf and the hearing people (Color figure online)

Result V of the Empirical Research: Communication Scene Experience Analysis of the Deaf and the Hearing People. During the investigation of the scene contact degree analysis, the testee need choose three scenes and rank by the order. Later during the data logging and analysis, the unchosen items is 0, and the three chosen items gets the score of 3, 2 and 1, then the average score is analyzed.

From Fig. 9 we could see: During the investigation of the scene contact degree analysis, the highest contact degree is the shopping mall both to the deaf and to the hearing, CSI (1.59) and CSI (1.90). Apart from this, the lowest one is the hospital, CSI (0.73) and CSI (0.72). The above information indicates that there are higher contact degrees in the daily scenes such as shopping mall, hospital and railway station etc., where there are more sign language happening. The margin scenes of schools tend to be the scenes with rare sign language. On the whole, the contact degree from the hearing people to the deaf is lower than that from the deaf to the hearing people, which reflects the low attention from the hearing people to the deaf and the necessity of the casual contact of the deaf and the hearing people.

2.3 The Iterative Process of the Service Designing

The service designing is one way of tackling the complexed problems on the whole [6], whose iterative designing procedure has three to seven steps with the multiple frames, and basically it is four steps of mining, locating, development and communication [7]. The iterative process of the four steps follows the ‘double diamond’ design process model mainly [8]. After the preliminary investigation, the background and demand of the users are shown, and there are the basically reliable information for the service location, then it’s the time for the designers to develop the service procedure and transmit the designing conception to the other stakeholders.

During the process of the service locating, the designers chose some easy and interesting sign language games to be the application carrier after testing several sign language education modes. During the later cooperative development process, the staff of Puji Public Service and other users were invited to attend the service experience with their feedback. According to the feedback, the design flow would return to the lo-fi model or case investigation step, which means the service designing development was carried on iteratively.

2.4 Lo-Fi Service Mode

During the process of the service design development, the lo-fi mode and hi-fi mode are the frequently used design tools [9].

Lo-fi mode is a kind of fast and low-cost establishing and testing method of service design [10], which has the pretty good effect when testing the user demand [11]. Based on the investigation result, the lo-fi prototype was developed under the cooperative design of the designing team and the stakeholders. Generally for the lo-fi prototyping, it includes tools as customer journey and personas etc. Because the net activity on the mobile net is mobile and based on the environment [12], so the renewal of the personal activity scene and the net information is more inseparable, then we chose the user trip drawing showing the experience process and effect as the main lo-fi mode, In the process of making the user experience, we determine the pain points and contact points according to the corresponding behavior generated by users at different stages, and obtain the corresponding design points. Sign language teaching APP and short video applications promote the equality of exchange between the deaf people and hearing people. Game experience also inspired the users to complete the goals of the determination, tapped the user's basic desires and needs. Finally, we will establish an effective information sharing platform based on these data (Fig. 8).

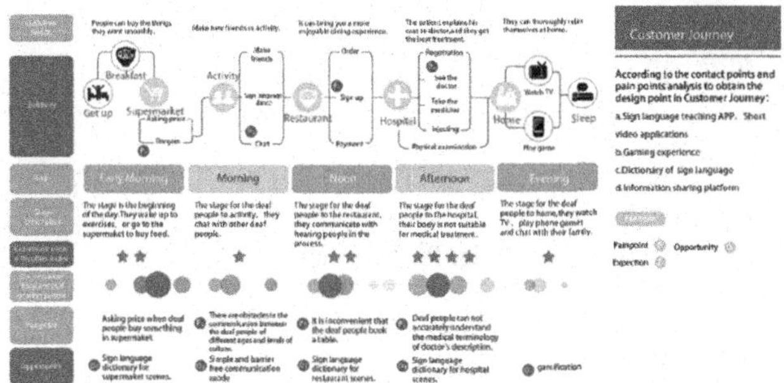

Fig. 8. Customer journey

At the same time, we are considered the different stakeholders and then analyze their attitude and vision according to the personas. Based on the views of existing situation of communication between the deaf people and the hearing people from the personas, namely, the deaf people, the hearing people and stakeholders, the analysis of user targets and their own smartphones consumption. We can draw the conclusion that the inability of expression of sign language has become the main barrier for communication. While the boring learning method of sign language and the lack of scenario-based learning of sign language constitute the main reason. Made the abstract service flow and scenes visible, possible for the people to understand the designing proposals intuitively, such as all kinds of stakeholders of volunteers, public service organizations, the deaf groups and the government departments (Fig. 9).

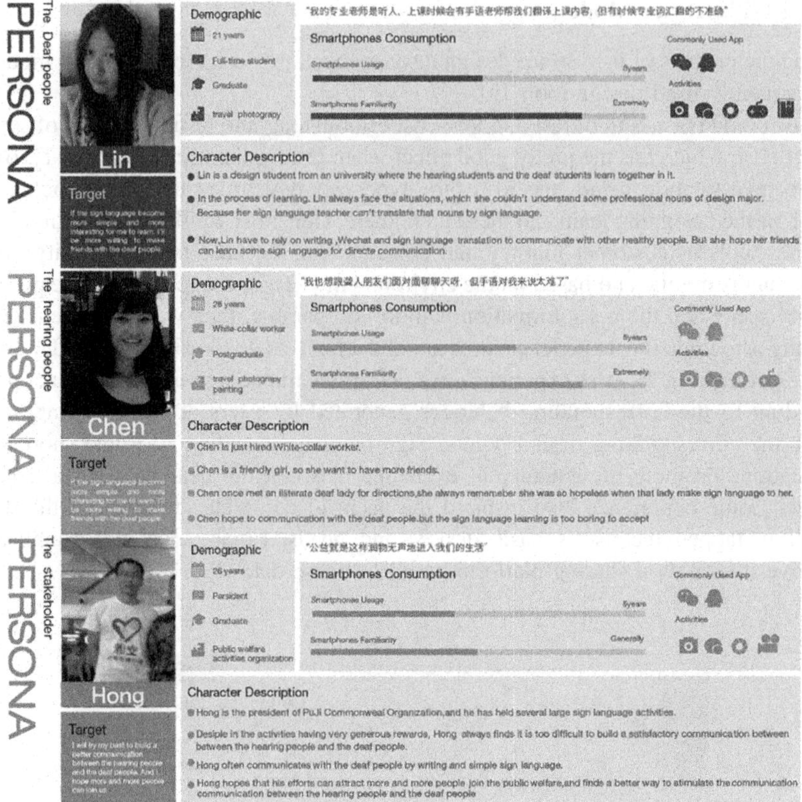

Fig. 9. Personas

2.5 Hi-Fi Service Mode

After the test of lo-fi mode on the service feasibility, design team needed to analyze the detail of the user experience on each link and also make the simulation test for service flow, which need to build hi-fi mode. Persona is a typical hi-fi service design tool, during which the designers and other participators play the roles of the service flow themselves, supposing the service existing, to experience the service result and the interactive relationship etc. [13]. More importantly, perona can help the designers to simulate and understand the different responses from different users under the same background [14]. The design team recorded some role play videos of designers themselves, which made the designers to have the personal experiences of the sign language educations, and the video itself displayed functions in the sign language App as one part of the designing materials.

Under the guidance of the theory, we analyze the data and extract the main demands then we make the interaction draft of "The taste of sign language". The taste of sign language is aimed to increase the communication between the deaf people and the hearing people. The main features include sign video teaching based on scenario classification, the entrance from the deaf world and the hearing one and the community for the purpose of interaction with the form of activities. On the content of the short videos they are elected with rating form. And it uses the game experience to enhance the interaction on the interactive mode. Apart from those, Positive and optimistic visual experience is expected to be available to users on the vision (Fig. 10).

Fig. 10. Interaction draft

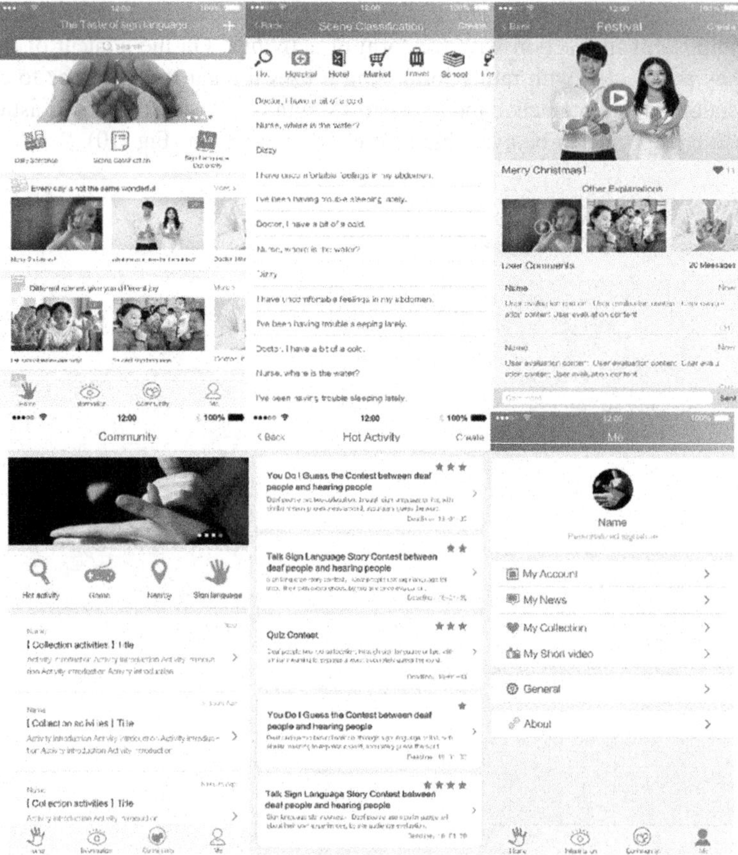

Fig. 11. Taste of sign language

3 Conclusion

After the analysis of all of the pain points and opportunity points, we found that the deaf and dumb circles are enclosed although they have the parties on certain days and there are the joint discussion about the news sign language explanation. Mainly the hobbies of the deaf are photography, painting, tour, dancing and playing cards. The sign language only exists in the special education school with the dialects. The national standard is not complete with the low acceptability, even many deaf people can not understand the national standard yet. There were some organizations online and offline of learning sign language for the hearing people with the low enthusiasm, stickiness and necessity. The activities of the Disabled Association are not for the deaf and dumb on purpose. The Deaf and Dumb Association is generally undertaken by the retiree, mainly making the retirement registration for the deaf and dumb. Up to now, there haven't been the real statistics of their profession, income and education levels. The specific data is counted in the community of the deaf and there haven't been the perfect statistics system (Fig. 11).

On the base of the sign language video resources, we make use of the video carrier (e.g. Meipai, iCastshow) to attract the hearing people to record their sign language. The user can get bonus after uploading the video, then he can share with others about his self-presentation as a partial social contact. The Taste of Sign Language (TTOSL) APP will post the contact information of the video uploaders (on their own will), correct the sign language in common sector with demonstration, then thumb-ups with motivation mechanism introduced. The user can build his own charity file through the uploading and sharing.

For the designing of The Taste of Sign Language, all the stakeholders were getting involved in the process of the beginning, investigation, lo-fi, hi-fi and the designing decision. The designing result makes the hearing people and the deaf to learn the sign language mutually and really with the short video, promoting the equal communication. Through recording the life little by little, sharing the thoughts, the online social scenes of the information times, the short video application motifs the 'performance' desire of the users, builds the empathy, gradually improves the user stickiness and helps the user to form the habit. The development and application of the service designing has provided new train of thought and solutions for public welfare undertakings.

References

1. Yangting, L.B.: Application of the service designing in the public service project. Pop. Lit. **24**, 107–108 (2011)
2. Phills, J.A., Deiglmeier, K., Miller, D.T.: Rediscovering social innovation. Stanf. Soc. Innov. Rev. **6**(4), 34–43 (2008)
3. Yu, Y.: "Xiaoyu" - Service Application Designing for the People with Hearing Impairment. Tsinghua University, Beijing (2013)
4. Chenhan, J., Wei, X.: Design strategy research on collaborative service for network traveling community. Package Eng. **14**, 83–87 (2015)
5. Davies, A., Simon, J.: How to grow social innovation: a review and critique of scaling and diffusion for understanding the growth of social innovation. In: 5th International Social Innovation Research Conference, September 2013
6. Stickdorn, M.: This is Service Design Thinking: Basics-Tools-Cases. BIS Publishers, Amsterdam (2012)
7. Best, K.: Design Management: Managing Design Strategy, Process and Implementation. AVA Publishing, New York (2006)
8. Council, D.: Eleven Lessons: Managing Design in Eleven Global Brands. The Design Council, London (2007)
9. Holmlid, S., Evenson, S.: Prototyping and enacting services: lessons learned from human-centered methods. In: Proceedings from the 10th Quality in Services Conference, QUIS, vol. 10 (2007)
10. Hinman,R.: Rachel Hinman in Conversation with Mark Jones, IDEO About Service Design (2007). http://adaptivepath.org/ideas/e000840/
11. Rudd, J., Stern, K., Isensee, S.: Low vs. high-fidelity prototyping debate. Interactions **3**(1), 76–85 (1996)

12. Zhenyu, W., et al.: Towards cloud and terminal collaborative mobile social network service. In: 2010 IEEE Second International Conference on Social Computing (SocialCom). IEEE (2010)
13. Suri, J.F.: Experience prototyping. In: Symposium on Designing Interactive Systems, Marion Buchenau (2000)
14. Simsarian, K.T.: Take it to the next stage: the roles of role playing in the design process. In: CHI 2003 Extended Abstracts on Human Factors in Computing Systems, pp. 1012–1013. ACM (2003)

Design Study of Patient-Oriented Information Service System for Ward Nurses Station by Taking Wuxi Fourth People's Hospital as a Case

Linghao Zhang(✉), Changfu Lv, Yun Feng, and Jiayu Zeng

Jiangnan University, No. 1800, Lihu Road, Binhu District, Wuxi, Jiangsu, China
wowo.zlh@163.com, {997842742,532751063,1561178483}@qq.com

Abstract. This paper discusses the present situation and the development in the field of the medical service in China. To make the wards information service as the consisting of different contact points of nursing service, it is helpful to optimize the complexity questions of the hospitalization experience. From the perspective of information service, it deeply analyses the business and the nursing information of the ward nurses station from service process and the contact point of information service. We also have took a research in Wuxi Fourth People's Hospital to get In-depth knowledge of the question and specific needs when hospitalized patients and nurses on the ward medical service which is researched through the user interviews of hospitalized patients, behavior observation, the service blueprint and some other methods. Then have summed up five categories such as service of handing of patients' admission and discharge, cost query, rehabilitation nursing, food ordering and personal center. Finally, it formulates the construction strategies including set up the service platform of doctor-patient information symmetry and provide diversified information service content, and also communication strategies including rich media replace text, using infographics design, as well as online information service platform design for patients.

Keywords: Information service · System innovation · Experience in hospital · Strategy · Online platform

1 Introduction

Medical industry is a significant part of social public services [1]. With the continuous progress of social economy and life quality, People's health awareness is also increasing. It attaches great importance on diagnosis and treatment level, external form and additional experience. However, public health service industries in our city are still in a stage of development. The Ward Nurses Station, which works as a unit of information service in the daily life of the ward, has many experience problem unresolved. Therefore, it will better achieve the patient centered design transformation of information service platform that recognizes complexity of information design in service system design way, analyses touch point and has an insight into the needs of stakeholders with using Internet technology to improve or optimize the process experience.

P.-L.P. Rau (Ed.): CCD 2016, LNCS 9741, pp. 717–728, 2016.
DOI: 10.1007/978-3-319-40093-8_71

2 Information Service System for Ward Nurses Station and Service Design Thinking

2.1 Information Service System and Related Problems in Ward Nurses Station

Nurses Station, which closely connects with pharmacy, charges and inspection services system, is an important part of hospital information system. It's used to support medics in clinical activities, collective and manage patients' data [2]. What's more, it enables nurse better deal with hospital bed quantity, nursing process and charge statistics. So, Ward Nurses Station, which is based on information service system, extends daily nursing care to patient clinic. It's a general name for the information service in the area of bed management, nursing administration and cost statistic, and medical order treatment (Fig. 1).

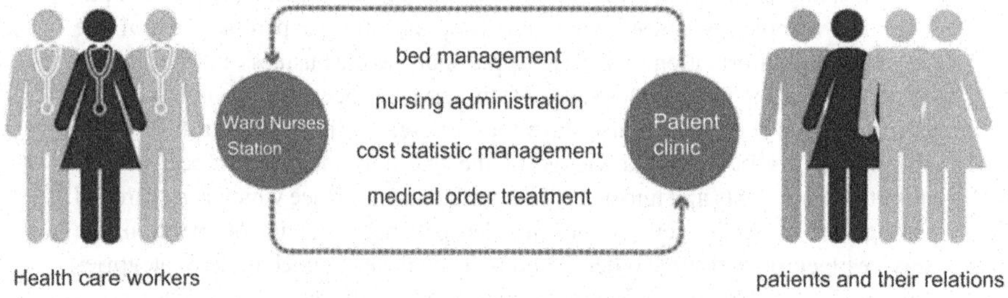

Fig. 1. Nursing station information service system

Traditional Nurses Station with the patient as the center, has simple information point. It is isolated that health care workers and clinical patients work as two parts. Thereby, patients are often in the state of information passive. It's mainly reflects in following aspects:

1. In the aspect of information management. Due to large and complex patients' information, nurses can not make targeted care. Furthermore, information asymmetry, which make patients in a passive situation, has been reflected in wards' information management; It also lead to low efficiency in bed management, nursing administration and cost statistic, and so on.
2. In the aspect of information acquisition, a large number of medical information is available in a single channel. Access to health knowledge, nursing information, examination of the documents, pain assessment information and daily room service is originally passed on orally which leads to poor information dissemination. In addition, it is hard for patients to understand some medicines' function and expense invoices.
3. In the aspect of information interaction. If they lacked efficiently communicate and interact with nurses, patients would recover hardly. Health care workers cannot get recovery related mental health and other privacy issues in time. What's more, there is no service platform to offer a relatively closed communication and interaction

which make nurses aware of patients' potentially mental disorders and then take the relevant measures.

2.2 Import of Service Design Thinking

As a result of an innovative strategy shift under the new situation [3], service system design is a collection of material product, service flow and information dissemination. Focusing on the structure of the whole system [4] and improving user experience can create more business value of the product when it is from the users' point of view. The traditional thinking of "production line model" is clearly unable to cope with the challenges of health care services. However, service design focus from on product to on value transfer, and make full use of Internet technology and human relations to achieve a simplified service, so that brings excellent service experience [5]. It often takes positive change as the goal, showing the power to change the vision and motivation of both sides, especially combines the value proposition of business thinking with the user service contact points in real condition [6]. What's more, through blending appropriate qualitative with quantitative thinking, new thinking in service design responds to the complex needs of consumers [7]. It includes the use of empathy insight into user needs, finding opportunities through the visual visualization and with the help of a prototype tool to realize serve mode.

Take Kaiser Permanente as an example, which has improved nurse handover information model. The ward nurses were divided into middle shift, day shift and night shift, so the unity and continuity of nursing information when they shift is essential for patients' rehabilitation. To face the problem, Kaiser Permanente and IDEO design company work together and hope to develop a systemic and effective solution which is easy to use and transfer of information by nurses for patient safety, quality of care and the efficiency of shift. IDEO conducted a continuous observation of the shift in the ward, and then understood the way of exchanging information among nurses. In addition, they found other factors which will affect results, such as the nursing process, the management of patients and the records of nursing. They revealed that every nurse has its own information priority standard and interaction manner. Thus, IDEO built an interaction framework and placed the entry point in the information transfer, patient interaction, information software and other aspects. Finally, combined with the specific needs of patients, which improved the work efficiency of the nurses and the safety of patients, they established a set of commonly used information interactive template for care information expression and importance ranking.

It can be seen in the medical service progress that patient needs penetrate the whole life cycle of service system. Contact point of patients, health care workers, family members and other stakeholders' relationship is the focus of designing and exploration which can be improved and integrated into a systematic and implemental solution.

3 Research Process

3.1 Analysis of Nursing Process in Ward Nurses Station

From the beginning to the end, each patient in entire business process will have a close relationship and interact with the hospital ward nurses station. Nursing process is a process of information exchange in the patients receiving the system. Nursing information flow is complex, and service projects of different patients are not the same. One day in nursing station usually includes following: patients admission, admission assessment, grading nursing, nursing rounds, patients discharge and other major processes. In addition to these basic nursing operation, it needs to cooperate with ward nurse station information system to collect and input information module relevant to patients, so as to better serve them. The whole process of nursing information is shown in Fig. 2.

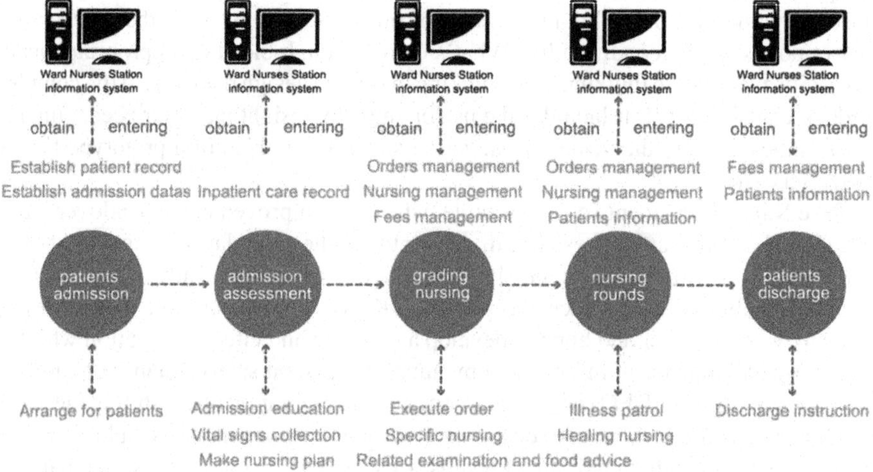

Fig. 2. Nursing process of nursing station in ward

From the perspective of service system, the hospitalization process is an entirety, and each different nursing service is a sub process of it. The goal of these sub processes is to make patients satisfied with the hospital services. Meanwhile, doctors, nurses and other stakeholders have to meet the needs of patients. Therefore, to improve hospital management efficiency and experience, we need to do first is optimizing the sub process of the service system, and then bring along improvement of the whole service system experience.

3.2 Analysis of Information Service Contact Points in Ward Nurses Station

All part of services in medical process can be regarded as a contact point. Including tangible and intangible continuous system elements and spatial information, even participants' behavior and emotion [8]. It could be an equipment (Nurse PC) or a service link

(Vital Signs Collection, Execution Order…), each contact point is the key point to improve the patients' experience. Only by improving contact point design can we enrich and make the process more coherent. The contact points help the designer to find out the service that has the problem, to define and enhance the patient's needs and the existing services and products, and then promote interaction between station and patients.
Admission Assessment. At first, getting patient information, which contain patient's disease situation, enable hospital to meet their reasonable needs and propagate admission process, ward environment, inpatient care attention and equipment use-methods. Subsequently, the medical staffs need to carry out the nursing assessment, and measure patients with vital signs information. According to collections which contain patient's health condition [9], they can provide an instruction for nursing plan and advice.

Many contact points are associated with ordering information checking and executing. Through taking and consulting medical orders in nursing information system station, nurse prints out the order items and list of drugs in the ward today be executed, and check on distribution of drugs from dispensing room. Meanwhile, making the implementation records and medication nursing records, doctors can read and check the system. At present, the information system in nursing station can't track the medical advice life cycle. Without health care information, patients cannot get the information of individual nursing project.

The collection of vital signs is the contact point of the information service. The nurses measure the vital signs according to the nursing grade and the patient's condition every day. In general, the nurse should first confirm the identity of the patient, and then measure the vital signs specifically. After all of these, they will input all the relevant data and their collector into the nursing station information system. So far, this process is complicated, and way of information acquisition is single.

Nursing rounds, including the patient's mental expression and conscious state, diet and nutrition, etc. To grasp the latest information of the clinical situation and get in touch with patients' families and doctors timely for emergent problems, nurses usually perambulate three or four times around wards during their daily work. There are great possibilities for improving accuracy and efficiency of patients' pain degree collection, as well as information interaction.

Inpatient information management, which contain doctor's orders information management, such as its contents, execution situation and so on; Nursing information management, such as nursing records, nursing quality, nursing evaluation and so on; Beds information management, such as patients and beds conditions; Cost information management, such as the hospitalization expense list, care and treatment and so on. Every day, nurses need to effectively manage these information through clinical acquisition and ward nurse station shared. At present, information management workload is heavy, and information obtain experience for patients needs to be optimized.

Food ordering is also an important part of the system. According to the doctor's diet advice, the information will be sent to nutrition, and put dietary requirements and restrictions on a car beside patient's bedside, as a basis for the food allocation. Lack of diet education information, the current service process is too messy to make patients understand and follow the diet plan.

Therefore, it is necessary to build the online information service platform of nurse station by Internet technology, which transmits data to desktop information system of ward nurse station through WLAN. It is a supplementary and extended information service platform for patients beside bed. On one hand, it will provide patients with related service and information handily. On the other hand, it can effectively promote the interaction between patients and medical staff, since it is an information communication service platform for patients and medical personnel which is set up in the bed.

3.3 The Analysis and Research of Ward Nurses Station Information Service System About Fourth People's Hospital in Wuxi

Based on the analysis above, we set out from the nursing station in the Fourth People's Hospital in Wuxi. Through a series of survey methods, such as target user interview, satisfaction survey and behavior observation, we inquired the basic situation and existing problems of information service. At the same time, we summed up the pain points and potential needs of patients and medical staff during the ward nursing service process, and obtains the information content and specific form. The whole research is divided into three stages.

In the first stage, a preliminary interview with 2 nurses in the Department of general surgery of Wuxi Fourth People's Hospital was conducted to understand the basic situation and needs of the patients during hospitalization. To understand the patients' inner feelings, and difficulties of their accompanying family members and medical staffs, we classified the content of the interview. Finally, we merged them into six major categories, which include inpatient rehabilitation nursing, hospital daily service, patient information management, ordering and diet guidance, medical treatment and cost and project inquiry. Next, to re-examine the issue which contains six aspects, then investigation the

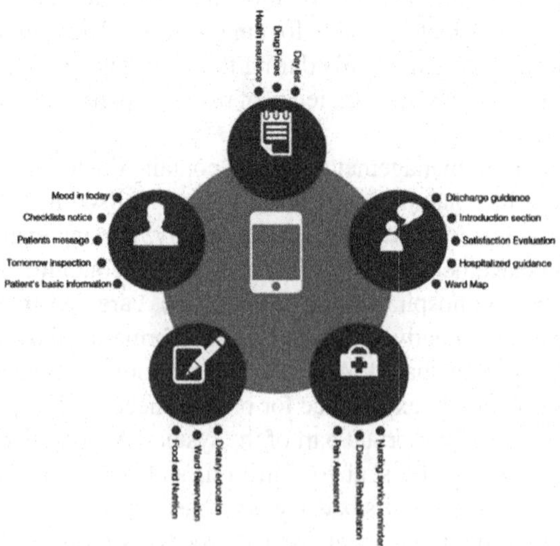

Fig. 3. Deeply interview summary

quantifying of user satisfaction, to screening and verification the common question of patients and medical staff thinks. The results showed that patients are agree with the pain points and issues about costs and project inquiries, inpatient rehabilitation care, hospital daily service, patient information management, ordering, diet and other aspects. It Illustrated these aspects deserve optimization and improvement.

Then the second phase, to had a depth user interviews for the 10 patients, family members of patients and five health care workers, the five questions on a stage of further exploration, and design needs further in-depth and refinement. The results are shown in Fig. 3.

Then the third phase, the observation of nurses one day nursing behavior, in order to be more scientific to explore nursing services and issue in ward area, and to identify problems in the ward area between nurses and patients, the project as a spectator to observed nursing behavior of the day from morning to night of a nurse in Wuxi Fourth People's Hospital, and had in-depth conversation for some problems. The results through the service blueprint and working pressure map (Fig. 4) and analysis the relevant contact points. As can be seen, health care workers working in the day care pressure index were higher, especially nine o'clock to fourteen o'clock, and there are some problems about the interaction with the patient's feelings, information acquisition and execution efficiency.

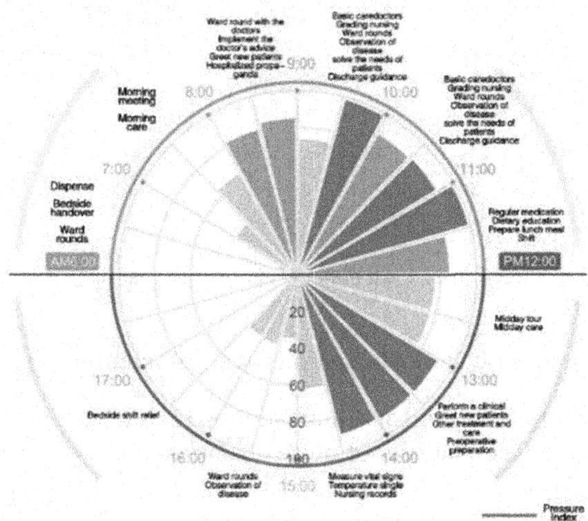

Fig. 4. Deeply interview summary

Subsequently, had an in-depth conversation with the department's head nurse, from a professional view and through the entire user experience map to have an intuitive and holistic understanding of the hospitalization process, Thereby further clear demand: improving the patient's ability to obtain medical information initiative, on the other hand to improve the nurses working efficiency; the nurses station information service online platform also can include service terminal, wechat platform, information manuals; and improve the ward electronic information construction level.

4 Strategies and Outputs of Ward Nurses Station Information Service System Design

Through research, analysis and summary, established the whole direction of the ward nurse station information service system (Fig. 5), by through the establishment of the nurses' station assisted information online platform, redesigned and improved the existing nursing station information systems, services in the patient's bed management, care management and expense management modules which is component by the partial service terminals, wechat platform and other aspects, as a supplement to the main nursing station, information services extended to the patient bedside, it effectively enhance the interaction with the patient and focus on optimizing contents of hospitalization information, improve the interactive of information, presenting information and other aspects, Then connected service platform and the entire hospital information system to build the whole information service system as taking patients as the core.

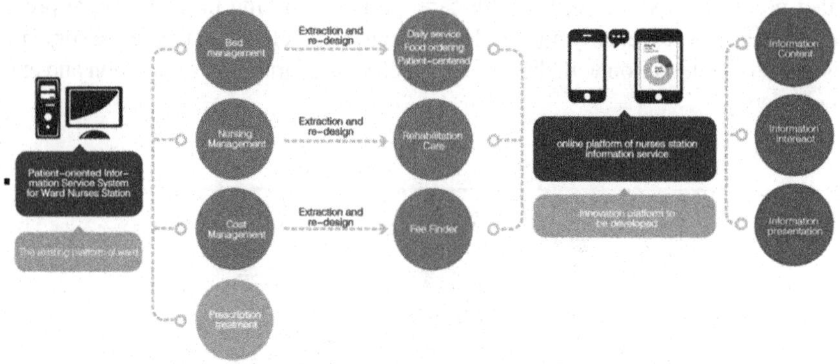

Fig. 5. The direction of ward nursing station information service system

4.1 Establish Doctor and Patients Symmetrical Information Service Platform

Equality between doctors and patients information acquisition, patient ward can provide online information service platform of nurse station, and it is connected to the main nursing station, it could share information, thus provide some beds, fees, nursing care and other medical services information for patients, to facilitate patient search; Secondly, the information platform also taking into account the state of the patient's condition and personal fitness, and push some medical information with the individual property features, then personalized interactive information, such as the rehabilitation of fracture information, daily mood message and attendance, and then provide reasonable services to meet patients' needs. Meanwhile, the medical staff and patients are in the same information service system, they can constantly exchange information and interaction between them, and to some extent, it realized real-time information sharing.

4.2 Provide Diversified of Information Services

Provides the daily costs list of hospitalization by electronic way, and will provide the list of hospital costs of yesterday, and timely to correct any errors. Take the form of the list to design the information, it mainly to provide information on: cost type, project name, price and specifications, quantity and amount. Each item of information is in a column, left-aligned, and the cost of the same type attribute would be restructure and collation. The Important usual pharmaceutical signed by five-pointed star-mark, and the patient can view the drug effects by click on pop-ups. Drug market take the same form of the list to design the information, navigation position could provide the first level information, that the drug category (medicine, Chinese medicine and herbal medicine), and the secondary market have more detailed information.

Provide rehabilitation care information, such as fracture departments provide recovery after fractures and how to avoid secondary fractures; obstetrics and gynecology departments can provide care knowledge of nurse babies, and post-natal care, etc. Information arranged in the form of a springboard layout style, then the information use rich media formats, combined with the specific rehabilitation topics picture or video guidance information, that patients can also be read by clicking the module (Fig. 6).

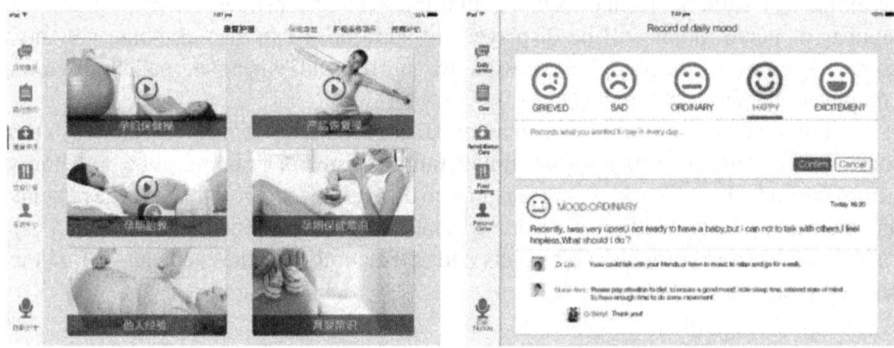

Fig. 6. Rehabilitation nursing module **Fig. 7.** Daily attendance message

Provide the nurse service project every day, namely the completed project and unfinished project of the nurse service in each day, and what is the specific implementation of nurse service projects, like executor, execution time and doctor's care programs, include Long-term program or care program. When patients are in full screen view by follow the care program, it will automatically switch to a different thumbnail view of different days, then patients can click on the appropriate date to see the corresponding care programs.

Also provides daily hospitalization services information, including: Admission and discharge guidance, departments and medical staff, ward maps. The information, use rich media formats, are arranged in the form of a springboard layout style, to combine the pictures, in line with the guidance of the subject matter of admission, could reflect the theme of feature as much as possible. In addition, making a reservation by the way of information, presentation of recipes by combining the pictures, then using a list or gallery.

4.3 Build Multi-faceted Clinical Interaction of Nurse-Patient

It is necessary to build an interactive platform to leave comments, through a wireless local area network technology and real-time connect the ward nurses station, patients could leave voice or text massage the relevant issues about hospitalization in the information platform, in the another way, the medical staff could arrange fragmented time, and reply the patients' massages by wireless network.

Construct the interactive platform of mood (Fig. 7), the moods are all use cartoon face, and the color will occur after select. And then by choosing different cartoon expressions to reflect their feelings, and leave their doubts and the massage they want to say, then nurses could screening some patients in a bad mood for targeted psychological care through the platform, it is enhance the interaction and communication of nurses and patients.

Construct satisfaction evaluation interactive platform for nurses care satisfaction rating during hospitalization, every nurse using point to praise and comment way, breaking the traditional form of complex multiple-choice questions. After the point, the number of nurse' point will be displayed, In addition it can also combine patients' comment to write the detail evaluation for nurse, and when the patient reviews completed, the icon style will change.

Safety reminder platform that can automatically remind patients and nurses, in the form of dialog, it is important to push timely information. For example, about two hours to turn the body, knock back, urging the nurse to do a turn over care, but also urge patients and their families. In addition, for some special cases of emergency, patients could use "nurse call" feature to make voice calls and interaction with the medical staff of the nursing station at the first time.

4.4 Improve the Service of the Ward Details Service Information Design

Beside to pay attention to the patient's condition care, the hospital also follow others service during hospitalization, it also related to the rehabilitation of the disease and satisfaction. For example, it can provide accommodation information, magazines of disease care, milk and supper for the family members who accompanying the patient. For patients, the hospital can provide convenient setting during hospitalization, decompression soothing music. Whenever the patient was discharged or catch up with holiday time, the hospital can prepare for some small gift: a free cup of coffee ticket, an illness rehabilitation manual or notebooks. Through these, it can shows the hospital take much count of each patient's hospitalization experience, it provide a positive opportunity for interaction between patients and medical staff.

4.5 With the Interactive Tools of Non-text to Improve the Efficiency and the Experience of the Transmission of Information

For the convey of medical information, if we want to break the traditional paper-based text communication, it should to use some rich media forms, like image, audio, animation, etc. and present the medical information to patients abundantly and efficiently, then to guide patients through the sound operation, vividly shows recovery points and methods of disease. It is helpful for patients who have different cultural level, and for elderly patients are more easily understood and accepted.

To clearly the convey theme of medical information, guide patients interact with them. It should provide a visual hierarchy information for patients, refined medical information, to have a guiding force, and combined with rich media formats, enjoys popular support language to make resonance, let patient involved, to guide actively cooperate with treatment.

Active use the information visualization and data visualization, make the information and data restructuring and consolidation, then it also can be deleted and hided, etc. And converted to radius graphics or cartoon faces, also can combined with humorous language, it is easy to people understanding, thus making the patient to be more willing to accept, use cold warm color to distinguish the information attribute, the warm colors are important and positive elements, it could use line graph, pie and bar chart to presentation and comparison the data. To facilitate patients comparison and understanding.

5 Conclusion

This paper from the perspective of services system design to analysis ward nurses stations' information service system and its status, from the service process and the contact point to rediscover the complex issues and constitute of the ward nurses station information service system, then through user research of Wuxi four hospital ward nurses station in three stages, and insight and summarized the pain points demand and priorities when medical care in the ward. Then use the strategies of establish doctor and patients' symmetrical information service platform, provide diversified of information services, build multi-faceted clinical interaction of nurse-patient, improve the service of the ward details service information design, to with the interactive tools of non-text to improve the efficiency and the experience of the transmission of information to construction of new information service system, then the final output will help to improve patient satisfaction of patient-centered services and hospital efficiency in health care services, and it also provides a new reference for other hospitals ward management. It highlights the patient centered service concept, becoming the development direction of medical service in the future [10].

References

1. Nan, S., Baixia, L.: Research on healthy aging and medical care services in LiaoNing province. Contemp. Econ. **24**, 38–39 (2009)
2. Baidu Baiku: Clinical Information System (2015). http://baike.baidu.com/view/1537878.htm

3. Xin, L., Jikun, L.: Chances and challenges: the concept and practice of product service system design. Creativity Des. **05**, 15–17 (2011)
4. Cheng-lein, T.: Touch the service touchpoints. Decoration **06**, 13–17 (2010)
5. Polaine, A., Lovlie, L., Reason, B.: Service Design and Innovative Practice. Tsinghua University Press, Beijing (2015). p. 21
6. Polaine, A., Lovlie, L., Reason, B.: Service Design and Innovative Practice. Tsinghua University Press, Beijing (2015). p. 184
7. Vogel, C.M.: Definition of design thinking. In: Health Design Seminar in Jiangnan University (2014)
8. Shan, C.: Research on the touchpoints of the design services: centering on touchpoints application in the design of public service in South Korea. Ind. Des. Res. **03**, 111–114 (2015)
9. Lei, Y.: Clinical application of mobile medical system. In: The Proceedings of Inner Mongolia Medical University, pp. 177–181 (2014) (S1)
10. Mingyao, Z.: The history of "patient-centered" mode. Chin. J. Med. Hist. **03**, 15–17 (2003)

Measuring Chinese Medical Beliefs of Chinese Adults

Runting Zhong, Pei-Luen Patrick Rau(✉), and Shuyu Li

Department of Industrial Engineering, Tsinghua University, Beijing 100084, China
rpl@mail.tsinghua.edu.cn

Abstract. The study aims at developing an instrument measuring Chinese medical beliefs held by Chinese adults. In an online survey, participants were asked to rate their agreement with 35 Chinese medical beliefs. 257 valid responses from Chinese adults were collected. Exploratory factor analysis indicates that Chinese medical beliefs of Chinese adults are loaded onto seven factors of preventive diet, traditional health practices, preferences of TCM and western medicine, energy concept in TCM, medicated diet, pathogenic factor, and TCM hesitation. The study points out some Chinese medical beliefs held by Chinese adults.

Keywords: Chinese medical beliefs · Culture · TCM · Instrument

1 Introduction

Culture influences people's health-seeking behaviors, so we should pay attention to it in the health-care service design. In China, traditional Chinese medicine (TCM) is widely adopted among Chinese people. TCM is a unique medical system, which stemmed from ancient times [1] and thrives until today. It influences Chinese people's (even Asians') perceptions and behaviors related to health and medical service in many ways. For example, a woman needs "doing the month" after childbirth, meaning that she must observe a period of confinement and taboos and that she must not wash her hair during the period of confinement [2].

Nowadays, most doctors in China are educated under Western medical educational systems. Doctors are often unaware of the complex Chinese culture that influences their patients' responses to care [3]. Discrepancies of medical beliefs between doctors and patients would probably lead to distrust in healing process. Despite that researchers have noticed the impact of Chinese medical beliefs on Chinese immigrants' behavior [2, 4–7], there are few explicit ways to measure people's Chinese medical beliefs to our knowledge.

This study aims at developing an instrument measuring Chinese medical beliefs held by Chinese adults. The instrument will help doctors understand patients' medical beliefs, thus provide specific treatment to patients.

P.-L.P. Rau (Ed.): CCD 2016, LNCS 9741, pp. 729–736, 2016.
DOI: 10.1007/978-3-319-40093-8_72

2 Literature Review

2.1 TCM Concepts

TCM concepts are summarized as the foundation of the instrument. The concepts include Yin-yang, Five phases, Taoism, Confucianism and Buddhism.

Yin-Yang. The yin and yang are complementary opposite forces. Everything has both the yin and yang aspects. They control the relationship between humans and environment together with the "qi" energy [8]. In the health context, an imbalance in these two forces or in the 'qi' results in illnesses [9]. Food has its cold or hot characteristics. Thus, Chinese patients usually take special foods and herbs according to the season to balance either yin or yang in order to enhance their energy [3].

Five Phases. According to this theory, all phenomena in the universe are the products of the movement of five qualities: wood, fire, earth, metal and water. The organs correspond to each of the phase. For example, liver corresponds to wood, heart to fire, spleen to earth, lung to metal, and kidney to water. Organs interacts each other in illness. Thus, patients would ask for medication to protect the organs related to their target organ [3].

Taoism. The Taoism philosophy advocates *non-action*, or 'let-it-be'. According to this philosophy, one should not overdo anything [3]. Taoism emphasizes the importance of keeping harmony with nature. It is believed that being harmony with nature will provide peace of mind, and promote good health [10].

Confucianism. The Confucian philosophy plays an important role in Chinese society. It reminds people that they are destined by heaven to complete their mission. The Confucianism advocates *chung-yung*, which asks people to maintain a neutral position when examining all phenomena [3]. This belief may contribute to Chinese patients' hesitation about receiving Western medicine surgery, since they consider Western treatments too aggressive to incorporate with the natural recovery speed [9, 11].

Buddhism. Buddhism believes fate and "inn kuo" (cause and effect) are the key factors of health [12]. Most Chinese Buddhists with malignant disease usually attributes the cause of disease to their sin, and they tend to have self-blame responses [3]. Buddhism has pessimistic thoughts, which may make the doctor and patient lack confidence.

Guided by these philosophies, people with Chinese medical beliefs may have special considerations for dietary, medicine, daily practices and so on.

2.2 Influence of Chinese Medical Beliefs

There are different aspects of Chinese medical beliefs. Lai et al.'s investigates 12 cultural health beliefs held by older Chinese in Canada, and these beliefs are loaded onto three factors about traditional health practices, beliefs about traditional Chinese medicine, and beliefs about preventive diet [7]. In a study conducted in Malaysia, researchers interviewed 50 Malaysian Chinese from the general public and 50 Chinese medical students about 22 items. It was found that there was a discrepancy in the extent of these beliefs among the general public and Chinese medical students [2].

Chinese medical beliefs influence Chinese immigrants' utilization of health-care service like mammography screening [13, 14], cancer services [5], and mental illness services [15]. Yeo et al. found that Chinese-Australians maintained traditional Chinese beliefs about cancer, such as explaining it as karma or retribution, despite their high acculturation [5]. Another example was that Chinese were not very aware of mental illness. They interpreted it more as somatic symptoms [16]. Researchers argued that these perceptions were possible barriers to access of appropriate health service.

Though quite a few studies are conducted abroad, Chinese medical beliefs held by Chinese adults are rarely found in China, where TCM originates. So this study was carried out to measure the Chinese medical beliefs held by Chinese adults living in China.

3 Research Questions and Methods

3.1 Research Questions

The following research questions are proposed for this study.

Q1: What are Chinese medical beliefs held by Chinese people?

First, items that could be representative of Chinese medical beliefs should be selected.

Q2: What is Chinese adults' agreement with these Chinese medical beliefs?

Chinese adults' agreement with Chinese these items are measured to identify the degree to which Chinese medical beliefs are endorsed by Chinese adults.

Q3: What are the dimensions of the Chinese medical beliefs?

To understand the underlying structure of the items measuring Chinese medical beliefs, factor analysis could be used to identify the dimension of Chinese medical beliefs.

3.2 Questionnaire Design

Questionnaire survey was adopted as the research method. The questionnaire consisted of two parts. The first part was to collect demographic information of the participants and their experiences in using TCM, including gender, age, occupation, profession, education level, marital status, birthplace, current residence, frequency of visiting TCM last year, place of visiting TCM, causes of visiting TCM and cumulative time of taking TCM.

The second part was to measure Chinese adults' agreement with Chinese medical beliefs. In this study, the items measuring Chinese medical beliefs were selected from Chew et al.'s [2] and Lai et al.'s studies [7]. The researchers also added 5 items about Chinese medical beliefs according to life experience. The Chinese medical beliefs were about cause of disease, diet taboo, daily habit, folk prescription, and attitude towards TCM.

The items were measured by 7-point Likert scales. 1 represents strongly disagree, 7 represents strongly agree, and 4 represents neutral or never heard of this item. The translations were checked by one undergraduate student majoring in English. Then the questionnaires were plot tested by two human factors engineering PhD students to prevent ambiguity. A few adjustments were made, such as adding the interpretation of professional word "wind" in TCM. As a result, a questionnaire is constructed with 35 items measuring Chinese medical beliefs. One of the 35 items is reverse item (Item 19).

3.3 Participants

The questionnaires were uploaded on sojump, an online questionnaire system. Then the online questionnaires were distributed via Wechat, a social media in China. RMB 2-worth of "Red Packet" was rewarded to each participant. Ultimately this study collected 293 responses, among which 257 questionnaires were valid.

The final sample consisted of 101 Chinese males and 156 Chinese females. The mean age of the participants is 25.2 years old (SD = 5.5). The oldest is 52 years old and the youngest is 18 years old. More than 80 % report an undergraduate education level or above. More than 80 % report that they are unmarried. The sample covers various occupation and profession.

About frequency of visiting TCM last year, 63 % report that they didn't visit TCM last year. 33.1 % visited TCM 1~5 times last year. 2.3 % visited TCM 6~10 times. 1.6 % visited TCM more than 10 times. Among the 95 participants visiting TCM last year, 40.0 % visited in large hospitals, 25.3 % in community hospitals, 38.9 % in clinic and 20.0 % in other places. Most of the participants (55.8 %) visited TCM because of chronic disease. Nearly 75 % of the participants have ever taken TCM.

4 Results

4.1 Agreement with Chinese Medical Beliefs

To identify the degree to which Chinese medical beliefs are endorsed by Chinese adults, we summarize the mean and standard deviation of each item. Table 1 presents 10 Chinese medical beliefs with highest agreement in this study. For example, "9. Eating too much deep-fried food will cause *Shanghuo.*" (M = 5.89, SD = 1.32) "*Shanghuo*" is a widely a term in TCM, with common symptoms like sore throat, feeling hot and dry, or getting pimples. This statement is highly agreed among Chinese adults. The item with second highest agreement is "1. Certain diseases are caused by 'too much heat' or 'too much coldness' in the body (disruption of yin-yang balance)." (M = 5.67, SD = 1.35) This item is the explanation of illness based on the yin-yang theory. The item with third highest agreement is "11. Soup is good for health." (M = 5.63, SD = 1.27) This is a dietary norm to maintain health.

Table 1. 10 Chinese medical beliefs with highest agreement

Item of Chinese medical beliefs	Mean	SD
9. Eating too much deep-fried food will cause *Shanghuo*	5.89	1.32
1. Certain diseases are caused by 'too much heat' or 'too much coldness' in the body (disruption of yin-yang balance)	5.67	1.35
11. Soup is good for health	5.63	1.27
24. Drinking pear water can cure cough	5.52	1.24
27. Traditional Chinese herbal medicine can balance yin and yang in the body	5.45	1.35
14. Consuming certain food like garlic and ginger can help dispel wind from the body	5.44	1.40
18. One should avoid eating seafood after surgical operation.	5.40	1.43
26. Drinking momordica grosvenori tea can clear the lung and decrease internal heat	5.39	1.31
12. When you are not feeling well, it is better for you to have plain congee	5.24	1.48
22. One will get headache at an older age if going to bed without properly drying his or her hair after washing	5.21	1.50

The Chinese medical beliefs with lowest agreement includes: "33. If you have taken TCM prior to visiting your doctor, would you be uncomfortable to reveal to your doctor that you have taken TCM prior to the consultation?" (M = 2.78, SD = 1.8) This item is measuring the hesitation attitude towards TCM. It turns out that patients don't mind talking about TCM to their doctors, perhaps because TCM is well-known around Chinese people in China. "2. Fever is due to excessive heat inside the body" (M = 3.19, SD = 1.58) and "13. One should consume less amount of rice or totally abstain from taking rice when having fever" (M = 3.43, SD = 1.63) also receive low agreement, perhaps because these two items violate the interpretation of fever with modern medicine–fevers are commonly caused by bacterial/viral infections.

4.2 Exploratory Factor Analysis

We used exploratory factor analysis to explore the factor structure of the remaining 34 items of Chinese medical beliefs, after removing the reverse item. The results of the Kaiser–Mayer–Olkin (KMO) test and Bartlett's test of sphericity were .893 and $\chi 2 = 3698.2$ ($p < .001$), suggesting being suitable for factor analysis.

In the factor extracting and screening phase, the following rules were adopted: extracting components with eigenvalues larger than 1 as principal component; deleting items with loadings smaller than .45 on all common factors; deleting factors containing only one item [17, 18]. 6 items were dropped according to the rules above. For example, one item about combining both TCM and modern medicine together was dropped because it was the only item in the factor. Verimax rotation with Kaiser normalizing rotation was used acquire a meaningful explanation of the model.

Finally, 28 items were retained. The 28 items composed of seven factors and explained 61.7 % of the total variance. The seven factors were named as preventive diet, traditional health practices, preferences of TCM and western medicine, energy concept in TCM, medicated diet, pathogenic factor, and TCM hesitation. The seven factors accounted for 17.3 %, 9.0 %, 8.4 %, 8.2 %, 7.3 %, 6.5 %, and 5.0 % of the variance, respectively.

Preventive diet describes about folk prescription and dietary restrictions during one's illness, such as "drinking momordica grosvenori tea can clear the lung and decrease internal heat" and "consuming certain food like garlic and ginger can help dispel wind from the body."

Traditional health practices describe about traditional practices that Chinese like to follow. Typical example is women's confinement in childbirth, which is commonly known as "zuo yue zi" in Chinese.

Preference of TCM and western medicine describes people's preference when facing TCM and western medicine. Items in this factor are about choosing TCM alone as the initial treatment choice and hesitation in receiving western medicine.

Energy concept in TCM describes the interpretation of energy in TCM, like "wind" or excessive heat could cause related illness.

Medicated diet consists of beliefs about Chinese herbal medicine and tonic food. It is believed homology of medicine and food, namely, choosing appropriate food can act as medicine and enhance the immunity.

Pathogenic factor describes about the cause of disease, such as "having too much cold food or drink will cause dizziness" and "exposure to rain water can cause respiratory tract infection".

TCM hesitation is vague, consisting of only two items. One is about patient's hesitation in telling doctors that s/he has taken TCM prior to the consultation. The other is consuming less amount of rice when having fever.

5 Discussion

The study aims at developing an instrument measuring Chinese medical beliefs held by Chinese adults. By exploratory factor analysis, seven factors are identified about preventive diet, traditional health practices, preferences of TCM and western medicine, energy concept in TCM, medicated diet, pathogenic factor, and TCM hesitation. Factor 1 to Factor 6 are reliable with acceptable internal consistency (Cronbach's $\alpha > .60$). However, Factor 7 (TCM hesitation) is vague, with low reliability (Cronbach's $\alpha = .396$). This factor could be revised or removed in the future.

The study points out some Chinese medical beliefs physicians should notice in medical practice and communication. The instrument will help in the following aspects. First, the instrument could serve as a way to measure the extent to which people hold Chinese medical beliefs. Physicians educated under Western medical system also need to know what Chinese medical beliefs the patients have so that they could answer patients' questions and make appropriate treatment plan. Second, as we identify seven factors about Chinese medical beliefs, the instrument could further measure people's acceptance with TCM in different subscales, such as dietary, traditional practices. Third, the instrument could be used to identify which subscale has a good predict effect on people's medical choice.

There are a few limitations of this study, suggesting improvement direction of the instrument. First, the samples are mainly younger Chinese adults and the education level is relatively high. Since age may influence Chinese medical beliefs according to [19], sampling from more general population including different age levels and education background should be adopted in future study. Besides, the validity of the instrument is not yet verified. In-depth interview with TCM experts should be required to verify whether the items in each factor are representative enough as Chinese medical beliefs. What's more, Chinese medical believers and Western medical believers could be invited to prove the validity of the instrument. The future study could examine the impact of age, education level, overseas experience on Chinese medical beliefs.

6 Conclusion

In this study, we preliminarily develop an instrument measuring Chinese medical beliefs held by Chinese adults. Exploratory factor analysis indicates that the Chinese medical beliefs are loaded onto seven factors of preventive diet, traditional health practices, preferences of TCM and western medicine, energy concept in TCM, medicated diet, pathogenic factor, and TCM hesitation. The study points out some Chinese medical beliefs held by Chinese adults. Physicians should pay attention to these Chinese medical beliefs in medical practice and communication.

Acknowledgement. This study was funded by a Natural Science Foundation China grant 71188001.

References

1. Unschuld, P.U.: Huang Di Nei Jing Su Wen: Nature, Knowledge, Imagery in an Ancient Chinese Medical Text. University of California Press, Berkeley (2003)
2. Chew, K.S., Tan, T.W., Ooi, Y.T.: Influence of Chinese cultural health beliefs among Malaysian Chinese in a suburban population: a survey. Singapore Med. J. **52**(4), 252–256 (2011)
3. Shih, F.J.: Concepts related to Chinese patients' perceptions of health, illness and person: issues of conceptual clarity. Accid. Emerg. Nurs. **4**(4), 208–215 (1996)
4. Ma, G.X.: Between two worlds: the use of traditional and Western health services by Chinese immigrants. J. Community Health **24**(6), 421–437 (1999)
5. Yeo, S.S., Meiser, B., Barlow-Stewart, K., Goldstein, D., Tucker, K., Eisenbruch, M.: Understanding community beliefs of Chinese-Australians about cancer: initial insights using an ethnographic approach. Psycho-Oncology **14**(3), 174–186 (2005)

6. Green, G., Bradby, H., Chan, A., Lee, M.: "We are not completely Westernised": dual medical systems and pathways to health care among Chinese migrant women in England. Soc. Sci. Med. **62**(6), 1498–1509 (2006)
7. Lai, D.W., Surood, S.: Chinese health beliefs of older Chinese in Canada. J. Aging Health **21**(1), 38–62 (2009)
8. Ariff, K.M., Beng, K.S.: Cultural health beliefs in a rural family practice: a Malaysian perspective. Aust. J. Rural Health **14**(1), 2–8 (2006)
9. Ho, D.Y., Spinks, J.A., Yeung, C.S.H. (eds.): Chinese Patterns of Behavior: A Sourcebook of Psychological and Psychiatric Studies. Praeger Publishers, Westport (1989)
10. Chen, Y.C.: Chinese values, health and nursing. J. Adv. Nurs. **36**(2), 270–273 (2001)
11. Kleinman, A.: Social cultural and historical themes in the study of medicine in Chinese societies. In: Medicine in Chinese Cultures, pp. 75–653. DHEW Publication (NIH) (1975)
12. Chen, Y.L.D.: Conformity with nature: a theory of Chinese American elders' health promotion and illness prevention processes. Adv. Nurs. Sci. **19**(2), 17–26 (1996)
13. Wu, T.Y., West, B., Chen, Y.W., Hergert, C.: Health beliefs and practices related to breast cancer screening in Filipino, Chinese and Asian-Indian women. Cancer Detect. Prev. **30**(1), 58–66 (2006)
14. Liang, W., Wang, J.H., Chen, M.Y., Feng, S., Lee, M., Schwartz, M.D., Mandelblatt, J.S.: Developing and validating a measure of Chinese cultural views of health and cancer. Health Educ. Behav. **35**(3), 361–375 (2008)
15. Liu, C.H., Meeuwesen, L., van Wesel, F., Ingleby, D.: Beliefs about mental illness among Chinese in the west. Int. J. Migr. Health Soc. Care **9**(3), 108–121 (2013)
16. Lin, K.M.: Traditional Chinese medical beliefs and their relevance for mental illness and psychiatry. In: Kleinman, A., Lin, T.Y. (eds.) Normal and Abnormal Behavior in Chinese Culture, pp. 95–111. Springer, Dordrecht (1981)
17. Hair, J.F., Anderson, R.E., Tatham, R.L., Black, W.C.: Multivariate Data Analyses with Readings. Englewood Cliffs, New Jersey (1995)
18. Stiggelbout, A.M., Molewijk, A.C., Otten, W., Timmermans, D.R.M., Van Bockel, J.H., Kievit, J.: Ideals of patient autonomy in clinical decision making: a study on the development of a scale to assess patients' and physicians' views. J. Med. Eth. **30**(3), 268–274 (2004)
19. Xu, J., Yang, Y.: Traditional Chinese medicine in the Chinese health care system. Health Policy **90**(2–3), 133–139 (2008)

Culture for eCommerce and Business

Every Day for an Active Self-promotion: The Dialogue Between the Shower Gel Packaging on the Shelf of a Point of Sale and the Consumer

Mu-Chien Chou(✉) and Weng-Kit Chong

Department of Bio-Industry Communication and Development, National Taiwan University, No. 1, Sec. 4, Roosevelt Road, Taipei 10617, Taiwan, ROC
{choumc, b01610055}@ntu.edu.tw

Abstract. When a consumer walks into a point of purchase, their eyes start to search for the product they want. This study aims to investigate into the applications of the signs on shower gel package. For the mainstream applications, we have the following findings: In terms of packaging shape, press type is the mainstream of bottle head, while the body is largely rectangular solid. In terms of color, white is the mainstream. For the text on the package, we have at least six types of major text information, such as brand name, skin improvement effect, ingredient, aroma, attribute and volume. For text presentation, original characters are the mainstream. For packaging patterns, plant is the mainstream application, and realistic depiction is another mainstream in their presentation. In terms of packaging material, shower gel bottles are mainly made of non-transparent plastics. In this study, we have conducted a more extensive research, analyzing the applications of signs on the shower gel package in the market, and will make them available to designers or marketers as a reference.

Keywords: Shower gel · Packaging design · Consumption-related sign

1 Introduction

Fast Moving Consumer Goods (FMCG) refer generally to the products with short service life, fast consumption and high frequency of purchase in the market [1]. FMCG commonly appear in our daily lives, frequently seen and highly dependable. They seem to have become one of the largest, most profitable and rapidly growing industries in the world [2]. In Taiwan, the purchase rate of cleaning supplies goes up to 56.34 %, ranking the highest in all FMCG categories. Among them, shower gel has the highest at 60.33 %, above shampoo (55.61 %) and facial cleanser (53.08 %) [3]! Obviously, cleaning supplies in Taiwan, with high development potential, deserve our exploration, especially shower gel. The trait to grab consumer attention has become a necessary condition for a product to stand out from a variety of similar ones and then taken into consideration by the consumer [4]. However, how does a product successfully attract the attention of consumers? Packaging is the carrier and key used to perform this function [5, 6].

P.-L.P. Rau (Ed.): CCD 2016, LNCS 9741, pp. 739–751, 2016.
DOI: 10.1007/978-3-319-40093-8_73

When a consumer enters a point of purchase, they can often see all types of products. Armstrong and Kotler [7] pointed out that a typical supermarket sells as many as 15,000 kinds of items on average. Each consumer, however, can browse only about 300 items per minute, and just two-thirds of them have access to consumer attention [8]. Therefore most people tend to see the information provided on the package as the main clue for product selection and purchase [9]. Packaging not only provides product information, but also plays as the basis of determining the properties of its product in the consumer's purchase decision process [10–12]. A packaging sign, if clear enough in its design and classification, can even help simplify this process [13, 14]. Many studies have also found that any sign on the package is likely to induce consumers to make a purchase [11, 15]. In contrast, few academics have focused their research on the investigation of the signs on shower gel package. Accordingly, this study has the following two aims. First, to launch an extensive collection, observation and investigation into the applications of the signs on shower gel package. Second, on the basis of past literature, to analyze the trend of packaging signs that may affect the consumer's attention and purchase behavior.

2 Literature Review

When a consumer has decided what to buy in a store, when they will see is various brands of products greeting to them. This selection process is like a man/woman wooing their object, starting to introduce and promote themselves, using all means to pursue and go with them. How does the consumer select their favorite from those aggressive competitors? First impression! This idea is a total combination of all physical features and their advantageous impressions. Therefore, this leading product must be able to attract the consumer's attention by virtue of its appearance (facial features, body). Product appearance, known as packaging, has some signs on it to form the leading product and help the consumer with their evaluation. "Functions and importance of packaging", "communication of signs on the package" and "signs and elements on shower gel packaging" are discussed in the literature review of this study.

2.1 Functions and Importance of Packaging

Packaging has a protective effect for the contents of the product, which is the most important and basic function [7, 16]. Packaging isolates the product from external environment, keeping it out of hazardous factors. In addition, packaging can split the contents of the product into proper share for the convenience of easy carrying, as well as for efficient transport and storage [17–19]. Packaging is known as a "silent salesperson" [20], and plays a vital role from the perspective of sales promotion. Product packaging can attract consumer attention through a variety forms and visual techniques of colors, signs and advertising, while such information as the product features, directions for use, brand names and product images can also be conveyed for better communication with the consumer [19], and noticeable differentiation that helps the consumer make a quicker purchase decision among all kinds and sorts of product categories [21]. Accordingly, this study aims to explore more about the applications of packaging signs.

2.2 Communication of Signs on the Package

Sight is one of human's most important sensory functions [22], and packaging is the first step of the consumer's contact with the product. Successful packaging can grab their eyeballs [23]. Information and signs on the package provide clues for the consumer to make a judgment on product quality [24], and shape the consumer's expectation for product properties, smells and experience, stimulating their purchase behavior [25, 26]. Signs are everywhere and comprehensive in category [27]. The so-called "sign" is a kind of physical characterization. It needs to be identified by the user and then received through human organs to both interpret what it refers to and create effective communication [28]. In short, signs are a vehicle used to convey meaning. They represent certain things and concepts, and make sense after understood and interpreted in different context [27]. Swiss linguist Ferdinand de Saussure (1857–1913) was the first scholar to study signs as a new subject. He found signs are composed by two elements – the signifier and the signified, a "dual relationship." The signifier refers to the specific image of a sign. It can be perceived and received by the human senses; the signified is concept formed by a sign on the human mind. Signs contain two-axis interactions, namely paradigmatic axis and syntagmatic axis [28]; in the actual process of communication, the two of them need to be closely combined and are indivisible [29]. The paradigmatic axis is characteristic of analyzing its constituent elements, while the syntagmatic axis is used for sign extension, and to show full meaning of the signs. This study aims to only generalize and analyze the content of "signifier" on the package of a shower gel bottle and its presentation.

2.3 Sign Elements on Shower Gel Package

In the purchase decision process of most consumers for low-involvement products, packaging signs have become an important basis of whether they will make a purchase [30]. Although the signs on the package are plentiful, research on the packaging of cleaning products for personal use, such as shower gel, has been scarce. However, many elements of the signs on the package can still be explored. Smith and Taylor [31] noted that the shape, size, color, pattern, material and smell are the six essential elements for creating effective packaging. In addition, many scholars believe that the study of signs on the package should focus on the four elements of color, shape, text and pattern [9, 32, 33]. In addition to the shape, text, color, and pattern as the subjects of study, Silayoi and Speece [30] treated product information and packaging technique as his research priorities. Kuvykaite et al. [34] included not only the shape, color and pattern, but also package size, material, brand, country of origin, producer and product information into the packaging elements to be explored. Moreover, Adam and Ali [35] also added packaging size and material, on top of the four basic elements of shape, type, color and pattern, into their discussion. In this study, we have summarized the literature and taken the top five frequently-viewed elements – shape, color, text, pattern and material – as the subjects of study. Our later analysis of the signs on shower gel packaging is in accordance with the above subjects.

3 Research Methods

3.1 Sample Collection

In Taiwan, people most often buy shower gel in a hypermarket [36, 37], and Carrefour has been ranked No. one in the retail store option over the last five years. Therefore, in this study we visited 3 different Carrefour hypermarkets in Taipei for a cross reference of the item, with the shower gel packaging recurring in the stores being the sample of collection. As imported shower gel is filling up the market, according to our preliminary observation, we excluded package information shown other than in Chinese or English to avoid complexity of the language (such as the text message on the label). We had a total of 219 samples.

3.2 Sample Survey

A two-stage survey is adopted in this study. The first stage was conducted by natural observation method, with preliminary investigation into the signs on the shower gel package. The second stage went with summarization and analysis based on the top five packaging elements. In terms of styling, Wang and Sun's [38] research was used as a basis to explore the applications of signs on the bottle head and body. In terms of color, based on Chang et al. [39], the color tickets in PCCS (Practical Color Co-ordinate System) offered by Japan Color Research Institute were used as the standard to explore the sign trends. In terms of text, studies have shown that front label, compared with the back label, is more likely to affect a consumer's purchase decision [40, 41]; for the signs of text message, this study focuses only on the front label of shower gel packaging for information collection and discussion. In addition, with Wu's [42] research as the basis, we explored sign applications about text presentation. In terms of patterns, after observing the types of illustrations, with Meyer and Laveson's [43] research as the basis, sign applications about the illustration styles were also surveyed. In terms of materials, with Vilnai-Yavetz and Koren's [44] research as the basis, sign applications about material transparency were explored as well.

3.3 Data Statistics and Analysis

After observing, recording and photographing the sign applications on the above-mentioned shower gel packaging, we developed a coding book using Microsoft Excel. We also marked the sign categories corresponding to the samples and calculated the frequency using descriptive statistics, so as to render the result of data analysis.

4 Result and Analysis

4.1 Summary and Analysis of Shape Sign Applications

In the observation of this study, we found that the head of the shower gel bottle can be divided into press type, flip-cap and screw-cap types. Among them, press type is the mainstream in the applications of shower gel bottle head (196/89.5 %), followed by flip-cap (17/7.76 %) and screw-cap (6/2.74 %) types. In addition, the body of shower gel bottle can be sorted, according to their shapes, into rectangular solid, trapezium, cylinder, square, handle, S-shaped, 3-shaped, fat belly, C-shaped and irregular type (see Table 1). For the percentage of all bottle shapes, rectangular solid is the mainstream in

Table 1. Description and application of shower gel bottle shapes

No.	Shape	Image	Description	Total/ Percentage (%)
1	Rectangular Solid		Bottle shoulders are about 90 degrees, or sagging at 30 to 45 degrees. Bottle lines appear straight and rectangular, with a slender surface.	54/24.66
2	Trapezium		Bottle shoulders are about 90 degrees, or sagging at 30 to 45 degrees. Bottle shape gradually slants inwards from the shoulders to the bottom, with the whole bottle shaped like letter V.	17/7.76
3	Cylinder		Bottle shoulders are like arcs. Bottle lines appear straight and rectangular in shape, with the whole bottle shaped like a cylinder.	31/14.16
4	Square		Bottle shoulders appear level or sagging at 30 to 45 degrees. Bottle lines appear straight and rectangular in shape, with the whole bottle being shorter like a square.	16/6.85
5	Handle		Designed with an opening on the corner of the bottle as a handle.	17/7.76
6	S-Shaped		Arc shape appears from the bottle shoulders to the upper half, indenting in the lower half, and curving outward at the bottom of the bottle. The curves on each side of the bottle appear an S shape.	19/8.68
7	3-Shaped		Bottle shoulders are in arc shape that indents in the upper half, and curves outward at the lower half of the bottle. The curves on each side of the bottle appear a "3" shape.	22/10.05
8	Fat Belly		Bottle lines curve outward from the shoulders to the body, and slightly indent at the bottom of the bottle. The bottle is shaped like a big fat belly.	13/5.94
9	C-Shaped		Bottle lines on both sides of the upper half curve outward, and indent below the middle. Bottle lines in the middle are slightly rounded, with thin shoulders and bottom, showing a C shape on both sides of the bottle.	21/9.59
10	Irregular Type		Bottle curves on the both sides are varied and irregular, showing a wavy shape.	10/4.57

(Source: The study)

the applications of shower gel bottle body (24.66 %), followed by cylinder (14.16 %), 3-shaped (10.05 %), C-shaped (9.59 %), S-shaped (8.68 %), trapezium and handle type (7.76 % for each) square (6.85 %), fat belly(5.94 %) and irregular type (4.57 %).

4.2 Summary and Analysis of Color Sign Applications

The classification in this study is based on the color tickets in PCCS offered by Japan Color Research Institute. After preliminary observation, the number is reduced to 15 categories. For a precise judgement in this study, the largest block in a colored area of shower gel package is our target. We observed that the mainstream colors of shower gel packaging are white (81/36.99 %), followed by blue (21/9.59 %), pink (16/7.31 %), orange (15/6.85 %), purple (14/6.39 %), green (13/5.94 %), brown and yellow green (10/4.57 % for each), grey and black (9/4.11 % for each), yellow (8/3.65 %), red and violet (4/1.83 % for each), red purple (3/1.37 %), and olive (2/0.91 %).

4.3 Summary and Analysis of Text Sign Applications

In the observation of this study, we found that text signs on the package can be divided, according to their information properties, into 17 categories shown below: brand name, year of the brand, product's special name, manufacturer's name, ingredient, skin improvement effect, psychological effect, aroma, applicable object, attribute, recommendation and certification, technique, place of origin, volume, product uniqueness, product number and additional information (see Table 2), with each bottle package containing 5.59 types of information on average. For mainstream applications of the text messages on a shower gel package, brand name (97.26 %) appears on almost every package, followed by skin improvement effect (86.76 %), ingredients contained (57.53 %), aroma (53.9 %), attributes and volume (42 % for each), psychological experience (27.4 %), product's special name (22.83 %), the applicable object (19.2 %), manufacturer's name (16.9 %), product uniqueness (15.98 %), place of origin (15.53 %), year of the brand (11.42 %), recommendation and certification (10.5 %), product number and ingredients not contained (9.13 % for each), technique (3.65 %), and additional information (3.2 %).

After our observation, we only analyzed the presentation of the most noticeable text – key information of the product – on the shower gel package. Original characters are the mainstream application of text sign on shower gel package (150/68.5 %), followed by variant characters (59/26.9 %) and the hand-painted characters (8/4.60 %). In addition, we further cross-referenced text information and text presentation. No. 1 is brand name as the key information (152/69.41 %), followed by skin improvement effect (25/11.42 %), ingredients (12/5.48 %), product's special name and aroma (11/5.02 % for each), attribute (4/1.83 %), as well as the psychological effect and applicable object (2/0.91 %).

Table 2. Definition and application of text information on shower gel bottles

No.	Text information	Definition and description	Total/Percentage (%)
1	Brand name	Refers to the text that can be recognized and read by the consumer, suggesting that the product belongs to a specific brand, and that the consumer can link the product with the spirit and values implied and conveyed by the brand	213/97.26
2	Year of the brand	Refers to the year when the brand was established. A brand with a long history facilitates consumer's trust for the brand	25/11.42
3	Product's special name	Refers to the special, non-regulated terms created for the product. This is to differentiate products of the same brand yet different series	50/22.83
4	Manufacturer's name	Refers to the product maker's name by which the consumer can link the product with the spirit or symbolic meaning implied by the manufacturer	37/16.90
5	Ingredients contained	Refers to the ingredients of the product contents. It suggests the effect of the product or the specific aroma that will adhere to the skin after use	126/57.53
	Ingredients not contained	Refers to the ingredients excluded from the product contents. The ingredients generally refer to the chemical substances that will damage the skin	20/9.13
6	Skin improvement effect	Refers to the ability of the product to bring sensible or insensible improvement and feelings to the user's skin after use	190/86.76
7	Psychological effect	Refers to the ability of the product to bring positive feelings to the user's mental condition after use	60/27.40
8	Aroma	Refers to the specific aroma of the product	118/53.90
9	Applicable object	Refers to the products being applicable to the user with certain physical characteristics	42/19.20
10	Attribute	Refers to the product or its ingredients having a particular attribute or quality can be judged by the consumer, such as being natural	92/42.00
11	Recommendation and certification	Refers to the product being certified by an authority, so as to win the consumer's trust	23/10.50
12	Technique		8/3.65

(*Continued*)

Table 2. (*Continued*)

No.	Text information	Definition and description	Total/Percentage (%)
		Refers to the know-how in the process of raw materials to finished products	
13	Place of origin	Refers to the site where the product was made, or the source of its ingredients. It generally refers to a particular country or region	34/15.53
14	Volume	Refers to the volume or weight of the contents	92/42.00
15	Product uniqueness	Refers to the attributed and ingredients of a product, whose properties are distinct from other those of other competitors, such as "originating" a formula	35/15.98
16	Product number	Refers to the product code or bar code printed on the package	20/9.13
17	Additional information	Refers to the product information other than that provided above	7/3.20

(Source: The study)

4.4 Summary and Analysis of Pattern Sign Applications

After observation, we found that the patterns of shower gel packaging can be divided, according to their qualities, into the following nine categories: personal figure, fruit, animal, plant, natural phenomenon, water imagery, protective imagery, abstract image and no image (see Table 3). Among them, plant is the mainstream application of

Table 3. Pattern sign applications for shower gel bottles

No.	1	2	3	4	5	6	7	8	9
Schematic Diagram									
Illustration Category	Personal Figure	Fruit	Animal	Plant	Natural Phenomenon	Water Imagery	Protective Imagery	Abstract Image	No Image
Total/ Percentage (%)	33/ 15.07	17/ 7.76	13/ 5.94	80/ 36.53	8/ 3.65	16/ 7.31	8/ 3.65	33/ 15.07	11/ 5.02

(Source: The study)

Table 4. Combination of Paradigmatic axis and syntagmatic axis in the application of the signs on shower gel package.

Sign elements on shower gel package								
	Shape		Color	Text		Pattern		Material
	The bottle head	The bottle body	Color tickets	Text sign	Mainstream application of text sign	Illustration category	Illustration style	Visual representation
Paradigmatic axis	Press type	Rectangular solid	Pink	Brand name	Original characters	Personal figure	Photographic depiction	Transparent
	Flip-cap type	Trapezium	Red	Year of the brand	Variant characters	Fruit	Realistic depiction	Non-transparent
	Screw-cap type	Cylinder	Orange	Product's special name	Hand-painted characters	Animal	Symbolic depiction	
		Square	Brown	Manufacturer's Name		Plant	Pure Text	
		Handle	Yellow	Ingredients contained		Natural phenomenon		
		S-Shaped	Olive	Skin improvement effect		Water imagery		
		3-Shaped	Yellow green	Psychological effect		Protective imagery		
		Fat belly	Green	Aroma		Abstract image		
		C-Shaped	Blue	Applicable object		No image		
		Irregular type	Violet	Attribute				
			Purple	Recommendation and certification				
			Red purple	Technique				
			White	Place of origin				
			Grey	Volume				
			Black	Product uniqueness				
				Additional information				
				Additional information				
	Syntagmatic axis							

(Source: The study)

pattern sign on shower gel package (36.53 %), followed by personal figure and abstract image (15.07 % for each), fruit (7.76 %), water imagery (7.31 %), animal (5.94 %), no image (5.02 %), natural phenomenon and protective imagery (3.65 % for each). In terms of the illustration style, most of the patterns on shower gel packaging are using realistic depiction (100/45.66 %), followed by symbolic depiction (69/31.51 %) and photographic depiction (39/17.81 %); pure text is low in percentage (11/5.02 %).

4.5 Summary and Analysis of Material Sign Applications

After observation, we found that most of the shower gel packaging is made of plastics. According to its visual representation, it can be divided into "transparent" and "non-transparent" categories. Our analysis shows that the majority of our samples are non-transparent (164/74.89 %) and those with transparent materials account for only a quarter (55/25.11 %).

4.6 Total Summary of Packaging Sign Applications

In the summary of the application trends and surveys mentioned above, we are presenting a finding that the same concept of paradigmatic axis and syntagmatic axis is used in an identical brand of shower gel. This helps promote not only the diversity of the packaging signs, but also differentiation among products of different targets. In conclusion, we have applied the two axes of semiotics in this study (see Table 4).

5 Conclusion and Suggestion

With the full development of fast moving consumer goods, successful arousal of consumer's desire to make a purchase lies in the signs on the package being able to draw the consumer's attention. This study is focused on the applications of signs on the shower gel package. In terms of packaging form, press type is the mainstream of bottle head. For the bottle shape, rectangular solid is the mainstream. In terms of color, white is the mainstream of sign applications, based on the PCCS color system developed by Japan Color Research Institute. For the text on the package, we found at least six types of text information on average, seen as the mainstream, contained in the package of each shower gel brand. They are brand name, skin improvement effect, ingredient, aroma, attribute and volume. For the presentation of text, original characters are the mainstream. For packaging patterns, plant is the mainstream application, and realistic depiction is another mainstream in their presentation. In terms of packaging material, shower gel bottles are generally made of plastics, and our analysis found that most of them are non-transparent.

As this study is limited by such factors as time, budget, short-handedness and so on, there is still some room for improvement, including further study and discussion on many related issues. We are hereby making some points for future research: (1) For the research on personal cleaning supplies, we only explored shower gel packaging. We suggest a study and comparison in the future for other personal cleaning products, such as shampoo, facial cleanser, toothpaste and so on. (2) For the scope of the sample collection, we made sample collection for this study only in hypermarket Carrefour. We suggest a broader range of collection for the future, such as a large chain supermarket or other outlets, so that the collected samples will become closer to the actual market. (3) For the classification of samples, this research is based on personal subjective observation. We suggest a further classification where focus groups with different perspectives are invited or interviews with experts are held, so that a different or even more interesting result might be obtained. (4) For consumer testing, we suggest reference for the future to the survey result in the above combination of sign application on shower gel package, as well as a discussion about how the consumer interpret these signs, or what signs can excite their attention, stimulate their information search and have them make a purchase decision.

References

1. Majumdar, R.: Product Management in India. Prentice-Hall, New Delhi (2007)
2. Groothedde, B., Ruijgrok, C., Tavasszy, L.: Towards collaborative, intermodal hub networks: a case study in the fast moving consumer goods market. Transp. Res. Part E: Logistics Transp. Rev. **41**(6), 567–583 (2005)
3. Ho, T.-C.: An Analysis of Taiwan's Consuming Power in 2012 from Trendgo+ Market Research Database (2013). http://life.trendgo.com.tw/epaper/5548. [in Chinese, semantic translation]
4. Creusen, M.E., Schoormans, J.P.: The different roles of product appearance in consumer choice. J. Prod. Innov. Manag. **22**(1), 63–81 (2005)
5. Wang, R.W.Y., Chou, M.C.: Differentiation in the arched surface of packaging: its influence on the findability of logo typography displays. Displays **32**(1), 24–34 (2011)
6. Underwood, R.L., Klein, N.M., Burke, R.R.: Packaging communication: attentional effects of product imagery. J. Prod. Brand Manag. **10**(7), 403–422 (2001)
7. Armstrong, G., Kotler, P.: Marketing: An Introduction, 12th edn. Pearson Education, Boston (2014)
8. Stahlberg, M., Maila, V.: Shopper Marketing: How to Increase Purchase Decisions at the Point of Sale, 2nd edn. Kogan Page Publishers, London (2012)
9. Solomon, M.R., Marshall, G.W., Stuart, E.W.: Marketing Real People Real Choices, 7th edn. Prentice Hall, Boston (2011)
10. Clement, J.: Visual influence on in-store buying decisions: an eye-track experiment on the visual influence of packaging design. J. Mark. Manag. **23**(9–10), 917–928 (2007)
11. Poturak, M.: Influence of product packaging on purchase decisions. Eur. J. Soc. Hum. Sci. **3** (3), 144–150 (2014)
12. Vazquez, D., Bruce, M., Studd, R.: A case study exploring the packaging design management process within a UK food retailer. Brit. Food J. **105**(9), 602–617 (2003)
13. Chou, M.C., Wang, R.W.Y.: Displayability: an assessment of differentiation design for the findability of bottle packaging. Displays **33**(3), 146–156 (2012)
14. Loken, B., Ward, J.: Alternative approaches to understanding the determinants of typicality. J. Consum. Res. **17**(2), 111–126 (1990)
15. Barber, N., Almanza, B.A.: Influence of wine packaging on consumers' decision to purchase. J. Foodservice Bus. Rese. **9**(4), 83–98 (2007)

16. Prendergast, G., Pitt, L.: Packaging, marketing, logistics and the environment: are there trade-offs? Int. J. Phys. Distrib. Logistics Manag. **26**(6), 60–72 (1996)
17. Dyllick, T.: Ecological marketing strategy for toni yogurts in Switzerland. J. Bus. Ethics **8** (8), 657–662 (1989)
18. Robertson, G.L.: Good and bad packaging: who decides? Int. J. Phys. Distrib. Logistics Manag. **20**(8), 37–40 (1990)
19. Simms, C., Trott, P.: Packaging development: a conceptual framework for identifying new product opportunities. Mark. Theor. **10**(4), 397–415 (2010)
20. Sara, R.: Packaging as a retail marketing tool. Int. J. Phys. Distrib. Logistics Manag. **20**(8), 29–30 (1990)
21. Chaudhary, S.: The role of packaging in consumer's perception of product quality. Int. J. Manag. Soc. Sci. Res. **3**(3), 17–21 (2014)
22. Sinnett, S., Spence, C., Soto-Faraco, S.: Visual dominance and attention: the colavita effect revisited. Percept. Psychophys. **69**(5), 673–686 (2007)
23. Chou, M.C., Wang, R.W.Y.: The findability of food package design: what can catch your eye? Bull. Japan. Soc. Sci. Des. **59**(3), 11–20 (2012)
24. Rigaux-Bricmont, B.: Influences of brand name and packaging on perceived quality. Adv. Consum. Res. **9**(1), 472–477 (1982)
25. Ares, G., Deliza, R.: Studying the influence of package shape and colour on consumer expectations of milk desserts using word association and conjoint analysis. Food Qual. Prefer. **21**(8), 930–937 (2010)
26. Rebollar, R., Lidón, I., Serrano, A., Martín, J., Fernández, M.J.: Influence of chewing gum packaging design on consumer expectation and willingness to buy. An analysis of functional, sensory and experience attributes. Food Qual. Prefer. **24**(1), 162–170 (2012)
27. Hall, S.: This Means This, This Means That: A User's Guide to Semiotics, 2nd edn. Laurence King, London (2012)
28. Fiske, J.: Introduction to Communication Studies, 2nd edn. Routledge, London (2010)
29. Culler, J.: Ferdinand de Saussure. Cornell University Press, New York (1986)
30. Silayoi, P., Speece, M.: Packaging and purchase decisions: an exploratory study on the impact of involvement level and time pressure. Brit. Food J. **106**(8), 607–628 (2004)
31. Smith, P.R., Taylor, J.: Marketing Communications: An Integrated Approach, 4th edn. Kogan Page, London (2004)
32. Ampuero, O., Vila, N.: Consumer perceptions of product packaging. J. Consum. Mark. **23** (2), 100–112 (2006)
33. Vila, N., Ampuero, O.: The role of packaging in positioning an orange juice. J. Food Prod. Mark. **13**(3), 21–48 (2007)
34. Kuvykaite, R., Dovaliene, A., Navickiene, L.: Impact of package elements on consumer's purchase decision. Econ. Manag. **14**, 441–447 (2009)
35. Adam, M.A., Ali, K.: Impact of visual packaging elements of packaged milk on consumers buying behavior. Interdisc. J. Contemp. Res. Bus. **5**(11), 118–160 (2014)
36. TrendGo Consultant Co., Ltd.: Trendgo+'s Annual Survey on Taiwan's Consumer Life: Personal Cleaning Supplies – Shower Gel. New Taipei City, Taiwan (R.O.C.), TrendGo Consultant Co., Ltd. (2014). [in Chinese, semantic translation]
37. Pollster Online Market Survey: Pollster Biweekly Survey on Personal Bathing Habit and Consumer Behavior (2015). . http://www.pollster.com.tw/Aboutlook/lookview_item.aspx?ms_sn=2707. [in Chinese, semantic translation]
38. Wang, R.W.Y., Sun, C.-H.: Analysis of interrelations between bottle shape and food taste. In: Design Research Society-International Conference 2006, drs2006_0054, Lisbon, Portugal (2006)

39. Chang, Z.-H., Huang, Y.-C., Chen, J.-H.: The theoretical discussion and validation of color preference in gender. J. Commercial Des. **15**, 57–76 (2011). [in Chinese]
40. Thomas, A., Pickering, G.: The importance of wine label information. Int. J. Wine Mark. **15** (2), 58–74 (2003)
41. Siegrist, M., Leins-Hess, R., Keller, C.: Which front-of-pack nutrition label is the most efficient one? The results of an eye-tracker study. Food Qual. Prefer. **39**, 183–190 (2015)
42. Wu, J.-Y.: A study on emotion dimensions and event-related potential by packaging pictorial characters. Unpublished Master's thesis, in Department of Industrial and Commercial Design., National Taiwan University of Science and Technology, Taipei City, Taiwan (R.O. C.) (2008). [in Chinese]
43. Meyer, R.P., Laveson J.I.: An experience-judgement approach to tactical flight training. In: Proceedings of the Human Factors and Ergonomics Society Annual Meeting. Sage Publications (1981)
44. Vilnai-Yavetz, I., Koren, R.: Cutting through the clutter: purchase intentions as a function of packaging instrumentality, aesthetics, and symbolism. Int. Rev. Retail Distrib. Consum. Res. **23**(4), 394–417 (2013)

Transforming Branding Strategies from Product to Service: A Case Study About Yangshan Tourism Branding

Yin Liang(✉), Han Han, and Davide Fassi

Politecnico Di Milano – Design Department, Via Durando 38/a, 20158 Milan, Italy
{liang.yin,han.han,davide.fassi}@polimi.it

Abstract. With the development of service economy, some companies enter new service business such as tourism, culture or leisure industry. Traditional companies then become a product-service complex which works in a product service system.

Yangshan Peach is a traditional brand of agricultural products company group in China. Under the development in recent years, it is becoming a regional brand involving tourism and culture experience. In this case, new branding strategy should be designed. This paper is to analyze the branding process of Yangshan from product to service then to get insight about the brand equity and brand engagement. The relationship between customer and service brand equity has been concluded in case study analysis.

Keywords: Brand · Service branding · Brand-customer relationship · Brand equity · Brand engagement

1 Research Background

As the rise of the service economy is changing the framework of conventional business, some traditional product companies have been converting into product-service complex (Wilson et al. 2008) with the changing of brand value and brand engagement, the meaning of brand and method of branding have also been changed. Being different from product brands, service brands are executed as somehow heterogeneous, intangible and inseparable from the service provider. As delivering a consistent experience seems more important than before, designers are suggested to think differently about branding strategies (Llopis 2014).

1.1 Theory Background

As De Chernatony and Dall'Olmo Riley (1997) stated, "a brand is the link between firms' marketing activities and consumers' perceptions of functional and emotional elements in their experience with the product and the way it is presented". This link can

P.-L.P. Rau (Ed.): CCD 2016, LNCS 9741, pp. 752–760, 2016.
DOI: 10.1007/978-3-319-40093-8_74

be viewed in terms of the relationship between consumers and brands and that understanding consumer-brand bonds in terms of relationship marketing principles will assist marketers in enhancing brand value (Jillian et al. 2002).

Service brand is about more than relationship between companies and customers, it could also include relationship between all stakeholders (Bollen and Emes 2008). For example, customer behavior could be seen as branding which expressing the meaning of service. Because of this, the brand equity of service tends to be redefined. Brand awareness and brand meaning can be seen as fundamental factor of service brand equity (Berry 2000). Service Branding Model (Fig. 1) also differs in degree from product branding model.

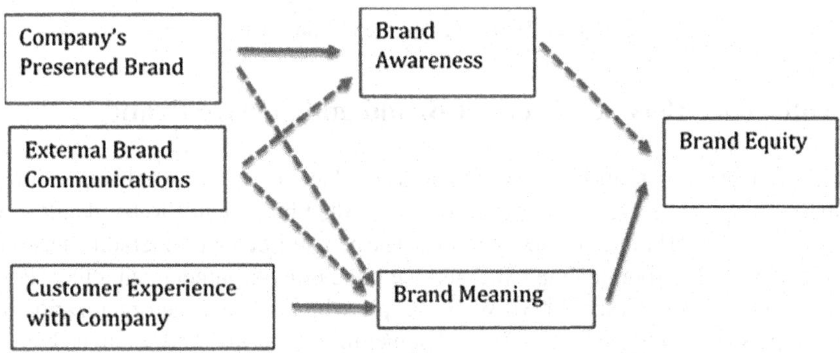

Fig. 1. Service branding model (Berry 2000)

1.2 Yangshan: Brand Not Only About Peach

Yangshan is one of the largest peach farmland in China, Jiangsu province, Wuxi, which is approximately 14000 hectares. People have planted peach there for more than 700 years and now there are about 13000 peach farmers and 700 companies.

Yangshan as a brand of peach represents a style of life: keep health and enjoy the nature. Volcano geopark locates in the west of Wuxi where is famous for its beautiful four hills, geological Heritage, cultural spots and botanic garden. As the Yangshan Volcano brings mineral rich tephra to farmland, peaches can be planted without chemical fertilizer, which means Yangshan Peach is organic.

With 41 % forest coverage and volcanic landform, Yangshan is an ideal place for leisure tourism, especially for those citizens living nearby. In another aspect, average lifetime of the peach trees is around 12 years which means farmers do not have income during the time period they plant new peach trees. Because of this, farmers always take part in the local cooperative which offer different jobs to local people.

With the development of tourism, catering and family outing service, Yangshan is no longer merely a product brand but a brand of service system which represents culture and lifestyle.

"Happy Farmhouse" (Fig. 2) is a new tourism project developed in recent years. People experience local culture and social relationship through events held by the hosts.

Yangshan Happy Farmhouse is supported by Yangshan Cooperative which organize farmers to grow organic food and build view point. Farmers will also host tourist in their house and enjoy Peach Festival together.

Fig. 2. Happy farmhouse in Yangshan

2 Difference Between Product Brand and Service Brand

Classic product brand is about product itself, as product doesn't answer back customers and perform the same every experience with a product brand tends to be identical. On the contrary, service brands are about people. The people's behavior including customer attitude, image of corporate employee, service price or environment can affect service branding (O'cass and Grace 2003). When people who represent the organization lose their tempers, get tired and anxious, and sometimes have just had enough that day, experience with a service brand is therefore different.

2.1 People as Brand

People were the first brands; faces were the first logos (Malone 2010). The way humans respond to brands could be seen as an extension of how they instinctively perceive or behave towards one another.

In the case that the person representing the brand doesn't perform properly, the relationship between the brand and the customer may collapse. The implication of this is that service-based companies have to focus on their internal employees to a greater extent than product-based companies.

2.2 Service Brand as a Relationship Partner

As conventional concepts of brand is refer to customer attitude, satisfaction, loyalty, and brand personality (Fournier 1994). The rising of service industry extends the understanding of brand dynamics. Service brand, as contributing-relationship partner of the consumers could be considered in a relationship dyad.

Designers, especially service designers, attempt to humanize and anthropomorphize brands. In this case, Yangshan local brands are described in media ads as having warm-hearted and positive personalities. However, a relationship in a person-to-person sense takes these perceptions a step further in that a relationship requires interaction and results in qualified statements about how the other person's personality interacts with our own.

Blackston (1992, 2000) conceptualizes the brand as a person with whom the consumer may choose to have a relationship. For service brand, it means which social network customers hope to build and which lifestyle they want to have.

3 Brand Equity from Product to Service

As what has been introduced in the previous sections of this paper, Yangshan Peach has been trying to develop several methods to access larger market potentials. The peach company historically worked on the products with local specialty subjecting to the mode of traditional agriculture industry, which made them as mass production supplier for retail sites mainly within regional market. While during the recent years the company has been making continuous efforts enhancing its market performance through transformation from traditional agriculture strategies to a more integrated scale, that is, branding level, or in another word, through the transformation from a product brand to a service brand. The efforts include redesign for visual presentations (e.g. logo and package, etc.), adjustment of pricing strategies (raise the price for high-quality and limited products), extension of product lines (postcards, souvenirs, etc.), and even development to tourism industry (agri-tainment activities e.g. Happy Farmhouse), which all target to provide stronger brand experience for sense of uniqueness and distinctive quality.

Such strategic transformation the company practice for its market development from product-focused to service-focused indicate an urgent need for enhancement of its brand equity through strategic branding design catering its special strengths. Brand equity from the marketing arena refers to a concept focusing on the relationship between the brand and its customers, which has been defined and interpreted by various scholars with different approaches. Feldwick (1996) tried to simplify it as a total value of a brand as a separable asset resulted from the attachment between brand and consumers. Aaker raised discussion (Aaker 1992) on the importance of brand equity significantly creating

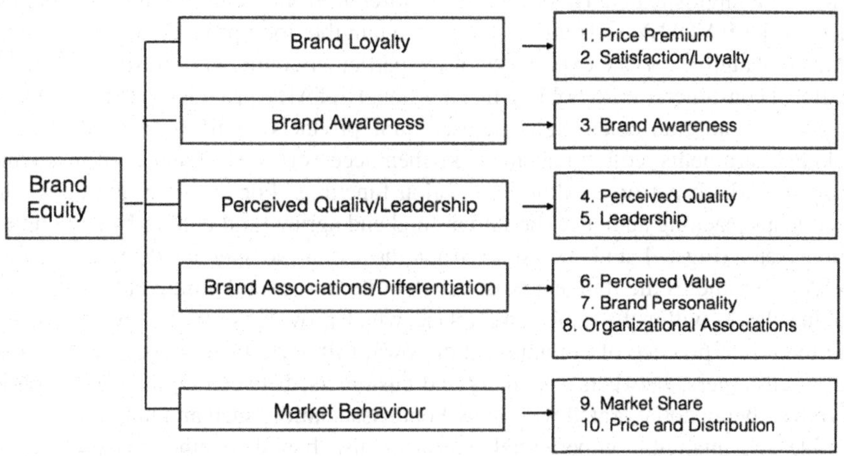

Fig. 3. Asker's brand equity 10

value to both the brand and its customers, and later in his book Managing Brand Equity (Aaker 2009) summarizes a Brand Equity 10 model (Fig. 3) which indicates five dimensions that drive the understanding as well as strategies for brand equity enhancement. All the dimensions direct to the end of strengthening brand-consumer relationship, which can be formed from the holistic experience the brand offer to the consumers. This hence is able to provide theoretical rationale for the strategic branding design for Yangshan Peach, which interpret its brand pursuit as to enhance the brand equity by reaching better brand-consumer relationship through experience building.

3.1 Experience Matters—Peach, Not Only a Product for Eat, a Case of EATALY

Holbrook and Hirschman (1982) originally suggested the vital impact on consumption practice that involves consumers' participation with feelings of fun and fantasy engaging both environmental and self-input from consumers' experiential point of view. Extended from this issue, later scholars explored types of models addressing the importance of customer experience in different academic fields. Schmitt's studies on experiential marketing specifically reveal strong insights for marketing and communication strategies regarding on effectively staging holistic brand-consumer experience encountering not only sensory and emotional responses but also engaging critical, behavioral and social practices (Schmitt 1999). At this point, the case of EATALY illustrates an inclusive example for Yangshan Peach when dealing with the issue on how to transform the food concept from product of traditional agricultural industry into an integrative service level of experience through multiple channels.

EATALY is the world largest Italian marketplace concentrating on all food-concept-related products and activities including not only retail of products like food and beverage but also services like dining and cooking school. It was found in 2003 in Turin, and now has developed worldwide points of sales including New York City, Istanbul, San Paulo, and Tokyo, etc. As what is stated in their official description, their target is to promote "eating Italian food, living the Italian way", which has been fully indicated by its name linguistically. Therefore, being different from the traditional food marketplaces, what EATALY sells are no longer the tangible food products from Italy only, but also intangible service experience of the particular culture and lifestyle of Italy, to the global consumers. With holding this mission, EATALY provides extensive product categories from traditional Italian agricultural products to lifestyle products (e.g. cooking instruments, coffee machines, kitchen accessories, etc.) and even magazines and books which perform cultural education functions. For example, the books and round maps teaching audience the Italian food and agricultural culture by seasons and regions, etc. (Figs. 4 and 5). Apart from the extensive merchandise assortments, EATALY promotes the Italian atmosphere by offering several dining options and also cooking classes within the same marketplace, which provides service platforms to facilitate the social practice of communication toward lifestyle factors between the brand and its customers, between customers and customers, between culture and cultures. Moreover, being collaborated with Slow Food Association, such an integration of both tangible and intangible experiential interfaces also bound together to co-create the philosophy and value with its customers regarding the issue of "sustainability, responsibility, and sharing" through consumption practice. Hence, this integrative strategy practically interpret Schmitt's model (2000) of experiential marketing in dimensions of sense, feel, think, act, and relate with deep degree of brand-consumer adhesion, which effectively fulfills the power of brand equity engine. This case thereby discloses brighter possibilities of insights for Yangshan Peach to strategically transform itself from a product brand to a service brand by providing holistic channels for brand-consumer experience, especially when combining its existing strengths when considering the cultural tourism factors introduced in previous parts.

Fig. 4. Books about Italian food

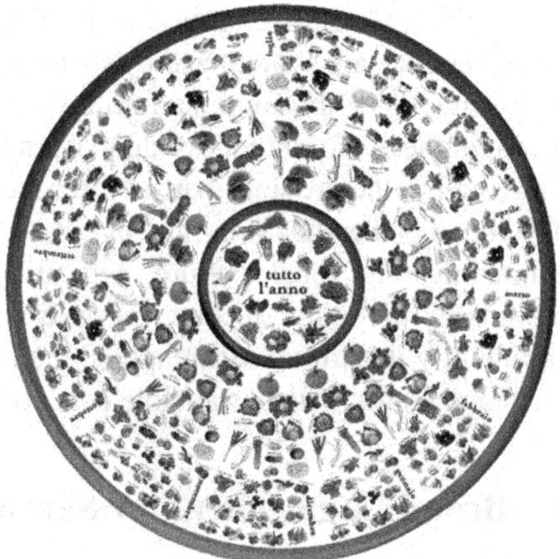

Fig. 5. Agricultural culture and region map

3.2 Brand Community Building—Peach, Not Only a Concept About Eat

The strategies for brand innovation by enhancing brand-consumer experience discussed above suggested a possible pathway to construct the contact between the brand and its customers from both tangible and intangible interfaces especially within the marketplace. Apart from such direct strategies, the brand-consumer relationship should also be nurtured from indirect channels. Brand community then no doubtfully serves this function that leverage the brand equity by strengthen the attachment between the brand and the consumers. Studies have driven abundant focus on how the customer-centric brand community building exercises large positive impact on brand loyalty, brand awareness, and brand association, etc. (McAlexander et al. 2002, 2003; Jang et al. 2008; Schau et al. 2009). The concept demonstrates a set of social relationship structured by shared consciousness, values, identities, ritual and traditions, co-created by both the brand and its customers, which equips the brand asset emotionally and socially (Muniz and O'Guinn 2001).

In terms of branding for food, Wright et al. (2006) started to look from the influence of virtual brand community building by the study of "my Nutella The Community" project, which shows the empowerment of consumers by cultivating themselves to express their relationship with Nutella narrating their personal stories for the goal of self-expression for its emotional attachment to the brand. In this case, each consumer as participant passionately shares his/her subjective experience toward the brand that is regarded as his/her extended self, and the brand community then becomes the pool feasts individualism through the virtual campaign. Compared to this case, more classical cases that have been discussed by years of brand community studies are from vehicle brands such as Harley Davison, Mini, Mercedes, etc., which strategically formed not only virtual communities but also member clubs integrating both on-line and off-line activities, both products and services exclusively for the members. For example, H.O.G club of Harley Davison in different countries organize various types of riding activities catering for consumers' diversities, during which the enhancement of brand-consumer relationship is experientially tighten up, meanwhile it also offers platforms for consumers and relative parties socializing with one another. Therefore, the brand and the experience are symbolized by social meanings which connect self with product, self with self, self with group, and group with group, for pursuance of individualism and belongingness, commonness and distinction. Combining the experiential strategies suggested in the previous part of the paper, Wuxi Yangshan Peach has the potential to develop membership program by providing series of experience-oriented activities communicating local culture, educating innovative agricultural philosophy, and promoting particular leisure lifestyle toward its target consumers, by which the community is built up to strengthen the brand-consumer relationship so as to enhance the brand equity with sustainable concern.

4 Brand Engagement for Service

Service brands elevate themselves by injecting a service element into their DNA to create a richer and more multi-dimensional brand experience. Yangshan create new channels for customer service including both online and offline. First they cooperate with Tujia which is an online tourism service system to build up a plant form sharing user experience and publishing news. Then, to enhance customer engagement, self-service tourism will be supported by local companies. In this case, Yangshan brand act as an umbrella for the whole service system, enabling efficient marketing with brand in a solution-driven way. This is then a more customer-centered process instead of putting focus too much on the brand itself.

4.1 Customer Engagement in Service

In service process, customer engagement exists in a full spectrum of experiences. It is no longer a series of one-off experiences—it is an ongoing dialogue. One aspect of this spectrum is the relationships that customers form with each other. The peer-to-peer relationships are core to the social web. As the rapid development of internet, customers will not just be interacting with companies, they will talk amongst themselves, sharing their perspectives across. For this, Yangshan cooperated with many internet enterprises to build up a huge information platform.

4.2 Real Brand Engagement

Through serious of interactive activities in Yangshan, customers get multiple experience in a well-designed customer journey.

With awareness a given, service providers will link "engagement" to how well the brand is perceived versus their category's ideal, rather than just counting "likes" or leveraging imagery. Hosts of Happy Farmhouse is core member of service system who receive feedback from both customers and providers so that they are able to evaluate the customer experience through multiple aspects.

4.3 Brand as Mutually Beneficial Relationship

Yanshan try to build up a well-developed friendship based on interdependent needs and mutual respects. This friendship is a two-way street. On one hand, during the online platform and co-design process, customers feel heard, and they can see their role in Yangshan as a social actors. At the same time, Yangshan get feedback, and have the opportunity to improve their business, thereby by attracting more customers.

5 Conclusion

Branding strategies for service-focused brand is quite different from traditional branding. User experience is vital and branding could be anytime and anywhere. As a designer, we should stay in the forefront of customers' minds and analyze all the stakeholders in a big map with service design tools.

With service brands, customers have a wider lens to access multiple offerings. As they take all stakeholders into consideration, it's necessary to sharp brand image for designers.

Brand Engagement and brand equity is the vital factors in this process. Service design methodology can help designers to get insights of stakeholders and find the opportunities through the studies on brand-consumer relationship.

References

Aaker, D.A.: The value of brand equity. J. Bus. Strategy **13**(4), 27–32 (1992)

Aaker, D.A.: Managing Brand Equity. Simon and Schuster, New York (2009)

Berry, L.: Cultivating service brand equity. J. Acad. Mark. Sci. **28**(1), 128–137 (2000)

Bollen, A., Emes, C.: Understanding customer relationships: how important is the personal touch? (2008)

Blackston, M.: A brand with an attitude: a suitable case for treatment. J. Market Res. Soc. **34**, 231–241 (1992)

Cova, B., Pace, S.: Brand community of convenience products: new forms of customer empowerment-the case "My Nutella The Community". Eur. J. Mark. **40**(9/10), 1087–1105 (2006)

Dall'Olmo Riley, F.: The service brand as relationships builder. Br. J. Manag. **11**(2), 137–150 (2000)

De Chernatony, L., Dall'Olmo Riley, F.: Brand consultants' perspectives on the concept of the brand. Mark. Res. Today **25**(February), 45–52 (1997)

Feldwick, P.: Do we really need "brand equity?". J. Brand Manag. **4**(1), 9–28 (1996)

Fournier, S.: A Consumer-Brand Relationship Framework for Strategy Brand Management (1994)

Holbrook, M.B., Hirschman, E.C.: The experiential aspects of consumption: Consumer fantasies, feelings, and fun. J. Consum. Res., 132–140 (1982)

Jang, H., Olfman, L., Ko, I., Koh, J., Kim, K.: The influence of on-line brand community characteristics on community commitment and brand loyalty. Int. J. Electron. Commer. **12**(3), 57–80 (2008)

Llopis, G.: 6 Brand Strategies Most CMOs Fail To Execute, source (2014). http://www.forbes.com/sites/glennllopis/2014/03/10/6-brand-strategies-that-most-cmos-fail-to-execute/#2715e4857a0b5808e0567611

Sweeney, J.C., Chew, M.: Understanding consumer-service brand relationships: a case study approach. Australas. Mark. J. **10**(2), 26 (2002)

Malone, C.: What Are Social Media Good For? Putting a Face to a Brand, source (2010). http://adage.com/article/cmo-strategy/marketing-social-media-helps-put-a-face-a-brand/145324/

McAlexander, J.H., Kim, S.K., Roberts, S.D.: Loyalty: the influences of satisfaction and brand community integration. J. Mark. Theor. Pract. **11**, 1–11 (2003)

McAlexander, J.H., Schouten, J.W., Koenig, H.F.: Building brand community. J. Mark. **66**(1), 38–54 (2002)

Muniz Jr., A.M., O'guinn, T.C.: Brand community. J. Consum. Res. **27**(4), 412–432 (2001)

O'cass, A., Grace, D.: An exploratory perspective of service brand associations. J. Serv. Mark. **17**(5), 452–475 (2003)

Schau, H.J., Muñiz Jr., A.M., Arnould, E.J.: How brand community practices create value. J. Mark. **73**(5), 30–51 (2009)

Schmitt, B.H.: Experiential Marketing: How to Get Customers to Sense, Feel, Think, Act, Relate. Simon and Schuster, New York (2000)

Wilson, A., Zeithaml, V., Bitner, M.J., Gremler, D., Zeithaml, V.A., Bitner, M. J. Gremler, D.D.: Services Marketing: Integrating Customer Focus Across the Firm (2008)

Mobile Technology Use Among Sales People in Insurance Industry

Ming-Hsin Lu[1(✉)], Hsiu-Ping Yueh[1], and Weijane Lin[2]

[1] Department of Bio-Industry Communication and Development, National Taiwan University, Taipei, Taiwan
{f01630002,yueh}@ntu.edu.tw

[2] Department of Library and Information Science, National Taiwan University, Taipei, Taiwan
vjlin@ntu.edu.tw

Abstract. In recent years, implementing mobile IT management and application are important organizational development strategies for international enterprises. This study aims to explore the insurance salesperson's usage behavior of mobile technology and their attitude toward using mobile technology in workplace by the case study method. A total of 72 valid questionnaires were collected from local employees of an insurance company in Taiwan. The results showed: (1) Smartphones were more often used to support instant communication tasks and read individual's learning resources and (2) were viewed as more helpful to support most tasks than tablets besides reading official learning resources. (3) Using mobile devices in workplace were regarded to improve information communication, images and individual's workflow efficiency. The findings provided information for companies' managers to design a more productive mobile workplace especially for sales departments that have high mobility employees.

Keywords: Mobile technology · Mobile enterprise · Mobile workers · Sales

1 Introduction

In recent years, implementing mobile IT management and application have been an important organizational development strategy for international enterprises [1]. As reported in Accenture's 2014 mobility survey, companies were moving aggressively to adopt mobile technologies and are developing formal strategies [2]. According to iThome's 2015 annual CIO survey, the insurance industry had the highest willingness to implement mobile technology in workplace among other industries in Taiwan [3]. This survey also showed that sales departments often adopted mobile technologies earlier than the other divisions in insurance industry.

Many reports and researches has verified the benefits of implementing mobile technology in the workplace. Accenture [2] showed that more than 45 % senior decision-makers for digital strategy and technologies in companies considered that implementing multiple mobile technologies in workplace could create revenue opportunities, increase product/service development speed and customer engagement,

P.-L.P. Rau (Ed.): CCD 2016, LNCS 9741, pp. 761–768, 2016.
DOI: 10.1007/978-3-319-40093-8_75

and also enable rapid responses to customer demands [4]. Mobile technology not only provided the anytime anywhere learning environment to enhance employees' work capability but also facilitated immediate service to clients and finally made company get rid of the existing energy-intensive business environment, to create a low-carbon economy [5–7]. Yueh et al. [8] found that using smartphone on work tasks had a positive impact on individual perceived work performance.

The most revenue in an insurance company is from sales departments. The salesperson should provide efficient service to clients anytime and anywhere to increase individual performance and companies' revenue. Their work is of high mobility and need instant information. As mentioned previously, the advantages of mobile technology support the salesperson's work tasks and improve the workflow. When organizational managers target the specific individual requirements depending on job roles and tasks, a better fit between the type of mobile technology and job demands is likely to increase productivity [9]. Motivated by the aforementioned phenomenon, this study aims to explore the insurance salesperson's usage behavior of mobile technology and their attitude toward using mobile technology in workplace. In doing so, this study provides two main contributions. First, it deliver information for companies' managers to design a more productive mobile workplace especially for sales departments which have high mobility employees. Second, the results shed light on the relevance issue of mobile workplace research.

2 Methods

This study adopted the survey method to collect empirical data from the employees in a regional business establishment of a leading insurance company in Taiwan, which has implemented mobile technology of iPad to support the salesperson's work tasks from 2012. All participants are from the sales department. A total of 72 valid questionnaires were collected from local employees using paper questionnaires.

This study investigated participants' demographic information, attitude toward advantages and applications of mobile technology measured by a 6-point Likert scale, anchored by 1 (strongly disagree) and 6 (strongly agree). The questionnaire also inquired participants' actual mobile technology using experiences measured by a 5-point Likert scale. The using experiences survey investigated users' using frequency (0 = never use, 4 = always use) and perceived usefulness (0 = unhelpful, 4 = very helpful) of various tasks (i.e. making a phone call, using e-mail, checking personal schedule and browsing web pages editing files) in works.

For data analysis, descriptive statistical analysis was applied to report the overall status. In addition, paired-samples T test and Cohen's d effect size was used to analyze the difference using experience between smartphones and tablets.

3 Results

3.1 Demographics and the Using Experiences of Mobiles

The samples were composed of 80.3 % females and 19.7 % males, and nearly 70 % samples' age were above 35. Above 65 % of participants have worked in this companies more than five years (46, 65.7 %). Over 90 % of the participants (67, 96 %) held high school diplomas and 42 % of the participants (29, 42 %) held bachelor degrees.

Almost all participants have smartphones (70, 97 %). The proportion of operating system run on smartphones is iOS:Android = 1:3.5. Compared to the possession rate of smartphone, 81.9 % of the participants have tablets, and more than half of them use iPads. Most employees responded they have adopted mobiles over 1 years (51, 77.1 %) and used them more than twice a day (50, 71.4 %). The respondents considered mobile devices were easy to use (M = 5.01, SD = 1.014). Most of the employees bought their own mobiles personally (28, 45.2 %) or obtained discount to buy mobiles from the company rather (27, 43.5 %) than got allotment of mobiles from the company (5, 8.1 %).

Table 1 shows the using frequency rating of smartphones for different work tasks by the participants in this study. When participants responded the using frequency of smartphones for a task was more than 0, their perceived usefulness of smartphones for the tasks could be analyzed (Table 2). As can be seen in Table 1, participants regarded five tasks – make a phone call, browse web pages, use e-mail and manage individual's schedule– were more usually supported by smartphones (mean > 2.5). Table 2 shows smartphones were useful to support work tasks (mean > 2.5). Participants considered most tasks – make a phone call, use e-mail, browse web pages, read official learning resources, manage individual's schedule, finish work tasks and read individual learning resources–especially could be efficiently supported by smartphones (mean > 3).

Table 1. Using frequency rating of smartphones for work tasks

Tasks	Using frequency (N = 72)	
	Mean	SD
Make a phone call	3.25	1.110
Browse web pages	2.89	1.240
Use e-mail	2.65	1.425
Finish work tasks	2.55	1.302
Manage individual's schedule	2.52	1.403
Edit files	2.46	1.362
Take notes	2.43	1.359
Read official learning resources	2.39	1.405
Read individual learning resources	2.38	1.405

Table 3 reports the using frequency rating of tablets for various work tasks by the participants in this study. Table 3 shows the main task supported by tablets is browsing

Table 2. Perceived usefulness rating of smartphones for work tasks

Tasks	Perceived usefulness		
	n	Mean	SD
Make a phone call	67	3.54	0.628
Use e-mail	59	3.38	0.699
Browse web pages	66	3.32	0.805
Read official learning resources	59	3.16	0.843
Manage individual's schedule	61	3.14	0.828
Finish work tasks	61	3.03	0.803
Read individual learning resources	59	3.02	0.683
Edit files	62	2.94	0.978
Take notes	61	2.93	0.883

web pages (mean > 2.5). Table 4 shows tablets were usefulness to support work tasks (mean > 2.5). Participants regarded some tasks – read official learning resources, browse web pages, use e-mail, and read individual learning resources–could be efficiently supported by smartphones (mean > 3).

Table 3. Using frequency rating of tablets for work tasks

Tasks	Using frequency (N = 72)	
	Mean	SD
Browse web pages	2.64	1.507
Use e-mail	2.48	1.493
Read individual learning resources	2.37	1.467
Finish work tasks	2.37	1.477
Read official learning resources	2.35	1.475
Edit files	2.25	1.471
Manage individual's schedule	2.15	1.443
Take notes	2.14	1.497
Make a phone call	1.67	1.613

This study summarizes participants' mobile devices usage behavior in workplace in Tables 1, 2, 3 and 4. The results shows the using frequency and perceived usefulness of tablets for work tasks both are generally lower than smartphones.

Table 4. Perceived usefulness rating of tablets for work tasks

Tasks	Perceived usefulness		
	n	Mean	SD
Read official learning resources	56	3.29	0.768
Browse web pages	59	3.19	0.83
Use e-mail	58	3.17	0.831
Read individual learning resources	56	3.17	0.784
Finish work tasks	56	3.17	0.716
Edit files	57	2.93	0.882
Make a phone call	42	2.92	0.87
Manage individual's schedule	55	2.89	0.806
Take notes	56	2.73	0.946

3.2 The More Efficient Mobile Technology to Support Various Work Tasks

To verify which mobile device is regarded as more efficient to support different work tasks, this study analyzed using frequency and perceived usefulness of smartphones and tablets for work tasks by T-test for paired samples and Cohen's *d*. All variables were below the guidelines for skewness and kurtosis (<3 and <10, respectively) recommended by Kline [10]. The participants who both used smartphones and tablets to support a task were analyzed (the using frequency is more than 0).

Table 5 shows the paired t-tests result for using frequency of smartphones and tablets for work tasks. As can be seen in Table 5, using frequency of smartphones for three tasks – make a phone call ($M = 3.48$, $p < 0.001$), manage individual's schedule ($M = 2.89$, $p < 0.05$) and read individual learning resources ($M = 2.73$, $p < 0.05$) – are significant higher than tablets with an effect size of $d = 0.627$, 0.326 and 0.332 respectively. Table 6 reports the paired t-tests result for perceived usefulness of smartphones and tablets for work tasks. According to the results in Table 6, perceived usefulness of smartphones for four tasks – make a phone call ($M = 3.50$, $p < 0.001$), manage individual's schedule ($M = 3.08$, $p < 0.001$), read individual learning resources ($M = 3.50$, $p < 0.001$) and finish work tasks – are significant more useful than tablets with an effect size of $d = 0.578$, 0.480, 0.463 and 0.578 respectively. Although perceived usefulness of smartphones for three tasks – use e-mail ($M = 3.47$, $p = 0.654$, $d = 0.256$), edit files ($M = 3.41$, $p = 0.096$, $d = 0.224$) and take notes ($M = 3.10$, $p = 0.107$, $d = 0.223$) – are not significant more useful than tablets on the p values, their effect size of d shows smartphones are a little more useful for supporting these three tasks than tablets.

3.3 Advantages of Using Mobile Technology in Workplace

Table 7 presents employees' perceived impact of using mobile technology in workplace. As the result in Table 7, participants considered using mobile technology in

Table 5. Paired t-tests (*P* values) result for using frequency of smartphones and tablets for work tasks

Tasks		Smartphones		Tablets		T value	df	Sig.	d
	n	Mean	SD	Mean	SD				
Make a phone call	42	3.48	0.591	2.87	0.994	4.060	41	0.000*	0.627+++
Use e-mail	55	3.17	0.831	3.02	0.843	1.249	54	0.217	0.168
Manage individual's schedule	52	2.89	0.806	2.89	0.808	2.346	51	0.023*	0.326
Edit files	57	3.19	0.830	3.13	0.844	0.424	56	0.673	0.056
Take notes	54	2.93	0.882	2.74	0.900	1.143	53	0.164	0.192
Read individual learning resources	54	2.73	0.946	2.67	0.966	2.445	53	0.018*	0.332+
Read official learning resources	51	3.17	0.784	3.09	0.828	−0.204	50	0.839	0.028
Finish work tasks	51	3.29	0.768	3.05	0.826	0.144	50	0.886	0.085

$^{*}p < 0.05$; $^{+}$small effect; $^{++}$medium effect; $^{+++}$large effect

Table 6. Paired t-tests (*P* values) result for perceived usefulness of smartphones and tablets work tasks

Tasks	n	Smartphones		Tablets		T value	df	Sig.	d
		Mean	SD	Mean	SD				
Make a phone call	42	3.50	0.582	2.92	0.870	3.742	41	0.000*	0.578+++
Use e-mail	55	3.47	0.654	3.20	0.845	1.897	54	0.063	0.256+
Manage individual's schedule	52	3.30	0.722	2.91	0.815	3.467	51	0.001*	0.480++
Edit files	57	3.41	0.725	3.19	0.835	1.964	56	0.096	0.224+
Take notes	54	3.10	0.900	2.89	0.881	1.640	53	0.107	0.223+
Read individual learning resources	54	3.08	0.784	2.71	0.947	3.402	53	0.001*	0.463++
Read official learning resources	51	3.12	0.553	3.18	0.730	−0.636	50	0.528	0.089
Finish work tasks	42	3.50	0.582	2.92	0.870	3.742	41	0.001*	0.578++

$^{*}p < 0.05$; $^{+}$small effect; $^{++}$medium effect; $^{+++}$large effect

workplace has positive influences. Using mobile devices in workplace not only can support the communication among colleagues (M = 5.10, SD = 0.981), the company (M = 5.08, SD = 1.003) and clients (M = 5.01, SD = 1.068), but also enhance the company (M = 5.00, SD = 0.890) or individuals' professional image (M = 4.94, SD = 1.005) and improve personal work management (M = 5.00, SD = 0.964) and completion (M = 4.99, SD = 0.986).

Table 7. Influence on using mobile technology in workplace

Item (N = 72)	Mean	SD
Using a mobile device makes me communicate with my colleges more easily in the workplace	5.10	0.981
Using a mobile device is helpful for communicating with my company in the workplace	5.08	1.003
Using a mobile device is helpful for communicating with clients in the workplace	5.01	1.068
Using a mobile device in the workplace will improve company's image	5.00	0.890
Using a mobile device can improve my work management in the workplace	5.00	0.964
Using a mobile device is helpful for finishing my work in the workplace	4.99	0.986
Using a mobile device in the workplace will improve my individual image	4.94	1.005

4 Discussion

The participants of this study were senior sales in the insurance company and have substantial experience of using mobile devices. They generally perceived mobile devices as highly easy to use and regarded using mobile devices in workplace can improve information communication, images and individual's workflow.

The results of descriptive statistics shows the using frequency and perceived usefulness of smartphone for work tasks both are generally higher than tablets generally. Only the perceived usefulness of tablets for reading official learning resources is higher than smartphones. The results of *T*-test and effect size of *d* reports that the participants significantly more often used smartphones to support instant communication tasks and read individual's learning resources and considered smartphones are more helpful to support most tasks besides reading official learning resources.

According to these findings, this study proposes that smartphones have higher mobility and more functions to support instant communicating and creating and managing individual's work information than tablets in workplace. The screen size of smartphones become bigger than bigger but still smaller than tablets, so when the applications are more various and accessible, smartphones' mobility could be more helpful for supporting sales' work tasks.

This study is a pilot study to explore sales' mobile technology using behavior in workplace. Future studies should increase the sample size and compare the mobile technology using behavior between the field and indoor jobs to propose more specific suggestions for a high productive mobile workplace design.

References

1. Dimension Data. http://www.slideshare.net/DimensionData/the-2015-mobile-workforce-report-rise-of-the-mobile-worker-55884128
2. Accenture. http://www.accenture.com/SiteCollectionDocuments/Lcal_China/PDF/Accenture-Mobility-Research-Report-2014.pdf

3. iThome. http://www.ithome.com.tw/article/94091
4. Accenture. https://www.accenture.com/t20150805T060328__w__/us-en/_acnmedia/Acccenture/Conversion-Assets/Microsites/Documents14/Accenture-Growing-The-Digital-Business-Acn-Mobility-Research-2015.pdf
5. Donnelly, K.: Learning on the move: how m-learning could transform training and development. Develop. Learn. Organ. **23**, 8–11 (2009)
6. Unhelkar, B., Murugesan, S.: The enterprise mobile applications development framework. IT Prof. **12**, 33–39 (2010)
7. Lu, M.-H., Yueh, H.-P., Lin, W.: Exploring the key factors for cooperate implementation of mobile technology. In: The 15th IEEE International Conference on Advanced Learning Technologies, Research Paper (2015)
8. Yueh, H.-P., Lu, M.-H., Lin, W.: Employees' acceptance of mobile technology in a workplace: An empirical study using SEM and fsQCA. J. Bus. Res. (2015)
9. Köffer, S.: Designing the digital workplace of the future–what scholars recommend to practitioners. In: The 36th International Conference on Information System, Completed Research Paper (2015)
10. Kline, R.B.: Principle and Practice of Structural Equation Modeling. Guilford, New York (2005)

Cross-Cultural Conflict Management in Taiwan-Funded Enterprises in Mainland China

Lin Ma[1], Xin Wu[1], Zhe Chen[1(✉)], and Fuyuan Shi[2]

[1] Beihang University, Beijing, China
zhechen@buaa.edu.cn
[2] Wuhan University, Wuhan, China

Abstract. As the quantity of Taiwan-funded enterprises investing in mainland China keeps increasing, management problems caused by cultural differences between the mainland and Taiwan have drawn attention from both academic and business circles. Though they are of the same origin, Taiwan culture and mainland culture have formed their individual characteristics due to different social evolution for more than a century. In this study based on Hofstede's Culture Measurement Model, cultural conflicts in Taiwan-funded enterprises in mainland China are systematically analyzed from the three levels of values, institution and management behavior through the interview analysis of three Taiwan-funded enterprises. Starting with the strategy of collaborating in conflict management, specific and constructive solutions to the problems mentioned above are proposed accordingly.

With the deepening of cross-Strait relations, numerous Taiwan companies invest in mainland China. They face cultural conflicts brought by cultural differences between the mainland and Taiwan when Taiwan-funded enterprises copy Taiwan management mode to mainland China. This problem has a significant impact on company development. Difference in values between people in the mainland and Taiwan caused by different histories, social patterns and economic systems will necessarily provoke cultural conflicts. Cultural conflicts damage the harmonious relationships between the management and staff, weaken team cohesiveness, and are not in the interest of global strategy implementation by Taiwan-funded enterprises. It is an important topic of conflict management how to understand cross-Strait cultural differences, to solve cultural conflicts in Taiwan-funded enterprises, and to help enterprises gain sustainable competitiveness.

Keywords: Cross-cultural conflict · Collaborating · Taiwan-funded enterprises

1 Cross-Cultural Conflicts

Conflicts are everywhere. Conflicts will be provoked when individuals in an organization have disputes in such aspects as objectives, emotion and interest (Bendersky and Hays 2012). Cross-cultural conflicts refer to disputes caused by cultural differences (Jassawalla et al. 2004).

The cultural model built by Hofstede (1984) has been widely applied in research on cross-cultural management. Hofstede divided culture measurement into three levels.

P.-L.P. Rau (Ed.): CCD 2016, LNCS 9741, pp. 769–776, 2016.
DOI: 10.1007/978-3-319-40093-8_76

(1) The Values Level: It consists of three dimensions, namely personal ideology, work attitude and demand for power; (2) The Institution Level: It refers to the human resources management mechanism; (3) The Management Behavior Level: It refers to the behavior guidance of the management. Based on Hofstede's Culture Measurement Model, cultural conflicts in the operation of Taiwan-funded enterprises in mainland China are discussed in this paper respectively from the three levels of values, institution and management behavior.

The five strategies of conflict management are respectively: (1) Competing, in which one side wins and the other loses; (2) Avoiding, in which both conflicting parties put off conflict indefinitely; (3) Compromising, in which the conflicting parties give up elements of their position in order to establish an acceptable solution; (4) Accommodating, in which one side meets the demand of the opposing side at the expense of their own interests; (5) Collaborating, in which both parties work together to find a win-win solution (Rahim 1983; Thomas 1992). Existing studies show that the strategy of collaborating in conflict management not only effectively buffers conflicts but also maximizes advantages of both parties to achieve satisfactory results (Rahim 2002).

2 Research Methods

In this paper, with three Taiwan-funded enterprises in Beijing as research objects, an in-depth discussion is made on cultural conflicts in the operation of Taiwan-funded enterprises in mainland China. We interviewed 56 people in total, among whom there were 6 senior managers, 15 middle managers, 16 junior managers and 19 employees. Interviews were conducted separately to dispel the concerns of interviewees. The average interview time was 20 min per person. All interviews were conducted with the semi-structured interviewing technique. The interview outline was prepared according to the three levels in Hofstede's Culture Measurement Model. Additional questions could be asked on a case-by-case basis to gain insight into the status of corporate cultural conflicts. Some interviews were recorded with the permission of the interviewees.

Four Ph.D. students processed the interview transcription and encoded the transcription in two groups according to the following criteria: (1) Sentences were classified in accordance with the three levels in Hofstede's Culture Measurement Model; (2) Sentence description must be clear and definite; (3) Original sentences were used as far as possible; (4) Each code was meaningful. After coding, two groups of Ph.D. students discussed and modified their coding results until they reached agreement under the guidance of a lecturer.

3 Analysis of Cultural Conflicts in Taiwan-Funded Enterprises

3.1 The Values Level

Personal Ideology. It is found in the interviews that managers and employees in Taiwan-funded enterprises, who have a strong sense of organization, generally consider the overall interests of the organization. Most of them are ready to sacrifice private interests for public affairs. Employees from Taiwan have a stronger sense of belonging to their companies and are willing to grow with their companies. Interviewees said employees from Taiwan generally had a stronger sense of belonging than their mainland counterparts though young employees of the new age showed a much weaker sense of belonging than before in recent years.

Compared with their Taiwan counterparts, mainland employees tended to change their jobs and places of residence more frequently. Besides, they generally did not maintain stable and long-term relationships with their colleagues. Most mainland employees chose to leave for a better job if there was a company offering a better salary and benefits. Interviewees also said that after accumulating certain working experience and interpersonal connections, some employees resigned immediately and started homogeneous companies to compete with their former companies.

Attitude at Work. In Taiwan-funded enterprises, compared with their Taiwan colleagues, mainland employees are more willing to accept risky and challenging tasks. Mainland employees generally regard the challenges as good opportunities to fully show their work ability and talent. Only by firmly seizing these opportunities can their strengths and talents be recognized by colleagues and managers. However, Taiwan managers are comparatively conservative and are not willing to accept high-risk tasks or jobs. They are generally worried that uncertain risks will influence their positions. This is closely related to the influence of long-term colonization on Taiwan, which results in that people generally lack the sense of security. They are often reluctant to undertake tasks beyond their normal scope of work and would like to reduce the risks in finishing the tasks.

Power Distance. Mainland subordinates have a relatively weaker perception of power distance to their superiors, especially the young generation born after 1980, who have higher education backgrounds and rich knowledge, and are profoundly influenced by foreign cultures (especially western cultures), thus advocating freedom and equality. They have insightful views and opinions regarding problem solving and do not accept the absolute authority of their superiors. They often actively raise their doubts and opinions if they think the solutions of their superiors are to be improved. Employees from Taiwan, however, have a stronger perception of power distance. According to the stereotyped ideology in their minds, differences in social wealth and power have been institutionalized and legalized. There is a strict hierarchy between superiors and subordinates in an enterprise. In communication, ranks are emphasized and people with different ranks stay away from each other. A superior would like his subordinates to accept his ideas and act according to his way of thinking. He seldom takes the doubts and suggestions of his subordinates but regards them as disrespect to him.

3.2 The Institution Level

Human Resources Planning. HRP (*Human Resources Planning*) focuses on the analysis of future human resources supply and demand, according to which recruitment and training plans are prepared. HRP is drafted in all of the interviewed Taiwan-funded enterprises. According to the interviews, Taiwan-funded enterprises paid more attention to short-term HRP due to the lack of knowledge about mainland labor laws and regulations. As the market environment changes, long-term HRP is generally not executed though prepared.

Recruitment and Selection. The HR managers from the interviewed companies all complained that it was difficult to recruit talents in mainland China. It is mainly because of comparatively less attractive salaries and benefits as well as limited career development prospects. Taiwan-funded enterprises attach great importance to work attitude. Employees from Taiwan are also highly loyal and dedicated. This phenomenon is popular in Taiwan-funded enterprises. The relationship between a mainland employee and his company is, however, more like a contractual relationship, i.e. "I work as much as I am paid". A mainland employee usually resigns if the salary given by his company fails to meet his expectations. That's also why mainland employees recruited by Taiwan-funded enterprises often resign after they are mature, though these enterprises invest a lot to train them in the preliminary stage. Taiwan-funded enterprises widely complain that they cannot retain talents as employees are not loyal enough. Mainland employees, however, complain that Taiwan-funded enterprises offer low salaries but tiring jobs. This phenomenon is mainly caused by cultural differences between the two sides.

Salary and Incentive Systems. Taiwan-funded enterprises generally offer much lower salaries than US and European enterprises. As the interviews shows, it is because Taiwan-funded enterprises pay much attention to the training of employees who can share a common fate with them. Therefore, they tend to recruit new college graduates and spend much money on staff training. This type of corporate culture, though it is the values of Taiwan-funded enterprises, can hardly integrate with mainland employees nor attract or retain outstanding employees. On the other hand, the interviewed companies pay salaries to mainland employees according to the local wage level, but to employees from Taiwan according to the Taiwan wage level which is generally much higher than the former. Mainland employees, thus, find the salary system unfair. In addition, the large wage gap between Taiwan managers and ordinary employees also dissatisfies mainland employees. Mainlanders generally canonize economic egalitarianism but disapprove a large wage gap between managers and ordinary employees. This is closely related to the years of "Communal Pot" system. Therefore, the large wage gap between superiors and subordinates, to some extent, hits the morale of subordinates and is not in the interest of smooth and effective work.

Training. Besides skills training, Taiwan-funded enterprises also provide mainland employees with training on working habits, behavior and attitude and so on. As the interviews show, though mainland and Taiwan are from the same root, mainland employees may misunderstand their Taiwan managers due to cultural and conceptual differences because languages, customs and habits around mainland China, which has a vast territory, are significantly different.

Career Development. In the interviewed companies, 100 % of the senior managers are from Taiwan and only about 30 % of the middle managers are mainlanders. The CEOs of the three companies all said that they would rather appoint Taiwan managers. On one hand, it is related to the quality of mainland employees. On the other hand, they cannot promote too many mainland employees considering the mentality of employees from Taiwan. This not only hits the morale of mainland employees, but also makes Taiwan-funded enterprises less attractive to outstanding mainland talents.

3.3 The Management Behavior Level

Centralization. From the interviews, it can be seen that Taiwan-funded enterprises attach great importance to qualifications and social status. In the interviewed companies, managers and ordinary employees have meals in separate areas. It reflects the corporate culture that values qualifications and social status. Many employees from Taiwan regard this treatment as a symbol of status. In Taiwan-funded enterprises, significant authority is granted to managers. Compared with mainland employees, Taiwan managers have a stronger concept of centralization. Subordinates must absolutely follow the decisions of their superiors even when they know these decisions are wrong.

The ferocious and stern attitude of quite a few Taiwan managers has been formed in their long period of rigid labor management in Taiwan. Most incumbents (male) in Taiwan enterprises and public institutions have served in the army and experienced military life. Current Taiwan-funded enterprises still retain a distinct hierarchical patriarchal culture as military life features result-orientation, hierarchy and the obedience of superior orders. Mainland employees, however, may regard it as an insult to their characters or an infringement of their rights since they have been taught that "All men are created equal" for a long time.

Institutionalization. All the interviewed companies emphasized that it was important to impose severe company rules and regulations. Employees are regulated by discipline and will be severely punished if they make mistakes. Nobody can escape his responsibility for any excuse. According to the interviewed companies, various rules and regulations made by a company are not for the convenience of managers but used to regulate employee behavior and to facilitate the healthy development of the company. They disapproved the governance of a company in the "Tender Management" method. If an employee did not receive due punishment after making a mistake, managers would fall into an extremely passive state when similar events happened again. Mainland employees, however, generally focus on feelings and interpersonal relationships and find Taiwan-funded enterprises impersonal. On the contrary, employees from Taiwan think that mainland employees are too flexible and unprincipled facing the regulations.

4 Collaborating in Conflict Management

It is especially important to handle them with the strategy of collaborating in conflict management after the cultural conflicts in Taiwan-funded enterprises in mainland China are identified. A brand-new organizational culture that integrates both cultures can be formed only when two different cultures admit and value their differences and respect, supplement and coordinate with each other. This unified culture is not only highly stable but also has the advantage of "hybridization". It is, therefore, the optimal choice for Taiwan-funded enterprises in mainland China to reduce cultural barrier cost and to improve economic efficiency by absorbing the essence of different cultures through collaborating and forming a unique corporate culture and management style.

4.1 Enhancing Communication at the Values Level

According to the analysis above, there are large gaps between mainland and Taiwan employees in terms of ideology, attitude and power cognition at the values level. Conflicts happen if they fail to understand and communicate with each other properly. Taiwan-funded enterprises, therefore, should usually organize various activities and guide employees of different cultural backgrounds to positively and actively integrate themselves into the local living and cultural environment through formal and informal parties. They should also create conditions for the two employee groups' to understand each other's cultural backgrounds, values and expressions, so as to improve interpersonal relationships, strengthen communication and remove prejudice, and to create an atmosphere of mutual trust, sincere cooperation and open communication. Especially, senior managers should enhance their interaction with mainland employees to improve their affinity; encourage employees to make suggestions so as to absorb all useful ideas; build consensus and good working relationships among employees with the idea of solving problems, to correct the imperfections of paternalistic leadership. Many scholars have pointed out that trust accumulates when regular communication and timely feedback increase. Taiwan businessmen, therefore, must build a mutual-trust relationship between Taiwan and mainland employees through such open communication.

4.2 Strengthening Cultural Training at the Institution Level

According to the interview results, cultural conflicts at the institution level in Taiwan-funded enterprises in mainland China mainly lie in the following four aspects: environmental policy, employee competency, salaries and staff promotion. Training is the most effective way to solve these cultural conflicts. First of all, strengthen timely training of senior managers on mainland environmental policy to help managers seize opportunities and make correct decisions. Second, especially strengthen the training of employees' sense of belonging and cohesiveness to help mainland employees realize the long-term investment of their companies in their personal development and to improve staff loyalty. Third, continue strengthening staff cultivation and personal ability trainings to help mainland employees grow. Fourth, organize training of team awareness for all the staff. It is because they regard each other as out-group members that so many inharmonious and unpleasant cases occur between Taiwan employee teams and mainland employee teams. It is, thus, necessary to increase the contact between the two groups and to actively create opportunities for all to interact with each other with ease after work. As they understand each other better, previous prejudices will fade away gradually. Last, train a large pool of outstanding talents with cross-cultural management ability by seizing the opportunity of cross-cultural training. They are aware of mainland China's actual conditions and skilled at communication with subordinates, trust and support their subordinates, and have rich professional knowledge, personality charm and strong managerial ability. The rapid and stable development of a company depends on these highly qualified managers.

4.3 Improving Localization at the Management Behavior Level

Cultural conflicts at the management behavior level are particularly reflected in the totalitarian thoughts of Taiwan managers and institutional control. The localization of managers is an effective solution to these conflicts. Taiwan-funded enterprises must enhance the training and appointment of mainland managers, especially senior and middle managers. Mainland managers who know mainland cultural traditions and way of thinking can communicate and work collaboratively with their subordinates, regulate employees' behavior and improve employees' capability and quality. Besides, mainland managers, most of whom have a higher education background, can realize efficient management of a company as they have a profound understanding of western management methods and can understand and implement management ideas of their Taiwan bosses well. Overall expenses on expatriate managers, therefore, will be reduced and the working enthusiasm of mainland employees will also be raised.

Staff localization is an optimal solution to cross-cultural management conflicts. The following two measures must be taken to realize staff localization. On one hand, "No Ceiling" policy should be implemented for the promotion of local talents. A company with human-based management shall never allow the existence of regional, racial, gender or age discrimination in human resources management. Only when there is enough development space can Taiwan-funded enterprises attract high-caliber and outstanding local talents. On the other hand, the policy of "equal pay for equal work" should be applied to local talents. Only when local talents are treated equally without discrimination can the sense of belonging of local staff be strengthened and can excellent employees be retained.

5 Conclusion and Discussion

Taiwan-funded enterprises, as an important component of the pluralistic economy of mainland China, have made outstanding contributions to the economic development of mainland China. It is of important practical significance to analyze the cross-cultural conflicts in the actual management process in Taiwan-funded enterprises, to find out the reasons and seek solutions, and to help Taiwan-funded enterprises establish their management modes in the mainland cultural environment.

In this paper, cultural conflicts in Taiwan-funded enterprises in mainland China are discussed respectively at the three levels of values, institution and management behavior through field research, interviews and literature analysis. In conclusion, there are four types of cultural conflicts: staff loyalty, salary system, centralized management style and localization of managers. Due to problems such as strict hierarchy, paternalistic management mechanism, unreasonable salary system and "Glass Roof" for mainland employees, Taiwan-funded enterprises become less attractive in staff recruitment with an increasing churn rate of mainland employees and the complaints of Taiwan managers about the low loyalty and dedication of mainland employees.

Based on the strategy of collaborating in conflict management, this research identifies the correct solution to cross-cultural conflicts in Taiwan-funded enterprises. First of all, managers of Taiwan-funded enterprises should build a mutual-trust relationship between mainland and Taiwan employees by usually creating various opportunities for open communication between them. Second, Taiwan-funded enterprises should pay attention to cross-cultural training to improve the cross-cultural communication ability, team awareness and competence. Besides, they should also train a pool of outstanding talents with cross-cultural management ability. Third, Taiwan-funded enterprises should accelerate the localization of managers to strengthen the sense of belonging of local staff and to raise their working enthusiasm. Taiwan-funded enterprises should try to build a unified vision, strengthen the construction of cohesion, and help themselves gain competitive advantages through open and inclusive organizational cultures.

Acknowledgements. This work has been supported by a grant from the National Natural Science Foundation of China (Project Number: 71502009).

References

Bendersky, C., Hays, N.A.: Status conflict in groups. Organ. Sci. **2**, 323–340 (2012)

Hofstede, G.: Culture's Consequences: International Differences in Work-Related Values, vol. 5. Sage Publications, Beverly Hills (1984)

Jassawalla, A., Truglia, C., Garvey, J.: Cross-cultural conflict and expatriate manager adjustment: an exploratory study. Manag. Decis. **7**, 837–849 (2004)

Rahim, M.A.: A measure of styles of handling interpersonal conflict. Acad. Manag. J. **2**, 368–376 (1983)

Rahim, M.A.: Toward a theory of managing organizational conflict. Int. J. Confl. Manag. **3**, 206–235 (2002)

Thomas, K.W.: Conflict and conflict management: reflections and update. J. Organ. Behav. **3**, 265–274 (1992)

The Thinking Model and Design Process of Empathic Design: Cases Studies of Counter Design

Shu-Huei Wang(✉) and Ming-Shean Wang

Department of Digital Design, MingDao University,
Wen-Hua Rd, 52345 Changhua, Taiwan
angelawang36@gmail.com, wangms@mdu.edu.tw

Abstract. Empathic design is an emerging issue in the field of design, adopts the human-oriented concept and emphasizes the position of the design object and an in-depth understanding of the potential needs of users to design the products, services and environment users really need. Designers may design products that satisfy the needs of users by exercising empathy and an in-depth understanding of the potential demands of users. Four designers of S brand were aimed as the object of this study and an in-depth interview was made to understand the thinking processes of designers. The thinking models of these four designers were constructed respectively to explore the empathic design process. This research methodology included the grounded theory, data and literature analysis and comparative case analysis of researches on cross-presentation of empathic design conceptual models. The empathic design models of these four designers were analyzed by the grounded theory and a total of 367 concepts, 75 sub-categories and 24 categories were generated, including P1 with 87 concepts, 17 sub-categories and 6 categories, P2 with 68 concepts, 18 sub-categories and 6 categories, P3 with 89 concepts, 19 sub- categories and 6 categories and P4 with 123 concept, 21 sub-categories and 6 categories.

Keywords: Empathic design · Empathic design thinking model · Design thinking · Design process · Counter design

1 Introduction

People emphasize the spiritual significance of consumption and emotional resort in the era of experience consumption. Consequently, the human factor is tremendously focused during the design process such as human-centered design, user-centered design and consumer-centered design. The main core issues are to realize the real demands of consumers and to confirm whether users are satisfied with the designed products and services. Market surveys and focus groups and so on were the common methods to collection consumer information on earlier days. Designers also conducted participant design to explore consumer behaviors or observe in the lab. However, when people were aware of being observed, their true colors would not be revealed causing the difficulty in excavating the real problems. Designers need to develop empathy towards users (to feel how the users feel) and understand the potential demands of users so as to

P.-L.P. Rau (Ed.): CCD 2016, LNCS 9741, pp. 777–787, 2016.
DOI: 10.1007/978-3-319-40093-8_77

satisfy user requirements. As a result, methods of literature review, case study, in-depth interviews and grounded theory are adopted in this research. Four designers of S brand were aimed as the object of study and in-depth interviews were made to understand the thinking processes of the designers. Thus, the thinking models of these four designers were constructed and analyzed and the conceptual model of empathic design was demonstrated by probing the process, analysis of the grounded theory, summarization of literature reviews and comparison and analysis of studies.

2 Literature Review

1. **User-centered Design:** Norman took the psychological aspect for emotional design recently and used the concepts of designers and users as examples to develop a successful and identical psychological model commonly shared by designers and users. The conceptual models of the designers and the users as shown in Fig. 1 communicate through products and products communicate the messages of systematic images. Norman and Draper (1986) proposed user-centered design (UCD) and Norman (1988) defined UCD as a philosophy in compliance with demands and interests of users to produce a usable and understandable product.

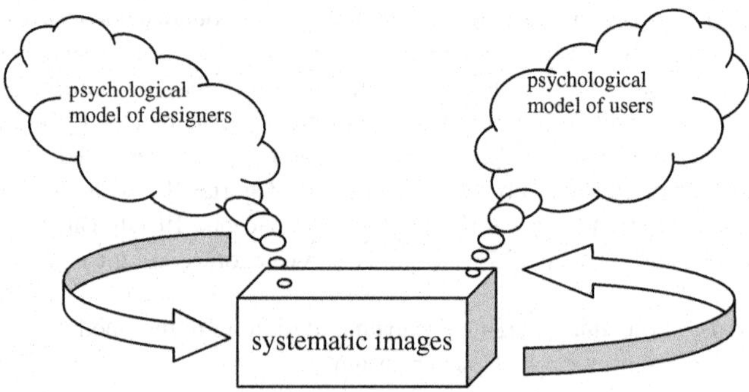

Fig. 1. Conceptual model (Norman 2005:94)

It is critically important to know the expectations and needs of users prior to launching a new product in particular. Thus, designers can't just resort to their own experiences and expertise to design similar products. More related information from consumers is required. For instance, users can be invited to try new products and describe their ideas and defects about such products as a reference for designers. Users are like co-designers, which is unprecedented. We name such approach of data collection as user-centered design currently. The most common questions include "What does the user want?" "Why does the user want this?" and "What does the user expect?" etc.

2. **Role Playing:** Tim Brown, the CEO of IDEO, mentioned the true experience of Kristian Simsarian, a designer of IDEO, being a patient in an emergency room at a seminar on serious play in 2008. Altay Sendil, another designer of IDEO, used to

have his hair on the chest removed and experience the moment when the dressing patch was removed as the pains chronic patients felt. These experiences are role playing, which is a powerful sensation that helps designers to think when designing. In other words, designers experience the things they are about to design through playing the roles (Brown 2008). After designers experience in person, they can apply it to find out the products, services and environment that suit users best.

3. **Scenario-oriented Design Approach:** Acer introduced scenario design from IDEO in 1990, which was like the mind map of users. Scenarios or stories that are transformed from rational data are the most touching. Designers explain events and texture and integrate sense and sensibility via storytelling and scripts as well as visualizing imagination through different scenarios so as to understand various needs of the users (Yu et al. 2001). The process of script design is illustrated in Fig. 2. Four steps of producing a script, including introduction, elucidation of the theme, transition to another viewpoint and summing up are utilized to set up a story. Designers then absorb the related information and convert it to a communication tool so as to design the products, services and environment that meet demands of the users.

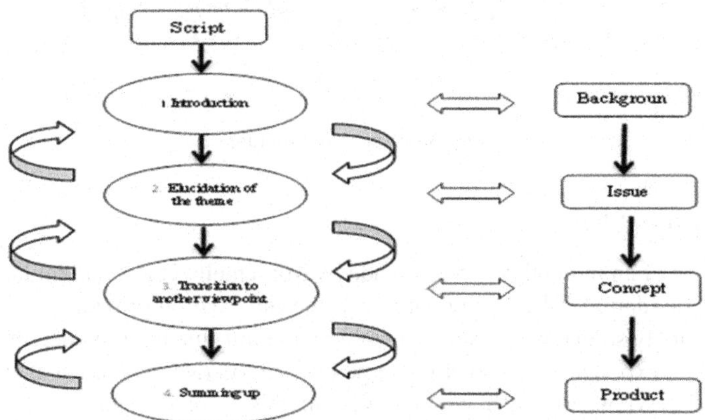

Fig. 2. Process of script design (amended from Yu et al. 2001, P: 13)

4. **User Experience (Prototypes):** it is a term to test use and satisfaction of a product and is usually used for software or marketing testing. Norman (1999) described it as a process of product development that starts with users and their needs rather than with technology. Kuniavsky (2003), one of the initiators of Adaptive Path, said in his book Observing the User Experience that how to apply it extensively to more user research techniques of high efficiency. Rubinoff (2004) considered user experience was based on four elements, including brand, use, function and satisfaction, which provided a key to success. Paluch (2006) mentioned on his website that user experience was the description of a user about the feature of any product when using it, which could extend to cars, cellphones, magazines or kids' toys. The

significance is how the user feels about the product or service and how to put it into words. Reiss (2009) defined user experience (UX) as a sum of a series of interactions in his blog.

3 Methodology

In-depth interviews, design of question items, case study, analysis of the grounded theory, an understanding of the problems related to empathic design and literature review were conducted in this research. The design processes of four designers (two designers and two senior designers) from the same brand were compared and analyzed. The in-depth interviews were analyzed and summarized by the grounded theory to develop the empathic design model (Fig. 3).

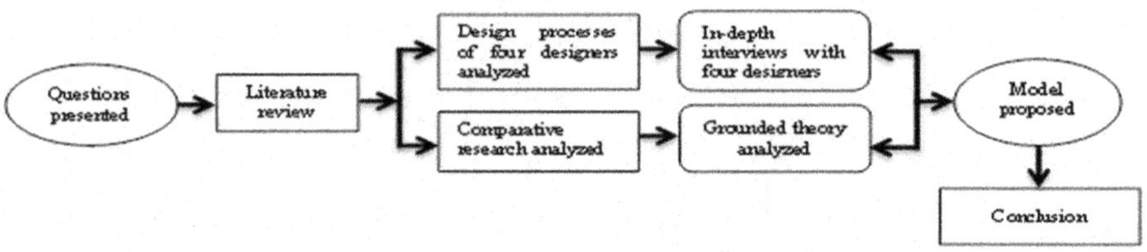

Fig. 3. Research structure

3.1 Method of Study

The definition of an in-depth interview made by Minichiello et al. was similar to that by Taylor and Bogdan (1984). The research and the information provider encounter face to face repeatedly so that the views expressed by the information provider about his/her own way, life, experience or scenario can be understood (Minichiello et al. 1996). The qualitative interview approach was adopted in this research and a semi-structured interview was made with individual designer on his/her design process.

3.2 Object of Study

Purposive sampling was adopted to choose the object of study and the researcher judged and selected the samples. There were four people to be interviewed with, who were the designers of brand S (including two designers and two senior designers). The products, services and management concepts of brand S are customer-oriented, 100% customer satisfaction and complete sincerity. The theme under study is correlated to the features of the population. The profile of these four designers who applied empathy to truly understand the real needs of users and meet their demands is listed in Table 1.

Table 1. Basic information of objects of study

No.	P1	P2	P3	P4
Gender	Male	Female	Male	Female
Age	32(69)	42(59)	52(49)	50(51)
Education	University	University	Senior High School	University
Years of Service	5 years	4 years	26 years	24 years
Project Design	Showcase Design	Showcase Design	Showcase Design	Showcase Design
Date of Interview	Sep. 15, 2008	Sep. 15, 2008	Sep. 15, 2008	Sep. 15, 2008
Brand Outlet	Watsons	Watsons	Specialty Shop	Department Store
Experience of Design	8 years	19 years	28 years	29 years

4 Results and Discussion

The case of brand S was studied and their designers were served as the objects of study. They have more than one thousand showrooms around the island and their outlets are mainly in the department stores, specialty shops and cosmeceutical stores. Four of their five showcase designers were interviewed due to the huge quantity of their stores. How these four designers applied empathy to design will be examined carefully in this research. Cases of these four designers who put themselves in customers' shoes will be analyzed and their thinking models in design will be generalized.

4.1 Comparative Research Analysis

The individual design process, ideas and implementation of these four designers are compared and analyzed with eight question items and summarized in Table 2. The comparison is concluded as follows:

The design process of the designers is summarized as the following: the same places of the brand are that (1) designers investigate prior to design, including site surveys, measurement, understanding customer segments and communication with users; (2) designers communicate with people participating in the design project over the design plan, 3D drawing and 3D virtual drawing during the design process; (3) designers coordinate and communicate with collaborative manufacturers over implementation; and (4) designers inspect and review upon completion for design evaluation.

The different places are that: (1) designers interview with users face to face for an in-depth understanding of users' needs and experience the product and the service process in person for investigation before design; (2) presentation of design details, consideration of costs, drawing communication and creative implementation during the design process differ; (3) completion schedule differences, production costs, design

Table 2. Comparison of four designers

Designer / Question Item	P1	P2	P3	P4
1. Individual design process	•To cope with reality with ideas •To extend the theme •To achieve consensus with the proprietor	•Channel demands •Functional design •To integrate with company rules •To execute the ideas	•To confirm individual position •To survey the surroundings •To realize special needs •To measure •To confirm user needs •To design	•Customer needs •To collection information •To set up the theme •Individual views and opinions
2. Thought reflected in design	•To discuss limitations with the superior •To master the features of works	•Standardized design •Functional adjustment •Design of new concepts •Division of channels •To satisfy customer needs •To meet company concepts	•Site survey •Subjective thought •3D simulation chart •To visit similar stores •To apply images to reduce communication differences	•Local designers and originators •To merge into the local market •To set up the framework •To satisfy the details of the local market •To divide various market differences •To integrate popularity and life with design •The idea of a lounge bar
3. Understanding of user's need	•Users may present their needs directly. •Sometimes the proprietor is not the user. •Designers need to put themselves in others' shoes to meet their needs. •Right thing for the right person	•To think if I were the customer •To expect the environment the proprietor will provide •To visit friends •To compare different aspects	•Emotional needs of users •Sensible needs of users •More problems of perceptual needs •To explore commercially •Specialty position •To respect the proprietor's opinions	•To measure •Users are service personnel and customers. •Design is based on good looks, usability and operation needs. •Design is aimed at usability, convenience and joy.
4. Empathic methods	•Accumulation of experiences prevents making mistakes. • To analogize by individual's experience	•To assume yourself as a user •To pretend to be a customer in a store •To experience the purchase process •To experience the feelings about different products •To experience the whole process in person •To go through directly	•To feel instinctively •To sit still and let yourself go •To think over the overall design demands	•To treat yourself as a consumer •To receive service at the showcase actually •To experience the service process in person •To understand the strengths and weaknesses of design •To provide modified ideas •To be a consumer •To experience indirectly •To receive service and experience the process

5.Creation through empathy	•Renew To renew by communicating with users continuously •To present questions •To ponder on solutions for optimum •Attraction	•To treat yourself as a consumer •To exercise in practice to know more about customers' needs •To be more considerate while designing •Intimate presentation •To be aware of presentation of details	•Budgets and cultural backgrounds •Designers integrate needs and aesthetics with specialty. •Designers are responsible for coordinating the surroundings. •Empathy and communication with users	•To treat yourself as a consumer to experience •To experience different brands
6. Putting themselves in customers' shoes	•Users are the service personnel at the showcase. •To satisfy their needs is to satisfy customers' needs.	•Designers are humans as well. •They are customers, too. •To see from the angle of general customers •To think from the position of the person in need	•To aim at customers' demands •Customer-oriented	•The key to skin is to prepare a skin care room. •Special service •Restricted and time limited service •100% customer satisfaction •To be in customer's position
7. Other design methods	•Problems proposed by customers •Make-up trial and sincere conversation •How to make customers comfortable	•The number of consideration perspectives	•Proprietors' trust •Designers need to take proprietors' demands into consideration.	•Complete experience •Privacy and safety of open space
8. Difficulty in breakthrough	•Dilemmas and conflicts •Designers take the users' aspects and convince their superiors.	•Struggles between ideality and reality •Production costs •Time urgency •Professional design behavior •Market surveys require time testing. •Breakthroughs of new ideas and types •To obtain a balance	•Huge differences in thoughts •Proprietors' satisfaction •Designers and proprietors have the same position. •To surprise the proprietors •To beautify and integrate •Mutual satisfaction	•To develop creativity fully •Design costs •Corporate cultures •Special effects •To apply the Japanese ideas first •To set up the title and the theme for company annual plan

limitations and integration of creative design for design execution are different; and (4) designers taking part in inspection upon completion and reporting for the stage of design evaluation vary.

4.2 Analysis Result of Grounded Theory

Open coding is to retrieve the terms (schema) related to the subject from data collected through in-depth interviews and the schema is condensed to several categories, which become concepts or themes (cognitive structure) that symbolize special meanings of the data. As these four designers were interviewed respectively, the in-depth interviews and the grounded theory are analyzed and summed up as follows: 367 concepts in total with 75 sub-categories and 24 categories. These main and sub-categories are then introduced to the individual empathic design thinking model (Table 3).

P1 has 87 concepts, 17 sub-categories and 6 categories, whose design process is illustrated in Fig. 4. P2 has 68 concepts, 18 sub-categories and 6 categories, whose

Table 3. Decoding table of four designers

Main category	Sub-category	Main category	Sub-category	Main category	Sub-category	Main category	Sub-category
P1 **1. Source of design concepts**	1.Designer's own thinking	**P2** **1.Understand the differences in channel design concepts.**	1.Know division of channels.	**P3** **1. Verify one's own position.**	1. Authority in the company	**P4** **1.Beginning of design**	1Functions of local designers
	2.People that are served give design ideas directly.		2. Great differences in brand channel design		2.Who to face		2. Cultural differences
			3. Maintain the brand image.				3. Popular living culture
2.Understand design limits	1.Discuss with the superior in advance.	**2. standards.**	1.Standardized design	**2.Preparations prior to design**	1. Survey the conditions of the marketplace.	**2. Understand customers' requirements.**	1.Understand customers' needs.
	2.Understand design problems.		2.Basic requirements		2. Verify users' requirements.		2. Corporate management strategies
	3. Achieve a consensus with the proprietor.		3.Meet various requirements.		3.Conduct visualized communication before design.		3.Cost consideration
3.Understand requirements of people involved	1. Requirement proposer	**3.Empathic design methods**	1.Observe the marketplace.	**3. Empathic design methods**	1.Instinctive design	**3. Empathic design methods**	1.Division of markets
	2. Understand communication requirements.		2.Place oneself in others' position.		2. Listen to the proprietor's needs.		2. Process of experiencing in person
			3Experience in person.		3. Sensible and perceptual needs		3. Assume the roles of customers.
			4. On-site practice		4. Understand the background of the proprietor.		4Association
			5.different angles		5. Methods to achieve a consensus		5.Cultural habits
4. Empathic design methods (sensible & emotional thinking)	1.Place oneself in others' position.	**4.Considerate design**	1.Consider customers' requirements.	**4.Satisfy aesthetics.**	1.Express beauty and taste.	**4. Set up subjects and collect data.**	1.Thematic fashion design
	2.Functional consideration		2.Consequences resulted from careless consideration				2. Concept of lounge bar
	3. Ergonomic consideration				2. Integrate environmental aesthetics.		3.Concept of nightclubs
5.Maintain features (during the design process)	1. Design the uniqueness of the brand.	**5. Cost control**	1. Brand management strategies				4.Design details
	2. Visual presentation of posters		2. consideration	**5. Project design**	1.Case design	**5.Present personal opinions.**	1.Personal creative views
	3.consideration		3. requirements		2.Professional design		2. Innovative design
	4.Lighting effects				3. Cost consideration		3. Design problems
6Compromise between brand and service	1.Maintenance of brand image	**6.Design specialty**	1.Professional design		4Implementation		
	2.Selection of image or service		2.Better living design	**6. Proprietor's satisfaction**	1. Special cases	**6. Serve customers to accomplish their satisfaction and joy.**	1.Merge into the environment of the department store.
	3. Accumulation of design experiences				2. Satisfy the proprietor with specialty.		2.Activities
					3Have the same position as the proprietor.		3.Quality of service

design process is shown in Fig. 5. P3 has 89 concepts, 19 sub-categories and 6 categories, whose design process is illustrated in Fig. 6. P4 has 123 concepts, 21 sub-categories and 6 categories, whose design process is shown in Fig. 7.

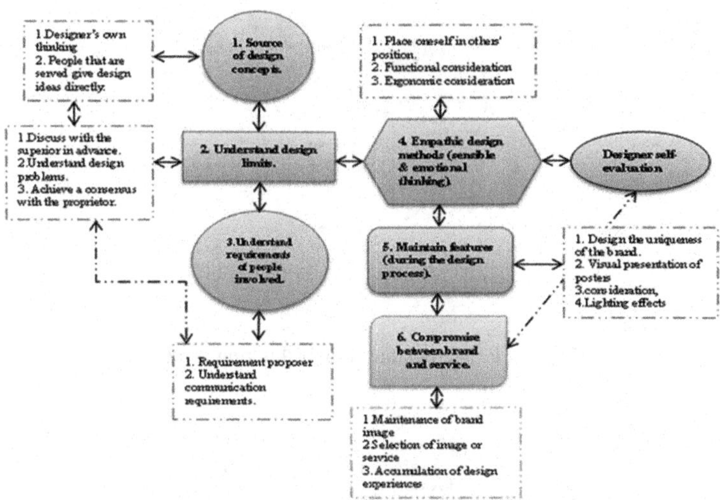

Fig. 4. P1's empathic design thinking model

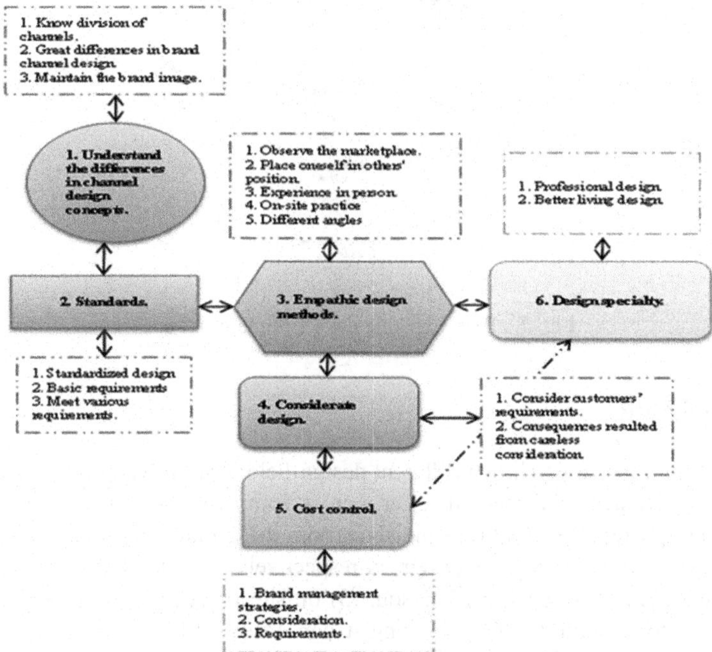

Fig. 5. P2's empathic design thinking model

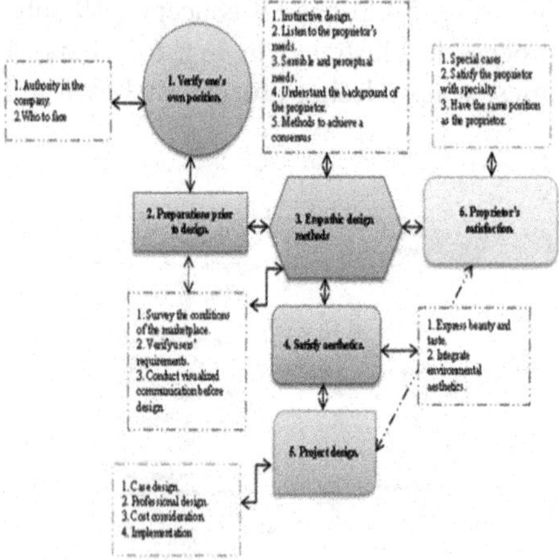

Fig. 6. P3's empathic design thinking model

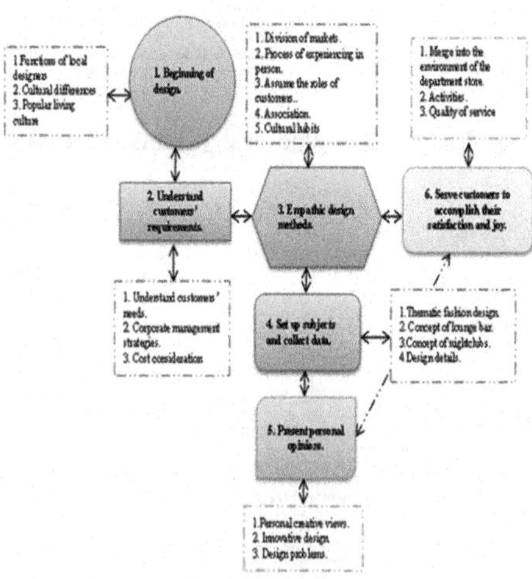

Fig. 7. P4's empathic design thinking model

5 Conclusion

It is found from the research that different design fields lead to various applications of empathic design steps and methods after a cross comparison of empathic design theories and design practice. As far as the showroom design area is concerned, empathic design ways used by these four designers respectively include (1) putting oneself in other's shoes, (2) experiencing in person, (3) on-site practice, (4) instinctive design, (5) listening to customers, (6) achieving a consensus and (7) association. Finally, empathic design in the showcase design domain is defined as follows: problems are located from the showcase design locale and designers provide satisfactory service to customers via empathic design methods like putting oneself in other's position, experiencing in person, on-site practice, and listening to customers, etc.

References

Minichiello, V., Aroni, R., Timewell, E., Alexander, L.: In Depth Interviewing, 2nd edn. Addison Wesely Longman Australia Pty Limited, South Melbourne (1996)

Norman, D.A., Draper, S.W. (eds.): User Centered System Design: New Perspectives on Human-Computer Interaction. Lawrence Erlbaum Associates, Hillsdale (1986)

Norman, D.A.: The Psychology of Everyday Things. Basic Books, New York (1988)

Norman, D.: Invisible Computer: Why Good Products Can Fail, the Personal Computer Is So Complex and Information Appliances Are the Solution. MIT Press, Cambridge (1999)

Norman, D.A.: Translation Reviewed by Wang, H.-S., translated by Wung, C.-L., Cheng, Y.-P., Chang, C.-C. Emotional Design, 1st edn., vol. 94. Garden City Publishers, Taipei (2005)

Taylor, S.J., Bogdan, R.: Introduction to Qualitative Research Methods. Wiley, New York (1984)

Brown, T.: Serious Play, the Art Center Design Conference 2008 (at TED.com), Art Center College of Design South Campus Pasadens, California, USA (2008)

Yu, T.-C., Lin, W.-C., Wang, C-C.: Scenario-Oriented Design: New Design Methods for Information Products and Services, pp. 11, 13. Garden City Publishers, Taipei (2001)

Reiss, E.: A definition of "user experience". http://www.fatdux.com/blog/2009/01/10/a-definition-of-user-experience/ (2009). Accessed 05 May 2009

Paluch, K.: What Is User Experience Design. http://www.montparnas.com/articles/what-is-user-experience-design/ (2006). Accessed 05 May 2009

Kuniavsky, M.: User Expectations in a World of Smart Devices [Online PDF]. http://www.adaptivepath.com/ideas/essays/archives/000272.php (2003). Accessed 05 May 2009

Rubinoff, R.: How To Quantify The User Experience. http://www.sitepoint.com/article/quantify-user-experience/ (2004). Accessed 05 May 2009

The Emotional Experience of Inquiry Feedback Delaying in Online e-Commerce Platform Service Design: A Case Study from Chinese Customers

Hao Tan[1(✉)], Wei Li[2], and Jiahao Sun[2]

[1] State Key Laboratory of Advanced Design and Manufacturing for Vehicle Body, Hunan University, Changsha, China
htan@hnu.edu.cn

[2] School of Design, Hunan University, Changsha, China
{liwei2014, sunjiahao2015}@hnu.edu.cn

Abstract. In online e-Commerce platform service design, feedback delaying occurs in different service scenarios, which has become one of the key issues of the current service design and user experience study. Based on the previous research on the feedback delaying during interaction, we took the Chinese consumer as an example and focused our research on the inquiry feedback service delaying when the servants answer the consumer's questions in online e-Commerce platform. We adopted the methods of protocol analysis and emotional scales and arranged different feedback delays into the inquiry tasks and obtained the consumer's oral reports and subjective rating scores. We analyzed the levels of emotion and experience and gained the quantitative indicator of emotional experience. At last, we proposed a correlation model between different feedback delaying and emotional experience levels in online e-commerce platform, which produced a trial design guide of feedback delaying service design in online e-commerce platforms.

Keywords: Feedback delaying · Online inquiry · Emotional experience · Online e-commerce platform · Service design

1 Introduction

Feedback online is one of the most important issues in service design on e-commerce platform. During e-commerce serving, the feedback delaying is a kind of time delay when the user operates and waits for the service system or servicer's feedback resulting in the impact of the user's emotional experience, which is an essential issue in service design and user experience research. In early 1993, Nielsen has proposed the impacts of three kinds of time delay (0.1 s, 1 and 10 s) on user's emotional perception, which is the earliest study about the impact of time delay on the quality of user perception in the field of HCI. In 2003, the International Telecommunication Union established Recommendation ITU-T P.800.1 standard based on the delay of voice calls. This standard focused how the quality of PSTN or CS voice type can affect user experience.

P.-L.P. Rau (Ed.): CCD 2016, LNCS 9741, pp. 788–799, 2016.
DOI: 10.1007/978-3-319-40093-8_78

Furthermore, an experience quality has been proposed based on five-point scale ranging from excellent to bad. In 2012, Lorentzen et al. put forward the difference impacts between initial delay and interrupt delay on user experience of service and product and built related theoretical model. Reichl et al. (2010) observed a distinct sensitivity of user perception to response and download times in interactive services on the web. Egger et al. (2012) also presented the delay impact on the quality of experience on web services. By the year of 2014, Ericsson APP coverage whitepaper presented the impact on the user experience within 10 s delay.

Our experiment took the Chinese consumer as an example, participants were recruited and asked to complete three different shopping tasks on one or two online e-commerce platforms. On the basis of our previous research method of the verbal analysis with Chinese language (Tan and Sun 2015), we analyzed the levels of emotion and experience from the consumer's oral reports and gained the quantitative index of emotional experience. Moreover, with the consumer's subjective scores in emotional scales, a correlation model between different inquiring feedback delaying and the different emotional experience levels in online e-commerce platform was designed, which produced a trial guide of feedback delaying service design in online e-commerce platform and help to promote the online e-commerce service experience.

2 Experiment

2.1 Participants

In this research, we invite 47 participants in total (21 male and 26 females). All participants had online shopping experience with different length of time. Their ages ranged from 18 to 51. 10 of the participants took part in the experiment 1 (5 male and 5 females). 17 of the participants took part in the experiment 2 (7 male and 10 females). 20 of the participants took part in the experiment 3 (9 male and 11 females).

2.2 Experimental Arrangement

The research was divided into three experiments. In Experiment 1, use the timer and bell to record the point of the limit time. In Experiment 2, the participants were asked to narrate their feelings using think aloud protocol and use the recording equipment to record the experimental condition. In Experiment 3, the participants need to rate the emotion scale.

2.3 Experiments

Experiment 1. To simulate the real online shopping environment, we made three kinds of web pages (food, clothing and office supplies) based on Taobao pages. Every participant need to complete three tasks. In each task the participant selects a product the experimenter specified. Then the participant need ask the customer service whether the products are in stock and wait for the reply. When the participant send the message, experimenters started timing and marked the time point as T0 (=0). The participants rang when they start to feel impatient, experimenters marked this time point as T1. Finally, the experimenters calculated average of T1 (Fig. 1: Experiment 1 process).

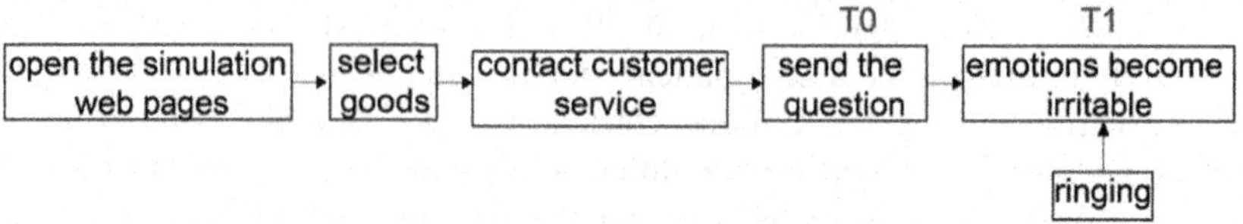

Fig. 1. Experiment 1 process

Experiment 2. Experiment 2 had n parts and in each part the participants can ask any questions to the customer service. They need to wait for the answers for different length of time in different parts. During the experiment their verbal reports were recorded.

In experiment 1 we got the limit time T1. Based on this limit time we divided the waiting time into several parts. In these parts participants need to wait different length of time. Each neighboring parts has a difference of 3 s. So for each part the waiting time is 3 s (first part), 6 s (second part)…T2 (n part) (Fig. 2).

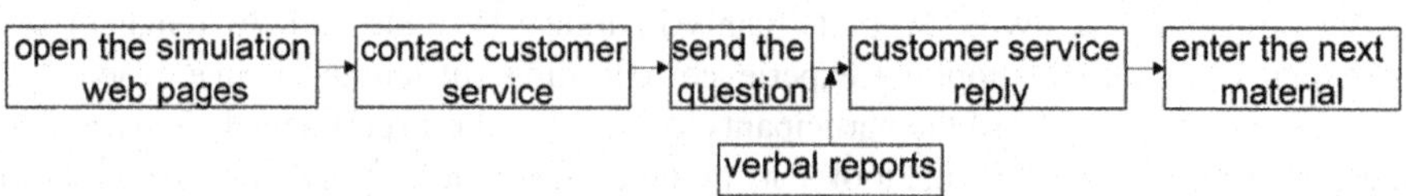

Fig. 2. Experiment 2 process

Process Methods and Measurements of Verbal Report. Direct extraction method: adjective and adverbs of degree that appeared explicitly in sentences were directly extracted (Table 1).

Table 1. Direct extraction

Participants exact words	Extracted adjectives	Adverbs degree	Level
I wait a little long	Long	A little	Lower
This reply is relatively fast	Fast	Relatively	Medium grade
Why does he not reply, so slow	Slow	So	High level
Too slow!	Slow	Too	Extreme
It's pretty fast	Fast	Pretty	High level

Situational Extraction. Sometimes the feedback from participants did not contain any obvious adverbs or adjectives. One way we could judge the participants' attitude in this case is that judge through colloquial descriptions (including exclamatory and interrogative sentences) and intonation combined with the context in which the language was uttered. Once interpreted, this raw data was translated into adjective-dominated declarations (Table 2).

Table 2. Situational extraction

Participants exact words	Extracted adjectives	The adverbs of degree	Level
Wow, he replied!	*Quick*	*Very*	High level
Why didn't he reply?	Slow	Pretty	High level
Is he next to the computer?	Slow	So	High level
He can't surf the Internet?	Slow	too	Extreme
Is this automatic reply?	Fast	Pretty	High level

Verbal Language Environment Extraction. Another way to judge participants' attitude in the case that the feedback we got did not contain any obvious adverbs or adjectives was through the analysis of participants' verbalized assumptions, comparisons, suggestions, and expectations. After being analyzed, this language was translated into adjective-dominated declarations (Table 3).

Table 3. Verbal language environment extraction

Participants exact words	Extracted adjectives	The adverbs of degree	Level
I feel impatient, I will ask it again and again	Slow	Very	High level
I hope this store has an automatic response	Slow	So	High level
Do they have a lot of customers?	Slow	So	High level

Incidence-Description Extraction. The third way we could judge participants' attitude using feedback without any obvious adverbs or adjectives was through participants' descriptions of the test process. We analyzed the movement and brain function of the participants. Following analysis, the data was also translated into adjective-dominated declarations (Table 4).

Classification of Adjectives. The data—adjectives and adverbs—were then coded in accordance with the guidelines set forth by Ma Shi When Tong. First, adjectives were classified according to whether they were positive or negative. If an adjective expressed a relatively pleasant position (such as "good" or "easy"), it was coded as positive (+). If an adjective expressed a relatively unfavorable position, such as tension or worry, it was coded as negative (−). After classifying the adjectives, the total amount of each

Table 4. Incidence-description extraction

Participants exact words	Extracted adjectives	The adverbs of degree	Level
I want to do something else when I wait for the answers, if nothing can be done like this, so that is waste of my time	Long	Very	High level
I think I've been waiting all the time	Slow	Too	Extreme
He is a responsible customer service	Quick	So	High level

kind of adjective was determined. In our analysis here, this amount is expressed by the number n occurrences of each adjective type.

Adverbs were coded differently. Because the participants' reports were recorded in Chinese and, for the sake of accuracy, analyzed in Chinese, the processing of adverbs made reference to the local grammar. According to the XinHua Dictionary, adverbs of degree can be divided into four categories: intense, high, moderate, and low. According to these categories, adverbs extracted from the data were arranged on a Likert scale with eight levels. Intense, high, moderate, and low positive adverbs were assigned 4, 3, 2, and 1 points, respectively. Likewise, intense, high, moderate, and low negative adverbs were assigned −4, −3, −2, and −1 points, respectively. Neutral adverbs were assigned 0 points (Table 5).

Table 5. Research degree adverbs of degree

Level of gradable adverb	Level of gradable adverb in paper
Extreme	Too, extremely
High level	Also, very, quite, pretty, especially, utterly, fully, so, fairly, such, particularly, incomparable
Medium grade	Relatively, even more, still more
Lower	Slightly, a little

Experiment 3. In Experiment 3, the participants will complete the n parts same as Experiment 2 and when they complete each part, they have to rate the affective dimensions using the Self-Assessment Manikin (Fig. 3).

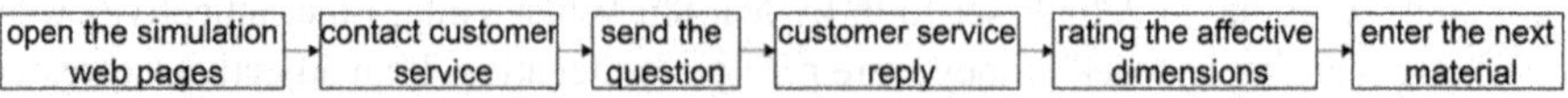

Fig. 3. Experiment 3 process

The Self-assessment Manikin. The participant need to rate their emotion in 9 levels (upset and calm). 1 is very irritable, 9 is very calm, 5 is the intermediate emotion between irritable and calm. Assessment materials are the Self-Assessment Manikin by Bradley and Lang (1994).

3 Results

3.1 Experiment 1

This study tested what is the last straw of subjects when they wait for the Customer Services reply in three kinds of products respectively.

When buying food item online (such as Three Squirrels), subjects' average impatience time T1 is 31.9 s. While buying Office Supplies online (such as Deli), the average impatience time T1 is 31.3 s. As for the clothing category which took Sundance as an example, T1 is 33.3 s (Experimental result has listed in the following Fig. 4).

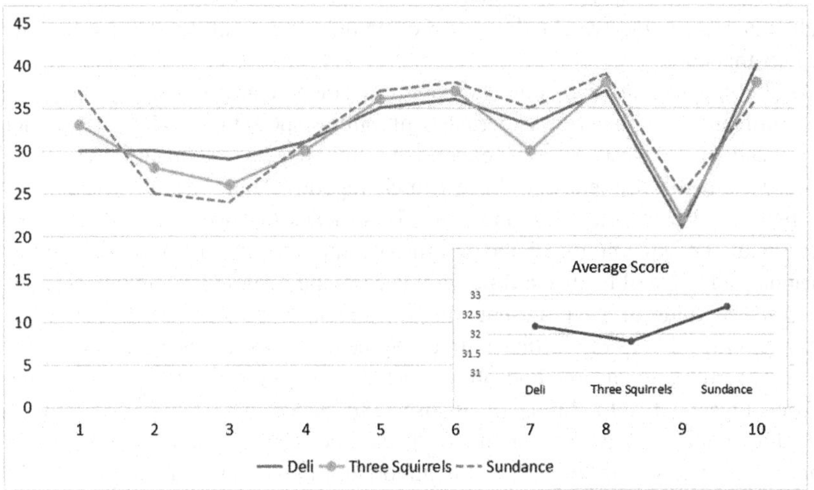

Fig. 4. Limit waiting time of the participants

3.2 Experiment 2

In experiment 2, the subjective experience of 11 tests used the same experimental materials, the only difference between these tests is the time of customer services reply. While testing, the experimenter recorded the subjective verbal reports, then analyzing the emotion of these reports. At last, calculating average of subjects' positive and negative emotion then divided into five levels.

The first thing to be done in this experiment is determining the positive and negative tendencies of user experience. For instance, user A said: "wow! It replies me so fast!" So the positive emotion can be identified from a response like this. Secondly, using the grading scale above, adverbs of degree were added to the existing positive and negative adjective tallies, and weighted at a value of 4, 3, 2, or 1 according to which of the four adverb categories they belonged to. According to the method of emotional analysis based on verbal Chinese (Tan and Sun 2015), we calculated the user experience using this formula.

$$S_{UX} = \frac{1}{N}\sum_{i=1}^{m}(n_i \bullet a_i) \tag{1}$$

Where

$$N = \sum_{i=1}^{m} n_i \tag{2}$$

means the total number of all adjectives belonging to the same category, n_i represents the number of occurrences of a certain grade in a certain adjective, a_i on behalf of the represented the weight value of that grade. M is 4 on behalf of the four different weights, and S_{ux} is the weighted average of participants' evaluations of different tests based on this data.

As the experiment only aims to explore a single factor's, namely the feedback time's influence on the user experience of online shopping, and every participant experienced all 11 tests of this experiment, the results are ideal. The adjectives extracted from the original data have a high repetitive rate and all of them can be classified into 2 categories: fast and slow. This means that we can easily rule out the influence of the uncertainty of the weight of other factors and focus on the unidimensional influence of feedback time. In this case, the confidence coefficient α identity in 1. And the value of S_{ux} represents the overall user experience of specific tests.

It is obvious that as the feedback time lengthen, user experience gradually becomes worse. According to the method above, the highest score (3.09) appears when the feedback time is 3 s. In this case, all user experience are positive. And the figure reached the bottom at −3.16 when the feedback time is 31 s. So the overall range of the participants' score is 3.09 to −3.16. It is important to note that when the feedback time increased to 9 s, negative user experience appears, then positive and negative user experience coexist for the next 9 s until the feedback time lengthened to 18 s, all participants turned into negative emotion. The experimental data has shown in Table 6 and Fig. 5 listed below.

3.3 Experiment 3

We got the average scores of the affective dimensions from the participants (Table 7), then divided these scores into five levels (Table 8, Fig. 6).

At the same time, according to the scale of the test, we analyzed the score trend of customer service reply time for different shopping experience (Fig. 7), by the table can

Table 6. The experimental data of experiment 2

Experimental material	Reply	Average Score		Final average score
1st experimental material	3 s	+3.09	0.00	+3.09
2st experimental material	6 s	+2.75	0.00	+2.75
3st experimental material	9 s	+2.70	−1.00	+0.85
4st experimental material	12 s	+2.63	−1.00	+0.815
5 st experimental material	15s	+1.00	−1.80	−0.40
6st experimental material	18 s	0.00	−1.67	−1.67
7st experimental material	21 s	0.00	−1.89	−1.89
8st experimental material	24 s	0.00	−2.22	−2.22
9st experimental material	27 s	0.00	−2.38	−2.38
10 st experimental material	30 s	0.00	−3.00	−3.00
11st experimental material	33 s	0.00	−3.16	−3.16

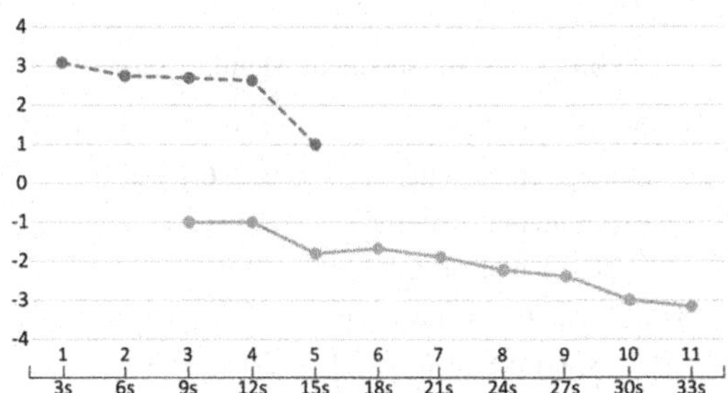

Fig. 5. Trend of self-assessment Manikin scores

be seen, in the same waiting time, Love Heart user's score is higher, the lowest score were Pink crown users. The overall trend according to the score from high to low is Heart users, Gold diamond users, Gold crown users, Pink crown users.

3.4 Analysis on the Results

By comparing the analysis results of the user's oral reports and scale scores, which prove the consistency of the user oral reports and subjective rating scale (Fig. 8).

According to the experiments, user's average limit waiting time is about 32.2 s. According to the user's oral report and scale score, users' emotion changes when waiting for the reply can divided into five grades. From the verbal reports, the level five to the level four is the transition stage of emotion, behind the third grade, start from grade four the users only have negative emotions (about 15 s). The third level was the user's positive and negative emotion change level. In summary, we divided the point of user's emotional change into three stages (Fig. 9), the first stage is 0–8 s and the second stage is 9–17 s, and the third stage is after 18 s.

Table 7. The experimental data of experiment 3

Experimental material	The time of receiving reply	The final average score
1st experimental material	3 s	8.35
2st experimental material	6 s	7.75
3st experimental material	9 s	6.60
4st experimental material	12 s	5.90
5 st experimental material	15 s	5.10
6st experimental material	18 s	4.35
7st experimental material	21 s	3.45
8st experimental material	24 s	2.95
9st experimental material	27 s	2.45
10 st experimental material	30 s	1.65
11st experimental material	33 s	1.36

Table 8. Self-assessment Manikin score

Level	Experimental material	The time of receiving reply
5	1st, 2st experimental materials	3 s, 6 s
4	3st, 4st experimental materials	9 s, 12 s
3	5st, 6st experimental materials	15 s, 18 s
2	7st, 8st, 9st experimental materials	21 s, 24 s, 27 s
1	10st, 11st experimental materials	30 s, 33 s

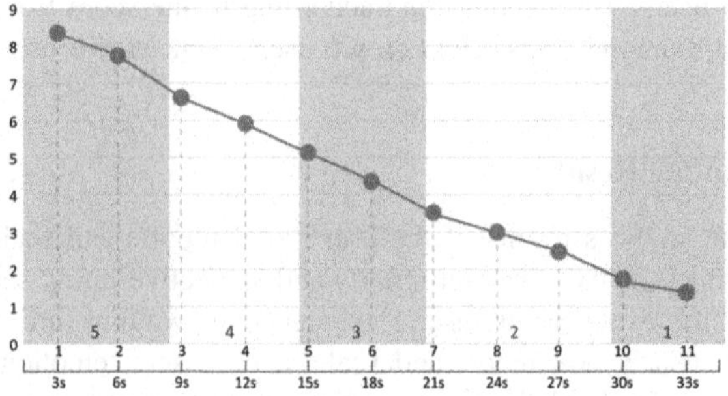

Fig. 6. Self-assessment Manikin score and levels

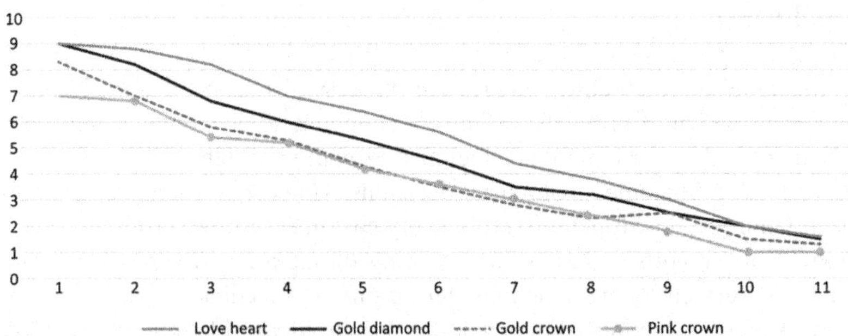

Fig. 7. Score-based trends in different shopping experience

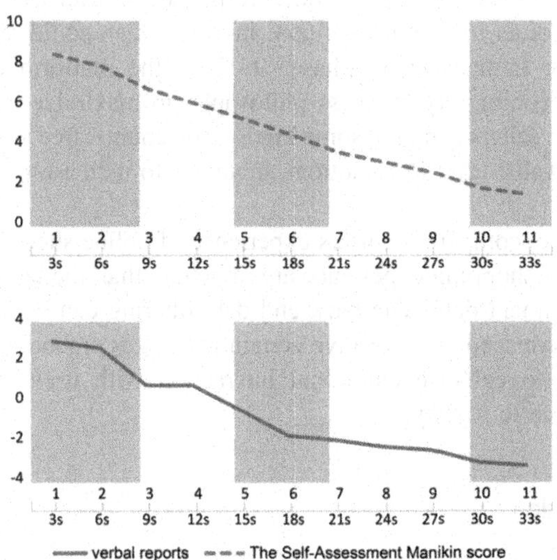

Fig. 8. Oral report and subjective rating scale

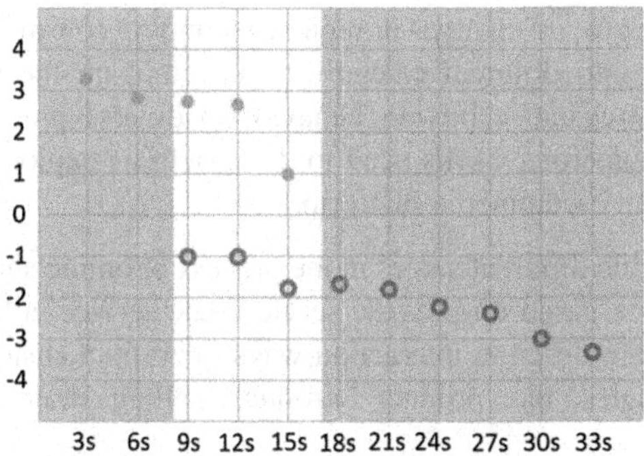

Fig. 9. Emotion change stages

4 Conclusion

Online shopping is a complex interactive process, as a whole, each procedure (browsing information of products, asking for shopping advice, purchasing orders and so on.) will affect the user experience feelings. Providing a high quality of service is a key point to affect customers' purchase decisions. However, when facing numerous customers' inquiries, it is difficult to reply every customer in time. From the analysis of the results of oral reports and subjective scoring through experiments, we found that users have different emotional reactions during different feedback delays which result in different shopping feelings. For resolving this problem, different interaction measures can be designed in each period to improve the user experience of shopping service. Form the emotional model experiment based on phased emotional experiences, we can make targeted services designed by different interactions. For example, in the initial stage (0–8 s) to give customers quick response, we translate common issues to digitally encode in order to give users fuzzy answer, which could resolve a number of customer problems. In the second phase (9–17 s), the platform can provide some information of the commodity business philosophy to maximize the users' residence time. After 18 s, the sellers can give some kinds of discounts, free postage, membership services and other value-added promotions strategies to increase the user's propensity to buy.

At the same time, compare the users experience of online shopping, it is obviously that users with more shopping experience are impatient than the less experienced users based on our experiment data. The back-end data filtering can be set to certain privileges for more experienced users or give certain privileges embodied in the consulting platform interface, to enhance emotional interaction with users and promote their emotional experience to loyalty.

5 Future Work

Experimental study in this article is limited to the Chinese online shopping platform, so there are still several problems need to be solved. At first, we will subdivide consult situations and shopping segments for the specific situation of each different process, and observe mood changes in different feedback delays under different situations, to discover user feedback mood changes in separate shopping consultations. Secondly, we will divide products into different categories, and compare the differences between different types of merchandise buying behavior in diverse product categories. Furthermore, there are numerous works need to do to help us explore more details about the user experience on e-commerce platform.

- More research on the different stages in the process of online shopping, compare the different experience based on pre-sale service, sale service, after-sale service.
- Design and compare different interaction ways to abstract customers in the website from different angles, like product introduce, selling strategy then measure its validity.

Acknowledgments. We would like to express our gratitude to Xuyi Wei, Shihui Xu and Honghong Qin who helped us during the experiment. The research was supported by National Key Technologies R&D Program of China (2015BAH22F01), National Natural Science Foundation of China (61402159/60903090), Hunan Provincial Social Science Foundation of China (2010YBA054), the State Key Laboratory of Advanced Design and Manufacturing for Vehicle Body Funded Projects.

References

Nielsen, J.: Usability Engineering. Academic Press, Boston (1993)

Hossfeld, T., Egger, S., Schatz, R., Fiedler, M., Masuch, K., Lorentzen, C.: Initial delay vs. interruptions: between the devil and the deep blue sea. In: QoMEX, Visual User Experience 1, vol. 27, pp. 1–6 (2012)

International Telecommunication Union. Mean Opinion Score (MOS) Terminology. ITU-T P800.1 (2003)

Reichl, P., Egger, S., Schatz, R., D'Alconzo, A.: The logarithmic nature of QoEand the role of the weber-fechner law in QoE assessment. In: Proceedings of the 2010 IEEE International Conference on Communications, pp. 1–5 (2010)

Egger, S., Reichl, P., Hossfeld, T., Schatz, R.: Time is bandwidth? Narrowing the gap between subjective time perception and quality of experience. In: IEEE ICC 2012 - Communication QoS, Reliability and Modeling Symposium (ICC 2012 CQRM), Ottawa, Ontario, Canada (2012)

A Whitepaper from Ericsson, Facebook and XL Axiata: Measuring and Improving Network Performance. https://fbcdn-dragon-a.akamaihd.net/hphotos-ak-xap1/t39.23656/10734295_270843076447514_1952370192_n.pdf

Loiacono, E.T., Watson R.T., Goodhue, D.L.: Web qual: a measure of website quality. In: Proceedings of the Winter Educator's Conference, American Marketing Association, Chicago, pp. 432–437 (2004)

Christie, B.: Research finds life is a three second experience. BMJ **342**(5), d750 (2011)

Tan, H., Sun, J.: Differences between the user experience in automatic and driverless cars. In: IASDR Interplay, 1975–1983 (2015)

Ma, J.: Ma Shi Wen Tong. Business Press, Shanghai (2010)

Bradley, M.M., Lang, P.J.: Measuring emotion: the self-assessment Manikin and the semantic differential. J. Behav. Ther. Exp. Psychiatry **25**, 49–59 (1994)

Design for Transition to a Circular Economy

Hao Yang(✉)

College of Design and Innovation, Tongji University, Shanghai, China
barbaray@163.com

Abstract. There are problems and challenges in transition to a circular economy in China. The challenges may vary from micro scope to macro scope: the micro scope, that of individual behavior, relates to the consumption habits in one's everyday life; the meso scope, that of groups where the individual may still have some influence, involves the companies and organizations with their ways of producing and delivering their products and services; the macro scope, that of ecosystem, which means seeing the natural domain and human society as a whole system. Alternative to the government-oriented reform, companies should take the lead in the transition from bottom-up. There are catalysts needed to get companies change. Design, with its various capabilities, could provide "activation energies".

Keywords: Reusing and sharing · Value creation · Empathy · Context · Product service system design

1 Introduction

A circular economy is an alternative to a traditional linear economy (make, use, dispose) in which we keep resources in use for as long as possible, extract the maximum value from them whilst in use, then recover and regenerate products and materials at the end of each service life [1]. The transition towards a circular economy has the potential to change the situation that economy growth is heavily dependent on resource consumption in China. It works to decouple the economic development and the resource consumption. Circular economy approaches save industry money through reduced cost of resources and energy, generate revenue from waste streams and retention of value in existing infrastructure, as well as assets through new business models such as leasing.

The development of circular economy thoughts originated in 1966, when Boulding presented the idea in his spacecraft economy, a shift way of thinking from the traditional open system to a circulation of closed loop of materials; in 1989, with Pearce putting forward the use of the word "Circular Economy" in English, and the rising of Industrial Ecology in the 1990's, research on circular economy formed its imposing manner; since 2010, In UK, the Ellen MacArthur Foundation (hereinafter referred to as EMF) has led the upgrading to an optimized version, with the joint efforts from enterprise and higher education.

3R, namely reduce, reuse, and recycle, is the operation principle of circular economy. There are two directions of development followed this 3R principle. The one focuses

P.-L.P. Rau (Ed.): CCD 2016, LNCS 9741, pp. 800–807, 2016.
DOI: 10.1007/978-3-319-40093-8_79

on recycle, mainly related to waste management; the other one underlines reuse, as Stahel and other, claiming a new economic system.

Over the past decade in China, the main approaches to transit to the circular economy are mostly from top down and government took the initiatives. For example, from 2001 to 2011, in ten years, 60 state-level eco-industry parks had been constructed to demonstrate the systemic circulation of ecological industrial organization. However, to truly realize the circular economy transformation, especially at the city level, enterprises should be the leading force. Different from the government, with large amount of investments to stimulate the transformation, seeking out consistently profitable model with the framework and concept provided by circular economy and design innovation, is the key for enterprises to success. In addition to developing venous industry of recycling, the tendency today is towards to develop second-hand goods exchange, sharing economic or collaborative consumption. Many projects that are currently operating need to be connected in order to form a systemic circulation. Bottom up projects initiated by companies should become major contributors.

To realize this systemic transformation, the challenges may vary from micro scope to macro scope: the micro scope, that of individual behavior, relates to the consumption habits in one's everyday life; the meso scope, that of groups where the individual may still have some influence, involves the companies and organizations with their ways of producing and delivering their products and services; the macro scope, that of ecosystem, where the natural domain and human society should be regarded and researched as a whole system.

These are enormous challenges; we are facing the notion of complex interaction, iteration and uncertainty. What is calling is a systemic approach which unifies and concentrates on the interaction between elements and the effects of those interactions, and integrates the relationships during the course of time.

Design, with its nature of solving problem through synthesis, has potential to take up the challenges from various scopes mentioned above through interventions in various levels of system and at various action points in processes to build up a regenerative cycle in a new ecosystem.

In UK, the interdisciplinary collaboration in the innovation to accelerate the transition to circular economy is emphasized, and design is regarded as one of the three main driven forces. In the book The Circular Economy: A Wealth of Flows, a publication by EMF in 2015, circular economy is defined as: "one that is restorative by design, and which aims to keep products, components and materials at their highest utility and value, at all times." The highlight of design is obvious. Design is put at the key position to the implementation of circular economy.

2 Challenges in Closing the Loop of Reuse

Walter Stahel stated reuse as good strategy: "The linear model turned services into products that can be sold, but this throughput approach is a wasteful one. In the past, reuse and service-life extension were often strategies in situations of scarcity or poverty and led to products of inferior quality. Today, they are signs of good resource husbandry and smart management." [2].

Where living standards are low, sharing may well be the only way to afford commodities. At the beginning of the 20th century in Europe, shared cooking and washing facilities were typical in the apartment buildings; people were used to waiting in turn to use something. After the Second World War, the quick growth of economy changed the situation, and the microwave and the washing machine are considered to be basic needs for every household. Today in China, shared electric appliance and facilities could be found at many places in less developed areas, such as remote rural villages and city slums; while in the modern cities, shared facilities are rare in new built communities, and every family has their own household appliances.

In the era of consumption, a kind of consumer habit has been cultivated that people are inclined to possess a product in order to use it at any time one wants to, and to define one's own status, even the product is not useful for him. In a recent survey in China's rural area, videos were recorded of the 24-h daily behavior in the household; a phenomenon was discovered that the refrigerator in the kitchen was seldom used and always empty, but in the village where this survey was taken place, every household had at least one refrigerator. Villagers bought refrigerator as it was perceived as a sign of modern life style and got ambivalence to it after figuring out they do not need it as they easily access to fresh food.

Normally, a consumer makes the choice between leasing and temporarily using a product supplied by a provider and buying a product for owning it, depending on consideration of the following aspects:

- Relative affordability
- Functionality and usage
- Freedom and convenience
- Identity and status

The first two are commonly considered together. When buying is expensive and the product is only needed for once or for a very short period of time, chances are that the product will be rented rather than be bought. But, if renting is barely cheaper than buying, and the product provided not attractive or well maintained, it will be the opposite. In many cases, the last two aspects are more decisive. With the traditional linear model, companies try to sell more goods to generate profit. For example consumers are encouraged to possess a whole set of kitchen appliances and utensils, even some tools are barely used. They buy for the convenience that they can use it whenever they want. The reason they buy these sought of tools is also because renting is not as easily accessed as buying in today's community. Another example is that companies upgrade their products frequently and consumers are incited to buy the new series when their old version products are still working well. In these cases, people buy to show who they are. People own much more than they use which is why it is so difficult to compete with economic material growth. Sharing and renting somehow have to find their way in. New business models for sharing and reusing are to be designed, and consumer habits and behaviors should be carefully studied and considered.

In China, from rural to urban areas, a lot of bottom-up social innovation practices have been emerged, kinds of sustainable products and sharing services are provided by small start-ups, and certain companies are exploring into new business models to get profit through maximizing the product usage and extending its service life. But regarded to China's overall economic scale, these practices are still in a state of fragmented. On the contrary to these emerging practices, most of the existing mainstream businesses still maintain a certain market, and the products they provide are closely connected to the consumers' habits and unsustainable ways of living. They take a wait-and-see attitude to transition to the new circular model, and regard that reform will be beneficial only when the company getting privilege by policies and/or getting large amount of investigation from government.

At the same time, most of the company's internal structures of organization are bound to the linear economic model, transformation means more than just researching and developing innovative sustainable products and services, it also means that the company needs internal organization reform. Moreover, comparing to many start-ups and social companies initiated by designers, where open design is regarded as the main approach to achieve innovative outcomes, those traditional companies with linear business models oversee the design capabilities. Their understandings of design are still staying in the design 1.0 era. Many of them only look into the technical sphere to find innovative solutions when they are seeking ways of change. For a time, mainly in the top-down approaches, companies adopted new technologies to produce more eco-friendly products, for which more cost added to purchase new materials and pay for new crafting processes. In many ways, the perception of sustainability has come to a notion of high cost and low profit. For lacking of understanding of design and underestimating design's capability, many companies ignored possible opportunities to gain profit and growth when developed sustainable business models and delivered products and services in sustainable ways.

In China, design thinking and open innovation should be introduced to the mainstream companies, such as textile, home appliances manufacturers. Design thinking and open design methods could help them to change mindset and reform their internal organizational structure, to become more innovative and more adaptable to the present situation of rapid transformation. Via ongoing efforts in co-creation practices, they will find the way to change and growth; and become successful adopter of the new economy.

3 Capabilities of Design for Enabling the Transition

There are "activation energies" required to get business to change. Could design offer the energies in need? Mainly in three ways design could be beneficial and act as catalyst to the transition.

The value creation by design could be one of these "activation energies". Design always has the capability to recognize unusual opportunities to create value, particularly intangible one [3]. Intangible value creation in the process of service is enabled by design of the product service system. Experience, social connection, and other kinds of intangible values are the reason consumer would like to adopt the sharing and renting than the buying.

When Uber, a smart car service provider, came to China, it launched an event of "celebrity drives for you". People were excited in taking Uber cars for the opportunity of meeting celebrities. Although it was only a temporary service provided, it highlighted and made it visible that the trip with Uber has different experience from taking a taxi or driving by oneself. It is about serendipity to meet with interesting people, interesting cars and at the same time a convenient and relax trip. It was this intangible value which other kind of services don't offer. As a series services similar to this are emerging in the market, people are more and more considering taking alternative way when travel.

In a community creation project in an old area in Shanghai city last winter, designer built up a small playground at the street corner for children living in the community using abandoned bike racks at the site. It was also taken as a neighborhood interaction space by the residents when completed. The project had a very low budget for moving the bike racks to shape the game installation, changing the surface color for a vivid appearance for the kid's preference, and wrapping up the steel frame with shockproof packaging material to achieve security, but a completely different experience were gained, and a whole new service life was given to the used bike racks. It is the design eyes see the shape of bike rack and the space it formats usually provide the use of parking bikes could, in another way, be used as a space for children to climb and play.

Recently, Alibaba added a new application Idle Fish to its successful app group served as a platform for users to exchange second-hand items; it connects to Taobao, the successful C2C online shopping platform founded in May 2003 by Alibaba, and shares many existing resources in Taobao application, to provide the accessibility of second-hand transactions. On this platform, many items were formerly purchased from Taobao, product information is already available and easily to forward to the second hand trading platform, great convenience is offered smartly. And through this platform, people interested in similar products or related topics in everyday life exchange ideas, stories and photos, social connections are thus built up. In this context, reusing and sharing are no longer signs of negative status, but a kind of culture of social interaction. Experience and the social connection are the two examples of mindset shift engine which make the reusing and sharing valuable choices to consumers.

The second "activation energy" design could provide is empathy. Companies normally think of users in terms of market segments. Normally in a consumer questionnaire, preferences are separate and cannot provide an integrated image for consumer to choose, they can only rely on the image they try to form up by the limited information provided and with reference to the existing products on the market. These surveys can hardly be helpful as people make decisions finally in an integrated way. And they are especially weak when encountering the case that designers try to change the consumer behavior by design intervention. People may not tell you how they will make an alternative choice. The current situation is that, though many have the awareness of the environmental crisis and sustainability, they will still stay with the old ways of living as long as the market provides the same kind of services as before. With the stereotype image of the access model services, directly asking question to the customers can only get similar answers showing the current phenomenon. Design process can explore the potential needs people do not know to ask. By an approach of observation of what people do and with methods of user study it could lead to real insights.

There are successful examples of understanding users by design empathy and coming up with new business opportunity. TU Delft IDE student Sarah Bork carried out her graduation project at Interface®. Interface® is floor covering provider and an early Access Model adopter. Sarah researched related services provided by other companies such as cleaners, architects and installers. In her research, she figured out nuance differences between users, this helped her to come up with differentiated Product Service System, with three types of users: "high image", "true green & functional", and "fast movers". Distinguishing between different kinds of users doubles the economic lifespan of carpet tiles from 7 to 14 years, leading to a match of economic and technical lifespan. Lowering recycling frequency and offering more pricing flexibility improves interface's financial performance [4].

Then comes to the third "activation energy" design is capable to contribute to make the change. It is the ability to visualize ideas. By visualizing and prototyping ideas, giving abstract ideas concrete images and shapes, design makes the stakeholders see possibilities in an integrated way, and enables user tests in a transformed context. Even in the case of no new product is needed, for example the sharing or reusing of an existing product, visualizing the activities and interaction between users and stakeholders, involving all elements in the context and environment services provided, designers and co-creators can discuss and compare different options. With a set stage for the test, user behavior could be studied in the new context transformed by the new service provided. And this is vital for innovative ideas which do not have reference in the current situation.

4 Changing Contexts in Design

Establishing product service system by design is the key to accelerate the transition and enable the circulation of reusing and sharing. A "product-service-system" is a blend of products, communication strategies, services and spaces that are used in an integrated way to offer comprehensive, ethical solutions to complex demands [5]. Designing product service system for access business model under the principle of reuse for a circular economy, the design principles and contexts are shifting.

The center of the product-service-system is the people (users, suppliers, employees, or stakeholders in general) who interact with all these multiple design components, which are part of the system as well. Not only users but all people, and their activities, interactions needed to be considered in the systems. Different with the products designed for individual owning for a long time, when coming to the design for a product of service, for example a product for share and reuse, the contexts it will be used in are varied. For example, differentiated demanding and preferences will occur when designing a table for rental in a co-working space, as the user will work in a collaborative mode and may have different interactions with the table and with other people working together with him in such context. And the return of the table after use, the disassembly and/or repair by the providers, the material and resource effectiveness are all important issues to be considered, to ensure each link in the process of circulation being connected easily and fluently. The principles for this design goal are as followed: ease of maintenance and repair, ease of dis- and reassemble, adaptability and upgradability, standardization and compatibility. In addition to this, understanding that the human activities and behaviors are influenced by the instant environment and the context is also fundamental for working with the context for a product service system. Complex interaction, iteration and uncertainty are the notion may designers encounter. A dynamic and systemic vision is needed when comes to the context of a product service system for an access business model.

In case study of the sharing and reusing service in China, it shows that the adopter and user of those services are a very specific group of people. These are neither the normally range of demographic characteristics nor a propensity to buy things within the categories of interest to a company. These are people with intention to collaborate and who are more open to the sustainable way of living, and they are all match the storytelling of the specific service. Thus it can be seen that the development and operation of a specific sharing and reuse service model need to find its specific user group. It requires solid field survey and user study, as well as working and creating together with the potential users to generate real vital system of products and services.

Work on complex projects goes beyond the knowledge of one person to require the knowledge and skills of people from different disciplines. They need to coordinate their activities and synthesize their knowledge. Here, designers are to be working together with experts from ends of market, business and technology, as well as together with potential users and possible stakeholders. Designers will not only work on the products or the graphics which are the traditional orders for design discipline, they are to be working on the synthesis of the activities and knowledge of all the participators. They will design and generate new tools and methods to communicate with experts, users and stakeholders, to ensure their ideas and potential needs are properly communicated; and they will need also to provide convenient tools and friendly interfaces in order to create more open and innovative atmosphere for all the people working together.

5 Conclusions

Apart from the market, looking to the current situation in design education in China, could we say that the framework and worldview of circular economy has taken its place in what we understand of design and the general sense of problem solving? There is a good reservoir of teachers and many enthusiastic learners who wish to see change for the better, a more prosperous, thriving world and citizens active in their democracies. This has been true for the decade but it is hard to say that it has operated to create more than in a piecemeal fashion.

Design schools or colleges can serve as a special agency, playing an important role in promoting enterprises' transformation to circular economy. It is not just because the design schools and colleges are the incubator for cultivating the future talents in design, but also because they are the active agencies for innovation practices, researches and experiments, collaborating with enterprises, scientific research institutions, technology development department and government. They are to work in the context of the big picture demand of the circular economy in world view, pedagogy, skills and aptitudes as well as new knowledge, and for the integrated systems which could work on the larger scale to create circular cities.

References

1. http://www.wrap.org.uk/search/gss/circular%20economy
2. Webster, K.: The Circular Economy a Wealth of Flow. Ellen MacArthur Foundation Publishing, Isle of Wight (2015)
3. Whitney, P.: Design and the economy of choice. J. Des. Econ. Innov. **1**, 57–78 (2015)
4. Bakker, C., den Hollander, M., van Hinte, E., Zijlstra, Y.: The Product That Last. TU Delft Library, Delft (2014)
5. http://www.design.polimi.it/pssd/?lang=en

To Save or Not to Save? Let Me Help You Out: Persuasive Effects of Smart Agent in Promoting Energy Conservation

Guo Yu, Pei-Luen Patrick Rau(✉), Na Sun, and Xiang Ji

Department of Industrial Engineering, Institute of Human Factors and Ergonomics, Tsinghua University, Beijing 100084, China
rpl@mail.tsinghua.edu.cn

Abstract. In public places, people's energy conservation decisions and behaviors are easily suppressed by contextual and/or personal factors. To perform and maintain energy-saving behaviors, people need to be empowered both externally and internally. This research explored how a smart agent could help. The first study revealed that when a smart agent empowered people externally by offering help, people would be more active and resolute in decision-making and more likely to save energy, while some would be unaffected and decide to use energy. The second study found that the acknowledgement of behavioral impact could significantly facilitate people's evaluation processes and enhance their self-efficacy, but such effects would be moderated by the time cost of a task, which was proved positively correlated with the perceived task difficulty. Both theoretical and practical implications for energy conservation were discussed, and six guidelines for smart agent design were proposed.

Keywords: Energy conservation · Self-efficacy · Persuasive agent · Empowerment · Behavioral impact

1 Introduction

As the internet of things is burgeoning, there have been more possibilities that we can promote energy conservation by building an intelligent home or office environment (Roalter et al. 2010) since energy use could be visualized, monitored, and controlled with ease.

The advantages of an intelligent energy-saving environment would not be fully exploited if human factors were omitted. For instance, if notifications or feedbacks were not properly designed, it would hardly boost people's awareness of energy use (Anker-Nilssen 2003). Furthermore, however powerful an intelligent system is, we should remember that it will take time for the system to spread and get fully implemented, and any system could fail, hence people's own determination and efforts are indispensable in intensifying and sustaining their optimal performance in energy conservation. Therefore, this research tried to find out what design features of the system could make energy conservation noticeable in a certain context, easy to achieve, and durable without external aids, as well as how would people react to those features and why would they

P.-L.P. Rau (Ed.): CCD 2016, LNCS 9741, pp. 808–815, 2016.
DOI: 10.1007/978-3-319-40093-8_80

do so? Two empirical studies were conducted to answer these questions and a set of guidelines for persuasive agent design were proposed.

2 Literature Review

2.1 Motivators and Barriers to Energy-Saving Behavior

Most models think that user's environmentally behavior is determined by user's environmental consciousness or environmental concern (H'Mida et al. 2008). Two groups of factors would influence user's intension and behavior. One is internal/psychological factors, including user's value, attitude, knowledge, skill and ability, and perceived self-efficacy. The other is external/situational factors like social norms (Griskevicius et al. 2010), information, and other external incentives (Sahakian and Steinberger 2011). There are also some barriers. A model that explains the barriers between environmental concern and actual action (Kollmuss and Agyeman 2002) identified three barriers as individuality, responsibility, and practicability. Specially, individuality refers to barriers caused by passive attitudes (i.e., laziness, lack of environmental concerns) and personal needs (i.e., keeping warm at home) (Van Raaij and Verhallen 1983).

2.2 Self-efficacy and Behavioral Change

Self-efficacy refers to the self-appraisal to one's own capability of coping with a certain task. People would eschew the predicament which they reckon as beyond their coping capabilities, but confidently undertake what they judge themselves capable of managing (Bandura 1977). To obtain information in forming perceived self-efficacy, people would generally refer to performance attainments, vicarious experiences, verbal persuasion and physiological states (Bandura 1982). To make information instructive, cognitive appraisal should be activated, hence cues or indicator should be provided (Bandura 1981). People's self-efficacy also have a causal relationship with their action (Bandura et al. 1982). Empirical studies have proved the performance of actions to vary in response to different levels of perceived self-efficacy. Meanwhile, this causation between perceived self-efficacy and action performance could be a mutually enhancing process: At first, people's prejudgment about their self-efficacy and coping capabilities would partly determine how much efforts they would devote, then their skill acquisition and performance mastery, if satisfying, would boost their self-efficacy in return (Bandura 1982), thereby shaping a positive feedback cycle.

2.3 Persuasion and Energy Conservation

Persuasive technologies have brought new possibilities into energy conservation. One method is to visualize the energy use, enabling people to monitor energy use and get timely feedback of behavioral impact (Fischer 2008; Pierce and Paulos 2012). But many energy monitors have usability problems like users feeling "money were seeping out" as the digits flickering, or feeling routine activities like heating water being disturbed.

After a period of use, people got used to it gradually, so the feedback was no longer incentive (Hargreaves et al. 2010). Both problems could be explained by self-efficacy. People obtained more pressure than efficacy from the system, so the external incentives failed to translate into people's interests in saving energy. Therefore two features could be added to strengthen the persuasive effects of energy monitors. Firstly, let the monitor act as an embodied conversational agent (Kirby et al. 2010) that could provide recommendations in explicit or implicit ways (Xiao and Benbasat 2007). It could result in less decision time, less cognitive load, higher decision quality and higher self-confidence, hence people would gain more self-efficacy. Secondly, let the agent execute simple and repetitive tasks for people, so people would feel perceive tasks easier, and their behavioral intention can increase along with the increasing sense of control.

3 Research Framework

Based on the literature above, some hypotheses were proposed regarding user's perceived necessity of energy use, the empowerment of agent and the time cost which lead to user's perceived task difficulty and self-efficacy, as well as user's behavioral impact which leads to the evaluation process and user's perceived self-efficacy.

Necessity:

H1.1: In public places, when people need to make decision and perform action in person, they do not have obvious consensus on the necessity of a certain energy use.
H1.2: In public places, the perceived necessity of using energy would not change whether or not a smart agent could provide help, while the perceived necessity of saving energy would increase if the agent could provide help.

Empowerment and Time Cost:

H2.1: In public places, people would be more active and resolute in making decision when being served by a smart agent that could provide help compared to the one that could not.
H2.2: In public places, people would be more likely to save energy when being served by a smart agent that could provide help compared to the one that could not.
H3.1: The perceived time cost and perceived difficulty of a task would be positively correlated with the actual time cost of the task.
H3.2: The time cost of a task would moderate the effect of acknowledgement of behavioral impact.

Behavioral Impact:

H4.1 The acknowledgement of behavioral impact would reduce the time people spent in the evaluation processes.
H4.2 The acknowledgement of behavioral impact would enhance people's self-efficacy-related perceptions.

4 Study 1 – Empowerment

4.1 Methodology

Study 1 explored how people's decisions of using/saving energy would be influenced by a smart agent. 48 students of Tsinghua University (22 females, 26 males; average age = 24.48, SD = 2.24) were invited as participants. A primary-secondary task methodology was adopted in the experiment: Participants were told that their primary task was to watch a 30-min video then answer 5 questions about it. During their watching, a smart agent named Intelligent Energy-Saving Environment would interact with them on SNS, and participants were free to reply or not.

This independent variables include the Empowerment of agent and the Scenario of energy use. Empowerment was a two-level between-subject factor, classified as In Person level (Participants were both the decision maker and performer, while the Intelligent Energy-Saving Environment acted as a reminder) and Agent level (they system acted both the reminder and performer, while participants merely made decisions). Scenario was a within-subject factor with seven levels like turning off unused lights in the corridor and turning off unused water heater in the lab. To measure the influence of the Intelligent Energy-Saving Environment on the participants, their voluntary responses to the reminders were collected as an indicator of their behavioral intention. For either group, on receiving the same message, participants could choose "Save" decision, "Use" decision or "Not Decide".

4.2 Results

Chi-square test was done among the numbers of participants in the In Person group choosing "Save" decision, "Use" decision and "Not Decide" on each of the seven scenarios. It was found that in the first six scenarios, the incidence of the three types of decisions show no significant difference (all $ps > .05$), while in the seventh scenario, the incidence of S to prevail over that of U or N significantly ($p = .01$). Therefore, H1.1 was partly supported for the first six scenarios, and was not supported by the seventh scenario (Turning off unused printer in the lab). Paired t-test was done on the number of participants choosing "Use" decision between the In Person and the Agent groups. The difference was not significant ($t = 0.464$, $p = .659 > .05$), therefore the first part of H1.2 was supported. Then nonparametric test was adopted to compare the mean. There was significant between two groups ($p = .001 < .01$). Hence H2.1 was supported. For the number of participants choosing "Save" decision, paired t-test was adopted. The difference between two groups was significant ($p = .011 < .05$), indicating people made more energy-saving decisions when the smart agent could help, and hence the second part of H1.2 and H2.2 were both supported.

5 Study 2 – Self-efficacy

5.1 Methodology

Study 2 explored how people's evaluation processes and self-efficacy in energy conservation could be influenced by task difficulty and behavioral impact. 24 students of Tsinghua University (12 females, 12 males; average age = 22.4, SD = 1.24) were invited as participants. A prototype of mobile App named Energy-Saving Building would send each participant six task reminders, showing that some appliances were still on in some classrooms that had not been scheduled a class, and asked s/he to go there and have a checkup, then evaluate task from several aspects.

Independent variables include the Acknowledgement of behavioral impact as a between-subject factor, and the Time Cost of a task as a within-subject factor. Participants were divided into two groups. The Energy-Saving Building App would only show one group (denoted as Unshown) how many appliances they turned off without specific information of behavioral impact, whereas it would show the other group (denoted as Shown) how many appliances they had just turned off and how much energy they could conserve on each appliance. Among the six tasks assigned to each participant, three tasks took 25 s (Short) and the other three took 50 s (Long). For hypotheses testing, both objective and subjective data were collected to measure how the two factors would affect participants' evaluation processes and the perceptions related with self-efficacy.

5.2 Results

Nonparametric test of Mann-Whitney U was adopted to compare the difference. The correlation of actual time cost and perceived time cost was .627 ($p < .001$), of actual time cost and perceived difficulty was .490 ($p < .001$), and that of perceived time cost and perceived difficulty was .428 ($p < .001$). A task that took shorter time had resulted in a significantly smaller estimate of time cost compared with a task that took longer (22.74 s < 46.66 s, $U = 428.000$, $p < .001$), and similarly, a shorter task generally received a lower rating on task difficulty than a longer task (3.23 < 4.24, $U = 1190.500$, $p < .001$). Therefore H3.1 was supported. When the time cost was short (25 s), only two measurements manifested difference between two groups, whereas under longer time cost (50 s), eight measurements were significantly influenced ($p < .05$). Therefore, the hypothesis H3.2 was supported.

When the task took a longer time (50 s), all the time measurements of the Shown group were significantly smaller than the Unshown group, including the time spent on evaluating the time cost, behavioral impact, task difficulty, behavioral meaningfulness, and sense of achievement (all ps < .05). Therefore, H4.1 was supported in that the acknowledgement of behavioral impact had reduced the time in people's evaluating process. Similarly, when the time cost was long, the subjective ratings given by the Shown group on the self-efficacy-related measurements were significantly higher than the Unshown group, including the perceived behavioral impact, perceived behavioral meaningfulness, and the sense of achievement (all ps < .05). Hence H4.2 was supported for the acknowledgement of behavioral impact had enhanced people's self-efficacy.

6 Discussion

From the perspective of user's experience, it's important how users would perceive the energy-saving tasks, especially their understanding on whom that took credit after saving the energy? This question calls for the concept of agency in the field of cognitive neuroscience (Moore and Haggard 2008). Humans are also agents: They have the capacity to take actions intentionally to change the external world, and they could consciously experience such capacity through their actions. The experience of agency is, therefore, "person's sense of being in control of their actions and through this control of being responsible for, or having ownership of, the consequences of those actions" (Coyle et al. 2012). Meanwhile, people would also experience agency when interacting with an intelligent system. Empirical studies have proved that the more assistance a system provides, the less sense of agency a user would gain. Arguably, in this research, participants aided by the Intelligent Energy-Saving Environment would experience lower agency and think, "The energy was actually saved by the intelligent system", while the Energy-Saving Building would make people believe that "It was me that saved the energy!" The Intelligent Energy-Saving Environment and the Energy-Saving Building would produce disparate experience in the user-agent interaction, and result in different behavior and self-efficacy in energy conservation. At current stage we could not predict which one would be better: the Intelligent Energy-Saving Environment could make tasks much easier, but people could neither experience much agency nor gain much self-efficacy; the Energy-Saving Building could enhance self-efficacy and agency, but such incentives might satiate users in long-term.

Design Guidelines: Based on the findings and theoretical basis, the following six design guidelines for smart agent were proposed, which are designed to persuade people to save energy.

- Give users a nudge, remind them and hint the necessity.
- Let users feel the power of control, and believe the positive outcomes are all due to their decisions.
- Understand users in different situations, and assign tasks according to users' habits, level of self-efficacy, and current situation.
- Retain reasonable uncertainty.
- Present behavioral impact.
- Keep the history, and create something new.

7 Conclusion

To promote user's energy conservation behavior in public places, this research focused on the persuasive effects of smart agent and carried out two empirical studies. The first study found that when an agent could empower people with control, people would be more active and determined in decision-making and more likely to make energy-saving decisions. The second study found that providing information about behavioral impact would facilitate people's evaluation processes and enhance their self-efficacy, and those effects would be moderated by the time cost of task, which was positively correlated to the perceived task difficulty. Then this research discussed who should take credit after saving the energy and proposed six guidelines for persuasive agent design.

Acknowledgments. The authors would like to acknowledge the sponsorship provided by the National Natural Science Foundation China grant 71188001.

References

Anker-Nilssen, P.: Household energy use and the environment: a conflicting issue. Appl. Energy **76**(1), 189–196 (2003)

Bandura, A.: Self-efficacy: toward a unifying theory of behavioral change. Psychol. Rev. **84**, 191 (1977)

Bandura, A.: Self-referent thought: a developmental analysis of self-efficacy. In: Social Cognitive Development: Frontiers and Possible Futures, pp. 200–239 (1981)

Bandura, A.: Self-efficacy mechanism in human agency. Am. Psychol. **37**(2), 122–148 (1982)

Bandura, A., Reese, L., Adams, N.E.: Microanalysis of action and fear arousal as a function of differential levels of perceived self-efficacy. J. Pers. Soc. Psychol. **43**(1), 5–21 (1982)

Coyle, D., Moore, J., Kristensson, P.O., Fletcher, P., Blackwell, A.: I did that!: measuring users' experience of agency in their own actions. In: Proceedings of the 2012 ACM Annual Conference on Human Factors in Computing Systems, pp. 2025–2034. ACM (2012)

Fischer, C.: Feedback on household electricity consumption: a tool for saving energy? Energy Effi. **1**(1), 79–104 (2008)

Griskevicius, V., Tybur, J.M., Van den Bergh, B.: Going green to be seen: status, reputation, and conspicuous conservation. J. Pers. Soc. Psychol. **98**(3), 392–404 (2010)

H'Mida, S., Chávez, E., Guindon, C.: Determinant of pro-environmental behaviors within individual consumers. J. Econ. Lit. Classif. M **31**, 1–12 (2008)

Hargreaves, T., Nye, M., Burgess, J.: Making energy visible: a qualitative field study of how householders interact with feedback from smart energy monitors. Socio-Econ. Trans. Towards Hydrogen Econ. – Find. Eur. Res. Regul. Pap. **38**(10), 6111–6119 (2010). doi:10.1016/j.enpol.2010.05.068

Kirby, R., Forlizzi, J., Simmons, R.: Affective social robots. Robot. Auton. Syst. **58**(3), 322–332 (2010)

Kollmuss, A., Agyeman, J.: Mind the gap: why do people act environmentally and what are the barriers to pro-environmental behavior? Environ. Educ. Res. 8(3), 239–260 (2002)

Moore, J., Haggard, P.: Awareness of action: inference and prediction. Conscious. Cogn. **17**(1), 136–144 (2008)

Pierce, J., Paulos, E.: Beyond energy monitors: interaction, energy, and emerging energy systems. In: Proceedings of the 2012 ACM Annual Conference on Human Factors in Computing Systems, pp. 665–674. ACM (2012)

Roalter, L., Kranz, M., Möller, A.: A middleware for intelligent environments and the internet of things. In: Yu, Z., Liscano, R., Chen, G., Zhang, D., Zhou, X. (eds.) UIC 2010. LNCS, vol. 6406, pp. 267–281. Springer, Heidelberg (2010)

Sahakian, M.D., Steinberger, J.K.: Energy reduction through a deeper understanding of household consumption. J. Ind. Ecol. **15**(1), 31–48 (2011)

Van Raaij, W.F., Verhallen, T.M.: A behavioral model of residential energy use. J. Econ. Psychol. **3**(1), 39–63 (1983)

Xiao, B., Benbasat, I.: E-commerce product recommendation agents: use, characteristics, and impact. MIS Q. 31(2), 137–209 (2007)

The Innovation Research of Takeaway O2O Based on the Concept of Service Design

Mei Yu Zhou, Pei Xu(✉), and Pei Long Liang

School of Art Design and Media, ECUST, M.BOX 286, NO. 130, Meilong Road, Xuhui District, Shanghai 200237, China
zhoutc_2003@163.com, {987375724,798491428}@qq.com

Abstract. With the status of service industry in the social and economic increasing, service design is received widespread attention. Touch point is an important part of service design, that is the dynamic interaction between the user and the service system, which affects the user's overall perception of the level of service. Takeaway Online to Offline as a vertical kind of special life service, the essence of which is to meet the needs of users, providing the most optimized dining solution. But there are many problems in the process of development of Takeaway Online to Offline, for instance, the food is not delivered on time, the food is not health, which seriously affect the quality of service. In order to explore the optimization direction of the Takeaway Online to Offline service, this paper, basing on the theory of touch point, fully analyses the touch point of the process of takeout online to offline service from the perspective of service design, and puts forward the methods and suggestions of optimization of service experience, which includes two aspects. On the one hand, from macro level, that is establishing reasonable division system, shaping brand image and perfecting the mechanism of evaluation. On the other hand, from micro level, that is establishing food community and reward system, indicating the operating state of peak period of business operators, and designing behavior of personnel distribution.

Keywords: Takeaway from online to offline · Service design · Touch point

1 An Exploration of Service Models of Takeaways O2O

With the increasing prevalence of smart phones and rapid development of internet, O2O service has gradually entered people's lives. At present, Takeaway is the most popular O2O service. According to permanent data, Takeaway is expected to amount to RMB120 billion in China in 2015, and there will be more than 0.2 billion online users [1]. Stimulated by such market environment, internet companies have successively made plans and practised. In 2013, "Alibaba" Group launched a mobile catering platform known as "Taodiandian". In the mean time, "Meituan "launched its takeaway services online based on its advantages in group purchase. In 2014, "Baidu Waimai" (Takeaway) was launched online, and the website "Dianping" strategically invested 80 million US dollars to become a shareholder of "ele.me". The takeaway industry that has been constantly invested has tended to

P.-L.P. Rau (Ed.): CCD 2016, LNCS 9741, pp. 816–823, 2016.
DOI: 10.1007/978-3-319-40093-8_81

achieve explosive development. Internet enterprises try to connect users with sellers in all possible ways, so competition has become extremely fierce (Fig. 1).

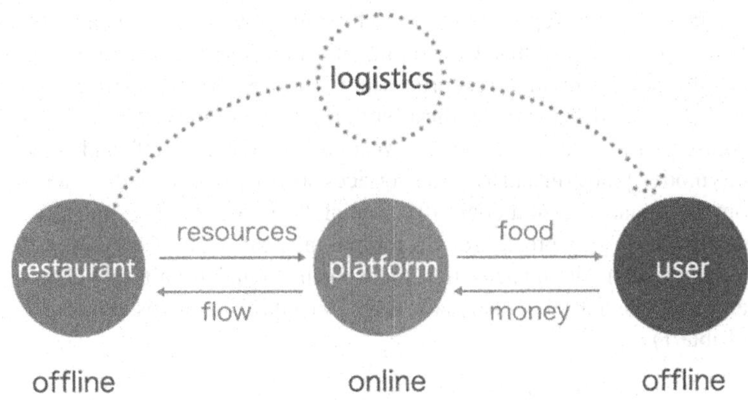

Fig. 1. Takeaway O2O platform

Table 1. The brief introduction of the development model of Takeaway O2O

Takeaways	Target	Model	Brief introduction
Ele.me	Universities	Platform	Online/offline integrated operation
Meituan	All	Platform	Take advantage of resources of group buying
Taodiandian	All	Platform	"Taobao + Tmall" model
Baidu waimai	All	Platform	Map-based takeaway platform
WaimaiChaoren	White-collars, foreigners	Platform + logistics	Global food ordering platform
Shanghai Daojia	Urban families	Platform + logistics	Delicious takeaway food for families
Line0	Urban white-collars	Platform + logistics	Catering service providers
Etaoshi	All	Platform + logistics	One-stop platform of catering functions
SHBJ	All	Platform + logistics	LBS-based SHBJ catering services
Dianwoba	Middle/high-end	Platform + logistics	Extensive takeaway websites
Yes, I Deliver	White-collars	Platform	Ordering takeaway by cell phone

Due to uncertainties of takeaway products and complexity of target groups, takeaway market is still highly fragmented. According to availability of independent logistics distribution system, its service model may be divided into two categories as follows. One is light platform represented by Meituan (i.waimai.meituan.com), ele.me (www.ele.me) and Baidu waimai. Concerning this model, services are provided through platforms without logistics and food processing. They deliver orders received online to sellers and have food distributed by third-party logistics companies. The other is heavy model represented by platforms such as "WaimaiChaoren", "line0" and "etaoshi". As regards this model, platform and logistics services are provided without food processing. Apart from these mainstream models, differentiated service strategies are also explored by some platforms to seek breakthroughs for making profits. By connecting sellers with users through thematic dating activities, the website "5qnc" hasn't only enriched UGC (User Generated Content), but also made users' social relationships closer and services stickier (Table 1).

2 Outstanding Problems with Development of Takeaway O2O

To maximize interests of users and businesses, takeaway platforms strive to provide the best services. In spite of different service models, they have met some common problems that greatly impact quality of their services in the course of their development.

1. Worrying Safety and Hygiene of Takeaway. Food safety and hygiene have been always pain points of takeaway industry. For instance, to rapidly expand their scale, Takeaway O2O platforms like "ele.me" haven't developed strict procedures to review food providers joining in their platforms. As a result, these platforms are mixed with some merchants who are unqualified for providing food. Additionally, administrative departments' supervision over takeaway platforms is inadequate that they fail to appropriately cope with users' complaints. After investigating and analyzing takeaway platforms, it is discovered from the perspective of collaborative innovation that a complete scientific food and beverage safety and hygiene management system, including some incentives and legal regulations, focusing on internal drives of service platforms and supported by external supervision, shall be established, in order to improve users' acceptance of takeaway safety, on the grounds that takeaway safety and hygiene don't only impact brand image and business performances of takeaway platforms, but also arouse people's worries about the whole industry of Takeaway O2O.

2. Backward Construction of Logistics Services. At present, light model is major service model of mainstream companies of Takeaway O2O. In other words, only platforms are built, while food and beverage are delivered by third-party logistics companies. In this case, food delivery is completely out of companies' control. As a result, problems about untimely food delivery and food safety may be easily caused. Users complain about these problems most frequently, which happen for several reasons as follows. On one hand, it is so complex and time-consuming to make independent logistics distribution available that takeaway companies are reluctant to invest money in that respect, but concentrate more on increasing their online orders. On the other hand, crazy price subsidy has consumed most cash of companies, so no more capital is available for logistics construction. However, food delivery is an important part of online services and a major factor for users' perceived experience of services. Therefore, it is a crucial aspect to be explored in creatively designing services of Takeaway O2O.

3. Crazy Price Support and Unreasonable Resource Allocation. As a high-frequency and low-price industry, Takeaway O2O is highly attractive for users in terms of its price, so all takeaways consider price support as an important development strategy. It is just because of this that takeaways have cost much money for competition in this respect. For instance, the website "ele.me" has launched an event of free lunch for 200, 000 people together with Focus Media. In addition, it adopts policies of differential subsidy like RMB10 off for a consumption of RMB20 and RMB30 off for a consumption of RMB50. According to measurements, this platform spends a huge amount of about RMB0.1 billion every month in such events. Besides, both Baidu Waimai and Meituan are crazy about another round of financing. Thus, such "money-burning wars" becomes increasingly more intense and never appears to be suppressed at all. Although such crazy acts of "money burning" make the Takeaway O2O appear to be quite bustling, it is actually crisis-ridden. First of all, it is impossible to develop customer loyalty by price support. Once these subsidies are suspended, users will turn to other catering platforms. Next, price support is an unsustainable means involving no technologies, because much money is invested for subsidizing price of food and beverage that corresponding companies will permanently suffer losses and this will be unfavorable for sustainable development. Furthermore, insufficient resources are available from other parts of takeaway services to improve construction and lead to poor quality of the services on the whole. Price support may merely contribute to temporary rapid increase in orders, but can't be permanently practised in a sustainable manner. Only improving quality of differentiated catering services is the right development strategy for Takeaway O2O. For this purpose, resources, particularly money shall be allocated by takeaways more reasonably and efficiently. In terms of resource output, priorities are given to optimizing technologies and systems and considering core pain points for "rapid delivery" of takeaway services.

Current Takeaway O2O is still a growing market facing various problems. In the mean time, core pain points of Takeaway O2O haven't been effectively solved, and development strategies differ among takeaways. Although quality of takeaway services has been improved to certain extent after fierce market competition, on the whole, many innovative aspects of such services are worthy of exploration. Therefore, with constant expansion of businesses, better seamless experiences of catering services will be brought to users if online and offline services can be better integrated. This will not only become a key concern of takeaways, but also an important driving force for development of the whole Takeaway O2O towards correct directions.

3 Analysis on Touchpoints of Takeaway O2O

3.1 Service Touchpoints and Customer Journey Map

Like system design, service design highlights being user centered and concerned about situation of the whole service system. In the field of design, there is still no unified definition of service design. According to definition of the International Association of Societies of Design Research, service design means setting services from the standpoints of customers for the purpose of guaranteeing service interfaces. From users' points of view, services may be classified into useful, usable and good services, while they may be categorized to be efficient and distinct by service providers [2]. However, enterprises like IBM consider that service design means designing different touchpoints of users based on timeline via creative methods and processes while making constant adjustments of interactions between service providers and ultimate users. LIVE WORK, as a famous service design company in England, pointed out in 2010 that in designing services, existing design ideas, technologies and methods were incorporated into the field of services to develop innovative ideas that could effectively satisfy users' requirements for all elements by comprehensively considering multiple dimensions such as environment, products and emotions.

In the process of designing services, concept of service design is always involved no matter what methods and means are adopted. As key points for interactions between users and service systems, service touch points have significant impacts upon users' perception of services [3]. Based on forms, touch points may be divided into physical touch points, digital touch points, emotional touch points, invisible touch points and integrated touch points. A service system may have multiple such touch points. Once a user consecutively experiences several touch points of a platform, he or she will have an overall impression on services of the platform. It is thus clear that touch point design is essential for designing services of a platform.

As a major tool for designing touch points, customer journey map is a graphic method for displaying information. A complete and effective customer journey map generally includes requirements, scenarios, interactions, users' mental state and system state and so on. This method is helpful for designers to understand real feelings of users to discover pain points and opportunities of services in different stages of experience, so as to make the entire service system user-centered [4].

3.2 Analysis on Touch Points of Takeaway O2O and Innovation Strategies

After analyzing and summarizing touch points of Takeaway O2O service system, they are visually presented through a customer journey map, as shown in Fig. 2. Three modules of systematic innovative design are gained by summing up and analyzing seven main touch points.

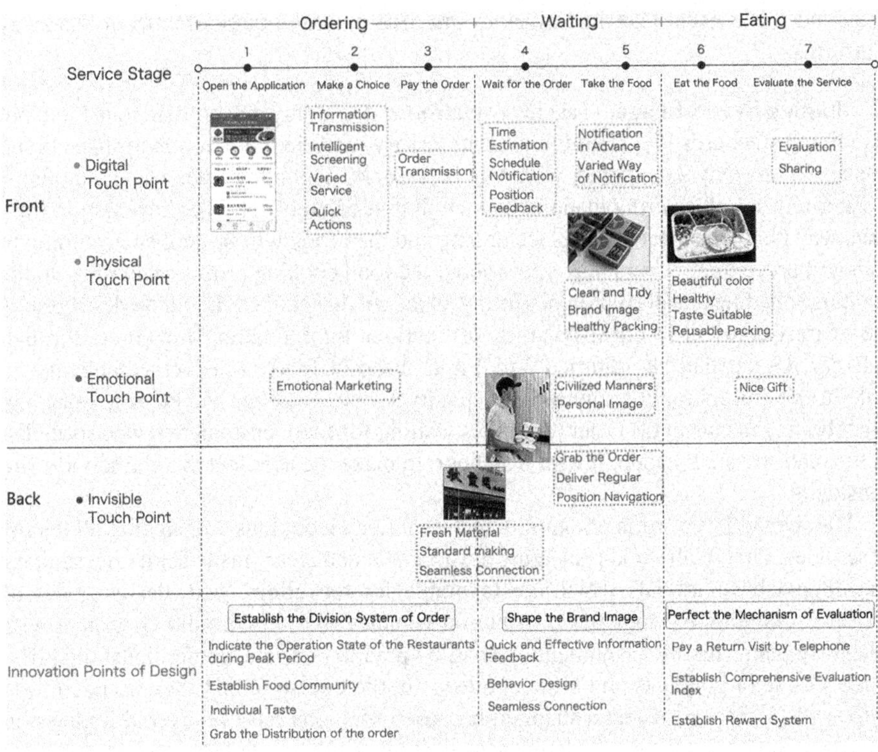

Fig. 2. Customer journey figure of Takeaway O2O

(1) Establishing an Information Diffluence Mechanism for Food Ordering. In users' waiting for food, the major pain point consists in unpunctual delivery of takeaway. This problem shall be solved from a systematic perspective. To be exact, a reasonable diffluence mechanism shall be established for the stage when users order food. It may be specifically executed from three perspectives. Firstly, a function shall be set up for food reservation by means of marketing, in order that users won't order food in rush hours. Secondly, state information of catering service providers is displayed on a real-time basis. Operation state of a catering service provider may be divided into two categories, including good and crowded. In this way, users may have certain psychological expectations in ordering food, and can accept even if food delivery is postponed. Operation state of a catering service provider may be known from data feedbacks of orders. Thirdly, sub-platforms shall be constructed for delicious food and beverage to accumulate content of users and explore characteristic delicious food for small groups of customers, so as to reduce their ordering pressure in rush hours. Meanwhile, personalized food may be customized according to tastes of users. Additionally, information about takeaways shall be effectively communicated. For instance, information of pictures shall be real and presented as far as possible, so as to help users make quick decisions. No matter what mechanism is utilized, the major objective is to minimize risks and make users take initiatives to improve natural experiences from takeaway platforms.

(2) Shaping Brand Image. Takeaway platforms don't only deliver delicious food, but also living standards [5]. Therefore, it is necessary to make more efforts to shape brand images. This may be started with two keywords, including speed and emotions. Concerning speed, catering manufacturers will immediately get order information from takeaway platforms once users place orders, and then food will be cooked according to standard procedures. Users may know about the food cooking process according to the cooking schedules displayed on platforms. Once food is cooked, it will be delivered by the nearest couriers to corresponding destinations by competing for orders through delivery. Users shall be informed 2 to 5 min ahead of food and beverage delivery, in order to give users rapid seamless high-quality service experiences. Provided that any user chooses to cancel his order during his waiting for food, customer service specialist of the platform shall handle it within an hour, to make the user feel that the services are considerate.

The second keyword is emotion, which requires meticulously designing all details of services. First of all, food packaging must be neat and clean, made from safe, sanitary and degradable materials which are favorable for recycling. Next, design styles of couriers' clothing and logistics distribution vehicles shall be visually consistent with takeaway platforms. At last, attention shall be paid to couriers' professional qualities, namely code of conducts and basic etiquettes in the course of distribution. Each food delivery is a process of brand shaping, because users may have an overall impression on services of the takeaway platform in dealing with the platform and its couriers. Therefore, brand building is an important measure for increasing user satisfaction, user flow and corporate benefits.

(3) Improving Evaluation System. At present, Takeaway O2O platforms usually consider destination of their services is to deliver food and beverage to users. In contrast, from the perspective of service sustainability, it is the beginning of another service when users begin to have the food or beverage delivered [6], on the grounds that users won't make the most important comments on takeaway quality until their eating. Food manufacturers and takeaway platforms must track users' dining feedbacks. Thus, a complete evaluation system shall be established to improve overall services. Users' perception is mainly impacted by three aspects as follows. Firstly, relationship between users and food which are concerned about takeaway nature and food quality is the most important factor. If takeaway is unsanitary in terms of quality, users may choose the report function of a takeaway platform. Under this situation, both food manufacturers and service platforms shall actively solve the problems to appease users. If users have a low opinion of takeaway, manufacturers and service platforms have to interview the users to seriously take their advices and strive to improve quality of takeaways [7]. Secondly, people's contact. In other words, concerning standards for distribution personnel, indexes shall be constructed to evaluate services of distribution personnel and incorporated into the evaluation system. Evaluation results shall be connected with performance appraisal of distribution personnel, to promote constant improvement of their services. Thirdly, connections between people and products, which matter about usability of products on takeaway platforms. Once all services are based on indexes, effective complete service evaluation and feedback systems need to be established, in order to constantly improve user satisfaction. Additionally, touch points of reward functions may be introduced, namely users can reward businessmen and distribution personnel at fixed amount if they feel takeaway is sold with high quality and distributed at fast pace after they have the food. Besides, the rewarded amount may be allocated according to the proportion designated by users, so as to encourage businessmen to constantly improve quality of their takeaways and distribution, for the final purpose that users can have sustainable delightful experience from services.

4 Conclusions

In light of problems with design of Takeaway O2O platforms, service touch points of these platforms are completely analyzed and designed based on concepts of service design. In the mean time, three systematic innovative design modules are put forward to construct a diffluence mechanism, shape brand image and improve evaluation system. As O2O service platforms, takeaways shall understand multiple factors such as pain points of users' demands, application environment, service content and touch points during design, in order to appropriately plan service procedures of Takeaway O2O, pay close attention to natural experiences of users and systematically analyze all details of catering services, particularly offline services and their touch points which are crucial for designing services for Takeaway O2O platforms. As regards innovative design of Takeaway O2O, it is more necessary to highlight user-centered system innovation. In other words, better dining experiences are provided for users by overall intervention with "products and services" to improve customer satisfaction.

References

1. Official website of iResearch. http://www.iresearch.com.cn/view/229060.html
2. Baidu Baike (Baidu Encyclopedia). http://baike.baidu.com/view/3640801.htm
3. Luo, S., Zhu, S.: Service Design, p. 91. China Machine Press, Beijing (2011)
4. Zhang, L.: Exploration of system design strategies for online platform services in communities applicable to retirement. Design **2**, 139–141 (2015)
5. Harada, S.: Branding, 1st edn. Jiangsu Fine Arts Publishing House (2009). (Japan)
6. Chen, Y.: Takeaway O2O: win "the Last Kilometer". Shanghai Informatization **1**, 42–45 (2015)
7. Duan, H.: State analysis and optimization for O2O E-commerce based on takeaway ordering software. Guide of Sci-tech Magazine **24**, P252 (2014)
8. Pinhanez, C.: Services as customer-intensive systems. Des. Issues **25**(2), 3–13 (2009)
9. Hollins, B.: About service design. Des. Council **24**(12), 33–34 (2003)
10. Deng, C.-L.: Touch the service touch points. Zhuangshi **6**, 13–17 (2010)

Author Index

Printed in the United States
By Bookmasters

Printed in the United States
By Bookmasters